ANTIQUE MAP PRICE RECORD & HANDBOOK FOR 1997-1998

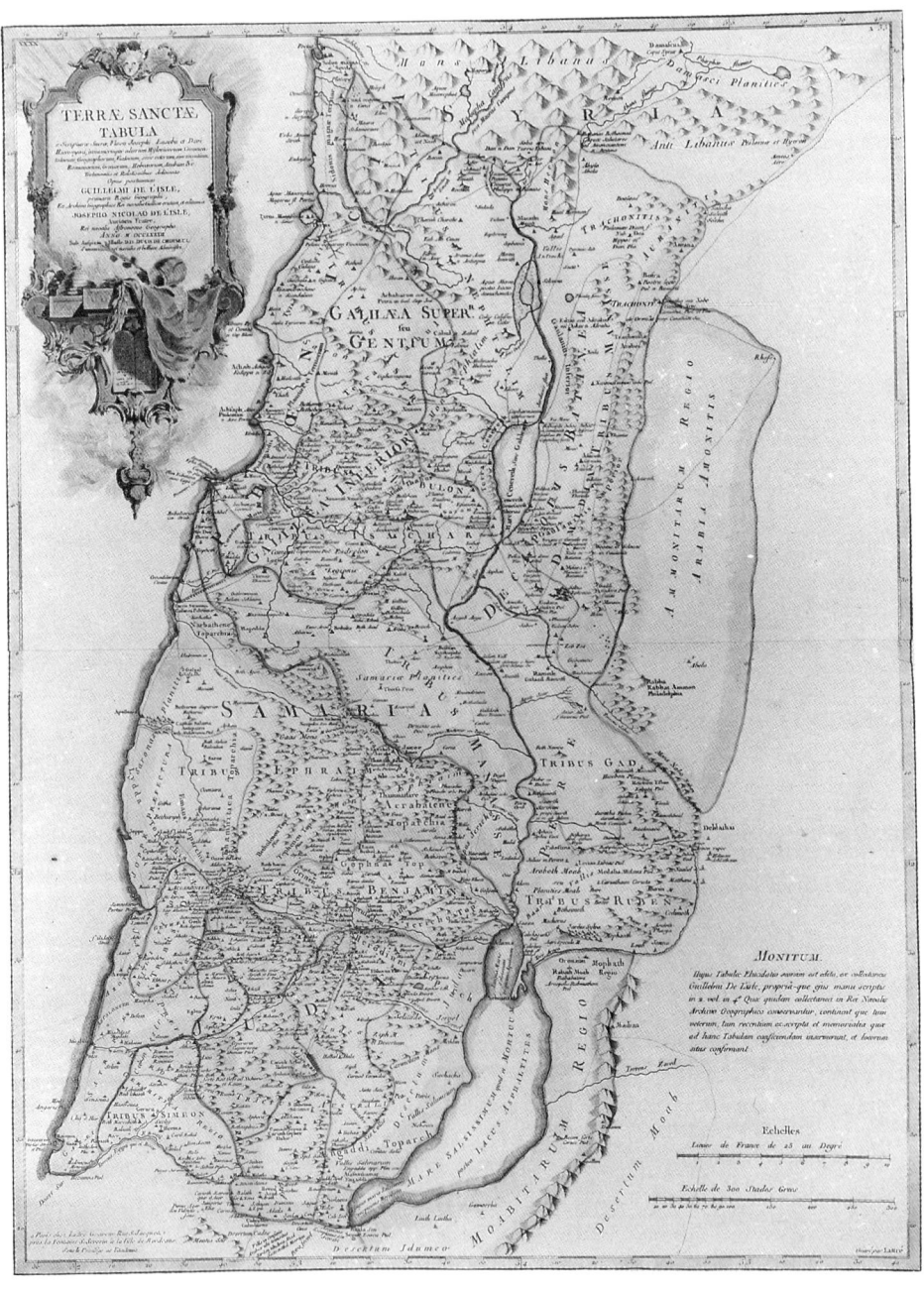

Terræ Sanctæ Tabula, 1782, a posthumous work of Guillaume De L'Isle (1675-1725), edited by his younger brother, Joseph Nicolas (1688-1768) engraved and published in *Atlas Moderne* by Lattré in 1783 and thereafter. This map of the Holy Land, almost entirely in Latin, was published in two sheets shown here joined. Broad outline color delineates the areas of the tribes. 26x19½ inches overall, the scale of about 6 miles to the inch permits exquisite detail.
(Courtesy of Amherst Antiquarian Maps, Amherst, Massachusetts.)

ANTIQUE MAP PRICE RECORD & HANDBOOK FOR 1997-1998

Including SEA CHARTS, CITY VIEWS, CELESTIAL CHARTS, BATTLE PLANS and GLOBES

Compiled and edited
by
Jon K. Rosenthal and Bernice M. Rosenthal

Amherst, Massachusetts
Kimmel Publications
1998

Copyright © 1998 by Jon K. Rosenthal. All rights reserved.

Portions of introductory remarks originally copyrighted by David C. Jolly.

Volume 15

ISBN 0-9638100-4-9   ISSN 1070-8421

Library of Congress Catalog Card Number 94-640696

Printed in the United States of America

Volumes 1 and 2 appeared as *Antique Maps, Sea Charts, City Views, Celestial Charts & Battle Plans: Price Guide and Collectors' Handbook* (ISSN 0747-7597)

Volumes 3 through 10 appeared as *Antique Maps, Sea Charts, City Views, Celestial Charts & Battle Plans: Price Record & Handbook* (ISSN 0749-4971)

Volumes 11 through 14 appeared as *Antique Map Price Record & Handbook* (ISSN 1070-8421)

Ordering information appears on Page 402. Requests for information, communications to the editor, discovery of errors, and all other correspondence should be sent to:

Jon K. Rosenthal
Kimmel Publications
P.O. Box 12
Amherst, Massachusetts 01004, USA

CONTENTS

PREFACE	vi
NOTICE TO ALL READERS	viii
NEWS AND COMMENTS	1
HOW TO USE THE *PRICE RECORD*	5
Standard Form of Map Entries	
Factors Affecting Value	
CARTOGRAPHIC REFERENCES	7
NEW BOOKS REVIEWED	10
Cumulative Index of Books Reviewed – 12	
MAP DEALER QUESTIONNAIRE	16
DIRECTORY OF DEALERS	17
United States Dealers – 18	
International Dealers – 27	
On Dealers' Catalogues – 33	
CUMULATIVE FREQUENCY DISTRIBUTION	35
OF MAP-MAKERS with Sketches of Map-Makers	
PRICE LISTING	73
Abbreviations Used – 307	
REFERENCES CITED	308
TITLE INDEX	314
GEOGRAPHICAL INDEX	382
ORDERING INFORMATION; Other Publications	402
CURRENCY CONVERSION TABLES	404
CATALOGUE CODES	405

PREFACE

The fifteen volumes of Antique Map Price Record published to date have included over 70,000 records of cartographic material for sale. In this, our first biennial volume, we have had time to enlarge the sample by more than a thousand entries over the previous edition. For the first time, auction records are presented along with offerings from dealer's catalogues. This has been undertaken only after a great deal of consideration. We readily acknowledge that we are reporting on two different kinds of enterprises and markets where the only thing in common is the type of material for sale. Elaboration of some of the differences can be found in *Notice to All Readers* (page viii)

ACKNOWLEDGMENTS

Antique Map Price Record is made possible only by the generous supply of catalogues that are provided to us by antiquarian map dealers and auctioneers of antique maps. We are grateful to all who have contributed. Every time we have posed a question to a professional in the antique map trade we have always received a complete and cordial answer. It is with regret that we have not been able to represent every contribution that has come our way. Multi-lingual Thomas Aalund, of Trade Winds Gallery in Mystic, Connecticut continues to help out with languages we don't understand. Acknowledgments previously given to Bernice Massé Rosenthal are now coming from her as she has agreed to co-author this volume. It's about time she got credit. She's certainly worked hard over the years. I could not have produced any of the volumes without her help.

Jon K. Rosenthal

WARNING!

Users of this work are warned that typographical errors may be present, and that prices for some items may not reflect the price that would be set by a majority of dealers. The publisher disclaims responsibility for any consequences of such errors and anomalies. Price information is given as an approximate guide to market values, and should be used with caution. An expert should always be consulted before making purchases or sales.

To Tiffany and Chelsea

NOTICE TO ALL READERS

We need to emphasize that the price information that is presented here is of two kinds. The first type is the asking prices of antique map dealers. The second are auction prices realized (including buyers premium) from sales of antique cartographic material. These are two completely different ways of trading merchandise. The only thing in common is the type of merchandise that is being bought and sold.

The reason for presenting what some may regard as disparate information in a single context is that dealers and auctions are both sources of antique maps and atlases for collectors, institutions and other dealers as well.

It has been argued that a map dealer's reported asking price may not be the price at which an item is sold or indeed, it may not be sold at all. An easy way to find out is to inquire. Similarly, in reporting what sold at auction, two categories are regularly omitted: The first are those mixed lots that cannot be appropriately described or compared to the material included in the *Price Record*. A second and more serious methodological problem is encountered when auction lots are passed, without a buyer. While we have certain knowledge of what some items fetched, others are simply not in the sample. In brief, without inside information (which by definition has limited circulation) there is no way to be certain that a record of prices is an accurate reflection of value.

There are other differences between a dealer and an auctioneer that should be borne in mind. Dealers maintain an inventory that is available over time. The objective of an auctioneer is to liquidate a stock of merchandise at a point in time. In general, the buyer is able to contemplate his purchase from a dealer in a more relaxed manner than in the competitive atmosphere of an auction which can demand quick decisions.

Both dealers and auction houses may produce catalogues that vary in the degree of comprehensiveness and accuracy in describing the item for sale. With both, transactions may occur at a distance by mail, phone, fax or e-mail, with no opportunity for personal inspection. What the purchaser buys is dependent on the quality of the description. Return privileges to auction houses are usually limited to misrepresentation of the merchandise; many map dealers allow returns for any reason, which can be taken to include *buyer's remorse*. Most dealers guarantee the authenticity of their wares.

We have found that there are numerous instances in which a price realized at auction is less than a dealer's asking price. Yet there are cases recorded in the current volume in which the auction price exceeds that of a dealer listing. What this demonstrates is that both markets are imperfect. To have missed a "good buy" at auction may only mean that the would-be purchaser was in the wrong place at the wrong time, and simply not in the market that day.

Readers are warned that asking prices and auction prices realized may not be comparable. Conclusions should be drawn with caution and questioned.

NEWS and COMMENTS

Bernice M. Rosenthal has joined her husband Jon as co-author of Volume 15, the first biennial edition of *Antique Map Price Record & Handbook for 1997-1998*.

This year's edition

For the first time, sales of more than 1,100 maps and atlases at auction are reported alongside offerings by map dealers. See <u>Notice to All Readers</u> at Page viii, opposite.

The current edition includes offerings from forty-eight catalogues issued by thirty map dealers. In addition the results of ten sales of over 1,000 maps and atlases at six auction houses are recorded. Together, there are 5,265 entries representing 694 mapmakers, with 16 additional generic categories. Included are more than 250 atlases (with a few facsimile atlases) and books with maps. The asking and sales prices total over $6,100,000, or about $1,160 per item (as compared with $870 a map in the 1996 edition). The rise in the average price can be attributed to the inclusion of some "big ticket" offerings, editorial reduction of redundancy at the lower priced end, and a moderate upward trend in prices across the board. Tracking atlas prices, we have noticed increases that bring into question the age-old practice of "separating out" individual maps for sale. Quoting from a catalogue, "Dealers are admonished that it is extremely unwise to disassemble any gilt edged atlas without further investigation." But generalizations can be misleading. To better determine the direction of prices, readers are referred to earlier editions of *the Price Record*.

We need to reemphasize that *Antique Map Price Record & Handbook* **is not a price guide**. David Jolly had the good sense to recognize what he was doing after two editions when he expunged the word "Guide" from the title and replaced it with "Record". The information in this book is gathered from published sources and **reported** as accurately as possible in a standard form to facilitate interpretation of the data.

We have had to make space for the additional entries and more robust information for each, including references when available. The "Glossary of Terms" and "Foreign Language Dictionaries" have been eliminated from this edition. Both sections have been identical for several years. The reader is referred to Volumes 11 through 14 for this information, all of which are still available from the publisher as of this date, but these are the only back issues still in print.

Auction Records

While we have heard some criticism of our decision to include auction records along side map dealer offerings, there are many more who welcome the idea. Again, all of this information is available to anyone who takes the trouble to find it. We are told that the user may not realize that some entries are asking prices and others are prices realized (with premiums included). There should be no confusion in the *Price Record* as to which is which since the code for auction sales is always prefixed with an "A", such as [A11 ...]. A more subtle complaint is that the novice may not understand that the purpose, objective and modus operandi of a dealer and an auctioneer are completely different as explained in <u>Notice to All Readers</u>. With the usual admonition, *caveat emptor*, we leave it to the intelligence of our readers to make their own interpretations of the information available and to seek out the enterprises that are trustworthy.

The Internet

In case it hasn't been noticed, "E-mail" and the World Wide Web are now common parlance, even for those who are still brave enough not to be wired. Where it has been provided or when we have been able to ferret out electronic addresses, they have been included in the listing of dealers. The press reports frequently on the upsurge of Internet commerce, a phenomenon that is likely to continue.

The conventional press is still reporting! We have wondered if we might be made obsolete. It is doubtful. The reason is that we have not found the web especially easy or efficient to use when one is trying to assemble a wide array of comparable data. As an analogy, our readers can probably extract more information in half-an-hour with a good newspaper than they can in a day with television news. Nevertheless, the *world wide web* works quite well in two ways: First, if the search is focused, the objective can be reached in a remarkably short time. Second, there is a quality of serendipity that ink on paper cannot match. We feel that print and electronic media are complementary. There is a place for both.

One site of interest to map dealers and collectors is MapHist. The URL address is:
> http://kartoserver.frw.ruu.nl/HTML/STAFF/krogt/maphist.htm

To skip this step, looking for "MapHist" through a search engine will produce almost the same result. This site is at the Universiteit Utrecht in The Netherlands. The audience is international in scope, with most communications in English. For those inclined to "surf the web", the possibilities here are endless. While this site is on the screen you will be given many options including instructions on securing a subscription to an E-mail discussion group on the history of cartography. One discussion we followed had to do with the accuracy with which one should measure an antique map (we'll stick with nearest centimeter and the nearest half-inch.) And we were mightily amused by the influence attributed to this publication in a comment suggesting that the convention of measuring height before width stemmed from David Jolly's practice. Should you join, you will find your E-mail box stuffed with all kinds of valuable and learned commentary on maps and cartography, but some of which falls into the category of junk mail. Should you be overwhelmed, there are instructions about how to "unsubscribe".

Another site at the University where you can find web sites for all kinds of entities relating to cartography is at Oddens's Bookmarks ("Oddens" through a search engine, or):
> http://kartoserver.frw.ruu.nl/html/staff/oddens/oddens.htm

Here you will find leads to map collections of the world, a calendar of cartographic events and exhibitions, and news of the preceding month. Of particular interest to our readers will be the pages listing sellers of antiquarian cartographic materials at:
> http://kartoserver.frw.ruu.nl/html/staff/oddens/sellers.htm#Antiq

While the listing of map dealers' web sites is not as complete as the one embedded in our dealer listing, it is liable to be more current than ours as time passes.

Of approximately 350 antique map dealers and auction houses listed in our directory, 97 had an E-mail address and 55 had a *World Wide Web* site. Some web pages lead to whole catalogues, complete with color illustrations. Others are simple notices that make ones presence known. There is little doubt that the numbers will increase rapidly in the coming months and years. What is also apparent is that addresses will change as clients utilize more sophisticated site developers and servers, for it is already apparent that dealers are securing their own domain names. With the volatility of internet addresses, the present existence of a web site or E-mail listing that can't be found at a later date could well mean that the internet service provider has changed. One can usually count on a search engine such as "Yahoo" to come to the rescue.

A *Condition* classification system for antiquarian maps?

Descriptions of condition that are found in catalogues of antique maps are about as subjective as it can get. One dealer's "excellent" might be another dealer's "good". A verbal description can do a lot to convey information about condition, but among a range of catalogues comparability has yet to be achieved. Some dealers omit condition statements entirely, presumably on the assumption that their reputation is sufficient - and often it is, especially with a return guarantee. Of necessity, auction catalogues generally have more extended descriptions of condition since misinformation can invalidate a sale.

Old World Mail Auctions has used the following *condition codes* in addition to a short descriptive statement. Their criteria are described below. We have included these letter grades when entering their items.

(A+) **Fine Condition**. Clean and bright, with crisp engraved lines. On sound paper with wide margins. Fine quality coloring.
(A) **Very good condition**. Clean and bright, with crisp engraved lines. On sound paper with no imperfections in the image. Small tears or minor discoloration in the margins only. Very good quality coloring.
(B) **Good condition**. No significant imperfections. Minor spotting, foxing, short separations on centerfold with no image loss, or overall age toning may be present. May have narrow margins but paper is still sound. Good coloring.
(C) **Fair Condition**. Noticeable imperfections. Scattered foxing or spotting. Long separations on centerfold or tears entering image which can be easily repaired. Color may be slightly faded.
(D) **Poor condition**. Needs significant repair and cleaning. Paper may be highly acid and brittle. Color may be faded.

We feel this is an admirable start that allows a reader to take in a generalized notion of condition at a glance. If anything, there is a bit of grade inflation at the top, with just a scant "+" between *Fine* and VG. Other dealers and auctioneers may not choose to adopt these standards, but it would be very helpful if they elaborated on their meaning of such terms as *mint, pristine, superb, excellent, very fine, fine, very good, good, fair, only fair* and *poor*. Can it get any worse?

What's happening with the money?

Antique Map Price Record uses the comparative values of money at the mid year prior to the year of publication, since this is about the midpoint in time of the catalogues that are used. For many years, prices have been given in U.S. dollars and Sterling. Starting this year, other original catalogue currencies are also given in the *Price Record*.

There are two reasons: First, to some degree, markets are somewhat separated between continents. A more significant reason is that economic globalization of finance has led to rapid adjustments in the relative values of the currencies. From 1994 to 1995 the

U.S. dollar was driven down relative to most European moneys. From then until midyear 1997 the dollar made a strong comeback against most of the world's currencies except the British pound and the Australian dollar. In the last year, European currencies have shown only a slight decline against the dollar, but weakness in the Japanese yen continues, now joined by Australian and New Zealand dollars.

Up to the moment exchange rates between any currencies can be obtained on the internet from **The Universal Currency Converter**™ at: http://www.xe.net/currency

George T. Goodspeed

Goodspeed's Book Shop was founded a century ago. In addition to rare books, they also sold manuscripts, fine arts and maps. George T. Goodspeed graduated from Harvard, got on the subway and took the only job he ever had and held it for seventy years. The store, which had become a Boston institution, closed in 1995 and George Goodspeed passed away in the spring of 1997 at the age of ninety-three.

Goodspeed's was old world. Its spacious rooms on Beacon Street, just down from the Common and the State House, had a sedate, hushed quality that one would expect in a shrine. It was not that their stock was unmatched, but rather that the low-keyed ambiance set it apart. The *Boston Globe* wrote of George Goodspeed's sharp eyes, encyclopedic mind and good taste. He said that the antiquarian book trade [first cousin to maps] "involves a smattering of bibliography, an occasional bit of detective work, and a good deal of horse trading." In a Harvard class report, he wrote, "I have developed few hobbies ... because the business in which I am lucky enough to find myself is so varied, so full of excitement, that I find almost all of my extra-curricular activities to be centered in it ... The antiquarian book trade is almost more by way of being a profession than a trade, or so at least those engaged in it like to believe."

My first visit to Goodspeed's was in my student days when I purchased a reproduction of the 1722 John Bonner map of Boston for $2.50 (no tax then). Pinned to the wall, it led me to understand the history and structure of the city across the river from where I was living. Years later I was to return for a copy of *Landmarks of Map Making* by Tooley, Bricker & Crone. Although it was an institution, it could not survive George Goodspeed. Is it that there is no longer a role for the place that it was? Boston is so radically changed in barely a generation: high rise, glitz and homogenization. Well, at least the downtown streets are still where they used to be. On this the Bonner map is still of help.

What's in the Future?

We are planning to compile the biggest and best *Price Record* yet for the Year 2000. It is going to be the **Classic Millenium Edition**. In order to make it the greatest we will need the continuing support of a wonderful corps of map dealers who continue to send us their catalogues. We are counting on the cooperation of auction establishments to help round out the record of activity. We encourage authors and publishers to submit cartobibliographical works for review and for use as references. We invite comment from readers regarding additional features they might like to find in the *Price Record & Handbook*. We intend to make the "Millenium Edition" a handbook and a reference book with information that is of value into the future.

HOW TO USE THE *PRICE RECORD*

Antique Map Price Record & Handbook is composed of six parts:
1. **Reference material and dealer listing.**
2. **Cumulative Frequency Distribution of Map-Makers.**
3. **Main PRICE LISTING with References cited.**
4. **Title index to main price listing.**
5. **Geographical index to main price listing.**
6. **Currency conversion table and catalogue codes.**

Most readers want to know if an old map of interest to them is listed in the *Price Record*. The first step is to see if any names appear on the map or view. If so, then try under that name in the main **Price Listing**. If not found there, then try the **Title Index**. If still not found, and if there were no entries in the main listing under the names on the map or view, then try the indexed **Cumulative Frequency Distribution of Map-Makers** to see if there were any entries under those names in past years.

Standard Form of Map Entries

The *Price Record* is organized by Map-Makers. Maps attributed to a particular map-maker are all listed under his name in the *Price Listing*. There are a number of special categories for maps not involving personal names or names of private companies. These include governmental entities such as *British Admiralty* or *U.S. Pacific R.R. Survey*, maps printed in non-Roman letters, including East Asian cartography, and various thematic or "catch-all" categories such as *Anonymous or Unknown, Manuscript Maps*; *Local and State Maps, U.S Civil War Maps* and *Railroad Company Maps* that were previously listed under the individual rail line. Maps from the early editions of Ptolemy's Geography are generally listed under Ptolemy; the later editions by Waldseemuller. Fries, Münster, Gastaldi, Ruscelli and Magini are listed under their names. Maps in Cyrillic characters are normally listed under their transliterated author and titles. A full listing of the thematic categories appears at the start of the "Cumulative Frequency Distribution" on Page 35. A typical entry follows:

BLAEU
MOLUCCAE INSULAE CELEBERRIMAE [1635] From *Theatre du Monde* .... 38x48cm (15x19")
Orig color. Excel. Ref: Koeman Bl 12.   [10] £330 $495

Map-Maker. The name is in boldfaced, large capital letters. Assigning an item to a particular name is somewhat arbitrary. For example, a map may have been surveyed by Smith, drawn by Jones, engraved by Black, published by White in an atlas edited by Brown, and then reissued in another atlas published by Green. There is no consistent standard for assigning a map to one of these names. The name assignments in this book generally follow custom. For example, maps from atlases published by Ortelius, the Blaeu family or Mathew Carey are usually assigned to Ortelius, Blaeu and Carey rather than to the name of a cartographer that might appear on the map itself.

Title. Given in bold capital letters. This is not always straightforward. Some maps have two titles, more than a single title cartouche, or a title repeated in another language. Maps without a title are supplied with a descriptive title in square brackets [ ]. In other cases a dealer might have paraphrased or abbreviated the title. Diacritical marks such as umlauts and accents are omitted here. Where appropriate, "U" and "V" are given in their intended form, for example, NOUA is transcribed as NOVA.

Date. Given next, in square brackets. It is usually the date given in the catalogue. This may be either the date of first appearance or the date of actual publication of the map or both.

Remarks. If present, these follow the date and may include the source of the map and any other brief information of relevance to the map in general.

Dimensions. Size is given to the nearest centimeter – height first and width second – followed, in parentheses, by dimensions rounded to the nearest centimeter and closest half-inch. Dimensions are usually for the outer neat line, but in some cases may represent the plate mark size, or the paper size. Diameters are expressed as a single figure.

Color. Antique maps come in a variety of color styles. They may be in full color (also called wash color or body color); full color to the primary subject; outline color of the political subdivisions; highlight color for features such as cities; map border color; cartouche color; any combination of the above heightened with gold, and not least -- uncolored. Before the printed color of the mid to late 19th-century, all coloring was by hand.

Condition. A condensed phrasing of the dealer's statement of condition is given. Some dealers say nothing of condition; others issue a blanket statement covering an entire catalogue except as noted. Expansive laudatory comments are omitted. Terms in general use describing condition are reported, – usually ranging from "mint" or "pristine" to "fair" and rarely "poor" – with the caveat that in the antiquarian map trade there is little agreement as to the meaning of the words. See a letter grade system in use by an auctioneer on Page 3.

References. Increasingly, dealers are making use of references to direct the reader to a further source of information or an illustration. When given, they are reported or if the compiler is certain of a reference, it is provided.

Catalogue Code. The number in square brackets (just before price) corresponds to the catalogue in which the map was offered for sale. The key can be found at the end of the book.

Price. The currency used in the catalogue appears in **bold** type. The price is given in both pounds and dollars or in a third currency if used in the catalogue. The conversion rates at mid-year 1997, used in computing the prices, are given at the end of the book. Note, however, that the fluctuations in currency values in the course of a year may significantly affect prices across borders. Although the same item may appear at different prices, it cannot be inferred that one is overpriced, or the other underpriced. Condition is extremely important and may not be adequately described in but a few words.

Factors Affecting Value

Historical importance. Maps which are pivotal in the history of exploration and cartography tend to be in great demand. Particularly sought after are maps that are the first to show some discovery or event.

Region depicted. This factor is probably most important in explaining the wide range in the price of maps from a given source, say an atlas by Ortelius, Blaeu, or Sanson. "World" maps are of global interest; demand is high and prices follow. Maps of other areas, which may be remote, less affluent or with alternative cultural interests, tend to be less expensive.

The Map-Maker. For similar maps, the popularity and style of the maker can strongly influence the price. This may be a reflection of scarcity, as well. For example, Ortelius and de Jode both produced similar maps at about the same time. Over 40 editions of Ortelius *Typus Orbis Terrarum* were published, far more than the two issues of de Jode's *Speculum Orbis Terræ*.

Age. For similar maps, the older map is generally the more valuable. But age as the sole basis of evaluation is risky, since some maps from the 1500s fetch far less than some from the 19th century.

Size. For maps of about equal age and subject matter, larger maps tend to be more valuable. Folio maps of an area will bring considerably more than miniature or pocket versions by the same map-maker. Larger maps allow for more detail and decoration.

Aesthetic qualities. A map with sea monsters, scrollwork, decorative borders, sailing ships, gargoyles, putti, have artistic merit in addition to cartographic information and may sell for a premium.

Color. Since most decorative maps look better colored, these are the maps in highest demand. Collectors seem to agree that original color commands a premium, but this is where agreement ends. Some prefer the original condition whether with color or without. Others may choose good modern color instead of an uncolored original. Most agree that no coloring is preferable to a bad, unskilled application of modern color. While sometimes it may be difficult to guarantee original color, it may be easier to confirm a suspicion of modern color.

Condition. Condition plays a major role in pricing. When a map is extremely rare, condition may be relatively unimportant, since choice may be simply "to have or to have not." With maps in greater supply, condition becomes a discriminating factor. Problems affecting appearance are more serious for a decorative map than for an item primarily of historical value. While very minor flaws, such as tiny spot stains or a slight crease, generally have only a minimal effect on value, more serious problems can cause a substantial disparity in price between copies of the same item.

CARTOGRAPHIC REFERENCES

The *general references* listed below may prove useful and interesting for the novice as well as the seasoned collector. The list is necessarily brief; there are scores, even hundreds, of fine books dealing with antique maps.

General References

Bagrow, Leo, *The History of Cartography,* Chicago: Precedent Publishing, Inc., 1985. R.A. Skelton, ed. This is perhaps the most highly regarded book on old maps, although not specifically about collecting.

Brown, Lloyd A., *The Story of Maps,* Boston: Little, Brown & Co., 1949. Reprinted by Dover Books, New York. A readable and scholarly history of map-making.

Howes, Wright, *U.S.iana* [1650-1950) A selective bibliography in which are described 11,620 uncommon and significant books relating to the continental portion of the United States, revised and enlarged edition, New York: R.R. Bowker, 1962.

Imago Mundi. The Journal of the International Society for the History of Cartography, a scholarly periodical with articles on early maps, reports and news. Back issues available. (Imago Mundi, Meadow Bank, 26 Lucastes Road, West Sussex, RH 16 1JW, U.K.)

Lister, Raymond, *Old Maps & Globes,* London: Bell & Hyman, 1979. An exceptionally fine introductory book. Ample material on early cartography, map-making techniques, and early globes is supplemented with a lengthy dictionary of map-makers and illustrations of about 200 watermarks.

Koeman, I.C., *Atlantes Neerlandici: Bibliography of terrestrial, Maritime and celestial atlases and pilot books, published in the Netherlands up to 1880,* 5 vols. Amsterdam: Theatrum Orbis Terrarum, 1967-71. A reprint is on the way.

Map Collector, The. 74 quarterly issues from 1977 to 1996. Highly polished and illustrated; articles of general and special interest on early maps and map collecting. Incorporated into *Mercator's World*, 1996.

Map Collectors' Series, London: The Map Collectors' Circle. 110 numbered issues in 11 volumes, 1964-1974.

Mickwitz, Ann-Mari, *The A.E. Nordenskiold Collection in the Helsinki University Library:* Annotated Catalogue of Maps Made up to 1800. 3 vols. Includes full collations of atlas maps in the collection and maps from books of travels and voyages which are seldom listed elsewhere. [Vol. 3 reviewed in 1986]

Moreland, C. & D. Bannister, *Antique Maps: A Collector's Handbook,* Oxford: Phaidon/ Christies, 1986. A superior reference, with many illustrations and much useful information. [reviewed in 1987]

Nordenskiöld, A.E., *Facsimile-Atlas to the Early History of Cartography,* Stockholm, 1889. Reprinted by Dover Publications, New York. A useful reference for those interested in maps of the 15th and 16th centuries. There are almost 200 illustrations of old maps.

Phillips, Philip L., *A List of Geographical Atlases in the Library of Congress,* Vols. I-IV, continued by Clara Egli LeGear, Vols. 5-9. Washington: Government Printing Office, 1909 through 1974. An exhaustive listing of the Library's extensive collection of atlases. Many are fully collated or with a list of maps pertaining to America. All volumes reprinted by Maurizio Martino, 746 Mansfield City Road, Storrs-Mansfield, CT 06268, USA.

Tooley, R.V., *Maps and Map-Makers,* New York: Crown Publishers, 1982, revised ed. Perhaps the most useful general purpose book for map collectors.

Tooley, R.V., *Tooley's Dictionary of Mapmakers* 1979, and Tooley's Dictionary of Mapmakers, Supplement 1985, New York: Alan R. Liss, Inc., & Amsterdam: Meridian Publishing Co. These books give information about almost any cartographer likely to be encountered. Recommended for all dealers and collectors. [reviewed in 1987]

Tooley, R.V., C. Bricker, & G.R. Crone, *Landmarks of Mapmaking*, New York: Thomas Y. Crowell, 1976. Numerous illustrations, including large folding color plates.

Wallis, H.M. & A.H. Robinson, eds., *Cartographical Innovations: An international handbook of mapping terms to 1900*, Tring: Map Collector Publications, Ltd., 1987. Contains a wealth of information on early mapping, with numerous references for further reading. [reviewed in 1988]

Woodward, David, editor, *Five Centuries of Map Printing*. An excellent discussion of the techniques of printing maps through the ages, from woodcut and copper plates to lithography and photography. Based on Nebenzahl lectures at the Newberry Library. Chicago: University of Chicago, 1975.

Index of Specialized References

These references have been cited by cataloguers or the editors in the "Price Listing". It is far from comprehensive. Full authors names and titles are given in the list of **"Cumulative References Cited"**, starting on Page 308.

World & generalized global

World
Shirley (World)

Illustrated References
Baynton-Williams [Investing]
Campbell (Earliest Maps)
Campbell (Early Maps)
Gohm (Antique Maps)
Humphreys [antique maps & charts]
Potter [antique maps]
Skelton (Decorative)
Tooley (Maps &Mapmakers)
Tooley et al (Landmarks)

By Subject
Blaeu
British Periodicals
Celestial

Charts

French atlases
Globes
Ortelius
Vaugondy family

Goss
Jolly
Snyder (Heavens);
    Stott; Warner
Howse & Sanderson;
    Whitfield
Pastoureau
Dekker & Van der Krogt
Van den Broecke
Pedley

Americas

Landis [European Americana]
Marcou [geology]
Marshall [Clements Library]
McCorkle (America Emergent)
Phillips (Maps in the LOC)

Suarez [mapping the discovery]
Tooley (America)
Winsor (Critical & Narrative)
Wolff [America: early world maps]

North America

Burden [definitive: 1511-1670]
Cumming (Discovery)
Cumming (Colonial America)
Cumming et al (Exploration)
Goss (North America)
Heidenreich & Dahl [French mapping]
Johnson [America explored]

Lunny [early maps]
Modelski (NA) [railroads]
Portinaro & Knirsch [illus, 1500-1800]
Schwartz & Ehrenberg
Sellers & Van Ee [1750-89]
Trudel [New France]

United States

Regions

Carolina	Karpinski (Carolina)
Florida	Lawson & Faupel
Former Spanish Possessions	Lowery
Great Lakes	Karpinski; Kaufman
Middle West	Karrow, R.W.
Pacific Coast	Wagner (NW)
Plains & Rockies	Luebke; Wagner-Camp
Southeast	Cumming (SE)
Southwest	Reinhartz & Colley
West	Wheat (TM);
Western Surveys	Schmeckebier

States & Cities

Alabama	Birmingham Public Library
Alaska	Falk,; Phillips (Alaska)
Colorado	Ellis
Connecticut	Thompson
DC, Washington	Phillips (Wash); Reps (Wash)
Hawaii	Fitzpatrick
Idaho	Preston
Kentucky	Clark, T.D; Sames
Maryland	Papenfuse & Coale; MD Hist. Soc.
MA, Boston	Boston Engineering Dept.
Michigan	Karpinski (MI)
MI, Detroit	Koerner
New Hampshire	Cobb (NH)
New Jersey	Snyder, J.P.
NY, New York	Haskell; Stokes
North Carolina	Williams & Johnson
Ohio	Smith, T.H.
PA, Philadelphia	Phillips (Phila); Snyder, M.P.
Rhode Island	Chapin
Texas	Day; Martin & Martin
Utah	Moffat
Vermont	Cobb (VT)
Virginia	Phillips (VA); Sames; Swem; Sanchez-Saavedra

By Subject

Amer. Revolution	Clark, D.; Nebenzahl (2)
Atlases	Le Gear
California Island	Leighley; McLauglin; Tooley (Amer)
Civil War	Stephenson (2)
City Views	Reps (3); Stokes & Haskell
Charts	Guthorn (Charts)
Congressional Publ.	Clausen & Friis
Early Amer. History	Fite & Freeman
Early Amer. Publ.	Wheat & Brun
Explorers' Routes	Ladd
General Land Off.	Kelsay
Geology	Marcou & Marcou
Gold Rush	Wheat (Gold)
Graff Collection	Storm (Graff)
Historical Geog.	Paullin & Wright
Map-makers	Ristow (Amer M&M)
Pilot Books	Campbell, J.F.
Railroads	Modelski

Other Western Hemisphere

Canada

Armstrong [art & discovery maps]
Dawson [Nova Scotia]
Dionne [Quebec]
Kershaw [early printed maps]
Lande [Canadiana at McGill]
Lemon [Maritimes]
Winearls [Upper Canada]

West Indies & Atlantic

Kapp (Central Amer)
Kapp (Jamaica)
Kapp (Panama)
Palmer (Bermuda)

Eastern Hemisphere

Europe

British Isles - Chubb; Shirley (2)
England, London - Howgego
England, Yorkshire - Rawnsley
Germany, Pfalz - Hellwig et al
Greece - Zacharakis; Soc. for Hellenistic Cartog.
Russia - Bagrow (Russia)
Wales - Booth
Poland - Buczek
Scotland - Moir; Royal Scottish Geog. Soc.

Asia & Pacific	Australia
Arabia - Tibbetts	Clancy (Australis)
Asia - Yeo	Clancy & Richardson
Cyprus - Stylianou	McCormick [1st views]
Holy Land - Laor; Nebenzahl (Holy Land)	Perry
India - Gole	Perry & Prescott
Japan - Campbell (Japan); Cortazzi; Walter	Schilder (Australia)
Philippines - Quirino	Tooley (Australia)

Africa - Norwich, Tooley (Africa)

NEW BOOKS REVIEWED

Philip D. Burden. *The Mapping of North America 1511-1670* Volume One. Rickmansworth, England: Raleigh Publications, 1996. ISBN 0-952773-0-9. 14x10 inches; xxxiv, 568 pp. 429 plates, a few in color. Cloth. ($195.00)

Every few years, a cartobibliographic work is produced that is incontrovertibly the definitive work on the subject, and likely to remain so for many decades. In the first of two planned volumes, Philip Burden has combed and expanded the records of maps of North America. We are told that under worldwide scrutiny, those extreme rarities that he may have missed can be counted on one hand. Not bad sleuthing; the author has rounded up over 99% of the suspects. While the theme focuses on printed maps depicting any part of North America, the precursors, including reference to pre-Columbian voyages and maps of the encounter period, are noted in an extensive introductory section.

As a demonstration of the exhaustive coverage, Burden has identified thirteen states of Munster's *Novae Insulae* of the Americas, which appeared in four languages with different titles: *Die neüwe Inselen ..., La table des Isles neufes ..., Tavola dell'isole nuoue ...* These maps, exhibiting the "Verrazano Sea" are distinguished from the 1588+ Petri editions of *Americae Sive No =/vi Orbis ...* where it is absent; details for identifying the issues to 1628 are provided. The charts and appendices set the standard for this kind of work. Included are family trees of derivative maps, a list of "lost" maps, California as an island (well covered beyond 1670 by McLaughlin), the first appearance of important place names, a chronology of events, a list of entries, and most important, a title index. This book is a must on the bookshelf of anyone even remotely interested in the early mapping of North America. In most instances, the "Burden" reference is checked and provided in this *Price Record* when the maps are offered for sale.

Unfortunately, there is a downside to many copies. This is in the construction of the book which weighs in at over 8 pounds (4 kg). Printed in Hong Kong, the signatures are beginning to separate where glued after less than two years of frequent use. The value of the reference is such that many owners will consider rebinding it when the time should arrive. In the meantime, readers can look forward with great anticipation to Volume Two. Without doubt attention will be paid to the physical integrity of the book because the period from 1670 to 1700 will be of at lease equal interest to aficionados and collectors as these are the maps that are still relatively obtainable. We can't wait. Bravo, Philip Burden.

T.M. Perry and Dorothy F. Prescott, compilers. *A Guide to Maps of Australia in Books Published 1780-1830*. Canberra: National Library of Australia, 1996. ISBN 0 642 25237 8. 10x7 inches; viii, 315 pp; a few illustrations. Cloth. (Aus$75.00 + shipping; Sales and Distribution, National Library of Australia, Canberra ACT 2600)

> For Australia, this guide to maps in books fills a need that is shared by many geographic entities: a listing of maps in books and not just atlases. While most works are European, Australian sources and the American Jedidiah Morse are included. Among the almost 600 maps cited are those in narratives of travels, in histories such as Cook's or La Perouse' voyages, and charts. Arranged chronologically, the cross-indexing by author of the source, map titles and geographic areas, and even titles of inset maps, facilitates use of the guide. The meaning and use of terms, place names like "Nuyt's Land" or descriptive phrases such as "Van Dieman's Land linked to New Guinea" are made clear. Before going to press, we have used our own geographic index to offer entries from the guide as a reference where possible. In the case of a map from a foreign language edition of Cook's voyages, we were unable to find a reference, but perhaps this was from our unfamiliarity with the indexing system or the subject matter. The guide will undoubtedly be of intense interest to cartophiles focusing on Australia, its surroundings and its emergent history. For others, it will serve as model for similar, much needed works on other parts of the world.

Gregory W. Williams & Allen S. Johnson. *Tar Heel Maps: Colony and State 1590-1995*. Rocky Mount: North Carolina Wesleyan College Press, 1996. ISBN 0-933598-56-4. 8½x10¾ inches; iii, 93 pp; 36 illustrations, some in multiple sections. Wrappers. ($22.00; College Store, North Carolina Wesleyan College, 3400 Wesleyan Road, Rocky Mount, NC 27804 or Gregory W. Williams, P.O. Box 654, Rehoboth Beach, DE 19971)

> The book is a catalogue of maps on exhibition at the college in 1996 with an essay on the historical background of North Carolina and the events which the maps portray. Far from exhaustive, the selections touch the highlights of any collection of the area: the White/De Bry map, the Dutch school, Ogilby, Morden, Moll, Mouzon, Homann, and a host of Americans. Speed is absent, however. What the exhibition might have lacked in breadth or depth, the authors have supplemented in the discussion relating to the maps. For example, the text cites twenty-one derivatives of the Tanner *New Universal Atlas* map which are represented by an 1852 Thomas, Cowperthwait issue. The introductory essay touches on emergent Carolina, its physical characteristics, settlement patterns, economic development, and Civil War situation. The book does not pretend to approach the comprehensiveness of a Cumming, but it provides a quick digest of the history and geography of the state that many will enjoy.

David Woodward. *Catalogue of Watermarks in Italian Printed Maps ca 1540-1600*. Chicago: University of Chicago Press, 1996. ISBN 0-226-90727-9. 9½x7 inches; 205 pp. Cloth. ($65.00).

> The prolific David Woodward, well known as editor of *The History of Cartography*, has returned to his work in watermarks and the tools used in their study. Watermarks are one of the bibliographer's methods for dating the paper of the period. 335 photographs of beta-radiograph images of watermarks are catalogued, mostly from sixteenth century Italian maps in composite atlases printed in Rome and Venice. These images reveal minute variations that are almost invisible to the eye. Entries include a

description of the watermark mould, with a description and numerical code based on the practice of the International Standard for the Registration of Watermarks published by the International Association of Paper Historians. The catalogue is organized by image categories of watermarks, with a line drawing supplement to aid in identification. One can scan for familiar names with the year of the paper: Lafreri, Duchetti, Forlani, Gastaldi - and some less well known.

Cumulative Index of Books Reviewed

The number in square brackets after the title is the year of review.

Akerman, J.R. & D. Buisseret, *Monarchs, Ministers & Maps: A cartographic exhibit at the Newberry Library* [1988]

Allen, P., *The Atlas of Atlases: The map maker's vision of the world* [1993]

Bagrow, L., *A history of cartography of Russia up to 1600* and *A history of Russian cartography up to 1800* [1990]

Bagrow, L. & R.A. Skelton, *History of cartography, 2nd ed.* [1987]

Bellec, F., *Océan des Hommes* [1989]

Beresiner, Y., *British County Maps: Reference and price guide* [1985]

Brandão, A.F., *Dialogues of the Great Things of Brazil* [1988]

Buczek, K., *The History of Polish Cartography from the 15th to the 18th Century* [1985]

Buisseret, D., *Tools of Empire: Ships and maps in the process of westward expansion* [1988]

Burden, P.D., *The Mapping of North America 1511-1670* Volume One [1998-98]

Cajori, F., *The Chequered Career of Ferdinand Rudolph Hassler* [1989]

Calissano, M, et al., *Architettura Rurale In Valle Stura: Il paesagio agricolo nel Cabreo Spinola di Campofreddo* [1988]

Campbell, T., *The Earliest Printed maps 1472-1500* [1989]

Campbell, T., *Early Maps* [1985]

Cobb, D. & N. Vick, eds., *Early Maps of Terra Sancta: Maps of the Holy Land* [1989]

Cobb, D., *New Hampshire Maps to 1900: An annotated checklist* [1989]

Conzen, M.P., ed., *Chicago Mapmakers: Essays on the rise of the city's map trade* [1986]

Cook, T., *Archival Citations* [1985]

Coppo, P., *Il Portolano* [1988]

Cotter, C., *A History of the Navigator's Sextant* [1989]

Dawson, J., *The Mapmaker's Eye: Nova Scotia through early maps* [1992]

Delano-Smith, C. and E. M. Ingram, *Maps in Bibles 1500 - 1600 An Illustrated Catalogue* [1994]

Delpar, H., ed., *The Discoverers: An encyclopedia of explorers and exploration* [1989]

Dilke, O.A.W., *Greek and Roman Maps* [1987]

Dörflinger, J., *Österreichische Karten des 18. und zu Beginn des 19. Jahrhunderts unter besonderer Berücksichtigung der Privatkartographie zwischen 1780 und 1820* [1991]

Dreyer-Eimbcke, O., *Die Entdeckung der Erde: Geschichte und Geschichten des kartographischen Abenteuers* [1991]

Dreyer-Eimbcke, O., *Island, Grönland und das nördlich Eismeer im Bild der Kartographie seit dem 10 Jahrhundert* [1990]

Dubreuil, L., *Early Canadian Topographic Map Series: The Geological Survey of Canada 1842-1949* [1992]

Dubreuil, L., *Sectional Maps of Western Canada, 1871-1955: An early Canadian topographic map series* [1992]

Dubreuil, L., *Standard Topographical Maps of Canada, 1904-1908* [1992]

Edwards, A.C. & K.C. Newton, *The Walkers of Hanningfield: Surveyors and mapmakers extraordinary* [1987]

Emlen, R.P., *Shaker Village Views: Illustrated maps and landscape drawings by Shaker artists of the nineteenth century* [1990]

Falk, M.W., *Alaskan Maps: A cartobibliography of Alaska to 1900* [1987]

Farrell, B. & A. Desbarats, *Explorations in the History of Canadian Mapping: A collection of essays* [1992]

Faupel, W.J., *A Brief and True Report of the New Found Land of Virginia: A study of the de Bry engravings* [1990]

Fell, R. T., *Early Maps of South-East Asia* [1993]

Gasset, J., ed., *Cartografia de Catalunya Dels Segles XVII i XVIII* [1989]

Globe, A., *Peter Stent, London Printseller, Circa 1642-1665: Being a catalog raisonné of his engraved prints and books with an historical and bibliographical introduction* [1987]

Goss, J., *Blaeu's The Grand Atlas of the 17th-Century World* [1992]

Goss, J., *The Mapmaker's Art: An Illustrated History of Cartography* [1994]

Graffagnino, J.K., *The Shaping of Vermont from the Wilderness to the Centennial 1749-1877* [1986]

Hadjipaschalis, A., *Cyprus: 2500 years of cartography* [1989]

Hale, E., *The Discovery of the World: Maps of the earth and the cosmos. From the David M. Stewart Collection* [1988]

Harley, J.B., assisted by E. Hanlon & M. Warhus, *Maps and the Columbian Encounter: An Interpretive Guide to the Travelling Exhibition* [1994]

Harley, J.B. & D. Woodward, *The History of Cartography Volume Two, Book One: Cartography in the Traditional Islamic and South Asian Societies* [1993]

Harris, H.M., *The Asiatic Fathers of America: Book one, The Chinese discovery and colonization of ancient America (2640 B.C. to 2200 B.C.); Book two, the Asiatic kingdoms of America (458 A.D. to 1000 A.D.)* [1988]

Heijden, H.A.M. van der, *The Oldest Maps of the Netherlands: An illustrated and annotated carto-bibliography of the 16th century maps of the XVII provinces* [1988]

Higman, B.W., *Jamaica Surveyed: Plantation maps and plans of the eighteenth and nineteenth centuries* [1990]

Holton, M., *The James W. Macnutt Collection of maps of the Gulf of St. Lawrence with Particular Emphasis on Prince Edward Island* [1991]

Jackson, J., R. Weedle & W. de Ville, *Mapping Texas and the Gulf Coast: The contributions of Saint-Denis, Oliván, and Le Maire* [1991]

Javorski, M., *The Canadian West Discovered: An exhibition of printed maps from the 16th to early 20th centuries* [1985]

Johnson, P., *Celestial Images: Astronomical charts from 1500 to 1900* [1986]

Jolly, D.C., *Maps in British Periodicals: Part I, major monthlies before 1800* [1990]

Jolly, D.C., *Maps in British Periodicals: Part II, annuals, scientific periodicals & miscellaneous magazines mostly before 1800* [1991]

Jolly, D.C., *Maps of America in Periodicals before 1800* [1989]

Jourdin, M.M. du, & M. de la Roncière, *Sea Charts of the Early Explorers, 13th to 17th Century* [1987]

Karrow, R.W. Jr. *Mapmakers of the Sixteenth Century and Their Maps: Bio-Bibliographies of the Cartographers of Abraham Ortelius, 1570* [1994]

Karamitsanis, A., ed., *From Terra Incognita to the Prairie West: A map exhibit* [1990]

Kaufman, K. (ed.), *The Mapping of the Great Lakes in the Seventeenth Century: Twenty-two Maps from the George S. & Nancy B. Parker Collection: A Portfolio with an Introduction and Commentary by Kevin Kaufman* [1994]

Kershaw, K.A., *Early Printed Maps of Canada I. 1540-1703* [1994]

King, G.L., *The Printed Maps of Staffordshire 1577-1850* [1990]

Klein, C., *Maps in Eighteenth-Century British Magazines: A checklist* [1990]

Koepp, D.P., ed., *Exploration and Mapping of the American West: Selected essays* [1988]

Konvitz, J., *Cartography in France, 1660-1848: Science, engineering, and statecraft* [1988]

Kroessler, J., *A Guide to Historical Map Resources for Greater New York* [1989]

Krogt, P.C.J. van der, *Advertenties Voor Kaarten, Atlassen, Globes e.d. in Amsterdamse Kranten 1621-1811* [1989]

Krogt, P.C.J. van der, *Old globes in the Netherlands: A catalogue of terrestrial and celestial globes made prior to 1850 and preserved in Dutch collections* [1986]

Lago, L. & C. Rossit, *Pietro Coppo Le "Tabulae" (1524-1526): Una preziosa raccolta cartografica custodita a Pirano. Note e documenti per la storia della cartografia* [1988]
Lanman, J., *Glimpses of History from Old Maps: A collector's view* [1991]
Lanman, J., *On the Origin of Portolan Charts* [1989]
Laor, E., *Maps of the Holy Land: Cartobibliography of printed maps, 1475-1900* [1988]
Larsgaard, M.L., *Map Librarianship: An introduction* [1990]
Lawson, S. & W.J. Faupel, *A Foothold in Florida; The Eye-Witness Account of Four Voyages made by the French to that Region and their attempt at Colonisation 1562-1568* [1994]
Lemon, D.P., *Theatre of Empire* [1990]
Lépine, Pierre, *Cartes Anciennes: cartes originales ou reproduites* [1994]
Lépine, P. & J. Berthelette, *Documents Cartographiques Depuis la Découverte de l'Amérique jusqu'à 1820: Inventaire sommaire* [1989]
Luebke, F, F. Kaye & G. Moulton, eds., *Mapping the North American Plains: Essays in the history of cartography* [1989]
Lyons, R., *The Conquest of Mexico by Hernan Cortez 1518-1521* [1988]
Mackal, R.P., *A Living Dinosaur? In search of Mokele-Mbembe* [1991]
Mackower, J., ed., *The Map Catalogue: Every kind of map and chart on earth and even some above it, 2nd ed.* [1991]
Manasek, F.J. *Uncommon Value: A Rare Book Dealer's World* [1995]
Martin, J.C. & R.S. Martin, *Maps of Texas and the Southwest, 1513-1900* [1987]
Martin-Merás, L. & B. Rivera, *Catologo de Cartografía Historica de España del Museo Naval* [1992]
McLaughlin, Glen, *The Mapping of California as an Island: An Illustrated Checklist* [1996]
Meinig, D.W., *The Shaping of America, Volume 1: Atlantic America, 1492-1800* [1987]
The Mercator Society, *English Mapping of America 1675-1715* [1989]
Mertz, H., *Pale Ink: Two ancient records of Chinese exploration in America*, 2nd ed. [1988]
Meurer, P.H., *Atlantes Colonienses: Die Kölner Schule der Atlaskartographie 1570-1610* [1990]
Michael, D.M.M., *The Mapping of Monmouthshire: A descriptive catalogue of pre-Victorian maps of the county (now Gwent) from Saxton in 1577 with details of British atlases published during that period* [1991]
Mickwitz, A.M., ed., *The A.E. Nordenskiöld Collection: Annotated catalogue of maps made up to 1800, vol. 3, Books containing maps, loose maps, addenda to vols. 1-2* [1986]
Monmonier, M., *Maps with the News: The development of American journalistic cartography* [1992]
Monmonier, M., *Drawing the Line: Tales of Maps and Controversy* [1995]
Mooney, J., *Maps, Globes, Atlases and Geographies through the Year 1800: The Eleanor Houston and Lawrence M.C. Smith Cartographic Collection at the Smith Cartographic Center, University of Southern Maine* [1992]
Moore, J.N., *The Mapping of Scotland: A guide to the literature of Scottish cartography prior to the Ordnance Survey* [1986]
Moreland, C. & D. Bannister, *Antique Maps: A collector's handbook, 1983 ed.* [1985]
Moreland, C. & D. Bannister, *Antique Maps: A collector's handbook, 1986 ed.* [1987]
Moulton, G.E., ed., *Atlas of the Lewis & Clark Expedition: The journals of the Lewis and Clark Expedition, Volume 1* [1987]
Mueller, G.F., *Bering's Voyages: The reports from Russia* [1988]
National Library of Ireland, *Ireland from Maps* [1985]
Nebenzahl, K., *Atlas of Columbus and the Great Discoverers* [1992]
Nebenzahl, K., *Maps of the Holy Land: Images of Terra Sancta through two millennia* [1988]
Noel, T.J., P.F. Mahoney & R.E. Stevens, *Historical Atlas of Colorado* [1994]
Norwich, O.I., *Maps of Africa: An illustrated carto-bibliography* [1986]
Pagani, L., (Introduction), *Cosmography: Maps from Ptolemy's Geography* [1993]
Pedley, M. S., *Bel et Utile: The work of the Robert De Vaugondy Family of mapmakers* [1993]
Pennick, N., *Lost Lands and Sunken Cities* [1989]
Perry, T.M. & and D.F. Prescott, compilers, *A Guide to Maps of Australia in Books Published 1780-1830* [1997-98]

Popescu-Spineni, Marin, *Rumänien in seinen Geographischen und Kartographischen Quellen* [1992]

Portinaro, P. & F. Knirsch, *The Cartography of North America 1500-1800* [1990]

Potter, J., *Country Life Book of Antique Maps: An introduction to the history of maps and how to appreciate them* [1990]

Public Archives of Canada, *National Map Collection* [1989]

Quaini, M., ed., *Carte e Cartografi in Liguria* [1988]

Quaini, M., *Piante delle Due Riviere della Serenissima Repubblica di Genova Divise ne' Commissariati di Sanita* [1987]

Reinhartz, D. & C.C. Colley, *The Mapping of the American Southwest* [1990]

Reps, J.W., *Views & Viewmakers of Urban America: Lithographs of towns and cities in the United States and Canada, notes on the artists and publishers, and a union catalog of their work, 1825-1925* [1985]

Rey, L., ed., *Unveiling the Arctic* [1987]

Ristow, W., *American Maps & Mapmakers: Commercial cartography in the nineteenth century* [1986]

Schulz, Juergen, *La Cartografia Tra Scienza e Arte: Carte e cartografi nel Rinascimento italiano* [1992]

Sertima, I. van, ed., *African Presence in Early America* [1989]

Shirley, R.W., *Early Printed Maps of the British Isles 1477-1650* [1994]

Shirley, R.W., *The Mapping of the World: Early printed world maps 1472-1700* [1985; 1995]

Sider, S., A. Andreasian & M. Codding, *Maps, Charts, Globes: Five Centuries of Exploration An Exhibition in Commemoration of the Columbus Quincentenary* [1993]

Simpson, A., *The Mysteries of the "Frenchman's Map" of Williamsburg, Virginia* [1987]

Society for the History of Discoveries, *Terrae Incognitae: The journal of the history of discoveries*, v.18 [1989]

Snyder, G., *Maps of the Heavens* [1985]

Stevens, A.R. & W.M. Holmes, *Historical Atlas of Texas* [1991]

Stommel, H., *Lost Islands: The story of islands that have vanished from nautical charts* [1987]

Suarez, T., *Shedding the Veil: Mapping the European discovery of America and the world based on selected works from the Sidney R. Knafel collection of early maps, atlases, and globes, 1434-1865* [1992]

Taliaferro, H.G., comp., *Cartographic Sources in the Rosenberg Library* [1991]

Tompkins, E., *Newfoundland's Interior Explored* [1990]

Tooley, R.V., *Dictionary of Mapmakers: Supplement* [1987]

Tooley, R.V., *Tooley's Handbook for Map Collectors: The map collector's vade mecum arranged by subjects and personalities alphabetically* [1988]

Van Ermen, E., *The United States in Old maps and Prints* [1992]

Vigeant, L., *Dealer's Thesaurus: 6,000 Ways to Describe Books and Historical Paper* [1994]

Wallis, H.M. & A.H. Robinson, *Cartographical Innovations: An international handbook of mapping terms to 1900* [1988]

Walsh, J., *Maps Contained in the Publications of the American Bibliography, 1639-1819: An index and checklist* [1990]

Walsperger, A., *Untitled World Map of 1448* [1988]

Walter, L. (ed.), *Japan A Cartographic Vision: European Printed Maps from the Early 16th to the 19th Century* [1995]

Warner, D.J., *The Sky Explored: Celestial cartography, 1500-1800* [1986]

Wheat, C.I. *Mapping the Transmississippi West* (reprint) [1995]

Williams, G. & A. Frost, eds., *Terra Australis to Australia* [1990]

Williams, G.W. & A.S. Johnson. *Tar Heel Maps: Colony and State 1590-1995* [1997-98]

Wolter, J.A., ed., *World Directory of Map Collections, 2nd ed.* [1988]

Wood, D., with J. Fels, *The Power of Maps* [1994]

Woodward, D., ed., *Art and Cartography: Six historical essays* [1988]

Woodward, D., *Catalogue of Watermarks in Italian Printed Maps ca 1540-1750* [1997-98]

Zögner, L., ed., *Bibliographia Cartographia: International documentation of cartographical literature*, vol. 11 [1986]

Zögner, L., *Von Ptolemaeus bis Humbolt. Kartenschätze der Staatsbibliothek Preußischer* Kulterbesitz: *Ausstellung zum 125 jährigen Jubiläum der Kartenabteilung* [1986]

MAP DEALER QUESTIONNAIRE

Note to Map Dealers: Volume 16, the next biennial edition *of Antique Map Price Record & Handbook for 1999-2000* will be the "Classic Millennium Edition". If you wish to be included in the "Directory of Dealers" in the Millenium Edition, <u>you must submit a completed map dealer questionnaire</u>. It is important that we assure our readers that the dealer information is accurate and up-to-date. Should it change before our deadline of September 30, 1999, please bring such alterations to our attention even if you have returned the questionnaire. Help us keep them current. Thank you in advance for your cooperation.

1. Your business name: _____

2. Your personal name: *(optional)* _____

3. Your preferred address: _____

   _____

   _____

4. Telephone number: _____

5. FAX number: _____

6. Electronic access:

   (E-Mail, www) _____

7. Check any that apply: (* revised)

   (a) _____ Do you maintain regular shop hours?

   (b) _____ Do you see customers by appointment only?

   (c) _____ Do you sell by mail order?

   (d) _____ Do you exhibit at fairs?

   (e) _____ Do you issue catalogues or price lists?

   *(f) _____ Do you do appraisals of antique maps for insurance or tax purposes?

   (g) _____ Do you conduct antique map auctions? How many per year? _____

8. If <u>over 50%</u> of your business is in Antique Maps, Sea Charts, City Views, Celestial Charts, or Battle Plans, please check here. (it will be noted) _____

9. If you have a cartographic specialty (i.e., American West, sea charts, Africa, etc.), indicate it briefly. If your stock is reasonably general, please note it. Limit your listing to cartographic material. Entries may be edited with regard to relevance and length.

   _____

10. If you are no longer in business or wish to discontinue your listing, check here. _____

Please return a photocopy of this form to:

Kimmel Publications, P.O. Box 12, Amherst, MA 01004, USA.   Fax (413) 256-6291

The deadline for inclusion in the 1999-2000 edition is <u>September 30, 1999</u>

DIRECTORY OF DEALERS

Twenty-six dealers contributed to the first edition of *Antique Map Price Record* series in 1983 and formed the nucleus of a "proto-directory". Over the years the listing grew to over 700 names of individuals or firms trading in old maps, but we found that many who were listed either participated marginally in the trade or didn't take the trouble to return a questionnaire. In 1996 the listing pared down to its present lean size of about 350 traders.

We are eager to add *bone fide* antique map dealers to the list at all times. We continue to need the cooperation of dealers world wide in assembling the data and keeping it current. Between editions, these names will be added to the dealer mailing labels that are available from Kimmel Publications (see Page 403 for ordering information). Please note our requirement that *dealers return a questionnaire every two years to be certain that a listing in the directory is continued*. We urge all dealers in antique maps to take a moment to return a copy of the *Map Dealer Questionnaire* (as on the previous page – Page 16) to us by September 30, 1999 for inclusion in the next edition of the *Antique Map Price Record & Handbook*. For your convenience, you may use the publisher's Fax Number, (413) 256-6291.

Apologies are extended to any dealers inadvertently omitted or mistakenly included. Dealers who are not yet listed should use the questionnaire which can be easily photocopied with our permission. Any errors should be called to the attention of the publisher so that corrections can be made in future editions.

IMPORTANT!

Inclusion of a name should not be regarded as an endorsement by the publisher, nor should omission be regarded as a lack of such endorsement.

Even though some entries do not indicate that an appointment is required, the information is not always complete, and even dealers with shop hours can be preoccupied with some activity such as preparation for a book fair. Therefore it is suggested that you either write or telephone before visiting.

When writing to dealers for catalogues or quotes, please remember that it is far more efficient for dealer and customer alike to give a detailed description of the desired material. Some dealers charge a small fee for their catalogues, many of which are held to scholarly standards and generously illustrated.

Kimmel Publications cannot attest to the accuracy of the information provided in the dealer listing. The publisher disclaims responsibility for any consequences of any errors, omissions or interpretation of the information provided.

United States Dealers in Alphabetical Order

† indicates that dealer's catalogue was used in the *Price Listing*
[>½] dealers indicated that over 50% of business is in antique maps or closely related

†**Acquitania Gallery**, Diane D. Vasica, 158 Carl St., San Francisco, CA 94117. (415) 664-2707, Fax same. by appt., mail order, lists/catalogues. California as an island; San Francisco.
Amherst Antiquarian Maps, P.O. Box 12, Amherst, MA 01004. (413) 256-8900, Fax (413) 256-6291, E-mail: navigateur@aol.com. by appt., mail order, fairs. General. [>½]
Sy Amkraut, 35 Winding Wood Rd. N., Rye Brook, NY 10573. (914) 939-1509, Fax same. by appt., mail order. General. [>½]
Anderson Antiquarian Maps, Eric B. Anderson, 4 Grant St., Norfolk, CT 06058. (860) 542-5472, Fax (860) 541-6919. by appt., mail order, fairs. Atlases & town maps of CT, MA, RI, ME, VT & NY. [>½]
Antipodean Books Maps & Prints, David Lilburne, 6 Depot Square, Garrison, NY 10524. (914) 424-3867, Fax (914) 424-3617, E-mail: antipbooks@highlands.com. shop hours, mail order, fairs, lists/catalogues, appraisal. Australia; South Pacific.
The Antiquarian Shop, George E. Chamberlain, 4246 N. Scottsdale Rd., Scottsdale, AZ 85251. (602) 947-0535, Fax (602) 947-7815. shop hours, mail order.
Antique Art Exchange, Tom Phillips, 361 Summit Boulevard, Birmingham, AL 35243. (205) 967-1700, Fax (205) 967-1708. shop hours, mail order. Alabama, Southeastern U.S.
Antique Geography, Joe Cline, 110 Pearl Street, Port Hueneme, CA 93041. (805) 986-0202. by appt., fairs. 19th century hand colored maps. [>½]
Antique Map Company, Richard D. Stout, 903 Driver Rd., P.O. Box 1274, Fort Payne, AL 35967. (205) 845-5171. by appt., mail order. Southeast, North America 1600-1860. [>½]
Antique Maps & Prints, Inc., Joseph & Bette Rubini, 5794 Sunset Dr., South Miami, FL 33143. (305) 665-5070, Fax same, daytime. shop hours, appraisal. General. [>½]
Antique Prints Ltd., Robert & Martha Seamans, 42 Central Ave., Rt. 1, Box 156, Ocean View, DE 19970. (302) 539-6702, Fax (302) 539-9057. by appt., mail order, fairs, lists/catalogues, appraisal. Chesapeake Bay area; VA, MD, DE, Washington, DC. [>½]
Antiques Americana, K.C. Owings, Jr., P.O. Box 19, North Abington, MA 02351. (617) 587-6441. by appt., mail order, lists/catalogues. General U.S., Civil War.
Appalachian Arts, Bernard Rogers, 22 Swiss Lane, Blue Ridge, GA 30513. (706) 632-8974, Fax same, E-mail: brogers@blrg.tds.net, Web: www.athens.net/~aarts. by appt., lists/catalogues. Also Bud Rogers; (941) 403-8986; E-mail: aarts@athens.net. 19th c. maps, charts & prints. [>½]
W. Graham Arader III, 435 Jackson St., San Francisco, CA 94111. (415) 788-5115, Fax (415) 788-5125. shop hours, fairs, lists/catalogues. General; World, Americas.
W. Graham Arader III, 29 E. 72nd St., New York, NY 10021. (212) 628-3668, Fax (212) 879-8714.
W. Graham Arader III, 1000 Boxwood Court, King of Prussia, PA 19406. (610) 825-6570, Fax (610) 825-2152. shop hours, mail order, fairs, lists/catalogues. General
W. Graham Arader III Gallery, Lori Cohen, 1308 Walnut St., Philadelphia, PA 19107. (215) 735-8811, Fax (215) 735-9864. shop hours, by appt., mail order, fairs, lists/catalogues. [>½]
W. Graham Arader III, Galleria One, 5015 Westheimer; Suite 2303, Houston, TX 77056. (713) 527-8055.
Argonaut Book Shop, Robert D. Haines, Jr., 786 Sutter St., San Francisco, CA 94109. (415) 474-9067, Fax (415) 474-2537. shop hours, mail order, fairs, lists/catalogues.
Argosy Gallery, 116 E. 59th St., New York, NY 10022. (212) 753-4455, Fax (212) 593-4784. shop hours, mail order.
†**Richard B. Arkway, Inc.**, 59 E. 54th St., #62, New York, NY 10022. (800) 453-0045, (212) 751-8135, Fax (212) 832-5389, E-mail: arkway@aol.com. shop hours, mail order, fairs, lists/catalogues, appraisal. General, America; maps, atlases globes. [>½]
Art Source International, 1237 Pearl, Boulder, CO 80302. (303) 444-3670, Fax (303) 444-4298. shop hours, mail order, lists/catalogues. Also: 413 E. Hyman Ave., Aspen, CO 81611; (303) 925-6850.
The Atlas, Thos. E. Greene, P.O. Box 3822, North Providence, RI 02911. (401) 353-1161. by appt., mail order, fairs, lists/catalogues. America; Rhode Island.
Bay Books, David N. Harbaugh, 27115 E. Oviatt Road, P.O. Box 40306, Bay Village, OH 44140. [bus.] (216) 892-9191; [res.] (216) 835-5444. shop hours, by appt., mail order, fairs. Local, special & general atlases.
The James K. Beier Co., 955 Harvey Ave., Brookfield, WI 53005. (414) 786-0176. by appt., mail order, fairs, appraisal. General; Civil War. [>½]
Bickerstaff's, Stephen P. Hanly, 3 Ellery Road, Waltham, MA 02154. (617) 899-5504, E-mail: bicks@shore.net. mail order, fairs, lists/catalogues. 18th c. New England maps & charts.
Bill George International, William G. Smith, 200 E. 66th St. (C-1702), New York, NY 10021. (212) 356-1448, Fax (212) 356-0955. by appt. appraisal. General; atlases, travel, exploration, 15-19 c. Also 1370 Broadway. [>½]

18

United States Dealers

The Bookpress, John Ballinger & John Robert Curtis, Box KP, Williamsburg, VA 23187. (804) 229-1260, Fax (804) 229-0498. shop hours, mail order, fairs, lists/catalogues. Colonial America; Virginia.

Branford Rare Books, John R. Elliott, Clocktower Antiques Group, 824 E. Main St. (Rte. #1), Branford, CT 06405. (203) 488-1919, Fax (203) 483-7477. shop hours, by appt., mail order, fairs. General.

Brenwassser Studio, Don Brenwasser, 509 Wellington Dr., Wyckoff, NJ 07481. (201) 891-7032, E-mail: brenwasser@internexus.com. by appt., mail order, lists/catalogues. General pre-1800. [>½]

Phyllis Y. Brown, Antique Prints, Maps & Books, 6325 Ellenwood, St. Louis, MO 63105. (314) 725-1434 & 725-1023. by appt., mail order, fairs, lists/catalogues. Also Ladue Galleries, #50. 8811 Ladue Rd., St. Louis.

Clive A. Burden Inc., P.O. Box 190, Bedford, NY 10506. (914) 234-6140. General. See England entry.

John Bouvier Maps & Prints, 11D Avilef St, St. Augustine, FL 32084. (904) 825-0920, Fax same. shop hours. General; Florida.

Buxbaum Geographics, Jeanne K. Buxbaum, Box 3746, Greenville P.O., Wilmington, DE 19807. (302) 994-2663, mail order, lists/catalogues. National Geographic Society maps.

California Book Auction Galleries, 220 San Bruno Ave., San Francisco, CA 94103. (415) 861-7500, ext 204, Fax (415) 553-8678. shop hours, by appt., lists/catalogues, appraisal, auction.

Camelot Books, Jim Kissko, 2403 Hillhouse Rd., Baltimore, MD 21207. (410) 448-1015, Fax same. by appt., mail order, fairs, lists/catalogues, appraisal. 19th c. America maps & atlases. [>½]

Cape James Antiquarian Books & Maps, Ltd., Kevin Moore & Greg Williams, 109 E. Fourth St., Lewes, DE 19958. (302) 227-9441, (302) 645-7224, Fax (302) 227-8847, E-mail: gwwmaps@shore.intercom.net. by appt., mail order, fairs, lists/catalogues. Mid-Atlantic; Delaware; North Carolina. [>½]

Thomas Edward Carroll, P.O. Box 398, Hatfield, MA 01038. (413) 247-9767. by appt., mail order, fairs. American Northeast, pre-1800. [>½]

Cartographic Arts, Luke & Patricia Vavra, P.O. Box 2202, Petersburg, VA 23804. (804) 861-6770, Fax (804) 861-3021, E-mail: carto@dogstar.com, Web: www.dogstar.com. by appt., mail order, fairs, appraisal. General; North America [>½]

† **Cartographics of Vermont**, Christopher Watters, P.O. Box 145, East Middlebury, VT 05740. (802) 388-6488, E-mail: christopher.d.watters@middlebury.edu. shop hours, mail order, lists/catalogues, appraisal. At Middlebury Antiques Center, East Middlebury; (802) 388-6229. 19 c. Wall & pocket maps, games, atlases, guides. [>½]

The Cartophile, William T. Clinton, 934 Bridle Lane, West Chester, PA 19382-2172. (610) 692-7697, Fax (610) 918-3990. by appt., mail order, fairs, appraisal. Pre-1870 atlases printed in America; early travels & exploration [>½]

El Cascajero, Anthony Gran, The Old Spanish Book Mine, 506 Laguardia Place, New York, NY 10012. (212) 254-0905. by appt., mail order, lists/catalogues.

JoAnn & Richard Casten Ltd., 4 Dodge Lane, Old Field, NY 11733. (516) 689-3018, Fax (516) 689-8909. by appt., mail order, fairs, lists/catalogues, appraisal. World, North America, Holy Land. [>½]

The Centuries, F.I. Mapes, Antique Maps and Prints, 517 St. Louis, New Orleans, LA 70130. (504) 568-9491. shop hours, mail order. General. [>½]

Chartifacts, Walter J. Auburn, P.O. Box 8954, Richmond, VA 23225. (804) 272-7120. by appt., mail order, fairs, lists/catalogues. U.S. Coast Survey, Coast & Geodetic Survey. [>½]

Chartwell Mapsellers, S.I. Miller, P.O. Box 1207, Huntsville, AL 35807-0207. (205) 536-1521, Fax (205) 534-0533, mail order, lists/catalogues. Southeast U.S., AL, TN. [>½]

Dennis Clare, 818 Duboce Ave., San Francisco, CA 94117. (415) 552-0437. by appt., mail order. U.S.; West. [>½]

Cleveland Antiquarian Books, William Chrisant, 13127 Shaker Sq., Cleveland, OH 44120. (216) 561-2665, Fax (216) 561-2771, E-mail: clantbks@aol.com. shop hours, appraisal.

Bob Coffin Books, 1139 S. Fifth Place, Las Vegas, NV 89104-1413. (702) 598-0982, Fax (702) 598-0985, E-mail: bcoffin@interloc.com. by appt., mail order, fairs, lists/catalogues, appraisal. Nevada, West.

Compass Rose Gallery, Curt & Marti Griggs, 671 Highway 179, Sedona, AZ 86336. (520) 282-7904, Fax (520) 282-3945, E-mail: oldmaps@sedona.net, Web: www.oldmaps.com. shop hours, lists/catalogues, appraisal. [>½]

Darvill's Rare Print Shop, P.O. Box 47, Eastsound, WA 98245. (360) 376-2351, Fax (360) 376-2391. shop hours, lists/catalogues. General; Pacific Northwest.

Deja View Antique Maps and Prints, Steve & Laurie Armistead, P.O. Box 61722, Vancouver, WA 98666. (360) 696-3252, E-mail: sarmis@teleport.com, Web: www.teleport.com/~sarmis/dejaview. by appt.

C. Dickens, Fine, Rare & Collectible Books, 3393 Peachtree Rd., N.E., Atlanta, GA 30326. (800) 548-0376, (404) 231-3825, Fax (404) 364-0713. shop hours, mail order.

Duck Creek Books, Jim Richards, P.O. Box 203, Caldwell, OH 43724. (614) 732-4856, E-mail: dukcreek@interloc.com. by appt., mail order, fairs, lists/catalogues.

† **Dumont Maps & Books of the West**, Andre & Carol Dumont, 301 E. Palace Ave., #1, P.O. Box 10250, Santa Fe, NM 87504. (505) 988-1076, Fax (505) 986-6114, E-mail: dumontbk@rt66.com / webart.com/dumont/index.html. shop hours, mail order, lists/catalogues. Trans-Mississippi West.

United States Dealers

V. & J. Duncan, Antique Maps, Prints & Books, Virginia & John Duncan, 12 E. Taylor St., Savannah, GA 31401. (912) 232-0338, Fax (912) 232-3489. shop hours, mail order.

Early American History Auctions, Inc., Dana Linett, Suite 205, 7911 Herschel Ave., La Jolla, CA 92037. (619) 459-4159, Fax (619) 459-4373, E-mail: auctions@earlyamerican.com, Web: www.earlyamerican.com. by appt., mail order, lists/catalogues. auction. North America, Western Hemi, World.

Einhorn Associates, Joseph J. Einhorn, P.O. Box 973, Orange, CT 06477. (203) 795-5830, Fax same. by appt., mail order, fairs, lists/catalogues, appraisal, auction. Also Antique Ctr, 67 Jefferson St., Stamford, CT.

Emerson Booksellers, Thomas & Mary Emerson, 18 Exchange St., Portland, ME 04101. (207) 874-2665. shop hours, mail order. [>½]

Far West Trading Company, 3422 Monroe Ave., Cheyenne, WY 82001. (307) 638-2396, E-mail: farwesttc@sisna.com, Web: www.sisna.com/farwesttc/farwest.htm.

Joseph J. Felcone Inc., P.O. Box 366, Princeton, NJ 08542. (609) 924-0539, Fax (609) 924-9078. by appt., mail order, fairs, lists/catalogues.

Clifton F. Ferguson, Antique Maps & Atlases, 4999 Meandering Creek Dr., Belmont, MI 49306. (616) 874-9297, Fax same. by appt., mail order, lists/catalogues. [>½]

First of Florida Maps, Ashby M. Moody, 4305 El Prado, Tampa, FL 33629. (813) 839-7098. by appt., appraisal. Florida.

† **Richard Fitch,** Old Maps, Prints & Books, 2324 Calle Halcon, Santa Fe, NM 87505. (505) 982-2939, Fax (505) 982-3148, E-mail: oldmaps@swcp.com. by appt., mail order, lists/catalogues, appraisal. North America & its subdivisions, especially sequences. [>½]

Fleetstreet, Christopher Charles, P.O. Box 11406, Bainbridge Island, WA 98110. (206) 842-7488, Fax (206) 842-7489. by appt., mail order, fairs, lists/catalogues, appraisal. Pacific Northwest.

Craig Flinner Gallery, 505 N. Charles St., Baltimore, MD 21201. (410) 727-1863, Fax (410) 727-1175. shop hours, fairs.

Front Street Antiques, John Tompkins, P.O. Box 565, Millbrook, NY 12545. (914) 677-9079, Fax (914) 677 6085. by appt., mail order, appraisal. General. [>½]

Gallery 515, Deborah McAfee & Michael Sisk, 515 E. Paces Ferry Rd., N.E, Atlanta, GA 30305. (404) 233-2911, Fax same. shop hours, mail order. General; American maps. [>½]

George D. Glazer, 28 East 72nd St., New York, NY 10021. (212) 535-5706, Fax (212) 988-3992, E-mail: Worldglobe@aol.com. shop hours, by appt., mail order, fairs, lists/catalogues. Globes; 19th c atlases & maps, esp US; celestial charts. [>½]

Goreham Collectibles, Dennis Goreham, 1539 East 4070 South, Salt Lake City, UT 84124. (801) 277-5119. by appt., mail order, fairs. General; American West.

Grace Galleries, Inc., Jacqueline Grace, RR 5, Box 2488, Brunswick, ME 04011. (207) 729-1329, Fax (207) 729-0385. by appt., mail order, lists/catalogues, appraisal. General; Great Britain; Nautical. [>½]

Graton & Graton, Waldo & Marilyn Graton, 1601 Oakwood Ave., Highland Park, IL 60035. (847) 432-4722, Fax same. by appt., fairs. [>½]

E. Greene Gallery, Edward Greene, 327 Washington St., Hoboken, NJ 07030. (201) 659-8033, Fax (201) 222-3349.

Haley & Steele, 91 Newbury St., Boston, MA 02116. (617) 536-6339, Fax (617) 536-2298, E-mail: oldprint@aol.com, Web: www.haleysteele.com.

Douglas N. Harding, Harding Book Shop, Route 1 North, Wells, ME 04090. (207) 646-8785, Fax (207) 646-8862. shop hours, mail order, fairs.

Heirloom Book Store, Judi & Jim McMeans, 4100 Atlanta Highway, Athens, GA 30622. (706) 369-7304. shop hours, mail order, fairs, lists/catalogues.

Herb's Old Prints, Herb Pape, P.O. Box 83, Warrenton, MO 63383. Off I-70, Warrenton exit.

Here Be Dragons, Ed Curley, P.O. Box 57520, Tucson, AZ 85732. (520) 326-3132. by appt., mail order. General; Arizona. [>½]

Heritage Antique Maps, 551 Christopher Lane, Doylestown, PA 18901. (215) 340-9662, Fax same, E-mail: maps1@HeritageAntiqueMaps.com, Web: www.HeritageAntiqueMaps.com. by appt., mail order, fairs. General. [>½]

Heritage Guild, P.O. Box 225, Lemont, IL 60439. (630) 257-7546, Fax (630) 257-7547. by appt., mail order, lists/catalogues. Baltic States, E. Europe, World

† **Heritage Map Museum,** James E. Hess, 55 N. Water St., P.O. Box 412, Lititz, PA 17543. (717) 626-5002, Fax (717) 626-8858, E-mail: heritage@carto.com, Web: www.carto.com. shop hours, auction. 15th-19th c. [>½]

Robert M. Hicklin Jr.,Inc., 509 E. St. John St., Spartanburg, SC 29302. (864) 585-3553. shop hours, mail order, lists/catalogues. Southeastern North America.

† **High Ridge Books, Inc.**, Fred Baron, P. O. Box 286, Rye, NY 10580. (914) 967-3332, Fax (914) 967-6056, E-mail: highridg2@usa.pipeline.com, Web: www.highridgebooks.com. by appt., mail order, fairs, lists/catalogues. 18 & 19 c. American atlases; separately published maps.

The Historian's Gallery, Robert C. Hill III, 3232 Cobb Parkway, Suite 207, Atlanta, GA 30339. (404) 843-2395, Fax same, E-mail: history@mindspring.com, Web: www.nr-net.com/history.

United States Dealers

Historic Urban Plans, Inc., Box 276, Ithaca, NY 14850. (607) 272-6277. by appt., mail order, lists/catalogues. Wholesale: town plans & views; American maps.

Historicana, Irvin Ungar, 1200 Edgehill Dr., Burlingame, CA 94010. (650) 343-9578, Fax (650) 579-6014. by appt., mail order, fairs, lists/catalogues. Maps of the Holy Land.

The Holy Land, Dr. Samuel Halperin, 3041 Normanstone Terr., N.W., Washington, DC 20008. (202) 965-4831, Fax (202) 965-1746, E-mail: shalperin@aypf.org. by appt., mail order, fairs, appraisal. Holy Land; Palestine. [> ½]

T.S. Hotter Gallery, Thomas J. Hotter, 94 Water St., Rockdale, Cambridge, WI 53523. (608) 423-9544. by appt., fairs. General. [> ½]

Houle Rare Books & Autographs, 7260 Beverly Blvd., Los Angeles, CA 90036. (213) 937-5858, Fax (213) 937-0091. shop hours, mail order, fairs, lists/catalogues.

† **Murray Hudson**, Antiquarian Books & Maps, 109 S. Church St., P.O. Box 163, Halls, TN 38040. (800)-748-9946, (901) 836-9057, Fax (901) 836-9017, E-mail: mapman@usit.net. shop hours, mail order, fairs, lists/catalogues, appraisal. General: wall & pocket maps, atlases, geographies, sea charts, globes; Southern & Western U.S. [> ½]

Indian Ocean Books, Maps & Prints, Larry W. Bowman, 458 Middle Turnpike, Storrs, CT 06268. (860) 486-3355, Fax (860) 486-3347, E-mail: bowman@uconnvm.uconn.edu. by appt., mail order, lists/catalogues. Indian Ocean; Madagascar & other islands; Zanzibar, etc.

† **Kit S. Kapp**, Antiquarian Maps, Box 64, Osprey, FL 34229. (813) 966-4181. by appt., mail order, lists/catalogues. Maps of the Americas. [> ½]

† **Kauai Fine Arts**, Paul & Mona Nicholas, P.O. Box 1079, Lawai, Kauai HI 96765. (808) 332-8508, (808) 335-3778, Fax (808) 332-9808, E-mail: kfa@brunias.com, Web: www.brunias.com. shop hours, mail order, fairs, lists/catalogues. Worldwide; Americas; Pacific; West Indies. [> ½]

Gary Kunkelman, American Maps & Prints, Box 6115, Wyomissing, PA 19760. (610) 678-6049, Fax (610) 670-6854, E-mail: amishwor@redrose.net. lists/catalogues.

Lahaina Printsellers Ltd., Alan Walker, 636 Luakini St., Lahaina, Maui, HI 96761. (808) 667-7843, Fax (808) 667-5634, E-mail: info@printsellers.com, Web: www.printsellers.com. shop hours, mail order, lists/catalogues. General; Cook memorabilia; Hawaiiana. [> ½]

The Lamp, William G. Mayer, 117 Evergreen Rd., Pittsburgh, PA 15238. (412) 963-0663. by appt., mail order, lists/catalogues. 19th c. American. [> ½]

Latitudes, Tom Lazor, 19 Novelty Lane, P.O. Box 66, Essex, CT 06426. (860) 767-3001. shop hours, mail order, fairs, appraisal. 17th-19th c maps & charts; Conn. River & Nantucket views. [> ½]

Don Leeper, Antique Maps & Atlases, 3645 N.W. Glenridge Dr., Corvallis, OR 97330. (541) 758-3242, Fax same. mail order, fairs, lists/catalogues. [> ½]

Edward J. Lefkowicz, Inc., P.O. Box 630, Fairhaven, MA 02719. (508) 997-6839, (800) 201-7901, Fax (508) 996 6407, E-mail: seabooks@saltbooks.com, Web: www.saltbooks.com/~seabooks. by appt., mail order, lists/catalogues. Sea charts.

Lighthouse Books, Michael Slicker, 1735 First Avenue North, St. Petersburg, FL 33713. (813) 822-3278, E-mail: lightbks@interloc.com. shop hours, mail order, fairs, lists/catalogues, appraisal. General; Florida & Caribbean.

Lincoln-Roberts Gallery, Lincoln W. Higgie, 411 Market St., San Diego, CA 92101. (619) 702-5884. shop hours, mail order, appraisal. World, U.S., to 19th century.

Little Hundred Gallery, Paul Whitfield, 1500 East Fourth Street, Charlotte, NC 28204. (704) 372-8322, Fax (704) 372-1954. by appt., mail order, lists/catalogues.

Lombard Antiquarian Maps & Prints, R.T. Lombard, Jr. & Sally C. Lombard, P.O. Box 281, Cape Elizabeth, ME 04107. (207) 799-1889, Fax (207) 799-9593, E-mail: rtl@lombardmaps.com, Web: www.lombardmaps.com. by appt., mail order, fairs, appraisal. General. [> ½]

Low Country Collectibles Gallery, George L. Timmons III, 32 Palmetto Bay Rd., Hilton Head Island, SC 29928. (803) 842-8543, Fax same. shop hours, fairs, appraisal. General; Southeastern U.S.

Phyllis Lucas Gallery, Peter B. Lucas, 981 Second Ave., New York, NY 10022. (800) 749 2545, Fax (212) 753 1441. shop hours, mail order.

Lyons Ltd. Antique Prints, Charles & Leila Lyons, 75 Arbor Road, Menlo Park, CA 94025. (800) Lyons Ltd; (650) 325-9010, Fax (650) 325-8332, E-mail: lyonsltd@gte.net, Web: www.dir-dd.com/lyons.html. shop hours, mail order, fairs, lists/catalogues.

G.B. Manasek, Inc., F.J. Manasek, Box 1204, Norwich, VT 05055-1204. (802) 649-1722, Fax (802) 649-2256, E-mail: manasekinc@aol.com. by appt., mail order, fairs, lists/catalogues. [> ½]

Prints Old & Rare / Manning's Books & Prints, Kathleen Manning, 580 M Crespi Dr., Pacifica, CA 94114. (415) 621-3565, (415) 355-6325, Fax (415) 355-1851. shop hours, mail order, fairs, lists/catalogues. Also 209 Corbett, San Francisco, CA 94044. [> ½]

The Map Store, Mike McGuire, 5821 Karric Square Dr., Dublin, OH 43016. (614) 792-6277, Fax (614) 792-9132. shop hours, mail order. General; Ohio. [> ½]

Map World, Dave Moser, 123-D N. El Camino Real, Encinitas, CA 92024. (619) 942-9642, in CA (800) 246-MAPS, Fax (619) 942-3229. shop hours, mail order, lists/catalogues. Pacific Rim, American West.

United States Dealers

Mappamundi, Eric Groot, 7006 York Road, Baltimore, MD 21212. (410) 828-6825, Fax (410) 828-6870. by appt., mail order. Pre-1750 maps. [> ½]

† **Maps of Antiquity**, Lynn Vigeant, 160 Midland Ave., Montclair, NJ 07042. (973) 744-4364, mail order, lists/catalogues, appraisal. Also May-Oct.: 1022 Route 6A, West Barnstable, MA 02668; (508) 362-7169. shop hrs. General; township maps of Northeastern states. [> ½]

Maps of Texas, Robert Storey, P.O. Box 12761, Austin, TX 78711. (512) 837-1915, Fax (512) 491-6177, E-mail: mapsoftx@earthlink.net / texas.data.net/mapsoftexas/.

Maps of the Holy Land, Howard I. Golden, 305 Madison Ave., 46th Floor, New York, NY 10165. (212) 682-2300, Fax (212) 922-1353, E-mail: manpartners@delphi.com. by appt., mail order, lists/catalogues. Holy Land. [> ½]

Margolis & Moss, David Margolis, P.O. Box 2042, Santa Fe, NM 87504. (505) 982-1028, Fax (505) 982-3256, E-mail: mmbooks@rt66.com. by appt., mail order, fairs, lists/catalogues.

Douglas W. Marshall, 545 University Pl., Grosse Pointe, MI 48230. (313) 882-6322, Fax (313) 974-7102. by appt., mail order. North America; Great Lakes. [> ½]

† **Martayan Lan Inc.**, 48 E. 57th St., New York, NY 10022. (800) 423-3741, (212) 308-0018, Fax (212) 308-0074, E-mail: martlan@aol.com, Web: www.dir-dd.com/martayan-lan.html/. shop hours, mail order, fairs, lists/catalogues, appraisal. General. [> ½]

Mickler's Antiquarian Books, Georgine J. Mickler, P.O. Box 660038, Chuluota, FL 32766-0038. (407) 365-3636, Fax (407) 365-8798. by appt., mail order, lists/catalogues. Florida related.

J.T. Monckton, Ltd., Jack Monckton, 1050 Gage St., Winnetka, IL 60093. (847) 446-1106, Fax (847) 446-1103, E-mail: mapman1050@aol.com. shop hours, mail order, lists/catalogues, appraisal. General; world. [> ½]

Kenneth Nebenzahl, Inc., Ken & Jossy Nebenzahl, P.O. Box 370, Glencoe, IL 60022. (847) 835-0515, Fax (847) 835-0519. by appt., mail order, fairs. World, America, Asian regions, 19th c. Trans-Mississippi West. [> ½]

New Albion Island Classics, Sally & Louis Lewis, P.O. Box 390, Diablo, CA 94528. (510) 893-7543, Fax (510) 452-2804. by appt., mail order. General. [> ½]

New World Maps, Inc., Charles R. Neuschafer, Apple Hill Road, Bennington, VT 05201-9544. (802) 442-2846, E-mail: charlieneu@aol.com / pages.prodigy.com/maproom. by appt., mail order, fairs, lists/catalogues. General; early highway maps. [> ½]

Cheryl M. Newby Inc., 5001 N. Kings Highway, Myrtle Beach, SC 29577. (800) 435-2733, (803) 449-4157, Fax (803) 449-1007. shop hours, mail order, lists/catalogues.

Newman's Books & Maps, Alfred W. Newman, 1414 Mariposa St., Vallejo, CA 94590. (707) 642-9091, Fax (707) 642-9275. by appt. Californiana. [> ½]

Nineteenth Century Imprints, Elisabeth Burdon, 2732 S.E. Woodward St., Portland, OR 97202. (503) 234-3538, Fax (503) 238 7988, E-mail: imprints@oldimprints.com, www.oldimprints.com. by appt., mail order, fairs, lists/catalogues. General: Northwest.

North Shore Arts, Bob & Marian Teplin, 339 Woodlyn Dr., Mequon, WI 53092. (414) 241-5704, Fax (414) 241-1126, E-mail: rteplin@execpc.com.

Northern Map Company, Miss Victoria Bates, P.O. Box 129, Dunnellon, FL 34430-0129. (800) 314-2474, Fax (352) 489-1002. shop hours, mail order, lists/catalogues. World & U.S. battle plans; American West; Railroad maps; Geneology. [> ½]

Oakdale Maps, Bill Landefeld, 2048 Lenape Unionville Rd., Kennett Square, PA 19348. (800) 291-1996, Fax (610) 347-2423, E-mail: oakdalemap@aol.com. by appt., mail order, fairs, appraisal. Americas; Africa. [> ½]

The Observatory, 235 Second Street, Juneau, AK 99801. (907) 586-9676, Fax (907) 586-9606, E-mail: deelong@alaska.net. shop hours, mail order, appraisal. General; Alaska; Siberia, Tartary. [> ½]

Oinonen Book Auctions, Richard E. Oinonen, P.O. Box 470, Sunderland, MA 01375. (413) 665-3253, Fax (413) 665-8790, , lists/catalogues. auction. Occasional maps.

Old Ink, Jan Hanna, 25 High Street, Belfast, ME 04915-1511. (207) 338-1209. by appt., mail order, fairs. General. Also at Seaport Antique Mall, Rt. 1, Searsport, ME

† **The Old Map Gallery**, Paul F.Mahoney, 1746 Blake St., Denver, CO 80202. (303) 296-7725, Fax (303) 296-7936, E-mail: oldmapgallery@denver.net, Web: www.oldmapgallery.com. shop hours, mail order, fairs, lists/catalogues, appraisal. [> ½]

† **Old Maps and Prints**, Preston & Petra Figley, P.O. Box 2234, Fort Worth, TX 76113. (817) 923-4535, Fax (817) 923-9375. by appt., mail order, lists/catalogues, appraisal. North America, West, Southwest, Texas. [> ½]

† **The Old Print Gallery, Inc.**, Judith Blakely, 1220 31st St., N.W., Washington, DC 20007. (202) 965-1818, Fax (202) 965-1869. shop hours, mail order, lists/catalogues, appraisal. General.

† **The Old Print Shop, Inc.**, Harry, Robert & Kenneth Newman, 150 Lexington Ave., New York, NY 10016. (212) 683-3950, Fax (212) 779 8040. shop hours, fairs, lists/catalogues, appraisal. General; the Americas.

† **Old World Mail Auctions**, Curt & Marti Griggs, 671 Highway 179, Sedona, AZ 86336. (800) 664-7757; (520) 282-3944, Fax (520) 282-3945, E-mail: owma@oldmaps.com, Web: www.oldmaps.com. auction. [> ½]

Orbis Maps, Katherine McCormick, 1050 Barlow Rd., Hudson, OH 44236. (440) 528-0566. by appt., mail order, fairs, lists/catalogues, appraisal. General; Ohio. [> ½]

United States Dealers

Overlee Farm Books, Martin Torodash, Box 1155, Stockbridge, MA 01262. (413) 637 2277. by appt., mail order, lists/catalogues. Cartographic reference works; atlases. [> ½]

Pacific Book House, 435 Atkinson Dr., Honolulu, HI 96814.

Pacific Shore Maps, Richard Cloward, 5664 Menorca Dr., San Diego, CA 92124-1104. (619) 571-2031, Fax same, E-mail: psmaps@electriciti.com, Web: www.electriciti.com/psmaps. by appt., mail order, fairs, lists/catalogues. Pacific Rim countries; Coast Survey; Southwest U.S. [> ½]

† **Ridler Page Rare Maps**, 205 King St., Charleston, SC 29401. (803) 723-1734, Fax same. shop hours, mail order, lists/catalogues, appraisal. General; Southeast. [> ½]

Pageant Book & Print Shop, Shirley Solomon, 114 W. Houston St., New York, NY 10012. (212) 674-5296, Fax (212) 674-2609. Web: www.pageantbooks.com. shop hours, fairs. N.Y.C. & metropolitan area.

Paulus Swaen Old Maps & Prints, Pierre W.A. Joppen, P.O. Box 1238, Indian Rocks Beach, FL 34635. (813) 596 8734, Fax same. by appt., mail order, fairs, lists/catalogues. see Netherlands entry. [> ½]

Scott Petersen, P.O. Box 384, Kenilworth, IL 60043. (847) 251-4909, Fax (847) 251-6907, E-mail: swpetersen@compuserve.com. by appt., mail order, lists/catalogues. General; mostly historical manuscripts.

† **The Philadelphia Print Shop, Ltd.**, Christopher W. Lane & Donald Cresswell, 8441 Germantown Ave., Philadelphia, PA 19118. (215) 242-4750, Fax (215) 242-6977, E-mail: philaprint@philaprintshop.com, Web: philaprintshop.com. shop hours, mail order, fairs, lists/catalogues, appraisal. General.

The Portsmouth Bookshop, Brian DiMambro, 1 Islington St., Portsmouth, NH 03801. (603) 433-4406, Fax (603) 433-0901. shop hours, mail order. General, c.1750-1880.

† **Primitive Pieces**, Christoper G. Muscavage, 537 W. Franklin St., Slatington, PA 18080. (610) 760-0470, E-mail: ppieces@pdt.net. by appt., mail order, fairs, lists/catalogues. General. [> ½]

The Prints & The Pauper, Roger Genser, P.O. Box 5133, Santa Monica, CA 90409-5133. (310) 392-5582. by appt., mail order, fairs, lists/catalogues, appraisal. General; pre-1800 Western Hemisphere.

Ptolemaeus Antiquarian Maps, Charts & Plans, Bruce F. DeVine, 1243 Rossmoyne Ave., Glendale, CA 91207. (818) 507-1201. by appt., mail order, fairs, appraisal. General 16-19 c. [> ½]

Charles Edwin Puckett, 3767 Forest Lane, Suite 124-445, Dallas, TX 75244-7100. (214) 351-3242, Fax (214) 351-3018, E-mail: cepuckett@compuserve.com. by appt., mail order, fairs, lists/catalogues. Early World, New World, America, Southwest, Texas. [> ½]

William Reese Co., 409 Temple St., New Haven, CT 06511. (203) 789-8081, Fax (203) 865-7653, E-mail: coreese@reeseco.com, Web: www.reeseco.com. by appt., mail order, fairs, lists/catalogues. American West.

Reid & Wright Books, Rodger Reid, 287 New Milford Turnpike, New Preston, CT 06777. (860) 868-7706, Fax (860) 868-1242, E-mail: reidbook@snet.net. shop hours, appraisal. General.

Riddell Rare Maps & Fine Prints, Royd Riddell, 2607 Routh St., Dallas, TX 75201. (214) 953-0601, Fax 214-953-0869, E-mail: map@why.net. shop hours, mail order, fairs, lists/catalogues, appraisal. World, Americana, Western, Texana, RR & geological; 16 19th c. [> ½]

† **George Ritzlin**, Maps & Prints, 469 Roger Williams Ave., Highland Park, IL 60035. (847) 433-2627, Fax (847) 433-6389. shop hours, by appt., mail order, fairs, lists/catalogues, appraisal. General, 15-19th c.; cartographic reference books. [> ½]

River Gallery, Maureen Kahoun, 61 W. Clinton St., Joliet, IL 60431. (815) 749-5996, Fax (708) 349-1038. shop hours, fairs, lists/catalogues. [> ½]

Cedric L. Robinson, Booksellers, Cedric L. & William F. Robinson, 597 Palisado Ave., Windsor, CT 06095. (860) 688-2582. by appt., mail order, lists/catalogues, appraisal. General pre-1900; Western hemisphere.

† **George Robinson**, Old Prints & Maps, 124-D Bent St., Taos, NM 87571. (505) 758-2278, Fax (505) 758-1606. shop hours, mail order, lists/catalogues, appraisal. General; early miniature maps. [> ½]

Robert Ross, Antiquarian Maps,, Views & Related Books, P.O. Box 8362, Calabasas, CA 91372. (818) 348-7867, Fax same, E-mail: rossmaps@earthlink.net, Web: www.abaa-booknet.com/usa/ross. by appt., mail order, fairs, lists/catalogues, appraisal. [> ½]

Barry Lawrence Ruderman, Old Historic Maps & Prints, 6141 Soledad Mountain Road, La Jolla, CA 92037. (619) 551-8500, Fax (619) 456-4095, E-mail: blr@raremaps.com, Web: www.raremaps.com. by appt., mail order, fairs, lists/catalogues, appraisal. [> ½]

Ken Sanders, Books, P.O. Box 26707, Salt Lake City, UT 84126. (801) 467-1490, Fax (801) 467-1495. by appt., mail order, fairs, lists/catalogues. American West; Utah, the Mormons.

John Scopazzi Gallery, Jill A. Scopazzi, 130 Maiden Lane, San Francisco, CA 94108-5302. (415) 362-5708, Fax same. shop hours, by appt.[> ½]

Sherwood's Gallery, 2618 Briar Ridge Dr., Houston, TX 77057-4534. (713) 974-3700. shop hours, by appt., mail order, lists/catalogues. America; Texas. [> ½]

Dorothy Sloan, Rare Books, P.O. Box 49670, Austin, TX 78765-9670. (512) 477-8442, Fax (512) 477-8602, E-mail: sloanbooks@dsloan.com, Web: www.dsloan.com. by appt., mail order, lists/catalogues, appraisal, auction.

Solomon's Antique Maps, Ed Solomon, 1641 N.W. 19th Terrace, CB 131 46A, Delray Beach, FL 33445. (951) 274-4545, mail order, lists/catalogues, appraisal. Pre-1850 maps; geographies; map references. [> ½]

United States Dealers

The Jean Spedden Gallery, Ltd., 73 Broad St., P.O. Box 13446, Charleston, SC 29422-3446. (803) 571-0199.
David R. Spivey, Books, Old Maps, Fine Art, 825 Westport Road, Kansas City, MO 64111. (816) 753-0520, Fax (816) 753-6140, E-mail: spiveybook@delphi.com. shop hours, mail order, fairs.
Carolyn Staley - Fine Prints, 313 First Avenue South, Seattle, WA 98104. (206) 621-1888, Fax (206) 325-9046. shop hours, mail order, fairs, lists/catalogues, appraisal. Very small stock.
Harry L. Stern, Ltd., Suite 2506, 919 N. Michigan Ave., Chicago, IL 60611. (312) 337-1401, Fax (312) 214-2510. by appt., mail order, appraisal. Maps & charts of the Americas. [>½]
†**Thomas & Ahngsana Suarez**, Rare Maps & Prints, 225 Warren Avenue, Hawthorne, NY 10532. (914) 741-6155, Fax (914) 741-6156, E-mail: suarez@mci2000.com+. by appt., mail order, fairs, lists/catalogues, appraisal. World, America, Far East.
Susan Benjamin Rare Prints & Maps, Benjamin & Susan Caughey, Fig Tree Farms, 13721 W. Telegraph Ave., Santa Paula, CA 93060. (805) 933-3193, Fax same, E-mail: suben@west.net. shop hours, mail order, fairs, lists/catalogues. [>½]
Bernard Sussman, 565 Sanctuary Dr., B104, Longboat Key, FL 34228. (941) 383-5823, Fax same, E-mail: photour@aol.com. by appt. General. [>½]
Swan Creek Maps Prints & Books, P.O. Box 972, Maumee, OH 43537. (419) 866-4989, E-mail: oldmap@aol.com. mail order, lists/catalogues, appraisal. Pre-1700 maps & atlases. [>½]
†**Swann Galleries, Inc.**, 104 E. 25th St., New York, NY 10010. (212) 254-4710, Fax (212) 979-1017, E-mail: SwannSales@aol.com. auction.
Sykes & Flanders, P.O. Box 86, Weare, NH 03281.
William R. Talbot Fine Art, 129 W. San Francisco St., P.O. Box 2757, Santa Fe, NM 87504. (505) 982-1559, Fax (505) 820-1044. shop hours, mail order, lists/catalogues, appraisal. General 16-19th c.; Amer. West; Texas. [>½]
Henry G. Taliaferro, 110 W. 80th St., New York, NY 10024. (212) 595-0289.
Taylor Clark Gallery, George Clark, 2623 Government St., Baton Rouge, LA 70806. (504) 383-4929, Fax (504) 383-3043. shop hours, by appt., mail order, appraisal. Louisiana Territory & State; Gulf Coast; southern states.
Jeffrey Thomas, Fine & Rare Books, 49 Geary St., Suite 230, San Francisco, CA 94108. (415) 956-3272, Fax (415) 956-2738, E-mail: finebks@jeffreythomas.com. shop hours, mail order, fairs, lists/catalogues. Few maps.
Trade Winds Gallery, Thomas K. Aalund, 20 W. Main St., Mystic, CT 06355. (860) 536-0119. shop hours, mail order. [>½]
Unicorn Bookshop, James Dawson, P.O. Box 154, Trappe, MD 21673. (410) 476-3838. shop hours, mail order. Maryland, Chesapeake Bay.
Paul Victorius Framing Shop, Richard B. Freeman, 1413 University Ave., Charlottesville, VA 22903. (804) 296-3456, (804) 293-3342. shop hours.
Washington Square Gallery Ltd., Joseph N. Pattison IV, 221 Chestnut St., #100, Philadelphia, PA 19106. (215) 923-8873, Fax (215) 592-8989, E-mail: iciconst@erols.com. shop hours, mail order, fairs, lists/catalogues. General.
†**Waverly Auctions Inc.**, Dale A. Sorenson, 4931 Cordell Ave., Bethesda, MD 20814. (301) 951-8883, Fax (301) 718-8375. shop hours, by appt., lists/catalogues, appraisal, auction.
Ann H. Wells, Rare Tennessee Maps, 117 Prospect Hill, Nashville, TN 37205. (615) 383-2767, Fax same. by appt., mail order, lists/catalogues, appraisal. Tennessee.
The World Map Co., Randall A. Detro, 2407 Highway 18 (rear), P.O. Box 340, Edgard, LA 70049-0340. (504) 497-3042, Fax (504) 497-8757. by appt., mail order, fairs, lists/catalogues, appraisal. General from 1500; World, North America pre-1820. [>½]
The Yellow Room, Jonathan Blackman, 511 N. Robertson Blvd., West Hollywood, CA 90048. (310) 274-3190, Fax (310) 274-0129, E-mail: globemeister@msn.com, Web: www.globemeister.com. shop hours, by appt., mail order. Globes.
Yellowhouse Gallery, John H. Sandberg, 2902 S. Virginia Dare Trail, P.O Box 554, Nags Head, NC 27959. (252) 441-6928, E-mail: yelnag@pinnacle.com, Web: www.yellowhousegallery.com. shop hours, mail order. Civil War maps. [>½]
Yesterday's Gallery, P.O. Box 154, East Woodstock, CT 06244. (860) 928-1216, mail order, fairs. General.
Yesteryear Book Shop, Inc., Frank Walsh & Polly Fraser, 3201 Maple Dr., N.E., Atlanta, GA 30305. (404) 237-0163, Fax (404) 365-0441. shop hours, mail order, fairs, lists/catalogues, appraisal. General, 17-19 c.; Southeastern U.S., Georgia.
Yu Heng Art Co., Donald Sheff, 303 East 57th St., Suite 38E, New York, NY 10022. (212) 838-2126, Fax (212) 867-8122, E-mail: 71670.3626@compuserve.com. by appt., mail order. World, 15-17 c.; New York, 16-18 c.; Celestials. [>½]

United States Dealers by State and City

For complete information, see United States dealers in Alphabetical Order above.

ALABAMA
Birmingham	Antique Art Exchange
Fort Payne	Antique Map Company
Huntsville	Chartwell Mapsellers

ALASKA
Juneau	The Observatory

ARIZONA
Scottsdale	The Antiquarian Shop
Sedona	Compass Rose Gallery
Sedona	Old World Mail Auctions
Tucson	Here Be Dragons

CALIFORNIA
Burlingame	Historicana
Calabasas	Robert Ross, Antiquarian Maps
Diablo	New Albion Island Classics
Encinitas	Map World
Glendale	Ptolemaeus Antiquarian Maps
La Jolla	Early American History Auctions
La Jolla	Barry Lawrence Ruderman
Los Angeles	Houle Rare Books & Autographs
Menlo Park	Lyons Ltd. Antique Prints
Pacifica	Manning's Books & Prints
Port Hueneme	Antique Geography
San Diego	Lincoln-Roberts Gallery
San Diego	Pacific Shore Maps
San Francisco	Acquitania Gallery
San Francisco	W. Graham Arader III
San Francisco	Argonaut Book Shop
San Francisco	California Book Auction Galleries
San Francisco	Dennis Clare
San Francisco	John Scopazzi Gallery
San Francisco	Jeffrey Thomas
Santa Monica	The Prints & The Pauper
Santa Paula	Susan Benjamin Rare Prints
Vallejo	Newman's Books & Maps
W. Hollywood	The Yellow Room

COLORADO
Boulder	Art Source International
Denver	The Old Map Gallery

CONNECTICUT
Branford	Branford Rare Books
E. Woodstock	Yesterday's Gallery
Essex	Latitudes
Mystic	Trade Winds Gallery
New Haven	William Reese Co.
New Preston	Reid & Wright Books
Norfolk	Anderson Antiquarian Maps
Orange	Einhorn Associates
Storrs	Indian Ocean Books & Maps
Windsor	Cedric L. Robinson, Booksellers

DELAWARE
Lewes	Cape James Antiquarian Books
Ocean View	Antique Prints Ltd.
Wilmington	Buxbaum Geographics

DISTRICT OF COLUMBIA
Washington	The Holy Land
Washington	The Old Print Gallery, Inc.

FLORIDA
Chuluota	Mickler's Antiquarian Books
Delray Beach	Solomon's Antique Maps
Dunnellon	Northern Map Company
Indian Rocks	Paulus Swaen Old Maps & Prints
Longboat Key	Bernard Sussman
Osprey	Kit S. Kapp
St. Augustine	John Bouvier Maps & Prints
St. Petersburg	Lighthouse Books
South Miami	Antique Maps & Prints, Inc.
Tampa	First of Florida Maps

GEORGIA
Athens	Heirloom Book Store
Atlanta	C. Dickens
Atlanta	Gallery 515
Atlanta	The Historian's Gallery
Atlanta	Yesteryear Book Shop, Inc.
Blue Ridge	Appalachian Arts
Savannah	V. & J. Duncan

HAWAII
Honolulu	Pacific Book House
Lahaina, Maui	Lahaina Printsellers Ltd.
Lawai	Kauai Fine Arts

ILLINOIS
Chicago	Harry L. Stern, Ltd.
Glencoe	Kenneth Nebenzahl, Inc.
Highland Park	Graton & Graton
Highland Park	George Ritzlin
Joliet	River Gallery
Kenilworth	Scott Petersen
Lemont	Heritage Guild
Winnetka	J.T. Monckton, Ltd.

LOUISIANA
Baton Rouge	Taylor Clark Gallery
Edgard	The World Map Co.
New Orleans	The Centuries

MAINE
Belfast	Old Ink
Brunswick	Grace Galleries, Inc.
Cape Elizabeth	Lombard Antiquarian Maps
Portland	Emerson Booksellers
Wells	Douglas N. Harding

MARYLAND
Baltimore	Camelot Books
Baltimore	Craig Flinner Gallery
Baltimore	Mappamundi
Bethesda	Waverly Auctions Inc.
Trappe	Unicorn Bookshop

MASSACHUSETTS
Amherst	Amherst Antiquarian Maps
Boston	Haley & Steele
Fairhaven	Edward J. Lefkowicz, Inc.
Hatfield	Thomas Edward Carroll
N. Abington	Antiques Americana
Stockbridge	Overlee Farm Books
Sunderland	Oinonen Book Auctions
Waltham	Bickerstaff's

MICHIGAN
Belmont	Clifton F. Ferguson
Grosse Pointe	Douglas W. Marshall

MISSOURI
Kansas City	David R. Spivey
St. Louis	Phyllis Y. Brown
Warrenton	Herb's Old Prints

NEVADA
Las Vegas	Bob Coffin Books

NEW HAMPSHIRE
Portsmouth	The Portsmouth Bookshop
Weare	Sykes & Flanders

NEW JERSEY
Hoboken	E. Greene Gallery
Montclair	Maps of Antiquity
Princeton	Joseph J. Felcone Inc.
Wyckoff	Brenwassser Studio

NEW MEXICO
Santa Fe	Dumont Maps & Books
Santa Fe	Richard Fitch
Santa Fe	Margolis & Moss
Santa Fe	William R. Talbot Fine Art
Taos	George Robinson

NEW YORK
Bedford	Clive A. Burden Inc.
Garrison	Antipodean Books Maps & Prints
Hawthorne	Thomas & Ahngsana Suarez
Ithaca	Historic Urban Plans, Inc.
Millbrook	Front Street Antiques
New York	W. Graham Arader III
New York	Argosy Gallery
New York	Richard B. Arkway, Inc.
New York	Bill George International
New York	El Cascajero
New York	George D. Glazer
New York	Phyllis Lucas Gallery
New York	Maps of the Holy Land
New York	Martayan Lan Inc.
New York	The Old Print Shop, Inc.
New York	Pageant Book & Print Shop
New York	Swann Galleries, Inc.
New York	Henry G. Taliaferro
New York	Yu Heng Art Co.
Old Field	JoAnn & Richard Casten Ltd.
Rye	High Ridge Books, Inc.
Rye Brook	Sy Amkraut

NORTH CAROLINA
Charlotte	Little Hundred Gallery
Nags Head	Yellowhouse Gallery

OHIO
Bay Village	Bay Books
Caldwell	Duck Creek Books
Cleveland	Cleveland Antiquarian Books
Dublin	The Map Store
Hudson	Orbis Maps
Maumee	Swan Creek Maps Prints & Books

OREGON
Corvallis	Don Leeper
Portland	Nineteenth Century Imprints

PENNSYLVANIA
Doylestown	Heritage Antique Maps
Kennett Square	Oakdale Maps
King of Prussia	W. Graham Arader III
Lititz	Heritage Map Museum
Philadelphia	W. Graham Arader, III Gallery
Philadelphia	The Philadelphia Print Shop
Philadelphia	Washington Square Gallery
Pittsburgh	The Lamp
Slatington	Primitive Pieces
West Chester	The Cartophile
Wyomissing	Gary Kunkelman

RHODE ISLAND
N. Providence	The Atlas

SOUTH CAROLINA
Charleston	Ridler Page Rare Maps
Charleston	The Jean Spedden Gallery, Ltd.
Hilton Head Is.	Low Country Collectibles Gallery
Myrtle Beach	Cheryl M. Newby Inc.
Spartanburg	Robert M. Hicklin Jr., Inc.

TENNESSEE
Halls	Murray Hudson
Nashville	Ann H. Wells

TEXAS
Austin	Maps of Texas
Austin	Dorothy Sloan, Rare Books
Dallas	Charles Edwin Puckett
Dallas	Riddell Rare Maps & Fine Prints
Fort Worth	Old Maps and Prints
Houston	W. Graham Arader III
Houston	Sherwood's Gallery

UTAH
Salt Lake City	Goreham Collectibles
Salt Lake City	Ken Sanders, Books

VERMONT
Bennington	New World Maps, Inc.
E. Middlebury	Cartographics of Vermont
Norwich	G.B. Manasek, Inc.

VIRGINIA
Charlottesville	Paul Victorius Framing Shop
Petersburg	Cartographic Arts
Richmond	Chartifacts
Williamsburg	The Bookpress

WASHINGTON
Bainbridge Is.	Fleetstreet
Eastsound	Darvill's Rare Print Shop
Seattle	Carolyn Staley - Fine Prints
Vancouver	Deja View Antique Maps & Prints

WISCONSIN
Brookfield	The James K. Beier Co.
Cambridge	T.S. Hotter Gallery
Mequon	North Shore Arts

WYOMING
Cheyenne	Far West Trading Company

International Dealers Alphabetically within Country

† indicates that dealer's catalogue was used in the *Price Listing*
[> ½] dealers indicated that over 50% of business is in antique maps or closely related

ARGENTINA
Enrique Martinez, Maps & Prints, Elfein 3951 - 6 p.E, CP. 1636. (54) 1 743 3342, Fax same.

AUSTRALIA
† **Gowrie Galleries Pty Ltd.**, Simon Dewez, 316 Oxford St., Woollahra, Sydney, NSW 2025. 9-387 4581 (02), Fax 9-389 0640 (02). E-mail: maps@sydney.net. shop hours, mail order, fairs, lists/catalogues, appraisal. World, pre-1800; Australia; Pacific; Southeast Asia [> ½]
Tim McCormick Rare Books, Box 391, Woollahra, Sydney, NSW 2025. 612 9363-5383, Fax 612 9326-2752. shop hours, mail order, fairs, lists/catalogues. Australiana.
Robert Muir, Old & Rare Books, 15 / 145 Stirling Highway, Nedlands, WA 6009. (09) 386 5842, Fax (09) 386 8211, E-mail: muir@merriweb.com.au, Web: merriweb.com.au/muir. shop hours, mail order, fairs, lists/catalogues, appraisal. Western Australia.
The Old Bookroom, Barbara & Sally Burdon, Belconnen Churches Centre, Benjamin Way, Belconnen, ACT 2617. (062) 251 5191, Fax (062) 251 5536. shop hours, mail order, fairs.
Gaston Renard Fine & Rare Books, Julien Renard, 51 Sackville St., Collingwood, Victoria 3066. +61 3 9417 1044, Fax +61 3 9417 3285, E-mail: booksaus@anzaab.com.au. shop hours, mail order, fairs, lists/catalogues.
† **Spencer Scott Sandilands**, 546 High St., East Prahran, Melbourne, Victoria 3181. 61(3) 9529 8011, Fax 61(3) 9521 1754. shop hours, mail order, fairs, lists/catalogues, appraisal. [> ½]
Terra Australis Antique Maps & Prints Pty Ltd, Nigel J. Tully, 2/10 Hazelbank Rd., Wollstonecraft, NSW 2065. 02-9929 6510. by appt., mail order, appraisal. Australia, Pacific, Japan. [> ½]
Ulimaroa, Prof. Robert Clancy, Box 48, New Lambton, NSW 2305. 6149-296 277, Fax 6149-252 169, by appt., mail order. Australia; Antarctic. [> ½]

BAHAMAS
Balmain Antiques, Jonathan C.B. Ramsay, F.R.G.S., 1st Fl., Masonic Bldg., 308 Bay St., P.O. Box N-9562, Nassau. 809-323-7421, Fax same. shop hours, mail order, fairs. Bahamas, West Indies. [> ½]

BELGIUM
Elisabeth Hermans, Old Prints, Grote Zavel, 8-9, B4, Grand Sablon, B 1000 Brussels. Fax 011.31.66.96. shop hours, appraisal. [> ½]
Antiquariaat Logenhaghen, Philippe Swolfs, Nieuwe Steenweg 31, 9140 Elversele. (32) 52.46.21.19, Fax same. by appt., mail order, fairs. [> ½]
Librairie Moorthamers, Av. Louise 230, Boite 6, 1050 Brussels. 02 647 8548, Fax 02 640 73332. shop hours.
Librairie au Vieux Quartier, Goffin Adrienne, 30, Rue de la Croix, B-5000 Namur. 32-81-22 19 94, Fax same. shop hours, mail order, lists/catalogues. Belgium

BERMUDA
Nicholas Lusher Art & Antiques, No. 68, Phase II, Washington Mall, 22 Church St., Hamilton. (441) 296-2232. shop hours, mail order, fairs, lists/catalogues. Bermuda.
Pegasus Print & Map Shop, Robert F.Lee, P.O. Box 1551, Hamilton 5. (809)-29-5-2900.
Anthony Pettit, P.O. Box FL 318, Flatts Village. (809) 292 2482, Fax (809) 295 5416.

CANADA
The Allery, Cathy Clatworthy, 145 Front Street East, Toronto, Ontario M5A 1E3. (416) 869-9393, Fax (416) 869-9669. shop hours, mail order, appraisal. General.
The Antiquarian Print Room, Caroline Duncan, 840 Fort St., 2nd Floor, Victoria, B.C. V8W 1H8. (250) 380-1343, Fax (250) 384-1805. E-mail: antiquarian@bc.sympatico.ca, Web: victoriabc.com/shopping/antiqmap.htm. shop hours, lists/catalogues. General.
Antique Map-Print Gallery, Prop. Brendan Moss, at "Le Magazin", 110-332 Water St., Gas Town, Vancouver, B.C. V6B 1B6. (250) 662-8171. shop hours, fairs. General, low & mid-priced; Pacific North West; Ireland; England.
The Astrolabe Gallery, John W. Coles, 112 Sparks St., Ottawa, Ontario K1P 5B6. (613) 234-2348. Fax same. shop hours, mail order, fairs. N. America; Canada.
Beach Antique Maps & Prints, Kate & Alec Parley, 3 First Brooke Road, Toronto, Ontario M4E 2L2. (416) 694-8119, Fax (416) 694-2462, E-mail: beachmp@ican.net, Web: home.ican.net/~beachmp. shop hours, mail order. Shop at Harbour Front Antique Market, 390 Queens Quay West, Toronto. [> ½]
Canadiana Fine Arts Ltd., 1208 Belavista Crescent S.W., Calgary, Alberta T2V 2B1. (403) 252-3421. shop hours, mail order. Canadian maps, pre-confederation.

27

International Dealers

Caston Cartographics, Wayne Caston, Antique Maps Division, P.O. Box 839, Waterloo, Ontario N2J 4C2, (519) 884-0314, Fax same.
Judaica Sales Reg'd, Isidore Baum, P.O.B. 55 - St. Martin, Laval, Québec H7V 3P4. (514) 687-0632, Fax (514) 687-3143. by appt., mail order, fairs, lists/catalogues. Holy Land.
Helen R. Kahn Antiquarian Books, P.O. Box 323, Victoria Station, Montréal, Québec. H3Z 2V8. (514) 844-5344, Fax (514) 499-9274, E-mail: hrkahn@core-net.com, Web: www.hrkahnbooks.com. by appt., mail order, fairs, lists/catalogues, appraisal.
Kershaw Old Maps & Prints, Ken Kershaw, 442 Wilson St. East, Ancaster, Ontario L9G 2C3. (905) 648-1991, Fax (905) 304-1037. shop hours, by appt., mail order, fairs, lists/catalogues.
D. & E. Lake Ltd., 239 King St. East, Toronto, Ontario, M5A 1J9. (416) 863-9930, Fax (416) 863-9443. shop hours, mail order, fairs, lists/catalogues. General; North America.
The Loose Page / Juilliard Antiques, J.M. Waibel, 1512 Marine Drive, P.O. Box 91158, West Vancouver, B.C. V7V 3N6. (604) 926-0809, Fax (604) 926-9966. mail order,. appraisal. Asia; Persia.
† **Neil D. MacDonald, Fine Books**, Suite 2B, 27 Davies Ave., Toronto, Ontario M4M 2A9. (416) 778-5332, Fax (416) 778-5327. mail order, lists/catalogues.
The Map Room, L. Sneyd, Exploration House, 18 Birch Ave., Toronto, Ontario, M4V 1C8. (416) 922-5153. shop hours, mail order, lists/catalogues,. appraisal. General maps & globes. [>½]
North by West, Dr. Iain C. Taylor, P.O. Box 70, Dartmouth, Nova Scotia, B2Y 3Y2. (902) 425-0668, Fax (902) 425-1338. by appt., mail order, fairs, lists/catalogues,. appraisal. North America; Atlantic & West Coasts. [>½]
Ptolémée Plus Antique Maps, David Chandler, 11860 Dépatie, Montréal, Québec, H4J 1W5. (514) 334-7418. by appt., mail order, fairs, lists/catalogues. General; New France, Canada. [>½]
Schooner Books, John D. Townsend, 5378 Inglis St., Halifax, Nova Scotia, B3H 1J5. (902) 423-8419, Fax same. shop hours, mail order, fairs, lists/catalogues. Canadiana specialty.
The Wayfarer's Bookshop, Suite 1307, 1323 Homer St., Vancouver, B.C. V6B 5T1. (604) 684-2996, Fax same
Ronald Whistance-Smith, Antique Maps & Prints, 14520 84 Ave. NW, Edmonton, Alberta, T5R 3X2. (403) 483-5858, Fax same, add *51. , by appt., fairs. Canada, British Isles, Austria-Hungary. [>½]
Joyce Williams, Antique Prints & Maps, Joyce Williams & Don Clark, 346 W. Pender St., Vancouver, B.C. V6B 1T1. (604) 688-7434, Fax (604) 530-3079. shop hours, appraisal. General; Western Canada, B.C., Arctic.
Thomas N. Yarmon, 8 King St. East, Toronto, Ontario, M5C 1B5. (416) 363-5086, Fax (416) 363-6845, E-mail: tyarmon@myna.com. by appt., mail order. [>½]

CHANNEL ISLANDS

Channel Islands Galleries Ltd., Trinity Square, Guernsey, Channel Islands. (0481) 723 274.
The Selective Eye Gallery, Warwick Blench, 50 Don St., Saint Helier, Jersey. JE2 4TR +44 1534-25281, Fax +44 1534 58789, E-mail: segart@itl.net, Web: www.desiderata.com/ Selective/. shop hours, mail order, lists/catalogues, appraisal.

DENMARK

Politikens Antikvariat, Peter Daugaard & Erik Finnerup, 37, Raadhuspladsen, DK-1785 Copenhagen V. +33 47 23 97, Fax +33 11 14 10, E-mail: antikvariat@online.pol.dk, Web: www.polantik.dk. shop hours, mail order, fairs, lists/catalogues, appraisal. General; Scandinavia, Arctica.
Kaabers Antikvariat, Alette Kaaber, Skindergade 34, 1159 Kobenhavn. (+45) 33 15 41 77, Fax (+45) 33 93 99 01. shop hours, mail order, lists/catalogues. General.

ENGLAND

Altea Antique Maps & Atlases, Mr. Massimo De Martini, 34 Wentworth Rd., London NW11 0RN. 0181-455 4132, Fax 0181-731 9723, E-mail: altea@dial.pipex.com, Web: dialspace.dial.pipex.com/town/place/pc80. shop hours, mail order, fairs, lists/catalogues. Gallery: Camden Passage Antique Market, 114 Islington High St., London. [>½]
† **Antique Atlas**, W.J. Faupel, 3 Halsford Lane, East Grinstead, West Sussex. RH19 1NY (01) 342-315-813, Fax (01) 342-318-058. by appt., mail order, lists/catalogues, appraisal. General; Americana. [>½]
Ash Rare Books, Laurence Worms, 25 Royal Exchange, Threadneedle St., London EC3V 3LP. 0171-626-2665, Fax 0171-623-9052. shop hours. General; London.
David Bannister FRGS, 26 Kings Rd., Cheltenham, Gloucestershire GL52 6BG. [44] 1242-514 287, Fax [44] 1242-513 890, E-mail: DB@AntiqueMaps.co.uk. by appt., mail order, fairs, appraisal. Early general. [>½]
† **Roderick M. Barron**, 21 Bayham Road, Sevenoaks, Kent TN13 3XD 1732-742 558, Fax same, E-mail: barron@centrenet.co.uk. by appt., mail order, fairs, lists/catalogues, appraisal. Early World, Americana; Asia, Southeast Asia, Far East. [>½]
Steve Bartrick Antique Prints & Maps, Gloucester Antique Centre, Severn Rd., Gloucester, GL1 2LE. (0) 1242 231691, Fax (0) 1242 697881, E-mail: enquiries@antiqueprints.com, Web: www.antiqueprints.com. shop hours.
Baynton-Williams Gallery, Roger Baynton-Williams, 37A High Street, Arundel, W. Sussex BN18 9EL. 01903-883 588, Fax same. shop hours, mail order, lists/catalogues, appraisal. [>½]

International Dealers

D.M. Beach, Anthony Beach, 52 High St., Salisbury, Wiltshire SP1 2PG. 01722-333 801, Fax 01722-333 720. shop hours. General [20% of large shop]

Thomas J. Booth, Antique Maps & Prints, 33 Beaconsfield Rd., Claygate, Esher, Surrey KT10 0PN. 01372-462 764, Fax 01372-462 161. by appt., mail order, appraisal. [>½]

Clive A. Burden Ltd., Elmcote House, The Green, Croxley Green, Rickmansworth, Herts WD3 3HN (0) 1923 772 387 / 778 097, Fax (0) 1923 896 520. by appt., mail order, fairs, lists/catalogues, appraisal. Americas, Australasia, S.E. Asia, U.K. [>½]

Christie's South Kensington, 85 Old Brompton Rd, London SW7 3JS. (0171) 321 3152, Web: www.christies.com. auction.

Coach House Books, M.K. & J.S. Ellingsworth, 17 A Bridge St., Pershore, Worcestershire WR10 1AJ. (01386) 552 801, Fax (01386) 561 389. shop hours, mail order, lists/catalogues. General; Great Britain; counties.

Ivan R. Deverall, Duval House, The Glen, Cambridge Way, Uckfield, Sussex TN22 2AB. (01825) 762 474, lists/catalogues.

Egyptophilia, Pierre Farid Kioumgi, Flat 7, 105 Gloucester Terrace, London W2 3HB. 0171-706 1399, Fax 34-71-639 254 (Spain). by appt., lists/catalogues. Eygpt, Arabia.

Susanna Fisher, Spencer, Upham, Southampton SO32 1JD. 01489-860 291, Fax 01489-860 638. by appt., mail order, lists/catalogues.

J.A.L. Franks Ltd., 7 New Oxford St., London WC1A 1BA. (0171) 405 0274, Fax (0171) 430 1259, E-mail: Jalfranks@btinternet.com. shop hours, mail order, fairs. General; miniatures. [>½]

Garwood & Voigt, Nigel Garwood & Rainer Voigt, 55 Bayham Road, Sevenoaks, Kent TN13 3XE. (01732) 460025, Fax (01732) 460026. by appt., mail order, fairs, lists/catalogues, appraisal. World, America, Asia, Europe, Germany.

Geldart Antique Maps and Prints, Jon Geldart, 13 Oakwood Rd., Wetherby, W. Yorkshire LS22 7QY. 01937-583 385, Fax same. by appt.. Yorkshire; Scotland. [>½]

Mrs. D.M. Green, 7 Tower Grove, Weybridge, Surrey KT13 9LX. 0932-241105.

F. & J. Hogan, 31 Tranmere Rd., Edmonton, London N9 9EJ. 0181-360-6146. shop hours, mail order, fairs, lists/catalogues. General; English speaking areas. [>½]

Stephanie Hoppen Ltd., 17 Walton Street, London SW3. 01-589-3678.

Simon Hunter Antique Maps, 3 Meeting House Lane, Brighton, Sussex BN1 1HB. +44 (0) 1273 746 983, Fax same. shop hours, mail order, fairs, lists/catalogues. General inexpensive. [>½]

InterCol London, Yasha Beresiner, 43 Templars Crescent, London N3 3QR. (181) 349 2207, Fax (181) 346 9539, E-mail: 100447.3341@compuserv.com. shop hours, mail order, fairs, lists/catalogues, appraisal. British counties; curiosities; playing cards. At 114 Islington High St., Camden Passage, London. [>½]

Lee Jackson, (formerly Avril Noble), 2 Southampton St., London WC2E 7HA. 0171-240 1970, Fax same. shop hours, mail order, fairs, appraisal. General. [>½]

Warwick Leadlay Gallery, 5 Nelson Road, Greenwich, London SE10 9JB. (0181) 858 0317, Fax (0181) 853 1773, lists/catalogues.

The Lyver & Boydell Galleries, 15 Castle Street, Liverpool, Merseyside L2 4SX. 0151 236 3256, Fax 0151-227 3293. shop hours, mail order, fairs, appraisal. U.K. county maps; Lancashire, Cheshire.

Magna Gallery, Martin Blant, 41 High St., Oxford OX1 4AP. 01865 245 805. shop hours, mail order, fairs, lists/catalogues, appraisal. English county maps. [>½]

The Map House of London, 54 Beauchamp Pl.,, Knightsbridge, London SW3 1NY. 0171-589 4325, 0171-584 8559, Fax 0171-589 1041, E-mail: maps@themaphouse.com, Web: www.themaphouse.com. , lists/catalogues.

Map World, Jeffrey Sharpe, 25 Burlington Arcade, London W1. 071-495 5377, Fax same. shop hours, appraisal. General. [>½]

Roger Mason, 86A Banbury Rd., Oxford. 0865-59380.

P.J. Morris Antique Maps, 11 The Orchard, Marston Green, West Midlands B37 7DH. (0121) 779 3718, mail order, lists/catalogues. General; British Isles. [>½]

Richard Nicholson of Chester, Stoneydale, Pepper St., Christleton, Chester CH3 7AG. 01244-336 004, Fax 01244-336 138, E-mail: richard@maps.u-net.com, Web: www.antiquemaps.com. General; British Isles. [>½]

O'Flynn Antiquarian Booksellers, D. Francis O'Flynn, 35 Micklegate, York YO1 1JH. 01904-641 404, Fax 01904-611 872. shop hours, mail order, lists/catalogues. General, 15 c.-1900. [>½]

Old Soke Books, Peter & Linda Clay, 68 Burghley Rd., Peterborough PE1 2QE. 01733-64147. shop hours, mail order, fairs. 18c. English county maps.

Paul Orssich, 117 Munster Road, Fulham, London SW6 6DH. 0171 736 3869, Fax 0171 371 9886, E-mail: paulo@orssich.com, Web: www.orssich.com. shop hours, mail order, fairs. Balearic Islands.

The O'Shea Gallery, 120A Mount St., Mayfair, London W1Y 5HB. 0171 629 1122, Fax 0171 629 1116.

Patterson & Liddle, 10 Margaret's Buildings, Brock St., Bath BA1 2LP. 01225-426 722, Fax same. shop hours, mail order. Local English counties.

International Dealers

† **Phillips**, Book Department, 101 New Bond St., London W1Y 0AS. 0171 468 8351, Fax 0171 465 0224, Web: www.phillips-auctions.com/auct/. Map sections in monthly auctions.
Postaprint, W.D.J. Bennett, Taidswood House, Iver Heath, Bucks SL0 0PQ. (+44) 01.895.833.720, Fax (+44) 01.895.834.890, E-mail: Postaprint@btinternet.com, Web: www.postaprint.co.uk. by appt., mail order, lists/catalogues. Office hours. Wide general stock. [>½]
† **Jonathan Potter Ltd.**, 125 New Bond St., London W1Y 9AF. 0171 491 3520, Fax 0171 491 9754, E-mail: jpmaps@ibm.net, Web: www.desiderata.com. shop hours, mail order, fairs, lists/catalogues. General; New World; reference books. [>½]
The Print Cellar, Elizabeth Tremlett, 35 Church St., Ashbourne, Derbyshire DE6 1AE. 01335-342 933. General; Derby & Staffordshire.
The Print Room, John Cumming, 37 Museum St., London WC1A 1LP. (0171) 430 0159, Fax (0171) 831 2874, lists/catalogues.
Professional Views, Philip J.B. Sharpe, 9 Chichester Rents, Chancery Lane, London WC2A 1EG. 171 404 0800, Fax 171 242 1321, E-mail: philip.sharpe@virgin.net. shop hours, mail order, fairs, lists/catalogues. General [>½]
Bernard Quaritch Ltd., 5-8 Lower John St., Golden Square, London W1R 4AU. 01-734-2983.
Sanders of Oxford Ltd., 104 High St., Oxford OX1 4BW. 01865 242 590, Fax 01865 721 748, Web: www.oxlink.co.uk/antiques/sanders.html. shop hours, mail order, fairs.
The Schuster Gallery, Thomas E. Schuster, 14 Maddox St., London W1R 9PL. 071-491 2208, Fax 071-491 9872. shop hours, mail order, fairs. Rare & expensive maps, early town views, panoramas & atlases.
† **Sotheby's Book Dept.**, 34-35 New Bond St., London W1A 2AA. (171) 408 5291, Fax (171) 408 5904, Web: www.sothebys.com. auction.
Stage Door Prints, A.L. Reynolds, 1 Cecil Ct., London WC2N 4E2. 0171-240 1683. shop hours. General.
Storeys Ltd., Timothy Kingswood, 3 Cecil Ct., Charing Cross, London WC2 4E2. 0171 836 3777, Fax 01689 850 274. shop hours, mail order, lists/catalogues. General.
The Swan Gallery, S. Lamb, 51 Cheap St., Sherborne, Dorset DT9 3AX. 01935-814 465, Fax 01308-868 195.
Thornburgh Gallery, Leslie Turner, 17 Nicholas St., York YO1 3EQ. 0904-413 000. by appt., mail order, fairs.
† **Tooley Adams & Co. Ltd.**, Stephen Luck, 13 Cecil Court, Charing Cross Road, London WC2N 4EZ. 0171 240 4406, Fax 0171 240 8058, E-mail: tooleys@btinternet.com, Web: www.btinternet.com/~tooleys. shop hours, mail order, fairs, lists/catalogues. General. [>½]
Jenny Wagstaff, Little Gables, Stoke Close, Stoke D'Abernon, Cobham, Surrey KT11 3AE. +44 (0) 1932 862 511, Fax +44 (0)1932 860 886.
Welland Antique Maps & Prints, R.A. Warner, Lawnwood, Little Bytham near Grantham, Lincs. NG33 4PX. (01780) 410 254.
Edna Whiteson Ltd., 301 Mutton Lane, Potters Bar, Hertfordshire EN6 2AT. 01707 647 716, Fax 01707 660 801. shop hours. by appt., mail order, fairs, lists/catalogues, appraisal. General, 17th-19th c. [>½]
Witch Ball Prints & Maps, Gina Daniels, 48 Meeting House Ln., Brighton, E. Sussex BN2 1HB. (01273) 26618.

FINLAND

Jan Strang, Jatasalmentie 1, FIN-00830 Helsinki. +358-0-755 4929, Fax same. by appt., mail order, fairs, lists/catalogues. Northern Europe. [>½]

FRANCE

Dudragne Librairie, Patrick Dudragne, 86 rue de Maubeuge, 75010 Paris. 33/1/48 78 5095, Fax 33/1/40 05 9804. shop hours, by appt., mail order, fairs, lists/catalogues, auction. Middle East; Palestine; France wine region; America. [>½]
D.R. Lyon Tableaux, - Gravures - Livres Anciens, B.P. 138, 06504 Menton CEDEX. 04 9357 5509, Fax same. by appt., mail order, fairs, appraisal. General; America; pre-1850 Atlases. [>½]
Marianne Katz-Moorthamers, 26 rue Olivier de Serres, 75015 Paris. 33-145 319 498, Fax 33-145 317 133. by appt., mail order, fairs, lists/catalogues. General [>½]
Friedrich Weissert, 22 rue de Savoie, 75006 Paris. 43-29-72-59, Fax 46-34-60-63. shop hours.

GERMANY

F. Dörling GmbH, Neuer Wall 40, 20354 Hamburg. (40) 374 9610, Fax (40) 374 96166, lists/catalogues, auction.
Kunstantiquariat am Gasteig, Adina Sommer, Rosenheimerstr. 8, 81669 München. 089/811 2250, 089/448 6260, Fax 089/811 1336. shop hours, mail order, fairs, lists/catalogues. Early maps & views. [>½]
Antiquariat Granier GmbH, Ilse Granier, Welle 9, D-33602 Bielefeld. (49) 521 6 71 48, Fax (49) 521 6 71 46. shop hours, mail order, fairs. [>½]
Auktionhaus Granier, Jochen Granier, Otto-Brenner Str. 186, D-33604 Bielefeld. (49) 521 28 50 05, Fax (49) 521 28 50 15. shop hours, mail order, lists/catalogues, auction.
Antiquariat Gebr. Haas Ohg, Posfach 1155, D-47547 Bedburg-Hau. (28) 21 6336, Fax (28) 21 6739.
Hartung & Karl, Karolinenplatz 5a, D-8000 Munchen 2.

International Dealers

Kunsthandlung Hattesen, Dr. Peter Goeritz, Holm 76, 24937 Flensburg. 461 / 25077, Fax 461 / 24334. shop hours. [>½]
Antiquariat Ruthild Jaeger, Dr. Eckhard Jaeger, Steinweg 17, D-21635 Lueneburg. 4131-42797, Fax (+49) 4131-42798. by appt., mail order, fairs, lists/catalogues. [>½]
Hans Horst Koch, Buch- und Kunstantiquariat, Ku'damm 216, D-1000 Berlin. 15 030-882-63-60.
Lueder H. Niemeyer, Dorfstrasse 4, D-27632 Pading-buettel. +49 (0) 47 42-21 17, Fax same. shop hours, mail order, lists/catalogues. Sea charts; wall maps.
Reiss & Sohn, Adelheidstrasse 2, D-61462 Königstein. 49-6174-1017, Fax 49-6174-1602, Web: www.reiss-sohn.de. auction.
Kunstantiquariat Monika Schmidt, Zentnerstr. 18; 5th floor, D-80798 München. (49-89) 272 4582, Fax (49-89) 222-315. by appt., mail order, fairs, lists/catalogues. [>½]
Antiquariat Hanno Schreyer, Georg Schreyer, Euskirchener Strasse 57, D-53121 Bonn. +49-228-62 10 59, Fax +49-228-61 30 29. by appt., fairs. 50,000+ items. [>½]
Antiquariat Stenderhoff, Theo Hobbeling, Alter Fischmarkt 21, 48143 Münster (02) 51 447 49, Fax (02) 51 515 26.
Venator & Hanstein KG, im Kunsthaus Lempertz, Cacilienstrasse 48, 50667 Koln (0) 221-2 57 54 19, Fax (0) 221-2 57 55 26. auction
† **H. Th. Wenner Antiquariat**, Heger Str. 2-3, 49074 Osnabrück. (0541) 33 103 66, Fax (0541) 201 113. shop hours, mail order, lists/catalogues, auction.
Zisska & Kistner, Buch-und Kunstauktionhaus, Unterer Anger 15, D-80331 München. (0) 89-26 38 55, Fax (0) 89-26 90 88, auction.

GREECE
Stavros Stavridis, Panaghitsas 20, Kifissia, 14562 Athens. 01-801 7079, Fax 01-808 6227. shop hours, mail order. Greece, Cyprus, Turkey.

HUNGARY
Cartographica Hungarica, Tibor Szathmary, Rudolf utca 1, H-2800 Tatabanya. 00-3634-333010, Fax same.

INDIA
Phillips Antiques, Farooq Issa, Opp. Regal Cinema, Museum, Bombay. 400 001 202 0564 / 282 0782, Fax 202 5579. shop hours. India.

IRELAND
Neptune Gallery, Andrew & Charlotte Bonar Law, 41 S. William St., Dublin 2. 1-671 5021, Fax same. shop hours, fairs, appraisal. Irish maps.

ITALY
Old Times, Le Stampe Antiche, Cesare Giannelli, Via Campo di Marte, 26, 06100 Perugia. 075/7520 18.
Libreria Antiquaria Perini, Ruth Perini, Via Amatore Sciesa 11, 37122 Verona. (045) 803 0073, Fax same.
Valeria Bella Stampe, Mrs. Valeria Bella, Via S. Cecilia 2, 20122 Milano. 02-7600 4413, Fax 02-7600 6505. shop hours, fairs, lists/catalogues.

MALTA
Paul Bezzina, Early Maps & Prints, 114 St. Lawrence St., Vittoriosa. 356-665 812. mail order.

The NETHERLANDS
De Ark, Dr. F. Muller, Suderein 40, 9255 LC Tietjerk. 31 511 432 146, Fax 31 511 432 135. by appt., mail order, fairs, lists/catalogues. Africa; Americas; Asia. [>½]
Asher Rare Books, Zeeweg 264, P.O. Box 258, NL-1970 AG Ijmuiden. +31 255 523 839, Fax +31 255 510 352, E-mail: Asher@Euronet.nl. .
J.L. Beijers B.V., Achter St. Pieter 140, 3512 HT Utrecht. 030-310958, Fax 030-312061. auction.
Cartographica Neerlandica, Dr. Marcel P.R. van den Broecke, Soestdijkseweg 101, 3721 AA Bilthoven. +31-30-220 2396, Fax +31-30-220 3326, E-mail: cart.neer@tip.nl, Web: www.tip.nl/users/cart.neer. by appt., mail order, fairs, lists/catalogues. Ortelius. [>½]
Antiquariaat S. Emmering B.V., Nieuwezijds Voorburgwal 309, 1012 RV Amsterdam. 31.20.623 1476, Fax 31.20.624 5487. shop hours. Holy Land, West Indies.
Leon Helmink, Plompetorengracht 8-G, 3512 CC Untrecht. +31 30 231 3531, Fax +31 65 127 5921, E-mail: helmink@worldonline.nl, Web: home.worldonline.nl/~helmink/index.html. .
B.M. Israel BV, Boekhandel en Antiquariaat, NZ Voorburgwal 264, 1012 RS Amsterdam. 020-624 7040; 020-622 5500, Fax 020-638 2355. shop hours, mail order, fairs. General. [>½]
Firma Loose, R. Loose, Papestraat 3, NL 2513 AV Den Haag. 31 70 346 0404. shop hours, fairs.
Paulus Swaen Old Maps & Prints, Pierre W.A. Joppen, Hofstraat 19, 5664 HS Geldrop. (040) 285 3571, (06) 5319 5323, Fax (040) 285 4075, E-mail: paulus@swaen.com, Web: http://www.swaen.com. by appt., mail order, fairs, lists/catalogues, Internet auctions, P.O.B. 317, 5660 AH Geldrop. see U.S. entry. [>½]

International Dealers

Robert Putman, Antiquarian Maps & Atlases, P.O. Box 70084, 1007 KB Amsterdam. (3102) 6.701.700, Fax (3102) 6.700.350, E-mail: putmap@wxs.nl, Web: www.nvva.nl/putman. by appt., mail order, fairs, lists/catalogues. General; sea charts. [>½]

NEW CALEDONIA
Galerie Ad Lib, Max Sheckleton, B.P. 362, 98845 Noumea Cedex. 687. 284 040, Fax 687. 272 636. by appt., mail order. South Pacific islands.

NEW ZEALAND
Anah Dunsheath, Antiquarian Booksellers, 6 High Street; P.O. Box 4181, Auckland. 64 9 379 0379, Fax 64 9 358 0181. shop hours, mail order, fairs, lists/catalogues. General; South Pacific.
Neil McKinnon Ltd., P.O. Box 847, Timaru. 368 81931, Fax 368 88068. by appt., mail order, lists/catalogues, appraisal, auction. Asia; Australasia; Canada. [>½]

NORWAY
Damms Antikvariat A/S, Claes Nyegaard, Christiana Torv, Akersgt. 2, N-0158 Oslo. +47-22-41-04-02, Fax +47-22-33-66-15. shop hours, mail order, lists/catalogues, appraisal. Arctic; Northern Hemisphere. [>½]

SCOTLAND
Billson of St. Andrews, 15 Greyfriars Garden, St. Andrews, Fife KY16 9HG. (01334) 475063.
The Carson Clark Gallery, Scotia Maps-Mapsellers, 173 Canongate, Edinburgh. EH8 8BN 0131-556-4710, Fax same.
Benny Gillies, 31-33 Victoria St., Kirkpatrick Durham, Castle Douglas. 01556 650 412. shop hours, mail order, fairs, lists/catalogues. Scotland.

SINGAPORE
Antiques of the Orient PTE Ltd., Julie Yeo, 21 Cuscaden Road #01-02, Ming Arcade, Singapore 249720. 65-733 0830, Fax 65-732 8652. shop hours, mail order, fairs, lists/catalogues, appraisal. Southeast Asia. [>½]

SOUTH AFRICA
Jeffrey Sharpe Rare Books, Victoria & Alfred Hotel, Shop No. 1, Waterfront, Cape Town. 021-254 641, Fax 021-790 1430. shop hours, appraisal. Africa. [>½]

SPAIN
Frame SL, Mapas Y Grabados Antiguos, General Pardiñas 69, Madrid 28006. (34.1) 411 3362, Fax (34.1) 564 1520, E-mail: armero@mailhost.nauta.es.
Gonzalo Fernandez Pontes, Nunez de Balboa 19, 28001 Madrid. 34-1-435 8000, Fax same. shop hours, mail order, lists/catalogues, appraisal. Spain; South America. [>½]

SWEDEN
K.M. Flodin & Co. AB, Sture Flodin, Vasterlanggatan 37, S-11129 Stockholm. +46 820 4881, Fax +46 820 6195. shop hours. General; Scandinavia. [>½]
Oson AB, Rolf Ottoson, Verkstadsvagen 21, 5-14170 Huddinge. +46-8-646 8918, Fax +46-8-646 9548. by appt., mail order. Scandinavia.

SWITZERLAND
Antik-Pfister, Old Prints & Maps, Mrs. Jackie Pfister, Antiquariat & Stichgalerie, Wattstr. 3 / Postfach 8129, CH-8050 Zurich 01 / 312 0993. shop hours. by appt., mail order, lists. General; Swiss maps & views.
Helmut Schumann AG, Schweizerische Antiquariat, Ramisstrasse 25, CH-8024 Zurich 01 251 02 72, Fax 01 252 79 61.

TAIWAN
Bipolar International Corp., Oliver Yeh, No.9, Alley 10, Lane 237, Wan Ta Road, 109, Taipei. 2-301 1000, Fax 2-307 7777. by appt., mail order, fairs. Formosa & China only, 1500-1900.

THAILAND
White Lotus Co. Ltd., Diethard Ande, G.O.P. Box 1141, Bangkok. 10501 662-2861100, Fax 662-2131975.

TURKEY
F. Muhtar Katircioglu, Karanfil Araligi 14, Levent, 80620 Istanbul. Anatolia, Ottoman Empire, Constantinople. [>½]

WALES
David Archer, The Pentre, Kerry, Newtown, Montgomeryshire SY16 4PD. 01686 670 382. by appt., mail order. British Ordnance Survey, 1805+ [>½]

On Antique Map Catalogues

The information in *Antique Map Price Record* is drawn from dealers and auction catalogues with prices realized. Dealers and auctioneers are invited to submit their catalogues for possible inclusion in the *Price Record*.

Catalogues vary widely in character. Some are based on extensive research; others are little more than stock lists. Some are graced with lovely color photographs that leave no doubt as to the identity and nature of the item for sale; others rely on text, with few if any illustrations. Most catalogues lie between the extremes. To be sure, preparation of a good catalogue is labor intensive, but it enables a dealer to project the scope and nature of his enterprise.

Appearance and spelling, especially <u>spelling</u>, are revealing as to the care a dealer has taken and his regard for his clientele. Ambiguity in terminology, exemplified by *margin* and *border*, is to be avoided. Conventions, such as height before width (or vice versa) should be made clear.

The organization of the catalogues should be apparent. Some methods in common use are:

1. Chronologically, beginning with the earliest item.
2. Alphabetically by map-maker.
3. Geographically, and chronologically within each region.
4. Geographically, and alphabetically by author within each region.

Regardless of which system is used, the following information should be provided for the customer. It is highly desirable, if not essential, for items included in *Antique Map Price Record*.

Map-Maker: There may be some ambiguity in map authorship. One might cite the cartographer, engraver, publisher, or others associated with the map production. Custom generally dictates the choice. For example, maps in Blaeu's atlases are generally attributed to Blaeu, regardless of engraver or cartographer.

Title: The title should be given verbatim and as fully as possible. A reason is that slight changes might reveal a variant. Bibliographical standards dictate copying the exact spelling and punctuation. With very long titles it is customary in such cases to omit some of the unnecessary verbiage. Ellipses (...) should be used to indicate portions omitted, but place names, dates, and personal names should be retained, since these are of most value in identifying the item. For purposes of the *Price Record*, it is essential to have the exact beginning of the title verbatim since that makes the alphabetical **Title Index** more useful. The following example is illustrative:

> A NEW & ACCURATE CHART OF THE WORLD. DRAWN FROM AUTHENTIC SURVEYS, ASSISTED BY THE MOST APPROVED MODERN MAPS & CHARTS & REGULATED BY ASTRONL. OBSERVATIONS.

A barely acceptable abbreviation might be:

> A NEW & ACCURATE CHART OF THE WORLD ...

Some confusing abbreviations would be:

> A NEW AND ACCURATE CHART OF THE WORLD ...   (& replaced by and)
>
> A NEW & ACCURATE CHART OF THE WORLD ETC.   (Etc. not really part of title)
>
> CHART OF THE WORLD   (Too vague, and no ellipses)
>
> ... CHART OF THE WORLD ...   (Better, but still too vague and hard to alphabetize)
>
> THE WORLD   (Much too vague to identify)

Common problems in title transcription include interchanging '*and*' and '*&*', or '*etc.*' and '*&c.*' or substituting '*U.S.*' for '*United States*'. Map titles can be a confusing mix of lettering styles which may not appear as correct when transcribed. Most dealers just use normal capitalization, or give the title in all capitals. It is a good idea to have the title set off in some manner – by quotes, underlining, boldface type, or some other method – since it is sometimes hard to tell where the title stops and the description begins. When a map has no title, a descriptive title can be supplied in brackets [ ].

Date: The date can be somewhat confusing. For example, a map from a 1587 edition of Ortelius could be dated as **1587**. However, the map may have first appeared in the 1570 edition, and last appeared in the 1612 edition. Ideally, one could explicitly state something like **1570 (1587)**. However, it is sometimes not possible for the dealer to determine the exact edition. In such cases, the date of first publication is often used. If one knows the range, but not the exact date, one might give **1570-1612**. Sometimes it is easier to just explain what is known about the date.

Source: It is helpful to know the source of a map if it was extracted from an atlas or other work. If known it should include the name of the author of that work, the publisher's name and place of publication. It is well to know if the map was published separately.

Dimensions: The dimensions should be given accurately in inches or metric units. Height first, and width second, is the most common system. Dimensions are usually measured to the outside of the border or neat line. When a title or signature appears outside of the border, i.e. in the margin, it is preferable to exclude this from the dimensions, but there is no standard system. Dimensions in the *Price Record* are rounded to the nearest centimeter and half-inch, although there is good reason to be more precise, especially with small maps.

Color: If it is known that coloring is original or "modern", it should be noted. Printed color should be mentioned to distinguish it from the presumption of hand coloring on older maps. When the land areas are wash colored, this is often referred to as *full color*. If the cartouche has been left uncolored on an otherwise fully colored map, it can be specifically mentioned. Outline color usually means that just the boundaries or coastlines are colored.

Condition: If the map is in reasonably typical condition for its age, condition is sometimes omitted. It is advisable to mention noticeable flaws. The customer deserves to know the quality of the paper and if there are tears, separations at the centerfold, spotting (foxing), offsetting, stains, narrow margins, and other flaws. Any repairs should be noted.

References: A huge store of reference books are now available on many facets and subcategories of antiquarian maps. Citation of a reference, especially one which provides a good illustration will do much to unambiguously identify the map and place it in context.

Commentary: This gives the dealer a chance to explain the significance of the map and why a collector should buy it. It is also an opportunity for the dealer to distinguish himself, to display his knowledge of his field and convey it to others.

Illustrations: Nothing sells like a picture. It arouses interest and provides information. Often, details can be checked with the aid of a magnifying glass. Illustrations form the core of some catalogues, accompanied by minimal text. There is little to compare to a professional photograph, but they are expensive and some sensitivity is needed in lay out. Of late, electronic methods of capturing images are advancing rapidly and competing with the conventional photo in dealer's catalogues.

Price: It can (and does) get omitted from time to time. Some dealers provide a separate sheet listing the prices for the items in their catalogue. In such cases, they may be subject to change on short notice.

CUMULATIVE FREQUENCY DISTRIBUTION OF MAP-MAKERS

The purpose of this section is to associate map-makers with the number of entries in the *Price Record* currently and cumulatively attributed to them. The biographical notes are provided to help link a map-maker with a place or time. In some cases the entry that appears may not be that of the most prominent map-maker with a particular surname. For broader and more detailed information, readers are referred to Tooley's *Dictionary of Mapmakers* and Moreland and Bannister's *Antique Maps*, both of which have been essential as a check on information provided for the *Price Record* and both of which are highly recommended.

The *Cumulative Frequency Distribution* table greatly simplifies a search through *Antique Map Price Record,* Volumes 11 throught 15, in quest of entries for a particular map maker and helps to direct one toward the greatest concentration of entries. The distribution for 1983 through 1992 will be found in Volumes 11, 12 and 13.

Total Entries for 1997-98: 5,265   Different Names and Categories in 1997-98: 710

Cumulative Entries since 1983: 70,628   Different Names and Categories since 1983: 2,369

The table includes several categories which are organized by other than the name of the map-maker. These include maps issued by infrequent publishers and organized by *genre*, manuscript maps and items of unknown attribution. Should the reader not find certain kinds of maps under the name of a map-maker, comparable items may turn up in one of the following categories:

Aeronautical Maps & Charts	Japanese Cartography	Military Maps
Anonymous & Unknown	Gov't Maps: Local & State	Mining Maps
Armenian Cartography	Gov' t Maps: National	Nautical Charts
Artifacts	Highway Maps	Puzzles & Games
Chinese Cartography	Local & State Maps	Railroad Company Maps
Company Maps	Local & State *Pocket* Maps	Real Estate & Promotional
Concept Maps	Local & State *Wall* Maps	Spanish-American War
Globes	Manuscript Maps	U.S. Civil War Maps

	Total	'83-'92	'93	'94	'95	'96	'97-8
Abert. U.S. Army; mid 1800s. see U.S. categories	1	1	.	.	.	.	.
Ackermann Lith. NY; mid 1800s. see U.S. categories	7	7	.	.	.	.	.
Adams & Son. USA; late 1800s	1	1	.	.	.	.	.
Adrichom. see Van Adrichem	.	.	.	.	.	.	.
Aeronautical Maps.	3	0	.	.	.	.	3
Ainslie. incl John. Scottish; late 1700s	5	4	.	.	1	.	.
Ainsworth, W. Glasgow; late 1800s	1	1	.	.	.	.	.
Alabern. Barcelona; mid 1800s	1	1	.	.	.	.	.
Alaska.	1	1	.	.	.	.	.
Albrizzi, Giambatista. Venice; mid 1700s	142	135	2	1	1	2	1
Alden. USA; wall maps; mid 1800s	2	2	.	.	.	.	.
Alexander. late 1800s	3	1	.	.	1	1	.
Allan. J.; mid 1800s	1	0	.	.	.	.	1
Allard, Carel (& family). Amsterdam; 1648-1709	56	38	6	4	5	.	3
Allardt, G.F. San Francisco; late 1800s	2	1	.	.	.	.	1
Allen: various; incl Wm. Allen & Co., London	9	8	.	.	.	1	.
Almon, John. London; late 1700s	2	2	.	.	.	.	.
Alting, Menso (younger). Amsterdam; early 1700s	2	1	.	.	1	.	.

	Total	'83-'92	'93	'94	'95	'96	'97-8
American Antiquarian Society.	4	4	.	.	.	.	.
American Bank Note Co.	3	2	.	.	.	.	1
American Ethnological Society.	3	1	.	1	.	.	1
American Geographical Society.	1	0	.	.	.	1	.
American Journal of Science.	5	3	.	1	.	1	.
American Litho. Co. NY; mid 1800s	3	3	.	.	.	.	.
American Philosophical Society.	3	0	.	2	.	.	1
American Publishing Co. Milwaukee; late 1800s	4	4	.	.	.	.	.
American Sunday School Union.	2	0	.	1	.	.	1
Amico. Bernardino; Florence; early 1600s	2	0	.	.	.	.	2
Amman, Jost. Zurich; 1539-91	1	1	.	.	.	.	.
Analectic Magazine. Phila; early 1800s	4	2	.	.	.	1	1
Anburey, Thomas. London.	3	3	.	.	.	.	.
Anderson: various. 1800s	8	7	.	.	.	.	1
Andreas, Alfred T. Chicago; late 1800s	25	17	1	3	2	2	.
Andrees. Germany; late 1800s	1	0	.	.	.	.	1
Andrews: incl John, England, 1736-1809; D.C. & Co, Israel, US; Lorran, HI, mid 1800s	23	12	.	.	3	6	2
Andrews & Dury. England; late 1700s	2	2	.	.	.	.	.
Andriveau-Goujon (families). Paris; mid 1800s	23	13	3	2	.	3	2
Andrus & Judd. Hartford; early 1800s	4	2	1	.	.	.	1
Angelo, Theodore G.N. Danish; early 1800s	1	1	.	.	.	.	.
Angelocrator, Daniel. Frankfurt; early 1600s	3	2	.	.	1	.	.
Annales des Mines. Paris	1	1	.	.	.	.	.
Annin & Smith. USA; early 1800s	2	2	.	.	.	.	.
Annual Register. England; mid 1700s	1	0	.	.	.	1	.
Anonymous or Unknown.	528	444	22	29	13	10	10
Ansart. Paris; mid 1800s	3	3	.	.	.	.	.
Anson, George. London; mid 1700s	37	22	3	6	2	1	3
Anthony. Providence; early 1800s	1	1	.	.	.	.	.
Antoine, Louis. Paris; mid 1800s	3	3	.	.	.	.	.
Apianus: Peter, early 1500s; Philip, mid 1500s; Germany	38	29	1	3	3	.	2
Appleton, D. & Co. incl Appleton's Journal. NY; late 1800s	45	36	2	.	3	2	2
Apthorp. USA; late 1800s	1	1	.	.	.	.	.
Aquila, Prospero dell'. Venice; late 1700s	2	2	.	.	.	.	.
Aragon, J. mid 1800s	1	1	.	.	.	.	.
Arbuckle [Bros.]; Coffee Co. late 1800s; map cards	6	2	.	.	.	1	3
Archaeological Americana. early 1800s	1	1	.	.	.	.	.
Archer, Joshua. London; mid 1800s	27	24	1	.	1	1	.
Arias Montanus, Benedictus. Spain; 1527-98	15	7	.	1	1	3	3
Armenian Cartography.	3	1	.	.	.	.	2
Armstrong. incl Mostyn John. Scottish; late 1800s	3	3	.	.	.	.	.
Arrowsmith: Aaron Sr; Jr; John; Samuel. London; early 1800s	387	315	27	11	8	8	18
Arrowsmith & Lewis. see Lewis & Arrowsmith, '83-'93	146	59	26	34	9	4	14
Artaria & Co. Vienna; early 1800s	3	2	1	.	.	.	.
Artifacts - Infrequent Publisher.	4	0	.	.	.	.	4
Aschbach. Penna; mid 1800s	3	1	.	1	.	1	.
Ashby, H. London; late 1700s	3	1	.	1	1	.	.
Asher.	1	1	.	.	.	.	.
Asher & Adams. NY; late 1800s	169	85	15	12	19	21	17
Asher & Co. mid 1800s	9	6	.	.	1	2	.
Aspin, Jehoshaphat. London; early 1800s	6	2	.	1	2	.	1
Astley Magazine.	1	0	1	.	.	.	.
Atcheson.	2	2	.	.	.	.	.
Atchison, Topeka & Santa Fe R.R.	1	1	.	.	.	.	.
Atkinson, S.C. Phila; mid 1800s	3	0	.	.	.	3	.
Atlantic Neptune. see Des Barres	.	.	.	.	.	.	.
Atlas Maritimus & Commercialis. see Cutler	.	.	.	.	.	.	.
Atwater, Caleb; Amer.; early 1800s	2	1	.	.	.	1	.
Atwood, J.M. Phila; mid 1800s	10	8	.	1	.	.	1
Aveline, Antonio. mid 1600s	2	1	.	.	.	.	1
Avery, H.M. Cleveland; late 1800s	1	1	.	.	.	.	.
Bachelder, John B. USA; mid 1800s	3	0	.	1	.	.	2
Bachiene, Willem Albert. Amsterdam. late 1700s	45	38	2	.	4	1	.
Bachmann, C. see Magnus, C.	10	6	.	.	3	1	.

Name	Total	'83-'92	'93	'94	'95	'96	'97-8
Back, Capt. (Adm.) George, R.N. 1796-1873.	1	0	.	.	.	1	.
Bacon. incl C.; G.W. & Co., London.	34	18	6	1	4	2	3
Baeck, Elias. Augsburg; 1679-1747	1	1	.	.	.	.	.
Baedeker (Company). Leipzig; late 1800s	15	14	.	.	.	1	.
Baffin, William. English; 1584-1622	2	1	.	.	1	.	.
Bailey & Co., O.H. urban views. see Bailey, 1990	14	5	2	3	.	1	3
Bailey & Hazen. NY	1	1	.	.	.	.	.
Bailleul, Gaspard. Gaspard, early 1700s; Francois, mid 1700s; France	2	1	.	.	.	.	1
Baillie, Alexander. Edinburgh; mid 1700s	1	1	.	.	.	.	.
Baines, John & Co. early 1800s	1	1	.	.	.	.	.
Baker: various; incl T.W.	8	4	.	.	1	2	1
Baker & Harper. Butte, MT; late 1800s	2	1	.	.	.	.	1
Balch. USA; late 1800s	1	0	.	.	1	.	.
Baldwin: various; incl Richard, Jr., London	18	17	.	.	.	.	1
Baldwin & Cradock. London; early 1800s. see S.D.U.K.	35	34	1	.	.	.	.
Baldwin & Thomas. Phila; mid 1800s	1	1	.	.	.	.	.
Ballino, Giulio. Italy; mid 1500s	1	1	.	.	.	.	.
Ballou,. Pictorial Drawing Room Companion. mid 1800s	6	5	.	.	.	1	.
Bancroft: various; mid 1800s	3	3	.	.	.	.	.
Bancroft & Knight. San Francisco; mid 1800s	2	2	.	.	.	.	.
Bankes, Thomas. London; late 1700s	8	5	.	.	3	.	.
Banks, J.H. & Co. London	1	0	.	1	.	.	.
Banvard, J. London; mid 1800s	1	1	.	.	.	.	.
Barber, J.W. Hartford; mid 1800s	1	0	.	.	.	1	.
Barbie du Bocage. Jean Denis, 1760-1825; Jean-Guillaume, 1795-1848. see Du Bocage to '90	7	0	.	.	.	.	7
Barclay, T. London; late 1800s	6	5	1	.	.	.	.
Barcleus.	1	1	.	.	.	.	.
Bardin, Wm. & J.M. globes; early 1800s	2	0	1	.	.	.	1
Barfield, J. London; early 1800s	1	1	.	.	.	.	.
Barker, William. William, Phila, late 1700s; Henry Aston, England, early 1800s	2	1	.	.	.	.	1
Barlaeus, Caspar (van Baarle). Amsterdam; mid 1600s.	1	1	.	.	.	.	.
Barlow. incl J. late 1800s	7	6	1	.	.	.	.
Barnes & Burr. NY; mid 1800s	9	9	.	.	.	.	.
Barnes, R.L. Phila	9	4	2	3	.	.	.
Barrow, Sir John. London; late 1700s	11	10	.	.	1	.	.
Burgoyne. John; English general; late 1700s	1	0	.	.	.	.	1
Barthelemy. Abbe Jean Jacques; France; 1716-95	1	0	.	.	.	.	1
Bartholomew: George; John; John (II); John George. late 1700s+	70	49	4	4	8	4	1
Bartlett: incl W.H. views, mid 1800s; J.R., London, mid 1800s.	19	17	1	.	.	.	1
Barton. incl C. Claremont, NH.	2	2	.	.	.	.	.
Bartram. Paris; late 1700s	1	0	.	.	1	.	.
Basire: James, mid 1700s; (II) early 1800s; (III) mid 1800s. English	8	7	.	.	.	1	.
Baskin, Forster & Co. Chicago	2	0	.	1	.	1	.
Batelli & Fanfani. Milan, early 1800s	3	3	.	.	.	.	.
Bates, Thomas. Dublin; late 1700s	2	0	.	.	.	2	.
Baudartius. early 1600s	12	12	.	.	.	.	.
Baudin, Admiral. Paris; early 1800s	1	1	.	.	.	.	.
Bauerkeller, George. mid 1800s	1	0	1	.	.	.	.
Baumgarten, Siegmund Jakob. Halle; mid 1700s	5	5	.	.	.	.	.
Bauza, Filipe. early 1800s	1	1	.	.	.	.	.
Bayly. London; late 1700s	2	1	.	1	.	.	.
Beadle, E.F. Buffalo; mid 1800s	1	1	.	.	.	.	.
Beaulieu, Sebastian de Pontault. France; late 1600s	2	2	.	.	.	.	.
Beautemps-Beaupre, Charles Francois. Paris	7	6	1	.	.	.	.
Beck & Pauli. urban views	2	2	.	.	.	.	.
Beechey. English; early 1800s	4	3	.	.	.	1	.
Beer, Johan Christoph. 1673-1753	33	1	.	.	31	1	.
Beers: (various companies) NY; late 1800s	109	26	.	25	26	14	18
Beers & Lake.	1	1	.	.	.	.	.
Beers, Comstock & Cline.	4	4	.	.	.	.	.
Beers, Ellis & Soule. USA; late 1800s	8	4	4	.	.	.	.
Beischlag. early 1800s	1	1	.	.	.	.	.
Belcher, Sir Edward. mid 1800s	1	1	.	.	.	.	.
Belden.	2	1	1	.	.	.	.
Beldin. incl H., late 1800s	5	5	.	.	.	.	.

Name	Total	'83-'92	'93	'94	'95	'96	'97-8
Belknap, Jeremy. NH, USA; late 1700s	1	0	.	.	.	1	.
Bell: A., Edinburgh; Peter, London; late 1700s; James, Glasgow; early 1800s see Scot's Magazine	18	14	.	.	2	.	2
Bellairs, L. London; mid 1800s	1	1	.	.	.	.	.
Bellere, Jean. Antwerp. late 1500s	1	1	.	.	.	.	.
Bellin. Jacques Nicolas. Paris; mid 1700s	482	482	.	.	.	.	.
(large) see Depot de la Marine	247	165	22	11	19	15	15
(small) see De Charlevois, Prevost d'Exiles	1201	723	123	118	79	94	64
Bellus. assoc with "Ostreichischer Lorberkranz".	10	0	.	6	.	3	1
Benard: Jacques Francois, Paris, early 1700s; Robert, France, late 1700s. see Cook	54	47	1	4	2	.	.
Benton, Henry. Hartford, mid 1800s	2	1	1	.	.	.	.
Berard. mid 1800s	1	1	.	.	.	.	.
Berey, Nicolas. France; mid 1600s	2	1	.	.	.	.	1
Bergen, Daniel & Gracey. Austin, TX; late 1800s	1	1	.	.	.	.	.
Berghaus, H. mid 1800s	7	1	1	1	3	.	1
Bernard, Jean Frederic. Amsterdam; mid 1700s	9	4	.	1	1	3	.
Bernhardt, L. Stockholm; mid 1800s	1	1	.	.	.	.	.
Bero, D. with Pierrugues. Bordeaux; early 1800s	1	0	1	.	.	.	.
Berry. William; London; fl 1669-1708.	10	8	.	.	.	1	1
Bertelli, Fernando. Venice; mid 1500s	12	8	1	.	.	1	2
Bertholon, C. late 1700s	5	3	.	1	1	.	.
Bertius, Pieter. Amsterdam; early 1600s	247	170	7	25	10	21	14
Betts, John. London; mid 1800s	18	7	5	1	1	1	3
Bevis, John. London.	1	0	.	1	.	.	.
Bew, John. late 1700s. see Political Magazine	8	8	.	.	.	.	.
Bezzera, P. Milan: mid 1800s	1	1	.	.	.	.	.
Bickham, George Jr. London; mid 1700s	4	3	.	1	.	.	.
Biddle, Edward C. mid 1800s	1	1	.	.	.	.	.
Bidwell, Oliver Beckworth. mid 1800s	2	0	.	.	1	1	.
Bien, Julius. lith; NY; mid 1800s	26	13	.	10	.	.	3
Bill, Henry. mid 1800s	2	1	.	.	.	1	.
Binet. Paris, publisher; mid 1800s	2	0	.	.	.	.	2
Bineteau. mid 1800s	1	1	.	.	.	.	.
Bingham, J. London; early 1700s	1	1	.	.	.	.	.
Bion, Nicolas. Paris; mid 1700s	4	1	1	.	.	2	.
Birga, A.,. Florentine Edifice Society.	1	0	.	1	.	.	.
Birkbeck, M. early 1800s	2	1	.	.	.	1	.
Blachford, William. London; mid 1800s	5	4	.	.	.	.	1
Black, Adam & Charles. Edinburgh; mid 1800s	161	121	9	6	11	7	7
Blackie. W.G. (& Son); Glasgow; Edinburgh; mid 1800s	34	26	1	1	1	.	5
Blackmore, William. mid 1800s	1	1	.	.	.	.	.
Blackwood, W. & Son. Edinburgh, London; mid 1800s	2	1	.	.	.	1	.
Blaeu: Willem Jans Zoon, 1571-1638; Joan, 1596-1673; Cornelius, 1610-48. Amsterdam	1648	1137	.	52 138	54	134	133
Blair, John. England; d 1782	21	14	.	.	1	.	6
Blanchard, Rufus. Chicago; mid 1800s	12	7	.	2	.	1	2
Blankaart, Nicolas. Leyden; mid 1600s	3	3	.	.	.	.	.
Blankman, Edgar. Constantia, NY; late 1800s	1	1	.	.	.	.	.
Blau, F.G. late 1800s	1	1	.	.	.	.	.
Blodget, Lorin. late 1800s	1	1	.	.	.	.	.
Blome, Richard. London; late 1600s	99	61	19	3	6	2	8
Blondeau, Alexandre. Paris; early 1800s	4	3	1	.	.	.	.
Bluhme. mid 1800s	1	1	.	.	.	.	.
Blundell, J. London(?); early 1700s	7	6	1	.	.	.	.
Blunt, Edmund. Newburyport, MA; NY; early 1800s	164	102	4	5	6	26	21
Boardman, Harvey. mid 1800s	2	2	.	.	.	.	.
Bochart & Knollis. English; late 1600s	1	0	.	.	.	.	1
Bocharti, Samuel. Leyden; late 1600s	1	0	1	.	.	.	.
Bock, H. early 1800s	1	1	.	.	.	.	.
Bode, Johann Ehlert. Hamburg; 1747-1826	11	0	.	.	11	.	.
Bodenehr (family). Augsburg; early 1700s	153	113	.	9	6	16	9
Bogart & Andrews. late 1800s	1	1	.	.	.	.	.
Bohn: Carl Ernst, Hamburg, late 1700s; Casimir, Washington, mid 1800s	12	8	.	1	1	2	.
Boileau de Bouillon, Gilles. Flemish; 1525-63	1	1	.	.	.	.	.
Boisseau, Jean. Paris; mid 1600s	12	7	1	3	.	1	.

Name	Total	'83-'92	'93	'94	'95	'96	'97-8
Boissevin, Louis. Paris; fl. 1652-1658.	1	0	.	1	.	.	.
Bolton, Solomon. London; late 1700s	12	2	3	2	2	1	2
Bond. wall map; mid 1800s	1	1	.	.	.	.	.
Bonferius. Jacobus; Paris; early 1700s	1	0	.	.	.	.	1
Bongars, J. early 1600s	1	0	.	.	1	.	.
Bonne, Rigobert. Paris; late 1700s	646	455	28	41	38	36	48
Bonner, William G. Millegeville, GA	1	1	.	.	.	.	.
Bonneville, Benj. L.E. de. USA; 1796-1878	8	1	.	1	3	2	1
Booth & Hulbert. mid 1800s	1	1	.	.	.	.	.
Borden, Simeon. Boston; mid 1800s	2	1	.	1	.	.	.
Bordiga, F. Venice; early 1800s	3	2	.	.	.	1	.
Bordone, Benedetto. Padua; 1460-1531	95	74	2	7	6	3	3
Borghi, A.B. early 1800s	9	7	.	1	1	.	.
Bormeester, Joachim. Amsterdam; late 1600s	1	1	.	.	.	.	.
Borthwick, J. London; mid 1800s	1	1	.	.	.	.	.
Bory de Saint-Vincent. J.B.M.G.; French naturalist; 1780-1846	1	0	.	.	.	.	1
Boschini, Marco. Venice; 1613-78	1	1	.	.	.	.	.
Bossi, Luigi. Milan; 1758-1835	1	1	.	.	.	.	.
Bossuet, J.B. Amsterdam; early 1700s	7	7	.	.	.	.	.
Botero, Giovanni. Italian; late 1500s	14	8	1	.	1	2	2
Bouchette, Joseph. London; early 1800s	40	36	2	1	1	.	.
Bougainville, Comte Louis Antoine de. French; 1729-1811	4	1	.	1	1	.	1
Boulton: Dennis & Co., Toronto; mid 1800; S., late 1700s	2	1	.	.	.	1	.
Bourgoin. Paris; mid 1700s	5	4	.	.	.	.	1
Bourrelier. mid 1800s	1	1	.	.	.	.	.
Boutatts, Gaspar. Vienna; late 1600s	1	1	.	.	.	.	.
Bowen. various. incl Emanuel, Thomas to '92	463	462	.	.	.	.	1
Bowen, Emanuel. London; mid 1700s. see Harris	124	0	31	15	16	13	49
Bowen, Thomas. London; late 1700s	24	0	5	6	3	2	8
Bowen & Gibson.	9	7	.	.	1	1	.
Bowen & Kitchin.	2	2	.	.	.	.	.
Bowles: Thomas, early 1700s; John, mid 1700s; Carington; late 1700s. London	93	72	7	2	4	1	7
Bowles, Samuel. USA.	1	1	.	.	.	.	.
Bowyer, R. early 1800s	2	0	.	.	2	.	.
Boydell, John. late 1700s	1	1	.	.	.	.	.
Boynton, George W. Boston; mid 1800s	9	7	2	.	.	.	.
Bradford, Thomas Gamaliel. Boston; NY; early 1800s. see Bradford & Goodrich, '90-'93	534	364	34	27	24	42	43
Bradley: Abraham Jr., Amer., early 1800s; William.& Co., Phila. late 1800s	114	70	7	13	12	6	6
Bradshaw, George. Manchester; 1801-53	3	1	.	.	2	.	.
Brandard, E.P. London; late 1800s	1	1	.	.	.	.	.
Braun & Hogenberg. late 1500s	770	521	24	34	88	35	68
Bretez, Philip. 1601-68; Louis, mid 1700s	3	1	.	.	1	.	1
Bridgens. H.F.; Amer., mid 1800s	1	0	.	.	.	.	1
Briet, Philip. Paris, 1601-68	6	3	.	1	1	1	.
Brightly & Kinnersley. Bungay, Suffolk; early 1800s	8	7	.	.	.	1	.
Brion, A. Forsley. late 1800s	4	3	.	.	.	.	1
Brion de la Tour, Louis. Paris; late 1700s	57	28	4	6	5	4	10
British Admiralty. see Admiralty to '93	686	485	66	9	115	5	6
British American Land Co. London; early 1800s	1	1	.	.	.	.	.
British Government. see Great Britain to '92; see Admiralty, Ordnance Survey	9	4	1	.	3	1	.
British Magazine.	1	1	.	.	.	.	.
British Ordnance Survey. see Ordnance Survey, to '92	17	7	.	.	9	1	.
Britton & Rey. San Francisco; mid 1800s	7	2	.	1	.	3	1
Britton Lith. late 1800s	1	1	.	.	.	.	.
Brockhaus, F.A. Germany.	2	0	.	2	.	.	.
Bromfield. Sacramento; late 1800s	1	1	.	.	.	.	.
Bromley, George & W.S. late 1800s	4	1	.	.	1	.	2
Bromme. Traugott; Stuttgart; 1802-66	1	0	.	.	.	.	1
Brooke, W.H., Amer., mid 1800s	2	2	.	.	.	.	.
Brookes, Richard. late 1700s	12	5	.	.	3	1	3
Brooking, Charles. early 1700s	1	0	.	.	.	1	.
Broughton, Capt. A. London; early 1800s	1	1	.	.	.	.	.
Brown: various; incl T.	8	6	1	1	.	.	.
Brown & Parsons. Hartford; mid 1800s	3	3	.	.	.	.	.
Browne: Christopher, London, late 1600s; E., late 1700s; H., early 1800s	15	10	.	1	.	.	4

Name	Total	'83-'92	'93	'94	'95	'96	'97-8
Bruce, James. late 1700s	2	0	2	.	.	.	.
Brue, Adrien Hubert. Paris; 1786-1832	95	75	6	3	2	8	1
Brunacci, Baldo. Pisa; early 1500s	2	1	.	1	.	.	.
Brunton, R. Henry. London; late 1800s	1	1	.	.	.	.	.
Bryan, W. NY; late 1800s	1	1	.	.	.	.	.
Bryant, A. London; early 1800s	7	7	.	.	.	.	.
Bryant Union.	2	0	1	1	.	.	.
Buache, Phillipe. Paris; 1700-73	63	35	4	12	3	3	6
Bucelini. Italy; mid 1600s	10	0	.	2	.	8	.
Buchanan, R. Edinburgh; early 1800s	1	1	.	.	.	.	.
Buchon, Jean Alexandre. Paris; 1789-1846	184	131	9	10	8	18	8
Buffier. mid 1700s	7	5	.	1	.	1	.
Buffon. late 1700s	1	0	.	.	1	.	.
Bufford, J.H. Boston; mid 1800s	12	8	.	1	.	3	.
Buisson. Paris; late 1700s	1	1	.	.	.	.	.
Bullock, William. early 1800s	2	2	.	.	.	.	.
Bunney & Gold. early 1800s	2	2	.	.	.	.	.
Buno. late 1600s	1	0	.	.	1	.	.
Bunting, Heinrich. Hanover; late 1500s	53	24	9	4	5	5	6
Burchell. early 1800s	1	1	.	.	.	.	.
Burckhardt. mid 1700s	2	0	.	.	.	.	2
Burder. London; early 1800s	1	0	.	.	1	.	.
Bureau of the Amer. Republics.	1	0	.	1	.	.	.
Burgess, Daniel & Co. NY; mid 1800s	19	17	1	1	.	.	.
Burleigh & Thomson. mid 1700s	1	1	.	.	.	.	.
Burleigh. litho. urban views. Troy, NY; late 1800s	5	1	1	1	2	.	.
Burnet. Thomas, England; 1635-1715	1	0	.	.	.	.	1
Burney, James. London; early 1800s	5	5	.	.	.	.	.
Burr, David H. NY; early 1800s	238	151	46	6	14	8	13
Burriel, Father Andres Marcos. Madrid; mid 1700s	1	1	.	.	.	.	.
Burritt, Elijah. US; mid 1800s	10	6	.	.	.	1	3
Busch, Georg Paul. Germany	1	0	.	1	.	.	.
Buschbeck, C. Berlin; late 1800s	1	1	.	.	.	.	.
Bushman, John. London; early 1800s	3	3	.	.	.	.	.
Bussemacher, Johannes. Cologne; late 1500s. see Quad	.	.	.	.	.	.	.
Butler, Samuel. English; early 1800s	14	9	.	.	.	2	3
Butterfield, Col. C. early 1800s	1	1	.	.	.	.	.
Byrne, P. Dublin; late 1700s	1	0	1	.	.	.	.
Byron, Commodore J. 1723-86	1	1	.	.	.	.	.
Cadell & Davies.	9	6	.	1	1	1	.
Cadell, Thomas. London; late 1700s	4	4	.	.	.	.	.
Cady & Burgess. NY; mid 1800s	1	1	.	.	.	.	.
Caillet. Paris; mid 1800s	1	1	.	.	.	.	.
Caimor, Balthasar. early 1600s	1	0	.	.	.	1	.
Caldwell, Joseph A. USA; late 1800s	3	0	.	.	.	1	2
California.	2	2	.	.	.	.	.
Callot, Jacques. Nancy; early 1600s	3	2	.	.	.	.	1
Calmet, Augustin. 1672-1757	9	5	1	.	3	.	.
Calvert. lith. Detroit; late 1800s	1	1	.	.	.	.	.
Camden, William. English; early 1600s. see Hole, Kip	65	54	1	.	6	1	3
Cammermeyer, A. late 1800s	1	1	.	.	.	.	.
Cammeyer. early 1800s	1	1	.	.	.	.	.
Camocio, Giovanni Francesco. Venice; mid 1500s	53	43	.	.	.	8	2
Campanius Holm, Tomas. Stockholm; late 1600s. see Holme, 1983	12	12	.	.	.	.	.
Canada Southern Rwy. Line.	1	1	.	.	.	.	.
Canadian Governments. see Canada to '92	19	11	.	.	1	1	6
Cantelli da Vignola, Giacomo. Modena; 1643-95	18	4	2	1	11	.	.
Canzler, Friedrich. early 1800s	1	1	.	.	.	.	.
Capewell & Kimmel. mid 1800s	1	1	.	.	.	.	.
Cappelen, J.W. Oslo; mid 1800s	1	1	.	.	.	.	.
Capper, Benjamin Pitts. London; early 1800s	10	10	.	.	.	.	.
Cardon, S. mid 1700s.	1	0	.	.	.	1	.
Carey, Mathew [& Son]. Phila; 1760-1839. see Lewis	491	323	40	51	17	41	19
Carey & Lea. Phila; early 1800s	345	227	18	20	28	22	30
Carey & Warner. early 1800s	2	2	.	.	.	.	.

Name	Total	'83-'92	'93	'94	'95	'96	'97-8
Carez, J. Paris; early 1800s	1	1	.	.	.	.	.
Carleton, Osgood. Boston; late 1700s	9	8	.	1	.	.	.
Carli, Pazzini. Siena; late 1700s	3	3	.	.	.	.	.
Carolus, Frans. Amsterdam; early 1700s	1	1	.	.	.	.	.
Caron. Francois, with VOC, d.1674; Cincinnati, late 1800s	3	1	.	.	.	1	1
Carpelan, W.M. Swedish; 1780-1830	1	0	1	.	.	.	.
Carr. Newport, RI; late 1800s	1	1	.	.	.	.	.
Carrigain, Phillip (NH Sec. of State).	3	0	.	1	.	1	1
Carter. incl Hosea B., late 1800s	3	3	.	.	.	.	.
Carteret, Philip, R.N. late 1700s	1	1	.	.	.	.	.
Cartwright, George W. NY; mid 1800s	2	2	.	.	.	.	.
Carver, Capt. Jonathan. London; late 1700s	6	2	.	1	1	.	2
Cary, John. London; c.1754-1835	294	210	9	11	28	7	29
Case, O.D. Hartford, CT	4	3	.	1	.	.	.
Case, Tiffany & Co. mid 1800s	6	3	.	.	.	2	1
Cassell: incl W., London, mid 1800s	6	4	.	.	.	.	2
Cassell & Galpin. London; mid 1800s	6	5	.	.	1	.	.
Cassini, Giovanni Maria. Rome; late 1800s	72	57	5	5	.	4	1
Castelli, D. early 1600s	1	1	.	.	.	.	.
Castellini. Italy	1	0	.	1	.	.	.
Castilla, A. de. Madrid; early 1800s	2	2	.	.	.	.	.
Catesby, Mark. English; c.1679-1749	5	3	1	.	.	1	.
Catlin, George; Amer., 1796-1872	4	4	.	.	.	.	.
Cavazza, J. Battista. Bologna; mid 1600s	5	3	1	.	.	.	1
Cave, Edward. London; 1691-1754	3	2	.	.	1	.	.
Cellarius, Andreas. Amsterdam; mid 1600s	127	69	2	11	1	36	8
Central Pacific R.R.	2	2	.	.	.	.	.
Century Atlas. late 1800s	29	10	12	3	1	1	2
Chabert, Joseph Bernard. French; mid 1700s. see De Chabert, '88 +	.	.	.	.	.	.	.
Chace, J. USA; mid 1800s	3	0	.	.	.	2	1
Chain & Hardy. Denver; late 1800s	1	1	.	.	.	.	.
Chambers, William & Robert. Edinburgh; late 1800s	17	13	.	.	.	3	1
Chamouin, Jean Baptiste Marie. Paris; early 1800s	7	2	.	2	2	.	1
Champlain, Samuel de. French; 1567-1635 [incl repro c.1850]	3	1	.	.	.	.	2
Chanlaire & Mentelle. Paris; early 1800s	12	11	.	1	.	.	.
Chanlaire, Pierre Gregoire. Paris; early 1800s	7	4	.	.	2	1	.
Chapin: A.M., Boston; William. NY; mid 1800s	4	3	.	.	.	1	.
Chapin & Taylor. mid 1800s	2	2	.	.	.	.	.
Chapman: incl John, London, late 1700s; Silas, USA, mid 1800s	25	15	2	2	.	2	4
Chapman & Hall; London; mid 1800s. See Society for the Diffusion of Useful Knowledge	18	17	1	.	.	.	.
Chapman & Silas. USA; mid 1800s	9	9	.	.	.	.	.
Chappe d'Auteroche. Abbe Jean; French; 1722-69	2	0	.	.	.	.	2
Chardin, Jean. French; 1643-1713	5	5	.	.	.	.	.
Chardon, C. Paris; mid 1800s	1	1	.	.	.	.	.
Charles, J. Dublin; early 1800s	2	2	.	.	.	.	.
Charlevoix. see De Charlevoix, '87 +; see Bellin	.	.	.	.	.	.	.
Chase, J. wall maps. US, mid 1800s	4	2	.	2	.	.	.
Chastenet-Puisegur, Comte Jacques de. late 1700s	2	2	.	.	.	.	.
Chatelain, Henry Abraham. French; early 1700s	255	162	10	15	22	20	26
Chedel, F. Paris	1	0	.	1	.	.	.
Chereau le Jeune. mid 1700s	1	0	.	1	.	.	.
Chetwind, Philip. late 1600s. see Heylin	15	14	.	.	.	.	1
Chevalier. M, late 1700s; Michel, French, 1806-79	3	0	1	1	.	.	1
Chicago, Burlington & Quincy R.R.	2	2	.	.	.	.	.
Chicago & Northwestern Rwy.	2	2	.	.	.	.	.
Chicago, Rock Island & Pacific Rwy.	2	2	.	.	.	.	.
Child, G. London; mid 1700s; VT gazetteer, late 1800s.	11	10	.	.	.	1	.
Childs: incl G., mid 1700s; O.W., NY, mid 1800s	1	1	.	.	.	.	.
Chinese Cartography.	3	1	.	1	1	.	.
Chiquet, Jacques. French; early 1700s	27	23	1	.	1	.	2
Choris. early 1800s	1	1	.	.	.	.	.
Church, A.F. Nova Scotia; late 1800s	2	2	.	.	.	.	.
Churchill, Awnsham. London; fl 1681-1728	6	3	.	3	.	.	.
Churruca. Don Cosmo de; late 1700s	1	0	.	.	.	.	1
Citti, Louis F. Richmond; mid 1800s	1	1	.	.	.	.	.

41

	Total	'83-'92	'93	'94	'95	'96	'97-8
Claesz, Nicolas. Amsterdam; early 1600s	1	1	.	.	.	.	.
Clarendon, Edward. history, early 1700s	16	16	.	.	.	.	.
Claret de Fleurieu. Paris	1	0	1	.	.	.	.
Clark: Mathew, USA, late 1700s; Richard, USA, mid 1800s	14	6	1	2	.	1	4
Clark & Tackabury. mid 1800s	2	1	.	.	.	.	1
Clark & Wagner. mid 1800s	1	1	.	.	.	.	.
Clarke Lith. Halifax; mid 1800s	1	1	.	.	.	.	.
Clarke & Stephenson. mid 1800s	1	1	.	.	.	.	.
Clason Map Co. Denver; early 1900s	3	0	1	.	1	.	1
Clayton Lith. mid 1800s	1	1	.	.	.	.	.
Clemens, E.J. late 1800s	1	1	.	.	.	.	.
Clerk, Thomas. Edinburgh; early 1800s	1	1	.	.	.	.	.
Cloesen, B. early 1700s	1	0	.	.	.	1	.
Cloppenburgh, H. Jan Evertsz. Amsterdam; early 1600s	29	7	1	.	5	1	15
Clouet. L'Abbe Jean Baptiste Louis. Paris; late 1700s	22	15	2	2	.	.	3
Cluny. late 1700s	2	2	.	.	.	.	.
Cluver, Philip. Leyden; early 1600s	178	128	5	11	17	7	10
Cobbett, W. early 1800s	2	2	.	.	.	.	.
Coccetus, J. early 1700s	1	0	1	.	.	.	.
Cochin, Nicolas. Paris; mid 1600s	7	7	.	.	.	.	.
Cochrane Co. early 1800s	1	1	.	.	.	.	.
Coello, Francisco. Spanish; 1820-98	6	4	1	.	.	1	.
Coggins, E.H. Phila; mid 1800s	2	1	.	.	.	.	1
Coghlan, Francis. London; mid 1800s	1	1	.	.	.	.	.
Colburn. H. London; mid 1800s	6	6	.	.	.	.	.
Colby: incl C.G., New Orleans, mid 1800s; George N., Maine, late 1800s	19	7	1	4	4	.	3
Colden, Cadwallader, London, 1688-1776; (grand son) New York, 1769-1834	2	1	.	.	.	1	.
Cole. Benjamin. London; early 1700s	19	17	1	.	.	.	1
Coles, T. London	1	0	.	1	.	.	.
Collin, L. French; early 1800s	1	1	.	.	.	.	.
Collins, Capt. Grenville. England; fl 1669-98	217	185	8	.	15	2	7
Collins, Henry George. London; mid 1800s	9	8	.	.	.	.	1
Collins, William [& Son]. London, Glasgow, Edinburgh; mid 1800s	5	5	.	.	.	.	.
Collins & Clark. wall maps; USA; mid 1800s	2	1	.	.	.	.	1
Collins & Son. London; late 1800s	2	1	.	.	.	.	1
Collot, Victor George Henri. French; early 1800s	13	10	1	.	.	.	2
Colnett, Capt. James. London; late 1700s	2	1	1	.	.	.	.
Colom. Jacob (father) 1600s; Arnold (son), mid 1600s; Dutch	44	30	2	2	6	2	2
Colorado & Red River Land Co. mid 1800s	1	1	.	.	.	.	.
Colton: Joseph Hutchins, NY, 1800-93; George Woolworth, NY, 1827-1901.	1120	917	97	106	.	.	.
Colton (Atlas Maps).	228	0	.	.	78	55	95
Colton (Pocket & Wall).	86	0	.	.	8	38	40
Columbian Magazine. late 1700s	4	4	.	.	.	.	.
Comettant, Oscar. traveler; French; mid 1800s	3	3	.	.	.	.	.
Comite Geologique. late 1800s	1	1	.	.	.	.	.
Commelin. Isaac; mid 1600s. see De Bry	1	0	.	.	.	.	1
Company Maps.	7	0	1	2	2	2	.
Comstock & Cassidy. Albany; mid 1800s	1	1	.	.	.	.	.
Conant, A. NY; mid 1800s	1	1	.	.	.	.	.
Concept Maps - Infrequent Publishers.	3	0	.	.	.	.	3
Condamine. see De la Condamine, '87 +	.	.	.	.	.	.	.
Conder, Thomas. London; late 1700s	29	24	3	.	.	1	1
Confederate States of America.	4	0	.	3	.	1	.
Conkey. late 1800s	1	0	.	.	1	.	.
Connecticut, State of.	1	1	.	.	.	.	.
Conover, A.B. lith. Milwaukee; late 1800s	1	1	.	.	.	.	.
Conradi & Van der Plaats. late 1700s	1	1	.	.	.	.	.
Conservancy, Thomas. English; late 1700s	1	1	.	.	.	.	.
Constable, Archibald. London, Edinburgh; early 1800s	6	5	.	.	1	.	.
Cook, Capt. James. London; late 1700s. see Hogg, Benard	236	147	18	28	16	11	16
Cooke: incl C., London, late 1700s; G., London, early 1800s; D.B., USA, mid 1800s; Lt. Col. Phillips St. G., U.S. Army, 1809-95	11	10	1	.	.	.	.
Cooper: incl H., London, early 1800s; John M., USA, mid 1800s; T.	6	4	2	.	.	.	.
Copley, Charles. mid 1800s	8	3	.	1	1	.	3
Coreal. early 1700s	1	1	.	.	.	.	.

	Total	'83-'92	'93	'94	'95	'96	'97-8
Cornelis, Lambert. Dutch; early 1600s	1	1	.	.	.	.	.
Cornell: incl Sarah Sophia, mid 1800s	9	6	1	.	1	.	1
Coronelli, Vicenzo Maria. Venice; late 1600s	445	301	21	36	21	23	43
Cotovicus, J. (also Kootwyck). Dutch; early 1600s	12	12	.	.	.	.	.
Count & Hammond. NY; mid 1800s	1	1	.	.	.	.	.
Cousen. mid 1800s	1	1	.	.	.	.	.
Cousin, Paul. late 1800s	1	1	.	.	.	.	.
Covens & Mortier. Amsterdam; early 1700s	284	228	4	17	11	10	14
Cowley: John, English, mid 1700s; R., London, late 1700s	25	24	1	.	.	.	.
Cowperthwait, Desilver & Butler. Phila; mid 1800s	7	3	.	.	.	1	3
Cowperthwait, H. Phila; mid 1800s. see Thomas, Cowpertwait & Co.	9	8	.	.	1	.	.
Cox, George. London; mid 1800s. see Society for the Diffusion of Useful Knowledge	7	6	1	.	.	.	.
Coxe, Rev. William. English; 1747-1828	3	3	.	.	.	.	.
Craddock & Joy. early 1800s	2	2	.	.	.	.	.
Crafts. incl Henry, mid 1800s; N.	4	2	1	1	.	.	.
Cram, George. Chicago; late 1800s	584	342	61	50	38	47	46
Cramer, John Anthony. England; early 1800s	1	0	1	.	.	.	.
Crantz, David. London; late 1700s	6	6	.	.	.	.	.
Craskell & Simpson, Thomas. English; mid 1700s	2	1	.	1	.	.	.
Crawford: incl C.G., NY, late 1800s	5	5	.	.	.	.	.
Crepy (Chez). Paris; mid 1700s	8	6	.	.	1	.	1
Crevecoeur. see De Crevecoeur, '87+	.	.	.	.	.	.	.
Crocker & Brewster. publisher; Boston; early 1800s	1	1	.	.	.	.	.
Crocker. San Francisco; late 1800s	5	3	.	2	.	.	.
Crofutt. USA; late 1800s	1	1	.	.	.	.	.
Croisey. engraver for Bellin (at Depot de la Marine??)	1	0	.	1	.	.	.
Crosman & Mallory. views; mid 1800s	3	0	1	1	.	.	1
Cross, Joseph. London; mid 1800s	6	4	1	1	.	.	.
Cruchley, George Frederick. London; mid 1800s	38	23	7	1	2	4	1
Cruikshanks, James. late 1800s	1	1	.	.	.	.	.
Cruttwell. gazetteer; London; late 1700s	1	1	.	.	.	.	.
Cuccioni. mid 1800s	1	0	1	.	.	.	.
Cullen, C. London; late 1700s	1	1	.	.	.	.	.
Cummings & Hilliard. early 1800s	9	2	1	.	4	1	1
Cummings, Jacob Abbot. Boston; early 1800s	1	1	.	.	.	.	.
Currier & Ives. USA; late 1800s	1	0	.	1	.	.	.
Currier, Nathaniel. NY; 1813-88	3	2	1	.	.	.	.
Curtice & Stateler. St. Paul, MN; late 1800s	1	1	.	.	.	.	.
Custodis [also Custis], David & Raphael. early 1600s	6	2	.	.	1	.	3
Cutler, Nathaniel; London, early 1700s; incl *Atlas Maritimus & Commercialis*.	13	11	1	.	.	1	.
D'Anania. Giovanni Lorenzo; Italy; c.1525-1602	1	0	.	.	.	.	1
D'Anville, Jean Baptiste Bourguignon. Paris; mid 1700s. see Santini	132	82	15	11	10	9	5
D'Apres de Mannevillette, Jean B.N.D. Paris; late 1700s	145	125	11	.	8	1	.
D'Entrecasteaux, Joseph Antoine Bruni. Gov. of Mauritius	3	0	.	2	1	.	.
D'Expilly, Jean Jos. Georges. French; 1719-93	14	13	1	.	.	.	.
Dablon, Claude. French; c.1618-97	1	1	.	.	.	.	.
Dahlberg, Count Erik J. Stockholm; 1625-1703	2	0	1	.	.	1	.
Daily Graphic. NY; late 1800s	4	3	.	.	.	.	1
Dal Re, Marc Antonio. Milan; early 1700s	1	1	.	.	.	.	.
Dalrymple, Alexander. London; late 1700s	22	15	2	.	5	.	.
Dampier, William. London; early 1700s	18	12	2	1	.	.	3
Dana, Charles A. mid 1800s	9	9	.	.	.	.	.
Danby, Thomas. US; early 1800s	1	0	1	.	.	.	.
Danckerts (family): Cornelis elder, younger; Hendrik; Justus. Amsterdam; 1600s	157	128	6	4	4	4	11
Danckwerth: Caspar; Joachim; mid 1600s	3	3	.	.	.	.	.
Danckwerth & Meyer. Husum; mid 1600s	2	2	.	.	.	.	.
Danet, Guillaume. Paris; early 1700s	13	4	.	2	.	5	2
Dapper, Olivier. Amsterdam; late 1600s. see Montanus, Ogilby	49	42	.	2	1	.	4
Darby, William. Penna; 1775-1854	2	0	.	2	.	.	.
Darton, William. London; early 1800s	20	13	5	1	.	.	1
Darton & Clark. London; mid 1800s	2	1	1	.	.	.	.
Darton & Harvey. London; early 1800s	2	1	.	.	.	1	.
Dashiell, S.L. USA; early 1800s	3	1	.	.	2	.	.
Daumont. publisher; Paris; mid 1700s	4	2	1	.	.	1	.
Davenport: various	7	7	.	.	.	.	.

Name	Total	'83-'92	'93	'94	'95	'96	'97-8
Davidszoon. Dirck; Holland; late 1600s	1	0	.	.	.	.	1
Davies, Benjamin Rees. London; early 1800s	4	2	.	.	1	1	.
Davis: incl Jefferson, US; A.M, US, late 1800s	4	0	.	.	.	.	4
Davison, C. Wright. Minneapolis; late 1800s	4	3	.	.	.	1	.
Daw. E; E.M. & Co.; London; late 1800s	1	0	.	.	.	.	1
Dawson: D., mid 1800s; - Brothers, Montreal, late 1800s	7	5	.	.	.	1	1
Day: incl Charles, Macon, late 1800s	1	1	.	.	.	.	.
Day & Haghe. lith. London; mid 1800s	3	3	.	.	.	.	.
Day & Sons. English; mid 1800s	5	5	.	.	.	.	.
De Aefferden. Don Francisco. Antwerp; 1653-1709	13	3	1	3	5	.	1
De Azara, Felix. French; 1746-1821	8	7	.	.	.	1	.
De Bar, Alexandre. London; late 1800s	1	1	.	.	.	.	.
De Beaurain, Jean Chev. Paris; 1696-1722	6	4	.	.	.	.	2
De Belleforest, Francois. France; 1530-83	21	15	1	2	1	2	.
De Belleyme, Pierre. Paris; 1747-1819	1	1	.	.	.	.	.
De Berey, Nicolas. Paris; mid 1600s	3	3	.	.	.	.	.
De Bouge, Jean Baptiste. Brussels; late 1700s	1	1	.	.	.	.	.
De Brahm, W. Gerard. 1717-99	1	1	.	.	.	.	.
De Bruyn, Cornelis. Delft; early 1700s	74	72	1	.	.	.	1
De Bry, Theordore. Frankfort; 1528-98	369	262	30	26	16	16	19
De Chabert, Joseph Bernard Marquis. Paris; late 1700s. see Chabert to '86	16	16	.	.	.	.	.
De Charlevoix, P.F. Xavier. Paris; mid 1700s. see Bellin (see Charlevoix to '86)	32	24	.	.	.	8	.
De Chastellux. late 1700s	4	3	1	.	.	.	.
De Cordova. mid 1800s	2	0	.	.	.	.	2
De Crevecoeur. Michel Guillaume St. Jean; French-American, 1735-1813 see Crevecoeur to '86	17	7	5	5	.	.	.
De Fer, Nicolas. Paris; 1646-1730	114	114	.	.	.	.	.
(large).	55	18	6	5	9	7	10
(small).	152	48	28	25	21	8	22
De Freycinet, Henri-Louis & Louis Claude Desaules. French, early 1800s. see Freycinet, '85	7	7	.	.	.	.	.
De Grado, Philip. Spanish; early 1700s	2	1	.	1	.	.	.
De Groot, J. Netherlands; late 1700s	4	0	.	1	1	2	.
De Herrera, Antonio. Madrid; early 1600s. see Herrera to '87	63	46	6	3	3	2	3
De Hondt, P. publisher; Hague; mid 1700s	2	2	.	.	.	.	.
De Hooghe, Romain. Amsterdam; late 1600s	1	1	.	.	.	.	.
De Huyser, J.C. views; late 1700s	1	0	.	1	.	.	.
De Jode: Cornelis, Gerard; Antwerp; late 1500s	80	69	2	3	2	1	3
De Jorio, Andre. early 1800s	1	0	.	1	.	.	.
De l'Isle, Guillaume (1675-1725) & family, Paris, 1700s Try Albrizzi, Buache, Covens & Mortier, Dezauche, Lotter	306	165	18	12	59	11	41
De la Bastide. late 1700s	1	1	.	.	.	.	.
De la Condamine, Charles Marie. Paris; 1701-74. see Condamine, '85	8	8	.	.	.	.	.
De la Croix. early 1700s. see Croix, '91	3	3	.	.	.	.	.
De la Feuille (family). Amsterdam; early 1700s. see La Feuille, '84	28	20	1	5	1	1	.
De la Hire, Phillippe. French; 1640-1718	1	1	.	.	.	.	.
De la Houve, Paul. publisher; Paris, early 1600s	2	0	.	.	1	1	.
De la Potherie, B. Paris; early 1700s	7	7	.	.	.	.	.
De la Rue, Phillipe. French; mid 1600s	16	6	2	1	5	.	2
De Laborde, Jean Benjamin. late 1700s	6	5	.	1	.	.	.
De Laet, Joannes. Leyden; early 1600s	78	52	5	3	14	.	4
De Laporte, Joseph. French; 1713-79	20	6	.	4	1	4	5
De Lat, Jan. Deventer; mid 1700s	14	8	.	1	1	2	2
De Lavaur. G.L.; mid 1800s	1	0	.	.	.	.	1
De Leth, Hendrik (elder & younger). Amsterdam; mid 1700s	12	7	1	2	2	.	.
De Marre. with Dutch East India Co.; 1696-1763.	1	0	.	.	.	1	.
De Monthuchon, H. Altona; late 1700s	1	1	.	.	.	.	.
De Nicolay, Nicholas. Lyons; mid 1500s	2	2	.	.	.	.	.
De Pages, Vicomte Pierre Marie Francois. French; 1748-93	1	1	.	.	.	.	.
De Pretot, Etienne Andre Phillipe. Paris; 1708-87	7	1	1	.	3	2	.
De Ram, Johannes. Amsterdam; 1648-93	2	1	.	1	.	.	.
De Redern,. Berlin; mid 1700s	2	0	.	.	.	2	.
De Reneville, Constantin. Rouen; early 1700s	12	0	.	.	.	11	1
De Rienzi, L.G. Demeuy. Paris; 1789-1843	1	1	.	.	.	.	.
De Solis y Ribadeneyra. see De Solis, '89	2	1	.	.	.	1	.

	Total	'83-'92	'93	'94	'95	'96	'97-8
De Ulloa, Antonio. mid 1700s	2	2	.	.	.	.	.
De Vaugondy. Gilles Robert, 1686-1766; Didier Robert, 1723-86; Paris. see Delamarche, Diderot	757	571	27	34	59	24	42
De Vou, Johannes. late 1600s	1	1	.	.	.	.	.
De Wit, Frederick. Amsterdam; late 1600s	422	296	16	37	10	27	36
De Witt, Simeon. US, 1756-1834	3	2	.	.	.	1	.
Dean & Munday. London; mid 1800s	1	1	.	.	.	.	.
Dearborn, Benjamin. Boston; early 1800s	7	5	.	1	.	1	.
Decker, Paul. early 1700s	1	1	.	.	.	.	.
Deffenbaugh & Burroughs. late 1800s	1	1	.	.	.	.	.
Delagrive, Abbe Jean. Paris; 1689-1757	2	0	.	1	.	.	1
Delahaye: incl Guillaume Nicolas; French; 1727-1802. see De La Haye, '89	3	2	.	.	.	.	1
Delamarche, Charles Francois. Paris; late 1700s. see De Vaugondy	81	64	2	4	1	2	8
Della Gatta, Francesco. publisher; Rome; mid 1500s	2	2	.	.	.	.	.
Demarest, Benjamin D. NY; late 1800s	1	1	.	.	.	.	.
Dember, G. Albany; mid 1800s	1	1	.	.	.	.	.
Den Schryver. Dutch (?); early 1700s	1	1	.	.	.	.	.
Denis, Louis. Paris; late 1700s	3	3	.	.	.	.	.
Denison, J. Boston; late 1700s	1	1	.	.	.	.	.
Denver & Rio Grande R.R.	1	1	.	.	.	.	.
Deposito Hidrografico.	1	1	.	.	.	.	.
Depot de la Marine. French Admiralty. Paris. see Bellin, Vincendon-Dumoulin	303	239	15	8	27	7	7
Depot General de la Guerre. Paris	2	1	1	.	.	.	.
Derfelden van Hinderstein, Gijsbert Franco. Dutch; 1783-1857	1	1	.	.	.	.	.
Deroy. views; French; mid 1800s	3	0	1	.	.	1	1
Des Barres, Joseph F.W. London; 1721(?)-1824	193	122	17	17	32	1	4
Desbordes, Charles. early 1700s	1	1	.	.	.	.	.
Desbruslins. father, son. mid 1700s	2	1	1	.	.	.	.
Desgranges. late 1600s	2	2	.	.	.	.	.
Desilver, Charles. Phila; mid 1800s	190	109	36	15	11	11	8
Desnos, Louis Charles. Paris; late 1700s	42	32	1	3	2	.	4
Desobry, Prosper. Amer., mid 1800s.	2	1	.	.	.	1	.
Desoer, F.I. late 1700s	1	1	.	.	.	.	.
Dessing, J. Nuremberg; mid 1700s	1	1	.	.	.	.	.
Dezauche, J.A. Paris; early 1800s	48	33	.	2	.	6	7
Dezobry E. Magdeleine et Cie. Paris; 19 c.	1	0	.	.	.	1	.
Dezoteux. French; late 1700s	5	5	.	.	.	.	.
Dheulland, Guillaume. Paris; 1700-70	1	0	1	.	.	.	.
Di Arnoldi, Fiamengo Aroldo. Bologna; early 1600s	3	2	.	1	.	.	.
Diamond Atlas. USA; mid 1800s	5	3	.	.	.	1	1
Dicey, William. with Cluer. London; mid 1700s	1	1	.	.	.	.	.
Diderot, Denis. encyclopedist, France; 1713-84. see De Vaugondy	121	67	.	15	12	16	11
Didot. publisher; Paris; late 1700s +	7	7	.	.	.	.	.
Dien.	1	1	.	.	.	.	.
Dilly, Charles. London; late 1700s	4	3	.	1	.	.	.
Dinsmore. mid 1800s	4	4	.	.	.	.	.
Direccion de Hidrografia. Spanish Admiralty	83	59	11	1	7	2	3
Disturnell, John. NY; 1801-77	18	11	1	2	.	4	.
Dixon, George. London; late 1700s	12	10	2	.	.	.	.
Dixson, T. London; early 1800s	1	1	.	.	.	.	.
Djurberg, Daniel. Swedish; 1744-1834	5	0	.	.	2	2	1
Dobson & Cobbett. Phila; late 1700s	1	1	.	.	.	.	.
Dobson, Thomas. Phila; late 1700s	1	1	.	.	.	.	.
Dockam, C. Augustine. Boston, mid 1800s	2	1	.	.	.	1	.
Dodd, Mead. late 1800s	1	1	.	.	.	.	.
Dodge. Grenville M., mid 1800s; R.P., mid 1800s	2	2	.	.	.	.	.
Dodsley, Robert. London; 1703-64	4	1	1	.	1	1	.
Dolendo, Bartholomew. Leyden; early 1600s	1	1	.	.	.	.	.
Dollar Weekly Tribune. late 1800s	1	1	.	.	.	.	.
Donaldson. Alexander, Edinburg mid 1800s; Thomas, late 1800s.	5	1	1	.	3	.	.
Doncker, Hendrik. Amsterdam; late 1600s	53	37	2	2	7	2	3
Doppelmayr, Johann Gabriel. Nuremberg; 1677-1750. see Homann	20	4	3	3	5	3	2
Dorr, Howland & Co. Worcester, MA; mid 1800s	2	1	.	.	.	.	1
Dou, Jan Jansz. Dutch; late 1600s	1	1	.	.	.	.	.
Doughty, Samuel. mid 1800s	2	1	.	.	.	.	1

45

	Total	'83-'92	'93	'94	'95	'96	'97-8
Douglas. C., Bristol, mid 1700s; George, late 1800s.	2	1	.	.	.	.	1
Dower, John. London; mid 1800s. see Teesdale	53	44	3	1	3	1	1
Drake, E.C. London; late 1700s	2	1	.	.	1	.	.
Drayton, Michael. London; early 1600s	56	55	.	.	.	1	.
Drew, Columbus. USA; late 1800s	3	1	1	.	.	.	1
Drinkwater, John. London; early 1800s	1	1	.	.	.	.	.
Drioux & Leroy. mid 1800s	2	1	.	.	.	.	1
Drioux, Claude Joseph. 1820-98	1	1	.	.	.	.	.
Dripps, Matthew. NY; late 1800s	18	9	.	6	1	1	1
Drummond, A. mid 1700s	1	1	.	.	.	.	.
Du Bocage. see Barbie du Bocage '97-8	4	0	.	.	.	.	.
Du Bosc, Claude. mid 1700s	2	2	.	.	.	.	.
Du Four. early 1800s	2	1	.	1	.	.	.
Du Halde, Jean Baptiste. Paris; 1674-1743	9	0	.	4	1	1	3
Du Pinet, Antoine. c.1510-66	2	1	.	.	.	1	.
Du Sauzet, Henri. Amsterdam; early 1700s, see De Sauzet, '85	7	7	.	.	.	.	.
Du Val, Pierre. Paris; mid 1600s	153	96	7	9	10	20	11
Du Vivier, F. Paris; late 1600s	1	1	.	.	.	.	.
Duchetti, Claudio. Rome; late 1500s	5	4	.	.	.	1	.
Dudley, Robert. Florence; mid 1600s	259	223	11	6	6	6	7
Dufertre, V. late 1800s	1	1	.	.	.	.	.
Duflot de Mofras, Eugene. 1810-84. see De Mofras to '88	25	24	.	.	.	1	.
Dufour, Adolphe Hippolyte. Paris; 1798-1865	77	52	3	3	5	3	11
Duluth News Co. late 1800s	1	1	.	.	.	.	.
Dumont d'Urville, Jules S.C. French; 1790-1842. see D'Urville, '85	28	6	.	.	.	19	3
Duncan, E. mid 1800s	2	2	.	.	.	.	.
Dunn, Samuel. London; late 1700s. see Laurie & Whittle, Sayer	38	27	3	1	1	1	5
Duperrey, Louis Isidore. French; 1786-1865	13	12	.	.	1	.	.
Dupont-Buisson. late 1700s	1	1	.	.	.	.	.
Dupuis. French(?); late 1700s	1	1	.	.	.	.	.
Durell, Philip. English; mid 1800s	3	2	1	.	.	.	.
Durocher, J. French; 1817-60	1	1	.	.	.	.	.
Dury, Andrew. London; fl 1742-78	12	10	.	.	1	.	1
Dury & Bell. mid 1700s	1	1	.	.	.	.	.
Dusacq & Cie. publisher; France; late 1800s	1	1	.	.	.	.	.
Dussieux, Louis Etienne. French; 1815-94	3	2	1	.	.	.	.
Dutton: incl Clarence, USA, 1841-1912; E.P., Boston, mid 1800s	10	7	1	1	.	.	1
Duval: lith. Phila; mid 1800s; incl P.S. & Son. see U.S. categories	10	7	2	.	.	.	1
Duvotenay, Thunot. French; 1796-1875	9	6	2	.	.	.	1
Dwight, Timothy. USA; early 1800s	2	2	.	.	.	.	.
Eastman, Capt. S. USA; mid 1800s	12	8	2	1	.	1	.
Ecker. early 1800s	1	1	.	.	.	.	.
Eckhoff & Riecker. NY; late 1800s	1	1	.	.	.	.	.
Eddy: incl John H., NY, early 1800s; R.H., Boston, mid 1800s	6	4	.	1	.	1	.
Edgar, William. mid 1700s	2	1	.	.	.	.	1
Edinburgh Magazine. mid 1700s	1	1	.	.	.	.	.
Edsall, D.A. late 1800s	4	3	.	.	.	1	.
Edwards, Bryan. London; late 1700s	108	84	2	9	6	7	.
Ehrenberg, Herman. USA; mid 1800s	1	1	.	.	.	.	.
Ehrmann, Theodor Friedrich. Weimar; early 1800s	4	3	1	.	.	.	.
Eldridge, George. late 1800s	15	1	.	.	.	13	1
Ellicott: Andrew, US, 1754-1820. also J.&B.	8	0	1	1	1	1	4
Elliot, A. London; late 1800s	2	1	.	1	.	.	.
Elliott: incl Wallace W.; Elliott Publ; Elliot Lith.; San Francisco; late 1800s	4	3	.	.	.	.	1
Ellis, John. London; late 1700s	16	16	.	.	.	.	.
Elwe, Jan Barend. Amsterdam; late 1700s	49	35	2	6	2	1	3
Ely. mid 1800s	1	1	.	.	.	.	.
Emery. views; USA; mid 1800s	1	0	1	.	.	.	.
Emmerlich. mid 1800s	1	1	.	.	.	.	.
Emmons, Samuel Franklin. USA; 1841-1911	2	1	.	.	.	.	1
Emory, Major William Hemsley; Amer., mid 1800s	2	1	1	.	.	.	.
Encyclopaedia Britannica.	2	2	.	.	.	.	.
Endicott & Co. lith; NY; mid 1800s	8	5	.	1	.	1	1
Engelmann Lith. early 1800s	1	1	.	.	.	.	.
Engelmann, Graf, Coindet & Co. early 1800s	1	1	.	.	.	.	.

Name	Total	'83-'92	'93	'94	'95	'96	'97-8
English Pilot. see Mount & Page	.	.	.	.	.	.	.
Enouy, J. early 1800s	1	0	1	.	.	.	.
Ensign: incl T. & E.H., NY, mid 1800s; D.W., Chicago, late 1800s	11	5	2	1	.	1	2
Ensign, Bridgman & Fanning. mid 1800s	19	13	.	1	1	2	2
Ensign & Bridgman. mid 1800s	1	1	.	.	.	.	.
Ensign & Thayer. mid 1800s	27	20	1	3	.	1	2
Entick, John. London; mid 1700s	11	10	1	.	.	.	.
Eriksson, Jon. late 1700s	1	1	.	.	.	.	.
Ertl, Anton Wilhelm. Munich; early 1700s	25	24	.	1	.	.	.
Eschinardi, Francisco. Rome; 1623-c.1700.	1	0	.	1	.	.	.
Espinosa y Tello, Jose de. traveller, Madrid; 1763-1815	1	1	.	.	.	.	.
Esquemeling, Alexandre Oliver. England; late 1600s	21	19	1	.	.	.	1
Etablissement Geographique de Bruxelles. mid 1800s	1	0	1	.	.	.	.
Ettling, Theodore. London; mid 1800s. see Weekly Dispatch	25	20	2	2	.	1	.
Euler. see Von Euler	.	.	.	.	.	.	.
Euling, T., London, mid 1800s	1	1	.	.	.	.	.
European Magazine. late 1800s	2	1	.	1	.	.	.
Evans, John. London; late 1700s	14	9	.	.	1	3	1
Everts, L.H. & Co. late 1800s	8	6	.	.	.	1	1
Everts & Richards. late 1800s	1	0	1	.	.	.	.
Everts & Stewart. late 1800s	7	4	.	.	.	.	3
Every Saturday. late 1800s	2	2	.	.	.	.	.
Ewen, Daniel. mid 1800s	2	1	.	.	.	.	1
Ewings, Thomas. Edinburgh; early 1800s	1	1	.	.	.	.	.
Exshaw, John. Dublin; mid 1700s	3	3	.	.	.	.	.
Faden, William. London; late 1700s. Try Tarleton	329	241	20	12	23	9	24
Fahlberg, Samuel. Sweden	2	0	.	1	.	1	.
Fairbanks, H. San Francisco; late 1800s	1	1	.	.	.	.	.
Fairburn, John. London; late 1700s	2	2	.	.	.	.	.
Family Times. London; mid 1800s	2	1	1	.	.	.	.
Fanning. NY; mid 1800s	1	1	.	.	.	.	.
Farmer, John. USA; 1798-1859	7	3	.	2	.	1	1
Farmer, Silas & Co. Detroit; late 1800s	4	4	.	.	.	.	.
Farnham, Thomas. NY; mid 1800s	3	2	.	.	.	1	.
Fassmann, D. early 1700s	3	1	.	1	.	1	.
Faulkner, G. Dublin; mid 1700s	15	15	.	.	.	.	.
Faure. early 1700s	1	1	.	.	.	.	.
Featherstonhaugh, G. mid 1800s	1	1	.	.	.	.	.
Felton, Parker & Barker. USA; mid 1800s	1	1	.	.	.	.	.
Fenner. early 1800s	2	2	.	.	.	.	.
Fenner, Sears & Co. London; early 1800s. see Hinton, et al	43	43	.	.	.	.	.
Ferguson: incl James, London, mid 1700s; A.M. & J., late 1800s	3	0	.	3	.	.	.
Ferraris. early 1800s	1	1	.	.	.	.	.
Fidalgo, Joaquin Francisco. Madrid; early 1800s	8	8	.	.	.	.	.
Fielding: incl John, publisher, London; Fielding & Walker; late 1700s	12	11	1	.	.	.	.
Filloeul. mid 1600s	1	0	1	.	.	.	.
Filson, John; Amer., c.1747-88	2	1	.	.	.	1	.
Finaeus, Orontius (Fine). French; 1494-1555	3	2	.	.	.	1	.
Findlay, Alexander. London; mid 1800s	18	14	2	.	.	.	2
Finley, Anthony. Phila; c.1790-1840	322	187	27	22	24	25	37
Finn. views; early 1900s	1	0	1	.	.	.	.
Fisher: incl H., London, early 1800s	12	9	1	.	1	.	1
Fisher & Son. London; early 1800s	2	0	.	.	1	1	.
Fisk: incl Fisk & Co., late 1800s; Fisk & See, NY, late 1800s	3	3	.	.	.	.	.
Fisk & Russell. NY; mid 1800s	3	3	.	.	.	.	.
Fitch, Asa. Albany; mid 1800s	1	1	.	.	.	.	.
Flamm. USA; late 1800s	2	0	2	.	.	.	.
Flamsteed, John. 1646-1719	7	7	.	.	.	.	.
Fleischmann. early 1700s	1	0	.	.	1	.	.
Fleming, S.A. Toronto; late 1800s	1	1	.	.	.	.	.
Flemming, Carl. Glogau; mid 1800s	29	19	.	2	4	4	.
Fleurieu. late 1700s	2	2	.	.	.	.	.
Flinders, Mathew. English; 1774-1814	2	1	.	.	.	.	1
Florianus, Antonius. Venice; mid 1500s	2	2	.	.	.	.	.
Florimi, Matteo. Siena; early 1600s	2	2	.	.	.	.	.

Name	Total	'83-'92	'93	'94	'95	'96	'97-8
Flushing & North Side R.R. NY; late 1800s	1	1	.	.	.	.	.
Foot, Thomas. London; late 1700s	2	2	.	.	.	.	.
Foppen. views; early 1900s	1	0	1	.	.	.	.
Forbes & Russell. Boston; mid 1800s	1	1	.	.	.	.	.
Forbes, Alexander. history; mid 1800s	1	1	.	.	.	.	.
Fores, Samuel W. publisher; London; late 1700s-mid 1800s	1	0	.	.	1	.	.
Forlani, Paolo de. Venice; mid 1500s	4	4	.	.	.	.	.
Forsell. Stockholm; early 1800s	1	0	.	.	.	.	1
Forster: incl G.; J.R., London, late 1700s	4	2	1	.	1	.	.
Forster & Maurice. Erie, PA; early 1800s	1	1	.	.	.	.	.
Foster: incl G.G., London, mid 1800s	5	3	.	.	1	1	.
Foster, John. Boston; 1648-81	1	0	.	.	1	.	.
Foster Groom. early 1900s	1	0	1	.	.	.	.
Fostes. Paris; mid 1800s	1	1	.	.	.	.	.
Fourdrinier, Peter. London; fl 1720-60	1	1	.	.	.	.	.
Fowler: George, Albany, early 1800s; T.M., late 1800s	3	1	.	.	.	2	.
Fowler & Moyer. views; late 1800s	9	5	.	2	.	2	.
Fox, Watson A. Buffalo; mid 1800s	1	1	.	.	.	.	.
Frank Leslie's Illustrated Newspaper. mid-late 1800s	24	16	.	1	3	4	.
Franklin: may incl Benjamin, Amer., 1700s; Sir John to '93 (see below)	27	23	2	.	.	2	.
Franklin (Globes). Troy, NY; late 1800s	1	0	.	1	.	.	.
Franklin, Sir John. English explorer, 1786-1847. see Franklin to '93	6	0	.	4	2	.	.
Franklin Mint. mid 1800s+	1	1	.	.	.	.	.
Fraser: incl J., London, late 1700s	2	2	.	.	.	.	.
Frazier. early 1700s	1	1	.	.	.	.	.
Fremin, A.R. Paris; mid 1800s	9	5	.	.	.	1	3
Fremont, John Charles. 1813-90.	25	6	2	1	2	6	8
French. J.H.; Phila; mid 1800s	1	0	.	.	.	.	1
French & Smith: incl French, Wood & Smith ('90); mid 1800s	6	4	.	1	.	.	1
Freycinet. see De Freycinet, '87+	.	.	.	.	.	.	.
Frezier, Amedee Francois. Paris; early 1700s	5	5	.	.	.	.	.
Fricx, Eugene Henri. Brussels; early 1700s. see De L'Isle	9	5	.	.	.	.	4
Fried. early 1800s	1	1	.	.	.	.	.
Friedenreich, P.C. Copenhagen; mid 1800s	1	1	.	.	.	.	.
Friederichs, J. mid 1800s	1	0	1	.	.	.	.
Fries, Lorenz. Strasbourg; c.1490-1532. See Ptolemy (1522-1541 Strassburg)	68	0	5	7	12	20	24
Fritz, Samuel. German; 1656-1725	2	1	.	.	.	.	1
Froiseth, B.A.M. USA, late 1800s	4	1	.	.	1	2	.
Fullarton, Archibald. Glasgow; Edinburgh; London; mid 1800s	263	225	12	14	6	4	2
Fuller, Thomas. English; mid 1600s	90	73	6	1	7	.	3
Funcke, David. Nuremberg; early 1700s	1	1	.	.	.	.	.
Furne (Cie). publisher; Paris; mid 1800s	5	4	.	1	.	.	.
Furst, Paul. Nuremberg; c 1605-1666	1	0	.	.	1	.	.
Gage, Isaac. mid 1800s	1	1	.	.	.	.	.
Galiani, M. late 1700s	1	1	.	.	.	.	.
Galiano & Valdes. voyagers; early 1800s	2	2	.	.	.	.	.
Galignani. Paris; mid 1800s	4	1	1	.	.	2	.
Gall & Inglis. Edinburgh; London; late 1800s	27	18	3	.	2	1	3
Galle: incl Philippe, late 1500; Cornelis, mid 1600s; Antwerp	15	11	1	2	.	1	.
Galluci, Gioavanni Paolo. Italy, fl 1569-97	3	1	.	.	1	1	.
Galt & Hoy. NY; late 1800s	3	2	1	.	.	.	.
Gamble, Wm. H. engr., Phila; mid 1800s	4	4	.	.	.	.	.
Gardiner, C.K. USA; mid 1800s	1	1	.	.	.	.	.
Gardner, James Sr. London; mid 1800s	7	7	.	.	.	.	.
Garneray. mid 1800s	3	0	2	.	1	.	.
Garnier, F. Paris; mid 1800s	23	8	1	2	1	10	1
Garran, Andrew. late 1800s	7	7	.	.	.	.	.
Gaskell, C.A. Chicago; late 1800s	12	6	2	2	.	2	.
Gast & Co. USA; late 1800s	7	1	.	.	.	.	6
Gastaldi, Giacomo. Venice; mid 1500s. see Ptolemy (1548)	38	1	4	6	11	3	13
Gaston, Samuel N. NY; mid 1800s	7	7	.	.	.	.	.
Gaston & Johnson. publisher; NY; mid 1800s	3	1	.	1	.	.	1
Gaubil, Antoine. 1689-1759	2	2	.	.	.	.	.
Gaudy, John. mid 1700s	1	1	.	.	.	.	.
Gaultier. Paris; early 1800s	1	0	1	.	.	.	.

Name	Total	'83-'92	'93	'94	'95	'96	'97-8
Gauthey. France, late 1700s	2	0	.	1	.	1	.
Gavarrete, Juan. late 1800s	1	1	.	.	.	.	.
Gavin, H. mid 1700s	1	1	.	.	.	.	.
Gavit & Duthie. mid 1800s	2	1	1	.	.	.	.
Gavit, John. printer; Albany; mid 1800s	2	2	.	.	.	.	.
Gazzettiere Americano. Coltellini, publisher; Livorno; mid 1700s	158	98	3	13	2	35	7
Gebauers, J.J.; Halle; mid 1700s	1	0	1	.	.	.	.
Geddes, James. Albany, NY; early 1800s	2	2	.	.	.	.	.
Geil. Samuel (incl Geil & Jones); Phila; mid 1800s	2	1	.	.	.	.	1
Geil, Leamings & Cathcart. Phila; mid 1800s	1	1	.	.	.	.	.
Gell, William. 1777-1836	2	0	1	1	.	.	.
Gemellis, John Francis. early 1700s	1	1	.	.	.	.	.
Gemma Frisius; Louvain; early 1500s. try Apianus	3	1	.	1	.	.	1
Gendron, Pedro. Madrid; mid 1700s	6	6	.	.	.	.	.
General Magazine of Arts & Sciences. mid 1700s	13	9	1	.	1	.	2
Gensoul, Adrien. publisher; San Francisco; mid 1800s	4	3	.	1	.	.	.
Gentleman's & London Magazine. mid 1700s	4	1	1	.	.	2	.
Gentleman's Magazine. 1700s	519	359	31	29	39	24	37
Genty. late 1700s	1	1	.	.	.	.	.
Gerritz, Hessel. 1581-1632.	3	2	.	.	.	.	1
Gerstmayr. German(?); late 1700s	3	3	.	.	.	.	.
Gibbes, Chas. Drayton. San Fran., late 1800s.	2	1	.	.	.	1	.
Gibson, John. London; mid 1700s. see Gentleman's Magazine	93	78	4	.	3	3	5
Gilbert: incl James, publisher, London, early 1800s.	5	4	.	.	.	1	.
Gill, J.K. Portland, OR; late 1800s	7	5	.	.	.	.	2
Gillet, George. USA; 1771-1853	1	1	.	.	.	.	.
Gilliam. Phila; mid 1800s	1	1	.	.	.	.	.
Gilman, E. Phila; mid 1800s	6	4	.	1	.	1	.
Gilpin, William. Phila; mid 1800s	11	7	.	1	1	1	1
Gilquin & Dupain. mid 1800s	2	2	.	.	.	.	.
Giustiniano. various	4	4	.	.	.	.	.
Glazier, Willard. Phila; late 1800s	1	1	.	.	.	.	.
Gleason: Pictorial Drawing Room Companion. Boston; mid 1800s	10	10	.	.	.	.	.
Globes.	17	0	.	.	.	9	8
Goad, Charles. late 1800s	32	25	.	.	7	.	.
Goeree, Jan. Amsterdam; early 1700s	5	5	.	.	.	.	.
Goering, A. Leipzig; late 1800s	3	3	.	.	.	.	.
Goggins, Joseph. late 1800s	1	1	.	.	.	.	.
Gold, Joyce. London; early 1800s. see Naval Chronicle	20	20	.	.	.	.	.
Goldbach. Christian Friedrich; German; 1763-1822	1	0	.	.	.	.	1
Goldthwait: incl J.H. mid 1800s; T.H., Boston mid 1800s	13	6	2	.	1	3	1
Gonzalez, Nicolas. Manilla, late 1800s.	1	0	.	.	.	1	.
Goodrich, Samuel Griswold (aka Peter Parley). Boston, 1793-1860	56	50	.	1	.	.	5
Goodwin, F. NY; mid 1800s	1	1	.	.	.	.	.
Goos (family): Abraham, c.1590-1643; Pieter, c.1616-75; Amsterdam	173	139	14	4	7	8	1
Gordon: incl Patrick, London, mid 1700s; P. Dublin; late 1700s	22	21	.	.	.	.	1
Gordon, T. engraver, Gordon's History. see Gordon to '93	1	0	.	1	.	.	.
Gordon, William. *History of Amer.*, 1788	6	0	.	.	.	.	6
Goschen, G. Leipzig; early 1800s	1	1	.	.	.	.	.
Gosse & Pinet. mid 1800s	7	7	.	.	.	.	.
Gottfried, aka Johann Philipp Abelin. mid 1600s	10	2	.	3	.	.	5
Gould, August. late 1800s	3	2	.	.	.	1	.
Gould, Jay. American tycoon; 1836-92.	1	.	.	1	.	.	.
Gourlay, Robert Fleming. mid 1800s	1	1	.	.	.	.	.
Government Maps: National. see U.S. categories; British; Canadian. try Title Index	2	0	.	.	.	.	2
Government Maps: Local & State. see Local & State Gov't to '96. try Title Index	29	0	4	6	2	5	12
Graham's Magazine. mid 1800s	1	1	.	.	.	.	.
Grand Magazine. late 1700s	2	2	.	.	.	.	.
Grand Magazine of Magazines. mid 1700s	6	2	4	.	.	.	.
Grand Magazine of Universal Intelligence. mid 1700s	3	2	.	.	.	1	.
Grant, A.A. (Cram licencee), USA, late 1800s	26	1	4	.	4	16	1
Graphic, The., late 1800s	6	2	.	2	.	.	2
Grattan & Gilbert. London mid1800s	5	4	.	.	1	.	.
Gratz. early 1800s	3	3	.	.	.	.	.
Gravier, Giovanni. mid 1700s	1	0	.	1	.	.	.

Name	Total	'83-'92	'93	'94	'95	'96	'97-8
Gravius, N.T. Amsterdam; mid 1700s	7	3	1	3	.	.	.
Gray & Johns. mid 1800s	1	1	.	.	.	.	.
Gray, Ormando Willis. Phila; late 1800s	297	165	27	43	22	24	16
Greenebaum & Sampson. Chicago; mid 1800s	1	1	.	.	.	.	.
Greenhow, Robert. USA; 1800-54. see Burr	2	1	.	.	.	.	1
Greenleaf. Moses, Portland, ME, early 1800s; Jeremiah, Brattleboro, VT; mid 1800s	132	101	8	8	6	5	4
Greenwood; publisher (various imprints): London; early 1800s	31	28	.	.	.	.	3
Gregory. late 1700s	5	1	1	.	2	1	.
Grenier. late 1700s	1	1	.	.	.	.	.
Gridley, Richard. mid 1700s	4	4	.	.	.	.	.
Grierson, George. Dublin; mid 1700s	18	10	1	.	7	.	.
Grigg, John. publisher, Phila, early 1800s	3	1	.	.	.	1	1
Grimmel. Russia; mid 1700s	1	0	.	.	1	.	.
Griswold. New Orleans; mid 1800s	6	6	.	.	.	.	.
Grose, Francis. c.1731-91	5	5	.	.	.	.	.
Gross. incl Rudolph, Germany, late 1800s	1	0	1	.	.	.	.
Grosse. late 1700s	2	2	.	.	.	.	.
Grundy, John (Sr & Jr). England; mid 1700s	1	1	.	.	.	.	.
Grynaeus, Simon. Basle; 1493-1541	8	6	.	.	1	.	1
Gugler Lith. Milwaukee; late 1800s	1	1	.	.	.	.	.
Guicciardini, Luigi. Antwerp; late 1500s	49	35	2	.	9	2	1
Guilquin & Dupain. Paris; mid 1800s	1	1	.	.	.	.	.
Guizot. Paris; mid 1800s	1	0	.	.	.	1	.
Gurney Cab Service. late 1800s	1	1	.	.	.	.	.
Gussefeld, Franz Ludwig. Nuremberg; late 1700s. see Homann	19	14	.	1	2	.	2
Gussfield. globe; early 1800s	1	0	1	.	.	.	.
Guthrie & Jones. early 1800s	3	0	.	.	3	.	.
Guthrie, William. London; late 1700s	39	28	.	3	1	2	5
Guyot.	2	0	.	.	.	1	1
Haasis & Lubrecht. late 1800s	3	2	1	.	.	.	.
Habermann, F.X. Augsburg; late 1700s	7	7	.	.	.	.	.
Hachette, Louis Christophe Francois. publisher, Paris; mid 1800s+	5	3	.	.	.	2	.
Hacke, Capt. William. voyages, late 1600s	2	1	.	1	.	.	.
Hadfield, W. London; mid 1800s	1	1	.	.	.	.	.
Haellstrom. Carl Peter; Finnish; 1774-1836	1	0	.	.	.	.	1
Haffner. M, Germany late 1600's; Johann Christoph, publisher, early 1700s	2	0	1	.	.	.	1
Hagaman & Markham. Auburn, NY; mid 1800s	1	1	.	.	.	.	.
Haines. includes D., Phila, early 1800s; S.	2	1	1	.	.	.	.
Hajeck, I.F. engraver; Germany; mid 1800s	1	0	.	.	.	1	.
Hale, Nathan. Boston; early 1800s	2	1	.	.	1	.	.
Hales, John Groves. Mass., 1785-1832	2	1	.	.	.	1	.
Haliburton, Thomas C. Halifax, NS; early 1800s. see Halliburton, '84	11	11	.	.	.	.	.
Hall: incl William, late 1700s; may incl Sidney	84	78	5	.	.	.	1
Hall, Ralph	1	0	.	1	.	.	.
Hall, Sidney. London; early 1800s	18	0	.	3	3	5	7
Halley, Edmund. English; 1656-1742	3	0	1	.	.	.	2
Halma, Francois. Amsterdam; Leeuwarden; early 1700s	2	2	.	.	.	.	.
Hals & Rydstrom. late 1800s	1	1	.	.	.	.	.
Hamelmann. late 1500s	2	1	.	.	1	.	.
Hamilton, Adams & Co. London; early 1800s	2	1	1	.	.	.	.
Hamilton, Alexander (of East India Co.). 1688-1723	1	0	.	.	1	.	.
Hammond. publisher; Chicago; late 1800s+	2	1	1	.	.	.	.
Handtke, Friedrich H. Glogau; 1815-79	6	2	1	2	1	.	.
Hanna, Capt. James. late 1700s	1	1	.	.	.	.	.
Hannibal & St. Joseph Short Line. late 1800s	1	1	.	.	.	.	.
Hansard & Sons. London, early 1800s	1	1	.	.	.	.	.
Happel. early 1700s	2	0	1	.	.	.	1
Hardesty, H.H. Chicago, Toledo, Richmond; late 1800s	32	10	5	4	4	3	6
Hardy, John. London; late 1700s	2	2	.	.	.	.	.
Harmon, C.P. Grants Pass, OR; late 1800s	1	1	.	.	.	.	.
Harper: incl J.J. NY, early 1800s	18	15	.	1	1	.	1
Harper Bros. (Harper & Bros) publisher, NY, mid 1800s	15	10	1	.	2	2	.
Harper's Weekly. NY; late 1800s	93	53	11	6	8	12	3
Harrewyn (family). Brussels; early 1700s	1	1	.	.	.	.	.
Harris, John. English; early 1700s. see E. Bowen	62	47	6	1	2	2	4

	Total	'83-'92	'93	'94	'95	'96	'97-8
Harrison: incl John E., London, late 1700s; George, Pitts, mid 1800s	47	30	.	.	14	.	3
Harrison & Sons. mid 1800s	2	1	.	.	.	1	.
Harrison & Warner. Phila; late 1800s	2	1	1	.	.	.	.
Hart. early 1800s	3	2	.	.	.	1	.
Hassenstein, Bruno. Berlin; 1839-1902	1	1	.	.	.	.	.
Hassler, Ferdinand Rudolph. U.S.C.S.; 1770-1843	1	1	.	.	.	.	.
Haszard, George T. P.E.I.; mid 1800s	1	1	.	.	.	.	.
Hatch. lith; NY; mid 1800s	1	1	.	.	.	.	.
Hauducoeur, C.P. late 1700s	1	1	.	.	.	.	.
Hausermann, R. France, late 1800s	1	0	.	.	.	1	.
Haven, John. USA; mid 1800s	3	2	.	.	1	.	.
Hawkes, W. publisher; London; late 1700s	2	2	.	.	.	.	.
Hawkins. incl Alfred, Quebec, mid 1800s	3	2	.	.	.	1	.
Hayden, Ferdinand Vandeveer; Amer., 1829-87	28	1	4	.	.	8	15
Hayward. John, Hartford; G., NY; mid 1800s	9	5	.	.	1	2	1
Hazard, Willis P. mid 1800s	2	1	.	.	.	1	.
Heaphy, Charles. New Zealand; mid 1800s	3	3	.	.	.	.	.
Hearne, Samuel. English, 1740-92	17	12	.	.	4	1	.
Heather, William. London; early 1800s	31	17	2	.	3	.	9
Hebner, John. London; early 1800s	1	1	.	.	.	.	.
Heck, G. mid 1800s	13	11	.	.	1	1	.
Heliotype Printing Co. Boston; late 1800s	1	1	.	.	.	.	.
Heller, C. mid 1800s	1	0	1	.	.	.	.
Hemback. late 1800s	1	1	.	.	.	.	.
Henderson: G., early 1800s; J., mid 1800s	2	2	.	.	.	.	.
Henn, Williams & Co. mid 1800s	3	2	.	.	.	1	.
Hennepin, Louis de, Amsterdam, 1640-1701	18	12	1	.	1	2	2
Henriol, J.N. Paris; mid 1800s	1	1	.	.	.	.	.
Henry, J. mid 1800s	2	1	.	.	1	.	.
Hentschell. late 1800s	1	1	.	.	.	.	.
Herberstein, Sigismund. Austrian; 1486-1566	3	1	.	2	.	.	.
Herbert, William. London; mid 1700s	80	61	12	1	1	2	3
Herder, B. Freiburg; mid 1800s	1	1	.	.	.	.	.
Heriot, George. traveler, early 1800s	9	8	.	.	.	1	.
Herisson, Eustache. Paris; early 1800s	13	10	2	.	.	.	1
Hermann Bros. San Jose, CA; late 1800s	1	1	.	.	.	.	.
Hermannides, Rutger. mid 1600s	1	1	.	.	.	.	.
Hermet. late 1800s	1	1	.	.	.	.	.
Herrera. see De Herrera, '88+	.	.	.	.	.	.	.
Herrman, Augustine. Bohemian, London; 1621-85	1	1	.	.	.	.	.
Hersbach. Caspar; early 1600s	1	0	.	.	.	.	1
Hertel. Nuremberg; late 1700s	1	0	.	.	.	1	.
Hesse, J. views; mid 1800s	1	0	1	.	.	.	.
Heubache, E. Chicago; late 1800s	1	1	.	.	.	.	.
Hewitt, N.R. London; early 1800s	1	1	.	.	.	.	.
Heydt, Johann Wolfgang. German; mid 1700s	2	1	.	.	1	.	.
Heylin, Peter. London, 1599-1662	11	6	1	4	.	.	.
Heyns: Pieter, 1537-98; Zacharias (son), 1566-1638; Amsterdam	3	0	.	2	.	1	.
Hickling, C. publisher; Boston; mid 1800s	1	1	.	.	.	.	.
Higginson, J.H. NY: mid 1800s	1	1	.	.	.	.	.
Highway Maps.	3	0	.	.	.	.	3
Hildburghausen Bibliographisches Institut. see Hildburg Institut to '91	113	22	.	8	66	4	13
Hildebrandt. views; mid 1800s	2	2	.	.	.	.	.
Hill: incl Samuel, Amer, early 1800s; A,J.; J.W., mid 1800s; H.; H.H. & Co, Decatur, IL; H.W. & Co.	6	4	1	.	.	.	1
Hill, Nathaniel. globes, c.1750	1	0	.	.	.	.	.
Hilliard d'Auberteuil. late 1700s	1	1	.	.	.	.	.
Hilliard, Gray & Co. Boston; early 1800s	1	1	.	.	.	.	.
Hills, John. US; fl. 1777-1817	4	2	.	.	.	2	.
Hilton. J. engraver; mid 1700s	2	1	.	1	.	.	.
Hind, Henry Youle. Canadian travels; mid 1800s	4	3	.	1	.	.	.
Hinrichs, O. Chicago; late 1800s	1	1	.	.	.	.	.
Hinshelwood, R. NY; mid 1800s	3	3	.	.	.	.	.
Hinton, John. London; mid 1700s. name used into 1800s	74	47	4	4	7	3	9
Hinton, Simpkin & Marshall. see Fenner, Sears. London; early 1800s	10	10	.	.	.	.	.

51

Name	Total	'83-'92	'93	'94	'95	'96	'97-8
Hitchcock: incl Edward, USA, mid 1800s; Charles, USA, late 1800s	4	4	.	.	.	.	.
Hobbs, J.S., London, mid 1800s	3	2	.	.	.	.	1
Hobbs & Wilson. charts; mid 1800s	2	2	.	.	.	.	.
Hodder & Stoughton,. publisher; London; mid 1800s	6	0	.	.	.	6	.
Hodges & Smith. Dublin; mid 1800s	1	0	1	.	.	.	.
Hodges, J. London; mid 1700s	1	1	.	.	.	.	.
Hoen & Co. lith; Baltimore; mid-late 1800s. see U.S. categories	7	5	.	1	.	1	.
Hoffman: Johannes. Nuremberg, 1629-98; W., Weimar, early 1800s	3	1	.	.	1	1	.
Hofmann. C.G.; Leipzig; mid 1700s;	1	0	.	.	.	.	1
Hogenberg, Frans. Cologne, 1535-90	4	4	.	.	.	.	.
Hogg, Alexander. London; late 1700s. see Cook	72	59	7	1	3	2	.
Holden's Dollar Magazine. mid 1800s	1	1	.	.	.	.	.
Hole, William. fl 1600-46. see Camden, Kip	37	29	1	5	2	.	.
Hollar, Wenceslaus. London; Bohemian, 1607-77	10	6	1	2	.	.	1
Holman, Thomas. printer, NY; mid 1800s	1	1	.	.	.	.	.
Holmes: incl J.B., NY, late 1800s; W.H., late 1800s	7	5	.	.	.	.	2
Holt, Warren. San Francisco; late 1800s	6	6	.	.	.	.	.
Holtrop, W. Amsterdam; late 1700s	6	6	.	.	.	.	.
Homann & Homann Heirs. Johann Baptist, Nuremberg, 1663-1724.	1201	766	169	54	75	44	93
Homann Heirs thereafter. see Doppelmayr; Gussefeld							
Home Insurance Co. NY; mid 1800s	5	5	.	.	.	.	.
Home Missionary Magazine. mid 1800s	1	0	.	.	.	1	.
Hondius (family): Jodocus (I) 1563-1612; (II) 1594-1629;	671	454	45	58	22	29	63
Henricus 1597-1651. Amsterdam (& London). see Jansson; Mercator							
Honter, Jan Coronensis. Kronstadt, Zurich; 1498-1549	41	37	1	2	.	.	1
Hood: incl Washington, US T.E., mid 1800s; R.V., London, mid 1800s	7	3	.	.	.	2	2
Hooker. early 1800s	2	2	.	.	.	.	.
Hooper & Berner. San Francisco; late 1800s	2	2	.	.	.	.	.
Hooper, Samuel. London; fl 1770-93.	2	2	.	.	.	.	.
Hopkins, G.M. Phila; late 1800s	15	4	.	1	3	3	4
Horatius, Andreas Antonius. Rome; early 1700s	1	1	.	.	.	.	.
Hornius, Georg. Dutch, 1620-70	3	3	.	.	.	.	.
Horsburgh, Capt. James, R.N. 1762-1836	17	14	.	1	2	.	.
Horwood, Richard. English; c.1758-1803	1	1	.	.	.	.	.
Hough, E. late 1800s	1	1	.	.	.	.	.
Houze, Antoine Philippe. Paris; mid 1800s	7	6	.	.	1	.	.
Howe, Henry. USA; mid 1800s	2	0	.	.	2	.	.
Howell: incl Reading, late 1700s; Mark, late 1800s	7	3	1	1	.	.	2
Howells, William C. Hamilton, OH; mid 1800s	1	1	.	.	.	.	.
Howen, A., lith; Baltimore, mid 1800s	1	1	.	.	.	.	.
Hoxford & Co. NY; mid 1800s	1	1	.	.	.	.	.
Hubbs, Edwin C. late 1800s	1	1	.	.	.	.	.
Huber. mid 1800s	1	1	.	.	.	.	.
Huberti, Adrien. engraver, views; late 1500s	4	4	.	.	.	.	.
Hughes: incl Michael, Phila, mid 1800s; William, London; mid 1800s	10	6	.	3	.	1	.
Hulett, J. London(?); mid 1700s	3	2	.	1	.	.	.
Hulsius, Levinus. Frankfort; late 1500s	15	13	.	.	2	.	.
Humboldt. see Von Humboldt, '87 +	.	.	.	.	.	.	.
Hume & Smollett. London; mid 1800s	1	1	.	.	.	.	.
Hunt & Randel. US; mid 1800s.	1	0	.	.	.	.	1
Hunt & Eaton. publisher, USA; late 1800s	12	10	.	.	.	1	1
Hunter, William S. Boston; mid 1800s	1	1	.	.	.	.	.
Huntington, F.J. NY; mid 1800s	4	3	.	.	1	.	.
Huntington & Willard. publisher; Hartford; early 1800s	1	1	.	.	.	.	.
Huot, Jean Jacques Nicolas. French; mid 1800s	3	2	.	1	.	.	.
Huquier. Paris; mid 1700s	1	1	.	.	.	.	.
Hurd, D.H. Boston; late 1800s	3	1	.	.	.	.	2
Husson, Pieter. publisher; Hague; 1678-1733	6	5	1	.	.	.	.
Hutawa, Edward & Julius, litho; St. Louis, mid 1800s	3	1	.	1	.	1	.
Hutchings, John.	1	1	.	.	.	.	.
Hutchins, Thomas. USA; 1730-89	4	3	1	.	.	.	.
Hutchinson; incl Thomas. London; mid 1700s	2	2	.	.	.	.	.
Hyde & Co. New York, late 1800s	8	6	.	1	.	1	.
Hydrographical Office. see British Admiralty	.	.	.	.	.	.	.
I.C.M.R. 1800s	1	1	.	.	.	.	.

Name	Total	'83-'92	'93	'94	'95	'96	'97-8
Iliff. late 1800s	1	1	.	.	.	.	.
Illman, T. & Sons. English; mid 1800s	7	5	.	2	.	.	.
Illustrated London News. mid 1800s +	82	63	2	.	6	4	7
Illustrated News. mid 1800s	6	6	.	.	.	.	.
Imbert, J. Leopold. Paris; late 1700s	4	3	.	.	.	.	1
Imray, James. English; mid 1800s	110	83	9	4	5	1	8
Ingersoll, Ernest. late 1800s	1	1	.	.	.	.	.
International Survey Co., Chicago, c.1900	2	0	.	1	.	1	.
Irving, Washington; American author, 1783-1859	4	2	.	1	1	.	.
Ivison & Blakeman. Chicago; late 1800s	2	2	.	.	.	.	.
Jackson: incl M., London, mid 1800s; P., London, early 1800s; Wm. A., NY	6	6	.	.	.	.	.
Jacobsz (aka Lootsman): Anthonie, c.1606-50; Jacob, Caspar, mid 1600s; Amst.	42	33	1	.	8	.	.
Jacottet, E. lith; late 1800s	1	1	.	.	.	.	.
Jaeger, Johann Wilhelm Abraham. Frankfurt; 1718-90	4	3	.	1	.	.	.
Jaillot, Alexis-Hubert. Paris; 1632-1712. see Mortier	263	193	12	15	12	7	24
James. incl Dr. Edwin (Long Exped.), early 1800s; J.A. & U.P.; W.	8	2	3	.	.	1	2
Jamieson, Alexander. early 1800s	19	0	.	1	.	18	.
Jansson, Jan. Amsterdam; 1588-1664. see Hondius; Mercator; Valk & Schenk	1186	805	117	63	56	50	95
Janvier, Jean. Paris; late 1700s	53	33	1	3	3	7	6
Japanese Cartography.	27	13	.	4	2	5	3
Jarves. mid 1800s	1	1	.	.	.	.	.
Jaugeon, N. Paris, late 1600s	2	0	.	.	.	2	.
Jean. publisher; Paris; early 1800s	2	1	1	.	.	.	.
Jefferys, Thomas. London; c.1710-71. see Laurie & Whittle; Sayer et al	428	316	20	14	33	24	21
Jefferys & Faden. late 1700s	3	1	.	1	.	.	1
Jeppe, Frederick. Pretoria; 1833-98	1	1	.	.	.	.	.
Jewett, Thomas & Co. USA; mid 1800s	2	1	1	.	.	.	.
Johnson, A.J. NY; mid 1800s. see variants to '89	628	351	49	47	70	40	71
Johnson & Browning. NY; mid 1800s. see Johnson	55	55	.	.	.	.	.
Johnson & Ward. NY; mid 1800s. see Johnson	128	128	.	.	.	.	.
Johnston. Incl Thomas, Boston, mid 1700s; W. & A.K., Edinburgh, mid 1800s	306	230	15	19	18	12	12
Johnstone. mid 1800s	1	1	.	.	.	.	.
Jollain: Claude; Francis; Gerard; Paris; 1600s	2	0	.	.	.	1	1
Joly, Joseph Romain. 1715-1805	1	0	1	.	.	.	.
Joslin. globes; Boston, mid 1800s	2	0	.	.	.	2	.
Jourdan & Defrenoy. late 1800s	2	1	.	.	.	1	.
Journeaux L'Aine. early 1800s	1	0	1	.	.	.	.
Jouvot. publisher, Paris; late 1800s	1	1	.	.	.	.	.
Judd, James. English; mid 1800s	1	1	.	.	.	.	.
Julien, Roth-Joseph. Paris, fl 1750-80.	2	0	.	1	1	.	.
Juta. publisher; Capetown; late 1800s	2	0	.	.	1	.	1
Kaempfer, Engelbert. German(?); 1651-1716	26	1	1	10	2	10	2
Kaerius. see Van den Keere	.	.	.	.	.	.	.
Kane, Elisha Kent. Phila; mid 1800s	3	2	.	1	.	.	.
Kearfott, J. Baker. late 1800s	3	3	.	.	.	.	.
Kearsley, George. publisher; London; late 1700s	2	2	.	.	.	.	.
Keefer, Thomas C. Montreal; mid 1800s	3	3	.	.	.	.	.
Keeler: J.M., San Fran, late 1800s; Wm. J., Washington, late 1800s	3	1	.	.	.	1	1
Keere. see Van den Keere	.	.	.	.	.	.	.
Keily, J. with J.W. Otley. New Jersey	1	0	.	1	.	.	.
Keller. Heinrich, Swiss, 1778-1862; mid 1800s; A., Dutch(?), late 1800s	5	1	1	.	2	.	1
Kellogg. lith, Hartford, mid 1800s	2	2	.	.	.	.	.
Kelly, Thomas. London; mid 1800s	30	25	3	.	1	1	.
Kemble, W. NY; mid 1800s	4	2	.	.	.	1	1
Kendall. Geo. W.; Amer journalis; 1809-67	3	0	.	.	.	.	3
Kennard. London; mid 1800s	1	1	.	.	.	.	.
Kensett, Thomas. New Haven; early 1800s	5	2	1	1	.	.	1
Kepler, Johann. German; 1571-1630.	1	1	.	.	.	.	.
Kepohoni. Hawaii; mid 1800s	2	1	.	1	.	.	.
Keur, Jacob & Hendrik. Dutch; mid 1700s	13	6	1	1	1	3	1
Key, John R. NY; mid 1800s	1	1	.	.	.	.	.
Keyser, Jacob. Amsterdam; early 1700s	6	6	.	.	.	.	.
Keystone Publishing Co. Chicago; late 1800s	1	1	.	.	.	.	.
Kiepert, Heinrich. Weimar; mid 1800s	8	3	4	.	1	.	.
Kilbourn, John. Columbus, OH; early 1800s	1	1	.	.	.	.	.

	Total	'83-'92	'93	'94	'95	'96	'97-8
Kilburn. Boston; mid 1800s	1	1	.	.	.	.	.
Kilian, George Christophe. engraver. Augsburg, 1709-80	13	0	.	5	.	4	4
Kimmel & Foster. mid 1800s	1	1	.	.	.	.	.
Kincaid, Alexander. late 1700s	3	1	1	.	1	.	.
King, Daniel. London; mid 1600s	1	1	.	.	.	.	.
Kingman Bros. Chicago; late 1800s	6	6	.	.	.	.	.
Kingsbury, Lt. J.P. US Army; mid 1800s	2	1	1	.	.	.	.
Kinnersley, E. Bungay, Suffolk; early 1800s	2	2	.	.	.	.	.
Kino, Eusebio Francisco. Spanish; 1644-1711	7	3	.	1	1	1	1
Kip, William. English; early 1600s. see Camden	35	31	.	.	.	1	3
Kircher, Athanasius. Amsterdam; mid 1600s	57	36	1	11	5	1	3
Kirkwood, James & Son. publisher; Edinburgh; early 1800s	2	2	.	.	.	.	.
Kitchin, Thomas. London; 1718-84	309	239	8	14	15	10	23
Klaproth, Heinrich Julius von. traveler; 1783-1835	1	1	.	.	.	.	.
Klauprech & Menzel. lith, Cincinnati; mid 1800s	1	1	.	.	.	.	.
Kleinknecht, L.V. mid 1800s	6	2	.	4	.	.	.
Klinckowstrom, Axel Leonhard. Stockholm; 1775-1837	1	1	.	.	.	.	.
Klockhoff, H. late 1800s	2	2	.	.	.	.	.
Knapton. mid 1700s	1	1	.	.	.	.	.
Knight, Charles. London; mid 1800s. see Society for the Diffusion of Useful Knowledge	14	14	.	.	.	.	.
Knipe, J.A. mid 1800s	3	1	.	.	.	.	2
Knox, James. early 1800s	2	1	.	.	1	.	.
Koch, Augustus. late 1800s	1	1	.	.	.	.	.
Kohl, A. late 1800s	1	1	.	.	.	.	.
Kok, J. Amsterdam; late 1700s	3	3	.	.	.	.	.
Kolb, Peter. (aka Kolben); 1675-1726	14	6	.	.	.	.	8
Koller, G. early 1700s	2	2	.	.	.	.	.
Kootwyck. see Cotovicus	.	.	.	.	.	.	.
Krayenhoff, Baron C.T.R. van. French; early 1800s	2	2	.	.	.	.	.
Kreffeldt, Mart. Karol. Dutch(?); mid 1500s	1	1	.	.	.	.	.
Krevelt, A. van. engraver, Amsterdam; late 1700s	5	3	.	.	.	2	.
Kruikius, Nicolas Samuelsz. Delft, 1678-1754	11	11	.	.	.	.	.
Krusenstern. Adam Johann von; Russia; 1770-1827	1	0	.	.	.	.	1
Kuchel, C.C. San Francisco; mid 1800s	1	1	.	.	.	.	.
Kurtz & Allison. late 1800s	1	1	.	.	.	.	.
La Harpe, Jean Francis de. 1739-1803	8	0	3	.	.	2	3
La Hontan, Baron Louis de. The Hague; London; 1666-1715. see Lahonton, '89	55	44	3	1	4	1	2
La Perouse, Comte Jean de. Paris; 1741-88. aka: Jean Francois de Galoup. see Robinson	150	81	24	8	19	12	6
La Pointe. engraver, late 1600s	1	1	.	.	.	.	.
La Rochefoucault-Liancourt, Francois A.F.. late 1700s	3	1	.	.	.	2	.
Labat, J.B. The Hague; early 1700s	7	6	1	.	.	.	.
Labelye, Charles. London; mid 1700s	1	1	.	.	.	.	.
Labillardiere. Jacques Julien Houton de; French; early 1800s	1	0	.	.	.	.	1
Lacoste, Charles. Paris; late 1800s	3	3	.	.	.	.	.
Ladies Repository. USA; mid 1800s	26	17	4	.	.	1	4
Lafitau. mid 1700s	9	0	.	.	8	1	.
Lafreri School (Antonio Lafreri). Rome. see Bertelli; Camocio; Duchetti; Forlani; Gastaldi; Rasciotti; Salamanca; Zaltieri	11	6	3	1	1	.	.
Lagniet. Jacques; Paris; mid 1600s	1	0	.	.	.	.	1
Lake et al. US; late 1800s	1	0	.	.	.	.	1
Lake Shore & Michigan Southern Rwy. late 1800s	2	2	.	.	.	.	.
Lallemand. Paris; mid 1800s	2	0	2	.	.	.	.
Lambert, J. traveler; early 1800s	5	4	1	.	.	.	.
Lamy, Bernard.	1	0	.	1	.	.	.
Lancelot, D. views; London; late 1800s	1	1	.	.	.	.	.
Lane: Nathaniel; also W, London; late 1700s	3	3	.	.	.	.	.
Lange: incl Henry, German, 1821-93; views, G.G., mid 1800s	7	3	2	.	1	.	1
Lange & Kronfeld. views; mid 1800s	1	0	1	.	.	.	.
Langenes, Barent. Amsterdam; late 1500s	19	7	3	3	2	3	1
Langhans, Paul. Gotha; late 1800s	1	1	.	.	.	.	.
Langley, Edward. London; early 1800s	12	12	.	.	.	.	.
Langlois, Hyacinthe. Paris; early 1800s	2	2	.	.	.	.	.
Langsdorff, G. Frankfort; early 1800s	2	2	.	.	.	.	.
Lanne. Longuet sucessor; Paris; late 1800s	1	0	.	.	.	.	1

	Total	'83-'92	'93	'94	'95	'96	'97-8
Lapie, Alexandre Emile & Pierre. Paris; early 1800s	89	44	6	10	5	7	17
Lapointe, D. Paris; mid 1600s	1	1	.	.	.	.	.
Laporte, Joseph de. late 1700s	11	1	.	1	1	1	7
Las Cases, Comte Emmanuel M.J.A.D. de. (aka Le Sage). 1766-1842.	2	2	.	.	.	.	.
Laso. Madrid; early 1700s	1	0	.	.	1	.	.
Lasor a Varea, Alphonsus. Padua; early 1700s. aka R. Savonarola.	124	76	.	24	.	14	10
Lathrop, H.P. New Orleans; mid 1800s	3	3	.	.	.	.	.
Latrobe, C.I. London; early 1800s	1	1	.	.	.	.	.
Lattre, Jean. Paris; late 1700s	35	23	4	.	6	1	1
Lauremberg, Johannes Wilhelm. Amsterdam, 1590-1658	8	8	.	.	.	.	.
Laurent; incl J., Paris, mid 1800s	6	3	.	2	1	.	.
Laurie: John, mid 1700s; Robert, 1755-1836; Richard Holmes, fl 1822-58; London	19	17	.	1	.	1	.
Laurie & Whittle. London; late 1700s+. see Dunn; Jefferys	339	224	37	17	42	11	8
Lavoisne, C.V. London; early 1800s	34	5	2	1	5	6	15
Law, John (Louisiana Co.). early 1800s	6	4	1	.	1	.	.
Lawrence, H.L. lith; NY; mid 1800s	1	1	.	.	.	.	.
Lawson, John. London; early 1700s	3	3	.	.	.	.	.
Lay: incl John, early 1800s	6	4	.	1	1	.	.
Lazius, Wolfgang. Hungarian; 1514-65	1	1	.	.	.	.	.
Le Beau, Claude. Amsterdam; mid 1700s	1	1	.	.	.	.	.
Le Bruyn, Cornelis. early 1700s	17	15	.	.	.	.	2
Le Clerc: Jean, Paris, 1560-1621; Sebastian, Paris, late 1600s	21	17	.	1	.	1	2
Le Gentil, G.I.H. French traveler; 1725-92	1	1	.	.	.	.	.
Le Maire, Jacque. early 1600s	1	0	1	.	.	.	.
Le Maitre. engraver; Paris; early 1800s	2	1	.	1	.	.	.
Le Moyne. Jacques; French; d.1587. see De Bry	2	0	.	.	.	.	2
Le Page du Pratz. Paris; mid 1700s	3	2	1	.	.	.	.
Le Rouge, George Louis. Paris, fl 1740-80	245	171	11	11	30	6	16
Le Sage (pseudonym for Las Casas); early 1800s	6	4	1	1	.	.	.
Le Temps. publication; Paris	1	1	.	.	.	.	.
Le Vasseur de Beauplan, Guillaume. 1595-1685	1	1	.	.	.	.	.
Lea: Philip, London, late 1600s; Isaac, Phila, early 1800s	25	21	2	.	.	.	2
Lea & Blanchard. publisher; Phila; mid 1800s	1	1	.	.	.	.	.
Lea & Overton. late 1600s	4	4	.	.	.	.	.
Leadville Daily Herald. late 1800s	1	1	.	.	.	.	.
Legrand. early 1800s	2	2	.	.	.	.	.
Leigh, Samuel. London; early 1800s	13	10	.	1	1	.	1
Leitch: incl R.P., views, mid 1800s; J. Leitch & Co., London, late 1800s	5	5	.	.	.	.	.
Lejeune, T. mid 1800s	1	1	.	.	.	.	.
Lemercier. French; late 1800s	3	2	.	.	.	.	1
Lescarbot. Marc; France; 1590-1630	1	0	.	.	.	.	1
Lester. incl Wm, New Haven, early 1800s; John S., Boston, late 1800s	3	1	.	.	.	1	1
Letts. publisher; London; late 1800s	16	9	.	1	.	4	2
Leval, P. Paris; early 1700s	1	1	.	.	.	.	.
Levanto, Francesco Maria. Genoa; mid 1600s	3	3	.	.	.	.	.
Levasseur, Victor. Paris; mid 1800s	124	69	4	13	6	11	21
Levi. mid-late 1800s	1	0	1	.	.	.	.
Lewis & Clark. explorers; USA; early 1800s	2	2	.	.	.	.	.
Lewis, Samuel & Co. London; mid 1800s	15	7	2	.	.	.	6
Lewis, Samuel. Phila; late 1700s. see Carey	27	26	.	.	.	.	1
Liebaux, Jean Baptiste. Paris; late 1600s	1	1	.	.	.	.	.
Liefrinck, Mynken. Antwerp; late 1500s	1	1	.	.	.	.	.
Ligon, Richard. mid 1600s	8	8	.	.	.	.	.
Lincoln & Edmands. mid 1800s	3	0	1	2	.	.	.
Lindeman. late 1700s	1	1	.	.	.	.	.
Lindenkohl, Adolph. USA; 1833-1904	3	0	.	.	.	3	.
Lindner, F.L. early 1800s	2	1	.	.	1	.	.
Lindsay & Blakiston. Phila; mid 1800s	1	1	.	.	.	.	.
Lindstrom.	1	1	.	.	.	.	.
Linforth, James. author; mid 1800s	2	2	.	.	.	.	.
Link, W.F., NY, late 1700s.	1	0	.	.	1	.	.
Linschoten. see Van Linschoten, '86+	.	.	.	.	.	.	.
Linton: incl H. & W.J., London, late 1800s	4	4	.	.	.	.	.
Lippincott; late 1800s	5	5	.	.	.	.	.
Lippincott & Grambo; publisher, Phila; mid 1800s	2	2	.	.	.	.	.

55

Name	Total	'83-'92	'93	'94	'95	'96	'97-8
Lirelli. late 1700s	1	1	.	.	.	.	.
Literary Magazine. late 1700s	1	1	.	.	.	.	.
Lizars (family): Daniel, fl 1776-1812; William Home, 1788-1859; Edinburgh	54	41	4	.	3	3	3
Lloyd: various, 1800s; may incl H.H.	67	47	7	2	5	4	2
Lloyd, H.H. NY; mid 1800s	17	0	.	7	.	6	4
Lobeck, Tobias. mid 1700s	29	29	.	.	.	.	.
Lobineau, D.G.A. Paris, early 1800s	2	0	.	1	1	.	.
Local & State Maps & Views -Infrequent Publishers. try Title Index	60	0	.	8	5	14	33
Local & State Pocket Maps -Infrequent Publishers. try Title Index	43	0	.	18	.	9	16
Local & State Wall Maps -Infrequent Publishers. try Title Index	42	0	.	23	4	5	10
Lockhead. Berwick publ; early 1800s	6	0	.	.	.	.	6
Lockman, John. mid 1700s	1	1	.	.	.	.	.
Lockwood, Benoni. USA; early 1800s	1	0	1	.	.	.	.
Lodge, John. London; late 1700s	46	42	1	.	2	.	1
Logan & Hartley. Canada; late 1800s	1	1	.	.	.	.	.
Logerot. publisher; Paris; mid 1800s	7	2	3	.	1	1	.
Loggan, David. English; late 1600s	2	2	.	.	.	.	.
London Benevolent Repository. mid 1800s	1	1	.	.	.	.	.
London Gazette. late 1700s	5	5	.	.	.	.	.
London Illustrated News. mid 1800s +	2	2	.	.	.	.	.
London Journal. mid 1800s	4	4	.	.	.	.	.
London Magazine. mid-late 1700s	307	213	19	23	24	17	11
London News. mid-late 1800s	21	21	.	.	.	.	.
London Printing & Publishing. mid 1800s	2	0	1	.	.	1	.
London Steam Boat Co. late 1800s	1	1	.	.	.	.	.
London Times. late 1800s +	6	6	.	.	.	.	.
Long: includes Maj. Stephen H., USA, 1784-1864; various others	3	3	.	.	.	.	.
Longchamps. S.G.; French; mid 1700s	5	1	.	.	1	.	3
Longman (Co.). London; mid 1800s	20	16	.	1	3	.	.
Longman & Rees. London; early 1800s	1	1	.	.	.	.	.
Longworth, D. early 1800s	1	0	1	.	.	.	.
Lootsman. see Jacobsz							
Lopez: Juan, late 1700s; Tomas, Madrid, 1730-1802	31	12	3	9	.	6	1
Lorrain: incl N., Paris, mid 1800s	5	3	1	.	.	1	.
Lothian, John. Edinburgh; fl 1825-46	6	5	.	.	.	.	1
Lotter (family): Tobias Conrad, 1717-77; Mathais Albrecht, 1741-1810; Augsburg	369	227	13	22	60	12	35
Lottery Magazine. late 1700s	3	1	1	.	.	.	1
Lottin, M. French; early 1800s	1	1	.	.	.	.	.
Loveringh, Jacobus. publisher; Amsterdam; mid 1700s	1	1	.	.	.	.	.
Lowden & Johnson. Sacramento; 'ate 1800s	1	1	.	.	.	.	.
Lowizio, George Moritz Lowitz. Nuremberg; mid 1700s	2	1	.	.	.	1	.
Lowry. mid 1800s	6	4	.	.	1	.	1
Lubrecht, Charles. mid 1800s	2	1	.	.	.	.	1
Lucas, Fielding. Baltimore; 1781-1854	222	145	20	19	25	4	9
Luffman: incl I, NY, early 1800s; John. London; early 1800s	32	29	1	.	.	1	1
Lufft: incl Hans Luft, Wittenberg, early 1500s	3	3	.	.	.	.	.
Lumsden. mid 1700s	1	0	1	.	.	.	.
Luther.	1	1	.	.	.	.	.
Lutke, Frederic. mid 1800s	1	0	.	.	.	1	.
Lyell, Charles. English; mid 1800s	1	1	.	.	.	.	.
MacLure & MacDonald. Glasgow; mid 1800s appears in '86,'87 as "MacClure"	5	5	.	.	.	.	.
MacDonald. mid 1800s	2	2	.	.	.	.	.
MacDougall & Southwick. Seattle; late 1800s	1	1	.	.	.	.	.
MacGregor, M.M., London, mid 1800s	2	2	.	.	.	.	.
MacKenzie: incl Murdoch, English, late 1700s; Alexander, London, early 1800s; William, London, Edinburgh	51	35	7	.	8	.	1
MacKinlay, A. London; late 1800s	7	6	1	.	.	.	.
MacPherson: A., London, early 1800s; D., Phila, early 1800s	6	4	.	1	.	.	1
Macrobius, Ambrosius Aurelius Theodosius. Roman, 399-423. Principal work: "In Somnium Scipionis".	3	0	.	1	.	1	1
Madison, Bishop James, D.D. Virginia, early 1800s.	4	1	.	.	.	2	1
Maescamp. early 1800s	1	1	.	.	.	.	.
Maffeius, Peter. Venice, Cologne; late 1500s	2	2	.	.	.	.	.
Magazine of Magazines. London; 1750-51	1	0	.	.	.	.	1
Maggi, C., editor, Turin, mid 1800s	2	2	.	.	.	.	.

Name	Total	'83-'92	'93	'94	'95	'96	'97-8
Magini, Giovanni Antonio. Venice, 1555-1617. see Ptolemy (1596-1621)	104	2	.	21	14	20	47
Magnelli. late 1700s	1	0	.	.	1	.	.
Magnus, Charles, lith; NY, mid 1800s	57	29	.	14	2	8	4
Maire, N. mid 1800s	1	0	1	.	.	.	.
Maitland, William. mid 1700s	1	1	.	.	.	.	.
Malby, T. England, mid 1800s	1	0	1	.	.	.	.
Malham, John. late 1700s	16	14	.	1	.	1	.
Mallery & Ward. San Francisco; late 1800s	1	1	.	.	.	.	.
Mallet, Alain Manesson. Paris; 1630-1706	610	410	52	46	52	35	15
Malte-Brun, Conrad. Danish, Paris; 1775-1826	79	64	1	3	2	8	1
Mandrillon, J. late 1700s	1	1	.	.	.	.	.
Manouvier, J. New Orleans; mid 1800s	1	1	.	.	.	.	.
Mansell, F. engraver; mid 1800s	1	0	1	.	.	.	.
Mante, Thomas. London; late 1700s	6	5	.	.	.	1	.
Manuscript Maps.	47	0	.	11	12	9	15
Marchand, Etienne. 1755-93	1	1	.	.	.	.	.
Marchenkov, Ivan; Russia, late 1700s	1	0	.	1	.	.	.
Marchetti, Pietro Maria. Brescia; late 1500s	3	3	.	.	.	.	.
Marcy, Capt. R.B. US; mid 1800s	3	2	.	.	.	1	.
Mariette: Pierre (I) 1603-57; (II) 1634-1716; Paris	10	3	1	.	3	3	.
Marks, S. NY; early 1800s	1	1	.	.	.	.	.
Marlin, J.F. views; mid 1800s	1	1	.	.	.	.	.
Marmocchi. Francesco; Italy' mid 1800s	1	0	.	.	.	.	1
Marryat. mid 1800s	1	1	.	.	.	.	.
Marsh, William S. publisher: Hartford; early 1800s	1	0	1	.	.	.	.
Marshall: John; USA; 1755-1835. incl Wm., mid 1600s, T.C., mid 1800s, London	129	81	2	10	9	12	15
Martell, Peter. 1701-61	1	1	.	.	.	.	.
Martenet, Simon J., publisher; Baltimore, mid 1800s	3	2	.	.	.	1	.
Martin: various; incl Benjamin, English, mid 1700s	5	4	.	.	.	.	1
Martin & Smith. NY, mid 1800s	1	1	.	.	.	.	.
Marzolla, Benedetto. Naples; mid 1800s	12	6	2	2	2	.	.
Mason: incl C. Allen, Portland, OR, late 1800s; L.D.V., late 1800s	2	2	.	.	.	.	.
Mason & Dixon. late 1700s	1	1	.	.	.	.	.
Maspero, M. Turin; early 1800s	3	3	.	.	.	.	.
Mast. with Crowell & Kirkpatrick; Phila, late 1800s	18	14	1	1	.	1	1
Mather: incl W.W., NY, mid 1800s	4	2	.	1	.	1	.
Mathews, Alfred E. late 1800s	4	3	.	.	.	.	1
Matthews, Northrup Co. publisher; Buffalo; late 1800s	31	29	.	1	.	1	.
Maundressi. late 1600s	2	2	.	.	.	.	.
Maurepas. late 1700s	1	1	.	.	.	.	.
Mauro, Fra. 1400s	1	0	.	.	1	.	.
Maverick, Peter; engraver for Isaac Riley; NY early 1800s.	2	0	.	1	.	.	1
Mawman, J. London; early 1800s	10	10	.	.	.	.	.
Maximilian of Wied. mid 1800s	2	1	.	.	.	.	1
Maxwell Land Grant Co. Denver; late 1800s	1	1	.	.	.	.	.
May, B. mid 1800s	1	1	.	.	.	.	.
Mayer, Johann Tobias, German, mid 1700s; incl J. & Co., mid 1800s	3	3	.	.	.	.	.
Maynard. London; late 1800s	2	1	.	.	1	.	.
McConnell, J.L. Phila; mid 1800s	1	1	.	.	.	.	.
McCulloch. London; mid 1800s	1	0	.	.	.	1	.
McElroy, Son & Brown. Brooklyn; late 1800s	3	1	.	.	.	.	2
McGregor: incl J., London; early 1800s	38	37	.	1	.	.	.
McIntyre: incl A. Edinburgh; late 1700s; H., Amer., mid 1800s	6	5	.	1	.	.	.
McLoughlin Bros. late 1800s	1	1	.	.	.	.	.
McMillan. late 1800s	2	2	.	.	.	.	.
McNally, F. NY; mid 1800s	17	15	.	.	.	.	2
Mead, Bradock (aka John Green). mid 1700s	1	0	.	1	.	.	.
Meares, John. voyager; late 1700s	31	25	1	.	.	1	4
Megarey, Henry I. NY; early 1800s	1	1	.	.	.	.	.
Meierus, J. late 1600s	1	1	.	.	.	.	.
Meijer, Peter. Amsterdam; late 1700s	4	3	1	.	.	.	.
Meisner, Daniel. Bohemian; 1585-1625	109	30	.	11	.	43	25
Meissas, Achille Pr. de. Paris; mid 1800s	2	2	.	.	.	.	.
Mela, Pomponius. Roman; 1st c. AD.	2	1	.	.	1	.	.
Melish, John. Phila; 1771-1822	78	55	5	6	4	5	3

	Total	'83-'92	'93	'94	'95	'96	'97-8
Melling, Antoine. views; Paris; early 1800s	3	3	.	.	.	.	.
Mendel Lith. Chicago; mid 1800s	1	1	.	.	.	.	.
Mendenhall, Edward & C.S; Cincinnati, late 1800s.	6	4	.	.	.	1	1
Mentelle, Edme; French, 1730-1815	8	5	1	.	1	1	.
Menzies. Edinburgh; late 1700s	1	0	1	.	.	.	.
Mercator (family), incl Gerard, Duisburg, 1512-94							
Rumold, c.1540-99 (folio) see Hondius; Jansson; Ptolemy (1578-1730)	673	416	57	55	95	18	32
Gerard (II) c.1565-1656 (small) see Purchas	472	317	18	35	24	15	63
Merchant, G.W. Albany, NY. Wall map.	1	0	.	1	.	.	.
Mercurio Peruano. late 1700s	1	1	.	.	.	.	.
Merian, Matthaus. Frankfort; 1593-1650	564	434	2	41	9	34	44
Merritt & Co. Leonidas. USA; late 1800s	1	1	.	.	.	.	.
Merula, Paulus. Leyden; 1588-1607	8	5	1	1	.	.	1
Messier, Charles. French; 1730-1817	2	0	.	.	.	2	.
Metellus, Natalius Sequanus. Cologne, 1520-97	6	2	1	1	.	1	1
Meyer: Philip, London; late 1600s; Hermann J; H., NY; mid 1800s; Joseph, Germany, 1796-1856	170	91	38	11	4	5	21
Mialhe. views; late 1800s	2	0	1	.	.	.	1
Michalet. Estienne; publ Paris; late 1600s	1	0	.	.	.	.	1
Michault, R. Paris; late 1600s	5	2	1	1	.	.	1
Michaux, Francois A. early 1800s	1	1	.	.	.	.	.
Michelin, F. NY: mid 1800s	1	1	.	.	.	.	.
Michelot, Henri. Paris; early 1700s	4	0	.	2	1	.	1
Michigan Central R.R. late 1800s Includes Michigan Central & Great Western Railway	2	2	.	.	.	.	.
Middleton, Charles T.; London, late 1700s	28	14	2	2	3	3	4
Migeon, J. Paris; late 1800s	12	10	.	1	.	1	.
Milbert, J. Paris; mid 1800s	3	2	.	.	.	.	1
Miles, Frederick B. & Co. Canada: late 1800s	9	9	.	.	.	.	.
Military Maps - Infrequent Publishers.	16	0	.	4	6	6	.
Millar: Andrew, London; mid 1700s; George H., London; late 1700s	20	20	.	.	.	.	.
Miller: William, London, early 1800s; J., NY, mid 1800s; J. Martin, Chic, late 1800s	6	4	.	.	.	2	.
Mills, Robert. USA; 1781-1855	1	1	.	.	.	.	.
Mills & Co., Des Moines, late 1800s	3	2	.	.	.	1	.
Milne. mid 1800s	2	1	1	.	.	.	.
Milton & Cheadle. mid 1800s	1	1	.	.	.	.	.
Mining Maps.	11	0	.	4	2	3	2
Missouri River, Ft. Scott & Gulf R.R.	1	1	.	.	.	.	.
Missouri, State of.	1	1	.	.	.	.	.
Mitchell, George. Phila; mid 1800s	1	1	.	.	.	.	.
Mitchell, John. English, Virginia; mid 1700s. see Le Rouge	13	9	1	2	.	1	.
Mitchell, Samuel Augustus. Phila; 1792-1868	1019	1019	.	.	.	.	.
Mitchell, S.A. (Atlas Maps 1859 & Earlier).	148	0	42	6	12	56	32
Mitchell, S.A. (Atlas Maps 1860 & Later).	337	0	56	95	53	71	62
Mitchell, S.A. (maps not in atlases).	74	0	5	22	16	10	21
Moffat, J. Edinburgh; early 1800s	4	4	.	.	.	.	.
Mogg, Edward. publisher; London; early 1800s	9	5	4	.	.	.	.
Moithey, Maurille Antoine. Paris; 1732-1810	10	4	.	1	.	2	3
Molini, Guiseppe. Italy; early 1800s	1	1	.	.	.	.	.
Moll, Herman. Dutch; London; fl 1678-1732	249	249	.	.	.	.	.
(large).	131	48	9	16	37	6	15
(small). see Thesaurus Geographicus	425	238	28	38	45	39	37
Mollhausen, Baldwin. London; mid 1800s	3	2	.	.	.	.	1
Mollo, Tranquillo; engr Vienna; fl 1800-30	1	0	.	.	.	.	.
Molyneux, Emery. fl 1587-1605	1	1	.	.	.	.	.
Monaldini, Vananzio. publisher; Rome; mid 1800s	4	3	.	.	.	.	1
Monarch Co. publisher; Chicago; late 1800s	19	19	.	.	.	.	.
Monath: various. Nuremberg; mid 1700s	4	3	.	.	.	1	.
Mondhare, L. publisher; Paris; late 1700s	4	1	.	3	.	.	.
Monin, Charles V. France, fl.1830-80.	15	12	1	.	.	1	1
Monin & Fremin. Paris; mid 1800s	4	4	.	.	.	.	.
Monin & Vuillemin. mid 1800s	1	1	.	.	.	.	.
Monk, Jacob. Baltimore; Phila; mid 1800s	19	11	2	1	.	2	3
Montanus, Arnoldus. Amsterdam; late 1600s. see Dapper; Ogilby	97	72	4	5	6	7	3
Monthly Chronologer. mid 1700s	3	2	.	.	.	1	.
Monthly Intelligencer. mid 1700s	3	3	.	.	.	.	.

	Total	'83-'92	'93	'94	'95	'96	'97-8
Montigny. mid 1700s	2	0	.	.	.	2	.
Montresor, John. English; late 1700s	10	4	1	3	2	.	.
Moon. mid 1800s	1	1	.	.	.	.	.
Moore. John Hamiliton, London, late 1700s; James B., Cincinnati, mid 1800s	8	7	.	.	.	.	1
Morales, Jose Pilar. mid 1800s	2	2	.	.	.	.	.
Morden, Robert. London; fl 1668-1703	500	318	26	79	29	31	17
Morden & Berry. early 1700s	2	2	.	.	.	.	.
Morden & Lea. late 1600s	1	1	.	.	.	.	.
Morgan: incl Wm. H., Phila, early 1800s; T.J. Amer., late 1800s	2	2	.	.	.	.	.
Morisot, Claude Bartholomew. Dijon; 1592-1661	2	0	.	1	.	.	1
Morrill, George. Boston; late 1800s	2	1	.	.	.	.	1
Morris: Lewis, mid 1700s; William (son), early 1800s	53	22	28	.	3	.	.
Morrison: various	7	7	.	.	.	.	.
Morrison & West. London(?); early 1800s	2	2	.	.	.	.	.
Morse: incl Jedidiah, Sidney to '92	210	210	.	.	.	.	.
Morse, Jedidiah; Amer., 1761-1826. see Stockdale	100	0	26	14	22	18	20
Morse, Sidney. NY: 1794-1871	19	0	3	5	3	4	4
Morse & Breese. NY; mid 1800s	144	98	11	7	8	15	5
Morse & Gaston. NY: mid 1800s	28	10	2	7	1	7	1
Mortier, Pierre. Amsterdam; 1661-1711. see Jaillot	382	253	7	15	68	11	28
Mortimer & Co. Ottawa; late 1800s	1	1	.	.	.	.	.
Mosting, Hermann. late 1600s	1	1	.	.	.	.	.
Mottram, C. mid 1800s	1	1	.	.	.	.	.
Moule, Thomas. London; mid 1800s	17	7	.	.	.	4	6
Mount & Page (with various partners), London; mid 1700s	311	253	8	7	18	6	19
Mouzon, Henry. 1741-1807	7	1	1	.	1	3	1
Moxon: James (elder & younger); Joseph. London; 1600s	19	14	1	.	4	.	.
Mudie, Robert, publisher; London, 1777-1842	2	1	.	.	.	1	.
Muller: Johann Ulrich (Mueller), Ulm, late 1600s; Gerard Friedrich, Russia, 1705-83	45	35	2	4	3	1	.
Munson. Cincinnati; mid 1800s	1	1	.	.	.	.	.
Munster, Sebastian. Basle; 1489-1552	940	532	47	45	103	90	123
Murphy & Co. Baltimore; late 1800s	1	1	.	.	.	.	.
Murray: incl John, London, early 1800s; incl Hugh, *Encyclopedia of Geography*	24	17	4	.	2	.	1
Murray, Heiss & McLaughlin. Cleveland; late 1800s	1	1	.	.	.	.	.
Mutlow, I. London; early 1800s	1	1	.	.	.	.	.
Myers, J.F. Halifax; mid 1800s	1	1	.	.	.	.	.
Myritius, Johannes. Ingolstadt; late 1500s. see Mauritius '87	0	2	1	1	1	.	1
Nagel & Weingartner. NY; mid 1800s	1	1	.	.	.	.	.
Narborough, John. 1640-88	1	1	.	.	.	.	.
National Geographic Society.	2	1	1	.	.	.	.
National Publishing Co. USA; early 1900s	1	0	.	.	1	.	.
National Soc. for Promoting Educ. of the Poor. London; mid 1800s	4	2	.	.	2	.	.
National Union Executive Committee. NY; mid 1800s	1	1	.	.	.	.	.
Nautical Charts - Infrequent Publishers.	1	0	.	1	.	.	.
Nautical Magazine. mid 1800s	2	2	.	.	.	.	.
Naval Chronicle; London; early 1800s. see Gold	20	14	2	1	1	2	.
Naymiller & Allodi. Italy, mid 1800s	1	0	.	.	.	.	1
Neal. Daniel; England; early 1700s	1	0	.	.	.	.	1
Neele (family): engraver, publisher; London; late 1700s+	23	19	.	3	1	.	.
Nell, Louis. Denver; late 1800s	7	5	.	1	.	.	1
Nelson, V.H. London; mid 1800s	1	0	.	.	.	1	.
Neptune Francois. see Depot de la Marine; Jaillot; Mortier	.	.	.	.	.	.	.
Neugebauer, Saloman; German, early 1600.	1	0	.	1	.	.	.
Nevers, Roderick. Hartford; mid 1800s	1	1	.	.	.	.	.
New England Lith. Co.	1	1	.	.	.	.	.
New York Manual. see Shannon, Valentine's Manual, N.Y. Manual to '92	2	2	.	.	.	.	.
New York Herald.	34	25	.	3	2	4	.
New York Illustrated News.	2	1	.	.	.	1	.
New York, State of	7	3	.	3	.	1	.
New York State Documentary History. Albany; mid 1800s. see Pease	7	0	5	.	1	1	.
New York Sun.	1	1	.	.	.	.	.
New York Tribune.	3	1	.	.	1	1	.
Newbery, Francis John; London; late 1700s	1	1	.	.	.	.	.
Newton, John; London, late 1600s	1	1	.	.	.	.	.
Newton & Berry. globes; London; early 1800s; incl Newton & Sons, mid 1800s	3	0	2	.	.	.	1

Name	Total	'83-'92	'93	'94	'95	'96	'97-8
Nichelson, William. English; mid 1700s. see Nicholson, '95	4	0	.	.	2	2	.
Nicholls, Sutton. London; early 1700s	1	1	.	.	.	.	.
Nicholson: incl W.L., Amer., US Post Office, late 1800s	7	5	.	.	1	1	.
Nicol, George. London; late 1700s	12	6	2	2	1	1	.
Nicolosi, Giovanni Battista. Rome; mid 1600s	9	7	.	.	1	1	.
Nieuhoff. early 1700s	4	2	.	2	.	.	.
Nolin, Jean Baptiste (the elder), 1657-1725; (Jr.) 1686-1762; Paris	72	44	7	8	5	3	5
Noll, E.P. Phila; late 1800s	1	1	.	.	.	.	.
Nolli. Italy; mid 1700s	1	0	.	.	.	1	.
Norden, John. English; 1548-c.1625	1	1	.	.	.	.	.
Nordenankar, Jan de. Sweden; 1722-1804	1	1	.	.	.	.	.
Norie, John William; London, 1772-1843	31	25	2	.	1	1	2
Norman, John. USA; late 1700s	2	1	1	.	.	.	.
Norris, Geo. E. Brockton, MA; late 1800s	1	1	.	.	.	.	.
Norris Peters Co. USA; late 1800s	4	0	1	1	.	2	.
Norris, Wellge & Co. Milwaukee; late 1800s	1	1	.	.	.	.	.
Northern Pacific R.R.	3	3	.	.	.	.	.
Northwest Publishing Co. US; late 1800s	1	0	.	.	.	.	1
Norwood, J.G. USA; mid 1800s	1	1	.	.	.	.	.
Nuremberg Chronicle. 1493. see Schedel	.	.	.	.	.	.	.
Nuttall & Dixon. early 1800s	2	2	.	.	.	.	.
Nuttall, Fisher & Dixon. early 1800s	4	4	.	.	.	.	.
Nutzhorn. late 1600s	1	1	.	.	.	.	.
Oakland Land, Loan & Trust Co. late 1800s	1	1	.	.	.	.	.
Oakley. Edward, architect & publisher, England; worked with Rocque's widow.	2	0	.	1	1	.	.
Oesfeld, Carl Ludwig von. 1781-1843	1	1	.	.	.	.	.
Ogilby, John; London, 1600-76. Try Dapper; Montanus	252	166	11	7	29	19	20
Olaus Magnus. Swedish, Rome; 1490-1558	1	1	.	.	.	.	.
Oldmixon, John. English; 1673-1742	1	1	.	.	.	.	.
Olearius, Adam. German; 1599-1671	1	1	.	.	.	.	.
Oliver & Boyd. Edinburgh; early 1800s	2	1	1	.	.	.	.
Oliver, John. English; late 1600s	1	1	.	.	.	.	.
Olmsted, Frederick Law. USA; 1822-1903	2	1	.	.	1	.	.
Olney: incl Jesse, NY, 1798-1872; A.N., mid 1800s	43	11	3	3	4	4	18
Ordnance Survey. see British Ordnance Survey, '93+	.	.	.	.	.	.	.
Orr: incl Orr & Smith, London, mid 1800s	4	1	.	.	2	1	.
Ortelius, Abraham; Antwerp, 1527-98	.	.	.	.	.	.	.
(folio).	1246	830	44	86	105	54	127
(miniature).	262	182	15	27	16	20	2
Osborne. England; mid 1800s	2	1	.	.	.	.	1
Ottens (family): Joachim; Reiner & Joshua; Amsterdam; early-mid 1700s	117	79	9	4	6	6	13
Overton: John, 1640-1713; Philip, d. 1751; Henry, fl 1706-64; London	22	9	3	2	2	2	4
Overton & Bowles. early 1800s	1	1	.	.	.	.	.
Overton & Morden. late 1600s	1	1	.	.	.	.	.
Owen, David Dale. Washington; mid 1800s	9	8	.	.	.	1	.
Owen & Bowen. London; mid 1700s	19	17	.	.	.	.	2
Owen's Magazine. mid 1700s	1	1	.	.	.	.	.
Oxford Magazine. mid 1700s	1	1	.	.	.	.	.
Paas. C., late 1700s	1	0	.	.	.	.	1
Pacific Coast Atlas. San Francisco; late 1800s	9	9	.	.	.	.	.
Packard & Bros. late 1800s	2	2	.	.	.	.	.
Padley, James Sanby. English; mid 1800s	1	1	.	.	.	.	.
Page: incl H.R., Chicago; Page & Smith, Amer., late 1800s	18	6	.	2	3	2	5
Palairet, Jean. England; 1697-1774	5	2	1	.	.	.	2
Palfrey, John Gorham. Boston, 1796-1881	2	2	.	.	.	.	.
Pallas. traveller; late 1700s	1	0	.	.	.	1	.
Panckoucke. Charles; publ Paris; early 1800s	1	0	.	.	.	.	1
Panter-Downes. views; London; mid 1800s	1	1	.	.	.	.	.
Paoli, Sebastiano. Rome; early 1700s	1	1	.	.	.	.	.
Papen, Augustus. Hannover; mid 1800s	2	2	.	.	.	.	.
Paris, Comte de. Louis Phillipe Albert d'Orleans; 1838-94	5	0	.	.	.	5	.
Parke, Lt. J.G., Amer., mid 1800s	1	1	.	.	.	.	.
Parker: Rev. Samuel, Utica, mid 1800s; incl Nathan, St. Louis, mid 1800s	16	9	1	1	.	3	2
Parley. mid 1800s	1	1	.	.	.	.	.
Parr, Richard. London; mid 1700s	1	1	.	.	.	.	.

	Total	'83-'92	'93	'94	'95	'96	'97-8
Parry, William Edward. London; early 1800s	20	19	.	1	.	.	.
Pate, William & Co. views; NY; late 1800s	1	1	.	.	.	.	.
Paulin & Chevalier. publisher; Paris; mid 1800s	1	1	.	.	.	.	.
Pawley, G. England; early 1800s	3	3	.	.	.	.	.
Payne, John. NY; late 1700s	83	50	10	2	8	7	6
Payot, Upham & Co. San Francisco; late 1800s	1	1	.	.	.	.	.
Peabody & Co. NY; mid 1800s	1	1	.	.	.	.	.
Pease & Niles. early 1800s	3	1	.	.	.	1	1
Pease Lith. Albany; mid 1800s. see N.Y. State Doc. History	2	2	.	.	.	.	.
Pease, R.H. lith. NY; mid 1800s. see N.Y. State Doc. History	11	10	.	.	.	.	1
Peck, Jacob. USA; mid 1800s	3	1	1	1	.	.	.
Pedemonte. early 1800s	1	1	.	.	.	.	.
Peeters, Jacques. Antwerp; late 1600s	43	28	.	1	1	10	3
Pelham, C. London(?); early 1800s	1	1	.	.	.	.	.
Pelton, C. Phila; mid 1800s	2	1	1	.	.	.	.
Pendleton, John B. lith., Boston; mid 1800s	2	2	.	.	.	.	.
Pennant. late 1700s	1	0	.	.	1	.	.
Pennsylvania, State of.	2	2	.	.	.	.	.
Pennsylvania Historical Society.	2	1	.	.	.	1	.
Pennsylvania Magazine. late 1700s	12	4	3	2	3	.	.
Penny Magazine. London; mid 1800s	1	1	.	.	.	.	.
Penny National Atlas. England; c.1830s	2	1	.	.	.	1	.
People's Atlas. Chicago; late 1800s	42	33	4	1	1	3	.
Perelle. Paris; late 1600s	3	2	1	.	.	.	.
Perkins, G. London; mid 1800s	1	1	.	.	.	.	.
Perrine, Charles O., Indianapolis, mid 1800s	4	2	.	.	.	1	1
Perrot, Aristide Michel. French; 1793-1879	5	3	.	.	1	.	1
Perry. early 1800s	2	0	.	.	1	1	.
Perry & Spaulding. Boston; late 1800s	2	2	.	.	.	.	.
Perthes, Justus. Gotha; mid 1800s	49	32	.	9	.	5	3
Petavius.	1	1	.	.	.	.	.
Petermann, Augustus Herman. Germany; mid 1800s	44	18	4	4	12	4	2
Petri, Edmund. London; late 1700s	1	0	.	.	.	.	1
Petri, Heinrich. Basle; 1508-79. see Munster	1	1	.	.	.	.	.
Petrini, Paolo. Naples; late 1600s	48	45	.	3	.	.	.
Petroschi, Giovanni. Rome; early 1700s	1	1	.	.	.	.	.
Peutinger, Konrad. Nuremberg; 1465-1547 (Peutinger Table)	1	0	.	1	.	.	.
Pharus-Verlag. Germany; early 1900s	1	0	1	.	.	.	.
Phelan. late 1800s	1	1	.	.	.	.	.
Phelipeau, Rene. Paris; late 1700s	7	7	.	.	.	.	.
Phelps, Humphrey. publisher; NY; early 1800s	22	13	.	2	.	2	5
Phelps & Ensign. publisher; NY; early 1800s	16	9	.	3	.	2	2
Phelps & Watson. mid 1800s	14	6	1	1	.	2	4
Philadelphia Publishing House. late 1800s	1	0	.	1	.	.	.
Philip: may incl George	126	124	.	.	2	.	.
Philip, George. Liverpool; London; mid 1800s	36	0	16	6	4	9	1
Philippe. late 1700s	1	1	.	.	.	.	.
Phillips: incl Richard, London, 1767-1840	24	21	1	.	.	.	2
Phinn, Thomas. Edinburgh; late 1700s	1	1	.	.	.	.	.
Phipps. Constantine John, English navigator, 1744-92	1	0	.	.	.	.	1
Piale, Luigi. Rome; mid 1800s	3	1	.	.	.	2	.
Picart: incl Hughes, engraver, early 1600s; Nicolas, Paris, mid 1600s	4	1	.	.	1	2	.
Picquet: various; incl Charles, Paris, early 1800s	8	4	.	.	1	3	.
Pictorial Times. London; mid 1800s	1	1	.	.	.	.	.
Pierce: various	1	0	.	.	.	1	.
Pietro. engraver; early 1800s	1	1	.	.	.	.	.
Pigafetta, Filippo; Rome, 1533-1603	3	2	.	.	1	.	.
Pigot, James & Co. Liverpool; London; early 1800s	17	15	.	.	.	.	2
Pike, Charles J. USA. mid 1800s	1	0	.	1	.	.	.
Pike, Zebulon. USA; 1779-1813. see U.S.	3	0	.	1	.	1	1
Pimentel, Manoel. Portugal, 1650-1719	3	0	.	.	.	3	.
Pine, John. London; early 1700s	2	2	.	.	.	.	.
Pingeling. mid-late 1700s	2	2	.	.	.	.	.
Pinkerton, John; Edinburgh, 1758-1826	94	61	.	5	23	5	.
Pinnock & Maunder; London; early 1800s	2	2	.	.	.	.	.

Name	Total	'83-'92	'93	'94	'95	'96	'97-8
Pinnock; mid 1800s	1	1	.	.	.	.	.
Piquet; Paris; mid 1800s	3	1	1	.	1	.	.
Pitt, Moses; London, late 1600s	50	33	2	2	4	2	7
Plancius, Petrus; Amsterdam, 1552-1622	27	17	2	1	4	1	2
Platen, Charles G. USA; late 1800s	1	1	.	.	.	.	.
Playfair, James. Edinburgh; early 1800s	5	4	.	.	.	.	1
Plon. late 1800s	2	0	.	.	2	.	.
Plot, Robert. England; 1640-96	2	1	.	.	.	.	1
Pluche. Paris; late 1700s	2	1	.	.	.	1	.
Pluth, F. Prague; early 1800s	2	2	.	.	.	.	.
Poirson, Jean Baptiste; Paris, 1760-1831	25	16	3	2	3	.	1
Political Magazine. London; late 1800s	90	69	8	6	2	1	4
Pomarede, Daniel. mid 1700s	1	1	.	.	.	.	.
Pomba, Cesar. Turin; mid 1800s	1	1	.	.	.	.	.
Pomeroy. publ US; late 1800s	2	0	.	.	.	.	2
Pont: may incl Timothy, fl 1579-1610	1	1	.	.	.	.	.
Pontanus. early 1600s	3	1	.	.	2	.	.
Pontoppidan. Christian Joachim; Denmark; 1739-1807	1	0	.	.	.	.	1
Poole Bros. Chicago; late 1800s	2	1	.	1	.	.	.
Poor, Henry V. NY; mid 1800s	1	1	.	.	.	.	.
Popple, Henry. London; early 1700s	46	33	4	1	3	2	3
Porcacchi, Tomaso; Venice, 1530-85	133	113	3	5	6	1	5
Porro, Girolamo; Venice, late 1500s	5	1	2	.	.	.	2
Port Folio; Phila, early 1800s	2	1	.	.	.	1	.
Porter: incl D., early 1800s; T.	2	1	1	.	.	.	.
Portlock, Nathaniel. London; late 1700s	3	3	.	.	.	.	.
Postel, Guillaume. France; 1510-85	1	0	.	.	1	.	.
Postlethwait, Malachy. 1700s	5	3	.	.	.	1	1
Pouchot, Capt. late 1700s	2	2	.	.	.	.	.
Poussin, G. mid 1800s	1	1	.	.	.	.	.
Powell, John Wesley. USA; 1834-1902	4	1	.	1	1	.	1
Pozzi. mid 1800s	1	1	.	.	.	.	.
Prang, Louis. USA; late 1800s	11	8	.	1	.	2	.
Presdee & Edwards. NY, late 1800s	3	2	.	.	.	1	.
Preuss, Charles. USA; 1803-54	2	2	.	.	.	.	.
Prevost d'Exiles, A.F. Paris; mid 1700s. see Bellin (small)	42	33	1	.	.	7	1
Price: Charles, London, fl 1680-1720; William, Boston, mid 1700s	3	2	.	.	.	.	1
Price & Senex. incl Price, Senex & Marshall; England, early 1700s	2	2	.	.	.	.	.
Prichard. James Cowles; 1786-1848	1	0	.	.	.	.	1
Prinald. engraver; mid 1700s	2	1	.	.	.	.	1
Prior, John. England; late 1700s	2	1	.	.	.	.	1
Probst, Johann Michael. George Bathasar, Johann Michael; Augsburg; 1700s	31	8	1	1	18	.	3
Prockter. J.; English engraver; fl 1750-76	1	0	.	.	.	.	1
Propper, George N. USA; mid 1800s	1	1	.	.	.	.	.
Proud. London; mid 1700s	1	1	.	.	.	.	.
Ptolemy (1478-1508 Rome)	10	3	.	2	3	2	.
Ptolemy (1482 Florence)	7	3	.	2	2	.	.
Ptolemy (1482-1486 Ulm)	20	17	.	.	.	.	3
Ptolemy (1511 Venice)	12	8	.	1	.	.	3
Ptolemy (1513-1520 Strassburg) see Waldseemuller	85	53	.	32	.	.	.
Ptolemy (1522-1541 Strassburg) see Fries, Waldseemuller	174	153	1	4	13	1	2
Ptolemy (1540-1552 Basle) see Munster	.	.	.	.	.	.	.
Ptolemy (1548 Venice) see Gastaldi, '94 +	85	78	7	.	.	.	.
Ptolemy (1561-1599 Venice) see Ruscelli, '94 +	333	245	88	.	.	.	.
Ptolemy (1578-1730 Mercator)	20	17	1	1	.	.	1
Ptolemy (1596-1621 Magini) see Magini, '94 +	132	121	11	.	.	.	.
Purcell, Joseph. 1700s	2	0	1	.	.	1	.
Purchas, Samuel; London, c.1575-1626. see Briggs, Hondius, Mercator	28	15	1	.	4	3	5
Purdy, John. England; 1773-1843	2	2	.	.	.	.	.
Putter, A. de. early 1700s	1	0	.	.	1	.	.
Puzzles & Games.	23	0	.	6	.	2	15
Quad, Matthias. Cologne; late 1500s	272	194	9	24	17	10	18
Quick, A.C. late 1800s	1	1	.	.	.	.	.
Radefeld, Carl Christian Franz; German, 1788-1874	37	28	1	4	1	3	.
Raignauld, Henry; French, early 1600s	5	5	.	.	.	.	.

Name	Total	'83-'92	'93	'94	'95	'96	'97-8
Railroad Company Maps. see Colton, Rand McNally & each RR to '92	101	.	15	8	17	20	41
Railway News. USA; late 1800s	4	4	.	.	.	.	.
Raimondi. Antonio; Peru, 1826-90	1	0	.	.	.	.	1
Rainaldi, Carlo. early 1600s	1	1	.	.	.	.	.
Raleigh, Sir Walter; English, c.1552-1618. see Hole	1	0	.	.	.	.	1
Ramble, Reuben. England; mid 1800s	27	27	.	.	.	.	.
Ramsay, D. Charleston; early 1800s	11	10	.	.	.	1	.
Ramsey, David. late 1700s	1	1	.	.	.	.	.
Ramsey, Milleet & Hudson. Kansas City; late 1800s	2	2	.	.	.	.	.
Ramusio, Giovanni Battista; Venice, 1485-1557	136	94	6	5	8	6	17
Rand, Avery & Co. late 1800s	5	2	.	.	.	1	2
Rand, McNally & Co. publisher; Chicago; 1862-present	446	353	46	47	.	.	.
Rand, McNally (Atlas Maps).	109	0	.	.	32	45	32
Rand, McNally (Pocket, Wall & Globes).	42	0	.	.	14	14	14
Ranney, Adolphus. NY; mid 1800s	3	2	.	.	.	.	1
Ransom & Doolittle. San Francisco; mid 1800s	2	2	.	.	.	.	.
Rapin de Thoyras, Paul ("Rapin"). 1661-1725. see Tindal	13	3	.	4	3	2	1
Rapkin, J. London; mid 1800s. see Tallis	5	1	1	1	1	1	.
Rasciotti, Donato of Brescia. Rome; late 1500s	1	1	.	.	.	.	.
Raspe, Gabriel Nikolaus; Nuremberg, 1712-85	7	4	1	1	1	.	.
Ratcliff. USA; late 1800s	1	1	.	.	.	.	.
Ratelband, Johannes; Amsterdam, 1715-93	20	10	.	5	.	3	2
Rathbone, Aaron. early 1600s	1	0	.	.	1	.	.
Ratino. views; late 1700s	1	1	.	.	.	.	.
Rau, Jacob. NY; late 1800s	1	1	.	.	.	.	.
Rauw, Johannes. Germany, late 1500s	11	0	.	.	.	4	7
Ravenstein. late 1800s	2	1	1	.	.	.	.
Rawlings, T. London; mid 1800s	2	2	.	.	.	.	.
Raymond, J. views; London; late 1700s	1	1	.	.	.	.	.
Raynal, Guillaume Thomas Francois. 1713-96	14	13	.	.	.	.	1
Real Estate & Promotional Maps.	39	0	4	4	5	10	16
Ream, Robert K. NY; mid 1800s	1	1	.	.	.	.	.
Reclus, Jean Jacques Elisee. 1830-1905	1	0	1	.	.	.	.
Rector, William. Phila; early 1800s	3	3	.	.	.	.	.
Reed: incl John A. Phila; late 1700s; Edwin D., Cincinnati, mid 1800s	2	2	.	.	.	.	.
Reed & Barber. Hartford; mid 1800s	3	3	.	.	.	.	.
Reed Parsons Co. USA; mid 1800s	2	2	.	.	.	.	.
Reese, George W. Buffalo; mid 1800s	1	1	.	.	.	.	.
Regnier & Cie. mid 1800s	1	1	.	.	.	.	.
Reichard, Christian Gottlieb Theophil; Weimar, 1752-1828	15	11	1	.	1	1	1
Reid: John, USA, late 1700s; incl Alexander, mid 1800s	55	43	7	1	.	3	1
Reilly. see Von Reilly, '84+	.	.	.	.	.	.	.
Reinecke, Johann Matthais Christoph. Halberstadt; 1768-1818. see Weimar Geog. Inst.	2	0	.	2	.	.	.
Reisch, Gregor. Freiberg, Strassburg; c.1470-1525	5	4	.	1	.	.	.
Reland. Adrien. Amsterdam; early 1700s	6	3	1	2	.	.	.
Remond, N. views; mid 1800s	1	1	.	.	.	.	.
Remquet, M. Paris; mid 1800s	1	1	.	.	.	.	.
Remy, Jules. mid 1800s	1	1	.	.	.	.	.
Renard, Louis. Amsterdam; early 1700s	61	39	3	6	3	6	4
Rennel.	1	1	.	.	.	.	.
Rennell, James; English, India; 1742-1830	4	1	2	.	.	1	.
Renner, J.C., German, mid 1800s	23	20	.	3	.	.	.
Renouard, Antoine Augustin. publisher; Paris; mid 1800s	10	8	.	1	.	.	1
Reyland. early 1700s	1	1	.	.	.	.	.
Reynolds: James, publisher, London, mid 1800s; incl R., Wm. C., mid 1800s	10	3	7	.	.	.	.
Rhode, Johann Christoph. Berlin; 1713-86.	3	1	.	1	.	.	1
Rice, G. Jay; St. Paul, MN, late 1800s	5	1	1	2	.	.	1
Richards. US; late 1800s	2	0	.	.	.	.	2
Richardson, F. views; Boston; mid 1800s	3	1	2	.	.	.	.
Ridge, John. Dublin; mid 1700s	5	4	.	.	.	1	.
Riedel. late 1700s	1	1	.	.	.	.	.
Riegel, Christophe; Nuremberg, late 1600s	43	40	.	1	.	2	.
Ringgold, Cadwaller. USA; 1807-67.	2	2	.	.	.	.	.
Risdon, Orange. Albany; early 1800s	2	2	.	.	.	.	.
Ritch, William G. views; late 1800s	1	1	.	.	.	.	.

Name	Total	'83-'92	'93	'94	'95	'96	'97-8
Rivelanti. Italy.	1	0	.	1	.	.	.
Rizzi-Zannoni, Giovanni Antonio. Italian; c.1736-1814. see Zannoni, '87	14	4	1	1	4	1	3
Robbins, O.W. USA; mid 1800s	1	1	.	.	.	.	.
Robert de Vaugondy. see De Vaugondy	.	.	.	.	.	.	.
Roberts: various; incl A.G., Paris, mid 1700s; H.	12	9	1	.	1	.	1
Robertson: various; incl William (History by); G.J., Cincinnati; mid 1800s; J.	5	4	.	.	.	1	.
Robinson, G.G. London; late 1700s	131	122	4	1	2	2	.
Robinson, Lewis; Vermont, mid 1800s	2	0	.	2	.	.	.
Robiquet, Aime; Paris, mid 1800s	3	2	.	1	.	.	.
Robson, T. Newcastle; late 1700s	1	1	.	.	.	.	.
Robyn, Jacob (Robijn). Amsterdam; late 1600s	7	4	1	1	.	1	.
Rocky Mountain News Co. mid 1800s+	1	1	.	.	.	.	.
Rocque, Jean, Mary Ann. London; mid 1700s	60	44	1	4	2	2	7
Roe Bros. St. John, N.B. Canada; late 1800s	29	29	.	.	.	.	.
Rogers: various	6	6	.	.	.	.	.
Rogers & Johnston. Edinburgh; mid 1800s	24	16	.	.	.	7	1
Rogers, Peet & Co. retailers; NY; late 1800s+	2	2	.	.	.	.	.
Roggeveen: Arent; Arnold. Amsterdam. Arent, d.1670; Arnold, fl.1675-1700.	1	0	.	1	.	.	.
Rollandet, Edward. Denver; late 1800s	3	2	.	1	.	.	.
Rollinson. late 1800s	2	2	.	.	.	.	.
Rollos, G. London; late 1700s	36	32	1	.	.	1	2
Romans, Bernard. London; late 1700s	1	1	.	.	.	.	.
Romanus, Adrianus. 1561-1615	1	0	.	.	1	.	.
Romolo Bulla. views; late 1800s	1	0	1	.	.	.	.
Root, C. views; NY; mid 1800s	1	1	.	.	.	.	.
Root & Tinker. views; late 1800s	1	1	.	.	.	.	.
Rosaccio, Guiseppe. Italian; c.1530-1620	23	14	.	4	3	1	1
Rose; early 1900s	1	0	.	.	1	.	.
Rose & Woolman; Phila, late 1800s	11	10	.	.	1	.	.
Ross: various	9	8	.	.	.	1	.
Rosselin. Paris; mid 1800s	2	1	.	.	.	1	.
Rossi: incl Giacomo Giovanni, publ, Rome, late 1600s; may incl Luigi (see below)	54	31	2	6	8	4	3
Rossi, Giovanni Battista de. Rome; 1576-1656. see De Rossi, '85-'86	3	3	.	.	.	.	.
Rossi, Luigi. Milan; early 1800s	17	0	1	15	.	.	1
Rota, Martino. Sebenico; late 1500s	2	2	.	.	.	.	.
Rouargue, F., views; Paris; early 1800s	1	1	.	.	.	.	.
Roussin. mid 1800s	2	1	1	.	.	.	.
Roux, Joseph. Marseilles; late 1700s	44	34	.	2	1	5	2
Rowe, Robert. London; 1775-1843	1	0	1	.	.	.	.
Royal Geographic Journal. London	4	3	.	.	1	.	.
Royal Geographical Society. London	24	6	2	.	10	5	1
Royal Magazine. London	10	8	.	.	1	1	.
Royal Society of London Philosophical Transactions. maps 1669-1797	1	0	.	.	.	1	.
Royce. late 1700s	1	1	.	.	.	.	.
Rubeis. J. de; Italy; early 1600s	1	0	.	.	.	.	1
Rudbeck, Olof. Sweden; late 1600s.	1	0	.	.	.	1	.
Rudolphi. early 1700s	6	5	.	.	.	1	.
Ruggles, Edward. USA; early 1800s	2	1	1	.	.	.	.
Rughesi, Fausto. Italy; late 1500s	1	1	.	.	.	.	.
Ruscelli, Girolamo. Venice; c.1504-66. see Ptolemy (1561-1599) to '93	98	0	.	11	24	28	35
Russel. late 1700s	1	1	.	.	.	.	.
Russell: John, London, late 1700s; incl various	136	108	7	3	3	1	14
Russian Government.	2	0	.	2	.	.	.
Russo, G. Italy; mid 1800s	3	3	.	.	.	.	.
Ruysch, Johannes. early 1500s	1	1	.	.	.	.	.
S.D.U.K. see Society for the Diffusion of Useful Knowledge	.	.	.	.	.	.	.
Sachse & Co. Baltimore; mid 1800s	2	1	.	.	.	1	.
Sackersdorff, Otto.	1	1	.	.	.	.	.
Sacrobosco. fl 1220-56 (republished early 1500s)	2	2	.	.	.	.	.
St. Albin. Charles de; France; mid 1700s	1	0	.	.	.	.	1
St. Aubin Lith. mid 1800s	1	1	.	.	.	.	.
St. Louis Republican. late 1800s+	1	0	1	.	.	.	.
St. Louis, Iron Mountain, & Southern R.R. late 1800s	1	1	.	.	.	.	.
Salamanca. Rome; mid 1500s	1	1	.	.	.	.	.
Salmon. incl Thomas, geographies; London; mid 1700s+	15	3	.	1	5	2	4

	Total	'83-'92	'93	'94	'95	'96	'97-8
Sampson, Davenport & Co. Boston; late 1800s	2	1	.	.	.	.	1
Sanderus: incl Antoine, Flemish, 1586-1654	7	7	.	.	.	.	.
Sands, John. publisher; Sydney; late 1800s	24	24	.	.	.	.	.
Sandys, George. early 1600s	1	1	.	.	.	.	.
Sanford & Everts. Phila; late 1800s	3	3	.	.	.	.	.
Sanford & Goodhue. Phila; late 1800s	1	1	.	.	.	.	.
Sanson, Nicolas. Paris; mid 1600s. sons: Adrian; Guillaume; Nicolas Fils	138	138	.	.	.	.	.
(folio) see Jaillot; Mortier	335	186	12	19	28	20	70
(small).	324	250	24	12	4	26	8
Santini, P. Venice; late 1700s	92	80	3	2	1	3	3
Sanuto, Giulio. engraver; Venice; 1540-80	2	1	.	1	.	.	.
Sarony Lith. Incl Sarony & Major; & with Knapp; mid 1800s	6	6	.	.	.	.	.
Sartine. late 1800s	20	7	1	.	4	5	3
Sauer, Martin. early 1800s	1	0	.	.	1	.	.
Saunders, H. Atlanta; late 1800s	1	1	.	.	.	.	.
Sauthier, Claude Joseph. late 1800s	3	1	1	.	1	.	.
Savage. U.S.; mid 1800s	1	0	.	.	.	.	1
Savery. Jacob [Savry]. Amsterdam, mid 1600s; Soloman, Dutch, 1594-1670	3	0	.	.	1	2	.
Saxton, Christopher; London, c.1542-1606	89	87	.	.	1	1	.
Sayer, Robert; London, 1725-94. see Jefferys	111	77	8	6	7	10	3
Sayer & Bennett; London, late 1700s. see Jefferys	256	197	24	10	12	7	6
Sayer & Jefferys; London, late 1700s	2	1	.	.	.	1	.
Schaus, William. NY; mid 1800s	2	1	.	.	1	.	.
Schedel, Hartmann; Nuremberg, 1440-1514. (Nuremberg Chronicle)	114	44	2	9	38	10	11
Schedler. late 1800s	1	0	.	.	1	.	.
Schenk: Pieter, 1645-1715; (Jr) c.1698-1775; Amsterdam	169	136	3	10	10	6	4
Scherer, Heinrich; Munich, 1628-1704	144	87	15	10	5	7	20
Schiller, Julius. Strassburg; early 1600s	3	0	.	.	3	.	.
Schleuen. mid 1700s	1	1	.	.	.	.	.
Schley, Jacob. mid 1700s. see Van der Schley, '87+	.	.	.	.	.	.	.
Schlieben, Wilhelm Ernst August. Leipzig; 1781-1839	3	3	.	.	.	.	.
Schmidt: icnl M.F., Berlin; O.E, Germany; early 1800s	4	4	.	.	.	.	.
Schmolder. Capt. B.von; Germany; mid 1800s	1	0	.	.	.	.	1
Schomburgk, Robert Hermann. Leipzig; mid 1800s	5	5	.	.	.	.	.
Schonberg. NY; mid 1800s	7	5	.	.	.	2	.
Schonsperger, Johann. Augsburg; late 1400s	4	0	.	.	.	2	2
Schoolcraft, Henry Rowe. USA; 1793-1864	24	17	2	.	.	3	2
Schott, C. NY; late 1800s	1	1	.	.	.	.	.
Schouten, Willem Cornelisz. Amsterdam; 1567-1625	6	6	.	.	.	.	.
Schoyer. U.S.; early 1800s	2	0	.	.	.	.	2
Schrader, Th. St. Louis; mid 1800s	1	1	.	.	.	.	.
Schraembl, Franz Anton. Vienna; 1751-1803	38	10	1	3	3	20	1
Schreiber: incl Johann C., 1700s; [son] Johann Goerg, 1676-1750; Leipzig.	33	7	1	3	21	1	.
Schropp & Co. Berlin; early 1800s	1	0	1	.	.	.	.
Schroter. Germany; mid 1700s	3	1	1	1	.	.	.
Schwabe, J. Leipzig; mid 1700s	1	1	.	.	.	.	.
Science (journal).	1	1	.	.	.	.	.
Scobie, Hugh. Toronto; mid 1800s	1	1	.	.	.	.	.
Scots Magazine. Edinburgh; mid-late 1700s	24	14	.	3	3	3	1
Scott, E. late 1700s	1	1	.	.	.	.	.
Scott, Joseph. Phila; late 1700s; may incl R.	77	50	14	9	.	3	1
Scull, William. late 1700s. see Sayer & Bennett	5	0	.	2	.	2	1
Scull & Heap. Phila; mid 1700s	5	4	.	1	.	.	.
Seale, Richard William. London; mid 1700s	52	32	2	4	5	3	6
Seaton, Robert. England; mid 1800s	1	1	.	.	.	.	.
Seile, Henry; Anna. London; mid 1600s	7	5	.	.	1	.	1
Selden & Johnson. late 1800s	1	1	.	.	.	.	.
Seligmann, Joh. Michael. Germany; mid 1700s	7	5	.	.	.	1	1
Seller, John. London; late 1600s	138	104	2	16	5	4	7
Seller & Price. London; early 1700s	1	0	.	.	.	1	.
Sellwood Real Estate Co. Portland; late 1800s	1	1	.	.	.	.	.
Senex, John. London; early 1700s	202	163	10	7	11	2	9
Serres, D. London; early 1800s	1	1	.	.	.	.	.
Seutter: George Matthaus. 1678-1757; (younger) 1729-60; Albrecht Karl, 1722-62; Augsburg	406	265	13	31	36	13	48

65

Name	Total	'83-'92	'93	'94	'95	'96	'97-8
Seyfart. Battle plans c.1763.	7	0	.	3	.	3	1
Shaffner, T. NY; mid 1800s	2	2	.	.	.	.	.
Shannon, Joseph. NYC Manual; late 1800s. see New York City Manual	5	4	.	.	.	.	1
Sharp. England; mid 1800s	3	1	.	.	2	.	.
Sharpe, J. mid 1800s	2	1	1	.	.	.	.
Shattuck. USA; early 1800s	1	1	.	.	.	.	.
Shaw. USA; late 1800s	1	1	.	.	.	.	.
Sheafer, P.W. Pottsville, PA; mid 1800s	2	2	.	.	.	.	.
Shearer, W.O. Penna; mid 1800s	1	1	.	.	.	.	.
Shelton & Kensett. Conn; early 1800s	2	2	.	.	.	.	.
Sherman & Smith. NY; mid 1800s	7	5	.	1	1	.	.
Sherwood & Jones. London; early 1800s	3	3	.	.	.	.	.
Sherwood, Neely & Jones. London; early 1800s	1	0	.	.	1	.	.
Shober & Carqueville Lith. Chicago; late 1800s	2	2	.	.	.	.	.
Shober, Charles. Chicago; late 1800s	2	1	.	1	.	.	.
Shobere, W. publisher; London; mid 1800s	1	1	.	.	.	.	.
Sickler, Friedrich Carl Ludwig. early 1800s	2	0	.	.	.	1	1
Sidman, T. London; mid 1800s	1	1	.	.	.	.	.
Sidney, J.S. Phila; mid 1800s.	1	0	.	1	.	.	.
Sifton, Praed. London; mid 1800s	1	1	.	.	.	.	.
Silver: incl Thomas, mid 1700s; S.W. & Co., late 1800s; London	3	3	.	.	.	.	.
Silvestre, Israel; Paris(?), 1621-91	1	1	.	.	.	.	.
Simonin & Hansen. late 1800s	1	1	.	.	.	.	.
Simons, Mathew. English; mid 1600s	1	1	.	.	.	.	.
Simplot, Alex. views; late 1800s	1	1	.	.	.	.	.
Sinclair, Thomas; lith., Phila, mid 1800s	3	2	.	1	.	.	.
Skelton, J. early 1800s	1	1	.	.	.	.	.
Skinner, A.B. Keene, NH; late 1800s	1	1	.	.	.	.	.
Slater. Isaac; London; mid 1800s. see Pigot	1	0	.	.	.	.	1
Slator, John & Thomas. USA; mid 1800s	1	1	.	.	.	.	.
Slatter, H. Oxford; early 1800s	1	1	.	.	.	.	.
Slezer. John; Scotland; late 1600s	1	0	.	.	.	.	1
Smedley, Samuel L. Phila; late 1800s	1	0	.	.	.	1	.
Smillie. USA; mid 1800s Bunker Hill panorama	2	2	.	.	.	.	.
Smith: various. may incl others separately listed, '93 +	99	93	.	.	.	3	3
Smith, Asa. mid 1800s	5	5	.	.	.	.	.
Smith, Charles. London; early 1800s	21	1	10	4	.	4	2
Smith, Fern & Co. mid 1800s	1	1	.	.	.	.	.
Smith, G.	3	0	.	1	1	1	.
Smith, John. English explorer; 1580-1631	3	0	1	1	1	.	.
Smith, John Calvin. NY: mid 1800s	7	0	.	3	.	2	2
Smith, Mason & Co. USA; mid 1800s	1	1	.	.	.	.	.
Smith, Roswell C. USA; mid 1800s	17	1	1	1	4	3	7
Smith, W. H. England; late 1800s	2	0	2	.	.	.	.
Smith & Jones. London; late 1700s	1	1	.	.	.	.	.
Smollett. history; England; mid 1700s	2	2	.	.	.	.	.
Smyth: various; incl W., London, mid 1800s	4	4	.	.	.	.	.
Snow & Co. San Francisco; late 1800s	3	1	.	.	1	1	.
Snyder & Black Lith. NY; late 1800s	1	1	.	.	.	.	.
Snyder, Van Vechten & Co. late 1800s	2	1	.	.	1	.	.
Society for Anti-Gallicians. London; mid 1700s	1	0	1	.	.	.	.
Society for the Diffusion of Useful Knowledge. London; 1800s	916	566	.	84	61	75	65	65
SDUK to '88. see Baldwin & Cradock; Chapman & Hall; Cox; Knight; Stanford; Letts							
Society for the Promotion of Christian Knowledge. London; mid 1800s	2	2	.	.	.	.	.
Society for the Propagation of the Gospel. mid 1800s	2	2	.	.	.	.	.
Society of Friends. USA; mid 1800s +	1	0	.	1	.	.	.
Sohr, Dr. Karl. Glogau; 1844-1901	2	0	.	1	.	1	.
Solinus, Caius Julius. late 1400s	7	6	1	.	.	.	1
Solis. Hernando de. Spain; early 1600s	2	0	.	1	.	.	1
Sonnenstern. Maximilian von; mid 1800s	1	0	.	.	.	.	1
Sotzmann. Daniel Friedrich; Germany; 1754-1840	2	0	1	.	.	.	1
Soulavie. mid 1800s	1	1	.	.	.	.	.
Soules, Francois. Paris; late 1700s	3	1	.	.	.	.	2
Souter, J. London; early 1800s	1	0	.	1	.	.	.
Southern Pacific Co.	3	3	.	.	.	.	.

	Total	'83-'92	'93	'94	'95	'96	'97-8
Spanish Admiralty. see Direccion de Hidrografia	.	.	.	.	.	.	.
Spanish-American War - Infrequent Publisher.	3	0	.	1	.	2	.
Sparrman, Anders. Swedish; late 1700s	1	0	.	.	.	1	.
Spaulding, J.R. Boston; late 1800s	1	1	.	.	.	.	.
Specht, Caspar. Utrecht; early 1700s	1	1	.	.	.	.	.
Speed, John. London; 1552-1629	1046	821	22	49	50	33	71
Speer, Capt. Joseph Smith. London; late 1700s	3	3	.	.	.	.	.
Spilsbury, J. London; late 1700s	1	1	.	.	.	.	.
Spirinx, Nicolas. Lyons; early 1600s	1	1	.	.	.	.	.
Sprange, Jasper. England; late 1700s	1	1	.	.	.	.	.
Sproule, G. English; late 1700s	1	0	1	.	.	.	.
Stackhouse, Thomas. publisher; London; 1706-84	20	13	2	1	4	.	.
Stalker, C. London; late 1700s	1	1	.	.	.	.	.
Standard Atlas. Chicago; late 1800s	16	11	5	.	.	.	.
Stanford, Edward. London; 1827-1904. see S.D.U.K.	124	65	43	5	6	3	2
Stannard & Son. London; late 1800s	1	1	.	.	.	.	.
Stansbury, A.J. USA; early 1800s. see U.S.	2	1	.	.	.	.	1
Stansby, Keily & Rea. Phila; mid 1800s	1	1	.	.	.	.	.
Starckman. engraver; mid 1700s	2	2	.	.	.	.	.
Starling, Thomas. London; early 1800s	25	20	1	2	2	.	.
Staveley, E. English; mid 1800s; with H.M. Wood, early 1800s	2	2	.	.	.	.	.
Stearns & Hitchcock. late 1800s	1	1	.	.	.	.	.
Stebbins: incl Henry S., USA, late 1800s; L.	10	2	4	2	.	1	1
Stedman: Charles; John Gabriel. London; late 1700s	86	55	15	10	1	3	2
Stedman, Brown & Lyons. Amer; late 1800s	1	0	.	.	.	.	1
Steinberger, L. Auugsburg; late 1600s	1	0	.	.	1	.	.
Stennett, R. London; early 1800s	1	1	.	.	.	.	.
Stent, Peter. London; mid 1600s	3	2	.	1	.	.	.
Stetter, Johan Jacob. Frankfurt; early 1700s	1	1	.	.	.	.	.
Steudner, Johann Philip. Augsburg; late 1600s	1	1	.	.	.	.	.
Stevens, Isaac Ingalls. USA; 1818-62	3	3	.	.	.	.	.
Stewart, John. London; late 1800s	1	1	.	.	.	.	.
Stieler, Adolph. Gotha; 1775-1836 (successors used name)	88	56	5	10	4	5	8
Stiger & Co.	1	0	1	.	.	.	.
Stockdale, John; London, 1739-1814. see Morse	63	47	6	3	2	1	4
Stocklein, Joseph. Augsburg; mid 1700s	3	1	.	1	.	1	.
Stoddard, S.R. Glens Falls, NY; late 1800s	3	2	.	.	.	.	1
Stone & Pomeroy. Phila; mid 1800s	1	1	.	.	.	.	.
Stone, W.J. engraver, USA, early 1800s	2	0	.	.	1	1	.
Stoner, J.J. views; USA; late 1800s	4	4	.	.	.	.	.
Stoopendaal, Daniel. Amsterdam; early 1700s	36	15	1	4	3	6	7
Stopius, Nicolaus. mid 1500s	1	1	.	.	.	.	.
Stouf. USA; late 1800s	1	1	.	.	.	.	.
Stow, John. London; early 1600s	23	23	.	.	.	.	.
Strabo. Greek; c.50 BC-25 AD	1	0	1	.	.	.	.
Strada, Famiano. early 1600s.	9	5	1	1	1	1	.
Stradanus. Johannes; Flemish; early 1600s.	1	0	.	.	.	.	1
Strahan & Cadell. late 1700s	1	1	.	.	.	.	.
Stratford. late 1700s	2	2	.	.	.	.	.
Streit, Friedrich Wilhelm. Germany; early 1800s	3	2	.	.	.	.	1
Striedbeck, Johann. Strassburg; mid 1700s	2	1	.	1	.	.	.
Strobridge & Co. Cincinnati; late 1800s	1	1	.	.	.	.	.
Strong, Ezra. Hartford; mid 1800s	1	1	.	.	.	.	.
Strype, John. London; early 1700s	11	6	5	.	.	.	.
Stuart: J.H. & Co., Maine; Oliver J., NY; late 1800s	2	2	.	.	.	.	.
Stucchi. Milan; early 1800s	1	0	1	.	.	.	.
Studer. mid 1800s	1	1	.	.	.	.	.
Studley, R.P. & Co. St Louis; late 1800s	1	1	.	.	.	.	.
Stukeley, William. England; early 1700s	2	1	.	1	.	.	.
Stukely.	1	1	.	.	.	.	.
Stulpnagel. see Von Stulpnagel, '87 +	.	.	.	.	.	.	.
Stumpf, Johann. Swiss; 1500-76	9	6	1	1	.	.	1
Sudlow, E. London; late 1700s	5	4	.	.	1	.	.
Suhr, Peter. German; mid 1800s	2	2	.	.	.	.	.
Sumner: incl - & Co.; William, Pitts, early 1800s; H.F., Hartford, mid 1800s	7	6	.	.	1	.	.

67

Name	Total	'83-'92	'93	'94	'95	'96	'97-8
Swallow, F.G. Boston; mid 1800s	1	1	.	.	.	.	.
Swanston, George H. mid 1800s	25	11	6	1	3	1	3
Sweden, Government of.	1	1	.	.	.	.	.
Sweet, Homer D.L. NY; late 1800s	1	1	.	.	.	.	.
Sweny, M.A. Liverpool; late 1800s	2	1	1	.	.	.	.
Swift, William Henry; US; early 1800s	1	0	.	.	.	.	1
Swinton, W. late 1800s	44	43	.	.	.	.	1
Synd,. late 1700s	1	1	.	.	.	.	.
Tackabury, George N. Toronto; late 1800s	5	5	.	.	.	.	.
Taintor; mid 1800s. incl Taintor Bros.	3	3	.	.	.	.	.
Taintor & Merrill; NY, late 1800s. incl Taintor Bros. & Merrill	13	10	.	3	.	.	.
Talbot, John. Leeds; early 1800s	4	3	1	.	.	.	.
Tallis, John (& various companies). London; Glasgow; Edinburgh; mid 1800s	828	672	15	21	56	31	33
Tanner, Henry Schenck; Phila, NY, 1786-1858	370	251	33	26	17	21	22
Tardieu (family). Paris; late 1700s-early 1800s	89	65	6	6	3	4	5
Tarleton, Banastre. London; late 1700s	6	5	.	.	.	.	1
Tassin. Nicolas. Paris(?); early 1600s	5	1	.	.	.	3	1
Tasso, G. Venice; early 1800s	3	0	.	.	1	2	.
Taunton. late 1800s	3	1	1	.	.	.	1
Tavernier, Melchior; 1564-1641 (& family); Paris, Antwerp	24	9	1	2	2	6	4
Taylor: various; incl Thomas (see below); David. NY; mid 1800s	17	15	.	.	2	.	.
Taylor, Thomas; London, fl 1670-1721	3	1	1	1	.	.	.
Taylor & Skinner. late 1700s	5	0	.	4	1	.	.
Teesdale, Henry. London; mid 1800s. see Dower	67	61	1	.	3	.	2
Tegg, T. publisher; London; mid 1800s	12	11	.	.	.	.	1
Teubet & Burty. mid 1800s	1	1	.	.	.	.	.
Texas & Pacific Rwy.	2	2	.	.	.	.	.
Texas, State of.	2	2	.	.	.	.	.
Thackara & Vallance. USA; late 1700s	1	1	.	.	.	.	.
Thacker, W. late 1800s	1	1	.	.	.	.	.
Thaxter, S. & Son. Boston; late 1800s	2	2	.	.	.	.	.
Thayer, Bridgman & Fanning. publisher; NY; mid 1800s	2	2	.	.	.	.	.
Thayer, Horace & Co. mid 1800s	2	1	.	.	.	1	.
Thayer. lith; Boston; mid 1800s	10	9	.	1	.	.	.
Theakston, S.W. Scarborough, UK; late 1800s	1	1	.	.	.	.	.
Therbu, L. late 1700s	2	0	.	.	1	1	.
Thesaurus Geographicus. see Moll	9	9	.	.	.	.	.
Thevenot, Melchisedech; Paris, 1620-92	19	12	.	.	2	2	3
Thevet, Andre. French; 1502-90	4	4	.	.	.	.	.
Thierry. engraver; Paris; early 1800s	5	4	.	.	.	1	.
Thissel, J. Phila; mid 1800s	1	1	.	.	.	.	.
Thomas & Andrews. publisher; Boston; late 1700s+	2	2	.	.	.	.	.
Thomas, Cowperthwait & Co. Phila; mid 1800s	507	361	19	37	24	28	38
Thompson: various; incl. Zadock, mid 1800s.	9	5	.	3	1	.	.
Thompson & Everts. USA; late 1800s	1	1	.	.	.	.	.
Thompson Bros. & Burr. USA; late 1800s	1	1	.	.	.	.	.
Thomson. John & Co; Edinburgh, fl 1813-69	492	392	15	18	28	16	23
Thornton: John, London, late 1600s; Samuel, early 1700s	22	17	1	2	1	.	1
Thrall, Willis. Hartford; early 1800s	3	2	.	1	.	.	.
Throop, O.H. USA; mid 1800s	3	2	1	.	.	.	.
Tilden, S.D. Hartford; late 1800s	3	1	.	1	.	1	.
Tilgmann, F. early 1900s	1	0	1	.	.	.	.
Tillotson & Son. late 1800s	1	0	.	.	1	.	.
Tindal, Nicolas; London, 1687-1774. see Rapin	50	43	.	1	5	1	.
Tirinus, Jacobus. Antwerp; mid 1600s	4	2	1	.	.	.	1
Tirion, Isaak. Amsterdam; mid 1700s. see Albrizzi	305	224	12	22	18	21	8
Titsingh, Isaac. early 1800s	1	1	.	.	.	.	.
Tombleson. London; mid 1800s	1	1	.	.	.	.	.
Toms, William Henry. London; mid 1700s	8	7	1	.	.	.	.
Topham. London; early 1800s	1	1	.	.	.	.	.
Torbett, C.W. London; early 1800s	2	2	.	.	.	.	.
Torniello, Augustine. Milan; late 1500s	13	8	1	.	4	.	.
Torrente, M. Madrid; early 1800s	1	1	.	.	.	.	.
Toudy, H.J. Phila; late 1800s	1	1	.	.	.	.	.
Toussaint. Paris; early 1800s	1	0	1	.	.	.	.

Name	Total	'83-'92	'93	'94	'95	'96	'97-8
Town & Country Magazine. London; late 1700s	4	1	.	.	.	1	2
Tramezini, Michaelo. Rome; Venice; mid 1500s	3	3	.	.	.	.	.
Tremaine, George C. Toronto; mid 1800s	2	2	.	.	.	.	.
Treuttel. late 1700s	1	1	.	.	.	.	.
Trine & Hills. Colorado; late 1800s	1	1	.	.	.	.	.
Troncoso, Diego. Mexico; late 1700s	1	1	.	.	.	.	.
Trusler, John. English; late 1700s	18	7	.	10	.	.	1
Trutch, J.W. Ottawa; late 1800s	1	1	.	.	.	.	.
Truxton, Thomas. late 1700s	2	1	.	.	.	.	1
Tschesky, K. Russian; early 1800s	2	2	.	.	.	.	.
Tunison, H.C. USA; late 1800s	28	11	3	6	1	5	2
Turner: James, Boston; mid 1700s; Charles, London; early 1800s	1	1	.	.	.	.	.
Tyson, Philip. Washington; mid 1800s	2	2	.	.	.	.	.
U.S. [Government] see Ackerman Lith.; Bien; Cowles; Duval Lith.; Fremont; Hayden Hoen & Co.; Powell; Wagner & McGuigan, individual surnames. try Title Index	1375	1018	87	47	33	71	119
U.S. Civil War - Infrequent Publishers. see U.S. Union & Confederate Armies	7	0	.	.	.	6	1
U.S. Coast & Geodetic Survey.	31	9	.	4	10	3	5
U.S. Coast Survey.	875	681	31	53	36	30	44
U.S. Election Map Co. San Francisco; late 1800s	1	0	.	1	.	.	.
U.S. Exploring Expedition. mid 1800s	36	21	3	3	2	5	2
U.S. Geological Survey.	72	6	7	19	18	11	11
U.S. Hydrographic Office.	3	0	.	.	1	1	1
U.S. Pacific R.R. Survey. mid 1800s	134	93	12	2	6	10	11
U.S. State Surveys. see Dept. of Interior, '83	422	211	41	40	36	50	44
U.S. Union & Confederate Armies Atlas. publ 1891-95. see Cowles, '91-'92.	75	27	.	5	13	22	8
U.S. War Department.	308	2	71	51	61	66	57
Ulloa: incl Ulloa & Juan, Spanish, 1716-95	2	1	1	.	.	.	.
Union Pacific R.R.	1	1	.	.	.	.	.
Universal Magazine. London; mid-late 1700s	109	73	7	1	10	6	12
Universal Museum Magazine. London; mid 1700s	7	4	.	1	.	2	.
Universal Traveller. mid 1800s	1	1	.	.	.	.	.
Vadianus, Joachim (von Watte). Swiss; 1484-1551	2	0	.	.	1	.	1
Valdes, Antonio. late 1700s	1	1	.	.	.	.	.
Valdis. Antonio; late 1700s.	1	0	.	.	.	.	1
Valdor, Joannes. Liege(?); early 1600s	1	1	.	.	.	.	.
Valegio & Diono. Italy; early 1600s	1	1	.	.	.	.	.
Valentine's Manual. NY; mid 1800s. see New York City Manual	7	5	.	.	.	.	2
Valentyn, François. Amsterdam; Dordrecht; early 1700s	43	16	3	5	2	9	8
Valeso. late 1500s	3	3	.	.	.	.	.
Valk: Gerard, c.1650-1726; Leonard, 1675-1755; Amsterdam	73	49	5	7	2	3	7
Valk & Schenk. Amsterdam; early 1700s	74	42	2	5	2	3	20
Vallance, J. Phila; 1770-1823	1	1	.	.	.	.	.
Van Adrichem, Christian. Cologne; 1533-85	7	3	.	.	2	.	2
Van Aelst, Nicolas. C.1527-1613	1	0	.	.	1	.	.
Van Alphen, Pieter. publisher; Rotterdam; mid 1600s	1	1	.	.	.	.	.
Van Baarsel. engraver; Netherlands; late 1700s	5	5	.	.	.	.	.
Van Call, Pieter. early 1800s	1	1	.	.	.	.	.
Van Campen, Jacob. Amsterdam; mid 1600s	1	0	.	.	1	.	.
Van de Passe. Crispyn; engr for Plantin; 1564-1637	1	0	.	.	.	.	1
Van den Aveele, Jan. Leiden; 1655-1722	1	0	.	.	.	1	.
Van den Hoeye, Rombout. Amsterdam; 1622-71	1	1	.	.	.	.	.
Van den Keere, Pieter. Amsterdam; 1571-1646	147	117	5	6	9	5	5
Van der Aa, Pieter. Leiden; 1659-1733	314	187	21	20	30	33	23
Van der Hagen. engraver; late 1700s	1	1	.	.	.	.	.
Van der Schley, Jacob. German; mid 1700s. see Schley, '83	22	10	1	1	1	8	1
Van Doetecum, Baptista (& family). Deventer; Haarlem; late 1500s	2	2	.	.	.	.	.
Van Geelkerken: Nicolaas, Amsterdam, early 1600s; & others	7	6	1	.	.	.	.
Van Harreveldt & Changuion. publisher; late 1700s	2	2	.	.	.	.	.
Van Jagen, C. & Jan. Amsterdam; mid 1700s	4	2	.	.	.	.	2
Van Keulen: Johannes, 1654-1715; Gerald, 1678-1727; etc. Amsterdam	330	220	31	29	19	18	13
Van Linschoten, Jan Huygen. Amsterdam; 1653-1610. see Linschoten to '85	93	59	6	6	9	4	9
Van Lochom, Michael. Paris; 1601-47	13	10	3	.	.	.	.
Van Loon: Herman, Gillis, Johannes; Amsterdam; mid 1600s	15	5	2	2	2	2	2
Van Meurs, Jacob. Amsterdam; 1620-80	13	7	.	1	1	.	4
Van Schagen, Gerrit Lucaszoon. Amsterdam; 1642-90	3	1	.	.	1	1	.

Name	Total	'83-'92	'93	'94	'95	'96	'97-8
Van Schoel: incl Hendrick, early 1600s	3	3	.	.	.	.	.
Van Spilbergen, Juris. Dutch; early 1600s. see Spilbergen, '84	3	3	.	.	.	.	.
Van Zouteveen. late 1800s	1	0	1	.	.	.	.
Vance, David H. wall maps; NY; early 1800s	1	0	.	1	.	.	.
Vancouver, Capt. George. English; 1758-98	44	27	6	.	2	7	2
Vandermaelen, Philippe Marie Guillaume. Brussels; 1795-1869	303	244	14	14	7	8	16
Varela y Ulloa, Josef. Madrid; late 1700s	2	2	.	.	.	.	.
Varin. late 1700s	1	0	.	.	1	.	.
Varle, P.C. French(?); early 1800s	3	3	.	.	.	.	.
Varte. late 1800s	1	1	.	.	.	.	.
Vascellini, G. Milan; late 1700s	1	1	.	.	.	.	.
Vaughan: David, mid 1800s; Robert, London, mid 1600s	3	1	.	1	.	.	1
Vaughan. Robert; English engraver; 1600-66	1	0	.	.	.	.	1
Vaugondy. see De Vaugondy	.	.	.	.	.	.	.
Velten, J. Karlsruhe; early 1800s	5	4	1	.	.	.	.
Venegas, Miguel. Madrid; mid 1700s	2	1	.	.	.	1	.
Verbiest, Pieter. Antwerp; mid 1600s	1	1	.	.	.	.	.
Verdun de la Crenne, Marquis Jean Rene Antoine de. mid 1600s	1	1	.	.	.	.	.
Verleger. early 1800s	2	2	.	.	.	.	.
Vertue, George. London; 1684-1756	2	2	.	.	.	.	.
Viele, Egbert L. NY, late 1800s	4	0	.	.	1	1	2
Villalpando, Juan Bautista. Spanish, Rome, 1552-1608	4	4	.	.	.	.	.
Villamena, Francesco. early 1600s	1	1	.	.	.	.	.
Villedieu. mid 1800s	1	0	1	.	.	.	.
Vincendon-Dumoulin, C.A. French; 1811-58. see Depot de la Marine	6	6	.	.	.	.	.
Vincent: various	3	3	.	.	.	.	.
Vincent, Brooks, Day & Son. late 1800s	11	11	.	.	.	.	.
Virtue, George. publisher; London; mid 1800s	30	24	.	1	1	.	4
Virtue, Yorston & Co. mid 1800s	15	11	.	.	.	4	.
Visscher: Claes Janszoon, 1587-1652; Nicolas, 1618-79; Nicolaes Jansz. II, 1649-1702; Amsterdam. see Schenk; Valk & Schenk	483	328	20	22	30	25	58
Vivien: incl Louis ... de Saint Martin, Paris, 1802-97	30	22	1	.	3	2	2
Vliet, Jesper. Milwaukee; mid 1800s	1	1	.	.	.	.	.
Volkamer, Johann Christoph. Nuremberg; 1644-1720	1	0	.	.	.	1	.
Volney. c. 1800	1	0	.	.	.	1	.
Von Breydenbach, Bernard. traveller; c.1440-97	3	2	.	.	1	.	.
Von de Sandrart, Jacob. German; 1630-1708	3	1	.	1	.	1	.
Von der Hayden. mid 1700s	1	1	.	.	.	.	.
Von Euler, Leonhard. Berlin; 1707-83	21	13	2	1	2	1	2
Von Humboldt, Alexander. German; 1769-1859. see Humboldt, '84	15	14	.	.	.	.	1
Von Kotzebue, Otto. Russian; 1787-1846	2	1	1	.	.	.	.
Von Leonard. Germany; mid 1800s.	1	0	.	.	.	.	1
Von Mechel, Christian. Basle; 1737-1817	1	1	.	.	.	.	.
Von Pufendorf. Nuremberg; late 1600s	5	5	.	.	.	.	.
Von Reilly, Franz Johann Joseph. Vienna; 1766-1820. see Reilly, '83	121	55	2	32	3	13	16
Von Schlieben, Wilhelm Ernst August. Leipzig; 1781-1839. See Schlieben, '89, '90	2	1	1	.	.	.	.
Von Siebold, Philip Franz Balthasar; German working for Dutch in Japan; 1796-1866	3	0	.	3	.	.	.
Von Spener, Harde. late 1700s	1	1	.	.	.	.	.
Von Staehlin, Jacob. German; late 1700s. see Staehlin, '83	1	1	.	.	.	.	.
Von Steinwehr, A.W.A.F. 1822-77	1	0	.	.	.	1	.
Von Stulpnagel. German; 1781-1865. see Stulpnagel to '86	15	8	3	.	2	2	.
Von Zach, Freiherr Anton. Austrian; 1747-1826. see Anton, 1986	1	1	.	.	.	.	.
Vorzet, E. France, late 1800s. see Paris, Comte de	1	0	.	.	.	1	.
Vose, J.W. NY; late 1800s	2	2	.	.	.	.	.
Vouillemont, Estienne. late 1600s	2	2	.	.	.	.	.
Vrients, Jan Baptista. Antwerp; late 1500s	6	4	1	.	.	.	1
Vuillemin, Alexandre A. Paris; mid 1800s	22	12	4	2	1	1	2
Wade, W. early 1800s	1	1	.	.	.	.	.
Wadsworth, Unwin & Browne. late 1800s	2	2	.	.	.	.	.
Waesberger. Johann; Jansson son-in-law; d.1681. see Jansson	1	0	.	.	.	.	1
Waghenaer, Lucas Janszoon. Leiden, Antwerp; 1533-1606	68	55	4	2	1	2	4
Wagner: incl Matthais, Ulm, 1648-94	2	0	.	1	.	1	.
Wagner & McGuigan, Phila; mid 1800s. see U.S. categories	1	1	.	.	.	.	.
Wahl. early 1800s	2	2	.	.	.	.	.
Waite, J.F. Chicago; late 1800s	38	30	7	.	1	.	.

Name	Total	'83-'92	'93	'94	'95	'96	'97-8
Wakefield. early 1800s	1	1	.	.	.	.	.
Walch, Johann. Germany, late 1700s	10	2	1	.	1	1	5
Waldseemuller, Martin. Lorraine; 1470-1521. see Ptolemy (1513-20)	17	0	1	4	4	2	6
Wales. late 1700s	2	1	1	.	.	.	.
Walker: Samuel Jr., Boston. mid 1800s; may incl J. & C., & others	61	57	.	.	2	2	.
Walker, George. Boston; late 1800s	15	0	3	9	2	1	.
Walker, H.B. late 1800s	6	0	.	.	.	2	4
Walker, J. & C. London; fl 1820-95	5	0	1	.	3	1	.
Walker & Miles. Canada; late 1800s	33	31	2	.	.	.	.
Wall, J. Sutton. Harrisburg, PA; late 1800s	2	1	.	.	.	.	1
Walling; Henry F. USA; 1825-88	66	29	8	6	7	7	9
Walling & Gray. Boston; late 1800s	42	10	4	15	2	5	6
Walling, Tackabury & Co. Boston; late 1800s	3	3	.	.	.	.	.
Wallis: various, England; early 1800s	16	12	2	.	.	2	.
Wallis & Reid. England; early 1800s	17	17	.	.	.	.	.
Walsh: various	2	2	.	.	.	.	.
Walter, J. London; late 1700s	3	3	.	.	.	.	.
Walther, Johann Georg. Frankfort; late 1600s	1	1	.	.	.	.	.
Walton, Robert. London; mid 1600s	9	4	2	.	1	.	2
Wangersheim, William. Chicago; late 1800s	6	6	.	.	.	.	.
Warburton. John. English; early 1700s	5	4	.	.	.	.	1
Ward: H., early 1800s; J., mid 1800s; London	5	5	.	.	.	.	.
Warden, D. Edinburgh; early 1800s	2	2	.	.	.	.	.
Ware. Richard; London; mid 1700s	8	3	.	.	1	.	4
Warner & Beers. USA; late 1800s	27	9	1	2	7	3	5
Warner & Hanna. USA; early 1800s	1	1	.	.	.	.	.
Warner & Higgins. USA; mid 1800s	1	1	.	.	.	.	.
Warner, Benjamin. USA; early 1800s	3	1	1	.	1	.	.
Warner, Higgins & Beers. USA; mid 1800s	2	2	.	.	.	.	.
Warren, William. USA; 1806-79	2	1	.	.	.	1	.
Waterlow. London; late 1800s	1	1	.	.	.	.	.
Waters & Son. NY; mid 1800s. see Harper's Weekly; N.Y. Herald	17	0	.	.	3	14	.
Watson, Gaylord. NY; late 1800s	44	32	3	4	3	1	1
Watts. views; USA; mid 1800s	1	1	.	.	.	.	.
Waud. views; USA; mid 1800s	3	3	.	.	.	.	.
Weale, John. London; mid 1800s	2	1	1	.	.	.	.
Weaver, H. mid 1800s	1	0	1	.	.	.	.
Weber, P. Karlsruhe; mid 1800s	4	4	.	.	.	.	.
Webster, John. NY; mid 1800s	1	0	.	1	.	.	.
Weed, Parsons. Albany; mid 1800s	2	2	.	.	.	.	.
Weekly Dispatch. London; mid 1800s. Try Dower; Ettling; Lowry; Weller	65	37	3	4	9	7	5
Weekly Herald. mid 1800s	1	1	.	.	.	.	.
Weigel, Christopher (the elder). Nuremberg; 1654-1725	52	28	1	10	8	2	3
Weiland, Carl Ferdinand. Weimar; 1782-1847. see Weimar Geog. Inst.	10	5	.	.	2	1	2
Weimar Geographisches Institut. Germany; early-mid 1800s	48	19	22	.	4	1	2
Weis, Jean Martin. Strassburg; late 1800s	1	1	.	.	.	.	.
Weiss. late 1700s	1	1	.	.	.	.	.
Weld, Isaac. traveler; late 1700s	14	10	1	.	1	1	1
Weller, Edward. London; late 1800s. see Weekly Dispatch	69	53	4	7	3	.	2
Wellge. USA; late 1800s	1	1	.	.	.	.	.
Wells: incl J., Chicago, mid 1800s; J.G., New York, mid 1800s	8	7	.	.	.	.	1
Wells, Edward. London; Oxford; 1667-1727. may incl J.	153	108	6	11	10	8	10
Wells & Rowley. Penna; late 1800s	1	1	.	.	.	.	.
Werner, W. lith; Leipzig; early 1800s	9	8	.	.	1	.	.
Wescoatt, N. USA; mid 1800s	3	1	.	.	1	1	.
West Shore. Portland, OR; late 1800s	7	7	.	.	.	.	.
Wetstein, R & G. Amsterdam; early 1700s	3	1	1	.	.	1	.
Weygand. early 1800s	2	2	.	.	.	.	.
Whitchurch, William. engraver; London; late 1800s	1	0	1	.	.	.	.
White & Kemble. USA; early 1900s	4	0	.	.	.	4	.
White, M.W. USA; late 1800s	5	3	.	1	1	.	.
White, W. Sheffield; mid 1800s	1	0	.	.	1	.	.
Whitefield, E. Chicago; mid 1800s	1	1	.	.	.	.	.
Whitelaw, James. Vermont; late 1700s	1	0	.	1	.	.	.
Whiting, E. USA; mid 1800s	1	0	.	1	.	.	.

	Total	'83-'92	'93	'94	'95	'96	'97-8
Whitney: incl Charles, Boston, mid 1800s; W.H., Phila, late 1800s	8	6	.	.	.	1	1
Whitney & Standish. Albany; mid 1800s	1	1	.	.	.	.	.
Whittaker, W.B. publisher; London; mid 1800s	1	1	.	.	.	.	.
Whymper, F. views; London; late 1800s	4	4	.	.	.	.	.
Wiggin, C.P. Pittsburgh; mid 1800s	2	2	.	.	.	.	.
Wight. England; mid 1700s	1	1	.	.	.	.	.
Wightman, Thomas. engraver; Boston; early 1800s	1	0	1	.	.	.	.
Wilcocke, S.H. London; early 1800s	2	2	.	.	.	.	.
Wild. publisher; Paris; mid 1800s	1	1	.	.	.	.	.
Wilgus, A.W. Buffalo; mid 1800s	1	1	.	.	.	.	.
Wilkes: incl J., London, early 1800s; Charles, USA, mid 1800s. see U.S. Exploring Expedition	21	14	1	1	3	2	.
Wilkie, J. & T. publisher; England; late 1700s	8	5	.	.	2	1	.
Wilkinson, Robert. London; fl 1785-1825	117	78	5	1	17	4	12
Will, Joh. Martin. engraver; Augsburg; late 1700s	1	0	.	.	1	.	.
Willard, Emma. 1787-1870; incl Asaph, mid 1800s; Hartford	6	2	.	.	1	1	2
Willdey, George. London; early 1700s	19	14	2	.	.	1	2
Willemsz, Marcus. Belgium; mid 1600s	1	1	.	.	.	.	.
Williams: incl A & Co.; Alexander; B; E.P.; J. David to '92; John; etc.	25	21	.	1	1	2	.
Williams, C.S. publisher; Phila; mid 1800s	12	8	1	.	.	.	3
Williams, J.David. People's Pictorial Atlas; USA; late 1800s	9	0	.	2	.	6	1
Williams, W: incl William, Utica, early 1800s; W. at NY, Phila, mid 1800s	15	7	2	.	1	3	2
Williamson, Lt. R.S. Robert, Dublin, mid 1700s; Lt. R.S., US Army, mid 1800s. see U.S.	3	2	.	.	.	.	1
Willis. views; mid 1800s	1	1	.	.	.	.	.
Willmann, Edward. views; Karlsruhe; mid 1800s	3	3	.	.	.	.	.
Willyams, Cooper. late 1700s	1	0	1	.	.	.	.
Wilmore, J.A. Richmond; late 1800s	5	1	1	1	1	.	1
Wilson: incl Charles, London, mid 1800s	21	16	4	.	1	.	.
Wilson, Capt. James. late 1700s	7	6	.	1	.	.	.
Winchell. USA; late 1800s	3	1	.	.	.	1	1
Winkelmanns Chronik. late 1600s	2	2	.	.	.	.	.
Winslow, E.N. Boston; late 1800s	1	1	.	.	.	.	.
Winterbotham, William. 1763-1829	13	6	2	.	2	2	1
Wislizenus, Dr. Frederick Adolphus. German-Amer., 1810-89	3	0	1	.	.	1	1
Witsen, Nicolaas. Amsterdam; early 1700s	1	1	.	.	.	.	.
Witter, Conrad. St. Louis; mid 1800s	1	1	.	.	.	.	.
Wolfe: incl John, publ., London, late 1500s; J.M. & Co, Omaha, late 1800s.	7	0	.	5	1	1	.
Wolff: incl Jeremias; Augsburg, 1663-1724; T., mid 1700s	2	2	.	.	.	.	.
Wood: incl Wm, c.1580-1639; also Wm. H., Jersey City, mid 1800s	2	2	.	.	.	.	.
Woodbridge, William Channing. Hartford; 1794-1854	16	7	1	1	1	3	3
Woodford, E.M. Phila; mid 1800s	5	3	.	.	.	2	.
Woodruff, Charles P. NY: late 1800s	1	1	.	.	.	.	.
Woodruff Mining Co. Calif; mid 1800s	1	1	.	.	.	.	.
Woodward, Tiernan & Hale. St. Louis; late 1800s	1	1	.	.	.	.	.
Woolman & Rose. see Rose & Woolman, '92	.	.	.	.	.	.	.
Wooten, Joseph. Manchester; early 1800s	1	1	.	.	.	.	.
Wright: various; incl Benjamin, English, late 1500s	6	6	.	.	.	.	.
Wyatt. England; early 1800s	1	1	.	.	.	.	.
Wyld: James, 1790-1836; (II) 1812-87; John Cooper, 1845-1907; London	318	238	31	9	17	10	13
Wytfliet, Cornelis. Louvain; late 1500s	120	50	7	15	9	16	23
Yeager, James. engraver; USA; early 1800s	4	3	1	.	.	.	.
Young: incl J., Washington, mid 1800s	4	4	.	.	.	.	.
Young, James H.; Phila; mid 1800s	8	5	3	.	.	.	.
Young & Brownlee. Canada; late 1800s	1	1	.	.	.	.	.
Young & Williams. USA; mid 1800s	1	1	.	.	.	.	.
Zahn, Johann. Nuremberg; late 1600s	8	4	.	.	.	.	4
Zakreski, Alex. San Francisco; mid 1800s	1	1	.	.	.	.	.
Zaltieri, Bolognini. Venice; fl 1550-80	1	1	.	.	.	.	.
Zatta, Antonio. Venice; fl 1757-97	475	356	15	22	43	25	14
Zeese. A.& Co.; Chicago; late 1800s	4	3	.	.	.	.	1
Zell, T. Ellwood. publisher; Phila; late 1800s	4	2	.	.	.	2	.
Ziegler & McCurdy. late 1800s	1	0	.	.	.	1	.
Ziegler, Jacob. Vienna; early 1500s	7	7	.	.	.	.	.
Zimmerman, E.F.W. USA; late 1800s	1	1	.	.	.	.	.
Zurner, Adam Friedrich. Amsterdam; 1680-1742	6	3	.	1	1	.	1

PRICE LISTING

Prices realized at auctions are indicated by the prefix "[A]" in the dealer code and include buyer's premium. Prices in **bold** type indicate the catalogue currency.

AERONAUTICAL MAPS

ARROW AIRWAYS, INC. [c.1920] Durie and Hinrichs. Northern NJ bird's-eye; large arrow points to Arrow's base, Paterson Airport. 36x51cm (14x20") Uncolored. Some soiling, but VG.   [25]   £75 **$125**

DOMESTIC AIR MAIL SERVICE IN THE UNITED STATES   [May 1, 1938]   Wash: P.O. Dept. 46x71cm (18x28") Full color. Some soiling one side; repairs verso.   [25]   £54 **$90**

RAND MCNALLY WORLD MAP FOR THE AIR AGE [c.1937] North polar projection; dissected & folded into case; corner hanging grommets. 112x112cm (44x44") Full color. VG.   [25]   £60 **$100**

ALBRIZZI

CARTA GEOGRAFICA DEL MESSICO O SIA DELLA NUOVA SPAGNA   [c.1740]   From *Atlante Novissimo*. After De L'Isle. 33x42cm (13x16½") B&W.   [27]   £118 **$195**

ALLAN

MAP OF NEW SOUTH WALES AND VICTORIA   [1853] Folding map bound with 23x22cm map of Sydney in orig cloth folder. 64x53cm (25x21") OL color. Superb.   [15]   £754 **$1,250**

ALLARD

ASIAE NOVA DISCRIPTIO ... ALLARD ... 1679   [1679] 44x54cm (17x21½") Color.
 [42] **Aus$1,450** £658 $1,092

NOVA TABULA INDIA ORIENTALIS HUGO ALLARDT EXCUDIT INDE KALVERSTRAET INDE WERRELT CAERTE [1697 (1705)] Orig publ in *Atlas Major*. Indian Ocean and adjacent lands. 45x56cm (17½x22") Orig color. Ref: Tooley (Australia) p.207, 49.   [13] **Aus$6,800** £3,088 $5,120

RECENTISIMA NOVA ORBIS SIVE AMERICAE SEPTENTRIONALIS ET MERIDIONALIS TABULA EX OFFICINA CAROLI ALLARD   [c.1700]   Insular Calif. 50x59cm (20x23½")   Orig color. Sm stain; else exc. Ref: McLaughlin 132; Tooley (Amer) p.127 #65.   [23]   £2,111 **$3,500**

ALLARDT

SALE MAP NO.3 - SALT MARSH AND TIDE LANDS SITUATE IN THE CITY OF SAN FRANCISCO, STATE OF CALIFORNIA   [1869]   G.H. Baker, lith. Unbacked, never folded map of lands south of China Basin. 52x59cm (20½x23") Uncolored.   [15]   £256 **$425**

AMERICAN BANK NOTE CO.

ALBANY & NEW YORK DAY STEAMERS   [c.1890]   Hudson River & adjacent detail. 51x20cm (20x8") Route in red. VG.   [25]   £30 **$50**

AMERICAN ETHNOLOGICAL SOCIETY

MAP OF A SECTION OF TWELVE MILES OF THE SCIOTO VALLEY, WITH ITS ANCIENT MONUMENTS [1854] From *Observations on the Aboriginal Monuments of the Mississippi Valley* ... Vol.II of the Transactions. Sarony & Major, lith. Chillicothe area. 25x19cm (10x7½") B&W. Furnished with 75 pp orig article, 19 in-text figures & another map. Ref: cf Smith (OH) p.44; Karrow 2-2423.   [12]   £112 **$185**

AMERICAN PHILOSOPHICAL SOCIETY

A CHART OF THE GULF STREAM   [1786]   As in *Transactions*. Accompanied letter from Benj. Franklin; James Poupard, sc. 20x25cm (8x10") B&W. Lt browning Ref: Phillips (M) p.592; cf Wheat & Brun 721.
 [A2]   £730 **$1,210**

AMERICAN SUNDAY SCHOOL UNION

A MISSIONARY MAP REPRESENTING THE EVANGELICAL CONDITION OF THE WORLD TO ACCOMPANY THE MISSIONARY MANUAL [c.1830] Phila. J.& W.W. Warr, engr. Sm wall map; continents keyed in gray tones; locates missionaries. 32x54cm (12½x21½") Oceans in wash color.   [15]   £211 **$350**

AMICO

DISRETIONE VERA DE LANTICA CITA DI GIERUSALEM   [c.1620]   23x29cm (9x11½") Ref: Laor 941.
 [A8]   £329 **$546**

LA VERA E REALE CITA DI GIERUSALEM COME SI TROVA OGI   [c.1620]   Bird's-eye view. 23x29cm (9x11½") Ref: Laor 940.   [A8]   £381 **$632**

73

ANALECTIC MAGAZINE
PLAN OF THE POSITION TAKEN BY GEN. BURGOYNE ON THE 10TH OF OCTR. 1777 IN WHICH THE BRITISH ARMY WAS INVESTED BY THE AMERICANS UNDER THE COMMAND OF GEN;. GATES AND SURRENDERED TO HIM ON THE 16TH OF OCTOBER THE SAME YEAR   [1818] Phila: Moses Thomas. Saratoga battle plan drawn by Isaac A. Chapman; Fairman, sc. 22x36cm (8½x14") B&W. Lt scattered foxing; 2 sm tears repaired verso; VG. Ref: Phillips (M) 784.   [35] £106 **$175**

ANDERSON
MAP OF THE RAILROADS OF PENNSYLVANIA AND NEW JERSEY AND PARTS OF ADJOINING STATES 1880 [1880] J.A. Anderson, Phila. Dissected, linen-mounted, folding map in modern buckram with orig label. RRs in red & blue. 81x120cm (32x47") Ref: Modelski (US) 296.   [15] £392 **$650**

ANDREES
CAPLAND UND ANGRENZENDE GEBEITE [1893] South Africa. 34x43cm (13½x17") Colonial status color coded. ["Verkehrskarte des Atlantischen Ozeans" offered at same price]   [40] £18 **$30**

ANDREWS
A PLAN OF THE CITY OF BATAVIA   [1774] Publ in John Andrews atlas of Town Plans of the World. 17x23cm (6½x9") Uncolored. Exc.   [4] **£140** $232
A PLAN OF THE CITY OF QUEBEC   [1761] 18x23cm (7x9½") Color. Exc.   [24] £166 **$275**

ANDRIVEAU-GOUJON
CARTE GENERALE DES INDES ORIENTALES INDIQUANT LES POSSESSIONS ANGLAISES [1837] 38x51cm (15x20") Color.   [39] £60 **$100**
MOUVEMENS APPARENS DU SOLEIL, THEORIE DES SAISONS   [1836] Earth's orbit. 46x58cm (18x23") Color. Exc. ["Revolution Annuelle de la Terre autour du Soleil" offered at same price] [39] £106 **$175**

ANDRUS & JUDD
AN ANCIENT OR BIBLE MAP, DESIGNED FOR THE USE OF BIBLE CLASSES, SUNDAY SCHOOLS AND PRIVATE FAMILIES [1832] Hartford. Folding in orig morocco folder. Mediterranean east of Italy, with Holy Land. 32x48cm (12½x18½") Full color. Sl fold junction separations; cover lt scuffed.   [15] £136 **$225**

ANONYMOUS or UNKNOWN
[GEOCENTRIC UNIVERSE]   [c.1510] From Virgil's *Aeneid*. Strasbourg. Orbits of sun, solar system & heavens, earth at ctr; a surround of scenes. 18x16cm (7½x6½")   [44] £286 **$475**
[UNITED STATES: GREAT LAKES AND MISSOURI AREA] [c.1750] German source; top left corner of 4 or 6 sheet map. Surface notes incl "Gros Meadows" in west, "1740" near Fort Wayne. Resembles, but distinct from Bellin 1745. 30x39cm (11½x15½")   [46] **£1,250** $2,073
[WORLD: MEDIEVAL]   [1491] From *Mer des Hystoires*. Woodblock, after map in *Rudimentum Novitiorum*, Lubec; sl reduced from 1488 French translation. Circular; 2 sheets joined, Diameter: 31cm (12") Uncolored. Ref: Shirley (W) 17.   [34] **£8,000** $13,265
[WORLD ON SILK]   [c.1800] Embroidered double-hemi, possibly after Carey's 1795 world; stitched broad floral surround in color gradations. 42x64cm (16½x25") Age-toned to bronze; sl fraying of silk; else VG.   [23] £1,508 **$2,500**
A MAP OF MR. BELL'S JOURNEY FROM MOSCOW TO PEKIN   [1763] Publ in Glasgow. Moscow, Tobolsk, Lake Baikal, Mongolia with nomadic tents, Beijing. 25x66cm (10x26") Some color.   [39] £81 **$135**
CINCINNATI, COVINGTON & NEWPORT   [c.1855] Litho view after drawing now in Ohio Historical Society. 26x39cm (10½x15½") Color. Fine. Ref: Reps (Views) 3059. Stokes & Haskell 86-B; Deak 708.   [28] £1,086 **$1,800**
GEOGRAPHIA MOSAICA GENERALIS CUM NOVISSIMA ORBIS TERRAQUEI FACIE ET COMMENTARIOUS [c.1690] Probably German source. Unconventionally arranged double hemis, insular Calif, with rich decor incl double-headed eagle & surround of armorial shields. 32x36cm (12½x14") Color. Ref: Shirley (W) 563, pl.391.   [13] **Aus$3400** £1,544 **$2,560**
LUNDEN [ON SHEET WITH] ABILLTUNG VIE KONIGLICHE MAISTAT IN ENGELANDT [AND] DIE ARTIKEL DESS SPANISCEN HEYRATHS IUR: BEKRESSTIGET ANNO 1623 [c.1623] Possible Meissner attribution. Pre-fire view of London; 6 appearances of James I. 27x32cm (10½x12½") Crack in printing plate ctr, lower corners broken off.   [47] **£320** $531
SICILIA COLLA DISTENZIONE, DELLE NOVE DIOCESI ...   [1776-86] Possibly D.C. Ventimiglia, Sicily. Large scale with side panels listing "Signori Vicere di Sicilia" & "Dominanti di Sicilia". 49x71cm (19½x28") Uncolored.   [34] **£500** $829

ANONYMOUS or UNKNOWN continued

THE UNITED STATES, 1861 [c.1862] Eastern KS a square; elongated CO to the west. Color distinguishes free & slave states. 11x18cm (4½x7") [12] £45 **$75**

ANSON
A CHART OF THE PACIFIC OCEAN FROM THE EQUINOCTIAL TO THE LATITUDE OF 39½ D NO. [1748] America to Japan. 30x89cm (12x35") [22] £106 **$175**

A CHART SHOWING THE TRACK OF THE CENTURION ROUND THE WORLD [1748] From ... *Voyages*. By Seale. Mercator proj; insular Calif. 23x41cm (9x16") OL color. [13] Aus$800 £363 **$602**

PLAN DE LA BAYE DE MANILLE [1750] 20x25cm (8x10") OL color. Faint soil at vert fold; VG. Framed. [A9] £139 **$230**

APIANUS
CARTA COSMOGRAPHICA, CON LOS NOMBRES, PROPRIEDAD, Y VIRTUD DE LOS VIENTOS [1575] Antwerp. From second block of Apian/Frisius rendering. 23x31cm (9x12") [A7] £1,040 **$1,725**

CHARTA COSMOGRAPHICA, CUM VENTORUM PROPRIA NATURA ET OPERATIONE [c.1553] Gemma Frisius / Peter Apian. 19x27cm (7½x11") B&W. Good. Ref: Shirley (W) 96 [2nd woodblock]. [32] £1,387 **$2,300**

APPLETON
[BOOK WITH MAPS] APPLETONS' ILLUSTRATED HAND-BOOK OF AMERICAN TRAVEL [1857] T. Addison Richards. 12mo, gold-embossed cloth covers; 420 pp, 24 pp illustrated ads, 100 views in text, 40 folding maps, 4 in full color, & city plans. Sl tear along spine; sl tears & edge rumpling of 2 maps; good-VG. [5] £326 **$540**

VIEW OF CASTLE GARDEN, AND NEW YORK BAY [1869] Supplement to *Appleton's Journal*. South from lower Manhattan. 20x65cm (8x25½") B&W. [12] £151 **$250**

ARBUCKLE
[ATLAS] ARBUCKLES' ILLUSTRATED ATLAS OF FIFTY PRINCIPAL NATIONS OF THE WORLD [1889] Wraps; 24 pp. Colored maps with characteristic illustration, each about 8x13cm (3x5") Two sm chips on cover; back cover little loose. [25] £90 **$150**

[ATLAS] ARBUCKLES' ILLUSTRATED ATLAS OF THE UNITED STATES OF AMERICA [1889] NY: Arbuckle Coffee Co. Oblong quarto, pictorial wraps, cord ties; 12 pp with four state & territorial commemorative type maps per page. Color. Wrappers detached & chipped. [A10] £146 **$242**

[ARIZONA] [1889] Coffee company promotional trade card with sm map & scenes. Chromolitho. 8x11cm (3x4½") [12] £27 **$45**

ARIAS MONTANUS
ANTIQUAE IERUSALEM VERA ICNOGRAPHIA ... [1572-] Appeared in Polyglot Bible. 28x24cm (11x9½") Uncolored. Ref: Laor 945. [34] £540 **$896**

BENEDICT ARIAS MONTANUS SACRAE GEOGRAPHIAE TABULAM EX ANTIQUISSIMORUM CULTOR. FAMILIIS A MOSE RECENSITIS AD SACRORUM LIBROR EXPLICANDOR COMMODITATEM ANTUURPIAE IN PHILIPPI REGIS CATHOLICI GRATIAM DESCRIBEBAT AO MDLXXI [1571] In Plantin Polyglot Bible *Biblia Sacra, Herbraice, Chaldaice, Graece & Latine* ... 32x53cm (12½x20½") B&W. Ref: Shirley (W) 125, pl.107. Schilder 20; Clancy p.54-5. [13] Aus$10,800 £4,905 **$8,132**

[SAME TITLE] [1571] [same source] Garden of Eden & flood scene below; insular Tierra del Fuego; lacks monsters & engraved sea. 34x50cm (13½x19½") B&W. Ref: Shirley (W) Corrigenda 125. [13] Aus$9,400 £4,269 **$7,098**

ARMENIAN CARTOGRAPHY
AMERIKA [IN SET WITH] AP'RIKE [AND] ASIA [AND] EWROPIA [1786 & 1787] Elia Endasian; printed at Armenian community, estab 1717, at St. Lazarus near Venice. After Cassini, Zatta, etc. Legends & cartouches in Armenian. Each 46x60cm (18½x24") Exc. Ref: John Carter Brown, *The Italians and the Creation of America* (1980) 122. [2] £5,729 **$9,500**

ARMENIAN MAP OF ASIA [ARMENIAN TITLED] [1787] E. Endasian; printed at Armenian community at St. Lazarus near Venice. After French cartography. 46x64cm (18x25") Uncolored. [34] £1,250 **$2,073**

ARROWSMITH
[ATLAS] AN ATLAS OF MODERN GEOGRAPHY FOR THE USE OF KING'S COLLEGE SCHOOL [1832] London: S. Arrowsmith & B. Fellowes. Octavo, orig half leather binding; 26 maps in orig OL color. Cover worn at edges; some maps have repaired tears, lt staining, sl fold separations; overall, contents VG. [33] £392 **$650**

ARROWSMITH continued

A MAP EXHIBITING ALL THE NEW DISCOVERIES IN THE INTERIOR PARTS OF NORTH AMERICA. INSCRIBED BY PERMISSION TO THE HONORABLE GOVERNOR AND COMPANY OF ADVENTURERS OF ENGLAND TRADING INTO HUDSONS BAY ...   [1814 / 1819] Most of N Amer. 122x140cm (48x55") Orig color. Map case backed with canvas; few canvas splits, no loss; some lt transfer; VG. Ref: Wheat (TM) 313; Tooley (Amer) p.79-80.   [A2]   £4,810 **$7,975**

A NEW MAP OF NORTH AMERICA SHEWING ALL THE NEW DISCOVERIES, 1791   [dated 1791] probably later. As in *Brookes Gazetteer*. With long River of the West 20x24cm (8x9½") Uncolored. VG.   [25]   £45 **$75**

ASIA   [1801]   Aaron & Samuel Arrowsmith. Dedicated to Maj. James Rennell. 4 sheets, each about 63x75cm (25x29½") Orig OL color. Binding folds flattened; fold cracks restored.   [46]   **£350** $581

CAPE OF GOOD HOPE   [1834-40]   48x60cm (19x23½") Orig OL color. Ref: Tooley (Africa) p.17.
[34]   **£180** $299

DETAILED MAP OF THE REVD. DR. LIVINGSTONE'S ROUTE ACROSS AFRICA ...   [1857]   Luanda, Angola to Zambesi mouth; route in red. 29x64cm (11½x25") Folds; VG.   [A9]   £31 **$52**

EASTERN FRONTIER OF THE COLONY OF THE CAPE OF GOOD HOPE, (AND PART OF KAFFIRLAND) FROM ALGOA BAY TO THE GREAT KEI RIVER...   [1848-51]   49x59cm (19½x23") Orig OL color. Ref: Tooley (Africa) p.20.   [34]   **£150** $249

LOWER CANADA, NEW BRUNSWICK, NOVA SCOTIA ... NEWFOUNDLAND   [1838]   NFL as inset. 61x48cm (24x19") Orig color.   [34]   **£220** $365

MAP OF ENGLAND AND WALES, SHOWING THE RAILWAYS, CANALS ...   [1852] By F. Mackenzie, printed by Hansard; 8 sheets forming single map emphasizing transportation, each 42x70cm (16½x27½") Orig OL color. Margin tears, printed area intact. Ex-lib.   [34]   **£340** $564

MAP OF TEXAS, COMPILED FROM SURVEYS RECORDED IN THE LAND OFFICE OF TEXAS AND OTHER OFFICIAL SURVEYS   [1843]   Maximum Texas republic. 60x50cm (24x20") Orig OL color. Few margin tears repaired; fine. Ref: Goss (NA) 75. Martin (TX) p.126-7.   [2]   £7,539 **$12,500**

MAP OF THE WINDWARD ISLANDS; COMPRISING BARBADOS, ST. VINCENT, GRENADA, TOBAGO, ST. LUCIA & TRINIDAD ...   [1842]   61x46cm (24x18") Color.   [18]   £100 **$165**

MEXICO   [1823]   From *New General Atlas*. Edinburgh: Archibald Constable. Incl present US Southwest. 20x25cm (8x10") OL color. Fine. Ref: Rumsey 34.   [12]   £96 **$160**

MEXICO   [1842]   Independent Texas (so bordered in B&W). 59x48cm (23½x19") Orig OL color.
[27]   £754 **$1,250**

THE SOUTH EASTERN PORTION OF AUSTRALIA   [1838]   52x64cm (20½x25") Orig OL color. Minor c'fold repair. Ref: Tooley (Australia) 96.   [34]   **£420** $697

THE WORLD FROM THE DISCOVERIES & OBSERVATIONS MADE IN THE LATEST VOYAGES & TRAVELS. DRAWN BY ARROWSMITH. ENGRAVED BY J. LODGE   [1798]   Probably from Bankes, *Universal Geography*. Double hemi. 23x45cm (9x18")   [19]   £75 **$125**

UNITED STATES   [1817]   West to Mississippi. 20x25cm (8x10") Uncolored. VG.   [26]   £54 **$90**

UPPER CANADA &C. ...   [1838]   63x50cm (24½x19½") Orig col. Minor c'fold reinforcement.   [34]   **£280** $465

VAN DIEMEN'S LAND ...   [1834]   Appeared in *London Atlas*. 61x50cm (24x20") Orig color. Ref: Tooley (Australia) 118.   [34]   **£250** $415

ARROWSMITH & LEWIS

CONNECTICUT   [1819]   20x25cm (8x10") B&W.   [22]   £54 **$90**

DELAWARE   [1805]   25x20cm (10x8") OL & wash color. Sm stain in map.   [40]   £51 **$85**

GEORGIA   [1804]   22x27cm (8½x10½") Uncol. VG. ["Virginia" offered at same price]   [26]   £72 **$120**

KENTUCKY   [1804]   Phila: Conrad. 22x27cm (8½x10½") Uncolored.   [26]   £106 **$175**

LOUISIANA   [1805]   Publ Boston. Based on French, pre-Lewis & Clark knowledge of area from Mississippi River to Pacific. 25x20cm (10x8") Uncolored. VG. Ref: Wheat (TM) 259.   [26]   £226 **$375**

LOUISIANA   [IN SET WITH]   BRITISH POSSESSIONS IN AMERICA   [AND]   SPANISH DOMINIONS IN NORTH AMERICA   [AND]   NORTH AMERICA   [1804]   Phila: Conrad. All about 27x22cm (10½x8½") All uncolored. All VG. Ref: Wheat (TM) 259, 260, 261, 262.   [26]   £452 **$750**

MISSISSIPPI TERRITORY   [1804]   Phila: Conrad. 22x27cm (8½x10½") Uncolored. VG.   [26]   £96 **$160**

NEW JERSEY   [1804]   Phila: Conrad. 27x22cm (10½x8½") Uncolored. VG.   [26]   £60 **$100**

NEW YORK   [1804]   22x27cm (8½x10½") Uncolored. VG.   [26]   £45 **$75**

OHIO   [1804]   Phila: Conrad. Earliest separate map of state. 27x22cm (10½x8½") Uncolored. VG. Ref: Smith (OH) illus 1805.   [26]   £166 **$275**

ARROWSMITH & LEWIS continued

OHIO [1805] From *New and Elegant General Atlas*. Boston: Thomas & Andrews. 25x20cm (10x8") B&W. Exc. Ref: Phillips (A) 708-53. Smith (OH) p.155. [12] £166 **$275**

SOUTH CAROLINA [1804] Phila: Conrad. Uncertain western border. 22x27cm (8½x10½") Uncolored. VG. ["North Carolina" offered at same price] [26] £54 **$90**

TENNESSEE [1804] Phila: Conrad. 22x27cm (8½x10½") Uncolored. VG. [26] £121 **$200**

UNITED STATES OF AMERICA [1805] Phila: Conrad. West to Mississippi. 22x27cm (8½x10½") Uncolored. VG. [26] £96 **$160**

ARTIFACTS - Infrequent Publishers

[TAROT CARD] CARTA VI SEGUONO LE COLONIE INGLESI [1779] Aniello Lamberti, Florence. Map, about 1¼x2" with text below, shows NE North America, New Jersey to Nova Scotia. On card 10x6cm (4x2½") Orig wash color. Exc. Ref: MCC 1972, No.87, p.23, #11. [2] £286 **$475**

A MOVABLE PLANISPHERE OF THE HEAVENS AT EVERY MINUTE ... [1862] Whitall. Star-finder designed to be use in place of Burritt's atlas. Revolving volvelle with revealing window. Paper on heavy cardboard with orig silk tabs. Diameter: 38cm (15") B&W. Surface dirt; minor wear; overall VG. [38] £271 **$450**

THE BARRITT-SERVISS STAR AND PLANET FINDER. NORTHERN HEMISPHERE. [1906] Leon Barritt & Garrett P. Serviss. Mechanical device; window shows visible sky by day & hour. 38x38cm (15x15") B&W. Occasional minor scratch & water stain; brass rivet in ctr replaced; o/w good. [32] £332 **$550**

[SAME TITLE] [1906] Rotating volvelle & revealing window. 38x38cm (15x15") B&W; red ecliptic line. Surface dirt; lower corner rivet lacking; gummed star pasted on corner; good. [38] £151 **$250**

ASHER & ADAMS

[ATLAS] ASHER & ADAMS' NEW COMMERCIAL, TOPOGRAPHICAL, AND STATISTICAL ATLAS AND GAZETTEER OF THE UNITED STATES [1872] NY. Folio; full & OL colored maps, half morocco. Backstrip defective, extremities worn. [A7] £902 **$1,495**

[ATLAS] ASHER & ADAMS' NEW TOPOGRAPHICAL ATLAS AND GAZETTEER OF NEW YORK ... [1870] 2nd ed (larger format than 1st, incl "Gazetteer of [NY] ... Sketch of Topography, Geology and History". Folio, orig gold stamped boards, recased. 16 maps. 3" tear in state map; o/w exc. Ref: Phillips (A) 2209; LeGear (US) 2399. [3] £407 **$675**

[SAME TITLE] [1871] Folio, half leather & cloth; 80 pp; 16 colored maps, some double page. Front cover detached, lacking spine; minor dampstain fore-edge some margins; contents VG. Ref: LeGear (US) 2400. [A10] £180 **$299**

[ATLAS] NEW TOPOGRAPHICAL ATLAS OF THE STATE OF NEW YORK [1869] Folio, publisher's half morocco; colored maps. Covers worn, sm hole one map. Ref: LeGear (US) 2398, calls for 16 maps. [A8] £208 **$345**

ASHER & ADAMS' CALIFORNIA & NEVADA NORTHERN PORTION [1872] 42x58cm (16½x23") Full color. Edges browned, few tears; margin corner chipped; good (B). [A3] £30 **$50**

ASHER & ADAMS' CALIFORNIA & NEVADA SOUTHERN PORTION [1872] 42x58cm (16½x23") Full color. Edges browned, few tears; one margin corner chipped; good (B). [A3] £29 **$48**

ASHER & ADAMS' COLORADO [1875] From ... *New Statistical and Topographical Atlas* ... 40x47cm (16x18½") Orig color by counties. Faint age toned strip at c'fold; o/w VG to fine. [14] £136 **$225**

ASHER & ADAMS' DAKOTA [1875] 58x41cm (23x16") Color by counties. Browned; no c'fold. [9] £60 **$100**

ASHER & ADAMS' KENTUCKY & TENNESSEE [1871] 41x58cm (16x23") Full color. [40] £39 **$65**

ASHER & ADAMS' TEXAS [1873] 57x41cm (22½x16") Full color. Browned; good. [16] £121 **$200**

ASHER & ADAMS' TEXAS WESTERN PORTION [1874] West of 98 deg longitude; Panhandle not shown 57x41cm (22½x16½") Full color. VG. [16] £136 **$225**

ASHER & ADAMS' WASHINGTON [1874] 39x57cm (15½x22½") Color. [40] £51 **$85**

ASHER & ADAMS' WYOMING [1875] 41x57cm (16x22½") Orig color. Faint age toning along c'fold; o/w VG to fine. [14] £136 **$225**

CALIFORNIA & NEVADA (NORTHERN PORTION) [1873] 42x58cm (16½x23") Full orig color. Some c'fold browning; but VG. [36] £57 **$95**

MAINE AND PART OF QUEBEC [1871] From *New Statistical and Topographical Atlas*. Incl adjacent regions. 41x56cm (16x22") Full pastel color. Lt toning at c'fold; good (B). [A4] £21 **$35**

MONTANA (EASTERN PORTION) [1873] 41x57cm (16x22½") Full orig color. VG. [36] £57 **$95**

TEXAS [1871] Eastern part. 56x41cm (22x16") Full color. Minor lt foxing; good (B). [A4] £30 **$50**

ASPIN

A CHART OF NEW SOUTH WALES, VAN DIEMEN'S LAND &C   [ON SHEET WITH]   SURVEYS IN THE INTERIOR OF NEW SOUTH WALES   [1821]   50x60cm (19½x23½")   Orig OL color.   Ref: Clancy (Australis) 9.32, ill. p.162.   [13]   **Aus$1,100**   £500 $828

ATWOOD

MAP OF THE WESTERN STATES   [1848 (1853)]   Publ by Thayer, Bridgman & Fanning.   Pocket map with covers. Ohio to Iowa. 45x58cm (18x23")   Full orig col. Some splitting along folds, o/w good.   [32]   £603   **$1,000**

AVELINE

LONDINUM URBS PRAECIPUA REGNI ANGLAE   [c.1700]   Attribution uncertain. Appears to be Italian copy, after Aveline, of London view from South, before the fire, with 10 point key. 37x50cm (14½x19½") Sl restoration; laid on archival tissue.   [46]   **£1,450** $2,405

BACHELDER, J.B.

HOLYOKE AND SOUTH HADLEY FALLS [MA] ... NO.13   [1856]   From *Album of New England Scenery*. NY: Endicott & Co.   Panoramic view; keyed features incl dam, mills, Mt. Tom, etc. Tinted lithograph. 25x39cm (10x15½")   Ref: Reps (Views) 1476.   [offered as same price: "Manchester [NH] ... No.1", "Marblehead ... No.5]   [12]   £392   **$650**

MAP OF THE BATTLEFIELD OF GETTYSBURG JULY 1ST 2ND 3RD 1863 [SET OF 3 MAPS FOR EACH DAY OF BATTLE]   [1876]   1st ed. Commemorative plans publ by authority of Sec. of War. Bien, engraver; Endicott, printer. Each 74x69cm (29½x27½")   Color. Sm margin repairs; faint stain remnant lower margin; VG. Ref: Stephenson (CW-1) 325; Phillips (M) p.299.   [29]   £905   **$1,500**

BACON

BACON'S NEW MAP OF THE SEAT OF WAR IN VIRGINIA AND MARYLAND. SHOWING THE INTERESTING LOCALITIES AROUND RICHMOND, WASHINGTON, BALTIMORE &C.   [1862]   "Bacon's New Shilling War Map." Separately issued. 60x46cm (23½x18")   Orig color.   [34]   **£340** $564

BACON'S NEW PLAN OF BRIGHTON AND HOVE   [c.1890]   Linen-backed map folding into orig cloth covers with gold title; street index within 58x94cm (22½x37")   Printed color. Good.   [11]   £51   **$85**

SERIO-COMIC WAR MAP FOR THE YEAR 1877. BY F.W.R.   [1877]   London: G.W. Bacon. 1st state. European countries in caricature; Russia as octopus. 43x47cm (17x18½")   Orig color. Some restoration. Ref: Hill, *Cartographical Curiosities* 57.   [46]   **£395** $655

BAILEY, O.H., & CO.

MIDDLETOWN, CONN. REVISED 1877 EDITION   [1877]   Bird's-eye view. 60x71cm (23½x28")   Uncolored. Sh tear 1" from lower edge; VG. Ref: Reps (Views) 569.   [15]   £573   **$950**

NEW HARTFORD, CONN.   [1878]   Bird's-eye view. 50x62cm (19½x24½")   Uncolored. Age-toning; repaired 1" tear into rt side, no loss. Ref: Reps (Views) 581.   [15]   £513   **$850**

VIEW OF ROCKVILLE, CONN. 1877   [1877]   Bird's-eye litho printed by J. Knauber & Co., after "G.S." 6 factory views; 51 item key. 50x65cm (20x26")   Color. Repaired tear lf just into image; o/w fine. Ref: Reps (Views) 608.   [28]   £452   **$750**

BAILLEUL

NOUVELLE MAPPEMONDE ...   [(1750) c.1772]   Attributed to Francois Bailleul (le jeune). Double hemi; elaborate decor. 52x72cm (20½x28½")   Color. Exc. Ref: Baynton-Williams illus p.46-7.   [4]   **£4,500** $7,462

BAKER

SKETCH MAP OF THE PROVINCE OF SOUTHLAND, NEW ZEALAND   [1865]   John H. Baker, Southland. Incl Steward Is. 82x52cm (32½x20½")   Lacks top rod; sm hole near top; fine.   [15]   £302   **$500**

BAKER & HARPER

MAP OF SILVER BOW COUNTY, MONTANA - JULY 1ST, 1897   [1897]   Linen-backed pocket map in orig cloth folder. Contours with elevations. 56x88cm (22x34½")   Full color by town & school districts.   [15]   £422   **$700**

BALDWIN

A NEW AND ACCURATE MAP OF THE WORLD, COMPREHENDING ALL THE NEW DISCOVERIES IN BOTH HEMISPHERES CAREFULLY BROUGHT DOWN TO THE PRESENT TIME ...   [1786]   From *Baldwin's New & Universal System of Geography*.   Double hemi; 5 sm spheres; garlanded scrolls & cartouche. 29x46cm (11½x18")   Minor repair.   [19]   £286   **$475**

BARBIE DU BOCAGE

BRITANNIA ANTIQUA [1781-88] From German ed, *Voyage Anarcharsis*. 24x18cm (9½x7") OL color. Sm tear ctr lf margin into neatline. [21] **Can$40** £17 $29

CARTE REDUITE DE LA MER DES INDES, ET D'UNE PARTIE DE CELLE DU SUD ... [1800] Prepared with J.J.H. De Labillardiere for account of search for La Perouse. Cape of Good Hope to New Zealand, with South Asia. 48x70cm (19x28") Uncolored. [34] **£520** $863

[SAME TITLE] [1800] From *Relation du Voyage a la Recherche de la Perouse* ... Orient, with Australia & New Zealand. 48x70cm (18½x28") OL color. [13] **Aus$1,180** £536 $888

GERMANIA ANTIQUA [1781-88] From German ed, *Voyage Anarcharsis*. 18x24cm (7½x9½") OL color. Sm tear lower c'fold; some browning at c'fold. ["Gallia Antiqua" & "Hispania Antiqua" offered at same price] [21] **Can$30** £13 $22

LACONIA UND DIE INSEL CYTHERA [1781-88] From German ed, *Voyage Anarcharsis*. 26x20cm (10x8") Lf margin trimmed. ["Messina" offered at same price] [21] **Can$50** £22 $36

VERSUCHEINER TOPOGRAPHIE VON SPARTA ... [1781-88] From German ed, *Voyage Anarcharsis*. 31x19cm (12x7½") Lf margin trimmed. [21] **Can$60** £26 $43

VINDELICIA, RHAETIA, NIRICUM, PANNONIA ET LILLYRICUM [1781-88] From German ed, *Voyage Anarcharsis*. 19x24cm (7½x9½") OL color. Sm tear lower c'fold; margin staining, image unaffected. [21] **Can$30** £13 $22

BARDIN

TO THE HONORABLE SIR JOSEPH BANKS ... THIS NEW BRITISH TERRESTRIAL GLOBE ... TO THE YEAR 1821 ... [IN SET WITH] NEVIL MASKELYNE, D.D, F.RS ASTRONOMER ROYAL THIS NEW CELESTIAL GLOBE CONTAINING THE POSITIONS OF NEARLY 6000 STARS, CLUSTERS, NEBULAE ... [1821] Globe pair: diameter 46cm (18"); overall height 120cm (47"). On orig swirled 3-legged wooden stands, with stretchers supporting magnetic compasses; brass fittings, horizon & meridian rings. Moderate patina, good clarity; repair in western U.S., some loss; repaired cracks at poles; other minor faults & repairs; overall VG. [23] £39,201 **$65,000**

BARKER

A VIEW OF THE GRAND HARBOUR OF MALTA. WITH PART OF THE CITY OF LA VALETTA, THE CAPITAL OF THE ISLAND [c.1813] I. Adlard, Printer, 23 Bartholomew-close. Woodcut broadsheet. 22x26cm (8½x10") Tape stain outside printed area. [46] **£150** $249

BARTHELEMY

[BOOK WITH MAPS] RECUEIL DE CARTES GEOGRAPHIQUES, PLANS, VUES ET MEDAILLES DE L'ANCIENNE GRECE, RELATIFS AU VOYAGE DU JEUNE ANACHARSIS [1790] Paris. Quarto, morocco gilt; 31 maps, some in OL color, & plates. Scattered minor foxing & browning. [another, "... Troisieme Edition" (1790) sold for $149] [A8] £121 **$201**

BARTHOLOMEW

TEXAS, NEW MEXICO, & INDIAN TERRITORY ... [1870] Phila: T. Elwood Zell. Insets: Chicago, New Orleans areas. 29x41cm (11½x16") Printed color. VG. [16] £60 **$100**

BARTLETT, J.R

GENERAL MAP SHOWING THE COUNTRIES EXPLORED & SURVEYED BY THE UNITED STATES & MEXICAN BOUNDARY COMMISSION, IN THE YEARS 1850, 51, 52 & 53, UNDER THE DIRECTION OF JOHN R. BARTLETT ... [1854] Issued in Bartlett's *Personal Narrative of Explorations and Incidents* ... Map by Colton. 38x49cm (15x19½") Laid on archival paper; few brown spots; o/w VG. Ref: Wheat (TM) 798. [8] £256 **$425**

BEERS

[ATLAS] ATLAS OF LIVINGSTON CO. NEW YORK [1872] F.W. Beers. Sm folio; 45 pp. Covers detached; few sh tears, frayed edges, pencil marks verso 2 maps; contents VG. Ref: LeGear (US) 2454, calls for 31 maps. [A10] £77 **$127**

[ATLAS] ATLAS OF LONG ISLAND, NEW YORK ... [1873] F.W. Beers; NY: Beers, Comstock & Cline. Folio. leather-backed cloth; 34 double-page colored maps, with insets, etc., incl 13½x52" Long Island. Covers detached; some loose signatures; margins sl toned/foxed; few maps foxed; interior mostly clean. Ref: LeGear (US) 2681, calls for 99 maps. [A10] £763 **$1,265**

[ATLAS] ATLAS OF LUZERNE COUNTY, PENNSYLVANIA ... [1873] D.G. Beers; publ by A. Pomeroy & Co. Folio; 71 map plates. Covers soiled & worn, front reattached with tape; contents tight; lt foxing title; tears on Carbondale fold out; o/w maps VG or fine. Ref: LeGear (US) 3042. [A2] £199 **$330**

BEERS continued

[ATLAS] ATLAS OF NEW YORK AND VICINITY [1867] F.W. Beers et al. Folio, publisher's half sheep; colored maps, litho views. Covers worn, hinges cracked or weak; several maps loose; minor foxing & soiling. [Editor: catalogue does not indicate which variant] [A8] £520 **$862**

[ATLAS] ATLAS OF ONEIDA COUNTY, NEW YORK [1874] NY: D.G. Beers. Sm folio, cloth. Colored lithographed maps. Needs rebinding; maps clean. Ref: LeGear (US) 2470, calls for 50 maps. [A7] £83 **$138**

[ATLAS] ATLAS OF WAYNE COUNTY PENNSYLVANIA [1872] NY: Pomeroy & Co. Folio; new end papers, spine & corners. Cover restored; some margin soiling; overall maps clean. Ref: Le Gear (US) L3063. [A1] £133 **$220**

[ATLAS] ATLAS OF WINDSOR COUNTY. VERMONT [1869] F.W. Beers; NY: Beers, Ellis & Soule. Sm folio, leather back & cloth; 47pp; 36 colored maps, 15 views on 5 pp. Spine mostly lacking, barely attached. Ref: LeGear (US) 3291. [A10] £139 **$230**

[ATLAS] ATLAS OF WORCESTER COUNTY [MA] [1870] NY: F.W. Beers. Sm folio; quarter sheep. Colored maps. Needs rebinding. Ref: LeGear (US) 1585, calls for 85 maps. [A7] £69 **$115**

[SAME TITLE] [1870] F.W. Beers. Folio, quarter sheep. Backstrip perished; hinges starting; internally clean. [A8] £191 **$316**

[ATLAS] COUNTY ATLAS OF LITCHFIELD [CT] [1874] F.W. Beers. Folio; colored maps. Boards, spine chipped, worn; complete. Ref: LeGear (US) 555; calls for 44 maps. [A8] £381 **$632**

[ATLAS] COUNTY ATLAS OF MIDDLESEX [CT] [1874] F.W. Beers. Folio; colored maps. Joints weak; spine scuffed & torn; complete. Ref: LeGear (US) 556; calls for 45 maps. [A8] £451 **$747**

[ATLAS] COUNTY ATLAS OF MIDDLESEX [MA] [1875] F.W. Beers. Folio; colored maps. Covers detached; spine worn; complete. Ref: LeGear (US) 1577, calls for 102 maps, many on verso. [A8] £277 **$460**

[ATLAS] COUNTY ATLAS OF TIOGA PENNSYLVANIA [1875] NY: F.W. Beers. Folio; new end papers spine & corners; Covers rubbed; contents tight, clean; occas smudge; a map with margin chipping; else VG. Ref: Le Gear (US) L3060. [A1] £299 **$495**

[ATLAS] STATE ATLAS OF NEW JERSEY [1872] F.W. Beers. Folio, half sheep; most maps in color. Covers worn; preliminary edges chipped, maps generally clean. Ref: LeGear (US) 2306, calls for 76 maps. [A8] £485 **$805**

MAP OF LAKE GEORGE & VICINITY [1876] F.W. Beers; NY: J.B. Beers & Co. Pocket map in gold-embossed cloth folder. 79x55cm (31x21½") Color by townships. Sl dull cover; fold separations; VG. [5] £175 **$290**

MAP OF THE STATE OF CONNECTICUT [1884] J.B. Beers, NY. Linen-backed folding map, not dissected, no folder. Full color by town. 116x127cm (45½x50") Exc. [15] £302 **$500**

MAP OF THE STATE OF NEW JERSEY [1872] From *State Atlas of New Jersey*. NY: Beers, Comstock & Cline. Highly detailed. 56x36cm (22x14") Color. Lt offsetting; else fine. Ref: LeGear (US) 2306. [12] £90 **$150**

[SAME TITLE] [1872] Beers, Comstock & Cline. Folding map in orig cloth folder, with sh pastedown Beers catalogue. Full color by town. 55x34cm (21½x13½") Superb. [15] £166 **$275**

BELL

[GEOGRAPHICAL SYMBOLS] [c.1810] Two fictitious maps on sheet exemplifying use of cartographic symbols. 23x18cm (9x7") B&W. Lt foxing; good (B). [A3] £26 **$43**

NEW SOUTH WALES AND VAN DIEMAN'S LAND [1837] As in *A New and General Atlas* ... Allen Bell & Co. Based on Wilkinson. 28x35cm (11x13½") Orig color. [13] **Aus$590** £268 **$444**

BELLIN (Large)

CARTE DE L'AMERIQUE SEPTENTRIONALE DEPUIS 28 DEGRE DE LATITUDE JUSQU'AU 72 [1755] State 2. 56x86cm (22x34") OL color. Repaired c'fold split; Japan paper backing; a rust spot; VG. Ref: MCC Heidenreich & Dahl #19; MCC 96, #764. [38] £905 **$1,500**

[SAME TITLE] [1755] 58x91cm (23x36") [A7] £1,387 **$2,300**

[SAME TITLE] [1755] Most of present US & Canada. 58x89cm (23x35") OL col. [A8] £1,040 **$1,725**

CARTE DE LA PARTIE ORIENTALE DE LA NOUVELLE FRANCE OU DU CANADA ... [1744] Labrador to Boston to James Bay. 40x56cm (15½x22") New OL color. Lt offsetting; Top lf margin trimmed close; sm tear to neatline; else fine. [14] £392 **$650**

CARTE REDUITE DE L'ISLE D'ANTIGUE ... [1750] 56x42cm (22x16½") B&W. [20] £528 **$875**

CARTE REDUITE DE L'ISLE DE SAINT CHRISTOPHE [1758] For Depot de la Marine. 61x95cm (24x37½") Scattered soiling; sl scuffing along vert fold. [A7] £225 **$373**

CARTE REDUITE DES COSTES ORIENTALES DE L'AMERIQUE SEPTENTRIONALE ... [1757] Isle Royale to NYC. Boston inset. 55x89cm (21½x35") OL color. Upper margin repairs; lt discolored c'fold strengthened; overall VG. Ref: MCCS 96, #739. [37] £1,206 **$2,000**

BELLIN (Large) continued

CARTE REDUITE DES DETROITS DE MALACCA SINCAPOUR ET DU GOUVERNEUR ... [1755] As in *Neptune Francois*. Under direction of Depot de la Marine. 55x89cm (21½x35"). Color. Exc. [4] £1,150 $1,907

[SAME TITLE] [1740] Close up of Singapore approaches; recognition views. 55x88cm (22x34½") Color. Side margins extended, sl loss neatlines; else exc. [23] £1,025 $1,700

CARTE REDUITE DES ISLES BRITANNIQUES ... CONTENANT L'IRELAND [1763] 86x55cm (33½x21½") Color. Lt browning & spotting. [A6] £322 $534

CARTE REDUITE DES MERS COMPRISES ENTRE L'ASIE ET L'AMERIQUE APELEES PAR LES NAVIGATEURS MER DU SUD OU MER PACIFIQUE [1742 (1756)] 56x84cm (22x33½") Uncolored. Good. [32] £905 $1,500

ESSAY D'UNE CARTE REDUITE, CONTENANT LES PARTIES CONNUEES DU GLOBE TERRESTRE ... [1748] 52x71cm (20½x28") OL color. [A7] £485 $805

KARTE VON LUISIANA, DEM LAUFE DES MISSISSIPI UND DEN BENARCHBARTEN LAENDERN [1755] Publ Leipzig. Covers present U.S., Atlantic to Rockies. 39x55cm (15½x21½") [11] £513 $850

PARTIE OCCIDENTALE DE LA NOUVELLE FRANCE OU DU CANADA ... [1755] Nuremberg. 41x52cm (16½x20½") B&W. VG. Ref: Heidenreich & Dahl 16, 20; Johnson (Amer Expl) p.195; MCCS 96, #684; Karpinski (MI) 57. [37] £1,086 $1,800

PLAN DE LA BAYE DE RIO-JANEIRO [c.1765] 51x34cm (20x13½") [A7] £225 $373

BELLIN (Small)

AMERIQUE MERIDIONALE [1787] 31x20cm (12x8") ["Carte du Nouv. Rme. de Grenade, de la Noule. Andalousie et de la Guyane ..." offered at same price] [11] £36 $60

CARTA DELLA NUOVA INGHILTERRA, NUOVA YORKE, PENSILVANIA [c.1750] After Bellin; Italian source, probably Venice. 22x32cm (8½x12½") [A7] £104 $172

CARTE D'UNE PARTIE DE L'AMERIQUE SEPTENTRIONALE, POUR SERVIR A L'INTELLIGENCE DU MEMOIRE SUR LES PRETENTIONS DES ANGLOIS AU SUJET DES LIMITES A REGLER AVEC LA FRANCE [1760s] Labrador to Carolinas, focusing on boundary disputes. 36x46cm (14x18½") Margins trimmed, just ample. [A7] £83 $138

CARTE DE L'AMERIQUE ET DES MERS VOISINES [dated 1763 (1764)] From *Le Petit Atlas Maritime* ... Mercator projection. 46x30cm (18x12") B&W. Exc. Ref: Phillips (A) 3508-2 [12] £232 $385

CARTE DE L'ARCHIPEL DE ST. LAZARE OU LES ISLES MARIANES ... [1750] Large Guam inset. 23x15cm (9x6") B&W. [20] £136 $225

CARTE DE L'EMPIRE DU JAPON ... [1752] 21x31cm (8½x12½") Color. Exc. Ref: Cortazzi (Japan) p.50; Walter (Japan) #101. [23] £452 $750

[SAME TITLE] [1752] From Prevost d'Exile, *Histoire Generale* ... 22x32cm (8½x12½") [46] £280 $465

CARTE DE L'EMPIRE DU MEXIQUE [1754] From Prevost d'Exile, *Histoire Generale* ... 20x29cm (7½x11½") OL color. [27] £51 $85

CARTE DE L'ENTREE ... DE LA RIVIERE DE CANTON [1752] From Prevost d'Exile, *Histoire Generale* ... Pearl River estuary. 26x20cm (10x8") Color. Fine. [4] £100 $166

CARTE DE L'ENTREE DE LA RIVIERE DE CANTON ... [1764] Incl site of Hong Kong. 26x20cm (10x8") ["Plan du Port et la Ville de Nangasaki" offered at same price] [11] £151 $250

CARTE DE L'ISLE D'HAYTI AUJOURD'HUI L'ESPAGNOLE, OU L'ISLE DE ST. DOMINIGUE AVEC LES ISLES VOISINES ... [dated 1754 (+?)] From Prevost d'Exile, *Histoire Generale* ... Hispaniola & nearby islands. 22x33cm (8½x13") B&W. Fine. [12] £96 $160

CARTE DE L'ISLE DE CEYLON [1764] 26x20cm (10½x8") [11] £45 $75

CARTE DE L'ISLE DE LA GRENADE [1754] 22x17cm (8½x6½") Orig wash color. [11] £51 $85

CARTE DE L'ISLE DE LA JAMAIQUE [1758] 21x32cm (8½x12½") New OL color. VG. [14] £136 $225

CARTE DE LA BAYE DE HUDSON [1744] From Charlevoix, *Histoire et Description ... de la Nouvelle France*. Desbruslins, sc. Differs from "Histoire Generale" map. 21x29cm (8x11½") B&W. Minor offsetting; fine. Ref: Storm (Graff) 650; Howes C-307; cf Phillips (A) 10267-4. [35] £90 $150

CARTE DE LA FLORIDE, DE LA LOUISIANE ET PAYS VOISINS ... [1757] Most of present US. 22x30cm (8½x12") Uncolored. Fine. [A2] £139 $231

[SAME TITLE] [1757] 22x30cm (8½x12") Full color. Exc. [36] £211 $350

CARTE DE LA LOUISIANE ET PAYS VOISINS ... [1757] 23x30cm (9x12") Minor browning; else good. [7] £136 $225

CARTE DE LA RIVIERE DE LA PLATA [1754] 19x28cm (7½x11") [11] £36 $60

BELLIN (Small) continued

CARTE DES COSTES DE LA FLORIDE FRANCOISE   [1744]   From Charlevoix, *Description Generale de la Nouvelle France*.   Cape Fear to St. Augustine.   20x14cm (8x5½")   B&W.   Partly remargined lf; fine.   Ref: Cumming (SE) 259. [31]   £148 **$245**

CARTE DES COSTES, DE PERSE, GUSARAT, ET MALABAR TIREE DE LA CARTE FRANCOISE DE L'OCEAN ORIENTAL   [1740]   25x20cm (9½x7½")   B&W.   Lt title impression; trimmed to 1/8" at binding edge; else clean (A).   [A3]   £26 **$43**

CARTE DES HAVRES DE KINGSTOWN ET DE PORT ROYAL   [1758]   25x37cm (10x14½")   Full color.   Ref: Kapp (Jamaica) 78.   [20]   £407 **$675**

CARTE DES ISLES DE JAVA, SUMATRA, BORNEO &C., LES DETROITS DE LA SONDE MALACA ET BANCA GOLPHE DE SIAM &C.   [1757]   25x29cm (10x11½")   [11]   £75 **$125**

CARTE DES LACS DU CANADA ...   [1744]   1st ed.   29x46cm (11½x18")   Exc.   [44]   £1,086 **$1,800**

CARTE DES PROVINCES DE NICARAGUA ET COSTA RICA   [1764]   20x17cm (8x6½")   [11]   £57 **$95**

CARTE DU COURS DU FLEUVE DE ST. LAURENT DEPUIS QUEBEC JUSQU'AU LAC ONTARIO ...   [1757 (1780)]   From La Harpe's *Albrege de l'Histoire Generale des Voyages*.   19x28cm (7½x11")   B&W.   Couple minor spots; o/w fine.   Ref: Sellers & Van Ee 227.   [21]   **Can$140**   £61 $101

CARTE DU COURS DU FLEUVE DE ST. LAURENT DEPUIS SON EMBOUCHURE JUSQU'AU DESSUS DE QUEBEC   [1757 (1780)]   From La Harpe's *Albrege de l'Histoire Generale des Voyages*.   19x30cm (7½x11½")   B&W.   Fine.   Ref: Sellers & Van Ee 229.   [21]   **Can$160**   £70 $116

[SAME TITLE]   [1757]   From *Histoire Generale* ...   19x29cm (7½x11½")   B&W.   Fine (A+).   [A3]   £60 **$99**

CARTE DU GOLPHE DU MEXIQUE ET DES ISLES DE L'AMERIQUE   [1754]   27x38cm (10½x15")   A false margin; sh repaired tear into graticule.   [German ed; Leipzig, 1756, offered at same price]   [11]   £136 **$225**

[SAME TITLE]   [1754]   27x38cm (11x15")   Full color.   Minor stains; else VG.   [36]   £226 **$375**

CARTE DU GOLPHE DU MEXIQUE ET DES ISLES DE L'AMERIQUE POUR SERVIR A L'HISTOIRE GENERALE DES VOYAGES   [1754]   From Prevost d'Exile, *Histoire Generale* ...   Also Dutch title.   27x37cm (11x14½")   B&W.   Clean.   [21]   **Can$325**   £142 $236

CARTE REDUITE DE LA MER DU SUD POUR SERVIR A L'HISTOIRE GENERALE DES VOYAGES ...   [1753]   From *Histoire Generale* ...   21x36cm (8½x14")   Color.   Ref: cf Tooley (Australia) 158 (Petit Atlas ed.)   [Dutch 1757 version with additional title "Gereduceerde Kaart van de Zuider-Zee ..." offered at Aus$520]   [13]   **Aus$590**   £268 $444

CARTE REDUITE DES PARTIES SEPTENTRIONALES DU GLOBE, SITUEES ENTRE L'ASIE ET L'AMERIQUE ...   [1758]   From *Histoire Generale* ...   Unknown areas left blank.   21x34cm (8½x13½")   B&W.   Fine.   [12]   £136 **$225**

CARTE REDUITE DES TERRES AUSTRALES   [1753]   In *Histoire Generale des Voyages*.   New Guinea, Australia & bulky New Zealand west coast.   20x28cm (8x11")   B&W.   Ref: Tooley (Australia) 156, pl.9; Clancy (Australis) ill.p.93.   [13]   **Aus$1,750**   £795 $1,318

CARTE REDUITE DU GLOBE TERRESTRE   [1764]   In vol.1, *Le Petit Atlas Maritime* ...   Mercator proj.   22x34cm (8½x13½")   Orig wash color.   [13]   **Aus$390**   £177 $294

CARTE REDUITE DU GOLPHE DU MEXIQUE ET DES ISLES DE L'AMERIQUE   [1764]   From *Le Petit Atlas Maritime* ...   21x31cm (8x12")   on 12½x18½" sheet.   B&W.   Lt spot; else fine.   Ref: Phillips (A) 3508-47.   [12]   £151 **$250**

[SAME TITLE]   [c.1765]   24x32cm (9½x13")   Color.   Browned overall.   [A7]   £173 **$287**

GRUNDRISS DES HAFENS VON ACAPULCO   [1756]   Publ Leipzig.   14-item key.   19x15cm (7½x6")   ["... Port Royal ... Campeche Bay" offered at same price]   [11]   £21 **$35**

GRUNDRISS VON NEU-ORLEANS NACH DEN MANUSCRIPTEN IN DEM SCHATZE DER KARTEN DER MARINE. VON N.B. INGR. DE LA M. 1744   [1755]   Publ Leipzig.   18-item key.   19x28cm (7½x11")   [11]   £256 **$425**

GRUNDRISS VON PORT ROYAL IN ACCADIA ... ANNAPOLIS ROYALE [NOVA SCOTIA]   [1755]   Publ Leipzig.   19x28cm (7½x11")   ["... Hafens Dauphin ..." (St. Anne), "... Hafens la Haive ..." (Mahone Bay), "... Bay Chedabuctu ..." (Gaysborough) & "... Hafen von Plaisance ..." (NFL) offered at same price]   [11]   £45 **$75**

ISLE DE MADAGASCAR AUTREMENT ISLE DE ST. LAURENT   [c.1757]   29x23cm (11½x9")   Uncolored.   VG.   [14]   £81 **$135**

KARTE VON ACCADIA ...   [1755]   Publ Leipzig.   20x32cm (8x12½")   [11]   £75 **$125**

KARTE VON DEM EYLANDE HAYTI HEUTIGES TAGES ESPAGNOLA ODER DIE INSEL ST. DOMINGO NEBST DEN BENACHBATEN EYLANDEN   [1756]   Publ Leipzig.   Hispaniola with nearby islands.   22x33cm (8½x13")   ["Le Port Marianne ... Cube", 1754, offered at same price]   [11]   £45 **$75**

KARTE VON DEM FLUSS RICHELIEU UND DEM SEE CHAMPLAIN ...   [1755]   Publ Leipzig.   Incl Montreal.   30x14cm (12x5½")   [11]   £36 **$60**

BELLIN (Small) continued

KARTE VON DEN KUSTEN DES FRANZOSISCHEN FLORIDA [1755] Publ Leipzig. Cape Fear to St. Augustine. 20x14cm (8x5½") Ref: Cumming (SE) 259. [11] £75 **$125**

KARTE VON DEN LAENDER NICARAGUA UND COSTA RICA [1756] Publ Leipzig. 20x17cm (8x6½") ["Karte der ... Tabasco, Chiapa, Verapaz, Guatimala, Honduras und Yucatan" offered at same price] [11] £36 **$60**

KARTE VON DEN UMLIEGENDEN GEGENDEN DER STADT MEXICO [1756] Publ Leipzig. 20x16cm (8x6") ["Karte von dem See von Mexico ..." & "Grundriss ... Stadt Vera Cruz ..." offered at same price] [11] £24 **$40**

KARTE VON DER ERDENGE PANAMA UND DEN PROVINZEN VERAGUA, TERRA FIRMA UND DARIEN [1756] Publ Leipzig. 20x29cm (7½x11½") [11] £45 **$75**

KARTE VON DER HUDSONS BAY [1755] Publ Leipzig. 20x28cm (8x11") ["Karte von dem Ende der Hudsons-Bay" (James Bay) offered at $30] [11] £24 **$40**

KARTE VON DER INSEL MONTREAL ... [1755] Publ Leipzig. 24x31cm (9½x12") [11] £136 **$225**

KARTE VON L'ISLE ROYALE [c.1760] After Bellin by G.C. Kilian. 18x26cm (7x10") Old color. [48] **DM 450** £155 $257

KARTE VON MEXICO [1756] Publ Leipzig. 16 to 24 deg. 20x29cm (7½x11½") [11] £30 **$50**

KARTE VON NORD-AMERICA ... [1755] Publ Leipzig. 28x35cm (11x13½") [11] £112 **$185**

LA RIVIERE DU DETROIT DEPUIS LE LAC SAINTE CLAIRE JUSQU'AU LAC ERIE [1764] Inset plan of Detroit, "earliest printed delineation of the city." 20x32cm (8x12½") B&W. Strong impression; fine. Ref: Karpinski (MI) LXXX, illus p.164. [38] £905 **$1,500**

PLAN DE LA BAYE DE RIO-JANEIRO [1764] 21x32cm (8½x12½") Wash color. [41] £60 **$100**

PLAN DE LA BAYE DE ST. YAGO DANS L'ISLE DE CUBE [1754] Harbor chart. 21x16cm (8½x6½") ["Baye de Matance ... Cube" offered at same price] [11] £51 **$85**

PLAN DE LA VILLE DE BOSTON ET SES ENVIRONS [1763-64] Publ in *Petit Atlas Maritime*. Reference key at lf. 17x27cm (6½x10½") Ref: Phillips (A) 3508, v.1-31. Tooley (Amer) p.208, #105. [22] £136 **$225**

PLAN DE LA VILLE DE BUENOS-AYRES [1754] 18x27cm (7x10½") [11] £45 **$75**

PLAN DE LA VILLE DE LOUISBOURG DANS L'ISLE ROYALE [1764] From *Petit Atlas Maritime*. 20x34cm (8x13½") OL color. Exc. Ref: Phillips (M) p.365. Sellers & Van Ee 340. [21] **Can$295** £129 $214

PLAN DE LA VILLE DE QUEBEC [1761] 20x28cm (8x11") Color. Exc. [24] £151 **$250**

PLAN DE LA VILLE ET DU PORT DE MACAO [1764] 21x17cm (8½x6½") Partial color. By sight, fine. Framed. [A9] £118 **$196**

PLAN DU BASSIN DE QUEBEC ET DE SES ENVIRONS [1744] 20x28cm (8x11") Printer's ink top rt corner, crisp, clean. [14] £136 **$225**

PLAN DU PORT ET VILLE DE LOUISBOURG DANS L'ISLE ROYALE [1755] Publ Leipzig. 19x28cm (7½x11") ["Karte von l'Isle Royale" offered at same price] [11] £51 **$85**

SUITE DES ISLES ANTILLES 1 PARTIE [1764] From *Le Petit Atlas Maritime* ... St. Lucie to Grenada. 22x16cm (9x6½") Color. Ref: Phillips (A) 3508, v.1-80. ["... 2 Partie", Guadeloupe to Martinique, offered as same price] [18] £100 **$165**

BELLUS

ABRISS DER STADT FRANCKENTHAL, WIE SOLCHE VON DEM VICE GENERAL DON GO...ALO FERNANDES DE CORDOVA BELAGERT WORDEN. 1621 [1627] From *Ostreichischer Lorberkranz*. 27x32cm (10½x12½") Sm lacuna & c'fold tear; lacuna at title restored with text. [48] **DM 500** £173 **$286**

BEREY

CARTE DE L'AMERIQUE CORIGEE ET AUGMENTEE ... [1658] Publ Paris. Based on Blaeu & Hondius; polar insets; surround of text. 40x51cm (15½x20") Color. Ref: Burden 328. [34] **£1,650** $2,736

BERGHAUS

UBERSICHT VON NORD-AMERICA ... [1887] From *Physikalischer Atlas*. Gotha. Geologic map; 12 insets detailing volcanoes, national parks, etc. Litho & hand color. 33x41cm (13x16") [12] £106 **$175**

BERRY

THE PROVINCE OF LEINSTER SURVEYED ... [c.1689] After Wm. Petty's survey. Separately issued. 44x56cm (17x22") Color. Margin restoration. ["... Connought ..." offered at £360] [34] **£380** $630

BERTELLI

ISOLA DE' RHODI   [c.1570]   Often in Lafreri atlases. 20x15cm (8x6")   Orig blue wash color. Trimmed close. Ref: Zacharakis 218, pl.32.   [2]   £844   **$1,400**

ISOLA DE ZANTE   [c.1570]   Often in Lafreri atlases. 20x15cm (8x6")   Orig blue wash color. Trimmed close. Ref: Zacharakis 205.   ["Isola de Scharpanto" offered as same price]   [2]   £603   **$1,000**

BERTIUS

[PORTRAIT]   PETRUS BERTIUS COLLEGII ILLUSTR.ORDINUM REGENS   [c.1620]   Unknown source; possibly French origin. 14x10cm (5½x4")   Uncolored. Dark impression; exc.   [4]   £150   **$249**

ABISSINORUM IMPERIUM   [1602]   Prester John after Ortelius. 8x13cm (3½x5")   OL color. Age-toned; show-through in margins; else VG.   [38]   £90   **$150**

CARTE DE L'AMERIQUE CORIGEE ET AUGMENTEE ... PAR P. BERTIUS 1662   [1639-1662] Publ Paris. Based on Blaeu & Hondius; polar insets. 27x36cm (10½x14")   Uncol. Ref: Burden 256, state 3.   [34]   **£800** $1,327

DANTZIG   [1616]   View. 15x20cm (6x8")   [48]   DM 700   £242 $401

FREIBERG IN MEISSEN   [1616]   Bird's-eye view. 15x20cm (6x8")   [48]   DM 80   £28 $46

HIBERNIA   [1598-1602]   From *Tabularum Geographicarum* ...   2nd state of Langenes-Bertius map. 9x12cm (3½x5")   Orig color.   [34]   **£140** $232

MOLUCCAE INSULAE   [1602]   Spice islands. 9x13cm (3½x5")   [11]   £75   **$125**

[SAME TITLE]   [1609]   8x13cm (3½x5")   Color. Fine.   [37]   £75   **$125**

NORVEGIA ET SUECIA   [1632]   With Finland and Baltics. 14x18cm (5½x7½")   [48]   DM 320   £110 $183

RUFACH   [1616]   Alsatian town; bird's-eye view. 14x19cm (5½x7½")   [48]   DM 200   £69 $114

SITTEN   [1616]   Sion, Switzerland view. 14x19cm (5½x7½")   [48]   DM 300   £104 $172

STRASBURG   [1616]   View. 14x20cm (5½x7½")   [48]   DM 450   £155 $257

TERRA NOVA   [1602]   From ... *Contractarum* ... *Edita Secunda*.   Newfoundland & adjacent. 9x12cm (3½x5")   Orig color.   [11]   £172   **$285**

TYPUS ORBIS TERRARUM   [1616 (1618)]   Like Hondius' oval of 1598. 10x13cm (4x5½")   Color. VG. Ref: Shirley (W) 290.   [37]   £271   **$450**

BETTS

MEXICO INCLUDING CALIFORNIA AND TEXAS   [c.1849]   Publ in *Betts Family Atlas*. TX bordered as republic; statehood boundaries outlined. 38x30cm (15x12")   Orig OL color.   [27]   £163   **$270**

NORTH AMERICA   [1844]   Part of *The London Series of Sixpenny Maps*. Minimum independent TX. 36x41cm (14x16")   Full color.   [9]   £100   **$165**

WESTERN AUSTRALIA   [1843]   From *Family Atlas*. "Van Diemen's Land" inset. 29x38cm (11½x15") Orig OL color. Ref: Tooley (Australia) 470.   [34]   **£150** $249

BIEN

[ATLAS]   ATLAS OF THE STATE OF NEW YORK PREPARED UNDER THE DIRECTION OF JOSEPH R. BIEN ... [1895]   Large folio, cloth; 36 (of 37) mostly double-page printed color maps, lacks state map. Covers worn, soiled; title browned; contents VG. Ref: LeGear (US) 2401.   [A10]   £180   **$299**

GEOLOGICAL MAP OF NEW JERSEY   [1889]   Part of *Atlas of the State of New Jersey*. 89x62cm (35x24½") Full printed color.   [22]   £54   **$90**

THE STATE OF NEW JERSEY   [1889]   Based on U.S. Coast & Geodetic Survey. Extensive road detail; without elevations. 89x63cm (35x25")   Printed earth tone color.   [1888 version, "New Jersey", with elevations & fewer placenames offered at $60]   [22]   £45   **$75**

BINET

ETATS-UNIS   [1844]   With Republic of Texas. 19x24cm (7½x9½")   OL color. Foxed; repaired tears rt margin; fair.   ["Amerique Nord", same condition, offered at same price]   [16]   £90   **$150**

MEXIQUE   [1844]   With Republic of Texas. 24x19cm (9½x7½")   OL col. Lt staining; good.   [16]   £121   **$200**

BLACHFORD

TO THE MERCHANTS & SHIP OWNERS OF THE UNITED KINGDOM OF GREAT BRITAIN & IRELAND, THIS CHART OF THE INDIAN & PACIFIC OCEANS ... IS ... DEDICATED   [1848]   Blue-backed chart. 4 insets, 3 coastal views, incl Port Jackson. 98x181cm (38½x71½")   Minor tears; lt soiling & damage to backing; an inset apparently cut out & replaced early; VG.   [15]   £211   **$350**

BLACK

[ATLAS] BLACK'S GENERAL ATLAS: A SERIES OF FIFTY-FOUR MAPS FROM THE LATEST AND MOST AUTHENTIC SOURCES [1841] Folio, cloth boards, corner & spine leather; steel plate engravings Sidney Hall. Orig OL color. Maps VG or fine, many with orig tissue guards; sl margin soiling early pages; covers rubbed, scuffed; sl giving on spine. [14] £814 **$1,350**

ASIA [1860] 42x54cm (16½x21½") Printed color. [40] £39 **$65**

BLACK'S ROAD & RAILWAY TRAVELING MAP OF ENGLAND [1882] Dissected, cloth back, folded into orig cloth case. 81x66cm (32x26") Minor marks, but VG; case exc. [25] £45 **$75**

ENGLAND AND WALES [1859] Edinburgh: A.& C. Black. On two sheets, each 41x56cm (16x22") Printed color. [40] £45 **$75**

IRELAND [1859] 51x41cm (20x16") Substantial color. VG. [25] £42 **$70**

MEXICO [1840] From early ed, *General Atlas*. Maximum Texas; 2 Buenaventura Rivers; Guatemala inset. 25x37cm (10x14½") OL color. Pristine. Ref: Phillips (A) 777-49. [12] £151 **$250**

PRUSSIA [1860] Edinburgh: A.& C. Black. Incl East Prussia, Pomerania & adjacent. 26x38cm (10½x15") Color. [40] £24 **$40**

BLACKIE

MEXICO [1860] From W.G. Blackie, *Imperial Atlas* … J.W. Lowry, engr. Shows "Gadsden or Arizona" in horiz form. 34x50cm (13½x19½") Pale wash color. Ref: cf Phillips (A) 3556. [12] £51 **$85**

[SAME TITLE] [c.1860] Incl Texas, with Galveston to Houston RR. 34x50cm (13½x19½") OL color. VG. [16] £106 **$175**

THE UNITED STATES, OF NORTH AMERICA. (GENERAL MAP) [1860] *Imperial Atlas of Modern Geography*. Drawn by Lowry. 34x50cm (13½x19½") Orig OL col. Fine. Ref: Phillips (A) 3556. [12] £151 **$250**

THE UNITED STATES OF NORTH AMERICA, PACIFIC STATES [ON SHEET WITH NORTH ATLANTIC] [1860] From *Imperial Atlas* … Drawn by Lowry. OR, WA (& NE) Territories to Rockies. Separate border each map. 34x25cm (13½x10") OL color. Fine. Ref: cf. Phillips (A) 3556. [12] £54 **$90**

UNITED STATES [c.1840] West to large IA & WI Terr. 48x37cm (19x14½") Full color. Lt toning & margin split at fold; good (B). [A3] £52 **$87**

BLAEU

[ATLAS] NOVUS ATLAS SINENSIS A MARTINO MARTINIO SOC.IESU DESCRIPTUS ET SEREN. ARCHIDUCI LEOPOLDO GUILIELMO AUSTRIACO DEDICATUS [1655] 1st western atlas of China & Japan. Folio, later vellum binding; 17 maps in orig color & gold highlighting, incl China, 15 provinces & Japan. Ref: Koeman Bl 154. [3] £11,459 **$19,000**

[CHINA & JAPAN: COMPLETE SET OF 17 FOLIO MAPS] [(1655) 1662] From Martino Martini's *Atlas Sinensis*. as incorporated into Vol.X of Atlas Maior. With gold heightened title page. Orig color, later additions. Exc. Ref: Koeman Bl 52 (418); Walter (Japan) 34, 35, 36. [4] £4,850 **$8,042**

[FACSIMILE ATLAS] LE GRANDE ATLAS OU COSMOGRAPHIE BLAVIANE [(1663) publ 1967-68] Amsterdam. 12 folio volumes (441 of 1,000 copies of "third centenary edition"), orig imitation vellum; numerous colored & plain maps. [A6] £1,725 **$2,861**

[TITLE PAGE] THEATRUM ORBIS TERRARUM [1655] Willem & Jan Blaeu; sectional title for Part One. [no dimens] Color. [A7] £208 **$345**

AEBUDAE INSULAE SIVE HEBRIDES [1625] 38x53cm (15x21") OL color. [A7] £97 **$161**

AETHIOPIA INFERIOR, VEL EXTERIOR [1635] 38x50cm (15x19½") OL color. Ref: Tooley (Africa) frontispiece. [A7] £156 **$258**

[SAME TITLE] [1635-62] 38x50cm (15x19½") Full early & later color. Faint soiling margins; some sh margin tears; hinge residue top edges verso; overall VG. Ref: Tooley (Africa) frontispiece, p.29. [A9] £226 **$374**

[SAME TITLE] [1640] 38x50cm (15x19½") Old color. Sm rough spots; sl browning, some foxing. Ref: Norwich #154. [48] DM 990 £342 **$567**

AETHIOPIA SUPERIOR VEL INTERIOR; VULGO ABISSINORUM SIVE PRESBITERI IOANNIS IMPERIUM [1649] 38x50cm (15x19½") New color. Faint age toning along c'fold; 1" fold separation at top margin; o/w VG. [A1] £382 **$633**

[SAME TITLE] [c.1640] 39x50cm (15½x20") OL color. Some overall darkening. [A8] £156 **$258**

AFRICAE NOVA DESCRIPTIO [1630] Side and top panels. 41x56cm (16½x22") Full orig color. Exc. Ref: Tooley (Africa) pl.18. Norwich 32. [2] £2,292 **$3,800**

AFRICAE NOVA DESCRIPTIO. AUCT: GUILJELMO BLAEUW [(1618-30) c.1640] Side and top panels. 44x55cm (17½x21½") Color. Sh repaired tear top margin; sm reinforcement lower c'fold margin; overall fine. Ref: Tooley (Africa) p.29, pl.18. Norwich 32. [4] £2,500 **$4,146**

BLAEU continued

AMERICAE NOVA TABULA   [1633]   In Van Metern's *Meteranus Novus*.   Willem Blaeu.   Variant borders probably due to masking.   36x46cm (14½x18½")   [A7]   £1,803   **$2,990**
[SAME TITLE]   [c.1660]   Carte a figures.   42x56cm (16½x22")   OL color.   Some gray-grained surface from worn plate; sl evident verso fold reinforcement.   [A8]   £2,636   **$4,370**
AMERICAE NOVA TABULA. AUCT: GUILJELMO BLAEUW   [c.1640]   Carte a figures.   41x56cm (16x22")   Full orig color. Fine. Ref: Burden 189; Goss (NA) 26.   [23]   £4,523   **$7,500**
ANNANDIA PRAEFECTURA   [1657]   Dumfries, Scotland.   58x51cm (23x20")   OL color. Browning on image.   [A7]   £97   **$161**
ARGOW CUM PARTE MERID ZURICHGOW   [1640]   After Mercator.   38x50cm (15x19½")   Old color. Few rust & mold spots; browning.   [48]   DM 990   £342   **$567**
ARRAGONIA REGNUM ...   [c.1640]   NE Spain.   41x52cm (16x20½")   OL color; decor in full color. Minor toning; c'fold creasing & repaired c'fold margin split; VG (A).   [A3]   £249   **$413**
ASIA NOVITER DELINEATA AUCTORE GUILJELMO BLAEUW   [(1617-30) c.1640]   Top & side panels.   42x55cm (16½x21½")   Color. Fine. Ref: Koeman Bl 7A (3).   [4]   **£2,750** $4,560
[SAME TITLE]   [1640]   Top & side panels.   41x55cm (16½x22")   Full color. Exc.   [45]   £2,051   **$3,400**
BARONIA UDRONE IN COMITATU CATHERLOUGHE   [1654]   Carlow.   38x25cm (15x10")   Orig OL color.   [34]   **£280** $465
BRANDEBURGUM MARCHIONATUS, CUM DUCATIBUS POMERANIAE ET MEKELENBURGI   [1640]   40x53cm (15½x21")   Old color.   [48]   DM 860   £297   **$492**
BRITANNIA PROUT DIVISA FUIT TEMPORIBUS ANGLO-SAXONUM PRAESERTIM DURANTE ILLORUM HEPTARCHIA   [c.1645]   From Vol. IV, *Theatrum*. After Speed; side panels.   42x53cm (16½x21")   Color. Filled worming in 2 sm side panels areas & lower margin; overall fine   Ref: Shirley (BI to 1650) 549 & 617, pl.151.   [4]   **£1,300** $2,156
[SAME TITLE]   [1645-1662]   Side panels.   42x53cm (16½x20½")   Orig color. Ref: Shirley (BI to 1650) 549.   [34]   **£1,850** $3,068
CALIAECIA REGNUM   [c.1635]   38x50cm (15x19½")   OL color. Repaired margin tears; else fine (A).   [A3]   £249   **$413**
CANIBALES INSULAE   [1662]   Puerto Rico to Trinidad.   42x53cm (16½x21")   Color.   [18]   £528   **$875**
CHINA VETERIBUS SINARUM REGIO NUNC INCOLIS TAME DICTA   [1640]   With Korea & Japan.   41x50cm (16x19½")   Old color. Sl browning; 2 sm spots.   [48]   DM 1,800   £621   **$1,030**
COMITATUS GLATZ AUTHORE JONA SCULTETO   [c.1640]   41x50cm (16x19½")   Modern full color. Minor damp stain; good (B).   [A3]   £113   **$188**
CONNACHTIA VULGO CONNAUGHTY   [1654]   38x50cm (15x19½")   Orig OL color.   [34]   **£400** $664
CYPRUS INSULA   [1642]   38x51cm (15x20")   Orig color, later additions. Sl color offset; c'fold restored. Ref: Stylianou 112; Koeman Bl 27a.   [46]   £780   **$1,294**
DEVONIA ...   [1645 or later]   Numerous coats of arms.   39x50cm (15½x19½")   Color.   [A5]   **£230** $382
DUCATO OUERO TERRITORIO DI MILANO   [1640]   38x51cm (15x20")   Old color. Uniformly browned.   [48]   DM 560   £193   **$320**
ESSEXIA COMITATUS   [1645]   From vol.4, *Novus Atlas*. Coats of arms at lf.   42x52cm (16½x20½")   Orig color; gold highlight.   [11]   £286   **$475**
[SAME TITLE]   [1645]   From *Theatrum* ...   42x53cm (16½x21")   Color. Laid down. Ref: Koeman Bl 42A, 20.   [42]   Aus$650   £295   **$489**
EUROPA RECENS DESCRIPTA ...   [1630]   Top & side panels.   41x55cm (16½x22")   Orig color. Exc. Ref: Potter illus p.99.   [2]   £2,111   **$3,500**
EXTREMA AMERICAE VERSUS BOREAM, UBI TERRA NOVA NOVA FRANCIA, ADIACENTIAQUE   [c.1660]   Only Blaeu map of Canada.   46x56cm (18x22")   Partial color. Soft crease; mounted on flexible sheet. Ref: Lepine 306.   [A8]   £555   **$920**
FLANDRIAE TEUTONICAE PARS ORIENTALIOR   [1640]   38x50cm (15x20")   Old color. Browning.   [48]   DM 560   £193   **$320**
GALLIA VETUS   [c.1640]   Roman period France.   38x50cm (15x19½")   OL color. Margin c'fold split; lt margin toning; VG (A).   ["Lemovicum" (Limoge) sold at same price]   [A3]   £186   **$308**
GALLIA VETUS, AD IUL CAESARIS COMMENTARIA   [1640]   After Ortelius.   39x50cm (15½x19½")   Old color.   [48]   DM 160   £55   **$91**
GERMANIAE VETERIS TYPUS   [c.1640]   Historical map.   38x48cm (15x19")   Col.   [48]   DM 580   £200   **$332**
[SAME TITLE]   [c.1650]   38x48cm (15x19")   Full modern color. Fine (A+).   [A4]   £329   **$545**

BLAEU continued

GRANATA ET MURCIA REGNA [1640] 38x50cm (15x20") Old color. Lt browning; some foxing.
[48] **DM 550** £190 $315

GUIANA SIVE AMAZONIUM REGIO [c.1640] With Parime Lacus. 37x49cm (14½x19½") Orig color. Faint toning; o/w VG to fine. [A2] £249 **$413**

GUINEA [c.1640] 39x53cm (15x20½") OL color. Minor toning; repaired margin split; VG (A).
[A3] £349 **$578**

HELLAS SEU GRAECIA SOPHANI [c.1640] 36x50cm (14½x19½") Newer OL col. Fine. [14] £392 **$650**

[SAME TITLE] [1634 - c.1640] 38x50cm (15x19½") Orig OL color. [34] £550 $912

INDIA QUAE ORIENTALIS DICITUR ET INSULAE ADIACENTES [1635] India to Japan & New Guinea. 41x50cm (16½x20") Orig color. Exc. Ref: Quirino p.81. [24] £1,206 **$2,000**

[SAME TITLE] [(1635) 1640] 41x50cm (16x19½") Color. Sh lower c'fold split closed with verso reinforcement; overall fine. Ref: Schilder (Australia) #40. [4] £1,200 $1,990

[SAME TITLE] [1640] India to S Japan & W Australia. 42x51cm (16½x20") Orig color with later additions. Repaired sm split lower c'fold. Ref: Koeman Bl 17. [46] £1,350 $2,239

INSULAE AMERICANAE IN OCEANO SEPTENTRIONALI CUM TERRIS ADIACENTIBUS [1635] West Indies. 38x52cm (15x20½") Full color. [20] £1,659 **$2,750**

[SAME TITLE] [1635] West Indies: Chesapeake to Orinoco. 38x52cm (15x20½") Orig color. Exc. Ref: Burden 242; Portinaro & Knirsch pl.86. [24] £1,206 **$2,000**

[SAME TITLE] [c.1635] 38x52cm (15x20½") Orig color. Pair minor stains lower c'fold; else fine. Ref: Burden 242. [45] £663 **$1,100**

[SAME TITLE] [1635 (1640)] 38x52cm (15x20½") Old OL color. Lt spotting margin; good. Ref: Koeman Bl 56 (78). [28] £905 **$1,500**

[SAME TITLE] [c.1640] 38x52cm (15x20½") OL & feature color. Mildew stain & paper loss top lf margin, image unaffected; tiny repair lf edge; else VG. Ref: Portinaro & Knirsch pp.178-9. [A10] £520 **$863**

INSULAE BALEARIDES ET PYTIVSAE [1647] 39x51cm (15x20") Wash & OL color. Scattered dampstaining; some show through; VG. Ref: Phillips (A) 3421, v.1-23. [35] £136 **$225**

[SAME TITLE] [c.1647] 38x49cm (15x19½") Orig OL col. Sm rust spot; else clean; VG (A). [A4] £139 **$230**

KREMLENAGRAD, CASTELLUM URBIS MOSKVAE [1662] Appeared in *Atlas Major*. The Kremlin; 32 point key; some Cyrillic lettering. 38x49cm (15x19½") Orig wash color. Laid on tissue to reinforce verdigris weaknesses. Ref: Koeman Bl 56. [46] £560 $929

LAGENIA; ANGLIS LEINSTER ... [1654] 38x50cm (15x19½") Orig OL color. [34] £480 $796

[SAME TITLE] [1654] 39x50cm (15½x19½") Orig OL col. Exc. Ref: Koeman Bl 49. [29] £362 **$600**

[SAME TITLE] [1654] From vol. 5, *Theatrum* ... SE Ireland. 40x50cm (15½x19½") Color. Ref: Koeman Bl 50, 52. [42] **Aus$550** £250 $414

LE GOUVERNEMENT DE L'ISLE DE FRANCE [1647] 41x52cm (16x20½") OL col. Fine. [14] £256 **$425**

LEODIENSIS DIOECESIS [1640] 38x50cm (15x20") Old color. Lt browning. [48] **DM 590** £204 $338

LIVONIA VULGO LYEFLAND [c.1640] 38x50cm (15x20") Old color. [48] **DM 800** £276 $458

LOTHARINGIA DUCATUS; VULGO LORRAINE [c.1640] 38x50cm (15x20") Color. [48] **DM 580** £200 $332

MAGNAE BRITANNIAE ET HIBERNIAE TABULA [1631] 39x50cm (15x19½") Orig OL color. Ref: Shirley (BI to 1650) 423; pl.128. [11] £332 **$550**

MAGNI DUCATUS LITHUANIAE ... [1650] 44x53cm (17½x21") Orig color. Lt time toned. Ref: Koeman I, Bl 29B. [2] £332 **$550**

MAGNI MOGOLIS IMPERIUM [c.1663] From *Atlas Major*. N India & adjacent. 41x52cm (16x20½") Orig color. Age toned. [46] **£230** $382

MAPPA AESTIVARUM INSULARUM, ALIAS BARMUDAS DICTARUM ... [1630] 40x53cm (16x21") Orig color. Exc. Ref: Campbell (Early) pl.23. Palmer (Bermuda) p.8-9. [24] £1,508 **$2,500**

MOLUCCAE INSULAE CELEBERRIMAE [(1630) c.1650] 37x49cm (14½x19") Orig col. Fine. [4] £285 $473

MOMONIA ... ANGLICE MOUNSTER [1654] 38x50cm (15x19½") Orig OL color. [34] £450 $746

MONTGOMERIA COMITATUS ET COMITATUS MERVINIA [1645] 38x50cm (15x19½") Color. VG+ Ref: Skelton (County) 28. [38] £241 **$400**

NATOLIA, QUAE OLIM ASIA MINOR [c.1640] 38x50cm (15x19½") Orig OL color. Lt surface soiling; o/w VG to fine. [A2] £83 **$138**

NOVA AEGYPTI TABULA [1662] North Nile & Red Sea. 44x54cm (17½x21") OL color. Side margin edges bit tattered. [A8] £294 **$488**

BLAEU continued

NOVA BELGICA ET ANGLIA NOVA [c.1635] 39x50cm (15½x20") Color. Exc. Ref: Burden 241; Goss (NA) #28. [45] £1,508 **$2,500**

[SAME TITLE] [1640+] 40x51cm (15½x20") OL col. Sl toned overall; few edge chips. [A8] £1,248 **$2,070**

[SAME TITLE] [c.1650] North to rt. 38x49cm (15x19½") Full color. Good. [32] £1,327 **$2,200**

NOVA ET ACCURATISSIMA TOTIUS TERRARUM ORBIS TABULA. AUCTORE JOANNE BLAEU [1662] As in *Atlas Maior*. Double hemi; insular California. 40x54cm (15½x21½") Color. Ref: Shirley 428; pl.315. [13] Aus$15,000 £6,812 **$11,295**

NOVA TOTIUS TERRARUM ORBIS GEOGRAPHICA AC HYDROGRAPHICA TABULA ... [1606 - c.1630] Carte-a-figures. 40x54cm (16x21½") Full orig color. Side margins extended, no loss printed surface; exc. Ref: Shirley (W) 255, pl.201 (1606). [2] £7,539 **$12,500**

[SAME TITLE] [1606 (1630-58)] State 4; Carte-a-figures: allegorical sun, moon, planets; 4 classical elements; 4 seasons; 7 ancient wonders. 41x55cm (16x21½") Color. [13] Aus$15,800 £7,175 **$11,897**

[SAME TITLE] [c.1635-57] Carte-a-figures: allegorical sun, moon, planets; 4 classical elements; 4 seasons; 7 ancient wonders. 40x54cm (16x21½") Color. Crease along part of c'fold; else exc. [23] £7,237 **$12,000**

NOVA VIRGINIAE TABULA [1630 & later] 38x48cm (15x19") Full orig color. Exc. [36] £1,628 **$2,700**

[SAME TITLE] [1632] 37x48cm (15x19") Orig col. Exc. Ref: Tooley (Amer) p.161-2. [24] £1,206 **$2,000**

[SAME TITLE] [1640] 37x48cm (15x19") Orig color. Faint watermarks in margin onto image; o/w exc. Ref: Burden 193; Portinaro & Knirsch p.158. [A1] £1,327 **$2,200**

[SAME TITLE] [1650] State 2 of Hondius plate. 37x48cm (15x19") Orig col. Minor split near c'fold; o/w exc. Ref: Burden 193; Tooley (Amer) p.162; Portinaro & Knirsch p.158. Van Ermen p.20. [14] £1,508 **$2,500**

[SAME TITLE] [c.1650] 37x48cm (15x19") Full color. Fine. [32] £1,146 **$1,900**

NOVUS XVII INFERIORIS GERMANIAE PROVINCIARUM TYPUS [c.1640] 40x50cm (15½x19½") Tan toning; couple lt brown stains. [A2] £315 **$523**

ORCADUM ET SCHETLANDIAE INSULARUM ACCURATISSIMA DESCRIPTIO [1656 (+)] 40x53cm (15½x21") Color. Minor dampstaining into image. [A7] £97 **$161**

PADERBORNENSIS EPISCOPATUS DESCRIPTIO NOVA [1640] 38x50cm (15x19½") Old color. [48] DM 1,450 £501 **$830**

PALATINATUS AD RHENUM [1640] 41x50cm (16½x19½") Old color. Some browning & rust spots. Ref: Hellwig et al, 36.3. [48] DM 1,350 £466 **$773**

[SAME TITLE] [c.1650] 41x50cm (16x19½") Full color. Repaired margin fold split; minor toning; VG (A). [A4] £133 **$220**

PARAGUAY, O PROV. DE RIO DE LA PLATA CUM REGIONIBUS ADIACENTIBUS TUCUMAN ET STA. CRUZ DE LA SIERRA [1647] 37x48cm (14½x19") OL color. Overall surface soiling; lt water stains. [A1] £116 **$193**

PARS FLANDRIAE TEUTONICAE OCCIDENTALIOR [1650] 40x50cm (15½x19½") Later OL color. Moderate browning sides, esp lower rt corner; else VG. [A9] £59 **$98**

[SAME TITLE] [c.1650] 40x50cm (15½x19½") OL color. Scattered obtrusive browning; side margins extended. [A8] £121 **$201**

PARTE ALPESTRE DELLO STATO DI MILANO CON IL LAGO MAGGIORE DI LUGANO E DI COMO [1665] 38x51cm (15x20") [41] £181 **$300**

PERCHENSIS COMITATUS [ON SHEET WITH] COMITATUS BLESENSIS [c.1662] Each about 38x23cm (15x9") Full color. VG (A). [A4] £267 **$442**

PORTUGALLIA ET ALGARBIA QUAE OLIM LUSITANIA [1635] 38x50cm (15x19½") OL col. [A7] £121 **$201**

PRUSSIA ACCURATE DESCRIPTA ... [1635] Former East Prussia region. 38x50cm (15x19½") Orig color. Superb. [24] £332 **$550**

[SAME TITLE] [c.1640] Old East Prussia. 26 symbols keyed. 38x50cm (15x19½") Old OL color. Heavy paper; sl age-toned; else fine. [38] £271 **$450**

QUARTA PARS BRABANTIAE CUJUS CAPUT SYLVADUCIS [1640] 41x52cm (16x20½") Color. Paper browned, moldy. [48] DM 880 £304 **$504**

REGIONES SUB POLO ARCTICO [1645] 2nd state. 41x53cm (16x21") Orig OL color. Lt toning; o/w VG to fine. Ref: Burden 252. Whitfield p.78-9. [A2] £763 **$1,265**

RENDSBURGUM CHILONIUM ET BORDESHOLMA [1662] Reissue of Johannes Mejer 1652 map in Danckwerth Schleswig-Holstein atlas. 41x61cm (16x24") Full color. Early mounting on old sheet; exc. [41] £211 **$350**

RIVIERA DI GENOVA DI LEVANTE [1640] Genoa to Carrara. 40x50cm (15½x20") Color. [48] DM 580 £200 **$332**

BLAEU continued

RUSSIAE VULGO MOSCOVIA DICTAE PARS AUSTRALIS   [1647]   39x53cm (15½x21")   Orig color. Lower c'fold split taped on front margin. Ref: Koeman Bl 29.   [47]   £380 $630

RUSSIAE VULGO MOSCOVIA DICTAE PARTES SEPTENTRIONALIS ET ORIENTALIS. AUCTORE ISACCO MASSA   [1647]   42x54cm (16½x21½")   Orig color. Ref: Koeman Bl 29.   [47]   £270 $448

RUSSIAE, VULGO MOSCOVIA DICTAE, PARTES SEPTENTRIONALIS ET ORIENTALIS [IN SET WITH] RUSSIAE VULGO MOSCOVIA, PARS AUSTRALIS   [1635]   Each 38x53cm (15x21")   Orig col. Exc.   [24]   £724   **$1,200**

SABAUDIA DUCATUS ...   [1631]   38x48cm (15x19")   OL color. VG.   [37]   £181   **$300**

SECUNDA PARS BRABANTIAE CUIUS URBS PRIMARIA BRUXELLAE   [1640]   42x52cm (16½x20½")   Old color. Few brown spots.   [48]   DM 490   £169   **$280**

TABULA ISLANDIAE AUCTORE GEORGIO CAROLO FLANDRO   [1635]   38x50cm (15x19½")   [11]   £452   **$750**

[SAME TITLE]   [c.1630]   38x50cm (15x19½")   Col, believed newer; gold highlights. Fine.   [14]   £874   **$1,450**

TABULA MAGELLANICA, QUA TIERRAE DEL FUEGO, CUM CELEBERRIMIS FRETIS A F. MAGELLANO ET I. LE MAIRE DETECTIS NOVISSIMA ET ACCURATISSIMA DESCRIPTIO EXHIBETUR...   [1635]   42x54cm (16½x21")   OL color.   [A7]   £329   **$546**

[SAME TITLE]   [1635]   41x53cm (16x21")   Orig & later col. Margin reinforcements; else exc.   [24]   £452   **$750**

[SAME TITLE]   [1640 (1660+)]   41x53cm (16½x21")   Later OL color. Near fine. Ref: Humphreys p.141.   [A9]   £260   **$431**

TARTARIA SIVE MAGNI CHAMI IMPERIUM   [1635 (+)]   38x50cm (15x19½")   OL color.   [another with OL color, minor dampstaining top margin sold for $201]   [A7]   £208   **$345**

[SAME TITLE]   [c.1640]   39x50cm (15x19½")   Old color.   [48]   DM 900   £311   **$515**

TERRA SANCTA QUAE IN SACRIS TERRA PROMISSIONIS OLIM PALESTINA   [1629]   38x50cm (15x19½")   OL color. Ref: Laor 106.   [A8]   £485   **$805**

[SAME TITLE]   [1642]   38x50cm (15x19½")   Orig color; later additions. Upper c'fold split restored. Ref: Laor 106. Koeman Bl 32a.   [46]   £750   **$1,244**

TERRITORII BERGENSIS ACCURATISSIMA DESCRIPTIO   [1663]   Alkmaar region, Holland. 42x55cm (16½x21½")   Later full color. Minor soiling; sl fraying & margin edge tears; else VG.   [A9]   £146   **$242**

TERRITORIUM METENSE ... LE PAIS MESSIN   [1640]   39x50cm (15½x19½")   Old col.   [48]   DM 650   £224   **$372**

TURCICUM IMPERIUM   [1640]   41x52cm (16x20½")   Old col. Sl brown tone; 2 sm spots.   [48]   DM 900   £311   **$515**

ULTONIA; HIBERNIS CUI-GUILLY; ANGLIS ULSTER   [1654]   Northern Ireland. 38x50cm (15x19½")   Orig OL color.   [34]   £520   **$863**

ULTRAIECTUM DOMINIUM   [1640]   38x50cm (15x19½")   Old color. Few rust & mildew spots.   [48]   DM 580   £200   **$332**

URBIS MOSKVAE   [1662]   Appeared in *Atlas Major*. City plan acquired from Hessel Gerritz in 1613. Some Cyrillic lettering. 38x48cm (15x19")   Orig wash col; some greens lt browned. Ref: Koeman Bl 56.   [46]   £560   **$929**

VALENTIA REGNUM   [c.1645]   39x50cm (15½x20")   Uncolored. Lt brown spot; o/w VG to fine. ["Legionis Regnum et Asturiarum Principatus" (OL color) sold at same price]   [A2]   £50   **$83**

VENEZUELA, CUM PARTIS AUSTRALIS NOVAE ANDALUSIAE   [1640]   37x48cm (14½x19")   Contemp color. Framed.   [A6]   £172   **$286**

VIRGINIAE PARTIS AUSTRALIS, ET FLORIDAE PARTIS ORIENTALIS, INTERJACENTIUMQ REGIONUM NOVA DESCRIPTIO...   [1638+]   39x50cm (15x20")   OL color. Sl toned overall; scattered minor foxing. Ref: Burden 253 Cumming (SE) 41; Goss (NA) 31.   [A8]   £589   **$977**

[SAME TITLE]   [1640]   38x50cm (15x20")   Orig color. Exc.   [24]   £1,206   **$2,000**

[SAME TITLE]   [c.1640]   38x50cm (15x19½")   Orig color. Fine.   [14]   £1,508   **$2,500**

[SAME TITLE]   [1644-45]   38x50cm (15x19½")   Orig color. Fine.   [A1]   £995   **$1,650**

[SAME TITLE]   [1650]   Blank verso. 38x50cm (15x20")   Contemp OL color.   [A6]   £575   **$954**

XAINTONGE ET ANGOUMOIS   [c.1635]   39x50cm (15½x20")   Color. VG.   [38]   £181   **$300**

ZEELANDIA COMITATUS ...   [1635]   38x50cm (15x19½")   Orig color. Exc.   ["Carte du Bourdelois du Pays de Medoc ..." on sheet with "Principatus Benearnia ..." (France) offered at same price]   [24]   £302   **$500**

ZEELANDICA COMITATUS   [1640]   38x50cm (15x19½")   Old color. Lt browning, few rust spots, some foxing.   [48]   DM 980   £338   **$561**

BLAIR

[ATLAS] FOURTEEN MAPS OF ANCIENT AND MODERN GEOGRAPHY FOR THE ILLUSTRATION OF THE TABLES OF CHRONOLOGY AND HISTORY [1768] London. Folio, calf & marbled boards; 20 pp. Maps by Thomas Kitchin incl eastern North America, West Indies, Europe, Palestine, etc. Hinges loose; worn; lt offsetting to couple maps; generally clean. Ref: Phillips (A) 3305. [21] **Can$1,450** £634 $1,051

A MAP OF NORTH AMERICA FROM THE LATEST SURVEYS AND MAPS BY JOHN BLAIR LLD & F.R.S. AS A SUPPLEMENT TO HIS TABLES OF CHRONOLOGY [1779] The U.S. & adjacent Canada to Great Plains, without FL peninsula. 42x57cm (16½x22½") B&W. VG to fine. [A1] £249 **$413**

[SAME TITLE] [1779] Apparently after Kitchin. 42x58cm (16½x22½") Near mint. [11] £513 **$850**

A MAP OF THE EAST INDIES FROM THE LATEST AUTHORITIES AND OBSERVATIONS [1779] India to Malaysia. 42x56cm (16½x22") Near Mint. [11] £196 **$325**

A MAP OF THE WEST INDIES AND MIDDLE CONTINENT OF AMERICA FROM THE LATEST OBSERVATIONS [1779] 42x58cm (16½x23") [11] £196 **$325**

A MAP OF THE WORLD WITH THE LATEST DISCOVERIES ... [1779] Double hemi; shows Cook's discoveries. 41x70cm (16x27½") Near mint. [11] £513 **$850**

BLANCHARD, R.

BLANCHARD'S GUIDE MAP OF CHICAGO ... [1878] Attached to orig paper wrappers. 69x48cm (27x19") Orig wash color. Few fold reinforcements; else fine. [24] £724 **$1,200**

CHICAGO INVESTMENTS [1873] Baldwin, Walker & Co. Octavo folding street map of city in orig wrappers. 43x31cm (17x12") Color. Sh clean separation at several folds. [A8] £225 **$373**

BLOME

A DRAUGHT OF THE SEA COAST AND RIVERS OF VIRGINIA, MARYLAND [1672] As in *A Description of the Island of Jamaica ... Territories in America* ... Chesapeake to Bay of Fundy. VA & MD delineated. 20x25cm (7½x10") Color. [34] **£520** $863

A GENERALL MAPP OF CAROLINA. DESCRIBEING ITS SEA COAST AND RIVERS [1672] As in *A Description of the Island of Jamaica* ... 15x22cm (6x8½") Color. Ref: Cumming (SE) 69. [34] **£600** $995

A MAPP OF ITALY [c.1688] Dedication cartouche reworked in plate; part of Calabria sacrificed. 29x39cm (11½x15½") Color. [39] £106 **$175**

A MAPP OF THE KINGDOME OF IRELAND [1673] From 1st ed, *Britannia*. R. Palmer, sc. Title & 4 dedication cartouches. 37x38cm (14½x15") Narrow margins; sm split in binding fold. Ref: Chubb 99. [46] £350 **$581**

A NEW & EXACT MAPP OF YE ISLE OF IAMAICA AS IT WAS LATELY SURVEYED ... 1671 [1672] From *A Description of the Island of Jamaica* ... West Indies inset. 28x32cm (11x12½") Margins trimmed; sm loss lower lf & rt margin, image unaffected; age toning; creasing; but good. Ref: Kapp (Jamaica) 42. [21] **Can$375** £164 $272

[SAME TITLE] [1671] West Indies inset. 28x33cm (11x13") Exc. [44] £724 **$1,200**

GEOGRAPHY [WORLD] [1686] From *The Gentleman's Recreation*. Concepts of geography diagramed on a sheet with sm double hemi world. 24x38cm (9½x15") Col. Ref: Shirley (W) 479; pl.351. [13] **Aus$680** £309 $512

LONDON [c.1673] 17x28cm (6½x11") By sight, fine. Framed. Ref: Howgego 15. [A9] £180 **$299**

BLUNT

[CHESAPEAKE BAY ENTRANCE] [1822] From *American Coast Pilot*. 18x21cm (7x8") Uncolored. VG. [14] £75 **$125**

[LITTLE EGG HARBOR, NJ] [1841] From same source. 14th ed. 13x21cm (5x8½") [17] £66 **$110**

[NEWPORT HARBOR, RI] [1827] From same source, 11th ed. 20x22cm (8x9") B&W. [1833 ed offered at $90] [17] £60 **$100**

BOSTON BAY [1822] From same source. 10x18cm (4x7") Uncol. Lt age toning; VG. [14] £45 **$75**

BOSTON HARBOUR ... [1850] From same source. 21x26cm (8½x10") Color. [17] £81 **$135**

[SAME TITLE] [1854] From same source. [no dimens] Modern color. [22] £54 **$90**

CAPE ANN HARBOUR SURVEYED BY THE REV. C. FETCH & T. MALLONE ESQ. IN 1819 ... [1827] From same source. Gloucester, MA. 22x19cm (9x7½") Color. [1837 ed offered at $75; 1840 ed offered at $70] [17] £51 **$85**

CAPE POGE AND ADJACENT SHOALS [MA. [1822] From same source. Eastern Martha's Vineyard and Chappaquiddick. 10x18cm (4x7") Uncolored. VG. [14] £45 **$75**

[SAME TITLE] [dated 1827] From same source. Diagonal orientation; Vineyard & upper Cape. 10x18cm (4x7") [22] £72 **$120**

BLUNT continued

CHESAPEAKE BAY ENTRANCE   [1827]   From same source. 1st issue of "Entrance" area only chart. 18x21cm (7x8") B&W. Few faint spots; near fine. Ref: Guthorn (Charts) p.87.   [Delaware River & Bay offered at same price]   [35]   £90 **$150**

HARBOUR OF ANNIS SQUAM IN IPSWICH BAY   [1827]   From same source. 11x18cm (4½x7") Color. [1850 ed offered at $70; 1854 ed offered at $65]   [17]   £54 **$90**

ISLES OF SHOALS [NH]   [1827]   From same source. 11th ed. 23x19cm (9x7½") B&W.   [12th ed (1833), color, offered at $85]   [17]   £45 **$75**

LITTLE EGG HARBOR [NJ]   [1827]   From same source, 11th ed. 12x20cm (4½x8") B&W. Part lower margin trimmed close by binder; near fine. Ref: Howes (US) F-421. Guthorn (Charts) p.75   [35]   £121 **$200**

NEW PORT HARBOR [RI]   [1838]   From same source. 21x19cm (8½x7½") B&W. [1854 ed offered at $85] [17]   £57 **$95**

PLAN OF PORTLAND HARBOUR.   [1827]   From *American Coast Pilot*. 18x10cm (7½x4") Color. [1833 ed offered at $75]   [17]   £48 **$80**

PLAN OF PORTSMOUTH HARBOUR   [1837]   From same source, 13th ed. 18x19cm (7½x7½") Color. [1850 ed offered at $65]   [17]   £48 **$80**

[SAME TITLE]   [Dated 1816] From same source. 10x18cm (4x7") B&W. Ref: cf Cobb (NH) 86.   [22]   £45 **$75**

PORTLAND HARBOUR FOR BLUNT'S COAST PILOT   [1856]   From same source. 13 buoys added. 20x11cm (8x4½") Color.   [17]   £27 **$45**

THE BAHAMA BANKS AND GULF OF FLORIDA   [1844]   1st ed. Blue-backed chart. 97x124cm (38x49") Lt soiling; stain at ctr; minor edge tears. Ref: cf Guthorn (Charts) p.156. [1848 ed, linen backing over blue, offered at $1,000]   [15]   £754 **$1,250**

THE BAY AND RIVER OF DELAWARE   [1809]   From *American Coast Pilot*. 18x21cm (7½x8½") Full color. VG.   [36]   £106 **$175**

THE COAST OF THE UNITED STATES, SHEET NO.2 FROM CAPE LOOKOUT TO CAPE CANAVERAL FROM U.S. COAST SURVEYS   [1865]   Blue-backed chart. Lighthouses in yellow & red. 78x118cm (30½x46½") Minor loss outside border lower lf; few sh repaired tears; VG.   [15]   £256 **$425**

BOCHART & KNOLLIS

A NEW & EXACT MAPP OF THE ISLAND OF JAMAICA ...   [1684]   From *Laws of Jamaica*. Charles Bochart & Humphrey Knollis; printed for Charles Harper. 1st map of Jamaica to show roads. 3 sheets, each about 56x42cm (22x16½") Some OL col. Heavy restoration with loss at edges. Ref: MCC 42.   [46]   **£1,650** $2,736

BODENEHR

[ATLAS] PROVINCIARUM EUROPAE GEOGRAPHICA DESCRIPTIO   [1679]   Augsburg. Tall 12mo; full orig leather binding; double title page; 34 maps on spherical projection, 2 of all Europe, 32 of parts fitting together; 26 pp placenames. OL color. Fine.   [11]   £754 **$1,250**

BREISACH WIE ES AO. 1697 BEY SCHLIESSUNG DES RYSWYCKISCHEN FRIDENS GESTANDEN   [c.1720] Fortification plan with legend. 17x33cm (6½x13")   [48]   **DM 150** £52 $86

CARTA HYDROGRAPHICA ODER ALGEMEINE WELT UND COMMERCIEN CARTE   [1710]   Mercator projection; insular Calif. 15x23cm (6x9") Color.   [13]   **Aus$720** £327 $542

DER GANTZE WELT KRETS IN SEINEN ZWEY GROSSEN BEGRISSEN ...   [1704 - 1715]   Double hemis; sm polar hemis; insular Calif. 15x13cm (6x5") Orig color.   [11]   £136 **$225**

FREIBURG IM BRISGOW   [c.1720]   Fortification plan. 16x29cm (6½x11½")   [48]   **DM 290** £100 $166

LANDAU   [c.1720]   Fortification plan with legend. 16x22cm (6½x8½")   [48]   **DM 290** £100 $166

ST. OMER MITT NAHE ANLIEGENDER GEGEND   [c.1720]   16x27cm (6½x10½")   [48]   **DM 60** £21 $34

TRAPANO IN SICILIEN   [c.1720]   View from sea. 16x19cm (6x7½")   [48]   **DM 120** £41 $68

WISMAR   [c.1720]   Plan with legend. 16x23cm (6x9")   [48]   **DM 140** £48 $80

BOLTON

NORTH AMERICA. PERFORMED UNDER THE PATRONAGE OF LOUIS DUKE OF ORLEANS ... BY THE SIEUR D'ANVILLE. GREATLY IMPROVED BY MR. BOLTON. ENGRAVED BY R.W. SEALE ...   [1751]   As in *Postlethwayt's Dictionary of Commerce*. 4 sheets joined, 81x85cm (32x33½") Color. Ref: Sellers & Van Ee 13. Lowery 382; Wagner (NW) 552; Wheat (TM) 127; Phillips (M) p.571.   [34]   **£1,400** $2,322

SOUTH AMERICA PERFORMED UNDER THE PATRONAGE OF LOUIS   [1755]   Publ in *Postlethwayt's Dictionary of Commerce*. After D'Anville; Kitchin, sc. 3 sheets joined, 120x75cm (47x29½") Color.   [34]   **£400** $664

BONFRERIUS

TABULA GEOGRAPHICA TERRAE SANCTAE [c.1717] Leeuwarden: Halma. Multi-sheet map joined, 39x115cm (15½x45½") Scattered lt offsetting; few soft partial creases. Ref: cf Laor 117 & 118. [A8] £416 **$690**

BONNE

[ATLAS] ATLAS DE TOUTES LES PARTIES CONNUES DU GLOBE TERRESTRE [1780] Geneva: J.L. Pellet. Sm folio, new quarter leather binding; 50 double page maps. Exc. Ref: Phillips (A) 652. [33] £1,267 **$2,100**

AFRIQUE ... [1787] 21x32cm (8½x12½") ["L'Asie" offered at same price] [11] £30 **$50**

AMERIQUE MERIDIONALE [c.1780] 32x22cm (12½x8½") B&W. Fine (A+). [A4] £48 **$79**

AMERIQUE SEPTENTRIONALE ... [1780] From Raynal, *Atlas de Toutes les Parties Connues* ... Geneva. 22x32cm (8½x12½") B&W. Ref: Phillips (A) 652-25. [12] £96 **$160**

[SAME TITLE] [c.1780] From *Atlas de Toutes les Parties* ... 21x31cm (8½x12") OL color. Minor browning outer margins; o/w fine. Ref: Wheat (TM) 187; Sellers & Van Ee 170. [21] Can$150 £66 **$109**

[SAME TITLE] [1787] 21x31cm (8½x12½") Sl weak impression. [11] £75 **$125**

CARTE DE L'EMPIRE DE LA CHINE, DE LA TARTARIE CHINOISE, ET DU ROYAUME DE COREE: AVEC LES ISLES DU JAPON [c.1780] 32x21cm (12½x8") B&W. Printer's crease; else fine (A+). ["Carte de l'Empire de Russie en Europe et en Asie" sold at same price] [A4] £37 **$61**

[SAME TITLE] [1787] Incl Japan. 32x21cm (12½x8") ["La Presqu' Isle de l'Inde" & "Carte de l'Arabie, du Golfe Persique, et de la Mer Rouge, avec l'Egypte, la Nubie et l'Abissinie" offered as same price] [11] £45 **$75**

CARTE DE L'ISLE DE LA JAMAIQUE [1780] 22x32cm (8½x12½") B&W. Fine (A+). [A4] £70 **$116**

[SAME TITLE] [1787] 20x31cm (8x12½") [11] £48 **$80**

CARTE DE L'ISLE DE ST. DOMINGUE UNE DES GRANDES ANTILLES [1780] From *Atlas de Toutes les Parties Connues du Globe Terrestre* ... 21x31cm (8½x12½") B&W. Strong impression; Fine. Ref: Phillips (A) 652-37. [35] £45 **$75**

[SAME TITLE] [1787] 21x31cm (8½x12½") [11] £30 **$50**

CARTE DE LA LOUISIANE, ET DE LA FLORIDE [1778] 32x21cm (12½x8½") Newer color. Few margin tears; o/w fine. [A2] £150 **$248**

[SAME TITLE] [1782] 32x21cm (12½x8½") Orig OL color. Some stains. [36] £151 **$250**

[SAME TITLE] [1787] 32x21cm (12½x8½") On thin paper. [11] £112 **$185**

CARTE DE LA PARTIE NORD, DES ETATS UNIS, DE L'AMERIQUE SEPTENTRIONALE [1780] From *Atlas de Toutes les Parties Connues du Globe Terrestre* ... 21x32cm (8½x12½") Fine. [1787 edition (3mm ink stain in sea area) offered at same price] [11] £75 **$125**

[SAME TITLE] [1783] 23x33cm (9x13") Uncolored. VG. [25] £96 **$160**

CARTE DE LA PARTIE SUD DES ETATS UNIS DE L'AMERIQUE SEPTENTRIONALE [1780] Chesapeake to GA. 22x32cm (8½x12½") Ref: Sellers & Van Ee 1406. [11] £75 **$125**

[SAME TITLE] [c.1780] VA to GA. 21x31cm (8½x12½") Color. Fine. [A1] £100 **$165**

[SAME TITLE] [c.1785] Chesapeake to GA, west to Appalachians. 21x31cm (8½x12½") B&W. On fine paper; VG (A). [A4] £130 **$215**

CARTE DES COTES DE BARBARIE [c.1770] Paris. 32x46cm (12½x18") OL color. [A7] £42 **$69**

CARTE DES ISLES ANTILLES OU DU VENT AVEC LA PARTIE ORIENTALE DES ISLES SOUS LE VENT [1787] Lesser Antilles. 32x21cm (13x8") [11] £60 **$100**

CARTE DES REGIONS ET DES LIEUX DONT IL EST PARLE DANS LE NOUVEAU TESTAMENT [c.1771] Paris: Lattre. Insets: Jerusalem; Judaea. 30x44cm (12x17½") Color. Stain; else exc. Ref: Laor 121. [24] £271 **$450**

[SAME TITLE] [c.1780] 30x44cm (12x17½") OL color; uncolored cartouche. Spotting margin, couple spots near c'fold; tiny worm track in inset; overall clean, crisp (B). Ref: Laor 121. [A3] £62 **$103**

CARTE DU CANAL DE MOZAMBIQUE, CONTENANT L'ISLE DE MADAGASCAR ... AVEC LES COTES D'AFRIQUE, LE CAP DE BONNE ESPERANCE [1787] Inset of Cape region. 21x32cm (8½x12½") [11] £48 **$80**

CARTE DU GOUVERNMENT DE GUIENNE ET GASCOGNE, AVEC CELUI DE BEARN ET BASSE NAVARRE [1785] 41x29cm (16x11½") OL color. Minor damp staining at c'fold, else fine (B). [A3] £62 **$103**

CARTE GENERALE DES ISLES ... [BOURBON; ISLE DE FRANCE; RODRIGUES] [c.1780] French Indian Ocean islands. 21x32cm (8x12½") B&W. Fine (A+). [A4] £28 **$46**

CARTES DE SUPPLEMENT POUR LES ISLES ANTILLES [1782] Virgin Islands at top; 2 rows of 4 Caribbean island charts below. 24x35cm (9½x14") Color. [18] £106 **$175**

L'ANCIEN ET LE NOUVEAU MEXIQUE, AVEC LA FLORIDE ET LA BASSE LOUISIANE. PARTIE OCCIDENTALE [IN SET WITH] ... PARTIE ORIENTALE [1780] Both with "Pays des Cenis". 35x23cm (13½x9½") Full modern color. VG. [16] £302 **$500**

BONNE continued

L'ANCIEN MONDE ET LE NOUVEAU EN DEUX HEMISPHERES   [1780] From *Atlas des Toutes les Parties ...* Paris: Pellet. 22x41cm (9x16"). Color. Ref: Phillips (A) 5992-1.   [19]   £96 **$160**

[SAME TITLE]   [1780]   24x42cm (9½x16½") OL col. Soft creases; minor dampstaining.   [A7]   £208 **$345**

[SAME TITLE]   [1787]   21x41cm (8½x16") ["Planisphere Suivant la Projection de Mercator" offered at same price]   [11]   £75 **$125**

[SAME TITLE]   [c.1780] "Etats Unis" named. 21x41cm (8½x16") B&W. On heavy paper.   [27]   £75 **$125**

L'EMPIRE DE LA CHINE D'APRES L'ATLAS CHINOIS, AVEC LES ISLES DU JAPON   [c.1760] Probably from Lattre's *Atlas Moderne ...*   31x45cm (12½x17½") Orig OL color.   [11]   £151 **$250**

L'ISLE DE CUBA   [1787]   Incl Caymans, FL keys, part of Bahamas. 21x32cm (8½x12½")   [11]   £45 **$75**

LA BASSE GUINEE CONTENANT LES ROYAUMES DE LOANGO, DE CONGO, D'ANGOLA ET DE BENGUELA, AVEC LA CAFRERIE OCCIDENTALE ET LA MERIDIONALE, OU LE PAYS DES HOTENTOTS   [c.1780]   36x23cm (14x9") B&W. Few tiny spots; else VG (B).   [A4]   £29 **$48**

LA PRESQU'ISLE DE L'INDE AU DELA DU GANGE   [1787]   From *Atlas Encyclopedique*. SE Asia & Indonesia. 24x35cm (9½x13½"). Wash color.   [13]   **Aus$180** £82 $135

LES ETATS UNIS DE L'AMERIQUE SEPTENTRIONALE PARTIE OCCIDENTALE ...   [c.1770]   Lake Superior & Mississippi Basin. 35x23cm (13½x9½"). Newer color. Some soft printer's wrinkles. Ref: Sellers & Van Ee 794.   [A2]   £119 **$198**

LES ISLES ANTILLES ET LE GOLFE DU MEXIQUE   [1787]   21x32cm (8½x12½")   [11]   £112 **$185**

LES ISLES PHILIPPINES, CELLE DE FORMOSE, LE SUD DE LA CHINE, LES ROYAUMES DE TUNKIN, DE COCHINCHINE, DE CAMBOGE, DE SIAM, DES LAOS; AVEC PARTIE DE CEUX DE PEGU ET D'AVA   [1780] From *Atlas de Toutes les Parties Connues du Globe Terrestre ...* Andre, sc. 21x31cm (8½x12½") B&W. VG (A).   [A4]   £65 **$107**

[SAME TITLE]   [1787]   Incl Indo-China. Insets: Guam; Marianas. 21x32cm (8½x12½") ["Carte des Isles de la Sonde et des Isles Moluques" offered at same price]   [11]   £75 **$125**

N'LLE GALLES MERID'LE OU COTE ORIENTALE DE LA NOUVELLE HOLLANDE ...   [ON SHEET WITH] PARTIE DE LA COTE DE LA NOUVELLE GALLES MERIDIONALE   [AND]   ESQUISSE DE LA TERRE VAN-DIEMEN   [AND]   BAIE BOTANIQUE   [AND]   ENTREE DE LA RIVIERE ENDEAVOUR   [1788]   From *Atlas Encyclopedique*. 4 maps by Cook. 24x35cm (9½x13½"). Orig color. Ref: Clancy (Australis) ill. p.98; cf Tooley (Australia) 233 & 234.   [13]   **Aus$440** £200 $331

PARTIE DU NORD DE L'AMERIQUE SEPTENTRIONALE POUR SERVIR A L'HISTOIRE PHILOSOPHIQUE ET POLITIQUE DES ETABLISSEMENS ET DU COMMERCE DES EUROPEENS DAN DEUX INDES   [c.1780] Eastern North America. 28x21cm (11x8") OL color. VG (A).   [A3]   £106 **$176**

PARTIE MERIDIONALE DE L'ANCIEN MEXIQUE OU DE LA NOUVLE ESPAGNE   [c.1780]   S Mexico to Panama. 21x32cm (8x12½") B&W. Old c'fold repair verso; good (B).   [A4]   £20 **$33**

[SAME TITLE]   [1783]   From Raynal's *Atlas de Toutes les Parties Connues du Globe Terrestre ...* South to Panama. 21x32cm (8x12½") B&W. Fine (A+).   [A3]   £27 **$44**

PARTIE OCCIDENTALE DU CANADA, CONTENANT LES CINQ GRANDS LACS, AVEC LES PAYS CIRCONVOISINS   [1780]   With trade routes, Indian tribes, forts. 22x32cm (8½x12½") 2 minor worm holes repaired, no loss. Ref: Seller & Van Ee 173.   [7]   £90 **$150**

[SAME TITLE]   [1780]   22x32cm (8½x12½") Ref: Seller & Van Ee 173.   [11]   £136 **$225**

[SAME TITLE]   1780]   With trade routes, Indian tribes, forts. 21x31cm (8x12½") OL & wash color.   [41]   £136 **$225**

BONNEVILLE

MAP TO ILLUSTRATE CAPT. BONNEVILLE'S ADVENTURES AMONG THE ROCKY MOUNTAINS ...   [1850]   As in vol.X, *The Works of Washington Irving* NY: Putnam/Colton. Mississippi to Pacific. 28x45cm (11x18") Lt toning folds; old repair binding tear; overall VG (A). Ref: Howes (US) I-85.   [A4]   £201 **$333**

BORDONE

[ATLAS]   ISOLARIO DI BENEDETTO BORDONE NEL QUAL SI RAGIONA DI TUTTE LE ISOLE DEL MONDO   [1537]   Sm folio; full modern calf. Wood cut maps: 6 double-page & 108 smaller in text. Greece map trimmed close; o/w exc. Ref: Incl "Terra de Lavaratore" Burden 8. Sabin 6420.   [3]   £9,046 **$15,000**

[WEST INDIES: ST. CROIX & ANTIQUA TO DOMINICA]   [1534]   From *Isolario ...*   Wood engraving on quarto page. 10x15cm (4x6") Ref: Sabin 6419.   [18]   £293 **$485**

SCILAM   [1528]   From *Isole del Mondo*. Ceylon. 8x14cm (3x5½")   [11]   £51 **$85**

BORY de SAINT-VINCENT

[ATLAS] VOYAGE DANS LES QUATRE PRINCIPALES ISLES DES MERS D'AFRIQUE [1804] Paris. Sm folio atlas vol; 58 maps & plates; quarter roan. Sl dampstaining throughout. [A7] £416 **$690**

BOTERO

ASIA [c.1595] Rome. 20x24cm (8x9½") Lf margin trimmed almost to rule. [A7] £156 **$258**
REGNUM CHINAE [(1596) c.1600] Appeared in Metellus' *Asia Tabulis Aenets*. 15x21cm (6x8") Uncolored. Exc. [4] £495 **$821**

BOUGAINVILLE

PLAN OF ACARRON BAY SITUATED AT THE EAST POINT OF THE MALOUINE ISLANDS [ON SHEET WITH] A VIEW OF FORT ST. LOUIS AT ACCARON BAY [1773] From English ed of voyages. Probably Stanley, Falkland Islands. 26x24cm (10½x9½") [40] £42 **$70**

BOURGOIN

CARTE UNIVERSELLE DE PTOLOMEE [1750] Eastern hemi combines Ptolemaic & modern world. Bourgoin, sc. 14x19cm (5½x7½") Color. [13] Aus$220 £100 **$166**

BOWEN

A MAP OF BOSTON COUNTY OF SUFFOLK AND THE ADJACENT TOWNS [c.1830] From Abel Bowen, *A Picture of Boston*. 31x31cm (12x12") Orig wash & OL color. Some folds repaired; rice paper backing; good. Ref: Phillips (M) p.155. [31] £172 **$285**

BOWEN, EMANUEL

[WORLD] [1765] Conventional double hemi with oblique hemi over Middle East & geometric diagrams. 18x30cm (7x12") Color. [19] £87 **$145**

A CORRECT DRAUGHT OF THE NORTH POLE AND OF ALL THE COUNTRIES HITHERTO DISCOVERED, INTERCEPTED BETWEEN THE POLE AND THE PARALLEL OF 50 DEGREES ... [1764] 39x44cm (15½x17½") [11] £112 **$185**

A MAP OF INDIA ON THE WEST SIDE OF THE GANGES ... [1764] Indian peninsula. 32x23cm (12½x9") ["India, As Described ... before the Fifth Century" offered at same price] [11] £36 **$60**

A MAP OF THE DISCOVERIES MADE BY CAPTN. WILLM. DAMPIER IN THE ROEBUCK IN 1699 [c.1760] New Guinea area. 20x32cm (8x12½") [11] £136 **$225**

A MAP OF THE KINGDOM OF IRELAND FROM YE LATEST & BEST OBSERVATIONS [1744] R.W. Seale, sc. 48x38cm (19x15") Orig OL color; full color cartouche. Folds as issued, lt toning at a fold; narrow margins; lt image transfer, Irish Sea; minute pinhole blank area; o/v VG to fine. [A1] £103 **$171**

A NEW & ACCURATE CHART OF THE WORLD ... [1744] 36x57cm (14x22½") Newer OL color. Crease at lower corners; faint age toning c'fold; o/w VG. [A2] £630 **$1,045**

A NEW & ACCURATE MAP OF ALL THE KNOWN WORLD ... [c.1750] Double hemi. 31x54cm (12x21") Side margins trimmed to platemark; few closed tears into image; some soiling, graying; paper-backed. [A8] £277 **$460**

A NEW & ACCURATE MAP OF ASIA DRAWN FROM ACTUAL SURVEYS ... [c.1752] 34x42cm (13½x16½") Sm separations c'fold ends; sm tape repair; o/w good. [21] Can$220 £96 **$159**

A NEW & ACCURATE MAP OF LOUISIANA, WITH PART OF FLORIDA AND CANADA, AND THE ADJACENT COUNTRIES ... [c.1750] 34x42cm (13½x16½") Uncolored. C'fold sl rubbed, soiled, 2" separation; margin soiled; tiny spot at ctr; faint vert line in image rt. [A10] £208 **$345**

A NEW & ACCURATE MAP OF SCOTLAND OR NORTH BRITAIN [c.1744] Table of shires & boroughs. 42x35cm (16½x13½") OL color. Fold split; imperfect repair; else clean; good (B). [A4] £63 **$105**
[SAME TITLE] [1744] 43x36cm (17x14") Later full col. Lt toning & uplifting at c'fold; VG+. [35] £81 **$135**

A NEW & ACCURATE MAP OF THE ISLAND OF ANTIGUA OR ANTEGO, TAKEN FROM SURVEYS, AND ADJUSTED BY ASTRONL. OBSERVATIONS [1744] 32x23cm (12½x9") Full color. [20] £211 **$350**

A NEW & ACCURATE MAP OF THE ISLANDS OF NEWFOUNDLAND, CAPE BRETON, ST. JOHN AND ANTICOSTA; TOGETHER WITH THE NEIGHBOURING COUNTRIES OF NOVA SCOTIA, CANADA, &C. [c.1744] 35x43cm (14x17") Color. [A7] £83 **$138**

A NEW & ACCURATE MAP OF THE NORTH POLE, WITH ALL THE COUNTRIES HITHERTO DISCOVERED SITUATED NEAR OR ADJACENT TO IT ... [1747] 38x43cm (15x16½") Top margin trimmed to platemark; sl browning at fold; washed, 6 text words partially bleached. [A8] £139 **$230**

A NEW & CORRECT MAP OF THE NETHERLANDS OR LOW COUNTRIES ... [c.1747] From *Rapin's History of England*. 43x34cm (17x13½") Full old color. Fine. [1] £241 **$400**

BOWEN, EMANUEL continued

A New and Accurate Chart of the West Indies with the Adjacent Coasts of North and South America ... [1764] Chesapeake to Spanish Main. 37x45cm (14½x18") [11] £256 **$425**

A New and Accurate Chart of the Western or Atlantic Ocean ... [1764] 37x45cm (14½x17½") [11] £172 **$285**

A New and Accurate Map of America ... Exhibiting the Course of the Trade Winds both in the Atlantic & Pacific Oceans [1744-48] From John Harris' *Navigantium ... Voyages and Travels*. London. 36x44cm (14x17½") B&W. 2 vert folds as issued; VF. Ref: Marshall I-108-2-6. [12] £196 **$325**

A New and Accurate Map of America Drawn from the Most Approved Modern Maps and Charts ... [1764] 35x45cm (13½x17½") [11] £256 **$425**

A New and Accurate Map of Europe ... [1764] 37x45cm (14½x17½") [11] £57 **$95**

A New and Accurate Map of Italy Drawn from the Latest and Best Authorities, and Regulated by the Most Approved Astronl. Observations [n.d.] Insets of volcanoes. 31x22cm (12½x8½") OL color. Fine. [14] £211 **$350**

A New and Accurate Map of Paraguay, Rio de la Plata, Tucumania Guarias &c. [1747] 36x43cm (14x17") OL color. [A7] £139 **$230**

A New and Accurate Map of Portugal Comprised from the Latest Improvemts. and Adjusted by the Most Authentic Astronl. Observats. [1746] 31x22cm (12½x8½") OL color. Fine. [14] £136 **$225**

A New and Accurate Map of Switzerland with Its Allies and Subjects, Composed from Its Most Approv'd Maps &c. and Regulated by Astronoml. Observatns. [1746] Geneva inset. 32x22cm (12½x9") OL color. Fine. [14] £211 **$350**

A New and Accurate Map of Terra Firma and the Caribbe Islands Drawn from the Most Approved Modern Maps & Charts ... [17747] Cuba to Amazon Basin. 36x43cm (14x17") Color. [18] £256 **$425**

A New and Accurate Map of the Empire of Japan ... [1744] Publ in *A Complete System of Geography*. State 2. 36x43cm (14x17") B&W. Exc. Ref: Cortazzi pl.81; Campbell (Japan) 61; Walter 92. [4] **£800** $1,327

A New and Accurate Map of the Kingdom of Hungary and Principality of Transilvania with the Bordering Countries Drawn from the Best Authorities Assisted by the Most Approved Modern Maps ... [1744] 34x42cm (13½x16½") OL color. Lt age toning along c'fold; some lt surface soiling; faint image transfer in blank areas; VG. [A1] £66 **$110**

A New and Accurate Map of the Kingdoms of Naples & Sicily ... [c.1744] 31x22cm (12½x8½") OL color. Fine. [A1] £66 **$110**

A New and Accurate Map of the World Drawn from the Best Authorities and Regulated by Astronomical Observations: Describing the Course of Each of the Following Circum-Navigators Vizt Ferdinand Magellan, Sr. Francis Drake and Commodore Anson [1764] Oval proj; title above. 29x55cm (11½x21½") [11] £332 **$550**

A New and Correct Chart of All the Known World Laid Down According to Mercator's Projection. Exhibiting All the Late Discoveries & Improvements: the Whole Being Collected from the Most Authentic Journals, Charts &c [1748] 36x46cm (14½x18") [11] £226 **$375**

A New and Correct Map of Africa Drawn from the Most Approved Modern Maps and Charts ... [1748] Winds & currents shown. 37x45cm (14½x17½") [11] £106 **$175**

A New and Correct Map of North America ... West India Islands [c.1755 - 1779] With John Gibson, sc; frequently reissued with revisions. 102x115cm (40x45½") Orig OL color. Good. Ref: Tooley (Amer) p.82, 49g. [34] **£2,200** $3,648

A New and Exact Map of Asia ... [1764] 37x46cm (14½x18") [11] £112 **$185**

A New General Map of America, Drawn from Several Accurate Particular Maps & Charts ... [c.1744] 35x42cm (14x16½") Color. Faint image transfer in c'fold blank areas; few lt spots; o/w fine. [A1] £332 **$550**

A New Map of Georgia with Part of Carolina, Florida, and Louisiana ... [1748] 1st map to feature Georgia; west to Mississippi R. 36x48cm (14½x19") Pristine. Ref: Cumming (SE) 267. [24] £1,327 **$2,200**

An Accurate Chart of the Mediterranean and Adriatic Seas with the Archipelago and Part of the Black Sea [1748] 29x59cm (11½x23½") [11] £75 **$125**

[SAME TITLE] [1748] Portolan style from Rochelle to Crimea. 29x58cm (11½x23") OL color. Lf margin trimmed close; else fine. [37] £226 **$375**

An Accurate Map of Italy ... [1764] From Guthrie's *General History of the World*. 24x22cm (9½x9") Lower lf margin cut away; image unaffected; o/w clean. [21] Can$110 £48 $80

BOWEN, EMANUEL continued

AN ACCURATE MAP OF THE COUNTY OF SURREY ... [c.1760] London: Sayer; printed for C. Bowles. Linen-backed, folding into orig slip case. 36x72cm (14x28½") Orig OL color. Wear at folds & case, no loss. [11] £106 **$175**

AN ACCURATE MAP OF THE EAST INDIES EXHIBITING THE COURSE OF THE EUROPEAN TRADE BOTH ON THE CONTINENT AND ISLANDS ... [1764] India to the islands. 37x45cm (14½x18") [11] £196 **$325**

AN ACCURATE MAP OF THE MOREA TOGETHER WITH NEIGHBOURING COUNTRIES IN GREECE; ALSO THE ISLANDS ... [1764] 22x32cm (8½x13") [11] £60 **$100**

AN ACCURATE MAP OF THE WEST INDIES [c.1760] 36x42cm (14x16½") Color. Minor browning lower margin. [A7] £173 **$287**

AN ACCURATE MAP OF THE WORLD LAID DOWN FROM THE MOST APPROVED MAPS & CHARTS & REGULATED BY ASTRONL. OBSERVATIONS BY EMAN. BOWEN 1747 [1747] Double hemi. 15x25cm (6x10") Color. [19] £142 **$235**

CAMBRIDGE SHIRE, DIVIDED INTO HUNDREDS [1767] From *Atlas Anglicanus*. 32x23cm (12½x9") Orig OL color. [11] £106 **$175**

DRAUGHTS AND PLANS OF SOME OF THE PRINCIPAL TOWNS AND HARBOURS BELONGING TO THE ENGLISH, FRENCH, AND SPANIARDS IN AMERICA AND THE WEST INDIES [1747] 13 maps & plans on sheet. 36x43cm (14x17") [A6] £517 **$858**

DURHAM [1767] From *Atlas Anglicanus*. Emanuel & Thomas Bowen, sc. 22x32cm (8½x12½") Orig OL color. Good. [11] £54 **$90**

NUOVA ESATTA CARTA DELL' ASIA ... [c.1780] Italian engraving (Rome?) of 1747 Bowen map. 34x42cm (13½x16½") Uncolored. [34] £360 **$597**

THE GALLAPAGOS ISLANDS DISCOVERED AND DESCRIBED BY CAPT. COWLEY IN 1684 [1764] 32x21cm (12½x8½") ["A Map of Marco Polo's Voyages and Travels in the 13th Century ..." offered at same price] [11] £90 **$150**

THE WORLD INCLUDING THE DISCOVERIES MADE BY CAPT. COOK [1782] Double hemi; north polar inset. 27x45cm (10½x18") Color. [19] £256 **$425**

BOWEN, THOMAS

A MERCATOR CHART OF THE WORLD ... [1778] American NW coast "according to the Japanese". 34x45cm (13½x18") Full color. VG+. [38] £302 **$500**

A NEW & ACCURATE CHART OF THE WESTERN OR ATLANTIC OCEAN, DRAWN FROM THE MOST APPROVED MODERN MAPS &C. BY THOS. BOWEN 1778 [1778] With adjacent lands. 22x27cm (8½x10½") [11] £51 **$85**

A NEW & ACCURATE MAP OF NORTH AMERICA ... [1778] Incl sketchy Sea & River of the West. 27x43cm (10½x17") OL color. A crease; else VG. [38] £232 **$385**

A NEW & ACCURATE MAP OF NORTH AMERICA; DRAWN FROM THE MOST AUTHENTIC MODERN MAPS [1779] From *Middleton's Complete System of Geography*. 27x43cm (10½x17") Later full color. Faint soiling top margin & c'fold; else clean, fresh. Framed. [A10] £111 **$184**

A NEW AND ACCURATE CHART OF THE WESTERN OR ATLANTIC OCEAN, DRAWN FROM THE MOST APPROVED MODERN MAPS ETC. BY THOS. BOWEN 1778 [1778] From *Middleton's Geography*. 21x27cm (8½x10½") B&W. Top margin trimmed to neat line; bit browned & creased; o/w/ good. [21] Can$120 £52 **$87**

NEW & ACCURATE MAP OF NORTH AMERICA INCLUDING NOOTKA SOUND: WITH THE NEW DISCOVERED ISLANDS ON THE NORTH EAST COAST OF ASIA [c.1790] 26x43cm (10½x17") Uncolored. VG. [A2] £349 **$578**

THE WORLD INCLUDING THE DISCOVERIES OF CAPT. COOK AND OTHER CIRCUMNAVIGATORS ... [c.1794] From *Bankes Geography*. Double hemi; North Polar inset. 34x46cm (13½x18") Later full color. VG. [25] £181 **$300**

THE WORLD, INCLUDING THE LATE DISCOVERIES, BY CAPTN. COOK AND OTHER CIRCUM NAVIGATORS [1779] Double hemi; North Polar inset. 27x46cm (10½x18") [11] £452 **$750**

BOWLES

A MAP OF THE MOST INHABITED PART OF NEW ENGLAND CONTAINING THE PROVINCES OF MASSACHUSETTS BAY AND NEW HAMPSHIRE WITH THE COLONIES OF CONECTICUT AND RHODE ISLAND ... [c.1765] 1st ed of Bowles reduction of Jefferys 4-sheet map. 64x52cm (25½x20½") Color. Margins trimmed but ample, sides remargined; soft crease near orig fold; sh closed tears. Ref: Tooley (Amer) p.69, #32. [A8] £3,052 **$5,060**

BOWLES continued

A NEW AND EXACT MAP OF THE ISLAND OF ANTIGUA IN AMERICA ACCORDING TO AN ACTUAL AND ACCURATE SURVEY MADE IN THE YEARS 1746, 1747 & 1748. DESCRIBING THE LIMITS & BOUNDARIES OF THE SEVERAL PARISHES, WITH THE CHURCHES ... [1748-49] By Robert Baker. English Harbour inset. "Printed for Carington Bowles ... & Wilkinson ... Price 10s 6d". On 4 joined sheets 114x142cm (45x56") Orig OL boundary color. Minor brown spot under title; exc. [20] £12,967 **$21,500**

A NEW AND EXACT MAP OF THE ISLAND OF ST. CHISTOPHER IN AMERICA ACCORDING TO AN ACTUAL AND ACCURATE SURVEY MADE IN THE YEAR 1753. DESCRIBING SEVERAL PARISHES, WITH THEIR RESPECTIVE LIMITS, CONTENTS & CHURCHES ... [1753] By Samuel Baker. "Printed for Carington Bowles ... & John Bowles ... Price 10s 6d". On 4 joined sheets 114x142cm (45x56") Orig OL boundary color. Exc. [20] £11,157 **$18,500**

A NEW CHART OF THE VAST ATLANTIC OR WESTERN OCEAN [1771] 46x56cm (18x22") OL color. Scattered foxing; bit browned along fold. [A8] £191 **$316**

BOWLES'S EUROPEAN GEOGRAPHICAL AMUSEMENT, OR GAME OF GEOGRAPHY; DESIGNED FROM THE GRAND TOUR OF EUROPE, BY DR. NUGENT [1770] Segmented, mounted on linen as issued, with orig slipcase, pasted title. 102 stops on Grand Tour listed at sides. 48x68cm (19x27") Orig wash color. Case scuffed; linen worn at intersections; map exc. [24] £724 **$1,200**

BOWLES'S NEW POCKET MAP OF THE FOLLOWING INDEPENDENT STATES OF NORTH AMERICA, VIZ. VIRGINIA, MARYLAND, DELAWARE, PENNSYLVANIA, NEW JERSEY, NEW YORK, CONNECTICUT & RHODE ISLAND ... LEWIS EVANS [1784] Post-Revolutionary issue. 50x64cm (19½x25") Full orig wash color. Exc. Ref: H.N. Stevens, *Lewis Evans His Map*, XVII. [23] £1,960 **$3,250**

THE BRITISH & FRENCH DOMINIONS IN NORTH AMERICA ... [c.1755] 43x56cm (17x22") Full orig color. Exc. [36] £1,628 **$2,700**

BRADFORD

[ATLAS] A COMPREHENSIVE ATLAS GEOGRAPHICAL, HISTORICAL & COMMERCIAL [1835] T.G. Bradford. Quarto, orig calf; 180 pp; maps, incl Texas, with orig OL color. Corners sl worn; hinges rubbed; some foxing; superior copy. [16] £1,357 **$2,250**

[UNITED STATES: 15 CITY PLANS] [1835] From *Comprehensive Atlas* ... 25x19cm (10x7½") Wash color. [40] £21 **$35**

AFRICA [1835] Ctr is "... Unexplored". 19x25cm (7½x10") OL color. [40] £21 **$35**

ALABAMA [1838. probably 1842] From *Universal Illustrated Atlas*. Bradford & Goodrich (as Plate no.36.) 36x29cm (14x11½") Color. Sl dampstain lower margin; else exc. Ref: Birmingham Pub. Lib. 38; cf Phillips (A) 783.34. [12] £106 **$175**

[SAME TITLE] [1842] 36x29cm (14½x11½") Color by county. Occas foxing margins; VG. [5] £72 **$120**

[SAME TITLE] [1842] 24x19cm (9½x7½") OL color. [40] £45 **$75**

ARKANSAS [1842] 28x36cm (11x14") Color by county. Occas foxing margins; VG. [5] £66 **$110**

CHINA, JAPAN &C. [1835] From *Comprehensive Atlas* ... 20x25cm (8x10") OL color. Lt foxing margins, minor spots image; VG (A). [A4] £9 **$15**

DELAWARE [1838] From *Illustrated Atlas* ... By Fielding Lucas; Boynton, sc. 36x29cm (14½x11½") Orig color. Faint darkening bottom rt; o/w fine. [14] £136 **$225**

FLORIDA [1842] 36x29cm (14x11½") Color by county. Occas foxing margins; staining around panhandle; VG. ["Louisiana" offered at same price] [5] £84 **$140**

GEORGIA [1838] From *Illustrated Atlas*. Boynton, sc. 36x32cm (14x12½") OL color. Some lt surface soiling; o/w VG to fine. [14] £96 **$160**

[SAME TITLE] [1838 (1841)] From S.G. Goodrich, *General Atlas of the World* ... (Goodrich later Bradford's partner) Updated from 1838. 36x29cm (14x11½") Full color (incl slate blue). Damp stain upper rt margin; else exc. Ref: Johnsen (GA) 188; Phillips (A) 6092. [12] £106 **$175**

IOWA AND WISCONSIN [1842] 36x29cm (14½x11½") Color by county. Occas foxing margins; VG. [5] £109 **$180**

ITALY [1835] From *Comprehensive Atlas* ... 25x20cm (10x8") OL color. Lt toning; little margin foxing; VG (A). [A3] £22 **$36**

KENTUCKY [1838] From *Illustrated Atlas*. 29x37cm (11½x14½") Orig OL color. Fine. [A1] £40 **$66**

LOUISIANA [1838] From *Illustrated Atlas*. 29x36cm (11½x14½") Orig color by parishes. Fine. [A2] £96 **$160**

MAP OF THE UNITED STATES AND TEXAS ... [c.1839] Stiles, Sherman & Smith. Hartford: Burgess. TX at ctr. Inset: Mexico & Guatimala. 27x45cm (10½x17½") Full col. Browned, waterstained; fair. [16] £196 **$325**

BRADFORD continued

MARYLAND [1838 (!841)] From S.G. Goodrich, *General Atlas* ... (Goodrich later Bradford's partner.) 29x36cm (11½x14") Full color. Spots lower margin; else perfect. Ref: cf Papenfuse & Coale p.72; Phillips 6092-27. [12] £90 **$150**

[SAME TITLE] [1842] From *Illustrated Atlas*. 29x36cm (11x14") Color by county. Occas foxing margins; VG. [PA, NC, SC, GA, KY, OH, IN, IL offered at same price] [5] £60 **$100**

MISSISSIPPI [1838 (1841)] From S.G. Goodrich, *General Atlas* ... (Goodrich later Bradford's partner). 37x29cm (14½x11½") Full color. Ref: Phillips (A) 6092-37. [12] £81 **$135**

MISSISSIPPI & ALABAMA [1835] From a quarto atlas. 20x25cm (8x10") Orig OL col. VG. [14] £84 **$140**

MISSOURI [1842] Undivided Platte County. 29x36cm (11½x14") Color by county. Occas foxing margins; VG. ["Michigan" offered at same price] [5] £96 **$160**

NEW HAMPSHIRE [1838] From *Illustrated Atlas ... of the United States*. 37x28cm (14½x11") Full color. Fine. Ref: Cobb (NH) 130. [12] £90 **$150**

[SAME TITLE] [1838 (1841)] From S.G. Goodrich, *General Atlas* ... (Goodrich later Bradford's partner). Belknap & Carroll Counties present. 36x29cm (14x11½") Full color. Minor dampstain upper rt corner; else fine. Ref: Phillips (A) 6092-11; cf Cobb (NH) 140. [12] £75 **$125**

NEW YORK [1835] 20x25cm (8x10") Orig OL color. 2 margin tears repaired with archival tape; o/w VG to fine. [14] £90 **$150**

NEW YORK [1838] 28x36cm (11x14½") Orig color by counties. VG to fine. [A1] £66 **$110**

NORTH AMERICA [1838] From *Illustrated Atlas*. Independent Texas. 37x28cm (14½x11") OL color. Ref: Phillips (M) p.602. [12] £96 **$160**

PHILADELPHIA [1842] 36x28cm (14x11") Color. Occas foxing margins; VG. [5] £78 **$130**

SOUTH CAROLINA [1838] From *Illustrated Atlas*. 29 counties. 28x37cm (11x14½") Color. On heavy paper; fine. Ref: cf Karpinski (Carolina) 154. [12] £112 **$185**

[SAME TITLE] [1838] 29x36cm (11½x14") Full orig color. Exc. [36] £151 **$250**

[SAME TITLE] [1838] From *Illustrated Atlas*. 29x37cm (11½x14½") Orig OL color by counties. Lt margin soiling upper lf; lt watermark on back; o/w VG to fine. [A1] £50 **$83**

TENNESSEE & KENTUCKY [1835] From *Comprehensive Atlas* ... 20x25cm (8x10") Orig OL color. Exc. [36] £90 **$150**

TEXAS [1842] Texas Republic; shows land grants & "Austin's Colony". 36x29cm (14x11") Color. Occas foxing margins; VG. [5] £356 **$590**

UNITED STATES [1835] With sm Texas republic. 20x25cm (8x10") OL color. Few sm stains; good. [16] £106 **$175**

[SAME TITLE] [1836] With Republic of Texas, large Iowa & Oregon Territories. 20x25cm (8x10") OL color. Some staining & spots; good. [16] £136 **$225**

UNITED STATES [1838] To Pacific; TX is part of Mexico. 36x58cm (14½x23") Orig color. C'fold split sl into image repaired verso; faint image transfer; sl surface soiling; o/w VG. Ref: Wheat (TM) 430. Van Ermen 50. [A2] £249 **$413**

UNITED STATES, EXHIBITING THE RAILROADS & CANALS [1835] 1st ed. 19x25cm (7½x9½") OL color. Few spots margin; VG (A). [A4] £65 **$107**

VERMONT [1838] Boynton, sc. 36x29cm (14x11½") OL color by counties; VG. ["New Jersey" offered at same price] [14] £106 **$175**

[SAME TITLE] [1838] From *Illustrated Atlas*. 28x39cm (11x15½") Full color. On heavy paper, wide margins; clean, bright. Ref: Phillips (A) 11028-25. [12] £112 **$185**

[SAME TITLE] [1838] From *Illustrated Atlas*. 29x37cm (11½x14½") Orig OL color by counties. Lt soiling upper rt margin; lt watermark on back; o/w VG to fine. [A1] £63 **$105**

WASHINGTON [ON SHEET WITH] CINCINNATI [AND] NEW ORLEANS [AND] LOUISVILLE [1838] 4 city plans. 29x36cm (11½x14½") Full color. Ref: Tooley (Amer) pl.113. [22] £33 **$55**

WESTERN HEMISPHERE [IN SET WITH] EASTERN HEMISPHERE [1835] From *Comprehensive Atlas* ... Each 24x19cm (9½x7½") Orig OL color. Fine. [36] £121 **$200**

[SAME TITLE] [1841] Goodrich edition of Bradford atlas. Each Diameter: 29cm (11½") Full color. Little foxing; overall nice. [40] £60 **$100**

BRADLEY Try *Mitchell, S.A. (Atlas Maps 1860 & Later)*

COLORADO [1886] 42x57cm (16½x22½") Full orig color. Exc. ["Dakota" (ND & SD) offered at same price] [36] £75 **$125**

COUNTY AND TOWNSHIP MAP OF DAKOTA [1882] 36x29cm (14x11½") Orig color. Fine. [14] £39 **$65**

BRADLEY continued

COUNTY AND TOWNSHIP MAP OF MONTANA IDAHO AND WYOMING   [1887]   37x55cm (14½x21½")
Color.   [10]   £81   **$135**

MONTANA, IDAHO AND WYOMING   [1886]   Much detail. 38x56cm (15x22")   OL color.   [7]   £90   **$150**

RAILROAD MAP OF THE UNITED STATES TOGETHER WITH THE VARIOUS STEAMSHIP LINES ALONG THE SEABOARD   [1889]   37x58cm (14½x23")   RRs in orange, o/w uncolored.   [22]   £24   **$40**

UTAH AND NEVADA   [1894]   38x57cm (15x22½")   Full color. VG (A).   [A3]   £33   **$55**

BRAUN & HOGENBERG

[FACSIMILE ATLAS] BESCHREIBUNG UND CONTRAFACTUR DER VORNEMBSTER STAET DER WELT   [1965] Plochingen, Germany.   1574 German ed in 6 folio volumes, imitation leather gilt. Complete color.
[A7]   £659   **$1,092**

[FACSIMILE ATLAS] CIVITATES ORBIS TERRARUM   [1965]   Germany: Muller und Schindler. Orig publ 1572-1618.   6 folio vols; leatherette & gilt ctr & corner panels. Printed color.   [21]   **Can$1,750**   £765 $1,269

[SAME TITLE]   [1966]   Cleveland & NY.   6 volumes in 3; folio; wrappers, contents loose as issued, 3 cloth-backed folding cases. Some color duplicate plates.   [A7]   £485   **$805**

[SAME TITLE]   [1966]   Cleveland.   Folio, 3 vols, cloth; reproduction of 1572-1618 ed at Amsterdam University. Ex lib; inked shelf numbers; ink stamp titles.   [A8]   £347   **$575**

ADEN, ARABIAE FOELICIS EMPORIUM CELEBERRIMI NOMINIS, QUO EX INDIA, AETHIOPIA ...   [ON SHEET WITH] MOMBAZA [AND] QUILOA [AND] CEFALA   [c.1572]   Aden in upper half. 33x47cm (13x18½"). Full color, bit oxidized. Sh repaired tear; good (B).   [A4]   £216   **$358**

AELST. - ALOSTUM, URBS FLANDRIAE IMPERATORIAE FIRMISSIMA   [1588]   Bird's-eye view. 33x42cm (13x16½")   Old color.   [48]   DM 450   £155   **$257**

ALEXANDRIA   [c.1572]   36x48cm (14½x19")   Color.   [A7]   £347   **$575**

ALEXANDRIA, VETUSTISSIMUM AEGYPTI EMPORIUM, AMPLISSIMA CIVITAS ...   [1575-]   36x48cm (14½x19")   Uncolored.   [34]   £450   **$746**

ALTEN STETTIN   [c.1600]   Bird's-eye view. 34x48cm (13x19")   Color.   [48]   DM 1,400   £483   **$801**

AMSTELODAMUM ...   [1617]   2nd B&H plan; shows new canals since 1572 version. 27x39cm (11x15½") Orig color. Lower c'fold reinforced; VG.   [23]   £724   **$1,200**

AMSTELREDAMUM, NOBILE INFERIORIS GERMANIAE OPPIDUM ...   [c.1572]   From Part I, *Civitates Orbis Terrarum*. Bird's-eye view. 33x48cm (13x19")   Color. Exc.   [4]   £775 $1,285

ANTIQUAE URBIS ROMAE IMAGO ACCURATISS: [1588]   From Part IV, *Civitates Orbis Terrarum*. 2 sheets joined. 68x50cm (27x19½")   Color. Exc.   [4]   £1,350 $2,239

[SAME TITLE]   [1588]   From *Civitates* ...   269 item key. Two sheets joined 69x50cm (27x19½")   Full orig color. Exc.   [23]   £1,809   **$3,000**

ANVERPIA   [c.1572]   From *Civitates Orbis Terrarum*. 34x48cm (13½x18½")   Orig color. Lt paper toning.
[4]   **£600** $995

ARRAS. ATREBATUM, FERTILISSIMAE ARTESIA URBS PRIMARIA, ELEGANTISSIMO SITU ...   [c.1580] Bird's-eye view. 35x47cm (13½x18½")   Old color.   [48]   DM 390   £135 $223

AUGUSTODUNUM [ON SHEET WITH] NOVIODUNUM   [1590]   Bird's-eye view of Autun & Nevers, side by side. 34x42cm (13½x16½")   Color. Sl margin foxing.   [A1]   £123   **$204**

[SAME TITLE]   [c.1575]   From *Civitates Orbis Terrarum*. 34x42cm (13x16½")   Full later color. Lt foxing margins; 2 spots in image; else fine (A).   [A3]   £219   **$363**

BARCELONA, BARCINO, QUE VULGO BARCELONA DICITUR   [ON SHEET WITH] ECIJA   [c.1572]   From *Civitates* ... 32x47cm (13x18½")   Full color. Strong impression; VG (A). Ref: Goss (Euro Cities) pl.6.   [A4]   £265   **$440**

BASILEA   [c.1580]   Basle bird's-eye view. 37x38cm (14½x15")   Old color. Sh margin tear at c'fold restored.   [48]   DM 2,300   £794 $1,317

BRIGHTSTOWE   [c.1580]   34x44cm (13½x17")   Mounted; 2 faint marks at c'fold. ["Nordovicum" in similar condition sold at same price]   [A5]   £138 $229

BRUXELLA, URBS AULICORUM FREQUENTIA, FONTIUM COPIA, MAGNIFICENTIA PRINCIPALIS AULAE ...
[c.1572]   From Part I, *Civitates Orbis Terrarum*. 33x47cm (13x18½")   Color. Exc.   [4]   £650 $1,078

[SAME TITLE]   [1572]   34x48cm (13½x18½")   Color. VG. Ref: Goss (Euro Cities) pl.12.   [24]   £844   **$1,400**

BYZANTIUM, NUNC CONSTANTINOPOLIS   [1572]   32x48cm (13x19")   Full orig color. a verdigris area reinforced; else exc.   [24]   £1,809   **$3,000**

CAIRUS, QUAE OLIM BABYLON; AEGYPTI MAXIMA URBS   [1572]   33x48cm (13x19")   Full orig color. Exc.
[44]   £905   **$1,500**

BRAUN & HOGENBERG continued

CANDIA [ON SHEET WITH] LA CITA DE CORPHU [1590] Bird's-eye views. [no dimens] Color. Sl cropped lower margin. [A6] £287 $476

CANTEBRIGIA [c.1575] 33x45cm (13x17½") Repairs, occas in pen facsimile. Framed. [A5] £196 $325

CANTUARBURY [1588] 29x43cm (11½x17") Color. Lt toned. some foxing; else VG. [23] £452 **$750**

CIVITAS EXONIAE [c.1580] 31x40cm (12½x15½") Color. Mounted; few tears & repairs; a sm hole. [A5] £104 $173

CIVITATIS ESSENSIS EXACTISS. DESCRIP. [c.1580] 14x42cm (5½x16½") Old color. [48] DM 3,400 £1,174 $1,946

DANORUM MARCA, UES CIMBRICUM, AUT DANIAE REGNUM ... [1585-] From *Civitates Orbis Terrarum*. Denmark, after Mark Jorden. 38x46cm (15x18") Orig color. Edges cut close, as usual; minor restoration & sm c'fold split. Ref: Baynton-Williams p.28, color illus. [46] £1,200 $1,990

EDENBURG [c.1580] 34x45cm (13½x18") Contemp color. C'fold repairs, occas in pen facsimile. Framed. [A5] £253 $420

GOA FORTISSIMA INDIAE URBS IN CHRISTIANORUM POTESTATEM ANNO SALUTIS 1509 DEVENIT [ON SHEET WITH] DUI [AND] AZAAMURUM [AND] ANFA [1572-] From *Civitates* ... Indian & Moroccan cities. 33x46cm (13x18") Uncolored. [34] £480 $796

HAEC EST NOBILIS & FLORENS ILLA NEAPOLIS ... [1572 (1574)] Bird's eye view. 33x46cm (13x18½") Color. A crease; else fine. [37] £573 **$950**

HIEROSOLYMA, CLARISSIMA TOTIUS ORIENTIS CIVITAS IUDAEE METROPOLIS [1572] From *Civitates Orbis Terrarum*. 2 aerial views: Biblical period; 16th c, each with reference table. 34x49cm (13½x19½") Color. Lower c'fold reinforced; else exc. Ref: Laor 1039. [24] £784 **$1,300**

[SAME TITLE] [c.1580] 33x42cm (13x16½") [A5] £506 $839

LACUS AGNIANUS [ON SHEET WITH] LA CAVERNA DE SIBYLLA CUMANA [c.1585] From *Civitates* ... Lake & cave near Naples. 33x47cm (13x18½") Full old color. [39] £332 **$550**

LEYDA, BATAVORUM LUGDUNUM, VULGO LEYDEN [c.1580] Bird's-eye view; 4 sm views. 34x48cm (13½x18½") Old color. [48] DM 500 £173 $286

LIER. - LIRA, ELEGANS ET AMOENUM BRABANTIAE OPP. [1588] Bird's-eye view. 32x40cm (12½x15½") Old color. Sh wrinkle at lf; sm hole. [48] DM 400 £138 $229

LILLE INSULA [c.1580] From *Civitates Orbis Terrarum*. 32x43cm (12½x17") Impression bit weak; o/w VG. [21] Can$375 £164 $272

LILLE. INSULA. RYSSELE [c.1580] Bird's-eye view. 33x43cm (13x17") Old color. Sh c'fold split restored. [48] DM 500 £173 $286

LONDINUM FERACISSIMI ANGLIAE REGNI METROPOLIS [1572] As in *Civitates Orbis Terrarum*. 33x48cm (13x19") Color. Reinforced printer's crease lower lf; else exc. Ref: Howgego 2. Goss (Euro Cities) pl.31. [24] £1,930 **$3,200**

[SAME TITLE] [1572] 33x48cm (13x19") Orig color. Exc. Ref: Howgego 2. [44] £2,292 **$3,800**

[SAME TITLE] [c.1572-73] From Part I, *Civitates Orbis Terrarum*. 32x47cm (13x18½") Uncolored. Exc. Ref: Howgego 2. [4] **£2,000** $3,317

LUTETIA VULGARI NOMINE PARIS, URBS GALLIAE MAXIMA, SEQUANA NAVIGABILI FLUMINE IRRIGATUR ... [c.1572] From Part I, *Civitates Orbis Terrarum*. 33x47cm (13x18½") Uncol. Exc. [4] **£825** $1,368

[SAME TITLE] [1572] 34x48cm (13½x19") Color. Minor reinforcement bottom c'fold; exc. Ref: Goss (Euro Cities) pl.44. [24] £1,327 **$2,200**

[SAME TITLE] [1572] 34x48cm (13½x19") Orig color. Outstanding. [44] £1,568 **$2,600**

MEXICO, REGIA ET CELEBRIS HISPANIAE NOVAE CIVITAS ... [1572+] Bird's-eye view; from sheet with Cusco. 27x23cm (10½x9") Color. [11] £353 **$585**

MEXICO REGIA ET CELEBRIS HISPANIAE NOVAE CIVITAS... [ON SHEET WITH] CUSCO REGNI PERU IN NOVO ORBE CAPUT ... [c.1572] From Part I, *Civitates Orbis Terrarum*. City views. 32x47cm (13x18½") Uncolored. Minor reinforcement lower c'fold margin; fine. [4] **£800** $1,327

[SAME TITLE] [1572-75] From same source. City views. 27x48cm (10½x19") Col. [34] £750 $1,244

MONACHIUM UTRIUSQUE BAVARIAE CIVITAS PRIMAR [1586] Munich. 28x49cm (11x19½") Color. C'fold tear backed. [48] DM 1,700 £587 $973

MONS [c.1580] From *Civitates* ... Bird's-eye view. 36x46cm (14x18") Later full color. Mild soiling margin & verso; few tiny edge chips; hinging residue verso. [A9] £104 **$173**

MUNDEN - MUNDENSIS, AD VISURGUM FLU. SAXONIAE URBIS, GENUINA DELINEATIO [1588] 30x48cm (11½x19") Color. [48] DM 1,540 £532 $881

BRAUN & HOGENBERG continued

NAMUR CUM ELEGANTISSIMA AD MOSAE FLUME CIVITAS [1572-1618] From *Civitates Orbis Terrarum*. 34x43cm (13½x17") Impression bit weak; o/w VG. [21] **Can$400** £175 **$290**

NORDOVICUM, ANGLIAE CIVITAS [c.1580] Norwich, bird's-eye view; 2 large coat-of arms. 29x42cm (11½x16½") Old color. [48] **DM 830** £287 **$475**

NULLUS IN ORBE LOCUS BAIIS PRAELUCET AMOENIS [c.1580] Ancient city near Naples. 34x49cm (13x19½") Old color. [48] **DM 750** £259 **$429**

PENIGK MISNIAE OPPIDUM [1617] 33x46cm (13x18") Old color. [48] **DM 750** £259 **$429**

PRAGA REGNI BOHEMIAE METROPOLIS / PALATIUM IMPERATORUM PRAGAE QUOD VULGO RATZIN APPELLATUR [c.1598] From *Civitates Orbis Terrarum*. 2 views. 36x49cm (14x19½") Color. Fine. [4] **£850** **$1,410**

ROMA [1575] Bird's eye view. 33x48cm (13x19") Full color. Fine. [37] **£905** **$1,500**

[SAME TITLE] [c.1572] From Part I, *Civitates* ... 33x49cm (13x19") Uncolored. Exc. [4] **£800** **$1,327**

SANT JUAN DEL FORATCHE ... JERENNA ... [1588-] From *Civitates Orbis Terrarum*. 5 views of San Juan on Guadalquivir, Jerenna, 3 Roman tombs, & towers at side, one cutaway with Hoefnagel ascending on horseback. 38x49cm (15x19½") Color. [34] **£400** **$664**

STOCKHOLM / STOCHOLM [c.1588] From *Civitates Orbis Terrarum*. 2 panoramic views. 32x47cm (13x18½") Uncolored. Exc. [4] **£700** **$1,161**

TRAIECTUM. - TRAIECTUM CLARA ET VETUS EST EPISCOPALIS CIVITAS [c.1580] Utrecht bird's-eye view. 33x48cm (13x19") Old color. [48] **DM 850** £293 **$486**

VALENCHIENNES. - VALENCENA, QUONDAM CYGNORUM VALLIS, URBS HAN. PERELEGAS, ET VALDE MAGNIFICA [c.1580] Bird's-eye view. 36x39cm (14x15½") Old color. [48] **DM 450** £155 **$257**

VENETIA [1572] Bird's-eye view; 153-item key. 36x50cm (14½x19½") Color. Minor c'fold reinforcement; else exc. Ref: Goss (Euro Cities) pl.55. [24] **£1,930** **$3,200**

VIENNA AUSTRIA METROPOLIS ... [c.1580] 15x48cm (6x19") Old color. [48] **DM 1,200** £414 **$687**

WARBORCH. WARBURGUM, ELEGANS WESTPHALIAE OPP. [c.1580] 18x48cm (7x18½") Old color. [48] **DM 1,400** £483 **$801**

WEINMAR. - WINMARIA, FERTILISS. THURINGIAE URBS PRAESTANTISSIMA VULGO WEINMAR [c.1580] Bird's-eye view. 35x48cm (14x19") Color. [48] **DM 1,200** £414 **$687**

ZURYCH. TIGARUM SIVE TUREGUM, CAESARI, UT PLERIQUE EXISTIMANT, TIGURINUS PAGUS, VULGO ZURYCH [1581] From *Civitates* ... 37x48cm (14½x19") Full color. Fine. Ref: Goss (Euro Cities) p.126-7. [14] **£1,327** **$2,200**

BRETEZ

PLAN DE PARIS COMMENCE L'ANNEE 1734 ... LEVE ET DESINE PAR LOUIS BRETEZ GRAVE PAR CLAUDE LUCAS / ET ECRIT PAR AUBIN [1739] Large folio of mottled calf in atlas form with 20 bound sheets & key sheet; shows every structure; if assembled map would be 12x8 feet. Turgot was dedicatee. Binding rebacked; exc. [23] **£7,237** **$12,000**

BRIDGENS

[ATLAS] BRIDGENS' ATLAS OF LANCASTER COUNTY PENNSYLVANIA [1864] Lancaster: D.S. Bare. Folio, new end papers & cloth spine; marbled boards, sl rubbed. Incl foldout county map, one tape repair. Contents clean; tight; VG. Ref: Le Gear (US) L3037; Phillips (A) 5017. cf Ristow (Amer M&M) p.404. [A1] **£216** **$358**

BRION

MAP OF HARRISBURG CITY [1875] Folding map; issued without covers, similar to atlas maps, but on heavier paper. Color by wards. 79x111cm (31x44") Worn; lt damage along folds. [15] **£75** **$125**

BRION DE LA TOUR

AFRIQUE [c.1750] Text at sides, map 28x27cm (11x10½") OL color. Lt toned at c'fold & separations to border; good (B). [A4] **£50** **$83**

CARTE DES ETATS-UNIS D'AMERIQUE ET DU COURS DU MISSISSIPI ... [c.1790] Appeared in vol.116, *Histoire Universelle*. "Frankland" marked for Franklinia. 23x27cm (9x10½") Uncolored. Ref: cf TMC 72, p.15, no.3 [34] **£280** **$465**

CARTE DES ISLES ANTILLES DANS L'AMERIQUE SEPTENTRIONALE ... [1782] Historical note upper rt. 52x75cm (20½x29½") Orig OL color. lt waterstain upper lf; o/w good. [28] **£534** **$885**

BRION DE LA TOUR continued

CARTE DU THEATRE DE LA GUERRE ENTRE LES ANGLAIS ET LES AMERICAINS: DRESSEE D'APRES LES CARTES ANGLAISES LES PLUS MODERNES   [1778] Northeast US; 2nd of 3 states. 75x51cm (29½x20") Orig OL color. Age toning, occas lt foxing; lt dampstain bottom margin sl past neatline; minor margin tears; soft creasing near horiz fold. Ref: Nebenzahl (Battle Plans) 121.   [A2]   £2,388   **$3,960**
HEMISPHERE ORIENTAL   [1780] 27x30cm (10½x12") Color. Ref: cf Tooley (Australia) p.317.
[13]   Aus$680   £309 $512
HISTOIRE DE LA DECOUVERTE DES MONDE NOUVEAU ET INCONNU ... 1761   [1761] From *Atlas Methodique*. Paris: Desnos. Polar double hemi; "Sea of the West"; text at sides; elaborate border. 38x52cm (15x20½") Color.   [19]   £181   **$300**
L'AMERIQUE   [1764] Paris: Desnos. Orig text at sides removed, amended text mounted on folio sheet by publisher. 22x34cm (9x13½") Color.   [A7]   £104   **$172**
LA JUDEE OU PALESTINE DRESSE POUR L'INTELLIGENCE DE L'HISTOIRE SAINTE   [1767] Paris: Desnos. 28x32cm (11x12½") Color. Top & bottom margins trimmed close as usual. Ref: Laor 131.   [A8]   £48   **$80**
LE DANEMARK DIVISE PAR PROVINCES ET DIOCESES   [c.1760] On 13x20" sheet with text at sides, map 24x25cm (9½x10") Full color. Lt toning at c'fold; good (B).   [A4]   £31   **$52**
NOUVEAU MEXIQUE, LOUISIANE, CANADA ET NLLE. ANGLETERRE   [1766] Most of North America; elaborate border. 27x30cm (10½x11½") Full color. Fine (A+).   [A3]   £349   **$578**

BRITISH ADMIRALTY

[GREAT LAKES, 7 CHARTS: ONE OF EACH LAKE; STRAITS OF MACKINAC; RIVER ST. MARY]   [c.1890] Complete set, after U.S. Coast Survey. Most about 54x96cm (21½x38") Fine.   [15]   £1,206   **$2,000**
ENTRANCES TO AUCKLAND HARBOUR   [1857-1863] Hydrographic Office. Linen-backed. 46x62cm (18½x24") Stained, soiled, a tear.   [A6]   **£115**   **$191**
FLORIDA STRAIT, NORTH PART   [1877 (revised 1880)] Compiled from Admiralty & U.S.C.S. surveys 99x66cm (39x26") Uncolored. Some lt spotting; good.   [25]   £256   **$425**
MORANT POINT TO PORT ROYAL   [1876 (1881)] SE Jamaica. 65x99cm (26x39") Full col.   [20]   £407   **$675**
PORT ROYAL AND KINGSTON HARBOURS   [1876] 65x94cm (25½x37") Full color.   [20]   £467   **$775**
ST. GEORGE HARBR. ... [GRENADA]   [1858 (1861)] 64x99cm (25x39") Full color.   [20]   £286   **$475**

BRITTON & REY

THE TELEGRAPH HILL OBSERVATORY, SAN FRANCISCO, CALIFORNIA   [1883] In Fred Marriott's *News Letter*. 3-color litho view with hand coloring. 41x64cm (16½x25") Traces of orig folds; rice paper backing; fine.   [28]   £844   **$1,400**

BROMLEY

[ATLAS] ATLAS OF THE CITY OF PHILADELPHIA, COMPLETE IN ONE VOLUME   [1910] Elephant folio; half leather; 4 pp street index, 53 double-page maps, 52 wards surveyed. Color. Binding poor; dampstained throughout; overall about good.   [1927 "Atlas of the City of Philadelphia, Wards 24, 27, 34, 40, 44 & 46 ..." offered as same price]   [35]   £60   **$100**
[ATLAS] ATLAS OF WESTCHESTER COUNTY, NEW YORK   [1881] NY: G.W. & W.S. Bromley. Folio; half morocco. Colored maps. Leather tips absent; backstrip torn; internally clean. Ref: LeGear (US) 2505, calls for 64 maps.   [A7]   £173   **$287**

BROMME

POST-KANAL-UND EISENBAHNKARTE DER VEREINIGTEN STAATEN VON NORD-AMERIKA. NACH SMITH, TANNER, MITCHELL UND DEN BERICHTEN DES GENERAL-POSTAMTS BEARBEITET VON TRAUGOTT BROMME ...   [1855] German language pocket map of U.S. folding into 16mo roan cover. Inset: "Oregon, California und der Mormonen-Staat Deseret". 55x67cm (22x26½") OL color. VG.   [16]   £724   **$1,200**

BROOKES

[BOOK WITH MAPS]   A GENERAL GAZETTEER; OR COMPENDIOUS GEOGRAPHICAL DICTIONARY ... [1830] London: J. Richardson et al; 15th ed. Half calf & marbled boards; xvi, 776; 8 folding maps, incl double hemi world, 5 continents, East & West Indies. Hinges loose; worn; some browning to maps; o/w VG.   [21]   Can$250   £109 $181
[BOOK WITH MAPS]   BROOKES'S GENERAL GAZETTEER IMPROVED   [1806] Richard Brookes (English); Phila: Jacob Johnson. Octavo, full leather with orig leather spine label; 8 maps. Lib labels inside front cover & trace on spine.   [33]   £332   **$550**
A MAP OF THE WORLD FROM THE BEST AUTHORITIES   [1795] Publ in Brookes' Gazetteer, London. Double hemi. 15x28cm (6x11") Full color.   [41]   £106   **$175**

BROWNE

A NEW MAP OF JAMAICA ... FROM ACTUAL SURVEYS MADE BY MR. SHEFFIELD AND OTHERS, FROM THE YEAR 1730 TO THE YEAR 1749   [1755] By Patrick Browne; sold by John Bowles. 1st state of two. Joined multi-sheet map, 68x127cm (27x50") Full orig color. Some repaired tears & fold reinforcement; o/w good. Ref: Kapp (Jamaica) 42.   [32] £3,015 **$5,000**

A NEW MAP OF ROME SHOWING ITS ANCIENT AND PRESENT SITUATION   [1710] Corner insets. 49x58cm (19x23") Color. Framed.   [A6] £184 $305

A NEW MAPP OF THE KINGDOM OF ENGLAND SHOWING ITS ANTIENT AND PRESENT GOVERNMENT   [c.1760] Christopher Browne; John Harris, sc; Carington Bowles & Robert Sayer. Quarto, half calf, sl rubbed; wall map on 15 sheets, 3 double-page; 6 as two joined sheets. Contemp color.   [A6] £529 $877

NORTH BRITAIN OR SCOTLAND 1708. A NEW MAPP OF SCOTLAND, THE WESTERN, ORKNEY, AND SHETLAND ISLANDS. BEGUN BY APPOINTMENT OF ROB.T MORDEN, FINISHED AT YE CHARGE AND BY DIRECTION OF C. BROWNE   [1708] 56x48cm (22x19") Counties by orig OL color. Some brown staining.   [46] £750 $1,244

BRUE

CARTE GENERALE DU GLOBE TERRESTRE   [1827] Paris: Goujon & Andriveau. Double hemi; dissected, linen-backed. 163x246cm (64x97") OL color.   [A6] £172 $286

BUACHE

A PHYSICAL PLANISPHERE WHEREIN ARE REPRESENTED ALL THE KNOWN LANDS AND SEAS N.TH OF THE GREAT CHAINS OF MOUNTAINS WCH. TRAVERSE THE GLOBE FROM THE NORTH POLE. ADAPTED TO MONSR: BUACHE'S MEMOIRE READ AT THE R. ACADEMY OF SCIENCES.   [1757] With copy of Buache's address. 31x29cm (12½x11½") Browning at folds; trimmed close at rt as issued; VG (A). Ref: Jolly GENT-104   [A3] £131 **$218**

CARTE DES NOUVELLES DECOUVERTES AU NORD DE LA MER DU SUD, 1750   [1752] Buache with J.N. De L'Isle. 1st state. With "West Sea". 46x65cm (18x25½") Orig OL color. Minor c'fold restoration. Ref: Tooley (Amer) p.34, #101. Schwartz & Ehrenberg p.157-61.   [34] £1,000 $1,658

CARTE DES NOUVELLES DECOUVERTES AU NORD DE LA MER DU SUD, TANT A L'EST DE LA SIBERIE ET DU KAMTCHATKA, QU A L'OUEST DE LA NOUVELLE FRANCE. DRESSEE SUR LES MEMOIRES DE MR. DEL'ISLE PROFESSEUR ROYAL ET DE L'ACADEMIE DES SCIENCES   [1750 / 1752] 1st issue. With "Mer ou Baye l'Ouest" 44x64cm (17½x25") OL color. C'fold off ctr with strip; folded in 3 sections; 4 faint spots, one foxing. Ref: Schwartz & Ehrenberg p.161, pl.94; Tooley (Amer) p.34, cf pl.22.   [1] £2,714 **$4,500**

CARTE DES TERRES AUSTRALES ...   [1754] Southern hemi with plausible Antarctica; text surround. 24x30cm (9½x12") Orig color. Exc.   [43] £814 **$1,350**

CARTE DU GLOBE TERRESTRE OU LES TERRES DE L'HEMISPHERE MERIDL. SONT SUPPOSEES ETRE VUES A TRAVERS CELLES DE L'HEMISPHERE SEPTENTL ...   [1746 / 1778] Paris: Dezauche. Superimposed polar projections; Shows "Sea of the West"; notes at sides. 25x33cm (10x13") Old color.   [19] £232 $385

PLANISPHERE PHYSIQUE OU L'ON VOIT DU POLE SEPTENTRIONALE ...   [c.1750] Polar projection. 36x44cm (14x17½") Orig color. Exc. Ref: Potter illus p.178.   [43] £513 **$850**

BUCHON *Dimensions sometimes include text around map*

[ATLAS]   ATLAS GEOGRAPHIQUE, STATISTIQUE, HISTORIQUE ET CHRONOLOGIQUE DES DEUX AMERIQUES ET DE ILES ADJACENTES; TRADUIT DE L'ATLAS EXECUTE EN AMERIQUE D'APRES LESAGE ... [1825] French ed of Carey & Lea, 7 new maps. Folio, marble-paper boards, quarter calf, gold title on spine; 51 maps (as called for, some out of order) in orig wash color. Joints weak; maps exc. Ref: Phillips (A) 1176.   [24] £4,523 **$7,500**

CARTE GEOGRAPHIQUE, STATISTIQUE ET HISTORIQUE DE L'INDIANA   [1825] With text surround, 18x24"; map 28x21cm (11x8½") Orig color. Lt soiling sm area of text; o/w VG.   [A1] £133 $220

CARTE GEOGRAPHIQUE, STATISTIQUE ET HISTORIQUE DE LA GEORGIE   [1826] On 18x24" sheet with text, map 28x23cm (11x9") Full orig color. VG. [NC, SC offered at same price]   [36] £166 $275

CARTE GEOGRAPHIQUE, STATISTIQUE ET HISTORIQUE DE MICHIGAN   [1825] Text at sides. Map 36x27cm (14x10½") on 21x27" sheet. OL col. Exc. Ref: Karpinski (MI) 98; Phillips (A) 1176-40.   [12] £226 $375

CARTE GEOGRAPHIQUE, STATISTIQUE ET HISTORIQUE DU CONNECTICUT   [1825] French ed of Carey & Lea. On 18x24" sheet with text surround, map 24x29cm (9½x11½") Color. Fine. Ref: Thompson (CT) 71.   [14] £136 $225

CARTE GEOGRAPHIQUE, STATISTIQUE ET HISTORIQUE DU NEW HAMPSHIRE   [1825] Young & Delleker, sc. Overall 18x24" with text; map 30x24cm (12x9½") Color. Fine. Ref: Cobb (NH) 101.   [14] £136 $225

BUCHON continued

CARTE GÉOGRAPHIQUE, STATISTIQUE ET HISTORIQUE DU TERRITOIRE D'ARKANSAS   [1825]   Incl western territories to Rockies. Text at sides. 36x36cm (14½x14½") on 20x26" sheet. Area & OL color. Faint toning at c'fold; fresh, clean.   [A10]   £160   **$265**

ETATS-UNIS D'AMERIQUE   [1825]   French ed of Carey & Lea. Resembles Melish. 43x53cm (17x21")   Orig color. VG to fine.   [A2]   £498   **$825**

BUNTING

AFRICA TERTIA PARS TERRAE   [(1581) c.1600]   From *Itinerarium Sacrae Scripturae*.   26x34cm (10x13½") Color. Fine. Ref: Norwich 17.   [4]   **£565** $937

AFRICA TERTIA PARS TERRAE SEPTENTRIO   [c.1581]   Hanover. German text verso. 26x34cm (10x13")   [A7]   **£347** $575

ASIA SECUNDA PARS TERRAE IN FORMA PEGASIR   [(1581) c.1600]   Asia as Pegasus. 24x35cm (9½x14") Color. Some text see-through; fine.   [4]   **£800** $1,327

DIE EIGENTLICHE UND WARHAFFTIGE GESTALT DER ERDEN UND DES MEERS. COSMOGRAPHIA UNIVERSALIS   [1581 (c.1600)]   From *Itinerarium Sacrae Scripturae*. 27x36cm (10½x14") Color. Mid c'fold reinforcement; minor infilling binding holes. Ref: Shirley (W) 143, pl.120.   [4]   **£900** $1,493

EUROPA PRIMA PARS TERRAE IN FORMA VIRGINIS   [(1581) c.1600]   Europe as Queen. 24x35cm (9½x14") Color. Minor text see-through; fine.   [4]   **£850** $1,410

[SAME TITLE]   [1581] 26x37cm (10½x14½")   Color. Mounted on rice paper; c'fold reinforced; repaired tear; VG. Ref: MCC #1, no.2.   [23]   £724   **$1,200**

BURCKHARDT

ASIA   [c.1760]   Hungarian text. 33x38cm (13x15") Uncolored.   [34]   **£460** $763

EUROPA   [c.1760]   In Hungarian. 33x37cm (13x14½") Uncolored.   [34]   **£320** $531

BURGOYNE

[BOOK WITH MAPS]   A STATE OF THE EXPEDITION FROM CANADA ... WITH A COLLECTION OF AUTHENTIC DOCUMENTS   [1780]   London: Almon. 2nd ed. 2 octavo volumes, new facsimile bindings, text in full leather, 6 maps (& 2 overlays) folded into half leather. Exc. Ref: Howes (US) B968 Sabin 9255.   [33]   £1,930   **$3,200**

BURNET

[WESTERN HEMISPHERE]   [1681 / 1684]   From *The Theory of the Earth* ...   Insular Calif. Diameter: 20cm (8")   Exc. Ref: McLaughlin 77, state 2; Shirley 507.   [2]   £392   **$650**

BURR

ARKANSAS   [1835 (1836)]   From *New Universal Atlas*. Miller Co. in SW. 27x32cm (10½x12½") Pastel color. Sl dampstain lf margin; else mint. Ref: Phillips (A) 771-50.   [12]   £112   **$185**

MAP ILLUSTRATING THE PLAN OF THE DEFENSES OF THE WESTERN FRONTIER, AS PROPOSED BY MAJ. GEN. GAINES, IN HIS PLAN DATED FEB 28TH, 1838   [1838]   From Gaines report, *The Defence of the Western Frontier* ... By D. Burr; litho by P. Haas. 60x37cm (23½x14½") B&W with forts in red. On thin paper; nice. Ref: Wheat (TM) 432.   [1]   £181   **$300**

MAP OF ILLINOIS WITH PARTS OF INDIANA, OUISCONSIN, &C.   [1836 (1837)]   From *Report on the Illinois Central Rail-Road Company*.   24th Cong, 2nd Sess, House Doc No.121. 60 counties. 44x33cm (17½x13") B&W. Fine. Ref: Claussen & Friis 168.   [12]   £112   **$185**

MAP OF THE STATE OF ALABAMA   [1834 (1836)]   From *New Universal Atlas*. 32x27cm (12½x10½") Full color. Fine. Ref: Birmingham Pub. Lib. 23.   [12]   £142   **$235**

MICHIGAN   [dated 1836]   From *New Universal Atlas*. Toledo is in MI. 32x27cm (12½x10½") Full color. Mint. Ref: Karrow 5-1968.   [12]   £232   **$385**

NEW YORK   [1832 (1836)]   From *New Universal Atlas*. 25x32cm (10x12½") OL color. Ref: cf Phillips (A) 771-36.   [12]   £106   **$175**

NORTH AMERICA   [c.1835]   Pl.29 in Greenleaf's *A New Universal Atlas*.   Brattleboro: G.R. French. 32x27cm (12½x11") Full color. Good. Framed.   [16]   £181   **$300**

OREGON TERRITORY   [1836]   As in *New Universal Atlas*. NY: Illman & Pilbrew. 27x32cm (10½x12½") Color. Clean, bright. Ref: Wheat (TM) 402.   [8]   £211   **$350**

BURR continued

THE NORTH-WEST-COAST OF NORTH AMERICA AND ADJACENT TERRITORIES COMPILED FROM THE BEST AUTHORITIES UNDER THE DIRECTION OF ROBERT GREENHOW TO ACCOMPANY HIS MEMOIR ON THE NORTH-WEST COAST ... DRAWN BY DAVID H. BURR [1840] Trans-Mississippi west; some imaginary geography. 41x54cm (16x21½") Folded; some foxing; else VG. Ref: Wheat (TM) 447. [10] £151 **$250**

[SAME TITLE] [1840] 41x54cm (16x21½") Catalog excerpt taped to verso; faint toning along folds; sh tear repaired; VG. Ref: Wheat (TM) 447. [A10] £69 **$115**

THE WORLD, BASED ON MERCATOR'S PROJECTION ... [1850] Boston: John Haven. Folding map; inset promoting transcontinental RR by W.L. Dearborn. 43x53cm (17x21") OL color. Lacks wrapper; holes at fold intersections; stained. [15] £226 **$375**

UNITED STATES [1833] NY: J.H. Colton & Co. Pocket map in orig leather folder. 7 insets. 44x53cm (17½x21") OL color. Front cover detached, scuffed; a fold separation; generally fine. [15] £814 **$1,350**

WEST INDIES, WITH PART OF GUATEMALA [1834] NY: Colton. Folds into orig sm 12mo roan case. 48x58cm (19x22½") OL color. [A7] £416 **$690**

BURRITT

[ATLAS] ATLAS DESIGNED TO ILLUSTRATE BURRITT'S GEOGRAPHY OF THE HEAVENS [1856] NY: F.J. Huntington. Oblong folio; 9 celestial charts, 6 with wash color; illustrated wraps. Covers lt soiled; 1st signature detached; plates clean, bright. With H.V. Mattison, *The Geography of the Heavens*; NY: Mason Bros. 12mo; quarter leather & cloth; 343 pp; covers waterstained; spine chipped; text vol good. [35] £136 **$225**

[ATLAS] ATLAS, DESIGNED TO ILLUSTRATE THE GEOGRAPHY OF THE HEAVENS ... NEW EDITION [1835] 8 maps, 7 with color; folio, Orig wrappers stained; scattered foxing & browning. [another with defective orig wrappers, browning & foxing, several leaves dampstained sold at $345] [A7] £260 **$431**

NORTHERN CIRCUMPOLAR MAP FOR EACH MONTH IN THE YEAR [IN SET WITH] SOUTHERN CIRCUMPOLAR MAP FOR EACH MONTH IN THE YEAR [1835] Each Diameter: 30cm (12") Orig color. Some lt foxing; o/w fine. [A1] £106 **$176**

BUTLER

[ATLAS] AN ATLAS OF ANCIENT GEOGRAPHY [1841] Phila: Lea & Blanchard. Marbled boards, leather spine; 21 OL color maps 23x15cm (9x6") Covers worn, loose; some pages detached; maps clean, bright; 3 with sh fold splits; 1 with lib stamp margin; all else fine (B). [A4] £128 **$212**

[ATLAS] AN ATLAS OF MODERN GEOGRAPHY [1830s] Samuel Butler, London. Octavo, half roan; 23 maps, most in OL color. Cover worn; scattered soiling & browning; double-hemi bit tattered. ["Atlas of Antient Geography" (Phila: 1843) sold at same price] [A8] £55 **$92**

AQUARIUS, PISCIS NOTUS AND CAPRICORNUS [1831] Publ U.S. 17x22cm (6½x8½") Substantial orig color. VG. ["Cepheus, Ursa Minor and Draco" offered at same price] [25] £30 **$50**

CALDWELL

[ATLAS] CALDWELL'S ILLUSTRATED, HISTORICAL, COMBINATION ATLAS OF CLEARFIELD COUNTY, PENNSYLVANIA [1878] Folio, half morocco & cloth; folding county map, 38 colored plat maps, numerous views, 19 pp business directory. Covers worn; front joint split; endpapers soiled; a laid-in folding county map with cellophane tape repairs; contents clean. Ref: LeGear (US) 3022. [A9] £347 **$575**

[ATLAS] CALDWELL'S ILLUSTRATED, HISTORICAL, COMBINATION ATLAS OF JEFFERSON COUNTY, PENNSYLVANIA [1878] Folio; new end papers, spine & end points. Incl large Brookville map. Occas margin smudges to maps; covers rubbed; tight; VG. [A1] £183 **$303**

CALLOT

SIGE DE BREDA. ISRAEL SILVESTRE EX PARISIJS ... [1628] Battle scene & vignettes merging into plan. 6 joined sheets, 120x140cm (47x55") Color. Framed. [42] Aus$12,500 £5,677 **$9,412**

CAMDEN

[ATLAS] BRITANNIA ... [1695] Swale & Churchill; 1st ed of Edmund Gibson's translation. Folio; later half calf, rebacked & repaired; 50 maps by or after Morden & others; portrait & 9 plates. Occas spotting or browning, mostly margin; some lt offsetting; few sh tears; 4 maps with sm holes; few text leaves with pen marginalia. Ref: Chubb 113. [A5] **£1,725** **$2,861**

[ATLAS] BRITANNIA: OR A CHOROGRAPHICAL DESCRIPTION OF GREAT BRITAIN AND IRELAND, TOGETHER WITH THE ADJACENT ISLANDS [1722] 2nd Edmund Gibson ed; folio, 2 vols, half calf; 50 maps (of 51, lacks Norfolk) by Robert Morden, Andrew Johnston & others; illustrations, 10 pp coins, etc. Covers detached, vol.2 lacks upper cover; sm worm hole early pp; 2 maps shaved at margins. Ref: Chubb 115. [A6] **£1,380** **$2,289**

CAMDEN continued

[ATLAS] BRITANNIA: OR A GEOGRAPHICAL ACCOUNT DESCRIPTION OF THE FLOURISHING KINGDOMS OF ENGLAND, SCOTLAND, AND IRELAND [1806] Stockdale; 2nd Gough ed. Folio, 4 vols; 103 plates, 53 maps (46 in color). Half calf worn & distressed; spines & covers detached or lacking; few margin tears & repairs; sold as is. [A6] £690 **$1,144**

CAMOCIO

MARGARITIN [c.1572] Lafreri School siege map of settlement in western Greece. 17x21cm (6½x8½") Uncolored. [39] £121 **$200**

SPALLATO [c.1572] Lafreri School map of Split, Dalmatia. 15x20cm (6x8") Uncolored. [39] £151 **$250**

CANADIAN GOVERNMENTS

A GENERAL MAP OF THE NORTHEWESTERN PART OF THE DOMINION OF CANADA [1898] Ministry of the Interior. Topographical map; relief by hachures. 91x122cm (36x48") Color. Lt age toning; corner/fold separations; brittle paper; in library sleeve; VG+. [6] £45 **$75**

MAP OF MANITOBA [1902] Ministry of the Interior. 91x122cm (36x48") Color. Lt age toning; corner/fold separations; brittle paper; in library sleeve; VG. [6] £12 **$20**

MAP OF MANITOBA SHEWING PROVINCIAL GOVERNMENT LANDS FOR SALE [1908] Winnipeg. 91x122cm (36x48"). Col. Lt age toning; corner/fold separations; brittle paper; in library sleeve; VG. [6] £51 **$85**

MAP OF PART OF THE PROVINCE OF ONTARIO, CANADA [1873] By W.J.S. Howell, for Dept. of Agriculture & Public Works, Ottawa. Silked, text on reverse; promotional map for distribution in U.K. 47x70cm (18½x27½") Uncolored. [15] £241 **$400**

MAP OF THE DOMINION OF CANADA AND PART OF THE UNITED STATES [1883] Dept. of Railroads. 2 sheets, 91x122cm (36x48") Color. Lt age toning; corner/fold separations; brittle paper; in library sleeve; VG. [6] £24 **$40**

MAP OF THE YUKON TERRITORY [1905] Geol. Survey of Canada. 91x122cm (36x48") Color. Lt age toning; corner/fold separations; brittle paper; in library sleeve; VG. [6] £12 **$20**

CAREY, MATHEW

[ATLAS] CAREY'S GENERAL ATLAS, IMPROVED AND ENLARGED: BEING A COLLECTION OF MAPS OF THE WORLD AND QUARTERS, THEIR PRINCIPAL EMPIRES, KINGDOMS, &C. [1814] Phila. Folio, 19th century boards rebacked & recased. 58 mostly double-page maps in orig OL color, incl 1st issue of new western territories. Few maps trimmed; few tears repaired, no loss; title page tear backed; overall VG. Ref: Phillips (A) 722. Sabin 10858. [3] £7,539 **$12,500**

[SAME TITLE] [1814] Phila. Folio; full period leather binding (17x11"); 58 mostly double-page maps, 28 of U.S. interest. Orig OL color. Occasional sm tear, minor staining and/or foxing; title & 2 text pp with vert crease & partly torn; moderate binding wear; overall VG. [32] £9,951 **$16,500**

A CHART OF THE WEST INDIES, FROM THE LATEST MARINE JOURNALS AND SURVEYS [1794] 28x40cm (11x15½") New OL color. Few margin tears; occas faint toning; o/w VG. Ref: Wheat & Brun 687. [A2] £100 **$165**

A MAP OF THE DISCOVERIES MADE BY CAPTS. COOK & CLERKE IN THE YEARS 1778 & 1779 BETWEEN THE EASTERN COAST OF ASIA & THE WESTERN COAST OF NORTH AMERICA ... [1795] 19x28cm (7½x11") New OL color. Occas faint soiling; o/w fine. [A2] £86 **$143**

A MAP OF THE TENNASSEE GOVERNMENT FORMERLY PART OF NORTH CAROLINA TAKEN CHIEFLY FROM SURVEYS BY GENL. D. SMITH. & OTHERS [1794] State 1. 24x52cm (9½x20½") Uncol. Tear 2" into blank area below & fold split repaired verso; o/w VG to fine. Ref: Wheat & Brun 650. [A2] £663 **$1,100**

A MAP OF THE UNITED STATES: COMPILED CHIEFLY FROM THE STATE MAPS AND OTHER AUTHENTIC INFORMATION BY SAML. LEWIS, 1796 [1802] 64x90cm (25½x35½") Tears into image closed on verso; sm portion remargined lf side. Ref: cf Wheat & Brun 123, 132, 133, 137. [A7] £659 **$1,092**

A NEW MAP OF THE UNITED STATES OF AMERICA, FROM THE LATEST AUTHORITIES [1814] From Carey's General Atlas. To Mississippi River. 32x43cm (12½x17") OL color. C'fold reinforced verso; faint foxing mostly margins; else clean. [A10] £146 **$242**

CONNECTICUT FROM THE BEST AUTHORITIES [1795] 1st state. Doolittle, del & sc. 30x37cm (12x15") Uncolored. Exc. Ref: Thompson (CT) 36; Wheat & Brun 284. [2] £211 **$350**

[SAME TITLE] [1795] From *The General Atlas for Carey's Edition of Guthrie's Geography Improved*. Doolittle, del & sc. 30x37cm (12x14½") B&W. Folds, intersection pinholes; old repair at tear 2" into map; lt offsetting; overall nice. Ref: Wheat & Brun 284. Thompson I-36; Phillips (A) 1172-6. [12] £226 **$375**

DELAWARE FROM THE BEST AUTHORITIES [1795] State I. 41x23cm (16x9") Uncolored. Bit faint foxing; o/w fine. Ref: Wheat & Brun 483. [A2] £133 **$220**

CAREY continued

KENTUCKY [1818] Probably from *General Atlas*. 26x48cm (10x18½") OL color. Margins toned/ soiled; image toned; else VG. Ref: Phillips (M) p.351. [A9] £160 **$265**

PLAT OF THE SEVEN RANGES OF TOWNSHIPS BEING PART OF THE TERRITORY OF THE UNITED STATES N.W. OF THE RIVER OHIO ... [1814] *General Atlas*. 61x34cm (24x13½") OL color. Glue browning at seam causing faint offsetting below c'fold; minor soiling margins; catalog excerpt taped to verso; overall VG. Ref: Phillips (A) 722-28; cf Wheat & Brun 677. Reps (West). [A10] £38 **$63**

SCOTLAND WITH THE PRINCIPAL ROADS FROM THE BEST AUTHORITIES [1795] 36x28cm (14x11") Orig OL color. Some printer's creases, some past border; occas lt soiling; else VG to fine. [A1] £43 **$72**

SOUTH CAROLINA [1804] From *American Pocket Atlas*. 15x19cm (6x7½") Full color. Lt staining lf margin; sm orig crease. Ref: cf Wheat & Brun 603. [another, 1808 ed, possibly proof copy with only state boundary colored, offered at same price] [15] £90 **$150**

THE STATE OF MARYLAND, FROM THE BEST AUTHORITIES. BY SAMUEL LEWIS [1795] State I. Counties named, no boundaries. 28x42cm (11x16½") Uncolored. Minor faint foxing; o/w fine. Ref: Wheat & Brun 510. [A2] £315 **$523**

THE STATE OF NEW JERSEY, COMPILED FROM THE MOST AUTHENTIC INFORMATION [1795] From American ed, *Guthrie's Geography Improved ...* By Lewis. 47x30cm (18½x12") Orig color. Age tone, browning at c'fold. Ref: Wheat & Brun 414. [1] £211 **$350**

[SAME TITLE] [1795] State I. 47x30cm (18½x12") Uncolored. Faint toning along lower horiz fold; repaired ½" tear bottom lf; o/w VG to fine. Ref: Wheat & Brun 414; Phillips (M) p.489. [A2] £216 **$358**

UPPER TERRITORIES OF THE UNITED STATES [1813-14] From *American Pocket Atlas*. (not in first 3 editions.) 20x15cm (8x6") Ref: Karpinski (MI) 21; Karrow (MW) 1-0789; Phillips (A) 1370-12a or 4523-12a. [12] £166 **$275**

[SAME TITLE] [1814] Illinois not on lake. 20x15cm (8x6") B&W. Few lt stains; else VG. [37] £181 **$300**

CAREY & LEA   *Dimensions sometimes include text around map*

[ATLAS] **FAMILY CABINET ATLAS** [1832] 1st American ed; said to be American ed of Starling 1831 atlas. Octavo, quarter calf with marbled boards; 48 colored maps, 4 plates, directories. Shaken, split spine, torn cover; contents dampstained & warped; no foxing; needs rebinding. Ref: Phillips (A) 762. [6] £250 **$415**

BRITISH POSSESSIONS IN NORTH AMERICA [c.1822] From ... *American Atlas*. On sheet with text, map 25x36cm (9½x14") Full color. Lt offsetting; fold split, only text affected; good (B). [A4] £73 **$121**

GEOGRAPHICAL, HISTORICAL AND STATISTICAL MAP OF AMERICA [1822] 2 maps with surround of text: "North America ...", 9x8"; "South America ..." 9x7"; on sheet 42x52cm (16½x20½") Full color. C'fold split in text, old repair; lt foxing; good (B). [A4] £66 **$110**

GEOGRAPHICAL, STATISTICAL AND HISTORICAL MAP OF BRAZIL [1827] Young & Delleker, sc. 30x22cm (12x9") with text surround 17x21". Color. Lt age toning along c'fold; VG. [14] £136 **$225**

GEOGRAPHICAL, STATISTICAL AND HISTORICAL MAP OF COLOMBIA [1822] Incl Venezuela. Yeager, sc. 30x22cm (12x9") with text surround 17x21". Color. Lt age toning along c'fold; VG. ["... Peru" (1827) offered at same price] [14] £121 **$200**

GEOGRAPHICAL, STATISTICAL AND HISTORICAL MAP OF CONNECTICUT [1827] Text surround on 3 sides. 25x29cm (10x11½") Full orig color. Fine [37] £166 **$275**

GEOGRAPHICAL, STATISTICAL, AND HISTORICAL MAP OF HAYTI, FORMERLY HISPANIOLA OR ST. DOMINGO [1827] From ... *American Atlas*. Text at bottom of full sheet 42x52cm (16½x20½") Full color. Lt browning at c'fold; VG (A). [A4] £50 **$83**

GEOGRAPHICAL, STATISTICAL AND HISTORICAL MAP OF INDIANA [1827] On 17x21" sheet with text, map 28x22cm (11x8½") Color. Some age toning along c'fold. [14] £121 **$200**

GEOGRAPHICAL, STATISTICAL AND HISTORICAL MAP OF JAMAICA [1822] On 17x21" sheet with text, map 29x31cm (11½x12") Archival tape repairs at c'fold ends; 5mm hole lower border near c'fold; o/w VG to fine. [14] £142 **$235**

GEOGRAPHICAL, STATISTICAL AND HISTORICAL MAP OF KENTUCKY [1827] From ... *American Atlas ...* 3rd ed. On 16½x20½" sheet with text below & extra text sheet; map 29x46cm (11½x18") Mint. Ref: Sames & Woods p.142; Phillips (A) 1177-27. [12] £151 **$250**

GEOGRAPHICAL, STATISTICAL AND HISTORICAL MAP OF LOUISIANA [1822] From ... *American Atlas*. With text surround, 17x21", map 29x32cm (11½x13") Orig color. Lt age toning along fold, separation below repaired with archival tape; few sm lt spots in text, margins & blank area; o/w VG to fine. [A1] £100 **$165**

GEOGRAPHICAL, STATISTICAL, AND HISTORICAL MAP OF MASSACHUSETTS [1823] On 16½x20½" sheet with text below. 30x47cm (12x18½") Full color. [22] £121 **$200**

CAREY & LEA continued

GEOGRAPHICAL, STATISTICAL, AND HISTORICAL MAP OF MEXICO [1826] 38x37cm (15x14½") Full color. Tears lower margin; dust soiled; good. [16] £302 **$500**

GEOGRAPHICAL, STATISTICAL, AND HISTORICAL MAP OF MICHIGAN TERRITORY [c.1822] 1st separate map of Mich. Terr. 37x27cm (14½x10½") Full color. Minor toning; japan tissue repair to fold split; VG (A). Ref: Karpinski (MI) 91. [A4] £384 **$636**

GEOGRAPHICAL, STATISTICAL AND HISTORICAL MAP OF MISSISSIPPI [1827] 3rd ed; 21 counties, 17 listed. 29x23cm (11½x9") with text, 16½x20½" overall. Color. [12] £196 **$325**

GEOGRAPHICAL, STATISTICAL AND HISTORICAL MAP OF NEW HAMPSHIRE [1822] From ... *American Atlas*. On 17x21" sheet with text, map 30x22cm (12x9") Color. Lt margin age toning; VG. Ref: Cobb (NH) 96. [14] £196 **$325**

GEOGRAPHICAL, STATISTICAL, AND HISTORICAL MAP OF NEW JERSEY [1822] From ... *American Atlas*. 13 counties; text on 3 sides. On 16½x20½" sheet, map 29x23cm (11½x9") Full color. Mended splits c'fold ends; else clean. Ref: Phillips (M) p.489; Phillips (A) 1373a-16. [12] £166 **$275**

GEOGRAPHICAL, STATISTICAL AND HISTORICAL MAP OF NEW YORK [1822] From ... *American Atlas*. With text, 17x21"; map 30x46cm (11½x18") Orig color. Few margin tears, one to neatline; lt marks in margin; o/w VG to fine. [A1] £150 **$248**

GEOGRAPHICAL, STATISTICAL AND HISTORICAL MAP OF NORTH AMERICA [1822] From ... *American Atlas*. With text on 3 sides, 17x21"; map 35x34cm (14x13½") Orig color. Some lt image transfer; fold separation into text repaired verso with archival tape; o/w VG to fine. [A1] £166 **$275**

[SAME TITLE] [c.1822] From ... *American Atlas*. Text on 3 sides, map 35x34cm (13½x13") Full color. Lt foxing, mostly margins; japan paper repair to fold splits VG (A). [A4] £100 **$165**

GEOGRAPHICAL, STATISTICAL, AND HISTORICAL MAP OF OHIO [1822] Text & data at sides; 59 counties. Overall 42x52cm (16½x20½") Orig color. Lower c'fold split; o/w very nice. [1] £90 **$150**

[SAME TITLE] [1822] From ... *American Atlas*. Text on 3 sides. Color. 30x24cm (12x9½") on 16½x20½" sheet. Sh c'fold end splits repaired; else fine. Ref: Phillips (M) p.628; Phillips (A) 1373a. [12] £136 **$225**

GEOGRAPHICAL, STATISTICAL AND HISTORICAL MAP OF RHODE ISLAND [1827] From ... *American Atlas*. 3rd ed. On 16½x20½" sheet with text, map 29x21cm (11½x8½") Color. Mended lower c'fold split; else fine. [12] £121 **$200**

GEOGRAPHICAL, STATISTICAL, AND HISTORICAL MAP OF THE DISTRICT OF COLUMBIA [c.1822] From ... *American Atlas*. With surround of text, map 27x27cm (10½x10½") Full color. Some foxing in text; japan tissue repair to c'fold split; VG (A). [A4] £119 **$198**

GEOGRAPHICAL, STATISTICAL AND HISTORICAL MAP OF THE LEEWARD ISLANDS [1822] Anguilla to Dominica; on sheet with text, overall 42x52cm (16½x20½") Color. ["... Windward Islands" offered at same price] [18] £100 **$165**

GEOGRAPHICAL, STATISTICAL AND HISTORICAL MAP OF UPPER AND LOWER CANADA, AND THE OTHER BRITISH POSSESSIONS IN NORTH AMERICA [1823] With text, 17x21"; map 25x52cm (10x20½") Orig color. Lt age toning along c'fold; VG. [A1] £63 **$105**

GEOGRAPHICAL, STATISTICAL, AND HISTORICAL MAP OF VERMONT [1823] 31x24cm (12½x9½") on 16½x20½" sheet with text. Full color. [22] £121 **$200**

MAP AND DESCRIPTION OF THE PRINCIPAL MOUNTAINS, &C. THROUGHOUT THE WORLD [1822] Incl explanatory text. 42x52cm (16½x20½") B&W. [A1] £73 **$121**

MEXICO AND GUATIMALA [1832] From 1st ed, *Family Cabinet Atlas*. 9x14cm (3½x5½") With Xeroxed index page. Color. Fine. Ref: Phillips (A) 762-90. [12] £51 **$85**

UNITED STATES OF AMERICA [c.1822] 42x54cm (16½x21") Full color. Deacidified; japan paper backing to close fold split & margin tears; good (B). [A4] £431 **$714**

CARON

DIERECHTE SEE-KARTE VON DER ZELEGENHEIT DER LANDES IAPAN [1663-72] From Caron & Shorten's book on Siam & Japan. 14x23cm (5½x9") Uncolored. Trimmed to edge of printed area; mounted on old paper; sm tear repaired. Ref: Walter (Japan) 115. [34] **£2,100 $3,482**

CARRIGAIN, P.

NEW HAMPSHIRE BY RECENT SURVEY ... [1816] 1st official map of state. 155x117cm (61x46") Orig color. Mounted on new rice paper; segmented & joined; sl loss; for its kind VG. Ref: Ristow (Amer M&M) p.96. [24] £3,619 **$6,000**

CARVER

A NEW MAP OF NORTH AMERICA [1779] From Dublin ed, *Travels through the Interior Parts of North-America*. Not a repeat of London ed map. 43x55cm (17x21½") Uncolored. [34] £850 $1,410

A PLAN OF CAPTAIN CARVER'S TRAVELS IN THE INTERIOR PARTS OF NORTH AMERICA IN 1766 AND 1767. [1778] From Jonathan Carver, *Travels through the Interior Parts of North America* ... Region west of Great Lakes. 26x34cm (10½x13½") B&W. Fine. Ref: Wheat (TM) 175; Howes C-215; Streeter 1772. Cumming (Exploration) p.79. [12] £513 **$850**

CARY, JOHN

[ATLAS] CARY'S ACTUAL SURVEY OF THE COUNTRY FIFTEEN MILES ROUND LONDON [1786] Octavo, speckled calf, rebacked; general map & 50 detailed colored maps; index. [A6] £391 $649

[ATLAS] CARY'S NEW AND CORRECT ENGLISH ATLAS [1787] Quarto, tree calf; general map & 46 county & regional maps in OL color. Lt offsetting; upper cover detached. Ref: Chubb CCLX. [A6] £460 $763

[SAME TITLE] [1793] Quarto, recent half calf; 46 regional & county OL color maps on 47 sheets. Contents page stained; occas margin soiling. Ref: Chubb 261. [A6] £414 $687

[ATLAS] CARY'S TRAVELLER'S COMPANION, OR A DELINEATION OF THE TURNPIKE ROADS OF ENGLAND AND WALES [1791] Octavo; title, ads, market towns listed; 43 OL color maps on 23 plates. Cover rebacked with orig spine & clasp. Ref: Chubb 274. [A6] £184 $305

[PUZZLE] A NEW MAP OF IRELAND, DIVIDED INTO ITS PROVINCES AND COUNTIES: ALSO, THE OPPOSITE COAST OF SCOTLAND AND WALES [1842] Full color jigsaw puzzle map with orig wooden box identified as "Edlin's New Dissected Map of Ireland", publ by E.C. Edlin, London. 47x52cm (18½x20½") Mahogany pieces sl warped; exc. [15] £513 **$850**

A NEW CHART OF THE WORLD, ON MERCATOR'S PROJECTION; EXHIBITING THE TRACKS AND DISCOVERIES OF THE MOST EMINENT NAVIGATORS, OF THE PRESENT PERIOD [1811] 46x51cm (18x20½") Orig color. Minor spot above N. Amer; faint age toning along c'fold; VG. [A1] £299 **$495**

A NEW MAP OF AFRICA, FROM THE LATEST AUTHORITIES [1811] 47x53cm (18½x21") Full orig color. Lt transference ocean area; VG. Ref: Tooley (Africa) p.35. MCC 47, p.30. [37] £181 **$300**

A NEW MAP OF AMERICA [1806] 46x52cm (18½x20½") Col. Browned along vert fold. [A7] £121 **$201**

A NEW MAP OF CHINA, FROM THE LATEST AUTHORITIES [1811] 47x51cm (18½x20½") Orig color. Separation at lower fold margin; VG to fine. [A1] £146 **$242**

A NEW MAP OF FRANCE, AGREEABLE TO ITS DIVISION INTO PROVINCES, AS PREVIOUS TO THE REVOLUTION FROM THE LATEST AUTHORITIES [1806] 46x52cm (18x20½") Orig color by provinces. Fine. [14] £136 **$225**

A NEW MAP OF IRELAND, DIVIDED INTO ITS PROVINCES AND COUNTIES [1799] 50x56cm (19½x22") OL color. [A8] £139 **$230**

A NEW MAP OF NOVA SCOTIA, NEWFOUNDLAND ... [1828] 46x52cm (18x20½") Full col. [41] £60 **$100**

A NEW MAP OF PART OF THE UNITED STATES OF NORTH AMERICA, CONTAINING THOSE OF NEW YORK, VERMONT, NEW HAMPSHIRE, MASSACHUSETTS, CONNECTICUT, RHODE ISLAND, PENNSYLVANIA, NEW JERSEY, DELAWARE, MARYLAND, AND VIRGINIA ... [1811] Incl ME. 46x52cm (18x20½") Orig color. Lt water stains lower rt ocean & cartouche area; o/w VG. [A2] £199 **$330**

[SAME TITLE] [1811] 52x58cm (20½x23") Color. Sl browned in ocean coastal areas. [A8] £173 **$287**

A NEW MAP OF SWISSERLAND, DIVIDED INTO ITS CANTONS AND DEPENDENCIES, INCLUDING THE GRISONS &C. &C. [1799] 46x52cm (18x20½") Orig color. VG to fine. [14] £196 **$325**

A NEW MAP OF THE RUSSIAN EMPIRE, DIVIDED INTO ITS GOVERNMENTS; FROM THE LATEST AUTHORITIES [1811] Much detail; with adjacent regions. 46x100cm (18x39½") Color. ¾" lower c'fold margin split; VG. [14] £166 **$275**

A NEW MAP OF THE UNITED STATES OF AMERICA, FROM THE LATEST AUTHORITIES [1806] To Mississippi River. 46x51cm (18x20") Full color. Faint toning margins; else clean. [A10] £208 **$345**

A NEW MAP OF THE WEST INDIA ISLES ... [1803] 46x51cm (18x20½") Orig full color. Sl fold darkening; VG. Ref: Phillips (M) p.1060. [16] £302 **$500**

A NEW MAP OF UPPER AND LOWER CANADA FROM THE LATEST AUTHORITIES ... [1807] 46x51cm (18x20") OL color. Fine. [37] £513 **$850**

AFRICA [1813] 23x29cm (9x11½") Orig color. Lt surface soiling; o/w fine. [14] £90 **$150**

AMERICA [1813] 28x23cm (11x9") Orig OL col. Occas faint surface soiling; o/w VG to fine. [A2] £80 **$132**

ARABIA [1808] 23x28cm (9x11") Orig col. Occas lt foxing & surface soiling; o/w fine. [A1] £100 **$165**

CAPE OF GOOD HOPE [1813] 23x28cm (9x11") Orig color. Fine. [14] £90 **$150**

CARY continued

CARY'S NEW MAP OF ENGLAND AND WALES, WITH PART OF SCOTLAND [1794] 1st ed. 6-part, dissected, linen-backed folding map with Wm. Faden labels on each map, in orig slipcase. Full color by county. 219x196cm (86x77") [15] £513 **$850**

CARY'S NEW POCKET PLAN OF LONDON, WESTMINSTER AND SOUTHWARK ... [1790-1811] Not dissected or mounted. Ran 18 editions to 1836. 40x60cm (16x23½") Orig OL color. Ref: Howgego 192, state 12. [34] **£500** $829

IRELAND [1813] 28x23cm (11x9") Orig col. Occas surface soiling; few brown spots; o/w fine. [A1] £96 **$160**

SICILY [1813] 23x28cm (9x11") Orig color. VG to fine. [14] £90 **$150**

THE UNITED STATES OF AMERICA [1808] West to Mississippi River, with maximum NW Terr. & Georgia. 28x23cm (11x9") Orig color. Faint foxing; o/w fine. [14] £136 **$225**

THE WEST INDIA ISLANDS [1808] 23x28cm (9x11") Orig color. Lt margin soiling; o/w fine. [14] £90 **$150**

CASE, TIFFANY & CO.

MAP OF THE UNITED STATES [1851] Folding map. Incl Mexico & part Central America, vignette of Washington & Capitol. 62x65cm (24½x25½") Color. [A7] £242 **$402**

CASSELL

CALIFORNIA AND OTHER WESTERN STATES OF THE UNITED STATES [1865] Oregon border to Baja; WA & OR inset. 43x30cm (17x12") Old OL color. Top margin sl crumpled; else VG. [38] £90 **$150**

CASSELL'S LARGE MAP OF LONDON. NEW EDITION, CORRECTED TO THE PRESENT TIME [1866] Cassell, Peter & Galpin. Parts I-III. Folio, orig wrappers; large colored wall map in 9 double-page mapsheets; 9 inches/mile. [A6] **£632** $1,048

CASSINI

LA NUOVA OLANDA E LA NUOVA GUINEA ... [1798] 35x48cm (14x19") Orig OL color. Ref: Tooley (Australia) 288, pl.15. [13] **Aus$4,200** £1,907 $3,162

CAVAZZA

NOVA TOTIUS TERRARUM ORBIS GEOGRAPHICA AC HYDROGRAPHICA TABULA [1642 (1643)] "Brachia" (curved arm-like shapes) at sides to be cut out for diurnal measure. 35x55cm (14x21½") Uncolored. Sm repair upper c'fold; o/w good. Ref: Shirley (W) 357. [32] £5,277 **$8,750**

CELLARIUS

COELI STELLATI CHRISTIANI HAEMISPHAERIUM PRIUS ... [1660] 1st ed. Western sky delineated with Christian figures. 43x51cm (17x20½") Full orig col, heightened in gold. Exc. Ref: Snyder (Heavens) pl.55; Warner p.53-4. ["Hemisphaerium Stellatum Austral ...", same description, offered at same price] [2] £3,317 **$5,500**

HAEMISPHAERIUM STELLATUM AUSTRALE AEQUALI SPHAERARUM PROPORTIONE [1660 (1708)] Schenk & Valk. 3rd state of three. Southern constellations superimposed on terrestrial western hemi; insular Calif. 43x51cm (17x20") Orig full color. Good. Ref: Burden 347; McLaughlin (Celestial #1). [32] £1,809 **$3,000**

HAEMISPHAERIUM STELLATUM AUSTRALE ANTIQUUM [1660] 44x52cm (17½x20½") Color. Clean tear vert fold lower margin just to image. [A7] £1,526 **$2,530**

HAEMISPHAERIUM STELLATUM BOREALE CUM SUBJECTO HAEMISPHAERIO TERRESTRI [(1661) 1708] Schenk & Valk. Northern constellations superimposed on terrestrial hemi. 43x51cm (17x20") Orig full color. Thin paper area on reverse; sm repaired hole; fair. [32] £1,146 **$1,900**

HEMISPHAERII BOREALIS COELI ET TERRAE SPHAERI CASCENOGRAPHIA [1660] 1st ed. Northern sky. 43x50cm (17x20") Full orig color, heightened in gold. Exc. Ref: Snyder (Heavens) pl.55; Warner p.53-4. ["Hemisphaerium Scenographicum Australe ...", same description, offered at same price] [2] £3,317 **$5,500**

HEMISPHAERIUM ORBIS ANTIQUI CUM ZONIS CIRCULIS ET SITU POPULORUM DIVERSO [(1661) 1708] Schenk & Valk. Eastern hemi with surround decor of astronomical devices. 41x51cm (16x20") Color. [13] **Aus$2,800** £1,272 $2,108

PLANISPHAERIUM BRAHEUM [c.1708] Schenk & Valk. Brahe solar system. 42x42cm (16½x16½") Color. [A7] £1,040 **$1,725**

SITUS TERRAE CIRCULIS COELESTIBUS CIRCUNDATAE [(1661) 1708] From *Atlas Coelestis* ... Schenk & Valk. 43x51cm (17x20") Color. Faint c'fold toning; overall VF. [4] **£1,850** $3,068

CENTURY ATLAS

OKLAHOMA AND INDIAN TERRITORY [1897] 27x38cm (10½x15") Orig color. VG. [14] £27 **$45**

TEXAS, WESTERN PART AND PANHANDLE [1902] 38x27cm (15x10½") Full color. [27] £42 **$70**

CHACE
MAP OF ROCKINGHAM COUNTY, NEW HAMPSHIRE   [1857]   Linen-backed wall map. 144x143cm (56½x56½") Full color. Lacks bottom rod; lt water damage; minor chipping; cracking & surface wear; age-toned; good. Ref: Cobb (NH) 239.   [15]   £422   **$700**

CHAMBERS
[ATLAS] ATLAS TO ACCOMPANY CHAMBERS'S ENCYCLOPOEDIA   [1869]   Phila: J.B. Lippincott. Quarto; cloth binding; 40 maps. Cover loose, worn at corners, torn at hinges; some maps with minor stains & browning; overall good. Ref: Phillips (A) 4351a.   [33]   £106   **$175**

CHAMOUIN
MAPPE-MONDE SUR LA PROJECTION REDUITE DE MERCATOR   GRAVE PAR CHAMOUIN ...   [1805]   Mercator proj; Australia at ctr. 29x45cm (11½x17½") Color.   [13]   Aus$430   £195 $324

CHAMPLAIN
LE BEAU PORT   [1613]   As in *Les Voyages du Sieur de Champlain*. Gloucester, MA. 15x25cm (6x10") Strengthened with Japan paper, some loss; lt browned. Ref: Burden 168.   [2]   £1,025   **$1,700**

PORT FORTUNE [CHATHAM, MA]   [1613]   "Picto-map" of Stage Harbor, Cape Cod. 20x25cm (8x10") Lt toning; mounted on rice paper; chipping along rt margin, sm area loss; fair-good. Ref: Burden 175.   [23]   £1,628   **$2,700**

CHAPMAN
CHAPMAN'S SECTIONAL MAP OF THE SURVEYED PART OF MINNESOTA   [1872]   Silas Chapman; Milwaukee. Folding map in orig cloth folder. 72x64cm (28½x25") Full col. Folder worn; internally fine.   [15]   £271   **$450**

CHAPMAN'S TOWNSHIP MAP OF WISCONSIN   [1874]   Silas Chapman Milwaukee. Folds into stiff case. 69x53cm (27x21") Full color by counties. Minor problems only, map & case.   [25]   £196   **$325**

MAP OF THE CITY OF MILWAUKEE   [1882]   Silas Chapman, Milwaukee. Folds into orig 16mo cloth case. 51x44cm (20x17") Color. Minor separation at several intersections.   [A8]   £225   **$373**

SECTIONAL MAP OF MINNESOTA   [1855]   Folded into case. Shows S part & W Wisconsin. 74x56cm (29x22") Orig color. Occas lt toning at folds; o/w fine.   [A2]   £265   **$440**

CHAPPE D'AUTEROCHE
KAMTSCHATSKISCHES MEER ...   [c.1780]   Believed from *Voyage en Siberie*. Incl SW Alaska. Voyages traced. With text, 17x27cm (6½x10½") Full orig color. Exc.   [36]   £271   **$450**

NORDLICHER THEIL DES GROSSEN SUD MEERS   [c.1780]   North Amer west coast. 23x16cm (9½x6½") Uncolored. VG.   [36]   £226   **$375**

CHATELAIN
CARTE CONTENANT LE ROYAUME DU MEXIQUE ET LA FLORIDE ...   [n.d.]   From *Atlas Historique*. Great Lakes to Panama. 40x52cm (16x20½") OL color. Exc.   [36]   £573   **$950**

CARTE DE L'ETA DU ROYAUME DE DANNEMARCK ET DIVERSES OBSERVATIONS POUR CONDUIRE AL INTELLEGENCE DEL' HISTORIE ET DU GOUVERNMENT DE CE ROYAUME   [c.1720]   Copenhagen view; 2 sm views. 33x44cm (13x17½") Sh upper c'fold separation at margin; o/w VG to fine.   [A1]   £199   **$330**

CARTE DE L'ISLE DE JAVA   PARTIE OCCIDENTALE, PARTIE ORIENTALE ...   [1719]   Publ in Vol.V, *Atlas Historique*. Extensive text panels. 2 sheets joined, 38x87cm (15x34") Color. Fine. Ref: Koeman Cha 6 (9).   [4]   £895 $1,484

CARTE DE LA NOUVELLE FRANCE   [1719 or later.]   Amsterdam. 43x50cm (17x20")   [A7]   £520   **$862**

CARTE DE LA NOUVELLE FRANCE, OU SE VOIT LE COURS DES GRANDES RIVIERES DE S. LAURENS & DE MISSISSIPI ... DE LA FLORIDE, DE LA LOUISIANE, DE LA VIRGINIE, DE LA MARIE-LANDE, DE LA PENSILVANIE, DU NOUVEAU JERSAY, DE LA NOUVELLE YORCK ...   [1719]   50x55cm (19½x21½") Full color. Exc.   [24]   £1,628   **$2,700**

[SAME TITLE]   [1719]   1st state. 42x50cm (16½x19½") Lt browned along fold.   [A8]   £1,318   **$2,185**

[SAME TITLE]   [1719 or later.]   Paris. Inset: Quebec map & view; vignettes. 42x50cm (16½x19½") Sl browning at 2 sm spots.   [A7]   £694   **$1,150**

[SAME TITLE]   [1720]   50x55cm (19½x21½") Full color. Exc.   [36]   £1,327   **$2,200**

CARTE DE LA PARTIE ... DU ROYAUME DE SUEDE AVEC UNE TABLE DES PROVINCES ET VILLES PRINCIPALES   [c.1710]   Two overlapping sheets headed "Meridionale" & "Septentrionale", each 39x45cm (15½x17½") Strong impression.   [11]   £232   **$385**

CHATELAIN continued

CARTE DES ANTILLES FRANCOISES ET DES ISLES VOISINES DRESSEE SUR LES MEMOIRES MANUSCRITS [1719] As in *Atlas Historique* ... Guadeloupe to (upside down) Grenada, with Barbados. 48x33cm (19x13") Color. Ref: Phillips (A) 548, v.6-35. [18] £208 **$345**

CARTE DU CANADA ... [1720] Great Lakes region to north of Hudson Bay. 41x52cm (16x20½") Uncolored. Exc. [36] £543 **$900**

CARTE DU PLAN DU VENISE, L'ETAT DE SA NOBLESSE, ... [1720] Half bird's-eye view; half text. 38x47cm (15x18½") Full color. Exc. Ref: Cassini, *Piante e Vedute Propettiche di Venezia*, #59. [36] £573 **$950**

CARTE GENEALOGIQUE POR CONDUIRE A L'HISTORIQUE DES ROIS DU NORD, LA CARTE DE LEURS ETATS, LEURS ARMES ET DES REMARQUES POUR CONDUIRE A L'INTELLIGENCE DE L'HISTOIRE DU NORD [c.1710] Incl 2 maps: "... Royaume de Suede ..." & "... Royaume de Gothie"; genealogical tree. 2 sheets, 38x97cm (15x38") Tear into text joined, no loss. [11] £151 **$250**

CARTE GENERALE DU ROYAUME DE FRANCE [1720] Provincial delineation. 13x17cm (5½x6½") OL & wash color. [40] £36 **$60**

CARTE POUR SERVIR L'INTELLIGENCE DE L'HISTOIRE DE GUSTAVE ADOLPHE, DE CHRISTINE, DE CHARLES GUSTAVE ET DE CHARLES XII [c.1710] Incl 2 maps: "... Conquestes ... en Pologne" & "... en Allemagne"; Bergen view; text below. 35x44cm (13½x17½") [11] £106 **$175**

CARTE TRES CURIEUSE DE LA MER DU SUD CONTENANT DES REMARQUES NOUVELLES ET TRES UTILES NON SEULEMENT SUR LES PORTS ET ILES DE CETTE MER, MAIS AUSSY SUR LES PRINCIPAUX PAYS DE L'AMERIQUE TANT SEPTENTRIONALE QUE MERIDIONALE ... [1719] Americas with opposite continental regions; insular California; many vignettes & insets. 4 sheets joined. 81x140cm (32x55½") Color. Few minor mends; overall exc. Ref: Tooley (Amer) p.130, #80; Schwartz & Ehrenberg pl.85. Leighly pl.xx. [24] £9,046 **$15,000**

DESCRIPTION DE L'ISTHME DE DARIEN, DES PROPRIETEZ DU PAYS ET DE LA VILLE DE PANAMA; A LA QUELLE ON A JOINT UNE DESCRIPTION CURIEUSE DES DIVERSES PLANTES, OISEAUX POISSONS LES PLUS RARES QUIT SE TROUVENT DANS LA NOUVELLE HOLLANDE [c.1720] Sm Panama map (3x5"); 6 panels of flora & fauna. 37x43cm (14½x17") Uncolored. Fine. [A2] £57 **$94**

L'AMERIQUE SEPTENTRIONALE SUIVANT MR. DELISLE DE L'ACADAMIE DES SCIENCES [1717] Paris: L'Honore & Chatelain. 14x17cm (5½x6½") B&W. Strong impression; fine. [35] £75 **$125**

L'EMPIRE DU JAPON TIRE DES CARTES DES JAPONNOIS ... [1719] As in Vol.V, *Atlas Historique*. After Reland. 66 provinces in European & kanji script. 36x44cm (14x17½") Color. Exc. Ref: Walter (Japan) 70; Cortazzi pl.74; MCC 36 #46; Koeman Cha 6 (12). [4] £1,250 **$2,073**

[SAME TITLE] [1720] From *Atlas Historique*. Nagasaki inset. 38x43cm (15x17") Uncolored. Exc. [36] £1,206 **$2,000**

LES INDES [1717] L'Honore & Chatelain. East Indies & Indo-China. 13x17cm (5x6½") B&W. Fine. [35] £27 **$45**

MAPPEMONDE OU DESCRIPTION GENERALE DU GLOBE TERRESTRE [c.1719] Double hemi; insular Calif; explorer's tracks; references below 34x44cm (13½x17½") OL color. Exc. [36] £573 **$950**

NOUVAUX MAPPEMONDE OU GLOBE TERRESTRE AVEC DES TABLES ET DES REMARQUES [1720] From *Atlas Historique* ... Double hemi. text surround referencing rivers & lakes. 48x69cm (19x27") Uncolored. Repaired tears lower text area; VG. [36] £965 **$1,600**

[SAME TITLE] [1732] As in *Atlas Historique*. Double hemi; index above & below; overall 46x66cm (18x26") Color. Tissue backed. [19] £558 **$925**

NOUVELLE CARTE DE L'AMERIQUE SEPTENTRIONALE ... [1720] From *Atlas Historique* ... Table at side; overall 47x59cm (18½x23½") OL color. Exc. [36] £573 **$950**

VUE DE STOCKHOLM &C. [c.1710] On plate entitled "Carte de la Maison du Roy ..." 35x45cm (13½x17½") [11] £136 **$225**

CHETWIND

AMERICAE DESCRIPTIO NOVA [IN SET WITH] **AFRICAE** [AND] **ASIAE** [AND] **EUROPAE** [1666] From Heylyn's *Cosmography*. Shows insular Calif. Each about 34x33cm (13½x13") All narrow margins, Asia cropped with sl loss; some creasing. Ref: McLaughlin 39. [A6] £920 **$1,526**

CHEVALIER

[BOOK WITH MAPS] **DESCRIPTION OF THE PLAIN OF TROY: WITH A MAP OF THAT REGION DELINEATED FROM AN ACTUAL SURVEY** [1791] Edinburgh: T. Cadell. Quarto; (xvi), 154, (10); 4 maps. Marbled boards: worn; NYHS stamps on title & preface; edge chips & some browning to maps. [21] Can$220 £96 **$159**

CHIQUET

LE GLOBE TERRESTRE REPRESENTE EN DEUX PLANS ... [1729] Publ in *Nouveau et Curieux Atlas*. Double hemi; insular Calif. 16x22cm (6½x8½") Color. Framed. [13] **Aus$840** £381 $632

LE NOUVEAU ET CURIEUX ATLAS GEOGRAPHIQUE ET HISTORIQUE, OU LE DIVERTISSEMENT DES EMPEREURS, ROY, ET PRINCES ... [c.1719] Oblong quarto, limp velum; 27 maps & plates in orig OL color, incl America with insular Calif; 4 pp index. Cover worn; soiling binding & plates, some foxing; VG. Ref: Phillips (A) 4279; McLaughlin 191. [24] £2,322 **$3,850**

CHURRUCA

PLANO GEOMETRICO DEL PUERTO CAPITAL DE LA ISLA DE PUERTO RICO LEVANTADO EN 1794 [1794] Harbor chart; soundings, sailing directions. 44x58cm (17½x23") Exc. [2] £1,689 **$2,800**

CLARK

CLARK'S MAP OF LITCHFIELD CTY, CONNECTICUT. FROM ACTUAL SURVEYS BY G.M. HOPKINS, JR. [1859] Richard Clark; Phila. Wall map; inset maps & views. Full color by town. 155x135cm (61x53") Wear & chipping, minor loss near top; lacks bottom roller; fine. Ref: Phillips (M) p.360. Thompson (CT) 184. [another, damage top 4" with considerable chipping, some loss; sides edged with masking tape, offered at $650] [15] £452 **$750**

MAP OF FAIRFIELD COUNTY, CONNECTICUT [1858] Richard Clark; Phila. 2nd ed with changes. Insets. 132x150cm (52x59") Lt age toning; exc. Ref: Thompson (CT) 176; Phillips (M) p.276. [15] £1,055 **$1,750**

MAP OF THE TOWN OF BRISTOL, HARTFORD COUNTY, CONNECTICUT. FROM ORIGINAL SURVEYS BY E.M. WOODFORD ... [1852] Wall map; 11 bldg views. Full color by district. 106x84cm (41½x33") Lt chipping, staining near top; generally good. Ref: Thompson (138). [15] £452 **$750**

MAP OF THE TOWN OF NORWALK, FAIRFIELD COUNTY, CONN. [1851] Richard Clark, Phila. Wall map. 113x90cm (44½x35½") Damage, chipping at top; VG, below top 5" superb. [15] £392 **$650**

CLARK & TACKABURY

NEW TOPOGRAPHICAL MAP OF THE STATE OF CONNECTICUT [1860] Linen-backed wall map with orig rollers; 9 insets. 220x138cm (86½x54½") Col. Minor deterioration; a sm hole; VG. Ref: Thompson (CT) 181. [15] £543 **$900**

CLASON MAP CO.

CLASON'S GUIDE MAP OF NEBRASKA [1917-18] Publ Denver. With green folder 36x71cm (14x28") Counties in green OL color; highways in red. VG. [26] £30 **$50**

CLOPPENBURGH

CHINA [1630-32] With Japan & NW America. 18x25cm (7x9½") Color. [34] £380 $630

DESCRIPTION DES ISLES BERMUDAS / MAPPA AETIVARUM INSULARUM [1630] Based on Speed. 19x25cm (7½x10") Color. Fine. [43] £452 **$750**

DU DESTROIT DE MAGELLAN [1630] From Mercator Minor Atlas. 18x25cm (7½x10") Color. ["Peru" (western South America) offered at same price] [39] £121 **$200**

GERMANIAE NOVA AC ACCURATA DESCRIPTIO ... [1630] Panels all around, incl German city views. 45x56cm (18x22") Early color. Fold reinforcements; else exc. Ref: MCC 35, #10b. [24] £1,689 **$2,800**

HISPANIAE NOVAE NOVA DESCRIPTIO [1630] From enlarged ed Mercator Minor Atlas. 19x25cm (7½x10") [39] £136 **$225**

IAPONIA [1630-32] From Cloppenburgh's *Atlas Minor*. Reduced Jodocus Hondius map. 18x24cm (7x9½") Color. [34] £720 **$1,194**

INDIA ORIENTALIS [1630-32] Reduced version of Hondius. 19x26cm (7½x10") Color. [34] £350 **$581**

PERSICI VEL SOPHORUM REGNI TIPUS [1630-32] Reduced version of 1606 Hondius. 19x26cm (7½x10") Color. [34] £200 **$332**

REGNI BOHEMIAE NOVA DESCRIPTIO [1618 - c.1630] By Van den Keere, with new imprint; separately published. 39x50cm (15½x20") Uncolored. [34] £850 **$1,410**

SEPTENTRIONALIUM TERRARUM DESCRIPTIO [1630-32] From 2nd ed, *Atlas sive Cosmographicae* ... Reduced version of Mercator; 4 arctic islands. 18x25cm (7x10") Uncolored. [34] £420 **$697**

TABULA GEOGRAPHICA IN QUA OMNES REGIONES URBES, OPPIDA, LOCA ET FLUVII ISRAELIAE DESCRI. [1643] D. Mathes; H. Doetecum, sc. Area of modern Israel; 15-panel surround. 28x50cm (11x19½") A false margin; backed with tissue. ["... Urbes, Oppida, et Locale Scribuntur ..." (Italy to Holy Land) offered at same price] [11] £271 **$450**

CLOPPENBURGH continued

TURCICI IMPERII IMAGO   [1630-32]   Reduced version of Jodocus Hondius. 19x25cm (7½x10")   Color. Ref: Tibbetts 80.   [34]   **£400**   **$664**

TYPUS ORBIS TERRARUM   [1630-1689]   In *Gerardi Mercatoris Atlas ... Jodoci Hondij*.   Double hemi. 19x26cm (7½x10½")   B&W.   Ref: Shirley (W) 334.   [13]   **Aus$2,200**   **£999**   **$1,656**

VIRGINIAE ITEM ET FLORIDAE AMERICAE PROVINCIARUM NOVA DESCRIPTIO   [1630]   19x25cm (7½x10") Full color. Exc. Ref: Burden 227   [44]   **£332**   **$550**

CLOUET

[NORTH AMERICA: EASTERN]   [1767]   Text at sides. 32x56cm (12½x22")   Orig color.   [46]   **£180**   **$299**

DES MERS ON APPELLE MER CETTE VASTE ETENDUE ... DE LA SURFACE DE LA TERRE ...   [1780]   From *Geographie Moderne* ...   Double hemi; border text; overall 32x56cm (13x22")   Color. Ref: Phillips (A) 3519-9.   [19]   **£109**   **$180**

DES ZONES LES TROPIQUES ET LES CERCLES POLAIRES DIVISENT LA TERRE ...   [1780]   From *Geographie Moderne* ...   Double hemi; border text; overall 32x56cm (12½x22")   Color. Ref: Phillips (A) 3519-4.   [19]   **£87**   **$145**

CLUVER

ACHAIA QUAE ET HELLAS HODIE LIVADIA   [c.1680]   Insets: Thebes; Athens. 20x25cm (8x10")   VG.   [A9]   **£49**   **$81**

CHERSONESI QUAE HODIE NATOLIA DESCRIPTIO   [c.1680]   20x26cm (8x10")   Uncolored. Fine. ["Daciarum Moesiarum et Thracie ..." & "Hellas seu Graecia ..." offered at same price]   [22]   **£42**   **$70**

ITALIA NOVA   [c.1680]   26x30cm (10½x12")   Uncolored. Fine.   [22]   **£90**   **$150**

ITALIAE GALLICAE SIVE GALLIAE CISALPINAE   [c.1680]   20x25cm (8x10")   Uncol. Fine.   [22]   **£39**   **$65**

NOVA TOTIUS GERMANIAE DESCRIPTIO   [c.1680]   26x33cm (10½x13")   Uncolored. Fine.   ["Prussiae Nova Tabula" offered at same price]   [22]   **£60**   **$100**

PELOPONNESUS NUNC MOREA   [c.1680]   21x25cm (8½x10")   Uncolored. Fine.   ["Macedoniae et Thessallae", "Scythia et Tartaria Asiatica" & "Campanie Samnii Apulliae Lucaniae Brutiorum ..." offered at same price]   [22]   **£36**   **$60**

REGNI DANIAE ACCURATISSIMA DELINEATIO   [c.1680]   21x25cm (8½x10")   Uncolored. Fine.   ["Germaniae Cisrhenanae ..." offered at same price]   [22]   **£48**   **$80**

SARMATIA ET SCYTHIA RUSSIA ET TARTARIA EUROPAEA   [c.1680]   23x25cm (9½x10")   Uncolored. Fine.   ["Hodiernae Belgicae ...", "... Pannoniae et Illyrici .." & "Vindeliciae Norici, Couterminacum" offered at same price]   [22]   **£45**   **$75**

SCYTHIA ET SERICA   [1706]   20x30cm (8x12")   Later pale OL color. Lt toning; good (B).   [A4]   **£34**   **$57**

SUEVIA QUAE CIS CODANUM SUITSINUM   [c.1680]   18x25cm (7½x10")   Uncolored. Fine.   [22]   **£51**   **$85**

COGGINS

AN EAST PROSPECT OF THE CITY OF PHILADELPHIA   [c.1854]   Litho repro of Heap's 18th c. view on sheet with Jefferys' map & view of Independence Hall. 56x90cm (22x35½")   Modern stiff archival backing; chipping in surface of view.   [15]   **£211**   **$350**

COLBY

MISSOURI   [1857]   Publ in *Diamond Atlas*. 15x13cm (6x5")   Full col. Margin spots; good (B).   [A3]   **£10**   **$17**

NEW JERSEY AND EASTERN PENNSYLVANIA   [1857]   Same source   15x13cm (6x5")   Full color. Margin staining; good (B).   [A3]   **£8**   **$14**

OHIO   [1857]   Same source. 15x13cm (6x5")   Full col. Margin staining; few spots; VG (B).   [A3]   **£6**   **$10**

COLE

A GENERAL VIEW OF THE CITY OF LISBON, THE CAPITAL OF THE KINGDOM OF PORTUGAL   [c.1769]   From *Geographical Dictionary*. View from harbor before 1755 earthquake. 15x28cm (6x11")   B&W. Fine.   [31]   **£118**   **$195**

COLLINS, GREENVILLE

[ENGLAND: THE SEVERN OR CHANNELL OF BRISTOLL]   [1693]   Clear 1st ed. 45x56cm (17½x22")   [34]   **£300**   **$498**

COLLINS, GREENVILE continued

[IRELAND: CARLINGFORD LOUGH] [1693] From *Great Britain's Coasting Pilot*; 1st ed. 42x32cm (16½x12½") [34] £240 $398

[IRELAND: DUBLIN BAY] [1693] From same source; 1st ed. 45x56cm (17½x22") [34] £340 $564

[ISLE OF MAN] [1693] Clear 1st ed. H. Moll, sc. 45x56cm (17½x22") [34] £400 $664

CARRECK-FERGUS [mid 18th c.] From *Great Britain Coasting Pilot.* 46x56cm (18x22") [A7] £121 $201

PLYMOUTH TO THE RT. HON.BLE ARTHUR EARLE OF TORRINGTON [1693] Clear 1st ed. 45x56cm (17½x22") [34] £320 $531

THIS CHART OF KINGSALE HARBOUR [1693] From *Great Britain's Coasting Pilot.* 1st ed. 45x58cm (17½x22½") [Chart of Carrickfergus Lough offered at same price] [34] £320 $531

COLLINS, H.G.

[ATLAS] THE TRAVELLING ATLAS OF ENGLAND AND WALES [1850] Octavo, morocco; general map, 44 colored regional & county maps. Cover worn; maps loose. Ref: Chubb 529. [A6] £230 $382

COLLINS & CLARK

MAP OF THE CITY OF BRIDGEPORT, CONN. FROM ORIGINAL SURVEYS BY SIDNEY & NEFF ... [1850] Phila. Wall map, linen-backed; 12 bldg views. 94x90cm (37x35½") Well worn; damage top left; lacks rollers. Ref: Thompson (CT)124. [15] £211 $350

COLLINS & SON

COLLIN'S STANDARD MAP OF LONDON [c.1885] Folding map dissected & mounted on linen, with accompanying booklet. 74x85cm (29x33½") Color. [39] £106 $175

COLLOT

GENERAL MAP OF NORTH AMERICA [(1797) 1805-26] From *Voyage dans l'Amerique Septentrionale.* 100 English ed & 300 French ed published. 58x84cm (23x33") B&W. Sm repairs to orig folds; fine. Ref: Howes C-601; Streeter 1789. [29] £2,352 $3,900

PLAN OF CAPE GIRARDO [1824-26] From English ed, *Journey in North America* ... (see Howes for rarity.) 27x16cm (11x6½") Fine. Ref: Howes (US) C-601. [15] £603 $1,000

COLOM

DE CARYBSCHE EYLANDEN VAN DE BARBADOS TOT DE BOCHT VAN MEXICO TOE NU EERST VYGEGEVEN DOOR ARONOLD COLOM TOT AMSTERDAM ... [c.1654] Incl SE present U.S. 53x64cm (21x25") Orig color. Bit lt foxing; else exc. Ref: Burden 320. Koeman IV, p.114-7. [23] £6,031 $10,000

NOVA TOTIUS TERRARUM ORBIS GEOGRAPHICA AC HYDROGRAPHICA TABULA AUCT. IACOBUS COLOM [c.1650] Separately issued; double-hemi; insular Calif; like Hondius, but Tycho Brahe & Copernicus portraits. 39x53cm (15½x21") Full orig color. Margins reinforced; toned; else VG. Framed. Ref: Shirley (W) 381. [23] £3,920 $6,500

COLTON (Atlas Maps)

[ATLAS] COLTON'S GENERAL ATLAS ... [1860] J.H. Colton, NY. Folio, half morocco. Colored maps. Extremities loose, text block about loose; some maps loose or soiled at edges; few sm tears in several margins; appears complete. [A8] £1,248 $2,070

[ATLAS] COLTON'S GENERAL ATLAS OF THE WORLD [1886] NY: G.W. & C.B. Colton. Folio; 212 images on 142 map sheets; half sheep. Internally clean, tight; joints reinforced; backstrip defective; extremities rubbed. [A7] £1,179 $1,955

[TITLE PAGE] AMERICAN ATLAS [c.1855] 6 Indians regard activities of whites from a bluff. 46x36cm (18x14") B&W. Spotting outside image; corner creased. [27] £54 $90

ARKANSAS [1855] 33x41cm (13x16") Orig color by counties. Lt margin age toning; o/w fine. [A1] £63 $105

[SAME TITLE] [1855] 32x41cm (12½x16") Full color. Some margin tears; clean; VG (A). [A4] £50 $83

AUSTRIA [1855] Incl Hungary & part of Balkans. 32x40cm (13x15½") Orig color. Lt margin age toning; o/w fine. [14] £78 $130

CANADA WEST OR UPPER CANADA [1855] 32x40cm (13x15½") Full col. Fine (A+). [A4] £40 $66

CENTRAL AMERICA [1884] Double page sheet, 41x69cm (16x27") Color by provinces. [40] £39 $65

CHINA [c.1855] 2 uncolored insets 32x40cm (13x16") Orig col. Lt edge toning; o/w fine. [14] £84 $140

[SAME TITLE] [1855 (1859)] 30x37cm (11½x14½") Creases; close rt margin. [21] Can$60 £26 $43

CITY OF BALTIMORE [1855 (1856)] 33x39cm (13x15½") Orig pastel color. Top margin uneven; clean. [27] £33 $55

COLTON (Atlas Maps) continued

CITY OF NEW ORLEANS [ON SHEET WITH] CITY OF LOUISVILLE [1855] 39x33cm (15½x13") Full orig color. Exc. [36] £57 **$95**

COLTON'S CALIFORNIA [1855, publ 1860] From Johnson & Browning, *New Illustrated ... Atlas ...* San Francisco inset. 39x32cm (15½x12½") Color. [12] £96 **$160**

COLTON'S CITY OF BALTIMORE ... [1860] From Johnson & Browning, *New Illustrated ... Atlas ...* Dated 1855. 32x39cm (12½x15½") Color. Ref: Gohm (Antique) p.77. [12] £39 **$65**

COLTON'S COMMON SCHOOL GEOGRAPHY. MAP NO.12. UNITED STATES [1874] Geo. W. Colton; NY: Sheldon & Co. 26x21cm (10½x8½") Partial printed color. Good [16] £27 **$45**

COLTON'S COMMON SCHOOL GEOGRAPHY REFERENCE MAP OF THE UNITED STATES SECTION 10 [TEXAS] [1880] Geo. W. Colton; NY: Sheldon & Co. Verso: Section 9, WI & MI. 30x24cm (12x9½") Full color. Lt browned; good. [16] £45 **$75**

COLTON'S GEORGETOWN AND THE CITY OF WASHINGTON, THE CAPITAL OF THE UNITED STATES OF AMERICA [1861] Vignettes. 33x41cm (13x16") Color by wards. [40] £45 **$75**

COLTON'S HAWAIIAN GROUP OR SANDWICH ISLANDS [1860] Sm insets: New Zealand; Samoa; Fiji; Society Islands; Marquesas; Galapagos. 40x32cm (16x13") B&W. Lt uniform age toning; lt offsetting from next page; little lt minor foxing; o/w VG. [14] £60 **$100**

COLTON'S ILLINOIS [1855] Chicago area inset. 40x32cm (15½x13") Orig color by counties. Lt uniform age toning; VG to fine. [14] £87 **$145**

COLTON'S INDIANA [1855] 40x33cm (16x13") Orig color by counties. Faint uniform age toning; o/w fine. [14] £84 **$140**

COLTON'S KANSAS AND NEBRASKA [1861] Eastern parts. 64x43cm (25x17") Full col. [41] £90 **$150**

COLTON'S KENTUCKY AND TENNESSEE [dated 1859] From Johnson & Browning, *New Illustrated ... Family Atlas ...* Publ 1860. Plate 38. 32x42cm (12½x16½") Brilliant color. [12] £51 **$85**

COLTON'S MAINE [1860] From Johnson & Browning, *New Illustrated ... Atlas.* Dated 1859; Plate 9, with Colton border. Knox County lacking. 39x32cm (15½x12½") Color. [12] £54 **$90**

COLTON'S MAP OF BOSTON AND ADJACENT CITIES [1855] J.H. Colton. 40x32cm (16x13") Orig color. Lt stain upper lf margin to border; VG. [14] £69 **$115**

COLTON'S MICHIGAN [IN SET WITH] COLTON'S LAKE SUPERIOR [1857] Full coverage of MI. Each 41x34cm (16x13½") Full color. VG. [26] £54 **$90**

COLTON'S OREGON, WASHINGTON, IDAHO, MONTANA AND BRITISH COLUMBIA [1869] Incl WY. 42x69cm (16½x27") Full color. [41] £75 **$125**

COLTON'S PERSIA AND ARABIA [1869] Shows caravan routes. 32x39cm (12½x15½") Color. [40] £27 **$45**

COLTON'S SOUTH CAROLINA [1857] Charleston area inset; decorative border. 41x34cm (16x13½") Full color. VG. ["... North Carolina" & "... Alabama" offered at same price] [26] £42 **$70**

COLTON'S TERRITORIES OF NEW MEXICO ARIZONA COLORADO NEVADA AND UTAH [1855 (1863)] Transitional period; 2 AZ counties. 33x39cm (13x15½") Color by counties. [8] £121 **$200**

COLTON'S TERRITORIES OF NEW MEXICO AND UTAH [1855 (1861)] NM-AZ division made north & south; proto-Colorado named "Colona". 32x39cm (12½x15½") [41] £136 **$225**

COLTON'S TEXAS [1864] 32x27cm (12½x10½") Yellow tint. VG. [26] £48 **$80**

[SAME TITLE] [1873 (1876)] G.W. & C.B. Colton, NY. 4 insets. 46x71cm (18x28") Full color. Weak c'fold; rebacked. [26] £106 **$175**

COLTON'S THE UNITED STATES OF AMERICA [1861] Unusual western territories. 39x66cm (15½x26") Full color. [41] £112 **$185**

COLTON'S UNITED STATES OF AMERICA [1859] Publ by Johnson & Browning. Transitional western territories, incl "Colona" in present CO. 39x67cm (15½x26½") Orig color. Few marks & repaired tears margin; minute dark area & hole Pacific; fox spot NV & TX; older archival tape c'fold reinforcement of 4" split. [A2] £232 **$385**

COLTON'S WASHINGTON AND OREGON [dated 1853 (1860)] From Johnson & Browning, *New Illustrated ... Family Atlas ...* Plate 53. Maximum WA to Rockies, abutting Nebraska Terr. 32x41cm (12½x16") Color. Tiny sulfide spot. [12] £81 **$135**

[SAME TITLE] [1859] Incl present Idaho. 32x40cm (13x16") Orig color. VG to fine. [14] £151 **$250**

COLTON'S WISCONSIN [1855] 1st ed; blank verso. Milwaukee inset. 40x33cm (16x13") Orig color. Some lt edge toning; VG. ["Minnesota" & "Ohio" offered at same price] [14] £90 **$150**

[SAME TITLE] [1857] Plain border. 41x34cm (16x13½") Full color. VG. [26] £42 **$70**

COLTON (Atlas Maps) continued

COLTON'S WISCONSIN [1859 (1860)] From Johnson & Browning, *New Illustrated ... Family Atlas ...* Plate 48. 55 counties. 39x32cm (15½x12½") Fine. Ref: Karrow (MW) 6-1797. [12] £75 **$125**

CONNECTICUT WITH PORTIONS OF NEW YORK AND RHODE ISLAND [1855] 32x39cm (13x15½") Orig color by counties. Lt margin soiling; fine. [14] £90 **$150**

CUBA JAMAICA AND PORTO RICO [1855] 1st ed; no text verso. Inset: "Porto Rico". 33x41cm (13x16") Orig color. Few lt foxing spots, mainly margin; overall VG. [14] £100 **$165**

EUROPE [1855] 32x40cm (13x16") Col. Lt margin age toning; lt crease lower rt corner; VG. [14] £90 **$150**

FLORIDA [1857] Inset of Keys. 41x34cm (16x13½") Full color. Bright; VG. [26] £54 **$90**

HINDOOSTAN OR BRITISH INDIA [1855] 40x32cm (15½x12½") Full color. VG (A). [A3] £15 **$25**

INDIANA [1861] 39x32cm (15½x12½") Full color. [40] £42 **$70**

IOWA [1855] 1st ed. 30x41cm (12x16") Orig color. [27] £36 **$60**

J.H. COLTON'S COLORADO AND NEW MEXICO [1865] From *Colton's Atlas of the Union.* 28x22cm (11x8½") Full color by counties. [25] £60 **$100**

J.H. COLTON'S MAP OF FLORIDA [1865] Probably from *Colton's Atlas of the Union.* South in 2 insets. 28x20cm (11x8") Full color. VG. [26] £36 **$60**

J.H. COLTON'S MAP OF NEBRASKA, DAKOTA AND MONTANA [1865] Incl CO, NM, parts of KS, OK, UT, ID, AZ, and WY as part of Dakota 28x20cm (11x8") Full color. VG. [26] £45 **$75**

KANSAS [1866 (1872)] 2 Wichitas; 2 Ft. Dodges. 42x61cm (16½x24") Full color. Dampstaining upper & lower margins; o/w fine. Ref: Karrow (MW) 13-0655. [12] £75 **$125**

LAKE SUPERIOR AND THE NORTHERN PART OF MICHIGAN [1855] 1st ed; blank verso. 33x40cm (13x16") Orig color by counties. VG to fine. [14] £93 **$155**

LOUISIANA [1855] 1st ed; blank verso. 32x39cm (13x15½") Orig color by counties. Bit of faint foxing; o/w fine. [14] £100 **$165**

MAP OF BOSTON AND ADJACENT CITIES [1856] Back Bay streets outlined. 37x30cm (14½x12") Color. [22] £54 **$90**

MASSACHUSETTS AND RHODE ISLAND [1855] Boston area inset. 32x41cm (13x16") Orig col. [27] £36 **$60**

[SAME TITLE] [1861] Boston area inset. 33x41cm (13x16") Full color. [40] £45 **$75**

MEXICO [1855] From *Atlas of America ...* J.H. Colton; 1st ed. 33x39cm (13x15½") Color. Fine. With text page. Ref: Phillips (A) 10269-54. [12] £51 **$85**

MICHIGAN [1884] 62x44cm (24½x17½") Full color. [40] £42 **$70**

MINNESOTA [1855] Incl present Dakotas to Missouri R. 33x41cm (13x16") Full color. VG. [26] £72 **$120**

[SAME TITLE] [1855] Western boundary is Missouri River. 32x41cm (12½x16") Full color. [39] £90 **$150**

[SAME TITLE] [c.1855] From *General Atlas.* J.H. Colton. State II, incl part Dakotas. 33x41cm (13x16") Full color. Pristine. [State IV, dated 1855, offered as same price] [12] £106 **$175**

MISSISSIPPI [1855 / 57] J.H. Colton. 37x29cm (15x11½") Full orig color. VG. [36] £75 **$125**

NEBRASKA AND KANZAS [1855] NE north to Canada & west to Rockies. 32x39cm (12½x15½") Color. Offsetting from facing sheet; o/w good. [8] £118 **$195**

[SAME TITLE] [1857] Nebraska north to Canada & west to Rockies. Plain border. 29x37cm (11½x14½") Color. [39] £121 **$200**

NEW MAP OF THE STATE OF TEXAS COMPILED FROM J. DECORDOVA'S LARGE MAP [1855] 43x66cm (17x26") Color. Lt offsetting in margin & Gulf; some sm dark spots; o/w fine. [14] £151 **$250**

[SAME TITLE] [1855] 1st ed. 41x62cm (16x24½") Full color. VG. [1861 ed offered at same price; 1866 ed offered at $225] [16] £166 **$275**

[SAME TITLE] [1855, publ 1857] From 1st ed, *General Atlas ...* Plain border version. 113 counties. 39x64cm (15½x25") Color. Superb. Ref: Day (TX) 445A; Phillips (A) 6129-37, 38. [12] £166 **$275**

[SAME TITLE] [1857] Plain border. 41x66cm (16x26") Color. Bright; VG. [26] £121 **$200**

[SAME TITLE] [1856 (1861)] NY: Johnson & Browning. 42x65cm (16½x26") Full orig color. Exc. [27] £196 **$325**

NORTH AMERICA [1855] Maximum Nebraska Terr. 40x34cm (16x13½") Orig color. Minute spot; VG. [A1] £73 **$121**

[SAME TITLE] [1857] 34x41cm (13½x16") Full color. Exc. [26] £54 **$90**

NORTH CAROLINA [1855] 32x39cm (13x15½") Orig pastel color. Even browning; sm border tears repaired. [27] £45 **$75**

[SAME TITLE] [dated 1855] From J.H. Colton, *General Atlas* 32x40cm (12½x16") Full col. [12] £36 **$60**

COLTON (Atlas Maps) continued

NORTH CAROLINA [1869] Beaufort Harbor inset 32x41cm (12½x16½"). Color. [40] £45 **$75**

NORTHERN AMERICA - BRITISH, RUSSIAN & DANISH POSSESSIONS IN NORTH AMERICA [1855] J.H. Colton. Canada, etc. 32x40cm (12½x15½") Full color. Rough top margin, tears to border; good (B). [A4] £37 **$61**

[SAME TITLE] [1869] Canada & Alaska. 33x41cm (13x16") Full color. [40] £42 **$70**

OREGON, WASHINGTON, CALIFORNIA, COLORADO, NEVADA, UTAH, NEW MEXICO AND ARIZONA [1863] Bay area inset. 32x27cm (12½x10½") Full color. VG. [26] £54 **$90**

PHILADELPHIA [1855] 40x32cm (16x13") Orig color. Lt margin soiling; ½" margin tear with archival tape verso repair; o/w fine. Ref: Van Ermen 58. [14] £66 **$110**

SOUTH AMERICA [1855] J.H. Colton. 39x33cm (15½x13") Orig color. Fine. ["Brazil and Guayana" & "Colton's Patagonia / Falkland Islands / South Georgia Islands / South Orkney or Powell's Group" offered at same price] [14] £84 **$140**

TERRITORIES OF NEW MEXICO AND UTAH [1855] 1st ed; blank verso. Incl AZ, most of CO and NV. 31x40cm (12½x15½") Color by counties. Clean. Ref: Wheat (TM) 832, frontis. [8] £151 **$250**

[SAME TITLE] [1857] Plain border. 33x41cm (13x16") Full color. VG. [26] £151 **$250**

TERRITORIES OF WASHINGTON AND OREGON [1855] Both territories east to divide. 34x41cm (13½x16") Full color. Exc. [26] £90 **$150**

TEXAS [1853 / 1856] Single page, without truncations. 32x40cm (12½x16") Full color. Margins browned & spotted; good. [16] £151 **$250**

TEXAS AND INDIAN TERRITORY [1857] From *Colton and Fitch's Modern School Geography*. 20x17cm (8x6½") Pale yellow color. VG. [38] £51 **$85**

[SAME TITLE] [1862] From Colton & Fitch, *Modern School Geography*. NY: Ivison, Phinney & Co. Surround of text. 20x17cm (8x7") Yellow tone. Margins browned; good. [16] £30 **$50**

THE ENVIRONS OF LONDON [1855] 33x41cm (13x16") B&W. Margin tear repaired on verso with archival tape; Lt margin age toning; o/w fine. [14] £75 **$125**

THE TERRITORIES OF NEW MEXICO & UTAH [c.1860] Incl AZ, most of CO and NV. Note, "Southern Boundary of N. Mexico by A.B. Gray ..." 30x37cm (12x14½") Orig color. Few minor margin tears repaired verso with archival tape; o/w fine. [14] £196 **$325**

THE TERRITORIES OF WASHINGTON AND OREGON [1853] To Continental Divide. 33x39cm (13x15½") Color by counties. Fine. [8] £90 **$150**

THE UNITED STATES OF AMERICA [1857] Plain border. 41x66cm (16x26") Full col. VG. [26] £145 **$240**

UNITED STATES OF AMERICA [1855+] WV separate from VA; large Dakota Terr. 39x66cm (15½x26") Color. Lt narrow age toned strip along c'fold; VG to fine. [14] £166 **$275**

VERMONT [1855] From 1st ed, *General Atlas*. 41x32cm (16x12½") Full color. Ref: Phillips (M) 972. [22] £45 **$75**

[SAME TITLE] 1869] 39x33cm (15½x13") Color by towns. ["Ohio" offered at same price] [40] £42 **$70**

VIRGINIA [1855] 32x40cm (13x15½") Orig color by counties. Fine. ["Alabama" & "Kentucky and Tennessee" offered at same price] [14] £90 **$150**

[SAME TITLE] [1855] 1st ed. 2 insets. 30x37cm (12x14½") Full orig color. Exc. [36] £90 **$150**

[SAME TITLE] [1857] Plain border. 41x34cm (16x13½") Full color. VG. [26] £48 **$80**

WASHINGTON AND OREGON [1855/57] East to Rockies; decorative border. 29x38cm (11½x15") Full orig color. VG. [36] £90 **$150**

COLTON (Pocket & Wall Maps; Maps not from Atlases)

COLTON'S DELAWARE AND MARYLAND [1863] Pocket map in orig cloth folder; DC inset with forts. Full color by counties. 28x40cm (11x16") Some fold junction separations; lt soiling & wrinkling; good. [15] £106 **$175**

COLTON'S ILLINOIS [1865] G.W. & C.B. Colton, NY. Folding map in orig cloth folder. Full color by county; uncolored Chicago inset. 39x32cm (15½x12½") Sm holes at some fold junctions; fine. [15] £241 **$400**

COLTON'S KANSAS [1866] G.W. & G.B Colton. Folding map with covers. 39x57cm (15½x22½") Full orig color. Some fold splits; o/w good. [32] £347 **$575**

COLTON'S KENTUCKY AND TENNESSEE [1863] J.H. Colton. Folds into orig 16mo cloth case. 35x42cm (14x16½") Color. Case dampstained; map clean. [A8] £294 **$488**

COLTON'S LOUISIANA [1874] Atlas map in pocket form, updated from 1855, in orig cloth. Full color by parish. 32x38cm (12½x15") Orig binding backwards; superb. [15] £226 **$375**

COLTON'S MAP OF THE STATE OF TEXAS [1866 (1877)] Folding map in orig covers. 38x39cm (15x15½") Full orig col. Some spotting; minor splitting at folds; glue stain where tipped on to cover. [32] £965 **$1,600**

COLTON (Pocket & Wall Maps; Maps not from atlases) continued

COLTON'S MASSACHUSETTS & RHODE ISLAND [1855] Boston: E.P. Dutton. Reissue of atlas sheet as pocket map folding into orig cloth boards, gilt embossed. 32x39cm (12½x15½") Full color. Covers lt rubbed; map fine (A+). [A3] £146 **$242**

COLTON'S MASSACHUSETTS AND RHODE ISLAND [1870] G.W. & C.B. Colton; NY. Pocket ed of atlas map in orig cloth folder. Full color by county. 32x39cm (12½x15½") Mild foxing; generally exc. [15] £75 **$125**

COLTON'S NEW BRUNSWICK, NOVA SCOTIA, PRINCE EDWARD ID., & CAPE BRETON ID. [1855] Pocket map in orig cloth folder; reissue of atlas map. Full color by county. 42x59cm (16½x23") Sl splitting top spine; minor edge tears; separations at some fold junctions. [15] £196 **$325**

COLTON'S NEW MAP OF MISSOURI, COMPILED FROM THE U.S. SURVEYS AND OTHER AUTHENTIC SOURCES [1869] G.W. & C.B. Colton; NY. Pocket map in orig cloth folder; never an atlas map. Full color by county. 53x69cm (21x27") Exc. [15] £211 **$350**

COLTON'S NEW RAILROAD AND COUNTY MAP OF THE UNITED STATES [1869] G.W. & C.B. Colton; NY. Folding map in orig cloth folder. East to Great Plains; inset to Pacific. Full color by county. 74x102cm (29x40") Minor tears at fold junctions; VG. [15] £452 **$750**

COLTON'S NEW TOPOGRAPHICAL MAP OF THE STATES OF VIRGINIA, WEST VIRGINIA, MARYLAND & DELAWARE AND PORTIONS OF OTHER ADJOINING STATES [1879] G.W. & C.B. Colton. Folds into orig 12mo cloth case. 80x113cm (31½x44½") Color. [A8] £589 **$977**

COLTON'S PENNSYLVANIA [1875] Folds into 5x3½" folder; gold stamped title. 32x40cm (12½x16") Orig color. VG. [A2] £106 **$176**

COLTON'S RAILROAD & TOWNSHIP MAP OF MASSACHUSETTS, RHODE ISLAND AND CONNECTICUT [1853] Folding pocket map; lacks covers. 55x64cm (21½x25½") Full orig color. Stain ctr lf margin where glued to covers; minor stain & weakness along folds; o/w good. [32] £467 **$775**

COLTON'S RAILROAD AND TOWNSHIP MAP OF NEW ENGLAND, WITH PORTIONS OF THE STATE OF NEW YORK, THE BRITISH PROVINCES. &C. [1853] NY: J.H. Colton. Dissected, linen-backed folding map; scenes at corners. Full color by county. 134x116cm (53x45½") Linen extensively repaired with modern tape. Ref: Modelski (US) 107; Phillips (M) p.473. [2nd ed, 1855, with extensive modern tape repairs offered at $1,000] [15] £754 **$1,250**

COLTON'S RAILROAD & TOWNSHIP MAP OF THE WESTERN STATES COMPILED FROM THE UNITED STATES SURVEYS ... [1858] J.H. Colton. Pocket map on banknote paper in gold embossed covers covering OH, IN, IL, MI, WI, MN, IA & MO; scrolled border & vignettes. 84x100cm (33x39½") Color by county. Sl rubbed cover edges & corners; near new except corner separation, browned fold, sm museum tape repaired tear; VG. [5] £513 **$850**

COLTON'S ROAD MAP OF THE COUNTIES OF PUTNAM AND DUCHESS NEW YORK [1890] G.W. & C.B. Colton. Pocket map in cloth folder. 64x32cm (25x12½") Color. Cover sl rubbed & soiled, corners bent; map sl foxed; VG. [5] £115 **$190**

COLTON'S TOWNSHIP MAP OF THE STATE OF MINNESOTA [1869] NY: G.W. & C.B. Colton. Pocket map on banknote paper folded into gold-embossed cloth cover. 58x43cm (23x17") OL & full color by county. Cover sl soiled & edges rubbed; map has fold separations; sl margin staining; good-VG. [5] £235 **$390**

CUBA, JAMAICA AND PORTO RICO [1856] Separately published atlas map in cloth cover. 31x39cm (12x15½") Full color. Superb. [15] £271 **$450**

ENGLAND AND WALES [1886] G.W. & C.B. Colton. Litho pocket map on banknote paper folded into gold-embossed 12mo folder 62x41cm (24½x16") Color by shire. Cover good, edges rubbed & spine torn; map fine. [6] £136 **$225**

EUROPE [1888] G.W. & C.B. Colton. Litho pocket map on banknote paper folded into gold-embossed 12mo folder. 65x83cm (25½x32½") OL & full col. Cover good with only torn end paper; map fine. [6] £169 **$280**

GENERAL MAP SHOWING THE COUNTRIES EXPLORED & SURVEYED BY THE UNITED STATES & MEXICAN BOUNDARY COMMISSION IN THE YEARS 1850, 51, 52 & 53 ... JOHN R. BARTLETT ... [c.1854] With most of American west. 39x49cm (15½x19½") Fine. Ref: Wheat (TM) 798. [A10] £146 **$242**

GEORGETOWN AND THE CITY OF WASHINGTON, THE CAPITAL OF THE UNITED STATES [1870] G.W. & C.B. Colton; NY. Pocket ed of atlas map in orig cloth folder. Full color by ward. 35x40cm (14x15½") Sm split lower spine; 2 sm lib blind stamps; fine. [15] £211 **$350**

GUIDE THROUGH OHIO, MICHIGAN, INDIANA, ILLINOIS, MISSOURI, WISCONSIN, IOWA, MINNESOTA, NEBRASKA & KANSAS [1857] In "Colton's Western Tourist and Emigrant's Guide"; cloth; 147 pp + 37 pp Colton catalog + indexes. Map by J.C. Smith in color, with vignettes, 51x70cm (20x27½") Boards bit faded; minor toning text; lt foxing end sheets, one torn; map mint; overall VG (A). [A3] £449 **$745**

MAP OF ILLINOIS [1854] Folding pocket map in gold embossed 5x3½" cloth cover. Chicago inset. 39x30cm (15½x12") Orig color. Lt stain where pasted into covers; else clean, fine. [38] £181 **$300**

COLTON (Pocket & Wall Maps; Maps not from atlases) continued

MAP OF THE CENTRAL PACIFIC RAILROAD. THE WESTERN PORTION OF THE MAIN TRUNK OF THE GREAT NATIONAL RAILROAD ROUTE ACROSS THE CONTINENT [c.1867-70] 19x76cm (7½x30") Full color by state; RRs in blue & red.   [39] £87 **$145**

MAP OF THE CHESAPEAKE AND OHIO RAIL ROAD AND ITS CONNECTIONS [1873] G.W. & C.B. Colton. Inset of trans-continental routes. 39x108cm (15½x42½") Full color. Few point tears; 2 clean fold separations; VG+. Ref: Modelski (US) 366.   [35] £60 **$100**

MAP OF THE UNITED STATES, MEXICO, &C. SHOWING THE VARIOUS LAND AND WATER ROUTES FROM THE ATLANTIC CITIES TO CALIFORNIA. COMPILED BY J.H. COLTON [1849] Frontis map, still in *Last Leaves of American History: ... the Mexican War and California*. Emma Willard; NY: Putnam. Octavo, cloth; stained, discolored, spine ends chipped, tips frayed; foxed. Map uncolored. 32x51cm (12½x20½") Toned along folds; narrow lf margin; 2 ink spots Tex/Mex region. Ref: Wheat (TM) 594. [A10] £77 **$127**

MAP OF THE UNITED STATES, THE CANADAS ... [1854] J.H. Colton, NY. Pocket map, dissected, on limp linen; US west to KS; insets: New England; N. Amer; Panama. OL color by state. 74x62cm (29x24½") Fine. [15] £302 **$500**

MAP SHOWING THE PACIFIC RAILWAYS AND THEIR BRANCHES ... 1887] Prepared for U.S. Pacific Railway Comm. Shows Trans-Mississippi West. Many RRs in color. 57x84cm (22½x33½") Folded; minor separations; crisp, bright paper. [10] £226 **$375**

[SAME TITLE] [1887] U.S. west of Chicago. 58x84cm (23x33") RRs in color. VG. [26] £151 **$250**

MAP TO ILLUSTRATE CAPT. BONNEVILLE'S ADVENTURES AMONG THE ROCKY MOUNTAINS [1849] CA gold regions marked. 28x46cm (11x18") B&W. Lower rt margin trimmed just within neat line; edge tears repaired; good+. [38] £136 **$225**

MASSACHUSETTS AND RHODE ISLAND [1854] Folding map with orig cloth folder. Boston inset. Full color by county. 31x40cm (12½x15½") Hinge torn; mild foxing; generally exc. [15] £106 **$175**

MINNESOTA [1857] On banknote paper, in Nathan H. Parker, "The Minnesota Handbook, for 1856-57 ..."; cloth; 159 pp. Map incl eventual eastern Dakotas. 32x37cm (12½x14½") Lt foxing to book, mostly end papers, & bit faded. Lt spot on map, else VG (A). [A3] £329 **$545**

NEBRASKA AND KANSAS [1855] J.H. Colton. Folding map with orig covers. Inset: Gadsden Purchase. 8 scattered vignettes. 69x51cm (27½x20½") Full orig color. Sl fold splits repaired; good. [32] £2,111 **$3,500**

NEW GUIDE MAP OF THE UNITED STATES & CANADA WITH RAILROADS, COUNTIES, ETC. [1862] Pocket map; insets. OL color by state. 77x93cm (30½x36½") Exc. [15] £302 **$500**

NEW MAP OF THE STATE OF TEXAS AS IT IS IN 1875 [c.1874] Laid into J.M. Morphis's *History of Texas*. 5 insets. 49x65cm (19½x26") Full col. Old backing with surveyor's cloth, some wrinkles; VG. [16] £226 **$375**

NEW TOWNSHIP MAP OF THE STATE OF FLORIDA [1876] G.W. & C.B. Colton. Pocket map; orig cloth; insets incl West Indies, Havana, Bermuda. Color by county. 69x68cm (27x27") Some separation at fold junctions; fine. [15] £452 **$750**

TEXAS [1857] Linen-backed pocket map folding into cloth boards; similar to atlas sheet, decorative border. 32x38cm (12½x15") Full color. Scattered foxing; lib stamp front cover; good (B). [A3] £278 **$461**

THE UNITED STATES OF AMERICA [1856] Issued in a guide; fine paper, elaborate border. 48x71cm (19x28") VG. [26] £196 **$325**

COMMELIN

TIJPUS FRETI MAGELLANICI QUOD GEORGIUS SPILBERGIUS CUM CLASSE LUSTRAVIT [1646] Copy of De Bry. 15x43cm (6x17") Exc. [43] £332 **$550**

CONCEPT MAPS - Infrequent Publishers

RADIO STATIONS MAP OF THE UNITED STATES AND MEXICO, SHOWING AT A GLANCE LOCATION, CALL LETTERS AND FREQUENCY OF ALL STATIONS [1933] RCA, NY. In support of "Radio Tour" game of picking up distant stations; verso information. 46x61cm (18x24") Full color. Minor repairs. [25] £45 **$75**

TEMPERANCE MAP [1838] Folding map in 5" folder. Fictitious geography divided into sobriety & inebriation; places incl "Rum Lake" & "Tranquility I." 31x35cm (12½x14") Orig color. Few fold-point separations; few minor tears & wormholes near folds; sl image transfer; occas lt foxing. [A1] £156 **$259**

THE BATTLE FRONT OF THE DRYS [1936] Modern Brewer, NY. Shows shade-coded areas of local option prohibition efforts after national repeal; breweries located. 69x107cm (27x42") B&W. Folded, creases present; some soiling mainly verso. [25] £90 **$150**

CONDER

NORTH AMERICA AGREEABLE TO THE MOST APPROVED MAPS AND CHARTS   [c.1778] From *Millar's New Complete & Universal System of Geography*. 33x38cm (13x15") OL color. Moderately browned. Framed. [A10] £97 **$161**

COOK

CARTE D'UNE PARTIE DE LA MER DU SUD CONTENANT LES DECOUVERTES DE VAISSEAUX DE SA MAJESTE ... [1774] From French ed, *An Account of the Voyages ... in the Southern Hemisphere*. Paris: Saillant et Nyon & Panckoucke. 37x67cm (14½x26½") Minor spotting.   [46] £280 **$465**

CARTE D'UNE PARTIE DE LA MER DU SUD CONTENANT LES DESCOUVERTES DE VAISSEAUX DES SE MAJESTE LE DAUPHIN, COMMODORE BYRON, LA TAMAR, CAPIT'NE. MOUATS, 1765, LE DAUPHIN, CAPIT'NE. WALLIS, LE SWALLOW, CAPIT'NE CATERET 1767 ET L'ENDEAVOUR, LIEUTENANT COOK   [1778] From *Voyages dans l'Hemisphere Australe*. 36x67cm (14x26½") OL col.   [13] Aus$1,380 £627 $1,039

CARTE DE L'HEMISPHERE AUSTRAL ...   [1778-] By Benard, in French ed of Cook's Voyages. 54x53cm (21x20½") Ref: Tooley (Australia) 335.   [34] **£400** $664

CARTE DE L'ISLE D'OTAHITI PAR LE LIEUTENANT J. COOK. 1769   [c.1774] From German ed of Cook. German & French titles. 23x41cm (9½x16") OL color. Fine.   [37] £121 **$200**

CARTE DE L'ISLE DE TAITI, PAR LE LIEUTENANT J. COOK, 1769   [c.1785] By Benard. 23x39cm (9x15½") B&W. Folds; dark impression.   [35] £100 **$165**

CARTE DE LA N'LE. GALLES MERID'LE ... N'LE HOLLANDE ...   [1773 / 1774] French ed. 36x77cm (14x30½") Orig wash color. Exc. Ref: Tooley (Australia) 342.   [45] £558 **$925**

CARTE DE LA NLE ZELANDE VISITEE EN 1769 ET 1770 PAR LE LIEUTENANT J. COOK COMMANDANT DE L'ENDEAVOUR VAISSEAU DE SA MAJESTE   [1774] French ed. 1st pub chart of Australian east coast. 38x48cm (15x19") B&W.   [13] Aus$1,600 £727 $1,205

[SAME TITLE]   [1774] From French ed, *An Account of the Voyages ... in the Southern Hemisphere*. Paris: Saillant, et Nyon & Panckoucke. 48x38cm (19x15") Very crisp.   [46] £860 $1,426

CHART OF NEW ZEALAND EXPLORED IN 1769 AND 1770 BY LIEUT. I. COOK ...   [1773] 1st ed of first published map of whole of New Zealand from Hawkesworth account of 1st voyage. 38x49cm (15x19½") Color. Ref: cf Perry & Prescott 1816.A10. cf Clancy (Australis) ill. p.117; Tooley (Australia) 322, pl.21   [13] Aus$1,950 £886 $1,468

CHART OF NEW-ZEALAND EXPLORED IN 1769 AND 1770 ... ENDEAVOR   [1772] 1st issue. 50x38cm (19½x15") Uncolored. Ref: cf Perry & Prescott 1816.A10.   [34] £1,350 $2,239

CHART OF PART OF THE COAST OF NEW SOUTH WALES FROM CAPE TRIBULATION TO ENDEAVOUR STRAITS BY J. COOK 1770   [1773] From Hawkesworth account of 1st voyage. 30x35cm (12x13½") B&W. Ref: Perry & Prescott 1773.05. cf Clancy (Australis) ill. p.97; Tooley (Australia) 327,344.   [13] Aus$490 £223 $369

CHART OF THE SANDWICH ISLANDS   [c.1790] Alexander Hogg; Condor, sc. 21x34cm (8x13") B&W. Lt toned; near fine.   [35] £211 **$350**

KAART VAN HET ZUIDER HALFROND VERTOONENDE DE KOERSEN VAN ENIGE DER BEROEMDSTE ZEE REIZIGERS DOOR KAPITEIN JAMES COOK   [1776] From Dutch ed of *Voyage toward the South Pole*. Southern hemisphere explorer's tracks. 53x53cm (21x21") B&W.   [13] Aus$800 £363 $602

KAART VAN VAN DIEMENS LAND OPGENOEMEN DOOR KAPITEIN FURNEAUX IN MAART 1773   [1794] From Dutch ed of account of 2nd voyage. 14x21cm (5½x8½") B&W.   [13] Aus$240 £109 $181

[SAME TITLE]   [1779] Amsterdam. 21x14cm (8½x5½")   [11] £36 **$60**

SCHELS VAN DE DONKERE BAAI IN NIEUW ZEELAND 1773   [1779] Resolution Bay. 20x38cm (8x15")   [11] £45 **$75**

COPLEY

CENTRAL AMERICA AND THE WEST INDIES FROM THE BEST AUTHORITIES   [1845] NY: Harper & Bros. Incl US gulf coast. Insets: Kingston; Havana. 33x50cm (13x19½") Full color. Fine.   [16] £121 **$200**

COAST OF THE UNITED STATES FROM NEW YORK TO CAPE FEAR   [1860] Blue-backed chart; 9 insets. 124x90cm (49x35½") Sm section out of top incl border & CT coast; else fine. Ref: cf Guthorn (Charts) p.11.   [15] £302 **$500**

MAP OF THE UNITED STATES, AND TEXAS   [1845] NY: Harper & Bros. Gazetteer illustration map; TX as republic. Insets: Boston, NY, Phila areas. 44x58cm (17½x23") Modern OL color. Tape stain; some lt foxing; good.   [16] £256 **$425**

CORNELL

KANSAS, COLORADO, TEXAS, &C. [c.1879] From *Cornell's Intermediate Geography*. Sarah S. Cornell; NY: D. Appleton. 25x21cm (10x8½") Sepia with red. Good. [16] £30 **$50**

CORONELLI Try *Nolin*

[ATLAS] PRIMA PARTE DELLO SPECCHIO DEL MARE [1698] 1st issued by F.M. Levanto, 1664. Folio, vellum; 138+ pp; 1 full page & 24 double-page charts on Mediterranean north shore, numerous woodcut illustrations. Binding worn; hinges broken; scattered staining, most charts clean; overall VG. Ref: Zacharakis 1242-53. [24] £8,745 **$14,500**

[GLOBE GORE: AFRICA, SOUTHEAST, & MADAGASCAR] [1692] For the 42" globe; figure symbolizes source of Nile. 41x28cm (16½x11") Orig color. sm stain; else exc. [23] £724 **$1,200**

[GLOBE GORE: AFRICA, SOUTHERN] [1692] For the 42" globe; sophisticated geography. 45x37cm (18x14½") Orig color. Lt foxed; VG. Ref: cf Norwich 52. [23] £1,206 **$2,000**

[GLOBE GORE: AUSTRALIA] [1688] For 110 cm (42") globe; Carpentaria Gulf west coast, Tasmania south coast. 41x28cm (16x11") Uncolored. Ref: Shirley (W) 537, pl.376. [34] **£480** $796

[GLOBE GORE: AUSTRALIA, EASTERN] [1692] For the 42" globe; sketchy Carpentaria & Tasmania. 47x30cm (18½x12") Orig color. Exc. [23] £1,025 **$1,700**

[GLOBE GORE: AUSTRALIA, NORTHERN] [1696] Incl parts of Indonesia; on full sheet of text with wide margins. 23x28cm (9x11") Mint. [44] £844 **$1,400**

[GLOBE GORE: NORTH AMERICA, CENTRAL; HUDSON'S BAY TO GULF OF MEXICO & FLORIDA] [1688] From *Libro dei Globi*. Shows Great Lakes & Mississippi River. 42x28cm (16½x11") Exc. Ref: Potter illus. p.145. [2] £1,568 **$2,600**

[SAME TITLE] [c.1698] For 42" globe. 43x25cm (17x10") B&W. Repaired margins; trimmed into map at bottom; fair; as is. Ref: Shirley (W) 537; Wheat (TM) 73. [31] £332 **$550**

[GLOBE GORE: NORTH AMERICA, EASTERN; DELAWARE TO NEWFOUNDLAND & CANADIAN ARCTIC] [c.1698] For 42" globe. 43x25cm (17x10") B&W. No lower margin; fine. Ref: Shirley (W) 537; Wheat (TM) 73. [31] £452 **$750**

[GLOBE GORE: NORTH AMERICA, NEW ENGLAND TO NORTHERN SOUTH AMERICA] [1688] From *Libro dei Globi*. Incl Caribbean. 42x28cm (16½x11") Exc. [2] £1,447 **$2,400**

[GLOBE GORE: NORTH AMERICA: INSULAR CALIFORNIA & SOUTHWEST U.S.] [1692] "Della California Alcuno ha credito ..." For the 110cm (42") globe. 47x30cm (18½x12") Orig color. Exc. Ref: Leighly 83. [23] £2,111 **$3,500**

[SAME TITLE] [c.1698] For the 42" globe; part insular Calif & New Mexico. 44x25cm (17½x10") B&W. No bottom margin; fine. Ref: Shirley (W) 537; Wheat (TM) 73. [31] £513 **$850**

[GLOBE GORE: PACIFIC, NEW ZEALAND] [1692] Sketch New Zealand. 44x29cm (17½x11½") Orig color. Streaking from unpolished plate; few stains; VG. [23] £724 **$1,200**

[GLOBE GORE: SOUTH AMERICA, SOUTHERN] [c.1690] La Plata Basin & Tierra del Fuego. 46x27cm (18½x10½") Minor browning. [A8] £416 **$690**

[GLOBE GORES: ASIA & PACIFIC: JAPAN, PHILIPPINES, WESTERN MICRONESIA] [1688] Matched pair, each 46x28cm (18x11") Exc. [44] £2,714 **$4,500**

[GLOBE GORES: ASIA & PACIFIC, SET OF THREE COVERING 1)BAY OF BENGAL TO MALAYSIA, 2) CHINA, WESTERN JAPAN & PHILIPPINES, 3) EASTERN JAPAN & MARIANAS] [c.1695] 3 uncolored gores, orig for 110cm diameter globe, reissued in sheet format. Each maximum 46x28cm (18x11") Invisible fill & reinstatement in easterly gore; o/w fine. Ref: Shirley (W) 537, pl.376. Walter (Japan) 44. [4] **£3,350** $5,555

[GLOBE GORES: NORTH AMERICA, SET OF THREE] [c.1688] Eastern Canada to most of insular Calif. For 110cm (42") globe; each 41x25cm (16½x10") Trimmed at Tropic of Cancer. Exc. [43] £1,508 **$2,500**

[PORTRAIT] VINC. CORONELLI MIN: CON COSMOGRAFO DELLA SERENIS REPUB DI VENETIA [c.1695] State I. 39x29cm (15½x11½") Uncolored. Exc. [4] **£385** $639

AEVI VETERIS USQUE AD ANNUM SALUTIS NON AGESIMUM SUPRA MILLES QUADRINGENTOS [1690] 46x62cm (18½x24½") Color & OL color. [A7] £277 **$460**

AMERICA MERIDIONALE ... [(1688) c.1692] 2 joined sheets, 60x87cm (23½x34½") Full color with minor offset. MS coordinate additions; VG. [4] **£900** $1,493

[SAME TITLE] [1696] Two unjoined sheets; overall 61x92cm (24x36") OL color. [A7] £1,179 **$1,955**

AMERICA SETTENTRIONALE COLLE NUOVE SCOPERTE SIN ALL ANNO 1688 ... [(1688) c.1692] As in *Atlante Veneto*. Insular Calif. Double sheet, 60x87cm (23½x34½") Full color. Some MS coordinate additions; VG. Ref: McLaughlin 103; Tooley (Amer) p.125, #57; Wheat (TM) 70. Cumming (Exploration) p.148. [4] **£4,500** $7,462

CORONELLI continued

AMERICA SETTENTRIONALE COLLE NUOVE SCOPERTE SIN ALL ANNO 1688 ... [1692] Insular Calif. 2 sheets joined, 60x88cm (24x34½") Uncol. Fine. Framed. [32] £5,277 **$8,750**

CANADA ORIENTALE NELL'AMERICA SETTENTRIONALE ... [1695] 45x60cm (18x24") Later color. Top margin trimmed close; o/w VG. Ref: Kershaw (Canada) 162. Armstrong 18. [2] £573 **$950**

CITTA DI VENETIA ... [1693] Bird's-eye view; surround of garland of arms. 2 joined sheets, 50x77cm (19½x30½") Exc. [24] £3,920 **$6,500**

CONTADO DI ZARA, PARTE DELLA DALMATIA DESCRITTO ... [1691-96] Crack in copperplate. 46x60cm (18x24") Color. [34] £480 **$796**

CORSO DEL FIUME DELL AMAZONI ... [1691-] Northern South Amer. 27x46cm (10½x18") Col. [34] £520 **$863**

ISOLA DE IAMES, A GIAMAICA, POSSEDUTTA DAL RE BRITANNICO DIVISA IN PARROCCHIE [1696] Publ in *Atlante Veneto*. Kingston absent. 22x29cm (8½x11½") OL col. Ref: Kapp (Jamaica) 36. [20] £528 **$875**

LE BERMUDE [ON SHEET WITH] FRISLANDA [AND] ISOLA DI MAYEN [AND] ISOLA DI TERRA NUOVA [1690] 4 maps on sheet; overall 46x61cm (18x24") [A6] £368 **$611**

MARE DEL NORD ... [c.1674] Atlantic & adjacent lands. 46x60cm (18x24") Remargined from platemark top & bottom, lt browning along fold; paper-backed. [A8] £347 **$575**

MARE DEL NORTE ... [1692] 46x60cm (18x24") OL color. [A7] £902 **$1,495**

MARE DEL SUD DETTO ALTRIMENTI MARE PACIFICO ... [c.1692] Insular Calif. 45x60cm (17½x23½") Uncolored. Sm wormhole mid ctr filled, no loss; o/w VF. Ref: McLaughlin 104; Tooley (Amer) p.125, #58. McLaughlin [4] £2,000 **$3,317**

PARTE DELLA NUOVA SPAGNE, O DEL MEXICO ... [1690] 45x60cm (18x24") Lt discoloration at fold. [A6] £207 **$344**

PARTE MERIDIONALE DEL REGNO D'INGHILTERRA [IN SET WITH] PARTE SETTENTRIONALE [1690] When joined 91x61cm (36x24") Lt browning at folds. [A6] £230 **$382**

PARTE SETTENTRIONALE DELL'IRELANDA DESCRITTA ... / IRLANDA PARTE MERIDIONAL ... [1693] Two sheets joined 90x62cm (35½x24½") Printer's crease lower sheet; else Exc. [23] £1,086 **$1,800**

[SAME TITLE] [c.1696] 89x62cm (35x24½") Color. Exc. [24] £1,327 **$2,200**

PARTIE OCCIDENTALE DEL MEDITERRANEO ... [1697] Adriatic to Gibraltar. 40x51cm (15½x20") Color. [34] £650 **$1,078**

PIANTA DELLA CITTA E FORTEZZA D'ATENE ... [c.1695] Athens. Separately printed broad ornate border. 45x60cm (18x24") C'fold reinforcement; VG. ["Bosforo Tracio ... Canale di Constantinopoli ..." offered at same price] [23] £724 **$1,200**

PLANISFERO DEL MONDO NUOVO, DESCRITTO DAL P. CORONELLI ... [1691] Western hemi; insular Calif. 46x61cm (18x24") B&W. Virtually flawless. Ref: Goss (NA) 43; McLaughlin 105. [27] £1,659 **$2,750**

PLANISFERO DEL MONDO VECCHIO DESCRITTO DAL P. CORONELLI [1696] Eastern hemi. 55x62cm (21½x24") Color. Ref: Shirley (W) 548, pl.383. [13] Aus$3,950 £1,794 **$2,974**

RAGUSI [1696] View of Ragusa, Sicily. Verso: Pastrouicci. 13x16cm (5x6½") [11] £51 **$85**

SCOTIA PARTE MERIDIONALE [IN SET WITH] PARTE SETTENTRIONALE [1690] When joined 91x62cm (36x24½") Lt browning at folds. [A6] £287 **$476**

TERRE ARTICHE ... [c.1696] 46x61cm (18x24") Lower margin trimmed to platemark; mounted on larger flexible sheet. [A8] £277 **$460**

COVENS & MORTIER   Try *De L'Isle*

ARCHIPELAGUE DU MEXIQUE, OU SONT LES ISLES DE CUBA, ESPAGNOLE, IAMAIQUE, &C ... [c.1720] 60x99cm (23½x39") Color. Exc. [23] £2,714 **$4,500**

CARTE DE LA LOUISIANE ET DU COURS DU MISSISSIPI DRESSEE SUR UN GRAND NOMBRE DE MEMOIRES ENTR'AUTRES SUR CEUX DE MR. LE MAIRE PAR GUILLME. DE L'ISLE DE L'ACADEMIE RLE. DES SCIENCES [c.1730] 44x60cm (17½x23½") Ref: Cumming (SE) 208. cf Martin (TX) p.98-9. [34] £1,400 **$2,322**

CARTE DU CONGO ET DU PAYS DES CAFRES [1730] Reengraved Dutch ed of 1708 De L'Isle map S of Equator. 50x61cm (19½x24") Orig wash color. Ref: Tooley (Africa) p.72. [46] £450 **$746**

CARTE GENERALE DU MARQUISAT DE MORAVIE [1757+] 51x64cm (20x25") OL color. Bit browned along fold. [A8] £121 **$201**

INSULA CORSICA ... [c.1730] 56x49cm (22x19½") Orig OL color. [46] £490 **$813**

L'AMERIQUE, DRESSE SUR LES N:OBSERVATIONS FAITES EN TOUTES LES PARTIES DE LA TERRE ... [c.1720] Wall map. 112x130cm (44x51½") Early full color heightened later. Joined, laid down, some restoration. [2] £19,601 **$32,500**

COVENS & MORTIER continued

L'AMERIQUE SEPTENTRIONALE ... [1757+] 48x58cm (19x23") OL color. Top margin trimmed, but ample; scattered browning; toned overall. [A7] £312 **$517**

L'ELECTORAT DE HANNOVER OU LES DOMAINES DU ROI DE LA GRANDE BRETAGNE EN ALLEMAGNE [1745] 59x52cm (23½x20½") Orig OL color. [11] £151 **$250**

L'HEMISPHERE MERIDIONAL POUR VOIR PLUS DISTINCTEMENT LES TERRES AUSTRALES. [1740-] After De L'Isle with updating & text after French Compagnie des Indes in 1739. 47x53cm (18½x21") Orig OL color. [46] £420 $697

NOUVELLE CARTE PARTICULIERE DE L'AMERIQUE OU SONT EXACTEMENT MARQUEES ... [1741] The NW sheet (of four) covering Hudson's Bay to Carolina with the Great Lakes, after Popple's 1733 twenty-sheet map of "The British Empire in North America" 57x52cm (22½x20½") Full wash & OL color. A margin reinforced; fine. [11] £1,055 **$1,750**

NOVA ET ACCURATA REGNI HUNGARIAE ... [c.1730] Based on De L'Isle. 46x57cm (18x22½") Orig body color. Lower c'fold split repaired; few scattered stains; faint pencil underlining; good+. [38] £181 **$300**

PLAN DE LA VILLE & DU FORT DE ST. PETERSBOURG ... [c.1730] 48x57cm (19x22½") Full orig color. Exc. [2] £1,930 **$3,200**

PLAN DU PORT DE LA VILLE ET DES FORTERESSES DE CARTHAGENE ... [1741] 50x60cm (20x23½") Top margin trimmed within platemark; sl browning; ex lib NYHS. [A7] £294 **$488**

PLAN NOUVEAU & TRES EXACT DE LA VILLE D'AMSTERDAM [1796 (1798)] Amsterdam: Mortier, Covens & Zoon. Dissected, contemporary linen backing, folding into cardboard case. Plan & bird's-eye views of public buildings, etc. [no dimens] VG. [38] £905 **$1,500**

COWPERTHWAIT, DESILVER & BUTLER

A NEW MAP OF ARKANSAS WITH ITS COUNTIES TOWNS, POST OFFICES, &C. [1856] Population & statistical data. 38x32cm (15x13") Orig color. 2 minor spots; o/w fine. [14] £84 **$140**

MAP OF MINNESOTA TERRITORY [1854] MN extends to Missouri River. 33x41cm (13x16") Orig color. Faint foxing; o/w fine. [A2] £159 **$264**

MAP OF THE STATE OF TEXAS FROM THE LATEST AUTHORITIES [1855] 33x40cm (13x16") Full color. Fine. [16] £332 **$550**

CRAM

[ATLAS] CRAM'S SUPERIOR ATLAS OF THE WORLD. INDEXED [1901] Sm Folio, cloth; printed color maps, many 2-page, on quality paper. Inner hinges cracked; edges frayed; Maps, contents VG. [A10] £104 **$173**

[ATLAS] CRAM'S UNRIVALED FAMILY ATLAS OF THE WORLD [1883 (1885)] Chicago. 12th ed. Folio, rebound in modern buckram with orig front cover laid down; 79 colored maps, 10 pp illustrations, 5 pp tables, diagrams. Tape repairs title & few leaves; minor margin dampstaining; ex lib; interior VG. [33] £151 **$250**

[SAME TITLE] [1886] Kansas City: Edwin Williamson. 16th ed. Sm folio; blindstamped cloth; 231 pp; numerous maps, printed color. Later spine & hinges; some overall soil; edges worn; title chipped, reattached with tape; mostly marginal soil & toning to contents. [A10] £55 **$92**

AFRICA [1883] From *Unrivaled Family Atlas* ... 24x32cm (9½x12½") Printed col. VG (A). [A3] £17 **$28**

ARKANSAS [1897] 31 RRs in strong color. 41x57cm (16½x22½") OL color. [40] £42 **$70**

CALIFORNIA [1883] From *Unrivaled Family Atlas*. Verso: NV. 47x30cm (18½x12") Printed color. Few lt stains; good (B). [A3] £13 **$22**

COLORADO [1883] From same source. 24x30cm (9½x12") Printed color. Sm spot; VG (A). [A3] £10 **$17**

[SAME TITLE] [1888] From *Cram's New American Railway Atlas*. 46x64cm (18x25") Some color. Strong impression. [26] £51 **$85**

[SAME TITLE] [1893] Verso: Nebraska. 26x33cm (10½x13") Full litho color by counties. Trimmed to bottom neatline; o/w VG to fine. [14] £24 **$40**

CRAM'S TOWNSHIP AND RAIL ROAD MAP OF ILLINOIS [c.1890] Folds into case. 58x41cm (23x16") Some soiling to case; map exc. [25] £90 **$150**

DALLAS, TEXAS [1893] Limits at Turtle Creek, Grand Ave. 33x25cm (13x10") Limited color. [27] £45 **$75**

EASTERN HALF OF TEXAS [1888] From *Standard Atlas* ... 41x56cm (16x22") Printed OL col. [22] £36 **$60**

EASTERN HALF OF TEXAS [IN SET WITH] WESTERN HALF OF TEXAS [1896] Verso: UT & NV; MN & AZ. Each 34x52cm (13½x20½") Full printed color. VG. [16] £75 **$125**

FLORIDA [1883] From *Unrivaled Family Atlas* ... Verso: AL. 30x25cm (12x10") Printed color. VG (A). ["New York", "Pennsylvania" & "Louisiana" sold at same price] [A3] £13 **$22**

CRAM

IDAHO [1883] From *Unrivaled Family Atlas* ... 13 counties. 30x25cm (12x10") Printed color. VG (A). ["Railroad and County Map of Michigan & Wisconsin" sold at same price] [A3] £11 **$19**

MAP OF THE OKLAHOMA COUNTRY IN THE INDIAN TERRITORY [1889] Present Oklahoma City region. 29x24cm (11½x9½") Printed OL color. [12] £51 **$85**

MAP OF THE UNITED STATES [1893] 30x46cm (12x18") Full litho color. [14] £33 **$55**

MASSACHUSETTS, RHODE ISLAND & CONNECTICUT [1883] From *Unrivaled Family Atlas*. Boston area inset. 24x29cm (9½x11½") Printed color. Good (B). [A3] £9 **$15**

MONTANA [1888] From *Cram's New American Railway Atlas*. 46x64cm (18x25") Counties in OL color. Strong impression. [26] £48 **$80**

[SAME TITLE] [1891-92] 16 counties; population table verso. 41x56cm (16x22") Pastel color. Fine. [offered at the same price: 1895-96 ed, probably by H.B. Walker, a Cram licensee] [12] £54 **$90**

NEVADA [c.1895] By H.B. Walker (Cram licensee). Hachures render range & basin topo. 56x41cm (22x16") Color. Pristine. [12] £54 **$90**

NEW RAIL ROAD & COUNTY MAP OF NEBRASKA [1882] From *Illustrated Family Atlas* ... 22x33cm (8½x13") Full color. Ref: Karrow (MW) 12-0509. [12] £54 **$90**

NEW RAIL ROAD AND COUNTY MAP OF SOUTHERN CALIFORNIA AND ARIZONA [1882] From *Unrivaled Family Atlas of the World*. 1st ed. Incl CA south of Monterey. 29x53cm (11½x21") Color. Perfect. Ref: Rumsey 4558. [12] £90 **$150**

NEW RAILROAD AND COUNTY MAP OF INDIAN TERRITORY, AND NORTHERN PART OF TEXAS [1882] From *Illustrated Family Atlas* ... 32x44cm (12½x17½") Hand color. Fine. Ref: Phillips (A) 901. [12] £106 **$175**

NEW RAILROAD AND COUNTY MAP OF SOUTHERN PART OF IDAHO [1882] Panhandle not covered. 29x24cm (11½x9½") Hand color. [12] £51 **$85**

OMAHA [1898] Whitmore to Wyman St. 33x27cm (13x10½") Printed color. [40] £18 **$30**

RAIL ROAD & TOWNSHIP MAP OF NEBRASKA [1878] Title bloc date, 1881. 69 counties. Printed OL color, state boundary hand colored. 42x55cm (16½x21½") Unfolded. Exc. [12] £90 **$150**

RAILROAD AND COUNTY MAP OF DAKOTA AND MANITOBA [1888] From *Standard Atlas* ... 56x41cm (22x16") Printed OL color. [22] £33 **$55**

RAILROAD AND COUNTY MAP OF LOUISIANA [1888] From *Standard Atlas* ... 41x56cm (16x22") Printed OL color. [MS, KS offered at same price] [22] £24 **$40**

RAILROAD AND COUNTY MAP OF MAINE [1888] Shows every station. 56x41cm (22x16") OL color. [NH & VT offered at $50] [22] £33 **$55**

RAILROAD AND COUNTY MAP OF MONTANA [1888] From *Standard Atlas* ... 41x56cm (16x22") Printed OL color. [NV offered at same price] [22] £36 **$60**

RAILROAD AND COUNTY MAP OF NEBRASKA [1888] From *Standard Atlas* ... 41x56cm (16x22") Printed OL color. [IN offered at same price] [22] £30 **$50**

RAILROAD AND COUNTY MAP OF NEW JERSEY [1888] All RRs & stations named; Hudson Co. inset. 57x41cm (22½x16½") Printed OL color. [22] £45 **$75**

RAILROAD AND COUNTY MAP OF TEXAS [1888] From *Cram Standard American Atlas*. Panhandle inset; with 2 sheets of index. 42x57cm (16½x22½") Printed OL color. Fine. [16] £81 **$135**

RAILROAD AND COUNTY MAP OF UTAH [1888] From *Standard Atlas* ... 41x56cm (16x22") Printed OL color. [ID offered at same price] [22] £27 **$45**

RAILROAD AND COUNTY MAP OF WASHINGTON [1888] From *Standard Atlas* ... 39x56cm (15½x22") Printed OL color. [OR offered at same price] [22] £39 **$65**

SECTIONAL MAP OF IOWA [1871] Pocket map on thick paper folded into gold-embossed covers with 3 pp data. 69x76cm (27x30") Color by county. Cover corners & spine sl torn; map lt soiled, stained on verso, fold & corner separations reinforced with museum tape; good. [5] £271 **$450**

SOUTH DAKOTA [1893] 26x33cm (10½x13") Full litho color by counties. Fine. [14] £24 **$40**

TEXAS [1883] Publ in *Unrivaled Family Atlas* ... Verso: AR; Indian Terr. 33x44cm (13x17½") Printed color. VG (A). ["Washington Ty." 9½x12", sold at same price] [A3] £20 **$33**

TEXAS ENGRAVED FOR THE PEOPLE'S PUBLISHING CO. [c.1889] Verso: AR; Indian Terr. 30x43cm (12x17") Printed OL color. VG. [16] £57 **$95**

UNITED STATES [1883] From *Unrivaled Family Atlas*. 29x46cm (11½x18") Printed color. Good (B). [A3] £17 **$28**

WESTERN HALF OF TEXAS [c.1887] Engraved for *Standard Atlas of the World*. Counties finally formed. 56x42cm (22x16½") OL color. VG. [16] £72 **$120**

CRAM continued

WESTERN HEMISPHERE [IN SET WITH] EASTERN HEMISPHERE [1883] From *Unrivaled Family Atlas* ... Each Diameter: 23cm (9"). Printed color. Good (B). [A3] £14 **$24**
WYOMING [1883] Publ in *Unrivaled Family Atlas*. 30x47cm (12x18½"). Printed color. 2 sm spots; still VG (A). [A3] £24 **$39**
WYOMING [c.1891-92] 12 counties. 41x56cm (16x22"). Pastel hand color. Fine. [12] £57 **$95**
YELLOWSTONE NATIONAL PARK [1893] 29x23cm (11½x9½") Fully printed in lt yellow. VG to fine. [14] £24 **$40**

CREPY

LA JAMAIQUE AUX ANGLOIS ... [ON SHEET WITH] LA BERMUDE AUX ANGLOIS ... [1767] 20x27cm (8x10½") Orig color. Exc. Ref: Kapp (Jamaica) 64; Palmer (Bermuda) p.11. [2] £332 **$550**

CROSMAN & MALLORY

PANORAMIC VIEW FROM BUNKER HILL MONUMENT [1848] James Smillie, sc. Octavo, recased, cloth. With folding keyed view; 16 pp text; & 2nd plate "Perspective view of Bunker Hill Monument". 15x112cm (6x44") Some wear at folds; o/w VG. Ref: cf Stokes & Haskell p.193. [21] **Can$375** £164 **$272**

CRUCHLEY

CRUCHLEY'S NEW PLAN OF LONDON SHEWING ALL THE NEW AND INTENDED IMPROVEMENTS ... [1836] 30-section linen-backed map with orig board cover & label. 46x86cm (18x33½"). Color. Sl toned; some separation between sections; sm chip present; ex lib NYHS. [A7] £104 **$172**

CUMMINGS & HILLIARD

[ATLAS] SCHOOL ATLAS TO CUMMINGS' ANCIENT & MODERN GEOGRAPHY [c.1810] 7th ed. Octavo, orig stiff printed wrappers; 8 maps in OL color incl double hemi world, 5 continents, US, Britain. Maps & cover toned; some foxing, browning at folds; good (B). [A3] £238 **$394**

CUSTODIS

BUDA CIVITAS [1627] D. Custos. View of Buda with King of Hungary's family tree 10 to 17th c; portraits, coats of arms, etc. 54x40cm (21½x15½") [48] **DM 650** £224 **$372**
COMITES TIROLENSES ... [1627] D. Custos. Innsbruck overall view with Count's family tree, 11th-17th c; with coats of arms & decoration. 54x40cm (21½x15½"). Sl weak lower impression. ["Saxones Anhaldini, Inclytiss. Pp. et Dnn. Pricibus Anhaldinis ... Saxoniae Angriae, et Westphaliae" offered at same price] [48] **DM 580** £200 **$332**
REGES NAVARRAE ... [1627] D. Custos. Town & troop encampments, with family tree. 40x25cm (16x10") 2 sm rust spots lf. [48] **DM 190** £66 **$109**

D'ANANIA

AMERICA [1582] As in *L'Universale Fabrica del Mondo*. State 1. 18x24cm (7x9½") Exc. Ref: Burden 54. [44] £332 **$550**

D'ANVILLE

[ATLAS] NOUVEL ATLAS DE LA CHINE, DE LA TARTARIE CHINOISE, ET DU THIBET: ... COREE ... [1737] Hague. Folio, full calf binding; 42 maps, incl "... Pays traverses par ... Beerings ..." Some browning in text; lt spotting on maps; generally VG. Ref: Phillips (A) 3189. [3] £7,237 **$12,000**
CANADA, LOUISIANE ET TERRES ANGLOISES [1755] From *Atlas General* ... Based on Mitchell. 4 sheets with margins, each about 48x54cm (19x21½") B&W. Edge chips to margins; creasing along c'fold; o/w VG. Ref: Cumming (SE) 296; Phillips (M) p.190. [21] **Can$2,850** £1,246 **$2,067**
CARTE DES ISLES DE L'AMERIQUE ET DE PLUSIEURS PAYS DE TERRE FERME [1731] Reduced from large chart. 31x44cm (12x17"). OL color. [11] £151 **$250**
CARTE PARTICULIERE DE LA COTE OCCIDENTALE DE L'AFRIQUE DEPUIS LE CAP BLANC JUSQU'AU CAP DE VERGA, ET DU COURS DES RIVIERES DE SENEGA ET DE GAMBIE [1751] W Africa between 9 & 21 deg north; details river courses. 70x100cm (27½x39½"). Uncolored. Orig folds; occas lt soiling & toning; fold-point separation, minor loss blank area; o/w VG. [A2] £73 **$121**
HEMISPHERE OCCIDENTAL OU DU NOUVEAU ... PAR LE S'R D'ANVILLE ... MDCCLXI ... [1761] 65x61cm (25½x24"). OL color. Printer's crease; else fine {A+}. [A3] £292 **$484**

DAILY GRAPHIC

MAP OF THE UNITED STATES SHOWING LAND GRANTS FOR RAIL AND WAGON ROADS. [Mar 8, 1880] Prepared under auspices of Dept. of Interior. 35x52cm (14x20½"). Color. [A7] £242 **$402**

DAMPIER

CARTE DU DETROIT DE MALACCA [1699] Malaysia, Singapore & Sumatra. 15x27cm (6x11") OL color. [44] £181 **$300**

REPRESENTATION DU COURS ORDINAIRE DES VENTS DE TRAVERSE QUI REGNENT SURE LES COTES, DANS LA GRANDE MER DU SUD [1699 - c.1710] From French ed, *Voyages and Descriptions.* Shows Pacific winds; insular Calif. 15x29cm (6x11½") Color. [13] **Aus$380** £173 $286

VOYAGE DU CAP'N DAMPIER, A LA N. HOLLANDE &C IN 1699 &C. [1703] In French ed, *A Voyage to New Holland ... 1699.* Most of Eastern hemisphere. 16x28cm (6½x11") Color. Ref: Clancy (Australis) ill. p.91. [13] **Aus$1,100** £500 $828

DANCKERTS

AFBEELDINGE VAN DE VEERTICH-JAARIGE REYSE DER KINDEREN ISRAELS [1721] 35x51cm (13½x20") Full wash & OL color. [11] £172 **$285**

DE GELEGENTHEYT VAN'T PARADYS EN'T LANDT CANAAN [1721] Cyprus to Persia. 35x51cm (13½x20") Full orig wash & OL color. Rt margin trimmed to neat line. [11] £211 **$350**

DE REYSE DES APOSTELS PAULI NA ROOMEN [1721] British Isles to Middle East. 37x52cm (14½x20½") Full orig wash & OL color. [11] £151 **$250**

DE STADT JERUSALEM [1721] Bird's-eye plan; 60-item key; view. 35x51cm (13½x20") Full orig color. 6cm tear into image joined, no loss. [11] £226 **$375**

HET BELOOFDE LANDT CANAAN [1721] 35x51cm (13½x20") Full orig & OL color. [11] £136 **$225**

INSULAE AMERICANAE NEMPE: CUBA, HISPANIOLA, JAMAICA, PTO RICO, LUCANIA, ANTILLAE VULGO CARIBAE, BARLO-ET-SOTTO VENTO. ETC. [c.1690] Incl FL peninsula. 50x58cm (19½x23") Orig color. [47] £980 **$1,625**

NORVEGIA REGNUM ... [c.1696] North to Frosten; Finmark inset. Full color. 58x50cm (23x19½") Fine. Ref: Koeman, Dan 4 (73). [37] £513 **$850**

NOVA TOTIUS TERRARUM ORBIS TABULA ... [c.1685] Double hemi; sm polar hemis; insular Calif; ornate decoration. 50x58cm (19½x23") OL color; scenes full color. Sl toned; sm abraded portion along fold; minor dampstaining; sl soiling. Ref: cf Shirley (W) 529. [A8] £2,358 **$3,910**

NOVI BELGII NOVAEQUE ANGLIAE NEC NON PENNSYLVANIAE ET PARTIS VIRGINIAE TABULA [1655 / c.1684] 2nd state; with Manhattan view. 46x54cm (18x21½") Uncolored. Strong impression. Exc. Ref: Tooley (Amer) p.285, pl.150. [2] £3,317 **$5,500**

NOVISSIMA ET ACCURATISSIMA TOTIUS ANGLIAE, SCOTIAE ET HIBERNIAE TABULA ... [1685] 50x57cm (19½x22½") Early OL color; full color cartouche. Sm printer's crease; else fine. Ref: Shirley (BI 1650-1750); Koeman II Dan 1. [37] £513 **$850**

NOVISSIMA ET ACCURATISSIMA TOTIUS ITALIAE CORSICAE ET SARDINIAE [1690] 50x58cm (19½x23") Full color. Exc. [24] £844 **$1,400**

DANET

CARTE GENERALE DE LA TERRE OU MAPPEMONDE ... [IN SET WITH] L'AFRIQUE ... [AND] L'AMERIQUE MERIDIONALE ET SEPTENTRIONALE ... [AND] L'ASIE ... [AND] L'EUROPE ... [1729-1732] Paris: L.C. Desnos. Ornate border; portraits; text panel lower lf. All about 49x72cm (19½x28½") Orig OL color, full later washes. Lt time toning to all; worming & infilling on continents; America has lower c'fold split closed & reinforced; overall fine. [4] £6,600 **$10,944**

L'AMERIQUE MERIDIONALE ET SEPTENTRIONALE ... [1731] Portraits, etc. in borders. 48x70cm (19x27½") Later color. Some repaired tears, no loss; good. [2] £2,714 **$4,500**

DAPPER

[BOOK WITH MAPS] DESCRIPTION EXACT DES ISLES DE L'ARCHIPEL, ET DE CHYPRE, RHODES, CANDIE, SAMOS, CHIO ... [1703] 1st French ed. Folio, leatherette-backed boards; 18 maps, 16 plates (some 2 on page), text illus. Browning throughout; some worming mainly margin affecting couple maps; repairs title & final leaf; 2 maps bound upside down. [A5] £1,725 **$2,861**

PERIGRINATIE OFTE VEERTICH IARIGE REYSE DER KINDEREN ISRAELS [1677] From *Naukeurige Beschrijving van Gantsch Syria en Palestyn.* Folding map. 39x47cm (15½x18½") Margins trimmed close; top margin chip within ruled border restored. Ref: Laor 232. [A8] £156 **$258**

ST. JAGO [1673] From German ed, Montanus *America.* View of Chile's capital. 13x15cm (5x6") Near fine. Ref: Howes (US) D-59. [35] £27 **$45**

VETUS MEXICO [1673] From German ed, Montanus *America.* Panoramic view. 28x34cm (11x13½") Lt browned at c'fold; early verso repairs; few sh margin tears; VG. Ref: Phillips (M) p.420; Howes (US) D-59. [35] £106 **$175**

DARTON
WORLD. ENGRAVED FOR WALKER'S GEOGRAPHY ... [1797] Double hemi; 6 very sm hemis. 18x34cm (7½x13½") Color. [19] £81 **$135**

DAVIDSZOON
NOVA TOTIUS TERRARUM ORBIS TABULA AUCTORE D.D. [1676] As in *Nieuwe Water - Werelt ofte Zee Atlas* ... Double hemi; insular Calif; with Great Wall of China in red. 40x58cm (15½x23") Color. Ref: Shirley (W) 477, pl.350. [13] **Aus$9,000** £4,087 **$6,777**

DAVIS
[ATLAS] ILLUSTRATED HISTORICAL ATLAS OF BERKS COUNTY, PENNA. [1876] A.M. Davis. Maps incl 50 of Berks Co., 13 of PA, US & continents; numerous illustrations; text. Orig receipt for $13 attached. [no dimens] Recased, old front cover laid on leather; cloth spine & points; edges rubbed; some tape repaired tears preliminary pp; occas lt foxing & soiling; maps generally VG. Ref: LeGear (US) 3010. [A2] £150 **$248**
[ATLAS] NEW ILLUSTRATED ATLAS OF LEHIGH COUNTY, PENNSYLVANIA [1876] A.M. Davis. 35 county maps; 13 of PA, US, continents. [no dimens] Covers soiled & worn, some edge rubbing; contents tight; maps lt toned, occas foxing & soiling; 2 Allentown maps with tears, tape repairs, one with loss; o/w generally VG. Ref: LeGear (US) 3041. [A2] £349 **$578**
OPERATIONS IN GEORGIA AND TENNESSEE [1881] From Jefferson Davis, *Rise and Fall of the Confederacy*. 22x19cm (8½x7½") B&W. Fine (A+). [A4] £11 **$19**
OPERATIONS IN MISSISSIPPI [1881] From Jefferson Davis, *Rise and Fall of the Confederacy*. 20x17cm (8x6½") B&W. Fine (A+). [A4] £7 **$12**

DAW
THE BRITISH ISLES, COMPILED FROM GOVERNMENT ORDNANCE [1872] Folding map, dissected, linen-backed in orig cloth folder. OL color by county. 153x141cm (60x55½") Exc. [15] £226 **$375**

DAWSON
DAWSON'S MAP OF THE DOMINION OF CANADA [1874] Folding map, linen-backed, in orig cloth folder. Cape Breton to lake Huron; insets, incl west to B.C. Printed by Bartholomew, Edinburgh. Full col. 54x81cm (21½x32") Some soiling; fraying & minor loss along folds. [1888 ed, fine, offered at $175] [15] £151 **$250**

DE AEFFERDEN
GLOBUS TERRESTRIS EX PROBATISSIMIS RECENTIORUM GEOGRAPHORUM OBSERVATIONIBUS CONSECTUSCIUM SYSTEMATE COPERNICANO ATQUE TYCHONICA ALUSQUE PHAENOMENIS [1709] In *El Atlas Abreviado*. Double hemi. 16x24cm (6½x9½") Color. [13] **Aus$990** £450 **$745**

DE BEAURAIN
CARTE DES DEUX REGIONS POLAIRES JUSQU'AU 45 DE LATITUDE [1778] From *Histoire Naturelle Generale*. Aldring, sc. Each pole to 45 deg; after Brion de la Tour. 44x23cm (17½x9") Color. [19] £87 **$145**
[SAME TITLE] [1800] Reissue of 1778 map. 19x28cm (7½x11") Color. [19] £54 **$90**

DE BRUYN
[CHIOS, GREECE] [1696] Publ in *Voyage au Levant* ... Panoramic view. 29x124cm (11½x49") B&W. Folds. [20] £1,357 **$2,250**

DE BRY   Try *Le Moyne*
[AFRICA] [1597] Pigafetta attribution. 2 separate full bordered sheets covering Tunisia to Arabia to Somalia to Cape of Good Hope, with Madagascar. Each about 28x41cm (11x16") Mint. [45] £2,714 **$4,500**
[BALI] [c.1600] 14x18cm (5½x7") Trimmed, mounted on tissue as issued; exc. [43] £211 **$350**
[BOOK WITH MAPS] GRAND VOYAGES ... FRANCOFORTI [c.1600] Set of 12 parts pertaining to America made from later sheets at hand. Sm folio, 19th c. blindstamped calf. Ref: Cumming (SE). Cutter, *Grand Voyages of De Bry*; Sabin 8784. [3] £66,341 **$110,000**
[SRI LANKA: CANDY] [c.1615] J.T. & J.I. De Bry. Bird's-eye view. 27x35cm (10½x14") [11] £106 **$175**
[TITLE PAGE: ATLANTIC AND ADJACENT LANDS] [1599] From 8th part, *Grand Voyages*. In regard to Drake, Cavendish & Raleigh. 9x14cm (3½x5½") Ref: Shirley (W) 130. [45] £226 **$375**
AMERICAE PARS MAGIS COGNITA. CHOROGRAPHIA NOBILIS & OPULENTAE PERUANAE PROVINCIAE, ATQUE BRASILIAE ... MDXCII [1592] As in Book III, *Grand Voyages*. 1st ed. 36x44cm (14½x17½") Sl wear at fold intersections; crease; overall bright, fine. Ref: Moreland & Bannister, illus p.249. [23] £3,317 **$5,500**

DE BRY continued

AMERICAE PARS, NUNC VIRGINIA DICTA, PRIMUM AB ANGLIS INVENTA SUMTIBUS DN. WALTERI RALEIGH ... MDLXXXV ... [1590] After John White. 30x42cm (12x16½") Printer's crease; else fine. Ref: Burden 76; Cumming (SE) 12; Fite & Freeman #26. [23] £8,142 **$13,500**

DESCRIPTIO HYDROGRAPHICA ACCOMODATA AD BATTAVORUM NAVIGATIONE IN JAVAM ... 1595 ... 1597 [1601] 2 plates joined 36x66cm (14x26") Uncolored. VF. [4] £2,750 **$4,560**

DIE CAPITEIN DRAKE DIE STATT S. DOMINICO IN DER INSEL HISPANIOLA GELEGEN EROBERT HAT [1599] Title above; town plan, ships in harbor, troops on land in 1586. 15x21cm (6x8½") [11] £151 **$250**

FERDINANDUS SOTTO TREIBT GRAFFE BUTEREN IN DER LANDTSCHASST FLORIDA [1593 / 1624] Scene of De Soto & company trying to extract treasure information by violence & torture. 15x19cm (6x7½") on folio text sheet. B&W. Fine. Ref: Cumming (Discovery) pl.108. [35] £211 **$350**

FLORIDAE AMERICAE PROVINCIAE RECENS & EXACTISSIMA DESCRIPTIO AUCTORE IACOBO LE MOYNE... [1591] 37x45cm (14½x17½") Dark impression; superb. Ref: Burden 79; Cumming (SE) 14; Cumming (Discovery) p.174-5. Schwartz & Ehrenberg pl.38. [24] £8,745 **$14,500**

INSULA D. HELENAE ... [1613] View with ships offshore. 21x28cm (8½x11") B&W. Trace of orig c'fold; fine. [29] £172 **$285**

NOVA TABULA INSULARUM IAVA, SUMATRAE, BORNEONIS ET ALIARUM MALLACCAM USQUAE ... [1599] Publ in Part II, *Minor Voyages*. Van Doetichum, sc. 36x43cm (14x17") Uncolored. Superb. Ref: TMC 9, illus p.9. [4] £3,500 **$5,804**

OCCIDENTALIS AMERICAE PARTIS, VELEARUM REGIONUM QUAS CHRISTOPHORUS COLUMBUS PRIMU DETEXIT TABULA CHOROGRAPHICAE MULTORUM AUCTORUM SCRIPTIS, PRAESERTIM VERO EX HIERONYMI BENZONI ... THEODORE DE BRY LEOD. ANNO M.D.XCIIII [1594] 32x42cm (12½x16½") Margins trimmed to & within border. [A8] £2,497 **$4,140**

TABULA GEOGRA. REGNI CONGO [c.1605] Based on Pigafetta's travels. 31x38cm (12x15") Close margins. [11] £232 **$385**

TABULA TERRAE NOVAE ZEMBLAE ... [c.1601] Illustrative of Barentz' 1596 voyage. 18x24cm (7x9½") [11] £211 **$350**

TABULAM HANC AEGYPTI, SI AEQUUS AC DILIGNES LECOT, CUM ALYS, QUAE HACTENUS PRODICUT ... [1590 / 1598] Reengraving of Pigafetta 2-sheet map in "Relatione del Reame di Congo". Most of Africa except western bulge. 55x41cm (21½x16") Superb. Ref: MCC 29, #134; cf Norwich #16. [23] £2,231 **$3,700**

VIRGINIA [1628] Frankfurt: Merian. Below: Erforshet und Beschreiben durch Captain Iohan Schmidt. 29x36cm (11½x14") On laid watermarked paper; c'fold separations repaired; lower lf corner reattached, tear barely visible; minor margin smudges; else VG. Ref: Burden 219. [A9] £1,179 **$1,955**

VIRGINIA ERFORSHET UND BESCHRIBEN DURCH CAPTAIN IOHAN SCHMIDT [1627] Accompanied 13th part, *Grand Voyages*. Publ Frankfort by Merian (De Bry's son in law). 29x36cm (11½x14") Exc. Ref: Burden 219; Tooley (Amer) p.163-4, #3. [23] £2,412 **$4,000**

DE CORDOVA

CARTE DU TEXAS POUR LES MISSION ET VOYAGES DE L'ABBE EM DOMENECH DRESSE D'APRES LES DOCUMENTS OFFICIELS TOPOGRAPHIQUES ET LES TRAVAUX DE J. CORDOVA [1857] From Abbe Domenech, *Journal d'un Missionaire au Texas et du Mexique*. Paris: Gaume Freres. After De Cordova, with TX west to Pecos. 44x36cm (17½x14") Orig partial color. Washed; VG. [16] £362 **$600**

DE CORDOVA'S MAP OF THE STATE OF TEXAS COMPILED FROM THE RECORDS OF THE GENERAL LAND OFFICE OF THE STATE BY ROBERT CREUZBAUR ... [1850] 2nd issue; "of the State" removed from title in 1851 printing. 85x78cm (33½x31") Full color. Restored; portion top lf panel replaced (1/8 of surface); appearance satisfactory; fair. Ref: Wheat (TM) 603; cf Day (TX) 1032A. Martin (TX) pl.39. [16] £4,523 **$7,500**

DE FER (Large)

DESCRIPTIO ACURATA TERRAE PROMISSAE PER SORTES XII ... [ON SHEET WITH] TERRE SAINTE MODERNE QUE LES TURCS ... [1720] 46x72cm (18x28½") Orig OL color. Fine. Ref: Laor 429. [2] £407 **$675**

L'AMERIQUE, MERIDIONALE, ET SEPTENTRIONALE ... [1699] 46x60cm (18x23½") Exc. Ref: McLaughlin 127, state 1; Tooley (Amer) p.126, #60. pl.51. [2] £1,508 **$2,500**

L'EUROPE [SHOULD READ "L'ASIE"] DIVISEE SELON L'ETENDUE DE SES PRINCIPALES PARTES ... [1736-1746] Reissued by son-in-law Danet. Wall map relaid on modern linen. Border panels. 105x154cm (41½x60½") OL color; panels & vignettes in full color. Minor repairs lf vert fold; old damage top & lower lf; surface loss at E. Africa; other sm repairs; overall VG. [4] £6,000 **$9,949**

L'ISLE ST. DOMINGUE OU ESPAGNOLE DECOUVERTE L'AN 1492. PAR LES ESPAGNOLS ... [1723] 43x58cm (17x23") Exc. [45] £513 **$850**

DE FER (Large) continued

LE GOUVERNEMENT GENERAL DE NORMANDIE DIVISE EN HAUTE ET BASSE   [1710]   Starckman, sc. 47x66cm (18½x26") Orig OL color. Lt browned overall; some worming.   [46]   £320 $531

LE GOUVERNMENT GENERAL DE CHAMPAGNE ET LA PROVINCI DE BRIE   [1710]   61x52cm (24x20½") Color. Lt age-toning; scattered stains; else VG.   [38]   £166   **$275**

LES ISLES BRITANNIQUES   [1714]   P. Starckman, sc. 4 sheets joined. 85x107cm (33½x42") Color. Few sm splits. Ref: Shirley (BI 1650-1750) 36.   [A6]   £299 $496

MAPPE-MONDE OU CARTE GENERALE DE LA TERRE DIVISEE EN DEUX HEMISPHERES SUIVANT LA PROJECTION LA PLUS COMMUNE OU TOUS LES POINTS PRINCIPAUX SONT PLACEZ SUR LES OBSERVATIONS ...   [1694 - 1717]   Double hemi; insular Calif; text surround; ornate decor. Shirley rating, "RRR" (rare & important). Map 77x109cm (30½x43") overall, 39x59½". Later color. Mounted with rollers on later linen; some loss. Ref: Shirley (W) 560, pl.390.   [2]   £21,108   **$35,000**

[SAME TITLE]   [(1694) 1760]   Reissue, with editions by Danet. Updated peninsular Calif; elaborate decor. 77x107cm (30½x42") Orig OL col, full later additions. Orig 8 panel dissection closely re-laid on modern linen; minor rubbing & chipping, little loss; overall fine. Ref: cf Shirley (W) 560, pl.390.   [4]   **£13,000** $21,556

PARTIE MERIDIONALE DE LA RIVIERE DE MISSISIPI ...   [1718]   Separately issued. Publ in connection with promotion of "Mississippi Bubble". 46x64cm (18½x25½")   OL color. Remargined, minor loss. surface attractive. Ref: Cumming (SE) 169.   [24]   £2,895   **$4,800**

DE FER (Small)   Try *Mortier*

CETTE CARTE DE CALIFORNIE ET DU NOUVEAU MEXIQUE EST TIREE DE CELLE QUI A ETE ENVOYEE PAR UN GRANDE D'ESPAGNE POUR ETRE COMMUNIQUEE A MRS. DE L'ACADEMIE ROYALE DES SCIENCES   [1700]   1st ed. Insular Calif; 314 settlements listed. 23x34cm (9x13½") Orig OL color. Ref: McLaughlin 134.   [27]   £1,055   **$1,750**

[SAME TITLE]   [1705]   Insular Calif; 314 placenames tabulated. 24x34cm (9½x13½") Ref: McLaughlin 134. Wagner (NW) 462; Wheat (TM) 78.   [46]   **£680** $1,128

[SAME TITLE]   [1705]   Insular Calif. 23x34cm (9x13½") Color, probably later. Paper tape margin reinforcement verso.   [A7]   £312   **$517**

ISLE ET ROYAUME DE SICILE   [1705]   23x33cm (9x13") Newer color. Margins extended on verso; VG.   [A2]   £63   **$105**

L'AMERIQUE MERIDIONALE ET SEPTENTRIONALE ...   [1700 (1717)]   Insular Calif. 22x32cm (8½x12½") B&W. Top & bottom margins trimmed. Ref: McLaughlin 135.   [27]   £422   **$700**

[SAME TITLE]   [1705]   Insular Calif. Inselin, sc. 23x34cm (9x13") Dark impression.   [46]   £420 $697

L'ASIE SUIVANT LES NOUVELLES DECOUVERTES DONT LES POINT PRINCIPAUX SONT PLACEZ ...   [1705] From *Atlas Curieux*. 22x32cm (9x12½") Color. Good.   [30]   £238   **$395**

LA PARTIE ORIENTALE DE L'ASIE OU SE TROUVENT LE GRAND EMPIRE DES TARTARES CHINOIS ET CELUY DU IAPON   [1703]   Engr for *Atlas Curieux*. C. Inselin, sc. 1st ed. 23x33cm (9x13") Orig OL color. Fine. Ref: Pastoureau Fer I (108) & Fer ID.   [4]   £240   **$398**

LA TERRE SAINTE. TIREE DES MEMOIRES DE M. DE LA RUE   [1705]   24x31cm (9½x12") Dark impression. Ref: Laor 271.   [46]   £180 $299

LE CANADA, OU NOUVELLE FRANCE ...   [1705]   Incl U.S. west to Mississippi R. 23x34cm (9½x13½") OL color. Fine.   [37]   £573   **$950**

LE CANADA, OU NOUVELLE FRANCE, LA FLORIDE, LA VIRGINIE, PENSILVANIE, CAROLINE, NOUVELLE ANGLETERRE ET NOUVELLE YORCK, L'ISLE DE TERRE NEUVE, LA LOUISIANE ET LE COURS DE LA RIVIERE DE MISISIPI   [1705] Van Loon, sc. 24x34cm (9½x13") Dark impression. sl stain in sea area.   [46]   £380 $630

LE DANEMARK SUIVANT DERNIER RELATIONS   [(c.1700)]   18x14cm (7x5½") Sl offsetting & browning; lf margin trimmed.   [21]   **Can$40**   £17 $29

LES COSTES AUX ENVIRONS DE LA RIVIERE DE MISISIPI ...   [1701]   Incl Cuba. 22x33cm (8½x13") OL color. Margins trimmed to outer border rule; some browning at top.   [A8]   £191   **$316**

LES COSTES AUX ENVIRONS DE LA RIVIERE DE MISISIPI. DECOUVERTES PAR MR. DE LA SALLE EN 1683, ET RECONNUES PAR MR. LE CHEVALLIER D'IBERVILLE EN 1698 ET 1699   [1705]   Carolinas to beyond Rio Grande. 22x32cm (9x13") Dark impression.   [46]   £360 $597

LES ENVIRONS DE VIENNE EN AUSTRICHE ...   [1705]   With bird's-eye view. 17x51cm (6½x20") Full color.   [1]   £271   **$450**

MADRID, VILLE CONSIDERABLE DE LA NOUVELLE CASTILLE ...   [1705] From *L'Atlas Curieux* ... 2 information tables. 23x33cm (9x13") B&W. Fine (A+).   [A4]   £53   **$88**

[SAME TITLE]   [1705]   26 item key. 23x33cm (9x13") Color. VG.   [38]   £90   **$150**

DE FER (Small) continued

MAPPE-MONDE OU CARTE GENERALE DE LA TERRE, DRESSEE SUR LES OBSERVATIONS DE MRS. DE L'ACADEMIE ROYALE DES SCIENCES ... [(1702) 1715-17] As in *L'Atlas Curieux* ... Double hemi; insular Calif; medallions of explorers. 23x34cm (9x13½") Col. Ref: Shirley (W) 601. [13] **Aus$1,350** £613 $1,016

MAPPE-MONDE OU CARTE UNIVERSELLE ... [1705] Insular Calif. OL color. 23x8cm (9x3½") [dimens in catalogue] Repaired tear lower margin sl into border; else VG. [37] £256 **$425**

PARTIE MERIDIONALE D'AFRIQUE OU SE TROUVENT LE BASSEE GUINEE ... L'ISLE DE MADAGASCAR [1705] S of equator. 22x32cm (8½x12½") Dark impression. [46] £180 **$299**

ROYAUME DE PORTUGAL [(c.1700)] 18x14cm (7x5½") Sl offsetting & browning; rt margin trimmed. [21] **Can$35** £15 $25

VEUE DES DARDANELLES DE CONSTANTINOPLE [1705] From *Atlas Curieux*. Bird's-eye view of Hellespont entrance to Sea of Marmara. 23x34cm (9x13½") B&W. Fine. [30] £238 **$395**

DE HERRERA

DESCRIPCION DE LAS YNDIAS DE NORTE [1601] Publ Madrid. 21x29cm (8½x11½") Exc. Ref: Burden 141. [43] £724 **$1,200**

DESCRIPCION DE LAS YNDIAS OCCIDENTALIS [1621 (1723)] Accompanied Torquemada's *Libros Rituales i Monarchia Indiana*. "Nuevo Mexico" & "Misisipi" added since 1st ed. 22x32cm (9x12½") Some color, probably later. Ref: Burden 140. Wagner (NW) 226. [10] £513 **$850**

DESCRIPTION DEL DESTRICTO DEL AUDIENCIA DE LA ESPANOLA 3 [1604 (+)] West Indies. 22x30cm (8½x11½") [A7] £416 **$690**

DE JODE

ASIAE NOVISSIMA TABULA [1578] From *Speculum Orbis Terrarum*. 1st ed. 34x44cm (13½x17½") Clean tear repaired, no loss; else VG. Ref: Koeman Jod1, 4; Allen (Atlases) p.49. [2] £6,634 **$11,000**

HESSIAE SEU CATTORUM NOBLISSIMORUM AC BELLICOSISSIMORUM ... [1593] 36x46cm (14x18") Old color. Ref: Koeman Jod 2. [48] **DM 3,000** £1,036 $1,717

QUIVIRAE REGNU CUM ALIJS VERSUS BOREA [1593] From *Speculum* ... 35x23cm (14x9½") Full color. Printer's crease; rt latitude scale rejoined; overall fine. [43] £5,126 **$8,500**

DE L'ISLE   Try Buache, *Covens & Mortier, Dezauche, Fricx, Lotter*

[ATLAS] ATLAS RUSSICUS MAPPA UNA GENERALI ET UNDERVIGINTI SPECIALIBUS VASTISSIMUM IMPERIUM RUSSICUM ... [1745 (1/58)] J.N. De L'Isle & Louis De L'Isle; St. Petersburg: Imperial Academy of Science. Folio; 20 maps with orig OL color + important extra, Mueller's map of the North Pacific showing Alaska. Heel of spine worn, boards scuffed, internally fine. Ref: Bagrow (Russia) 177-200; Breitfuss; Fite & Freeman 51; Phillips (A) 4060. [37] £9,046 **$15,000**

CARTE D'AFRIQUE [c.1750] Amsterdam: Covens & Mortier. 52x64cm (20½x25½") OL color. Top margin trimmed affecting several letters; minor browning at fold. [A7] £76 **$126**

CARTE D'AMERIQUE [1722] 50x62cm (19½x24½") OL color. Sl soiling overall; restoration upper margin. [A7] £555 **$920**

CARTE D'AMERIQUE ... CHEZ L'AUTEUR SUR LE QUAY DE L'HORLOGE [1722] 1st ed, 2nd state. 48x61cm (19x24") OL color. Lt damp stains corner; ink smudge margin; few sh tears to border repaired; VG (A). Ref: Tooley (Amer) p.13, #2, pl.1; Portinaro & Knirsch 114. [A3] £767 **$1,271**

CARTE DE L'EGYPT DE LA NUBIE DE L ABISSINIE &C. [c.1730] Covens & Mortier. NE Africa & Arabian peninsula. 50x58cm (19½x23") Orig OL color. VG. [A2] £232 **$385**

CARTE DE L'ISLE DE LA MARTINIQUE ... [1732] 46x58cm (18x23") OL color. [Covens & Mortier issue, c.1740, offered at same price] [20] £377 **$625**

CARTE DE L'ISLE DE LA MARTINIQUE COLONIE FRANCOISE DES ISLES ANTILLES DE L'AMERIQUE [1732] 47x60cm (18½x23½") Some orig line color. Sh c'fold split joined. [11] £196 **$325**

CARTE DE LA HONGRIE ... [1703] From 1st ed, *Atlas de Geographie*. 47x65cm (18½x25½") Full orig wash color. [1] £241 **$400**

CARTE DE LA LOUISIANE ET DU COURS DU MISSISSIPI DRESSEE SUR UN GRAND NOMBRE DE MEMOIRES ... [1718] 1st issue, without New Orleans; extent: New York to Rio Grande. 48x65cm (19x25½") Orig OL color. Exc. Ref: Schwartz & Ehrenberg pl.84. Martin (TX) p.98-9; [2] £5,729 **$9,500**

[SAME TITLE] [1718] 2nd issue; 1st map to name New Orleans. 48x65cm (19x25½") Orig OL color. Exc. [2] £4,523 **$7,500**

[SAME TITLE] [1718 (1730)] Amsterdam: Covens & Mortier. 3rd state. 44x60cm (17½x23½") Orig OL color. On heavy paper; orig off-center fold; lt browning lf. Ref: Cumming (SE) 208. [27] £1,176 **$1,950**

DE L'ISLE continued

CARTE DE LA LOUISIANE ET DU COURS DU MISSISSIPI DRESSEE SUR UN GRAND NOMBRE DE MEMOIRES ... A PARIS CHEZ L'AUTEUR LE SR. DELISLE SUR LE QUAY DE L'HORLOGE AVEC PRIVILEGE DU ROY JUN 1718 [1718] 1st ed, 1st state. New York to Rio Grande; New Orleans absent; 1st appearance of "Teijas". 48x65cm (19x25½") Orig OL color. Sm stain upper rt; else exc. Ref: Cumming (SE) 170; Schwartz & Ehrenberg pl.84. Martin (TX) pl.19. [24] £5,729 **$9,500**

CARTE DE LA TERRE FERME, DU PEROU, DU BRESIL ... [1716] Publ by "la Veuve [widow] de Paul Marret" for insertion in travel book. 47x63cm (18½x25") Uncolored. Protective added margins; tissue backing. ["Carte du Paraguay, du Chili, du Detroit de Magellan ..." from same source offered at £340] [34] **£360** $597

CARTE DE SUISSE [1780] Canton crests above. 49x62cm (19½x24½") Later color. [2] £452 **$750**

CARTE DES ANTILLES FRANCOIS ET DES ISLES VOISINES ... [1717] 1st ed. Guadeloupe to (upside down) Grenada, with Barbados. 64x37cm (25½x15") Color. [18] £226 **$375**

[SAME TITLE] [1730] Amsterdam: Covens & Mortier. Guadeloupe to (upside down) Grenada, with Barbados. 60x46cm (23½x18") Color. Ref: cf Phillips 3448, v.9-67. [18] £293 **$485**

[SAME TITLE] [1730] Amsterdam: Covens & Mortier. Guadeloupe to Barbados & Grenada. 59x44cm (23½x17½") OL color. Some lt surface soiling; lt text offset in blank area; overall VG. [A1] £106 **$176**

CARTE DES INDES ET DE LA CHINE ... [c.1730] Amsterdam: Covens & Mortier. India to Japan to Indonesia. 62x62cm (24½x24½") Orig col. Some restoration, mostly margins; sl weakness at folds. [46] **£680** $1,128

[SAME TITLE] [1740] Covens & Mortier. 61x61cm (24x24") Contemp OL color. [A6] £287 **$476**

CARTE DU CANADA OU DE LA NOUVELLE FRANCE ... [1703] 51x66cm (20x26") OL col. [A8] £589 **$977**

[SAME TITLE] [1703 (1730)] Amsterdam: Covens & Mortier. 49x57cm (19½x22½") B&W. Fine. Ref: Tooley (Amer) p.20; TMC 19, cover illus. [37] £905 **$1,500**

CARTE DU CANADA OU DE LA NOUVELLE FRANCE ET DES DECOUVERTES QUI Y ONT ETE FAITES DRESSEE SUR PLUSIERS OBSERVATIONS ... PAR GUILLAUME DE L'ISLE ... [1703 (1722)] Amsterdam: Covens & Mortier. 50x58cm (19½x23") Orig OL color; uncolored cartouche. On heavy paper. Ref: Tooley (Amer) p.20. [27] £905 **$1,500**

[SAME TITLE] [1703 / 1730] Amsterdam: Covens & Mortier. 49x57cm (19x22½") Orig OL color. Exc. Ref: Kershaw (Canada) 318; Tooley (Amer) p.20; Schwartz & Ehrenberg pl.80. [24] £724 **$1,200**

CARTE DU DUCHE DE BOURGOGNE ET DES COMTEZ EN DEPENDANS [c.1730] Covens & Mortier. Set of 2 maps, each about 48x64cm (19x25") Orig color. Fine. [A2] £150 **$248**

CARTE DU MEXIQUE ET DE LA FLORIDE DES TERRES ANGLOISES ET DES ISLES ANTILLES DU COURS ET DES ENVIRONS DE LA RIVIERE DE MISSISSIPI ... PAR GUILLAUME DEL'ISLE ... [1703] 48x65cm (19x25½") Orig OL color. Exc. Ref: Cumming 137; Wheat (Trans-Miss) 84; Schwartz & Ehrenberg, pl.82. Martin (TX) p.92-3. [2] £2,111 **$3,500**

[SAME TITLE] [1703 (1722)] Amsterdam: Covens & Mortier. 3rd state. 47x60cm (18½x24") Orig OL color. Sharp impression; on heavy paper. [27] £1,116 **$1,850**

CARTE PARTICULIERE DE LA HONGRIE DE LA TRANSILVANIE DE LA CROATIE ... [c.1740] Attributed as well to Schenk & Visscher. 48x57cm (19x22½") Full orig color. Exc. [2] £226 **$375**

HEMISPHERE SEPTENTRIONAL POUR VOIR PLUS DISTINCTEMENT LES TERRES ARCTIQUES [c.1730] De Leth imprint. Diam: 45cm (18") Full orig col. Lt offsetting; o/w VG. Ref: cf Wagner (NW) 504. [2] £332 **$550**

HEMISPHERE SEPTENTRIONAL POUR VOIR PLUS DISTINCTEMENT LES TERRES ARCTIQUES [IN SET WITH] HEMISPHERE MERIDIONAL POUR VOIR PLUS DISTINCTEMENT LES TERRES AUSTRALES [1714] Two polar projections. Each Diameter: 45cm (18") Orig OL color. Exc. Ref: Wagner (NW) 504. [2] £1,508 **$2,500**

[SAME TITLE] [1714] 1st ed. Each 47x47cm (18½x18½") Orig OL col. Heavy paper. [27] £1,176 **$1,950**

L'AFRIQUE ... [1700 (1708)] Quai de l'Horloge issue. 45x58cm (18x23") OL color. Fine. Ref: Norwich [37] £452 **$750**

L'AMERIQUE MERIDIONALE ... [1732] Amsterdam: Covens & Mortier. 48x58cm (18½x23") Orig OL color. Strong impression. [34] **£380** $630

L'AMERIQUE SEPTENTRIONALE ... [1700-1708] From *Atlas Nouveau*. Amsterdam: Mortier. 44x58cm (17½x23") OL color. Deacidified; japan paper backing closing margin tears, one 1½" into map; VG (A). [A4] £511 **$847**

L'AMERIQUE SEPTENTRIONALE DRESSEE SUR LES OBSERVATIONS ... [c.1740] Publ by Ottens. Peninsular Calif. 44x58cm (17½x23") Full orig color. Exc. [2] £588 **$975**

L'ESPAGNE ... [1730] Amsterdam: Covens & Mortier. 48x60cm (19x23½") OL col. Fine. [14] £226 **$375**

L'HEMISPHERE SEPTENTRIONAL POUR VOIR PLUS DISTINCTEMENT LES TERRES ARCTIQUES [c.1740] From *Nieuwe Atlas*. Amsterdam: Covens & Mortier. Extends to equator. 20x46cm (8x18") Orig OL color. Minimal offsetting; fine. Ref: Phillips (A) 595-2. [12] £332 **$550**

DE L'ISLE continued

LES ISLES BRITANNIQUES OU SONT LE ROYAUMES D'ANGLETERRE ... [1730 - 1733] Amsterdam: Covens & Mortier. 45x57cm (18x22½") OL color; B&W cartouche. VG to fine. [14] £528 **$875**

MAPPEMONDE A L'USAGE DU ROY PAR GUILLAUME DELISLE ... [1720] Double hemi; peninsular Calif; ribbon title. 44x67cm (17½x26½") OL color. Margins trimmed to border; c'fold reinforced, restored tear bottom rt blank area; o/w fine. [A1] £862 **$1,430**

MAPPEMONDE A L'USAGE DU ROY PAR GUILLAUME DE L'ISLE ... QUAI DE L'HORLOGE 15 APRIL 1720 [1720] Double-hemi. 44x67cm (17½x26½") Color. Minor repair; 2 close margins as issued. [19] £1,191 **$1,975**

ORBIS VETERIBUS NOTI TABULA NOVA ... 1714 [1731] Eastern hemi. Derosier, sc. 49x48cm (19½x19") OL color. Wide side margins sl trimmed; clean, fresh. [A9] £260 **$431**

THEATRUM HISTORICUM [1730] Amsterdam: Covens & Mortier. Europe; circular Western Hemi inset without detail. 48x65cm (19x25½") OL color. Lt image transfer in blank areas; o/w fine. [A1] £106 **$176**

DE LA RUE

REGNUM JUDEORUM IN FILIOS HERODIS MAGNI PER TATRARCHIAS DIVISUM AD TEMPORA CHRISTI DOMINI [1651] Paris: Mariette. 41x54cm (16x21") OL col. Lt browned along c'fold. Ref: Laor 418. [A8] £139 **$230**

TERRA PROMISSA IN SORTES SEU TRIBUS XII DISTINCTA SEU TABULA AD LIBRUM ISOVE [(1646) c.1730] Covens & Mortier reissue. 41x51cm (16x20½") Color. Fine. Ref: Laor 425. [39] £211 **$350**

DE LAET

[ATLAS] AMERICAE UTRIUSQUE DESCRIPTIO NOVUS ORBIS SEU DESCRIPTIONIS INDIAE OCCIDENTALIS LIBRI XVIII [1633] Antwerp; 1st Latin ed. Folio; orig gold-stamped calf binding, rubbed. 14 double page maps; illustrations. Ref: Sabin 38557. [3] £6,634 **$11,000**

AMERICAE SIVE INDIAE OCCIDENTALIS TABULA GENERALIS [1630] 28x35cm (11x14") Exc. Ref: Burden 229. [44] £452 **$750**

FLORIDA ET REGIONES VICINAE [1630] Map by H. Gerritsz. 28x36cm (11x14") Faint staining mostly margin; else exc. Ref: Burden 232; Cumming (SE) 34. [24] £1,508 **$2,500**

NOVA ANGLIA NOVUM BELGIUM ET VIRGINIA [1630] As in *Beschrijvinghe van West-Indien*. Bermuda inset. 28x36cm (11x14") Exc. Ref: Burden 231. [44] £2,533 **$4,200**

DE LAPORTE

CARTE DE LA NOUVELLE ANGLETERRE, NOUVELLE YORK, NOUVELLE JERSEY ET PENSILVANIE [c.1780] Minimum English possessions delineated; NJ extends to Canada. 18x22cm (7x8½") OL color. Surface dirt; VG. [38] £151 **$250**

CARTE DE LA VIRGINIE ET DU MARILAND [c.1780] 18x22cm (7x8½") OL color. C'fold & edge tears repaired; surface dirt; good. [38] £136 **$225**

L'EMPIRE DE LA CHINE AVEC LES ISLES DU JAPON [1781] With Korea & only SW Japan. 18x22cm (7x8½") [11] £57 **$95**

LES INDES ORIENTALES ET LEUR ARCHIPEL [1786] 18x22cm (7x8½") [11] £75 **$125**

MAPPE-MONDE OU DESCRIPTION DU GLOBE TERRESTRE [1786] Double hemi; rococo title. 18x22cm (7x8½") Color. [11] £151 **$250**

DE LAT

KAART VAN DE GEHEELE WERELD [1747] From *Atlas Portatif*. By Jacob Keizer. Insular Calif. 18x29cm (7x11½") Orig OL color. Good. Ref: Koeman Lat 7 (8). [29] £299 **$495**

KAARTJE VAN HET NOORDER-DEEL VAN AMERICA [1747] From *Atlas Portatif*. By Jacob Keizer. Insular Calif. 17x23cm (7x9½") Orig OL color. Good. Ref: McLaughlin 232. Koeman Lat 7 (12). [29] £299 **$495**

DE LAVAUR

NOUVEAU PLAN DE MOSCOU [c.1850] Moscow: Auguste Semen. Linen-backed folding map; 17 city districts; in French & Cyrillic. 56x64cm (22x25½") Color. Early pencil notes. [A7] £208 **$345**

DE RENEVILLE

IAVA MAIOR [1727] Java. 15x20cm (6x8") Exc. [44] £51 **$85**

DE VAUGONDY   Try *Delamarche, Diderot*

[ATLAS] ATLAS UNIVERSAL [1757] Gilles & Didier Robert de Vaugondy. Paris: Boudet Libraire Imprimeur. Folio, full contemporary calf: iv, 40; 108 double page maps with OL color. Binding wear, stain upper rt corner; hinges dry & starting. Maps have usual minor spots, offsetting or creasing; generally exc. Ref: Phillips (A) 619. Sabin 71864. [21] **Can$8,500** £3,718 **$6,164**

DE VAUGONDY continued

[ATLAS] ATLAS UNIVERSEL [1757-(58)] Folio, 2 vols, calf; 108 maps in OL color; 40 pp text Cover worn; occas lt soiling, mostly margin; 2 maps torn or frayed; dampstaining top rt corner map 29. [A5] **£5,290 $8,772**

[ATLAS] ATLAS UNIVERSEL PAR M. ROBERT GEOGRAPHE ORDINAIRE DU ROY, PAR M. ROBERT DE VAUGONDY SON FILS GEOGRAPHE ORD. DU ROY ... 1757 ... A PARIS ... [1757] 1st ed; "grand papier". Large folio, full calf; (3), 3-40 pp; 108 maps, orig OL color. Joints tender, firmly attached; modest wear; margins of several leaves dampstained; occas spotting; fresh, bright. Ref: Phillips (A) 619. Pedley. [24] £11,459 **$19,000**

AMERIQUE OU INDES OCCIDENTALES [1778] Insets: Martinique; Hispaniola. 52x64cm (20½x25½") OL color. 2 inkspots in image. [48] **DM 680** £235 $389

AMERIQUE SEPTENTRIONALE ... [1749] As in *Atlas Portatif Universel et Militaire*. 20x16cm (8x6½") Orig OL color. [34] **£150** $249

[SAME TITLE] [1775] Inset of NW. 48x59cm (19x23") OL color. Upper ctr stains. VF. [16] £528 **$875**

AMERIQUE SEPTENTRIONALE, DRESSEE SUR LES RELATIONS LES PLUS MODERNES DES VOYAGEURS ET NAVIGATEURS OU SE REMARQUENT ... LES ETATS UNIS ... PUBLIEE EN 1750 ET CORRIGEE EN 1783 ... [(1750) 1783] State 6; engraved new U.S. border. 48x58cm (19x23") Orig OL color. Exc. Ref: Pedley 450. [24] £2,714 **$4,500**

ARCHIPEL DES INDES ORIENTALES QUI COMPREND LES ISLES DE LA SONDE, MOLUQUES ET PHILIPPINES [1750] As in *Atlas Universel*. 48x59cm (19x23½") Orig color. [13] **Aus$1,000** £454 $753

CANADA, LOUISIANE, POSSESSIONS ANGL? ... [1778] 24x29cm (9½x11½") Col. Exc. [24] £121 **$200**

CARTE DE LA VIRGINIE ET DU MARYLAND DRESSEE SUR LA GRANDE CARTE ANGLOISE DE MRS. JOSUE FRY ET PIERRE JEFFERSON [1755] 1st French ed. 48x64cm (19x25½") OL color. Exc. [2] £905 **$1,500**

[SAME TITLE] [1755] 48x64cm (19x25") Orig OL color. Minor mend; else exc. [24] £1,146 **$1,900**

[SAME TITLE] [1755] 48x64cm (19x25½") OL color. Margins lt toned; brief tears rt margin; image clean. [A9] £659 **$1,093**

[SAME TITLE] [1755 (c.1760)] 48x64cm (19x25½") Orig OL color. Fine. Ref: Pedley 470 (unrecorded state 1a); Cumming (SE) 281.. [28] £814 **$1,350**

CARTE DU ROYAUME DE FRANCE [1758] 49x53cm (19½x21") OL color. [A8] £62 **$103**

COURS DU MISSISSIPI ET LA LOUISIANE [1749] As in *Atlas Portatif Universel et Militaire*. 20x16cm (8x6") Orig OL color. [34] **£200** $332

ETATS DU GRAND-SEIGNEUR EN ASIE, EMPIRE DE PERSE, PAYS DES USBECS, ARABIE ET EGYPTE ... [c.1760] 48x55cm (19x21½") Orig OL color. Lt foxing margins; o/w VG to fine. [A2] £100 **$165**

GOUVERNEMENT GENERAL DU DAUPHINE DIVISE PAR BAILLIAGES [1751] 49x51cm (19x20") OL color. [41] £112 **$185**

ISLE ROYALE [1749] As in *Atlas Portatif Universel et Militaire*. 16x24cm (6½x9½") Orig OL color. ["Partie du Mexique ou de la Nouvlle Espagne ..." offered at same price] [34] **£120** $199

L'EMPIRE DU JAPON ... [1750] 1st state. 48x54cm (19x21") Orig OL color. Mint. Ref: Walter (Japan) 86. [24] £905 **$1,500**

L'IRLANDE [1762] 24x22cm (9½x8½") Orig color. Lt brown spot in blank area; o/w fine. [A1] £63 **$105**

L'ISLE DE MARTINIQUE [1749] From *Atlas Portatif* ... Didier Robert de Vaugondy. 16x19cm (6½x7½") Orig OL color. [34] **£80** $133

LA JUDEE OU TERRE SAINTE, DIVISEE EN SES DOUZE TRIBES [1750] 48x59cm (19x23") OL color. Ref: Laor 667. [48] **DM 400** £138 $229

LES ISLES ANTILLES ... [1749] From *Atlas Portatif* ... Didier Robert de Vaugondy. 16x22cm (6½x9") Orig OL color. [34] **£100** $166

LES LACS DU CANADA ET NOUVELLE ANGLETERRE [1749] As in *Atlas Portatif Universel et Militaire*. Great Lakes. 17x22cm (6½x8½") Orig OL color. [34] **£280** $465

MAPPE MONDE OU DESCRIPTION DU GLOBE TERRESTRE ... [1752] Double hemi. 46x70cm (18x28") Wash color. Fine. Ref: Pedley #8, 1st state. [29] £1,055 **$1,750**

MAPPE MONDE SUIVANT LA PROJECTION DE CARTES REDUITES [1761] Mercator proj. 24x39cm (9½x15½") OL color. Lt toned; VG (A). [A4] £133 **$220**

MAPPE-MONDE DRESSEE SUIVANT LES NOUVELLES RELATIONS ET ASSUJETTIE AUX OBSERVATIONS ASTRONOMIQUES ... 1778 [1778] Double hemi; tracks of Tasman, Anson & "Galion N. Seignora 1743". 47x74cm (18½x29") Color. [19] £594 **$985**

MAPPEMONDE OU DESCRIPTION DU GLOBE TERRESTRE [1790] Double hemi; Cook's discoveries shown. 46x70cm (18½x28") New color. Fine. [14] £1,267 **$2,100**

DE VAUGONDY continued

NOUVELLE ANGLETERRE NLLE YORK, NLLE JERSEY, PENSILVANIE MARILAND ET VIRGINIE [1749] As in *Atlas Portatif Universel et Militaire*. 19x16cm (7½x6½") Orig OL color. [34] £220 $365

ORBIS VETUS IN ULTRAQUE CONTINENTE JUXTA MENTEM SANSONIANAM DISTINCTUS, NEC NON OBSERVATIONIBUS ASTRONOMICIS REDACTUS ... 1752 [1752] By Gilles (the son). Double hemi; with modern geography. 48x71cm (18½x28") Color. [13] **Aus$3,900** £1,771 $2,937

[SAME TITLE] [1752] Double hemi. 46x71cm (18½x28") Color. Ref: Phillips (A) 3524-1. [19] £522 **$865**

PART OF NORTH AMERICA, CONTAINING CANADA, THE NORTH PARTS OF NEW ENGLAND AND NEW YORK; WITH NOVA SCOTIA AND NEWFOUNDLAND [1762] Publ London, after De Vaugondy. Inset: ... Lakes of Canada" 21x29cm (8x11½") [11] £45 **$75**

PARTIE DE L'AMERIQUE SEPTENT? [SIC] QUI COMPREND LA NOUVELLE FRANCE OU LA CANADA ... [1757 / ?] 47x60cm (18½x23½") Orig OL color. Exc. Ref: Karpinski (MI) p.142. [24] £754 **$1,250**

[SAME TITLE] [1755] Great Lakes inset. 48x58cm (19x23") Orig OL color. Exc. [2] £513 **$850**

[SAME TITLE] [1755] From *Atlas Universel* ... Great Lakes inset. 48x60cm (19x23½") Orig OL color. Repair at inset; overall clean, bright. Ref: Holmden 33; Lepine 1400; Phillips 619-98. [12] £392 **$650**

PARTIE DE L'AMERIQUE SEPTENTRIONALE, QUI COMPREND LE COURS DE L'OHIO, LA NLLE. ANGLETERRE, LA NLLE. YORK, LE NEW JERSEY, LA PENSYLVANIE, LE MARYLAND LA VIRGINIE, LA CAROLINE [1755] 49x63cm (19½x25") OL color. [A7] £520 **$862**

[SAME TITLE] [1755 (c.1768)] 48x62cm (19x24½") Old OL color. Fine. Ref: Cumming (SE) 295. Pedley 469; Smith (OH) 7-14. [28] £573 **$950**

[SAME TITLE] [1763 & later] 48x61cm (19x24") OL & cartouche color. VG. [36] £724 **$1,200**

PARTIE DU CANADA OU SE TROUVENT LE FLEUVE ST LAURENT ET LA NOUVELLE ECOSSE [1749] As in *Atlas Portatif Universel et Militaire*. 16x21cm (6½x8½") Orig OL color. ["L'Acadie", "Isle de Terre Neuve", "Bayes d'Hudson et de Baffins et Terre de Labrador" and "Golfe de St Laurent, ... Terre Neuve" offered at same price] [34] £140 $232

PARTIE DU MEXIQUE ... OU SE TROUVE ... CALIFORNIE &C. [1749] As in *Atlas Portatif Universel et Militaire*. Incl present TX & CA. 16x20cm (6½x7½") Orig OL color. [34] £250 $415

PARTIE SEPTENTRIONALE DU ROYAUME DE NAPLES [1779] Venice: Santini. 49x60cm (19½x23½") OL color. Minor browning edges. [A8] £104 **$172**

TURQUIE D'ASIE, ARABIE, PERSE, TARTARIE INDEPENDANTE [1761] 23x21cm (9½x8½") Orig color. Lt foxing margins; o/w fine. [A1] £80 **$132**

DE WIT

[ATLAS] ATLAS [c.1680] Folio, stiff vellum binding; 52 maps in orig color, incl 4 continents. VG. Ref: Allen, *The Atlas of Atlases*. [3] £27,139 **$45,000**

[SOUTHERN HEMISPHERE] [1680] After Hondius & Jansson; lacks verso text. 43x48cm (17x19") Orig color. [13] **Aus$3,200** £1,453 $2,409

ACCURATISSIMA DOMINII VENETI IN ITALIA, DUCATUS PARMAE, PLACENTIAE MODENAE REGII ET MANTUAE EPISCOPATUSQ. TRIDENTINI TABULA QUAE EST LOMBARDIA INFERIOR [c.1690] 50x62cm (19½x24") Old color. [48] **DM 780** £269 $446

ACCURATISSIMA TOTIUS ASIAE TABULA ... [1670] 48x57cm (19x22½") Contemp col. [A6] £368 $611

[SAME TITLE] [c.1680] 49x58cm (19½x22½") OL col. Sl toned; glue remnants top margin. [A8] £416 **$690**

ASIAE NOVA DESCRIPTIO [(1660) c.1661] Carte-a-figures; costumes & cities. 44x56cm (17½x22") Color. Minor reinforcement lower c'fold; some placenames underlined; exc. [4] **£2,200** $3,648

CORECTISSIMA NEC NON NOVISSIMA DOMINII ET PROVINCIAE GRONINGAE ET OMLANDIAE [c.1690] 49x58cm (19½x23") Old color. [48] **DM 850** £293 $486

DANUBII FLUVII SIVE TURCICI IMPERII [1670] Centered on Greece. 50x61cm (20x24") Contemp body color. [A6] £299 $496

DUCATUS LUTZENBURGICI TABULA NUPERRIME IN LUCEM EDITA ... [c.1660] 46x56cm (18x22") OL color. Sh repaired margin fold splits; VG (A). [A4] £156 **$259**

DUCATUS PRUSSIAE TAM POLONO REGIAE, QUAM BRANDENBURGO ... [c.1695] N Poland & part Lithuania. 46x59cm (18½x23") Period color. Minor repairs. [42] **Aus$1,100** £500 $828

INDIAE ORIENTALIS NEC NON INSULARUM ADIACENTIUM NOVA DESCRIPTIO EDITA PER F. DE WITT [c.1700] Amsterdam: Mortier. Incl Japan. 50x60cm (20x23½") Full orig col. Fine. [23] £1,930 **$3,200**

INSULA CANDIA EJUSQUE FORTIFICATIO ... [c.1680] 6 insets. 46x54cm (18x21½") Full orig color. Exc. Ref: Zacharakis 2392. [23] £905 **$1,500**

DE WIT

INSULARUM MELITAE VULGO MALTAE GOZAE ET COMINI CORRECTISSIMA DESCRIPTIO [1707] Insets: Veletta; central Mediterranean. 46x56cm (18x22") Orig color. [47] **£950** $1,576

LITTORA BRASILIAE. PASCAERT VAN BRASIL [1670] 49x56cm (19x22") Contemp color. Framed. [A6] **£207** $344

MAGNI DUCATUS LITHUANIAE [c.1715] 45x52cm (17½x20½") OL color. [A7] **£139** $230

NOVA EUROPAE DESCRIPTIO [c.1660] Panels top & sides. 44x56cm (17½x22") Full color. C'fold margin break; exc. [1] **£965** $1,600

NOVA ORBIS TABULA IN LUCEM EDITA, A.F. DE WIT [1670] State 2 with putti & decorative border; double hemi; insular Calif. 48x57cm (19x22½") Orig color. Ref: Shirley (W) 499. [3rd state, 1680, "cum Privilegio ... Hollandiae et Westfrisia" offered at Aus$ 9,400] [13] **Aus$8,000** £3,633 $6,024

[SAME TITLE] [1680] Double Hemi; insular Calif. 48x56cm (18½x22") Col. Paper backing to take care of sm faults: sh tears, arsenic coloring surface disturbance. [A7] **£1,318** $2,185

NOVA PERSIAE, ARMENIAE NATOLIAE ET ARABIAE ... [c.1680] 47x56cm (18½x22") Full orig color. Lt toned; greens oxidized; VG. [23] **£724** $1,200

NOVA TOTIUS AMERICAE DESCRIPTIO AUCT F. DE WIT [c.1666] Separately issued; panels on 3 sides; insular Calif. 44x55cm (17½x22") Color. Reinforced vert crease in Atlantic; else exc. Ref: Burden 356; McLaughlin 24; Tooley (Amer) p.116, #18, pl.34. [24] **£3,619** $6,000

NOVISSIMA AC PRAE CAETERIS ALIIS ACCURATISSIMA REGNI ET INSULAE HIBERNIAE DELINEATO ... [c.1715] Amsterdam: Covens & Mortier. 58x49cm (23x19½") Full orig color by counties. Fine. [24] **£1,025** $1,700

NOVISSIMA ET ACCURATISSIMA SEPTENTRIONALIS AC MERIDIONALIS AMERICAE [c.1730] Covens & Mortier, reuse and altered title of worn 1710 De Wit plate. 44x54cm (17x21") Color. Sl toned. Ref: cf McLaughlin 49. [A7] **£902** $1,495

RECENTISSIMA NOVI ORBIS SIVE AMERICAE SEPTENTRIONALIS ET MERIDIONALIS TABULA ... [1690 - c.1710] Amsterdam: R. & J. Ottens. Insular Calif. 50x58cm (19½x23") Orig color. Ref: McLaughlin 178. [34] **£1,600** $2,653

[SAME TITLE] [c.1710] Ottens reissue. 50x58cm (19½x23") Orig wash color. Exc. [2] **£1,508** $2,500

REGNI NAVARRAE ACCURATA TABULA [c.1690] 38x50cm (15x19½") Old col. [48] **DM 300** £104 $172

REGNI POLONIAE ET DUCATUS LITHUANIAE, VOLINIAE, PODOLIAE, UCRANIAE, PRUSSIAE, LIVONIAE ET CURLANDIAE [1680] 35x50cm (14x19½") Orig color. Faint staining; else exc. [23] **£392** $650

REGNORUM CASTELLAE NOVAE, ANDALUSIAE, GRANADAE, VALENTIAE, ET MURCIAE [1680] 50x59cm (19½x23") Newer color. Fine. [14] **£311** $515

REGNUM HIBERNIAE DIVISUM IN QUATOUR PARTES QUAE PARTES SUNT ULTONIA CONACHIA, LAGENIA ET MOMONIA QUAE ET SUNT DIVISAE IN OMNES SUOS COMITATUS [1680-] 58x50cm (23x19½") Orig color. Ref: Moir p.177 [46] **£460** $763

TABULA COMITATUS ARTESIAE [c.1680] 46x55cm (18x21½") [39] **£90** $150

TABULA INDIAE ORIENTALIS EMENDATA A F DE WIT [1662] 46x57cm (18x22½") Orig color. [13] **Aus$2,400** £1,090 $1,807

[SAME TITLE] [1662] Lhuilier, sc. 46x56cm (18x22") Color. Exc. [4] **£875** $1,451

TABULA RUSSIA VULGO MOSCOVIA ... [c.1680] 45x56cm (18x22") Early color. Exc. [24] **£332** $550

TERRA NOVA AC MARIS TRACTUS CIRCA NOVAM FRANCIAM, ANGLIAM, BELGIUM, VENEZUELAM NOVA ANDALUSIAM, GUIANAM ET BRASILIAM. TERRA NEUF, ENDE CUSTEN VAN NIEUW VRANCKRYCK, NIEU ENGELAND, NIEU NEDERLAND, NIEU ANDALUSIA, GUIANA EN VENEZUELA [1680] 49x57cm (19x22") Contemp color. Cracking of green, sl loss; margins stained just to engraved area. [A6] **£299** $496

TETRACHIA DUCATUS GELDRIAE NEOMAGENSIS [c.1660] 45x56cm (17½x22") OL color. Sm wax spot; oxidized green; VG (A). [A4] **£116** $193

THE PLAN OF EDENBURGH EXACTLY DONE ... [c.1710] Orig drawn by Rev. James Gordon; De Wit's plan re-engraved by Andrew Johnston. 3 views. 2 sheets joined, 42x105cm (16½x41½") Uncol. [34] **£1,400** $2,322

TOTIUS FLUMINES RHENI ... [1671-80] 2 river sections on sheet. 46x53cm (18½x21") Full orig color. Age tone; spotting bottom rt. [1] **£332** $550

DELAGRIVE, J.

NEUVIE ME PLAN DE PARIS SES ACCROISSEMENS SOURS LE REGNE DE LOUIS XV ... [1737] 62x84cm (24½x33½") Orig col. Some fold reinforcement; few minor repairs; close all around; clean; VG. [23] **£1,327** $2,200

DELAHAYE
NOUVELLE CARTE DES MERS ... LE DETROIT DE BANCA ... DE MALAC   [c.1770]   As in *Le Neptune Orientale* ... Singapore & sea lanes. 49x67cm (19½x26"). Color.   [34]   **£500 $829**

DELAMARCHE   Try *De Vaugondy*
[ATLAS] PETIT ATLAS MODERNE OU COLLECTION DE CARTES ELEMENTAIRE ...   [1793]   Paris. Octavo; orig marble boards & leather spine; 2 celestial maps, 26 double-page maps as called for incl world & U.S. with Canada & Florida. Maps in OL color & near mint.   [11]   £754 **$1,250**
CANADA, LOUISIANE, ETATS-UNIS ... CORRIGES PAR LE CEN. LAMARCHE SON SUCCESSEUR   [1795] After Robert de Vaugondy. 24x29cm (9½x11½"). OL color. Sl dampstaining edges; mild foxing margins; penned notes rt margin.   [A10]   £146 **$242**
CARTE DE L'AMERIQUE MERIDIONALE   [1843]   43x30cm (17x12"). OL color. Minor margin stain; else fine (A).   [A4]   £7 **$11**
CARTE DE L'ETAT DU MONDE VERS LA FIN DU XVEME SIECLE   [1848-1850]   As in *Atlas Delamarche Geographie Moderne.* World, Mercator projection; Australia at ctr, named "Java la Grande plutard Nouvelle Hollande". 29x44cm (11½x17"). Color.   [13]   Aus$320 £145 **$241**
CARTE GENERALE DE L'AMERIQUE DIVISEE EN SES PRINCIPAUX ETATS ... PAR FX. DELAMARCHE SUCCESSEUR DE ROBERT DE VAUGONDY   [1818]   53x59cm (21x23½"). Modern OL color. Margin & fold repairs; good.   [16]   £302 **$500**
HOLLANDE ET BELGIUM   [1836]   Incl Luxembourg 41x29cm (16x11½"). OL col. Fine (A+).   [A3]   £26 **$43**
MAPPE-MONDE EN DEUX HEMISPHERES   [1846]   29x43cm (11½x17"). OL col. VG (A).   [A4]   £99 **$164**
MAPPE-MONDE PAR ROBERT DE VAUGONDY GEOGRAPHE CORRIGEE PAR DELAMARCHE SON SUCCESSEUR AN.IIIE DE LA REPUBLIQUE FRANCAISE   [1794]   From *Atlas Universel*. Double hemi. 26x43cm (10½x17"). Color. Ref: Phillips (A) 3524-17.   [19]   £220 **$365**

DEPOT DE LA MARINE   Try *Bellin (Large)*
[ATLAS] VOYAGE AUTOUR DU MONDE SUR LA FREGATE LA VENUS   [1845]   Du Petit-Thouars; Atlas Hydrographique only by de Tessan. Folio, half roan; 19 plans on 16 leaves. Cover extremities worn; occas lt browning & offsetting; title wanting. Ref: cf Sabin 21354,   [A5]   £782 **$1,297**
CARTE DE L'ILE DE LA JAMAIQUE EXTRAITE DES CARTES TOPOGRAPHIQUES ANGLOISES DE THOS. CRASKELL ... 1786   [1786]   58x86cm (23x34"). Full color. Ref: Kapp (Jamaica) 127.   [20]   £905 **$1,500**
CARTE DES COTES ORIENTALES DE CHINE ...   [1842]   Hong Kong marked; incl Korea & Formosa. 88x59cm (34½x23"). Uncolored.   [34]   £350 **$581**
CARTE GENERALE DE L'OCEAN ATLANTIQUE   [1786]   6th ed. Separately issued 3-sheet chart; text at sides. 62x90cm (24½x35½"). OL color.   [A8]   £312 **$517**
CARTE PARTICULIERE DU HAVRE DE BOSTON   [1780]   Joseph Bernard Chabert de Cogolin, after Des Barres. 58x86cm (23x34"). Orig OL color. 3" tear repaired, no loss; minor abrasion, no loss. Ref: Sellers & Van Ee 958.   [2]   £1,447 **$2,400**
CARTE REDUITE DE L'OCEAN OCCIDENTAL   [1742]   Atlantic north of equator. 55x80cm (21½x31½"). Full orig color. Fine (A+).   [A3]   £226 **$375**
CARTE REDUITE DES ILES ANTILLES [ON SHEET WITH] CARTE REDUITE DES DEBOUQUEMENTS DE ST. DOMINGUE ...   [1775]   Above: Virgin Islands to St. Vincent & Barbados; below: S Bahamas & N Hispaniola. 88x56cm (34½x22"). Color.   [18]   £317 **$525**

DEROY
VUE GENERALE DE LA HAVANE   [c.1851-78]   Paris: L. Turgis. From series "Ports de Mer d'Amerique". 37x50cm (15x20") Chromolitho, some hand tinting. Faint soiling & wear; else exc. Ref: cf Deak 747, 750, 764.   [24]   £2,111 **$3,500**

DES BARRES
[MASSACHUSETTS: NANTUCKET, MARTHA'S VINEYARD, ELIZABETH ISLANDS, UPPER & MIDDLE CAPE COD, BUZZARDS BAY & NARRAGANSETT BAY]   [Nov. 1st, 1781]   74x107cm (29x42"). Orig wash color. Exc. Ref: Sellers & Van Ee 988.   [2]   £5,729 **$9,500**
[TITLE PAGE] ATLANTIC NEPTUNE   [1778]   Swash lettering, "Charts ... of New England ..." 67x51cm (26½x20").   [11]   £60 **$100**
BAY OF SEVEN ISLANDS   [1778]   76x54cm (30x21½"). Color. Lower margin trimmed, some loss to rule; sl offsetting.   [A7]   £69 **$115**
THE COAST OF NEW ENGLAND   [1778]   2 sheets joined; Buzzards Bay to Passamaquoddy. 106x74cm (41½x29"). OL color. Minor browning.   [A7]   £1,942 **$3,220**

DESILVER

[TITLE PAGE] NEW UNIVERSAL ATLAS ... [1856] Scene: Columbus New World landing. Page size 43x35cm (17x14") Orig color. Lt toning & foxing; o/w VG to fine. [A2] £50 **$83**

A NEW MAP OF MICHIGAN [1856 (1858)] Horiz format; Isle Royale inset. ("714 Chesnut [sic] St." address) 33x41cm (13x16") Color. Immaculate. Ref: Karpinski (MI) 204. [12] £112 **$185**

A NEW MAP OF THE STATE OF ILLINOIS [1856 (1857)] Ford County lacking. 39x33cm (15½x13") Color. Ref: Karrow (MW) 4-1558. [12] £60 **$100**

A NEW MAP OF THE STATE OF SOUTH CAROLINA [dated 1858] From *New Universal Atlas*. By J.L Hazzard; reengraved 25% larger than previously; Charleston Harbor inset. 33x39cm (13x15½") Full color. Binding holes top margin; else fine. Ref: Phillips (A) 6135-19. [12] £90 **$150**

A NEW MAP OF THE UNITED STATES OF AMERICA [1856 (1859)] From *New Universal Atlas*. Philadelphia, but actually publ Cushing & Bailey, Baltimore; facsimile title page furnished. Insets: DC; CA gold region. 39x67cm (15½x26½") Full color. Immaculate. Ref: cf Phillips (A) 6135-5. [12] £226 **$375**

[SAME TITLE] [1856-59 (1862)] From *New Universal Atlas*. Title bloc date, 1859. Philadelphia: 1862; facsimile title page furnished. Insets: DC; CA gold region. Horiz AZ-NM border. 39x67cm (15½x26½") Full color. Splendid. [12] £271 **$450**

MAP OF NEW JERSEY COMPILED FROM THE LATEST AUTHORITIES [1859] Population & distance tables. 38x31cm (15x12½") Orig color. Faint margin soiling; o/w VG to fine. [14] £93 **$155**

MEXICO & GUATEMALA [1856 (1858)] *A New Universal Atlas*. Last appearance with 4 insets, incl "Guatemala or Central America". 31x38cm (12x15") Wash & OL color. Chipping lower rt margin; image near fine. Ref: Phillips (A) 4340. [35] £57 **$95**

DESNOS

AMERIQUE [1761] Full wash color. 29x24cm (11½x9½") in 15x21" border frame with text panels. VG. [37] £392 **$650**

CARTE PARTICULAIRE DE L'ISLE ET DES ENVIRONS DE CAYENNE, COLONIE FRANCAISE [c.1769] Decorative frame border. 38x55cm (15x21½") Orig wash color. Sm margin stains; VG. [30] £238 **$395**

L'AMERIQUE MERIDIONALE ET SEPTENTRIONALE ... [1781] Ornate border with portraits. 50x72cm (20x28½") Color. 2 sm brown spots. [A7] £1,179 **$1,955**

NLE. CARTE D'AMERIQUE [1781] 112x117cm (44x46") OL color. Extensively repaired; numerous verso fold reinforcements; dozen holes repaired; sold as is. [A7] £1,665 **$2,760**

DEZAUCHE   Try *De L'Isle*

[ATLAS] ATLAS GENERAL DE LA CHINE, DE LA TARTARIE CHINOISE, ET DU TIBET: CONTENANT ... PAR M. DANVILLE, PREMIER GEOGRAPHE DU ROI. A CHEZ DEZAUCHE GEOGRAPHE, SUCCESSEUR DES S.RS DELISLE ET PHILIPPE BUACHE ... [c.1790] Tall folio, new quarter calf, marble boards, gold tooled on spine, morocco label. 50 maps & plans incl 1st separate map of Korea, 9 Tibet maps, 14 plates. Lt damp-staining margin of few leaves; else clean, crisp. Ref: Tooley (M&M) p.107; cf Phillips (A) 3189. [24] £8,745 **$14,500**

CARTE D'AMERIQUE, DRESSEE POUR L'INSTRUCTION, PAR GUIL. DELISLE ET PHIL. BUACHE ... NOUVELLEMENT REVUE ... PAR DEZAUCHE [1800] Inset: Cook discoveries. 47x60cm (18½x23½") Old mounting on linen. Ref: Tooley (Amer) p.16, #16. [39] £302 **$500**

CARTE D'AMERIQUE, POUR L'INSTRUCTION. DRESSEE SUR LA MEM ECHELLE QUE CELLE DE GUIL. DELISLE ... [1801] 47x59cm (18½x23") OL color. VG (A). [A4] £153 **$254**

CARTE DU MEXIQUE ET DES ETATS UNIS D'AMERIQUE ... [1703-1783] Last re-issue of De L'Isle map. 48x65cm (19x25½") Orig OL color. Ref: cf Cumming (SE) 137. Martin (TX) p.92-3. [34] **£1,500 $2,487**

L'ITALIE [1809] After De L'Isle. 52x65cm (20½x25½") OL color. [A8] £208 **$345**

MAPPEMONDE A L'USAGE DU ROI ... [1785] After De L'Isle & Buache. Double hemi; shows Cook's tracks & "Etats Unis"; elaborate decor above. 45x65cm (17½x25½") Color. Crease at c'fold; else exc. [24] £1,508 **$2,500**

PLAN DE LA BAYE ET PORT DE RIO JANEIRO, SITUE A LA COSTE DE BRESIL ... LEVEE GEOMETRIQUEMENT PAR LE CAPASSI [1785] By P. Capassi. 73x51cm (28½x20") Binding folds flattened & laid on tissue for strength; faint stain in blank area. [46] **£280** $465

DIAMOND ATLAS

[ATLAS] THE DIAMOND ATLAS [1857] 2 large octavo vols, leather bindings, colored maps: American vol by Charles Colby, 239 pp, 55 maps; Oriental vol by Charles W. Morse; 239 pp; 32 maps. Fold out ethnographic chart; large Indiana map; appendices. Scattered foxing, insect damage to Oriental vol, VG; American volume shaken & more soiled with damp staining. [6] £413 **$685**

DIDEROT

CARTE DE LA CALIFORNIE ET DES PAYS NORD-OUEST SEPARES DE L'ASIE PAR LE DETROIT D'ANIAN ... [1772] From *Encyclopaedie*. By Robert de Vaugondy. 29x36cm (11½x14½") OL color. Lt uniform age toning; lower margin trimmed close to border; o/w VG. Ref: Wheat (TM) 159. [A1] £159 **$264**

[SAME TITLE] [1772] From *Encyclopaedie*. After maps by Visscher & Plancius, adapted by Vaugondy. 29x37cm (11½x14½") Uncolored. Ref: Wheat (TM) 159. Wagner (NW) 632; Phillips (A) 1195-4; Pedley 473. [22] £151 **$250**

CARTE DE LA CALIFORNIE SUIVANT I. LA CARTE MANUSCRITE DE L'AMERIQUE DE MATHIEU NERON PECCI OLEN DRESSES A FLORENCE EN 1604, II. SANSON 1656, III. DE L'ISLE AMERIQUE SEPT 1700, IV. LE PERE KINO JESUITE EN 1705, V. LA SOCIETE DES JESUITES EN 1767 [1770] From *Encyclopoedie*. Composite of 5 maps. 29x38cm (11½x15") B&W. Faint c'fold age tone; fine. Ref: McLaughlin 241, pl.76; Wheat (TM) 160; Fite & Freeman 52; Schwartz & Ehrenberg pl.76. Wagner (NW) 637; Tooley (Landmarks) p.215. [1] £392 **$650**

[SAME TITLE] [c.1770] From *Encyclopedie*. Early, possibly 1st ed. Robert de Vaugondy copies of 5 maps spanning 150 years. 29x36cm (11½x14") B&W. Fine. Ref: McLaughlin 241. [27] £362 **$600**

[SAME TITLE] [c.1780] From *Encyclopoedie*. Composite of 5 maps showing Calif as peninsula, to an island, and back again.. 29x39cm (11½x15½") Uncolored. VG. [36] £407 **$675**

CARTE DE PARTIES NORD ET EST DE L'ASIE QUI COMPREND LES COTES DE LA RUSSIE ASIATIQUE, LE KAMSCHATKA, LE JESSO, ET LES ISLES DU JAPON ... [1779] 30x38cm (12x15") ["Partie de la Carte du Capitaine Cluny ... en 1769" offered at same price] [11] £45 **$75**

CARTE DES PARTIES NORD ET OUEST DE L'AMERIQUE ... [1772-79] From *Encyclopaedie*. By Robert de Vaugondy. 30x38cm (12x15") Ref: Pedley 453. [7] £151 **$250**

CARTE GENERALE DES DECOUVERTES DE L'AMIRAL DE FONTE ET AUTRES NAVIGATEURS ESPAGNOLS, ANGLOIS ET RUSSES ... PAR M. DE L'ISLE ... [1772] From *Encyclopedie*. 30x38cm (12x15") Uncolored. Ref: Phillips (A) 1195; Wagner (NW) 637; Pedley 445. [22] £106 **$175**

[SAME TITLE] [1772] *Encyclopedie*. By Robert de Vaugondy. 38x29cm (15x11½") Full color. Margin laid in on binding edge; fine (A+). [A4] £239 **$396**

CARTE GENERALE DES DECOUVERTES DE L'AMIRAL DE FONTE REPRESENTANT LA GRANDE PROBABILITE D'UN PASSAGE AU NORD OUEST PAR T. JEFFERYS ... [1772] From *Encyclopedie*. By Robert de Vaugondy. 29x37cm (11½x14½") Full color. Margin laid in where bound; repaired margin tear; fine (A) Ref: Portinaro & Knirsch pl.159. [A4] £199 **$330**

PARTIE DE LA CARTE DU CAPITAINE CLUNY ... [c.1772] From *Encyclopedie*. Arctic America. 21x41cm (8½x16") Color. [39] £90 **$150**

DIRECCION DE HIDROGRAFIA

CARTA DE PARTE DE LAS COSTAS DEL NUEVO SANTANDER, LAS DE VERA CRUZ, TABASCO Y YUCATAN ... [1847] 61x100cm (24x39½") [11] £151 **$250**

CARTA ESFERICA DE LAS COSTAS ORIENTALES DE LA AMERICA SETENTRIONAL QUE COMPREHENDE DESDE NUEVA YORK HASTA EL GOLFO Y RIO S. LORENZO CON PARTE DE LA ISLA DE TERRANOVA CONSTRUIDA EN LA DIRECCION HYDROGRAPHICA... [1828] Corrections to 1839. 63x92cm (25x36") Lighthouses colored. [11] £473 **$785**

CARTA ESFERICA DE LAS COSTAS ORIENTALES DE LOS ESTADOS UNIDOS IN LA AMERICA SETENTRIONAL [1826] New York to Georgia. 61x90cm (24x35½") Sm fold tears & 4" tear. [2] £754 **$1,250**

DJURBERG

POLYNESIEN (INSELWELT) ODER DER FUNFTE WELTTHEIL VERSASST VON HERRN DANIEL DJURBERG NEU HERAUSGEGEBEN VON HERN F.A. SCHRAEMBL ... [1789] Schraembl reissue. Incl Hawaii. Djurberg adopted native name "Ulimaroa" for Australia. 47x71cm (18½x28") Color. Ref: Tooley (Landmarks) ill. p.264. cf Clancy (Australis) ill. p.100; Tooley (Australia) 447, pl.142. [13] Aus$2,600 £1,181 **$1,958**

DONCKER

OOSTERDEEL VAN OOST INDIEN ... [1659] Apparently from 1st ed, *De Zee-Atlas ofte Waterwaereld*. 53x61cm (21x24") Color. Fraying & damage at rt & corner, mainly in margin but some loss outer border reinstated & reinforced; verso reinforcement rt side of c'fold. Ref: MCC 66, #449; Koeman Don 1. [4] £2,500 **$4,146**

PASCAART VERTOONENDE DE ZEECUSTEN VAN CHILI, PERU, HISPANIA NOVA, NOVA GRANADA, EN CALIFORNIA [1600 (c.1672)] 2nd state; East at top; shows Central America east coast; insular Calif; Insets: New Zealand; N. Japan. 43x54cm (17x21") Orig col. Sm split lower c'fold; good. Ref: Burden 340; McLaughlin 21; Goss (NA) 35. [32] £2,111 **$3,500**

[SAME TITLE] [1659] 2nd state, 43x54cm (17x21½") Exc. [2] £2,292 **$3,800**

DOPPELMAYR   Try *Homann*
GLOBI COELESTIS IN TABULAS PLANAS REDACTI PARS I [IN SET WITH] ... PARS II [AND] ... PARS III [AND] ... PARS IV [AND] ... PARS V [AND] ... PARS VI [1742] From Homann's *Atlas Coelestis*. Set of 6 "gnomonic" chart (heavens shown as faces of a cube). Each 50x60cm (19½x23½"). Color. Exc. Ref: Warner (Sky) p.64-6. [4] **£1,500 $2,487**
PHAENOMENA IN PLANETIS PRIMARIIS   [c.1742]   Planetary orbits. 49x57cm (19½x22½")   Orig color. Good. [32] £724 **$1,200**

DORR, HOWLAND & CO.
MASSACHUSETTS   [1839]   18x30cm (7x11½")   Color. Repaired separation at fold; some browning.
[21] **Can$65** £28 $47

DOUGHTY
MAP SHOWING A DIVISION OF PART OF THE REAL ESTATE LATE OF NICHOLAS STUYVESANT, DEC'D, AMONG HIS HEIRS SITUATED IN THE 11TH WARD OF THE CITY OF NEW YORK   [1842]   Folding map of the East Village used as evidence in court. Color by lot. 54x76cm (21½x30") Separations, some large, along folds; some loss at title; MS notes [15] £392 **$650**

DOUGLAS
A PLAN SHEWING THE DIRECT ROADS ... FROM THE CITY OF BRISTOL   [1737]   C. Douglas; "Edw.d Ward Bookseller". Distance diagram from Bristol on schematic map; panel with post times in and out.. 23x23cm (9x9")   Uncol. [a simpler version, George Child, sc., without panel offered at £360] [34] £380 **$630**

DOWER
VAN DIEMAN'S LAND   [1831]   Publ in *General Atlas of the World*. London: Henry Teesdale. 37 numbered districts. 34x41cm (13x16½")   Orig OL color. Ref: Tooley (Australia) 200, p.314; Clancy (Australis) ill. p.159.
[13] **Aus$240** £109 $181

DREW
DREW'S NEW MAP OF THE STATE OF FLORIDA SHOWING THE TOWNSHIPS BY THE U.S. SURVEYS, THE COMPLETED & PROJECTED RAILROADS, THE DIFFERENT RAILROAD STATIONS AND GROWING RAILROAD TOWNS, THE NEW TOWNS ON THE RIVERS AND INTERIOR ... UP TO THE YEAR 1884   [1884] Jacksonville: Horace Drew. Pocket map folding into 6x4" cloth covers 61x64cm (24x25")   Full color. Near mint (A+). [A4] £562 **$932**

DRIOUX & LEROY
CARTE PHYSIQUE ET POLITIQUE DES ETATS-UNIS, CANADA ET PARTIE DU MEXIQUE   [1867]   From *Atlas Universel* ... Unique western territorial forms, incl horiz AZ-NM border; WV as "Kanawha"; incl AK inset. 29x42cm (11½x16½")   Full color. Fine. Ref: Phillips (A) 3562-73. [12] £112 **$185**

DRIPPS
MAP OF THE CITY OF NEW YORK, WITH STREET DIRECTORY, SHOWING HOUSE-NUMBERS, HOTELS, CHURCHES ...   [c.1883]   Folding map in orig cloth folder. Color by wards. 70x50cm (27½x20")   Ref: Haskell 1358. [15] £151 **$250**

DU HALDE
[BOOK WITH MAPS]   A DESCRIPTION OF THE EMPIRE OF CHINA AND CHINESE-TARTARY ... LONDON: PRINTED BY T. GARDNER ... FOR EDWARD CAVE ...   [1738 - 1741]   Separately issued parts bound in 2 vols; folio, early calf rebacked; 65 plates & maps. Summarized European knowledge of China; with maps based on Jesuit surveys. James Whatman bookplate; overall exc. [3] £5,729 **$9,500**
[TIBET]   [1738-41]   Tibet & environs at large scale on 9 sheets. [no dimens]   Some margin tattering; generally good. [45] £1,206 **$2,000**
THE KINGDOM OF KOREA   [CALLED BY THE CHINESE KAU-LI-QUAE ...]   [1738-41]   51x35cm (20½x14") Ragged rt margin; image unaffected. [45] £965 **$1,600**

DU VAL
CANADA   [1660 (1678)]   From *La Geographie Universelle*. NE North America. 10x12cm (4x5")   Color. Fine. Ref: Burden 351; Kershaw (Canada) 140. Pastoureau, Du Val XI; cf Karpinski (MI) p.37. [38] £211 **$350**
CARTE DE POLOGNE ET DES ETATS QUI EN DEPENDENT   [c.1685]   Attribution uncertain; publ by Nicolas Langlois 40x52cm (16x20½")   Old color. Good [28] £353 **$585**
CARTE DE SAVOYE   [c.1650]   36x48cm (14½x19")   Partial color. [A7] £208 **$345**

DU VAL continued

CARTE DES INDES ORIENTALES PAR P. DU VAL GEOGRAPHE ORDINAIRES DU ROY [1665] As in *Cartes des Geographie*. 1st state. Indian Ocean & adjacent lands. 39x54cm (15½x21½") Orig OL color. Ref: Tooley (Australia) pl.129; Schilder 86 p.415; Clancy (Australis) pp.86-7. [1677 ed offered at Aus$ 5,200] [13] **Aus$5,800** £2,634 **$4,367**

CARTE UNIVERSELLE DU MONDE ... PAR P. DU VAL GEOGRAPHE ORD'RE DU ROY [SOUTHERN SHEETS: TERRES AUSTRALES; AMERIQUE MERIDIONALE] [1679] Separately published; two of 4 untrimmed joinable sheets, each 41x58cm (16x22½") Orig OL col. Ref: Shirley (W) 489, cf pl.356. [13] **Aus$5,900** £2,679 **$4,443**

FLORIDA [1660 / 1678] Publ in Beer/Du Val atlas. Covers SE U.S. & part TX. 9x11cm (3½x4½") OL & wash color. [41] £172 **$285**

LE PLANISPHERE AUTREMENT LA CARTE DU MONDE TERRESTRE [1659] Double hemi. 41x80cm (16x31½") Orig OL color. Exc. Ref: Shirley (W) 420 [1660]. [2] £4,523 **$7,500**

LES COSTES DES ROYAUMES DE FEZ, ALGER, TUNIS ET TRIPOLI EN BARBARIE [1664] Unjoined 2-sheet map, 22x75cm (8½x29½") OL color. 2" spot on each; else VG (B). [A4] £107 **$177**

ORIENTALIORA INDIARUM ORIENTALIUM CUM INSULIS ADIACENTIBUS A PROMONTORIO C COMORIN AD IAPAN [1680] As in *Tabulae Maritimae ofte Zee-Karten*. East-oriented. 44x54cm (17½x21½") Ref: Perry pp.50-1; Clancy (Australis) pp.8-9, ill. p.83; Walter (Japan) 40. [13] **Aus$5,800** £2,634 **$4,367**

TERRA ANTARCTICA [1678] 3rd state; issued by Beer. 10x12cm (4x5") B&W. [13] **Aus$390** £177 **$294**

VIRGINIA ET INSULAE BERMUDES [1660 (1679)] From *Geographie Universalis pars Prior*. Middle Atlantic seaboard; sm Bermuda inset. 10x12cm (4x5") B&W. Narrow lf margin; good. Ref: Cumming (SE) 85. [31] £256 **$425**

DUDLEY

CARTA PARTICOLARE DEL ISOLE DI IAVA ... SUMATRA E BURNEO [1646] From *Arcano del Mare*. Antonio Lucini, sc. 48x75cm (19x29½") Uncolored. [34] £2,800 **$4,643**

CARTA PARTICOLARE DELLA BARBERIA OCCIDENTALE CHE COMINCIA CON IL CAPO GRUER E FINISCE CON IL CAPO MATAS ... DI AFFRICA CARTA III [1647] From *Dell' Arcano del Mare*. 48x74cm (19x29½") Uncolored. Mild toning & soiling at c'fold; else VG. [A10] £226 **$374**

CARTA PARTICOLARE DELLA COSTA AUSTRALE SCOPERTA DALL' OLANDESI ... [1646] From *Arcano dell Mare* ... 1st ed. Cape York peninsula; New Guinea joined to Australia. 38x47cm (15x18½") B&W. Ref: Tooley (Australia) pl.32; Tooley (M&M) ill. p.120; Schilder (Australia) 41. [13] **Aus$12,500** £5,677 **$9,412**

CARTA PARTICOLARE DELLA MALACCA ... SUMATRA ... BURNEO [1646] From *Arcano del Mare*. 49x75cm (19½x29½") [34] £3,000 **$4,975**

CARTA PRIMA GENERALE DELLA ASIA [c.1650] Antonio Francesco Lucini, sc. Recently discovered chart, after Dudley, but reduced in size. 24x38cm (9½x15") Exc. Ref: cf TMC #55, p.44. [2] £7,237 **$12,000**

CARTA QUINTA GENERALE DI EUROPA [1661] English Channel. Lucini, sc. 37x47cm (14½x18½") Folds strengthened; sm tear top margin. [A6] £230 **$382**

CARTA TERZA GENERALE DEL' ASIA [1646-47] From *Arcano del Mare*. 48x38cm (18½x15") Color. [An uncolored copy offered for sale at $ AUS 1,300] [42] **Aus$1,500** £681 **$1,129**

DUFOUR

AFRIQUE CENTRALE [c.1840] 25x32cm (9½x12½") Full pastel color. Fine (A+). [A3] £33 **$55**

AMERIQUE DU NORD ... [1854] Folding map, dissected, mounted on linen. Highly detailed. 90x64cm (35½x25") [39] £181 **$300**

[SAME TITLE] [1857] Territorial claims color-coded. 76x55cm (30x22") [11] £106 **$175**

[SAME TITLE] [1868] From *Atlas Universel* ... Paris: Armand Le Chevalier. 75x56cm (29½x22") OL color. Lt foxing; exc. Ref: Phillips (A) 852-37. [12] £211 **$350**

CARTE DE L'AMERIQUE [1842] Odd U.S. frontiers. Insets. 52x77cm (20½x30½") Orig OL color. All margins trimmed to neatlines; o/w VG to fine. [A1] £199 **$330**

ETATS-UNIS [c.1846] Planche 29 from *Geographie Moderne*. Paris: Renouard. Shows TX as republic. 24x38cm (9½x15") Full color. Some spotting; good. [16] £109 **$180**

ETATS-UNIS REGION DES TERRITOIRES [c.1853] Western territories. 32x24cm (12½x9½") Full color. Fine (A+). [A3] £106 **$176**

MAPPE-MONDE PLANISPHERIQUE PHYSIQUE ET HYDROGRAPHIQUE DRESSE PAR A.H. DUFOUR [1856] Mercator proj; orig color-coding of claims of 9 European powers. 55x75cm (21½x29½") [11] £90 **$150**

MEXIQUE ANTILLES ET CALIFORNIE [1858] Incl West Indies & most of US. 55x75cm (21½x29½") Orig OL color. [11] £196 **$325**

DUFOUR continued

MEXIQUE ANTILLES, ETATS-UNIS ... [1862] "Colona" in present Colorado; horiz NM-AZ division. 55x74cm (21½x29") OL color. C'fold & edges browned; o/w VG. [10] £241 **$400**

OCEANIE DRESSEE PAR A.H. DUFOUR [1857] Pacific & Rim, except far north. Insets; European claims color-coded. 55x75cm (21½x29½") [11] £90 **$150**

DUMONT D'URVILLE

[ATLAS] VOYAGE AU POLE SUD ET DANS L'OCEANIE [1847] Paris: Depot General de la Marine. Atlas Hydrographique. Folio; 57 maps loose in modern cloth boards. Browning & offsetting; c'fold tape repairs first 2 maps; cut down title attached to card. Ref: cf Sabin 21216. [A5] £1,840 **$3,051**

[ATLAS] VOYAGE DE LA CORVETTE L'ASTROLABE [1833] Atlas Hydrographique. Folio; 45 maps & plans loose in modern cloth boards. Some spotting & soiling; occas offsetting; few tears & repairs; inserted defective title from another part of work. Ref: cf Sabin 21210. [A5] £1,265 **$2,098**

CARTE GENERALE DE LA COTE SEPTENTRIONALE DE LA NOUVELLE GUINEE ... [1828] 58x87cm (23x34½") C'fold split joined; faint lib stamp. [11] £45 **$75**

DUNN

[ATLAS] A NEW ATLAS OF THE MUNDANE SYSTEM; OR, OF GEOGRAPHY AND COSMOGRAPHY: DESCRIBING THE HEAVENS AND THE EARTH ... CELESTIAL BODIES: THE VARIOUS EMPIRES, KINGDOMS, STATES, REPUBLICS; AND ISLANDS, THROUGHOUT THE KNOWN WORLD [(1778)-1786] London: Sayer & Bennett. Folio, full leather with raised bands & gold title; 6 celestial plates, 42 maps & charts in orig OL color. Most with sl offsetting & other minor blemishes; 2 with ms notes; 1 discolored with creases; o/w interior VG. [33] £4,342 **$7,200**

A GENERAL MAP OF THE WORLD, OR TERRAQUEOUS GLOBE, WITH ALL THE NEW DISCOVERIES AND MARGINAL DELINEATIONS, CONTAINING THE MOST INTERESTING PARTICULARS IN THE SOLAR, STARRY, AND MUNDANE SYSTEM, BY SAML. DUNN, MATHEMATICIAN [1794] 4 sheets in two parts, 105x123cm (41x48½") OL color. Soft fold; minor margin chipping, couple tears to border; for size, overall VG (A). [A4] £1,605 **$2,662**

A NEW MAP OF THE WORLD WITH THE LATEST DISCOVERIES BY SAMUEL DUNN, MATHEMATICIAN [1774] As in *A New Atlas of the Mundane System*. London: Sayer. 34x50cm (13½x20") Fold repair. Ref: Phillips (A) 3513-1. [19] £226 **$375**

GENERAL MAP OF THE WORLD, OR TERRAQUEOUS GLOBE, WITH ALL THE NEW DISCOVERIES ... [1787] From Sayer's *General Atlas*. Ornate double hemi; 10 insets, peripheral information; 2 sheets joined. 108x125cm (42½x49") Full color. Soiling around previous folds; generally VG. [15] £2,262 **$3,750**

SCIENTIA TERRARUM ET COELORUM, OR THE HEAVENS AND EARTH ASTRONOMICALLY AND GEOGRAPHICALLY DELINEATED AND DISPLAYED, CONTAINING THE MOST CURIOUS & USEFUL PARTICULARS IN THE SOLAR & MUNDANE SYSTEMS, FAITHFULLY ENUMERATED... [1780] London: Sayer & Bennett. Double hemi, with smaller hemis, insets & text. On four sheets, 104x124cm (41x48½") Orig OL color. Old folds, not distracting. [34] £2,750 **$4,560**

DURY

[ATLAS] A NEW, GENERAL AND UNIVERSAL ATLAS ... [1761] Sm oblong quarto; contemporary mottled calf; 38 maps on 39 heavy leaves, orig OL color. Binding sl scuffed, joints reinforced; internally exc. Ref: Phillips (A) 627. [23] £1,025 **$1,700**

DUTTON

MAP OF BOSTON (AS IT SHOULD BE) AND THE COUNTRY ADJACENT, WITH PROPOSED HARBOR IMPROVEMENTS, ETC. [1867] E.P. Dutton; publ at Boston Map Store. Pocket map on banknote paper folding into gold-embossed folder. 44x62cm (17½x24½") OL & full color. Sl spine tear; corners rubbed; sl browning along map folds; near fine. [5] £151 **$250**

DUVAL

PLAN OF THE TOWN OF PATTERSON, ON THE LINE OF THE PENNSYLVANIA RAILROAD, OPPOSITE MIFFLINTOWN, JUNIATA CO. [1852] Map printed on back of land indenture relating to sale by Penn RR. Map cut off but probably at orig extent; verso complete. 44x57cm (17½x22½") [15] £392 **$650**

DUVOTENAY

ETATS-UNIS [c.1849] Texas Republic bordered within US; huge Calif. 23x30cm (9x12") Full OL color. [27] £87 **$145**

EDGAR
THE PLAN OF THE CITY AND CASTLE OF EDINBURGH [1765] Reference table. 30x60cm (12x23½") Later full color. By sight, fine. Framed. [A9] £208 **$345**

ELDRIDGE
NEWPORT TO HALIFAX, CHART K [1909] Linen-backed chart; Narragansett Bay to Nova Scotia; little shore detail. 96x108cm (38x42½") [15] £136 **$225**

ELLICOTT
PLAN OF THE CITY OF WASHINGTON ... [c.1794-1807] In Scottish *Encyclopedia Perthensis*. 1st ed, watermarked "1794" (2nd ed, 1816). After Ellicott. 39x50cm (15½x19½") Later OL color. Folding map laid flat on thin paper; invisibly repaired tear upper ctr; fold & other minor repairs; appearance flawless. [27] £1,689 **$2,800**

PLAN OF THE CITY OF WASHINGTON ... [March 1792] Phila: Thackara & Vallance. 1st publication of Ellicott survey based on L'Enfant. 22x26cm (8½x10½") Lt toning & offsetting; overall exc. Ref: Wheat & Brun 527; Ristow (A La Carte) p.146. [24] £7,237 **$12,000**

PLAN OF THE CITY OF WASHINGTON, IN THE TERRITORY OF COLUMBIA, CEDED BY THE STATES OF VIRGINIA AND MARYLAND TO THE UNITED STATES OF AMERICA, AND BY THEM ESTABLISHED AS THE SEAT OF THEIR GOVERNMENT AFTER THE YEAR 1800 [1795] From Winterbotham, *An Historical ... View of the ... United States* ... Publ London. 40x53cm (15½x20½") Ref: Howes W-581. [11] £754 **$1,250**

[SAME TITLE] [1795] By J. Russell. 39x52cm (15½x20½") Uncolored. Folds as issued; margins trimmed to neatline; tear along fold into blank area repaired on verso; VG. Ref: Phillips (Wash) p.24. [14] £965 **$1,600**

ELLIOTT
BIRD'S EYE VIEW PLACERVILLE, CAL. ... [1888] Publ by *Placerville Weekly Observer*. Litho by Wallace W. Elliott. Surround of 24 scenic panels. Color. 52x72cm (20½x28½") View: 12x24". Lt backing; few light spots & surface abrasions restored; else exc. Ref: Reps (Views) 189. [12] £754 **$1,250**

ELWE
AMERIQUE SEPTENTRIONALE ... [1792] 48x60cm (18½x23½") Color. Vert fold reinforced on verso causing wrinkles on recto. [A7] £277 **$460**

[SAME TITLE] [1792] 47x58cm (18½x23") Full orig col. Minor c'fold repair; else VG. [36] £573 **$950**

MAPPE MONDE OU DESCRIPTION DU GLOBE TERRESTRE ET AQUATIQUE [1792] Final reissue, after Jaillot (1694) via Ottens. Double hemi; insular Calif. 46x61cm (18½x24") Orig color. Ref: cf. Shirley (W) 561, pl.13 (1st ed). [13] Aus$5,200 £2,361 **$3,915**

EMMONS
THE GOLD AND COAL FIELDS OF ALASKA, TOGETHER WITH THE PRINCIPAL STEAMER ROUTES AND TRAILS [Jan 1898] Almost entire territory; insets. 5-color litho. 60x72cm (23½x28½") Immaculate. Ref: Falk (AK) 1898-51; Phillips (AK) p.117. [12] £136 **$225**

ENDICOTT & CO.
MAP OF THE VILLAGE OF NIAGARA FALLS MADE FOR THE PROPRIETOR [c.1836] J.P. Haines; Endicott Litho. Real estate promotional broadside, 16x9½", with map 16x23cm (6½x9") Minor creasing; o/w VG. [21] Can$350 £153 $254

ENSIGN
ENSIGN'S TRAVELLER'S GUIDE AND MAP OF THE UNITED STATES CONTAINING THE ROADS, DISTANCES, STEAM BOAT AND CANAL ROUTES &C. [1845] T. & E.H. Ensign. Wall map; 15 inset maps, 5 historical vignettes, portraits of presidents, etc. 66x96cm (26x38") Orig color. Even shellac tone; one roller present, detached; minor edge fraying; one sm lt waterspot; minor scuffs, no loss; VG. [A2] £1,161 **$1,925**

[SAME TITLE] [1845] T. & E.H. Ensign. Wall map with rods; US west to Rio Grande, Texas in last year as largest republic; historical vignettes, portraits of presidents. 65x96cm (25½x37½") OL color. Cleaned; relined; good. [16] £1,086 **$1,800**

ENSIGN & THAYER
MAP OF MASSACHUSETTS, CONNECTICUT AND RHODE ISLAND COMPILED FROM THE LATEST AUTHORITIES ... [1850] Wall map with orig rod & rail. 13 inset city plans. 64x86cm (25x34") OL & full color by towns. Dull surface; damp stain at rt margin; split along horiz seam; VG. [5] £250 **$415**

MAP OF THE CITY OF NEW YORK, WITH ADJACENT CITIES OF BROOKLYN AND JERSEY CITY, & THE VILLAGE OF WILLIAMSBURG [1850] Folding map; 28 pp directory in orig cloth folder. 1st copyright by Phelps, 1844. OL color by ward. 41x51cm (16½x20") Exc. [15] £241 **$400**

ENSIGN, BRIDGMAN & FANNING

MAP OF CANADA EAST AND WEST   [1854]   Folding map in orig cloth folder; many updates since 1853 Thayer. Ontario main map; large Quebec inset. 65x51cm (25½x20") OL color. Exc.   [15]   £302 **$500**

OUR NATION'S CAMPGROUND   [c.1861]   Civil War broadside with Johnson map of Middle Atlantic & DC at ctr; several vignettes. 62x39cm (24½x15½") Color. Folded once; lt stains lf margin; generally fine.
[15]   £603 **$1,000**

ESQUEMELING

A MAP OF THE COUNTREY AND CITTY OF PANAMA ...   [1684]   Bird's-eye map showing troop movements. 17x28cm (6½x11") Color.   [11]   £151 **$250**

EVANS

TO SIR WATKIN WILLIAMS WYNN, BART., THIS MAP OF NORTH WALES IS RESPECTFULLY INSCRIBED [1797] Dissected, linen-backed folding map in orig slipcase with Wm. Faden label. 73x62cm (28½x24½") Full color. Lt soiling; 2 holes, one with minor loss.   [15]   £211 **$350**

EVERTS

[ATLAS]   NEW CENTURY ATLAS OF THE STATE OF NEW YORK. FROM OFFICIAL RECORDS ...   [1911] Large folio, half morocco & cloth; 229 pp; 58 colored maps, most double-page. Corners, spine ends worn; edges sl toned; contents VG. Ref: LeGear (US) 2402.   [A10]   £482 **$799**

EVERTS & STEWART

[ATLAS]   COMBINATION ATLAS MAP OF DAUPHIN COUNTY PENNSYLVANIA   [1875]   Folio. New cloth spine and corners. Couple minor chips title page; covers VG; contents clean & VG. Ref: LeGear (US) L3025.   [A1]   £249 **$413**

[ATLAS]   COMBINATION ATLAS MAP OF WASHTENAW COUNTY, MICHIGAN   [1874]   Folio, cloth, rebound; 30 colored plat maps; numerous views, 2 with pencil calculations. Michigan map missing Canadian corner. Ref: LeGear (US) 1879.   [A9]   £166 **$276**

[ATLAS]   COMBINATION ATLAS OF LANCASTER COUNTY PENNSYLVANIA ...   [1875]   Folio; quarter leather. Spine & corners rubbed & chipped; cloth covers sl worn; contents clean, tight. Ref: Le Gear (US) L3038.   [A1]   £265 **$440**

EWEN

MAPS OF THE WHARVES AND PIERS OF THE EAST [& HUDSON] RIVER   [1849]   3 linen-backed maps folding into orig cloth. Map 1: Hudson; Battery to 12th St. Map 2: East; Battery to Corlears Hook. Map 3: East; Corlears Hook to Dry Dock. 50x46cm (19½x18") Spine crudely repaired; leather tips perished; internally fine. Ref: Haskell 927, 928.   [15]   £452 **$750**

FADEN

[ATLAS]   LE PETIT NEPTUNE FRANCAIS; OR, FRENCH COASTING PILOT   [1793]   Quarto; 43 maps & plates of Channel, Bay of Biscay, French Mediterranean to Naples & Corsica; tree calf, rebacked; Extremities worn; top margin title excised (removing owner's name); sm scattering embossed lib stamps. Ref: Phillips (A) 5154.   [A7]   £277 **$460**

A CHART OF THE ARABIAN GULF OR RED SEA ... COMPOSED CHIEFLY FROM THE JOURNALS ... OF COLONEL JAMES CAPPER   [1781]   Louis Stanislas d'Arcy Delarochette. 4 sheets joined; laid on canvas. 117x88cm (46x34½") Some margin damage.   [47]   **£230** $382

A PLAN OF NEW YORK ISLAND WITH PART OF LONG ISLAND, STATEN ISLAND & EAST NEW JERSEY, WITH A PARTICULAR DESCRIPTION OF THE ENGAGEMENT ON THE WOODY HEIGHTS OF LONG ISLAND ... ON THE 27TH OF AUGUST 1776...   [1776]   5th issue of five. By Jefferys. With text below, 75x48cm (29½x19") Orig spot col. Rebacked; minor spotting; top margin trimmed close. Ref: Tooley (Amer) p.76, #41e.   [2]   £2,714 **$4,500**

[SAME TITLE]   [1776]   1st ed, 1st state of five; no text below. By Jefferys. 51x44cm (20x17½") Orig spot color. Fold repair, no loss; o/w fine. Ref: Nebenzahl (Amer Rev) map 12; Tooley (Amer) p.74, #41. Nebenzahl (Battle Plans) 107.   [2nd issue, with text below, exc condition offered as same price]   [2]   £4,423 **$7,500**

[SAME TITLE]   [Oct 19, 1776]   5th ed; treats British occupation of city; letterpress text below. Map size 52x44cm (20½x17½") on larger sheet. Color. Browned along horiz fold & repairable sl separation. Ref: cf Nebenzahl (Amer Rev) map 12.   [A8]   £2,219 **$3,680**

A PLAN OF THE ATTACK OF FORT SULLIVAN, NEAR CHARLES TOWN IN SOUTH CAROLINA   [1776] Dissected, mounted on 18th c. folding linen. 29x37cm (11½x15") Full orig color. Exc. Ref: Nebenzahl (Amer Rev) 8; Tooley (Amer) p.60-1, #14c. Nebenzahl (Battle Plans) 64.   [2]   £2,714 **$4,500**

FADEN continued

A PLAN OF THE OPERATIONS OF THE KING'S ARMY UNDER THE COMMAND OF GENERAL SR. WILLIAM HOWE, K.B. IN NEW YORK AND EAST NEW JERSEY, AGAINST AMERICAN FORCES COMMANDED BY GENERAL WASHINGTON, FROM THE 12TH OF OCTOBER TO THE 28TH OF NOVEMBER 1776 ... [1777] 1st ed. Westchester County action, by Sauthier. 72x48cm (28½x19") Full orig color. Exc. Ref: Nebenzahl (Amer Rev) map 13; Tooley (Amer) p.78, #45a. Nebenzahl (Battle Plans) 101, state 1. [2nd ed with ships off Tarrytown, orig spot color, exc., offered at $4,800] [2] £3,317 **$5,500**

A PLAN OF THE SURPRISE OF STONEY POINT BY A DETACHMENT OF THE AMERICAN ARMY COMMANDED BY BRIGR: GENL. WAYNE ... [1784] On Hudson River. 50x70cm (19½x27½") Orig wash color. C'fold repaired, sl surface loss; o/w VG. Ref: Nebenzahl (Amer Rev) map 32. [2] £2,111 **$3,500**

A PLAN OF THE TOWN OF NEWPORT IN RHODE ISLAND ... [1777] By C. Blaskowitz. 33x36cm (13x14") Dissected, re-joined & mounted; lt toned; minor repairs; in all VG. Ref: Nebenzahl (Battle Plans) 35. [23] £1,628 **$2,700**

A TOPOGRAPHICAL CHART OF THE BAY OF NARRAGANSET IN THE PROVINCE OF NEW ENGLAND ... TO WHICH HAVE BEEN ADDED THE SEVERAL WORKS & BATTERIES RAISED BY THE AMERICANS [1777] By Charles Blaskowitz. 93x63cm (36½x25") Exc. Ref: Schwartz & Ehrenberg pl.126; Nebenzahl (Amer Rev) map 16. Nebenzahl (Battle Plans) 34. [2] £3,317 **$5,500**

[SAME TITLE] [1777] Segmented, mounted on linen as issued. 93x63cm (36½x25") Lt staining; some wear to linen at folds; overall VG. Ref: Guthorn (Amer Rev) p.12. [24] £3,317 **$5,500**

ARGYLLSHIRE [1810] Langlands (George & Son); S.J. Neele, sc. 4 sheets joined & linen-backed. Insets & view. 148x120cm (58½x47") Color, faded. Some wear & soiling; 2 large tears; one roller only. [A6] **£414** $687

BATTLE OF BRANDYWINE IN WHICH THE REBELS WERE DEFEATED, SEPTEMBER THE 11TH 1777 ... UNDER THE COMMAND OF GENERAL SR. WILLM. HOWE ... [1778] 1st ed. 54x44cm (21½x17½") Orig spot color. Exc. Ref: Nebenzahl (Amer Rev) map 24. Nebenzahl (Battle Plans) 126. [2] £4,071 **$6,750**

COAST OF FRANCE AND ITALY FROM LA NAPOULE TO VILLAFRANCA [1805] From ... French Coasting Pilot. Incl French Riviera. 23x31cm (9x12½") Simple wash color. [39] £42 **$70**

COAST OF FRANCE FROM CAPE LA HAGUE TO ISLE BREHAT WITH ALL THE ADJACENT ISLANDS AND DANGERS [1805] From ... French Coasting Pilot. Incl Channel Islands & Mont St. Michel. 31x23cm (12½x9") Simple wash color. ["Coast of France from Isigny to Cape Carteret" offered at same price] [39] £39 **$65**

GEOMETRICAL SURVEY OF THE GULF OF NAPLES MADE BY ORDER OF THE KING OF THE TWO SICILIES [1793] Nautical chart. 23x36cm (9x14") Wash color. [39] £48 **$80**

GREECE, ARCHIPELAGO AND PART OF ANADOLI [1791] By de la Rochette. 53x74cm (21x29½") Color. [39] £181 **$300**

MAP OF THE REPUBLIC OF SWITZERLAND [1820] 58x60cm (23x24") Partial color. Some browning & offsetting. [A8] £69 **$115**

PLAN OF THE CITY AND ENVIRONS OF QUEBEC, WITH ITS SIEGE AND BLOCKADE BY THE AMERICANS ... [1776] 44x62cm (17½x24½") Full wash color. Fold splits reinforced; few repairs, sl loss; overall good. Ref: Nebenzahl (Amer Rev) 6. [24] £1,689 **$2,800**

PLAN OF THE CITY OF LONDON, DISTINGUISHING THE SEVERAL WARDS AS SKETCHED FROM MAITLANDS HISTORY OF LONDON [1819] 4th ed. 2 sheets dissected & backed on linen; when joined. 64x152cm (25x60") Color. [A6] **£575** $954

PLAN OF THE ENCAMPMENT AND POSITION OF THE ARMY UNDER HIS EXCELLY. LT. GENERAL BURGOYNE AT SWORDS HOUSE ON HUDSON'S RIVER NEAR STILLWATER [1780] 32x34cm (12½x13½") with loose 4x3½" overlay. Some color. Part top margin restored; repair into image top ctr; lt toned, lt margin soiling; signs of early lower margin separation at plate mark; VG. Ref: Nebenzahl (Amer Rev) map 22; Phillips (M) p.830,1, 5. Clark (Amer Rev) 14245; Nebenzahl (Battle Plans) 53. [35] £603 **$1,000**

PLAN OF THE OPERATIONS OF GENERAL WASHINGTON, AGAINST THE KING'S TROOPS IN NEW JERSEY ... [1777] Washington crosses the Delaware. Dissected, mounted on 18th c. folding linen. 29x39cm (11½x15½") Orig OL color. Exc. Ref: Tooley (Amer) p.72-3, #36b. Nebenzahl (Battle Plans) 119. [2] £2,714 **$4,500**

SWEDISH POMERANIA, WITH THE ISLAND OF RUGEN [c.1815] 58x60cm (23x24") OL color. Top margin trimmed close; sl browning; lt offset. [A8] £55 **$92**

THE CARIBBE ISLANDS AND GUAYANA ... [1776] By Delarochette; Jefferys, sc. North to Virgin Islands. 74x60cm (29x23½") Color. [18] £286 **$475**

FARMER

MAP OF THE SURVEYED PART OF MICHIGAN [1840] NY: J.H. Colton. Folding map in orig leather folder. Full color by county. 84x58cm (33x23") Minor separations at fold junctions; spine splitting, almost gone. Ref: Karpinski (MI) 141G, G2. [15] £814 **$1,350**

FINDLAY

THE WORLD WITH THE TRACKS & DISCOVERIES OF THE LATEST NAVIGATORS [1805] 23x43cm (9x17") Color. [19] £66 **$110**

WESTERN HEMISPHERE [IN SET WITH] **EASTERN HEMISPHERE** [1837] From Christopher Kelly, *Universal Geography*. Steel engraving on 2 sheets joined, 22x41cm (8½x16") Uncolored. [19] £30 **$50**

FINLEY

ALABAMA [c.1829] From *New General Atlas*. 29x22cm (11½x8½") Full color. Fine. Ref: cf Birmingham Pub. Lib. 15 & Phillips (A) 752-22. [12] £112 **$185**

BELGIUM [1825] Incl Luxemburg. 22x28cm (8½x11") Full color. Fine (A). [A4] £17 **$28**

CANADA [1831] Pocket map on banknote paper in leather folder; ad label pasted inside front cover. 22x28cm (8½x11") Color by province. Folder moderately worn; fold separations reinforced with museum tape; VG. [6] £166 **$275**

CONNECTICUT [1824] From *A New General Atlas*. 23x28cm (9x11") Color. Possible damp staining in set; else good. [ME, NH, VT, MA, RI, NJ offered at same price] [32] £51 **$85**

[SAME TITLE] [1826] From *A New General Atlas*. 22x28cm (8½x11") Color. Immaculate. Ref: Phillips (A) 6054-12. [12] £81 **$135**

DELAWARE [1826] From *A New General Atlas*. 29x22cm (11½x8½") Color. Lt foxing lower rt corner; spots top margin; else exc. Ref: Phillips (A) 6054-16. [12] £75 **$125**

GEORGIA [1824] From *New General Atlas ...* 29x22cm (11½x8½") Color. Possible damp staining in set; else good. [MD, SC, AL, MS, LA, TN, KY, OH, IN, IL offered at same price] [32] £51 **$85**

INDIANA [1826] From *New General Atlas*. Indian ranges in north. 29x22cm (11x8½") Full color. Brown spot lower rt margin; else fine. Ref: Phillips (A) 6054-26 [12] £112 **$185**

LOUISIANA [1826] From *New General Atlas*. 25 parishes. 22x28cm (8½x11") Full color. Minor ripple at ctr; else fine. [1831 ed offered at same price] [12] £112 **$185**

MAP OF FLORIDA ACCORDING TO THE LATEST AUTHORITIES [1826] From *New Amer. Atlas*. Incl 4½x9½" panel of American cities, mountains, etc. below. 41x25cm (16x10") Full orig color. Exc. Ref: Phillips (A) 1378, 13. [36] £392 **$650**

MAP OF LOUISIANA, MISSISSIPPI AND ALABAMA CONSTRUCTED FROM THE LATEST AUTHORITIES [1826] From pocket ed, *New American Atlas*. 43x55cm (17x21½") Full col. Middle third lf border discolored where attached to pocket atlas; else virtually perfect. Ref: cf Phillips (A) 1376-9 & Phillips (M) p.373. [12] £452 **$750**

MAP OF MAINE, NEW HAMPSHIRE AND VERMONT, COMPILED FROM THE LATEST AUTHORITIES [1826] From *New Amer. Atlas*. 43x53cm (17x21") Full orig color. VG. [36] £226 **$375**

MAP OF NORTH AMERICA ... [1826] From *New Amer. Atlas*. 53x43cm (21x17") Full orig color. C'fold split repaired; minor staining & offsetting; but VG. [36] £362 **$600**

MAP OF NORTH AND SOUTH CAROLINA AND GEORGIA, CONSTRUCTED FROM THE LATEST AUTHORITIES [1826] From *New Amer. Atlas*. 43x55cm (17x21½") Full orig col. Minor staining; c'fold wrinkle; else VG. [36] £362 **$600**

[SAME TITLE] [dated 1826] From pocket ed, *New Amer. Atlas*. Early county development; population table. 43x53cm (17x21") Full color. Middle third lf border sl discolored where attached; else exc. Ref: cf Johnsen (GA) 122; Phillips (A) 1378-8 [12] £452 **$750**

MAP OF THE STATE OF MISSOURI AND TERRITORY OF ARKANSAS COMPILED FROM THE LATEST AUTHORITIES [1826] From pocket ed, *New American Atlas*. AR incl most of present OK. 43x55cm (17x21½") Full color. Sl discoloring middle third lf border where attached; sm spot; sl browning at some folds; invisibly repaired intersection pinholes Ref: cf Phillips (A) 1378-12. [12] £513 **$850**

[SAME TITLE] [1826] From *New Amer. Atlas*. Incl most of present OK. 43x55cm (17x21½") Full orig color. Some offsetting, o/w VG. [36] £452 **$750**

MAP OF THE STATES OF OHIO INDIANA & ILLINOIS AND PART OF MICHIGAN TERRITORY ... [1826] From *New Amer. Atlas*. 43x55cm (17x22") Full orig color. Some offsetting, but VG. [36] £452 **$750**

MAP OF THE UNITED STATES, CONSTRUCTED FROM THE LATEST AUTHORITIES [1826] 43x56cm (17x22") Full orig color. Some offsetting; lower c'fold split repaired; o/w VG. [36] £452 **$750**

MAP OF VIRGINIA AND MARYLAND CONSTRUCTED FROM THE LATEST AUTHORITIES [1826] From pocket ed, *New Amer. Atlas*. Incl WV; DC inset. 43x55cm (17x21½") Full color. Some misfolds; middle third lf border sl discolored where attached; else fine. Ref: Sames & Woods p.142; Swem 520; cf Phillips (A) 1378-7. [12] £452 **$750**

[SAME TITLE] [1826] From *New Amer. Atlas*. Washington inset. 43x56cm (17x22") Full orig color. Some offsetting & staining; but good. [PA & DE, same size & condition, offered at $500] [36] £392 **$650**

FINLEY continued

MASSACHUSETTS [1826] From *A New General Atlas*. 23x29cm (9x11½") Color. Spotless. Ref: Phillips (A) 6054-10. [12] £54 **$90**

[SAME TITLE] [1831] Pocket map on banknote paper folded into gold-embossed leather cover. Incl parts of adjacent states; Boston inset. 22x27cm (8½x10½") Color by counties; Cover lt soiled & rubbed; map fold separations mended with loose old tape; lt stain near attachment; VG. [5] £226 **$375**

MISSISSIPPI [1829(?)] From *New General Atlas*. Date estimated from geography. 28x22cm (11x8½") Full color. "Museum" copy. Ref: cf Phillips (A) 752-28. [12] £112 **$185**

MISSOURI [1824] From 1st ed, *New General Atlas*. 28x22cm (11x8½") Color. Spot upper lf corner; else fine. Ref: Karrow (MW) 9-0755; Phillips (A) 4314-30; Ristow (Amer M&M) p.270. [12] £112 **$185**

[SAME TITLE] [1824] From *New General Atlas* ... 29x22cm (11½x9") Color. Possible damp staining in set; else good. [32] £57 **$95**

NEW YORK [1824] From *New General Atlas*. 23x28cm (9x11") Color. Possible damp staining in set; else good. [32] £45 **$75**

PENNSYLVANIA [1824] From *New General Atlas*. 22x28cm (8½x11") Color. Possible damp staining in set; else good. [32] £48 **$80**

[SAME TITLE] [1826-30] From *New General Atlas*. 51 counties. 22x28cm (8½x11") Color. Few margin spots; o/w fine. [12] £66 **$110**

THE WORLD ON MERCATOR'S PROJECTION [1824] From *New General Atlas*. 22x28cm (8½x11") Color. Possible damp staining in set; else good. [32] £48 **$80**

[SAME TITLE] [1828] From same source. 22x28cm (8½x11") Full pastel color. Fine (A+). [A4] £92 **$152**

[SAME TITLE] [1831] From same source. 22x28cm (8½x11") Full orig color. Exc. [36] £90 **$150**

UNITED STATES [1831] From same source. 28x22cm (11x8½") Full orig col. Some stains. [36] £106 **$175**

VERMONT [1824] From *A New General Atlas*. 28x22cm (11x8½") Pastel color. Ref: Cobb (VT) 192; Phillips (A) 4314-9. [12] £66 **$110**

[SAME TITLE] [c.1824] 28x22cm (11x8½") Color. Exc. [22] £75 **$125**

WESTERN HEMISPHERE [IN SET WITH] **EASTERN HEMISPHERE** [1824] From *New General Atlas*. Each about 27x23cm (10½x9") Color. Possible damp staining in set; else good. [32] £90 **$150**

[SAME TITLE] [1826] From *New General Atlas*. Color. Each 32x25cm (12½x10") [A7] £34 **$57**

FISHER

NORTH AMERICA [c.1815-20] 18x23cm (7x9") Full color. Fine. [12] £75 **$125**

FLINDERS

KAART VAN BASSES STRAAT [1801] From Dutch ed. 48x69cm (18½x27") B&W. Ref: Tooley (Australia-Tasmania) 227, pl.205. [13] **Aus$1,700** £772 **$1,280**

FORSELL

KARTA OFVAR SODRA DELEN AF SVERIGE OCH ORRIGE ... [1815-26] Southern Scandinavia, Trondheim east to Umea. Extreme detail; functions as sea chart. Dissected, mounted on linen; orig marbled slipcase, with linen ties. 231x163cm (91x64") Map with few lt stains & fold separations, VG+; slipcase scuffed, overall VG. [37] £452 **$750**

FREMIN

[PUZZLES: SET OF 8 - WORLD, 5 CONTINENTS, OCEANIA, FRANCE] [c.1842] To accompany Tardieu's atlas; each about 40-50 geographical colored pieces mounted on wood; in new box with world map on cover, sides lined with buckram. Each 34x46cm (13½x18") North America lacks 3 pieces, Africa one; waterstaining & rubbing to 2 others; lt foxing. [23] £1,508 **$2,500**

AMERIQUE SEPTENTRIONALE [c.1840] OR Terr extends north; TX separately outlined. 22x30cm (8½x11½") OL color. Lt toning; couple margin tears; VG (A). [A3] £60 **$99**

CARTE DE L'AMERIQUE ... [1836] 8 placenames in "Texas". 86x60cm (34x24") Orig OL color. Trivial soiling; good. [16] £302 **$500**

FREMONT   Try *U.S. Government*

[BOOK WITH MAPS] **REPORT OF THE EXPLORING EXPEDITION TO THE ROCKY MOUNTAINS IN THE YEAR 1842, AND TO OREGON AND NORTH CALIFORNIA IN THE YEARS 1843-'44** [1845] Marbled paper, later leather spine crudely attached; complete with 5 B&W maps & 22 plates; incl large 51½x30" map, deacidified & separations repaired. Covers rubbed; contents shaken & loose at front, scattered foxing, generally good (B). Ref: Storm (Graff) 1436. [A4] £796 **$1,320**

FREMONT continued

MAP OF AN EXPLORING EXPEDITION TO THE ROCKY MOUNTAINS IN THE YEAR 1842 AND TO OREGON & NORTH CALIFORNIA IN THE YEARS 1843-44   [1845]   From *Report of the Exploring Expedition* ...   Drawn by Preuss. 130x80cm (51x31½")   Some blue OL to water areas. Minor fold splitting; minor tear repaired; exc. Ref: Wheat (TM) 497; Ladd #223.   [27]   £513   **$850**

MAP OF OREGON AND UPPER CALIFORNIA   [1848]   By Charles Preuss; E. Weber & Co., Balt. OL color. 90x76cm (35½x29½")   Overall browning; sm holes at intersection folds.   [A7]   £1,318   **$2,185**

MAP OF OREGON AND UPPER CALIFORNIA FROM THE SURVEYS OF JOHN CHARLES FREMONT AND OTHER AUTHORITIES ... 1848   [1848]   Large version of this title; accompanied *Geographical Memoir upon Upper California*.   By Preuss. Shows entire West; 1st mention of "Golden Gate"; 1st record of Mormon Utah settlements. 84x67cm (33x26½")   Issued on poor paper; minor browning at folds; sm loss at blank corner; laid on archival paper. Ref: Wheat (TM) 559, illus opp p.56; Goss (NA) #77; Schwartz & Ehrenberg pl.171. Wheat (Gold) 40.   [8]   £513   **$850**

MAP OF OREGON AND UPPER CALIFORNIA FROM THE SURVEYS OF JOHN CHARLES FREMONT AND OTHER AUTHORITIES ... 1848   [1850]   By Preuss. Small version without Oregon publ by Congress to meet Gold Rush demand. 50x42cm (19½x16½")   Folded as issued; else clean, bright. Ref: Wheat (TM) 613. Wheat (Gold) 41; Wagner-Camp 150.   [8]   £226   **$375**

MAP TO ILLUSTRATE AN EXPLORATION OF THE COUNTRY, LYING BETWEEN THE MISSOURI RIVER AND THE ROCKY MOUNTAINS, ON THE LINE OF THE NEBRASKA OR PLATTE RIVER ...   [1843]   Fremont's 1st expedition to Rockies; Kit Carson as guide; Preuss as cartographer. 36x83cm (14x32½")   One edge trimmed close, sl neat line loss; o/w bright. Ref: Wheat (TM) 464.   [9]   £151   **$250**

[SAME TITLE]   [1843]   By John C. Fremont; Weber & Co., Baltimore, lith. Some rivers & lakes in blue. 36x84cm (14x33")   Narrow lf margin; minor misfolds; repaired 7" tear in mostly blank area. Ref: Wheat (TM) 464.   [12]   £232   **$385**

[SAME TITLE]   [1860]   Fremont's 1st Expedition. 36x83cm (14x32½")   Some color. Exc.   [41]   £181   **$300**

FRENCH

MAP OF ULSTER COUNTY, NEW YORK   [1858]   Wall map; insets. Full color by town. 147x147cm (58x58") Widespread chipping, some printed surface loss; fair. Ref: Phillips (M) p. 857.   [15]   £241   **$400**

FRENCH & SMITH

THE STATE OF NEW YORK, FROM NEW & ORIGINAL SURVEYS   [1860]   Wall map; 2nd ed. 168x183cm (66x72")   Torn, chipped top rt & along top, some loss; below top 6" VG. Ref: cf Ristow (Amer M&M) chap.22.   [15]   £452   **$750**

FRICX   Try *De L'Isle*

CARTE D'AFRIQUE   [1730]   Based on De L'Isle 1722 revision separating Niger & Senegal. 48x61cm (19x24") Orig body color. Lt surface dirt; 2 sm paper weakness strengthened verso; else VG.   [38]   £362   **$600**

CARTE D'AMERIQUE   [1722]   Re-engraving after De L'Isle. 48x60cm (19x23½")   Full orig body color. Ref: cf Tooley (Amer) p.13, #3.   [39]   £543   **$900**

CARTE PARTICULIERE DES ENVIRONS DE DUNKERQUE, BERGUES, FURNES, GRAVELINES, CALAIS ... [c.1725]   44x56cm (17½x22")   Color. Upper c'fold sl toned; mild surface soiling mainly margins & ocean; side edges sl chipped; overall VG.   [A10]   £132   **$219**

L'ASIE   [1730]   By De L'Isle. 44x58cm (17½x23")   Full color.   [39]   £332   **$550**

FRIES   Try *Ptolemy (1522-1541, Strassburg)*

[AMERICAS]   [1522-1535]   From ... *Geographia*. Strasbourg. After Waldseemuller's 1513 map on reduced scale; shows east coasts of New World, W Africa & Iberia. 29x43cm (11½x16½")   Uncolored. Minor restoration. Ref: Burden 4   [34]   £5,200   **$8,622**

[SAME TITLE]   [1522 (1535)]   From ... *Geographiae*. After Waldseemuller's 1513 map; latitude markings. 29x37cm (11½x15")   Minor mend at ctr; fine impression.   [45]   £3,920   **$6,500**

[ARMILLARY SPHERE]   [1522 (1525)]   Sphere & 12 windheads. 27x27cm (10½x10½")   Exc.   [45]   £256   **$425**

[ASIA: EAST]   [(1522) 1535]   Verso title. "T.A. Superioris Indiae". Trechsel edition. 1st post-Ptolemaic map of Far East. Trapezoidal, 29x46cm (11½x18")   Uncolored. Sm repair top margin; o/w exc. Ref: Pastoureau, Ptolemee E (44).   [4]   £2,150   **$3,565**

[ASIA: SOUTHERN]   [1522 (1541)]   After Waldseemuller. Extent: African east coast, India, SE Asia. 29x44cm (11½x17½")   Couple minor margin tears; VF.   [44]   £724   **$1,200**

[BRITISH ISLES]   [1522 (1535)]   After Waldseemuller. 28x41cm (11x16")   Patched wormhole at ctr; else exc.   [44]   £844   **$1,400**

FRIES continued

[FACSIMILE ATLAS] CARTA MARINA UNIVERSALIS 1530 [1926] Munich. Oblong folio; 12 maps; orig wrappers. Sh tears at edges. [A7] £260 **$431**

[PTOLEMAIC WORLD] [1522 (1535)] From *Geographia*. Strasbourg. 1st Servetus issue. Open Indian Ocean. 30x46cm (12x18") Exc. Ref: Shirley (W) 47. [43] £1,086 **$1,800**

[SAME TITLE] [1522 (1535)] Servetus edition. 30x46cm (12x18") B&W. Dark impression; sl margin soiling; faint area darkening at vert fold & sm separations; old hand brown ink words in margin have broken through leaving 3 slivers open; else VG. Ref: Shirley (W) 47. [A1] £995 **$1,650**

[SAME TITLE] [1522 / 1535] Servetus edition. 30x46cm (12x18") Newer color. Verso repair of minor separations along vert fold; faint surface soiling; few soft printer's creases into border; o/w VG. Ref: Shirley (W) 47. [14] £2,111 **$3,500**

[SOUTHEAST ASIA & EAST INDIES] [1522 (1541)] Incl primitive India, Ceylon, "Java Minor", etc. 30x43cm (12x17") Color. Exc. [45] £1,327 **$2,200**

[WORLD] [1522 (1535)] Old world with South America & Hispaniola; banner title, elaborate border. 31x47cm (12½x18½") Minor c'fold split mended; else VF. Ref: Shirley (W) 48. [45] £2,171 **$3,600**

OCEANI OCCIDENTALIS SEU TERRAE NOVAE TABULA [1522 (1535)] After 1513 Waldseemuller map. 29x43cm (11½x17") Exc. Ref: Burden 4. [43] £4,523 **$7,500**

TABU. MODER. INDIAE [1522-1535] Waldseemuller's 1513 map reduced; Indian Ocean lands. 34x44cm (13x17½") Uncol. Sm c'fold split repaired; minor ms reinstatement. Ref: Tibbetts 16. [34] **£1,650** $2,736

TABU. NOVA ASIAE MI. [1522 / 1535] Servetus edition. Asia Minor. 26x38cm (10½x15") B&W. Lt verso text show through; o/w VG to fine. [A1] £265 **$440**

TABU. NOVA PARTIS APH'RI [1522-1535] Waldseemuller, sl reduced. 32x40cm (12½x15½") Color. Minor c'fold repairs. Ref: cf Norwich 286. [34] **£580** $962

TABU. NOVA PARTIS APHRI [1522 (1535)] After 1513 Waldseemuller with added vignettes. 30x42cm (12x16½") plus title banner. Exc. [43] £905 **$1,500**

[SAME TITLE] [1522 / 1535] Servetus ed. Credible northern Africa with bulge; numerous coastal place names. 28x40cm (11x15½") Uncolored. Faint toning, few stitch hole marks along vert fold, no loss; minor foxing; overall VG. [A2] £498 **$825**

TABULA I ASIAE [1522 / 1535] Servetus edition. Ptolemaic Turkey. 29x44cm (11½x17½") B&W. Lt age toning along fold; a minute pin hole; lt verso text show through; o/w fine. [A1] £332 **$550**

TABULA ORBIS CUM DESCRIPTIONE VENTORUM [1522 / 1541] Old world with South America & Hispaniola; elaborate border. 34x48cm (13½x19") Possibly early color. Minor mend top c'fold; else exc. Ref: Shirley (W) 48. [23] £2,895 **$4,800**

TABULA TERRE SANCTAE [1522 / 1535] From ... *Geographiae*. Servetus ed. 27x41cm (11x16") Uncolored. Few stitch holes along fold; o/w VG. Ref: Laor 612. [14] £965 **$1,600**

TABULA VI ASIAE [1522 / 1535] From ... *Geographiae*. Servetus ed. Ptolemaic Arabia 27x43cm (11x17") Uncolored. VG. [14] £1,086 **$1,800**

[SAME TITLE] [1525] Johannes Gruninger. 31x46cm (12x18") Ref: Tibbetts p.41. [47] **£650** $1,078

TYPUS ORBIS DESCRIPTIONE PTOLEMAEI [(1522) 1541] From *Claudii Ptolemaei ... Geographiae*. Orig publ Strasbourg, but this ed Vienna with plate corner missing. 30x46cm (12x18") Color. Ref: Shirley (W) 47. [another uncolored copy offered at Aus$ 3,600] [13] **Aus$4,800** £2,180 $3,614

FRITZ

COURS DU FLEUVE MARAGNON AUTREMENT DIT DES AMAZONES [c.1770] Engr by Canu for Jesuit *Lettres Edifiantes*. Northern South Amer; whole Amazon basin; missions marked. 21x33cm (8½x13") B&W. Fine. Ref: Phillips (M) p.100 (1781). [30] £112 **$185**

FULLARTON

[BOOK WITH MAPS] THE PARLIAMENTARY GAZETTEER OF ENGLAND AND WALES ... FORMING A COMPLETE COUNTY-ATLAS OF ENGLAND [1844] Octavo, 12 vols, cloth; 5 folding & 42 double-page maps, 3 plates. Sl shaken. [A6] £299 **$496**

THE WORLD IN HEMISPHERES WITH COMPARATIVE VIEWS OF THE HEIGHTS OF THE PRINCIPAL MOUNTAINS AND ... RIVERS ON THE GLOBE [1860] By Swanston. 43x53cm (17x21") Color. [19] £66 **$110**

FULLER

AEGYPTUS ANTIQUA [c.1650] 30x34cm (11½x13½") [A7] £76 **$126**

PARS REGNI MOAB [1650] From *Pisgah Sight of Palestine*. Scenes, incl battles. 28x33cm (11x13") B&W. Fold split to neatline; else fine (A). [A4] £116 **$193**

FULLER continued

TERRAE ISRAEL [1650] To accompany *A Pisgah Sight of Palestine*. 34x50cm (13½x19½") Side margins trimmed. [A8] £208 **$345**

GALL & INGLIS

[PUZZLE] EUROPE [c.1850] "Peacock's New Double Dissection ..."; 2-sided jigsaw puzzle/map with orig wooden box. Recto: Europe, color by country; verso: 6 colored history of England scenes. 32x38cm (13x15") Well preserved. [15] £905 **$1,500**

[PUZZLE] MAP OF THE WORLD ON MERCATORS PROJECTION [c.1840] Jigsaw puzzle, complete with about 50 pieces. Full color by continent. 47x52cm (18½x20½") Minor soiling & rubbing; lt scattered surface loss. [15] £392 **$650**

AUSTRALIAN COLONIES AND NEW ZEALAND XLVII [1851] Several insets. 47x58cm (18½x22½") Orig color. Ref: Tooley (Australia) 662, pl.47. [13] **Aus$140** $64 $105

GARNIER

NOUVEAU PARIS MONUMENTAL. ITINERAIRE PRATIQUE DE L'ETRANGER DANS PARIS [c.1900] Garnier Freres. Bird's-eye view; streets & 100+ buildings appear. 53x69cm (21x27") Full color. Magnifique. [25] £54 **$90**

GAST & CO.

A NEW MAP OF NEBRASKA SHOWING COUNTIES, CITIES, TOWNS, RAILWAYS AND RAILWAY STATIONS [1880] Omaha. Folding map in stiff printed wrappers with U.P.RR ad. 22x40cm (8½x16") Uncolored. [15] £181 **$300**

MAP OF SAN JACINTO CO. [TX] [c.1879] August Gast & Co., St. Louis. Issued by Texas GLO. From files of Houston, Eastern & West Texas Ry. Co. 53x44cm (21x17½") Laid on linen. Some pencil notations; browned; good. ["Angelina County ...", "... Wharton County" & "Freestone County ..." (1888) offered at same price] [16] £302 **$500**

MAP OF SAN SABA CO. [TX] [c.1879] August Gast & Co., St. Louis. Issued by Texas GLO. 48x56cm (19x22") Worn, sm fold losses; backed & restored; good. ["McCulloch Co." (fair) offered at same price] [16] £241 **$400**

MAP OF THE LANDS OWNED BY THE NEW YORK & TEXAS LAND COMPANY, LIMITED [c.1880] August Gast & Co., St. Louis. Land east of Lubbock. [no dimens] Partial yellow tone. Restored; good. [16] £332 **$550**

OFFICIAL MAP OF EL PASO TEXAS [1899] Geo. C. Wimberly, city engineer; August Gast Bank Note & Litho. Co., St. Louis. 300 feet/inch. Adopted by City Council. Dissected, laid on linen. 130x140cm (51½x55½") Full color. Folded; lt waterstains at folds; good. [16] £1,508 **$2,500**

STATE OF SEQUOYAH [1905] D.W. Bolich; St. Louis: Aug. Gast Bank Note & Litho. Indian Terr. divided into 48 proposed counties; "Great Seal of the State of Sequoyah" below title 41x38cm (16x15") Color litho. Lf margin trimmed almost to neat line; archivally reinforced folds; VG. [A10] £555 **$920**

GASTALDI

[ATLAS] LA GEOGRAPHIA ... AGGIUNTEUI DI MESER IACOPO GASTALDI ... [1548] Octavo, vellum; 26 Ptolemaic & 34 new copper engraved maps incl new world. Some gatherings loose; spine defective; occas lt dampstaining & soiling mostly margin; some tears & repairs, mainly at c'folds; worming of guards, maps unaffected; map 55 lacks corner to border. Ref: Phillips (A) 369. [A5] **£5,980** $9,916

[ATLAS] LA GEOGRAPHIA DI CLAUDII PTOLEMAEI ... AGGIUNTEUI DI MESER IACOPO GASTALDI ... [1548] Octavo. 26 Ptolemaic & 34 new copper engraved maps incl new world. Munster's name censored in title page, re-entered in MS, as usual. Ref: Nordenskiold (Fac) p.25, #28; Phillips (A) 369. Sabin 26705. [3] £9,650 **$16,000**

AFRICA NOVA TABULA [1548] Southern Africa. 13x17cm (5½x7") Exc. [45] £407 **$675**

CARTA MARINA NOVA TABULA [1548] 13x18cm (5x7") Exc. Ref: Shirley (W) 88; Suarez 24. [44] £905 **$1,500**

GERMANIA NOVA TABULA [1548] 13x17cm (5x7") Newer OL color. Faint age toning at fold; o/w VG. [14] £181 **$300**

HISPANIA NOVA TABULA [1548] From Ptolemy, *Geographia*. 13x17cm (5x6½") B&W. Lt toned at c'fold; some text show through; VG. Ref: Phillips (A) 369. [35] £90 **$150**

ISOLA CUBA NOVA [1548] 13x17cm (5x6½") Exc. [44] £573 **$950**

NUEVA HISPANIA TABULA NOVA [1548] First printed map of New Spain; insular Yucatan. 13x17cm (5½x7") Exc. Ref: Burden 17. [43] £1,447 **$2,400**

TABULA ASIAE IIII [1548] Ptolemaic Holy Land. 14x18cm (5½x7") Uncolored. Fold repair verso, minor loss. [25] £136 **$225**

GASTALDI continued

TABULA EUROPAE II [1548] Ptolemaic Spain & Portugal. 13x17cm (5x7") B&W. Lt age toning along vert fold; some lt foxing; o/w VG. [14] £166 **$275**

TIERRA NOVA [1548] From *La Geografia di Claudio Ptolemeo* ... 1st pocket atlas; 1st printed map of South America alone. 13x17cm (5x7") Uncol. Lt impression; sm wormhole at c'fold repaired. [34] £450 **$746**

TIERRA NUEVA [1548] Primitive American east coast. 13x17cm (5½x7") Exc. [23] £1,628 **$2,700**

UNIVERSALE NOVO [1548] Venice. Reduced version of 1546 map. Six wind gods. 13x17cm (5x7") B&W. Some surface dirt; overall VG. Ref: Shirley 87. [37] £754 **$1,250**

GASTON & JOHNSON

A NEW MAP OF OUR COUNTRY PRESENT AND PROSPECTIVE. COMPILED FROM GOVERNMENT SURVEY AND OTHR RELIABLE SOURCES [1854] Wall map; North America to Venezuela. Color by county. 142x156cm (56x61½") Lt chipping top; sm hole; waterstained rt edge; some varnish yellowing; VG. Ref: Wheat (TM) 806; Phillips (M) p.905. [15] £663 **$1,100**

GAZZETTIERE AMERICANO

CARTA ESATTA RAPPRESENTANTE IL CORSO DEL FIUME PARAGUAY E DI PAESI AD ESSO VICINI [1763] Incl Buenos Aires, Potosi, etc. 23x26cm (9x10") OL & wash color. [41] £54 **$90**

CARTA RAPPRESENTANTE IL PORTO DI BOSTON [1763] Livorno: 22x18cm (8½x7") Color added. Ref: Phillips (A) 1161. [22] £151 **$250**

NUOVA E CORRETTA CARTA DELL'INDIE OCCIDENTALI ... [1763] 27x34cm (10½x13½") OL & wash color. [39] £136 **$225**

NUOVA ED ESATTA CARTA DELLA AMERICA RICAVATA DALLE MAPPE, E CARTE PIU APPROVATE [1763] Livorno: Coltellini. 34x28cm (13½x11") B&W. Trace foxing; fine. [12] £136 **$225**

PIANO DI PORTO BELLO [1763] 20x25cm (8x10") B&W. Ref: Phillips (A) 1161. ["Piano della Citta Rada e Porto di Chagre" offered at same price] [20] £51 **$85**

PLANO DEL PORTO E DEGLI STABILIMENTI DI PENSACOLA [1777] From Masi ed, entitled *Atlante dell' America*. Livorno. 20x27cm (8x11") Uncolored. Exc. Ref: Phillips (A) 1167-13. [36] £226 **$375**

PLANTA DELLA CITTA DI SANT' IAGO CAPITALE DEL REGNO DEL CHILI [1763] 28 landmarks keyed. 23x20cm (9x8") Full wash color. Ref: Phillips (A) 1161. [39] £54 **$90**

GEIL

MAP OF SARATOGA CO. NEW YORK [1856] Samuel Geil, Phila. Wall map; 15 inset maps; 7 views. Full color by town. 145x96cm (57x38") Age toning; chipping; staining at title; fair. Ref: Phillips (M) p.785. [15] £302 **$500**

GEMMA FRISIUS

CHARTA COSMOGRAPHICA CUM VENTORUM PROPRIA NATURA ET OPERATIONE [1544 (1553)] State 2 of three. Woodcut cordiform map. (title word spelled "Operavione" in catalogue illustration) 20x29cm (8x11½") Exc. Ref: Shirley (W) 96. [43] £1,447 **$2,400**

GENERAL MAGAZINE OF ARTS & SCIENCES

A MAP OF NEW ENGLAND & YE COUNTRY ADJACENT, EXTENDING NORTHWARD TO QUEBEC, & WESTWARD TO NIAGARA, ON LAKE ONTARIO; SHEWING GEN: SHIRLEY AND GEN: IOHNSON'S ROUTS, & MANY PLACES OMITTED IN OTHER ... [1755] 20x18cm (8x7") Ref: Jolly GENMAS-70. [A7] £156 **$258**

AN ACCURATE MAP OF PARAGUAY, TUCUMANIA, CHACO, RIO DE LA PLATA, &C. WITH PART OF BRASIL FROM 20 TO 37 DEGREES SOUTH LATITUDE. LAID DOWN FROM THE MOST APPROVED MODERN MAPS WITH IMPROVEMENTS BY EMAN: BOWEN GEOGR. TO HIS MAJESTY. [1756] 28x42cm (11x16½") Color. Ref: Jolly GENMAS-71. [34] £200 **$332**

GENTLEMAN'S MAGAZINE

A CHART OF THE BALTIC SEA, GULFS OF FINLAND AND BOTHNIA, WITH THE SOUND, DRAWN FROM THE BEST MAPS & CHARTS BY T. JEFFERYS, GEOGRAPHER TO HIS ROYAL HIGHNESS THE PRINCE OF WALES. [1748] With complete March issue. 24x26cm (9½x10½") B&w. couple sm worm holes; still fine (A). Ref: Jolly GENT-55. [A4] £77 **$127**

A GENERAL MAP OF THE DISCOVERIES OF ADMIRAL DE FONTE & OTHERS, BY M. DE L'ISLE. [1754] Errant geography: Northwest Passage, West Sea, and island east of Kamchatka. B&W. 19x25cm (7½x10") B&W. Usual narrow rt margin; else exc. Ref: Jolly GENT-88; Falk (AK) 1754-1. [12] £136 **$225**

A MAP OF CONNECTICUT AND RHODE ISLAND, WITH LONG ISLAND SOUND, &C. [1776] 17x23cm (7x9") B&W. Folds as issued; fine. Ref: Jolly GENT-249; Phillips (M) p.246; Thompson I-25; Guthorn (Amer Rev) 152-7. [12] £90 **$150**

GENTLEMAN'S MAGAZINE continued

A MAP OF PHILADELPHIA AND PARTS ADJACENT, BY N. SCULL AND G. HEAP [1777] 2nd ed. 34x29cm (13½x11½") Ref: Jolly GENT-256. [11] £232 **$385**

A MAP OF THAT PART OF AMERICA WHICH WAS THE PRINCIPAL SEAT OF WAR, IN 1756. [1756] (Attribution provided by compiler. Jolly notes ambiguity.) 22x34cm (9x13½") Partial color. Lacks sm part lower lf where removed from source. Ref: Jolly GENT-102. [A7] £104 **$172**

A MAP OF THE BRITISH AMERICAN PLANTATIONS, EXTENDING FROM BOSTON IN NEW ENGLAND TO GEORGIA; INCLUDING ALL THE BACK SETTLEMENTS IN THE RESPECTIVE PROVINCES, AS FAR AS THE MISSISSIPI. BY EMAN: BOWEN GEOGR: TO HIS MAJESTY. [1754] 22x27cm (8½x11") B&W. Sh lf margin extension; fine. Ref: Jolly GENT-89; Sellers & Van Ee 708; cf Cumming (SE) 272, dated 1749. [29] £220 **$365**

A MAP OF THE COUNTRY ROUND PHILADELPHIA INCLUDING PART OF NEW JERSEY NEW YORK STATEN ISLAND & LONG ISLAND. [1776] 18x22cm (7x8½") B&W. Lt toned; VG+. Ref: Jolly GENT-247; Phillips (M) p.699. Klein G76.6. [35] £133 **$220**

A MAP OF THE ISLAND OF JAMAICA. [1762] 11x20cm (4½x8") Uncolored. VG. Ref: Jolly GENT-158 [25] £36 **$60**

A MAP OF THE NEW GOVERNMENTS, OF EAST & WEST FLORIDA. [1763] 20x25cm (8x10") B&W. Sm tear to neatline, archival tape repair; faint text transfer. Ref: Jolly GENT-171; Cumming (SE) 336. [A1] £179 **$297**

A MAP OF THE SOUTH POLE, WITH THE TRACK OF HIS MAJESTY'S SLOOP RESOLUTION IN SEARCH OF A SOUTHERN CONTINENT [1776] T. Bowen, sc. With accompanying text. 22x21cm (8½x8½") Ref: Jolly GENT-241. [39] £75 **$125**

A MAP OF THE WORLD, ON MERCATORS PROJECTION. [1755] With related article. 18x28cm (7x11") B&W. Close top margin as issued; fine (A+). Ref: Jolly GENT-94. [A4] £153 **$254**

A NEW PROJECTION OF THE EASTERN HEMISPHERE OF THE EARTH ON A PLANE (SHEWING THE PROPORTIONS OF ITS SEVERAL PARTS NEARLY AS ON A GLOBE) BY J. HARDY, (W.M. & TEACHER OF MATHEMATICS) AT EATON COLLEGE. [1776] Thomas Bowen, sc. 21x21cm (8½x8½") B&W. Lt offsetting; 2 binding holes; good (B). Ref: Jolly GENT-242. [A3] £17 **$28**

A NEW PROJECTION OF THE WESTERN HEMISPHERE OF THE EARTH ON A PLANE (SHEWING THE PROPORTIONS OF ITS SEVERAL PARTS NEARLY AS ON A GLOBE) ... [IN SET WITH] A NEW PROJECTION OF THE EASTERN HEMISPHERE OF THE EARTH ON A PLANE ... [1776] 2 cleaved hemis by J. Hardy, Master at Eton. Each about 21x23cm (8½x9") OL col. Some foxing. Ref: Jolly GENT-242 & 244. [39] £148 **$245**

A PARTICULAR MAP, TO ILLUSTRATE GEN. AMHERSTS, EXPEDITION, TO MONTREAL; WITH A PLAN OF THE TOWN & DRAUGHT OF YE ISLAND. [Oct. 1760] 18x23cm (7x9") B&W. Fine. Ref: Jolly GENT-145. [29] £106 **$175**

A PLAN OF BRIDGE TOWN, IN THE ISLAND OF BARBADOES. [1776] City plan, after 1766 fire. 10x19cm (4x7½") B&W. Ref: Jolly GENT-188. [20] £136 **$225**

A PLAN OF THE HARBOUR OF CHEBUCTO AND TOWN OF HALIFAX. [1750] With porcupine. 22x27cm (8½x10½") Full color. Ref: Jolly GENT-70. [11] £271 **$450**

[SAME TITLE] [1750] The "Porcupine" map. 22x27cm (8½x10½") B&W. Lower lf margin extended; else fine. Ref: Jolly GENT-70; AMPR 1984, illus. Dawson (NS) p.114; Lemon (NS) p.65. [12] £196 **$325**

A PLAN OF THE SIEGE OF THE HAVANA, DRAWN BY AN OFFICER ON THE SPOT. 1762. [1762] 20x25cm (8x10") Uncolored. Lf edge trimmed close. Ref: Jolly GENT-163; Phillips (M) 312. [25] £75 **$125**

A PLAN OF THE TOWN AND CHART OF THE HARBOUR OF BOSTON EXHIBITING A VIEW OF THE ISLANDS, CASTLES, FORTS AND ENTRANCES INTO THE SAID HARBOUR [1775] 26x34cm (10½x13") Margins just ample. Ref: Jolly GENT-232. [A7] £121 **$201**

A VIEW OF AMSTERDAM [1748] Thomas Jefferys bird's-eye ; 42 buildings named. Comes with June edition. 17x39cm (6½x15") B&W. Bit browned; VG (A). [A4] £116 **$193**

A VIEW OF THE TOWN AND CASTLE OF ST. AUGUSTINE, AND THE ENGLISH CAMP BEFORE IT JUNE 20. 1740. BY THOS. SILVER [1740] Text below. 30x17cm (11½x6½") Ref: Jolly GENT-12. [11] £166 **$275**

[SAME TITLE] [1740] Birds-eye view. 30x17cm (11½x6½") Full color. VG. [36] £211 **$350**

[SAME TITLE] [1740] Birds-eye view. 30x17cm (11½x6½") Uncolored. Faint toning; o/w VG. [A2] £106 **$176**

AN ACCURATE MAP OF THE WEST INDIES. EXHIBITING NOT ONLY ALL THE ISLANDS POSSESS'D BY THE ENGLISH, FRENCH, SPANIARDS & DUTCH, BUT ALSO ALL THE TOWNS AND SETTLEMENTS ON THE CONTINENT OF AMERICA ADJACENT THERETO. [1740] Emanuel Bowen, sc. 29x39cm (11½x15") B&W. VG (A). Ref: Jolly GENT-6. [A4] £232 **$385**

GENTLEMAN'S MAGAZINE continued

AN EXACT MAP OF THE CRIM, (FORMERLY TAURICA CHERSONESUS) PART OF LESSER TARTARY, THE SEA OF ASOPH, AND THE ADJACENT COUNTRY OF THE KUBAN TARTARS; AS LAID DOWN BY THE CZARINA'S GEOGRAPHERS; EXHIBITING THE MARCH OF THE RUSSIAN ARMIES... [1739] 23x32cm (9x12½") Closed tear at trimmed rt margin. Ref: Jolly GENT-3. [21] Can$40 £17 $29

CHART OF THE ANTARCTIC POLAR CIRCLE, WITH THE COUNTRIES ADJOINING, ACCORDING TO THE NEW HYPOTHESIS OF M. BUACHE [1763] 20x22cm (7½x8½") OL col. Ref: Jolly GENT-166. [11] £136 $225

PLAN OF ST. LUCIA, IN THE WEST INDIES: SHEWING THE POSITIONS OF THE ENGLISH & FRENCH FORCES WITH THE ATTACKS MADE AT ITS REDUCTION IN DECR. 1778. [1779] Thomas Bowen, sc. 19x25cm (7½x10") B&W. Lt offsetting; VG. Ref: Jolly GENT-266; Phillips (M) p.768. Klein G79.2. [35] £75 $125

PLAN OF THE CITY AND HARBOUR OF HAVANNA. [1762] 11x20cm (4½x8") Uncolored. VG. Ref: Jolly GENT-162. [25] £45 $75

SKETCH OF THE COUNTRY ILLUSTRATING THE LATE ENGAGEMENT IN LONG ISLAND [1776] 20x31cm (7½x12½") B&W. Exc. Ref: Jolly GENT-248. Guthorn (Amer Rev) 152-6. [12] £136 $225

[SAME TITLE] [1776] Shows NYC & much of Long Island. 19x30cm (7½x12") [41] £136 $225

THE AUSTRIAN & FRENCH NETHERLANDS AGREEABLE TO THE BARRIER CONCLUDED AT ANTWERP, AND RELATIVE TO THE PRESENT WAR. [1744] Bound into June issue. 11x20cm (4½x8") B&W. VG (A). Ref: Jolly GENT-23. [A4] £55 $91

THE BRITISH GOVERNMENTS IN NTH. AMERICA LAID DOWN AGREEABLE TO THE PROCLAMATION OF OCTR. 7. 1763. [1763] By Gibson. Bermuda inset. 20x23cm (8x9½") B&W. Ref: Jolly GENT-170; Fite & Freeman #55. [20] £293 $485

[SAME TITLE] [1763] By Gibson. Bermuda inset. 20x23cm (8x9") Ref: Jolly GENT-170; Fite & Freeman pp.218-21, illus. [26] £133 $220

THE EAST INDIES DRAWN FROM THE LATEST DISCOVERIES, BY T. JEFFERYS, GEOGRAPHER, TO HIS ROYAL HIGHNESS THE PRINCE OF WALES. [1748] Incl whole June issue. India to Japan to N Australia. 23x26cm (9x10½") B&W. VG (A). Ref: Jolly GENT-58. [A4] £199 $330

THE GEOGRAPHY OF THE GREAT SOLAR ECLIPSE OF JULY, 14. MDCCXLVIII. EXHIBITING AN ACCURATE MAP OF ALL PARTS OF THE EARTH IN WHICH IT WILL BE VISIBLE WITH THE NORTH POLE ACCORDING TO THE LATEST DISCOVERIES. BY G. SMITH ESQR. [1748] Surround of 24 panels of eclipse images. 30x44cm (12x17") Ref: Jolly GENT-59. [11] £136 $225

THE SIEGE OF RHODE ISLAND, TAKEN FROM MR. BRINDLEY'S HOUSE, ON THE 25TH OF AUGUST, 1778. [1779] 13x21cm (5x8½") Ref: Phillips (M) p.743. [11] £45 $75

[SAME TITLE] [1779] 13x22cm (5x8½") B&W. Key text not present. Not in Jolly. [12] £75 $125

GERRITZ

PASCAERT VANDE CARIBES EYLANDEN; CURIOOSLYCK BETROCKEN, MET OCTROY VANDE HO. MO. HEEEREN DE STATEN GENERAEL DER VEREENIGHDE NEDERLANDEN, ENDE DEN E.E. HEEREN BEWINTHEBBEREN DER GHEOCTROYEERDE WEST INDISCHE COMPAGNIE ... HESSEL GERRITS, AO 1631 [1631] One of 2 known copies. Printed on vellum; internal company chart. 50x70cm (20x28") Orig color. Some staining & soiling; overall near exc. Ref: Wieder IV, 107; *Imago Mundi* VI, p.49-66. [23] £33,170 $55,000

GIBSON

A MAP TO EXPLAIN THE HISTORY OF THE ASSYRIANS. BABYLONIANS, MEDES, & PERSIANS [1764] From Guthrie's *General History of the World*. 24x21cm (9½x8½") OL color. Vert crease; sl trimmed margins; minor browning. [21] Can$75 £33 $54

A NEW AND ACCURATE MAP OF AFRICA DRAWN & ENGRAVED FROM THE BEST AUTHORITIES [1771] 20x23cm (8x9") Uncolored. VG. [25] £36 $60

A NEW AND ACCURATE MAP OF NORTH AMERICA DRAWN & ENGRAVED FROM THE BEST AUTHORITIES [1771] 15x20cm (6x8") Uncolored. VG. [25] £45 $75

A NEW AND ACCURATE MAP OF THE PROVINCES OF PENSILVANIA, VIRGINIA, MARYLAND AND NEW JERSEY [1762] Issued in *The American Gazetteer*. London. Many surface notes. 28x34cm (11x13½") Uncolored. [39] £392 $650

GREECE WITH THE NORTHERN PROVINCES NEAR THE DANUBE [1764] From Guthrie's *General History of the World*. 20x18cm (8x7") Lower lf margin cut away; image unaffected; closed sm lower c'fold tear. [21] Can$90 £39 $65

GILL

NEW SECTIONAL, TOWNSHIP AND COUNTY MAP OF WASHINGTON   [1889]   J.K. Gill, Portland; L.M. Snyder & Co., lith, Chicago. Full color by county. 70x53cm (27½x21") Lacks folder; soiling; minor fold junction separations; 2 fold tears lf edge, sl loss. [15]   £271   **$450**

OREGON & WASHINGTON TER.   [dated 1878]   By R.A. Habersham; A.M. Askevold, Chicago, lith. 88x69cm (34½x27") Full color. Fine. Ref: Phillips (M) p.644. [12]   £181   **$300**

GILPIN

MAP ILLUSTRATING THE SYSTEM OF PARCS, AND THE DOMESTIC RELATIONS OF THE GREAT PLAINS, THE NORTH AMERICAN ANDES, AND THE PACIFIC MARITIME FRONT   [1873]   53x57cm (21x22½") Full color. Smoke stains rt edge; lt water stain along fold; orig outside fold darkened; narrow margins. [1]   £151   **$250**

GLOBES   Try *Bardin, Newton & Berry*

[12 INCH GLOBE]   [1896]   W. & A.K. Johnston, London & Edinburgh. On bronze base. Diameter: 30cm (12") Half dime size chip near Arabia; fine. [36]   £573   **$950**

[GLOBE]   [c.1880]   English or American miniature ivory globe in turned dark wood case of treen ware style. Diameter: 3cm (1") Fine. [37]   £573   **$950**

[GLOBE]   [n.d.]   Ivory globe with brass fittings on brass and wood pedestal. Victorian era (?) in antique style with English & Latin place names. Diameter: 5cm (2") 3" high overall. Opens to reveal sun dial and brass gnoman. Red & black inks highlight incised portions. Verdigris touch on brass; else fine. [37]   £603   **$1,000**

A NEW AMERICAN TERRESTRIAL GLOBE, ON WHICH THE PRINCIPAL PLACES OF THE KNOWN WORLD ARE ACCURATELY LAID DOWN, WITH THE TRACED ATTEMPTS OF CAPTAIN COOK   [1811]   James Wilson, Bradford, VT. First dated American globe. Modern wooden stand to replicate original; metal pinions at pole; brass meridian ring. Diameter: 33cm (13") 12 colored gores, bit darkened; lacks paper calendar/zodiac; 2 cracks in surface; still fine. Ref: Warner 135; Yonge 65-67. [15]   £7,539   **$12,500**

GEOGRAPHIA 8 INCH TERRESTRIAL GLOBE   [19th c.]   Geographia Ltd., London. Diameter: 20cm (8") Clean, usual lt brown cast; few lt flecks, information unaffected; else VG. [A1]   £796   **$1,320**

KUNSTLICHER MECHANISCHER GLOBUS ZUM GEBRAUCH DES KLEINEN GEOGRAPHER   [c.1850]   F.G. Schulz, Stuttgart. 6 segments, 7x4", linked by linen bands, with tasseled ribbons bend into classroom globe; tucks into titled cardboard cover with text. Orig wash color. Rust spot on cover; exc. [27]   £1,568   **$2,600**

MALBY'S TERRESTRIAL GLOBE COMPILED FROM THE GLOBES OF THE SOCIETY FOR THE DIFFUS.N OF USEFUL KNOWLEDGE   [1883]   Housed in acorn-shaped wood case with mountings for travel & display. Diameter: 8cm (3½") Color. Clean, clear; repaired crack; else exc. [24]   £2,533   **$4,200**

NEW EIGHT-INCH TERRESTRIAL GLOBE   [1891]   Rand, McNally, Chicago. Orig tripod heavy metal stand, lacks hardware at top. Color by country. Diameter: 20cm (8") Minor loss from adhesion, Russia & Greenland; sm blemishes elsewhere; age darkening; generally exc. [15]   £603   **$1,000**

GOLDBACH

[ATLAS]   NEUESTER HIMMELS-ATLAS ...   [1819]   Weimar. Oblong quarto, orig boards, leather spine, printed label. 56 charts; white stars on black background from relief copper plates. Ref: Warner (Sky) p.96. [3]   £543   **$9**

GOLDTHWAIT

RAILROAD MAP OF NEW ENGLAND AND EASTERN NEW YORK   [1849]   Wall map mounted on linen with top rail & apparent orig half round lower. Boston inset. 60x50cm (23½x19½") OL color by state. Lt soiled; dull finish, needs cleaning; occas vert wrinkle; sl ragged margins; o/w VG. Ref: Modelski (US) 102. [5]   £238   **$395**

GOODRICH

[BOOK WITH MAPS]   A NATIONAL GEOGRAPHY, FOR SCHOOLS; ILLUSTRATED WITH 220 ENGRAVINGS, AND 33 MAPS; WITH A GLOBE MAP, ON A NEW PLAN ...   [1846]   NY: Huntington & Savage. Tall quarto, salmon boards; 108 pp; 2 hemi maps pasted together, laid in front cover, form the "globe". OL color. Front cover rubbed, loss, spine broken. [16]   £452   **$750**

[BOOK WITH MAPS]   PETER PARLEY'S GEOGRAPHY FOR BEGINNERS ...   [1845]   NY: Huntington & Savage. Square 16mo; 160 pp; 18 maps, 150 engravings. North America shows Texas Republic. Lacks rear board; contents tight, VG. [16]   £106   **$175**

MEXICO, TEXAS, GUATIMALA & WEST INDIES   [1845]   From *Parley's First Book of History, Combined with Geography* ... Boston: Jenks, Hickling & Swan. Attributed to Boynton. 11x16cm (4½x6½") Partial color. Browned; good. [16]   £72   **$120**

THE PACIFIC REGION   [1854]   With "Mesilla" for proto-AZ in southern NM. 18x15cm (7x8") on 10x8" sheet with text. VG. [26]   £36   **$60**

GOODRICH continued

UNITED STATES [1854] Large western territories; "Mesilla", proposed name for AZ, shown south of Gila R. 25x38cm (10x15") Full color. VG. [26] £72 **$120**

GOOS

DE WEST CUSTEN VAN YERLANDT BEGINNENDE VAN CORCKBEG TOT AEN SLYNHOOFT [1650] As in *Zeespiegel*. Portolan style chart of SW Ireland. 44x43cm (17x17") Color. Trimmed & remargined; little time stained. Ref: Koeman Goos 17, 51. [42] **Aus$1,400** £636 $1,054

GORDON

[BOOK WITH MAPS] GEOGRAPHY ANATOMIZ'D: OR, THE GEOGRAPHICAL GRAMMAR ... NINETEENTH EDITION ... WITH A SET OF NEW MAPS, BY MR. SENEX [1749] London. Thick octavo; many maps; contemporary calf. [A7] £294 **$488**

GORDON, WILLIAM

NEW HAMPSHIRE, VERMONT, &C. [1788] From *History of the American War*. T. Conder. 36x34cm (14x13½") Uncolored. Offsetting; narrow lf margin. [36] £166 **$275**

NEW YORK ISLAND, & PARTS ADJACENT [1788] From Gordon, *History of an ... Account of the Late War*. 26x17cm (10½x6½") OL color. Repaired margin tear; else fine. Ref: Sabin 28011. [37] £271 **$450**

THE JERSEYS, &C.&C. [1788] T. Conder. 30x23cm (12x9") Narrow lf margin; some offsetting. [36] £151 **$250**

THE PART OF VIRGINIA WHICH WAS THE SEAT OF ACTION [1788] From Gordon's *History*. T. Conder. 18x25cm (7x10") Uncolored. Some offsetting. [36] £121 **$200**

THE UNITED STATES OF AMERICA [1788] From Gordon's *History*. T. Conder. 29x29cm (11½x11½") Uncolored. Some offsetting; narrow rt margin. [36] £151 **$250**

YORKTOWN AND GLOUCESTER POINT AS BESIEGED BY THE ALLIED ARMY [1788] From Gordon's *History*. T. Conder. 29x21cm (11½x8½") Uncolored. Minor stains & offsetting; narrow lf margin. [36] £151 **$250**

GOTTFRIED

DELINEATIO PRAELII INTER SER. SUECORUM REGEM ET ... GENERAL. COM.A TILY 7. SEPTEMB. AI. 1631 PROPE LIPSIA COMMISSI [1632] From *Inventarium Sueciae*. 27x38cm (10½x15") Fold restored. [48] **DM 80** £28 $46

FRANCFURT AM MAYN [1632] From *Inventarium Sueciae*. Bird's-eye view with Sachsenhausen. 18x30cm (7x11½") [48] **DM 780** £269 $446

LUBEC [1632] From *Inventarium Sueciae*. On folio leaf, 7x13cm (3x5½") [48] **DM 350** £121 $200

STOCKHOLM [1632] From same source. View. 7x14cm (3x5½") on folio sheet. [48] **DM 220** £76 $126

WITTENBERG [1632] From *Inventarium Sueciae*. View. 8x14cm (3x5½") [48] **DM 180** £62 $103

GOVERNMENT MAPS: LOCAL & STATE

[ATLAS] PENNSYLVANIA MAPS ACCOMPANYING THE REPORT OF THE SECRETARY OF INTERNAL AFFAIRS ON THE BOUNDARIES OF THE COMMONWEALTH [1887] Phila. 20 litho folding maps in orig cloth folding covers, title & index glued inside; incl Mason-Dixon survey, etc. [no dimens] Covers worn; some sm tears at folds; maps exc. [33] £112 **$185**

ADIRONDACK MAP, 1909 [1909] NY Forest, Fish & Game Comm. 4 maps, folded into covers, each 84x76cm (33x30") OL color; ownership color coded. Exposed fold worn on one map. [25] £84 **$140**

FORT BEND COUNTY [TX] [1873] Texas GLO. Photo map by C.W. Pressler; drawn by A.C. Jessen. Owners shown with pencil & ink MS changes. 46x53cm (18x21") Purple stamp lower rt; photopaper laid on cotton, sm fold & margin losses; repairs; good. [16] £271 **$450**

HAWAII [IN SET WITH] KAUAI [AND] LANAI [AND] MAUI [AND] MOLOKAI [AND] OAHU [c.1900] Hawaii Government Survey. Various sizes. Litho color. [A8] £191 **$316**

MAP OF BEXAR COUNTY [1878] Texas GLO. By Otto Groos; Heliotype Printing Co., Boston, litho. County at present size; San Antonio at ctr; shows land owners.. 57x66cm (22½x26") Good. [16] £362 **$600**

MAP OF WISCONSIN PUBLISHED BY THE STATE BOARD OF IMMIGRATION [1895] Issued in sm booklet extolling WI. 51x58cm (20x23") Mildly soiled booklet. [25] £36 **$60**

MCCULLOCH COUNTY [TX] [1904 / 1917] General Land Office, Austin. Retraced by W.P. Doty, Brady. Oil leases; land holdings. 53x41cm (21x16") B&W. Folding. [27] £57 **$95**

NEW MAP OF FLORIDA, 1880 [1880] Publ by Bureau of Immigration. Souvenir map by Rand, McNally on reverse of broadside. 50x32cm (19½x12½") Printed OL color. Top margin chipped & browned into image; browned along some folds; some show through. [A10] £160 **$265**

GOVERNMENT MAPS: LOCAL & STATE continued

NEW YORK STATE RESERVATION AT NIAGARA   [c.1890] NY State Commissioners. One side of tourist brochure. 33x33cm (13x13") Substantial color. Sm fold tear repaired. [25]   £30 **$50**

RAILROAD MAP OF OHIO   [1898-99] Under direction of R.S. Kayler; Columbus Litho Co. Pocket map mounted on linen, folded into elongated octavo gold-embossed cloth covered boards. 80x71cm (31½x28") RRs In color. Sl soiled linen backing; end paper torn; VG. [5] £112 **$185**

SKETCH OF THE STATES OF MASSACHUSETTS, CONNECTICUT AND RHODE ISLAND AND PARTS OF NEW HAMPSHIRE & NEW YORK EXHIBITING THE SEVERAL RAIL ROAD ROUTES COMPLETE, CONSTRUCTING, CHARTERED & CONTEMPLATED   [1846] Publ by order of Massachusetts Legislature. Incl Long Island. 46x51cm (18x20") B&W. Sh tears repaired; lt soiling; VG. Ref: Modelski (US) 100. [35] £90 **$150**

TOPOGRAPHICAL MAP SHOWING THE LOCATIONS OF THE SUTRO TUNNEL AND THE COMSTOCK LODE   [1866] State of Nevada; by Chas. F. Hoffman. 36x28cm (14x11") Substantial color. VG. [25] £60 **$100**

GOVERNMENT MAPS: NATIONAL (not U.S. or Canada)

A GENERAL MAP OF IRELAND TO ACCOMPANY THE REPORT OF THE RAILWAY COMMISSIONERS SHEWING THE PHYSICAL FEATURES AND GEOLOGICAL STRUCTURE OF THE COUNTRY   [1839] Richard Griffith; publ Dublin & London. 6 sheets joined & linen-backed on orig rollers in orig wooden case. 180x146cm (71x57½") Color. Some soiling lower edge. [A6] £920 **$1,526**

GOVERNMENT MAP OF NICARAGUA FROM THE LATEST SURVEYS ORDERED BY PRESIDENT PATRICIO RIVAS AND GENL. WILLIAM WALKER   [1856] NY: A.H. Jocelyn. 80x64cm (31½x25") Color. Folded, third of folds separated; old linen stabilization; minor loss probable. [A7] £242 **$402**

GRANT

AFRICA   [1886] 56x41cm (22x16") Printed color. [40] £24 **$40**

GRAPHIC, THE

BIRD'S EYE VIEW OF CAIRO LOOKING NORTH EAST   [1882] Publ London. Incl the Pyramids to Suez. 41x56cm (16x22") Full soft color. VG. [26] £54 **$90**

MAP OF THE NORTH POLAR REGION   [1876] From U.S. Hydrographic Office Chart No.68. Dissected into 15 panels, linen-mounted; folds into octavo marbled wraps. Wrangell Land profile. 62x79cm (24½x31½") Red highlights. Some fold separations. [A10] £188 **$311**

GRAY

BOSTON AND ADJACENT CITIES   [1883] By H.F. Walling. [no dimens] Full orig col. Exc. [36] £75 **$125**

CALIFORNIA AND NEVADA   [c.1878] Insets; verso: San Francisco; OR & WA. 66x41cm (26x16") Full color. VG. [25] £72 **$120**

GRAY'S ATLAS MAP OF TEXAS [ON LEAF WITH] GRAY'S ATLAS MAP OF ARKANSAS   [1873] Each about 31x38cm (12½x15") Full color. VG. [16] £106 **$175**

GRAY'S NEW MAP OF BALTIMORE   [1883] 38x30cm (15x12") Full orig color. Exc. [36] £57 **$95**

GRAY'S NEW MAP OF MASSACHUSETTS RHODE ISLAND AND CONNECTICUT   [1881] 39x64cm (15½x25") Full color. [22] £30 **$50**

GRAY'S NEW MAP OF RICHMOND ...   [1883] 34x43cm (13½x17") Wards in full orig col. Exc. [36] £75 **$125**

GRAY'S NEW MAP OF SAINT LOUIS   [1883] Frank A. Gray. 41x33cm (16x13") Full orig color. VG. [Chicago offered at same price] [36] £57 **$95**

GRAY'S NEW MAP OF TEXAS AND THE INDIAN TERRITORY   [1878] 7 insets. 41x66cm (16x26") Full color. VG. [A10] £174 **$288**

[SAME TITLE]   [c.1881] 7 insets. 41x66cm (16x26") Full color. VG. [25] £90 **$150**

[SAME TITLE]   [1883] 43x66cm (17x26") Full orig color. Exc. [36] £136 **$225**

MAP OF THE UNITED STATES SHOWING THE PRINCIPAL GEOLOGICAL FORMATIONS BY CHAS. H. HITCHCOCK, PH.D., PROFESSOR OF GEOLOGY IN DARTMOUTH COLLEGE   [1874] 5 zones color keyed. 41x66cm (16x26") [40] £54 **$90**

MARYLAND, DELAWARE AND THE DISTRICT OF COLUMBIA   [1881] Insets, incl large DC. 41x67cm (16x26½") Color. Ref: Phillips (Wash) 290. [22] £45 **$75**

NEVADA   [1884] Carson City inset. 38x30cm (15x12") Pastel color. Exc. [27] £24 **$40**

SAN FRANCISCO   [1883] 38x30cm (15x12") Full orig color. VG. [36] £75 **$125**

UNITED STATES   [1879] 39x69cm (15½x27") Full printed color. [27] £42 **$70**

UNITED STATES OF AMERICA   [1877] Alaska inset. 39x67cm (15½x26½") Full color. Faint water stain. [40] £27 **$45**

GREENHOW

MAP OF THE WESTERN AND MIDDLE PORTION OF NORTH AMERICA [1844] To illustrate *History of Oregon and California* ... By George H. Ringgold; incl some Fremont information. 57x65cm (22½x26") Folded; some offsetting; still good. Ref: Wheat (TM) 481. [10] £211 **$350**

GREENLEAF

ARKANSAS [1842] From *New Universal Atlas*. Jeremiah Greenleaf. Direct descendant of Burr. Miller Co. in SW. 28x32cm (11x12½") Color. Perfect. Ref: Phillips (A) 784-50. [12] £96 **$160**

NEW HOLLAND AND NEW ZEALAND [1848] Little interior detail. 28x33cm (11x13") Full color. VG (A). [A4] £66 **$110**

NORTH AND SOUTH CAROLINA [1842] From *New Universal Atlas*. Jeremiah Greenleaf (based on Burr). 27x32cm (10½x12½") Full color. Exc. Ref: Phillips (A) 784-51. [12] £90 **$150**

OREGON TERRITORY [1842] From *New Universal Atlas*. Based on Burr. Extends east to Rockies & beyond 54 deg. north, with adjacent coverage. 27x32cm (10½x12½") Full color. Pristine. Ref: Phillips (A) 784-48. [12] £226 **$375**

GREENWOOD

[ENGLAND: SOMERSETSHIRE] [1809] On 4 sheets, dissected, mounted on linen, folding into octavo roan slipcase; when joined, 131x178cm (51½x70½") Color. Case worn, rubbed. [A6] **£207** $344

MAP OF THE COUNTY OF CAMBRIDGE FROM AN ACTUAL SURVEY MADE IN THE YEARS 1832 & 1833 [1834] From *Atlas of the Counties of England*. J. & C. Walker, sc. Ely cathedral engraving. 57x72cm (22½x28") Orig color. ["... County of Berks ..." offered at same price] [11] £90 **$150**

MAP OF THE COUNTY OF SOMERSET FROM ACTUAL SURVEY MADE IN THE YEARS 1820 & 1821 [1822] Dissected into 70 panels on two linen-backed sheets, folding into orig morocco gold tooled slip case. 132x185cm (52x73") Printed color. Exc. [11] £232 **$385**

GRIGG

MEXICO AND GUATIMALA [1830] John Grigg's "Malte-Brun" atlas. J.H. Young, sc. Texas as "New Estramadura". 20x25cm (8x10") Orig full color. VG. [16] £151 **$250**

GRYNAEUS

[BOOK WITH MAPS] NOVUS ORBIS REGIONUM AC INSULARUM VETERIBUS INCOGNITARUM, UNA CUM TABULA COSMOGRAPHICA ... [1532] Paris: Jean Petit. Folio; 514 pp; with 1st ed world map by Orontius Fine. "Nova, et Integra Universi Orbis Descriptio", double cordiform polar projection woodcut. 31x41cm (12x16½") Bound in French morocco, lots of gilt, in modern box, minor wear spine ends, joints bit shaken; minor soiling scattered leaves; limited lt waterstain; exc. Ref: Shirley (W) 66, state 1; Suarez 19. Sabin 34102; Karrow (16c) p.179-80, 27/4.4. [24] £41,011 **$68,000**

GUICCIARDINI

ARNHEM [c.1570] Bird's-eye plan. 23x34cm (9x13") B&W. Fine (A+). [A4] £88 **$146**

GUSSEFELD

CHARTE DER XV VEREINIGTEN STAATEN VON NORD-AMERICA ... [1800] Publ Weimar. "Franklin" marked. 47x52cm (18½x20½") Orig OL color. Ref: TMC 72, p.17, no.12. [34] **£580** $962

CHARTE UBER DIE XIII VEREINIGTEN STAATEN VON NORD-AMERICA ... [1784] After Homann. 45x58cm (17½x22½") Orig wash & OL color. [27] £513 **$850**

GUTHRIE

[ATLAS] AN ATLAS TO GUTHRIE'S GEOGRAPHICAL GRAMMAR [c.1797] Octavo, worn quarter leather binding; 28 maps with orig OL color by B. Baker, J. Russell & maybe others. Some lt transferring. [33] £513 **$850**

[BOOK WITH MAPS] GUTHRIE'S UNIVERSAL GEOGRAPHY, IMPROVED ... [1795] London. New enlarged ed. Quarto, leather in handmade burlap jacket; 24 B&W maps, incl NE US & Canada, eastern US, lacks The Sphere. Covers worn, detached; some maps sl foxed. [A10] £146 **$242**

THE BRITISH COLONIES IN NORTH AMERICA ... [1795] From *Atlas to Guthrie's System of Geography* ... London. 33x33cm (13x13") Orig OL color. Fine. Ref: Lepine 798; Phillips (A) 6006-21. [12] £136 **$225**

THE UNITED STATES OF AMERICA, ACCORDING TO THE TREATY OF PEACE OF 1784 [c.1785] 18x20cm (7x8") OL color. VG. [38] £151 **$250**

THE WEST INDIES FROM THE BEST AUTHORITIES [c.1800] From *Guthrie's Geography*. 19x32cm (7½x12½") OL color. Faint foxing; VG (A). [A4] £20 **$33**

GUYOT

THE WORLD IN HEMISPHERES [1875] Wash: Scribner Armstrong; Speller, sc. Double hemi & 4 sm hemis. 20x27cm (8x10½") Color. [19] £30 **$50**

HAELLSTROM

KARTA OFVER SVERIGE OCH NORRIGE [1815] Stockholm. 92x64cm (36½x25") Color. 25cm tear into image closed with thick paper; sm margin tears; ½cm worming along fold; ex lib NYHS. [A7] £208 **$345**

HAFFNER

ASIA [1684] From *Interioria Orientis Detecta*. M. Haffner. Map on visual scroll; plants below. 27x34cm (10½x13½") Uncolored. [34] £650 **$1,078**

HALL

[WORLD IN SET WITH 4 MAPS OF TERRA AUSTRALIS] [1605 (1643)] From Dutch ed of *Mundus Alter*. 5 maps with fanciful divisions of a southern continent. [no dimens] Ref: Shirley (W) 251, pl.198. [43] £422 **$700**

HALL, SIDNEY

CENTRAL AMERICA AND THE WEST INDIES FROM THE LATEST AND BEST AUTHORITIES [1840] London: Longman & Co. Linen backed pocket map. Incl Southern U.S & Republic of Texas to Amazon. 31x51cm (12½x20") VG. [16] £226 **$375**

MAP OF ROUTES TO THE PRINCIPAL MINING DISTRICTS IN THE CENTRAL STATES OF MEXICO [1829] Sidney Hall, London, based on information from diplomat Henry George Ward. Villas, pueblos, haciendas, ranchos, mines identified. 41x55cm (16x21½") Some wash color. [39] £121 **$200**

MEXICO AND GUATIMALA. CORRECTED FROM ORIGINAL INFORMATION COMMUNICATED BY SIMON A.G. BOURNE ESQ. [1828 (1830)] From 1st ed, *New General Atlas*. 41x51cm (16x20") OL color. Ref: Wheat (TM) 381; Phillips (A) 756-46. [12] £302 **$500**

NORTH AMERICA [c.1840] Large Texas republic. 37x26cm (15x10½") Later OL col. VG. [16] £90 **$150**

THE WORLD. ... BY S. HALL [1845] London: Longman & Co. Double hemi & 3rd sphere; with co-tidal lines. 22x39cm (8½x15½") Color. [19] £45 **$75**

UNITED STATES [c.1850] English school atlas map; TX incl Indian Terr. 19x26cm (7½x10½") Full color. Good. [16] £75 **$125**

WESTERN HEMISPHERE [c.1838] London: Longman, Orme & Co. Diameter: 42cm (16½") OL color. Lf margin chipped; good. [16] £181 **$300**

HALLEY

[WORLD] [c.1740] 52x144cm (20½x57") Full orig color. Sm mend lower c'fold; else exc. [44] £6,634 **$11,000**

TABULA TOTIUS ORBIS TERRARUM [1760] Similar to Mount & Page; Mercator proj; insular Calif; winds & magnetic influence indicated. 20x48cm (8x19") Color. [13] **Aus$480** £218 **$361**

HAPPEL

[WORLD. SET OF TWO HEMISPHERES] [1687] As in Matthaeus Wagner, *Mundis Mirabilis* ... Ulm. Insular Calif. On separate sheets, each 29x29cm (11½x11½") Color. Ref: Shirley (W) Corrigenda & Addenda 535A. [13] **Aus$7,400** £3,361 **$5,572**

HARDESTY

[ATLAS] **HISTORICAL ATLAS OF THE WORLD** [1876] Charles H. Jones & Theodore F. Hamilton, Chicago. Folio, roan backed cloth; colored maps. Extremities worn; preliminaries wrinkled. Ref: cf Phillips (A) 4136, calls for 49 maps. [A8] £451 **$747**

[ATLAS] **HISTORICAL HAND ATLAS ... GENERAL SURVEY OF THE WORLD ... MAP OF GALLIA COUNTY, AND HISTORIES OF LAWRENCE AND GALLIA COUNTIES, OHIO** [1882] Folio; 6 biblical maps, 51 US maps, 4 large tipped-in maps of NY, IL, OH, TX & Indian Terr., all in printed color; historical text; litho scenes & views. Irregular pagination (300+ pp). Rebound in three-quarter calf with orig gold-embossed cover; age toned; lt smudging at edges; occas tape repair; overall VG. [6] £392 **$650**

[BOOK WITH MAPS] **HARDESTY'S HISTORICAL AND GEOGRAPHICAL ENCYCLOPEDIA, ILLUSTRATED** [1883] Chicago; Toledo. Folio, half morocco; 314 & 29 pp colored maps, large oilskin paper maps of NY, OH, IL, TX & Indian Terr, CA & NV. Hinges sl cracked; superior. [16] £663 **$1,100**

[TEXAS: WESTERN PART] [1883] By Rand, McNally. 49x33cm (19½x13") Full printed color. Fine. [16] £90 **$150**

HARDESTY continued

MAP OF NEW MEXICO [1883] As in *Hardesty's Historical and Geographical Encyclopedia*. Printed by Rand McNally, issued under license. 51x36cm (20x14") Full color indicates land grant status. VG. [25] £60 **$100**

NORTHERN CALIFORNIA [1883] San Jose northward. 48x34cm (19x13½") Printed color by counties. Fine (A+). [A4] £43 **$72**

HARPER

MAP OF THE UNITED STATES AND TEXAS [c.1840] NY: Harper Brothers. 44x57cm (17½x22½") B&W. Trimmed to neatline for binding; some sm spots; good (B). [A3] £55 **$91**

HARPER'S WEEKLY

ASPEN AND ITS SURROUNDINGS - FROM A PHOTOGRAPH BY W.H. JACKSON & CO., DENVER COLORADO [Jan 19, 1889] 38x51cm (15x20") Uncolored. Nice. [26] £81 **$135**

PANORAMIC VIEW OF THE CITY OF TORONTO, CANADA WEST [Sept 8, 1860] After Wm. Armstrong drawing. 23x34cm (9x13½") B&W. Perfect. [12] £51 **$85**

POLITICAL MAP OF NEW JERSEY [Oct. 6, 1888] 1872 to 1884 national & state results by counties. Printed red & black. 36x24cm (14x9½") Fine. [12] £30 **$50**

HARRIS

A MAP OF THE COUNTY OF KENT [1719] John Harris; London. Dover view; border with 118 coats of arms. 2 sheets joined, 57x82cm (22x32") Color. [34] **£1,675 $2,778**

A PLAN OF THE CITY OF CANTON ON THE RIVER TA HOO [1764] 28x21cm (11x8") [11] £90 **$150**

A PROSPECT OF THE CITY OF GENOA [1764] Bird's-eye view. 18x37cm (7x14½") [11] £45 **$75**

PLANS OF THE OLD & NEW CITY OF NORTH PEKING YE METROPOLIS OF CHINA [1764] Plan of old city. 32x20cm (12½x7½") ["Tunxo in the Province of Peking" & "A Prospect of the Town of Batavia ..." offered at same price] [11] £45 **$75**

HARRISON

A GENERAL STEREOGRAPHIC MAP ON THE PLANE OF THE MERIDIAN [1783] Double hemi cut at Ferro. Woodman & Mutlow, sc 14x19cm (5½x7½") [19] £45 **$75**

A NEW MAP OF NORTH AMERICA [1785] 19x27cm (7½x10½") OL color. [9] £136 **$225**

A PARTICULAR MAP OF THE AMERICAN LAKES, RIVERS ETC. PAR LE SR. D'ANVILLE ... [1790] 51x71cm (20x28") B&W. Trace of foxing; fine. Ref: Marshall I-411-2-6. [12] £332 **$550**

HAYDEN, F.V. Try *U.S.*

DRAINAGE MAP OF COLORADO [1877] 65x89cm (25½x35") Some browning at folds; separations at junctions: generally VG. [7] £90 **$150**

ECONOMIC MAP OF COLORADO [1877] Publ in *Atlas of Colorado*. 76x94cm (30x37") Printed color. [27] £151 **$250**

[SAME TITLE] [1878] Color-keyed agriculture & minerals; topo not shown. 65x90cm (25½x35½") Folded; some browning & reinforcements, no loss. ["General Geologic Map ..." offered at same price] [10] £90 **$150**

[SAME TITLE] [1881] USGS. 76x94cm (30x37") Color indicates natural resources. VG. [25] £106 **$175**

MAP OF THE ELK MOUNTAINS COLORADO FROM SURVEY BY G.B. CHITTENDEN IN 1874 WITH GEOLOGY BY F.V. HAYDEN AND W.H. HOLMES [1876] Hayden Survey. Color & background printing indicates geology. Inset sketches. 48x25cm (19x10") VG. [26] £54 **$90**

MAP OF THE SHOSHONE GEYSER BASIN, WEST END OF SHOSHONE LAKE, YELLOWSTONE NATIONAL PARK [1878] After J.E. Mushbach notes & sketches; issued by Surveys. 61x88cm (24x34½") [40] £27 **$45**

MAP OF THE SOURCES OF THE SNAKE RIVER, WITH ITS TRIBUTARIES TOGETHER WITH PORTIONS OF THE MADISON AND YELLOW STONE ... [c.1875] Incl Jackson Hole area. 28x25cm (11x10") Uncolored. Folds as issued; VG. [25] £48 **$80**

NORTH-WESTERN COLORADO AND PART OF UTAH [1877] From *Atlas of Colorado*. Colored geological map. 57x88cm (22½x34½") [40] £60 **$100**

PART OF CENTRAL WYOMING [1877] Geologic map in color with contour lines; Rawlins to Lander. 65x85cm (25½x33½") Folded; minor browning & separations. [10] £75 **$125**

PRELIMINARY MAP OF CENTRAL COLORADO SHOWING THE REGION SURVEYED IN 1873 AND 1874 [1876] Hayden Surveys; by J.T. Gardner, G.B. Becker, Henry Gannett, A.D. Wilson, S.B. Ladd. Topo by hachures. 64x56cm (25x22") Uncolored. Repaired tear. [26] £72 **$120**

HAYDEN, F.V. continued

PRELIMINARY MAP OF THE EASTERN BASE OF THE ROCKY MOUNTAINS ... [1874] Pueblo to WY line. 121x26cm (48x10½") Folded; VG. [10] £106 **$175**
[SAME TITLE] [1874 (1876)] 122x28cm (48x11") Uncolored. Some repairs verso. [25] £75 **$125**
THE MOQUI MESAS [1876] Hopi Indian country. 19x34cm (7½x13½") [10] £45 **$75**
UPPER GEYSER BASIN, FIRE HOLE RIVER ... 1871 [1872] Incl Old Faithful. 28x25cm (11x10") Uncolored. Folded as issued; VG. ["Lower Geyser Basin ..." & "... Shoshone Geysers ..." offered at same price] [25] £24 **$40**
YELLOWSTONE NATIONAL PARK [1882] Hayden Surveys, *U.S. Geographical and Geological Survey of the Territories*. Issued with 12th Annual Report. 109x61cm (43x24") Full color. VG. [25] £75 **$125**

HAYWARD

HAYWARD'S MAP OF THE CITY OF BROOKLYN [1843] Folding map with worn cloth cover. Wards delineated; Brooklyn Heights view. 34x49cm (13½x19½") OL color. Few fold separations; else VG. [38] £211 **$350**

HEATHER

A NEW CHART OF HOLLAND WITH THE ENTRANCES TO THE SCHELD, &C. ... [1802] By Norie; J. Stephenson, sc. Insets. 63x79cm (25x31") Occas color. Narrow orig top margin. [47] £380 **$630**
A NEW CHART OF THE CATTEGAT AND BALTIC OR EAST SEA BY WILLIAM HEATHER 1801 [1801] Skagerack to Gulfs of Riga, Finland & Bothnia; 6 harbor insets. 94x123cm (37x48½") Edges discolored; sm fold split. [47] £780 **$1,294**
A NEW CHART OF THE GULF OF FINLAND SURVEYED BY ORDER OF THE EMPEROR OF RUSSIA AND KING OF SWEDEN WITH ADDITIONS AND IMPROVEMENTS BY WILLIAM HEATHER 1802 [1802] 5 harbor insets; recognition drawings. 2 sheets joined. [no dimens] Sm c'fold split; edges discolored. [47] £860 **$1,426**
SOUS'S CHART OF THE CATTEGAT [1801] Inset: The Sound. 64x78cm (25x30½") Narrow orig margins; edges discolored; minor rust marks at c'fold. [47] £480 **$796**
TO EVAN NEAPEAN ... THIS CHART OF THE SOUND AND GROUNDS IS HUMBLY DEDICATED ... [1801] The Oresund. 64x77cm (25x30½") Narrow orig margins. [47] £540 **$896**
TO THE MERCHANTS AND MASTERS OF VESSELS EMPLOYED IN THE COASTING TRADE, &C. THIS CHART OF THE EAST COAST OF ENGLAND AND SCOTLAND FROM THE HUMBER TO ABERDEEN IS MOST RESPECTFULLY DEDICATED ... [1798] Harbor insets. 62x77cm (24½x30½") Sm c'fold split; edges discolored. [47] £340 **$564**
TO THE MERCHANTS AND MASTERS OF VESSELS EMPLOYED IN THE COASTING TRADE, &C. THIS CHART OF THE EAST COAST OF ENGLAND IS MOST RESPECTFULLY DEDICATED ... [1802] By Norie; J. Stephenson, sc. Orford Ness to Spurn Head. 63x74cm (25x29") Narrow top margin; 2 sm spots at c'fold. [47] £320 **$531**
TO THE RIGHT HONORABLE LORD DUNCAN ... THIS CHART OF THE COASTS OF HOLLAND AND ENGLAND ... [IS] DEDICATED [1799] Drawn by Norie. 64x77cm (25x30½") Occas color. Top margin age-toned. [47] £380 **$630**
TO THE RIGHT HONORABLE THE MASTER ... TRINITY HOUSE. THIS CHART OF THE DOWNS AND MARGATE ROADS ... [IS] DEDICATED ... [1797] By Norie. 62x78cm (24½x31") Lights in red. [47] £290 **$481**

HENNEPIN

A MAP OF A LARGE COUNTRY NEWLY DISCOVERED IN THE NORTHERN AMERICA SITUATED BETWEEN NEW MEXICO AND THE FROZEN SEA ... [1698] From English ed. East coast to west of Mississippi River. 37x43cm (14½x17") Several folds, fold tear reinforced verso; narrow side margins; lt foxing/toning. [A10] £555 **$920**
CARTE D'UN NOUVEAU MONDE, ENTRE LE NOUVEAU MEXIQUE ET LA MER GLACIALLE ... [1683 / 1698] From *Nouveau Voyage d'un Pais Plus Grand que l'Europe*. Five near-correct Great Lakes. 29x47cm (11½x18½") Exc. Ref: Karpinski (MI) p.94-5; Kaufman (Gt.Lakes) #13. [24] £2,111 **$3,500**

HERBERT

A NEW MAP, OR CHART IN MERCATORS PROJECTION OF PART OF EUROPE, ASIA AND AFRICA [c.1720 - 1763] 1st publ by Senex. 62x79cm (24½x31") Color. Laid on tissue. [34] £1,000 **$1,658**
A NEW MAP, OR CHART IN MERCATORS PROJECTION OF THE ETHIOPIC OCEAN WITH PART OF AFRICA AND SOUTH AMERICA [c.1720 - 1763] By Senex, with revisions. Covers most of South America. 62x79cm (24½x31") Minor paper defects. [34] £650 **$1,078**
A NEW MAP, OR CHART IN MERCATORS PROJECTION, OF THE WESTERN OR ATLANTIC OCEAN, WITH PART OF EUROPE, AFRICA AND AMERICA [c.1720 - 1763] Orig publ by Senex; revisions described; separately issued. 62x79cm (24½x31") Color. [34] £1,450 **$2,405**

HERISSON
CARTE GENERALE ET ROUTIERE DU ROYAUME DE FRANCE [1816] 40-section linen-backed map with orig board slipcase. 131x186cm (51½x73") OL color. Several joints cracked; exc. [A8] £451 **$747**

HERSBACH
EIGENTLICHE VERZEICHNUS, DIESES IM ... JAHR 1618 ... [1619] Celestial chart with comet track. 30x25cm (12x10") Exc. Ref: De La Lande, *Bibliographie Astronomique*, p.178. [2] £1,146 **$1,900**

HIGHWAY MAPS
HIGHWAY MAP OF COLORADO [c.1928] Highway Map Co., Topeka, KS. Blue ink on off white paper. Road service listed at side; ads verso. 41x66cm (16x26") VG. [26] £27 **$45**

ROAD MAP OF HENNEPIN AND RAMSEY COUNTIES WITH ADJACENT PORTIONS OF ANOKA, WRIGHT, CARVER, SCOTT, DAKOTA AND WASHINGTON COUNTIES, MINNESOTA [c.1910] P.M. Dahl, Minneapolis. 43x53cm (17x21") Full color. Old folds with minor repairs. [25] £45 **$75**

STATE HIGHWAY DEPARTMENT'S OFFICIAL AUTOMOBILE ROAD MAP OF THE STATE OF OREGON [1923] Road surfaces color coded. 33x51cm (13x20") Substantial color. VG. [26] £24 **$40**

HILDBURGHAUSEN BIBLIOGRAPHISCHES INSTITUT
[**AUSTRIA: VORALBERG; TIROL. & LIECHTENSTEIN**] [c.1870] Extent: Lake Constance; Innsbruck; Bozen; Chur. 16x21cm (6x8½") [48] DM 130 £45 **$74**

AMERICA 1841 [1841] 26x21cm (10½x8") OL color. Rough rt edge; soft fold; VG (A). [A4] DM 48 **$79**

BLICK VOM TELEGRAPH HILL AUF DIE STADT, DEN HAFEN UND DIE BAY [c.1850-60] Steel engraved view. [no dimens] Color. [48] DM 190 £66 **$109**

BRASILIEN [c.1850] After Radefeld. 25x20cm (10x7½") OL color. [48] DM 110 £38 **$63**

BRITISCHES NORD-AMERICA [c.1850] After Radefeld. 22x26cm (8½x10½") OL col. [48] DM 120 £41 **$68**

DIE REPUBLIK POLEN NACH IHREM BESTANDE IM JAHRE 1772 UND DAS KONIGREICH POLEN SEIT DEM JAHRE 1815 [c.1850] Insets: Warsaw; Vilna area. 18x25cm (7½x10") Old color. [48] DM 100 £35 **$57**

FRANKREICH [c.1850] By Radefeld. 20x26cm (8x10") OL color. [48] DM 20 £7 **$11**

HANNOVER [c.1855] Plan with legend. Lithocolor. 16x14cm (6½x5½") [48] DM 180 £62 **$103**

KARTE VON DEM DEUTSCHEN MEERE UND DEN ANGRANZENDEN THEILEN DES ATLANTISCHEN OCEANS ... [c.1850] Bay of Biscay to Norway; insets. 28x22cm (11x8½") Old col. Browning. [48] DM 80 £28 **$46**

NEUESTE KARTE VON NORDAMERIKA IN 4 BLATTERN [1867] Newfoundland & Vancouver to Panama; several insets. 4 sheets in orig folder, each about 34x43cm (13½x17") OL col. Lt foxing. [48] DM 180 £62 **$103**

SPANIEN UND PORTUGAL [c.1850] 21x26cm (8½x10½") OL color. [Turkey in Europe; "Graecia Antiqua" offered at same price] [48] DM 20 £7 **$11**

VEREINIGTE STAATEN VON NORD-AMERICA UND MEXICO [c.1850] By Radefeld. 19x26cm (7½x10") OL color. [48] DM 50 £17 **$28**

VERGLEICHENDE UBERSICHT BEKANNTER HOHEN UND ORTE DER ERDE UBER DER MEERES-FLACHE [c.1850] By Renner. 400 mountains. 22x26cm (8½x10") [48] DM 20 £7 **$11**

HILL
A MAP OF CAPE COD, AND THE PARTS ADJACENT [1791] Appeared in *The Massachusetts Magazine*. S. Hill, Boston. Shoreline map, Cape Ann to Narragansett Bay, with the islands; accompanied article proposing a Cape Cod canal. 32x27cm (12½x11") Lower rt margin replaced; few mends; overall VG. Ref: Wheat & Brun 209. [24] £1,086 **$1,800**

HINTON
A GEOLOGICAL MAP OF THE UNITED STATES [1831] From *The History and Topography of the United States*. Engraved by Fenner, Sears & Co. 24x39cm (9½x15½") Color. Few foxing spots; o/w fine. [28] £112 **$185**

[**SAME TITLE**] [1832 (1842)] From *History and Topography of the United States*. Coast to coast; 9 colors only to Rockies. 25x39cm (10x15½") Vert folds as issued. Ref: Howes (US) H512. [12] £106 **$175**

MAP OF MAINE, NEW HAMPSHIRE AND VERMONT [1832] Hinton, Simpkin & Marshall, 36x25cm (14½x10") Uncolored. Ref: Cobb (NH) 114. [22] £39 **$65**

MAP OF THE STATE OF MISSOURI [1832] London: Hinton, Simpkin and Marshall. 25x37cm (10x14½") Uncolored. Ref: Karrow (MW) 9-0771. [22] £84 **$140**

MAP OF THE STATES OF KENTUCKY AND TENNESSEE [1831] From *The History and Topography of the United States*. 25x39cm (10x15½") Uncolored. [22] £72 **$120**

HINTON continued

MAP OF THE STATES OF MISSOURI AND ILLINOIS [1832] From *History and Topography of the United States*. Hinton, Simpkin & Marshall. Southern two-thirds IL only. 28x37cm (11x14½") B&W. Lt foxing; date trimmed below by binder; else exc. Ref: Karrow 9-0772. [12] £81 **$135**

MAP OF THE STATES OF NORTH & SOUTH CAROLINA [1832] From same source. Charleston inset. 25x40cm (10x16") Uncolored. Ref: Karpinski (Carolina) 155,156. [22] £81 **$135**

MAP OF THE STATES OF PENNSYLVANIA AND NEW JERSEY [1832] Hinton, Simpkin and Marshall. 15 NJ counties; Phila inset. 25x39cm (10x15½") Uncolored. Ref: Simonetti 351. [22] £42 **$70**

MAP OF THE UNITED STATES OF AMERICA AND NOVA SCOTIA, &C. &C. [1832] Hinton, Simpkin & Marshall. Inset: US claims in northwest to 54-40. 25x39cm (10x15½") Newer color. Fine. [A2] £119 **$198**

HOBBS

A GENERAL CHART OF THE INDIAN AND PART OF THE PACIFIC OCEANS, SHEWING THE VARIOUS PASSAGES TO & FROM CHINA, AUSTRALIA, NEW ZEALAND, &C. [1851] 5 insets; 3 joinable sheets, overall 110x199cm (43½x78½") MS tracks & notes; scattered mildew; modern rebacking; generally VG. [15] £211 **$350**

HOFMANN

NOVA DELINEATIO URBIS ET TEMPLI HIEROSOLYMARUM ... [c.1740] 19x28cm (7½x11") Color. Exc. Ref: Laor 1037. [24] £196 **$325**

HOLLAR

A NEW MAP OF BARKSHIRE WITH ALL THE HUNDREDS, PARKES AND OTHER PLACES THEREUNTO BELONGING [c.1715] London: Henry Overton. 1666 etching; reduced Speed map with Windsor Castle. 37x50cm (14½x19½") Orig OL color. Sl browning at c'fold. Ref: Pennington "Hollar" 658. [46] £780 $1,294

HOLMES

[NEW YORK CITY] MAP SHOWING ALL THE FARM AND BOUNDARY LINES OF THE ESTATES AS THEY EXISTED ... APTHORPES [ETC.] [c.1870] NY: Mayer, Merkel & Ottmann. NYC, 70th to 84th St, west of CPW. 69x98cm (27x38½") Color. Minor wrinkling; lacks sm part top lf corner to image; closed tears; mounted on stiff sheet. [A7] £104 **$172**

A NEW MAP OF KANSAS [1859] W.H. Holmes; Phila: Desilver. Separately issued. Incl present CO to Rockies; Indian battle areas identified. 42x69cm (16½x27") Color. Lt browned, more darkened at vert fold & side margins. [A8] £1,942 **$3,220**

HOMANN & HOMANN HEIRS   Try *Doppelmayr*

[ATLAS, COMPOSITE] [dated 1705-1750] By Homann Heirs, Schenk, Valk, Visscher, others. 19 maps incl World, America, Gt. Britain, etc. Folio, half sheep; 53x34cm (21x13½") Contemp color; cartouches mostly B&W. Covers worn; tears, repairs; creasing, occas spotting; c'fold splits 7 maps; dampstaining corners Asia & Africa; Germany defective. [A5] £3,680 $6,102

[CONTINENTS, 4 MAPS ON SINGLE SHEET: AFRICA, AMERICAS; ASIA; EUROPE] [c.1711] J.B. Homann. Each about 17x21cm (6½x8½") Color. Minor dampstain margin into one image. [A8] £694 **$1,150**

[PORTRAIT] IOANNES BAPTISTA HOMANN SAC. CAES. REGO. CATH. MAJ. GEOGRAPHUS, NEC NON REGIAE SCIENTIARUM SOCIETIS BEROLINENSIS MEMBRUM ... [c.1760] After Johann. Kenckel painting; Johann Wilhelm Winter, sc. 38x27cm (15x10½") Uncolored. Fine. [4] £350 $581

ACCURATE VORSTELLUNG DER HOCH FURSTL. BISCHOFFL. RESIDENZ UND HAUPT-STADT WURTZBURG ... [1723] J.B. Homann. 49x58cm (19x23") Partial contemp color. C'fold tear. Framed. [A5] £173 $287

ACCURATER GRUNDRISS U: GEGEND DER KONIGL: GROSS BRITTANNISCHEN HAUPT UND RESIDENZ-STADT LONDON ... [c.1710] J.B. Homann. Environs of London; views. 50x59cm (19½x23") Orig body color by hundreds. Ref: Howgego 58. [47] £650 $1,078

[SAME TITLE] [c.1710] J.B. Homann. Environs of London; 5 views. 50x59cm (19½x23") Orig body color. Ref: Howgego 58. [46] £540 $896

[SAME TITLE] [c.1720] J.B. Homann. Views. 49x58cm (19½x23") Full wash & OL col. [11] £392 **$650**

[SAME TITLE] [c.1720] J.B. Homann. 5 insets. 49x58cm (19½x23") Orig wash color on map; B&W insets. Exc. [23] £724 **$1,200**

ACCURATER PROSPECT UND GRUNDRIS DER KONIGL: GROS-BRITTANISCH: HAUPT UND RESIDENZ STADT LONDON ... [c.1700] J.B. Homann. Map, post-fire view, 2 building views. 50x59cm (19½x23") Orig body color. Ref: Howgego 51b. [47] £1,360 $2,255

HOMANN & HOMANN HEIRS continued

AFRICA SECUNDUM LEGITIMAS PROJECTIONIS STEREOGRAPHICAE REGULAS ... [c.1740] By J.M. Haas; publ by Homann Heirs. Ornate B&W cartouche. 47x56cm (18½x22") Orig color. Fine. Ref: Norwich 83. [A2] £315 **$523**

AMERICA SEPTENTRIONALIS A DOMINO D'ANVILLE IN GALLIS EDITA NUNC IN ANGLIA COLONIIS IN INTERIOREM VIRGINIAM DEDUCTIS NEC NON FLUVII OHIO CURSU ... [1756] Extensive text. 46x51cm (18x20") Full color. [27] £377 **$625**

[SAME TITLE] [1756] Homann Heirs. 48x52cm (18½x20½") OL color. Horiz crease to fold map into quarters. [another with sh separation lower fold margin sold at $488] [A7] £555 **$920**

AMERICAE ... [1746] Homann Heirs. 50x58cm (19½x22½") Color. Minor browning & soiling; sm stains ocean areas & top margin. [A8] £381 **$632**

AMERICAE MAPPA GENERALIS ... MDCCXXXXVI [1746] By J.M. Haas. Peninsular Calif. 49x56cm (19½x22") Orig body color. Ref: Wheat (TM) 237, misdated 1796. [47] £780 **$1,294**

[SAME TITLE] [1746] 46x53cm (18x21") Orig color. Faint uniform age toning; 2 sm wormholes blank area; minor ink transfer; faint printer's crease off c'fold. Not examined outside vacuum wrap. [A1] £730 **$1,210**

[SAME TITLE] [1746] Homann Heirs. 46x53cm (18½x21") Orig color. VG. [A2] £630 **$1,045**

[SAME TITLE] [1746] 47x54cm (18½x21½") Orig wash col. Fine. Ref: Wagner (NW) 555. [31] £513 **$850**

AMPLISSIMAE REGIONIS MISSISSIPI SEU PROVINCIAE LUDOVICIANAE A R.P. LUDOVICO HENNEPIN FRANCISC MISS IN AMERICA SEPTENTRIONALI ANNO 1687. DETECTAE, NUNC GALLORUM COLONIIS ET ACTIONUM NEGOTIIS TOTO ORBE CELEBERRIMAE... [1714] After De L'Isle. 48x58cm (19x23") Full orig color. Exc. Ref: Goss (NA) 49. cf Cumming (SE) 170. [24] £1,930 **$3,200**

[SAME TITLE] [1720] J.B. Homann. Early printing; edge bound, without c'fold. 49x58cm (19½x23") Full orig color. Exc. Ref: Cumming (SE) 170; Goss (N Amer) 49. [2] £1,176 **$1,950**

ASIA SECUNDUM LEGITIMAS PROJECTIONIS STEREOGRAPHICAE ... [1744] Homann Heirs. 50x56cm (19½x22") Full color. [20] £528 **$875**

BAVARIAE CIRCULUS ET ELECTORAT [c.1720] 56x47cm (22x18½") Color. [39] £211 **$350**

CARTA GEOGRAPHICA ... LO STATO DELLA REPUBLICA DI GENOVA ... DER STAAT VON DER REPUBLIC GENOVA, NACH SEINER EINTHEILUNG IN DIE OST- U. WEST-REVIER [1743] Homann Heirs. Monaco to La Spezia, old color; below: B&W plan & view of Genoa. 51x58cm (20x23") Sh wrinkle at margin; lower c'fold tear restored. [68] **DM 900** £311 **$515**

CARTE DE L'ISLE DE LA MARTINIQUE DRESSEE PAR MR. BELLIN ... [1762] Homann Heirs. 47x56cm (18½x22") Full color. [20] £377 **$625**

CARTE DE LA TERRE SAINTE DIVISEE SELON LES DOUZE TRIBUS D'ISRAEL [1750] Homann Heirs. 50x75cm (20x29½") Color. [A8] £416 **$690**

CARTE DES POSTES D'ALLEGMANE ET DE PAYS VOISINS. NEUE VERMEHRTE POST CHARTE DURCH GANTZ TEUTSCHLAND ... VON HERRN JOH. PETER NELL [c.1710] Folds into sm octavo stiff covers. 44x56cm (17½x22") OL color. Covers soiled & worn; map age toned, minor wear to creases; soiled verso; VG. [6] £238 **$395**

CASTILIAE NOVAE PARTS ORIENTALIS PROVINCIAS CEUNCA ET GUADALAXARA [1781] Homann Heirs. SW Spain. 52x44cm (20½x17") Orig OL color. Lt toning; else fine (A). [A3] £83 **$138**

CIRCULI FRANCONIAE PARS ORIENTALIS ... [c.1740] Nuremberg at ctr. 56x49cm (22x19") Full orig color. Oil stain & sh tear lf margin just into map; o/w good. [11] £136 **$225**

DAS CASPISCHE MEER [ON SHEET WITH] DAS LAND KAMTZADALIE SONST JEDSO [c.1720] J.B. Homann. 2 maps, vert cartouche between. 49x58cm (19½x23") Orig wash color. Exc. [43] £181 **$300**

[SAME TITLE] [c.1720] J.B. Homann. 50x58cm (19½x23") Wash & OL color. [A7] £139 **$230**

DIE GEGEND UM PRAG, ODER DER ALTE PRAGER KREYS ... [1742] Homann Heirs. French title also. 51x58cm (20x23") Contemp color. Sl soiling margin. [A6] **£172** $286

DIE INSELN MALTA UND GOZZO [1808] Homann Heirs. With Valetta plan. 50x59cm (19½x23") Orig color; later additions. [46] **£1,050** $1,741

DOMINIA ANGLORUM IN AMERICA SEPTENTRIONALI. SPECIALIBUS MAPPIS LONDINI PRIMUM A MOLLIO EDITA, NUNC RECUSA AB HOMANNIANIS HERED / DIE GROS-BRITANNISCHE COLONIE-LAENDER IN NORD-AMERICA [c.1710] Homann Heirs. 4 maps after Moll: Newfoundland & Nova Scotia; New England; Virginia & Maryland; Carolina, 51x55cm (20x21½") Orig wash color. Ref: Cumming (SE) 233. [47] £550 **$912**

[SAME TITLE] [1740] 51x56cm (20x22") Body color. Sl creasing at fold. [A6] £391 **$649**

[SAME TITLE] [c.1763] Homann Heirs. 50x55cm (19½x22") Orig color. Fold split to lower neatline; o/w fine. Ref: Cumming (SE) 233. Van Ermen p.70-1. [A1] £415 **$688**

HOMANN & HOMANN HEIRS continued

DUCATUS BRUNSUICENSIS IN TRES SUOS PRINCIPATUS CALENBERGICUM SC. GRUBENHAG. ET GUELPHERBITANUM DISTINCTE DIVISI, NEC NON ESPISCOPATUS HILDESIENSIS, PR. HALBER. COMITATUS SCHAUENBURGICI ... [c.1720] J.B. Homann. 51x60cm (20x23½") Color. [48] DM 450 £155 $257

DUCATUS STIRIAE [c.1720] J.B. Homann. 50x59cm (19½x23") Old color. [48] DM 550 £190 $315

ERFORDIAE PRIMARIAE THURINGIAE URBIS ... ERFURTH, DER HAUPT STADT IN THURINEN NEUESTER ... GRUNDRISS [1745] Plan with legend & view. 52x58cm (20½x22½") Old col. [48] DM 1,500 £518 $859

EUROPA CHRISTIANI ORBIS DOMINA ... [c.1710] 48x57cm (19x22½") Old color. Repaired tear bottom c'fold; fine. [1] £482 $800

HEMISPHAERIUM COELI AUSTRALI [c.1730] J.B. Homann. 50x60cm (19½x23½") Color. [A8] £555 $920

HIBERNIAE REGNUM [c.1680] J.B. Homann. (date from catalogue) 58x49cm (23x19½") Color. Sm spot offshore; sl soiling; minor browning at folds. [A7] £242 $402

HIBERNIAE REGNUM TAM IN PRAECIPUAS ULTONIAE, CONNACIAE, LACENIAE ET MOMONIAE ... [c.1720] J.B. Homann. 56x48cm (22x19") Orig color. Sm ink stain Irish Sea; o/w fine. [14] £513 $850

[SAME TITLE] [c.1720] 57x48cm (22½x19") Orig color. Some lt margin soiling; part of border added in facsimile; sm margin tear at horiz c'fold; o/w VG to fine. [A1] £199 $330

IMPERIUM TURCICUM IN EUROPA, ASIA ET AFRICA [c.1720] J.B. Homann. Wash & OL color. 51x61cm (20½x24") Scattered soiling, mostly margins. [A7] £104 $172

INSULA CRETA HODIE CANDIA ... [c.1720] Crete & islands to north. 48x58cm (19x22½") Orig wash & OL color. Lower margin sl soiled. [11] £151 $250

INSULAE CORSICAE [1735] 56x50cm (22x19½") Old color. Brown spots lf. [48] DM 690 £238 $395

IUDAEA SEU PALAESTINA OB SACRATISSIMA REDEMTORIS VESTIGIA HODIE DICTA TERRA SANCTA PROUT OLIM IN DUODECIM TRIBUS DIVISA SEPARATIS AB INVICEM REGNIS IUDA ET ISRAEL ... COLLECTA EX TABULIS GUIL. SANSONIJ ... [1707] Publ in J.B. Homann's 1st atlas; reprinted thereafter. 48x57cm (19x22½") Color. Fine. Ref: Laor 340. [14] £724 $1,200

[SAME TITLE] [1707] 48x55cm (19x21½") Orig col. Few stains; else exc. Ref: Laor 340. [24] £513 $850

MAPPA GEOGRAPHICA ... INDIAE OCCIDENTALIS ... [1740] After 1731 D'Anville map. Gulf, Caribbean & adjacent; inset maps & view. 58x48cm (23x19") Orig OL color. Fold lt browned; sl wrinkling one border. [27] £513 $850

MAPPA GEOGRAPHICA PROVINCIAE NOVAE EBORACI AB ANGLIS NEW YORK DICTAE EX AMPLIORI DELINEATIONE AD EXACTAS DIMENSIONES CONCINNATA IN ARCTIUS SPATIUM REDACTA CURA CLAUDII JOSEPHI SAUTHIER ... [1778] Homann Heirs, after Lotter-Sauthier. Two unjoined sheets, overall 76x58cm (30x23") OL color. Minor browning. [A7] £520 $862

MAPPA SPECIALIS PRINCIPATUS HALBERSTADIENSIS ... [1750] Homann Heirs. 50x56cm (19½x22") Old color. [48] DM 490 £169 $280

MAPPE MONDE QUI REPRESENTE LES DEUX HEMISPHERES [1746] Homann Heirs. With polar & astronomical diagrams. 46x55cm (18½x21½") Color. Occas lt soiling; VG. [14] £1,206 $2,000

MARCHIONATUS MORAVIAE CIRCULI ZNOYMENSIS ET IGLAVIENSIS [c.1720] J.B. Homann. 50x59cm (19½x23½") Color. Scattered soiling. [A7] £121 $201

MARCHIONATUS MORAVIAE CIRCULUS OLOMUCENSIS [c.1720] Dimensions for each of a pair of sheets: 50x58cm (19½x23") Old color. [48] DM 390 £135 $223

NEU VERMEHRTE POST CHARTE DURCH GANTZ TEUTSCHLAND [c.1730] J.B. Homann. 49x58cm (19½x23") OL color. Margins trimmed, but ample; sm tears closed on verso. [A8] £69 $115

NEU VERMEHRTER CURIOSER MEILEN-ZEIGER DER VORNEHMSTEN STAEDTE IN EUROPA BESONDERS IN TEUTSCHLAND, WIE VIEL GEMEINE TEUTSCHE MEILEN SOLCHE VONEINANDER ENTLEGEN [1731] Homann Heirs. Mileage table between 100+ European cities. 47x56cm (18½x22") Old color. Weak impression cartouche area; 2 sm spots. [48] DM 440 £152 $252

[SAME TITLE] [1731] Distance table. 45x53cm (18x21") Orig color. Lt dampstain; lt color transfer from red line. [A2] £66 $110

NEUE WELT KARTE WELCHE AUF ZWOO KUGELSLASCHEN DIE HAUPT THEILE DER ERDE ... [1784] Double hemi. 48x57cm (19x22½") Orig color. [13] Aus$2,200 £999 $1,656

[SAME TITLE] [1784] Homann Heirs. 48x56cm (19x22") Color. Minor repair. [19] £377 $625

NOVA ANGLIA SEPTENTRIONALI AMERICAE IMPLANTATA ANGLORUMQUE COLONIIS FLORENTISSIMA GEOGRAPHICE EXHIBITA ... [1720] J.B. Homann. 49x58cm (19½x23") Orig body color. Ref: Goss (NA) #50; Portinaro & Knirsch pl.116. [47] £780 $1,294

[SAME TITLE] [1730] J.B. Homann. 49x58cm (19½x23") Orig color. Exc. [24] £844 $1,400

HOMANN & HOMANN HEIRS continued

NOVA MARIS CASPII ET REGIONIS USBECK ...   [1735-] Homann Heirs. 49x59cm (19½x23") Orig color. [34] **£400** $664

PALAESTINA IN XII TRIBUS DIVISA CUM TERRIS ADIACENTIBUS DENUO REVISA & COPIOSIR REDDITA. STUDIO IOHANNIS CHRISTOPH. HARENBERG ...   [1750] Homann Heirs. 44x52cm (17½x20½") Orig full color. Margin staining; image clean, VG (A). Ref: Laor 325.   [A3] £302 **$501**

PARTIE OCCIDENTALE DE LA NOUVELLE FRANCE OU DU CANADA. PAR MR. BELLIN ...   [1755] After Bellin 1745 map. 43x53cm (17x21") Exc.   [2] £905 **$1,500**

[SAME TITLE]   [1755] Homann Heirs, after Bellin. 44x55cm (17½x21½") OL color.   [A7] £902 **$1,495**

PER INCLYTI CIRCULI SUEVICI ... SUEVIAE UNIVERSAE DESCRIPTIONEM   [c.1750] Homann Heirs. 1st ed. Southwestern Germany and adjacent in 8 parts on 7 sheets. Overall 144x135cm (56½x53") OL color.   [48] **DM 12,000** £4,143 $6,870

PRINCIPATUS CATALONIAE NEC NON COMITATUUM RUSCINONENSIS ET CERRETANAIE NOVA TABULA   [c.1735] J.B. Homann. 48x56cm (19x22") Orig body color.   [46] **£340** $564

PROSPECT UND GRUND-RISS DER KAYSERL RESIDENZ-STADT WEIN ...   [c.1720] Vienna area & view. 50x58cm (19½x22½") Orig body color. Dark impression.   [46] **£540** $896

PROSPECT UND GRUNDRISS DER WELTBERUHINTEN KONIGLICHE HAUBT STADT PARIS   [c.1730] J.B. Homann. Plan & view, both keyed. 49x57cm (19½x22½") Orig wash color. Good.   [29] £905 **$1,500**

REGNI BOHEMIAE, DUCATUS SILESIAE, MARCHIONATUS MORAVIAE ET LUSATIAE   [c.1730] 47x56cm (18½x22") Full orig color. Old fold split repair; clean, sound; good (B).   [A4] £66 **$109**

REGNI GALLIAE SEU FRANCIAE ET NAVARRAE ...   [1741] Homann Heirs; after De L'Isle. 48x57cm (19x22½") Orig color. Faint foxing rt corners; lt water stain onto cartouche; o/w fine.   [A2] £73 **$121**

REGNI MEXICANI SEU NOVAE HISPANIAE LUDOVICIANAE, N. ANGLIAE, CAROLINAE, VIRGINIAE, ET PENSYLVANIAE NEC NON INSULARUM ARCHIPELAGI MEXICANI IN AMERICA SEPTENTRIONALI ACCURATA TABULA ...   [c.1720] J.B Homann. 48x57cm (19x22½") Orig color. Trimmed to neatlines; rebacked; minute hole repaired; o/w VG to fine. Ref: Van Ermen 22.   [A2] £597 **$990**

[SAME TITLE]   [c.1720] J.B. Homann. 49x57cm (19½x22½") Col. Lt browning at fold.   [A7] £520 **$862**

[SAME TITLE]   [1725] As in *Atlas Novus*. 48x57cm (18½x22½") Full color.   [20] £1,357 **$2,250**

[SAME TITLE]   [c.1745] From Homann Heirs' *Atlas Geographicus* ... Based on De L'Isle. 47x56cm (18½x22") Orig wash col. Ref: Van Ermen Cumming (SE) 137; Van Ermen p.42; Martin (TX) p.96.   [12] £905 **$1,500**

REGNI SUICIAE ...   [c.1740] Incl Finland, Baltics, most of Norway. 49x56cm (19½x22") Full orig wash & OL color. Margins sl frayed.   [11] £136 **$225**

REGNORUM HISPANIAE ET PORTU GALLIAE TABULA GENERALIS DE L'ISLIANA   [c.1730] J.B. Homann. 47x57cm (18½x22½") Orig color. Faint foxing rt corners; waterstain lower lf; o/w fine.   [A2] £116 **$193**

REGNORUM HUNGARIAE, DALMATIA, CROATIAE, SCLAVONIAE, BOSNIAE, SERVIAE ET PRINCIPATUS TRANSYLVANIAE ...   [1720] J.B. Homann. 48x57cm (19x22½") Newer color. Fine.   [14] £329 **$545**

REGNUM PORTUGALLIAE DIVISUM IN QUINQUE PROVINCIAS MAJORES ...   [1736] J.B. Homann. 59x45cm (23x18") Orig color. Lt waterstain top lf onto cartouche & lower margin; margin tear top lf; o/w fine.   [A2] £133 **$220**

S.R.I. CIRCULUS RHENANUS INFERIOR SIVE ELECTORUM RHENI COMPLECTENS TRES ARCHIEPISCOPATUS, MOGUNTINUM COLONIENSEM ET TREVIRENSEM, PALATINATUM RHENI, COMIT. BEILSTEIN NEWENAER, INF. ISENBERG ET REIFERSCHEIT   [1731] 58x49cm (23x19½") Orig wash & OL color. Lf margin sl oil stained; few joined tears affecting graticules; few tiny ink spots; o/w good.   [11] £151 **$250**

SCANDINAVIA COMPLECTENS SUECIAE DANIAE & NORVEGIAE REGNA ...   [c.1720] Incl Finland, Baltics. 48x57cm (19x22½") Color; B&W cartouche.   [41] £181 **$300**

STATUS MUTINENSIS IN SUAS DITIONES ...   [c.1740] Homann Heirs. 48x51cm (19x20") Old color.   [68] **DM 380** £131 $217

STATUUM MOROCCANORUM ...   [1737] With Canaries & Madeira; Marrakech & Meknes views. 49x55cm (19½x21½") Orig body color.   [46] **£320** $531

STATUUM TOTIUS ITALIAE ...   [c.1720] J.B. Homann. 48x57cm (19x22½") Orig color, later cartouche additions. VG.   [24] £588 **$975**

[SAME TITLE]   [c.1720] J.B Homann. 49x57cm (19½x22½") Old color.   [68] **DM 550** £190 $315

TABULA MARCHIONATUS BRANDENBURGICI ET DUCATUS POMERANIAE ...   [c.1730] 48x56cm (19x22") Full orig wash & OL color.   [11] £90 **$150**

THEATRUM BELLI ... IN PARTIBUS REGNORUM SERVIAE ET BOSNIAE (CARTOUCHE TITLE) [IN SET WITH] REGNUM BOSNIAE ... - REGNI SERVIAE (TITLE ABOVE)   [c.1740] Homann Heirs. Incl 15 insets. Each map about 54x57cm (21½x22½") Old color. Narrow top & bottom margins.   [48] **DM 780** £269 $446

HOMANN & HOMANN HEIRS continued

TOTIUS AMERICAE SEPTENTRIONALIS ET MERIDIONALIS NOVISSIMA REPRAESENTATIO ... [c.1700+] Non-insular Calif: uncertain NW America. 49x59cm (19½x23") Color. [42] **Aus$2,500** £1,135 $1,882

[SAME TITLE] [c.1720-32] J.B. Homann. Corrected map; peninsular Calif. 48x57cm (19x22½") Orig wash color. Lower c'fold repair; good. [31] £844 **$1,400**

[SAME TITLE] [c.1730] J.B. Homann. 49x57cm (19½x22½") OL color. Sl soiling margins; lower fold split closed on verso. [A7] £694 **$1,150**

[SAME TITLE] [[1740] J.B. Homann. 48x58cm (19x22½") Restoration at lower fold & side margins; backed. [A6] £264 $438

UKRANIA QUAE ET TERRAE COSACCORUM CUM VICINIS WALACHIAE, MOLDAVIAE, MINORIS TARTARIAE PROVINCIIS [1720] J.B. Homann. 47x56cm (18½x22") Orig color. VG to fine. [14] £317 **$525**

URBIS ROMAE VETERIS ACCURATA DELINEATIO [c.1710] J.B. Homann. 48x58cm (19x23") Orig color. 2 minute brown spots near ctr; o/w fine. [14] £513 **$850**

VIRGINIA, MARYLANDIA ET CAROLINA IN AMERICA SEPTENTRIONALI ... [1730] J.B Homann. 48x58cm (19x22½") Orig color. Faint discoloration along c'fold; else exc. Ref: Cumming (SE) 156, pl.46. Morrison fig.27. [24] £1,086 **$1,800**

HONDIUS   Try *Jansson, Mercator*

[ATLAS] ATLAS MINOR ... [1631] Amsterdam: Jan Jansson. German text. Oblong quarto; morocco-backed boards, scuffed; pp. vi + 600 + xvi, index; frontis, 143 maps as called for. Inner hinges strained. Ref: Koeman Me 198. [47] £4,400 $7,296

[PORTRAIT] GERARDUS MERCATOR ... IUDOCUS HONDIUS ... [(1613) c.1620] Double portrait by Coletta Hondius. 39x46cm (15½x18") Color. Minor c'fold repair, verso reinforcement. [4] £950 $1,576

[SAME TITLE] [c.1630] From Mercator *Atlas*. 38x44cm (15x17½") Full color. Exc. [44] £905 **$1,500**

AEGYPTUS [1607] 15x18cm (6x7½") B&W. Faint margin time toning; o/w fine. [A1] £116 $193

AFRICAE NOVA TABULA [c.1632] Top & side panels. Early example (date removed after 1640). 41x55cm (16x21½") Dark impression. Lt age-toned. Ref: Tooley (Africa) p.54. [46] **£2,950** $4,892

AMERICA [1606] 37x50cm (14½x19½") Full color. Exc. Ref: Burden 150. [45] £3,317 **$5,500**

[SAME TITLE] [1606-1609] With Brazilian native brewing scene. 38x51cm (15x20") Color. Minor c'fold reinforcement. [34] **£4,200** $6,964

[SAME TITLE] [1606 / 1616] 37x50cm (15x19½") Col. C'fold restoration; else VG. [14] £2,593 **$4,300**

[SAME TITLE] [1606 (1619)] 37x50cm (15x20") Faded orig color. Old repair lower ctr crease; good. [32] £2,563 **$4,250**

AMERICA MERIDIONALIS [1606-33] From Mercator-Hondius *Atlas*. 36x49cm (14x19½") Uncolored. Fine. [34] £850 $1,410

AMERICA NOVITER DELINEATA ... [1641] Insets: Arctic; Greenland. Henricus Hondius had Jodocus borders removed to fit into atlas. 37x50cm (15x20") Orig color. Exc. Ref: Burden 192 (state 4); Goss (NA) 27; Tooley (Amer) p.299. [2] £1,508 **$2,500**

[SAME TITLE] [1641] 38x50cm (15x19½") OL col. Sl toned; minor browning margins. [A8] £2,081 **$3,450**

AMERICA NOVITER DELINEATA AUCT JUDOCO HONDIO [1659] From Pierre D'Avity, *Les Estats, Empires, Royaumes et Principautez du Monde*. Carte-a-figures. 41x55cm (16½x21½") Uncolored. Good. Ref: Burden 333. [2] £2,714 **$4,500**

[SAME TITLE] [1659] Paris: Pierre D'Avity. Folded into a volume. 41x54cm (16x21½") Color. Creased, reinforced at some folds; side margins extended; fair. Ref: Burden 333. [24] £2,322 **$3,850**

AMERICAE DESCRIP. [1607] From Mercator-Hondius *Atlas Minor*. 15x20cm (6x8") OL color. Exc. Ref: Burden 153. [43] £392 **$650**

ASIA RECENS SUMMA CURA DELINEATA. AUCT IUD HONDIO [1642] Publ in Boisseau's *Theatre des Galles*. Dedication replaced by "Yerzo Insula Nova Recognita" 38x49cm (15x19½") Blank verso. [46] £850 $1,410

ASIAE NOVA DESCRIPTIO AUCTORE JODOCO HONDIO IN ASIA PRIMI PARENTES NOSTRI ADAMUS ET EVA A DEO CONDITI: ... EXCUSUM IN AEDIBUS AUCTORIS. ANIAN FRETUM ET FRETUM JOANIS DAVIS [1606] As in *Atlas sive Cosmographicae* ... Mercator updated. 38x50cm (15x20") Color. C'fold repair; remargined. Ref: Koeman Me 15, 127. [42] Aus$1,950 £886 $1,468

CAMBRIA SIVE WALLIA [1607] From *Historia Mundi*. 15x20cm (6x8") Uncolored. VG. [25] £109 **$180**

CHINA [(1606) 1607] Mercator-Hondius atlas. Insular Korea. 34x45cm (13½x17½") Uncolored. Fine. Ref: Koeman ME 26A (134). [4] **£1,500** $2,487

HONDIUS continued

CHINA [1606-1609] Jodocus Hondius. With Japan, insular Korea & NW America. 34x46cm (13½x18") Uncolored. [34] **£1,700** $2,819

DE HEMELSCHE CLOOT [1599 (1609)] From Dutch ed, Langenes' *Caert-Thresoor*. Double hemi; word "Iehova" between. 9x13cm (3½x5") Full color. VG. Ref: Shirley (W) 211. Koeman Lan 8. [38] **£286** $475

EUROPA EXACTISSIME DESCRIPTA ... [1631-1633] Early edition. 38x50cm (15x20") Col. [34] **£750** $1,244

GERMANIA [1607] From Mercator-Hondius *Atlas Minor*. 15x19cm (6x7½") Newer color. Fine. ["Prussia" offered at same price] [14] **£166** $275

GRAECIA [c.1630] Mercator-Hondius Atlas. 36x47cm (14x18½") Orig color. VG. Ref: Zacharakis 1447. [24] **£452** $750

GUINEAE NOVA DESCRIPTIO [c.1606] 35x49cm (13½x19½") Orig color. Lower margin c'fold separation repaired; VG to fine. Ref: Norwich 316. [14] **£359** $595

HISPANIAE NOVAE NOVA DESCRIPTIO [1636] Mercator-Hondius. 13x19cm (5½x7½") Newer color. Lt margin toning; VG. [A1] **£119** $198

IAPONIA [1606] Mercator-Hondius. 34x45cm (13½x17½") Orig color. Mint. [44] **£2,714** $4,500

[SAME TITLE] [c.1606] From Mercator-Hondius atlas. 34x44cm (13½x17½") Full orig color. Exc. Ref: Walter (Japan) IV.1, 22. [2] **£2,714** $4,500

[SAME TITLE] [1606-28] Insular Korea, with qualifying note. 34x44cm (13½x17½") Orig color. Ref: Walter (Japan) 22. [34] **£2,500** $4,146

INDIA ORIENTALIS [(1606) 1613] From Mercator-Hondius Atlas. 36x49cm (14x19½") Color. Verso reinforcement of sh lower c'fold split; fine, crisp. Ref: Koeman Me22. [4] **£1,250** $2,073

[SAME TITLE] [1613] 36x49cm (14x19") Full orig color. Few stains; VG. Ref: Quirino p.80. [24] **£1,327** $2,200

[SAME TITLE] [1606-23] Plate added to Mercator's *Atlas*. 36x49cm (14x19") Color. [34] **£1,500** $2,487

INDIA QUAE ORIENTALIS DICITUR, ET INSULAE ADIACENTES [1633] From *Atlas Novus* ... 40x49cm (15½x19½") Uncolored. Minor repairs at c'fold. [42] **Aus$3,500** £1,589 $2,635

[SAME TITLE] [1639] From *Atlas Novus* ... 40x49cm (15½x19½") Color. Ref: Koeman Me 93B, 84. [42] **Aus$1,950** £886 $1,468

INSULAE INDIAE ORIENTALIS [1620] From Mercator-Hondius *Atlas Minor*. 14x20cm (5½x7½") Newer color. 1cm wormhole lower rt margin; o/w fine. [14] **£196** $325

INSULAE INDIAE ORIENTALIS PRAECIPUAE IN QUIBUS MOLUCCAE CELEBERRIMAE SUNT ... [(1606) 1619] From Mercator-Hondius Atlas. 35x48cm (13½x19"). Color. Good. [4] **£1,525** $2,529

MAGNAE BRITANNIAE ET HIBERNIAE TABULA ... 1631 [1633] Publ in *Atlas ou Representation du Monde Universel*. 38x50cm (15x20") Dark impression. Ref: Shirley (BI to 1650) 435. [46] **£460** $763

MAPPA AESTIVARUM INSULARUM ALIAS BARMUDAS DICTARUM ... [1633-] 40x52cm (15½x20½") Color. Some c'fold restoration. [34] **£1,400** $2,322

[SAME TITLE] [1639] Amsterdam: Jansson (but Jansson's name absent). 40x52cm (15½x20½") Orig color. Minor lower c'fold split; faint ink stamp show through. Ref: cf Palmer (Bermuda) pl.XI. [46] **£1,150** $1,907

MARCHIONATUS MORAVIAE ... HONDIUS [1636] From Mercator-Hondius-Jansson Atlas. 38x54cm (15x21½") Color. Ref: Koeman Me 41A, 71. [42] **Aus$750** £341 $565

NOVA EUROPAE DESCRIPTIO [1630] Jodocus Hondius. 37x50cm (14½x20") Color. [A6] **£460** $763

[SAME TITLE] [c.1640] 38x50cm (15x19½") Orig thick OL color. Age toned; restored upper c'fold splits. Ref: Koeman Me 136a. [46] **£950** $1,576

NOVA EUROPAE DESCRIPTIO AUCTORE IODOCO HONDIO [1606 / ?] Mercator-Hondius Atlas. 38x50cm (15x19½") Full orig color. Exc. Framed. [24] **£1,809** $3,000

NOVA TOTIUS TERRARUM ORBIS GEOGRAPHICA AC HYDROGRAPHICA TABULA AUCT. HENR: HONDIO [1630] 1st state of 4; insular Calif. 38x55cm (15x21½") Full orig color. Fine. Ref: Shirley (W) 336. [44] **£5,729** $9,500

[SAME TITLE] [1630 (1633)] H. Hondius; 1st state of 4; insular Calif; ornate decor.. 38x54cm (15x21½") Full color. VG. Ref: Shirley (W) 336. [32] **£5,428** $9,000

[SAME TITLE] [1630 / 1641] State 2; double hemi; insular Calif; shows Australia. 38x54cm (15x21½") Full orig color. C'fold repairs, no loss. VG Ref: Shirley (W) 336. Schilder (Australia) 39. [2] **£5,729** $9,500

[SAME TITLE] [1630-1641] From *Gerardi Mercatoris et I Hondii Atlas*. Double hemi; insular Calif. 38x55cm (15x21½") Orig color. [another 1636 B&W copy offered at Aus$ 11,000] Ref: Shirley (W) 336, col pl.256. [13] **Aus$12,800** £5,813 $9,638

HONDIUS continued

NOVA VIRGINIAE TABULA   [1630-33]   Centered on Chesapeake Bay. 38x49cm (15x19½") Uncolored. Ref: Burden 228.   [34] **£1,500** **$2,487**

[SAME TITLE]   [1630 / 1633] 38x49cm (15x19½") Orig color. Exc. Ref: Burden 228.   [2] £1,327 **$2,200**

PARADISUS   [1635]   From Thomas Cotes, *Historia Mundi*. London: Michael Sparke & Samuel Cartwright. A reuse of "Atlas Minor" plates, also used in "Purchas His Pilgrims". Set in Middle East, on page of text, 15x19cm (6x7½") Ref: Koeman vol.2, p.508.   [46] **£78** $130

PERSICI VEL SOPHORUM REGNI TYPUS   [1606-33] 36x50cm (14x20") Color.   [34] **£450** $746

POLUS ANTARCTICUS HENRICUS HONDIUS EXCUDIT   [1639] As in *Le Nouveau Theatre du Monde ou Nouvel Atlas*. 1st ed; polar hemi. 43x49cm (17x19½") Orig color. Ref: Tooley (Australia) pl.124 & 246; Clancy (Australis) p.84-5.   [2nd ed, by Jansson, 1650, offered at Aus$ 2,800]   [13]   **Aus$2,250** £1,022 $1,694

REGNI VALENTIAE TYPUS   [1638] Mercator-Hondius. 34x47cm (13½x18½") Full color. [41] £208 **$345**

TABULA GEOGRAPH IN QUA EUROPA, AFRICA, ASIAQ. ET CIRCUMIACENTIUM INSULARUM ORA MARITIMA ACCURATA DESCRIBUNTUR ...   [1615] Engraved for Pondanus' *Rerum et Urbis Amstelodamensium Historia*. 27x42cm (10½x16½") Col. Minor reinforcement at old fold lower ctr. Ref: Norwich 28. [4] **£1,250** **$2,073**

TABULA ISLANDIAE   [1631 / c.1638] By Carolus Flandro. 38x49cm (15x19½") Some splitting lower margin; o/w good.   [32] £814 **$1,350**

TARTARIA   [1606-33] From Mercator-Hondius *Atlas*. 34x50cm (13½x19½") Color.   [34] **£650** $1,078

[SAME TITLE]   [c.1613] 36x49cm (14x19½") OL color. Lt toned; scattered soiling, sh repaired tear top margin.   [A8] £191 **$316**

TURCICI IMPERII IMAGO   [1648] Mercator-Hondius. 15x20cm (6x8") Uncolored. Exc.   [25] £96 **$160**

TYPUS ORBIS TERRARUM   [1607]   From *Atlas Minor Gerardi Mercatoris a Hondi* ... Double hemi. 14x20cm (5½x7½") Orig wash color. Ref: Shirley (W) 259, pl.204.   [13] **Aus$990** £450 $745

VIRGINIAE ITEM ET FLORIDAE AMERICAE PROVINCIARUM NOVA DESCRIPTIO   [1606] 34x48cm (13½x19") Full orig color. Exc. Ref: Burden 151; Cumming (SE) 26; Goss (NA) 23.   [45] £1,568 **$2,600**

[SAME TITLE]   [c.1606] Mercator-Hondius Atlas. 34x48cm (13½x19") B&W. Sm area of lt inking; minor c'fold tear repaired; superb (A+).   [A3] £1,022 **$1,694**

[SAME TITLE]   [1606-1609] 34x49cm (13x19") Color.   [34] **£1,600** $2,653

[SAME TITLE]   [(1606) 1619]   Mercator-Hondius Atlas. 34x49cm (13x19½") Orig color. Sm reinforcement patch lower c'fold margin; sl separation top c'fold; o/w VF.   [4] £1,675 **$2,778**

HONTER

UNIVERSALIS COSMOGRAPHIA TIGURI IVE MDXLVI   [1546] Cordiform world. 13x16cm (5x6½") Usual stitching at ctr repaired; else fine. Ref: Shirley 86.   [44] £844 **$1,400**

HOOD

MAP OF THE UNITED STATES TERRITORY OF OREGON WEST OF THE ROCKY MOUNTAINS, EXHIBITING THE VARIOUS TRADING DEPOTS OR FORTS OCCUPIED BY THE BRITISH HUDSON BAY COMPANY, CONNECTED WITH THE WESTERN AND NORTHWESTERN FUR TRADE   [1838] 44x52cm (17½x20½") B&W. Tear at hinge; age toned top & side; sm spot ctr. Ref: Wheat (TM) 434, illus.   [1] £232 **$385**

[SAME TITLE]   [1838]   44x52cm (17½x20½") Few sh top margin tears repaired verso, sm damp stains; faint foxing; else clean, fresh. Ref: Wheat (TM) 433.   [A10] £111 **$184**

HOPKINS

[ATLAS]   CITY ATLAS OF SCHENECTADY, NEW YORK   [1880] Folio, leather back & cloth; 19 mostly double-page maps with some color, 2 views. Spine worn; contents fresh, bright. Ref: LeGear (US) 2664.   [A10] £180 **$299**

CHATTANOOGA AND VICINITY   [1914] G.M. Hopkins & Co., Phila. Pocket map. Walden's Ridge inset. 53x74cm (21x29") Full printed color. VG.   [36] £90 **$150**

DRIVING MAP OF ALLEGHENY COUNTY PENNSYLVANIA   [1886] Folding map on thin paper in 8 sections. Color by towns. 85x85cm (33½x33½") Sm holes at 2 fold junctions.   [15] £151 **$250**

MAP OF THE CITIES OF PITTSBURGH, ALLEGHENY, AND THE ADJOINING BOROUGHS   [1872] G.M. Hopkins. Folds into orig 12mo cloth case. 48x60cm (18½x23½") Color.   [A8] £329 **$546**

HOWELL

A MAP OF THE STATE OF PENNSYLVANIA   [1811] Phila: Kimber & Conrad & Jonson & Warner. Printed by Vallance. 54x84cm (21½x33") Uncolored. 3 sh tears into surface; exc. Ref: Ristow (Amer M&M) p.108.   [15] £1,809 **$3,000**

HOWELL continued

A MAP OF THE STATE OF PENNSYLVANIA [1817] Phila. Many additions to plate since 1811. 54x84cm (21½x33") Uncolored. Backed; good. Ref: Ristow (Amer M&M) p.108. [15] £1,659 **$2,750**

HUNT & EATON

MAP OF TEXAS, OKLAHOMA AND INDIAN TERRITORY [c.1895] 29x23cm (11½x9") Full printed color. VG. [16] £27 **$45**

HUNT & RANDEL

MAP OF TEXAS COMPILED FROM SURVEYS ON RECORD IN THE GENERAL LAND OFFICE OF THE REPUBLIC, TO THE YEAR 1839, BY RICHARD S. HUNT AND JESSE F. RANDEL [1839] Shows Houston; title above Texas star; inset of Rio Grand to Pacific. 80x61cm (31½x24") Partial color. Orig a pocket map, now laid on japan paper; fold & tear losses recolored; orig cover & guide book not present; good. Ref: Day (TX) p.28-9. [16] £10,554 **$17,500**

HURD

NEW YORK TO NORWALK ISLANDS, LONG ISLAND SOUND [1893] After U.S. Coast Survey. 43x69cm (17x27") Color. Ref: Phillips (A) 1476. [17] £87 **$145**

NORWALK ISLANDS TO SOUTHWEST LEDGE LONG ISLAND SOUND [1893] After U.S. Coast Survey. 43x69cm (17x27") Color. Ref: Phillips (A) 1476. [17] £75 **$125**

ILLUSTRATED LONDON NEWS

[LONDON: VIEW FROM SOUTH BANK OF THAMES LOOKING NORTH] [1845] Wood engraving; linen-backed. Image 29x119cm (11½x47") Creases along folds. [A6] £172 **$286**

[NEW YORK CITY VIEW] [Nov 24, 1855] Woodcut bird's-eye view. 24x36cm (9½x14½") B&W. [22] £45 **$75**

[NEW YORK CITY VIEW WITH BROOKLYN BRIDGE] [June 2, 1883] Bridge at ctr, seen from Manhattan. 21x30cm (8½x12") Uncolored. [22] £45 **$75**

BIRDSEYE VIEW OF THE CITY OF WASHINGTON, WITH THE CAPITOL IN THE FOREGROUND [May 25, 1861] View to west; new Capitol dome in process; partial Washington Monument. 34x51cm (13½x20") B&W. Immaculate. Ref: Reps (Wash) p.135. [12] £136 **$225**

LONDON, FROM THE SOUTH SIDE OF THE THAMES [1861] Image 43x131cm (17x51½") Color. Some staining along folds. [A6] £253 **$420**

PANORAMA OF THE CITY OF MEXICO [1863] B&W. Two panels, designed to make continuous scene, 17x99cm (6½x39") Immaculate. [12] £45 **$75**

WILMINGTON AND CAPE FEAR RIVER, NORTH CAROLINA [1865] Civil War defenses, etc., at 3 miles/inch. 34x24cm (13½x9½") B&W. VG (A). [A3] £40 **$66**

IMBERT

CARTE DES POSSESSIONS ANGLOISES DANS L'AMERIQUE SEPTENTRIONALE POUR SERVIR D'INTELLIGENCE A LA GUERRE PRESENTE TRADUITE DE L'ANGLOIS, PAR J. LEOPOLD IMBERT. 1777. A PARIS CHEZ MONDHARE RUE ST. JACQUES PRES ST. SEVERIN [1777] West Indies inset. 56x75cm (22x29½") OL color. Numerous extraneous soft creases. [A7] £555 **$920**

IMRAY

BRITISH ISLANDS TO PETSHORA BAY [CHART NO.1] SCOTLAND TO NORWAY COMPRISING THE NORTH PART OF THE NORTH SEA [1877] Blue-backed chart; incl Faroes, Hebrides, Orkneys & Shetlands; 2 insets. 106x139cm (41½x54½") Exc. [15] £75 **$125**

CARIBBEAN SEA [1878] Blue-backed chart; 20 insets. 104x206cm (41x81") Long repaired tear from rt margin; fine. [15] £226 **$375**

CHART OF THE BAY OF BENGAL, INCLUDING PLANS OF THE PRINCIPAL HARBOURS [1858] Blue-backed chart; 11 insets. 102x171cm (40x67½") Fine. [15] £75 **$125**

CHART OF THE GULF OF MEXICO AND WINDWARD PASSAGES INCLUDING THE ISLANDS OF CUBA, HAITI, JAMAICA, PUERTO RICO AND THE BAHAMAS [1875] Lighthouses in color. 105x192cm (41½x75½") Divided into 3 orig sheets; modern rebacking. Minor damage at top, no loss. [15] £513 **$850**

ENGLAND & SCOTLAND - COAST NORTHWARD OF FLAMBOROUGH HEAD [1878] Blue-backed chart; north to Orkneys; 24 insets. 105x203cm (41½x80") [15] £90 **$150**

HAITI [1875] Blueback chart of Hispaniola; some inland detail. 64x100cm (25½x39½") Repaired long tear at lf into map, sl loss; minor chipping top. [15] £136 **$225**

IMRAY continued

SOUTH ATLANTIC   [1875]   Blue-backed; 15 insets. Winds in printed color. 100x158cm (39½x62") Lt soiling; pencil notes & tracks; VF.   [15]   £75 **$125**

THE IRISH OR ST. GEORGE'S CHANNEL COMPILED FROM THE MOST RECENT SURVEYS   [1876]   Blue-backed; 12 insets. 189x103cm (74½x40½") Text leaf pasted on backing; exc.   [15]   £121 **$200**

JAILLOT

AMERIQUE MERIDIONALE DIVISEE EN SES PRINCIPALES PARTIES OU SONT DISTINGUES LES UNS DES AUTRES LES ESTATS ...   [1781 (sic)]   46x64cm (18x25")   OL & wash color.   [39]   £226 **$375**

AMERIQUE SEPTENTRIONALE ...   [c.1695] Standard folio ed. 47x58cm (18½x23") Old OL color. Age-toned; some foxing; sm edge tear & 4" tear through Isthmus & Carib repaired; overall good+.   [37]   £754 **$1,250**

AMERIQUE SEPTENTRIONALE DIVISEE EN SES PRINCIPALES PARTIES ... PAR SR. SANSON   [1674]   Title above: "L'Amerique Septentrionale ..."   Insular Calif. 56x87cm (22x34") Full color. Fine. Ref: McLaughlin 55; Tooley (Amer) p.121, pl.44. MCC 8, 37.   [1]   £2,895 **$4,800**

AMERIQUE SEPTENTRIONALE DIVISEE EN SES PRINCIPALES PARTIES OU SONT DISTINGUES LES UNS LES AUTRES ESTATS ...   [1674 / 1692]   55x88cm (21½x34½") Full orig color. C'fold repair, no loss; o/w exc. Ref: McLaughlin 101; Tooley (Amer) p.121, #37. pl.44. Leighly 87; Wagner (NW) 432.   [2]   £2,714 **$4,500**

[SAME TITLE]   [1692]   Insular California. 55x86cm (21½x34")   OL color. Stain traces lower margin & S. Atlantic; c'fold splits repaired; else VG.   [37]   £1,508 **$2,500**

[SAME TITLE]   [1694]   After Sanson; insular Calif. 45x63cm (18x25") Orig col. Exc.   [24]   £1,930 **$3,200**

BASSE PARTIE DE L EVESCHE DE MUNSTER, ET LE COMTE DE BENTHEM   [1700]   After Sanson. 44x57cm (17x22½")   Color.   [48]   **DM 1,800** £621 $1,030

CARTE DE LA MANCHE ...   [1692]   59x79cm (23½x31½") Orig OL color. Some surface dirt; scattered stains mainly in margins; else VG.   [38]   £302 **$500**

CARTE DES ROYAUMES D'ANGLETERRE D'ECOSSE ET D'IRLANDE   [1712-1715]   Inselin, sc. Hydrographical emphasis. 64x85cm (25x33½") Orig OL color. Old fold repairs. Ref: Shirley (BI 1650-1750) p.72, state 3.   [34]   **£1,400** $2,322

IUDAEA SEU TERRA SANCTA ...   [1692]   Cartouche notes offer for sale by Mortier, Amsterdam. 54x85cm (21½x33½")   Color. Few chips, tears at edges.   [A8]   £329 **$546**

IUDAEA SEU TERRA SANCTA QUAE HEBRAEORUM SIVE ISRAELITARUM IN SUAS DUODECIM TRIBUS DIVISA ...   [c.1677]   After Sanson. 58x84cm (22½x33½")   OL color. Ref: Laor 367.   [A8]   £971 **$1,610**

L'AFRIQUE DIVISEE SUIVANT L'ESTENDUE DE SES PRINCIPALES PARTIES ... PAR LE SR. SANSON ...   [1674]   56x86cm (22x34") OL color. Exc. Ref: Tooley (Afr) p.56, pl.41.   [44]   £603 **$1,000**

L'EUROPE DIVISEE SUIVANT ...   [1697]   Shows Ferro & "Premier Meridien". 2 sheets joined, 51x87cm (20x34½") Old OL col, refreshed; recent cartouche color. Scattered stains; c'fold repaired; overall good+.   [38]   £362 **$600**

LA PROVENCE   [1695]   From *Atlas Francois* ...   46x64cm (18x25") Orig OL color.   [34]   **£360** $597

LE CERCLE DE WESTPHALIE DIVISE EN TOUS LES ESTATS ...   [c.1720]   Amsterdam: Covens & Mortier. 60x45cm (23½x18") Orig OL col. ["Le Cercle de la Haut Saxe ..." offered at same price]   [11]   £90 **$150**

LE DUCHE DE LUXEMBOURG ...   [1696]   58x69cm (23x27") Orig OL color; uncolored cartouche. Lt surface dirt; else fine.   [38]   £302 **$500**

LE ROYAUME DE HONGRIE   [1691]   Incl Balkans. 55x86cm (21½x34")   Orig OL color. Some lt image transfer; o/w VG to fine.   [14]   £323 **$535**

MAPPE-MONDE GEO-HYDROGRAPHIQUE, OU DESCRIPTION GENERALE DU GLOBE TERRESTRE ET AQUATIQUE, EN DEUX PLANS-HEMISPHERES ...   [1687]   Double-hemi; insular Calif. 55x90cm (22x35½") Full color. Creasing at c'fold; else exc. Ref: Shirley (W) 536.   [24]   £3,317 **$5,500**

[SAME TITLE]   [1691]   Double-hemi; insular Calif. 53x91cm (21x36")   OL color. Repaired c'fold splits; few edges repaired to neat line; few lt stains; overall good. Ref: Shirley (W) 462.   [37]   £1,357 **$2,250**

PARTIE DE LA NOUVELLE FRANCE ...   [1685]   1st state; Newfoundland to Great Lakes with all Hudson Bay. 46x64cm (18x25½") Uncolored. Ref: Kershaw (Canada) 170.   [34]   **£1,200** $1,990

PARTIE DU DUCHE DE MILAN, LA PRINCIPAUTE DE PIEMONT ...   [1695]   From *Atlas Francois* ...   46x64cm (18x25") Orig OL color.   [34]   **£350** $581

PRINCIPAUTE DE CATALOGNE ...   [1685-1695]   Publ in *Atlas Francois* ...   Based on Sanson. 46x64cm (18x25") Orig OL color.   [34]   **£320** $531

ROYAUME D'IRLANDE DIVISE EN SES PROVINCES. SUBDIVISE EN SHIRERIES OU COMTES ...   [1693]   Updated & enlarged after Sanson. 89x62cm (35x24½")   OL color by counties. Strong impression.   [11]   £573 **$950**

TABULA REGNI POLONIAE, DUCATUS LITHUANIAE ...   [c.1740]   47x60cm (18½x23½") Full orig color. Exc.   [2]   £286 **$475**

JAMES

A New Map Of Mexico, California & Oregon [1848] Publ in *Doniphan's Expedition*. 33x23cm (13x9½") Ref: Wheat (TM) 546. Day (TX) 107. [7] £51 **$85**

Map of the Country Drained by the Mississippi [dated Feby. 1823] From English ed, *Account of an Expedition from Pittsburgh to the Rocky Mountains* ... Differs from American ed by combining east & west portion and extending only to 46° N. 38x52cm (15x20½") B&W. Fine. Ref: Wheat (TM) p.80, note 28. [12] £754 **$1,250**

JANSSON Try *Hondius, Mercator, Valk & Schenk*

[ATLAS] **Atlas sive Cosmographie Meditationes de Fabrica Mundi et Fabricati Figura.** Amsterdam: Johannes Janssonius van Waesberge [1673] 4th & last series of reduced Mercator atlases (larger than others) by Cloppenburgh. Large oblong quarto, vellum; 180 maps by Van den Keere, orig col. Lacks 4 maps listed in MS index. Exc. Ref: Shirley (W) 334. Koeman Me 205. [3] £17,490 **$29,000**

Aegyptus Antiqua [n.d.] Ancient Egypt; attributable to Du Val. 38x52cm (15x20½") Color. Ref: Koeman Me 177A, 14. [42] **Aus$1,200** £545 $903

Aeneae Troiani Navigatio ad Virgilij Sex Priores Aeneidos [c.1677] As in *Accuratissima Orbis Delineatio* ... Eastern Mediterranean with journeys of Aeneas & Ulysses. 40x50cm (15½x19½") Period color. Ref: Koeman Me 177A, 30. [42] **Aus$950** £431 $715

Aethiopia Inferior vel Exterior ... [1639-] 38x50cm (15x19½") Orig color. [46] £520 $863

Africae Antiquae ... Europae Asiaeque Adiacentium Regionum ... [1658] North Africa historical map; 2 cartouches, coins. 38x53cm (15x21") Old repair of tear at lf. [48] **DM 380** £131 $217

America Noviter Delineata [c.1645] Polar insets. 38x50cm (15x19½") Orig color. VG. Ref: Burden 207; McLaughlin 6; Wheat (TM) 45. [14] £1,809 **$3,000**

America Septentrionalis [1636] Insular Calif. 46x55cm (18½x22") Color. Lf margin extended, sl loss; overall VG to exc. Ref: Burden 245; McLaughlin 6; Wheat (TM) 45; Goss (NA) 30; Tooley (Amer) pl.28. [23] £1,930 **$3,200**

[SAME TITLE] [1639] Issued in *Nouvel Atlas*. 1st state. Insular Calif. 47x57cm (18½x22½") Orig or old OL color; later cartouche color. Faint tide mark at bottom; narrow margin; few sh tears to neat line. [9] £1,960 **$3,250**

[SAME TITLE] [c.1694] Amsterdam: Schenk & Valk. Orig publ 1636 by Hondius; 3rd & last state. Insular Calif. 46x55cm (18½x21½") Full orig color. [47] **£2,300** $3,814

Americae Descriptio [1661] Engr by Goos for 1628 *Atlas Minor* Peninsular Calif; no Great Lakes. 14x20cm (5½x8") Ref: Burden 221 (illus). [46] £240 $398

Arragonia Regnum [c.1695] By Joao Baptista Labanna, Royal Portuguese geographer. Publisher uncertain; used by both Jansson & Blaeu. 41x51cm (16x20") Full wash & OL color. [11] £166 **$275**

Belgii Novi, Angliae Novae, Et Partis Virginiae Novissima Delineatio [1651 / c.1660] 1st ed, 2nd state of Jansson-Visscher series. 44x52cm (17½x20½") Full orig color. Lt time toned; o/w/ exc. Ref: Burden 305 state 2; Tooley (Amer) p.283, #2, pl.145. Stokes (Manhattan) v.1, p.143-6. [2] £3,317 **$5,500**

[SAME TITLE] [1657] 1st state & 1st in Jansson-Visscher series of present Northeast. 44x51cm (17½x20½") Color. Exc. Ref: Burden 305; Tooley (Amer) p.283, pl.144. [23] £3,317 **$5,500**

Belgii Veteris Typus ex Conatibus Geographicis ... [n.d.] 39x48cm (15½x19") Color. Ref: Koeman 177A, 36. [42] **Aus$1,350** £613 $1,016

Bohemia in suas Partes Geographice Distincta ... [1636] From Mercator-Hondius-Jansson Atlas. 41x47cm (16x18½") Color. Ref: Koeman Me 41A, 69. [42] **Aus$950** £431 $715

Britannia Prout Divisa fuit Temporibus Anglo-Saxonum, Praesertim Durante Illorum Heptarchia [(1646) c.1650] Panels at sides. 42x53cm (16½x21") Color. Few edge chips & margin repairs; verso reinforcement lower c'fold margin; generally fine. Ref: Shirley (BI to 1650) 577. [4] **£1300** $2,156

[SAME TITLE] [c.1646] Panels at sides. 41x53cm (16½x21") Orig OL color. C'fold split repaired; good. [2] £1,146 **$1,900**

Buckingamiae Comitatus cum Bedfordiensi; vulgo Buckinghamshire and Bedfordshire [1646] From *Atlas Novus*. Verso text from Camden's Britannia. 40x50cm (16x20") Color. A county line burned through, reinforced verso & retouched. [11] £211 **$350**

Champagne [1637] 36x49cm (14½x19½") Age-toned; else VG. [38] £181 **$300**

Comitatus Lancastrensis. The Countie Palatine of Lancaster [1638] 1st state. 38x51cm (15x20") Orig color. Some creasing & restoration at c'fold. Ref: Koeman Me 69. [47] £390 **$647**

Creta Iovis Magni, Medio Jacet Insula Ponto ... [c.1677] As in *Accuratissima Orbis Delineatio* ... Ancient Crete. 38x49cm (15x19½") Color. Ref: Koeman Me 177A, 18. [42] **Aus$950** £431 $715

JANSSON continued

CYPRUS, INSULA LAETA CHORIS, BLADORUM ET MATER AMORUM   [c.1677]   As in *Accuratissima Orbis Delineatio* ...   34x47cm (13½x18½")   Color.   Ref: Koeman Me 177A, 17.   [42]   **Aus$1,750**   £795 $1,318

DESCRIPTIO PERIGRINATIONIS D. PAULI, APOSTOLI, EXHIBENS LOCA FERE OMNIA TAM IN NOVO TESTAMENTO QUAM IN ACTIS APOSTOLORUM MEMORATA ...   [c.1677]   As in *Accuratissima Orbis Delineatio* ...   36x51cm (14x20")   Color.   Ref: Koeman Me 177A, 12.   [42]   **Aus$750**   £341 $565

DIMIDA TRIBUS MANASSE ... TRIBUS RUBEN, ET GAD ... PARS MAXIMA TRIBUS IUDA ... [TRIBUUM EPHRAIM ...], [TRIBUS ASER ...], [TRIBUS SIMEON ...]   [1658]   As in *Novus Atlas* ...   6 sheets joined, 85x178cm (33½x70½")   Color.   Ref: Koeman Me 177A, 6-11.   [42]   **Aus$12,500**   £5,677 $9,412

DUCATUS LUTZENBURGICUS   [1628]   Mercator-Jansson.   Oval map; arabesque border.   12x17cm (4½x7")   Color.   [48]   **DM 480**   £166 $275

DUCATUS SILESIAE LIGNICIENSIS.   [1647]   With Liegnitz view.   39x48cm (15½x19")   Old color.   [48]   **DM 590**   £204 $338

ERYTHRAEI SIVE RUBRI MARIS PERIPLUS ...   [c.1677]   As in *Accuratissima Orbis Delineatio* ...   South Asia; incl North polar inset.   40x47cm (15½x18½")   Color.   ["Lumen Historiarum. Per Orientem, Illustrandis Biblijs Sacris ..." offered as same price]   Ref: Koeman Me 177A, 15.   [42]   **Aus$1,450**   £658 $1,092

EUROPAM, SIVE CELTICAM VETEREM   [c.1677]   As in *Accuratissima Orbis Delineatio* ...   Early Europe.   36x47cm (14x18½")   Color.   Ref: Koeman Me 177A, 51.   ["Africae Propriae Tabula ..." & "Tabula Itineris Decies Mille Graecorum ..." offered at same price]   [42]   **Aus$750**   £341 $565

GEOGRAPHICA SACRA. OPHIRAM REGIONEM ...   [c.1677]   As in *Accuratissima Orbis Delineatio* ...   After Ortelius; Near & Middle East region.   36x48cm (14½x19")   Color.   Ref: Koeman Me 177A, 2.   ["Argonautica" offered at same price]   [42]   **Aus$650**   £295 $489

GERMANIAE VETERIS NOVA DESCRIPTIO   [c.1677]   As in *Accuratissima Orbis Delineatio* ...   38x47cm (15x18½")   Color.   Ref: Koeman Me 177A, 50.   [42]   **Aus$950**   £431 $715

GUIANA SIVE AMAZONUM REGIO   [1647]   38x50cm (15x19½")   Old color.   [48]   **DM 950**   £328 $544

HELLAS, SEU GRAECIA UNIVERSA ...   [1650]   46x56cm (18½x22")   Orig color, later additions.   C'fold reinforced; else exc.   Ref: Zacharakis 1275.   [24]   £513   **$850**

HISPANIAE VETERIS DESCRIPTIO   [c.1677]   As in *Accuratissima Orbis Delineatio* ...   Ancient Iberia. 37x50cm (14½x19½")   Color.   ["Veteris Pannoniae ...", "Attica, Megarica ...", "Thraciae Veteris ...", "Insular Aliquot Aegaei ..." & " ... Patriarcharum Abrahami ..." offered at same price]   Ref: Koeman Me 177A, 33.   [42]   **Aus$1,250**   £568 $941

HUNGARIA REGNUM ...   [1637]   As in *Appendix Atlantis*.   42x51cm (16½x20")   Period color. Faded.   Ref: Koeman Me 44, 30.   [42]   **Aus$950**   £431 $715

HUQUANG, KIANGSI, CHEKIANG, AC FOKIEN, PROVIN: SIVE PRAEFECTURAE REGNI SINEN   [1705]   Schenk & Valk reissue.   36x52cm (14½x20½")   Orig wash color.   Without problems.   [47]   **£350** $581

IAPONIAE NOVA DESCRIPTIO   [1636+]   2nd state of Hondius map; new title cartouche; galleon replaces junk.   34x44cm (13½x17½")   Clean.   Ref: Walter (Japan) 23.   [46]   **£1,350** $2,902

IMPERII SINARUM NOVA DESCRIPTIO. AUCTORE JOH VAN LOON   [1658-]   47x52cm (18½x20½")   Orig OL color.   Ref: Koeman Me 90B.   [46]   **£720** $1,194

IMPERIUM ROMANUM AUTH PHIL. BRIETE SOCIET IESU   [c.1677]   As in *Accuratissima Orbis Delineatio* ...   38x52cm (15x20½")   Color.   Ref: Koeman Me 177A, 54.   [42]   **Aus$1,525**   £693 $1,148

INDIA QUAE ORIENTALIS DICITUR ET INSULAE ADIACENTES   [1638]   As in *Atlas Novus ... Janssonium & ... Hondius*.   39x48cm (15½x19")   Orig color.   [13]   **Aus$2,400**   £1,090 $1,807

[SAME TITLE]   [1644]   As in *Des Nieuwen Atlantis Aenhang* ...   40x50cm (15½x19½")   Color.   Ref: Koeman Me 75A, 103.   [42]   **Aus$2,750**   £1,249 $2,071

[SAME TITLE]   [1649]   By Henricus Hondius.   India to S Japan & W Australia.   40x49cm (15½x19½")   Orig color. Some browning; old lower c'fold repair.   Ref: Koeman Me 136a.   [46]   **£1,250** $2,073

INDIAE ORIENTALIS NOVA DESCRIPTIO   [1633]   As in *Atlas ou Representation du Monde* ...   39x50cm (15½x20")   Orig color.   Ref: Schilder (Australia) 24.   [13]   **Aus$2,100**   £954 $1,581

[SAME TITLE]   [1633]   As in *Appendix* ...   39x50cm (15½x20")   Color.   [42]   **Aus$2,500**   £1,135 $1,882

[SAME TITLE]   [1639]   Henricus Hondius.   40x51cm (15½x20")   Full orig color. Lt browned; lower c'fold split repaired.   Ref: Clancy & Richardson p.77-9, illus.   [47]   **£1,250** $2,073

INSULAE BORNEO ET OCCIDENTALIS PARS CELEBES ...   [1657]   42x53cm (16½x21")   Mint.   [44]   £844   **$1,400**

INSULAE IAVAE CUM PARTE INSULARUM BORNEO SUMATRAE ...   [1657]   42x52cm (16½x20½")   Contemp color.   [A6]   **£471** $781

JANSSON continued

INSULARUM MOLUCCARUM NOVA DESCRIPTIO [1633] 1st ed. 38x50cm (15x19½") Old OL color. Age-toned; lower margin repaired; else VG. Ref: Koeman Me35. [37] £392 **$650**

[SAME TITLE] [c.1650] 38x50cm (15x19½") Area & OL color. Sl toned; minor soiling. [A8] £329 **$546**

ITALIAE ANTIQUAE NOVA DELINEATIO ... [c.1677] As in *Accuratissima Orbis Delineatio ...* Ancient Italy. 38x50cm (15x19½") Color. Ref: Koeman Me 177A, 39. [42] **Aus$1,950** £886 $1,468

IUDAEAE SEU TERRAE ISRAELIS TABULA GEOGRAPHICA; IN QUA LOCORUM IN VETERI ET NOVO TESTAMENTO CELEBRATISSIMORUM SITUS ACCURATE DESCRIPTI [n.d.] 36x48cm (14x19") Color. Ref: Laor 373, illus. Koeman Me 177A, 4. [42] **Aus$1,500** £681 $1129

LE DUCHE D'ANIOU [1630] 37x49cm (15x19½") Full color cartouches. On heavy paper; lt age-toning; else VG. [38] £151 **$250**

LUMEN HISTORIARUM PER OCCIDENTEM EX CONATIBUS FRAN. HARAEI ANTVERPIAE [c.1677] As in *Accuratissima Orbis Delineatio ...* Mediterranean lands north to Germany. 38x48cm (15x19") Color. Ref: Koeman Me 177A, 56. ["... Pontus Euxinus ..." offered at same price] [42] **Aus$950** £431 $715

MAPPA AESTIVARUM INSULARUM, ALIAS BARMUDAS DICTARUM ... [1647-] Jansson's name on scale cartouche. 40x52cm (15½x20½") Orig color. Minor split lower c'fold. Ref: Palmer (Bermuda) pl.XI. [46] **£1,350 $2,239**

[SAME TITLE] [c.1647] 39x51cm (15½x20½") Orig color. Lt time toned; VG. Ref: Palmer (Bermuda) p.14. [2] £1,146 **$1,900**

MAR DEL ZUR HISPANIS MARE PACIFICUM [1650] From *Atlantis Majoris Quinta Pars ...* Insular Calif. 44x54cm (17½x21½") Col. Ref: Burden 292; McLaughlin 11; Tooley (Amer) pl.30; Potter p.129.. [42] **Aus$3,000** £1,362 $2,259

[SAME TITLE] [1650 (1657)] 44x54cm (17½x21½") OL color. Exc. [45] £1,689 **$2,800**

MEKLENBURG DUCATUS [1647] 36x48cm (14½x19") Old color. [48] DM 580 £200 $332

NOVA & ACCURATA TUSCIAE ANTIQUAE DESCRIPTIO ... [c.1677] As in *Accuratissima Orbis Delineatio ...* Ancient Tuscany. 35x50cm (14x19½") Color. Ref: Koeman Me 177A, 41. ["Latium" offered at same price] [42] **Aus$1,450** £658 $1,092

NOVA BARBARIAE DESCRIPTIO [1650] 35x52cm (14x20½") Contemp color. [A6] £92 **$153**

NOVA BELGICA ET ANGLIA NOVA [1647] Reissue of 1636, with Blaeu's decor. 39x50cm (15½x20") Color. Exc. Ref: Burden 247; Cumming (SE) 43; Morrison fig.10. [24] £1,206 **$2,000**

NOVA ET ACCURATA POLI ARCTICI ... [1637] 41x52cm (16x20½") Color. Lt staining; else exc. Ref: Burden 250. [24] £844 **$1,400**

NOVA HISPANIA ET NOVA GALICIA [1664] 34x48cm (13½x19") OL color. [41] £271 **$450**

NOVA ZEMLA, WAYGATS, FRETUM NASSOVICUM, ET TERRA SAMOIEDUM ... [c.1650] 41x50cm (16x19½") Later full color. Faint toning/soiling margins; else VG. [A9] £125 **$207**

ORBIS TERRARUM VETERIBUS COGNITI TYPUS GEOGRAPHICUS [1650] Ancient world on full global coordinate oval with much vacant area. 40x51cm (16x20") Color. Faint soiling; o/w fine. Ref: Shirley (W) 385. [A1] £730 **$1,210**

[SAME TITLE] [1657] In *Nieuwen Atlas ofte Werelt ...* 40x51cm (16x20") Color. [19] £392 **$650**

[SAME TITLE] [c.1677] As in *Accuratissima Orbis Delineatio ...* Ancient world as known. 40x50cm (15½x19½") Color. Ref: Shirley (W) 385. Koeman Me 177A, 1A. [42] **Aus$1,750** £795 $1,318

PALESTINA SIVE TERRAE SANCTAE DESCRIPTIO ... [1630] As in *Maioris Appendix ...* Panels top & bottom. 44x56cm (17½x22") Color. Ref: Laor 372. Koeman Me 31A, 80. [42] **Aus$3,000** £1,362 $2,259

[SAME TITLE] [1658] 43x57cm (17x22½") Full orig color. Lower c'fold repaired; o/w exc. Ref: Laor 372. Nebenzahl (Holy Land) pl.43. [2] £2,231 **$3,700**

PATRIAE ANTIQUAE INTER JULY ET CAROLI MAGNI [c.1652] By Hermann Ewich, Amsterdam. 48x61cm (18½x24") [A7] £83 **$138**

POLONIAE NOVA ET ACURATA DESCRIPTIO [1638] New map added to *Nieuwen Atlas*. Continuation of Mercator-Hondius atlas. 39x50cm (15½x20") Color. Few creases; minor mend; else exc. Ref: Koeman Me 69, 489. [24] £302 **$500**

PRINCIPATUS WALLIAE PARS BOREALIS VULGO NORTH WALES [1646] 41x51cm (16x20") OL & highlight color. Mild soiling margins; lower c'fold split repaired verso; image clean. [A9] £139 **$230**

RUSSIAE, VULGO MOSCOVIA ... [c.1658] Jansson-Waesberger. 42x54cm (16½x21") OL col. [A7] £242 **$402**

SALTZBURG [1657] As in *Theatrum Exhibens Illustriores Principesque Germaniae ...* Minor repairs. 38x48cm (15x18½") Period color. Minor repairs. Ref: Koeman Ja 13, 36. [42] **Aus$950** £431 $715

JANSSON continued

SICILIAE VETERIS TYPUS ... GOOS SCULPSIT [1630] As in *Atlantis Maioris Appendix* ... Ancient Sicily. 39x49cm (15½x19½") Color. ["Italia Gallica sive Gallia Cisalpina ..." offered at same price] Ref: Koeman Me 177A, 45. [42] **Aus$1,550** £704 $1,167
[SAME TITLE] [1666] 38x48cm (15x19") Full orig color. Age toned; else VG. [36] £332 **$550**
SITUS TERRAE PROMISSIONIS [c.1652] After Van Adrichom. 38x50cm (15x19½") OL color. Minor browning margins. Ref: Laor 24. [A8] £294 **$488**
SUMATRAE ... [1657] Incl Singapore; north to left. 43x52cm (17x20½") Mint. [45] £1,146 **$1,900**
SUMATRAE ET INSULARUM LOCORUMQUE ... CIRCUMIACENTIUM TABULA NOVA [1650] In Part V, *Atlas Novus*. Chart; north to left; little interior detail. 42x52cm (16½x20½") Orig color, later additions. Verso reinforcement to verdi gris deterioration around cartouche edges; o/w exc. [4] £500 $829
TABOR CIVITAS ANNO 1621 OBSESSA ET CAPTA [1657] As in *Urbium Totius Germaniae Superioris* ... Bird's-eye topographical map of siege. 34x45cm (13½x17½") Color. Rebacked. Ref: cf Koeman Ja 13, 59. [42] **Aus$825** £375 $621
TABULA ANEMOGRAPHICA SEU PYXIS NAUTICA VENTORUM NOMINA SEX LINGUIS REPRAESENTANS. [1650] As in *Atlantis Majoris Quinta Pars* ... Circular diagram of 32 winds named in 6 languages. 44x56cm (17½x22") Color. Ref: Koeman Me 164, 1. [42] **Aus$650** £295 $489
TABULA MAGELLANICA QUA TIERRAE DEL FUEGO [1652 (-1660)] 41x53cm (16x21") Color. Tiny restoration of lower lf neatline; good. Ref: Koeman Me 84 (93). [30] £573 **$950**
TERRA AUSTRALIS INCOGNITA [1663] Circular map of southern hemi. 43x49cm (17x19½") Sl spotted. [A6] £218 $362
TERRITORIO DI CREMONA [1647] 38x48cm (15x19") Old color. [48] **DM 690** £238 $395
ΘPAKH. THRACIAE VETERIS TYPUS [c.1660] 36x48cm (14x19") Color. [39] £151 **$250**
TRACTUUM BORUSSIAE, CIRCA GEDANUM ET ELBINGAM AB INCOLIS WERDER APPELLATI CUM ADIUNCTA NERINGIA, NOVA ET ELABORATISSIMA DELINEATIO [1646] 41x49cm (16½x19½") Old color. [48] **DM 900** £311 $515
TURCICUM IMPERIUM [1658-] 42x52cm (16½x20½") Orig color with gum arabic; full color cartouche. [46] **£680** $1,128
TYPUS FRISIAE ORIENTALIS ... [1630-1633] 38x50cm (15x19½") Uncolored. [34] **£320** $531
TYPUS ORBIS TERRARUM [1628 (1661)] As in Cluver's *Introductionis in Universam Geographicam* ... Double hemi; insular Calif. 15x20cm (5½x8") Col. Ref: cf Shirley (W) 325 & 426. [13] **Aus$1,400** £636 $1,054
URBIS ROMAE [1657] After Braun & Hogenberg. 38x51cm (15x20") Color. [A7] £329 **$546**
VALENTIA REGNUM. COTESTINI. PTOL. EDENTANI PLIN. [1647] West at top. 35x48cm (14x19") Orig wash & OL color. [11] £166 **$275**
VETUS DESCRIPTIO DACIARUM NEC NON MOESIARUM. PETRUS KAERIUS CAELAVIT [c.1677] As in *Accuratissa Orbis Delineatio* ... 36x48cm (14x19") Color. Ref: Koeman Me 177A, 47. [42] **Aus$625** £284 $471
VIRGINIAE PARTIS AUSTRALIS ET FLORIDAE PARTIS ORIENTALIS, INTERJACENTIUMQ REGIONUM NOVA DESCRIPTIO [1639] 38x50cm (15x19½") Orig color. VG. Ref: Burden 254; Cumming (SE) 42; Phillips (M) p.978. [2] £1,146 **$1,900**
[SAME TITLE] [1639+] Blank verso. 39x50cm (15½x20") Orig color. Sm lower c'fold discoloration; else VG. [38] £905 **$1,500**
[SAME TITLE] [c.1650] 38x50cm (15x20") Col. Sm repaired tear just affecting engraving. [A6] £517 $858
XUNTIEN ALIAS QUINZAY [1657] City plan of Hangzhou. 42x52cm (16½x20½") Color. [A7] £225 **$373**

JANVIER

L'AMERIQUE DIVISEE EN SES PRINCIPAUX ETATS, ASSUJETIE AUX OBSERVATIONS ASTRONOMIQUE ... [1769] With West Sea; Choffard vignette of stream side. 47x65cm (18½x26") OL col. VG. [16] £392 **$650**
L'AMERIQUE DIVISEE PAR GRANDS ETATS ... [dated 1762] From Lattre', *Atlas Moderne* ... With "West Sea". 30x44cm (12x17½") Orig OL color. Clean, bright. Ref: Phillips (A) 629-32. [12] £211 **$350**
[SAME TITLE] [1772] 30x44cm (12x17½") Wash color. [11] £136 **$225**
L'ITALIE [c.1780] 32x46cm (12½x18½") OL color. [A8] £69 **$115**
MAPPE MONDE OU DESCRIPTION DU GLOBE TERRESTRE ... 1775 [1775] From *Atlas Moderne* ... Paris: Lattre & Delalain. Double hemi; elaborate cartouche. 30x46cm (12x18") Color. Ref: cf Phillips (A) 5986-2. [19] £280 **$465**
[SAME TITLE] [1775] Double-hemi. 30x44cm (12x17½") OL color; B&W cartouche. MS "1775" in lower margin; VG (A). [A4] £292 **$484**

JAPANESE CARTOGRAPHY

[JAPAN: KYOTO] [1864] Folding into 16 parts showing city, waterways & mountains; pictorial wraps. 58x88cm (23x34½") Full orig color. Wraps sl soiled; MS notes; exc. [2] £513 **$850**

[WORLD] NANSENBUSHU BANKOKU SHOKA NO ZU [1710 / ?] 1st Buddhist world map, India & China centered, in Chinese & Japanese using European knowledge; Europe & South America as islands. 114x142cm (45x56") folding into 7x9" wrappers. Minor fold wear; wraps scuffed; else exc. Ref: Cortazzi p.36, pl.48. [23] £3,317 **$5,500**

KOISHIKAWA [1854] Woodcut Tokyo plan; Japanese text. Folds into octavo blue paper covers. 46x51cm (18x20") Printed color. Some wormholes in image; else VG. [A9] £226 **$374**

JEFFERYS Try *Laurie & Whittle, Sayer, Sayer & Bennett*

[ATLAS] THE AMERICAN ATLAS ... [1776] London: Sayer & Bennett. Large folio, modern calf; 22 maps on 29 sheets in orig OL color, incl Fry-Jefferson, Mouzon & "Most Inhabited Parts of New England". Some foxing. Ref: Phillips (A) 1166. [3] £33,170 **$55,000**

A CHART OF THE ENTRANCE INTO ST. MARY'S RIVER TAKEN BY CAPTN. W. FULLER NOV. 1769 [ON SHEET WITH] PLAN OF AMELIA ISLAND IN EAST FLORIDA [AND] A CHART OF THE MOUTH OF NASSAU RIVER [1770] 51x61cm (20x24") Full orig color. Fine. [32] £1,206 **$2,000**

A CHART OF THE STRAITS OF MAGELLAN [1775] London: Sayer. 52x70cm (20½x27½") OL color. Top margin trimmed to border with disturbance; minor offsetting. [A7] £121 **$201**

A MAP OF THE MOST INHABITED PART OF NEW ENGLAND, CONTAINING THE PROVINCES OF MASSACHUSETS BAY AND NEW HAMPSHIRE, WITH THE COLONIES OF CONNECTICUT AND RHODE ISLAND, DIVIDED INTO COUNTIES AND TOWNSHIPS ... [1755 / c.1768] 4 sheets joined, 104x98cm (41x38½") Orig OL color. Staining upper rt sheet; else exc. Ref: Tooley (Amer) p.71, 33d; Goss (NA) 66. Cumming (Colonial Amer) p 45-7; Benes #12. [24] £2,925 **$4,850**

[SAME TITLE] [Nov. 29, 1774] 4 sheets joined into two; if joined 104x98cm (41x38½") Orig OL color. Repaired 5" tear at ctr; some folds reinforced; good. Ref: Goss (NA) 66. Stevens & Tree 33e; Cumming (Colonial Amer) p 45-7; Phillips (A) 1165. [29] £1,930 **$3,200**

[SAME TITLE] [1774] Attributed to Braddock Mead. Segmented, mounted on linen. 104x99cm (41x39") Exc. Ref: Goss (NA) 66; Tooley (Amer) p.70-1, #33. [2] £2,352 **$3900**

A NEW MAP OF NOVA SCOTIA ... [1750] Insets: Halifax map; city view. 32x42cm (13x16½") Wide margin edges tissue-backed on verso, closing tears lower margin, map unaffected. [A7] £121 **$201**

A VIEW OF AMSTERDAM [n.d.] 17x39cm (6½x15½") Vert creasing; o/w exc. [21] Can$300 £131 **$217**

AN EAST PROSPECT OF THE CITY OF PHILADELPHIA; TAKEN BY GEORGE HEAP FROM THE JERSEY SHORE, UNDER THE DIRECTION OF NICOLAS SCULL SURVEYOR GENERAL OF THE PROVINCE OF PENNSYLVANIA [1756] Later of 2 states. View above, as titled; city plan, the battery & state house engravings below. 49x91cm (19½x36") Glued to stiff cardboard, 2 lateral tears possibly extruding glue, insignificant loss as tears are clean or in areas of no text; should be seen; not returnable. Ref: Snyder (Phila) p.45-7; Phillips (Phila) 439. [A1] £1,493 **$2,475**

AN EXACT CHART OF THE RIVER ST. LAWRENCE ... [1775] Robert Sayer. Insets; 2 sheets joined, 59x92cm (23x36") OL color. [A6] £172 **$286**

ANTIGUA SURVEYED BY ROBERT BAKER, SURVEYOR GENERAL OF THAT ISLAND [1775] Issued for *West India Atlas*. English Harbour inset. 50x62cm (19½x24½") Full color. [20] £1,055 **$1,750**

GRENADA DIVIDED INTO ITS PARISHES, SURVEYED BY ORDER OF HIS EXCELLENCY GOVERNOR SCOTT [1775] 2nd title in French; mostly French names. 46x61cm (18x24") B&W. [20] £573 **$950**

JAMAICA FROM THE LATEST SURVEYS [1775] Kingston & Bluefields harbor insets. 46x61cm (18½x24") Full color. Ref: Kapp (Jamaica) 101. [20] £739 **$1,225**

PLAN OF THE CITY AND HARBOUR OF THE HAVANA [1768] Fortifications & buildings keyed. 22x27cm (8½x10½") Uncolored. VG. Ref: Phillips (M) p.313. [25] £136 **$225**

THE COAST OF WEST FLORIDA AND LOUISIANA, BY THOS. JEFFERYS GEOGRAPHER TO HIS MAJESTY ... [1775] From *West India Atlas*. 1st issue. 48x63cm (19x25") Later color. [27] £1,025 **$1,700**

THE COAST OF WEST FLORIDA AND LOUISIANA, BY THOS. JEFFERYS GEOGRAPHER TO HIS MAJESTY [JOINED WITH] THE PENINSULA AND GULF OF FLORIDA OR CHANNEL OF BAHAMA WITH THE BAHAMA ISLANDS, BY THOS. JEFFERYS ... [1775] From *American Atlas*. Printed for Robert Sayer.. 48x123cm (19x48½") Orig OL color. Fine. Ref: Tooley (Amer) p.65-6, #26b. [28] £1,086 **$1,800**

[SAME TITLE] [1775] 47x122cm (18½x48") Orig OL color. VG. Same ref. [36] £1,689 **$2,800**

THE ISLAND OF CUBA WITH PART OF THE BAHAMAS BANKS & THE MARTYRS [1775] 50x63cm (20x25") Dampstaining top margin; minor browning edges. [A8] £260 **$431**

JEFFERYS continued

THE WINDWARD PASSAGE WITH THE SEVERAL PASSAGES, FROM THE EAST END OF CUBA, AND THE NORTH PART OF ST. DOMINGO [1775] As in *West India Atlas*. 50x64cm (19½x25") B&W. [20] £754 **$1,250**
[SAME TITLE] [1775] From *The West India Atlas*. Shows Bahama chain. 47x63cm (18½x24½") B&W. Fine Ref: Sellers & Van Ee 1735; Phillips (A) 2699. [28] £452 **$750**
THE WORLD AGREEABLE TO THE LATEST DISCOVERIES ... [1754] Double hemi. 19x39cm (7½x15") Color. Minor repair. [19] £172 **$285**

JEFFERYS & FADEN

A PLAN OF PORT ROYAL IN SOUTH CAROLINA. SURVEY'D BY CAPN. JOHN GASCOIGNE ... [c.1773] 1st state of four. Shows Hilton Head. 71x58cm (28x23") Uncolored. Fine. Ref: Tooley (Amer) p.96, #71a. [32] £1,809 **$3,000**

JOHNSON

[ATLAS] JOHNSON'S NEW ILLUSTRATED FAMILY ATLAS OF THE WORLD WITH DESCRIPTIONS ... [1865] NY: Johnson & Ward. Folio; quarter leather. Covers soiled, spine tight but leather dry & rubbed; maps clean with even toning, occas offsetting; margin tear in New Brunswick, clean tear in Calif & SW states. [A1] £548 **$908**
[SAME TITLE] [1866] A.J. Johnson; NY. Folio, orig gold stamped cloth binding; 66 maps & plates; orig color. VG. Ref: Phillips (A) 4346. [3] £724 **$1,200**
[SAME TITLE] [1884] A.J. Johnson. Folio; colored maps. Covers worn, leather points & spine rubbed; c'fold separations into image, US, Western states & N Amer; tear in Germany; most maps VG to fine. [A2] £663 **$1,100**
[ATLAS] JOHNSON'S NEW ILLUSTRATED (STEEL PLATE) FAMILY ATLAS OF THE WORLD ... [1862] NY: Johnson & Ward. Folio, 46x38cm (18x15") Full colored maps. Front cover loose, lacks spine; binding tight; contents generally clean, bright, but 1st few pages toned with chipping; good (B). [A4] £803 **$1,331**
[SAME TITLE] [1862] A.J. Johnson. NY. Folio; many maps; half roan. Cloth tape rebacking; lacks leather tips; o/w worn; internally clean. [A7] £902 **$1,495**
[SAME TITLE] [1863] By Richard Swainson Fisher. Folio, publisher's half morocco; with Peninsula Campaign sheet. Covers worn, numerous tears, chips to text leaves; few tears to several maps; occas browning, margin soiling. [A8] £451 **$747**
[SAME TITLE] [1864] A.J. Johnson; NY. Folio; 65 maps & plates; orig color. Orig gold stamped cloth binding, broken; interior sl soiled; generally good. Ref: Phillips (A) 843. [3] £573 **$950**
[SAME TITLE] [1864] A.J. Johnson. NY. Folio; many maps; half morocco. Sl dampstain front cover, lacks a leather tip, extremities lt rubbed; internally clean. [A7] £1,179 **$1,955**
[SAME TITLE] [1866] A.J. Johnson. NY. Folio; many maps; half morocco. Extremities worn; internally clean. [A7] £763 **$1,265**
[BOOK WITH MAPS] A CHRONOLOGICAL HISTORY OF THE CIVIL WAR IN AMERICA. ILLUSTRATED WITH A.J. JOHNSON'S AND J.H. COLTON'S STEEL PLATE MAP AND PLANS OF SOUTHERN STATES AND HARBORS ... [1863] NY: Johnson & Ward. Octavo, orig cloth; 160 pp; with 8 (of 10) maps. Cover edges worn, front hanging by cord, spine ends chipped; maps, text VG. Ref: Phillips (A) 1350. [A10] £139 **$230**
ARKANSAS, MISSISSIPPI, AND LOUISIANA [c.1864] From *New Illustrated Family Atlas* ... Johnson & Ward. 61x44cm (24x17") Full color. VG (A). [A3] £42 **$70**
DELAWARE AND MARYLAND [1864] From *New Illustrated Family Atlas* ... Johnson & Ward. 32x41cm (12½x16") Full color. Fine (A+). [A3] £43 **$72**
GEORGETOWN AND THE CITY OF WASHINGTON [1862] From Johnson & Ward, *New Illustrated Family Atlas*. 3 vignettes. 32x38cm (12½x15") Full color. Ref: Phillips (Wash) p.45. [12] £45 **$75**
[SAME TITLE] [1864] From *New Illustrated Family Atlas* ... Johnson & Ward. 3 vignettes. 32x40cm (12½x15½") Full color. Little lt offsetting; good (B). [A3] £60 **$99**
GEORGIA AND ALABAMA [1863] From *New Illustrated Family Atlas* ... Johnson & Ward. 2 vignettes. 43x61cm (17x24") Full color by counties. Couple lt spots; good (B). [A4] £33 **$55**
[SAME TITLE] [c.1864] Johnson & Ward. 40x57cm (15½x22") Full color. Fine (A+). [A3] £33 **$55**
JAPAN NIPPON, KIUSIU, SIKOK, YESSO AND THE JAPANESE KURILES [c.1864] Johnson & Ward. Insets incl Bay of Nagasaki. 32x39cm (12½x15½") Full color. VG (A). [A3] £37 **$61**
JOHNSON'S ASIA [1867] A.J. Johnson. 39x55cm (15½x22") Orig color. A ½" margin tear; VG to fine. [14] £78 **$130**
JOHNSON'S AUSTRALIA AND EAST INDIES [1867] New Zealand inset. 57x43cm (22½x17") Orig color. Some lt foxing blank areas; watermark bottom rt; o/w VG. [14] £48 **$80**

JOHNSON continued

JOHNSON'S CALIFORNIA TERRITORIES OF NEW MEXICO AND UTAH [1862] A.J. Johnson. "Arrizona" [sic]; horiz NM-AZ division. 43x61cm (17x24") Full color. C'fold split, sm loss just to top border; soft fold; good (B). [A4] £219 **$363**

[SAME TITLE] [1866 (given)] Johnson & Browning. 43x61cm (17x24") Orig col. Separation lower c'fold touching border; o/w VG to fine. [A1] £133 **$220**

JOHNSON'S CALIFORNIA, TERRITORIES OF NEW MEXICO, ARIZONA, COLORADO, NEVADA AND UTAH [1863-64] A.J. Johnson. 43x62cm (17x24½") Full color. Faint c'fold spotting; VG++. Ref: Phillips (A) 840, 58-59. [35] £166 **$275**

JOHNSON'S CALIFORNIA, WITH UTAH, NEVADA, COLORADO, NEW MEXICO AND ARIZONA [1863] Johnson & Ward. 43x61cm (17x24") Full color. Bright. [26] £106 **$175**

JOHNSON'S CUBA JAMAICA AND PORTO RICO [1863] From *New Illustrated Family Atlas* ... Johnson & Ward. Insets: Puerto Rico; Havana. 32x39cm (12½x15½") Full color. Lt damp stain; margin spotting; good (B). [A4] £24 **$39**

[SAME TITLE] [1864] Johnson & Ward; Insets: Puerto Rico; Havana. 33x40cm (13x16") Lt minor foxing in sea areas; o/w VG to fine. [14] £57 **$95**

JOHNSON'S DELAWARE AND MARYLAND [c.1863] Johnson & Ward. 3 vignettes; DC inset. 32x39cm (12½x15½") Full color. 2 margin tears; VG (A). [A4] £28 **$46**

[SAME TITLE] [1865] DC inset. 33x41cm (13x16") Color. [40] £39 **$65**

[SAME TITLE] [1867] A.J. Johnson; entered by Colton, 1855. B&W inset of DC. 32x40cm (12½x16") Orig color. VG to fine. [14] £75 **$125**

JOHNSON'S EUROPE [1864] A.J. Johnson. 42x57cm (16½x22½") Orig color. Some lt foxing blank areas; o/w VG to fine. [14] £78 **$130**

JOHNSON'S FLORIDA [1863] Johnson & Ward. 32x39cm (12½x15½") Orig color. Some lt margin age toning; o/w VG to fine. [1867 ed offered at same price] [14] £75 **$125**

JOHNSON'S GLOBULAR WORLD [1867] A.J. Johnson. Double hemi. 41x59cm (16½x23") Orig color. Lt age toning along edges & c'fold; o/w VG to fine. [14] £90 **$150**

JOHNSON'S JAPAN [1866] 32x39cm (13x15½") Orig color. Lt margin age toning; VG [14] £72 **$120**

JOHNSON'S MAINE [1862] From *New Illustrated Family Atlas* ... Johnson & Browning. 39x32cm (15x12½") Full color by counties. Margin tear to border; VG (A). [A4] £19 **$31**

JOHNSON'S MAP OF NEW YORK AND THE ADJACENT CITIES [c.1862] 41x65cm (16x25½") Color. [22] £51 **$85**

JOHNSON'S MAP OF THE VICINITY OF RICHMOND, AND PENINSULAR CAMPAIGN IN VIRGINIA ... [1864] From *New Illustrated Family Atlas*. Johnson & Ward. 45x67cm (17½x26½") Orig col. VG to fine. [A2] £133 **$220**

JOHNSON'S MAP OF THE WORLD ON MERCATOR'S PROJECTION. [1862] From *Illustrated Family Atlas* ... NY: Johnson & Ward. 41x64cm (16x25") Full color. Fine (A+). [A3] £63 **$105**

JOHNSON'S MEXICO [1863] Johnson & Ward. Most of southern US shown. 31x39cm (12½x15½") Orig color. Lt margin soiling; o/w VG to fine. ["... Central America" offered at same price] [14] £60 **$100**

JOHNSON'S MINNESOTA AND DAKOTA [1861] Johnson & Browning, NY. Dakota to Missouri River. 32x39cm (12½x15") Full orig color. [36] £90 **$150**

[SAME TITLE] [1863] Johnson & Ward. 31x39cm (12½x15½") Color. VG to fine. [14] £81 **$135**

JOHNSON'S NEBRASKA, DAKOTA, COLORADO & KANSAS [1862] Dakota to Rockies. 32x39cm (12½x15") Color. Deacidified; encased in mylar. [22] £75 **$125**

JOHNSON'S NEBRASKA, DAKOTA, COLORADO, IDAHO & KANSAS [1864] Johnson & Ward. 32x39cm (12½x15½") Orig color. VG. [14] £106 **$175**

[SAME TITLE] [1863] Johnson & Ward. No county divisions; immense ID west of Dakota. 32x40cm (12½x15½") Color. [12] £60 **$100**

[SAME TITLE] [1863] From *New Illustrated Family Atlas* ... Johnson & Ward. ID Terr incl MT & WY. 31x39cm (12x15") Full color by state. Spot in border; some margin dampstain; good (B). [A3] £33 **$55**

[SAME TITLE] [1864] Shows part of maximum Idaho. 32x39cm (13x15½") [22] £72 **$120**

[SAME TITLE] [1864] Huge Idaho. 33x41cm (13x16") Full color. VG. [26] £48 **$80**

JOHNSON'S NEBRASKA, DAKOTA, IDAHO AND MONTANA [1867] Incl WY. 43x59cm (17x23") Full color. Minor discoloration on border. [26] £72 **$120**

JOHNSON'S NEW JERSEY [1862] 21 counties. 40x32cm (16x12½") Color. [22] £42 **$70**

JOHNSON'S NEW MAP OF THE STATE OF TEXAS [1860-1861] Johnson & Browning; early ed. 43x62cm (17x24") Full orig color. [27] £166 **$275**

JOHNSON continued

JOHNSON'S NEW MAP OF THE STATE OF TEXAS [c.1861] From *New Illustrated Family Atlas* ... Johnson & Ward. 41x62cm (16x24½") Full color. Few margin tears & chipping, sm margin loss just to border; else clean; VG (A). [A4] £146 **$242**
[SAME TITLE] [1863] Johnson & Ward. 41x58cm (16½x23") Full col. Margin repair; VG. [16] £145 **$240**
[SAME TITLE] [1863-65] Johnson & Ward. 41x56cm (16x22") Full orig color. A rust spot. [27] £151 **$250**
[SAME TITLE] [1864] Johnson & Ward. 42x62cm (16½x24½") Full orig color. On good paper; faint tide mark lf half; else VG. Ref: cf Day (TX) 1416 & 1511. [37] £100 **$165**
JOHNSON'S NEW MILITARY MAP OF THE UNITED STATES SHOWING THE FORTS, MILITARY POSTS &C. WITH ENLARGED PLANS OF SOUTHERN HARBORS FROM AUTHENTIC DATA OBTAINED AT THE WAR DEPARTMENT [1864] Johnson & Ward. 43x61cm (17x24") Full color. Bright. [26] £48 **$80**
JOHNSON'S NORTH AMERICA [1862] 56x44cm (22x17½") Full color. [22] £51 **$85**
JOHNSON'S ONTARIO, OF THE DOMINION OF CANADA [1867] From *New Illustrated Family Atlas* ... 42x58cm (16½x23") Full color. Fine (A+). [A4] £17 **$28**
JOHNSON'S TEXAS [1866] A.J. Johnson. 39x55cm (15½x21½") Full color. VG. [16] £136 **$225**
JOHNSON'S WESTERN HEMISPHERE [AND] JOHNSON'S EASTERN HEMISPHERE [1861] NY: Johnson & Ward. 38x67cm (15x26½") Color. [19] £57 **$95**
JOHNSON'S WORLD ON MERCATOR'S PROJECTION [1870] Banknote border. 41x58cm (16x23") Full color. [40] £54 **$90**
KENTUCKY AND TENNESSEE [1865] From *New Illustrated Family Atlas* ... A.J. Johnson. 2 vignettes. 42x58cm (16½x23") Full color. Fine (A+). [A4] £27 **$44**
MICHIGAN AND WISCONSIN [c.1864] From *New Illustrated Family Atlas* ... Johnson & Ward. 44x61cm (17½x24") Full color. C'fold split repaired with archival tape; good (B). [A3] £21 **$35**
MINNESOTA AND DAKOTA [c.1864] From *New Illustrated Family Atlas* ... Johnson & Ward. 31x40cm (12½x15½") Full color. VG (A). [A3] £48 **$79**
MISSOURI AND KANSAS [1863] From Johnson & Ward, *New Illustrated ... Atlas* ... Eastern KS only; 3 vignettes. 43x58cm (17x23") Full color. Sh tears repaired in & through lower border; else fine. Ref: Phillips (A) 840-52/53 [12] £60 **$100**
MOUNTAINS & RIVERS [1862] Johnson & Ward. Massed mountains of the world rise from lower lf; rivers are at upper rt. 42x61cm (16½x24") Wash brown & blue. [27] £45 **$75**
NEW MILITARY MAP OF THE UNITED STATES SHOWING THE FORTS, MILITARY POSTS, &C. WITH ENLARGED PLANS OF SOUTHERN HARBORS ... [1861 (c.1864)] From *New Illustrated Family Atlas* ... Shows states & territories, not military depts. 44x60cm (17x23½") Full color. Fine (A+). [A4] £116 **$193**
NEW YORK AND THE ADJACENT CITIES [1862-63] Johnson & Ward. 41x66cm (16x26") Pastel color. Repaired 1" tear into Hoboken; overall VG. [27] £48 **$80**
NORTH AMERICA [1865] From *New Illustrated Family Atlas* ... 56x43cm (22x17") Full color. Fine (A+). [A4] £59 **$98**
NORTH AND SOUTH CAROLINA [c.1863] Johnson & Ward. Vignettes. 43x61cm (17x24") Full color. Lt damp stain margin; VG (A). [A3] £44 **$73**
THE HOLY LAND AND ITS BORDERS [c.1860] J. Hugh Johnson, Edinburgh. 57x47cm (22½x18½") Color litho. [A8] £48 **$80**
UNITED STATES [1864] From *New Illustrated Family Atlas* ... Transitional western territory configurations. 42x58cm (16½x23") Full color. Fine (A+). [A4] £92 **$152**
WASHINGTON, OREGON AND IDAHO [1863] Johnson & Ward. With part of present MT & WY. 31x39cm (12½x15½") Color. Mint. [12] £60 **$100**
[SAME TITLE] [c.1864] Johnson & Ward. With part of present MT & WY. 31x39cm (12½x15½") Full color. Fine (A+). [A3] £73 **$121**

JOHNSTON   Try *Globes*

[ATLAS] A SCHOOL ATLAS OF ASTRONOMY ... [1856] Edinburgh & London. Sm 4to; 18 double-page printed color plates. Half-leather scuffed; internally VG. [37] £151 **$250**
[ATLAS] THE NATIONAL ATLAS OF HISTORICAL, COMMERCIAL, AND POLITICAL GEOGRAPHY ... [1850] Tall folio, half leather & cloth; 46 double-page maps in OL color, incl 2 world, 4 North America, 18 Europe, 7 Asia, 5 Pacific & Australia, etc. Covers worn, soiled, front loose; leather worn, spine cracking & lifting; index edge chipped; maps VG. [A2] £730 **$1,210**
AUSTRALIA [c.1883] From *Globe Encyclopaedia Atlas*. 23x30cm (9x12") Printed color. Fine (A+). [A4] £19 **$31**

JOHNSTON continued

BASIN OF THE BALTIC [1862] By Keith Johnston; Edinburgh: Blackwood. Baltic rim regions. 44x57cm (17½x22½") Hand & printed color. [40] £45 **$75**

CENTRAL AMERICA AND WEST INDIA ISLANDS [c.1883] From *Globe Encyclopaedia Atlas*. W. & A.K. Johnston. 23x30cm (9x12") Printed color. VG. [A4] £10 **$17**

CHINA [1850] 50x60cm (19½x23½") Orig OL color; Hong Kong in red. Stain top margin; else VG. [38] £90 **$150**

ISLANDS IN THE PACIFIC OCEAN - SHEET 8 [c.1854] From A.K. Johnston, *National Atlas*. Folding linen-backed map with marbled paper cover; incl Australia, New Zealand, New Guinea, New Hebrides. 50x61cm (19½x24") OL color. Orig owner pasted relevant newspaper articles on linen panel; VG (A). [A3] £66 **$110**

NORTH AMERICA [c.1845] Edinburgh & London. Texas as republic. 60x50cm (24x19½") Orig OL color. VG. [38] £151 **$250**

NORTH AMERICA [c.1883] From *Globe Encyclopaedia Atlas*. 30x23cm (12x9") Printed color. Fold split repaired with archival tape; good (B). [A4] £10 **$17**

THE WORLD IN HEMISPHERES [1868] Blackwood & Son. 39x57cm (15½x22½") Color. [19] £57 **$95**

UNITED STATES AND TEXAS [c.1845] Niagara River inset; dates of foreign recognition of independent Texas. 50x61cm (19½x24") Orig OL color. Fine. Ref: Day (TX) 1431. [37] £362 **$600**

UNITED STATES OF NORTH AMERICA (WESTERN STATES) [c.1870] Coverage west of Mississippi. 44x57cm (17½x22½") Printed color. Fine (A+). [A4] £53 **$88**

JOLLAIN

CARTE DU ROYAUME DE SIAM ... [1686 (c.1775?)] Possibly a Dezauche reprint. 48x33cm (19x13") Color. Blackening at top cartouche, possibly color oxidation; 2 spots in cartouche; o/w good. [45] £905 **$1,500**

JUTA

STANDARD RAILWAY MAP OF SOUTH AFRICA ... [1907] Distributed by Central South African Railways; stops named, operators color coded. 96x75cm (38x29½") Orig color. Marginal damage restored. [34] £150 $249

KAEMPFER

MAPPA SPECIALIS ITINERIS ... AB URBE NANGASAKI ... [IN SET WITH] ... **AB URBE SIMONSEKI OSACCAM ...** [AND] ... **AB URBE OSAKA AD URBEM MIACO ...** [AND] ... **A PAGO FAMMAMATZ AD URBEM IEDO** [1777] Re-engraving of 1727 maps. 4 route maps of Dutch journey: Nagasaki to Kokura; Simonseki to Osaka; Osaka to Kyoto to Hamamatsu; Hamamatsu & Tokyo. All more or less 30x30cm (12x12") Color. Close side margins where bound newly reinstated; o/w exc. Ref: Walter (Japan) 104A-F; MCC 36 #48. [4] £950 $1,576

PLAN DE JEDO. [1758] Tokyo. Dheulland, sc. 32x32cm (12½x12½") B&W. VG (A). [A4] £133 **$220**

KEELER

THE NATIONAL MAP OF THE TERRITORY OF THE UNITED STATES, FROM THE MISSISSIPPI RIVER TO THE PACIFIC OCEAN [1867] William H. Keeler, Washington. Mounted on linen, folds into orig large 4to title stamped cloth case; text page laid inside front cover. 124x151cm (49x59½") Orig color. Creases at folds; generally exc. Ref: Howes (US) K-22; Storm (Graff) 2281; Wheat (TM) 1170. [24] £1,809 **$3,000**

KELLER

CANTON ZURICH [1856] Linen-backed 10-section map. 55x40cm (21½x16") Partial color. Ex lib NYHS. [A7] £42 **$69**

KEMBLE

TEXAS IN 1836 [1844] 21x24cm (8½x9½") Couple minor spots; o/w VG. [21] **Can$45** £20 $32

KENDALL

[ATLAS] **ATLAS OF THE HEAVENS; SHOWING THE PLACES OF THE PRINCIPAL STARS, CLUSTERS AND NEBULAE; DESIGNED TO ACCOMPANY THE URANOGRAPHY; OR, A DESCRIPTION OF THE HEAVENS** [1855] E. Otis Kendall; publ by E.H. Butler. 17 celestial views, B&W, about 22x41cm (8½x16") Covers worn, separated; pages loose; occas lt foxing margin; views VG to fine. [A2] £90 $149

[BOOK WITH MAPS] **NARRATIVE OF THE TEXAS SANTA FE EXPEDITION** [1846] NY: Harper & Bros. Two 12mo vols, orig cloth, rebacked & spines preserved, with slip box; map and all plates present. Good. Ref: Howes (US) K-75. [16] £573 **$950**

TEXAS AND PART OF MEXICO & THE UNITED STATES SHOWING THE ROUTE OF THE FIRST SANTA FE EXPEDITION ... W. KENDALL [1844] Geo. W. Kendall. 41x29cm (16x11½") VG. Ref: Storm (Graff) 2304. [16] £332 **$550**

KENSETT
To the Officers of the Army and Citizens of the United States This Map of Upper and Lower Canada and United States Contiguous... [1812] Amos Doolittle, sc. Border regions, Quebec to Lake Superior. 35x46cm (14x18½") Tear repaired; imprint almost obscured. Ref: Karpinski (MI) p.208. [2] £2,111 **$3,500**

KEUR
Perigrinatie Veertich-Iarize Reyse der Kinderen Israels ... [c.1700] Topical vignettes below. 30x45cm (12x18") Col. Sm lower margin; minor discoloration; else VG. Ref: cf Laor 807. [38] £271 **$450**

KILIAN, G.C.
Die Belagerung von Colberg Angegriffen durch den Russischen General V. Palmbach und Defendirt durch den Preussi. Obristen Bar v. Heyden von 3ten Oct. 1758 bis 1. Nov. da die Belagerung Aufgehebt Wurde [c.1760] Plan with troop positions & legend. 16x24cm (6½x9½") Partial color. [48] DM 420 £145 **$240**

Gegend am Rhein im Clevischen, wo die Alliirte Armee ... den 2. Juny 1758 Ubergangen [1760] Troop positions with legend. 16x26cm (6½x10") Old color. [48] DM 380 £131 **$217**

General Charte von den Mitternachte America und Sonderlich denen darin Befindliche Franzos Colonien ... [c.1730] From *Atlas Curieux*. Attributable to Bodenehr. North America; insular Calif; cartouche portrait of "Mississippi Bubble" Law. 17x25cm (7x10") Fine. Ref: McLaughlin 236, State 2. [43] £573 **$950**

Grund Riss und Kon. Preuss. Belagerung der Stadt Breslau vom 8. bis 20. Dec. 1757 [1760] Siege, troop positions, with legend. 18x28cm (7x11") Partial color. Narrow lf margin. [48] DM 320 £110 **$183**

KINO
Passage par Terre a La Californie Decouvert par le Rev. Pere Eusebe-Francois Kino Jesuite depuis 1698 jusqu'a 1701 ... [c.1770] From later ed of *Lettres Edifantes*. 1st publ 1705. 23x20cm (9x8") B&W. Part remargined at lf; fine. Ref: Wheat (TM) 89; Schwartz & Ehrenberg pl.75. Cumming (Exploration) 236, pl.379; Lowery 250. [29] £362 **$600**

KIP
[ASIA] [1665] As in Raleigh's *History of the World*. Shows Ark on Mt. Ararat; passage of Ophir & Hauilah. 25x38cm (10x15") B&W. [20] £136 **$225**

[Holy Land] [1665] From Raleigh's *History of the World*. 28x38cm (11x15") B&W. [20] £112 **$185**

[Middle East] [1665] From Raleigh's *History of the World*. Incl Cyprus, Mesopotamia, Arabia. 30x38cm (12x15") B&W. [20] £93 **$155**

KIRCHER
Hydrophylacium Africae ... [1678] Southern Africa & Madagascar. 34x41cm (13½x16½") [A7] £347 **$575**

Mappa Fluxus et Reflxu Rationes in Isthmo America; No in Freto Magellanico, Cateris; Que Americae Littoribus Exhibens [1665] Shows ocean currents. 34x41cm (13½x16½") Uncolored. [41] £392 **$650**

Tabula Geodoborica Itinerum a Varijs in Cataium ... [1667] From book on China; illustrates land & sea trade routes from Middle East to China. 27x35cm (10½x13½") Uncolored. [34] £320 **$531**

KITCHIN Try *London Magazine, Sayer*
A Compleat Map of the British Isles [1787] London: Sayer. 64x50cm (25x20") OL color. Scattered lt foxing & offsetting. [A7] £139 **$230**

A Correct Map of the Island of Jamaica. [1766] 11x19cm (4½x7½") [11] £51 **$85**

A Map of Essex [1749] From Kitchin & Jefferys *Small English Atlas*. Publ 1749-85. 12x14cm (4½x5½") [11] £36 **$60**

A Map of the Circle of Lower Saxony [c.1760] 22x26cm (9x10") [48] DM 110 £38 **$63**

A Map of the River Gambia from Eropina to Barrakunda by Captain John Leach in 1732 [1745] Drawings of 3 insects on same page. 20x32cm (8x12½") Uncolored. [41] £45 **$75**

A Map of the West Indies and Middle Continent of America from the Latest Observations [1768] 41x57cm (16x22½") OL & wash color. [41] £166 **$275**

A New & Accurate Map of China, Drawn from Surveys Made by the Jesuit Missionaries ... [1764] 34x41cm (13½x16") [11] £106 **$175**

[Same Title] [1764] 34x41cm (13½x16") Color. Exc. [24] £271 **$450**

KITCHIN continued

A New and Accurate Map of the British Dominions in America, According to the Treaty of 1763; Divided into the Several Provinces and Jurisdictions   [1763-] To accompany *Universal History of the World*. 52x63cm (20½x24½") Col. Ref: Sellers & Van Ee 104. Tooley (Amer) p.44.   [34]   **£1,400** **$2,322**

A New and Correct Map of Scotland or North Britain   [1787] London: Sayer. 4-sheet map; horiz parts joined; not vertically; overall 128x107cm (50½x42") OL color. Minor foxing & browning; fold intersection separations; sh margin tears just into image.   [A7]   **£173** **$287**

A New Map of England Divided into Its Counties ... [18th c.] From Barnard's *New Complete & Authentic History of England*. 36x33cm (14x13") Minor edge chips; sl creasing; o/w VG.   [21]   **Can$160** **£70** **$116**

A New Map of Ireland Divided into Provinces, Counties &c.   [1777] London: Sayer & Bennett. 64x56cm (25x22") Provinces by full color. Exc.   [36]   **£513** **$850**

A New Map of the Kingdom of Poland   [1787] London: Sayer. 50x66cm (19½x26") OL color.   [A7]   **£104** **$172**

A New Map of the Northern States Containing the Kingdoms of Sweden, Denmark, and Norway   [1788] London: Sayer. 50x66cm (19½x26") OL color. Minor browning & offsetting.   [A7]   **£69** **$115**

British Dominions in America Agreeable to the Treaty of 1763 ...   [1777] London: Dury. Issued separately (?); tab remnant suggests extraneous binding into something. 44x54cm (17½x21½") OL color.   [A7]   **£3,884** **$6,440**

Europe   [1787] London: Sayer. 4-sheet map; horiz parts joined, not vertically; overall 107x125cm (42x49") OL color. Several hard creases; margin tears, some loss; 16cm tear along fold; scattered browning; other faults.   [A7]   **£139** **$230**

Italy   [1786] London: Sayer. 60x52cm (23½x20½") OL color. Sh tear just into image; surface disturbance with sm hole; several soft creases.   [A7]   **£121** **$201**

Messico o Nuova Spagna   [c.1780] From Italian ed of *Dr. Robertson's History of America*. 28x37cm (11x14½") OL & wash color.   [39]   **£136** **$225**

North America   [1777] Publ in Guthrie, *A New Geographical ... Grammar*. 18x23cm (7x9") B&W. 2 sm acid burns; trimmed close to lower neat line; VG.   [35]   **£45** **$75**

Scotland with the Roads, from the Latest Survey ...   [c.1785] 36x33cm (14½x13") Old OL color. VG.   [38]   **£151** **$250**

The ... Russian Empire   [1788] London: Sayer. Two joined sheets. 50x128cm (19½x50½") OL color. 17cm tear into image fairly well closed; rt margin trimmed to platemark; several soft creases; minor foxing.   [A7]   **£294** **$488**

The World from the Best Authorities   [1767] 18x37cm (7½x14½") Color.   [19]   **£160** **$265**

West Indies, Agreeable to the Most Approved Maps & Charts   [1782] Publ in Millar's *New Complete & Universal System of Geography*. 34x38cm (13½x15")   [11]   **£90** **$150**

KNIPE

Geological Map of Scotland, Lochs, Mountains, Islands   [1859] I.A. Knipe. 107x81cm (42x32") Orig color.   [34]   **£380** **$630**

Geological Map of the British Isles and Part of France   [1847] J.A. Knipe. 1st ed. 4 sheets dissected & linen backed, folding into octavo roan slipcase. 161x138cm (63½x54½") Color. Case sl rubbed.   [A6]   **£632** **$1,048**

KOLB

Caarte van de Beyde Afgelegenste Colonien Drakensteen   [1727] From 1st Dutch ed, *Naauwkeurige en Uitvoerige Beshryving van de Kaap de Goede Hoop*. Amsterdam: Balthazar Lakeman. About 30x40cm (12x15½") Uncolored.   [34]   **£215** **$357**

Caarte van de Colonie van de Kaap   [1727] From 1st Dutch ed, *Naauwkeurige en Uitvoerige Beshryving van de Kaap de Goede Hoop*. Amsterdam: Balthazar Lakeman. About 30x40cm (12x15½") Uncolored. Ref: Norwich 217.   [34]   **£245** **$407**

Caarte van de Colonie van Stellenbosch   [1727] From 1st Dutch ed, *Naauwkeurige en Uitvoerige Beshryving van de Kaap de Goede Hoop*. Amsterdam: Balthazar Lakeman. About 30x40cm (12x15½") Uncolored.   [34]   **£225** **$373**

Caarte van de Kaap Goede Hoop   [1727] From 1st Dutch ed, *Naauwkeurige en Uitvoerige Beshryving van de Kaap de Goede Hoop*. Amsterdam: Balthazar Lakeman. St. Helena Bay to Mossel Bay. About 30x40cm (12x15½") Uncolored.   [34]   **£285** **$473**

KOLB continued

CAARTE VAN DE OOST-KUST VAN AFRICA ... AAN KAAP DE GOEDE HOOP [1727] From 1st Dutch ed, *Naauwkeurige en Uitvoerige Beshryving van de Kaap de Goede Hoop*. Amsterdam: Balthazar Lakeman. Cape Aguilhas to Mozambique. About 30x40cm (12x15½") Uncolored. [34] £250 **$415**

CAARTE VANDE KAAP DE GOEDE HOOP LEGGENDE IN'T ZUYDER GEDEELTE VAN AFRICA [1727(?)] Shows Hottentot camps. 30x38cm (12x15") ["Gezigt van de Kaap de Goede Hoop" offered at same price] [11] £106 **$175**

CARTE DE LA COLONIE DE STELLENBOSCH [1727(?)] 30x38cm (12x15") [11] £112 **$185**

CARTE VAN DE COLONIE VAN DE KAAP [1727(?)] 30x38cm (12x15") [11] £90 **$150**

KRUSENSTERN

[ATLAS] ATLAS IUZHNAGO MORIA [1824] 2nd ed of atlas of South Pacific surveys as part of circumnavigation. Folio, paneled morocco, gilt & blind-tooled; 18 maps, incl New Zealand & parts of Australia. Exc. Ref: cf Phillips (A) 3242, 1-15. [24] £7,539 **$12,500**

LA HARPE

CARTE DES DECOUVERTES ... LA MER PACIFIQUE ... PAR LE CAPTAINE COOK EN 1774 [c.1780] Tracks dated. 36x46cm (14x18½") OL color. VG. [37] £60 **$100**

CARTE DU GREENLAND [dated 1770 (1780)] By Laurent. Incl distorted Iceland. 19x25cm (7½x10") Wash color. [40] £45 **$75**

ETATS UNIS ET GRANDES ANTILLES [c.1816] US west to Mississippi Valley. 30x23cm (12x9") OL color. VG. [25] £48 **$80**

LA HONTAN

CARTE GENERALE DE CANADA [1703] From Tome Second, *Memoires de l'Amerique Septentrionale ou la Suite des Voyages ...* 23x39cm (9x15½") Offsetting; sm closed outer lf margin tear. Ref: Kershaw (Canada) 291. Armstrong #19; TMC 19. [21] **Can$625** £273 $453

PROFIL DE LA VILLE DE QUEBEC ET DE SES ENVIRONS ATTAQUEE PAR LES ANGLOISE EN L'ANNE 1691 [1728] From Tome Premier, *Memoires de l'Amerique Septentrionale ou la Suite des Voyages ...* 19x20cm (7½x8") B&W. Offsetting. Ref: Phillips (M) p.731. [21] **Can$160** £70 $116

LA PEROUSE

CARTE DES DECOUVERTES FAITES EN 1787 DANS LES MERS DE CHINE ET DE TARTARIE ... [SHEETS 1 AND 2] [1797] Track from Manila around Formosa & through Sea of Japan. Each 49x68cm (19½x27") [11] £196 **$325**

CARTE DES PARTIES DES ILES SANDWICH ... [ON SHEET WITH] CARTE DES ILES SANDWICH ... [1797] 1st ed. 68x49cm (26½x19½") Wash col. some creasing; else exc. Ref: Fitzpatrick (HI) p.26. [24] £1,025 **$1,700**

[SAME TITLE] [1797] 2 maps: before and after 1786 La Perouse mapping. 69x50cm (27x19½") Color. [46] £320 **$531**

CARTE GENERALE D'UNE PARTIE DE LA COTE DU NORD-OUEST DE L'AMERIQUE RECONNUE PAR LES FREGATES FRANCAISES LA BOUSSOLE ET ASTROLABE ... [1797] From *Atlas du Voyage de La Perouse*. 68x49cm (27x19½") B&W. Fine. [29] £332 **$550**

CARTE PARTICULIERE DE LA COTE DU NORD-OUEST DE L'AMERIQUE ... EN 1786 ... [1797] From orig French ed. Monterey Bay almost to Columbia River. 50x69cm (19½x27") Exc. Ref: Howes (US) L 93. [43] £271 **$450**

CHART OF THE PARTS OF THE SANDWICH ISLANDS ... [ON SHEET WITH] CHART OF THE SANDWICH ISLANDS ... [1798] 50x38cm (19½x15") Exc. [45] £543 **$900**

LABILLARDIERE

[BOOK WITH MAPS] AN ACCOUNT OF A VOYAGE IN SEARCH OF LA PEROUSE [1801] Atlas vol only. Large quarto; half calf marble boards; incl "A Chart of the Indian Ocean and Part of the South Seas ..." & 41 (of 43) natural history plates. [11] £452 **$750**

LADIES REPOSITORY

NEW HAVEN (FROM PERRY HILL) [1854] View. 11x20cm (4½x8") ["New Bedford" offered at same price] [41] £36 **$60**

NEW ORLEANS FROM THE LOWER COTTON PRESS [(1852) 1854] View, based on Smith Bros. litho. 11x18cm (4½x7½") ["Louisville ..." offered at same price] [41] £36 **$60**

PITTSBURGH AND ALLEGHENY [Apr 1854] View by B.F. Smith; steel engraving by Wellswood. 11x18cm (4½x7") B&W. Fine. Ref: Deak p.437. [12] £45 **$75**

PORTLAND, MAINE [1854] View. 13x20cm (5x8") [41] £39 **$65**

LAGNIET
CARTE DE L'ISLE CAYENNE [1652] 31x40cm (12½x16") Orig OL color. Exc. [2] £1,146 **$1,900**

LAKE et al
[ATLAS] AN ILLUSTRATED ATLAS OF WASHINGTON COUNTY, MARYLAND [1877] Lake, Griffing & Stevenson, Phila. Folio, half morocco; profusion of maps in color. Backstrip perished; joints reinforced; maps clean. [A8] £156 **$258**

LANEE
CHEMINS DE FER DE L'EUROPE CENTRALE [1890] Dissected into 21 panels, folded into octavo marbled case. Rail and ship routes, British Isles to Russia to Mediterranean. 46x64cm (18x25") Color. Case shaken, lacks spine piece; lt age-toned; ink trace lower corner; VG-fine. [6] £96 **$160**

LANGE
[ATLAS] SCHUL-ATLAS ZUM UNTERRICHT IN DER ERDUNDE [1866] Liechtenstern, T.F. & H. Lange. Tall quarto; 44 maps. Maps colored. Cloth covers sunned & soiled; inside hinge loose. [A1] £100 **$165**

LANGENES
IAPAN [1598 (1609)] 9x13cm (3½x5") Exc. Ref: Walter (Japan) 7. [43] £317 **$525**

LAPIE
CARTE D'AFRIQUE [1829] 43x56cm (17x22") Some color. VG. [25] £90 **$150**
CARTE DE L'AMERIQUE SEPTENTRIONALE [1829] 53x41cm (21x16") Some color. VG. [25] £136 **$225**
CARTE DE L'ITALIE [1831] 56x43cm (22x17") Some color. VG. [25] £54 **$90**
CARTE DE L'OCEANIE CONTENANT L'AUSTRALIE, LA POLYNESIE ET LES ILES ASIATIQUES ... [1829] As in *Atlas Universel*. 39x54cm (15½x21½") Orig OL color. Ref: Tooley (Australia) 836. [13] Aus$480 £218 $361
[SAME TITLE] [1829] 43x56cm (17x22") Some color. VG. [25] £72 **$120**
CARTE DE LA PALESTINE OU TERRE SAINTE [1833] 56x43cm (22x17") Some col. VG. [25] £72 **$120**
CARTE DE LA PLATA DU CHILI ET DE LA PATAGONIE [1828] 53x39cm (21x15½") OL color. Bit lt foxing, surface soil; overall VG (B). [A3] £12 **$20**
CARTE DES ANTILLES DU GOLFE DU MEXIQUE ET D'UNE PARTIE DES ETATS VOISONS [1829] 43x56cm (17x22") Some color. VG. [25] £90 **$150**
CARTE DES ETATS UNIS D'AMERIQUE [1838] Heart-shaped Texas Republic. 39x55cm (15½x21½") Orig OL color. [27] £232 **$385**
CARTE DES ETATS-UNIS D'AMERIQUE, DU CANADA, DU NOUVEAU BRUNSWICK ET D'UNE PARTIE DE LA NOUVELLE BRETAGNE [dated 1832] From *Atlas Universel* Lallemand, engr. Highly detailed except in Southwest. 39x53cm (15½x21") OL color. Pristine. [same title, engraved by Tardieu, dated 1854 with more information, offered at same price] Ref: Phillips (A) 765-43. [12] £226 **$375**
CARTE DES ETATS-UNIS D'AMERIQUE, DU CANADA, DU NOUVELLE BRUNSWICK ET D'UNE PARTE DE LA NOUVELLE BRETAGNE [1832] Paris: Eymery Frager. U.S. coast to coast. 41x53cm (16x21") OL color. VG. Ref: Wheat (TM) 428. [25] £196 **$325**
CARTE DES ETATS-UNIS DU MEXIQUE [1829] Incl present TX, AZ NM, CA, CO, NV, UT; Central America inset. 54x39cm (21x15½") Orig OL color. VG to fine. [A1] £216 **$358**
[SAME TITLE] [1829] 53x41cm (21x16") Some OL color. [25] £211 **$350**
[SAME TITLE] [1829] 53x39cm (21x15½") Orig OL color. [27] £238 **$395**
[SAME TITLE] [dated 1842] From *Atlas Universel* ... Texas Republic to Nueces; Central America inset. 54x39cm (21x15½") OL color. Fine. Ref: Phillips (A) 787-44. [12] £226 **$375**
ETATS-UNIS DE L'AMERIQUE SEPTENTRIONALE ... [1810] To Mississippi R. 22x29cm (8½x11½") Modern OL color. Lt even toning; 2 worm holes; good (B). [A3] £117 **$194**
SYSTEMS PLANETAIRES [1832] Armillary sphere & astronomical diagrams. 41x81cm (16x32") Uncolored. Some soiling. [25] £54 **$90**

LAPORTE
CARTE DE LA NOUVELLE ANGLETERRE, NOUVELLE YORK, NOUVELLE JERSEY, ET PENSILVANIE [1781] 18x22cm (7x8½") [11] £106 **$175**
CARTE DE LA VIRGINIE ET DU MARILAND [1781] 18x22cm (7x8½") [11] £151 **$250**
CARTE DES PAYS BAS COMPRENANT LE BRABANT, GUELDRE, LIMBOURG, LUXEMBOURG, HAYNANT, NAMUR, FLANDRE, CAMBRESIS ET ARTOIS [1781] 18x22cm (7x8½") OL color. [40] £36 **$60**

LAPORTE continued

Golfe du Mexique Assujetti aux Observations Astronomiques [1781] 18x22cm (7x9") [11] £90 **$150**
Isle de la Jamaique [1781] 18x22cm (7x8½") [11] £75 **$125**
La Russie d'Europe [1781] 18x23cm (7x9") OL color. [40] £42 **$70**
Les Couronnes du Nord Comprenant les Royaumes du Suede, Norwege, et Danemarck [1781] Incl Finland. 18x22cm (7x8½") OL color. [40] £45 **$75**

LASOR A VAREA

Amorfortia Dioecesis Ultrarectensis Oppidum ... [1713] Bird's-eye view. 9x13cm (3½x5") on text sheet. [48] DM 120 £41 **$68**
Argentina [Strasbourg] [1713] Bird's-eye view. 8x12cm (3½x5") [48] DM 190 £66 **$109**
Cassel [1713] View. 9x13cm (3½x5"); verso: Kaschau/Slowakei view. [48] DM 480 £166 **$275**
Di Hungaria et Transilvania Tavola Novissima [1713] 14x20cm (5½x8") [48] DM 130 £45 **$74**
Francfordia [1713] View, Frankfort / Oder, on text page. 9x14cm (3½x5½") [48] DM 320 £110 **$183**
Husenum [1713] View on text sheet with legend. 9x13cm (3½x5½") [48] DM 450 £155 **$257**
Moscovia, Urbs, Regionis eius de Nominis Metropolitica ... [1713] Bird's-eye view. 9x14cm (3½x5½") [48] DM 150 £52 **$86**
Piccola Tartaria [1713] 10x15cm (4x5½") on text sheet. [48] DM 60 £21 **$34**
Toledo [1713] Bird's-eye view. 8x13cm (3½x5") [48] DM 120 £41 **$68**
Torino Metropoli del Piamonte [1713] View. 12x18cm (5x7") Old lining. [48] DM 200 £69 **$114**

LATTRE

Mappe-Monde Geo Spherique ou Nouvelle Carte Ideale ... [1760] By Louis Claude de Vezou. 50x74cm (19½x29½") Full orig color. Exc. [2] £2,111 **$3,500**

LAURIE & WHITTLE   Try *Jefferys*

A Chart of the Straits of Malacca and Sincapore ... [1794] In *Complete East India Pilot and Oriental Navigator*. By Jefferys. 61x83cm (24x32½") Full color wash. Exc. [4] £1,000 **$1,658**
A New and Correct Map of Scotland or North Britain [1794] 4-sheets joined. 129x108cm (51x42½") OL color. Some browning along joints, minor separations where joined. [A7] £225 **$373**
A New Chart of the Coast of North America from Port Royal Entrance to Matanza Inlet Exhibiting the Coast of Georgia [1809] Separately issued for use at sea. Insets: Nassau & St. Mary's River entrances; St. Augustine. 72x51cm (28½x20½") Formerly dissected, mounted on rice paper; some offsetting; good-VG. [23] £2,895 **$4,800**
A New Map of North America, with the West India Islands ... 1783 [1794] By Pownall. Insets: Calif; Hudson's Bay. 4 sheets joined, 102x117cm (40x46") Full color. Sl creasing margins. [A6] £391 **$649**
Asia and Its Islands [1799] After D'Anville. 4 sheets joined, 102x119cm (40x47") Full col. [A6] £184 **$305**
Graeciae Pars Septentrionalis [1794] After De L'Isle. 48x64cm (18½x25") OL color. Sl offset & browned. [A8] £69 **$115**
The East Indies with the Roads [1794] By Jefferys. 4 sheets joined, 106x136cm (42x53½") Title on overslip. Full color. Some margin creasing. [A6] £644 **$1,068**
The Straits of Sincapore with Those of Drion, Sabon, Mandol, &ca and South Part of Malacca Straits. Improved and Corrected from the Observations of Captn. John Hall ... and Other Navigators [1799] Large scale. 43x58cm (17x23") Mint. [43] £1,447 **$2,400**

LAVOISNE

[Atlas] A Complete Genealogical, Historical, Chronological, and Geographical Atlas ... by M. Lavoisne First American Edition ... Philadelphia: Published by M. Carey and Son. 1820 [1820] Folio; many diagrams & 33 maps. Orig color. Orig boards detached; few maps split at folds; lib stamp title page & sm piece missing, no text loss. Ref: Phillips (A) 5527. [3] £573 **$950**
Canaan, with Part of Egypt, during the Residence of the Israelites in the Desert [ON SHEET WITH] Canaan, Subsequent to Its Conquest by the Israelites, and Its Division among the Tribes [1820] From 2nd American ed, *Genealogical, Historical ... and Geographical Atlas* ... 1st U.S. ed of map. Two maps with text surround; with five related folio sheets with text & tables. 25x24cm (10x9½") Full color. VG (A). [A3] £74 **$123**
China and the Tributary Kingdom of Corea [1820] From *A Complete Genealogical ... and Geographical Atlas* ... 1st ed; Kneass, Young, sc. With most of Japan. 22x27cm (8½x10½") Full color. Lt c'fold browning; VG. [35] £39 **$65**

LAVOISNE continued

GEOGRAPHICAL AND HISTORICAL MAP OF AFRICA [1820] From 2nd American ed, *Genealogical, Historical ... and Geographical Atlas ...* 28x29cm (11x11½") Full color. On heavy paper; sl toning at c'fold; VG (A). [A3] £124 **$206**

[SAME TITLE] [1821] Phila: Carey. On 16x20" sheet with text; map 29x30cm (11½x11½") Orig col. Lower c'fold separation repaired on verso; sh top margin tear into blank area repaired verso. [14] £142 **$235**

GEOGRAPHICAL AND STATISTICAL MAP OF ENGLAND [1820] From 2nd American ed, *Genealogical, Historical ... and Geographical Atlas ...* Phila: M. Carey & Son. With 3 text & tabular folio sheets. 38x34cm (15x13½") Full color. C'fold split repaired with archival tape; VG (A). ["... Italy", "... Sweden" on sheet with "... Denmark", "... Asia" & "... China" sold at same price] [A3] £40 **$66**

GEOGRAPHICAL AND STATISTICAL MAP OF IRELAND [1820] From 2nd American ed, *Genealogical, Historical ... and Geographical Atlas ...* Phila: M. Carey & Son. With text & tabular folio sheet. 35x33cm (13½x13") Full color. C'fold split repaired with archival tape; few lt stains in sea; VG (A). [A3] £87 **$145**

GEOGRAPHICAL AND STATISTICAL MAP OF POLAND [1820] From 2nd American ed, *Genealogical, Historical ... and Geographical Atlas ...* Phila: M. Carey & Son. Subtitle, " Poland, Prussia and Hungary ..."; text surround; with text folio sheet. 30x28cm (11½x11") Full color. Sh c'fold split repaired with archival tape; VG (A). [A3] £30 **$50**

GEOGRAPHICAL AND STATISTICAL MAP OF SCOTLAND [1820] From 2nd American ed, *Genealogical, Historical ... and Geographical Atlas ...* Phila: M. Carey & Son. With text & tabular folio sheet. 34x31cm (13½x12½") Full color. C'fold split repaired with archival tape; VG (A). [A3] £53 **$88**

GEOGRAPHICAL, HISTORICAL AND STATISTICAL MAP OF AMERICA [1820] From 2nd American ed, *Genealogical, Historical ... and Geographical Atlas ...* 2 maps with surround of text: "North America ..." (8x9") & "South America ..." (7x9"); printed surface dimensions about 44x53cm (17½x21") Full color. Archival tape repair to c'fold split; spot in text; VG (A). [A3] £99 **$164**

GEOGRAPHICAL MAP OF THE WORLD WITH THE TRACKS OF THE MOST CELEBRATED NAVIGATORS [1820] From 1st US ed, *Complete Genealogical, Historical ... Atlas*. Phila: M. Carey & Son. 1st state. On 17x22" sheet with text; double hemi, each Diameter: 25cm (9½") Full wash color. Faint offsetting; sm early repair text area; VG+. Ref: Phillips (A) 131. [35] £90 **$150**

[SAME TITLE] [1820] From 2nd American ed, *Genealogical, Historical ... and Geographical Atlas ...* Phila: M. Carey & Son. Double hemi; text below; with 4 folio sheets on history of world. 27x51cm (10½x20") Full color. Few lt spots in text; VG (A). [A3] £116 **$193**

[SAME TITLE] [1821] From same source. 1st state; 1st issue. 2 maps with surround of text: "North America ..." and "South America ..." by E. Paguenaud. On sheet with text, 41x55cm (16x21½") Full wash color. Faint offsetting; sh c'fold separation; VG+. Ref: Phillips (A) 131-67. [35] £90 **$150**

MAP OF POLAND, PRUSSIA AND HUNGARY, INDICATING THE PLACES RENDERED CELEBRATED BY SIEGES AND BATTLES [1820] From *A Complete Genealogical ... and Geographical Atlas ...* 1st ed; Kneass, Young, sc. Post-partition Poland. 29x29cm (11½x11½") Full color. Lt scattered foxing; lt toned; VG+. ["Geographical and Historical Map of Africa" offered at same price] [35] £45 **$75**

MAP OF SOUTH AMERICA [1820] From 2nd American ed, *Genealogical, Historical ... and Geographical Atlas ...* Attributed to E. Paguenaud. 41x32cm (16½x12½") Full color. VG (A). [A3] £29 **$48**

LE BRUYN

A DRAUGHT OF THE CITY OF JERUSALEM [1739] Bird's eye view from English ed of Le Bruyn; text below. B&W. 8x22cm (3½x9") Fine. [37] £106 **$175**

A MAP OF YE HOLY LAND [1740s] From English ed. 28x54cm (11x21½") Close lf margin. [A8] £69 **$115**

LE CLERC

ORBIS TERRAE NOVISSIMA DESCRIPTIO [1602] Double hemi, after Mercator; J. Hondius, sc. 33x51cm (13x20") Uncolored. Exc. Ref: Shirley (W) 233, pl.185. [2] £3,317 **$5,500**

[SAME TITLE] [1602 (1633)] Double hemi; J. Hondius, sc. 33x52cm (13x20½") Color. Ref: Shirley (W) 233, pl.185. [13] **Aus$9,000** £4,087 **$6,777**

LE MOYNE

FLORIDAE AMERICAE PROVINCIAE RECENS & EXACTISSIMA DESCRIPTIO AUCTORE IACOBO LE MOYNE ... [1591] Publ by De Bry. 37x45cm (14½x18") Sm tear repaired, no loss; exc. Ref: Burden 79; Schwartz & Ehrenberg pl.38; Goss (NA) 16. [2] £7,539 **$12,500**

[SAME TITLE] [1591] 37x46cm (14½x18") Exc. Same refs: [44] £7,539 **$12,500**

LE ROUGE

[ATLAS] ATLAS GENERAL [dated 1742-1749] Folio, modern cloth; 149 (of 153) maps, most in OL color, cartouches B&W. Maps loose, lacks World, Europe, Asia, Spain; worming throughout mainly along c'fold; tape repairs, occas damp staining mostly margin; 2 maps defective; sold as it. [A5] **£8,050** $13,348

[BOOK WITH MAPS] RECUEIL DES FORTIFICATIONS FORTS ET PORTS DE MER DE FRANCE LAVE' AU PINCEAU. A PARIS PAR LE ROUGE ... [c.1760] Octavo, mottled calf boards, gold tooled spine, orig morocco label; 89 plates, incl New Orleans, Quebec, Louisbourg. Binding bit worn; rebacked; internally exc. Ref: Phillips (A) 2975. [24] £1,206 **$2,000**

A MAP OF THE MOST INHABITED PART OF NEW ENGLAND CONTAINING THE PROVINCES OF MASSACHUSETS BAY AND NEW HAMPSHIRE WITH THE COLONIES OF CONECTICUT AND RHODE ISLAND ... 1777 [1777] After Jefferys. 4 sheets joined, 101x97cm (40x38") Orig OL color. Ref: cf Goss (NA) 66 (Eng. ed). [34] **£3,200** $5,306

AMERIQUE SEPTENTRIONALE AVEC LES ROUTES, DISTENCES EN MILES, VILLAGES ET ETABLISSEMENS FRANCOIS ET ANGLOIS PAR LE DOCTEUR MITCHEL ... A PARIS PAR LE ROUGE ... 1777 ... CORIGEE EN 1776 PAR M. HAWKINS ... [c.1783] Shows engraved outline of U.S. Overall 52x76" in 8 sheets joined to form four, each 132x48cm (52x19") Orig OL color. Staining at few folds; else exc. Ref: Ristow (A La Carte) p.102-13 [24] £7,237 **$12,000**

AMERIQUE SUIVANT LE R. P. CHARLEVOIX JTE. MR. DE LA CONDAMINE ET PLUSIEURS AUTRES NOUV LE OBSERVATIONS [1746] 49x64cm (19½x25") Orig OL color. [27] £573 **$950**

CANADA ET LOUISIANE [1755] Eastern North America; Mississippi & Missouri basin insets; sm Niagara view. 62x51cm (24½x20") OL color. [A7] £2,358 **$3,910**

CARTE DES TROUBLES DE L'AMERIQUE ... NEW YORK ... NEW JERSEY [1778] *Atlas Ameriquain Septentrionale.* After Sauthier. 71x52cm (28x20½") Color. [34] **£850** $1,410

DE L'EMPIRE DE LA CHINE [c.1748] 31x32cm (12x13") overall 12x22" with engraved side text panels. Color, pale blue paper. VG. [38] £90 **$150**

ISLES MOLUQUES [1748] 20x27cm (8x10½") Orig OL color. [11] £75 **$125**

L'IRLANDE [c.1750] 28x21cm (11x8½") Orig wash & OL color. [11] £75 **$125**

LA BARBADE ... [ON SHEET WITH] ISLE ST. CHRISTOPHLE ... [1748] 27x20cm (10½x8") Orig OL color. Ref: MCC 21 (Campbell) no.30, pl.13. [34] **£170** $282

LA GUADELOUPE ... [1753] Inset: Bourbon. 47x55cm (18½x21½") OL color. [20] **£377** $625

LA MARTINIQUE PAR LES INGENIEURS ANGLAIS LORSQU'ILS EN ETOIENT POSSESSEURS PAR JEFFERYS 1775 ... 1779 [1779] Inset: Cul de Sac Royal. 46x60cm (18x23½") B&W. [20] **£528** $875

MAPPE MONDE QUI COMPREND LES NOUVELLES DECOUVERTES FAITES JUSQUA CE JOUR [IN SET WITH] L'AFRIQUE SUIVANT LES NOUVELLES OBSERVATIONS [AND] AMERIQUE MERIDIONALE [AND] L'AMERIQUE SEPTENTRIONALE [AND] L'ASIE ... [AND] L'EUROPE ... [1746/48] From *Atlas Nouveau Portatif a l'Usage des Militaires, et du Voyageur.* 6 maps, each 22x30cm (8½x11½") Later full color. World has margin browning, paper added to margins; North America has old c'fold repair; others fine (A). [A3] £1,659 **$2,750**

PROVINCE DE NEW-YORK ... PAR MONTRESOR ... 1777 [1777] In 4 sheets, 141x91cm (55½x36") Orig OL color. Sm lt water stain; exc. Ref: Phillips (A) 1212-13 [2] £1,628 **$2,700**

[SAME TITLE] [1777] From French ed of Jefferys' "American Atlas". 4 sheets joined to make two, then folded; overall 144x91cm (56½x36") Orig OL color. Sm stain upper sheet; split & worm holes near folds; o/w good. [32] £1,809 **$3,000**

LEA

A MAPP OF JERUSALEM ... [c.1690] 32x47cm (12½x18½") Col. Fold repairs. [42] **Aus$1,950** £886 $1,468

A NEW MAP OF CAROLINA BY PHILIP LEA ... [c.1690] Thornton-Morden-Lea 2nd state, based on Gascoyne of 1682. 54x45cm (21x17½") Orig OL color. Sm hole in ctr repaired; o/w good. Ref: Cumming (SE) 104. [32] £7,237 **$12,000**

LEIGH

PLAN OF THE BATTLE OF WATERLOO, OR, MONT ST. JEAN, JUNE 18TH, 1815 [n.d.] Samuel Leigh. Folds into 12mo marble boards. 44x51cm (17½x20") Partial color. Mild toning & offsetting; few sh repaired fold splits. [A10] £90 **$150**

LEMERCIER

ARLES [c.1860] From *Voyage Aerien en France.* Paris: A. Hauser. Litho bird's-eye view by Villeman after A. Guesdon. 29x44cm (11½x17½") Color. Fine. ["Bordeaux" offered at same price] [29] £293 **$485**

LESCARBOT
FIGURE DU PORT ROYAL EN LA NOUVELLE FRANCE [1609] From *Histoire de la Nouvelle France*. 1st state. 14x24cm (5½x9½"). Good. Ref: Burden 158. [2] £1,508 **$2,500**

LESTER
MAP OF NEW LONDON AND WINDHAM COUNTIES IN CONN. FROM ACTUAL SURVEY ... [1833] New Haven. Linen-backed. 10 insets. OL color by town. 82x70cm (32½x27½"). Some wear; generally good. Ref: Thompson (CT) 88. [15] £573 **$950**

LETTS
THE UNITED STATES NO.12 [1880] Coverage of parts of MT, WY, NE & Dakota. 32x39cm (12½x15½") Printed OL color. [39] £60 **$100**

UNITED STATES, WEST & MEXICO, NORTH [c.1875] From *Letts's Popular Atlas*. 32x40cm (12½x15½") Printed OL color. Good. [16] £51 **$85**

LEVASSEUR
[ATLAS] ATLAS NATIONAL ILLUSTRE DES 86 DEPARTEMENTS ET DES POSSESSIONS DE LA FRANCE [1854] Folio, quarter sheep; 100 double-page maps in OL col. Extremities worn; internally clean. [A8] £589 **$977**

AFRIQUE [c.1860] Surround of vignettes. 30x46cm (12x18"). Map in full color. VG. [25] £96 **$160**

ALGERIE, COLONIE FRANCAISE [1868] From *Atlas Nationale*. Surround of uncolored scenes. 29x43cm (11½x17"). Map in full wash color. Fine (A+). [A4] £38 **$63**

AMERIQUE MERIDIONALE [c.1860] Surround of scenes. 30x46cm (12x18"). Map in full color. Nice. [26] £109 **$180**

AMERIQUE SEPTENTRIONALE [c.1845] Pictorial surround. Texas as Republic. 30x46cm (12x18"). Map in full color. Exc. Ref: Tooley (M&M) pl.89. [25] £136 **$225**

[SAME TITLE] [c.1845] Pictorial surround. 28x43cm (11x17"). [38] £151 **$250**

[SAME TITLE] [c.1845] Independent TX. 32x45cm (12½x17½") Orig OL color. [46] **£140** $232

[SAME TITLE] [c.1845] Texas as Republic. 28x43cm (11x17") Map in OL color. [A1] £133 **$220**

[SAME TITLE] [c.1845] From *Atlas National*. Texas as Republic; pictorial surround. 28x43cm (11x17") OL color. Margin stain lf; map fine; VG (A). [A3] £199 **$330**

[SAME TITLE] [1847] From *Atlas National*. Texas as Republic; pictorial surround by Raimond Bonheur. Overall 11x17", map 18x20cm (7x8") Orig wash color to map. Ref: Tooley (M&M) pl.89. [27] £136 **$225**

[SAME TITLE] [1861] From *L'Atlas Nationale Illustre*. TX still a republic. 28x43cm (11x17") Full color. Ref: Tooley (M&M) pl.89. [1] £121 **$200**

ASIE [c.1850] From *Atlas Nationale*. Surround of vignettes. 28x43cm (11x17") Map in full color. Fine (A+). [A4] £124 **$206**

[SAME TITLE] [c.1850] 29x43cm (11x17") Full color. Fine (A+). [A3] £113 **$187**

[SAME TITLE] [c.1860] 30x46cm (12x18") Full color on map. VG. [25] £106 **$175**

COLONIES FRANCAISES (EN AFRIQUE) [1868] From *Atlas Nationale*. Incl Senegal, Madagascar, Goree. Surround of uncolored engravings. 28x42cm (11x16½") Map in full wash color. Couple sh margin tears; else clean; fine (A). [A4] £60 **$100**

COLONIES FRANCAISES (EN AMERIQUE) [1841] 4 maps: Newfoundland; St. Pierre & Miquelon Islands; St. Martin & St. Barts; Guyana; surround of tropical scenes. Overall 30x43cm (12x17") Color. [18] £54 **$90**

COLONIES FRANCAISES, MARTINIQUE, AMERIQUE DU SUD [c.1860] Wide border of vignettes. 30x46cm (12x18") Island in full color. VG. [Map of Guadeloupe & other islands offered at same price] [25] £48 **$80**

DEPT. DE LA SEINE [c.1860] Paris at ctr; decorative surround. 30x46cm (12x18") Map in full color. VG. [25] £48 **$80**

EUROPE [c.1860] Surround of vignettes. 30x46cm (12x18") Countries in full color. VG. [25] £96 **$160**

OCEANIE [1845] Pictorial surround. 30x42cm (12x16½") Orig color. Exc. [24] £151 **$250**

[SAME TITLE] [c.1860] Pacific with Australia, S.E. Asia. Surround of scenes. 30x46cm (12x18") Full color on map. VG. [25] £145 **$240**

LEWIS Try *Carey*

THE TRAVELLERS GUIDE. A NEW AND CORRECT MAP OF THE UNITED STATES, INCLUDING GREAT PORTIONS OF MISSOURI, UPPER & LOWER CANADA, NOVA SCOTIA, NEW BRUNSWICK, THE FLORIDAS, SPANISH PROVINCES & C. ... BY SAMUEL LEWIS [1819] Wall map on rollers 75x105cm (29½x41½") Orig color; golden hue. Shellac worn top & lf margins; water marking top margin & staining top lf corner; few lt surface rubbings, no loss; minute flake missing from Gulf. Ref: Wheat (TM) 332. [A2] £3,980 **$6,600**

LEWIS, SAMUEL & CO.

CARLOW [1846] From *Lewis's Atlas Comprising the Counties of Ireland*. Paper size 30x24cm (12x9½") OL color. Good. [Also offered at same price: Armagh; Cavan; Longford; Meath; Roscommon; Tyrone; Westmeath] [32] £51 **$85**
DUBLIN [1846] From same source. Paper size 30x24cm (12x9½") OL color. Good. [32] £60 **$100**
GALWAY [1846] From same source. Paper size 30x24cm (12x9½") OL color. Good. [Clare; Cork; Kildare; Kilkenny; Mayo; Tipperary offered at same price] [32] £57 **$95**
KERRY [1846] From same source. Paper size 30x24cm (12x9½") OL color. Good. [Donegal; Waterford offered at same price] [32] £60 **$100**
LONDONDERRY [1846] From same source. Paper size 30x24cm (12x9½") OL color. Good. [Kings; Leitrim; Monaghan; Queens offered at same price] [32] £48 **$80**
WEXFORD [1846] From same source. Paper size 30x24cm (12x9½") OL color. Good. [Antrim; Down; Fermanagh; Louth; Sligo; Wicklow offered at same price] [32] £54 **$90**

LIZARS

PALESTINE [1831] Shows regions of 12 tribes. 23x18cm (9x7½") Color. [40] £36 **$60**
PLAN OF THE CITY OF WASHINGTON AND THE TERRITORY OF COLUMBIA [1819] From D.B. Warden, vol. 3, *A Statistical ... and Historical Account of the United States*. Edinburgh: W. & D. Lizars. 34x35cm (13½x13½") B&W. Fold splits repaired verso. Ref: Phillips (Wash) p.29. [12] £166 **$275**
UNITED STATES OF AMERICA [c.1810] 40x46cm (15½x18") Color. Some folds lower edge closed with archival tape; margins trimmed; some offsetting. [A7] £156 **$258**

LLOYD

LLOYD'S NEW MAP OF UNITED STATES, THE CANADAS AND NEW BRUNSWICK ... [1864] Wall map, unbacked, printed both sides, with orig rods. Full color by county. Verso: "Lloyd's Map of the Southern States". Uncolored. 95x126cm (37½x49½") Sm hole; tear near top; rod connection repaired & reinforced. Ref: Stephenson (CW-2) 46, 138. [15] £452 **$750**
LLOYD'S RAILROAD, TELEGRAPH & EXPRESS MAP OF THE EASTERN STATES TO ACCOMPANY LLOYD'S ... MAP OF THE UNITED STATES & CANADAS [1863] J.T. Lloyd, NY. RR's & stations; 3 insets; cautionary note about H.H. Lloyd. 66x95cm (26x37½") Uncolored. [15] £256 **$425**

LLOYD, H.H.

COUNTY MAP OF COLORADO, UTAH, NEW MEXICO, AND ARIZONA [1875] From a supplement to unidentified state or county atlas; in title bloc, "Atlas of the United States". 41x36cm (16x14") Full color. [12] £112 **$185**
COUNTY MAP OF TEXAS AND INDIAN TERRITORY [1875] From H.H. Lloyd & Co.'s *Atlas of the United States*. Chicago/NY: Warner & Beers. 42x39cm (16½x15½") Full color. Bright, fine. [16] £136 **$225**
OREGON, AND THE TERRITORY OF WASHINGTON. [1872] From Walling & Gray, *New Topographical Atlas of the State of Ohio*. Cincinnati. Supplement to atlas; in title bloc, "Atlas of the United States". 38x29cm (15x11½") Full color. Fine. Ref: LeGear (US) 2740. [12] £51 **$85**
PACIFIC STATES AND TERRITORIES [1868] From *Atlas of the State of Ohio*. NY: Walling, Stebbins & Lloyd. Supplement to atlas; in title bloc, "Atlas of the United States". 66x37cm (26x14½") Full color. Sh c'fold end splits mended; else fine. Ref: LeGear (US) 2739; Phillips (A) 1389 & 2346. [12] £121 **$200**

LOCAL & STATE MAPS & VIEWS - Infrequent Publishers

[**ATLAS, SCHOOL EXERCISE**] [c.1847] M.A. Quincy. Sm quarto, stiff marbled wraps; 5 pp text, 11 pp finely inked maps, incl New England, its 6 states, US, 2 hemis, Africa & unfinished Asia. [6] £591 **$980**
[**ATLAS**] **ILLUSTRATED ATLAS OF ALLEGAN COUNTY MICHIGAN** [1895] Racine: Kace Publ Co. Folio, half leather & cloth; 98 pp, numerous colored maps, incl US by Rand, McNally & MI. Covers worn, detached; title loose, chipped; lt soil & toning to contents; maps with few tears, sm loss state map. [A10] £277 **$460**
[**BOOK WITH MAPS**] **MAP AND PROFILES OF NEW-YORK STATE CANALS** [1858] Van Renssalaer Richmond; Albany: C.V. Benthuysen. Map & 10 profiles in gold-embossed cloth folder. 57x99cm (22½x39") Route & profiles in color. Presentation copy from J. Wesley Smith. Folder lightened, corners rubbed, endpaper cracked; map has sl corner separations; lt browning along folds; VG. [5] £157 **$260**
[**LONDON: IMPROVEMENTS TO THE DOCKS AROUND THE TOWER OF LONDON**] [c.1800] R. Metcalf. London: Surveyor's Office, Guildhall. With roads & lanes from Tower to Royal Exchange Inset: Isle of Dogs. 54x61cm (21½x24") Orig color. [46] £220 **$365**
[**MASSACHUSETTS: BOSTON VIEW**] [c.1860] Druck u Verlag V.F. Silber, Berlin. View of city from rural East Boston. 28x35cm (11x14") Col. Lt spot in sky; previous mounting remnant; else exc. [22] £332 **$550**

LOCAL & STATE MAPS & VIEWS continued

A MAP OF THE CITY OF PHILADELPHIA [1897] J.L. Smith 102x76cm (40x30") Full wash color by wards. Few sm point tears; o/w fine. [35] £45 **$75**

A MAP OF THE WONDROUS ISLE OF MANHATTAN [1926] Washington Square Bookshop. Labeled isometric bird's eye view. 64x102cm (25x40") Full color. Minor fold & tear repairs verso. [26] £90 **$150**

BERLIN [GERMANY] [c.1860] Balloon perspective; after Loeillot, by F. Sala; Mercier, lith. 36x56cm (14x22") [48] **DM 5,500** £1,899 **$3,149**

BIRD'S EYE VIEW OF BOSTON HARBOR AND SOUTH SHORE TO PROVINCETOWN SHOWING STEAMBOAT ROUTES [c.1900] Boston: Murphy. Key in booklet that contained map. 48x38cm (19x15") Full color. VG. [26] £48 **$80**

BIRD'S-EYE VIEW OF FULTON, N.Y. [1880] H.H. Rowley & Co., Hartford. 61x76cm (24x30") Uncolored. Sl discoloration near top. Ref: Reps (Views) 2533. [15] £392 **$650**

BIRD'S EYE VIEW OF PHILADELPHIA [c.1859] J.L. Locher. 50x70cm (20x28") Orig color. Lt scattered foxing. [A1] £1,327 **$2,200**

CITY OF FORT SCOTT [KS] [c.1875] Unknown source; probably for real estate promotion. 69x79cm (27x31") Full color. Creased down ctr; else crisp, bright. [9] £226 **$375**

DUNEDIN, N.Z. [July 1875] Publ as supplement to *The Illustrated Australian News*. Bird's-eye wood engraving of South Island city drawn by A.W. Cooke. 35x65cm (14x26") Color. Some folds repaired; rice paper backing; VG [30] £332 **$550**

GEOGRAPHICAL TOPOGRAPHICAL AND RAILROAD MAP OF CALIFORNIA [1908] California State Board of Trade, San Francisco. On thin polished paper. RR's in red. 64x50cm (25x19½") Printed color. Folded, couple separations repaired with archival tape; pinholes in margins; clean; VG (A). [A3] £52 **$87**

LUGDUNUM BATAVORUM ... [1675] Leiden city plan by C. Hagen. Surround of 16 building views, bird's-eye view below. Separately published; mounted on linen. 79x88cm (31½x35") Toned; cropped top & bottom; for its kind, good. [24] £2,714 **$4,500**

MAP OF MADISON AND THE FOUR LAKE COUNTRY [WI] [1854] Bayard Taylor & Horace Greeley endorsements; promotional map. 43x69cm (17x27") Uncolored. On thin paper; was folded, sm loss; o/w VG. [25] £151 **$250**

MAP OF MOOSEHEAD LAKE AND NORTHERN MAINE, EMBRACING THE HEADWATERS OF THE PENOBSCOT, KENNEBEC AND ST. JOHN RIVERS. SPECIALLY ADAPTED TO THE USES OF SPORTSMEN AND LUMBERMEN [dated 1879] Probably from *Woods & Lakes of Maine*. By Lucius L. Hubbard. 58x47cm (23x18½") B&W. On parchment-like paper; flawless. [12] £81 **$135**

MAP OF PROPERTY BELONGING TO NICH.S LUQUER IN THE 6TH WARD OF THE CITY OF BROOKLYN TO BE SOLD AT AUCTION BY JAMES BLEECKER & SONS ... [1835] W. Norris, NY, Lith. Broadside showing hundreds of lots reclaimed from Gowanus Bay & Luquer's mill pond. 46x61cm (18x24") B&W. Occas tears, sl loss at corner folds; lt pencil marks, soiling; good. [6] £353 **$585**

MAP OF THE CITY OF WASHINGTON .. [1892] To accompany B. de Keim's *Washington, What to See and How to See It*. . 42x50cm (16½x19½") Uncolored. VG. [36] £57 **$95**

MAP OF THE LANDS INCLUDED IN THE CENTRAL PARK, FROM A TOPOGRAPHICAL SURVEY, JUNE 17TH 1856 [c.1856] Ferd. Mayer, NY. 2 plans folding into boards: Land designated for park; Proposed development plan (not adopted.) Signed Egbert Viele. Uncolored. 111x57cm (43½x22½") Separations along folds, no loss. [15] £392 **$650**

MAP OF THE WHITE MOUNTAINS [1873] Boston: Snow and Bradlee. Relief map of plastic-like substance mounted on board; in orig cloth-backed boards. 22x27cm (8½x10½") Map box loose in binding. [A8] £139 **$230**

MAP SHOWING THE ROUTE OF THE CHAMPLAIN TRANSPORTATION CO'S STEAMERS, THE GATEWAY TO THE COUNTRY [1903] Lake Champlain & Lake George Line. On verso of time table; shows connecting RRs. 69x41cm (27x16") Some color. Old folds; VG. [25] £45 **$75**

MAPA OFICIAL DEL ESTADO DE SONORA [MEXICO] [1918] Hermosillo: Leon y Romo. Folds into 7x4" boards. 9 "distritos" with printed OL color; many place names; RRs shown; waterways, but no topo. 107x94cm (42x37") 3" tear at binding; boards worn; brittle paper; not for casual use. [8] £51 **$85**

MEXICO, FROM THE AZOTEA OF THE HOUSE OF H.M.S MISSION, SAN COSME. [1829] Litho from Mrs. H.G. Ward's drawing looking toward volcanoes; landmarks identified. 18x39cm (7x15½") [39] £72 **$120**

NEUES PANORAMA DES RHEIN VON MANNHEIM BIS COLN ... [c.1850's-60's] Frederick Herchenhein. Panorama in oblong octavo, red cloth & gilt, folding out to 223cm (88"), with views of cities, etc.; with English appendix. A fold repair. [21] **Can$300** £131 **$217**

LOCAL & STATE MAPS & VIEWS continued

NEWARK [NJ] (EAST OF MULBERRY ST. 1820-5) [c.1854] Bird's-eye retrospective; 38 references. 65x51cm (25½x20") Uncolored. Repaired long tear from top margin. In plain 19c. frame. Ref: Reps (Views) 2370. Deak 325. [15] £513 **$850**

NOUVEAU PLAN ROUTIER DE LA VILLE ET FAUXBOURGS DE PARIS [1789] Paris: Esnauts & Rapilly. Dissected, mounted on cloth, folds to 6½x6½". Streets & landmarks listed & keyed. Insets. 56x79cm (22x31") Lt toned, front & back panels more; cloth frayed & toned at some folds; faint foxing. [A10] £180 **$299**

PANORAMA DU MONT-RIGHI ... VOM RIGIBERG ... [c.1840] L.P. De Wyher; Lucerne. Etching & aquatint; shows landscape from Zug to Lucerne; with smaller views and map. 53x53cm (21x21") B&W. [34] £300 **$498**

PLAN OF FALMOUTH HEIGHTS. FALMOUTH, MASS. [1873] E. Boyden & Sons, Boston. Planning map, with 6 views. 53x83cm (21x32½") B&W. Folded, wear along folds; MS "X"s through some lots. [15] £211 **$350**

PLAT OF BOISE CITY, CAPITAL OF IDAHO [c.1885] Planning type map. 56x74cm (22x29") Uncolored. Minor edge damage; separations at some fold junctions. [15] £603 **$1,000**

REVISED MAP OF BELMONT TERRACE, TOWN OF BABYLON, SUFFOLK CO. N.Y., SURVEYED SEPTEMBER 1906 BY WM. ELLISON C.E. SURVEYOR, HICKSVILLE L.I. N.Y. [1907] NY: Colonial Press. Sepia print; 1"=160 ft. 46x130cm (18x51") Few soft creases while rolled; 2 sm holes rt margin; VG+. [35] £60 **$100**

SAN JOAQUIN, THE GATEWAY COUNTY OF CALIFORNIA [c.1900] Sierra Art and Engineering, San Francisco. Chamber of Commerce brochure; bird's-eye; Stockton at ctr. 64x48cm (25x19") Full color. VG. [25] £72 **$120**

VUE PERSPECTIVE DE LA VILLE DE NICE [c.1780] Vue d'optique. 29x42cm (11½x16½") Full orig color. Fine. [24] £452 **$750**

LOCAL & STATE POCKET MAPS - Infrequent Publishers

GUIDE MAP OF MINNEAPOLIS MINNESOTA [1891] Manz & Co., Minneapolis. Folds into sm red case; pictures of 14 buildings; promotionals on verso. 61x43cm (24x17") Substantial color. VG. [25] £72 **$120**

HOLBROOK'S MAP OF THE CITY OF NEWARK NEW JERSEY [1872] A. Stephen Holbrook; Newark. Pocket map in orig cloth folder. Full color by ward. 51x46cm (20x18") Exc. [15] £347 **$575**

MAP OF BUCKS COUNTY, PENNSYLVANIA [1898] James D. Scott, Doylestown, PA. In orig printed wrappers. Full color by town with highlighting. 63x41cm (25x16") Near mint. [15] £106 **$175**

MAP OF CAPE MAY CITY AND SEA GROVE [NJ] [1878] Wilson & Rose; Phila. With orig cloth folder; all bldgs shown; owners identified. 85x48cm (33½x19") Full color. Near mint. [15] £302 **$500**

MAP OF LANCASTER CITY, PA. AND SUBURBS [1900] L.B. Herr & Son, Lancaster. In stiff wrappers. 61x50cm (24x20") Uncolored. [15] £60 **$100**

MAP OF LONG ISLAND [1897] Brooklyn: Hyde & Co. 2nd ed. 3 large linen-backed maps folding into oblong sm folio album. [no dimens] Cover worn; some separations at fold intersections. [A8] £347 **$575**

MAP OF THE CITY OF BROOKLYN AND VILLAGE OF WILLIAMSBURGH, SHOWING THE SIZE OF BLOCKS AND WIDTH OF STREETS AS LAID OUT BY THE COMMISSIONERS [1877] Richard Butt; NY. Repro of Benjamin Demorest 1846 map. Dissected wall map, linen-backed, as folding map in orig half leather folder. Full color by farm. 78x120cm (30½x47") Scuffed, spine broken. Ref: Phillips (M) p.176. [15] £392 **$650**

MAP OF THE CITY OF BUFFALO [1901] Buffalo Electrotype and Engraving Co. In stiff paper wraps; color shows parks, public transport, expo site. 64x43cm (25x17") Case sl worn; VG. [26] £45 **$75**

NEW MAP OF BROOKLYN AND VICINITY, PUBLISHED FOR THE BROOKLYN DIRECTORY [1879] Lain & Co.; Brooklyn. Newtown Creek to Flatbush; orig cloth folder reinforced. 67x55cm (26½x21½") Uncolored. Many fold separations; some repaired. [15] £151 **$250**

POCKET MAP AND SHIPPERS GUIDE OF KANSAS [1911] Berry Publishing Co., Kansas City, MO. In protective case. 38x66cm (15x26") Full color. Minor edge repair; map & case VG. [25] £45 **$75**

ST. LOUIS WORLD'S FAIR, LOUISIANA PURCHASE EXPOSITION, MAY TO DECEMBER, 1904 [1904] Missouri Commission. Folds into stiff wraps. MO exhibits highlighted in red. 25x46cm (10x18") Exc. [26] £36 **$60**

STREET AND ROAD MAP OF SAN JOSE AND VICINITY, CALIFORNIA [1921] McMillan & McMillan, San Jose. Folded into case; key at sides. 38x51cm (15x20") Uncol. Some sm chips to case; map VG. [25] £45 **$75**

STREET NUMBER MAP OF CHICAGO [1894] E.A. Cummings & Co., Chicago. Lawrence Ave to 71st St. Folds into case with index. 86x61cm (34x24") Car lines in color. VG. [25] £45 **$75**

THE ONLY CORRECT MAP OF THE CITY OF CLEVELAND ISSUED IN 1876 [1876] Robison, Savage & Co., Cleveland, printed in large red across map. Folding map; orig cloth with tie. Ward line printed in red. 50x73cm (19½x28½") Exc. Ref: Phillips (M) p.237. [15] £513 **$850**

LOCAL & STATE POCKET MAPS continued

THE PHAT BOY'S DELINEATIONS OF THE ST. LAWRENCE RIVER   [1885]   E.F. Babbage, Rochester, NY. Folds into stiff wrappers; bird's-eye view from Montreal to Kingston, Ont; verso with ads on 20 panels. Uncolored. 16x240cm (6x94½").   [15]   £573 **$950**

WRIGHT'S MAP OF KANSAS CITY   [1884]   H.T. Wright, KC. In orig stiff purple wrappers. Full color by addition. 61x51cm (24x20")   Wraps chipped at corners; lacks text.   [15]   £226 **$375**

LOCAL & STATE WALL MAPS - Infrequent Publishers

1905 REVISED AND REDUCED EDITION OF THE OFFICIAL MAP OF THE COUNTY OF SANTA CLARA, CALIFORNIA   [1905]   J.G. McMillan, San Francisco. After larger official ed by tax office; highly detailed; orig rollers. 100x144cm (39½x56½")   Uncolored. Mild chipping near bottom.   [15]   £302 **$500**

CHART OF THE SACRAMENTO & SAN JOAQUIN RIVERS SHOWING ALL LANDINGS TO SACRAMENTO AND STOCKTON AND ROADS LEADING TO THEM   [1901]   Punnet Bros., San Francisco. Blueprint style; landing owners identified. 66x85cm (26x33½").   [15]   £226 **$375**

MAP OF CHESHIRE CO., NEW HAMPSHIRE   [1858]   L. Fagan; Phila. Linen-backed wall map; 26 insets; 6 views. Full color by town. 139x142cm (54½x56")   Mild leeching; lt soling near top; generally good. Ref: Cobb (NH) 247.   [15]   £392 **$650**

MAP OF NEW HAVEN COUNTY, CONNECTICUT   [1856]   H. & C.Y. Smith, Phila. Linen backed with orig rods; 21 inset maps, 12 bldg views, incl Yale. 141x139cm (55½x54½")   Staining top lf; exc. Ref: Thompson (CT) 169.   [15]   £452 **$750**

MAP OF THE ADIRONDACK FOREST AND ADJOINING TERRITORY COMPILED FROM OFFICIAL MAPS AND FIELD NOTES   [1893]   J.B. Koetteritz, Albany. Signed by Samuel J. Tilden as Forest Commissioner. 174x143cm (68½x56½")   Full color. Some age toning.   [15]   £302 **$500**

MAP OF THE CITY OF TROY, NEW YORK   [1873]   Full color by ward. 213x180cm (84x71")   Extensive repaired damage, still chipping, defects top 6"; other minor chipping; lacks bottom roller; overall good.   [15]   £452 **$750**

MAP OF TOLLAND COUNTY CONNECTICUT, FROM ACTUAL SURVEYS   [1857]   William C. Eaton & H.C. Osborn; Phila. 12 views. 141x131cm (55½x51½")   Lt chipping top ctr, minor damage in "Stafford"; 2 sh tears; VG. Ref: Thompson (CT) 174.   [15]   £452 **$750**

MAP OF VERMONT & NEW HAMPSHIRE   [1849]   Lewis Robinson, Reading, VT (?); 1st publ 1828. Wall map with orig cloth backing & rollers. Full color by county. 73x58cm (28½x23")   Minor cracking, loss of surface, no loss of text; silk edging torn near top. Ref: Cobb (NH) 136. cf Ristow (Amer M&M) p.272.   [15]   £694 **$1,150**

MAP OF WASHINGTON COUNTY, NEW YORK   [1853]   By Morris Levey; Phila: James Scott & Robert P. Smith. Linen-backed with orig rods; 8 insets, 15 bldg views; Full color. 145x99cm (57x39")   Lt age toning & soiling; fine. Ref: Phillips (M) p.1047.   [15]   £452 **$750**

TOPOGRAPHIC MAP OF COLORADO, 1913   [1913]   Colorado State Geological Survey. Cloth backed, on rollers. 97x140cm (38x55")   Full soft color. Bright, not much use. ["Geologic ..." companion offered at same price; as a pair for $350]   [26]   £121 **$200**

LOCKHEAD

ENGLAND AND WALES   [1811]   From *A Compendius Gazetteer and Modern Geography*. 23x21cm (9x8½") Tear to neatline; spots. ["Map of Asia ...", "Scotland" & "Italy" offered at same price]   [21]   **Can$50**   £22 **$36**

IRELAND   [1811]   From same source. 23x19cm (9x7½")   Couple spots.   [21]   **Can$65**   £28 **$47**

NEW MEXICO NEW SPAIN WITH THE WEST INDIES   [1811]   From same source. 23x16cm (9x6½")   Brown spots.   [21]   **Can$50**   £22 **$36**

THE SEVEN UNITED PROVINCES WITH THE DUTCH AND AUSTRIAN NETHERLANDS   [1811]   From same source. 23x17cm (9x6½")   Minor browning.   ["Norway ...", "Sweden" & "France" offered at same price]   [21]   **Can$45**   £20 **$32**

THE UNITED STATES OF NORTH AMERICA WITH THE BRITISH TERRITORYS ACCORDING TO THE TREATY OF 1783   [1811]   From same source. 23x20cm (9x7½")   Browned.   [21]   **Can$65**   £28 **$47**

THE WORLD WITH THE LATEST DISCOVERIES   [1811]   From same source. Double hemi. 23x40cm (9x15½") Creases; spotting; 1½" closed tear lower rt margin to South Pole.   [21]   **Can$90**   £39 **$65**

LODGE

A NEW MAP OF NORTH AMERICA, FROM THE BEST AUTHORITIES   [1781]   From Dr. John Campbell's *Lives of the British Admirals*. Similar to Carver's map. 33x36cm (13x14")   B&W. Exc.   [12]   £286 **$475**

LONDON MAGAZINE

A CHART OF THE CHANNEL IN THE PHILIPINE ISLANDS, THROUGH WHICH THE MANILA GALEON PASSES, WITH A MAP OF MANILA ISLAND. [1763] 25x21cm (10x8½") Orig color (unusually so). Exc. Ref: Jolly LOND-227. [43] £271 **$450**

A MAP OF GUADELOUPE ONE OF THE CARIBBY ISLANDS IN THE WEST INDIES SUBJECT TO FRANCE. [1759] 13x20cm (5x8") Uncolored. VG. Ref: Jolly LOND-162. [25] £36 **$60**

A MAP OF THE BRITISH & FRENCH PLANTATIONS IN NORTH AMERICA. [1755] Long Island to Labrador. 21x26cm (8½x10½") B&W. Fine. Ref: Jolly LOND-96. [28] £160 **$265**

A MAP OF THE WESTERN PARTS OF THE COLONY OF VIRGINIA. [1754] Present WV, western NY & PA, eastern OH. 19x12cm (7½x5") B&W. Narrow side margins; else exc. Ref: Jolly LOND-85. Sames & Woods p.47; Swem 181. [12] £136 **$225**

A NEW MAP OF NORTH AMERICA FROM THE LATEST DISCOVERIES. 1763. [1763] 27x37cm (11x15") Browning; lf margin trimmed. Ref: Jolly LOND-222 Sellers & Van Ee 106. [21] **Can$200** £87 **$145**

A NEW MAP OF THE PROVINCE OF QUEBEC IN NORTH AMERICA; DRAWN FROM THE BEST AUTHORITIES: BY THOS. KITCHIN, GEOGR. [1764] 17x22cm (6½x8½") Sl offsetting of text. Ref: Jolly LOND-241. [11] £45 **$75**

A PLAN OF QUEBEC, METROPOLIS OF CANADA IN NORTH AMERICA [1759] 12x18cm (4½x7") Ref: Jolly LOND-164. [11] £45 **$75**

[SAME TITLE] [1759] 13x20cm (5x8") Uncolored. VG. [25] £27 **$45**

AN ACCURATE MAP OF THE CARIBBY ISLANDS, WITH THE CROWNS, &C. TO WHICH THEY SEVERALLY BELONG. BY T. KITCHIN GEOGR. [1759] Puerto Rico to Trinidad. 25x19cm (9½x7½") Uncolored. VG. Ref: Jolly LOND-161. [25] £54 **$90**

ISLAND OF ST. LUCIA [ON PLATE WITH] ISLAND OF ST. VINCENT [AND] CHART OF PART OF THE WINDWARD IS. BY T. KITCHIN SENR. [AND] ISLAND OF BARBADOS. [1782] 25x19cm (10x7½") Color. Ref: Jolly LOND-346. [18] £100 **$165**

THE ISLES OF MONTREAL, AS THEY HAVE BEEN SURVEY'D BY THE FRENCH ENGINEERS. [1761] 23x33cm (9x13") B&W. Sm extension lower lf margin; o/w pristine. Ref: Jolly LOND-196. Trudel p.116; Lepine 1143; Winsor (C&N) 8 p.133. [12] £151 **$250**

LONGCHAMPS

CARTE DES POSSESSIONS FRANCOISES ET ANGLOISES DANS LE CANADA ET PARTIE DE LA LOUISIANE [1756] Inset: present SE U.S. Separately publ. 54x75cm (21½x29½") Color. Ref: Sellers & Van Ee 70. [34] **£2,400** **$3,980**

CARTE DES POSSESSIONS FRANCOISES ET ANGLOISES DANS LE CANADA ET PARTIE DE LA LOUISIANE ... PARIS, 1756 [1756] Inset: present SE U.S. 55x76cm (21½x30") Orig OL color. Margin repairs with some printed surface loss; o/w fine. Ref: Sellers & Van Ee 70. [2] £1,176 **$1,950**

DEPARTEMENT DU MONT BLANC ... DECRETE PAR LA CONVENTION NATIONALE LE 27 NOVEMBRE 1792 [c.1795] 64x50cm (25½x20") OL color. Sh margin tears & creases, image unaffected; ex lib NYHS. [A7] £139 **$230**

LOPEZ

CARTA MARITIMA DE LA ISLA DE CUBA, QUE COMPREHENDE LAS JURISDICCIONES DE FILIPINA, LA HAVANA ... MADRID, ANO 1783 [1783] Separate publication; linen-backed. 37x84cm (14½x33") Orig wash color. Fine. [43] £965 **$1,600**

LOTHIAN

MEXICO & GUATIMALA [1845] McDonald; Glasgow. Yellow squarish Texas Republic; atavistic names. 29x37cm (11½x14½") Orig OL color. [27] £133 **$220**

LOTTER

[ATLAS] ATLAS MINOR PRAEIPUA ORBIS TERRARUM IMPERIA, REGNA ET PROVINCIAS GERMANIAE ... [c.1760] Augsburg: Conrad Lotter. Oblong quarto, calf; title & 79 maps, full orig color. Exc. [3] £5,729 **$9,500**

[ATLAS] KURZGEFASETE GEOGRAPHIE ... VON TOBIAS LOBECK ... [2ND TITLE PAGE] ATLAS GEOGRAPHICUS PORTABILIS XXIX MAPPIS ORBIS ... ACCURATE EXPRESSIT TOBIAS CONRADUS LOTTERUS. DILINEAVIT ET EXECUDIT TOBIAS LOBECK ... [1762] Augsburg. Oblong octavo, gold tooled morocco, gilt edges; 29 orig color maps.. Exc. Ref: Phillips (A) 633. [3] £1,719 **$2,850**

LOTTER continued

A MAP OF THE MOST INHABITED PART OF NEW ENGLAND, CONTAINING THE PROVINCES OF MASSACHUSETS BAY AND NEW HAMPSHIRE, WITH THE COLONIES OF CONECTICUT AND RHODE ISLAND, DIVIDED INTO COUNTIES AND TOWNSHIPS ... LOTTER, IN AUGSBURG   [1775]   German ed of Jefferys map. 4 sheets joined, 102x97cm (40x38") Full orig color. Wear along vert crease; faint foxing; VG. Ref: Sellers & Van Ee 801.   [24]   £2,231 **$3,700**

A MAP OF THE PROVINCES OF NEW-YORK AND NEW-JERSEY, WITH A PART OF PENNSYLVANIA AND THE PROVINCE OF QUEBEC. FROM THE TOPOGRAPHICAL OBSERVATIONS OF C.J. SAUTHIER   [1777]   74x57cm (29½x22½") Orig wash color. Some faint foxing; sm stamp; else exc.   [24]   £2,292 **$3,800**

[SAME TITLE]   [1777]   75x56cm (29½x22") Orig wash & OL color. Ref: Phillips (M) p.505.
[27]   £1,116 **$1,850**

A MAP OF THE PROVINCES OF NEW-YORK AND NEW-YERSEY, WITH A PART OF PENNSYLVANIA AND THE PROVINCE OF QUEBEC. FROM THE TOPOGRAPHICAL OBSERVATIONS OF C.J. SAUTHIER   [1777]   Sauthier map reduced. In 2 sheets, 76x57cm (30x22½") Full orig color. Exc.   [2]   £1,146 **$1,900**

A PLAN OF THE CITY AND ENVIRONS OF PHILADELPHIA ...   [1777]   With State House view; based on Faden, retains English.. 60x45cm (24x18") Orig color. Exc. Ref: Nebenzahl (Battle Plans) #131; Snyder (Phila) #46.
[23]   £1,930 **$3,200**

[SAME TITLE]   [1777]   60x46cm (23½x18") Orig color. Good.   [32]   £2,051 **$3,400**

[SAME TITLE]   [1777]   60x46cm (23½x18") Orig color. Ref: Tooley (Amer) pl.132. Phillips (Phila) 168.
[A1]   £1,260 **$2,090**

[SAME TITLE]   [1777]   M.A. Lotter. 60x46cm (23½x18½") Wash & OL color. Margin trimmed; repaired tear into image; dampstaining lower lf corner; scattered soiling.   [A7]   £1,665 **$2,760**

AMERICA SEPTENTRIONALIS, CONCINNATA JUXTA OBSERVATIONES DNN ACADEMIAE REGALIS SCIENTIARUM ET NUNNULLORUM ALIORUM, ET JUXTA ANNOTATIONES RECENTISSIMAS, PER G. DE L'ISLE ...   [c.1780]   2nd plate. 45x57cm (18x22½") Orig wash color. Fine. Ref: Tooley (Amer) p.19, #34.
[29]   £663 **$1,100**

ASIA ...   [c.1760]   Tobias Conrad Lotter. 48x58cm (19x23") Full color. Exc.   [20]   £528 **$875**

BURGUNDISCHE CRAIS. WESTPHALISCHE CRAIS.   [1762]   From *Atlas Portatilis*. Benelux & adjacent. 10x12cm (3½x5") Old color.   [48]   DM 120   £41 **$68**

CARTE GEOGRAPHIQUE DU COMTE DE LA MARCK   [c.1760]   Ruhr region. 49x58cm (19½x23") Old color.
[48]   DM 1,480   £511 **$847**

CARTE NOUVELLE DE L'AMERIQUE ANGLOISE ...   [c.1770]   M.A. Lotter. Colonies by color; Indian lands shown. 60x49cm (24x19½") Wash & OL color. Browning along horiz fold; lacks sm portion rt margin fold; sm tear top just into border.   [A7]   £329 **$546**

COLOSSUS MONARCHICUS STATUS DANIELIS   [1765]   Allegorical figure; Daniel's interpretation of dream of Nebuchadnezzar; incorporates long list of monarchs. 58x49cm (23x19½") Orig body color. Restoration at c'fold. Ref: MCC 1 "Geographical Oddities" 26.   [46]   £320 $531

EUROPA REGNORUM   [c.1760]   50x58cm (19½x23") Old color. Brown spot; some placenames underlined.
[48]   DM 750   £259 **$429**

FIRENZA LA CAPITALE DI TOSCANA   [c.1770]   M.A. Lotter. City plan & view. 50x58cm (19½x23") Full color. Map in color.   [A7]   £1,318 **$2,185**

IMPERIUM RUSSICUM OMNISQUE TARTARIA   [1762]   From *Atlas Portatilis*. T.C. Lotter. With Japan. 10x12cm (3½x5") Old color.   ["Tabula Gener. Totius Belgii qua Provinciae XVII Infer. Germaniae olim sub S.R.I. Circulo Burgundiae" from same source offered at same price]   [48]   DM 80   £28 $46

LA PLUS GRANDE PARTIE DE LA MANCHE, QUI CONTIENT LES COTES D'ANGLETERRE ET CELLES DE FRANCE LES BORDS MARITIMES DE PICARDIE   [c.1760]   Extensive S England coverage. 49x57cm (19½x22½") Full orig color; red highlighted towns.   [11]   £211 **$350**

LIVONIAE ET CURLANDIAE DUCATUS CUM INSULIS ADJACENTIB.   [c.1760]   T.C. Lotter. 49x58cm (19x22½") Full color. Margin soiling; damp stain to border; couple tiny spots; 1" tear into map repaired; good (B).
[A4]   £143 **$237**

MAGNUS DUCATUS LITHUANIA ...   [c.1760]   T.C. Lotter. 48x57cm (19x22½") Full color. Margins tattered; surface soiling, few sm spots on map; good (B).   [A4]   £58 **$96**

MAPPA GEOGRAPHICA EXHIBENS ELECTORATUM BRANDENBURGENSEM, SIVE MARCHIAM VETEREM, MEDIAM ET NOVAM, NEC NON MARCHIAM UKERAM   [1758]   Berlin at ctr. 50x58cm (19½x22½") Orig wash & OL color. Lower margin tears just affect map.   [11]   £136 **$225**

NOVA MAPPA GEOGRAPHICA TOTIUS DUCATUS SILESIAE ...   [1758]   Breslau inset, 38-item key. 48x58cm (19x22½") Orig wash & OL color, cities in red.   [11]   £106 **$175**

LOTTER continued

NOVISSIMA ET ACCURATISSIMA HELVETIAE ...   [1761]   T.C. Lotter. 49x57cm (19½x22½")   Orig wash & OL color.   [11]   £271   **$450**

OPULENTISSIMUM SINARUM IMPERIUM JUXTA RECENTISSIMAM DELINEATIONEM IN SUAS PROVINCIAS DISTERMINATUM CURA ET SUMTIBUS   [c.1760]   50x57cm (19½x22½")   Orig body color. Vague printer's crease bottom lf.   [46]   **£680** $1,128

OSTERREICHISCHE CRAIS. CHURF. U. HERTZOGT. BAYERN   [1762]   From *Atlas Portatilis*. 10x13cm (3½x5")   Old color.   [48]   **DM 90**   £31 $51

PENSYLVANIA NOVA JERSEY ET NOVA YORK   [c.1760]   T.C. Lotter. 59x51cm (23x20")   Color.   [A7]   £763   **$1,265**

PENSYLVANIA NOVA JERSEY ET NOVA YORK CUM REGIONIBUS AD FLUVIUM DELAWARE IN AMERICA SITIS   [1777]   T.C. Lotter. Foreshortened eastern New England. 57x50cm (22½x19½")   Orig color. Fine.   [A2]   £1,924   **$3,190**

[SAME TITLE]   [1777]   T.C. Lotter. 57x49cm (22½x19½")   Orig color. VG to fine.   [14]   £1,809   **$3,000**

RECENS EDITA TOTIUS NOVI BELGII, IN AMERICA SEPTENTRIONALI SITI, DELINEATIO CURA ET SUMTIBUS TOB. CONR. LOTTERI ... AUGUST. VIND.   [1760]   With New York view. 50x58cm (19½x23")   Orig color. Few repaired tears, no loss; upper lf margin extended, facsimile addition 1 cm of border. Ref: Tooley (Amer) p.292, 5th state, #27.   [14]   £3,015   **$5,000**

REGNA PORTUGALLIAE ET ALGARBIAE, CUM ADJACENTIBUS HISPANIAE PROVINCIIS   [1762]   Brazil inset. 58x49cm (23x19½")   Old color.   [48]   **DM 580**   £200 $332

TABULA ANEMOGRAPHICA SEU PYXIS NAUTICA, VULGO COMPASS CHARTE   [c.1760]   T.C. Lotter. Compass card identifies 32 points, with windheads. 50x58cm (19½x22½")   Full color.   [A7]   £1,318   **$2,185**

TERRAE YEMEN MAXIMA PARS, SEU IMPERII IMAMI, PRINCIPATUS KAUKEBAN NEC NON DITIONUM HASCHID U BEKIL, NEHHM, CHAULAN, ABU ARISCH ET ADEN TABULA ...   [1774]   Jizan to Aden. 57x37cm (22½x14½")   Orig body color.   [46]   **£380** $630

TIROLIS COMITATUS CONTINENS EPISCOP. TRIDENTINUM ET BRIXIENSEM NEC NON COMIT. BRIGANTINUM, FELDKIRCH SONNEBERG ET PLUDENTIN   [1761]   49x58cm (19½x22½")   Orig wash & OL color; cities in red. 2 margin tears just to map supported verso, no loss.   [11]   £232   **$385**

LOTTERY MAGAZINE

A DRAUGHT OF THE HARBOUR OF HALIFAX IN NOVA SCOTIA BY AN OFFICER ON BOARD THE RAINBOW SR. GEO. COLLIER.   [1777]   17x23cm (7x9")   Ref: Jolly LOT-4.   [11]   £172   **$285**

LOWRY

THE WINDWARD OR SOUTH CARIBBEAN ISLANDS   [1852]   Martinique to Trinidad with Barbados. 47x34cm (18½x13½")   Color.   [18]   £51   **$85**

LUBRECHT

LUBRECHT'S CALIFORNIA   [1885]   From *Pictorial and Comprehensive Atlas of the World*. 32x28cm (12½x11")   Color. Fine.   [12]   £60   **$100**

LUCAS

GEORGIA   [1816]   37 counties. 27x21cm (11x8½")   OL color. Minor surface soiling.   [22]   £136   **$225**

ILLINOIS   [1823]   From *General Atlas* ... 30 counties. 30x23cm (12x9")   Wide OL pastel color. Fine. Ref: Karrow (MW) 4-1417; Phillips (A) 742-72.   [12]   £226   **$375**

MAINE   [1823]   From *General Atlas* ... 9 counties; far northern border; Portland the capital. 30x24cm (12x9½")   Wide OL pastel color. Lt foxing blank area; else fine. Ref: Phillips (A) 742-50.   [12]   £106   **$175**

MARYLAND   [1823]   From *General Atlas* ... 19 counties; Baltimore inset, 8½x9½"; map 28x50cm (11x19½")   Wide OL pastel color. Lt time-toned; margin repair lower c'fold; lt dampstains lower margin corners; else exc. Ref: Papenfuse & Coale fig 58; Morrison fig 58; Ristow (Amer M&M) fig 17-2; Phillips (M) p.396.   [12]   £232   **$385**

[SAME TITLE]   [1823]   From *General Atlas* ... Large Baltimore inset, incl DE.. 29x50cm (11½x20")   Orig wash color. C'fold repair; fine. Ref: Phillips (A) 742-60. Papenfuse & Coale fig.58.   [31]   £332   **$550**

NEW HAMPSHIRE   [c.1816]   6 counties. 27x21cm (11x8½")   Color, bit dimmed. Clean, bright. Ref: Cobb (NH) 93 [Lewis/Tanner].   [22]   £75   **$125**

NTH CAROLINA   [1823]   From *General Atlas* ... 28x48cm (11x19")   Wide OL pastel color. Dampstaining lower corners; moderate offsetting; overall exc. Ref: Phillips (A) 742-62.   [12]   £226   **$375**

LUCAS continued

UNITED STATES [1823] From *General Atlas* ... Immense Oregon Terr. 29x48cm (11½x19") Full color. Mild toning margins; else clean. Ref: Phillips (A) 742-49. [A10] £160 **$265**

[SAME TITLE] [1823] Extends to Pacific. 29x48cm (11½x19") Full orig color. Minor spotting; but VG. [36] £166 **$275**

LUFFMAN

[ATLAS] A NEW POCKET ATLAS AND GEOGRAPHY OF ENGLAND AND WALES [1803] Octavo, modern cloth; 54 colored miniature circular maps, text below, Lacks index map; one with printer's crease; 11 maps cropped edges, some text loss, one lacks corner; one with overlip; some soiling. Ref: Chubb 308. [A6] **£1,380 $2,289**

MacKENZIE

A MAP OF AMERICA, BETWEEN LATITUDES 40 AND 70 NORTH, AND LONGITUDES 45 AND 180 WEST, EXHIBITING MACKENZIE'S TRACK FROM MONTREAL TO FORT CHIPEWYAN & FROM THENCE TO THE NORTH SEA IN 1789, & TO THE WEST PACIFIC OCEAN IN 1793 [1801] 45x79cm (18x31") Trimmed to neat lines; fold repairs. [11] £151 **$250**

MacPHERSON

SPANISH DOMINIONS IN N. AMERICA [1821] London: Sherwood, Neely, Jones. Panama to 38th parallel. 19x24cm (7½x9½") Full color. Lib stamp Pacific O; else clean; good (B). [A3] £66 **$110**

MACROBIUS

[BOOK WITH MAPS] DE SOMNIUM SCIPIONIS ... [1528] (Dream of Scipio), Venice. Macrobius, a Roman, flourished 399-423 A.D. With map of ancient world, 7x7cm (2½x2½") Ref: Shirley (W) 13. [44] £558 **$925**

MADISON

OHIO [1805] Bishop James Madison. NW corner of 9-sheet "Map of Virginia ..." Ohio as 19x17" inset; shows "New Connecticut", Ohio Co. purchase & some counties. 59x58cm (23½x23") Faintly toned; some margin chipping. [A10] £146 **$242**

MAGAZINE OF MAGAZINES

A MAP OF THE BRITISH EMPIRE IN AMERICA, FROM THE HEAD OF HUDSONS BAY TO THE SOUTHERN BOUNDS OF GEORGIA [1750] Extracted from 8vo format; lacks publisher's imprint 26x32cm (10½x13") Hand color & OL, with some disturbance. Ref: Jolly MOM-2 [A7] £156 **$258**

MAGINI

[ATLAS] GEOGRAPHIAE UNIVERSAE TUM VETERIS TUM NOVAE ABSOLVTISSIMVM... [1597] Cologne: Keschedt. Large octavo, probably 19th c leather rebinding; 27 Ptolemaic, 37 reduced Mercator maps engraved by Porro, uncolored. Leather dry & rubbed, spine ends torn; internally tight; some worming cover & end papers; sl foxing & toning throughout; maps generally VG to fine. Ref: Phillips (A) 404. [A2] £3,450 **$5,720**

AFRICA [1597-98] From *Geografia*. Venice: Galignani. 13x17cm (5x6½") on sheet with text. B&W. Fine. Ref: Phillips (A) 405. [30] £178 **$295**

[SAME TITLE] [1596 / 1616] Porro, sc. 13x17cm (5x7") Color. [41] £96 **$160**

[SAME TITLE] [1596-1621] 12x17cm (5x6½") Color. Browning; repaired loss lower lf neatline; o/w VG. [21] **Can$130** £57 $94

AMERICA [1597] 13x17cm (5x6½") Color. Lt show through rt margin. Ref: Burden 97. [14] £513 **$850**

[SAME TITLE] [1597-98] From *Geografia*. Venice: Galignani. 13x17cm (5x6½") on sheet with text. B&W. Fine. Ref: Phillips (A) 405. [30] £407 **$675**

ASIA [1596-1621] 12x17cm (5x6½") Color. Minor browning; o/w VG. [21] **Can$130** £57 $94

[SAME TITLE] [1597-98] From *Geografia*. Venice: Galignani. 13x17cm (5x6½") on sheet with text. B&W. Fine. Ref: Phillips (A) 405. [30] £181 **$300**

BRITANICAE INSULAE [1597-98] From *Geografia*. Venice: Galignani. 13x17cm (5x6½") on sheet with text. B&W. Fine. Ref: Phillips (A) 405; Shirley (BI to 1650) 199. [30] £166 **$275**

EUROPA [1597-98] From *Geografia*. Venice: Galignani. 13x17cm (5x6½") on sheet with text. B&W. Fine. Ref: Phillips (A) 405. [30] £160 **$265**

[SAME TITLE] [c.1621] 13x16cm (5x6½") Color. Browning; lower lf margin repaired; few creases; o/w VG. [21] **Can$120** £52 $87

GALLIAE REGNUM [1597-98] From *Geografia*. Venice: Galignani. 13x17cm (5x6½") on sheet with text. B&W. Fine. Ref: Phillips (A) 405. ["Pedemontium Monsferratus et Liguria" & "Forum Iulii et Histria" offered at same price] [30] £87 **$145**

MAGINI continued

GERMANIA [1597] 14x17cm (5½x6½") B&W. Strong strike; faint age toning; o/w fine. [A1] £73 **$121**
[SAME TITLE] [1597-98] From *Geografia*. Venice: Galignani. 13x17cm (5x6½") on sheet with text. B&W. Fine. ["Italia" offered at same price] Ref: Phillips (A) 405. [30] £136 **$225**
GRAECIA [1597-98] From *Geografia*. Venice: Galignani. 13x17cm (5x6½") on sheet with text. B&W. Fine. ["Candia Insula, olim Creta" offered at same price] Ref: Phillips (A) 405. [30] £142 **$235**
HELVETIA [1597-98] From *Geografia*. Venice: Galignani. 13x17cm (5x6½") on sheet with text. B&W. Fine. Ref: Phillips (A) 405. ["Moscoviae Imperium", "Hispaniae Regnum" & "Portugalliae Regnum" offered at same price] [30] £112 **$185**
HISPANIAE REGNUM [1597] 13x17cm (5x6½") B&W. Lt toned; VG. Ref: Phillips (A) 404. [35] £54 **$90**
INDIA ORIENTALIS [1596] 1st issue. With North Amer west coast. 13x18cm (5½x7") Exc. [44] £220 **$365**
[SAME TITLE] [1597-98] From *Geografia*. Venice: Galignani. With American NW coast. 13x17cm (5x6½") on sheet with text. B&W. Fine. Ref: Phillips (A) 405. [30] £166 **$275**
MOSCOVIAE IMPERIUM [1617] As in *Geographiae* ... 13x17cm (5½x7") Color. [42] **Aus$295** £134 $222
NEAPOLITANUM REGNUM [1597-98] From *Geografia*. Venice: Galignani. 13x17cm (5x6½") on sheet with text. B&W. Fine. Ref: Phillips (A) 405 ["Marca Anconae, olim Picenum" offered at same price]. [30] £90 **$150**
ORBIS TERRAE COMPENDIOSA DESCRIPTIO ... MERCATOR ... [1596 (1597-98)] Venice: Galignani; Porro, sc. Double hemi. 15x24cm (6x9½") B&W. Fine. Ref: Shirley (W) 194. [30] £573 **$950**
PALAESTINA, VEL TERRA SANCTA [1597-98] From *Geografia*. Venice: Galignani. Nile to Beirut. 13x17cm (5x6½") on sheet with text. B&W. Fine. Ref: Phillips (A) 405. [30] £178 **$295**
PALESTINAE SIVE TOTIUS TERRAE PROMISSIONIS ... [1596] 1st ed; from the Ptolemy. Israelites' route from Egypt to Holy Land. 13x17cm (5x7") B&W. Fine. [37] £181 **$300**
POLONIAE REGNUM [1597] Text on verso. 13x17cm (5x7") Newer color. Fine. [14] £166 **$275**
[SAME TITLE] [1597-98] From *Geografia*. Venice: Galignani. 13x17cm (5x6½") on sheet with text. B&W. Fine. Ref: Phillips (A) 405. ["Hungaria et Transilvania", "Sardinia et Sicilia" & "Natolia olim Asia Minor" offered at same price] [30] £106 **$175**
PTOLEMAEI TYPUS [1596 (1597-98)] Ptolemaic World. 13x17cm (5½x7") on sheet with text. B&W. Fine. Ref: Shirley (W) 193. [30] £166 **$275**
[SAME TITLE] [1597 / 1617] Arnhem: Jansson. Ptolemaic world; verso: title page. 13x17cm (5½x7") Newer color. VG to fine. Ref: Shirley (W) 201. [A2] £150 **$248**
SCANDIA, SIVE REGIONES SEPTENTRIONALES [1597-98] From *Geografia*. Venice: Galignani. 13x17cm (5x6½") on sheet with text. B&W. Fine. Ref: Phillips (A) 405. [30] £178 **$295**
[SAME TITLE] [1597 / 1617] Arnhem: Jansson the Elder. 13x17cm (5x7") Newer color. Top of first title words clipped; o/w VG. Ref: Burden 98. [A2] £150 **$248**
TABULA APHRICAE I [1597-98] From *Geografia*. Venice: Galignani. Ptolemaic northwest Africa. 13x17cm (5x6½") on sheet with text. B&W. Fine. Ref: Phillips (A) 405. ["... Asia II" (Ptolemaic Georgia & Caucasus) offered at same price] [30] £87 **$145**
TABULA ASIAE IIII [1597-98] From *Geografia*. Venice: Galignani. Ptolemaic Holy Land. 13x17cm (5x6½") on sheet with text. B&W. Fine. Ref: Phillips (A) 405. [30] £112 **$185**
TABULA ASIAE VI [1597-98] From *Geografia*. Venice: Galignani. Ptolemaic Arabia. 13x17cm (5x6½") on sheet with text. B&W. Fine. Ref: Phillips (A) 405. [30] £118 **$195**
TABULA ASIAE IX [1597-98] From *Geografia*. Venice: Galignani. 13x17cm (5x6½") on sheet with text. B&W. Fine. ["... Asiae VIII" (Ptolemaic Tartary) offered at same price] [30] £75 **$125**
TABULA ASIAE XI [1597-98] From *Geografia*. Venice: Galignani. Ptolemaic southeast Asia. 13x17cm (5x6½") on sheet with text. B&W. Fine. Ref: Phillips (A) 405. [30] £96 **$160**
TABULA ASIAE XII [1597-98] From *Geografia*. Venice: Galignani. Ptolemaic Taprobana. 13x17cm (5x6½") on sheet with text. B&W. Fine. Ref: Phillips (A) 405. ["... Aphricae III" (Ptolemaic Egypt) offered at same price] [30] £106 **$175**
TABULA EUROPAE IIII [1597-98] From *Geografia*. Venice: Galignani. Ptolemaic Germany. 13x17cm (5x6½") on sheet with text. B&W. Fine. Ref: Phillips (A) 405. ["... Europae VII" (Sicily, Sardinia) & "... Asiae I" (Asia Minor) offered as same price] [30] £90 **$150**
TABULA EUROPAE VI [1596] Ptolemaic Italy. 1st ed. 13x18cm (5x7") B&W. Fine [37] £106 **$175**
[SAME TITLE] [1597-98] From *Geografia*. Venice: Galignani. Ptolemaic Italy. 13x17cm (5x6½") on sheet with text. B&W. Fine. ["... Asiae V" (Ptolemaic Persia) offered at same price] [30] £100 **$165**
TABULA EUROPAE X [1597-98] From *Geografia*. Venice: Galignani. Ptolemaic Greece & Crete. 13x17cm (5x6½") on sheet with text. B&W. Fine. Ref: Phillips (A) 405. [30] £118 **$195**

MAGINI continued

TABULA EUROPAE PRIMA [1597-98] From *Geografia*. Venice: Galignani. Ptolemaic Great Britain. 13x17cm (5x6½") on sheet with text. B&W. Fine. Ref: Phillips (A) 405. [30] £121 **$200**

TARTARIAE IMPERIUM [1597-98] From *Geografia*. Venice: Galignani. 13x17cm (5x6½") on sheet with text. B&W. Fine. Ref: Phillips (A) 405. [30] £211 **$350**

[SAME TITLE] [1598] From Ptolemy, *Geografia* ... Incl NW North America & relocated Japan. 13x17cm (5x6½") on 11x7½" sheet. B&W. Pristine. Ref: Phillips (A) 405. [12] £196 **$325**

TUSCIA [1597-98] From *Geografia*. Venice: Galignani. 13x17cm (5x6½") on sheet with text. B&W. Fine. ["Latium ...", "Lombardia ..." & "Aegyptus" offered at same price] [30] £100 **$165**

UNIVERSI ORBIS DESCRIPTIO [1596 (1597-98)] Oval projection after Ortelius, 13x17cm (5x7") on sheet with text. B&W. Orig printed overlapping title. Fine. Ref: Shirley (W) 195, pl.158. [30] £302 **$500**

UNIVERSI ORBIS DESCRIPTIO AD USUM NAVIGANTIUM [1596] 1st ed., after Mercator's 1569 map. 13x17cm (5x7") B&W. Strong impression; fine. Ref: Shirley (W) 196. [37] £362 **$600**

[SAME TITLE] [1596 (1597-98)] From *Geographicae Universae*. Porro, sc. "Carta Marina" after Mercator. 13x17cm (5x7") on sheet with text. B&W. Fine. Ref: Shirley (W) 196, pl.159. [30] £413 **$685**

MAGNUS, C.

FORTRESS MONROE, OLD POINT COMFORT AND HYGEIA HOTEL, VA. [1861] Bird's-eye view printed by E. Sachse & Co., Baltimore. 46x71cm (18x28"). Color. Fine. [31] £754 **$1,250**

MAP OF THE CITY OF ALBANY [c.1860] On double 10x8½" sheet. 13x20cm (5x8") Col. Fine. [12] £81 **$135**

ONE HUNDRED & FIFTY MILES AROUND RICHMOND [1864] 11th ed; 1/3000. Circular map; 9 sm circular maps (omits Natchez inset), 66x77cm (26x30½") Printed red & blue. Never folded; dry, fragile; tears, minor marginal restoration; good. [12th ed offered for $850] [16] £573 **$950**

PANORAMA OF THE MISSISSIPPI VALLEY AND ITS FORTIFICATIONS ... [c.1863] 4-part map of river, St. Louis to mouth; 4 city views; mounted on linen as issued. 60x64cm (23½x25") Orig wash color. Close top margin; few stains; of its kind, exc. Ref: Stephenson (CW-2) 42.5. [24] £905 **$1,500**

MALLET

AMERIQUE SEPTENTRIONALE [1684] Publ Frankfurt. Insular Calif. 15x11cm (6x4½") OL color. VG Ref: McLaughlin 81-2. [38] £121 **$200**

[SAME TITLE] [1686] Insular Calif. 17x11cm (6½x4½") OL color. Stains in margin; else VG. Ref: McLaughlin 81. [37] £136 **$225**

ANGRA [1685 / 1719] German ed. Bird's-eye of Azores city. 14x9cm (5½x3½") Full col. Fine. [35] £39 **$65**

CAMBALU OR PEKING [1683] View, city in distance. 14x9cm (5½x3½") Later full color. Fine. Ref: Phillips (A) 3447, v.2-p.15. [35] £33 **$55**

I. DE ST. HELENE [1683] From *L'Univers*. View with ships offshore. 15x10cm (6x4") B&W. Sm orig printing loss lower lf; good. [29] £51 **$85**

ISLE DU JAPON [1683] 14x10cm (5½x4") B&W. Ref: MCC 36, No.30. [A2] £66 **$110**

ISLE MOLUCOUES [1683] 15x10cm (6x4") B&W. VG. [37] £51 **$85**

ISLES CARIBES [1685] Puerto Rico, the Lesser Antilles, Spanish Main. 15x10cm (6x4") B&W. [20] £106 **$175**

ISLES DES LARRONS [1683] Bird's-eye of Marianas. 14x9cm (5½x3½") Later full color. Fine. Ref: Phillips (A) 3447, v.2-p.77. [35] £39 **$65**

LA FLORIDE [1686] Present Southeastern U.S. 15x11cm (6x4½") OL color. Surface dirt; else fine. Ref: Cumming (SE) 106. [37] £166 **$275**

MEXIQUE [1685] Mexico City view. 15x10cm (6x4") B&W. [20] £81 **$135**

MEXIQUE OU NOUVELLE ESPAGNE [1685] 15x10cm (6x4") B&W. [20] £93 **$155**

NOUVEAU MEXIQUE ET CALIFORNIE [1683] Insular Calif. 14x10cm (5½x4") Color. Ref: McLaughlin 87 (1). Phillips (A) 3447-V,333. [12] £332 **$550**

[SAME TITLE] [1684] Frankfurt. 14x10cm (5½x4") Color. Fine. Ref: McLaughlin 87-2. [38] £226 **$375**

PAYS DES CARIBES DE GUIANE [1686] Frankfurt: Zunner. Sketchy Lesser Antilles to Amazon Basin. 15x10cm (6x4") Color. [18] £42 **$70**

MALTE-BRUN

PLAN DE STUTTGART [1880] Paris: Rouff. Chromolitho. 24x33cm (9½x13") [48] DM 200 £69 **$114**

MANUSCRIPT MAPS

[ATLAS] MAPS, VII P. RIVETT [1871] By Palmer Rivett, n.p. (Norfolk, England?); School atlas exercise. Quarto; 14 maps in ink & OL watercolor; some signed and/or dated. US map 9x16", others 4½x6½". Few tears in home-made paper covers; internally VG+. [38] £573 **$950**

[ESTATE PLAN OF THE] LANDES OF WILLIAM HUNT OF DALEHILL IN THE PARRISH OF TISEHURST IN THE COUNTIE OF SUSSEX [c.1630] By William Gier. Roads, buildings, fields, woods, orchards, copses illustrated. 58x72cm (23x28½") Orig ink & watercolors on vellum; compass rose heightened with gold. [23] £4,523 **$7,500**

[KOREA] [17th or 18th c.] On mulberry paper from "Chanha-do" atlas. Seoul, in red, is capital; 84 localities, each with ruler. 29x34cm (11½x13") Orig color. Framed. [13] Aus$2,200 £999 **$1,656**

[PENNSYLVANIA: BEDFORD COUNTY] [1785] By Thomas Nickroy. 4 survey maps on one leaf showing land owners near Little Yough River in Brothers Valley Township, possibly as grants to soldiers. 20x31cm (8x12½") [15] £151 **$250**

[WORLD: CIRCULAR, KOREAN TITLE] [17th or 18th c.] Abstract & imaginary "Chonha-do" map on mulberry paper. 29x34cm (11½x13") Orig color. Framed. Ref: Simon Dewez, *The Australian Collector*, June 1997. [13] Aus$4,800 £2,180 **$3,614**

A MAP OF THAT PART OF BUCKS COUNTY RELEASED BY THE INDIANS TO THE PROPRIETARIES OF PENNSYLVANIA IN SEPTEMBER 1737 AS BY A FORMER AGREEMENT MADE WITH SAID INDIANS BY THE EXTENT OF A MAN'S WALK IN A DAY AND A HALF FROM THENCE ... TO THE DELAWARE RIVER [mid 19th c.] Anonymous. Illustrates "Walking Purchase" by Thomas & Richard Penn using fast pacers. 63x43cm (24½x17") Pen, ink & watercolor on silk. Early ctr strengthening, some silk loss, image unaffected; linen backed early; trimmed close to neatline; sm loss upper lf just beyond neatline; VG+. [35] £754 **$1,250**

BLOCK 16 G.H. & S.A. RY. FOLEY COUNTY ... [c.1890] Galveston, Houston & San Antonio RR lots on Rio Grande north bank, showing dimensions & topo. India ink on drafting paper laid on cotton. 50x65cm (19½x25½") Blue tinted water. Rolled; VG. ["Map of Gonzales County" offered at same price] [16] £452 **$750**

FRANCE [1878] Josselin Ernest, 11 year-old student. Departments delineated; towns located. 36x50cm (14x19½") Watercolor. VG (A). [A4] £50 **$83**

H. & T.C. RW. CO.'S BLOCKS NOS. 6, 7 & 8. IN PRESIDIO CO. [TX] [1889] By J.L. Mikich. Marfa area, precisely drafted. Possibly the orig from which copies were lithographed. Pencil additions. 68x62cm (27x24½") Stain top rt; browned, lf margin sl waterstained; purple stamp "Land Department"; laid on canvas; rolled; good. [16] £603 **$1,000**

MAPA DE LA CIUDAD DE LA HABANA Y LOBLACIONES DE SUS ALRDEDORES. L DIBUJO JUAN DE OLMEDILLAS [c.1765] Cruz Cano Olmedilla? Havana & vicinity for Auditor General, in pen, ink & watercolor on paper in red velvet binding with gold lock. 30x44cm (12x17½") Some wear & splitting at joint; official stamp, some rubbing to map; for its kind, exc. [24] £8,443 **$14,000**

PLAN DE LA VILLE ET RADE DE CARTAGENE ET DU FORT DE ST. LAZARE [23 Apr 1701] Manuscript map with color & signed in cartouche "Par Jacques Bureau" on sheet 53x74cm (21x29") Orig MS or early copy from published copy. Clean repairable vertical tear in half. NYHS lib stamp. [A7] £832 **$1,380**

PLAN DE LONGUVY [1686] By Guerin Cadet, Longuvy. Pen & ink drawing toward lf. On sheet 42x56cm (16½x22") [A7] £208 **$345**

PLAN OF COBLENTZ WITH THE CITADEL OF EHRENBREISTEIN AND THE FORTIFICATIONS ON BOTH BANKS OF THE RHINE. [1841] By A. Cimbolton after sketches by J.H. Humphrey. Pen & ink with orig wash & OL color. Large inset of citadel. 78x94cm (30½x37") Contemporary linen-backed paper little soiled. [11] £271 **$450**

PLANO DE LA RIA Y PUERTO DEL FERROL [1754] Linen backed 2-sheet map. Fortification in red; 8 fortification insets. 44x112cm (17x44") [A7] £416 **$690**

THIS CHART EXHIBITING THE TRACKS OF THE DISCOVERY AND ANTELOPE, WITH THE EXACT SITIATION OF THE PARACELS, IS RESPECTFULLY DEDICATED ... BY ... DANIEL ROSS, AND PHILIP MAUGHAN LIEUTENANTS OF THE BOMBAY MARINE 1808 [c.1808] Probably a duplication of a printed chart. Backed on orig linen. 64x64cm (25x25") Exc. [43] £422 **$700**

MARMOCCHI

[ATLAS] ATLANTE DI GEOGRAFICA-STORICA UNIVERSALE [1845] Florence. Folio; 35 OL color maps, 30 costume plates, 30 uncolored views; quarter sheep. Worn, lacks backstrip. [A7] £225 **$373**

MARSHALL

[ATLAS] ATLAS TO MARSHALL'S LIFE OF WASHINGTON [1832] Phila: J. Crissy. Octavo, orig paper boards; 10 double-page maps & plans with some color. Endpapers foxed; transferring on maps. Ref: Howes (US) M317. [33] £286 **$475**

MARSHALL continued

A MAP OF THE COUNTRY WHICH WAS THE SCENE OF OPERATIONS OF THE NORTHERN ARMY; INCLUDING THE WILDERNESS THROUGH WHICH GENERAL ARNOLD MARCHED TO ATTACK QUEBEC [1832] From *Life of Washington*. 25x19cm (10x7½") OL color. Ref: Clark (Amer Rev) 46150. [22] £45 **$75**

BOSTON ET SES ENVIRONS [1807] From French ed, *Life of Washington*. Paris: Dentu. 21x32cm (8½x12½") [47] £85 $141

CARTE DES PROVINCES MERIDIONALES DES ETATS-UNIS [1807] From French ed, *Life of Washington*. Paris: Dentu. 35x51cm (14x20") Binding folds flattened. [47] £95 $158

ILE DE NEW-YORK. PARTIE DE LONG-ISLAND OU DE L'ILE LONGUE, ET POSITIONS DES ARMEES AMERICAINE ET BRITANNIQUE, APRES LE COMBAT LIVRE SUR HAUTEURS, LE 27 AOUT 1776 [1807] From French ed, *Life of Washington*. Paris: Dentu. 41x26cm (16x10") Trimmed to top lf border due to binding. [47] £130 $216

INVESTISSIMENT ET ATTAQUE D'YORK, DANS LA VIRGINIE [1807] From French ed, *Life of Washington*. Paris: Dentu. 21x23cm (8½x9") [47] £35 $58

PARTIE DE L'ETAT DE RHODE-ISLAND, ET POSITION DES ARMEES AMERICAINE ET BRITANNIQUE, AU SIEGE DE NEWPORT, ET A L'AFFAIRE DU 29 AOUT 1778 [1807] From French ed, *Life of Washington*. Paris: Dentu. 44x26cm (17x10") Trimmed to top lf border due to binding. [47] £70 $116

PARTIE SEPTENTRIONALE DU NEW-JERSEY, ET POSITIONS DES ARMEES AMERICAINE ET BRITANNIQUE APRES LE PASSAGE DE LA RIVIERE DU NORD, EN 1776 [1807] From French ed, *Life of Washington*. Paris: Dentu. 40x26cm (15½x10") Trimmed to upper rt border due to binding. [47] £90 $150

PAYE SITUE ENTR FROG'S POINT ET CROTON RIVER, ET POSITION DES ARMEES AMERICAINE ET BRITANNIQUE, DEPUIS LE 12 OCTOBRE 1776, JUSQU'AU 28 DU MEME MOIS QU'ELLES ENGAGERANT LE COMBAT SUR LES PLAINES BLANCHES [1807] From French ed, *Life of Washington*. Paris: Dentu. 42x23cm (16½x9") [47] £65 $108

PLAN OF THE COUNTRY FROM FROGS POINT TO COTTON RIVER SHEWING THE POSITIONS OF THE AMERICAN & BRITISH ARMIES FROM THE 12TH OF OCTOBER 1776 UNTIL THE ENGAGEMENT ON THE WHITE PLAINS ON THE 28TH [1806] From *Life of Washington*. 1st ed; London; Richard Phillips. 41x22cm (16½x8½") B&W. [12] £96 **$160**

[SAME TITLE] [1807] From *Life of Washington*. London: R. Phillips. Troop positions in blue & red. 42x22cm (16½x8½") OL color. VG. [36] £166 **$275**

SIEGE DE CHARLESTON [1807] From French ed, *Life of Washington*. Paris: Dentu. 21x32cm (8½x12½") [47] £65 $108

THEATRE DES OPERATIONS DE L'ARMEE DU NORD ET DESERT QUE LE GENERAL ARNOLD TRAVERSE EN MARCHANT CONTRE QUEBEC [1807] From French ed, *Life of Washington*. Paris: Dentu. 25x22cm (10x8½") Trimmed to border lower lf due to binding. [47] £48 $80

THEATRE DES OPERATIONS DES ARMEES AMERICAINE ET BRITANNIQUE EN 1776 ET 1777, DEPUIS LE RIVIERE DE RARITON, DANS LE JERSEY DE L'EST, JUSQU'A LE TETE DE L'ELK DANS LE MARYLAND [1807] From French ed, *Life of Washington*. Paris: Dentu. NJ to MD. 25x39cm (10x15½") [47] £85 $141

THEATRE DES OPERATIONS LES PLUS IMPORTANTES DE L'ARMEE DU SUD, DANS LA VIRGINIE, DANS LES DEUX CAROLINES, ET DANS LA GEORGIE [1807] From French ed, *Life of Washington*. Paris: Dentu. 36x26cm (14x10") Trimmed to lf border due to binding. [47] £68 $113

MARTIN

[BOOK WITH MAPS] THE UNIVERSAL GAZETTEER: OR, A DESCRIPTION OF THE ... KNOWN WORLD [1771] Benjamin Martin; London: Strahan. 3rd ed. Octavo, orig full leather, rehinged; 7 maps by Gibson incl World, 5 continents, Germany. World lacks 2" at lf; N Amer & S Amer lack ½" in Atlantic; o/w VG. [33] £106 **$175**

MAST, CROWELL & KIRKPATRICK

ATLAS MAP OF TEXAS ... [1886] From 9th ed, *Peoples' Atlas*. Verso: AR & Indian Terr. 30x43cm (12x17") Red & green OL. VG. [16] £60 **$100**

MATHEWS

THE SEIGE OF VICKSBURG. MAJOR GENERAL U.S. GRANT, COMMANDING, REPRESENTING THE POSITION OF THE SEVENTH DIVISION OF MAJ. GEN. JOHN A. LOGAN'S DIVISION OF MAJ. GEN. J.B. MCPHERSON'S ARMY CORPS [1863] One of 4 views of Vicksburg battle. 35x60cm (14x23½") Damage & discoloration, rt corners; sm loss bottom lf; signs of wear & exposure. [another of set in similar condition offered at same price] [15] £513 **$850**

MAVERICK, P.
PLAN OF THE CITY OF NEW YORK, WITH RECENT AND INTENDED IMPROVEMENTS [1807] Attributed to Wm. Bridges. 31x33cm (12x13") Margins trimmed to neat line; minor loss at fold intersections; minor staining; few sh repairable tears; paper-backed; sold as is. [A8] £381 **$632**

MAXIMILIAN of WIED
MAP TO ILLUSTRATE THE ROUTE OF PRINCE MAXIMILIAN OF WIED IN THE INTERIOR OF NORTH AMERICA FROM BOSTON TO THE UPPER MISSOURI, ETC, IN 1823, 33, & 34 [c.1840] Text in French, German, English. Insets: Great Falls; Itaska Lake. 42x80cm (16½x31½") Some OL & route color. A vert fold faintly toned; verso repair of 10" branching tear (barely visible) & fold separation; archival paper backing; else good. Ref: Wheat (TM) 445. [A10] £902 **$1,495**

McELROY, SON & BROWN
MAP OF KINGS COUNTY SHOWING THE AVENUES, STREETS, BASINS, BULKHEAD LINES, RAILWAYS &C. ... [1875] Folding map with covers. 77x64cm (30½x25") Some splitting at folds; two panels browned where tipped into covers; o/w good. [32] £452 **$750**

MAP OF KINGS COUNTY SHOWING THE AVENUES, STREETS, BASINS, BULKHEAD LINES, RAILWAYS &C. OF THE COUNTY TOWNS [1875] Folding map in orig folder, repaired. Full color by ward. 78x62cm (30½x24½") Sm tears at folds. Ref: Phillips (M) p.176. [15] £241 **$400**

McNALLY
NEBRASKA, KANSAS, DAKOTA AND COLORADO [1862-63] As in *McNally System of Geography*. School geography. 23x28cm (9x11") Full color. Some edge soiling. [26] £45 **$75**

TEXAS [1859] From *McNally's System of Geography*. 21x27cm (8½x10½") Full col. VG. [16] £51 **$85**

MEARES
PIC DE LANTAO, PRES DE L'ENTREE DU BOCCA TIGRIS ... [1794] View of island west of Hong Kong 17x23cm (6½x9") Colored. Exc. [4] £265 **$440**

VUE DE L'ENTREE DU BOCCA TIGRIS ... [1794] A Pearl River narrow. 17x23cm (6½x9") Uncolored. Exc. [4] £200 **$332**

VUE DE L'ILE TIGER ... [1794] On upper Pearl River. 17x23cm (6½x9") Uncolored. Exc. [4] £175 **$290**

VUE DE LA VILLE DE MACAO [1794] From French ed of Voyages. 25x49cm (10x19½") Uncolored. Trace of old folds; exc. [4] £350 **$581**

MEISNER
ANTORFF [1623] From *Schatzkastlein*. Antwerp view . 10x15cm (4x6") [48] DM 320 £110 **$183**

ARNHEIM. IN GELDERN [1638] From *Sciographia Cosmica*. View. 10x15cm (4x6") [48] DM 250 £86 **$143**

BRIGHTSTOWE IN ENGELLANDT [1638] From same source. Bird's-eye view with figures. 10x15cm (4x6") ["Chester in Engelland" offered at same price] [48] DM 200 £69 **$114**

COBURG IN SACHSEN [1638] From same source. View. 10x15cm (4x6") [48] DM 800 £276 **$458**

DORTMUNDT. IN WESTPHALEN [1638] From same source. View with figures. 10x15cm (4x6") Sh lower lf tear to platemark repaired. [48] DM 1,300 £449 **$744**

EDENBURCK IN SCHOTTL. [1638] From same source. View. 10x15cm (4x6") [48] DM 280 £97 **$160**

EINSIDLEN IN SCHWEITZ [1638] From same source. Abbey view. 10x15cm (4x6") [48] DM 900 £311 **$515**

GENDT. IN FLANDERN [1638] From same source. 10x15cm (4x6") [48] DM 200 £69 **$114**

GRANATA IN HISPANIA [1638] From same source. View with Alhambra & figure. 10x15cm (4x6") ["Corduba in Hisp." offered at same price] [48] DM 220 £76 **$126**

HAAGE. IN HOLLANDT [1638] From same source. View with figures & Noah's ark. 10x15cm (4x6") [48] DM 350 £121 **$200**

HALL IN SACHSEN [1638] From same source. View. 10x15cm (4x6") [48] DM 680 £235 **$389**

HALL IN SCHWABEN [1637] From same source. View. 10x15cm (4x6") [48] DM 900 £311 **$515**

HOMBURG. NASSAW SARBR. [1638] From same source. View of Saarland castles with figures. 10x15cm (4x6") Sm blemish. [48] DM 900 £311 **$515**

INSPRUGK IN TYROL [1638] From same source. Innsbruck view. 10x15cm (4x6") [48] DM 550 £190 **$315**

LAMBACH [AUSTRIA] [1638] From same source. View. 10x15cm (4x6") [48] DM 300 £104 **$172**

NEGROPONTE IN MOREA [1638] From same source. View of Chalkis, Greece with figures. 10x15cm (4x6") [48] DM 170 £59 **$97**

MEISNER continued

NON EX QUOVIS LIGNO FIT MERCURIUS - AMACAO IN CHYNA [(1624) 1638] As in *Thesaurus Philo. Politicus ... Schatzkastlein*. Macao bird's-eye view with foreground figures. 10x15cm (4x6") Uncolored. Exc.
[4] **£235** $390

NURNBERGK [1626] From *Ostreichischer Lorberkrantz*. View. 10x15cm (4x6") [48] **DM 720** £249 $412

OFEN [BUDA] IN UNGARN [1638] From *Sciographia Cosmica*. View with Venus & Cupid. 10x15cm (3½x6")
[48] **DM 390** £135 $223

PASSAW. IN NIEDER BAYERN [1637] From same source. View with figures. 10x15cm (4x6") Repaired tear.
[48] **DM 600** £207 $343

PHILIPSBURG ZU BRAUBACH [1638] From same source. View from Rhine with figures. 10x15cm (4x6")
[48] **DM 380** £131 $217

PIACENZA IN ITALIA [1638] From same source. Bird's-eye view. 10x15cm (4x6") [48] **DM 200** £69 $114

REIMS IN CHAMPANIEN [1638] From same source. View. 10x15cm (4x6") [48] **DM 180** £62 $103

ULRICHSTEIN AM VOGEL [1638] From same source. View. 10x15cm (4x6") [48] **DM 380** £131 $217

WETZSLAR [1638] From same source. View with figures. 10x15cm (4x6") [48] **DM 1,100** £380 $630

MELISH

[BOOK WITH MAPS] A GEOGRAPHICAL DESCRIPTION OF THE UNITED STATES, WITH THE CONTIGUOUS BRITISH AND SPANISH POSSESSIONS, INTENDED AS AN ACCOMPANYMENT TO MELISH'S MAP OF THESE COUNTRIES [1816] Octavo; red leather spine & corners with marbled boards;182 pp. Incl maps of areas around Boston, NYC, Phila; Harrisburg. Tight; contents sl age toned & foxed; some worm holes, text sl affected; else VG.
[A1] **£232** $385

CHARLESTON AND ADJACENT COUNTRY [1837] 17x10cm (6½x4") Wash color. [40] **£39** $65

UNITED STATES OF AMERICA COMPILED FROM THE LATEST & BEST AUTHORITIES BY JOHN MELISH [1820] From 2nd American ed, *Lavoisne's Genealogical, Historical ... & Geographical Atlas*. With text folio sheet relating to map. 43x54cm (17x21½") Full color. Close orig lower margin; c'fold repair Ref: Wheat (TM) 338.
[A3] **£438** $726

MENDENHALL

MENDENHALL'S ROAD MAP OF WISCONSIN [1900] Folding photolithographic map in paper covers showing tourist & "Through Bicycle Routes"; Milwaukee inset. 61x51cm (24x20") OL color. Covers scuffed; map fine.
[38] **£75** $125

MERCATOR (Folio) Try *Hondius, Jansson*

[ATLAS] GERARDI MERCATORIS ATLAS SIVE COSMOGRAPHICAE [1630] Amsterdam: Hondius. Folio, orig gold stamped vellum binding with orig cloth ties. 164 maps. On quality paper; pristine. Ref: Koeman Me 29B.
[3] **£57,294** $95,000

[ATLAS] L'APPENDICE DE L'ATLAS DE GERARD MERCATOR ET IUDOCUS HONDIUS: CONTENANT DIVERSES NOUVELLES TABLES ET DESCRIPTIONS ... [1633] Folio; vellum binding. 104 maps in orig full & OL color; 1st to incl 59 new maps, some replacing plates sold to Blaeu. Ref: Shirley (W) 336. Keuning, *The History of the Atlas*; Imago Mundi IV, p.50-3; Koeman Me 35
[3] **£51,323** $85,000

ABISSINORUM SIVE PRETIOSI IOANNIS IMPERIU [1606 (1628)] From Mercator-Hondius *Atlas* ... Congo inset. 34x49cm (13½x19"). Orig color. Minor margin repairs; good.
[31] **£392** $650

AFRICA EX MAGNA ORBIS TERRE DESCRIPTIONE GERARDI MERCATORIS DESUMPTA, STUDIO & INDUSTRIA G.M. IUNIORIS [1595-1633] 38x46cm (15x18½") Color. Ref: Norwich 21. [34] **£850** $1,410

AMERICA SIVE INDIA NOVA AD MAGNAE GERARDI MERCATORIS AVI UNIVERSALIS IMITATIONEM IN COMPENDIUM REDACTA. PER MICHAELEM MERCATOREM DUYSBURGENSEM [1595] Western hemi; 3 sm corner circular maps. 37x46cm (14½x18") Later color. Exc. Ref: Burden 87; Goss (NA) 19.
[2] **£3,317** $5,500

[SAME TITLE] [1595 / ?] 37x46cm (14½x18") Full orig color. Exc. [24] **£3,920** $6,500

[SAME TITLE] [1595-1609] Amsterdam: Hondius. 37x46cm (14½x18½") Uncol. [34] **£4,800** $7,959

ANGLIA, SCOTIA ET HIBERNIA [1624] 33x41cm (13x16") Contemp color. Lt browning top edge.
[A6] **£172** $286

ASIA EX MAGNA ORBIS TERRAE DESCRIPTIONE GERARDI MERCATORIS DESUMPTA, STUDIO ET INDUSTRIA G.M. IUNIORIS [1595] 38x46cm (15x18½") Orig color. [13] **Aus$2,600** £1,181 $1,958

[SAME TITLE] [1595] From *Atlas*. 37x46cm (15x18") Color. Exc. [43] **£1,086** **$1,800**

MERCATOR (Folio) continued

CANDIA CUM INSULIS ALIQUOT CIRCA GRAECIAM [1623] Mercator-Hondius. Sm inset maps of Corfu, Zante, Milo, Nicsia, Santorini, Scarpanto 34x48cm (13½x18½") Later OL color. Minor soiling margins; 2 hinge stains top edge. [A9] £180 **$299**

CHINA [1606+] Mercator-Hondius . E-W Japan; insular Korea; shows "Americae Pars". 34x46cm (13½x18") Early col. Sl soiled; margins all around, but trimmed into verso text. Ref: Potter p.122-23. [11] £1,055 **$1,750**

GALLIA [1585 (1628)] 36x41cm (14x16½") OL color. Even age-tone; margin stains; else VG. Ref: Koeman, Me 28A. [37] £286 **$475**

HISPANIAE NOVAE NOVA DESCRIPTIO [1606+] From 1st Hondius ed, *Atlas sive Cosmographicae* ... 38x51cm (15x20") Color. Moderately toned. [A8] £277 **$460**

HUNGARIA REGNUM SUMPTIBUS HENRICI HONDY PER GERARDUM MERCATOREM ... [1636] From Mercator-Hondius-Jansson Atlas. 37x44cm (14½x17") Col. Ref: Koeman Me 41A, 74. [42] Aus$1,350 £613 **$1,016**

INDIA ORIENTALIS [1613] Amsterdam: Jodocus Hondius. India, China & Philippines. 36x48cm (14x19") Orig color; gold highlights. Age toned; upper c'fold split repaired. Ref: Koeman Me 23a. [46] £1,800 **$2,985**

IRLANDIA REGNUM [1613] Amsterdam: Henry Hondius. 34x42cm (13½x16½") Orig color by counties. Sm ink stamp in sea area. Ref: Koeman Me 22. [46] £450 **$746**

IRLANDIAE REGNUM [c.1630] 34x48cm (13½x18½") Color. Browned. [A8] £277 **$460**

ITALIA [c.1589] 37x47cm (14½x18½") Full orig color. VG. [2] £513 **$850**

ORBIS TERRAE COMPENDIOSA DESCRIPTIO QUAM EX MAGNA UNIVERSALI ... [1587 / 1602] Double-hemi; text below. 36x52cm (14x20½") Full orig color. Exc. Ref: Shirley (W) 157. [2] £3,920 **$6,500**

[SAME TITLE] [1587 - c.1605] Publ in ... *Strabonis Rerum Geographicarum* ... Double-hemi; text below; fine plate crack just starting. 29x52cm (11½x20½") Color. Ref: Shirley (W) 157. [13] Aus$8,900 £4,042 **$6,702**

[SAME TITLE] [1587-1623] Double-hemi. 29x52cm (11x20½") Clear, distinct engraving. Color. Ctr crease repaired, no loss. Ref: Shirley (W) 157. [34] £5,200 **$8,622**

ORBIS TERRARUM TYPUS DE INTEGRO MULTIS IN LOCIS EMENDATUS [1643] Double hemi Mercator 1587 derivative, updated by Plancius 1590, with credit to "D.R.M. Mathes". 29x52cm (11½x20½") Verso fold restoration, minute facsimile work, not visible on recto. [11] £2,322 **$3,850**

RUSSIA CUM CONFINIJS [1595 (1628)] 36x46cm (14x18½") Full color. Margin stains; else fine. Ref: Koeman Me 28A. [37] £302 **$500**

SCLAVONIA, CROATIA, BOSNIA CUM DALMATIAE PARTE [1636] From Mercator-Hondius-Jansson Atlas. 36x46cm (14x18½") Period color. Ref: Koeman Me 41A, 77. [42] Aus$950 £431 **$715**

SEPTENTRIONALIUM TERRARUM DESCRIPTIO [1595-1609] Hondius; 2nd state. Polar projection with polar islands. 37x39cm (14½x15½") Uncolored. Ref: Burden 88. [34] £1,800 **$2,985**

[SAME TITLE] [1595-1613] 36x39cm (14½x15½") Color. Good. [46] £1,350 **$2,239**

[SAME TITLE] [c.1595-1620] 38x40cm (15x15½") OL color. Sh tear lower margin closed on verso. [A7] £1,248 **$2,070**

SEPTENTRIONALIUM TERRARUM DESCRIPTIO PER GERARDUM MERCATOREM CUM PREVELEGIO [1595] 1st ed, 1st state. Polar projection with 4 polar islands. 37x39cm (14½x15½") Later color. Exc. Ref: Burden 88; Campbell (Early) p.22-3. [2nd ed, 1606/13, orig color, c'fold strengthened, o/w exc. offered at $2,800] [2] £2,352 **$3,900**

TAB. XII. ASIAE, TABROBANAM REPRAESENTANS [c.1695] From Mercator's Ptolemaic geography. 35x36cm (14x14") Ref: Koeman Me 19. [46] £230 **$382**

TARTARIA [c.1606] From Mercator-Hondius *Atlas*. Northern Asia. 34x50cm (13½x19½") Full color. Restored; deacidified; margin tears repaired; backed with japan tissue; VG (A). [A3] £502 **$833**

VIRGINIAE ITEM ET FLORIDAE AMERICAE PROVINCIARUM, NOVA DESCRIPTIO [1606 (1609)] Amsterdam: Hondius. 34x43cm (13½x17") B&W. Strong impression; 2 repaired tears into map; else VG. Ref: Burden 151; Cumming (SE) 26. [38] £814 **$1,350**

MERCATOR (Small)

[ATLAS] **ATLAS MINOR, DAS IS / EIN KURSZE JEDOCH GRUNDTLICHE DESCHREIBUNG DER GANSZEN WELT** ... [1609] Amsterdam: Hondius. Oblong quarto, orig vellum binding; (6) 676 pp, (9), 150 maps (4 extra). Covers stained & worn at extremities; lt toning & occas staining; strong impressions; for its kind, exc. Ref: Koeman Me 188. [23] £7,840 **$13,000**

[ATLAS] **ATLAS MINOR. DAS IST: EIN KURTZE JEDOCH GRANDLICHE BESCHREIBUNG DER GANTZEN WELT** ... [1631] Amsterdam: Jansson; German ed. Oblong quarto; stiff vellum; 143 maps by Goos & Van den Keere. Spotting on title page, German text pasted over Latin; o/w exc. Ref: Koeman Me 199. [3] £7,539 **$12,500**

MERCATOR (Small) continued

[ATLAS] ATLAS MINOR. DAS IST: EIN KURTZE JEDOCH GRANDLICHE BESCHREIBUNG DER GANTZEN WELT ... [1651] Amsterdam: Jansson; German ed. Oblong quarto; stiff vellum with ties. 215 maps, the most complete; Goos & Van den Keere, sc. Minor water staining last few leaves; exc. Ref: Phillips (A) 5940. Koeman Me 203. [3] £9,650 **$16,000**

ABISSINORUM REGNU [1608] From Mercator-Hondius *Atlas Minor*. About 15x18cm (6x7") Color. Good. Ref: Koeman Me 187. ["Fessae Regnum" offered at same price] [30] £87 **$145**

ALSATIA SUPERIOR [1623] From Mercator-Hondius *Atlas Minor*. Basle-Strasbourg region. 14x18cm (5½x7") Full orig color. VG (A). [A4] £63 **$105**

ANGLIA [1607] As in *Atlas Minor* ... Mercator-Hondius. 14x18cm (5½x7") Color. Ref: Koeman Me 186, 17. ["Eboracum Lincolnia" offered at same price] [42] Aus$325 £148 **$245**

[SAME TITLE] [1607(+)] From Mercator-Hondius *Atlas Minor*. Amsterdam: Jansson. 15x19cm (6x7½") Orig body color. Lt age-toned. Ref: Shirley (BI to 1650) 284. Koeman Me 186. ["Cambria sive Wallia" offered at same price] [47] **£180** **$299**

[SAME TITLE] [1608] From Mercator-Hondius *Atlas Minor*. About 15x18cm (6x7") Color. Good. Ref: Koeman Me 187. [30] £148 **$245**

ANGLIA SCOTIA ET HIBERNIA [1607(+)] From Mercator-Hondius *Atlas Minor*. Jansson. 14x18cm (5½x7½") Orig body color. Lt age-toned. Ref: Shirley (BI to 1650) 285. Koeman Me 186. [47] **£210** **$349**

[SAME TITLE] [1608] From Mercator-Hondius *Atlas Minor*. About 15x18cm (6x7") Color. Good. Ref: Koeman Me 187. [30] £136 **$225**

AUSTRIA ARCHIDUC [1608] From Mercator-Hondius *Atlas Minor*. About 15x18cm (6x7") Color. Good. Ref: Koeman Me 187. ["Saltzburg Carinthia", "Morea", "Slavonia Croatia Bosnia Dalmat", "Provincia", "Brabantia" & "Albruzzo et Terra di Lovorno" offered at same price] [30] £87 **$145**

BERRY [1623] From *Atlas Minor*. 13x17cm (5x6½") Full orig color. VG (A). [A3] £67 **$111**

BURGUNDIAE DUCA. [1623] From *Atlas Minor*. 14x18cm (5½x7") Full orig color. Lt toning; overall fine (A). [A3] £82 **$136**

CANDIA [1608] From Mercator-Hondius *Atlas Minor*. About 15x18cm (6x7") Color. Good. Ref: Koeman Me 187. [30] £136 **$225**

CEILAN INSULA [1607] Mercator-Hondius. 15x18cm (6x7½") Uncolored. Fine. [A2] £80 **$132**

[SAME TITLE] [1608] From Mercator-Hondius *Atlas Minor*. About 15x18cm (6x7") Color. Good. Ref: Koeman Me 187. [30] £112 **$185**

CHINA [1608] From Mercator-Hondius *Atlas Minor*. About 15x18cm (6x7") Color. Good. Ref: Koeman Me 187. [30] £136 **$225**

CUBA INSUL [ON SHEET WITH] HISPANIOLA [AND] HAVANA PORTUS [AND] I.JAMAICA [AND] I.S. IOANNIS [AND] I.MARGARETA [1610] Mercator-Hondius. 14x18cm (5½x7½") Color. [41] £136 **$225**

[SAME TITLE] [1625] From *Purchase: His Pilgrims*. Mercator-Hondius map. 14x19cm (5½x7½") Full color. [18] £166 **$275**

DESIGNATIO ORBIS CHRISTIANI [1607] 1st state. World, with religions diagramed. 15x19cm (6x7½") B&W. Fine. Ref: Shirley (W) 260. [35] £232 **$385**

EBORACUM LINCOLNIA ... [1607+] From Mercator-Hondius *Atlas Minor*. Incl Lincolnshire, Yorkshire, Derbyshire, Staffordshire, Nottinghamshire, Leicestershire, Rutland & Norfolk. 13x17cm (5x6½") [11] £51 **$85**

FRETUM MAGELLANI [1608] From Mercator-Hondius *Atlas Minor*. About 15x18cm (6x7") Color. Good. Ref: Koeman Me 187. [30] £112 **$185**

GRAECIA [1607] As in Mercator-Hondius *Atlas Minor* ... 14x18cm (5½x7") Color. Ref: Koeman Me 186, 120. ["Slavonia, Croatia, Bosnia, Dalmat." offered at same price] [42] Aus$325 £148 **$245**

HASSIA [1623] From Mercator-Hondius *Atlas Minor*. 14x18cm (5½x7") Full color. Age toned; couple tears repaired with archival tape; VG (A). [A4] £47 **$78**

HIBERNIA V. TABULA [1608] From Mercator-Hondius *Atlas Minor*. About 15x18cm (6x7") Color. Good. ["Udrone" & "Ultonia Oriental" offered at same price] Ref: Koeman Me 187. [30] £87 **$145**

HISPANIA NOVA [1608] From Mercator-Hondius *Atlas Minor*. About 15x18cm (6x7") Color. Good. ["America Meridionalis" offered at same price] Ref: Koeman Me 187. [30] £148 **$245**

HOLLANDIA [1608] From Mercator-Hondius *Atlas Minor*. About 15x18cm (6x7") Color. Good. Ref: Koeman Me 187. [30] £118 **$195**

HUNGARIA [1608] From Mercator-Hondius *Atlas Minor*. About 15x18cm (6x7") Color. Good. ["Prussia", "Bavaria", "Flandria", "Tuscia", "Sicilia", "Corsica, Sardinia", "Regni Valentiae Typus", "Natolia" & "Persicum Regnum" offered at same price] Ref: Koeman Me 187. [30] £100 **$165**

MERCATOR (Small) continued

INDIA ORIENTALIS [1608] From Mercator-Hondius *Atlas Minor*. About 15x18cm (6x7") Color. Good. Ref: Koeman Me 187. [30] £148 **$245**

[SAME TITLE] [1610] From Minor Atlas. India to Philippines. 14x18cm (5½x7½") Color. ["China" offered at same price] [41] £121 **$200**

INSULAE CUBA HISPANIOLA &C. [1608] From Mercator-Hondius *Atlas Minor*. About 15x18cm (6x7") Color. Good. Ref: Koeman Me 187. [30] £166 **$275**

INSULAE INDIAE ORIENTALIS [1608] From Mercator-Hondius *Atlas Minor*. About 15x18cm (6x7") Color. Good. Ref: Koeman Me 187. [30] £172 **$285**

IRLANDIA [1608] From Mercator-Hondius *Atlas Minor*. About 15x18cm (6x7") Color. Good. Ref: Koeman Me 187. [30] £166 **$275**

ISLANDIA [1608] From Mercator-Hondius *Atlas Minor*. About 15x18cm (6x7") Color. Good. Ref: Koeman Me 187. [30] £166 **$275**

LITHUANIA [1607] As in *Atlas Minor* ... Mercator-Hondius. 14x18cm (5½x7") Color. Ref: Koeman Me 186, 34. [42] Aus$650 £295 $489

[SAME TITLE] [1610] From Minor Atlas; large Lithuania. 13x18cm (5½x7") Color. [41] £60 **$100**

LIVONIA [1608] From Mercator-Hondius *Atlas Minor*. About 15x18cm (6x7") Color. Good. ["Portugallia olim Lusitania" offered at same price] Ref: Koeman Me 187. [30] £106 **$175**

LOTHARINGIA SEPTENTR. [1623] From Mercator-Hondius *Atlas Minor*. Moselle region. 13x20cm (5x7½") Full orig color. Couple sm margin holes; VG (A). [A4] £60 **$99**

MAPPA AESTIVARUM INSULARUM ALIAS BARMUDAS DICTARUM [1632] From *Atlas Minor*. Issued by Hondius, then Waesburg. No text verso. 20x25cm (8x10") Full color. [20] £754 **$1,250**

NORTHUMBR. CUMBERLADIA [1621] From Mercator-Hondius *Atlas Minor*. Final ed. 14x19cm (5½x7½") ["Westmorland, Castria, Cestria &c." offered at same price] [11] £24 **$40**

NOVA VIRGINIAE TABULA ... [1632] Van den Keere, sc. 18x25cm (7½x10") Margins ½"+/-; rt margin & border sl tattered & reinforced; sm loss, image unaffected; clean. Ref: Tooley (Amer) p.164. [A9] £166 **$276**

PALATINATUS RHENI [1608] From Mercator-Hondius *Atlas Minor*. About 15x18cm (6x7") Color. Good. Ref: Koeman Me 187. ["Bohemia", "Brandenberg et Pomerania" & "Saxoniae Superioris" offered at same price] [30] £81 **$135**

PARADISUS [1608] From Mercator-Hondius *Atlas Minor*. About 15x18cm (6x7") Color. Good. Ref: Koeman Me 187. [30] £136 **$225**

PEREGRINNATIO ISRAELITARU IN DESERTO [1608] From Mercator-Hondius *Atlas Minor*. About 15x18cm (6x7") Color. Good. Ref: Koeman Me 187. [30] £106 **$175**

PEREGRINNATIO PAULI [1608] From Mercator-Hondius *Atlas Minor*. About 15x18cm (6x7") Color. Good. Ref: Koeman Me 187. [30] £118 **$195**

PERIGRINATIO PAULI IN QUA ET OMNIA LOCA QUORUM FIT MENTIO IN ACTIS ET EPISTOLIS APOSTOLORUM ET APOCALYPSI, DESCRIBUNTUR [1610] As in Mercator-Hondius *Atlas Minor* ... 15x19cm (6x7½") Color. Ref: Koeman Me 188, 151. [42] Aus$225 £102 $169

PERSICUM REGNUM [1607] 14x19cm (5½x7½") Uncolored. VG to fine. [A2] £66 **$110**

[SAME TITLE] [1610] From Minor Atlas. 14x18cm (5½x7½") Color. [41] £60 **$100**

POLONIA ET SILESIA [1607] From Mercator-Hondius *Atlas Minor* ... 14x18cm (5½x7") Color. Ref: Koeman Me 186, 100. [42] Aus$450 £204 $339

POLUS ARCTICUS CUM VICINIS REGIONIBUS [1606 / 1610] From Mercator-Hondius *Atlas Minor*. 3 circular insets & title. 13x19cm (5x7½") Color. [41] £151 **$250**

ROMANDIOLA CUM D. PARMENSI [1610] From Minor Atlas. 14x18cm (5½x7") Color. [41] £60 **$100**

ROMANI IMPERII IMAGO [1607] Mercator-Hondius. 15x19cm (6x7½") Uncol. VG. [A2] £150 **$248**

RUGIA [1623] From *Atlas Minor*. 14x16cm (5½x6") Full col. Minor toning; else fine (A). [A3] £66 **$109**

SCAVONIA [1635] Incl Dalmatia, Croatia, Bosnia, Serbia. 14x19cm (5½x7½") [11] £30 **$50**

SCOTIAE TABULA II [1607(+)] From Mercator-Hondius *Atlas Minor*. Amsterdam: Jansson. Southern Scotland. 14x19cm (5½x7½") Orig body color. Lt age-toned. [47] **£130** $216

[SAME TITLE] [1608] From Mercator-Hondius *Atlas Minor*. About 15x18cm (6x7") Color. Good. Ref: Koeman Me 187. ["Scotia Tabula III" & "Anglesey, Wight, Garnsey, Iarsey" offered at same price] [30] £100 **$165**

SCOTIAE TABULA III [1607(+)] From Mercator-Hondius *Atlas Minor*. Amsterdam: Jansson. Northern Scotland. 15x19cm (6x7½") Orig body color. Lt age-toned. [47] **£110** $183

SICILIA [1607] Mercator-Hondius. 14x19cm (5½x7½") Uncolored. VG. [A2] £150 **$248**

MERCATOR (Small) continued

SUECIA ET NORWEGIA [1608] From Mercator-Hondius *Atlas Minor*. About 15x18cm (6x7") Color. Good. Ref: Koeman Me 187. ["Daniae Regnum", "Russia cum Consinus", "Zeelandia", "Hispania", "Graecia", "Macedonia ..." & "Alexandri Magni Expeditio" offered at same price]   [30]   £112   **$185**

TAURICA CHERONESUS [1623] From *Atlas Minor*. Russia, Ukraine & Crimea. 13x17cm (5x6½") Orig full color. Fine (A+).   [A3]   £91   **$151**

ULTONIA, CONATIA, ET MEDIA [1628] North Ireland. 14x20cm (5½x7½") Color.   [48]   DM 130   £45   **$74**

VIRGINIA ET FLORIDA [1610] From Mercator-Hondius *Atlas Minor*. 15x19cm (6x7½") Col.   [41]   £271   **$450**

WIRTENBERG [1610] From Minor Atlas. 15x19cm (6x7½") Color.   [41]   £60   **$100**

MERIAN

[BOOK WITH MAPS] TOPOGRAPHIA CIRCULI BURGUNDICI [BOUND WITH] TOPOGRAPHIA GALLIAE. PART 1 [1654/1655] Folio; 12 + 3 double-page maps, 84 (of 85) + 112 city and town views; 19th c. half calf. 30x20cm (12x8") Extremities rubbed; covers loose; internally bright, clean; ex lib NYHS.   [A7]   £3,329   **$5,520**

[BOOK WITH MAPS] TOPOGRAPHIA GALLIAE. PARTS 2 - 8 [1656/1657] Thick quarto; together 6 parts (of 13) in one; 140 double-page maps, city plans & views, 19 single-page plates. Vellum cover stained; several leaves loose; o/w clean; ex lib NYHS.   [A7]   £1,665   **$2,760**

[FACSIMILE ATLAS] TOPOGRAPHIA GERMANIAE [1964] Kassel & Basel: Barenteiter. Orig publ 1650. 17 quarto vols; profusion of folding views of 17th c German cities. Register volume lacks d/j; o/w as new.   [21]   **Can$2,250**   £984   **$1,632**

[GERMANY: PHILIPPSBURG] [1639] From *Theatrum Europaeum*. Fortress plan. 18x26cm (7½x10")   [48]   DM 200   £69   **$114**

AMERICA NOVITER DELINEATA [1631-] Earlier & larger of two versions. 36x44cm (14x17½") Uncolored. Sharp impression. Ref: Burden 235.   [34]   **£2,850**   **$4,726**

AMERICA NOVITER DELINEATA [1638] 28x36cm (11x14") B&W. Fine. Ref: Wheat (TM) 43; Tooley (Amer) p.299. Wagner (NW) 329.   [29]   £473   **$785**

[SAME TITLE] [c.1638] Smaller version. 28x36cm (11x14") Two sm margin tears. Ref: Wheat (TM) 43; Tooley (Amer) p.299.   [47]   £450   **$746**

ASCHAFFENBURG [1646] Southwest view with Swedish troops, 1631. 11x32cm (4½x12½") Narrow lower margin.   [48]   DM 1,300   £449   **$744**

BATTENBERG [1646] View with Kellerburg. 9x17cm (3½x6½")   [48]   DM 260   £90   **$149**

BELAGERUNG UND EROBERUNG DER VOSTUNG DEMIN, DURCH IHRO CHURFURSTL. DURCHL. ZU BRANDENBURG. ANNO 1676 EINGENOMEN WORDEN [1682] From *Theatrum Europaeum*. 26x36cm (10x14") Sides trimmed to neat line.   [48]   DM 180   £62   **$103**

BOURDEAUX [1652] From same source. View from 2 plates. 24x68cm (9½x27")   [48]   DM 890   £307   **$509**

BRUSSEL, DIE HAUPT-STADT DES HERTZOGTUMS - BRABANT, UND RESIDENTZ DES GUVERNEURS DES KONIGES IN SPANIEN. [1702] From same source. Fortification plan. 19x28cm (7½x11")   [48]   DM 120   £41   **$68**

CHINA VETERIBUS SINARUM REGIO NUNC INCOLIS TAME DICTA [1638] Insular Korea; 3 Japanese islands. 27x34cm (10½x13½") Color. Sm repaired tear lower lf, verso reinforcement; o/w fine.   [4]   £300   **$498**

[SAME TITLE] [c.1655] Incl Japan & insular Korea. 28x35cm (11x14")   [47]   £330   **$548**

CIVITAS LOANDAE S. PAULI [1649] From Gottfried's ... *Archontologia* ... Angola city plan. 30x38cm (11½x15") Old repair, rt margin replacement.   [48]   DM 100   £35   **$57**

CIVITATIS AVENIONIS OMNIMQ VIARUM ET AEDIFICIORUM EIUS PERFECTA DELINEATIO. 1635 [1649] From Gottfried's ... *Archontologia* ... Avignon bird's-eye view. 27x34cm (10½x13½") Sh margin tear at c'fold restored.   [48]   DM 480   £166   **$275**

CONSTANTINOPOLIS [1635 - 1638] From *Neuwe Archontologia Cosmica*. Panoramic view; 29 item key. 20x70cm (8x27½") B&W. Old fold strengthened; invisibly repaired 4" tear; o/w fine.   [30]   £1,086   **$1,800**

DAS SCHLOSS BRANDEYSS IN BOHME, UND VERSCHANTZUNGEN DES SCHWEDISCHE VELDS ... 1640 [1650] Part of the town, the Elbe, fortifications with profile. 21x32cm (8½x13") Sm wrinkle; sl c'fold glue stain.   [48]   DM 130   £45   **$74**

DIEPE [1649] From Gottfried's ... *Archontologia* ... Dieppe view. 12x32cm (4½x13") Narrow lower margin.   [48]   DM 180   £62   **$103**

EIGENTLICHE CONTRAFACTUR DER STATT BREYSACH, WIE SOLCHE VON MITTAG GEGEN MITTERNACHT AN ZU SECHEN [1644] 22x34cm (8½x13½") Fold tear repaired.   [48]   DM 500   £173   **$286**

EIGENTLICHER GRUNDTRISS DER STATT EGER WIE DIESELBE VON ... CAROL GUSTAFF WRANGEL DEN 14. JUNY 1647 BELAGERT UD DE 5 JULY MIT ACCORD EINGENOHME WORDEN [1647] From *Theatrum Europaeum*. 30x38cm (11½x15")   [48]   DM 350   £121   **$200**

MERIAN continued

GOA [1649] From Gottfried's ... *Archontologia* ... View. 28x36cm (11x14") Sl c'fold glue stain. [48] **DM 160** £55 $91

HISPANIA REGNUM [1638] From Gottfried's ... *Archontologia* ... 27x36cm (10½x14") Some placenames underlined in ink. [48] **DM 290** £100 $166

INDIA ORIENTALIS ET INSULAE ADIACENTES [c.1650] 27x36cm (10½x14") Early MS notes on Dampier's voyage; exc. [45] £392 **$650**

INSULA CANDIA OLIM CRETA [1672] From *Theatrum Europaeum*. With plans of Spinalonga, Suda, Chania, Rethymnon & E. Mediterranean inset. 31x42cm (12x16½") Ref: Zacharakis 1511. [48] **DM 450** £155 $257

LAUENAU [1654] 20x38cm (8x15") [48] **DM 200** £69 $114

LONDON [1638] From Gottfried's ... *Archontologia* ... View; 43-item key. 2 sheets joined as issued. 22x70cm (9x27½") Ref: Howgego, p.7. [48] **DM 2,000** £691 $1,145

[SAME TITLE] [c.1650] Pre-fire view; 43-item key. 2 sheets joined as issued. 23x70cm (9x28") Binding holes flattened; sm tear lf margin. Ref: Howgego, p.7. [47] **£1,250** $2,073

MAGNAE BRITANNIAE ET HIBERNIAE TABULAE [1630] 28x36cm (11x14") [A7] £156 **$258**

MAINZ [1698] From *Theatrum Europaeum*. Fortification plan & 1689 siege with legend. 30x41cm (11½x16") [48] **DM 480** £166 $275

NOBILIS FLUVIUS ALBIS ... [1633] From *Theatrum Europaeum*. Elbe, with Hamburg view. 2 plates joined, 18x104cm (7x40½") [48] **DM 1,400** £483 $801

NOVA TOTIUS TERRARUM ORBIS GEOGRAPHICA AC HYDROGRAPHICA TABULA [1638-] With Merian signature; fine engraving. 26x35cm (10½x14") Uncolored. Ref: Shirley (W) 345. [34] **£1,200** $1,990

PARYS [c.1630] Bird's-eye view; 56 item key. 26x69cm (10½x27½") Exc. [23] £1,086 **$1,800**

PROSPECT DER STATT UNDT VESTUNG HARBURG [1654] View near Hamburg on 2 plates. 26x74cm (10x29") Sh margin tear repaired. [48] **DM 1,680** £580 $962

PROSPECTUS TEMPLI CATHEDRALIS ... EIN SEHR ANMUHTIGER PROSPECT DES MUNSTERS, UND RHEINBRUCKEN ZU BASEL [1642] View along Rhine. 21x32cm (8½x13") Sm printer's wrinkle below lacks image. [48] **DM 1,300** £449 $744

REGENSPURG. - RATISBONA. REGENSPURG [1644] Bird's-eye with legend & overall view after Hollar. 29x36cm (11½x14") Remargined & upper neat line restored. [48] **DM 750** £259 $429

REPRAESENTATIO PUGNAE QUA ILL.MUS LUNEBURGENSIUM DUX GEORGIUS. GENERALIS SUECIUS ET CAMPIMARSCHALLUS KNIPHUSIUS COMIT. DE GRONSFELD ET MERODE. GENERALES CAESAREANOS 28 JUNY / 8 JULLY ANO 1633 PROPE OPPIDUM OLDENDORP AD VISURGIM FELICISSIME DEBELLAUIT [1639] From *Theatrum Europaeum*. 36x93cm (14½x36½") Two repaired tears. [48] **DM 980** £338 $561

ROMA [c.1630] Bird's-eye. 30x70cm (12x27½") Full color. Bottom & rt margins extended, no loss; else exc. [23] £905 **$1,500**

ROSTOCHIUM [1653] View. 14x36cm (5½x14") [48] **DM 500** £173 $286

TUBINGEN [1643] South view. 19x29cm (7½x11½") Sh fold tear restored. [48] **DM 1,800** £621 $1,030

VENETIA [c.1630] 29x71cm (11½x28") Some creasing; minor stains; else exc. [23] £1,206 **$2,000**

VUE GENERAL DE LA MAISON DU PLAISANCE, DE SA MAJESTE LE ROY DE PRUSSE, NOMME MON BYOUX, BATIE DEVANT BERLIN SUR LA SPREE [1717] From *Theatrum Europaeum*. View, "Mon Bijou" castle with gardens from the Spree. From 2 plates. 49x70cm (19½x28") Sh part top lf margin replaced; sh margin tear repaired; sh printer's wrinkle at rt; sl browning at rt & in sky. [48] **DM 2,200** £760 $1,259

WAHRE CONTRAFACTUR DER CHURFURSTLICHEN RESIDENTZ STATT HEIDELBERG [1645] North view over Neckar. 27x36cm (10½x14½") C'fold tear & lacuna restored. [48] **DM 980** £338 $561

WAHRER ABRISS DER BEYDEN KONIGLICHEN HAUBT ALT UND NEWSTATT PRAG, WIE DIESELBEN ... DEN 5. OCTOBRIS BELAGERT ... UNND DANN AM 2 NOVEMBRIS 1648 WIEDERUMBEN VERLASSEN UND QUITTIRET WORDEN [1652] From *Theatrum Europaeum*. Overall view of Swedish siege; portraits & decor. 30x58cm (11½x23") Remargined outside of image. [48] **DM 1,400** £483 $801

MERULA

TOTIUS ORBIS COGNITI UNIVERSALIS DESCRIPTIO [1605] From *Paulii G.F.P.N. Merulam Cosmographiae*. Circular insets: Japan; Ceylon; Iceland; St. Helena. 30x50cm (11½x19½") Color. Ref: Shirley (W) 254, pl.200. [13] **Aus$7,200** £3,270 $5,421

METELLUS

LIMES OCCCIDENTIS ET QUIVIRA ANIAN [1598] 3rd printed map of American northwest. 18x22cm (7x9") Fine. Ref: Burden 121. [43] £2,051 **$3,400**

MEYER

Berlin [c.1845] From *Hand Atlas*. Panoramic view below. 25x34cm (10x13½") Color. ["Plan von Munchen" & "Frankfurt" offered at same price] [22] £60 **$100**

Californien, Texas, und die Territorien New Mexico u. Utah [1852] Grassl, Hildburghausen. Heart-shaped Texas republic. 23x28cm (9x11") Orig wash OL color. [27] £196 **$325**

Die Staaten von Maine, New Hampshire, Massachusetts, Vermont, Connecticut, & Rhode I. [1850] Insets: Boston; Hartford; New Haven. 27x20cm (10½x8") OL & wash color. [40] £30 **$50**

Honolulu [c.1855] From *Universum*. View. 11x16cm (4½x6½") B&W. [12] £51 **$85**

Kansas City [1855] From C.A. Dana, *United States Illustrated*. View. 2 pp text furnished. 11x17cm (4½x6½") B&W. ["Louisville" & "Jefferson City (Missouri River)" from Meyer's Universum offered at same price] [12] £51 **$85**

Neapel [1845] From *Hand Atlas*. Panoramic view below. 35x39cm (14x15½") Color. ["Aachen" & "Lissabon" offered at same price] [22] £51 **$85**

Neueste Karte von Florida [1845] From *Handatlas*. 3 insets. 37x30cm (14½x12") Orig OL color. Fine. [27] £172 **$285**

Neueste Karte von Georgia [1845] From *Hand Atlas*. 37x30cm (14½x12") OL & full col. [22] £72 **$120**

[Same title] [1845] From *Handatlas*. 30x37cm (12x14½") Orig OL color. [27] £142 **$235**

Neueste Karte von Louisiana [1845] From *Hand Atlas*. New Orleans inset. 29x37cm (11½x14½") OL color. Ref: Tooley (Amer) pl.121. [22] £84 **$140**

Neueste Karte von Mexico [1845] From *Hand Atlas*. 30x37cm (12x15") Full earth tone color. [22] £196 **$325**

[Same title] [1845] From *Handatlas*. By Radefeld. Heart-shaped TX republic; Mexico to OR border. 29x37cm (11½x14½") Orig OL color. [27] £271 **$450**

[Same title] [1850] From *Grosser Zeitungs-Atlas*. Shows large "Deseret" & capital "Mormonfort". 29x36cm (11½x14") OL color. Faint soiling & toning margins; catalog excerpt taped to verso; image clean. [A10] £125 **$207**

Neueste Karte von Nord Carolina mit Seinen Canaelen, Strassen und Routen fur Dampfschiffe [1845] From *Hand Atlas*. Insets. 30x37cm (12x14½") OL & full color. [22] £81 **$135**

Neueste Karte von Tennessee [1845] From Joseph Meyer's *Hand-Atlas*. Hildburghausen. 61 counties. 30x37cm (12x14½") OL color. Pristine. [12] £106 **$175**

[Same title] [1845] From *Handatlas*. 30x37cm (12x14½") Orig wash & OL color. [27] £136 **$225**

Neueste Karte von Virginia [1845] From *Handatlas*. C&O Canal profile. 30x37cm (12x14½") Orig wash & OL color. [27] £118 **$195**

Nord-Americanische Freistaaten [1845] Publ in *Handatlas*. By C. Radefeld. Texas as a Republic. 29x36cm (11½x14") Orig OL color. Fine. [27] £226 **$375**

Rock Island City [IL] [c.1851] From C.A. Dana's *United States Illustrated*. View across river. 11x17cm (4½x6½") B&W. Fine. ["Fort Armstrong, am Mississippi", "Moline", "Burlington [IA] on the Mississippi", "Fort Snelling [MN]", "San Louis [MO] (Mississippi)" offered at same price] [12] £45 **$75**

San Francisco [1855] From Charles Dana, *United States Illustrated* ... View of crowded harbor. 11x16cm (4½x6½") B&W. Ref: Howes (US) D-45. ["Monterey" & "Sacramento ... 1850" offered at same price] [12] £54 **$90**

Texas ... [1846] From *Handatlas*. By Radefeld. TX borders reach to Santa Fe, WY, New Orleans; sketchy coverage of present southwest. 29x36cm (11½x14") Orig OL color. Superb. [27] £724 **$1,200**

MIALHE

Mapa Historico Pintoresco Moderno de la Isla de Cuba [1853] Bernardo May pirating of Frederic Mialhe's surround of views around map. 43x58cm (17x23") Sepia chromolitho. Fold reinforcements; else exc. [24] £2,111 **$3,500**

MICHALET

Les Deserts d'Egypte, de Thebaide d'Arabie, de Sirie [1693] Egypt to Asia Minor. 57x78cm (22½x30½") OL color. Sh tear into image at vert fold. [A7] £277 **$460**

MICHAULT

Costes et Rivieres de Virginie, de Mariland et de Nouvelle Angleterre [1674] One Great Lake. 19x24cm (7½x9½") Exc. [44] £332 **$550**

MICHELOT
NOUVELLE CARTE DE L'ARCHIPEL ... [1715] Publ Marseilles. Chart of Aegean islands & rim to Crete. 47x63cm (18½x25") Color. C'fold reinforced; else exc. Ref: Zacharakis 1518. [23] £905 **$1,500**

MIDDLETON
A VIEW OF MADRID THE CAPITAL OF SPAIN [1780] From *Middleton's Complete System of Geography*. 15x25cm (6x10") Color. Margin repair; fine. [31] £118 **$195**
A VIEW OF THE CITY OF VIENNA ... [1779] 16x26cm (6x10") ["A View of Madrid ..." offered at same price] [11] £45 **$75**
TERRESTRIAL GLOBE [ON SHEET WITH] CELESTIAL GLOBE [1779] Two globes on stands; 7 diagramatic spheres. 16x26cm (6½x10½") [11] £30 **$50**
THE WEST INDIES EXHIBITING THE ENGLISH, FRENCH, SPANISH, DUTCH & DANISH SETTLEMENTS ... [1779] Letter prefixes indicate colonial power. 19x28cm (7½x11") [11] £75 **$125**

MILBERT
CARTE POUR SERVIR A L'ITINERAIRE PITTORESQUE DU FLEUVE HUDSON ET DES PARTIES LATERALES DE L'AMERIQUE DU NORD [1826] From *L'Itineraire* ... By Jacques Milbert & H. Toquet. Northeast U.S. with map of Hudson above. 50x43cm (19½x17") Orig wash color. VG. [31] £172 **$285**

MINING MAPS
MAP OF GILPIN CO., COLO. [1891] E.E. Chase & S.A. Rank, Denver. Printed by J. Bien, NY. Mining claims by color. 63x101cm (25x40") Once folded, now flat. [15] £603 **$1,000**
MAP OF THE GOLDFIELD MINING DISTRICT, NYE AND ESMERALDA COUNTIES, NEVADA [1905] Elmer J. Chute, Goldfield, NV; printed by Rand, McNally, Chicago. Linen-backed folding map in stiff wrappers. Full color by claim. 61x58cm (24x23") Wraps extensively chipped; boards crudely repaired; wear at fold junctions; map good. [15] £226 **$375**

MITCHELL, S.A. (Atlas Maps 1859 & Earlier)
Try *Desilver, Tanner, Thomas, Cowperthwait & Co.*

[ATLAS] MITCHELL'S ATLAS OF OUTLINE MAPS [1839] Phila: Thomas, Cowperthwait. Quarto; 7 maps to be colored by students. Orig wrappers stained; fairly clean internally. [A7] £329 **$546**
[ATLAS] MITCHELL'S SCHOOL ATLAS [1840] 2nd issue. Phila: Thomas, Cowperthwait. Big quarto, salmon printed boards; 18 maps on 14 sheets by Young & Williams, maximum independent Texas appears on three. Covers darkened & shaken. [16] £362 **$600**
[SAME TITLE] [1849] Quarto; numerous colored maps; roan backed boards. Extremities worn; hinges cracked; some pen work, but maps clean. [A7] £156 **$258**
[SAME TITLE] [1855] Phila: Cowperthwait, Desilver & Butler. Big quarto; 32 colored maps; shows Gadsden Purchase line. Printed salmon boards shaken; some maps rubbed; generally good. [16] £172 **$285**
[ATLAS] NEW UNIVERSAL ATLAS [1846] 1st ed, 2nd state (Mitchell's name on title page without Tanner) Folio, orig half-morocco with marble boards; 117 map & plans. Exc. Ref: Phillips (A) 6103. [3] £3,920 **$6,500**
A NEW MAP OF ALABAMA WITH ITS ROADS & DISTANCES FROM PLACE TO PLACE, ALONG THE STAGE & STEAMBOAT ROUTES [1846] 1st ed. 36x29cm (14x11½") Full orig color. Exc. [36] £136 **$225**
A NEW MAP OF LOUISIANA WITH IT'S CANALS, ROADS AND DISTANCES FROM PLACE TO PLACE, ALONG THE STAGE AND STEAMBOAT ROUTES [1848-49] From *New Universal Atlas*. New Orleans inset. 31x39cm (12x15") Full wash color by parishes. Edges lt browned; fine. Ref: Phillips (A) 797-24. [35] £75 **$125**
A NEW MAP OF OHIO WITH ITS CANALS, ROADS & DISTANCES [1846] Cincinnati inset; canal profiles. 36x29cm (14x11½") Full orig color. Exc. [36] £121 **$200**
A NEW MAP OF THE WORLD [1846-48] Double hemi. 24x36cm (9½x14") Color. VG. [36] £106 **$175**
CANADA WEST FORMERLY UPPER CANADA [dated 1847] From *New Universal Atlas*. Lake Superior inset. 32x38cm (12½x15") Full color. Fine. Ref: Winearls 96-6; Phillips (A) 6104-4. [12] £54 **$90**
CITY OF NEW YORK [1846] Buildings referenced. 38x30cm (15x12") Full orig color. Exc. [36] £136 **$225**
CITY OF WASHINGTON [1846] From *New Universal Atlas*. 1st ed. 30x38cm (12x15") Full orig color. Exc. [36] £136 **$225**
CONNECTICUT [1846] From 1st ed, *New Universal Atlas*. Insets: Hartford; New Haven areas. 30x37cm (12x14½") Full orig color. Exc. [MD & DE with Baltimore inset offered at same price] [36] £136 **$225**
IOWA [1846] From *New Universal Atlas*. 1st ed. Transitional configuration. 41x33cm (16x13") Full color. Lt scattered foxing; narrow orig lf margin; else perfect. Ref: Karrow (MW) 8-0657; Phillips (A) 6103-34. [12] £151 **$250**

MITCHELL, S.A. (Atlas Maps 1859 & Earlier) continued

IOWA [1846] From *New Universal Atlas*. Incl southern MN. 41x33cm (16x13"). Full orig color. Exc. ["Wisconsin", same condition, offered at same price] [36] £178 **$295**

[SAME TITLE] [1847] 41x34cm (16x13½") Orig color. Occas lt surface soiling; o/w VG. [A2] £100 **$165**

MAP NO.3 MAP OF NORTH AMERICA ... TO ILLUSTRATE MITCHELL'S SCHOOL AND FAMILY GEOGRAPHY [c.1839] 1st ed. With maximum TX along north branch Arkansas River. 26x20cm (10½x8") Full color. Browned. [16] £90 **$150**

MAP NO.4 MAP OF THE UNITED STATES AND TEXAS ... [ON SHEET WITH] NO. 5 MAP OF MEXICO AND GUATIMALA [c.1839] 2nd issue. Maximum TX. 26x42cm (10½x16½") Orig full color. Stained; fold repair; pencil marking reverse; good. [16] £178 **$295**

MAP OF TEXAS ... [1846] From *New Universal Atlas*. 1st ed. 30x38cm (12x15") Full orig color. VG. [36] £332 **$550**

MAP OF THE CHIEF PART OF THE WESTERN STATES AND PART OF VIRGINIA [1839] From *Mitchell's School and Family Geography*. Covers OH, IN, IL, MO & KY, parts of VA, MI, IA & WI Terr. 26x41cm (10x16") Full color. Minor toning; some surface soil; sh c'fold split repaired with archival tape; good (B). [A3] £37 **$61**

MAP OF THE STATE OF TEXAS [1846] "No.13" engraved to illustrate *Mitchell's School and Family Geography*. 25x19cm (10x7½") Yellow toned. VG. [16] £151 **$250**

[SAME TITLE] [1846 (1848)] From *School and Family Geography*. Maximum statehood form; 35 counties. Yellow wash col. 27x20cm (10½x8") Immaculate. Ref: Day (TX) 128. [12] £121 **$200**

[SAME TITLE] [1846 / 1850] From *Mitchell's School Atlas*. Within present border; 36 counties. 27x20cm (10½x8") Full pale wash color. Lt toned; VG+. Ref: Phillips (A) 6111. [35] £75 **$125**

[SAME TITLE] [1852] Insets: Galveston area; panhandle. 20x28cm (8x11") Yellow tint. VG. [26] £48 **$80**

[SAME TITLE] [1853] "No.13", engraved to illustrate *Mitchell's School and Family Geography*. 20x27cm (8x10½") Orig full color. Lt browned; good. [1858 ed offered at $75] [16] £57 **$95**

MAP OF THE TERRITORIES [1850] Phila: Thomas, Cowperthwait. Shows MN, MO, Indian, NM (as a sliver) territories & large format TX. 16x14cm (6½x5½") Full color. VG. [16] £45 **$75**

THE WORLD ON AN EQUATORIAL PROJECTION [ON SHEET WITH] THE WORLD ON A POLAR PROJECTION [1852] Pair of sm double hemis from school geography. 29x20cm (11½x8") Color. [19] £36 **$60**

UNITED STATES [1847] From *New Universal Atlas*. West to MO, AR, LA, IA & MN Terr. 40x32cm (16x12½") Orig color. Occas lt surface soiling; o/w VG. [A2] £106 **$176**

UNITED STATES [1849-50] From *Mitchell's School Atlas*. Publ by Thomas, Cowperthwait; 3rd ed. Gold region inset. 27x42cm (10½x16½") Full wash color. Sh fold separations repaired; few spots; G+. Ref: Phillips (A) 6111. [35] £60 **$100**

WEST INDIES [1847] 30x38cm (12x15") Orig col. Lt surface soiling, faint foxing; o/w VG. [A2] £53 **$88**

WISCONSIN [1846] Entered by H.N. Burroughs. 23 counties. 40x33cm (16x13") Orig color. Crease top rt corner; o/w VG. [14] £96 **$160**

[SAME TITLE] [1847] 23 counties clustered in SE. 41x34cm (16x13½") Orig color. Lt surface soiling; o/w VG to fine. [A2] £199 **$330**

MITCHELL, S.A. (Atlas Maps 1860 & Later)

[ATLAS] MITCHELL'S ANCIENT ATLAS, CLASSICAL AND SACRED [1878] Phila: E.H. Butler. Sm folio, orig printed boards; 12 colored maps on 7 leaves. Covers worn & soiled; internally VG. [33] £45 **$75**

[SAME TITLE] [1860] Index & 7 maps dated 1844 (incl double-page Roman Empire) in full color. 24x30cm (9½x12") Maps fine; covers rubbed, lacks spine, but tight; good (B). [A3] £46 **$76**

[ATLAS] MITCHELL'S NEW GENERAL ATLAS ... [1860] Philadelphia. Folio; complete with 44 colored map sheets; half calf. Extremities lt rubbed. [A7] £1,526 **$2,530**

[SAME TITLE] [1862] Sm folio; many colored maps; half roan. Extremities rubbed; hinges starting; scattered foxing & soiling; generally clean. [A7] £555 **$920**

[SAME TITLE] [1864] Sm folio; many colored maps; half morocco. Extremities rubbed; hinges starting; minor foxing; sh tears title; generally clean. [1866 ed sold at same price] [A7] £694 **$1,150**

[SAME TITLE] [1864] Folio, publisher's half sheep; full complement of maps in OL color. Covers worn; scattered browning & soiling to maps. [A8] £763 **$1,265**

[SAME TITLE] [1868, one of 3 editions] "Containing Maps of the Various Countries of the World, Plans of Cities" Folio, cloth; 57 plates Front cover is separating; leather points & spine worn; end papers soiled; Title soiled, margin loss from silver fish (?), sl loss following 4 maps, German maps worn; generally VG [A2] £763 **$1,265**

MITCHELL, S.A. (Atlas Maps 1860 & Later) continued

[ATLAS] MITCHELL'S NEW GENERAL ATLAS ... [1869] Sm folio; many colored maps; half sheep. Extremities worn; internally clean, tight. [another, same ed, worn cover, cracked hinges, sh tears title, some browning & soiling sold for $1,265] [A7] £1,040 **$1,725**

[SAME TITLE] [1873] "Embraced in Seventy-Two Quarto Maps ... Forming a Series of One Hundred and Three Maps and Plans" Sm folio, half morocco, lettering brightened; colored maps. Moderate cover wear, spine repaired; maps lt toned, mostly margins. [A10] £590 **$978**

[SAME TITLE] [1875] Folio, publisher's half morocco; profusion of colored maps. Fine. [A8] £832 **$1,380**

[SAME TITLE] [1882] Phila. Folio, half morocco; 72 colored maps, some on verso. Covers sl worn. Ref: Phillips (A) 906. [A6] £230 **$382**

ARIZONA AND NEW MEXICO [1870] From *New General Atlas*. NM has 9 counties, AZ has 5. 28x36cm (11x14") Full color. Some margin chipping; VG (A). [A4] £65 **$107**

CALIFORNIA, OREGON, IDAHO, UTAH, NEVADA, ARIZONA AND WASHINGTON [1886] From *School Atlas*. 28x22cm (11x8½") Full color. Fine (A+). [A3] £24 **$39**

COLORADO [dated 1878] From *New General Atlas*. 30 counties. Verso: Indian Territory. 29x38cm (11½x15") Full color. [12] £60 **$100**

[SAME TITLE] [c.1892-94] From *New General Atlas*. Probably by Mitchell/Bradley licensee: A.Y. Huber or A.R. Keller or A.L. Smith. 53 counties. 28x37cm (11x14½") Full color. Fine. [12] £60 **$100**

COUNTY AND TOWNSHIP MAP OF ARIZONA AND NEW MEXICO [1892] Possibly publ by A.L. Smith. 34x52cm (13½x20½") Full color. [39] £60 **$100**

COUNTY AND TOWNSHIP MAP OF OREGON AND WASHINGTON [1882] 51x37cm (20x14½") Orig color. Fine. [14] £51 **$85**

COUNTY AND TOWNSHIP MAP OF UTAH & NEVADA [1881] 36x55cm (14x21½") Orig color. Fine. [14] £66 **$110**

COUNTY MAP OF CALIFORNIA [1860] From *New General Atlas*. Large inset: Great Salt Lake area. 34x27cm (13½x11") Color by counties. Fine. [7] £75 **$125**

COUNTY MAP OF COLORADO, WYOMING, DAKOTA, MONTANA [1877] 50x36cm (20x14") Full orig color. VG. [36] £75 **$125**

COUNTY MAP OF ENGLAND AND WALES [1864] From *New General Atlas*. 34x26cm (13½x10½") Orig color by counties. Fine. [14] £57 **$95**

COUNTY MAP OF FLORIDA [ON SHEET WITH] COUNTY MAP OF NORTH CAROLINA [AND] MAP OF SOUTH CAROLINA [1864] From *New General Atlas*. 29x35cm (11½x14") Orig color. Fine. [14] £60 **$100**

COUNTY MAP OF FLORIDA [ON SHEET WITH] MAP OF SOUTH CAROLINA [1860] From *New General Atlas*. SC as inset. 29x35cm (11½x14") Orig color. Fine. [14] £75 **$125**

COUNTY MAP OF GEORGIA AND ALABAMA [1860] 27x34cm (11x13½") Orig color by counties. Lt margin age toning; o/w VG. [14] £60 **$100**

COUNTY MAP OF MASSACHUSETTS, CONNECTICUT, AND RHODE ISLAND [1860] 29x36cm (11½x14") Orig color by counties. Fine. [14] £72 **$120**

COUNTY MAP OF MICHIGAN AND WISCONSIN [1860] 27x34cm (11x13½") Orig color by counties. Fine. [14] £51 **$85**

COUNTY MAP OF NOVA SCOTIA, NEW BRUNSWICK, CAPE BRETON ID. AND PR. EDWARD'S ID. [1860] From *New General Atlas*. 34x27cm (13½x10½") Full color. Some surface soil; else VG (B). [A4] £17 **$28**

COUNTY MAP OF TEXAS [1860] 27x34cm (10½x13½") Orig color. Fine. [14] £136 **$225**

[SAME TITLE] [c.1860] 1st ed. 27x34cm (11x13½") Full color. Good. [16] £96 **$160**

[SAME TITLE] [1867] 27x34cm (10½x13") Full color. Fine (A+). [A4] £86 **$143**

[SAME TITLE] [1872] 28x35cm (11x13½") Orig full color. [27] £112 **$185**

COUNTY MAP OF TEXAS, SHOWING ALSO PORTIONS OF THE ADJOINING STATES AND TERRITORIES [1873] 36x54cm (14x21½") Orig full color. [27] £106 **$175**

COUNTY MAP OF THE STATE OF CALIFORNIA [1874] 2 insets. 53x37cm (21x14½") Full color. Sh fold splits repaired with archival tape; VG (A). [1880 ed, fine, sold for same price] [A4] £73 **$121**

COUNTY MAP OF THE STATE OF ILLINOIS [1871] Springfield area inset. 34x28cm (13½x11") Color. [A10] £14 **$23**

COUNTY MAP OF THE STATE OF TEXAS, SHOWING ALSO PORTIONS OF THE ADJOINING STATES AND TERRITORIES [1879] With NM & Indian Terr. 36x54cm (14x21") Color by counties. [9] £136 **$225**

[SAME TITLE] [1879] By Gamble. 36x54cm (14x21½") Full col. Margin browned; good. [16] £109 **$180**

[SAME TITLE] [1887] Phila: Wm. M. Bradley & Bro. 36x54cm (14½x21½") Full col. VG. [16] £75 **$125**

MITCHELL, S.A. (Atlas Maps 1860 & Later) continued

COUNTY MAP OF UTAH AND NEVADA [1870] 29x36cm (11½x14") Full color. Few lt spots; good (B). [A3] £37 **$61**

COUNTY MAP OF VIRGINIA AND WEST VIRGINIA [dated 1860] 27x34cm (10½x13½") Orig color by counties. Fine. [14] £51 **$85**

MAP OF AFRICA, SHOWING ITS MOST RECENT DISCOVERIES [1860] 27x34cm (10½x13") Orig color. Lt margin age toning; o/w fine. [14] £60 **$100**

MAP OF BRAZIL, BOLIVIA, PARAGUAY, AND URUGUAY [ON SHEET WITH] MAP OF CHILI [1860] 27x34cm (10½x13½") Orig color. Fine. [14] £60 **$100**

[SAME TITLE] [1870] 27x34cm (10½x13½") Full color. Some margin chipping; VG (A). [A4] £7 **$11**

MAP OF CANADA WEST IN COUNTIES [1860] 32x39cm (12½x15½") Orig color. Fine. [14] £51 **$85**

MAP OF KANSAS, NEBRASKA AND COLORADO, SHOWING ALSO THE EASTERN PORTION OF IDAHO [1861] 29x36cm (11½x14") Orig color. Few margin tears; o/w VG. [14] £90 **$150**

MAP OF LOUISIANA, MISSISSIPPI, AND ARKANSAS [1860] 34x27cm (13½x10½") Orig color by counties. Lt margin soiling; o/w fine. [14] £69 **$115**

MAP OF MEXICO, CENTRAL AMERICA, AND THE WEST INDIES [1860] Insets: Bermuda; Panama RR; Cuba; Jamaica. 33x53cm (13x21") Wash & OL color. Lt toned at c'fold; VG+. Ref: Phillips (A) 831-40. [35] £45 **$75**

MAP OF NORTH AMERICA SHOWING ITS POLITICAL DIVISIONS, AND RECENT DISCOVERIES IN THE POLAR REGIONS [1860] From *New General Atlas*. 34x27cm (13x10½") Full col. Toned; VG (A). [A4] £23 **$38**

MAP OF OREGON, WASHINGTON, AND PART OF BRITISH COLUMBIA [1860] From *New General Atlas*. 1st ed. WA eastern border at Rockies abuts Nebraska Terr. (vs Dakotah in 1862.) 27x34cm (10½x13½") Full color. Immaculate. Ref: Phillips (A) 831-36. [12] £96 **$160**

MAP OF OREGON, WASHINGTON, IDAHO AND PART OF MONTANA [dated 1860] 27x34cm (11x13½") Color. [another version dated 1866, publ 1868, offered at $70] [22] £51 **$85**

MAP OF THE UNITED STATES AND TERRITORIES ... [c.1864] Montana present (1864). 34x53cm (13½x21") Color by states & terr. Folded; couple edge tears; else fine. [9] £90 **$150**

MEXICO, CENTRAL AMERICA AND THE WEST INDIES [1870] From *New General Atlas*. 4 insets. 33x55cm (13x21½") Full color. Fold splits repaired with archival tape. [A4] £28 **$46**

MINNESOTA AND DACOTAH [1860] From 1st ed, *New General Atlas*. Dakota to Missouri R. 27x34cm (10½x13½") Col. Dark impression; pristine. Ref: Karrow (MW) 7-0731; Phillips (A) 831-35. [12] £90 **$150**

NORTHWESTERN AMERICA SHOWING THE TERRITORY CEDED BY RUSSIA TO THE UNITED STATES [1880] Alaska. 29x37cm (11½x14½") Color. [40] £39 **$65**

[SAME TITLE] [1881] Reduced from U.S. Coast Survey map. 29x37cm (11½x14½") Orig color. 2 lt foxing spots; o/w VG to fine. [14] £75 **$125**

PLAN OF PHILADELPHIA [1860] 27x33cm (10½x13") Color by wards. [40] £33 **$55**

[SAME TITLE] [1860 / 1867] 28x33cm (11x13") Wash & OL color. VG+. [35] £18 **$30**

PLAN OF THE CITY OF PHILADELPHIA AND CAMDEN [1879] 37x56cm (14½x22") Full wash color. Near fine. [35] £18 **$30**

PLAN OF THE CITY OF WASHINGTON [1879] 28x36cm (11x14") Color by wards. ["Plan of New Orleans" offered at same price] [22] £27 **$45**

TERRITORY OF IDAHO [1880] 13 counties. 36x27cm (14x10½") Full color. [40] £51 **$85**

TERRITORY OF IDAHO 1876 [c.1878] Seemingly a photo reproduction of 1876 GLO map. 11 counties. 37x27cm (14½x10½") Ref: cf Preston (ID) p.24-5 & Kelsay p.152. [12] £60 **$100**

THE WORLD IN HEMISPHERES WITH OTHER PROJECTIONS &C. &C. [1860 / 1864] From *New General Atlas*. Double hemi. 28x33cm (11x13") Orig color. VG. [14] £66 **$110**

THE WORLD IN HEMISPHERES WITH OTHER PROJECTIONS ... CONSTRUCTED BY W. WILLIAMS [1867] 7 spheres total. 29x34cm (11½x13½") Color. [19] £36 **$60**

MITCHELL, S.A. (Pocket & Wall Maps; Maps not from atlases)

[BOOK WITH MAPS] ILLINOIS IN 1837; A SKETCH DESCRIPTIVE OF THE SITUATION ... ALSO, SUGGESTIONS TO EMIGRANTS ... [1837] 134 pp; map on banknote paper with "Cowperthwait" border, 38x31cm (15x12½") Orig paper covers browned, rubbed with cloth tape on loose spine; contents browned near covers; a page edge in facsimile; map toned, some dark foxing, some folds split; fair (C). [A3] £102 **$169**

MITCHELL, S.A. (maps not from atlases) continued

A NEW MAP OF TEXAS OREGON AND CALIFORNIA WITH THE REGIONS ADJOINING. COMPILED FROM THE MOST RECENT AUTHORITIES ... [1846] Folding map. 51x47cm (20x18½") Only blemish is rubbing out of some front cover words; internally exc; text fine; map exc. Ref: Wheat (TM) 520. Wheat (Gold) 29; Martin (TX) 36; Howes (US) M-685; Wagner-Camp 122b; [15] £3,619 **$6,000**

MAP OF THE STATES OF KENTUCKY AND TENNESSEE ... [1839] Sold by Thomas, Cowperthwait. Pocket map, with 3 insets, in orig embossed boards with owner's label. 45x53cm (17½x21") Full color. Covers lt rubbed; map mint; fine (A+). [A3] £420 **$696**

MAP OF THE UNITED STATES SHOWING THE PRINCIPAL TRAVELLING, TURNPIKE & COMMON ROADS ON WHICH ARE GIVEN THE DISTANCES IN MILES FROM ONE PLACE TO ANOTHER [1839] Folding map in orig leather folder. 8 insets. Full color by state. 59x45cm (23x17½") Map rebacked; several tears along folds with scattered lt chipping loss. [15] £362 **$600**

MITCHELL'S NATIONAL MAP OF THE AMERICAN REPUBLIC OR UNITED STATES OF NORTH AMERICA [1843] Wall map. 1st ed. Insets of 32 cities. Color by state. 86x62cm (33½x24½") Orig rollers. Lt waterstain top ctr & lower rt; VF. Ref: Streeter 3861 [15] £482 **$800**

[SAME TITLE] [1846] By J.H. Young; Brightly, sc. Folds into 12mo orig cloth book-style case with clasp; with Route-book; insets of extremities. 62x84cm (24½x33") Color. Sm hole at fold, map unaffected. [A6] £287 $476

MITCHELL'S NATIONAL MAP OF THE AMERICAN REPUBLIC, OR THE UNITED STATES OF NORTH AMERICA, TOGETHER WITH MAPS OF THE VICINITIES OF THIRTY-TWO OF THE PRINCIPAL CITIES AND TOWNS IN THE UNION [1843] 2 sheets, folding into cloth boards; map & broadside with descriptive text & data. each about 64x86cm (25x34") Full wash color. Both sheets toned overall; few sm point tears & fold separations repaired; cover spine missing; overall VG+. Ref: Phillips (M) p.896; Storm (Graff) 2838. Ristow (Amer M&M) p.310. [35] £573 **$950**

[SAME TITLE] [1843] Pocket map in 2 sheets; U.S. map in color on one, 32 cities & census data on other. Each about 64x88cm (25x34½") Few fold separations, archival tape verso repair; o/w VG to fine. [A1] £448 **$743**

[SAME TITLE] [1844] Wall map on rollers. West to TX; IA expands north & west; insets: extremities of ME & FL; surround of 32 cities. 93x115cm (36½x45½") Orig color. Lt toned, darker at top border; few cracks, no loss. [A2] £862 **$1,430**

MITCHELL'S NEW TRAVELER'S GUIDE THROUGH THE UNITED STATES, SHOWING THE RAILROADS, CANALS, STATE ROADS &C., WITH DISTANCES FROM PLACE TO PLACE [1860] Phila: Charles Desilver. By J.L. Hazzard & I.S. Drake. Issued to fold into guide. 56x73cm (22x29") Substantial color. Issued trimmed close; no fold breaks; occas age spotting. [26] £151 **$250**

MITCHELL'S TRAVELER'S GUIDE THROUGH THE UNITED STATES, A MAP OF ROADS, DISTANCES, STEAM BOAT AND CANAL ROUTES &C. BY J.H. YOUNG [1833] 2nd ed. With index & route guide, folding into orig morocco covers, orig label with owner's name. Extends west to MO; 9 inset city plans. 55x44cm (21½x17") OL color. Superb (A+). [A3] £329 **$545**

MITCHELL'S TRAVELERS GUIDE THROUGH THE UNITED STATES. A MAP OF ROADS, DISTANCES, STEAMBOAT AND CANAL ROUTES ETC. [1838] By J.H. Young. 16mo, gold-embossed covers; 78 pp text & gazetteer. Map on banknote paper; 8 inset city plans, 42x53cm (16½x21") OL color by state. Cover lt rubbed; sl loss at outer map fold; VG. Ref: Howes (US) 690. [5] £293 **$485**

NATIONAL MAP OF THE UNITED STATES [1843] 1st ed. Pocket map with leather folder. Separate sheet with 32 insets & data. Color. 86x62cm (33½x24½") Spine gone. Ref: Streeter 3861. [15] £482 **$800**

NEW NATIONAL MAP, EXHIBITING THE UNITED STATES [1860] Wall map of N.Amer; last ed; incl "Colona" in eastern CO, horiz AZ-NM border. Full color by county. 159x152cm (62½x60") Superb. [15] £754 **$1,250**

THE TOURIST POCKET MAP OF PENNSYLVANIA EXHIBITING ITS INTERNAL IMPROVEMENTS ROAD DISTANCES &C. [1838] Pocket map on banknote paper by J. H. Young folded into gold-embossed cover. 3 insets; canal profile. 32x38cm (12½x15") Color by county. Cover good, rubbed corners & edges; map has 2 sm stains, pinhole; VG. [5] £229 **$380**

THE TOURIST'S MAP OF THE STATE OF OHIO [1835] Folds into orig 16mo roan case. 39x32cm (15½x13") Color. Bit toned. [A8] £520 **$862**

THE TOURIST'S POCKET MAP OF THE STATE OF OHIO EXHIBITING ITS INTERNAL IMPROVEMENTS ROADS DISTANCE &C. [1839] Folds into cover; gold stamped title. 38x32cm (15x12½") Orig color. Few fold point & 1¼" separations, minor loss; lt toning at vert folds; bit of lower rt margin to border corner gone. [A2] £249 **$413**

THE TOURIST'S POCKET MAP OF THE STATE OF TENNESSEE [1839] Folds into orig 16mo roan case. 32x39cm (13x15½") Color. Lt toned; partial clean separation along a fold. [A8] £242 **$402**

MITCHELL, S.A. (maps not from atlases) continued

TRAVELERS GUIDE THROUGH THE UNITED STATES [1832] 1st ed. Folds into gilt titled 12mo roan cover; U.S. west to AR & MO; city plans; with letterpress sheet of travel data. 46x56cm (18x22"). Color. Map, sheet & cover restored; rice paper backing to map. [16] £754 **$1,250**

[SAME TITLE] [1834] J.H. Young & D. Haines, engr. Folds into orig 16mo morocco; issued with chart, prior to accompanying text; 9 insets. [no dimens] VF. [15] £452 **$750**

TRAVELER'S GUIDE THROUGH THE UNITED STATES, CONTAINING THE PRINCIPAL CITIES, TOWNS, &C. [1837] Folding map in orig 16mo leather with 78 pp text. US to beyond Mississippi; 9 insets. [no dimens] Map age-toned, lt stains; good; cover scuffed; overall fine. Ref: Howes (US) M-690. [15] £392 **$650**

MOITHEY

CARTE NOUVELLE DES POSSESSIONS ANGLOISES EN AMERIQUE DRESSEE POUR L'INTELLIGENCE DE LA GUERRE PRESENTE ET DIVISEE SUIVANT LES PRETENTIONS DES ANGLOIS [1777] 1st state. 49x70cm (19½x28"). Orig OL color. Trimmed close; laid on tissue; minor repairs. Ref: Sellers & Van Ee 155. [34] **£1,500 $2,487**

LE GLOBE TERRESTRE VU EN CONNEXE PAR LES DEUX POLES, L'EQUATEUR SERVANT D'HORISON [1787] From Pretot, *Atlas Universel pour l'Etude de la Geographie*. 23x41cm (9x16½"). Color. Ref: Phillips (A) 663-7. [19] £208 **$345**

PLAN GENERAL DE PARIS EN QUATRE DIVISIONS ... [IN SET WITH] DIVISION SUD-EST DE PARIS ... [AND] DIVISION SUD-OUEST ... [AND] DIVISION NORD-EST ... [AND] DIVISION NORD-OUEST ... [1787] Paris: Wallin le Fils. Never bound. 5 sheets, housed in contemporary board slipcase, each about 28x42cm (11x16½") Plan in OL color. Sm separations along 1st horiz fold; few minor spots; all VG. [21] Can$3,200 £1,400 **$2,321**

MOLL (Large)

A MAP OF THE WEST INDIES OR THE ISLANDS OF AMERICA IN THE NORTH SEA ... [c.1730] 2 sheets joined. 59x110cm (23x43½"). OL color. Folds closed on verso. [A7] £485 **$805**

A MAP OF THE WEST-INDIES OR THE ISLANDS OF AMERICA IN YE NORTH SEA; WITH YE ADJACENT COUNTRIES; EXPLAINING WHAT BELONGS TO SPAIN, ENGLAND, FRANCE, HOLLAND &C. ALSO YE TRADE WINDS, AND YE SEVERAL TRACTS MADE BY YE GALEONS AND FLOTA FROM PLACE TO PLACE ... [c.1719+] From *The World Described* ... Mexico City view; 5 insets. 58x100cm (23x39½") Orig OL color. Minor wear outer folds; 40% top rt margin shaved to border; overall exc. Ref: Marshall II-95-2-2; Phillips (A) 554-10 or 3469-10. [12] £905 **$1,500**

A NEW & CORRECT MAP OF THE WHOLE WORLD ... [c.1730] Mercator projection. 46x70cm (18x27½") [catalogue dimens] OL color. [A7] £1,110 **$1,840**

A NEW AND CORRECT MAP OF THE WORLD, LAID DOWN ACCORDING TO THE NEWEST DISCOVERIES ... [c.1730] From *The World Described* ... Double hemi; insular Calif; celestial diagrams. 57x97cm (22½x38½") OL color. Usual repaired folds; good. Ref: Phillips (A) 554-1. [30] £1,387 **$2,300**

A NEW AND EXACT MAP OF THE DOMINIONS OF THE KING OF GREAT BRITAIN ON YE CONTINENT OF NORTH AMERICA ... [c.1730] The "Beaver Map". 101x61cm (40x24") OL color. [A7] £1,387 **$2,300**

A NEW MAP OF THE NORTH PARTS OF AMERICA CLAIMED BY FRANCE UNDER YE NAMES OF LOUISIANA, MISSISSIPI, CANADA AND NEW FRANCE WITH YE ADJOINING TERRITORIES OF ENGLAND AND SPAIN ... 1720 [1720] From *A New and Compleat Atlas* ... 62x102cm (24½x40") Color. Some browning; paper bit brittle, separations along vert folds; substantially good. Ref: Phillips (A) 5961-9. Stevens & Stevens *The World Described*. [21] Can$2,900 £1,268 **$2,103**

[SAME TITLE] [1720] Incl present US; Insular Calif. 60x100cm (23½x39½") OL color. Fold partially closed on verso. [A7] £1,040 **$1,725**

[SAME TITLE] [1720] 60x101cm (24x40") OL color. Repaired & rebacked; some loss at folds & borders; fair. [15] £905 **$1,500**

TO HER MOST SACRED MAJESTY CAROLINA QUEEN OF GREAT BRITAIN, FRANCE AND IRELAND ... THIS MAP OF EUROPE ... [1708] 58x96cm (23x38"). Orig OL color. Some c'fold & side fold repairs, no loss; o/w VG. [2] £392 **$650**

TO THE RIGHT HONORABLE CHARLES EARL OF SUNDERLAND ... THIS MAP OF SOUTH AMERICA ACCORDING TO THE NEWEST AND MOST EXACT OBSERVATIONS IS MOST HUMBLY DEDICATED ... [1719] From *The World Described* ... Potosi view inset. 57x96cm (22½x38") OL color. Fold repairs; 2 repaired tears; good. Ref: Phillips (A) 554-11. [30] £452 **$750**

MOLL (Large) continued

TO THE RIGHT HONOURABLE JOHN LORD SOMMERS ... THIS MAP OF NORTH AMERICA ACCORDING TO YE NEWEST AND MOST EXACT OBSERVATIONS IS MOST HUMBLY DEDICATED BY ... HERMAN MOLL GEOGRAPHER [1719 (c.1720)] From *The World Described* ... The "Cod Fish" map. Insular Calif; 10 insets. 57x96cm (22½x38") Orig OL color. Tiny loss at rejoined fold; good. Ref: McLaughlin 192; Wheat (TM) 105; Tooley (Amer) p.130, #82; Schwartz & Ehrenberg pl.79; Phillips (A) 554-7. [30] £1,508 **$2,500**
[SAME TITLE] [c.1719] 59x97cm (23x38") OL color. Portion of fold closed. [A7] £832 **$1,380**
[SAME TITLE] [1720] The "Cod Fish" map. Insular Calif; 10 insets. 58x97cm (23x38½") Rebacked & repaired; loss at lf fold; rt fold reinforced; loss affects sm area cartouche & ocean [15] £1,206 **$2,000**
TO THE RIGHT HONOURABLE WILLIAM LORD COWPER, LORD HIGH CHANCELLOR OF GREAT BRITAIN, THIS MAP OF ASIA ACCORDING TO YE NEWEST AND MOST EXACT OBSERVATIONS IS MOST HUMBLY DEDICATED ... [1720] 7 inset maps. 58x95cm (22½x37½") OL color; cartouche in later full color. Faint browning vert folds, 4 sh separations repaired on verso; else fresh, clean. Framed. [A9] £555 **$920**
[SAME TITLE] [c.1720] T. Bowles, P. Overton & J. King. 58x96cm (22½x38") Color. Occas browning, fold repairs. [A5] £506 $839

MOLL (Small)

[ATLAS] A SET OF THIRTY SIX NEW AND CORRECT MAPS OF SCOTLAND ... [c.1728] 2nd published atlas of country. Oblong quarto. Orig OL color. Ref: Moir, vol.2, p.152, no.3. [34] **£2,200** $3,648
A CHART OF YE EAST INDIES. WITH THE COAST OF PERSIA, CHINA, ALSO THE PHILIPINA, MOLUCA AND SUNDA ISLANDS &C. [1745] Publ in *A Collection of Voyages and Travels* ... London: Thomas Osborne. 30x43cm (11½x17") [47] **£180** $299
A GENERAL AND PARTICULAR DESCRIPTION OF AMERICA ... [1709] Insular Calif. 18x19cm (7x7½") Narrow rt margin. [47] **£190** $315
A MAP OF NEW FRANCE CONTAINING CANADA, LOUISIANA &C. IN NTH. AMERICA. ACCORDING TO THE PATENT GRANTED BY THE KING OF FRANCE TO MONSIEUR CROZAT, DATED THE 14TH OF SEP. 1712, N.S. ... [1745] From *A Collection of Voyages and Travels* ... London: Thomas Osborne. Includes US to Rockies. 19x26cm (7½x10") Ref: Jolly (AMPR) v.2, p.16 illus. [47] **£260** $431
A MAP OF SWITZERLAND [1723] 18x19cm (7x7½") ["Poland" offered at same price] [11] £36 **$60**
A MAP OF THE NORTH POLE WITH ALL THE TERRITORIES THAT LYE NEAR IT, KNOWN TO US &C. ... [1739] To 60 deg north. 20x28cm (8x11") B&W. Dark impression; fine (A+). [A4] £118 **$195**
A NEW MAP OF NORTH AMERICA ACCORDING TO THE NEWEST OBSERVATIONS [1745] From *A Collection of Voyages and Travels* ... London: Thomas Osborne. Insular California. 18x26cm (7½x10") Ref: McLaughlin 225. [47] **£260** $431
A NEW MAP OF THE WORLD ... [1711 and later.] Double-hemi; sm polar hemi insular Calif. 18x28cm (7x11") Full color. [36] **£271** **$450**
A NEW MAP OF THE WORLD ACCORDING TO THE NEW OBSERVATIONS ... [1745] Publ in *A Collection of Voyages and Travels* ... London: Thomas Osborne. Double-hemi; insular Calif. 18x28cm (7½x11") Minor spotting. [47] **£260** $431
A VIEW OF YE GENERAL & COASTING TRADE-WINDS, MONSOONS OR YE SHIFTING TRADE WINDS THROUGH YE WORLD, VARIATIONS &C. [1745] London: Thomas Osborne. 19x53cm (7½x21") Narrow margin bottom lf due to binding. [47] **£130** $216
[SAME TITLE] [1752] From Awnsham & Churchill, *Collections of Voyages and Travels* ... 50 degrees either side equator; centered on Pacific. 18x52cm (7½x20½") B&W. Sm thin spot reinforced with archival tape; else pristine. Ref: cf Marshall II-98-1-2. [12] £166 **$275**
AMERICA [1723] Insular Calif. 17x19cm (6½x7½") [11] £211 **$350**
ARABIA ... [1745] Publ in *A Collection of Voyages and Travels* ... London: Thomas Osborne. 19x26cm (7½x10") [47] **£120** $199
CAROLINA BY H. MOLL GEOGRAPHER [c.1720] From *Atlas Minor*. VA Capes to northern FL; note regarding English claims. 20x28cm (8x11") OL color. Fine. [38] **£271** **$450**
CHILI MAGGELLANS-LAND ... [1723] Incl Patagonia. 16x18cm (6½x7½") ["Brasil, Divided into Its Captainships" offered at same price] [11] £30 **$50**
CHINA ACCORDING TO THE NEWEST AND MOST EXACT OBSERVATIONS [1745] Publ in *A Collection of Voyages and Travels* ... London: Thomas Osborne 18x26cm (7½x10") [47] **£95** $158
EUROPE [1723] Text below & verso. 17x19cm (6½x7½") ["Denmark" & "Moscovia or Russia" offered at same price] [11] £30 **$50**

MOLL (Small) continued

MEXICO OR NEW SPAIN DIVIDED INTO THE AUDIANCE OF GUADALAYARA, MEXICO, AND GUATIMALA FLORIDA [1723] 17x18cm (6½x7") [11] £151 **$250**

NEW ENGLAND, NEW YORK, NEW JERSEY, AND PENSILVANIA [1745] From *A Collection of Voyages and Travels* ... London: Thomas Osborne. 19x26cm (7½x10") [47] **£220** $365

PHILIPPINE ISLANDS AGREEABLE TO MODERN HISTORY [1730] 20x26cm (8x10") Later OL color. By sight, fine. Framed. [A9] **£180** **$299**

SAVOY AND PIEDMONT [1723] Geneva to Mediterranean with Milan. 21x18cm (8½x7") [11] £51 **$85**

SWEDEN AND NORWAY [1723] Incl Finland. 17x18cm (6½x7") ["Scandinavia ..." offered at same price] [11] £45 **$75**

TERRA FIRMA AND THE CARIBBE ISLANDS &C. [1723] Incl "Parime Lake". 16x19cm (6½x7½") [11] £75 **$125**

THE ARTIFICIAL SPHERE [1723] Armillary sphere; text above, below, on verso. 13x10cm (5x4") [11] £18 **$30**

THE DOMINIONS OF MOSCOVY OR RUSSIA [c.1730] 18x25cm (7x10") OL color. VG. [38] £75 **$125**

THE EAST PART OF INDIA OR INDIA BEYOND THE R. GANGES ... [c.1730] Engr for Salmon's *History*. East to Borneo. 18x26cm (7x10") Color. Exc. [4] **£125** $208

THE ENGLISH EMPIRE IN AMERICA, NEWFOUND-LAND, CANADA, HUDSONS BAY &C IN PLANO, HERMAN MOLL FECIT. [1709] On page with text. 22x18cm (8½x7") [46] **£180** $299

[SAME TITLE] [1723] Labrador to Florida; text below & verso. 21x18cm (8½x7") [11] £166 **$275**

THE GREAT PROVINCE OF RIO DE LA PLATA [1723] 17x19cm (6½x7½") ["Peru and the Amazones" offered at same price] [11] £36 **$60**

THE ISLE OF CALIFORNIA. NEW MEXICO. LOUISIANE. THE RIVER MISISIPI AND THE LAKE'S OF CANADA. HERMAN MOLL FECIT [1701-23] Most of present US; insular Calif. 16x18cm (6½x7½") Ref: McLaughlin 144; Wheat (TM) 109. [11] £302 **$500**

[SAME TITLE] [1709] Most of present US; insular Calif. 16x19cm (6½x7½") [46] **£260** $431

THE PHILIPPINE ISLANDS AND OTHER OF THE EAST INDIES [1745] Publ in *A Collection of Voyages and Travels* ... London: Thomas Osborne. 18x26cm (7x10") [47] **£150** $249

THE PRINCIPAL ISLANDS OF THE EAST INDIES ACCORDING TO YE NEWEST OBSERVATIONS ... [c.1730] 17x26cm (6½x10") Color. Exc. [4] **£145** $241

THE SCOTS SETTLEMENT IN AMERICA CALLED NEW CALEDONIA [1699-1729] 25x20cm (10x8") Early OL color. Hint of foxing; VG. [A9] £97 **$161**

THE WORLD IN PLANISPHERE [1723] Double hemi; North Polar hemi; insular Calif. 16x19cm (6½x7½") [11] £256 **$425**

VIRGINIA AND MARYLAND BY H. MOLL GEOGRAPHER [c.1720] Chesapeake Bay area. 27x20cm (10½x8") OL color. Fine. [38] £286 **$475**

VIRGINIA AND MARYLAND BY H. MOLL GEOGRAPHER 1729 [1729] From 1st ed, *Atlas Minor*. Chesapeake Bay area. 27x20cm (10½x8") B&W. Fine. Ref: Morrison fig.25; Papenfuse & Coale p.22-3; Sames & Woods p.34; Swem 144; Phillips (A) 574-47. [12] £256 **$425**

MOLLHAUSEN

MAP ILLUSTRATING BALDWIN MOLLHAUSEN'S TRAVELS FROM THE MISSISSIPPI TO THE COAST OF THE PACIFIC, IN THE YEARS 1853-1854 [1858] From English ed, *Diary of a Journey from the Mississippi to the Coast* ... Ft. Smith to San Francisco with elevation profile. 20x44cm (8x17½") Little orig color. Rice paper backing; fine. Ref: Wheat (TM) 956; Howes M-713. Wagner-Camp 305. [28] £136 **$225**

MOLLO

PLAN DE LA VILLE ... VIENNE ... [c.1825] Bird's-eye view. 37x44cm (14½x17½") B&W. [1] £121 **$200**

MONALDINI

PIANTA DELLA CITTA DI ROMA [1824] 32-section linen-backed map after Nolli; 16 architectural views at sides. 75x112cm (29½x44") [A7] £520 **$862**

MONIN

SUEDE NORVEGE ET DANEMARK [1834] From *Atlas Classique de la Geographie*. 40x28cm (16x11") OL color. VG (A). [A4] £35 **$58**

MONK

MONK'S NEW AMERICAN MAP EXHIBITING THE LARGER PORTION OF NORTH AMERICA EMBRACING THE UNITED STATES AND TERRITORIES, MEXICO AND CENTRAL AMERICA [1857] Wall map with orig rail & rod; drawn, engraved, printed by Hoen & Co. 122x155cm (48x61") OL & full color by state & terr. Sm holes, stains, tears near rail; ragged side edges affecting only margins; varnish broken intermittently; VG+. [5] £458 **$760**

NEW MAP OF THAT PORTION OF NORTH AMERICA, EXHIBITING THE UNITED STATES AND TERRITORIES, THE CANADAS, NEW BRUNSWICK, NOVA SCOTIA, AND MEXICO, ALSO CENTRAL AMERICA, AND THE WEST INDIA ISLANDS [1851] 1st ed. Baltimore. Linen-backed wall map; erroneous Rio Grande boundary. 142x150cm (56x59") Chipping near top, loss in Oregon Terr; fair. Ref: cf Wheat (TM) 757. [15] £302 **$500**

[SAME TITLE] [1854] Baltimore. Wall map; Gadsden Purchase not shown. 142x150cm (56x59") Exc. Ref: cf Wheat (TM) 757. [1853 edition with some cracks & stains, VG, offered at $750; another with minor cracks & age toning, good, offered at $850] [15] £573 **$950**

MONTANUS

[BOOK WITH MAPS] DE NIEUWE EN ONBEKENDE WEERELD OF BESCHRYVING VAN AMERICA EN 'T ZUID-LAND ... [1671] Amsterdam. Folio, blind stamped vellum; 70 plates in text, 31 folding views, 16 maps, 7 Portraits. Sobolesky book plate; almost pristine. Ref: Sabin 50086. [3] £10,856 **$18,000**

CANGOXUMA [(1669) 1680] Kagoshima panorama. 28x57cm (11x22½") Uncolored. Exc. Ref: Cortazzi pl.72 & 73. [4] £260 **$431**

VIRGINIAE PARTIS AUSTRALIS, ET FLORIDAE PARTIS ORIENTALIS ... [1671] Carolina focus. 29x36cm (11½x14") Uncolored. Fine. Ref: Johnson (Amer Expl) p.130, illus; Cumming (SE) 67; Howes (US) p.17. [32] £588 **$975**

MOORE

CHART PREPARED BY JAMES B. MOORE, TO ACCOMPANY HIS MEMORIAL TO CONGRESS RESPECTING THE SUBJECT OF STEAM COMMUNICATION WITH CHINA, JAPAN ETC. 1850 [1850] Publ Cincinnati. World with ship routes; San Francisco Bay inset. 71x97cm (28x38½") Few stains; lt toned; else exc. Ref: cf Sabin 50404 (map not cited). [24] £905 **$1,500**

MORDEN

A NEW MAP OF CAROLINA ... [1688] Differs from 1687 version; printed as "Page 74". 12x13cm (5x5") Orig OL color. Ref: Williams & Johnson (NC) fig.6. [11] £106 **$175**

BEDFORD SHIRE [1695] Publ in Camden's *Britannia*. 32x40cm (12½x15½") Color. ["Cheshire" & "Dorset Shire" also offered at same price] [42] **Aus$375** £170 **$282**

BRITANNIA ROMANA [1695] Publ in same source. 36x43cm (14x17") Color. [42] **Aus$550** £250 **$414**

ENGLAND [1695] Publ in Camden's *Britannia*. 36x43cm (14x17") Color. [42] **Aus$425** £193 **$320**

HAMPSHIRE [1695] Publ in same source. 36x42cm (14x16½") Color. [42] **Aus$550** £250 **$414**

MEXICO OR NEW SPAINE [1688] From *Geography Rectified* ... 11x12cm (4x5") on 8x6" sheet. B&W. Ref: Phillips (A) 498-546. [12] £121 **$200**

MIDLESEX [1695] From Camden's *Britannia*. 37x43cm (14½x17") Color. [42] **Aus$650** £295 **$489**

NEW ENGLAND AND NEW YORK BY ROBT. MORDEN [c.1675] 11x13cm (4½x5½") Exc. [44] £271 **$450**

NORTHUMBERLAND [1695] From Camden's *Britannia*. 42x36cm (16½x14") B&W. VG. [Westmoreland offered at same price] [38] £90 **$150**

NOTTINGHAM SHIRE [1695] From same source. 35x43cm (13½x17") Col. [42] **Aus$300** £136 **$226**

OXFORD SHIRE [1695] From Camden's *Britannia*. 42x36cm (16½x14") Color. ["Hertford Shire", "Somerset" & "Worcester Shire" offered at same price] [42] **Aus$450** £204 **$339**

ROTELANDIAE [1695] From Camden's *Britannia*. Rutland. 29x36cm (11½x14") Color. ["Huntington Shire" offered at same price] [42] **Aus$275** £125 **$207**

SURREY [1695] From Camden's *Britannia*. 36x43cm (14x17") Color. ["Leicester Shire", "Lincolnshire" & "Northampton Shire" offered at same price] [42] **Aus$425** £193 **$320**

SUSSEX [1695] From same source. 34x42cm (13½x16½") Col. Crease line. [42] **Aus$475** £216 **$358**

THE SMALLER ISLANDS IN THE BRITISH OCEAN [1695] From Camden's *Britannia*. Incl Isle of Wight, Channel Islands, Man, Farne & Scilly Islands. 36x42cm (14x16½") Color. [42] **Aus$425** £193 **$320**

WARWICK SHIRE [1695] From same source. 37x42cm (14½x16½") Color. [42] **Aus$325** £148 **$245**

WILT SHIRE [1695] Publ in Camden's *Britannia*. 34x42cm (13½x16½") Color. ["Buckingham Shire" & "Shrop Shire" offered as same price] [42] **Aus$350** £159 **$263**

MORISOT

AMERICAE SEPTENTRIONALIS CIRCUITUS [1643] From *Orbis Maritimi ...*, Dijon. With much of Pacific. 13x17cm (5x6½") with text on 14x8½" sheet. B&W. Fine. [12] £362 **$600**

MORRILL

A MAP OF THE OLD COLONY RAILROAD AND CONNECTIONS [c.1890] George S. Morrill, Boston. Wall map of MA east of Worcester, with boat connections; blueprint style; trackage shown in red & white. 100x97cm (39½x38"). Near mint. [15] £166 **$275**

MORSE, JEDIDIAH

[BOOK WITH MAPS] A COMPENDIUS AND COMPLETE SYSTEM OF MODERN GEOGRAPHY [1814] Abridgement of 1812 American Universal Geography. Period sheep; complete, 671 pp; 7 folding maps in color: world, 5 continents, solar system. 23x14cm (9x5½") Binding rubbed, sl loss upper spine; contents tight; maps toned, lt foxing, color bit faded; good (B). [A3] £165 **$273**

[BOOK WITH MAPS] A NEW GAZETTEER OF THE EASTERN CONTINENT; OR, A GEOGRAPHICAL DICTIONARY ... EUROPE, ASIA, AFRICA ... [1802] Charlestown: Samuel Etheridge. Octavo, orig full leather binding with new label; 18 maps. Some age browning & sl spotting; clean. [33] £271 **$450**

[SAME TITLE] [1802] Charlestown. Thick leather bound 8vo; 18 maps of Europe, Asia & Africa. Covers dry & rubbed; lt scattered foxing throughout. [A1] £66 **$110**

[BOOK WITH MAPS] GEOGRAPHY MADE EASY [1790] Boston: Isaiah Thomas. 2nd ed. 12mo, sheep; 8 maps. Need rebinding; primary title excised from page, most remains. [A8] £121 **$201**

[BOOK WITH MAPS] THE AMERICAN GEOGRAPHY ... [1794] London. Thick 4to, calf; 24 maps, lacks Kentucky. Needs rebinding; internally clean; moderate foxing to maps. Ref: Howes (US) M840. [A8] £1,110 **$1,840**

[BOOK WITH MAPS] THE AMERICAN UNIVERSAL GEOGRAPHY [1812] Boston: Thomas & Andrews. 6th ed. 2 octavo vols, orig full leather; maps incl world & continents. Rehinged; new facsimile labels, orig labels tipped into pockets; maps browned. [33] £271 **$450**

A CHART OF THE NTH. WEST COAST OF AMERICA, & THE NTH. EAST COAST OF ASIA, SHEWING THE DISCOVERIES THAT HAVE BEEN LATELY MADE IN THOSE PARTS [1802] From *American Universal Geography*. 1st ed. Alaska interior blank. 18x29cm (7x11½") B&W. Ref: Phillips (AK) p.34; Falk (AK) p.81. [12] £106 **$175**

A CORRECT MAP OF THE GEORGIA WESTERN TERRITORY [1798] From *American Gazetteer*. Alabama & Mississippi. 18x15cm (7x6") Uncol. Some offsetting; good. Ref: Wheat & Brun 618. [36] £166 **$275**

A GENERAL MAP OF NORTH AMERICA FROM THE BEST AUTHORITIES [1796] Publ in *The American Universal Geography* Boston: Thomas & Andrews. Doolittle, sc. 20x23cm (8x9") Uncolored. VG. Ref: Wheat & Brun 55. [26] £48 **$80**

A MAP OF GEORGIA, ALSO THE TWO FLORIDAS, FROM THE BEST AUTHORITIES [1796] From *American Universal Geography*. Boston: Thomas & Andrews. GA to Mississippi River. 19x32cm (7½x12½") B&W. VG. Ref: Wheat & Brun 614. [26] £121 **$200**

A MAP OF THE NORTH WESTERN TERRITORY [1796] From 3rd ed, *American Universal Geography,* Thomas & Andrews. 24x18cm (9½x7") Uncolored. Lt offsetting. Ref: Wheat & Brun 679. [15] £121 **$200**

[SAME TITLE] [1796] 18x24cm (7½x9½") B&W. Few scattered stains; o/w VG. [38] £211 **$350**

A MAP OF THE STATE OF KENTUCKY AND THE TENNESSEE GOVERNMENT COMPILED FROM THE BEST AUTHORITIES BY CYRUS HARRIS [1798 (given)] 20x29cm (8x11½") Uncolored. VG. Ref: Wheat & Brun 645. [26] £136 **$225**

A MAP OF THE UNITED STATES OF AMERICA [1802] Boston: Thomas & Andrews. 14x14cm (5½x5½") Uncolored. VG. [25] £36 **$60**

A NEW MAP OF NORTH AMERICA SHEWING ALL THE NEW DISCOVERIES [1797] From *The American Gazetteer*. 1st ed. By Samuel Hill. 19x23cm (7½x9") Staining in ocean area; rt margin trimmed. [21] Can$90 £39 **$65**

CHART OF THE NEW DISCOVERIES EAST OF NEW HOLLAND AND NEW GUINEA [1797] From *The American Gazetteer*. 1st ed. By B. Callender. Australia to Easter I. 16x24cm (6½x9½") Browning; offsetting. Ref: Wheat & Brun 911. [21] Can$40 £17 **$29**

MAP OF NORTH AND SOUTH CAROLINA [1796] Boston: Thomas & Andrews; by J. Denison; Doolittle, sc. 20x24cm (8x9½") B&W. VG. [26] £84 **$140**

MAP OF NORTH AND SOUTH CAROLINA BY J. DENISON [1796] From *Universal Geography*. Doolittle, sc. 20x23cm (8x9") Uncolored. Minor stains; good. Ref: Wheat & Brun 585 [36] £166 **$275**

MORSE, JEDIDIAH continued

MAP OF THE SOUTHERN PARTS OF THE UNITED STATES OF AMERICA ... [1797] From *The American Gazetteer*. 1st ed. By Abraham Bradley. West to Mississippi R. 20x38cm (8x15") Browning & few spots; double c'fold crease; 1½" closed tear lower rt into ocean area. Ref: Wheat & Brun #496. [21] **Can$130** £57 **$94**

WEST INDIES FROM THE BEST AUTHORITIES [1797] From *The American Gazetteer*. 1st ed. By Samuel Hill. 19x32cm (7½x12½") Browning & few spots; 2" closed tear lower lf to Nicaragua. Ref: Wheat & Brun 699. [21] **Can$120** £52 **$87**

MORSE, SIDNEY

[ATLAS] A NEW UNIVERSAL ATLAS OF THE WORLD, ON AN IMPROVED PLAN; CONSISTING OF THIRTY MAPS ... WITH COMPLETE ALPHABETICAL INDEXES BY SIDNEY E. MORSE, A.M. NEW HAVEN: ENGRAVED AND PUBLISHED BY N. & S.S. JOCELYN [1825] !st ed. Sm folio, ¾-morocco, orig boards & label. 30 maps, incl 10 of U.S. in orig color. Scuffed; some spotting & lt browning on maps. Ref: Phillips (A) 746. [3] £905 **$1,500**

[BOOK WITH MAPS] A SYSTEM OF GEOGRAPHY FOR THE USE OF SCHOOLS [1844] 1st ed. NY: Harper & Brothers. Big quarto, salmon printed boards; 72 pp, cerographic maps; Texas Republic appears on three. Sl cracking of hinge; a presentation copy; fine. [2nd ed, 1845, boards worn, offered at $500; another, 1849, offered at $400] [16] £452 **$750**

TEXAS [1844] From *A System of Geography for the Use of Schools*. NY: Harper & Bros. Surround of text. Reverse: Mexico, Guatemala & West Indies showing Texas republic. 13x14cm (5½x5½") Yellow toned wax engraving. Lt foxing; good. [16] £90 **$150**

UNITED STATES [1823] N. & S.S. Jocelyn, New Haven. Folding map on thin paper in marbled wrappers; extends coast to coast. 24x42cm (9½x16½") OL color. Sm tears at folds & junctions. Ref: Wheat (TM) 355. [15] £181 **$300**

MORSE & BREESE

FLORIDA [1842, publ 1846] From *North American Atlas*. 21 counties. Overprinted cerographic color. 36x28cm (14x11") Lt scattered foxing; o/w fine. [12] £81 **$135**

IOWA AND WISCONSIN CHIEFLY FROM THE MAP OF J.N. NICOLLET [1844 (1845)] From *Cerographic Atlas of the United States*. Extended territorial forms. Verso: Michigan. 30x38cm (12x15") B&W. Ref: Phillips (A) 1383-26; cf Karrow (MW) 8-0650. [12] £112 **$185**

MEXICO [1845] As in the *Cerographic Atlas*. Incl TX & Southwest; Central America & Yucatan inset. 30x38cm (12x15") Yellowish hue. Edge browning; minor foxing; else VG. Ref: Wheat (TM) 462. [9] £136 **$225**

NORTH CAROLINA [1844] 30x43cm (12x17") Color. ["Illinois" offered at same price] Ref: Williams & Johnson (NC) fig.23. [41] £51 **$85**

SOUTH CAROLINA [1843 (1846)] From *North American Atlas*. 29 counties. Printed yellow cerographic overtones. 30x38cm (12x15") Minor spot; o/w exc. Ref: Phillips (A) 1228-17. [12] £60 **$100**

MORSE & GASTON   Try *Diamond Atlas*

TEXAS [1857] From *The World in Miniature*. With 3 pp text. 16x13cm (6½x5") Full col. Fine. [16] £54 **$90**

MORTIER

[TITLE PAGE] LE NEPTUNE FRANCOIS [1700] Amsterdam. Neptune & chariot motif. 51x37cm (20x14½") Dampstained margins; repairs. [A8] £242 **$402**

BOUSSOLE DES VENTS [1700] From Amsterdam ed, *Le Neptune Francois*. Wind chart. 37x37cm (14½x14½") Color. Dampstaining, mostly margins just into top rt image. [A8] £555 **$920**

CARTE DES COSTES DE L'ASIE SUR L'OCEAN CONTENANT LES BANCS ISLES ET COSTES &C. [c.1700] India to Japan with East Indies. 2 sheets joined, 58x87cm (22½x34½") Wash color. Fine. [4] **$2,500** **$4,146**

CARTE GENERAL DE LA CAROLINE [1700] From Amsterdam ed, *Le Neptune Francois*. 57x46cm (22½x18½") OL color. Minor browning; removable mildew rt margin & image. [A8] £763 **$1,265**

CARTE GENERALE DE TOUTES LES COSTES DU MONDE ... [c.1703] *Suite du Neptune Francois*. Covens & Mortier. 1693 map reengraved by Baltasar Ruyter at larger scale; 2 sheets, each 58x50cm (23x19½") overall, 23x39". Orig color. Exc. Ref: cf Shirley (W) 559. Wagner (NW) 439. [2] £3,317 **$5,500**

CARTE NOUVELLE DE L'AMERIQUE ANGLOISE CONTENANT LA VIRGINIE, MARY-LAND, CAROLINE, PENSILVANIA, NOUVELLE JORCK, N. IARSEY N: FRANCE, ET LES TERRES NOUVELLEMENT DECOUVERTE ... PAR LE SIEUR S [1700] By Sanson. 59x91cm (23½x36") Full orig color. Tear rt margin, sm outer margin losses; good. Ref: Cumming (SE) 129. [32] £2,111 **$3,500**

MORTIER continued

CARTE PARTICULIERE DE ISTHMUS OU DARIEN QUI COMPREND LE GOLFE DE PANAMA &C. CARTAGENA, ET LES ISLES AUX ENVIRONS ... [1700] From Amsterdam ed, *Le Neptune Francois*. 62x86cm (24x34") OL color. Minor browning top edges; removable mildew side margins. Ref: Kapp (Panama) 31. [A8] £485 **$805**

CARTE PARTICULIERE DE L'AMERIQUE SEPTENTRIONALE OU SONT COMPRIS LE DESTROIT DE DAVIDS, LE DESTROIT DE HUDSON, &C. [c.1700] 60x84cm (23½x33") OL color. Browned overall; offsetting from cartouche, etc. [A7] £451 **$747**

CARTE PARTICULIERE DE LA CAROLINE ... [1700] From Amsterdam ed, *Le Neptune Francois*. 48x60cm (19x23½") OL color. Removable mildew lower margin just into image; top margin & sm upper part of map rejoined; paper-backed. Ref: Cumming (SE) 121. [A8] £832 **$1,380**

CARTE PARTICULIERE DE LA MER ROUGE ... [1700] From Amsterdam ed, *Le Neptune Francois*. 53x75cm (21x29½") OL color. [A8] £347 **$575**

[SAME TITLE] [1700] 55x76cm (21½x30") Orig OL color. Exc. Ref: Norwich 262. [44] £573 **$950**

CARTE PARTICULIERE DE VIRGINIE, MARYLAND, PENNSILVANIE, LA NOUVELLE JARSEY ORIENT ET OCCIDENTALE [1700] From Amsterdam ed, *Le Neptune Francois*. 54x84cm (21½x33½") OL color. Minor browning. [A8] £2,081 **$3,450**

CARTE PARTICULIERE DES COSTES DE CAP DE BONE ESPERANCE ... [1700] 56x80cm (22x31½") Exc. Ref: Norwich 266. [44] £543 **$900**

[SAME TITLE] [1700] From Amsterdam ed, *Le Neptune Francois*. 57x80cm (22½x31½") OL color. Dampstaining along fold in top margin & into image. [A8] £694 **$1,150**

DINANT [BELGIUM] [c.1705] Plan with fortifications. 21x28cm (8½x11") [48] **DM 60** £21 $34

GALLIAE ANTIQUAE [c.1705] 44x54cm (17½x21") Color by regions. ["Graeciae Antiquae" (sh repairable tear) & "Geographia Patriarchalis" sold at same price] [A8] £104 **$172**

HAMBORG, VILLE IMPERIALE D'ALLEMAGNE [c.1705] Fortification plan. 22x30cm (8½x11½") [48] **DM 400** £138 $229

LE CANADA OU PARTIE DE LA NOUVELLE FRANCE, CONTENANT LA TERRE DE LABRADOR, LA NOUVELLE FRANCE, LES ISLES DE TERRE NEUVE, DE NOSTRE DAME &C. [c.1700] 1st state. 57x79cm (22½x31") Orig OL color. Oxidized areas reinforced; else exc. Ref: Kershaw (Canada) 176.1. Karpinski (MI) p.117 [24] £1,086 **$1,800**

LE GOLFE DE MEXIQUE, ET LES ISLES VOISINE. DRESSE SUR LES RELATIONS LES PLUS NOUVELLES. ARCHIPELAGUE DU MEXIQUE OU SONT LES ISLES DE CUBA, ESPAGNOLA, JAMAICA, &C. DRESSE SUR LES RELATIONS LES PLUS NOUVELLES [1700] From Amsterdam ed, *Le Neptune Francois*. Carolina to South America. 60x85cm (23½x33½") OL color [A8] £832 **$1,380**

LE ROYAUME DE SIAM ... [1700] From Amsterdam ed, *Le Neptune Francois*. 79x56cm (31x22") OL color. [A8] £520 **$862**

[SAME TITLE] [c.1710] (illustrated as southern sheet) Covers Malaysia, Sumatra, Java, Borneo. 48x55cm (19x21½") Orig OL color. Exc. [11] £754 **$1,250**

LE ROYAUME DE SIAM AVEC LES ROYAUMES QUI LUY SONT TRIBUTAIRES, ET LES ISLES DE SUMATRA, ANDEMAON, ETC. ET LES ISLES VOISINE [1700] From *Neptune Francois*. Incl Java, Borneo. 79x55cm (31x22") Orig OL color. Fine. Ref: Koeman Mor 1.7. [24] £2,322 **$3,850**

MER DE SUD OU PACIFIQUE, CONTENANT L'ISLE DE CALIFORNE, LES COSTES DE MEXIQUE, DU PEROU, CHILI, ET LE DESTROIT DE MAGELLANIQUE &C. [1700] As in *Neptune Francois*. 60x74cm (23½x29½") Uncol. Exc. Ref: McLaughlin 137; Tooley (Amer) p.127, #64. Wagner (NW) 440. [2] £3,317 **$5,500**

[SAME TITLE] [1700] From *Neptune Francois*. 61x75cm (24x29½") Orig color. Mended minor tears lower margin; else exc. [43] £1,930 **$3,200**

[SAME TITLE] [1700] From Amsterdam ed, *Le Neptune Francois*. Insular Calif. 2 sheets joined, 60x75cm (24x29½") OL color. Repairable dampstaining top margin into image. Ref: McLaughlin 137. ["Carte des Costes de l'Asie sur l'Ocean ..." sold at same price] [A8] £832 **$1,380**

PLAN DES VIELLES ET NOUVELLE FORTIFICATIONS DE MALTHE [c.1705] La Valetta plan with fortifications 22x29cm (9x11½") Wrinkle at ctr. [48] **DM 350** £121 $200

QUEBEC, VILLE DE L'AMERIQUE SEPTENTRIONALE DANS LA NOUVELLE FRANCE [1702] From Villeneuve's *Les Forces de l'Europe* ... 1690 siege plan. 20x29cm (8x11½") Exc. Ref: Kershaw (Canada) #280, 1st state; Phillips (A) 537, vol.1, 160. [21] **Can$600** £262 $435

SICILIAE INSULAE [c.1705] 44x56cm (17x22") Color. [A8] £156 **$258**

MOULE

[ATLAS] THE ENGLISH COUNTIES DELINEATED: OR A TOPOGRAPHICAL DESCRIPTION OF ENGLAND [1837] Geo. Virtue. Quarto, 2 vols, half calf; 59 of 60 maps, town plans & plates, some folding; lacks London plan. Cover rubbed; occas staining, offsetting; 2 border sl cropped. Ref: Chubb 472. [A6] £632 $1,048
CITY AND UNIVERSITY OF OXFORD [1839] From *The English Counties Delineated.* Publ by Virtue. 24x19cm (9½x7½") Color. Sm tears lower rt corner & ctr lf; some browning. [21] Can$125 £55 $91
HAMPSHIRE [1837] From *English Counties Delineated.* Vignette & coat of arms. 20x26cm (8x10") Color. Margin may be trimmed. ["Isle of Wight", "Berkshire", "Buckinghamshire", "Cheshire", "Hertfordshire" & "Environs of Bath and Bristol" offered at same price] [11] £36 **$60**
MIDDLESEX [1837] From *English Counties Delineated.* Vignette & coat of arms. 20x26cm (8x10½") Color. Margin may be trimmed. ["Isle of Man", "Cambridgeshire", "Oxfordshire", "Devonshire", "Gloucestershire", "... East Riding" & "... North Riding" offered at same price] [11] £30 **$50**
SHROPSHIRE [1837] From *English Counties Delineated.* Vignette & coat of arms. 26x20cm (10½x8") Color. Margin may be trimmed. ["Leicestershire", "Northumberland", "Nottinghamshire", "Rutlandshire", "Westmoreland" & "Isle of Thanet" offered at same price] [11] £18 **$30**
WILTSHIRE [1837] From *English Counties Delineated.* Vignette & coat of arms. 27x21cm (10½x8½") Color. Margin may be trimmed. ["Bedfordshire", "Durham", "Herefordshire", "Lincolnshire", "Northamptonshire", "Staffordshire" & "Worcestershire" offered at same price] [11] £24 **$40**

MOUNT & PAGE

[ATLAS] THE ENGLISH PILOT THE FOURTH BOOK DESCRIBING THE WEST INDIA NAVIGATION ... PRINTED FOR THOMAS PAGE, WILLIAM AND FISHER MOUNT ... [1725] London: John Seller. Folio, full calf binding, spine & corners renewed. 25 maps. VG. [1761 ed with 28 maps offered for $24,000] Ref: Verner, *The English Coast Pilot.* [3] £16,887 **$28,000**
[ATLAS] THE ENGLISH PILOT FOR THE SOUTHERN NAVIGATION: DESCRIBING THE SEA-COASTS ... OF ENGLAND, SCOTLAND, IRELAND, HOLLAND, FLANDERS, SPAIN, PORTUGAL, TO THE STREIGHT'S-MOUTH; ... BARBARY ... CANARY, MADIERA, CAPE DE VERDE, AND WESTERN ISLANDS ... [1758] London: John Seller. Folio, orig calf; 21 charts. Front cover detached; some lt browning; tears in charts; generally good. Ref: Tooley (M&M) p.61. [3] £2,835 **$4,700**
A CHART OF NEW YORK HARBOUR ... [1784] Appeared in final 3 ed of *The English Pilot, Book IV.* 61x46cm (24x18") Wash color. Exc. [24] £1,689 **$2,800**
A CHART OF THE NORTH SEA FROM THE FORELANDS TO NORTH BERGEN, AND FROM THE SCAW TO THE ORKNEYS AND SHETLANDS [1777] From *The English Pilot.* J. Thompson. Sailing directions; 12 profiles. 4 sheets joined, 88x100cm (34½x39½") Few fold splits, supported on verso; occas margin chips; o/w good. [11] £226 **$375**
A CHART OF THE SEA COAST OF NEW FOUNDLAND, NEW SCOTLAND, NEW ENGLAND, NEW YORK, NEW JERSEY, WITH VIRGINIA AND MARYLAND [c.1750] London: W. & J. Mount and T. Page. 47x59cm (18½x23") Margins trimmed but ample; scattered soiling, minor toning; lower rt corner rounded to border rules; vert fold closed on verso. [A7] £659 **$1,092**
A CORRECT CHART OF HISPANIOLA WITH THE WINDWARD PASSAGE ... BY C. PRICE ... [c.1740] 48x60cm (18½x23½") Color. [34] £520 $863
A CORRECT CHART OF THE CARIBBEE ISLANDS ... [1755] 43x53cm (17x21") OL col. Exc. [45] £513 **$850**
[SAME TITLE] [1758] From *English Pilot.* Puerto Rico to Spanish Main; distorted Trinidad. 43x53cm (17x21") Color. [18] £392 **$650**
A LARGE CHART DESCRIBING YE STREIGHTS OF MALACCA AND SINCAPORE ... CAREFULLY CORRECTED AND COMPARED WITH THE FRENCH CHARTS PUBLISHED IN 1745 [(1703) c.1750] 44x54cm (17½x21½") Color. Verso reinforcement of sh splits at c'fold ends; sm margin repair lower rt; o/w fine. [4] £800 $1,327
A LARGE DRAFT OF THE ISLAND ANTEGUA [1728] From *Coasting Pilot.* 33x25cm (13x10") Outline color. [20] £271 **$450**
A MAP OF THE COAST OF NEW ENGLAND, FROM STATEN ISLAND TO THE ISLAND OF BRETON ... [c.1730] London: F. Mount, T. Page & W. Mount, Tower Hill. 62x80cm (24x31½") Some separation along folds & intersections; minor browning. [A7] £1,526 **$2,530**
A NEW & CORRECT CHART OF CUBA, STREIGHTS OF BAHAMA, WINDWARD PASSAGE, THE CURRENT THROUGH THE GULF OF FLORIDA, ... [1767] 46x64cm (18x25") OL color. Exc. [24] £905 **$1,500**
A NEW AND CORRECT CHART OF THE NORTH PART OF AMERICA FROM NEW FOUND LAND TO HUDSONS BAY [1689-1706 (1751)] As in Part IV, 1751 ed, *The English Pilot.* Thornton revised. 43x55cm (17x22") Exc. Ref: Kershaw (Canada) 221. [43] £513 **$850**

MOUNT & PAGE continued

A NEW AND CORRECT CHART OF THE SEA COAST OF NEW ENGLAND FROM CAPE CODD TO CASCO BAY ... [c.1750] London: W. & J. Mount and T. Page. 50x118cm (19½x46½") Some separation at few folds; minor loss at one intersection. [A7] £1,248 **$2,070**

A NEW AND CORRECT CHART OF THE WESTERN AND SOUTHERN OCEANS SHOWING THE VARIATIONS OF THE COMPASS ACCORDING TO THE LATEST AND BEST OBSERVATIONS [c.1755] As in *The English Pilot*. By Edmund Halley. With text at sides, 58x71cm (23x28") Good. [2] £2,111 **$3,500**

A NEW GENERALL CHART FOR THE WEST INDIES OF E. WRIGHT'S PROJECTION VUT. MERCATOR'S CHART [1789] Atlantic Ocean chart. 45x57cm (17½x22½") Wash color. Few oil stains in sea area. Ref: Phillips (A) 4460-2. [11] £196 **$325**

BAHAMA AND WINDWARD PASSAGE [1706] Appeared in one ed of *English Pilot, Book IV*. Incl S Florida & Greater Antilles. 43x53cm (17x21") C'fold reinforced; else VG. [24] £1,508 **$2,500**

BARBADOS [1721] 29x27cm (11½x10½") Wash color. Exc. [44] £332 **$550**

THE RIVER OF THAMES FROM LONDON TO THE BUOY OF YE NOURE [1779] From *The English Pilot*. The estuary; most of river course in large inset. 47x59cm (18½x23") Color. [11] £178 **$295**

MOUZON

AN ACCURATE MAP OF NORTH AND SOUTH CAROLINA WITH THEIR INDIAN FRONTIERS ... [1775] Sayer & Bennett. Four sheets, joined two & two. 100x141cm (39½x55½") Full orig color. VG. Ref: Cumming (SE) 450; Williams & Johnson (NC) fig.12. Williams & Johnson (NC) [36] £8,443 **$14,000**

MUNSTER *(similar maps may have different titles in various language editions)*

[ATLAS] LA COSMOGRAPHIE UNIVERSELLE [1556] 2nd French ed. Sm folio, paneled calf rebacked. Numerous woodcut maps, views, illus. First few leaves repaired, some letters affected; fine. Ref: Sabin 51398. [3] £21,108 **$35,000**

[BALKANS] [c.1580] Incl Macedonia, Bosnia, Bulgaria, Constantinople. In full sheet with German text. 15x19cm (6x7½") B&W. Lt stain in text; map clean, bright (A). [A3] £70 **$116**

[BOOK WITH MAPS] COSMOGRAPHEI ODER BESCHREIBUNG ALLER LAENDER ... [1556] Petri. Folio; pigskin over wooden board, brass catches & clasps, rear cover wormed; [10], 1233, [1] pp. 38 double-page city views, 10 (of 14?) double-page maps. Stains, minor worming beginning & end; rt part World map tipped to stiff paper; verso cellotape on Vienna view. Maps 3 & 4 from Latin ed; lacks maps 2, 5, 6, 12. Sold as is. [A7] £4,855 **$8,050**

[EUROPE] [c.1590] Untitled west-central Europe on full German text sheet. 12x15cm (4½x6") B&W. Sm stain margin into text; VG (A). [A3] £95 **$157**

[EUROPE AS A WOMAN] [c.1588] As found in *Cosmographia*. Anthropomorphic map orig designed in 1537 by Bucius; royal feminine figure with Iberia at head, Italy & Denmark as arms, etc. 25x17cm (10x6½") B&W. Little surface soil; Fine (A+). [A3] £292 **$484**

AFRICA LIBYA MORENLANDT MIT ALLEN KUNIGREICHEN SO ZU UNSERN ZEITEN DARIN GEFUNDEN WERDEN [1540 / c.1550] 1st modern map of continent. 25x34cm (10x13½") 16th century color. Exc. Ref: Norwich 2. [2] £1,086 **$1,800**

AFRICA, LIBYA, MORLAND, MIT ALLEN KUNIGREICHEN SO ZU UNSERN ZEITEN DARIN GEFUNDEN WERDEN [c.1545] 25x33cm (10x13") Uncolored. VG. Ref: Tooley (Africa) pl.65; Tooley (M&M) p.97. Norwich 2. [A2] £448 **$743**

AFRICA, LYBIA, MORENLANDT MIT ALLEN KOENIGREICHEN SO JETZIGER EIT DARUMB GEFUNDEN WERDEN [1590] From *Cosmographia*. By Petri, appeared after 1580. 31x36cm (12x14") 2 faint dampstains top rt & lf; o/w VG. Ref: Tooley (Africa) p.85, pl.66. Norwich 14. [14] £663 **$1,100**

AFRICA / LYBIA / MORLANDT ... [1540-45] 27x35cm (10½x13½") Uncol. Ref: Norwich 2. [34] £850 $1,410

AFRICA / LYBIA / MOZENLAND [c.1565] With elephant & cyclops. 26x34cm (10x13½") Few wormholes; portion vert fold thinned. [A8] £294 **$488**

AFRICA MIT SEINEN BEFUNDERN LANDERN / THIEREN / UND WUNDERBARLICH EN DINGEN [c.1550] Most of continent on leaf with German text. 12x16cm (4½x6") Full modern color. Sl toning; margin spot; VG (A). [A3] £131 **$218**

AFRICA MIT SEINEM BEFUNDERN LAENDERN THIEREN UND WUNDERBARLICHEN DINGEN [1572] Ptolemaic form. 13x16cm (5x6") New color. Fine. Ref: Norwich 5. [A1] £100 **$165**

ALDENBURG [1614] View on folio text sheet; verso: Magdeburg bird's-eye view. 12x16cm (5x6") [48] DM 280 £97 $160

AMERICAE SIVE NOVI ORBIS, NOVA DESCRIPTIO [c.1580] Without Verrazano Sea. 31x36cm (12x14½") Some text show-through. [A8] £820 **$1,360**

MUNSTER continued

AMERICAE SIVE NOVI ORBIS, NOVA DESCRIPTIO [1582 (1600)] From *Cosmographia* 32x37cm (12½x14½") B&W. Sm part of lower corners built up & reconstructed; good. [1] £724 **$1,200**
[SAME TITLE] [1588] Basle: Petri. Fine. Ref: Shirley (W) 67. [11] £573 **$950**
APHRICAE TABULA IIII [c.1565] On sheet 28x36cm (11x14") Color. Browning; minor wrinkling. [A7] £225 **$373**
BOHEMIAE NOVA DESCRIPTIO TABULA XVII [1552] 29x38cm (11½x15") Color. VG. [24] £166 **$275**
CALARIS SARDINIAE CAPUT [1554] Cagliari; bird's-eye view on folio sheet with legend. 18x18cm (7x7") [48] DM 190 £66 $109
CIVITAS COLONIE [1550+] View across Rhine; 23-item key. 17x37cm (6½x14½") [11] £196 **$325**
CIVITAS FLORENTINA ... [c.1550] Bird's-eye view. 22x36cm (8½x14") [11] £226 **$375**
CIVITAS FRANCKO FORDIANA [1550+] Bird's eye view. 25x40cm (9½x15½") Side margins trimmed to neat line, as issued. [11] £172 **$285**
CIVITAS VENETIO ... [c.1550] Bird's-eye view. 24x39cm (9½x15½") A margin trimmed close; o/w exc. [11] £211 **$350**
CONSTANTINOPOLITANAE URBIS EFFIGIES ... [1550+] Bird's-eye view. 20x38cm (8x15") [11] £151 **$250**
CONTRUSEHEUNG DER SURNEMMEN STATT VENIZIG ... [c.1580] Bird's-eye view. Title above, "La Cite de Venise ..." 27x38cm (10½x15") Color. Exc. [24] £724 **$1,200**
DAS ERST GENERAL INHALTEND DIE BESCHREIBUNG UND DEN CIRCKEL DES GANTZEN ERDTRICHS UND MORES [c.1550] 26x38cm (10½x15") Full color. C'fold reinforced; else exc. Ref: Shirley (W) 92. [24] £1,689 **$2,800**
[SAME TITLE] [c.1550] With Verrazano Sea. 28x37cm (11x14½") Full color. Loss of neatline at bottom c'fold; else VG. [36] £1,447 **$2,400**
[SAME TITLE] [1550 (-1578)] Munster's second world map with "Verrazano Sea" & "DK' initials for David Kandel. 26x38cm (10½x15") B&W. Sm c'fold repair; fine. Ref: Shirley 92, pl.78. [30] £1,387 **$2,300**
DAS HEILIG JUDISCH LANDT MIT AUSZTEILUNG DER ZWOLFF GESCHLECHTER [c.1544-46] 28x35cm (11x14") Pair sm worm holes. Ref: Laor 526. [47] **£240** $398
[SAME TITLE] [1545] 26x34cm (10x13½") Ref: Laor 526. [A8] £208 **$345**
[SAME TITLE] [1572] South at top. 25x34cm (10x13½") New color. Some lt margin staining; some lt spots in sea; o/w fine. Ref: Laor 526. [A1] £796 **$1,320**
DAS KUNIGREICH ENGELLANDT MIT DEM ANSTOSSENDEN RICH SCHOTTLANDT SO VOR ZEITEN ALBION UND BRITANNIA HAN GEHEISSEN [1544-46] Basle: Petri. From the Cosmography. 27x35cm (10½x14") Pair sm worm holes. Ref: Shirley (BI to 1650) 42. [47] **£360** $597
[SAME TITLE] [c.1565] 25x34cm (10x13½") Minor soiling margins. ["Die Laender Asie" sold at same price] [A8] £277 **$460**
[SAME TITLE] [1569] From German ed, *Cosmographia*. 25x34cm (10x13½") Uncolored. Faint age toning along fold; o/w VG to fine. Ref: Shirley (BI to 1650) 45. [A2] £299 **$495**
DE COMITATUS FLANDRIAE [c.1560] 12x15cm (4½x6") [11] £36 **$60**
DE LA COSMOGRAPHIE FLORENCE ... [c.1580] 25x36cm (10x14") Color. Exc. [24] £513 **$850**
DER STATT METZ CIRCKEL, MAWREN UND PORTEN UND FURNEMESTE GEBAW, SAMPT DER BELAGERUNG [1598] Plan with legend on folio sheet. 16x21cm (6½x8½") [48] DM 110 £38 $63
DESCRIPTION NOUVELLE D'EUROPE [1552] North at bottom. 25x34cm (10x13½") Uncolored. Exc. [39] £392 **$650**
DESCRIPTION NOUVELLE DES GAULES [1552] Translation chart at lf, Latin to French. 25x34cm (10x13½") Uncolored. [39] £151 **$250**
DIE ERST GENERAL TAFEL DIE BESCHZEIBUNG UND DEN CIRCKEL DES GANTZEN ERDTRICHE UND PEERS INNHALTENDE [1588] From Petri ed of *Cosmographen* ... Basle. 31x36cm (12x14") Color. Crisp line work. Ref: Shirley (W) 163, pl.134. [13] **Aus$2,200** £999 $1,656
DIE LAENDER ASIE NACH IHRER GELEGENHEIT BISZ IN INDIA WERDEN IN DISER TAFELN VERZEICHNET [1540] 1st separate map of continent. 25x33cm (10x13") VG. Ref: Gole (India) p.20-1, pl.2. [2] £573 **$950**
[SAME TITLE] [1540] Publ in *Cosmographiae Universalis*. 29x37cm (11½x14½") Color. Ref: Clancy (Australis) 64. [13] **Aus$1,500** £681 $1129
DIE NEUWE INSELEN / SO ZU UNSERN ZEITEN DURCH DIE KUNIG VON HISPANIA IM GROSSEN OCEANO GEFUNDEN SINDT [c.1544-46] Basle: Petri. German text. With Verrazano Sea. 28x35cm (11x14") Pair sm worm holes. Ref: Burden 12, state 3. (Note: spelling differs in various editions) [47] **£2,300** $3,814

MUNSTER continued

DIE NEUWEN INSELN / SO HINDER HISPANIAM GEGEN ORIENT / BEY DEM LANDT INDIE LIGEN [c.1557-58] With Verrazano's findings. 26x34cm (10½x13½") Full color. Near fine. Framed. Ref: Skelton (Decorative) pl.7. [1] £1,809 **$3,000**

DIE NEUWEN INSELN SO HINDER HISPANIEN GEGEN ORIENT BEY DEM LANDT INDIE LIEGEN [1540 / 1561?] Narrow "Verrazano Isthmus". 29x37cm (11½x14½") Color. Sl creasing; exc. Ref: Burden 12; Tooley (M&M) pl.80. Cortazzi pl.12. [24] £2,111 **$3,500**

DIE NEWEN INSELN, SO HINDER HISPANIAM GEGEN ORIENT, BEY DEM LANDT INDIE GELEGEN [1598] 31x36cm (12x14") [48] DM 1,800 £621 **$1,030**

DIE STATT AYGSBURG [c.1600] Augsburg view. 26x35cm (10x14") ["Die Statt Solothurn" & "Die Statt Freijberg" (in the East?) offered at same price] [11] £75 **$125**

DIE STATT FRANCKFURT [c.1600] View of Frankfurt-on-the-Oder. 20x29cm (8x11½") ["Die Statt Weissenburg" offered at same price] [11] £60 **$100**

DIE STATT GENFF [c.1600] Geneva bird's-eye view. 15x36cm (6x14") [11] £112 **$185**

DIE STATT HEYDELBERG [c.1600] Panoramic view on 2 joined sheets, 25x72cm (10x28") [11] £166 **$275**

DIE STATT MONTPELLIER [c.1600] Panoramic view; 28-item key. 10x31cm (4x12½") [11] £45 **$75**

DIE STATT PARIS ... [c.1580] Plan view. 28x35cm (11x14") Color. Exc. [24] £724 **$1,200**

DIE STATT ZURICH [c.1600] Bird's-eye view. 18x39cm (7x15½") Printer's crease. [11] £151 **$250**

EUROPA DAS EIN DRITTHEIL DER ERDEN / NACH GELEGENHEIT UNSERER ZEIT BESCHRIEBEN. [1540] South at top. 25x34cm (10x13½") Exc. Ref: Potter illus p.98. [2] £1,086 **$1,800**

[SAME TITLE] [1540 - c.1560] 27x34cm (10½x13½") Uncolored. [34] **£600** $995

EUROPA PRIMA NOVA TABULA [1540] South at top. 31x40cm (12x15½") sheet size. Area & OL color. Early MS notations side margin. [A8] £381 **$632**

[SAME TITLE] [c.1550] 27x34cm (10½x13½") Color. Lt toned; else exc. [24] £603 **$1,000**

FIGURA DEL MONDO UNIVERSALE [c.1540-52] Ptolemaic world; wind head surround; Italian text ed. 28x35cm (11x14") Ref: Shirley (W) 76. [46] **£560** $929

FRANCKFURT AN DER ODER ANNO DNI. 1548 [1552] As in *Cosmographiae Universalis*. Bird's-eye view. 21x30cm (8½x12") Uncolored. Minor repairs. [42] Aus$550 £250 $414

FREYBURG DER FURNEMMEN STATT IN UCHTLANDT WAHRE ABCONTRAFACTUR [1598] View. 11x29cm (4½x11½") [48] DM 320 £110 $183

GALLIA IIII NOVA TABULA [1542] France. 27x34cm (10½x13½") Color. Exc. ["... Europae VII" & "... Europae X" offered at same price] [24] £241 **$400**

GALLIAE REGIONIS NOVA DESCRIPTIO [1540+] 25x34cm (10x13½") ["Francia" (c.1600) offered at same price] [11] £60 **$100**

GEMEINE BESCHREIBUNG ALLER MITNACHTIGEN LANDER / SCHWEDEN / GOTHEN / NORWEGIEN / DENNMARCK & C. [1572] 25x34cm (10x13½") Uncolored. C'fold strengthened & stitch holes closed verso; lt brown spot, faint toning at c'fold; VG to fine. [A2] £299 **$495**

GERMANIA NEW TEUTSCHLANDE ... [c.1600] North at bottom. 31x36cm (12x14½") ["Bohemia", "Tabula Pomeraniae Secundum ..." & "Die Ander Tafel ... Strassburg ... Cobolentz ..." offered at same price] [11] £106 **$175**

GERMANIA VI NOVA TABULA [1552] 29x37cm (11½x14½") Color. C'fold discoloration; else exc. [24] £211 **$350**

HELVETIA PRIMA ET VIII [1552] On sheet 32x40cm (12½x15½") [A7] £347 **$575**

HELVETIAE MODERNA DESCRIPTIO [1550+] 26x35cm (10x13½") ["Nuova Graecia Secundum Omnes Civs Regiones & Provincias ..." offered at same price] [11] £211 **$350**

HISPANIAE REGIONIS NOVA DESCRIPTIO [c.1550] 25x34cm (10x13½") [11] £151 **$250**

INDIA EXTREMA XXIIII. NOVA TABULA [1552] Incl grid system. 29x37cm (11½x14½") B&W. [13] **Aus$1,800** £817 $1,355

ITALIA MIT DEN DREYEN FURNEMPFTEN INSELN CORSICA, SARDINIA UND SICILIA [c.1544-46] In German ed, *Cosmography*. 27x34cm (10½x13½") Pair sm worm holes. [47] **£180** $299

LA TABLE DE LA REGION ORIENTALE COMPRENANT LES DERNIERES TERRES & ROYAUMES D'ASIE [1570+] On sheet 28x36cm (11x14") Color. Ample unevenly trimmed margins; sh tear into image closed, recolored; vert fold partially reinforced on verso. [A7] £208 **$345**

LA TABLE DES ISLES NEUSUES, LESQUELLES ON APPELLE ISLES D'OCCIDENT & D'INDIE POUR DIVERS REGARDZ [1552] 1st French ed. Americas with "Verrazano Sea". 25x33cm (10x13") Exc. Ref: Burden 12, state 5; Kershaw (Canada) p.8, 4d. [2] £2,111 **$3,500**

MUNSTER continued

LA TABLE DU PAYS DE POMERAN, SELON LES PRINCIPAUTEZ, LES VILLES LES PLUS EXCELLENTES ... [1552] Rugen to Gdansk. City arms across top. 24x38cm (9½x15") Uncolored. [39] £136 **$225**

LAUERE DEPINTURA DI COLMARIA CITTA, & DEL CAMPO, CHE LA CIRCONDE [1555] Bird's-eye of Colmar & surroundings. 23x34cm (9x13") B&W. Fine (A+). [A4] £104 **$172**

MEYDENBURG [1598] Bird's-eye view on text sheet; verso: Wolfenbuttel view. 12x15cm (5x6") [48] **DM 280** £97 $160

MODERNA DISCRIZZIONE DELL' EUROPA [c.1558] South at top. 27x35cm (10½x14") Sm hole in border. [46] **£420** $697

MODERNA EUROPAE DESCRIPTIO [c.1550] South at top. 25x34cm (10x13½") [11] £151 **$250**

[SAME TITLE] [1558] 27x34cm (10½x13½") Old color. Top margin tear repaired; faint stain left by old tape. [1] £467 **$775**

NEUEW GRIECHENLANDT [c.1565] 26x34cm (10x13½") Paper restoration lower rt corner & top margin. [A8] £173 **$287**

NEUW INDIA / MIT VILEN ANSTOSSENDEN LENDERN / BESUNDER SCYTHIA / PARTHIA / ARABIA / PERSIA ETC. [1540-46] Basle: Petri. Modern Asia map 28x25cm (11x10") Pair sm worm holes. [47] **£680** $1,128

NOUVELLE DESCRIPTION DU PAYS DE SOUYSSE [1552] Western Switzerland & adjacent. 25x34cm (10x13½") Uncolored. [39] £151 **$250**

[SAME TITLE] [c.1560] On sheet 31x40cm (12x15½") [A7] £294 **$488**

NOVAE INSULAE XXVI NOVA TABULA [1540-45] Lacks the German, "Die Nuw Welt", seen 1544+. 27x34cm (10½x13") Ref: Burden 12, state 2. [34] **£3,000** $4,975

PARIS [c.1600] Bird's-eye view; elaborate border. 25x32cm (10x12½") [11] £106 **$175**

POLONIAE ET UNGARIAE NOVA DESCRIPTIO [1550+] Southern Poland to Black Sea 26x34cm (10x13½") [11] £90 **$150**

PREUSSEN [1554] On folio sheet with Latin text. 10x14cm (3½x5½") [48] **DM 380** £131 $217

PTOLEMAISCH GENERAL TAFEL ... [1540 (c.1545)] Modern world. 1st state, with Verrazano Sea & "Pacific" Ocean. 25x34cm (10x13½") Exc. [43] £1,809 **$3,000**

PTOLEMAISCH GENERAL TAFEL BEGREIFFEND DIE HALBE KUGEL DER WELT [1561] Ptolemaic Old World. 25x34cm (10x13½") Uncol. Faint age toning at vert fold; o/w VG. Ref: Shirley (W) 76. [A2] £763 **$1,265**

PTOLEMAISCH GENERAL TAFEL ... [1588] Basle. Ptolemaic map; 12 windheads. 30x36cm (12x14") B&W. VG. Ref: Shirley (W) 162. [37] £392 **$650**

PTOLEMAISCH GENERAL TAFEL [IN SET WITH] AFRICA [AND] AMERICAE [AND] ASIA [AND] EUROPA [c.1588] Each about 31x36cm (12x14") OL color. Various minor faults; Africa cleanly torn along vert fold. [A7] £1,665 **$2,760**

PTOLEMEISCH GENERAL TAFEL DIE HALBE KUGEL DER WELT BEGREIFFENDE [1540 (1588)] Publ in *Geographia Universalis vetus et Nova ... Ptolemaii ...* 25x34cm (10x13½") Color. Framed. Ref: Shirley (W) 76. [13] **Aus$2,600** £1,181 $1,958

ROMANAE URBIS SITUS, QUEM HOC CHRISTI ANNO 1549 HABET. [c.1550] Bird's-eye view; 19-item key below. 24x36cm (9½x14") Repaired tears into margins & key. [11] £112 **$185**

SARDINIA INSULA [c.1550] 26x15cm (10x6") [11] £45 **$75**

SITUS URBIS ROMAE [c.1600] 29x44cm (11½x17½") Side margins trimmed to neat lines as issued. [11] £54 **$90**

SOLOTHURENSIS CIVITATIS ... [1550+] Bird's-eye view. 23x30cm (9x12") [11] £136 **$225**

SUEVIA ET BAVARIA XI NOVA TABULA [1542] 27x34cm (10½x13½") Color. Good ["Slesiae Descriptio XV", "... Europae V", "... Europae IX" & "... Asiae V" offered at same price] [24] £151 **$250**

SUMATRA EIN GROSSE INSEL ... [1628] Incl S Malaysia; with elephant. 30x36cm (12x14½") [11] £347 **$575**

SYRIA CYPERN PALESTINA MESOPOTAMIA BABYLONIA CHALDEA UND ZWEY ARABIA MIT BERGEN WASSERN UND STATTEN [1572] Middle East; corresponds to "Tabula IIII Asiae". 25x33cm (10x13") New color. Lt age toning & repaired pin holes along c'fold; Ref: Laor 525. [A1] £597 **$990**

TABULA ASIA I [1542] Ptolemaic Turkey. 26x34cm (10½x13½") Color. Exc. ["Italia XIIII" offered at same price] [24] £286 **$475**

TABULA ASIAE X [1542 Ptolemaic India & environs. 26x34cm (10½x13½") Color. Exc.] [24] £136 **$225**

TABULA ASIAE XI [1540 (1542)] Ptolemaic Far East. 25x34cm (10x13½") Exc. [44] £271 **$450**

[SAME TITLE] [c.1550] 25x34cm (10x13½") Bit soiled. [11] £151 **$250**

TABULA ASIAE XII [1540 (1542)] Ptolemaic Taprobana with elephant. 26x34cm (10x13½") Mint. [44] £332 **$550**

MUNSTER continued

TABULA EUROPAE I [1540-] From *Geographia*. Ptolemaic British Isles. 26x33cm (10x13") Ref: Shirley (BI to 1650) 27. [34] £600 **$995**

[SAME TITLE] [c.1570] Ptolemaic British Isles. 30x33cm (12x13") sheet size. [A8] £139 **$230**

TABULA EUROPAE II [1542] Ptolemaic Iberia. 27x34cm (11x13½") Color. VG. ["Aphricae Tabula I" offered at same price] [24] £181 **$300**

[SAME TITLE] [1542] Ptolemaic Iberia. Trapezoidal, 26x34cm (10½x13½") OL color, full color waters. Lt toned; sm tape stains upper corners; wormholes top edge; c'fold reinforced verso. [A10] £243 **$403**

TABULA EUROPAE VIII [1552] Ptolemaic eastern Europe. 27x34cm (10½x13½") B&W. VG (A). [A4] £75 **$124**

TABULA GRECIAE [c.1550] 25x32cm (10x13") B&W. Lt age-toning; else fine. ["Tabula Siciliae et Sardinia" offered at same price] [38] £181 **$300**

TAVOLA DELL'ISOLE NUOVE ... [1571] The New World. Petri ed. Sheet size 32x41cm (12½x16") 3 sm wormholes restored lower margin; verso paper tape fold reinforcement. [A8] £1,110 **$1,840**

TAVOLA DELLA ORIENTAL REGIONE DELL' ASIA [c.1550] 25x33cm (10x13") Col. Exc. [24] £603 **$1,000**

TAVOLA, & DISCRIZZIONE UNIVERSALE DI TUTTA L'AFRICA [c.1565] On sheet 30x40cm (11½x15½") [A7] £156 **$258**

TERRA SANCTA XXIII NOVA TABULA [1545] 31x40cm (12x15½") Color. Sm closed tear bottom 5cm into image; 2 sm wormhole, visible if held to light. Ref: Laor 617. [A8] £208 **$345**

TOURS [c.1600] Bird's-eye view; ornamental border. 25x34cm (10x13½") [11] £60 **$100**

TRANSYLVANIA XXI NOVA TABULA [1542] 26x34cm (10½x13½") Color. VG. ["... Europae III", "... Asiae VII" & "... Asiae IX" offered at same price] [24] £121 **$200**

TYPUS ORBIS TERRARUM [1575] From French ed, *Cosmography*. Francois de Belle-Forest. Woodcut copy of Ortelius. 34x50cm (13½x19½") Uncolored. Closed fold splits & old reinforcement verso; inked longitudes along equator; fine printer's creases; few faint toned spots; o/w VG to fine. Ref: Shirley (W) 135. [A2] £2,455 **$4,070**

TYPUS ORBIS UNIVERSALIS [1550] Ovaloid projection; wind heads, monsters. 26x38cm (10½x15") Color. Ref: Shirley 92, Pl.78 [another, entitled "Das Erst General Inhaltend die Beschreibung und den Circkel des Gantzen Erdtrichs und Moses" offered at Aus$ 3,600]. [13] **Aus$4,200** £1,907 **$3,162**

[SAME TITLE] [c.1550] Oval projection; 12 wind heads; David Kandel's initials. 26x37cm (10½x15") B&W. Fine. Ref: Shirley (W) 92. [38] £1,206 **$2,000**

TYRUS [1554] View from sea on folio sheet with Latin text. 10x11cm (4x4½") [48] **DM 170** £59 **$97**

VALESIAE PRIOR ET VI NOVA TABULA [1542] 26x36cm (10½x14½") Color. Exc. ["Helvetia Prima Rheni ..." & "... Europae IIII" offered at same price] [24] £211 **$350**

VON DEM BANERLANDT [c.1598] From *Cosmographia*. Bavaria. 6x13cm (2½x5") on 8½x13" sheet with text. VG. ["Samartia" & "Von dem Landt Oestereich" offered at same price] [35] £36 **$60**

VON DEM ELSASS [c.1598] From *Cosmographia*. Rhine Valley, Strasbourg to Basle. 9x13cm (3½x5") on 8½x13" sheet with text. VG. [35] £39 **$65**

VON DEM PREUSSEN LANDT [c.1598] From *Cosmographia*. Gulf of Danzig region. 9x13cm (3½x5") on 8½x13" sheet with text. VG. ["Von dem Nortgow" (Bavaria & Bohemia) & "Hystereich" (Italy & Istria) offered at same price] [35] £48 **$80**

MURRAY

MAP TO ILLUSTRATE THE NARRATIVE OF ROBT. ADAMS' ROUTE IN AFRICA [1816] London: John Murray. N & W Africa. 50x37cm (19½x14½") OL color. Little offsetting; binding tear repaired with archival tape; good (B). [A3] £19 **$31**

MYRITIUS

UNIVERSALIS ORBIS DESCRIPTIO; COGIMUR E TABULA PICTOS EDISCERE MUNDOS [1590] 27x40cm (10½x15½") Minor worming repaired; o/w exc example. Ref: Shirley (W) 175, pl.142. Sabin 51650. [2] £4,523 **$7,500**

NAYMILLER and ALLODI

AMERICA SETTENTRIONALE [1867] Milan: Francesco Pagnoni. "Rep. di Texas" indicated. 42x33cm (16½x13") OL color. Lt soiling mostly margin; lacks lower lf margin corner; penciled place names. Ref: cf Phillips (A) 851. [A10] £38 **$63**

NEAL

[BOOK WITH MAPS] THE HISTORY OF NEW ENGLAND CONTAINING AN IMPARTIAL ACCOUNT OF THE CIVIL AND ECCLESIASTICAL AFFAIRS OF THE COUNTRY TO THE YEAR OF OUR LORD 1700 [1720] London. 2 vols, octavo; x, 712, xv; with folding map, "A New Map of New England According to the Latest Observations", printed for Clark, Ford & Cruttendon. 23x53cm (9x21") Full orig leather binding rebacked. Ref: Phillips (M) p.468. [11] £1,659 **$2,750**

NELL

NELL'S MAP OF COLORADO [1906] Louis Nell. Pocket map folded into 12mo gold-embossed cloth covers with 12 pp gazetteer. 72x99cm (28½x39") OL & full color by county. Cover lt rubbed; occas corner separation, repaired margin fold separation; VG. [5] £193 **$320**

NEWTON & BERRY

NEWTON'S NEW & IMPROVED TERRESTRIAL GLOBE. PUBLISHED BY NEWTON, SON & BERRY ... [c.1830] In black, shagreen covered case with clasps, lined with celestial charts. Diameter: 8cm (3") Color. Patina, areas of faint discoloration; else exc. [23] £3,920 **$6,500**

NICHELSON

A DRAUGHT OF THE GREAT BAY, BACK BAY AND HARBOUR OF TRINCOMALAY, ON THE ISLAND OF ZELOAN ... [1770] Two joined sheets, 91x98cm (36x38½") [11] £513 **$850**

DRAFT OF MATHEWERN BAY, ON THE NORTH SIDE OF THE ISLAND OF DIEGO RAYES ... [1770] Two joined sheets, 85x129cm (33½x51") [11] £232 **$385**

NOLIN   Try *Coronelli*

AMERIQUE OU LE NOUVEAU CONTINENT ... [1759] Inset of de Fonte's NW America. 46x69cm (18x27") Full orig color. Fine. Framed. [36] £1,025 **$1,700**

ARCHIPELAGUE DU MEXIQUE OU SONT LES ISLES DE CUBA, ESPAGNOLE, IAMAIQUE AVEC LES ISLES LUCAYES, ET LES ISLES CARIBES, PAR LE P. CORONELLI ... [1688] 45x60cm (17½x23½") Orig OL color. Few areas of weakening of plate; else exc. [23] £1,086 **$1,800**

ATLAS GENERAL A L'USAGE DES COLLEGES ET MAISONS D'EDUCATION ... 1783 ... A PARIS ... [1783] School atlas; retrograde geography. Quarto, quarter calf, paper over boards, worn; 48 maps in OL color & plates. A plate shaved at bottom; few faint stains; paper bright, fresh; internally exc. Ref: Phillips (A) 4297. [24] £3,438 **$5,700**

L'AFRIQUE DRESSEE SUR LES RELATIONS LES PLUS RECENTES ET RECTIFICES SUR LES DERNIERES OBSERVATIONS DEDIEE ET PRESENTEE A SA MAJESTI TRE CHRESTIENNE LOUIS XV [1740] Separately issued. 25[+] panels all around. 122x136cm (48x53½") OL color on map; full color on cartouche & panels. Mounted on orig linen; some fold wear; a stain; untreated; fresh. [23] £7,237 **$12,000**

LA TERRE SAINTE DIVISEE EN SES DOUZE TRIBUS [1756] 46x66cm (18½x26") OL color. Margins trimmed just beyond border. Ref: Laor 536. [A8] £139 **$230**

NORIE

A CHART OF THE SOUTHERN PART OF THE NORTH SEA SHEWING THE NAVIGATION FROM THE THAMES, HARWICH AND DOWNS, TO CALAIS, DUNKIRK, OSTEND ... [1853] Blue-backed; 2 insets. 126x79cm (50x31") Fine. [15] £106 **$175**

A NEW CHART OF THE CARRIBEAN ISLES CALLED ALSO THE WINDWARD & LEEWARD ISLANDS FROM PORTO RICO TO TRINIDAD [1828] Blue-back chart. 63x93cm (25x36½") Minor vert cracking; chips lower margin, one into bottom lf border; fine. [15] £271 **$450**

NORTHWEST PUBLISHING CO.

PLAT BOOK OF NODAWAY COUNTY MISSOURI [1893] Large folio; cloth; 37 of 38 colored maps; commemorative map laid in. Covers worn; crudely rebacked; sporadic margin soiling; occas edge wear; title torn; some pencil marks; maps mostly VG Ref: LeGear (US) 2137; Phillips (A) 2086. [A9] £111 **$184**

NUREMBERG CHRONICLE   See *Schedel*

OGILBY   Try *Montanus*

[BOOK WITH MAPS] AMERICA BEING THE LATEST, AND MOST ACCURATE DESCRIPTION OF THE NEW WORLD [1671] 3 folio volumes, old full leather bindings, gold tooling, raised bands, in half leather slipcase box; 19 maps, 31 views, 6 portraits, 57 full page engravings, etc. Cover worn at edges & spine, some hinge weakening; a view detached; images time toned, some spots, repaired tears, sm holes; interior generally clean. [33] £11,157 **$18,500**

OGILBY continued

ARX CAROLINA [1670] 28x35cm (11x14") Few mends. VG. [24] £271 **$450**

CHILI [1670] 29x36cm (11½x14") Later color. Minor crinkling & soiling lower third; reinforcement near lower c'fold verso. [A9] £125 **$207**

INSULAE AMERICANAE IN OCEANO SEPTENTRIONALI, CUM TERRIS ADIACENTIBUS [1671] From *America*. 28x36cm (11x14") Fine dark impression. [46] £380 **$630**

MAPPA AESTIVARUM INSULARUM ... [1670] Publ in *America* ... List of tribes below. 29x36cm (11½x14") Full color. [20] £1,357 **$2,250**

NOVA VIRGINIAE TABULA [1671] 29x36cm (11½x14") Color. Fine. Ref: Phillips (VA) p.41-2. [14] £1,086 **$1,800**

NOVI BELGII, QUOD NUNC NOVI JORCK VOCATUR, NOVAE QE ANGLIAE & PARTIS VIRGINIAE ... [1670] Derivative of Jansson-Visscher series. 29x36cm (11½x14½") Color. Exc. Ref: Tooley (Amer) p.289, #21, pl.157. [23] £905 **$1,500**

NOVISSIMA ET ACCURATISSIMA BARBADOS. DESCRIPTIO PER JOHANNEM OGILVIUM. COSMOGRAPHUM REGIUM [1671] As in *America*. 29x36cm (11½x14") OL color. [20] £694 **$1,150**

NOVISSIMA ET ACCURATISSIMA JAMAICAE DESCRIPTIO PER JOHANNEM OGILVIUM. COSMOGRAPHUM REGIUM [1671] Publ in *America*. Based on 1670 survey. 43x54cm (17x21") Full color. Ref: Kapp (Jamaica) 13. [20] £1,674 **$2,775**

PARAQUARIA VULGO PARAGUAY CUM ADJACENTIBUS [1671] 29x37cm (11½x14½") B&W. Lt foxing along c'fold; few faint spots blank areas; narrow top margin; VG. [A1] £83 **$138**

PORTO RICO [1671] San Juan view. 28x34cm (11x13½") Color. C'fold reinforced; minor repair; VG. [23] £513 **$850**

PORTUS ACUPULCO [1673] View. 28x36cm (11x14") [41] £211 **$350**

TABULA MAGELLANICA, QUA TIERRAE DE FUEGO ... [1670] Much decoration. 29x36cm (11½x14") Fine dark impression. [46] £380 **$630**

THE CITTY OSACCO - DE STADT OSACCO [(1669) 1670] From *Atlas Jappanensis*. 1st Western view; pirated from Montanus. 26x70cm (10x27½") Uncolored. Exc. ["Miako" (Kyoto) offered at same price] Ref: Cortazzi pl.73. [4] £500 **$829**

THE ROAD FROM BRISTOL ... TO EXETER ... [1675] From *Britannia*. Strip map in form of scrolls; pictorial roadside features. 33x43cm (13x17") Col. VG. [Bristol to Weymouth offered at same price] [38] £211 **$350**

THE ROAD FROM TINMOUTH ... TO ... CARLISLE [1675] From *Britannia*. Strip map in form of scrolls; pictorial roadside features. Incl Newcastle. 33x43cm (13x17") Color. VG. [London to Darby offered at same price] [38] £181 **$300**

THE ROAD FROM WELSHPOOL ... TO ... CARNARVAN ... [1675] From *Britannia*. Strip map in form of scrolls; pictorial roadside features. 33x43cm (13x17") Color. VG. [38] £196 **$325**

VENEZUELA CUM PARTE AUSTRALI NOVAE ANDALUSIAE [1671] From *America*. 29x36cm (11½x14") B&W. Fine. [30] £332 **$550**

VIRGINIAE PARTIS AUSTRALIS ET FLORIDAE PARTIS ORIENTALIS INTERJACENTIUMQ REGIONUM NOVA DESCRIPTIO [1671] 29x36cm (11½x14") Color. VG. Ref: Cumming (SE) 67. [38] £573 **$950**

[SAME TITLE] [1671] 29x36cm (11½x14") Color. Sl time-toned; VG. [29] £694 **$1,150**

OLNEY

[ATLAS] A NEW AND IMPROVED SCHOOL ATLAS ... [1831] D.F. Robinson. Quarto, yellow wraps; 12 colored maps incl double-page U.S. Worn wraps; maps soiled with dog-eared corners; only good. [6] £112 **$185**

[ATLAS] OLNEY'S SCHOOL ATLAS CONTAINING ... 13 MAPS ... [c.1841] NY: Robinson, Pratt & Co. Big quarto; 5 double page maps; Republic of Texas appears 3 times. Limp printed boards worn, stained; home made calico cover. [1848 ed, with 25 maps, offered at $550] [16] £271 **$450**

ENVIRONS OF NEW YORK [ON SHEET WITH] PHILADELPHIA AND TRENTON [AND] PORTLAND [AND] CHARLESTON [AND] BOSTON [AND] BALTIMORE AND WASHINGTON [1833] Incl 20 to 40 mile surroundings. 27x23cm (10½x9") Uncolored. VG. [New Orleans with Mobile, Savannah, St. Louis, Cincinnati & Chicago offered at same price] [25] £36 **$60**

MAP OF AFRICA ... [1864] From *Olney's Atlas* ... 22x28cm (8½x11") Full color. Few spots; close bottom margin; good (B). [A3] £16 **$26**

MAP OF CANADA [1864] From *Olney's Atlas* ... E & W Canada; inset of Maritimes. 22x28cm (8½x11") Lt full color. Few spots; good (B). [A3] £10 **$17**

MAP OF CANADA AND NEW-YORK [1864] From *Olney's Atlas* ... Incl New England states. 27x44cm (10½x17½") Full color. Few spots; surface soiling; good (B). [A3] £7 **$11**

OLNEY continued

MAP OF MICHIGAN, WISCONSIN AND MINNESOTA   [1864]   From *Olney's Atlas* ...   Eastern MN only. 22x28cm (8½x11") Full color. Good (B).   [A3]   £13   **$22**

MAP OF NORTH AMERICA   [1864]   From *Olney's Atlas* ...   28x22cm (11x8½")   Full color. Few spots; good (B).   [A3]   £19   **$32**

MAP OF NORTH AMERICA TO ILLUSTRATE OLNEY'S NEW SCHOOL GEOGRAPHY   [1829 (c.1842)]   Incl Texas Republic & maximum Oregon Terr. 25x22cm (10x8½") Full color. Sm ink spot near title; o/w VG.   [25]   £36   **$60**

MAP OF NORTH AMERICA TO ILLUSTRATE OLNEY'S SCHOOL GEOGRAPHY   [1858]   Sherman & Smith; NY: Pratt, Oakley & Co. 27x22cm (10½x9") Full color. VG.   [16]   £36   **$60**

MAP OF THE SOUTH WESTERN AND PART OF THE WESTERN STATES   [1858]   School geography. Sherman & Smith; NY: Pratt, Oakley & Co. 46x27cm (18x11") Full col. Minor stains; fold repair; good.   [16]   £60   **$100**

[SAME TITLE]   [1864]   From *Olney's Atlas* ...   Covers IL, MS, AR, MO, IA, parts of KS, TX, Indian Terr. 46x27cm (18x10½") Full color. Few spots; good (B).   [A3]   £6   **$10**

MAP OF THE SOUTHERN STATES   [1864]   From *Olney's Atlas* ...   Covers NC, SC, TN, AL, GA. part of FL. 27x44cm (10½x17½") Full color. Few spots; surface soiling; good (B).   [A3]   £23   **$38**

MAP OF THE UNITED STATES, CANADA, TEXAS AND PART OF MEXICO   [c.1844]   Sherman & Smith. Hartford: Robinson. 27x44cm (10½x17½") Full orig color. Good.   [16]   £166   **$275**

MAP OF THE UNITED STATES TO ILLUSTRATE OLNEY'S SCHOOL GEOGRAPHY   [1828 (1842)]   Independent TX; distance chart in location of future US southwest. 25x43cm (10x17") Full color. Minor age toning; quite bright.   [25]   £75   **$125**

MAP OF THE WORLD ON GLOBULAR PROJECTION   [IN SET WITH]   A CHART OF THE WORLD SHOWING ... THE GREAT PHYSICAL FEATURES OF THE GLOBE   [1855-64]   From *Olney's Atlas* ...   Globular in full color, bit faded; chart with little interior continental detail (for student testing?) Each about 30x47cm (11½x18½") Toning, some foxing; good (B).   [A3]   £31   **$51**

WESTERN TERRITORIES OF THE UNITED STATES   [1847 (1850)]   Publ in School Atlas. NW U.S. 28x44cm (11x17½") Full color.   [41]   £112   **$185**

[SAME TITLE]   [1864]   From *Olney's Atlas* ...   West from MN; south to Santa Fe. 28x44cm (11x17½") Full color. Few spots; good (B).   [A3]   £52   **$87**

ORTELIUS (Folio)

[ATLAS]   THEATRUM ORBIS TERRARUM   [1570]   1st ed, 2nd variant of 4. Folio, modern full calf; 53 maps, few reinforced at margins. VG. Ref: Phillips (A) 374. Koeman Ort 1B; Karrow (16c) p.4.   [3]   £27,139   **$45,000**

[SAME TITLE]   [1579]   1st Plantin ed. Folio, rebound in 17th c speckled calf; 83 mapsheets in orig color. Sl browning & toning throughout consistent with age; 3 leaves with wormholes & early repairs lower rt, text unaffected; some show-through of arsenic green. Ref: Koeman Ort 15A.   [A8]   £38,659   **$64,100**

[FACSIMILE ATLAS]   THEATRUM ORBIS TERRARUM   [1964]   Amsterdam. "First Series - Volume III". After 1570 Antwerp ed in Universiteitsbibliotheek, Amsterdam. Folio; cloth; dust jacket.   [A7]   £242   **$402**

[PORTRAIT]   SPECTANDUM DEDIT ORTELIUS MORTALIB.ORBEM ORBI SPECTANDUM GALLEUS ORTELIUM. PAPIUS   [1579]   Portrait by Galle in *Theatrum* ...   32x21cm (12½x8½") Color. Sm rust hole in forehead filled; o/w fine.   [4]   **£260** $431

ABRAHAMI PATRIARCHAE PEREGRINATIO ET VITA ...   [1590-]   Holy Land; surround of 22 medallions. Without pagination, from early "Addendum". 35x46cm (14x18") Uncol. Ref: Laor 547.   [34]   **£1,500** $2,487

[SAME TITLE]   [1590 / ?]   Surround of 22 medallions. 35x46cm (14x18") Color. Exc. Ref: Laor 547. Nebenzahl (Holy Land) 34.   [24]   £2,262   **$3,750**

AEGYPTUS ANTIQUA   [1595]   North at rt. 36x51cm (14x20½") Full color. Exc.   [45]   £332   **$550**

AENEAE TROIANI NAVIGATIO ...   [1594]   Voyages in Eastern Mediterranean. 35x48cm (13½x19") Color. Exc.   [24]   £513   **$850**

[SAME TITLE]   [1595]   From the *Parergon*.   Aeneas voyages in Eastern Mediterranean. 34x49cm (13½x19½") Margins trimmed but ample, verso text affected; sm brown spots.   [A7]   £225   **$373**

AFRICAE PROPRIAE TABULA   [1590]   34x48cm (13x19") Color. Sh margin tears; sl margin browning.   [A8]   £329   **$546**

AFRICAE TABULA NOVA   [1570]   37x50cm (15x20") Full orig color. VF. Ref: Tooley (Africa) p.84 color illus, 88. Norwich 10.   [45]   £1,327   **$2,200**

[SAME TITLE]   [c.1570]   37x50cm (15x20") Later color. Exc.   [2]   £754   **$1,250**

[SAME TITLE]   [1570 / ?]   37x50cm (14½x19½") Color. Exc.   [24]   £1,327   **$2,200**

ORTELIUS (Folio) continued

AFRICAE TABULA NOVA [1570 - c.1600] 37x50cm (14½x19½") Color. [34] **£950** $1,576
[SAME TITLE] [1571 or later] Issued before crack in plate. 38x50cm (15x20") Color. Moderate uniform toning; sh tears into image & at fold closed on verso. [A8] **£485 $805**
[SAME TITLE] [c.1580] 37x50cm (14½x19½") Orig color, later additions. Restored. Ref: Van den Broecke 8. [46] **£920** $1,526
AMERICAE SIVE NOVI ORBIS, NOVA DESCRIPTIO [1587] 3rd state; South American bulge removed. 36x48cm (14x19") Newer color. Fine. Ref: Burden 64; Portinaro & Knirsch pl.54. [14] **£3,015 $5,000**
[SAME TITLE] [1587] 36x48cm (14x19") Full orig color. Mint. [45] **£3,920 $6,500**
[SAME TITLE] [1588 or later] 36x48cm (14x19") Area & OL color. Sl toned; verso fold reinforcement. [A8] **£2,358 $3,910**
ANGLIAE REGNI FLORENTISSIMI NOVA DESCRIPTIO, AUCTORE HUMFREDO LHUYD DENBYGIENSE [1573-1587] From *Theatrum* ... 2nd state with corrected mileage scale. 38x47cm (15x18½") Orig color. Margin ink stain Ref: Shirley (BI to 1650) 98. [34] **£750** $1,244
[SAME TITLE] [1595] 38x48cm (15x18½") Orig color. Ref: Shirley (BI to 1650) 98. Van den Broecke 19; Koeman Ort 29. [46] **£560** $929
ANGLIAE, SCOTIAE, ET HIBERNIAE, SIVE BRITANNICAR:INSULARUM DESCRIPTIO [1570] 34x50cm (13½x19½") Early color. Framed. [A6] **£414** $687
[SAME TITLE] [1579] From *Theatrum* ... After Mercator; west at top. 34x50cm (13½x19½") Orig body color. Sm scuff marks in sea area. Ref: Shirley (BI to 1650) 86, pl.42. [47] **£720** $1,194
[SAME TITLE] [c.1590] 34x50cm (13½x19½") Color. Some c'fold wear, sl plate surface loss. Framed. [A5] **£322** $534
ARCHIPELAGI INSULARUM ALIQUOT DESCRIP. [c.1590] Crete & 10 other islands. 36x50cm (14x20") Color. Restoration at lower corners with pen facsimile. [A5] **£81** $135
ASIAE NOVA DESCRIPTIO [1570] From *Theatrum* ... 37x49cm (14½x19½") Orig color. Ref: Walter (Japan) 11C; Clancy (Australis) p.25. [13] **Aus$2,280** £1,035 $1,717
[SAME TITLE] [1570-] From *Theatrum* ... 1st state; faint "cum privilegio" lower lf. 37x49cm (14½x19½") Uncolored. [34] **£1,400** $2,322
AUSTRIAE DESCRIP. PER WOLFGANGUM LAZIUM [1598] 35x48cm (14x19") Full orig color. Exc. [23] **£392 $650**
AUSTRIAE DUCATUS CHOROGRAPHIA, WOLFGANGO LAZIO AUCTORE ... [1570] From *Theatrum* ... 34x47cm (13½x18½") Color. Ref: Koeman Ort 1A-1D, 27. [42] **Aus$1,500** £681 $1,129
BARBARIAE ET BILEDULGERID, NOVA DESCRIPTIO [c.1580] 33x50cm (13x20") Color. Ref: Koeman Ort 53. [48] **DM 980** £338 $561
BASILIENSIS TERRITORII DESCRIPTIO NOVA, AUCTORE SEBASTIANO MUNSTERO ... [1573] As in *Ein Zusatz bie dass Theatrum* ... North to Baden with part of Alsace. 32x24cm (12½x9½") Period color. [42] **Aus$850** £386 $640
BITURIGUM EXACTISS: DESCRIPTIO PER D. IOANNEM CALAMAEUM [1570] From *Theatrum* ... Central France. 31x31cm (12x12") Period color. Ref: Koeman Ort 1A, 1D. [42] **Aus$650** £295 $489
BRITANNICARUM INSULARUM TYPUS ... [1595] From *Theatrum* ... Reduction of earlier 2-sheet map; west at top. 36x50cm (14½x20") Colored cartouches. Fine. Ref: Shirley (BI to 1650) 186, pl.71. [14] **£513 $850**
[SAME TITLE] [1595] From *Theatrum* ... Ancient British Isles. 36x51cm (14½x20") Period color. [42] **Aus$3,500** £1,589 $2,635
BURGUNDIAE INFERIORIS, QUAE DUCATUS NOMINE CENSETUR, DES. 1584 [1584] From *Additamentum III* ... 37x46cm (14½x18") Color. Ref: Koeman Ort 18, 3. [42] **Aus$1,100** £500 $828
CAMBRIAE TYPUS [1584] 37x49cm (14½x19½") Contemp color. [A6] **£230** $382
CHINAE, OLIM SINARUM REGIONIS, NOVA DESCRIPTIO. AUCTORE LUDOVICO GEORGIO [1584] 1st printed European map of China. 37x47cm (14½x18½") Color. Exc. Ref: Walter (Japan) p.186, 11F; Tooley (M&M) pl.78. [24] **£2,231 $3,700**
CULIACANAE AMERICAE REGIONIS DESCRIPTIO ... [ON SHEET WITH] **HISPANIOLAE, CUBAE, ALIARUMQUE INSULARUM CIRCUMIACENTIUM, DELINEATIO** [1581] Greater Antilles; western Mexico. 36x50cm (14x19½") Bit toned; sl browned along fold. [A8] **£294 $488**
CYPRI INSULAE NOVA DESCRIPT. [1573] 36x50cm (14x19½") Lt darkening at vert fold; lt stains margin; 3 sm wormholes on image. [A8] **£329 $546**
[SAME TITLE] [1573 / 1598] 35x50cm (14x19½") Orig color. Fine. [23] **£724 $1,200**
DAPHNE [1598] Classical town in Asia Minor. 36x48cm (14½x19") Orig color. Exc. [23] **£452 $750**

ORTELIUS (Folio) continued

ERYN. HIBERNIAE, BRITANNICAE INSULAE, NOVA DESCRIPTIO. IRLANDT [1573] 36x48cm (14x19") Partial OL color. Lt darkening along vert fold. [A8] £381 **$632**

EUROPAE [1570 / ?] 34x46cm (13½x18") Color. Lower c'fold reinforced; else exc. [24] £905 **$1,500**

[SAME TITLE] [1612] From *Theatrum* ... 34x46cm (13½x18½") Color. Fine. [37] £603 **$1,000**

FLANDRIAE COMITATUS DESCRIPTIO [1592] 37x49cm (15x19½") Uncolored. Minor foxing & soiling, mostly margins; faint c'fold toning. [A9] £97 **$161**

FORI IULII ACCURATA DESCRIPTIO [1574] Venice to Trieste. 36x48cm (14x19") Early col. [11] £392 **$650**

FRANCIAE ORIENTALIS (VULGO FRANCKENLANT) DESCRIPTIO [c.1580] Franconia, Germany. 36x25cm (14½x10") Color. [48] DM 950 £328 **$544**

GALLIA [1612] Plancius map appeared only in Ortelius atlas from 1606 to 1612, publ by Vrients. 40x48cm (16x19") Color. Exc. [24] £1,508 **$2,500**

GALLIA VETUS [1595] Dated 1590. Ancient Gaul. 36x46cm (14x18½") Color. Fine. Ref: Koeman, Ort 25 (10). [37] £452 **$750**

GALLIAE REGNI POTENTISS: NOVA DESCRIPTIO, IOANNE IOLIVETO AUCTORE [1570-1573] From *Theatrum* ... Early ed. 34x46cm (13½x18") Color. Ref: Van den Broecke 34. [46] £320 **$531**

GERMANIA [c.1574] From *Theatrum* ... Central Europe. 36x51cm (14½x20") Col. Fine. [14] £452 **$750**

GORITIAE, KARSTII, CHACZEOLAE, CARNIOLAE, HISTRIAE, ET WINDORUM MARCHAE DESCRIP [1573] As in *Ein Zusatz bei dass Theatrum* ... 34x23cm (13½x9") Period color. [42] Aus$750 £341 **$565**

GRAECIAE UNIVERSAE SECUNDUM HODIE R'NUM SITUM NEOTERICA DESCRIPTIO [1598] 36x50cm (14x20") Full orig color. Printer's crease; exc. Ref: Zacharakis 1610. [24] £573 **$950**

HELVETIAE DESCRIPTIO AEGIDIO TSCHUDO AUCT. [1572] 34x46cm (13½x18") [A7] £208 **$345**

[SAME TITLE] [1574] 34x44cm (13½x17½") New color. Some margin age toning; sm worm hole near c'fold top margin; image fine. [14] £573 **$950**

HISPANIAE NOVA ... 1579 [1598] 34x50cm (13½x19½") Contemp color; green sl oxidized. [1598 edition, color, some staining below, sold at £230] [A6] £253 **$420**

HISPANIOLAE, CUBAE, ALIARUMQUE INSULARUM CIRCUMIACIENTIUM ... [1579-] 1st state; Tropic of Cancer is given as Capricorn until 1590. Bahamas to Mexico. 35x50cm (14x19½") Uncol. [34] £850 **$1,410**

HUNGARIAE DESCRIPTIO, WOLFGANGO LAZIO AUCT. [1598] 36x50cm (14x19½") Orig color. Exc. [23] £407 **$675**

IAPONIAE INSULAE DESCRIPTIO LUDOICO TEISERA AUCTORE ... [1595] 35x48cm (14x19") Full orig color. Exc. Ref: Cortazzi p.24-5; Walter (Japan) IV.1, 19. [2] £3,317 **$5,500**

[SAME TITLE] [1595] 35x48cm (14x19") Color. Exc. [45] £2,714 **$4,500**

[SAME TITLE] [(1595) c.1603] 1st atlas map of Japan. Insular Korea. 36x49cm (14x19") Color. Fine. Ref: Walter (Japan) 5; Cortazzi pl.2; MCC 36 #2. [4] £2,500 **$4,146**

ILLYRICUM [1572] Covers Croatia, Bosnia & Serbia. 37x48cm (14½x18½") Full color. Lt toning; lt printer's crease; margins trimmed to ½" from neat line; old MS in margin; VG (A). [A3] £265 **$440**

INDIAE ORIENTALIS INSULARUMQUE ADIACIENTIUM TYPUS [1570] From *Theatrum* ... 37x52cm (14½x20½") Orig color. Ref: Tooley (Australia) 937; Clancy (Australis) p.71. [13] Aus$3,300 £1,499 **$2,485**

[SAME TITLE] [1570] Incl NW American coast. 35x50cm (14x20") Full orig color. VF. Ref: Humphreys illus p.68. [45] £2,111 **$3,500**

[SAME TITLE] [c.1570] No text verso. 35x50cm (13½x19½") B&W. [20] £1,794 **$2,975**

[SAME TITLE] [(1570) 1598] From *Theatrum* ... 35x50cm (13½x19½") Orig color. Minor reinforcement lower c'fold; Sl creasing lower rt; lt margin waterstaining. Ref: Walter (Japan) 11D; Cortazzi pl.17; Koeman Ort 31; Van den Broecke 166. [4] £1,450 **$2,405**

[SAME TITLE] [1598] 35x50cm (14x19½") Full orig color. Fine. Ref: Quirino p.76. [23] £1,689 **$2,800**

INSULAR ALIQUOT AEGEAN ... [1584] 10 island, incl Cyprus, Rhodes, Lesbos. [no dimens] C'fold split repaired; else VG. Ref: Zacharakis 1456. [37] £513 **$850**

INSULARUM ALIQUOT MARIS MEDITERRANEI DESCRIPTIO [1570] 6 maps: Sicily, Sardinia, Corfu, Zerbi, Elba, Malta. 36x48cm (14½x19") Color. Fine. [37] £302 **$500**

[SAME TITLE] [c.1570] 6 maps: Sicily, Sardinia, Corfu, Zerbi, Elba, Malta. 36x48cm (14½x19") Sl browning at vert fold. [A7] £139 **$230**

[SAME TITLE] [c.1600] 6 maps: Sicily, Sardinia, Corfu, Zerbi, Elba, Malta. 36x48cm (14x19") Lt stains & darkening along vert fold & margins. [A8] £121 **$201**

ITALA NAME TELLUS GRAECIA MAIOR ERAT. [1624] From *Parergon*. Southern Italy; S at top. 34x48cm (13½x19") Ref: Van den Broecke 210. [46] £230 **$382**

ORTELIUS (Folio) continued

ITALIAE NOVISSIMA DESCRIPTIO ...   [1570 (1574)]   After Gastaldi. 36x51cm (14x20") Subtle color. Lt age-toned; else fine. Ref: Koeman, Ort 12.   [37]   £513   **$850**

[SAME TITLE]   [1584]   1st issue of new plate; based on Gastaldi. 36x55cm (14x21½") Full color. Exc. Ref: Van den Broecke 118.   [24]   £905   **$1,500**

LA FLORIDA [ON SHEET WITH] GUASTECAN [1584] Portion of folio sheet with 3 maps of Spain's New World empire. Florida 15x23cm (6x9") Full orig color. Exc. Ref: cf Schwartz & Ehrenberg pl.35 & Burden 57.   [44]   £452   **$750**

LA FLORIDA [ON SHEET WITH] PERUVIAE AURIFERAE REGIONIS TYPUS. DIDACO MENDEZIO AUCTORE [AND] GUASTECAN REG.   [1584] From *Theatrum* ... 3 maps: Spain's New World empire; 1st printed map of American Southeast. 33x46cm (13x18") Orig color. Exc. Ref: Burden 57; Cumming (SE) 5; Goss (NA) 13.   [24]   £1,206   **$2,000**

[SAME TITLE]   [1584 / 1612]   1st separate map of Florida. 34x46cm (13½x18½") Full orig color. VG. Ref: Cumming (SE) 5; Schwartz & Ehrenberg pl.35; Portinaro & Knirsch p.210.   [2]   £1,025   **$1,700**

LATIUM   [1624]   From *Parergon*. Ancient Latium. 36x46cm (14x18") Ref: Van den Broecke 209.   [46]   £230 $382

LEODIENSIS DIOCESIS TYPUS [n.d.] 38x49cm (15x19½") Orig col. Lt image transfer; o/w fine.   [A1]   £126   **$209**

LORRAINE. LOTHARINGIAE NOVA DESCRIPTIO   [1582]   34x50cm (13½x20") Color. Some lt soiling & occas lt foxing in margin; VG.   [A1]   £150   **$248**

LUTZENBURGENSIS DUCATUS ...   [1598]   36x49cm (14½x19½") Orig color. Exc.   [23]   £573   **$950**

[SAME TITLE]   [1602]   From Spanish ed, *Theatrum* ... 37x50cm (14½x19½") Full orig color. Ref: Van den Broecke 60 (3rd state).   [47]   **£390** $647

MARIS PACIFICI, (QUOD VULGO MAR DEL ZUR) CUM REGIONIBUS CIRCUMIACENTIBUS, INSULISQUE IN CODEM PASSIM SPARSIS, NOVISSIMA DESCRIPTIO [1589] From *Theatrum* ... 35x50cm (13½x19½") Orig color. Ref: Burden 74; Campbell (Early) pl.9. Tooley (Landmarks) p.200; Clancy (Australis) p.65; Goss (NA) 14.   [13]   **Aus$7,900**   £3,588 $5,949

[SAME TITLE]   [1589]   34x50cm (13½x19½") Full orig col. Mint.   [45]   £4,704   **$7,800**

[SAME TITLE]   [1590]   From *Theatrum* ...   34x50cm (13½x19½") Uncolored.   [34]   £4,600 $7,628

[SAME TITLE]   [1590 (1601)]   35x50cm (13½x19½") Full color. Faint c'fold darkening; few pinholes repaired; else fine. Ref: Wagner (NW) p.73; Cortazzi pl.21.   [38]   £3,166   **$5,250**

[SAME TITLE]   [1602] 35x50cm (13½x19½") Col. Exc. Ref: Wagner (NW) p.74, #156.   [23]   £3,317   **$5,500**

NATOLIAE, QUAE OLIM ASIA MINOR, NOVA DESCRIPTIO [ON SHEET WITH] AEGYPTI RECENTIOR DESCRIPTIO [AND] CARTHAGINIS CELEBERRIMI SINUS TYPUS [1603] 32x49cm (12½x19½") Later full color. Mild soiling margins & c'fold.   [A9]   £153   **$253**

PALAESTINAE SIVE TOTIUS TERRAE PROMISSIONIS NOVA DESCRIPTIO AUCTORE TILEMANNO STELLA SIGENENS   [1570]   Nile Delta to Beirut, with Exodus path. 34x46cm (13½x18") Orig color. VG to fine. Ref: Laor 540B.   [14]   £844   **$1,400**

[SAME TITLE]   [1570 (1608)]   3rd state. 34x46cm (13½x18") Subtle color. C'fold repaired; else VG. Ref: TMC 3, p.28-31.   [37]   £754   **$1,250**

[SAME TITLE]   [1579]   35x46cm (14x18") Wash & OL color.   [A7]   £451   **$747**

[SAME TITLE]   [1584]   34x46cm (13½x18") Orig color. Lt soiling margins & Mediterranean; 2 pinholes near c'fold repaired verso; o/w fine. Ref: Laor 540B.   [A1]   £862   **$1,430**

POLONIAE ...   [1570] From *Theatrum* ... 1st ed. 37x50cm (14½x19½") Orig color. Minor repairs; good. Ref: Koeman Ort 1A, 44.   [28]   £510   **$845**

POLONIAE FINITIMARUMQUE' LOCORUM DESCRIPTIO. AUCTORE WENCESLAO GODRECCIO POLONO ...   [1587]   As in *Theatre de l'Universe*. Greater Poland and adjacent. 38x50cm (15x20") Period color. Ref: Koeman Ort 22, 86.   [42]   **Aus$1,500**   £681 $1,129

PRESBITERI IOHANNIS, SIVE ABISSINORUM IMPERII DESCRIPTIO   [1573]   37x44cm (15x17½") Color. Exc. Ref: Tooley (Africa) p.89, illus.   [24]   £573   **$950**

[SAME TITLE]   [1588 or later] 37x44cm (14½x17½") Color. Beautiful.   [A8]   £763   **$1,265**

REGNI BOHEMIAE DESCRIPTIO   [c.1580]   34x52cm (13½x20½") Color.   [48]   **DM 600**   £207 $343

RUSSIAE, MOSCOVIAE ET TARTARIAE DESCRIPTIO ...   [1570]   35x45cm (14x17½") Color.   [A7]   £451   **$747**

SALISBURGENSIS JURISDICTIONIS   [1570]   With bird's-eye view. 34x44cm (13½x17") Color. Ref: Koeman Ort 28.   [48]   **DM 1,380**   £476 $790

SCHLAVONIAE, CROATIAE, CARNIAE, ISTRIAE, BOSNIAE ... AUCTORE AUGUSTINO HIRSVOGELIO   [1598]   33x46cm (13x18") Orig color. Fine.   [24]   £392   **$650**

ORTELIUS (Folio) continued

SEPTENTRIONALIUM REGIONUM DESCRIP. [1570] 36x49cm (14½x19½") North Atlantic lands; some imaginary. Full orig color. Fine. Ref: Moreland & Bannister illus p.55. [1] £1,327 **$2,200**
[SAME TITLE] [1570-95] 36x49cm (14x19½") Uncolored. [34] **£1,400** $2,322
[SAME TITLE] [c.1590] North Atlantic lands, incl NE North America; some imaginary. 36x50cm (14½x19½") Sm repair lower margin. [A8] £555 **$920**
SILESIAE TYPUS DESCRIPTUS ET EDITUS A MARTINO HEILWIG ... 1561 [1574] 28x38cm (11x15") New color. Few margin wormholes; some lt soiling; bottom corners added in facsimile; a lt crease in margin; at least ¼" margin all around. [A1] £90 **$149**
SUEVIAE CIRCULUS SIVE LIGA VULGO SCHWABISCHE KRAISS. DAVID SELTZLIN ... 1572 [1573] As in *Additamentium* ... SW Germany. 32x24cm (12½x9½") Color. [42] **Aus$750** £341 $565
TARTARIAE SIVE MAGNI CHAMI REGNI TYPUS [1570] From *Theatrum* ... With NW America coast. 35x47cm (14x18½") Orig wash color. Lt browning at fold. Ref: Burden 41; Wheat (TM) 16; Moreland & Bannister p.269, illus. [27] £814 **$1,350**
[SAME TITLE] [1570 / 1572] With NW America coast. 35x47cm (14x18½") Full orig color. Good. Ref: Wheat (TM) 16; Moreland & Bannister p.269, illus. Koeman Ort5-47. [2] £724 **$1,200**
[SAME TITLE] [1573] From *Theatrum* ... With NW America coast. [no dimens] Newer color. Cleaned; lower margin worm tracks repaired; VG. [14] £874 **$1,450**
[SAME TITLE] [1587] From *Theatrum* ... With NW America coast. Framed. 35x47cm (13½x18½") Contemp color. [A6] **£483** $801
[SAME TITLE] [1590 or later] With NW America coast. 36x48cm (14½x19") Color. [A8] £589 **$977**
[SAME TITLE] [c.1590] Incl California. 35x47cm (14x18½") Full color. [A7] £555 **$920**
TEMPE [1598] Mount Olympus. 36x48cm (14½x19") Orig color. Exc. [23] £573 **$950**
TERRA SANCTA A PETRO LAICSTAIN PERLUSTRATA, ET AB EIUS ORE ET SCHEDIS A CHRISTIANO SCHROT IN TABULAM REDACTA [1584] 37x50cm (14½x20") Orig color. Exc. Ref: Laor 543. Nebenzahl (Holy Land) pl.31. [23] £905 **$1,500**
TURCICI IMPERII DESCRIPTIO [1579-1584] 38x50cm (15x19½") Color. Ref: Tibbetts 42. [34] **£850** $1,410
TYPUS CHOROGRAPHICUS, CELEBRIUM LOCORUM IN REGNO IUDAE ET ISRAHEL. ARTE FACTUS A TILEMANNO STELLA SIGENENSI [1590 / ?] 36x46cm (14x18") Full color. Exc. Ref: Laor 546. [23] £905 **$1,500**
TYPUS ORBIS TERRARUM [1570] 1st state. 34x50cm (13½x19½") Full orig color. 2 sm repairs to ctr; toned; else fine. Ref: Shirley (W) 122. [43] £4,523 **$7,500**
[SAME TITLE] [1570+] From *Theatrum* ... 1st state; early crack in plate without repair dates from 1575-79. 34x49cm (13x19½") Orig color. Ref: Shirley (W) 122, pl.104. [13] **Aus$8,400** £3,815 $6,325
[SAME TITLE] [(1570) c.1575] From *Theatrum* ... 1st plate. 34x50cm (13x19½") Orig color with later additions. Minor verso reinforcement lower c'fold; 2 sm closed tears to border; Generally VG. Ref: Shirley (W) 122, pl.104. Van den Broecke 1. [4] **£4,000** $6,633
[SAME TITLE] [1587] 3rd plate. 36x48cm (14x19") Full color. Lower c'fold repair. Framed. Ref: Shirley (W) 158. [1] £3,317 **$5,500**
[SAME TITLE] [1587] From *Theatrum* ... 3rd plate; lacks S. Amer. bulge. 36x49cm (14x19") Color. Ref: Shirley (W) 158. [13] **Aus$7,800** £3,270 $5,421
[SAME TITLE] [1587 (1592)] 36x48cm (14x19") B&W. Superb. [27] £2,895 **$4,800**
[SAME TITLE] [1588] Spanish text ed; plate 2, state 2. 34x50cm (13x19½") Full contemporary color; cracking where thick. Tide marks upper corners; closed lower c'fold tear. Ref: Shirley (W) 122. Van den Broecke 2.2. [38] £3,015 **$5,000**
[SAME TITLE] [1606] Only English ed. Corrected South American shape. 36x49cm (14x19½") Orig color. Margins extended; c'fold repairs, some loss; fair-good. Ref: Shirley (W) 158. [23] £3,317 **$5,500**
TYPUS ORBIS TERRARUM [IN SET WITH] AFRICAE TABULA NOVA [AND] AMERICAE SIVE NOVI ORBIS NOVA DESCRIPTIO [AND] ASIAE NOVA DESCRIPTIO [AND] EUROPAE [1570] From *Theatrum* ... 5 maps, all about 36x48cm (14x19") Color. Minor worming lower margins of continental maps; overall VF. Ref: Shirley (W) 122, pl.104; Goss (NA) 11. Walter (Japan) 11B & 11C; Van den Broecke 1, 4, 8, & 9. [4] **£8,850** $14,675
UNGARIAE LOCA PRAECIPUA RECENS EMENDATA ATQUE EDITA, PER IOANNEM SAMBUCUM PANNONIUM, IMP. MS. HISTORICUM. 1579 [1579] Incl Transylvania. 35x50cm (13½x20") Color. Lt soiling margin & blank area; lower rt border corner not printed, orig plate presumed broken. [A1] £133 **$220**
UTRIUSQUE FRISIORUM REGIONIS NOVISS DESCRIPTIO 1568 [c.1620] No border or neat line on this copy. 34x51cm (13½x20") Color. [39] £181 **$300**
WESTPHALIAE TOTIUS [1579] 35x50cm (14x19½") OL color. [A7] £121 **$201**

ORTELIUS (Miniature)

[ATLAS] EPITOME DU THEATRE DU MONDE D'ABRAHAM ORTELIUS ... A ANVERS, DE L'IMPRIMERIE PLANTINIENNE POUR PHILIPPE GALLE. M.D.XC [1590] Sm oblong quarto, modern limp vellum; 94 maps. Strong impressions; exc. Ref: Koeman Ort 54. [3] £2,955 **$4,900**

[PORTRAIT] ABRAHAMUS ORTELIUS ANTUERPIANUS COSMOGRAPHUS NATUS AO MDXXVII [c.1595-1600] Possibly by Crispyn de Passe, Flemish engraver, from portrait album; modeled on Galle portrait facing rt. 14x10cm (5½x4") Uncolored. Exc. [4] £225 **$373**

OSBORNE

A MAP OF THE BRITTISH PLANTATIONS ON THE CONTINENT OF AMERICA [c.1745] From Salmon's *Modern History*. Seemingly based on Popple. 34x30cm (13½x12") B&W. Repaired margin tear to printed border; else VG+. [37] £271 **$450**

OTTENS

[GULF OF MEXICO] [c.1730] Coast of TX, LA & Mexico sheet from "Grand Theatre de la Guerre en Amerique". 45x57cm (18x22½") Orig color. [27] £1,508 **$2,500**

ASTRONOMISCHE HEMEL SPIEGEL [1738] Double hemi (apparently reworked 1655 A. Colom plate), with eclipse diagrams; affected areas shaded. With folio page by Symon Panser. 46x62cm (18½x24½") Orig color. Ref: cf Shirley (W) 395. [34] £3,400 **$5,638**

CARTE DES POSSESSIONS ANGLOISES & FRANCOISES DU CONTINENT DE L'AMERIQUE SEPTENTRIONALE [1755] French and Dutch titles at top. 46x56cm (18x22") Orig color. Ref: Sellers & Van Ee 58. [34] £1,200 **$1,990**

CARTE GENERALE DES ROYAUMES D'ESPAGNE & DE PORTUGAL ... [c.1740] 48x58cm (19x23") Full orig color. Exc. [2] £226 **$375**

CARTE NOUVELLE DE TOUT L'EMPIRE DE LA GRANDE RUSSIE [c.1735] Peter the Great dedication. 47x65cm (18½x25½") Color. Faint water stains. [41] £181 **$300**

FRIESLAND [c.1750] 33x42cm (13x16½") Wash & OL color. ["Over-Ijsel" & "Uitrecht" offered at same price] [11] £90 **$150**

L'EMPIRE D'ALLEMAGNE DIVISEE EN TOUS SES ETATS [1745] Reissue of Jaillot map. 48x61cm (19x24") Full color. [39] £181 **$300**

LES ISLES BRITANNIQUE ... [c.1745] Cartouche by Jaillot. 47x59cm (18½x23½") Full col. [39] £181 **$300**

NIEUW ALGEMEENE KAART VAN GROENLAND ET STRAET DAVIDS [1745] Arctic regions from North America to Nova Zemla. 2 joined sheets, 48x115cm (19x45½") Contemp color. Some staining. [A6] £402 **$667**

NIEUWE CAARTE VAN KAAP DE GOEDE HOOP ... VAN AFRICA ... [c.1740] Insets: Table Bay; Fort of Good Hope. 44x56cm (17½x22") Orig color. Ref: Norwich 163. [34] £450 **$746**

NOVISSIMA ET ACCURATISSIMA HELVETIAE ... [c.1740] 48x57cm (19x22½") Full orig color. Exc. [2] £528 **$875**

ORIENTALIORA INDIARUM ORIENTALIUM CUM INSULIS ADJACENTIBUS A PROMONTORIO C. CORMORIO AD IAPAN ... [1745] From *Tabulae Maritimae ofte Zee-Karten*. Title also in Dutch. Reissue of De Wit with Tasmania charted. 44x54cm (17½x21½") Orig color. Ref: cf Tooley (Australia) 1369 & 1370, pl.100; Clancy (Australis) ill. p.83. [13] **Aus$4,850** £2,203 **$3,652**

RUSSIAE ET NOVAE ZEMLAE MARITIMAE [before 1750] 49x56cm (19½x22") Wash & OL color. Sl surface loss along vert fold (when held to light); sm brown spot. [A7] £277 **$460**

OVERTON

A NEW AND ACCURAT MAP OF THE WORLD ... [1670] John Overton. Double hemi with sm celestial hemis; vignettes top & bottom; explorers portraits. 39x52cm (15½x20½") Margins trimmed just beyond platemark, but ample; sm surface tear closed on verso. Ref: Shirley (W) 456. [A7] £5,202 **$8,625**

A NEW AND EXACT PLAN OF THE CITY OF LONDON AND SUBURBS THERETO ... [1724] Sutton Nicholls, sc. Indices at sides; 3 sheets joined, 58x147cm (23x58") Orig OL col. Ref: Howgego 64. [47] £2,500 **$4,146**

A NEW MAPP OF THE CITTY OF LONDON MUCH INLARGED ... [1706] John Overton. Separately issued; 2 sheets joined, . 56x94cm (22x37") Uncolored. Restoration to frayed edges & old creases. Ref: Howgego 53. [34] £1,400 **$2,322**

GEOGRAPHIA SACRA, OR NEW & COMPENDIOUS MAPS OF THE HOLY LAND [c.1715] Separately issued two-sheet map containing 6 maps, 5 in color, Jerusalem uncolored. Sheets joined, 60x102cm (23½x40") Margins just ample; few repairable tears just into image. [A8] £971 **$1,610**

OWEN & BOWEN

[ATLAS] BRITANNIA DEPICTA: OR OGILBY IMPROVED [1720] T. Bowles & E. Bowen; 1st ed. Octavo, rebacked calf; 273 county & strip road maps. Ref: Chubb 147. [A6] £747 $1,239

[ATLAS] BRITANNIA DEPICTA OR OGILBY IMPROV'D ... [1736] 4th ed. Sm quarto, modern calf backed boards; 273 route maps on 137 leaves; 8 pp index. Occas sl spotting or staining. [A6] £632 $1,048

PAAS

MAP OF THE WORLD FROM THE BEST AUTHORITIES [1789] C. Paas, London. 19x36cm (7½x14") Color. [19] £81 **$135**

PAGE

COUNTY MAP OF TEXAS, NEW MEXICO, AND INDIAN TERRITORY [1875] From Page & Smith's *Combination Atlas Map of Shelby County, Ohio*. Border resembles H.H Lloyd map. Inset: southern TX. 37x56cm (14½x22") Full color. Repaired sh split lower c'fold, else fine. Ref: LeGear (US) v.2, 5971. [12] £172 **$285**

MAP OF TEXAS PUBLISHED BY H.R. PAGE & CO. [1887] Vert format; west TX upside down in inset. 66x42cm (26x16½") Color by counties. [39] £121 **$200**

MAP OF WASHINGTON TER. [dated 1883 (1887)] H.R. Page & Co., Chicago. 41x66cm (16x26") Full color by counties. [39] £90 **$150**

PAGE'S MAP OF COLORADO [1887] 41x66cm (16½x26") Full color by counties. [39] £96 **$160**

PAGE'S MAP OF KANSAS [1886] 41x67cm (16x26½") Full color by counties. [39] £87 **$145**

PALAIRET

A MAP OF NORTH AMERICA BY J. PALAIRET WITH CONSIDERABLE ALTERATIONS & IMPROVEM'TS FROM D'ANVILLE, MITCHELL & BELLIN [1762] L. Delarochette; publ by T. Bowles. 48x58cm (19x23") Full orig wash & OL color. Trimmed almost to neat lines; 4 folds; sl browning in sea areas; some ink MS notes. Ref: Sellers & Van Ee 115. [11] £1,116 **$1,850**

CARTE DES POSSESSIONS ANGLOISES & FRANCOISES DU CONTINENT DE L'AMERIQUE SEPTENTRIONALE [1763] Engraved by Kitchin. Shows English claims west to Mississippi. 41x57cm (16x22½") Full orig color by controlling power. Sl discoloration in ocean; o/w fine. Ref: Sellers & Van Ee 57; Tooley (Amer) p.62, #18; Phillips (M) p.579. [38] £1,960 **$3,250**

PANCKOUCKE

[ATLAS] DESCRIPTION DE L'EGYPTE - ATLAS GEOGRAPHIQUE ... SECONDE EDITION [1826] Paris. Folio, 72x55cm (28½x22") 52 double-page maps; orig wrappers. Minor foxing. [A7] £1,526 **$2,530**

PARKER

[BOOK WITH MAPS] JOURNAL OF AND EXPLORING TOUR BEYOND THE ROCKY MOUNTAINS [1844] Ithaca; 4th ed. Octavo, cloth; 416 pp; "Map of Oregon Territory", 1 plate. Cover corners, spine & hinges worn; ownership penned on endpapers; contents VG. [1] £241 **$400**

MAP OF OREGON TERRITORY [1838] 36x58cm (14x23") B&W. Thin paper, folds & wrinkles; rough hinge edge. Ref: Wheat (TM) 438. [1] £181 **$300**

PAYNE

A MAP OF NORTH AMERICA FROM THE LATEST AURTHORITIES [1802] Publ by I. Low, *Complete Encyclopedia*. Later state of 1799 map. 20x22cm (8x8½") Uncolored. Ref: cf Wheat & Brun 65. [22] £72 **$120**

AFRICA FROM THE BEST AUTHORITIES [1799] 18x22cm (7x8½") B&W. Few soft creases; lt offsetting; VG. Ref: Wheat & Brun 859. [35] £36 **$60**

GENERAL CHART ON MERCATOR'S PROJECTION [1798] From *Universal Geography*. NY: J. Low. Rollinson, sc. 18x23cm (7x9") B&W. Lt scattered foxing; VG+. Ref: Wheat & Brun 39; Phillips (A) 4303-2. [35] £48 **$80**

THE STATE OF NEW HAMPSHIRE COMPILED CHIEFLY FROM ACTUAL SURVEYS [1799] From ... *Universal Geography*. 30x18cm (12x7½") Clean, dark Ref: Wheat & Brun 190; Cobb (NH) 78. [22] £72 **$120**

THE STATE OF VIRGINIA FROM THE BEST AUTHORITIES. 1799 [1799] From *Payne's New Geography*. 19x25cm (7½x10") Mildly foxed; offsetting ctr. Ref: Wheat & Brun 574. [A10] £63 **$104**

THE WORLD FROM THE BEST AUTHORITIES [1798] From *Universal Geography*. NY: J. Low. Rollinson, sc. Double hemi, each Diameter: 19cm (7½") B&W. Lt offsetting; VG+. Ref: Wheat & Brun 40; Phillips (A) 4303-1. [35] £75 **$125**

PEASE

MAP OF FRENCH & ENGLISH GRANTS ON LAKE CHAMPLAIN [1849] 59x37cm (23x14½") Litho color. Some browning; sm repaired margin tear; creased; o/w clean, clear. [21] Can$120 £52 **$87**

PEASE & NILES
[BOOK WITH MAPS] HISTORY OF SOUTH AMERICA AND MEXICO ... [WITH] A GEOGRAPHICAL AND HISTORICAL VIEW OF TEXAS [1837] Hartford. Octavo, 2 vols in one; later ¾-leather with cloth; 5 maps & plates, incl folding bright color map of South America & "Mexico & Texas" as large republic. Maps backed. [16] £467 **$775**

PEETERS
COMITATUS FLANDRIAE [1692] 15x18cm (6x7½") Uncolored. Fine. ["... Artesiae", "... Hanoniae", "... Brabantiae" & "... Namurci" offered at same price] [22] £33 **$55**
COMITATUS HOLANDIAE [1692] 15x18cm (6x7½") Uncol. Fine. ["... Frisiae", "... Geldriae", "... Groeningae", "... Zelandiae", "... Zutphaniae", "Over-Yssel" & "Ultraiectini Domini" offered at same price] [22] £33 **$55**
DANE MARCK ET SUD-GOTHLANDE [1692] 13x16cm (5½x6½") Uncolored. Fine. [22] £33 **$55**

PERRINE
PERRINE'S NEW TOPOGRAPHICAL WAR MAP OF THE SOUTH [1864] Indianapolis. Folding map with 203, vi pp text history of war to date, orig boards. OL color by state; battles circled in red. 71x92cm (28x36½") One tear; a fold separation; spine gone. Ref: cf Stephenson (CW-2) 43.6. [15] £271 **$450**

PERROT
ETATS-UNIS [c.1825] MO is labeled "Jefferson". 14x18cm (5½x7½") OL color. Fine. [38] £90 **$150**

PERTHES   Try Stieler
DIE VITI - ODER FIJI INSELEN ... [1882] After Horne & British Admiralty. Insets; soundings. 43x51cm (17x20") Full color. VG. [26] £54 **$90**
ETHNOGRAPHISCHE KARTE VON NORDAMERICA [1846] For Berghaus Physical Atlas; publ Gotha. Shows TX as republic; details 34 Indian groups; inset of European language areas. 29x39cm (11½x15½") Full color. Fine. [16] £166 **$275**
POLYNESIEN UND DER GROSSE OCEAN ... ZUR ETHNOGRAPHISCHEN UBERSICHT VON DR. G. GERLAND [1872] 25x43cm (10x17") Some color. VG. [26] £36 **$60**

PETERMANN   Try Stieler
DIE GROSSEREN DER VITI - ODER FIJI INSELN [1861] After Wilkes. 20x24cm (8x9½") Full col. [26] £45 **$75**
LIEUT. WHEELER'S EXPEDITION NACH NEW-MEXICO & ARIZONA, 1873 [1874] From *Geographische Mittheilungen*. Gotha: Perthes. Tracks of Wheeler (in orange-brown) & predecessors. 25x19cm (10x7½") Full color. Fine. [12] £75 **$125**

PETRIE
ICHNOGRAPHY OF CHARLESTON ... FOR THE USE OF THE PHOENIX FIRE COMPANY OF LONDON ... [1788/90] City plan; "earliest American fire insurance map". 49x69cm (19½x27") Uncol. Backed; minor staining; narrow margins; overall VG for type. Ref: Ristow (Amer M&M) p.245-7, illus. [36] £7,237 **$12,000**

PHELPS
MILLER'S NEW MAP OF THE CITY OF NEW YORK [1857] Humphrey Phelps. Folding map in orig full cloth cover; street guides below & sides. 38x69cm (15x27") Full color. Ref: Haskell 1047. [15] £151 **$250**
NEW YORK CITY MAP [1857] Shows Central Park. 42x74cm (16½x29") Orig wash color. One mend; near exc. Ref: Haskell 1044. [24] £392 **$650**
PHELPS & ENSIGN'S MAP OF THE CITY OF NEW YORK [1841] Pocket map in *Stranger's Guide through the City of New York* ... Folds into cloth boards, gilt title; north to 14th St; tables list local features. 42x51cm (16½x20") Full color. Sm ink stain cover, MS date inside; map has few minor spots; sl discoloration where pasted in; else VG (A). [A3] £402 **$666**
PHELPS NEW-YORK CITY GUIDE AND CONDUCTOR [1857] NY: Ensign, Bridgman & Fanning. Folding map; gold-stamped embossed cloth covers; 95 pp guide book, 9 views. North to 88th St. 44x39cm (17½x15½") Full orig stencil color. Covers lt scuffed; map VG. [38] £181 **$300**
PHELPS'S NATIONAL MAP OF THE UNITED STATES, A TRAVELLERS GUIDE ... [1849/1857] Surround of presidents & state logos; western portion an inset. 53x64cm (21x25") Orig col. Stain; else exc. [24] £1025 **$1,700**

PHELPS & ENSIGN
PHELPS & ENSIGN'S TRAVELLER'S GUIDE, AND MAP OF THE UNITED STATES CONTAINING THE ROADS, DISTANCES, STEAM BOAT AND CANAL ROUTES &C. ... [1841] Coast to coast depiction; with orig rod & rail; insets: 15 cities, mountains & rivers, hemis, etc; below: 4 historic scenes, 10 presidents, etc. 43x97cm (17x38") Color by state & region. Sl ragged edges; sm hole in MN; VG. [5] £452 **$750**

PHELPS & ENSIGN continued

PHELPS & ENSIGN'S TRAVELLER'S GUIDE THROUGH THE UNITED STATES: CONTAINING STAGE, STEAMBOAT, CANAL & RAIL-ROAD ROUTES ... [1838] 1st ed. 16 sm insets; with 53 pp text. OL color by state. 55x43cm (21½x17") 2 sm holes along folds, sl loss; VG. [15] £513 **$850**

PHELPS & WATSON

HISTORICAL AND MILITARY MAP OF THE BORDER AND SOUTHERN STATES [1867] Folds into stiff paper wraps; 36 pp text. Full color by state; battle sites highlighted. 49x89cm (19½x35") Sl bumped, sl creasing; text detached; minor separations some folds; fine. [15] £362 **$600**

PHELPS AND WATSON'S HISTORICAL AND MILITARY MAP OF THE BORDER AND SOUTHERN STATES [1862 / 1867] Paper wraps, linen reinforced spine; 36 pp booklet listing Civil War battles. 64x88cm (25x34½") Color by state. Wraps lt soiled & cracked, corners bent; booklet loose, lt soiled; occas map fold separation; good-VG. [5] £256 **$425**

[SAME TITLE] [1863] From PA southward. 64x90cm (25x35½") Orig wash color. Sl fold wear; mounted on rice paper; for its kind, exc. [24] £905 **$1,500**

[SAME TITLE] [1864] Folds into orig case. Battles listed & marked by red dots. 64x89cm (25x35") Full orig color by states. Text pages, if any, not present. Trimmed close; minor soiling in MO; corners repaired; basically VG. [25] £226 **$375**

PHILIP, G.

THE ATLANTIC OCEAN [c.1890] Linen-backed pocket map in 12mo folder; 16 pp index. 60x50cm (23½x19½") Color by country. Cover corners bent; VG. [6] £84 **$140**

PHILLIPS

[BOOK WITH MAPS] AN EASY GRAMMAR OF GEOGRAPHY. INTENDED AS A COMPANION ... FOR SCHOOLS AND YOUNG PERSONS [1806] By Rev. J. Goldsmith (Richard Phillips pseudonym). 12mo, full leather, orig boards & new spine; 2 plates, 7 folding maps incl world, 5 continents, British Isles. VG. [33] £392 **$650**

A MAP OF THE RHINE FROM DUSSELDORF TO MAINZ OR MAYENCE [1807] 14x24cm (5½x9½") [48] **DM 60** £21 $34

PHIPPS

GEOGRAPHY. A MAP OF THE WORLD IN THREE SECTIONS DESCRIBING THE POLAR REGIONS TO THE TROPICS ... [1781] In *Voyage towards the North Pole*. Partial polar hemis, with equatorial supplement to tropics showing ecliptic & 12 zodiac symbols 23x42cm (9x16½") Color. [19] £172 **$285**

PIGOT

MIDDLESEX [1835] As in *Pocket Topography* ... St. Paul's vignette. 23x35cm (9x14") Orig OL color. Folds supported on verso, no loss. [11] £45 **$75**

SURREY [1837] Vignette. 23x35cm (9x14") Color. Strong impression. [11] £36 **$60**

PIKE, ZEBULON

PREMIERE PARTIE DE LA CARTE DE LA LOUISIANE [IN SET WITH] CARTE DE L'INTERIOR DE LA LOUISIANE ... NOUVEAU MEXIQUE ... PROVINCE DE TEXAS [1812] From French ed, *Account of Expeditions to the Sources of the ...Rivers*. Each about 43x41cm (17x16") First sheet orig folded; second sheet lt backed. [27] £1,086 **$1,800**

PITT

A MAP OF THE NORTH POLE AND THE PARTS ADJOINING [c.1680] 46x58cm (18x23") Orig color. Good. [32] £1,659 **$2,750**

EPISCOP. ULTRAIECTINUS [c.1680] With Jansson. 38x48cm (15x19") Highlight color. [A8] £121 **$201**

FLANDRIA NOVA DESCRIPTIO [c.1680] 48x56cm (19x22") Sm stain in image at lower fold. [A8] £90 **$149**

HUNGARIAE REGNUM [1680] 42x51cm (16½x20") OL color. Faint toning along c'fold; else fresh, clean. [A9] £146 **$242**

NOVA TOTIUS TERRARUM ORBIS GEOGRAPHICA AC HYDROGRAPHICA TABULA [1680] 1608 Van Den Keere plate reworked; surround of panels. 40x53cm (15½x21") Color. Exc. Ref: Shirley (W) 504, pl.362. [4] **£6,000** $9,949

NOVISSIMA ISLANDIAE TABULA [1680] 38x49cm (15x19") Color. Repaired tear crossing lower rt border through blank area almost to fold; top c'fold separation to border; o/w VG to fine. [14] £407 **$675**

Orbis Terrarum Nova et Accuratissima Tabula Auctore Ioanne a Loon [1680] Double hemi; insular Calif. 44x53cm (17½x21"). Color. Sl rubbing at fold; else exc. Ref: Shirley (W) 439. [24] £4,222 **$7,000**

PLANCIUS

Tabula Geographica, in qua Paradisus, nec non Regiones, Urbes, Oppida et Loca Describuntur; Quorum in Genesi Mentio Fit ... [1609] Surround of 15 vignettes of episodes from Genesis. 29x49cm (11½x19½") Minor stain lower margin; a soft crease. Ref: Laor 565. [A8] £1,179 **$1,955**

Tabula Geographica, in qua Paradisus, nec non Regiones, Urbes Oppida et Loca Describuntur: Quorum in Genesi Mentio Fit: Auct. D.R.M. Mathews [c.1650] Small Middle East map; several scenes. Reworking of Baptista van Doetechum plate, c.1590, for Plancius Bible by Joost Hartgers. 29x33cm (11½x13") Full color. Exc. [43] £1,086 **$1,800**

PLAYFAIR

North America [1821] States named in key. 44x53cm (17½x21") Col. Lt soiling; else VG. [10] £196 **$325**

PLOT

[Staffordshire] [1682] From Dr. Robert Plot's *Staffordshire*. By Joseph Browne. 65x54cm (25½x21½") Browning, few spots; margins trimmed; lower lf corner repaired; folds reinforced. Ref: cf Moreland & Bannister p.160. [21] **Can$800** £350 $580

POIRSON

Partie Septentrionale de l'Ocean Pacifique ou l'On A Marque les Descouvertes et les Routes de Mrs. de la Perouse et Cook. Par J.B. Poirson Ingenieur Geographe [c.1820] Tardieu, engr. 35x46cm (13½x18") Orig OL color. [12] £226 **$375**

POLITICAL MAGAZINE

A Draught of the Harbours of Port Royal and Kingston, in Jamaica. With the Fortifications Correctly Laid Down; Also All the Keys and Shoals Adjacent [1782] 26x38cm (10x15") Full color. Ref: Jolly POL-47; Kapp (Jamaica) 118. [20] £407 **$675**

A New and Accurate Chart of the Harbour of Boston, in New England. In North America. [1782] 22x17cm (9x6½") Uncolored. Mint. Ref: Jolly POL-63. [22] £136 **$225**

An Accurate Map of the Two Sicilies, Particularly Shewing the Places Destroyed by the Late Earthquakes. [1783] 32x24cm (12½x9½") Uncolored. VG. Ref: Jolly POL-72. [25] £30 **$50**

Map of the Islands of Martinico, Dominico, Guardalupe, St. Christophers &c. Shewing the Place of Adml: Rodney's Late Victory Over the French Fleet. [1782] Area of "Battle of the Saints" 24x28cm (9½x11") Color. Ref: Jolly POL-55; Phillips (M) p.1058. [18] £166 **$275**

POMEROY

[Atlas] Atlas of Lycoming County Pennsylvania ... under the Direction of Beach Nichols [1873] 38 map plates. [no dimens] Front cover detached with edge wear; few instance lt foxing; maps generally VG. Ref: LeGear (US) 3043. [A2] £249 **$413**

[Atlas] Atlas of Seneca County New York ... under the Direction of Beach Nichols [1872] Pomeroy, Whitman & Co. 16 maps, incl state & county. [no dimens] Covers rubbed, edge wear; contents tight; some red ink notes on blank margin of 2 maps; generally VG. [A2] £119 **$198**

PONTOPPIDAN

Det Sydlige Norge [in set with] Det Nordlige Norge [1785-1795] Not dissected, folded or mounted as usual. Two maps on 3 sheets, each about 53x69cm (21x27") Orig OL color. [34] **£400** $664

POPPLE

A Map of the British Empire in America ... [4 joined sheets: Connecticut River & eastern Long Island to Labrador] [1733] Vignettes of NYC, Quebec, etc. 100x98cm (39½x38½") [A8] £1,110 **$1,840**

A Map Of The British Empire In America ... [key sheet] [1733] Overall map showing proper alignment of all 20 sheets; insets & views at rt. 50x48cm (20x19") Orig OL color. Toned; minor repair; VG. [23] £2,714 **$4,500**

A Map of the British Empire in America ... [lower left quadrant: Gulf of Mexico & adjacent lands; title] [c.1740] Covens & Mortier reissue of Popple's 1733 map. All Florida, eastern Mexico to Panama. 68x49cm (26½x19½") Full orig OL color. Strong impression; heavy paper. Ref: Cumming (SE) 216. [27] £1,357 **$2,250**

PORCACCHI

[ATLAS] L'ISOLE PIU FAMOSE DEL MONDO ... IN VENETIA MDLXXVI [1576] 2nd (expanded) ed. Sm folio; full vellum; 47 maps & plans in text, incl "Mondo Nuovo" (North America). Part of last leaf missing; o/w VG. Ref: Phillips (A) 167. Sabin 64149. [3] £2,714 **$4,500**

[WORLD] ... LA CARTA DA NAVIGARE [1576] From 2nd of 8 editions of *L'Isole Piu Famose del Mondo*. Venice. Porro, engr. 10x14cm (4x5½") on 11½x8" sheet with text. B&W. Fine. Ref: cf Shirley (W) 128. Phillips (A) 167-198. [12] £271 **$450**

DESCRITTIONE DEL MAPPAMONDO [1572-] 11x15cm (4x5½") Uncol. Ref: Shirley (W) 127. [34] **£300** $498

DISCORSO INTORNO ALLA CARTA DA NAVIGARE [1572-] From *L'Isole Piu Famose del Mondo*. 11x14cm (4x5½") Uncolored. Ref: Shirley (W) 128. [34] **£300** $498

IL SITU DE' CURZOLARI [1590] Southern Greece; Patrai at ctr. 9x14cm (3½x5½") B&W. Fine (A+). [A3] £42 **$70**

PORRO

[ASIA] [c.1590] 18x24cm (7x9½") Color. [42] **Aus$1,500** £681 $1,129

[EUROPE] [1560-68] Appeared in Bertelli's *Civitatum Aliquot Insigniorum*. 11x15cm (4x5½") Uncolored. [34] **£1,400** $2,322

POSTLETHWAIT

NORTH AMERICA ... [1766] From *Universal Dictionary of Trade and Commerce*. One plate of multi-sheet map showing American Southwest & inset of NE Canada. 43x33cm (17x13") Col, probably later. [7] £166 **$275**

POWELL

THE WORLD AGREEABLE TO THE LATEST DISCOVERIES [1778] Publ London; T.K. Powell, sc. 16x26cm (6½x10½") Color. [19] £142 **$235**

PREVOST D'EXILES   Try *Bellin* (small)

STADT ST DOMINGO [1756] Bird's-eye view. 18x26cm (7x10") [11] £21 **$35**

PRICE

A NEW AND CORRECT MAP OF THE WORLD PROJECTED UPON THE PLANE OF THE HORIZON ... BY C. PRICE ... SOLD BY G. WILLDEY ... [1714] 64x102cm (25x40") Strong impression. Exc. Ref: cf Campbell (Early) p.68. [2] £5,729 **$9,500**

PRICHARD

ETHNOGRAPHICAL MAP OF NORTH AMERICA IN THE EARLIEST TIMES, ILLUSTRATIVE OF DR. PRICHARD'S NATURAL HISTORY OF MAN AND HIS RESEARCHES INTO THE PHYSICAL HISTORY OF MANKIND, SECOND EDITION, 1861 [c.1861] Color shows origin of 23 races. 61x48cm (24x19") VG. [Similarly titled companion maps of South America & Europe offered at $80; Asia at $100; Africa & Polynesia at $140] [26] £90 **$150**

PRINALD

A NEW MAP OF IRELAND ... [c.1760] 28x19cm (11x7½") OL color. VG. [37] £106 **$175**

PRIOR

MAP OF LEICESTERSHIRE [1779] Luffman, sc. 4 sheets joined, dissected & linen-backed. 112x120cm (44½x47") Contemp color. Lt soiling at folds; folds strengthened verso. [A6] **£391** $649

PROBST

NOVA ET ACCURATA TABULA REGNORUM SUP. ET INF. HUNGARIAE IT. SCLAVONIAE, BOSNIAE, SERVIAE, ALBANIAE. BESSARABIAE UT ET PRINCIP. TRANSILVANIAE, MOLDAVIAE, WALACHIAE, BULGAR ET ROMANIAE [1771] J.M. Probst. 50x59cm (19½x23") Old color. [48] **DM 350** £121 $200

NOVA MAPPA GEOGRAPHICA AMERICAE SEPTENTRIONALIS ... [1782] After Popple; insets of ports. 58x51cm (22½x20") Color. [A7] £416 **$690**

PARIS [c.1750] F.B. Werner Siles. Panorama; 50-item key. 34x97cm (13½x38½") Exc. [24] £2,714 **$4,500**

PROCKTER

A NEW AND ACCURATE MAP OF EAST AND WEST FLORIDA, DRAWN FROM THE BEST AUTHORITIES. [1765] Similar to same title in *London Magazine*. but differs: lacks "London Magazine" above; signed J. Prockter, engr; extends 40' further north. 19x20cm (7½x8") B&W. Lt offsetting; else fine. Ref: cf Jolly LOND-243. [12] £166 **$275**

PTOLEMY (1482-1486, Ulm)

NONA ASIE TABULA [1486] Ptolemaic Pakistan. [no dimens] Ref: Nordenskiold (Fac) p.16. [A2] £995 **$1,650**

SEXTA ASIE TABULA [1482] From Holle's ed of *Geographia*. 1st ed with strong orig color. Arabian peninsula 29x55cm (11½x21½") Negligible surface blemishes. Ref: Tibbetts 8. [34] £6,800 **$11,275**

TABULA MODERNA TERRA SANCTAE [1482] Ulm: Holle. 25x53cm (10x21") on larger sheet. Color. Sm chip & minor browning rt edge, image unaffected. Ref: Laor 603. [A8] £3,884 **$6,440**

PTOLEMY (1511, Venice)

OCTAVA EUROPAE TABULA [1511] Sylvanus, Venice. 39x46cm (15½x18") Two-color printing. Minor creasing; else exc. [24] £724 **$1,200**

SECUNDA EUROPAE TABULA [1511] On two sheets joined, 41x57cm (16x22½") Printed red & black. Exc. [24] £1,689 **$2,800**

UNDECIMA ASIAE TABULA [1511] 41x46cm (16x18½") Printed red & black. Exc. [24] £2,111 **$3,500**

PTOLEMY (1513-1520, Strassburg)   See *Waldseemuller*

PTOLEMY (1522-1541, Strassburg)   Try *Fries*

ASIAE TABULA PRIMA [after 1520] Asia Minor. 30x46cm (11½x18") Color at later date. [A7] £121 **$201**

TABULA NOVA PARTIS AFRICAE [c.1540] Lyons. 28x40cm (11x15½") Browning along vert fold; 2 sm wormholes top margin. [another, color, repaired clean slice through image, sl loss at fold, sold for $201] [A7] £242 **$402**

PTOLEMY (1540-1552 Basle)   See *Munster*
PTOLEMY (1548, Venice)   See *Gastaldi*
PTOLEMY (1561-1599, Venice)   See *Ruscelli*
PTOLEMY (1596-1621)   See *Magini*

PTOLEMY (1578-1730, Mercator)

TAB. XII. ASIAE. TAPROBANAM REPRAESENTANS [c.1695] Ceylon. 34x36cm (13½x14") OL color. [A8] £225 **$373**

PURCHAS

CHINA [1625] After Hondius. North at rt. 15x18cm (6x7½") on 13x8" text leaf. Full col. VG [38] £136 **$225**

HISPANIA [1625] 15x18cm (6x7½") on 13x8½" text leaf. Color. Fine. [38] £90 **$150**

TABULA CANANAEAE ... [1625] North to rt. 15x18cm (6x7½") on 13x8½" text leaf. Color. Fine. [37] £136 **$225**

THE NORTH PART OF AMERICA CONTEYNING NEWFOUNDLAND, NEW ENGLAND, VIRGINIA, FLORIDA, NEW SPAINE, AND NOVA FRANCIA, WTH YE RICHE ILES OF HISPANIOLA, CUBA, JAMAICA, AND PORTO RICO, ON THE SOUTH, AND UPON YE WEST THE LARGE AND GOODLY ISLAND OF CALIFORNIA... [1625] As in *Purchas His Pilgrims*. Very early insular Calif map. 29x36cm (11½x14") Minor creasing; else exc. Ref: Burden 214; McLaughlin 2; Fite & Freeman 35. [23] £7,237 **$12,000**

VIRGINIA ET FLORIDA [1625] Reduced from Hondius; large "Lacus dulci". 15x18cm (6x7½") on 13x8" leaf. Color. VG. Ref: Cumming (SE) 33. [37] £271 **$450**

PUZZLES and GAMES

[JIGSAW] BACON'S GEOGRAPHICAL ESTABLISHMENT [c.1885] Set of 8 dissected map puzzles of 20 squares each with own frame; made in Bavaria: England & Wales; Australia; India; World; Asia; Europe; Africa; N. Amer. Each 20x25cm (8x10") Litho color. Box scuffed & worn; map & puzzles VG+. [37] £256 **$425**

[JIGSAW] ENGLAND AND WALES [1904] Gall & Inglis; London. Map dissected by Wm. Peacock. Complete with own mat. Color. 43x34cm (17x13½") Stains; minor restoration; else good+. [37] £166 **$275**

[JIGSAW] EUROPE [c.1810] By Wm. Darton(?); apparently produced professionally, but no box or label. Full color by country. 46x49cm (18x19½") "Germany" piece in facsimile. [15] £452 **$750**

[JIGSAW] EUROPE [c.1890] George Philip & Son; London & Liverpool. Complete, with own mat. Color. 56x68cm (22x27") Stains, surface dirt; minor restoration; good+. [37] £271 **$450**

A MAP OF IRELAND. WARRANTED PERFECT IMPROVED DISSECTED MAPS COMBINING INSTRUCTION WITH AMUSEMENT [1796] J. Wallis; London. Mounted on mahogany, cut into 50 pieces along county lines & interlocking border pieces; with mahogany box & sliding cover, sl warped. [no dimens] OL color. A missing piece; mended side groove. [6] £247 **$410**

PUZZLES and GAMES continued

A TRAVELLING GAME OF INDIA DESIGNED TO AFFORD INSTRUCTION AND AMUSEMENT IN THE HOME CIRCLE [c.1840] Liverpool: Arthur Hewling; London: Thomas Hatchchard; Edinburgh: Oliver & Boyd. Oblong 8vo, cloth; 9-section map on linen, 60x47cm (23½x18½") With 34 (of ?) engraved game cards by J. Johnston. Litho color by British & Independent States. Covers soiled & about loose; map age-toned. [21] **Can$120** £52 $87

CLEMENS' MAP OF OHIO [1882] Rev. E.J. Clemens, Clayville, NY; G.W. & C.B. Colton. Jig-saw puzzle on ¼" wood cut along county lines; ad verso; wooden box, lacks half label. 29x37cm (11½x14½") Color by county. Box only good; sl soiled, occas surface buckling, sl loss Lake Erie; VG. [5] £175 **$290**

DISSECTED OUTLINE MAP OF THE UNITED STATES OF AMERICA [c.1910] Milton Bradley, Springfield, MA. Random cut puzzle, with box, but decorative top lacks sides. 25x36cm (10x14") [25] £72 **$120**

EUROPE FOR THE ELUCIDATION OF THE ABBE GAULTIERS' GEOGRAPHICAL GAMES [1832] By Jehoshaphat Aspin; publ by John Harris. 33x41cm (13x16") OL color. Closed tear upper rt margin to neatline; creased. [21] **Can$60** £26 $43

GAME OF UNCLE SAM'S MAIL [1893] Board game; McLaughlin Bros., NY. Map of U.S. with mail routes in red & black, folding into panels. Color. 48x86cm (19x34") Surface dirt, some rubbing; verso chipped; else VG. [37] £166 **$275**

MAPPEMONDE EN DEUX HEMISPHERES ET SOUS LA DIRECTION DE MR. J.G. BARBIE DU BOCAGE [c.1840] Paris: Bouasse-Lebel. Atlas map laid on heavy cardboard, incised into 28-piece jigsaw puzzle. Shows TX as republic. 24x33cm (9½x13") Orig partial color. Surface darkened; couple pieces stained; good. [16] £271 **$450**

OUTLINE MAP OF THE UNITED STATES [c.1901] Milton Bradley, Springfield, MA. 2 sided: U.S. with new possessions; world flags & 4 Uncle Sams. 41x51cm (16x20") Full color. Map complete; sl age soil; box present, but sides poor. [26] £72 **$120**

RAMBLES THROUGH OUR COUNTRY, AN INSTRUCTIVE GEOGRAPHICAL GAME FOR THE YOUNG [1890] American Publishing Co., Hartford. Paper game map on folded canvas, full of illustrated & colorful regional cliches for each state. 64x89cm (25x35") Full color. Minor loss at folds & some abrasions; overall splendid. [25] £256 **$425**

ROUND THE WORLD WITH NELLIE BLY [1890] McLoughlin Bros. Game board only; inward spiraling path of 72-day trip that beat Phineas Fogg. 41x42cm (16x16½") Chromolitho. Lt rubbed, few surface flecks; VG. [6] £115 **$190**

WALLIS'S NEW GEOGRAPHICAL GAME EXHIBITING A VOYAGE ROUND THE WORLD, A NEW GEOGRAPHICAL PASTIME. [1804] London. Dissected, linen-mounted, double-hemi world map, directions and rules in orig labeled slipcase. 48x64cm (19x25") Full orig color. Some surface dirt; few fold separations; else VG. [another, similar "... through the United Kingdom" (1811) offered at the same price] [37] £392 **$650**

QUAD

ANGLIAE REGNI FLORENTISSIMI NOVA DESCRIPTIO, AUCTORE HUMEREDO LHUYD DENBYGIENSE [1592] Cologne: Bussemacher. Nagel, sc. 18x27cm (7½x10½") Old color. Some age toning; sm hole restored. Ref: Shirley (BI to 1650) 172, pl.65. [47] £280 $465

APHRICA [1597] Text at left. 21x30cm (8½x11½") [A7] £139 **$230**

ASIA PARTIU ORBIS MAXIMA [1598 - 1608] From *Fasciculus Geographicus*. 21x30cm (8½x11½") OL color, probably later. Moderate toning & soiling; c'fold repairs verso & faint browning; overall VG. [A9] £260 **$431**

BURGUNDIAE INFERIORIS QUAE DUCATUS NOMINE CENSETUR DESC. [1592] 19x26cm (7½x10") C'fold restored. [48] **DM 180** £62 $103

CORSICA [1592] Latin text below. 24x32cm (9½x12½") [46] £350 **$581**

HIBERNIAE BRITANICAE INSULAE NOVA DESCRIPTIO. ERYN. IRLANDT [1596-1600] Issued in *Geographisch Handtbuch*. Bussemacher, sc. With Elizabeth I portrait. 22x30cm (8½x12") Color. Lt see-through of verso text. [34] £500 **$829**

[SAME TITLE] [1600] With Elizabeth I portrait. 22x30cm (8½x12") Exc. [45] £353 **$585**

ISLANDIA [1596 - c.1600] King Christian IIII portrait. 22x29cm (9x11½") Color. [34] **£1,200** $1,990

[SAME TITLE] [c.1600] 22x29cm (9x11½") Full color. Exc. [43] £558 **$925**

NOVI ORBIS PARS BOREALIS, AMERICA SCILICET, COMPLECTENS FLORIDAM, BACCALAON, CANADAM, TERRAM CORTERIALEM, VIRGINIAM, NOROMBECAM PLURESQUE ALIAS PROVINCIAS [1600] 23x30cm (9x11½") Exc. Ref: Burden 133; Cumming (SE) 24; Goss (NA) 22. [23] £1,508 **$2,500**

[SAME TITLE] [1600-] From *Geographisch Handtbuch*. After De Jode; Bussemacher, sc. 23x29cm (9x11½") Uncolored. Ref: Burden 133. [34] **£2,400** $3,980

QUAD continued

POLUS ARCTICUS SIVE TRACT, SEPTENTRIONALIS. COLONIAE, EX OFFICINA TYPOGRAPHICA JANI BUSSEMECHERS [1600] 21x28cm (8½x11") Exc. Ref: Burden 134. [44] £392 **$650**

PORTUGALLIAE QUE OLIM LUSITANIA, NOVISSIMA ET EXACTISSIMA ... [1592 - c.1600] Bussemacher, sc. 18x26cm (7x10½") Uncolored. [34] £300 **$498**

THURINGIA [1603] 22x27cm (8½x10½") [A8] £121 **$201**

TYPUS ORBIS TERRARUM, AD IMITATIONEM UNIVERSALIS GERHARDI MERCATORIS ... [1596] From *Europae Totius Orbis Terrarum*. Cologne. 22x32cm (8½x12½") B&W. Ref: Shirley (W) 197, pl.160. [13] **Aus$3,000** £1,362 **$2,259**

[SAME TITLE] [1596] Based on 1569 Mercator map. 22x31cm (8½x12½") Exc. [43] £1,146 **$1,900**

[SAME TITLE] [1597] 22x32cm (8½x12½") Missing top margin repaired; remargined at lf, neatline restored; sm lower margin tears backed. [48] **DM 2,200** £760 **$1,259**

[SAME TITLE] [1597] 22x31cm (8½x12½") Lt browned along fold & spots in margins. [A8] £1,526 **$2,530**

RAILROAD COMPANY MAPS

[OHIO, INDIANA & ILLINOIS] [1833] In Oct 12 issue of *American Railroad Journal, and Advocate of Internal Improvements*. D.K. Minor. 16 pp quarto. Wood engraved map shows proposed Mad River and Lake Erie RR, canals & National Road. 13x24cm (5x9½") B&W. Fine. [37] £151 **$250**

A GEOGRAPHICALLY CORRECT MAP OF THE STATE OF TEXAS ... [1876] Texas & Pacific Railway Co. Letterpress verso. 46x51cm (18x20") Yellow & blue. VG. [16] £271 **$450**

CALIFORNIA, LASTEST MAP OF THE STATE [c.1900] Trans-Continental Freight Co., Chicago, shippers (presumably by rail). 43x38cm (17x15") Uncolored. Folds; VG. [26] £36 **$60**

CHICAGO, MILWAUKEE, ST. PAUL AND PACIFIC RAILROAD [1926] With both intact rollers; full color, RR in red. 107x157cm (42x62") Minor repairs verso; sm worm hole blank area. [25] £151 **$250**

COAST TO COAST MAP OF THE DENVER & RIO GRANDE RAILROAD [1916] Appeared in Descriptive Time Table of the D&RG and Western Pacific. Shows band across US ctr; strip maps of routes with descriptions. 24x84cm (9½x33") Wear, but intact. [9] £45 **$75**

COLUMBUS [OH] SHOWING TERMINAL FACILITIES OF THE NORFOLK & WESTERN RAILROAD [1893] City plan; all streets named. 39x60cm (15½x23½") Rivers & RRs in color. [41] £48 **$80**

DENVER AND RIO GRANDE RAILROAD SYSTEM [c.1885] Printed color indicates 3 RR gauges; KS to CA inset shows connections. 36x44cm (14x17") VG (A). Framed. [A3] £91 **$151**

[SAME TITLE] [c.1890] Probably from annual report. Incl CO, UT, NM; topo shading; rail gauges indicated. 37x46cm (14½x18") Substantial color. Minor verso repair to old folds. [25] £72 **$120**

[SAME TITLE] [c.1895] From Stanley Woods' *Over the Range to the Golden Gate*. Mostly intermountain; inset to Pacific. Litho color indicates topo & rail gauges. 36x44cm (14½x17½") Fine. [12] £66 **$110**

MAP EXHIBITING THE EXPERIMENTAL AND LOCATED LINES FOR THE NEW-YORK AND NEW-HAVEN RAIL-ROAD [1845] P. Anderson, NY. 5 joined sheets. 47x315cm (18½x124") Foxing lf, minor damage rt end; exc. Ref: Modelski (US) 484. Modelski (NA) 9. [15] £1,508 **$2,500**

MAP OF FLORIDA [AND] SOUTHERN RAILWAY SYSTEM [1924] Inset shows the Southern System, FL lines in red; list of FL bound trains. Folds into stiff cardboard case. 76x46cm (30x18") VG. [26] £36 **$60**

MAP OF OREGON [1902] Southern Pacific Ry. Settlement promotional. 51x66cm (20x26") Full color. Minor repairs corners, sl loss; overall VG. [25] £84 **$140**

MAP OF THE CHICAGO, BURLINGTON AND QUINCY RAILROAD AND ITS CONNECTIONS [1878] CB&Q, Chicago. ME to CO; Chicago to Pacific inset; schedule & ads verso. 51x74cm (20x29") Blue ink. Folded as issued; VG. [25] £109 **$180**

MAP OF THE COTTON BELT ROUTE [1898] St. Louis Southwestern Railway Co of Texas; route map, timetable. 34x70cm (13½x27½") Yellow tone. VG. [16] £196 **$325**

MAP OF THE COUNTRY BORDERING THE BUFFALO & MISSISSIPPI AND OTHER LAKE RAILROADS [1846] By G.R. Baldwin; Boston: Bouve. 2 joined sheets, 37x99cm (14½x39") Few creases; o/w VF. [A7] £121 **$201**

MAP OF THE COUNTRY EMBRACING THE VARIOUS ROUTES SURVEYED FOR THE WESTERN & ATLANTIC RAIL ROAD OF GEORGIA [1837] J.F. Cooper; Washington. 19x55cm (7½x21½") Uncolored. Some stains. [36] £75 **$125**

MAP OF THE LIMA TOLEDO RAILROAD COMPANY AND CONNECTIONS [1926] Central Electric Traffic Assoc. Shows inter-urban trolley lines in red in OH, IN & southern MI; index verso. 51x56cm (20x22") Yellow background. Old folds. [25] £45 **$75**

RAILROAD COMPANY MAPS continued

MAP OF THE MISSOURI PACIFIC RAILWAY   [1882] Map as small ctr part of 16-panel timetable & promotional; all stops shown. 23x16cm (9½x6½") Some fold splits; minor separations at junctions; o/w near fine. [7] £136 **$225**

MAP OF THE NEW AND POPULAR ST. LOUIS AND TEXAS SHORT LINE!   [1878] St. Louis, Iron Mountain & Southern Railway. 2 maps on sheet; letter press verso. 48x80cm (19x31½") Full printed color. Agent's stamp; fine. [16] £241 **$400**

MAP OF THE NORTH WEST FROM EXPLORATIONS BY THE UNITED STATES ENGINEERS & ROYAL ENGINEERS AND UNION & NORTHERN PACIFIC R.R. SURVEYS   [1870] Julius Bien, NY. Nova Scotia to Vancouver, Nebraska to James Bay; N.P.RR in bold line; crop, mineral, temperature notations. 38x107cm (15x42") OL color. Rebacked; minor loss. [25] £226 **$375**

MAP OF THE OREGON RAILROAD AND NAVIGATIONAL COMPANY AND THE SOUTHERN PACIFIC COMPANY (LINES IN OREGON)   [1898] Chicago: Poole Bros. Shaded relief. 61x53cm (24x21") VG. [26] £45 **$75**

MAP OF THE ST LOUIS IRON MOUNTAIN AND SOUTHERN RAILWAY   [1878] US west to Rockies; AR & MO description on verso. 27x36cm (10½x14½") Folded as issued; generally VG. [7] £75 **$125**

MAP OF THE TEXAS & PACIFIC RAILWAY & CONNECTIONS   [c.1890] Vol.XLIX, Poor's Investors Supplement, NY. New Orleans to El Paso. 17x28cm (7x11") OL color. VG. [16] £60 **$100**

MAP OF THE TEXAS AND PACIFIC RAILWAY AND CONNECTIONS   [c.1875] Estimated date. Most of US, coast to coast; Iron Mountain, Missouri Pacific routes shown; timetables & Calif promotionals on verso. 39x71cm (15½x28") Printed color by states. Fragile; splitting at folds; 2 sm paper loss spots. [9] £118 **$195**

MAP OF THE UNITED STATES SHOWING THE ST. LOUIS, IRON MOUNTAIN & SOUTHERN RAILWAY, THE GREAT TRUNK LINE, CONNECTING THE NORTHERN RAILWAYS AT ST. LOUIS AND THE SOUTHERN RAILWAYS   [1878] 26x36cm (10x14") VG. [16] £90 **$150**

MAP OF THE WEST - BURLINGTON ROUTE   [1940] Chicago, Burlington & Quincy RR Co., Chicago. Full color printed on heavy stock with rollers, showing lines. 109x155cm (43x61") Exc. [26] £84 **$140**

MAP OF WESTERN CANADA, MANITOBA, ALBERTA, SASKATCHEWAN AND PART OF BRITISH COLUMBIA SHOWING SYSTEM OF LAND SURVEY AND LINES OF THE CANADIAN PACIFIC RAILWAY COMPANY   [1908] Chicago: Poole Bros. 109x74cm (43x29") Uncolored. Old folds but VG. [25] £36 **$60**

MAP SHEWING THE RAILROADS BETWEEN LAKE ERIE, NEW YORK & BOSTON ... TO ILLUSTRATE THE ROUTE OF THE NEW YORK AND ERIE RAILROAD   [1842] J.F. Smith, NY. Folding map in cloth folder. Lt wash OL color by state. 42x55cm (16½x21½") Browning lf side. [15] £136 **$225**

NEW TOWNSHIP MAP OF THE STATE OF ARKANSAS   [1878] Webber & Nowlin. Centerfold of 16 pp tabloid RR promotional showing swath of Memphis and Little Rock & Fort Smith and Little Rock Railways 36x39cm (14x15½") Poor quality paper, fragile; splitting along horiz fold, no loss. [7] £151 **$250**

NEW YORK CENTRAL LINES [c.1890] Buffalo: Mathew Northrup. 41x66cm (16x26") Uncol. VG. [25] £30 **$50**

NORFOLK AND WESTERN RAILROAD AND CONNECTIONS   [Jan 1, 1890] 700 track miles to Norton & Bristol, VA. 19x44cm (7½x17½") Printed color. [40] £21 **$35**

NORFOLK SHOWING THE PROPERTY AND LINES OF THE NORFOLK AND WESTERN RAILROAD AND PROPOSED BELT LINE   [1890] 29x44cm (11½x17½") Chromolitho. [41] £39 **$65**

NORTHERN PACIFIC RAILROAD   [1885] Litho by Bien & Co. Chicago to Pacific. 33x69cm (13x27") Full color; N.P. in red, others colored. VG. [25] £96 **$160**

OFFICIAL MAP OF THE UNION PACIFIC RAILWAY   [1886] Greater UP system on coast to coast band of most of US; printed color time zones. Verso: time tables, ads, advice. 41x109cm (16x43") Some misfolding; minor separations fold junctions; spotting on cover; sh repaired tear; no loss; good. [7] £196 **$325**

ROUTE OF THE WESTERN RAIL ROAD. WEST OF CONNECTICUT RIVER   [dated 1837] "Enlarged from the Map of State"; litho by Thomas Moore. Westfield River route. 48x65cm (19x25½") B&W. On thin tissue; lt scattered foxing; good. [12] £106 **$175**

SECTIONAL MAP NO.2 OF THE LANDS AND THE LINE OF THE TEXAS & PACIFIC RY. CO.   [1885] Land Department, T&P Ry. Co., Dallas. Midland-Big Springs area; Howard, Martin, Andrews, Midland, Tom Green counties. 36x52cm (14½x20½") Sm margin tears repaired; o/w clean; VG. [16] £302 **$500**

THE NORTHWEST PRESENTS THE GREATEST OPPORTUNITIES FOR SETTLERS OF ANY PORTION OF "UNCLE SAM'S" DOMAIN - FOR GRAINS, GRASSES, FRUIT, LIVESTOCK, AND MINERALS ...   [1898] Oregon RR & Navigation Co. promotional covering OR & WA. 62x52cm (24½x20½") Printed browns & blues. [41] £72 **$120**

THE PRINCIPAL TRANSPORTATION LINES WEST OF CHICAGO, ST. LOUIS & NEW ORLEANS   [c.1878] Unknown source. Rails thin out going west. 52x58cm (20½x23") Printed color. Folded as issued; minor separations at fold intersections. [7] £57 **$95**

RAILROAD COMPANY MAPS continued

THE TOURISTS IDEAL ROUTE, ROME, WATERTOWN & OGDENSBURG RAILROAD, THE ONLY ALL RAIL ROUTE TO THE THOUSAND ISLANDS [c.1890] R.W.& O. RR. Shows 1,000 Island region. 18x61cm (7x24") Substantial color. VG. [25] £45 **$75**

UNION PACIFIC SYSTEM OF THE ROCKY MOUNTAIN NATIONAL (ESTES) PARK, DENVER MOUNTAIN PARKS [1922] Chicago: Poole Bros. Denver to Grand Lake; shaded relief. 81x64cm (32x25") Color. VG. [26] £45 **$75**

W. & N.B.R.R [WILLIAMSPORT & NORTH BRANCH] EXTENSION FROM NORDMONT TO DOHM'S SUMMIT [1892] Anonymous manuscript. Pen & ink on silk. 20x38cm (8x15") Red & blue highlighting. Fine. [35] £45 **$75**

RAIMONDI

[ATLAS] MAPA DEL PERU [1898] Paris: Erhard Freres. 35 mapsheets (numbered to 32) in oblong folio, modern half calf, labeled "Atlas del Pero". Several wormed lower edge; most have lib stamp. Ref: cf Phillips (M) p.697. [A6] **£287** $476

RALEIGH, W.

[BOOK WITH MAPS] THE HISTORIE OF THE WORLD [1614] London: Walter Burre. Folio, calf, later morocco lettering piece, heavily worn; 6 double-page maps, 2 plates. Covers detached; some dampstaining; title mounted & loose, worn at edges; lacks leaf with Ben Jonson verse. [A8] £659 **$1,092**

RAMUSIO

[AFRICA] [1550] Most of Africa north of Tropic of Capricorn, except bulge; south at top. 22x14cm (9x5½") Exc. [45] £392 **$650**

[ASIA: SOUTHWEST] [1563] India to Arabia with Indian Ocean. 28x38cm (11x15") Exc. [45] £513 **$850**

[MEXICO CITY] [1556 (1606)] City, with whole lake. 27x17cm (11x7") Exc. [45] £271 **$450**

[NEW FRANCE] [1556] 1st ed; after Gastaldi. On sheet 30x39cm (12x15½") Worming along fold restored. [A7] £624 **$1,035**

[NORTHEASTERN NORTH AMERICA: CANADA & NEW ENGLAND] [1556 / 1606] After Gastaldi 27x37cm (10½x14½") Exc. Ref: Burden 25; Goss (NA) 8. [24] £1,508 **$2,500**

[SAME TITLE] [1556 (1606)] [no dimens] Wash color (early?). Exc. [45] £1,387 **$2,300**

LA NUOVA FRANCIA [1565] 2nd ed; codfish removed, trees reworked. 31x40cm (12x16") Restoration margins & sm facsimile areas at vert fold; sl browning at fold; mounted on larger sheet. Ref: Potter, illus p.141. [A8] £589 **$977**

LA TERRA DE HOCHELAGA NELLA NOVA FRANCIA [1556] 1st state of three; woodcut block destroyed by fire 1557; proto-Montreal. 25x37cm (10x14½") Ref: Kershaw (Canada) #16, pl.9. [43] £844 **$1,400**

[SAME TITLE] [1556 (1565)] Woodcut; proto-Montreal. 27x37cm (10½x14½") Exc. Ref: Kershaw (Canada) #17, pl.10. [44] £663 **$1,100**

PARTE DE L AFRICA [c.1565] Wood engraving; area below Tropic of Cancer; animals. 28x38cm (11x15") [A7] £139 **$230**

PRIMA TAVOLA [AFRICA] [1563] As in *Navigationi et Viaggi*. State 2, copperplate; possible Gastaldi attribution. All Africa; south at top. 27x39cm (11x15½") Few ctr margin worm holes; o/w exc. Ref: Sabin 67732. [11] £754 **$1,250**

[SAME TITLE] [1563] 28x39cm (11x15½") Sl separation at fold repaired. [A7] £329 **$546**

SUMATRA [(1556) c.1606] Woodblock engr for *Della Navigatione e Viaggi*. South at top. 27x37cm (10½x14½") Uncolored. Fine. [4] **£600** $995

[SAME TITLE] [1556 (1606)] 27x37cm (10½x14½") Exc. [44] £513 **$850**

UNIVERSALE DELLA PARTE DEL MONDO NUOVAMENTE RITROVATA [1556] Circular map; 1st printed map showing Coronado discoveries. 27x27cm (11x10½") Uncolored. Sm repaired worm holes; sl split at ctr crease; o/w good. Ref: Burden 24; Wheat (TM) 9. Wagner (NW) 35. [32] £2,111 **$3,500**

[SAME TITLE] [c.1565] From "Della Navigationi e Viaggi". On sheet 32x42cm (12½x16½") Sh clean separation along vert fold; staining top margin; image unaffected. [A7] £451 **$747**

[SAME TITLE] [1556 / 1565] After Gastaldi; Western hemi; 1st map showing Sierra Nevada & Coronado expedition. 29x30cm (11½x11½") Exc. Ref: Burden 24. [24] £1,206 **$2,000**

RAND, AVERY & CO.

BOSTON AND MAINE RAILROAD AND CONNECTIONS [c.1885] Publ Boston. Colored litho map of northeast US & adjacent Canadian provinces; dissected into 32 panels, mounted on linen, folded into quarto leather cover. 95x113cm (37½x44½") Lacks front cover; occas linen fold weakness & soiling verso; o/w VG.
[6] £106 **$175**

MAP OF EASTLAND CO. [TX] [1877] By F.G. Blau; printed for R.M. Elgin, Houston. 57x55cm (22½x21½") Corners torn where mounted; clean, fine. [16] £332 **$550**

RAND, McNALLY & CO. (Atlas Maps)

[ADVERTISEMENT FOR GLOBES] [1897] Atlas page. (12" table globe, $13.50; 30" floor globe, $200.00) 46x32cm (18x12½") [39] £27 **$45**

[ATLAS] RAND, MCNALLY & CO.'S INDEXED ATLAS OF THE WORLD ... [1884] Chicago. Imp quarto, full calf beveled boards, gilt; 918 pp., 93 maps present, 251 colored diagrams, etc. Deluxe presentation copy. Binding broken. [16] £603 **$1,000**

[SAME TITLE] [1888-89] Chicago: Continental Publishing Co. Thick big quarto, pebbled cloth over beveled boards; 751 pp; huge foldout maps on pocket maps stock of NY, PA, OH, TX. Printed color. Shaken, spine ends frayed; NY map torn, defective; overall restorable. [16] £905 **$1,500**

[TENNESSEE: MEMPHIS ON SHEET WITH CHATTANOOGA] [1892] Each 22x15cm (8½x6") on large sheet.
[40] £24 **$40**

[TEXAS: WESTERN PART] [1883] From *Indexed Atlas of the World*. 49x32cm (19x12½") Part printed color. Fine. [16] £66 **$110**

ARIZONA [1892] Many towns, mining camps, wagon roads. 48x33cm (19x13") Printed color. ["Oregon" (19x26") offered at same price] [40] £45 **$75**

CALIFORNIA [1895] 2 insets: central part; southern part. Verso: San Francisco. 23x30cm (9x12") Printed color. VG (A). [A4] £24 **$39**

COL. N.M., ARIZONA AND UTAH [c.1881-84] From unrecorded ed of *New Family Atlas*. 32x25cm (12½x10") Printed color. Fine. [12] £45 **$75**

DAKOTA [NORTHERN PORTION] [1882] From *Indexed Atlas of the World*. 32x47cm (12½x18½") With 5 pp, incl population tables (part facsimile). Printed OL & highlight color. Mint. Ref: Karrow (MW) 10-0223.
[12] £48 **$80**

HAWAII [1898] Islands shaded gray; printed blue water. Verso: AK; western Canada; NW states. 31x48cm (12x19") Fine. [12] £36 **$60**

INDIANA [1909] Probably from *Enlarged Business Atlas*. Congressional districts, RRs, electric service indicated. 5-color litho. 66x48cm (26x19") Mended 8" tear at rt; folds; o/w fine. [12] £54 **$90**

IRELAND [1898] From *Indexed Atlas*. 65x48cm (25½x19") Printed color. Couple margin tears; VG (A).
[A4] £14 **$24**

ISLAND OF LUZON - PHILIPPINE ISLANDS [1898] From *Universal Atlas*. Index at side. 31x23cm (12x9") Printed color. VG (A). [A4] £13 **$21**

MAP OF ALABAMA [1892] 66x48cm (26x19") Printed color. [40] £36 **$60**

MAP OF FLORIDA [1892] Insets. 48x66cm (19x26") Printed color. [40] £42 **$70**

MAP OF NORTH WEST TERRITORIES [CANADA] [1892] Incl present Alberta & Saskatchewan. 31x48cm (12½x19") [40] £30 **$50**

MAP OF TEXAS [1884] For *[Standard &] Poor's Manual of Railroads for 1885*. 22x25cm (8½x10") Printed color. Lt browned; good. [16] £45 **$75**

MAP OF THE MAIN PORTION OF BOSTON [1898] As in *Universal Atlas*. Verso: RI. 23x30cm (9x12") Printed color. VG (A). [A4] £14 **$24**

MASSACHUSETTS [1890] As in *Indexed Atlas*. Large Boston inset. 48x66cm (19x26") Printed color. Sh fold split; else fine (A). [A4] £25 **$42**

MILWAUKEE [1892] 48x31cm (19x12½") [40] £27 **$45**

NEW JERSEY [1892] With sheet identifying 78 RRs 50x32cm (19½x12½") Printed color. [40] £24 **$40**

NEW MEXICO [1888 (1892)] Limited printed OL color shows grants & reservations. 48x33cm (19x13") On heavy paper. [12] £60 **$100**

NORTH DAKOTA [1889 (1891)] 2 pp population table verso. 34x57cm (13½x22½") Printed OL color. Ref: cf Karrow (MW) 10-0281. [12] £54 **$90**

NORTHERN HEMISPHERE [ON SHEET WITH] SOUTHERN HEMISPHERE [AND] WESTERN HEMISPHERE [AND] EASTERN HEMISPHERE [1889] From *Atlas of the World*. With mountains & rivers. 32x23cm (12½x9½") Color. [19] £21 **$35**

RAND, McNALLY & CO. (Atlas Maps) continued

OKLAHOMA / INDIAN TERRITORY   [1892]   Lettered counties; gazetteer on verso. 30x48cm (12x19") Clean, bright.   [8]   £45   **$75**

RAND MCNALLY ... MAP OF NEW ORLEANS   [1894]   Inset of environs. 50x32cm (19½x12½")   Full printed color. VG.   [36]   £57   **$95**

RAND MCNALLY ... MAP OF ST. PAUL, MINNEAPOLIS AND ENVIRONS   [1894]   From *Indexed Atlas* ... Regional map with each city center below. 66x48cm (26x19")   Full printed color. VG.   [36]   £57   **$95**

STREET GUIDE MAP OF CHICAGO   [1896]   Rose-Hill Cemetery to Blue Island. 70x48cm (27½x19")   OL & highlight color.   [40]   £39   **$65**

TEXAS   [1892]   Greer Co. is "Unassigned Land". 48x66cm (19x26") Full color.   [40]   £60   **$100**

[SAME TITLE]   [1895]   Text information verso. 43x66cm (17x26") Full color.   [27]   £106   **$175**

[SAME TITLE]   [c.1898]   From *Indexed Atlas of the World*. Also titled "... New Business Atlas Map of Texas". 48x66cm (19x26") Full printed color. VG.   [16]   £72   **$120**

WEST VIRGINIA   [1892]   Panhandle inset. 33x50cm (13x19½")   [40]   £30   **$50**

RAND, McNALLY & CO. (Pocket & Wall Maps; Maps not from atlases)

[KANSAS]   [1885]   Promotional map for Angell Matthewson & Co., Bankers, Parsons, KS; blank verso. Full color by county. 33x51cm (13x20")   [15]   £90   **$150**

MAP OF DAKOTA 1885   [1885]   Folding giveaway map, presented by Western Loan & Trust Co., of Pierre. 34x49cm (13½x19½") Uncolored.   [another entitled "Official Map of Dakota", 1888, presented by Western Loan & Trust, full col by county, minor fold junction separations, offered at same price]   [15]   £241   **$400**

MAP OF THE ALL-WATER ROUTE FROM THE MISSISSIPPI TO NEW YORK AND THE EASTERN ATLANTIC   [1885]   For the Michigan and Mississippi Canal Commission. Eastern U.S. with proposal for "Hennepin" Canal from Davenport, IA to Illinois River. 53x67cm (21x26½")   Folded; else VG.   [10]   £90   **$150**

MISSOURI, KANSAS & TEXAS RAILWAY AND CONNECTIONS   [c.1890]   Folded annual report route map. 21x29cm (8x11½")   Full printed color. Lf margin trimmed close; VG.   [16]   £54   **$90**

NEW MAP OF THE AMERICAN OVERLAND ROUTE SHOWING ITS CONNECTIONS, AND LAND GRANTS OF 30,000,000 ACRES   [c.1880]   Publ for Union Pacific & Central Pacific RRs. Most of U.S. with route in black. 45x90cm (17½x35½")   Orig printed color. Minor fold repairs; rice paper backing; good.   [30]   £178   **$295**

NEW MAP OF THE UNITED STATES SHOWING THE COMPLETE RAILWAY SYSTEM OF THE TRANS-MISSOURI COUNTRY   [1882]   George Crofutt. On stiff polished paper; folds as issued. 67x112cm (26x44") Printed color. Few sm clean point tears; soft creases; near fine.   [35]   £106   **$175**

POCKET MAP AND SHIPPERS' GUIDE OF TEXAS   [1911]   Folding map with gazetteer. 66x94cm (26x37") Color by counties. Minor splitting, especially at fold intersections; generally good.   [7]   £90   **$150**

RAND-MCNALLY & COS. INDEXED COUNTY AND TOWNSHIP POCKET MAP AND SHIPPERS GUIDE OF KANSAS   [1892]   Folding map in orig booklet of 50+ pages, incl RR information. 48x66cm (19x26") Printed color.   [39]   £60   **$100**

RAND MCNALLY & COS. INDEXED COUNTY AND TOWNSHIP POCKET MAP AND SHIPPERS GUIDE OF SOUTH DAKOTA   [1906]   In orig 16 pp booklet; 13 RRs. 32x47cm (12½x18½") Full color.   [39]   £39   **$65**

RAND, MCNALLY & CO.'S INDEXED MAP OF MASSACHUSETTS   [1879]   Folds into stiff wraps with text. 51x41cm (20x16") VG.   [25]   £27   **$45**

RAND MCNALLY & CO'S INDEXED POCKET MAP OF ALASKA   [1906]   Folded into case as issued. 2 insets. 48x48cm (19x19")   Almost no wear.   [26]   £45   **$75**

RAND MCNALLY'S POCKET MAP AND SHIPPER'S GUIDE OF ARIZONA   [1899]   Folding map with 18 pp gazetteer. 48x32cm (19x12½")   RRs in red. Map & book show wear; else good.   [10]   £75   **$125**

ST. JOSEPH MISSOURI ... THE QUEEN CITY OF THE MISSOURI VALLEY   [1888]   Issued by Manufacturers' Bureau. 30x41" promotional sheet folded into 16 pp text, with "Map Showing the Rail Road Facilities of St. Joseph ..." 51x74cm (20x29") Color. Long separation through map ctr & at some corners; VG.   [5]   £157   **$260**

TOWNSHIP, COUNTY AND RAILROAD MAP OF DAKOTA   [1879]   Boundaries, rivers & RRs in OL color. 53x46cm (21x18") Covers sl soiled; map clean, bright.   [10]   £136   **$225**

RANNEY

MAP OF THE UNITED STATES   [1854]   Folding map with orig leather cover. Copyright names Rufus Blanchard. 48x74cm (19x29") Full color. Scorches at 3 fold intersections with sl separations.   [15]   £452   **$750**

RAPIN

PLAN OF THE TOWN AND FORTIFICATIONS OF GIBRALTAR   [c.1728]   39x60cm (15½x24")   [A8]   £121   **$201**

RATELBAND
PLATTE GROND VAN DE STERKE VESTING RHYNBERK, DEN 7DEN FEBRUARY 1703 DOOR DE GEALLIEERDEN
VEROVERD   [1735] Fortification plan. 16x28cm (6½x11") Old color.   [48] **DM 200** £69 $114
ZUYD AMERICA - L'AMERIQUE MERIDIONALE [1735] 14x19cm (5½x7½") Old col. [48] **DM 300** £104 $172

RAUW
[FRANCE: ROUEN]   [1597]   7x9cm (3x3½")   [48] **DM 260** £90 $149
[GERMANY: AACHEN]   [1597] View on text page. 7x9cm (3x3½")   [48] **DM 590** £204 $338
[GERMANY: MAINZ]   [1597] View on text sheet. 7x9cm (3x3½")   [48] **DM 550** £190 $315
[GERMANY: ROSTOCK] [1597] On half text page. 7x9cm (2½x3½")   [48] **DM 350** £121 $200
[POLAND: WROCLAW. (BRESLAU, SILESIA)]   [1597] 7x9cm (3x3½")   [48] **DM 800** £276 $458
[SWITZERLAND: ZURICH] [1597] View on text sheet. 7x10cm (2½x3½")   [48] **DM 900** £311 $515
WORMBS   [1597] View on text sheet. 7x9cm (3x3½")   [48] **DM 540** £186 $309

RAYNAL   Try *Bonne*
[BOOK WITH MAPS] HISTOIRE PHILOSOPHIQUE ET POLITIQUE DES ETABLISSEMENS ET DU COMMERCE DES EUROPEENS DANS LES DEUX INDES [INCLUDING] ATLAS DE TOUTES LES PARTIES CONNUES DU GLOBE TERRESTRE ... [1783-84] Neuchatel & Geneva: Jean-Leonard Pellet. 10 octavo text vols & quarto atlas. 49 maps by Rigobert Bonne, 32 on blue tinted paper. Spines a bit dry, sm chips & wear, loss at atlas head; internally clean. Margin stain to neat line 1st three maps; browning 1" into image final 10 maps; o/w VG. Ref: Phillips (A) 5995; cf 5992. Sabin 68081.   [21] **Can$2,800** £1,050 $1,740

REAL ESTATE & PROMOTIONAL MAPS - Infrequent Publishers
ALAMEDA COUNTY, CALIFORNIA [c.1915] Printed on one side of local brochure. Bird's eye view showing roads, topo & bay; Pleasanton at ctr. 38x56cm (15x22") on 18x31" sheet. Full color. VG.   [26] £54 **$90**
BROOKLAND AND ADDITIONS [DC] [c.1900] Lots for sale by McLachlen & Batchelder north of 13th St, & R.I. Ave. Folds into stiff wraps. 53x43cm (21x17") Case hinge split, but VG.   [25] £54 **$90**
LANDS OF THE MAXWELL IRRIGATED LAND CO. [NM] [1913] Aerial view from Cimarron toward Sangre de Cristos. With land contract attached with orig straight pin. 15x25cm (6x10") Folded; else VG. [9] £75 **$125**
LEONARD TRACT, TOWN OF BERKELEY, SALE, THURSDAY, 16TH MAY, 1878 [1878] H.A. Cobb, San Francisco. Recto: 20 blocks along Humboldt & Ellsworth, Dwight Way to Russell St.; verso: Berkeley, in relation to San Francisco. Silked. 45x56cm (17½x22") Uncolored.   [15] £211 **$350**
MAP OF ANGLESEA, FIVE MILE BEACH, CAPE MAY CO., N.J. [c.1880] Five Mile Beach Improvement Co. Pocket map in stiff printed wrappers; promotional for 1,000 platted acres at north. 82x56cm (32½x22") Uncolored. Wrappers chipped; map fine.   [15] £136 **$225**
MAP OF BASIC CITY, AUGUSTA COUNTY, VIRGINIA. NOVEMBER 1ST, 1890 [1890] D.C. Humphreys, Washington. Detailed planning map; inset with town location; Hotel Brandon view. Printed in red & black. 36x50cm (14x19½")   [15] £196 **$325**
MAP OF CHICAGO AND ITS SOUTHERN & WESTERN SUBURBS [1854] In 2" letters top margin, "Chicago. Land Office of N.P. Inglehart & Co." Blue Island Avenue in blue. Mounted on linen. 69x48cm (27x19") Folded into eighths. Few chips & abrasions; lt toned top fourth; else VG.   [A10] £260 **$431**
MAP OF THE CITY OF STAUNTON, AUGUSTA COUNTY, VIRGINIA [1891] Staunton Development Co., Roanoke. Views. 3-color chromolitho. 52x67cm (20½x26½") Bright, crisp.   [15] £362 **$600**
MAP OF THE CITY OF WASHINGTON, DISTRICT OF COLUMBIA [1882 penciled] Tyler & Rutherford, R.E. & Insurance Brokers & Agents, Wash. 36x46cm (14x18") Uncolored. Some repairs verso.   [25] £45 **$75**
MAP OF THE UPPER SOUND COUNTRY COMPRISING PARTS OF THE COUNTIES OF PIERCE. THURSTON, KITSAP, MASON AND KING, WASHINGTON [c.1895] Henry G. Plummer, Tacoma; Lith by Crocker, San Fran; Mason Mortgage Loan Co., publ. On very thin paper. by counties. 62x81cm (24½x31½") Broad OL color. Lt creasing lower border.   [15] £513 **$850**
MINNESOTA FARM LAND COMPANY [c.1890] Publ St. Paul. 53x66cm (21x26") Some color shows available land. Minor repairs to old folds; o/w VG.   [25] £75 **$125**
PALACIOS CITY MATAGORDA COUNTY TEXAS [c.1890] Palacios City Townsite Company. Plat from office of J.F. Hervey, Jennings, LA. On Tres Placios Bay. 40x40cm (16x16") Stains; pencil notations; good.   [16] £226 **$375**
PLAT OF COLUMBIA HEIGHTS [1881] John Sherman, Trustee, Lots for sale by M.M. Parker; north of Boundary St., between 12th & 14th. 91x51cm (36x20") Issued folded; VG.   [25] £45 **$75**
PLAT OF GRAMMAR'S ADDITION TO TAKOMA PARK [MD] [1890] H.L. Thornton & Wm. H. Saunders. (note of a lot sold for $1,100) 28x51cm (11x20") Uncolored. Folded as issued; VG.   [25] £30 **$50**

REAL ESTATE & PROMOTIONAL MAPS continued

SHAKER HEIGHTS, THE VAN SWERINGEN COMPANY [1920 penciled] Lots shown; owners named where built; parks green, transit red; streets brown. 43x61cm (17x24") Full color. VG.   [25]   £96 **$160**

TOWN SITE OF LA GLORIA [CUBA] [c.1902] Cuban Land and Steamship Co., NY. Printed both sides: Proposed town in color with American-English street names; verso: the region, uncolored. 61x67cm (24x26½") With deed to a prospect in Quincy, MA.   [15]   £286 **$475**

REICHARD

DER NOERDLICHE THEIL DES GROSSENWELT MEERES ... [1804] North Pacific rim, incl Sandwich Is. 51x67cm (20x26½") Orig OL color.   [34]   £320 **$531**

REID

VERMONT FROM THE LATEST AUTHORITIES [1796] From ... *American Atlas*. 42x34cm (16½x13½") B&W. Fine. Ref: Wheat & Brun 198. Cobb (VT) 127; Phillips (M) p.972.   [12]   £211 **$350**

RENARD

[FRONTISPIECE] PLANISPHERE REPRESENTANT TOUTE L'ETENDUE DU MONDE [1715] State 1 of two. Polar projection supported by Atlas; insular Calif; early Australia. 43x27cm (17x10½") Orig color. Exc. Ref: McLaughlin p.130, (title) 12.   [43]   £528 **$875**

[SAME TITLE] [(1715) c.1792] Reissue by Elwe. Polar projection on Atlas shoulders; insular Calif. 43x26cm (17x10") Orig OL color, later additions to surround. Exc. Ref: McLaughlin (title) 12.   [4]   **£480** $796

NOVA TOTIUS TERRARUM ORBIS TABULA EX OFFICINA L. RENARD AMSTELODAMI [1715] From *Atlas ... Maritimus ofte Zee Atlas*. De Wit 1668 reissue. Double hemi; sm polar hemis; insular Calif; decorative surround. 48x56cm (19x22") Color. Ref: Shirley (W) 444, pl.327.   [13]   **Aus$9,800** £4,451 **$7,379**

TOTIUS EUROPAE LITTORA NOVISSIME EDITA ... [1715] From *Atlas de la Navigation et du Commerce*. De Wit chart reworked; Morocco to Nova Zemlya to Iceland, with western Mediterranean. 71x89cm (28x35") Full orig color. Fold repaired; o/w exc. Ref: Potter illus p.63. Koeman Ren 1.   [2]   £2,714 **$4,500**

RENOUARD

MAPPE MONDE HISTORIQUE [1827] From *Mappemonde Voyageurs*. A. Moisy, sc. Text below. 28x57cm (11x22½") Color.   [19]   £66 **$110**

RHODE

THEATRUM BELLI IN AMERICA SEPTENTRIONALI [1755] 57x80cm (22½x31½") Orig OL color. Surface tears repaired, sl loss; o/w good. Ref: Sellers & Van Ee 59. Brown (Ohio) 23.   [2]   £2,352 **$3,900**

RICE, G.J.

RICE'S MAP OF MINNEAPOLIS MINNESOTA [1895] Folded into stiff wraps. 71x56cm (28x22") Some color. Case hinges split; corner repairs verso; sm loss at a fold; pencil notes.   [25]   £90 **$150**

RICHARDS

[ATLAS] RICHARDS STANDARD ATLAS OF THE CITY OF WORCESTER MASSACHUSETTS ... [1922] Large folio, half leather & cloth. Some stains boards, corners worn; front joint partially split; text repair; minor spotting contents. Ref: LeGear (US) 1751, calls for 1 + 31 maps.   [A10]   £83 **$138**

UTAH, AND THE OVERLAND ROUTES TO IT, FROM THE MISSOURI RIVER [1855] From *Route from Liverpool to G.S.L. Valley*. F.D. Richards. 29x47cm (11½x18½") OL color. Faint edge toning; else clean. Ref: Wheat (TM) 858.   [A10]   £146 **$242**

RIZZI-ZANNONI

CARTE GEO-HYDROGRAPHIQUE DU GOLFE DU MEXIQUE ET DE SES ISLES [c.1780] 31x45cm (12½x17½") Orig OL color.   [11]   £226 **$375**

LA SUISSE [1762] Border with canton arms. 33x47cm (13x18½") Full col. Soiling in margin. [A7] £90 **$149**

NUOVA CARTA DELL' ITALIA ... [1802] 2 joined sheets, 122x92cm (48x36") Sl browned; some weak spots; generally good.   [11]   £392 **$650**

ROBERT DE VAUGONDY   See *De Vaugondy*

ROBERTS

MAP TO ILLUSTRATE THE SKETCHES OF DAVID ROBERTS, ESQ: R.A. IN EGYPT AND NUBIA, 1849 [1856] Shows places he sketched & painted. 20x15cm (8x6") Some wash color.   [40]   £18 **$30**

ROCQUE
[BOOK WITH MAPS] A SET OF PLANS AND FORTS IN AMERICA [1765] Sm quarto, orig calf; 30 plates of French & Indian War period, incl Manhattan fold-out. Some offsetting in maps. Ref: Howes (US) A261. Sabin 79332. [3] £17,490 **$29,000**
A MAP OF THE KINGDOME OF IRELAND [1794] 4 sheets joined, 122x96cm (48x38") Col. [A6] £345 $572
A MAP OF THE KINGDOM OF IRELAND, DIVIDED INTO PROVINCES ... [1773] 4 joined sheets, 122x97cm (48x38") Orig OL color. [34] £460 $763
ENGLAND AND WALES DRAWN FROM THE MOST ACCURATE SURVEYS [1794] Laurie & Whittle. 4 sheets joined, 146x98cm (57½x38½") Color. [A6] £115 $191
PLAN OF THE HOUSE, GARDENS, PARK & HERMITAGE OF THE MAJESTIES, AT RICHMOND; AND OF THEIR R.H. THE PRINCE OF WALES, & THE PRINCESS ROYAL AT KEW [1734] London: John Bowles. Large scale plan; elevations of 12 buildings. 2 sheets joined, 58x90cm (23x35½") Some browning at folds; minor restoration. [46] £650 $1,078
SUSSEX [1746] Probably from *The Small British Atlas*. T. Read; publ by Rocque & Sayer; based on Moll & Budgens's survey. 16x20cm (6x7½") Partial color. [11] £45 **$75**
THE ENVIRONS OF LONDON REDUCED FROM AN ACTUAL SURVEY IN 16 SHEETS. BY THE LATE JOHN ROCQUE ... WITH NEW IMPROVEMENTS TO THE YEAR 1763 [1764] Publ by M.A Rocque. Extent: Tottenham High Cross-Woolwich-Morden-Hounslow; on 4 sheets, each 44x66cm (17½x26") Near mint. Ref: Howgego 124. [11] £1,508 **$2,500**

ROGERS & JOHNSTON
NEW YORK AND ITS ENVIRONS [1857] From *Atlas of the United States* ... Near circular map of NYC area centered on Narrows. 2-color litho. 19x17cm (7½x6½") on 12x7½" tinted background. [12] £54 **$90**

ROLLOS
A NEW MAP OF GERMANY DIVIDED INTO CIRCLES [1770] Incl Switzerland, Austria, Czech Republic. 20x29cm (8x11½") OL color. [40] £39 **$65**
AN ACCURATE MAP OF NORTH AMERICA DRAWN FROM THE SIEUR ROBERT, WITH IMPROVEMENTS [1760] Engraved by G. Rollos for *Geographical Dictionary*. After de Vaugondy. 19x29cm (7½x11½") B&W. Fine. [12] £106 **$175**

ROSACCIO
ORBIS TERRAE COMPENDIOSA DESCRIPTIO [1598-1713] From Lasor a Varea, *Universus Terrarum Orbis Scriptorum*. Double hemi. 17x25cm (7x10") Uncolored. Ref: cf. Shirley (W) 217 [34] £380 $630

ROSSI
ISOLE DELL' INDIA CIOE LE MOLUCCHE LE FILIPPINE E DELLA SONDA ... [1683] As in *Mercurio Geografico*. East Indies with "Nuova Olanda" & "Carpentaria". 45x58cm (17½x23") Color. Ref: Clancy (Australis) 6.21, ill. p.88. [13] **Aus$2,950** £1,340 $2,221
LE POSTE DELLA FRANCIA [1697] Double sheets joined, 67x56cm (26½x22") OL color. Toned; some dampstaining; faults repairable. [A8] £76 **$126**
ROMA ANTIQUA TRIUMPHATRIX ... [c.1690] Rossi, alias Rubeis. 279 item key; surround of 20 vignettes, each with explanatory text. 48x74cm (19x29") Full color. Exc. [23] £1,327 **$2,200**

ROSSI, L.
GRANDE OCEANO OUVERO QUINTA PARTE DEL MONDO [1820] As in *Nuovo Atlante Milano*. Pacific rim. 20x25cm (8x10") B&W. [13] **Aus$290** £132 $218

ROUX
BAIE DE ALMERIE [1799] 13x20cm (5x7½") B&W. Lt foxing; good (B). [A4] £15 **$25**
PLAN DE L'ISLE SPINE LONGUE SUR L'ISLE CANDIE [1779] 12x19cm (4½x7½") B&W. VG (A). [A3] £17 **$28**

ROYAL GEOGRAPHICAL SOCIETY
SKETCH OF PART OF THE HIMMA-LEH MOUNTAINS TO ILLUSTRATE THE PAPER BY CAPT. JOHNSON [1834] To the Jumna River headwaters. 20x17cm (8x6½") Routes in color. VG. [26] £24 **$40**

RUBEIS
RECENTIS ROMAE ICHNOGRAPHIA ET HYPSOGRAPHIA SIVE PLANTA ET FACIES ... [1756] Attributable also to Falda de Valle. 69x88cm (27x35") Color. Sl wear at fold intersection; else exc. [24] £1,809 **$3,000**

RUSCELLI

[ATLAS] LA GEOGRAFIA DI CLAUDIO TOLOMEO ALESSANDRINO NOUVAMENTE TRADOTTA DI GRECO IN ITALIANO DA GIROLAMO RUSCELLI ... [1561] Valgrisi; 1st ed of six. Quarto, vellum, recased, new end papers; 358+ pp; 27 Ptolemaic & 37 modern maps enlarged & updated from 1548 Gastaldi, incl 4 new. Minor margin waterstain on several maps; a margin repair; generally fresh. Ref: Sabin 66504; Phillips (A) 371. [24] £6,333 **$10,500**

[ATLAS] LA GEOGRAFIA DI CLAUDIO TOLOMEO ALESSANDRINO NUOVAMENTE TRADOTTA DI GRECO IN ITALIANO ... [1564] Quarto, old half sheep; 50 double-page maps. Foxing, soiling, stains mostly margin affecting some maps; lacks title & another leaf. Ref: Sabin 66504. [A8] £3,329 **$5,520**

AFRICA NUOVA TAVOLA [1561] Southern Africa; after Gastaldi. 18x24cm (7x9½") B&W. Faint age toning along fold; lt watermarks to image lower side margins; o/w fine. ["Africa Minor Nuova Tavola" (Barbary Coast) sold at same price] Ref: Tooley (Africa) p.46. [A1] £66 **$110**

[SAME TITLE] [1561-99] Southern Africa. 18x25cm (7x10") B&W. Fine (A+). [A3] £131 **$218**

AMERICA [1599] Venice. From the Ptolemy; Italian text verso. 19x25cm (7½x10") Sm repair lower vert fold. [A7] £242 **$402**

BRASIL NOVA TABULA [1599] Venice. From the Ptolemy. 20x26cm (7½x10") [A7] £277 **$460**

BRASIL NUOVA TAVOLA [1561] 18x25cm (7x10") B&W. Faint age toning along fold; lt image transfer blank areas; o/w fine. [A1] £110 **$182**

CARTA MARINA NUOVA TAVOLA [1561-] From *La Geographia*. Venice: Ziletti. 18x24cm (7½x9½") Ref: Shirley (W) 111. [34] £480 **$796**

[SAME TITLE] [1561] World, after Gastaldi. 19x25cm (7½x9½") Exc. Ref: Shirley 111. [43] £573 **$950**

DI HUNGARIA ET TRANSILVANIA [1599] 14x20cm (5½x8") B&W. Fine (A+). [A3] £55 **$91**

EUROPAE TABULA V [1561] Ptolemaic Italy. 18x25cm (7x9½") [11] £60 **$100**

EUROPAE TABULA VI [1561] From *Geographia*. Ptolemaic Italy. 18x25cm (7x9½") Uncolored. Paper separation along vert fold, no loss; VG to fine. [14] £196 **$325**

ESPOSITIONI [ARMILLARY SPHERE] [1561] 13x18cm (5x7") Wash color. [41] £45 **$75**

ISOLA CUBA NOVA [1561] From *La Geografica di Claudio Tolomeo* ... 1st ed. Incl Jamaica & Hispaniola. 18x25cm (7x9½") B&W. Light but good impression; VG (A). Ref: Phillips (A) 373. [A4] £210 **$349**

MOSCHOVIA NUOVA TAVOLA [1561] 4 groups of tents to east. 18x24cm (7x9½") B&W. Faint age toning along fold; o/w fine. [A1] £83 **$138**

NATOLIA NUOVA TAVOLA [1599] 19x26cm (7½x10") B&W. Couple worm holes margin; VG (A). [A4] f45 **$74**

ORBIS DESCRIPTIO [1561] From *La Geografia* ... Venice: Valgrisi. 1st ed. Double hemi; America joined to Asia. 18x26cm (7x10") Fine. Ref: Shirley (W) 110; Phillips (A) 371. [19] £449 **$745**

SCHONLADIA NUOVA [1561] From *Geographia di Claudio Tolomeo* ... 18x25cm (7x10") B&W. Lt toned at c'fold; near fine. Ref: Phillips (A) 371. [35] £196 **$325**

[SAME TITLE] [1561] 18x25cm (7x10") B&W. VG to fine. [A1] £123 **$204**

SEPTENTRIONALIUM PARTIUM NOVA TABULA [1562] North Atlantic lands; a "Zeno" derivative. 18x24cm (7x9½") C'fold restoration. [11] £211 **$350**

TABULA APHRICAE II [1599] Venice: Rosaccio. Ptolemaic North Africa. 19x25cm (7½x10") B&W. Fine. ["Tabula Africae III" (Ptolemaic Egypt) offered at same price] Ref: Phillips (A) 409. [35] £100 **$165**

TABULA APHRICAE III [1562] From *La Geographia di Claudio Tolomeo* ... 18x25cm (7x10") B&W. Fine (A+). [A4] £77 **$127**

TABULA APHRICAE IIII [1562] *La Geographia di Claudio Tolomeo* ... Ptolemaic conception of northern Africa past equator to Mountains of the Moon; hexagonal shape. 19x25cm (7½x10") B&W. Fine (A+). Ref: Norwich 292. [A4] £138 **$228**

TABULA ASIA IX [1562] 19x24cm (7½x9½") B&W. C'fold toning; VG+. Ref: Phillips (A) 372. [35] £72 **$120**

TABULA ASIAE IIII [1561] From *Geographia*. Ptolemaic Middle East. 18x24cm (7x9½") Uncolored. Faint age toning at vert fold; o/w fine. [14] £196 **$325**

TABULA ASIAE V [1561] 1st ed. Ptolemaic Persia. 19x25cm (7½x10") B&W. Lt c'fold toning; VG. Ref: Phillips (A) 371. [35] £90 **$150**

TABULA ASIAE VI [1561] Ptolemaic Arabia; trapezoidal form. 18x23cm (7x9½") Lt age toning along fold; o/w fine. [A1] £119 **$198**

TABULA EUROPAE I [1561] Ptolemaic British Isles; Scotland lies east-west. 18x25cm (7x10") B&W. Lt age toning along fold; some lt verso text show through; o/w fine. Ref: Shirley (BI to 1650) 67. [A1] £119 **$198**

RUSCELLI continued

TABULA EUROPAE V [1561] Ptolemaic southern Europe; Sicily to Danube. 18x26cm (7x10") B&W. Minor toning; VG (A). [A3] £74 **$122**
TABULA EUROPAE VI [c.1597] Ptolemaic Italy. Valgrisi ed, 15x18cm (6x7") Uncol. VG. [25] £106 **$175**
TAVOLA NUOVA D'ITALIA [c.1561] 19x25cm (7½x10") B&W. Age toned; barely visible tear in image; good (B). [A4] £37 **$61**
TAVOLA NUOVA DI GERMANIA [1561] 18x25cm (7x10") B&W. Faint age toning along fold; o/w VG to fine. [A1] £83 **$138**
TIERRA NUEVA [1561] 1st state; 1st issue. 18x25cm (7½x9½") Exc. Ref: Burden 30; Kershaw (Canada) 18a, pl.12; Goss (NA) 9. [44] £663 **$1,100**
[SAME TITLE] [1561] 19x26cm (7½x10½") Full old OL color, if not orig. [27] £452 **$750**
TOSCANA NUOVA TABULA [1561] 17x25cm (7x10") B&W. Even edge tone; VG (A). [A4] £50 **$83**

RUSSELL

A GENERAL MAP OF NORTH AMERICA DRAWN FROM THE BEST SURVEYS BY J. RUSSELL, 1794 [1795] 36x47cm (14½x18½") B&W. Fold separation repairs; rt margin repaired past neat line; image VG. Ref: Wheat (TM) 228; Phillips (A) 1363-1. Ristow (Amer M&M) p.153. [35] £106 **$175**
A GENERAL MAP OF NORTH AMERICA FROM THE LATEST OBSERVATIONS [1778] Eastern North America, incl US & Canada; incl distance table. 28x41cm (11x16") Uncol. Lower rt corner repaired. [26] £196 **$325**
A VIEW OF THE CITY OF MEXICO [1778] 18x20cm (7x8") Uncolored. VG. [26] £36 **$60**
AN EXACT MAP OF NEW ENGLAND, NEW YORK, PENSYLVANIA & NEW JERSEY FROM THE LATEST SURVEYS [1778] NYC to Canada; Cape Cod to Lake Erie. 19x25cm (7½x10") Uncolored. Lower rt corner repaired. [26] £84 **$140**
AN EXACT MAP OF NEW JERSEY, PENSYLVANIA, NEW YORK, MARYLAND & VIRGINIA FROM THE LATEST SURVEYS [1778] 19x25cm (7½x10") Uncolored. Lower lf corner repaired; o/w VG. [26] £96 **$160**
AN EXACT MAP OF NORTH AMERICA FROM THE BEST AUTHORITIES [1778] 25x38cm (10x15") Uncolored. Some repair lower rt corner. [26] £151 **$250**
AN EXACT MAP OF NORTH AND SOUTH CAROLINA, & GEORGIA WITH EAST AND WEST FLORIDA FROM THE LATEST DISCOVERIES [1778] 19x25cm (7½x10") Uncolored. VG. [26] £96 **$160**
AN EXACT MAP OF THE FIVE GREAT LAKES WITH PART OF PENSILVANIA, NEW YORK, CANADA AND HUDSONS BAY TERRITORIES FROM THE BEST SURVEYS [1778] 19x25cm (7½x10") Uncolored. Lower rt corner repaired; o/w VG. [26] £193 **$320**
AN EXACT MAP OF THE PROVINCE OF QUEBEC WITH PART OF NEW YORK, NEW ENGLAND FROM THE LATEST SURVEYS [1778] 19x25cm (7½x10") Uncolored. Exc. [26] £54 **$90**
MAP OF THE STATE OF KENTUCKY; WITH THE ADJOINING TERRITORIES [1794] From Winterbotham's *History of America*. London. Incl all KY, most of TN, some N.W. Terr. 38x46cm (15x18") Uncolored. Lt offsetting; weakness at some folds; lt discoloration lower margin; VG. [15] £452 **$750**
PLAN OF THE CITY OF WASHINGTON, IN THE TERRITORY OF COLUMBIA, CEDED BY THE STATES OF VIRGINIA AND MARYLAND TO THE UNITED STATES OF AMERICA ... [1796] From Winterbotham's *History of America*. London. 40x53cm (15½x21") Uncolored. [15] £1,055 **$1,750**
SOUTH WEST VIEW OF FORT GEORGE WITH THE CITY OF NEW YORK [1778] Tip of Manhattan; British ship in foreground. 18x20cm (7x8") Uncolored. Strong engraving. [26] £54 **$90**
THE WEST INDIES AND GULF OF MEXICO FROM THE LATEST DISCOVERIES AND BEST OBSERVATIONS [1778] 23x36cm (9x14") Uncolored. VG. [26] £84 **$140**
THE WORLD WITH THE LATEST DISCOVERIES TO THE PRESENT YEAR 1808 [1808] J. Russell, London. 22x43cm (9x17") Color. [19] £72 **$120**

SALMON

[BOOK WITH MAPS] A NEW GEOGRAPHICAL AND HISTORICAL GRAMMAR ... TWELFTH EDITION [1772] Octavo; many maps; calf. [13th ed, 1785; scattered dampstaining; sold for same price] [A7] £260 **$431**
[BOOK WITH MAPS] MODERN HISTORY [1744] Volume 1 only (of 3). Folio, sheep; 48 maps & plates by Herman Moll. Covers worn & loose. [A8] £485 **$805**
LA CITTA DI TREVERI, CAPITALE DELL' ARCIVESCOVATO [c.1740] Trier view. 16x22cm (6x9") [48] **DM 640** £221 **$366**
THE PLAN OF CONSTANTINOPLE [1739] From *Modern History*. Herman Moll, sc. View. 17x28cm (6½x11") B&W. Fine. [30] £87 **$145**

SAMPSON, DAVENPORT & CO.

MAP OF CAPE ANN [ON SHEET WITH GLOUCESTER, MA] [1885] Pocket map in orig gilt-stamped cloth folder. 31x52cm (12x20½") Full color. Fold repaired. [15] £121 **$200**

SANSON (Folio)   Try *Jaillot*

AFRICA VETUS [1667] Paris: Mariette. Classical placenames. 40x55cm (15½x21½") Orig OL color. Ref: Norwich 41. [34] £380 **$630**

AMERIQUE MERIDIONALE ... [1667-69] Guillaume Sanson revision. 40x56cm (15½x22") Orig OL color. [34] £450 **$746**

ANCIENS ROYAUMES DE KENT, D'ESSEX, ET DE SUSSEX ... [1654-1667] 36x48cm (14½x19") Color. [34] £400 **$664**

ASIA VETUS ... [1667] Modern outline; ancient divisions; classical & traditional names. 40x56cm (15½x22") Orig OL color. [34] £500 **$829**

ASIE ... [1650] 39x56cm (15½x22") Early OL color. Mild dampstains margin & lower lf image; lower margin corners chipped; some fraying along edges. [A9] £125 **$207**

ASIE. PAR N. SANSON D'ABBEVILLE GEOG. DU ROY ... [1650] Paris: Mariette. Insular Korea. 39x57cm (15½x22½") Color. Margin repairs; fine. [30] £513 **$850**

ATLANTIS INSULA, A NICOLAO SANSON ANTIQUITATI RESTITUTA NUNC DEMUN MAJORI FORMA DELINEATA, ET EN DECEM REGNA, IUXTA DECEM NEPTUNI FILIOS DISTRIBUTA ... EX CONATIBUS GULIELMI SANSON NICOLAI FILII... [1669] Insular Calif: Japan as "Iabadii". 39x56cm (15½x22") OL color; uncolored cartouche. Fine (A+). Ref: Burden 405; Mclaughlin 46. [A4] £657 **$1,089**

[SAME TITLE] [1730] Amsterdam: Covens & Mortier. Centered on Americas with most of adjacent oceans; 39x55cm (15½x21½") OL col. Few sm stains; a fold strengthened. Ref: McLaughlin 46. [A6] £517 **$858**

BALTIA, QUAE ET SCANDIA, FINNINGIA ... [1667-] Appeared in *Tables de la Geographie* ... Paris: Mariette. Ancient Scandinavia. About 40x52cm (15½x20½") Orig OL color. ["... Scandinavie; ou Sont Suede, Gotlande, Lapponie Suedoise ...", trimmed at top, offered at same price] [34] £380 **$630**

CARTE GENERAL DE LA CAROLINE. DRESSE SUR LES MEMOIRES LE PLUS NOUVEAUX PAR LE SIEUR S ... [c.1696] Amsterdam: Mortier. 57x46cm (22½x18½") Full orig color. Exc. Ref: Cumming (SE) 120. [24] £1,719 **$2,850**

[SAME TITLE] [c.1696] Amsterdam: Mortier. Based on Thornton - Morden. Charleston Harbor inset. 56x47cm (22x18½") Full orig color. Ref: Cumming (SE) 120. [36] £1,659 **$2,750**

[SAME TITLE] [c.1720] After Thornton-Morden Lea; reengraved by Mortier. 57x46cm (22½x18½") Later color. Exc. Ref: cf Cumming (SE) 120. [2] £1,689 **$2,800**

CARTE GENERALE DES INDES ORIENTALES ET DES ISLES ADIACENTES [c.1654] Paris: Pierre Mariette. India to S Japan & W Australia. 39x48cm (15½x19") Color. [46] £780 **$1,294**

CARTE PARTICULIERE DE LA CAROLINE DRESSE SUR LES MEMOIRES LE PLUS NOUVEAUX ... [c.1696] Amsterdam: Mortier. 46x59cm (18x23½") Orig OL col. Exc. Ref: Cumming (SE) 121. [36] £1,659 **$2,750**

[SAME TITLE] [c.1700] Amsterdam: Mortier. 48x59cm (19x23½") Later color. Exc. Ref: Cumming (SE) 121; Potter illus p.20. [2] £2,262 **$3,750**

CERCLE DE FRANCONIE ... [1667-] Appeared in *Tables de la Geographie* ... Paris: Mariette. About 40x52cm (15½x20½") Orig OL color. ["Haute Saxe ..." offered at same price] [34] £240 **$398**

COURS DU DANUBE DE BELGRADE JUSQUES AU PONT EUXIN [1667-] Appeared in *Tables de la Geographie* ... Paris: Mariette. About 40x52cm (15½x20½") Orig OL color. [34] £220 **$365**

DESCRIPTION DE LA TARTARIE TIREE ED PARTIE DE PLUSIEURS CARTES [1654-1667] From *Tables de la Geographie Ancienne et Nouveli* ... Paris: Mariette. 36x57cm (14x22") Orig OL color. [34] £350 **$581**

ERTZ-HERTZOGTHUMB OESTERREICH ... ARCHIDUCHE D'AUSTRICHE ... [1667-] Appeared in *Tables de la Geographie* ... Paris: Mariette. About 40x52cm (15½x20½") Orig OL color. Ref: Phillips (A) 4260-56. [34] £380 **$630**

ESTATS ET ROYAUMES DE FEZ ET MAROC [1667-] From *Tables de la Geographie* ... 36x52cm (14x20½") Orig OL color. [34] £340 **$564**

GEOGRAPHIAE SACRA [1679] 40x51cm (15½x20") OL color. [A8] £173 **$287**

GEOGRAPHIAE SACRAE EX VETERI, ET NOVO TESTAMENTO [1667] In *Tables de la Geographie* ... 40x52cm (15½x20½") Orig OL color. Ref: Laor 688. [34] £300 **$498**

GOUVERNEMENT GENERAL D'ORLEANS [1650] 40x53cm (15½x21") OL color; B&W cartouche. VG (A). [A4] £30 **$50**

GRAECIAE ANTIQUAE ... [1636] 41x55cm (16½x22") Old OL color. Sm margins; else fine. Ref: Zacharakis 1861. [37] £286 **$475**

SANSON (Folio) continued

HARMONIE OR CORRESPONDANCE DU GLOBE ... [1659] Double hemi; insular Calif. 38x52cm (15x20½") Full wash color. VG. [36] £467 **$775**

HAUTE ALLEMAGNE, DIVISEE PAR SES ESTATS ... [1667-] Appeared in *Tables de la Geographie* ... Paris: Mariette. About 40x52cm (15½x20½") Orig OL color. [34] **£300** $498

HAUTE ETHIOPIE OU SONT L'EMPIRE DES ABISSINS, LA NUBIE. [1667-] From *Tables de la Geographie* ... 36x52cm (14x20½") Orig OL color. [34] **£450** $746

HAUTE OU PETITE POLOGNE ... [1667-] Appeared in *Tables de la Geographie* ... Paris: Mariette. Cracow region. About 40x52cm (15½x20½") Orig OL color. [34] **£200** $332

HAUTE PARTIE DE LA BASSE SAXE ... [1667-] Appeared in *Tables de la Geographie* ... Paris: Mariette. About 40x52cm (15½x20½") Orig OL color. Ref: cf Phillips (A) 4260-63. ["Basse Partie de la Basse Saxe ..." offered at same price] [34] **£280** $465

HELSINGE, MEDELPADIE ANGERMANNIE, IEMPTIE, DALECARLIE ... [1667-] Appeared in *Tables de la Geographie* ... Paris: Mariette. About 40x52cm (15½x20½") Orig OL color. [34] **£300** $498

HEMISPHERE OCCIDENTAL DU GLOBE TERTRE VEU EN CONVEX ... [IN SET WITH] ... EN CONCAVE [c.1697 - 1705] Pierre Moullart Sanson, Paris. Insular Calif; one hemi seen from outside, other from inside; each 23x21cm (9x8½") Ref: cf Shirley (W) 591& 592; McLaughlin 125 & 126, state 2. [34] **£550** $912

HERTZOTHUMB POMMERN ... [1667-] Appeared in *Tables de la Geographie* ... Paris: Mariette. About 40x52cm (15½x20½") Orig OL color. Ref: Phillips (A) 4260-62. [34] **£250** $415

HUNGARIA REGNUM [1667-] Appeared in *Tables de la Geographie* ... Paris: Mariette. About 40x52cm (15½x20½") Orig OL color. [34] **£260** $431

ISLE D'AUPHINE ... NOMMEE ... MADAGASCAR [1667] 58x45cm (23x17½") Orig OL color. Lt stains at bottom c'fold. [34] **£420** $697

ISLE DE LA GUADELOUPE ... [1667] Paris: Mariette. 32x43cm (12½x16½") Orig OL col. [34] **£400** $664

KONIGREICH BOHEIM ... [1667-] Appeared in *Tables de la Geographie* ... Paris: Mariette. Prague environs. About 40x52cm (15½x20½") Orig OL color. Ref: Phillips (A) 4260-58. [34] **£250** $415

L'AFRIQUE OU LYBIE ULTERIEURE ... [1667-] From *Tables de la Geographie* ... 36x52cm (14x20½") Orig OL color. [34] **£360** $597

L'HYDROGRAPHIE OU DESCRIPTION DE L'EAU C'EST A DIRE DES MERS, GOLFES, LACS, DESTROITS ET RIVIERES PRINCIPALES ... DU GLOBE TERRESTRE [1652] Double hemi; insular Calif. 40x54cm (15½x21½") Color. Sl browning & soiling margins. [A7] £520 **$862**

L'INDE DECA ET DELA LE GANGE, OU EST L'EMPIRE DU GRAND MOGOL ... [1654-1667] Paris: Mariette. 35x55cm (13½x21½") Orig OL color. [34] **£300** $498

LA CHINE ROYAUME ... [1656] 41x54cm (16x21") OL color; later cartouche color. Faint soiling margins; else fresh, clean. [A9] £243 **$403**

LA LIVONIE DUCHE DIVISEE EN SES PRINCIPLES PARTIES ESTEN, ET LETTEN [1667-] Appeared in *Tables de la Geographie* ... Paris: Mariette. About 41x53cm (16x21") Orig OL color. [34] **£340** $564

LA LORRAINE, QUI COMPREND LES DUCHES DE LORRAINE ET DE BAR, ET LES BALLIAGES DES EVESCHES ET DES VILLES DE METZ, TOUL, ET VERDUN [c.1700] Mortier. 55x88cm (21½x34½") Orig color. VG. [A2] £166 **$275**

LA SOUABE ... [1667-] Appeared in *Tables de la Geographie* ... Paris: Mariette. About 40x52cm (15½x20½") Orig OL color. ["Palatinat du Rhin, Alsace, et Partie de Souabe, de Franconie &c." and "Estats de la Succession de Cleves et Juliers" offered at same price] [34] **£260** $431

LA TERRE ET LES ISLES MAGELLANIQUES ... [1668] 37x49cm (14½x19") OL color. Separation upper c'fold & tear lower c'fold repaired verso with archival tape; lt ink transfer blank areas; VG. [A1] £119 **$198**

LE CANADA OU NOUVELLE FRANCE ... [1656] 40x54cm (15½x21½") Orig OL color. Few faint stains; else exc. Ref: Burden 319; Schwartz & Eherenberg pl.62. Kaufman (Gt.Lakes) #3. [24] 2,352 **$3,900**

LE CHILI DIVISE EN SES TREIZE IURISDICTIONS ... [1667] 40x46cm (15½x18") Orig OL color. ["Le Paraguay ..." offered at £360] [34] **£380** $630

LE GOUVERNEMENT GENERAL DU DAUFINE, ET DES PAYS CIRCUMVOISINS OU SONT LA SAVOYE [1667] Incl Lyon, Geneva, Turin. 36x43cm (14x17") OL color. Fine (A+). [A4] £62 **$103**

LE NOUVEAU MEXIQUE, ET LA FLORIDE ... [1656] Iohanes Somer, sc. Insular Calif. 32x55cm (12½x21½") Contemporary OL color. Exc. Ref: McLaughlin 17; Tooley (Amer) p.115, #14, pl.31. Leighly pl.31. [1] £3,015 **$5,000**

SANSON (Folio) continued

LES DEUX POLES ARCTICQUE OU SEPTENTRIONAL, ET ANTARCTICQUE OU MERIDIONAL, OU DESCRIPTION DES TERRES ARCTICQUES ET ANTARCTICQUES; ET DES PAYS CIRCOMVOISINS JUSQUES AUX 45 DEGRES DE LATITUDE   [1657]   Double polar partial hemis. Jean Somer Pruthenus, sc. 38x53cm (15x21") Full orig color. Minor staining; else VG. Ref: See note Shirley (W) 408. [36]   £588 **$975**

[SAME TITLE]   [1657]   Paris: Mariette. Two hemis. 39x53cm (15½x21") Color. Sl browning along vert fold; minor browning & soiling mostly margin.   [A7]   £347 **$575**

[SAME TITLE]   [1657-67]   Partial polar double hemi. 38x53cm (15x21") Orig OL color. Ref: Kershaw (Canada) 144; see note Shirley (W) 408. Kershaw (Canada).   [34]   £400 **$664**

[SAME TITLE]   [dated 1679]   Jean Somer Pruthenus, sc. 39x53cm (15½x21") Color. Minor repair. Ref: Shirley (W) 408; Phillips (A) 4260-97.   [19]   £293 **$485**

LES ETATS DE LA COURONNE DE CASTILLE, ... ANDALOUSIE, GRANADE, ET MURCIE   [1667-]   Appeared in *Tables de la Geographie* ... Paris: Mariette. About 40x52cm (15½x20½") Orig OL color.   [34]   £350 **$581**

LES ETATS DE LA COURONNE DE PORTUGAL EN ESPAGNE   [1667-]   Appeared in *Tables de la Geographie* ... Paris: Mariette. About 52x40cm (20½x15½") Orig OL col. Ref: cf Phillips (A) 4261-71.   [34]   £400 **$664**

MEXIQUE, OU NOUVELLE ESPAGNE, NOUV.LLE GALLICE, IUCATAN &C. ET AUTRES PROVINCES JUSQUES A L'ISTHME DE PANAMA; OU SONT LES AUDIENCES DE MEXICO, DE GUADALAIARA, ET DE GUATIMALA [1656]   1st ed. 37x55cm (14½x22") Orig OL color. Exc. Ref: Kapp (Cent Amer) 10. Pastoureau San5.   [2]   £573 **$950**

[SAME TITLE]   [1656]   37x55cm (14½x22") Orig OL color. Exc.   [24]   £452 **$750**

PARTIE DE LA BARBARIE OU EST LE ROYAUME D'ALGER   [1667-]   From *Tables de la Geographie* ... 36x53cm (14x21") Orig OL color.   [34]   £260 **$431**

PARTIE DE LITHUANIE ... MINSK ...   [1667-]   Appeared in *Tables de la Geographie* ... Paris: Mariette. Chernobyl region. About 40x52cm (15½x20½") Orig OL color.   [34]   £120 **$199**

PARTIE DE TERRE FERME OU SONT GUIANE ET CARIBANE. AUGMENTEE ET CORRIGEE SUIVANT LES DERNIERES RELATIONS. PAR N SANSON D'ABBEVILLE ...   [1656 (1657)]   Paris: Mariette. 41x54cm (16x21") Old col. Lt vert crease; minor surface soil; good. Ref: cf Phillips (A) 486-29.   [30]   £332 **$550**

[SAME TITLE]   [1656-1667]   Trinidad to Amazon mouth with Lake Parime & Eldorado. 40x54cm (15½x21½") Orig OL color.   [34]   £350 **$581**

PARTIE MERIDIO.LE DU ROYAUME D'IRLANDE   [1690]   40x50cm (16x19½") Col. Lt toned. [A8]   £139 **$230**

PARTIE MERIDIONAL DO REYNO DE PORTUGAL   [1667-]   Appeared in *Tables de la Geographie* ... Paris: Mariette. About 40x52cm (15½x20½") Orig OL color. Ref: cf Phillips (A) 4261-73.   [34]   £320 **$531**

PARTIE MERIDIONALE DE L'INDE EN DEUX PRESQU'ISLES L'UNE DECA ET L'AUTRE DELA LE GANGE ... A PARIS CHEZ PIERRE MARIETTE ...   1654   [c.1654] India & Indo-China. 38x52cm (15x20½") Color. Sl margin staining.   [46]   £560 **$929**

PARTIE ORIENTALE DE LA LAPPONIE SUEDOISE ...   [1667-]   Appeared in *Tables de la Geographie* ... Paris: Mariette. About 40x52cm (15½x20½") Orig OL color.   [34]   £180 **$299**

PARTIE SEPTENTRIE DU ROYAUME D'IRLANDE   [1665]   40x49cm (15½x19½") Color. ["Partie Meridiole. ..." offered at £340]   [34]   £380 **$630**

PARTIE SEPTENTR.LE DU ROYAUME D'IRLANDE ...   [IN SET WITH]   PARTIE MERIDIO.LE DU ...   [1665] Paris: Mariette. Each 40x49cm (15½x19½") Orig OL color. Strong impression.   [11]   £754 **$1,250**

ROYAUME DE NORWEGE ...   [1667-]   Appeared in *Tables de la Geographie* ... Paris: Mariette. About 52x40cm (20½x15½") Orig OL color. Trimmed close at rt.   [34]   £400 **$664**

SUD-GOTLANDE, ET PAYS CIRCOMVOISINS   [1667-]   Appeared in *Tables de la Geographie* ... Paris: Mariette. About 40x52cm (15½x20½") Orig OL color.   [34]   £280 **$465**

TABULA NOVA TOTIUS REGNI POLONIAE ...   [c.1710]   Amsterdam: Visscher. 42x55cm (16½x22") Full orig wash & OL color.   [11]   £196 **$325**

TERRA PROMISSA IN SORTES SEU TRIBUS XII ...   [1667]   In *Tables de la Geographie* ... 40x52cm (15½x20½") Orig OL color.   [34]   £320 **$531**

SANSON (Small)

AMERICQUE SEPTENTRIONALE ...   [1683]   Insular Calif; open ended Great Lakes. 20x24cm (8x9½") Orig color. Fine.   [4]   £400 **$664**

AUDIENCA DE GUADALAJARA, NOVA MEXICO, CALIFORNIA &C.   [1656 (c.1657)]   State 4, from only Latin ed. Insular Calif. 20x24cm (8x9½") B&W. Sm spot; else fine, dark impression. Ref: McLaughlin 16 (4); Tooley (Amer) p.116. Leighly 9; Lowery 148.   [12]   £543 **$900**

SANSON (Small) continued

AUDIENCE DE GUADALAJARA, NOUVEAU MEXIQUE, CALIFORNIE, &C. ... [1657] 1st state. Insular Calif. 20x24cm (8x9½") Orig color. Exc. Ref: McLaughlin 16. [44] £724 **$1,200**
[SAME TITLE] [1683] Winter, sc. Insular Calif. 20x24cm (8x9½") Orig color. Fine. Ref: McLaughlin 89. [4] £450 **$746**
LA FLORIDE PAR N. SANSON D'ABBEVILLE ... [1657 (1662)] 18x25cm (7½x10") Orig OL color. Exc. Ref: Burden 326. [44] £332 **$550**
LA GRANDE TARTARIE [1652] 19x25cm (7½x10") Old OL color. Faint tide mark; else VG. [38] £75 **$125**
LES ISLES PHILIPPINES [ON SHEET WITH] ISLAS DE LOS LADRONES OU ISLE DES LARRONS ... [1652 (1683)] From new plate. 19x25cm (7½x10") Orig OL color. Exc. [43] £172 **$285**
'T GEBIEDT VAN GUADALAJARA, NIEW MEXICO EN CALIFORNIA ... [1657 (1683)] Dutch issue. 20x23cm (8x9½") Full color. Exc. Ref: McLaughlin 16, state 5. [43] £513 **$850**

SANTINI

CARTE GENERALE DU CANADA, DE LA LOUISIANE, DE LA FLORIDE, DE LA CAROLINE, DE LA VIRGINIE, DE LA NOUVELLE ANGLETERRE ETC. PAR LE SR. D'ANVILLE [1776] [no dimens] Orig OL color; pair of red lines intersect in NJ. Lt age toning along vert fold; o/w fine. [A2] £597 **$990**
GEORGIE, ARMENIE [1775] 38x56cm (15x22") OL color. [20] £347 **$575**
NOUVELLE MAPPE MONDE DEDIEE AU PROGRES DE NOS CONNOISSANCES ... [1784] Oblique double hemi, each showing maximum land and water respectively; text below. 46x64cm (18½x25") Early color. Few mends & stains; else VG. [24] £1,809 **$3,000**

SARTINE

CARTE REDUITE DES COTES ORIENTALES DE L'AMERIQUE SEPTENTRIONALE ... [1778] Coast chart with inland detail. 59x88cm (23½x34½") Wash color. [27] £1,086 **$1,800**
[SAME TITLE] [1780] NJ to Maritimes. 58x87cm (23x34½") OL color. Exc. [24] £1,327 **$2,200**
PLAN DE LA RIVIERE DU CAP FEAR DEPUIS LA BARRE JUSQUES A BRUNSWICK [1778] 58x42cm (23x16½") Full color. Minor repairs. [36] £844 **$1,400**

SAVAGE

TEXAS [c.1855] Wood engraved map. Panhandle inset. 12x20cm (5x8") B&W. VG. [37] £60 **$100**

SAYER Try *Jefferys, Kitchin*

A NEW MAP OF THE WHOLE CONTINENT OF AMERICA [1786] Thomas Pownall. 4-sheet map joined as two, overall 104x118cm (41x46½") OL color. [Laurie & Whittle 1794 version in full color sold for £391] [A6] £287 **$476**
COURSE OF THE RIVER MISSISSIPI, FROM THE BALISE TO FORT CHARTRES; TAKEN ON AN EXPEDITION TO THE ILLINOIS, IN THE LATTER END OF THE YEAR 1765 ... [1775] By Lt. John Ross. 112x34cm (44x13½") Orig OL color. Exc. Ref: Tooley (Amer) p.69; #31b; Goss (NA) 67. [24] £1,689 **$2,800**
THE PROVINCES OF NEW YORK AND NEW JERSEY, WITH PART OF PENSILVANIA, AND THE PROVINCE OF QUEBEC. DRAWN BY MAJOR HOLLAND ... CORRECTED AND IMPROVED ... BY GOVERN'R POWNALL [1776] [compiler's attribution] 3 sheets joined; Montreal to Delaware Bay; insets. 136x54cm (53½x21½") Wash & OL color. Lower margin trimmed to border with sm disturbance; browning along horiz areas where joined. Ref: Tooley (Amer) p.78, #44. [A7] £971 **$1,610**

SAYER & BENNETT Try *Jefferys, Kitchin*

[ATLAS] THE AMERICAN MILITARY POCKET ATLAS; BEING AN APPROVED COLLECTION OF CORRECT MAPS, BOTH GENERAL AND PARTICULAR, OF THE BRITISH COLONIES; ESPECIALLY THOSE WHICH NOW ARE, OR PROBABLY MAY BE THE THEATRE OF WAR; ... [1776] The *Holster Atlas*. Octavo, half calf with orig marble-papered boards, orig label. 6 maps, incl Roman's Southeast, Evans' Middle Colonies, Brassier's Lake Champlain. Unrestored; superb. Ref: Schwarz & Ehrenberg, p.190; Nebenzahl (Amer Rev) pp.11-17; Phillips (A) 1206 & 1343. [3] £9,650 **$16,000**
A CHART OF THE ENTRANCE OF THE RED SEA [1778] Based on D'Apres de Mannevillette. Gulf of Aden; insets. 33x65cm (13x25½") [11] £51 **$78**
A CHART OF THE INNER PASSAGE, BETWEEN THE COAST OF AFRICA AND THE ISLE OF MADAGASCAR, FROM D'ANVILLE AND D'APRES'S CHARTS COMPARED WITH THE ENGLISH JOURNALS [1780] 3 insets. 61x72cm (24x28½") Color. [46] £250 **$415**
A CHART OF THE RED SEA FROM GEDDAH TO SUEZ ... [1781] Northern part. After D'Apres de Mannevillette. Insets, profiles. 50x68cm (19½x27") C'fold split supported on verso. [11] £136 **$225**

SAYER & BENNETT continued

A GENERAL MAP OF THE NORTHERN BRITISH COLONIES IN AMERICA ... [1777] Folding map from "Holster Atlas". 66x48cm (26x19") OL color. Foxing & lt staining; sm tear with hole lf border; wear along folds; 3 sm holes at junctions; overall good. [15] £1,055 **$1,750**

THE PROVINCES OF NEW YORK AND NEW JERSEY, WITH PART OF PENSILVANIA, AND THE PROVINCE OF QUEBEC ... [1776] 6th issue. Pownall & Holland surveys; Montreal to Delaware Bay. 2 sheets joined, 103x52cm (40½x20½"). Color. Spotting & soiling margins; some sm tears. Ref: Tooley (Amer) p.78; Goss (NA) 69. [A6] £345 **$572**

SCHEDEL

[BOOK WITH MAPS] LIBER CHRONICARUM [1493] 1st ed. Folio, paneled sheep; 322 (of 326) leaves (lacking pp 164, 171, 263, 290) ; 28 (of 29) double-page maps, incl World, Europe; numerous illustrations. Lacks spine, clasps; numerous repairs & defects, worming & paperclip rust marks throughout, particularly double-page views; sold as is. [A5] £4,370 **$7,246**

[EUROPE: CENTRAL AND NORTHERN] [1493] From Latin ed, "Nuremberg Chronicle"; Ireland & Scandinavia to Black Sea. 40x58cm (15½x23"). Vert fold closures; sl browning; few sm wormholes margin. [A8] £1,803 **$2,990**

BAVARIA [1493] Composite, imaginary view of typical structures. With text, image 23x23cm (9½x9") Full color. Exc. [43] £211 **$350**

CONSTANTINOPOLIS ... [1493] 39x53cm (15½x21"). Color. Threadhole repairs; exc. [24] £1,327 **$2,200**

DAMIATA [1493 / 1500] Wolgemut, sc. Fanciful view of city at east mouth of Nile on verso of full folio sheet CCX; 3 saints on recto. View 14x24cm (5½x9½"). B&W. Sm early repair 3" from image; near fine. [35] £121 **$200**

FLORENCIA [1493] From *Nuremberg Chronicle*. Text above. 25x50cm (10x19½"). Color. Threadhole repairs; else exc. [24] £1,628 **$2,700**

HIEROSOLIMA [1493] German ed. 19x23cm (7½x9"). Long tear invisibly repaired, no loss. Ref: Laor 1123. [44] £513 **$850**

ROMA [1493] From the Nuremberg Chronicle. 23x54cm (9x21½"). Color. Exc. [45] £1,086 **$1,800**

SECUNDA ETAS MUNDI [1493] Wood engraving from Latin ed of Nuremberg Chronicle. 31x44cm (12x17½") on sheet 43x58cm. C'fold restored without loss. Ref: Shirley (W) 19. [A7] £5,549 **$9,200**

SENA [1493] Sienna; wood cut view from Nuremberg Chronicle. 20x22cm (8x9") on 17½x11½" text leaf. B&W. Old margin repairs; VG+. [37] £136 **$225**

TOLOSA [c.1493] Toulouse. From the Nuremberg Chronicles. 20x22cm (7½x8½"). Minor ink impression from verso; dark impression. [21] Can$250 £109 $181

SCHENK

ACCURATE GEOGRAPHISCHE DELINEATION DES ZUDEM CHURSAECHSISCHEN THUERINGEN GEHOERIGEN AMMTES LANGENSALTZA [1754] Road map. 47x56cm (18½x22"). OL color. [A8] £42 **$69**

AMERICAE TAM SEPTENTRIONALIS QUAM MERIDIONALIS IN MAPPA GEOGRAPHICA DELINEATIO...OPERA A.F. ZURNERI...EX OFFICINA PETRI SCHENKII ... [1705] 49x57cm (19½x22½"). Orig color. Mint. Ref: McLaughlin 166; Tooley (Amer) p.128, pl.53. [44] £1,327 **$2,200**

BELGII PARS SEPTENTRIONALIS ... VULGO HOLLANDIA ... [c.1700] The Netherlands; insets of commercial interests: Present northeast U.S. with New Amsterdam view ; SE Asia & East Indies. 48x60cm (19x24"). Orig & later color. Exc. [23] £1,086 **$1,800**

PLANISPHAERIUM COELESTE ... [c.1700] As bound into *Atlas Contractus*. Double polar hemis with sm diagrams. 48x56cm (19x22"). Orig color. Exc. Ref: Warner (Sky) Warner p.222-3. [4] £950 $1,576

SCHERER

[FRONTISPIECE] LAPPONUM MORES, HABITUS, ET CONVERSANDI AC VIVENDI RATIO [c.1710] From work on Lapps. 24x20cm (9½x7½"). [46] £180 $299

[PACIFIC OCEAN & NORTHERN RIM] [c.1700] As in *Atlas Novus*. East & west reversed; hemi inset also reversed; insular Calif. 23x43cm (9x17"). Uncolored. Exc. Ref: McLaughlin 159. [4] £600 $995

[SAME TITLE] [1703] 23x34cm (9x13½"). Exc. Ref: McLaughlin 159. [43] £452 **$750**

AFRICAE PARS AUSTRALIS [c.1700] S of Equator. 23x35cm (9x13½"). [46] £290 $481

AFRICAE PARS BOREALIS 1699 [c.1700] South to Congo. 24x36cm (9½x14"). Sm worm hole in printed margin. [46] £180 $299

AMERICA BOREALIS [c.1700] Insular Calif. 24x36cm (9½x14"). [A8] £451 **$747**

SCHERER continued

ARCHIPELAGI AMERICANI DELINEATIO GEOGRAPHICA   [1700]   Caribbean and surrounding rim. 23x34cm (9x13½"). Color.   [11]   £573 **$950**
[SAME TITLE]   [c.1700]   24x34cm (9½x13½")   C'fold sl browned.   [46]   £380 $630
DELINEATIO NOVA ET VERA PARTIS AUSTRALIS NOVI MEXICI CUM AUSTRALI PARTE INSULAE CALIFORNIAE SAECULO PRIORI AB HISPANIS DETECT.   [c.1700]   24x36cm (9½x14")   [46]   £480 $796
INSULAE INDICAE CUM TERRIS CIRCUMVICINIS   [c.1700]   East Indies to N Australia. 24x36cm (9½x14")   [A8]   £191 **$316**
NAVIGATIONES PRAECIPUAE EUROPAEORUM AD EXTERAS NATIONES   [c.1700]   World on oval projection; insular Calif. 23x34cm (9x13½")   Ref: Shirley (W) 631.   [A7]   £832 **$1,380**
PATRIARCHATUS IEROSOLYMITANUS COMPREHENDEBAT TRES PROVINCIAS I. PALESTINAM TRIPLICEM. II. IUDAEAM. III. ... PATRIARCHATUS ANTIOCHENUS CONTINEBAT PROVINCIAS V. I. SYRIAM ... II. CILICIAM ... III. INSUL. CYPRUM. IV. MESOPOTAMIAM. V. PHOENICIAM ...   [1702]   23x36cm (9x14")   Newer color. Fine. Ref: Laor 708.   [A2]   £73 **$121**
PROVINCIAE BOREALIS AMERICAE NON ITA PRIDEM DETECTAE AUT MAGIS AB EUROPAEIS EXCULTAE   [1703-20]   Insular Calif. 23x34cm (9x13½")   B&W. Immaculate. Ref: McLaughlin 160; Tooley (Amer) p.131, #86. Leighly 151.   [12]   £814 **$1,350**
REGIONUM CIRCUM POLARIUM LAPPAONIAE ISLANDIAE ET GROENLANDIAE NOVAE ET VETERIS NOVA DESCRIPTIO GEOGRAPHICA 1701   [1703]   NE America, NW Eurasia; rich decor. 23x35cm (9x13½")   B&W. Ref: Phillips (A) 3462-138,9.   [12]   £482 **$800**
[SAME TITLE]   [1701]   23x35cm (9x13½")   Uncolored.   [39]   £392 **$650**
REPRAESENTATIO GEOGRAPHICA ITENERIS MARITIMI NAVIS VICTORIAE ...   [1703]   North polar projection, side vignettes; Magellan's track marked; insular Calif. 23x36cm (9x14")   B&W. Dark, fine. Ref: Shirley (W) 626; Portinaro & Knirsch pl.103.   [12]   £663 **$1,100**
SOCIETAS IESU PER UNIVERSUM MUNDUM DIFFUSA PRAEDICAT CHRISTI EVANGELIUM   [1703]   North polar projection, corner vignettes; Jesuit missions marked globally; insular Calif. 23x36cm (9x14")   B&W. Dark, fine. Ref: Shirley (W) 629.   [12]   £603 **$1,000**
TYPUS TOTIUS ORBIS TERRAQUEI GEOGRAPHICE DELINEATUS ...   [1700]   In Part V, *Atlas Novus* ... World in a set of twelve gores; insular Calif. 22x35cm (8½x13½")   Color. Ref: Shirley 633, pl.437.   [13]   **Aus$1,680** £763 $1,265
[SAME TITLE]   [1700]   22x34cm (8½x13½")   B&W. Ref: Shirley 633; pl.437.   [27]   £663 **$1,100**
[SAME TITLE]   [1710]   22x34cm (8½x13½")   Ref: Shirley (W) 633.   [A6]   £299 $496

SCHMOLDER

NEUESTE SPECIAL-KARTE DER WESTLICHEN U. SUDLICHEN THEILE VON NORD AMERIK. DIE NEUESTEN GEBIETE DER UNION UND DIE VEREINIGTEN STAATEN VON MEXICO AUS DEU NEUESTEN QUELLEN VEROSTENTLICHT DURCH, MO LANDRATH CAPT. B. SCHMOLDER   [1848]   Litho by M. Frommann, Darmstadt. American west & most of Mexico. May not be Wheat (TM) 566. 43x57cm (17x22½")   Wash color. Repaired tear through Oregon; lt water stain lower third; strong, clear impression.   [A1]   £1,061 **$1,760**

SCHONSPERGER

[JERUSALEM]   [1496]   From pirated "mini-Schedel". 10x20cm (4x8")   Full color. Margins extended. Ref: Laor 1126.   [44]   £347 **$575**
NUREMBERG [ON SHEET WITH VIENNA]   [1497]   10x20cm (4x8")   Full col. Margins extended.   [44]   £226 **$375**

SCHOOLCRAFT

ETHNOGRAPHICAL MAP OF THE INDIAN TRIBES OF THE UNITED STATES A.D. 1600   [1853]   Orig in Schoolcraft's *History of the Indian Tribes*. Map by Eastman covers North America. 23x30cm (9x12")   Color.   [10]   £57 **$95**
MAP OF OREGON SHOWING THE LOCATION OF INDIAN TRIBES   [1852]   Publ in *History of the Indian Tribes* ... By Seth Eastman. 21x25cm (8x10")   OL color.   [41]   £87 **$145**

SCHOYER

MAP OF THE UNITED STATES DRAWN FROM THE MOST APPROVED SURVEYS   [1826]   US west to Rockies; eagle vignette. 41x51cm (16x20")   OL color. Previously folded; flattened, laid on paper; good.   [16]   £965 **$1,600**
MAP OF THE UNITED STATES DRAWN FROM THE MOST APPROVED SURVEYS   [1826]   Folding map; based on Finley's geography; publ New York. Eccentric & OL color. 42x52cm (16½x20½")   Rebacked, loss at folds; stain where previously glued into covers; only good.   [37]   £271 **$450**

SCHRAEMBL
DAS VORGEBIRG DER GUTEN HOFNUNG VERFASST VON HERRN L.S. DE LA ROCHETTE NEU HERAUSGEGEBEN VON HERRN. F.A. SCHRAEMBL ... [1789] Austrian version of 1782 Faden map. 51x33cm (20x13") Color. Ref: Tooley (Africa) p.42, cf pl.30. [46] **£360** **$597**

SCOTS MAGAZINE
A NEW CHART OF THE RIVER ST. LAWRENCE FROM THE ISLAND OF ANTICOSTI TO LAKE ONTARIO. A. BELL SCULPT. [Sept. 1759] 18x25cm (7x10") B&W. Fine. Ref: Jolly SCOT-23.   [29]   £106 **$175**

SCOTT
SOUTH CAROLINA [1795] From *United States Gazetteer*. 15x18cm (6x7½") Uncolored. Ref: Wheat & Brun 602. [22] £81 **$135**

SCULL
A MAP OF PENNSYLVANIA EXHIBITING NOT ONLY THE IMPROVED PARTS OF THAT PROVINCE, BUT ALSO ITS EXTENSIVE FRONTIERS ... [1778] Paris: Le Rouge. 66x131cm (26x51½") Orig OL color. Some fold reinforcement; else clean. [24] £2,865 **$4,750**

S.D.U.K.   See *Society for the Diffusion of Useful Knowledge*

SEALE
A MAP OF ANTIENT EGYPT [1764] From Guthrie's *General History of the World*. 24x21cm (9½x8½") Lower rt margin cut away & corner creased, sm closed tear; o/w clean.   [21] **Can$80** £35 **$58**

A MAP OF NORTH AMERICA WITH THE EUROPEAN SETTLEMENTS & WHATEVER ELSE IS REMARKABLE IN YE WEST INDIES ... [1745] Insular Calif. 37x47cm (15x18½") Exc. Ref: McLaughlin 228. [44] £724 **$1,200**

A MAP OF SOUTH AMERICA WITH ALL THE EUROPEAN SETTLEMENTS & WHATEVER ELSE IS REMARKABLE FROM THE LATEST & BEST OBSERVATIONS. R.W. SEALE, DELIN. ET SCULP. [1754] 47x37cm (18½x15") [41] £148 **$245**

A PLAN OF IUAN FERNANDES ISLAND IN THE SOUTH SEA ... [1748] From 1st ed, Anson's *Voyage*. Alexander Selkirk marooned here inspired DeFoe's Robinson Crusoe. 23x49cm (9x19½") OL color. Repaired tears; else VG. [37] £151 **$250**

TO THE MOST NOBLE THOMAS HOLLES PELHAM, DUKE OF NEWCASTLE ... THIS MAP OF THE COUNTY OF MIDDLESEX IS DEDICATED [c.1756] 1st state; publ alongside Bowen maps in Large English Atlas; with livery of City & 92 fully colored armorials of Free Companies at sides. 52x71cm (20½x28") Color. C'fold reinforced. [47] **£890** $1,476

VETERIS ORBIS CLIMATA EX STRABONE [c.1768] 20x30cm (8x12") Modern OL color. Couple tears & lib stamp in margin; good (B). [A3] £59 **$97**

SEILE
AN EXACT GROUND-PLOT OF YE CITY OF WORCESTER, AS IT STOOD FORTIFYD, 3. SEPT. 1651 [c.1669] London: Anna Seile. 28x36cm (11x14") Margins trimmed to border & mounted on larger sheet. [A7] £42 **$69**

SELIGMANN
CAROLINAE FLORIDAE NEC NON INSULARUM BAHAMENSIUM ... IOH. MICHAEL SELIGMANN NORIMBERGAE AO, 1755 [1755] As in Catesby, German ed, *Natural History of Carolina*. 43x58cm (17x23") Orig color. Few stains; else fine. Ref: Cumming (SE) 292. [24] £1,689 **$2,800**

SELLER
A CHART OF THE SEA COASTS OF NEW ENGLAND, NEW JERSEY, VIRGINIA, MARYLAND, AND CAROLINA FROM CAPE COD TO CAPE HATTERAS ... [1675] 1st ed. 43x53cm (17x21") Orig OL color. Exc. [2] £11,760 **$19,500**

A GENERAL CHART OF THE SOUTH SEA FROM THE RIVER PLATE TO DAMPIER'S STREIGHTS ON YE COAST OF NEW GUINEA [c.1705] Attribution uncertain; map-maker's name erased from cartouche; similar to Goos, Doncker & Van Keulen. 43x57cm (17x22½") Orig color. Trimmed at top & reinstated in manuscript. [13] **Aus$1,400** £636 $1,054

A MAPP OF THE FIVE ZONES [1685] Earth with no geographical features; sun, moon, clouds. 11x12cm (4½x4½") Orig wash color. [11] £45 **$75**

CORNWALL [1694] About 12x14cm (5x5½") [11] £60 **$100**

SELLER continued

DEVONSHIRE [1694] About 12x14cm (5x5½") ["Barkshire", "Bedford Shire", "Hant Shire", "Leicester Shire" & Worcester Shire" offered at same price] [11] £45 **$75**
OXFORD SHIRE [1694] About 12x14cm (5x5½") [11] £51 **$85**
PIXIX NAUTICA OR THE MARRINER COMPAS SHEWING THE NAMES OF THE POINTS [1685] Compass rose with winds from miniature atlas. 12x14cm (4½x5½") [11] £51 **$85**

SENEX

A MAP OF LOUISIANA AND THE RIVER MISSISSIPI [1721] 49x57cm (19x22½") [A7] £589 **$977**
A MAP OF OLD & NEW CASTILE FROM THE OBSERVATIONS OF RODRIGO MENDES SILVA AND OTHERS [c.1720] Central Spain. 44x55cm (17½x21½") Orig full col. Margin tears repaired; fine (A). [A3] £130 **$215**
A NEW AND CORRECT MAP OF THE WORLD ... [1728 - c.1740] Mary Senex. Double hemi; insular Calif. 15x29cm (6x11½") OL color. Minor damp stain; good (B). [A3] £248 **$411**
A NEW MAP OF AMERICA FROM THE LATEST OBSERVATIONS REVIS'D BY I. SENEX [1719] Insular Calif; speculative NW cartography. 48x56cm (19x22") Orig OL color; later (?) cartouche color. C'fold reinforcement; creasing; else exc. Ref: McLaughlin 193; Tooley (Amer) p.130, #81; [23] £1,327 **$2,200**
A NEW MAP OF INDIA & CHINA [c.1720] Publ in *New General Atlas*. 50x59cm (19½x23") Orig OL color. Exc. [4] £775 **$1,285**
A NEW MAP OF IRELAND FROM THE LATEST OBSERVATIONS [1720] 59x49cm (23x19½") Orig OL color by provinces. Verso support to verdi gris, appearance unaffected. [11] £332 **$550**
A NEW MAP OF THE CITY OF AMSTERDAM [1721] 288 streets & lanes keyed. 49x58cm (19½x23") Uncolored. [34] £400 **$664**
A NEW MAP OF THE WORLD FROM THE LATEST OBSERVATIONS ... [c.1720] Publ in *New General Atlas*. Double hemi; insular Calif. 42x52cm (16½x20½") Orig OL color. Sl c'fold toning; o/w exc. [4] £2,250 **$3,731**
STELLARUM FIXARUM HEMISPHAERIUM BOREALE ... [IN SET WITH] STELLARUM FIXARUM HEMISPHAERIUM AUSTRALE ... [1728] Probably from Knapton's *Atlas Maritimus Commercialis*. Each Diameter: 65cm (25½") B&W. Archival tissue repair of edge tears; show through of some brown stains; overall good+. Ref: Warner (Sky) p.242-3, illus p.5. [38] £905 **$1,500**

SEUTTER

[ATLAS] ATLAS MINOR, PRAECIPUA ORBIS TERRARUM IMPERIA, REGNA ET PROVINCIAS, GERMANIAE POSTISSIMUM [1744] Matthaus Seutter, Augsburg. Oblong quarto. later sheep; title & 67 OL color mapsheets (one more than called for), many by C.T. Lotter. 21x33cm (8½x13") Extremities rubbed; minor margin soiling from thumbing; Salzburg map trimmed, remounted; text leaf repaired. Ref: Phillips (A) 3494. [A7] £2,913 **$4,830**
[ATLAS] ATLAS TRES-EXACT DES PAIS BAS CATHOLIQUES [1758] Albrecht Karl & Matthaus Seutter, Augsburg. Oblong quarto, early wrappers; 2 titles & 23 (titles call for 24) colored mapsheets. Scattered staining, mostly in margin. [A7] £1,040 **$1,725**
ACCURATA DELINEATIO CELEBERRIMAE REGIONIS LUDOVICIANAE VEL GALLICE LOUISIANE OT CANADAE ET FLORIDAE ADPELLATIONE IN SEPTEMTRIONALE AMERICA DESCRIPTAE QUE HODIE NOMINE FLUMINIS MISSISSIPPI VEL ST. LOUIS ... [c.1730] Cartouche reflects John Law's Mississippi Bubble scheme. 49x57cm (19½x22½") Orig color. Mint. Ref: Portinaro & Knirsch pl.117. [23] £1,508 **$2,500**
ACCURATA DESIGNATIO CELEBRIS FRETI PROPE ANDALUSIAE CASTELLUM GIBRALTAR [1735] Insets of Cadiz, the Rock & other cities. 50x58cm (19½x22½") Body color. [A6] £276 $458
ARTESIA CUM FINITIMIS LOCIS VELUT SEDES AC THEATRUM BELLI ... [c.1730] After De L'Isle. 49x58cm (19½x22½") Old color. [48] **DM 200** £69 $114
ASIA CUM OMNIBUS IMPERIIS PROVINCIIS STATIBUS ET INSULIS ... [c.1730] 50x58cm (19½x22½") Full color. [20] £528 **$875**
ASIA CUM OMNIS IMPERIIS PROVINCIIS, STATIBUS ET INSULIS ... [c.1745] 49x57cm (19½x22½") Orig color. Minor margin waterstaining; lt c'fold toning. [4] **£525** $871
BELGIUM FOEDERATUM ... [c.1730] 50x57cm (19½x22½") Old color. Sm brown spot lower lf. [48] **DM 800** £276 $458
BORUSSIAE REGNUM ... [c.1730] 50x58cm (20x23") Old color. [48] **DM 1,300** £449 $744
CONSTANTINOPOLIS AMPLISSIMA, POTENTISSIMA, ET MAGNIFICENTISSIMA ... [c.1730] Bird's-eye plan & view. 49x57cm (19½x22½") Orig color. Repair lower rt, sm restored area; dark impression; VG. [24] £905 **$1,500**

SEUTTER continued

DIVERSI GLOBI TERR-AQUEI STATIONE VARIANTE ET VISU INTERCEDENTE ... [c.1720] Double hemi with smaller world hemis & diagrams; insular Calif. 50x57cm (19½x22½") Orig color. Verso sl reinforced. [43] £1,387 **$2,300**

[SAME TITLE] [c.1720] 50x58cm (20x23") Wash & OL color. Scattered lt browning mostly in margins; minor soiling. [A7] £1,248 **$2,070**

[SAME TITLE] [c.1745] Publ in *Atlas Novus*. Double-hemi & sm spheres; insular Calif. 49x57cm (19½x22½") Orig color, later additions. Fine. [4] £1,700 **$2,819**

IMPERIUM JAPONICUM ... [c.1740] After Reland 1715 map; with "privilege". 49x58cm (19½x23") Full color; B&W cartouche. Fine. Ref: Cortazzi pl.78. [1] £3,015 **$5,000**

INDIA ORIENTALIS CUM ADIACENTIBUS INSULIS NOVA DELINEATIONE ... [c.1740] As in *Atlas Novus*. 48x57cm (19x22½") Orig wash color, later additions; cartouche uncolored. Exc. [4] £950 **$1,576**

IUSTISSIMAE CAUSAE HEROICA VIRTUTE PROPUGNATAE GLORIOSISS: TRIUMPHI PRAEMIUM ... [1690+] Covers former Yugoslavia; Belgrade at ctr. 50x58cm (19½x23") Orig OL color. Sl soiled lower edge. [11] £151 **$250**

LE GOUVERNEMENT DE CHAMPAGNE. I.E. PRAEFECTURA GENERALIS CAMPANIAE IN ELECTIONES SUAS DIVISA [c.1730] Inset of Seine. 58x50cm (23x19½") Old color. [48] DM 380 £131 **$217**

LE PLAN DE PARIS SES FAUBOURGS ET SES ENVIRONS ... [1740] [no dimens] Orig color. A sm lt brown spot along fold. [A1] £199 **$330**

[SAME TITLE] [c.1760] Augsburg: T.C. Lotter. 50x57cm (19½x22½") Orig body color. [46] £480 **$796**

LE SETTE CHIESE DI ROMA ... DIE SIEBEN KITCHEN VON ROM, MIT IHREN VORNEHMSTEN HEILIGTHUMERN, STATIONEN UND ABLASS [c.1720] 9 images: 7 churches; sm city plan. 50x58cm (19½x23") Old color. Bottom & lower c'fold tears repaired. [48] DM 1,480 £511 **$847**

MAIESTAS AUSTRIACA [c.1730] 50x58cm (20x23") Color. Margins trimmed to just beyond platemark; scattered lt soiling; minor foxing margins. [A8] £191 **$316**

MAPP GEOGRAPHIAE NATURALIS ... [c.1735] Fictitious instructional map incorporating array of features & 40 symbols found in 18th century maps. 50x57cm (19½x22½") Orig color. Fine. [23] £724 **$1,200**

MAPPA CIRCULI RHENANI SUPERIORIS ... [c.1730] Koblenz & Frankfurt to Kassel. 49x57cm (19½x22½") Full orig color. Sl soiled lower margin. [11] £166 **$275**

MAPPA GEOGRAPHICA REGIONEM MEXICANAM ET FLORIDAM TERRAEQUE ADJACENTES UT ET ANTERIORES AMERICAE INSULAS ... [1740] T.C. Lotter, sc. 47x57cm (18½x22½") Col. VG-fine. [A1] £1,028 **$1,705**

MAPPAE IMPERII MOSCOVITICI PARS SEPTENTRIONALIS [c.1720] NW Russia. 49x57cm (19½x22½") Orig color. Fine. [A2] £83 **$138**

MARCHIONATUS MISNIAE [c.1730] By T.C. Lotter. 50x59cm (19½x23") Old color. Sm hole restored; narrow margin. [48] DM 280 £97 **$160**

NOVA ET ACCURATA TOTIUS REGNI SCOTIAE [1740] 58x49cm (23x19½") Old body col. Fine. [37] £362 **$600**

NOVA ET ACCURATISSIMA MARIS CASPII ... [c.1730] 49x57cm (19½x22½") Old color. Part of c'fold restored. Ref: Bagrow (Russia) S.127. [68] DM 550 £190 **$315**

NOVISSIMA ET ACCURATISSIMA DELINEATIO STATUS ECCLESIAE ET MAGNI DUCATUS HETRURIAE [c.1730] 50x58cm (19½x23") Old color. [48] DM 580 £200 **$332**

NOVISSIMA ICHNOGRAPHICA DELINEATIO MUNITISSIMAE URBIS ET CELEBERRIMI EMPORII OSTENDAE, IN COMITATU FLANDRIAE AUSTRIACAE SITAE, CUR ET COELA MATTHAEI SEUTTERI [c.1730] Ostend. 50x58cm (19½x23") Old color. [48] DM 1,600 £552 **$916**

NOVUS ORBIS SIVE AMERICA MERIDIONALIS ET SEPTENTRIONALIS ... [c.1745] As in *Atlas Novus*. Insular Calif. 49x57cm (19½x22½") Orig color. Exc. Ref: McLaughlin 211. [4] £1,000 **$1,658**

OPULENTISSIMUM SINARUM IMPERIUM ... [c.1740] Publ in *Atlas Novus*. 49x57cm (19½x22½") Orig color, with additions. Fine. [4] £525 **$871**

PALAESTINAE ACCURATA DESCRIPTIO GEOGRAPHICA ... [c.1741] Tobias Lotter, sc. 50x58cm (19½x22½") Orig color. Ref: Laor 721. [46] £540 **$896**

PENSYLVANIA NOVA JERSEY ET NOVA YORK CUM REGIONIBUS AD FLUVIUM DELAWARE IN AMERICA SITIS, NOVA DELINEATIONE OB OCULOS POSITA PER ... [c.1751] Eastern New England foreshortened. 57x49cm (22½x19½") Orig color. Exc. [24] £1,689 **$2,800**

PORTUGALLIA ET ALGARBIAE REGNA ... [c.1730] Inset: Brazil. 49x56cm (19x22") Full color. Old c'fold repairs; couple margin tears to border; else clean, crisp (B). [A3] £263 **$436**

PRAGA CELEBERRIMA ET MAXIMA TOTIUS BOHEMIAE ... [c.1730] Plan & view. 49x57cm (19½x22½") Orig color. Stain lower rt; else fine. [24] £1,206 **$2,000**

SEUTTER continued

RECENS EDITA TOTIUS NOVI BELGII, IN AMERICA SEPTENTRIONALI SITI, DELINEATIO CURA ET SUMTIBUS MATTHAEI SEUTTERI [1730 c.1757] T.C. Lotter. 5th state. Last of Jansson-Visscher sequence. With Manhattan view. 50x58cm (19½x22½") Orig color. Ref: Tooley (Amer) Campbell 27. [34] **£3,000** $4,975

REGNI JAPONIAE NOVA MAPPA GEOGRAPHICA ... [c.1740] After Kaempfer with Japanese motifs. 48x56cm (19x22") Orig color. Fine. Ref: Walter (Japan) 80. [24] £2,714 **$4,500**

REGNI JAPONIAE NOVA MAPPA GEOGRAPHICA ... KAEMPFERO [c.1740-] After Kaempfer with Japanese motifs. 49x56cm (19½x22") Orig color. Ref: Walter (Japan) 80. [34] **£3,000** $4,975

REPRESENTATION SYMBOLIQUE ... LES ATTAQUES DE L'AMOUR [c.1730] From allegorical map series depicting man in fortress under siege from bombardment & diversion of fair sex; heavily annotated about protection of the heart. 50x57cm (19½x22½") Orig color. Some restoration; some surface discoloration. [34] **£800** $1,327

SAXONIAE INFERIORIS CIRCULUS JUXTA PRINCIPATUS ... [c.1730] Holstein to Gottingen to Berlin. 50x58cm (19½x22½") Orig OL color. ["Ducatus Juliacensis, Cliviensis et Montensis ..." offered at same price] [11] £196 **$325**

SUPERIOR ET INFERIOR HASSIAE LANDGRAVIATUS ... [c.1730] 49x56cm (19x22") Orig OL color; cities in red. [11] £106 **$175**

TABULA NOVISSIMA ACCURATISSIMA REGNORUM ANGLIAE, SCOTIAE HIBERNIAE [c.1730] 58x50cm (23x19½") Old color. 2 sm rust spots. Ref: Shirley (BI 1650-1750) Seutter 1. [48] **DM 700** £242 $401

THEATRUM BELLI RUSSORUM VICTORIIS ... TURCICARUM ET TARTARICUM ... [c.1740] Ukraine region. 49x57cm (19½x22½") Orig wash & OL color. [11] £90 **$150**

THEATRUM BELLI RUSSORUM VICTORIIS ILLUSTRATUM SIVE NOVA ET ACCURATA TURCICARUM ET TARTARICUM ... [c.1730] 50x58cm (19½x22½") Old col. Sh wrinkle upper part. [48] **DM 280** £97 $160

TYPUS CHORO-TOPOGRAPHICUS REGIAE ... LUTETIAE PARISIORUM ... [c.1730] Paris & environs. 50x58cm (19½x22½") Color. Minor browning top margin & vert fold. [A7] £191 **$316**

VENETIA POTENTISSIMA ... [c.1730] Bird's-eye view; 2 Piazza de San Marco views. 50x57cm (20x22½") Full orig color. Fine. [24] £1,357 **$2,250**

WETTERAVIA CUM OMNIBUS INCLUSIS PRINCIPATIBUS ... [c.1730] Frankfurt to Giessen. 50x58cm (19½x23") Full orig wash & OL color. Faint water stain. [11] £211 **$350**

SEYFART

PLAN DER BELAGERUNG U. EINNAHME DER STADT U. VESTUNG WOLFFENBUTTEL IM MONAT OCT. 1761 [1763] Troop positions & legend. 20x28cm (8x11") Partial color. [48] **DM 490** £169 $280

SHANNON

MAP OF THE CITY OF NEW YORK [1868] Prepared for W.C. Rogers & Co. for Joseph Shannon's Manual of NY. Dimens as given, 97x20cm (38x8") Full color by wards. VG. [25] £45 **$75**

SICKLER

PLAN TOPOGRAPHIQUE DE LA CAMPAGNE DE ROME ... [1832] Dissected, mounted on canvas, folding into orig slipcase. Labeled as circulating from a library. 56x87cm (22x34½") Uncolored. [34] **£260** $431

SLATER

[ATLAS] SLATER'S NEW BRITISH ATLAS [1857] Folio, modern half calf; 3 linen-backed folding maps, England, Scotland, Ireland; 39 maps & circular London. Color. Ref: Chubb 429. [A6] **£1,035** $1,716

SLEZER

THE NORTH PROSPECT OF THE CITY OF EDINBURGH [c.1719] 2 sheets joined, 44x107cm (17½x42") Orig color. Minor surface defects. [34] **£1,500** $2,487

SMITH

[ATLAS] AN ATLAS OF ANCIENT GEOGRAPHY BIBLICAL AND CLASSICAL [1874] Tall oblong folio, 20x14"; half leather & cloth; 43 maps, many double page. OL color. Covers rubbed & soiled, point wear; some lt image transfer; o/w maps VG. [A2] £349 **$578**

MAP OF DELAWARE COUNTY, PENNSYLVANIA [1848] Wall map by Joshua W. Ash; Robert Piersall Smith, Phila, publ. 105x142cm (41½x56") Lacks rods; cracking & damage, sm loss; age toning; fair to good. Ref: cf Ristow (Amer M&M) p.348. [15] £452 **$750**

NEW POCKET MAP OF THE CITY OF PHILADELPHIA FROM THE LATEST CITY SURVEYS [1882] J.L. Smith, Phila. Pocket map folded into 12mo gold-embossed cloth covers. 83x67cm (32½x26½") Color by wards. Cover edges & corners rubbed; map has occas lt foxing, few corner separations; VG. [5] £136 **$225**

SMITH, C.

NORTH AMERICA [Jan 6, 1816] From *New General Atlas*. London. 27x35cm (10½x14") OL color. Ref: cf Phillips (A) 729-45 & 6042-49. [1826 ed, updated, full color, fine, offered at same price] [12] £151 **$250**
UNITED STATES [c.1825] Big Arkansas Terr. 36x36cm (14½x14") Col. Rt margin extended. [39] £160 **$265**

SMITH, J.C.

MAP OF THE STATE OF NEW YORK, SHOWING THE BOUNDARIES OF THE COUNTIES AND TOWNSHIPS, THE LOCATION OF CITIES, TOWNS & STAGE ROADS BY J. CALVIN SMITH [1855] NY: Disturnell. Orig pocket map; lacks case. Insets: NYC; St. Lawrence River. 48x61cm (19x24") Full color. VG. [25] £166 **$275**
MAP OF THE UNITED STATES OF AMERICA INCLUDING CANADA AND A LARGE PORTION OF TEXAS [1844] NY: Sherman & Smith; 1st ed, 2nd state. Mounted on cloth, lt varnished, with lower roller. Scrolled border 16 views & great seal. OL color by state & terr. 160x208cm (63x82") Top 6" shabby, sl damp stained & torn, pieces missing & surface detached; remainder with occas vert wrinkles, lt striping near vert seams, near fine; needs restoration. [5] £754 **$1,250**

SMITH, ROSWELL C.

LOUISIANA, MISSISSIPPI, ARKANSAS AND PART OF TEXAS [1861] From *Smith's New Geography ... for the Use of Common Schools*. Phila: Lippincott. 30x25cm (12x10") Full color. VG. [16] £57 **$95**
MAP NO.10. UNITED STATES [1854] From a school geography. Western U.S with large NE, WA, OR, UT & NM territories. 28x23cm (11x9") Full color. Minor edge wear. [26] £48 **$80**
MAP OF THE UNITED STATES AND CANADA DESIGNED TO ACCOMPANY SMITH'S GEOGRAPHY FOR THE SCHOOLS [1839] 1st ed. Stiles, Sherman & Smith. Hartford: Daniel Burgess. TX in large form. Inset: Mexico, Guatimala & Texas. 27x45cm (10½x17½") Full color. Waterstained. [16] £211 **$350**
NORTH AMERICA [1853] By David Burgess; to accompany Smith's Geography. 27x22cm (10½x8½") Full color. VG (A). [A4] £29 **$48**
SOUTHERN STATES [1835] From *Smith's Atlas for Schools* ... 1st ed. Southeast: NC to AR & LA, incomplete FL. 27x42cm (10½x16½") Full wash color. Near fine. ["Western States", OH to MO, offered at same price] Ref: Phillips (A) 318-6. [35] £24 **$40**
TEXAS [1853 (1856)] From *Geography for Schools*. Yellow wash color. 25x22cm (10x8½") [12] £54 **$90**
UNITED STATES [1835] From *Smith's Atlas for Schools* ... 1st ed. Hammond, sc. Coast to coast; large trans-Mississippi territories. 27x43cm (10½x17") Full wash color. Sh c'fold separation; dampstain top ctr; VG. Ref: Phillips (A) 318-3. [35] £54 **$90**

SOCIETY FOR THE DIFFUSION OF USEFUL KNOWLEDGE

[NORTH POLAR REGIONS] [1833] Incl Arctic continental rim. 28x28cm (11x11") OL color. [40] £36 **$60**
A MAP OF THE PRINCIPAL RIVERS SHEWING THEIR COURSES, COUNTRIES, AND COMPARATIVE LENGTHS [1834] Baldwin & Cradock. 39x31cm (15½x12½") OL color. [48] DM 60 £21 **$34**
AMSTERDAM [1835] Baldwin & Cradock. 32x38cm (12½x15") Exc. ["Berlin" & "Copenhagen" offered at same price] [11] £45 **$75**
ANTWERP [1832] Baldwin & Cradock. Plan with view & elevations. 30x40cm (12x15½") Exc. ["Bordeaux" offered at same price] [11] £36 **$60**
ASIATIC ARCHIPELAGO [1874] From *Complete Atlas* ... Indo-China & East Indies. 31x41cm (12½x16") OL color; oceans in blue wash. VG (A). [A3] £42 **$70**
ATHENS [1832] Baldwin & Cradock. Building elevations & views. 34x40cm (13½x15½") Orig OL & partial color. Exc. ["Turin" & "Parma" offered at same price] [11] £60 **$100**
[SAME TITLE] [1832] Ancient Athens; panoramas at top & sides; building elevations at bottom. 33x39cm (13x15½") OL & wash color. [39] £60 **$100**
BERLIN [1833] Elevation drawings of buildings at bottom. 29x37cm (11½x14½") Color. [39] £60 **$100**
BOSTON WITH CHARLESTOWN AND ROXBURY [1843] Pre-Back Bay. 37x29cm (14½x11½") Wash color. Ref: Tooley (Amer) pl.107. [41] £106 **$175**
BRITISH COLUMBIA, VANCOUVER ISLAND, &C. [1874] From *Complete Atlas* ... From Prince of Wales Is. south; east to Lesser Slave Lake. 32x38cm (12½x15") OL color. VG (A). [A3] £48 **$80**
[SAME TITLE] [1874] London: Stanford. 31x38cm (12½x15") Orig OL color. [11] £45 **$75**
CALCUTTA [1842] Chapman & Hall. 31x40cm (12½x16") Orig wash color. [11] £36 **$60**
CANTON [ON SHEET WITH] MACAO [AND] SKETCH OF THE RIVER FROM MACAO TO CANTON [1852] Canton street plan; Hong Kong inset. 30x25cm (12x15") OL color. Fine. [38] £90 **$150**

SOCIETY FOR THE DIFFUSION OF USEFUL KNOWLEDGE continued

CENTRAL AMERICA II. INCLUDING TEXAS, CALIFORNIA AND THE NORTHERN STATES OF MEXICO [1842] Chapman & Hall; Texas as Republic. 31x39cm (12x15½") Orig OL color. Ref: Wheat (TM) 460; Day (TX) 1472. [27] £220 **$365**

CIRCUMJACENT THE NORTH POLE [1874] From *Complete Atlas* ... "No.5"; to 45 deg north. 27x27cm (10½x10½") OL color. VG (A). [A3] £11 **$19**

CIRCUMJACENT THE SOUTH POLE [1874] From *Complete Atlas* ... "No.6"; to 45 deg south 27x27cm (10½x10½") OL color. VG (A). [A3] £26 **$43**

CONSTANTINOPLE [1840] 32x39cm (12½x15½") Orig partial color. Exc. [11] £45 **$75**

DRESDEN [1833] Baldwin & Cradock. 32x38cm (12½x15") Old color. Sh margin tears repaired. [48] DM 250 £86 **$143**

DUBLIN [1836] Baldwin & Cradock. Building elevations below. 29x40cm (11½x15½") Partial orig wash color. Exc. ["Edinburgh" offered at same price] [11] £51 **$85**

[SAME TITLE] [1843] Building elevations below. 29x39cm (11½x15½") Wash color highlights. ["Edinburgh" offered at same price] [41] £72 **$120**

EASTERN HEMISPHERE [IN SET WITH] **WESTERN HEMISPHERE** [1842] 2 sheets joined, overall 34x67cm (13½x26½") Color. [19] £66 **$110**

EMPIRE OF JAPAN [1874] Stanford. Insets: Nagasaki; "Yeso". 39x31cm (15½x12") Orig OL col. [11] £45 **$75**

FLORENCE [1835] Baldwin & Cradock. Building elevations below. 28x38cm (11x15") Orig partial color. Exc. ["Genoa" offered at same price] [11] £75 **$125**

IRELAND [1842] 41x33cm (16x13") Some OL color. VG. [25] £54 **$90**

ISLANDS IN THE INDIAN OCEAN [1874] From *Complete Atlas* ... 11 maps on sheet. 32x39cm (12½x15½") OL color. VG (A). [A3] £14 **$23**

LISBON [1833] With view & inset of region. 31x38cm (12x15") Orig partial color. Exc. ["Madrid" & "Oporto" offered at same price] [11] £51 **$85**

LONDON [1843] London: Chas. Knight. Folio strike. Extent: Kingsland-Blackwall-Kennington-Bayswater. 38x65cm (15x25½") Exc. Ref: Howgego 385. ["Brussels" offered at same price] [11] £60 **$100**

[SAME TITLE] [1843] 39x66cm (15½x26") Wash color highlights. [41] £133 **$220**

MOSCOW [1836] 33x36cm (13x14") Orig OL color. Age-toned margins; else VG. [38] £75 **$125**

MUNICH [1832] Baldwin & Cradock. View at lower margin. 31x38cm (12x15") Orig partial color. Exc. ["Frankfurt" & "Hamburg" offered at same price] [11] £75 **$125**

NEW SOUTH WALES [1874] Stanford. Sydney inset. 39x33cm (15½x13") Orig OL color. ["The Islands of New Zealand" & "Western Australia ... & Tasmania" offered at same price] [11] £45 **$75**

NEW YORK [1843] City south of 42nd St; vignettes. 29x37cm (11½x15") Wash color. Ref: Tooley (Amer) pl.128. [41] £106 **$175**

NORTH AMERICA [1843] Large independent TX. 39x30cm (15½x12") Lt soiled. [9] £106 **$175**

NORTH AMERICA SHEET IV LAKE SUPERIOR REDUCED FROM THE ADMIRALTY SURVEY [1832] Baldwin & Cradock. 32x39cm (13x15") OL color. [48] DM 80 £28 **$46**

NORTH AMERICA SHEET V PARTS OF WISCONSIN AND MICHIGAN [1874] 30x38cm (12x15") OL color. VG (A). [A3] £25 **$41**

NORTH AMERICA SHEET V THE NORTH WEST AND MICHIGAN TERRITORIES [1833] London: Baldwin & Cradock. Lake Michigan region. 30x38cm (12x15") Pristine. OL color. Ref: Karpinski (MI) 120; Phillips (A) 753-35. [12] £106 **$175**

NORTH AMERICA SHEET VII PENNSYLVANIA, NEW JERSEY, MARYLAND, DELAWARE, COLUMBIA AND PART OF VIRGINIA [1833] 37x31cm (14½x12") OL color. Fine (A+). [A4] £50 **$83**

[SAME TITLE] [1833-40] London: J. & C. Walker. 37x32cm (14½x12½") Orig OL col. VG. [36] £75 **$125**

[SAME TITLE] [1874] From *Complete Atlas* ... 37x32cm (14½x12½") OL color. VG (A). [A3] £20 **$33**

NORTH AMERICA SHEET VIII OHIO, WITH PARTS OF KENTUCKY, VIRGINIA AND INDIANA [1874] 35x32cm (14x12½") OL color. VG (A). [A3] £19 **$32**

NORTH AMERICA SHEET X PARTS OF MISSOURI, ILLINOIS, KENTUCKY, TENNESSEE, ALABAMA, MISSISSIPPI AND ARKANSAS [1833] 31x39cm (12½x15½") OL color by counties. VG to fine. [14] £60 **$100**

NORTH AMERICA SHEET XI PARTS OF NORTH AND SOUTH CAROLINA [1874] 37x34cm (14½x13½") OL color. VG (A). [A3] £29 **$48**

NORTH AMERICA SHEET XIV FLORIDA [1834] London: Baldwin & Cradock. 41x30cm (16x12") Full color. Exc. [36] £166 **$275**

SOCIETY FOR THE DIFFUSION OF USEFUL KNOWLEDGE continued

NORTH AMERICA SHEET XIV FLORIDA [c.1863] Publ by Edward Stanford; J. & C. Walker., sc. 41x30cm (16x12") Orig OL color. Good. [28] £178 **$295**

[SAME TITLE] [1874] London: Stanford. 40x31cm (15½x12") Orig OL color. [11] £60 **$100**

NORTH AMERICA SHEET XV UTAH, NEW MEXICO, TEXAS, CALIFORNIA &C. [1874] London: Stanford. 31x39cm (12x15½") Orig OL color. [11] £90 **$150**

NORTH AMERICA SHEET XV UTAH, NEW MEXICO, TEXAS, CALIFORNIA &C. AND THE NORTHERN STATES OF MEXICO [1861] Stanford. Horiz NM-AZ division; large UT, KS & NE. 30x38cm (12x15") OL color. VG. [16] £211 **$350**

NORTH AMERICA SHEET XVI THE SOUTHERN PART OF MEXICO, ALSO BELIZE, GUATEMALA, SALVADOR, HONDURAS, NICARAGUA, AND COSTA RICA [1874] From *Complete Atlas* ... 32x39cm (12½x15½") OL color. VG (A). [A3] £24 **$39**

PALESTINE WITH THE HAURAN ... [1843] Wm. Hughes. 39x31cm (15½x12") OL color. VG (A). Ref: Laor 362. [A4] £34 **$56**

PALESTINE WITH THE HAURAN AND THE ADJACENT DISTRICTS [IN SET WITH] **ANCIENT PALESTINE** [1874] From *Complete Atlas* ... Each 39x32cm (15½x12½") OL color. Ref: cf Laor 362. [A3] £37 **$61**

PHILADELPHIA [1840] Vignettes; 96 landmarks identified. 29x38cm (11½x15") OL color. Ref: Moreland & Bannister illus. p.45. [22] £54 **$90**

POMPEII [1832] Baldwin & Cradock. 31x39cm (12x15½") Orig partial color. Good. [11] £57 **$95**

RUSSIA IN EUROPE [PART I THROUGH PART VIII] [1874] From *Complete Atlas* ... Complete set, incl general map & Sheet 8 inset index. 39x32cm (15½x12½") OL color. VG (A). [A3] £106 **$176**

SOUTH AFRICA [1874] London: Stanford. 16-item key. 31x39cm (12½x15½") Orig OL color. [11] £45 **$75**

STOCKHOLM [1836] Baldwin & Cradock. 33x40cm (13x15½") Orig partial color. Exc. [11] £75 **$125**

[SAME TITLE] [1838] Vignette of city. 32x39cm (12½x15½") Wash color. [41] £60 **$100**

THE ANTILLES OR WEST-INDIA ISLANDS [1874] From *Complete Atlas* ... 30x39cm (12x15") OL color. VG (A). [A3] £33 **$55**

THE AUSTRALIAN COLONIES. [1874] Insets; table of counties. 40x68cm (15½x27") Orig OL color. 2 sh margin tears. [11] £90 **$150**

THE BRITISH ISLANDS IN THE WEST INDIES [1835] London: Baldwin & Cradock. Jamaica & surround of 14 sm maps of islands & groups. 32x39cm (12½x15½") Color. [18] £57 **$95**

THE WORLD ON MERCATOR'S PROJECTION [1874] From *Complete Atlas* ... Two sheets joined, 39x66cm (15½x26") Blue OL wash around continents. VG (A). [A3] £34 **$57**

VENICE [1832] On 2 sheets, overall 38x59cm (15x23") Orig partial color. Exc. ["Milan" (single sheet) offered at same price] [11] £90 **$150**

[SAME TITLE] [1843] Vignettes; region inset. 38x58cm (15x23") Some wash color. [41] £133 **$220**

VIENNA [1833] Building drawings below. 34x37cm (13x14½") Partial color. Rough above top plate line. [1] £112 **$185**

[SAME TITLE] [1833] Building elevations below. 32x38cm (12½x15") Orig partial color. Exc. ["Geneva", "Marseille", "Naples" & "Syracuse with Remaining Vestiges of Its Five Cities" offered at same price] [11] £51 **$85**

WESTERN HEMISPHERE [c.1840] British Pacific North American claims advanced. Diameter: 33cm (13") OL color. [40] £51 **$85**

SOLIS

TIPUS ORBIS TERRARUM [1589 (1603)] In Botero's *Relaciones Universalis del Mondo* ... 34x50cm (13½x19½") Color. Ref: Shirley (W) 242, pl.192. [13] Aus$7,800 £3,542 **$5,873**

SONNENSTERN

MAPA DE LA REPUBLICAS DE AMERICA CENTRALE [1860] Folds into orig octavo cloth slipcase. 96x108cm (37½x42½") Color. Some staining at folds. [A6] **£368** $611

SOTZMANN

CONNECTICUT ... [1796] Hamburg: Bohn. Uncompleted state-by-state project initiated by Christoph Ebeling. 38x47cm (15x18½") Color. Soft crease through image; exemplary. [A7] £1,248 **$2,070**

SOULES

[BOOK WITH MAPS] HISTOIRE DES TROUBLES DE L'AMERIQUE ANGLAISE [1787] Paris: Buisson. 4 octavo vols, orig full leather binding with gold stamping; 3 folding maps. Rehinged. Ref: Howes (US) S770. Sabin 87290; Nebenzahl (Battle Plans) 185 & 198. [33] £844 **$1,400**

PLAN D' YORK EN VIRGINIE AVEC LES ATTAQUES ET LES CAMPEMES DE L'ARMEE COMBINEE DE FRANCE ET D'AMERIQUE [1787] 29x38cm (11½x15") Color. Exc. [24] £286 **$475**

SPEED

[ATLAS] ENGLAND, WALES, SCOTLAND AND IRELAND DESCRIBED AND ABRIDGED [1627] Geo. Humble. Oblong octavo, calf; 60 (of 64) maps by Van den Keere. Lower cover detached; some lt dampstaining; few margins trimmed, occas loss; Yorkshire repaired; ms notes Dorset verso; title soiled, rebacked, sl loss; signature & stamp front end paper. Ref: Chubb 12. [A5] £1,265 **$2,098**

[ATLAS] THE THEATRE OF THE EMPIRE OF GREAT BRITAIN ... TOGETHER WITH A PROSPECT OF THE MOST FAMOUS PARTS OF THE WORLD [1676] Bassett & Chiswell. Folio; 5 parts in 1 vol, 18th c mottled calf with gilt & morocco label in wooden box; 96 colored maps incl 28 from "Prospect". Lacks Great Britain; Holy Land & Garnsey duplicates. 12 maps with sh margin tears & repairs, tape repair Bermuda verso; few shaved margins; joints cracking, extremities worn. Ref: Chubb 27. [A5] £44,000 **$72,957**

[PORTRAIT] AET. M VIRI CLARISSIMI JOANNIS SPEED ... [1631] Posthumously engraved by Solomon Savery for atlases issued by Humble. Uncol. Close border, no loss; sm tear lower rt closed on verso. [4] £260 **$431**

A MAP OF NEW ENGLAND AND NEW YORK [1676] 38x50cm (15x19½") From *A Prospect ... of the World*. London: Bassett & Chiswell; F. Lamb, sc. Fine. Ref: Tooley (Amer) p.290-1, #23. [11] £1,508 **$2,500**

[SAME TITLE] [1676] 39x51cm (15x20") Color. [34] £3,600 **$5,969**

[SAME TITLE] [1676] 2 pp text on reverse. 38x51cm (15x20") Sm margin tear repaired. [46] £2,650 **$4,394**

A MAP OF VIRGINIA AND MARYLAND [1676] 2nd state (of 3); 9th & last Smith derivative. 38x50cm (15x20") Color. VG. Ref: Tooley (Amer) p.170, pl.78. Verner (VA) [31] £2,533 **$4,200**

A MAPP OF THE SOMMER ILANDS ONCE CALLED THE BERMUDAS LYING AT THE MOUTH OF THE BAY OF MEXICO ... [1627-76] From *A Prospect ... of the World*. A. Goos, sc. 40x54cm (15½x21") Color. Usual narrow side margins; sm rust hole filled. [46] £1,550 **$2,570**

[SAME TITLE] [1676] From same source. 40x53cm (16x21") Full color. [20] £1,297 **$2,150**

A NEW DESCRIPTION OF CAROLINA ... [1676] 37x51cm (15x20") Uncolored. Fine. Ref: Cumming (SE) 77; Goss (NA) #41. [32] £1,930 **$3,200**

[SAME TITLE] [1676] By Lamb after Ogilby; 2 pp text on reverse. 38x52cm (15x20½") Color. Some restoration at c'fold. [46] £1,750 **$2,902**

[SAME TITLE] [1676] By Lamb after Ogilby; text on verso. 37x50cm (14½x20") [47] £1,800 **$2,985**

[SAME TITLE] [1676] From *A Prospect ... of the World*. Incl Lederer fabrications. 39x51cm (15½x20") Full color. Sm stain; else VG. [36] £1,809 **$3,000**

A NEW MAPPE OF THE ROMANE EMPIRE NEWLY DESCRIBED BY JOHN SPEEDE [1626] In *Prospect ...* London: G. Humble. Carte a figures. 39x50cm (15½x19½") Border & OL color, faded. Moderately browned. [A9] £295 **$489**

[SAME TITLE] [1676] Based on Ortelius; panels top & sides; inset history text. 38x51cm (15x20") OL color; full color panels. 2 sm obscured rust spots ctr; overall VG. [37] £573 **$950**

A NEWE MAPE OF TARTARY ... [(1626) 1627-76] 39x50cm (15½x19½") Color. Ink inscription in blank cartouche; o/w fine. [4] £595 **$987**

AFRICAE, DESCRIBED, THE MANNERS OF THEIR HABITS, AND BUILDINGS: NEWLY DONE INTO ENGLISH BY J.S. ... [1627-76] From *A Prospect ... of the World*. London: Bassett & Chiswell. A. Goos, sc. Carte-a-figures. 40x52cm (15½x20½") Color. Sm lower c'fold split restored; o/w good. [46] £2,700 **$4,477**

AMERICA WITH THOSE KNOWN PARTS IN THAT UNKNOWNE WORLD BOTH PEOPLE AND MANNER OF BUILDINGS DISCRIBED AND INLARGED BY I.S. ANO 1626 [1626 / 1631] G. Humble; 1st state, 1st reissue. Border vignettes top and sides; insular Calif. 39x51cm (15½x20½") Color. Few sm margin mends; else exc. Ref: Burden 217; McLaughlin 3; Tooley (Amer) p.113. [23] £4,523 **$7,500**

[SAME TITLE] [1626 / 1631] Abraham Goos, sc. 1st ed, 2nd issue; border vignettes top and sides; insular Calif.. 39x51cm (15½x20") Some restoration, esp lf margin. Ref: Burden 217; McLaughlin 3; Tooley (Amer) p.113. Leighly 6. [2] £2,895 **$4,800**

[SAME TITLE] [1626 / 1676] Bassett & Chiswell. Calif. 40x52cm (16x20½") Sl browning along fold; verso fold reinforcement with paper tape; sm surface section abraded, letters disrupted. [A8] £2,358 **$3,910**

[SAME TITLE] [1626-1676] London: Bassett & Chiswell. 39x51cm (15½x20½") [34] £5,600 **$9,286**

SPEED continued

AMERICA WITH THOSE KNOWN PARTS IN THAT UNKNOWNE WORLD BOTH PEOPLE AND MANNER OF BUILDINGS DISCRIBED AND INLARGED BY I.S. ANO 1626 [1627 / 1676] 1st English printed map of Western Hemi. Modern, not recent color. 39x51cm (15½x20") Lower c'fold strengthened, margin repair. 2" stain lower ctr; overall VG. Ref: Leighly 6. [37] £3,619 **$6,000**

ASIA WITH THE ISLANDS ADIOYNING DESCRIBED ... [(1626) 1627-76] From *A Prospect of the Most Famous Parts of the World*. Panels at top and sides. 39x51cm (15½x20½") Color. Fine. [4] £2,750 $4,560

BOHEMIA ... [1676] Bassett & Chiswell. 42x52cm (16½x20½") Color. Cropped at lower border; strengthened at fold. [A6] £299 $496

BRITAIN AS IT WAS DEVIDED IN THE TYME OF THE ENGLISHE-SAXONS ESPECIALLY DURING THEIR HEPTARCHY [1611-76] Panels at sides. 38x50cm (15x20") Full color. Heavy paper, some waving, a thin area; exc. Ref: Shirley (BI to 1650) 317; Moreland & Bannister p.215. [1] £1,447 **$2,400**

BUCKINGHAM, BOTH SHYRE AND SHIRETOWNE DESCRIB. [1666] Sold by Bassett. Buckingham & Reading plans. 38x51cm (15x20") OL color. Sl toned, more at c'fold; sm edge chips; c'fold separation repaired verso; sl weak impression. [A9] £139 **$230**

CAMBRIDGESHIRE DESCRIBED WITH THE DEVISION OF THE HUNDREDS, THE TOWNES SITUATION, WITH THE ARMES OF THE COLLEGES OF THEAT FAMOUS UNIVERSITI [1627-32] London: George Humble. 38x52cm (15x20½") Color. Minor restoration at c'fold. [47] £1,150 $1,907

CANAAN ... [1611-1651] For use in *A Prospect ... of the World*. Jerusalem inset. 39x52cm (15½x20½") Color. C'fold split repaired. Ref: Laor 737. [34] £1,400 $2,322

CORNWALL [1611-16] London: Sudbury & Humble. Inset: Launceston view. 38x51cm (15x20") Fine. Ref: Chubb 24a; Skelton (County) 11. [47] £1,200 $1,990

CUMBERLAND [1627] Sudbury & Humble. Carlisle inset. 38x50cm (15x19½") Col. Framed. [A6] £391 $649

DEVONSHIRE WITH EXCESTER DESCRIBED [1676] London: Bassett and Chiswell. 38x51cm (15x20") Color. Margins trimmed but ample; third image dampstained; browned overall. [A7] £139 **$230**

[SAME TITLE] [1676] 38x51cm (15x20") Orig wash & OL col. Faint waterstains; o/w good. [11] £452 **$750**

DORCET SHIRE: [1627] London: G. Humble. From Miniature Atlas. About 8x12cm (3½x5") ["Bedford Shire:", "Chester:", "Hereford Shire:" & "Leicester Shire:" offered at same price] [11] £45 **$75**

GLOUCESTERSHIRE [1612] Sudbury & Humble. Insets. 38x51cm (15x20") Color. Repaired split upper fold; lt staining top corners. Framed. [A6] £552 $916

GREECE [1626-1665] From *A Prospect ... of the World*. 39x50cm (15½x20") Color. [34] £650 $1,078

[SAME TITLE] [(1627) 1676] From *A Prospect ... of the World*. London: Bassett & Chiswell. 40x51cm (15½x20") Top rt corner tip not printed due to plate damage; edges browned. [46] £680 $1,128

KENT [1627] Sudbury & Humble. Insets: Canterbury; Rochester. 38x50cm (15x19½") Color. Sm repair fold ends. Framed. [1676 ed, framed, sold for £460] [A6] £506 $839

LINCOLNE SHIRE: [1627] London: G. Humble. From Miniature Atlas. About 8x12cm (3½x5") ["Bark Shire:", "Essex County:", "Glocester Shire:", "Norfolke:", "Wight Island:" & "Wilt Shire:" offered at same price] [11] £60 **$100**

MAPPA AESTIVARUM INSULARUM ALIAS BERMUDAS [1676] Title repeated in English. 40x52cm (15½x20½") Color. Sides cropped, sl loss one margin; lt browning. [A6] £517 $858

MIDDLE-SEX: [1627] London: G. Humble. From Miniature Atlas. About 8x12cm (3½x5") [11] £75 **$125**

MIDLE-SEX DESCRIBED WITH THE MOST FAMOUS CITIES OF LONDON AND WESTMINSTER [1610-76] London: Bassett & Chiswell. Insets: London; Westminster; views. 40x51cm (15½x20") Color. Ref: Howgego 7 (inset). Skelton (County) 92. [47] £950 $1,576

NOTTINGHAM SHIRE [1627] London: G. Humble. From Miniature Atlas. About 8x12cm (3½x5") ["Northumber Land:" offered at same price] [11] £30 **$50**

OXFORDSHIRE DESCRIBED WITH YE CITIE AND THE ARMES OF THE COLLEDGES OF YT FAMOUS UNIVERSITY ... [1610] 38x52cm (15x20½") Later color. Age toned. Ref: Campbell (Early) p. 76-7. [2] £905 **$1,500**

SOMERSET-SHIRE DESCRIBED: AD IN TO HUNDREDS DEVIDED, WITH THE PLOTT OF THE FAMOUS AND MOST WHOLSOM WATERS AND CITIE OF THE BATHE [1611] From *Theatre of the Empire* ... 1st ed. 38x51cm (15x20") Period color. [42] Aus$1,450 £658 $1,092

SPAINE ... [1614] Humble. Carte a figures. 41x54cm (16x21") Color. Lower border sl cropped; few sm tears just affecting engraving. [A6] £345 $572

[SAME TITLE] [1626 (1676)] Bassett & Chiswell. Carte a figures. 42x54cm (16½x21½") Color. C'fold wear, sl plate surface loss; margins shaved. Framed. [A5] £276 $458

SPEED continued

SPAINE NEWLY DESCRIBED WITH MANY ADDITIONS, BOTH IN THE ATTIRES OF THE PEOPLE & THE SETUATIONS OF THEIR CHEIFEST CITYES BY JOHN SPEED 1626 [1627-76] From *A Prospect ... of the World*. London: Bassett & Chiswell. A. Goos, sc. Carte a figures. 42x54cm (16½x21½") Color. C'fold restored. [46] **£780** $1,294

SUFFOLKE, DESCRIBED ... [1610 (1676)] London: Bassett and Chiswell. 38x52cm (15x20½") OL color, probably later. Linen-backed. Ex lib NYHS. [A7] £139 **$230**

SUSSEX [1612] Sudbury & Humble. Inset: Chichester. 39x51cm (15x20") Color. Framed. [A6] £575 **$954**

THE COUNTIE AND CITIE OF LYNCOLN DESCRIBED WITH THE ARMES OF THEM THAT HAVE BENE EARLES THEREOF SINCE THE CONQUEST [1611] From *Theatre of the Empire* ... Jodocus Hondius, sc. 39x52cm (15½x20½") Period color. [42] **Aus$1,100** £500 $828

THE COUNTIE OF NOTTINGHAM DESCRIBED, THE SHIRE TOWNES SITUATION AND THE EARLS THEREOF OBSERVED [1627] From *Theatre of the Empire* ... 39x51cm (15x20") Color. [11] £172 **$285**

THE COUNTYE PALATINE OF CHESTER WITH THAT MOST ANCIENT CITIE DESCRIBED [1611-16] London: Sudbury & Humble. 39x51cm (15½x20") Fine. Ref: Chubb 24a; Skelton (County) 11. [47] **£1,100** $1,824

THE INVASIONS OF ENGLAND AND IRELAND WITH AL THEIR CIVILL WARS SINCE THE CONQUEST [1627-76] From *A Prospect ... of the World*. 38x51cm (15x20") Minor restoration to c'fold; dark impression. Ref: Shirley (BI to 1650) 397, pl.119. [46] **£1,280** $2,123

THE KINGDOME OF CHINA NEWLY AUGMENTED BY J.S. ... [1627] Humble. Carte a figures. 40x51cm (15½x20") Color. Corner repair with some facsimile. [A6] **£805** $1,335

[SAME TITLE] [(1626) 1627-76] From *A Prospect ... of the World*. 39x51cm (15½x20") Color. Repaired split lower c'fold, verso reinforcement, no loss; o/w fine. Ref: Cortazzi (Japan) pl.29. [4] **£2,300** $3,814

[SAME TITLE] [1626-76] From same source. *A Prospect ... of the World*. Carte a figures. 39x52cm (15½x20½") Color. Minor c'fold repairs; o/w good. [34] **£2,400** $3,980

[SAME TITLE] [1626 / 1676] Bassett & Chiswell. Carte a figures. 40x51cm (15½x20") OL color; full color side figures. Evenly browned. [A8] **£1,526** $2,530

[SAME TITLE] [1627-76] Engraved for *A Prospect ... of the World*. Carte a figures. Incl Japan & insular Korea. 40x52cm (15½x20½") Old color. Margins reinforced. [47] **£2,300** $3,814

THE KINGDOME OF ENGLAND [1610 / 1616] Jodocus Hondius, sc. 38x52cm (15x20½") Color. Margins extended, no loss; few tears repaired; attractive. Ref: Shirley (BI to 1650) 345, cf 318. [24] £1,206 **$2,000**

[SAME TITLE] [1632] From *Theatre of the Empire* ... London: Humble. The 2nd plate by A. Goos replacing Hondius original. 8 costumed vignettes. 40x52cm (15½x20½") Color, possibly old or orig. Restored split lower c'fold; minor spotting. Ref: Shirley (BI to 1650) 434. [46] **£1,450** $2,405

THE KINGDOME OF GREAT BRITAINE AND IRELAND [1610 (1611)] Sudbury & Humble. Insets: London; Edinburgh. 37x51cm (14½x20") Color. Verso c'fold repair. Framed. [A5] **£863** $1,431

[SAME TITLE] [(1611) 1614-16] 2 insets views. 38x51cm (15x20") Color. Sm lower ctr margin wormed area now filled; o/w fine. [1676 ed offered at same price] Ref: Shirley (BI to 1650) 343. [4] **£1,250** $2,073

THE KINGDOME OF PERSIA WITH THE CHEEF CITTIES AND HABITES DESCRIBED [1626-31] From *A Prospect ... of the World*. Carte a figures. 40x51cm (15½x20") Color. [34] **£800** $1,327

[SAME TITLE] [c.1627] Humble. 40x51cm (15½x20") OL color; full color side figures. Sl darkened. [A8] £451 **$747**

[SAME TITLE] [1676] 39x52cm (15½x20½") Orig OL color. Bit soiled & faded. [11] £271 **$450**

THE KINGDOME OF SCOTLAND [1627] Sudbury & Humble. 38x51cm (15x20") Color. Sl wear at folds; 2 sm holes. Framed. [A6] **£805** $1,335

THE MAPE OF HUNGARI NEWLY AUGMENTED BY JOHN SPEEDE [1627-76] From *A Prospect ... of the World*. London: Bassett & Chiswell. A. Goos, sc. Top & side panels. 40x52cm (15½x20½") Color. C'fold reinforced. [46] **£480** $796

[SAME TITLE] [1626] From *A Prospect ... of the World*. Top & side panels; A. Goos, sc. 40x51cm (15½x20") Color. Lower c'fold repair; good. [28] £663 **$1,100**

THE TURKISH EMPIRE [1626 / 1676] Bassett & Chiswell. Carte a figures. 40x52cm (15½x20½") OL color; full color side figures. Minor browning, especially along fold. [1626 ed, trimmed to platemark; scattered lt soiling, sold at $862] Ref: Potter illus p.119. [A8] £589 **$977**

WALES [1610-76] 14 side panels. 38x50cm (15x20") Ref: Booth (Wales) 9; Skelton (County) 92. [47] **£750** $1,244

[SAME TITLE] [1627] Sudbury & Humble. Side panels of town plans. 38x50cm (15x19½") Color. Narrow rt margin, strengthened at lower corner. Framed. [A6] **£506** $839

ST. ALBIN
HORIZON DE PARIS ... [1739] Hemisphere, diameter 22", centered on Paris; with text at sides, 60x81cm (24x32") Orig OL color. Exc. [2] £1,749 **$2,900**

STANFORD Try *Society for the Diffusion of Useful Knowledge*
STANFORD'S MAP OF THE SEAT OF WAR IN AMERICA (SHEET 1) [dated Aug 1861] Folding map, dissected, linen-backed in orig cloth folder; NE section of later 4-sheet map, NY to OH to VA. 69x56cm (27x22") Full color. Ref: cf Stephenson (CW-2) 17.55. [15] £241 **$400**

THE POSITION OF THE YUKON GOLDFIELDS ... CANADA [1897] Separately issued; laid on orig canvas. Incl Alaska, NWT, BC. 51x64cm (20x25") Orig color. Little wear along folds; old ink stains. [34] £260 $431

STANSBURY
[BOOK WITH MAPS] AN EXPEDITION TO THE VALLEY OF THE GREAT SALT LAKE OF UTAH [1852] Phila. 1st ed. Octavo, orig publisher's cloth; 57 plates; with 2 folding maps in separate book-style case. Maps spotted; spotting throughout; 2 plates torn. Ref: Howes (US) S-884. [A6] £172 $286

STEBBINS
THE STATE OF CONNECTICUT, WITH ALL THE NEW TOWNS, INCLUDING PARTS OF NEW YORK & NEW JERSEY [1858] L. Stebbins & Co. Wall map. Full color by towns. 74x99cm (29x39") Age-toned varnish; repaired tears & lt chipping, sm loss near top; lt water stain rt edge; VG. Ref: cf Thompson (CT) 180. [15] £452 **$750**

STEDMAN
PLAN OF THE SIEGE OF CHARLESTOWN IN SOUTH CAROLINA [1794] From ... *Amer War* ... 25x29cm (10x11½") Uncolored. VG. [36] £332 **$550**

SKETCH OF THE BATTLE OF HOBKIRKS HILL, NEAR CAMDEN, ON THE 25TH APRIL 1781 [1794] From ... *Amer War* ... 43x29cm (17x11½") Uncolored. 2 repaired tears into image. [36] £166 **$275**

STEDMAN, BROWN & LYONS
TEXAS [1878] From *Atlas of the United States*. Publ Baltimore. Counties with founding dates. 29x38cm (11½x15") Orig color. Chipped at edges. [27] £151 **$250**

STIELER Try *Perthes, Petermann*
[UNITED STATES: WEST] [1879] Most of trans-Mississippi west except south TX. 36x41cm (14x16") Clean, crisp. [7] £54 **$90**

DAENMARK MIT HOLSTEIN [1823] 29x34cm (11½x13½") OL & wash color. [40] £24 **$40**

DER SUDLICHE THEIL VON SUD-AMERICA [1840] 31x41cm (12½x16") OL & wash color. [40] £27 **$45**

DIE VEREINIGTEN STAATEN VON AMERIKA IN 6 BLATTERN - BL.4 [1873] From *Hand-Atlas*. SW section of US: Monterey to Colorado to Guaymas, Mex. Highly detailed. 33x41cm (13x16") OL color. Lower margin dampstain; else exc. [1897 ed offered at same price] [12] £96 **$160**

EUROPA [1839] Divided into river basins 29x36cm (11½x14") Color. [40] £18 **$30**

MEXICO UND CENTRO-AMERICA [1828] From early ed, *Hand-Atlas*. By von Stulpnagel; Gotha: Justus Perthes. 30x36cm (11½x14") OL color. Lt scattered foxing in margin; near fine. Ref: Phillips (A) 6039-11 or 6075-58. [12] £142 **$235**

POLYNESIEN UND DER GROSSE OCEAN [1873] East sheet. Insets: HI; Honolulu; etc. 33x41cm (13x16") Color. [40] £45 **$75**

VEREINIGTE STAATEN VON NORD-AMERICA [1834] 30x39cm (12x15½") OL color. Some margin foxing; VG. Ref: Wheat (TM) 406. [A1] £166 **$275**

STOCKDALE
A NEW MAP OF THE WEST INDIES FOR THE HISTORY OF THE BRITISH COLONIES [1793] As in Bryan Edward's *History of the West Indies*. 70x112cm (27½x44") Full color. [20] £754 **$1,250**

A REDUCED MAP OF THE EMPIRE OF GERMANY, HOLLAND, THE NETHERLANDS, SWITZERLAND, THE GRISONS, ITALY, SICILY, CORSICA AND SARDINIA [1800] 3 sheets, each 47x81cm (18½x32") Browning, off-setting, esp sheet 1 & 3; a margin trimmed; folds reinforced; NYHS stamps verso. [21] Can$350 £153 $254

NEW PHYSICAL, HISTORICAL ... MAP OF ENGLAND & WALES [1809] By John Andrew, London. Folding map, dissected, linen-mounted; with orig labeled slipcase. 133x162cm (52½x64") OL col. Superb. [15] £271 **$450**

SKETCH OF SYDNEY COVE, PORT JACKSON IN THE COUNTY OF CUMBERLAND, NEW SOUTH WALES, JULY 1788 [1788] In *Voyage of Governor Phillip to Botany Bay*. 1st publ map of Sydney Cove; shows layout of convict settlement; Capt. John Hunter's soundings. 45x52cm (17½x20½") Col. Ref: Perry & Prescott 1789.07. Clancy (Australis) illus. p.142; Tooley (Australia) 741, pl.168; McCormick pl.2. [13] Aus$2,000 £908 $1,506

STODDARD

MAP OF THE ADIRONDACK WILDERNESS [1901] S.R. Stoddard; engr & printed by Louis Neuman, NY. Pocket map in cloth folder. 10 mile concentric circles around Mt. Marcy. 77x61cm (30½x24") Color by county. Sl browned folds; near fine. [5] £160 **$265**

STOOPENDAAL

HET BELOOFDE LANDT CANAAN ... [c.1720] 36x46cm (14x18½") OL color. [A8] £173 **$287**
HET BELOOFDE LANDT CANAAN DOOR WANDELT VAN ONSEN SALICHMAEKER NEFFENS SYNE APOSTTELEN ... [c.1680] Orig in Dutch Bible. 32x46cm (12½x18") Uncol. Mild soiling at c'fold. [26] £115 **$190**
ORBIS TERRARUM TABULA RECENS EMENDATA ET IN LUCEM EDITA [c.1680] After Visscher; double hemi; 2 sm celestial hemis; insular Calif. 35x45cm (14x18") Early color. Exc. Ref: Shirley (W) 498. [24] £1,930 **$3,200**
[SAME TITLE] [1682] Double-hemi from Dutch Bible; similar & reduced from 1658 Visscher, but polar projections replaced with pre- & post-Copernican diagrams; decorative surround. 36x47cm (14x18½") Full color. Strong impression; one false margin fitted. [11] £1,357 **$2,250**
WERELT CAERT [c.1680] After Visscher's Bible map. Double-hemi; insular Calif. 30x43cm (12x17") Color. Fine. Ref: cf Shirley (W) 498. [A1] £1,725 **$2,860**
[SAME TITLE] [c.1690] Double-hemi; insular Calif. 29x46cm (11½x18") [A7] £763 **$1,265**
[SAME TITLE] [1716] Reduced version of Visscher; plate appears reworked from orig. Double-hemi; sm polar hemis; insular Calif; elaborate decor; 31x46cm (12x18") [11] £814 **$1,350**

STRADANUS

[TITLE PAGE] [1600] From *Nova Reperta*. Inventions & artifacts illustrated; sm Western Hemisphere map. 20x27cm (8x10½") Exc. Ref: Burden 139. [43] £724 **$1,200**

STREIT

CHARTE VON AUSTRALIEN ... [1817] 2 Sydney insets. 48x65cm (19x25½") Color. Fold reinforcement; abraded area; overall VG. Ref: cf Tooley (Australia) p.151. [24] £1,146 **$1,900**

STUMPF

EUROPA / DIE ERST TAFEL DESZ ERSTEN BUCHE [1584] Woodblock "upside-down" map. 29x39cm (11½x15½") B&W. 2 faint stamps top & bottom rt; faint ink notes in image; fine. [1] £603 **$1,000**

SWANSTON

OREGON AND CALIFORNIA [1848] 23x14cm (9x5½") OL color. Fine (A+). [A4] £50 **$83**
[SAME TITLE] [c.1849] Probably from *Gazetteer of the World*. Publ by Fullarton. Covers Rockies to Pacific. 23x15cm (9x6") Orig pastel color. Fine. [12] £81 **$135**
UNITED STATES ... SOUTH CENTRAL SECTION COMPRISING TEXAS, LOUISIANA, ARKANSAS, WESTERN TERRITORY [c.1856] Edinburgh: Fullarton. 41x53cm (16½x21") Orig wash pastel. [27] £90 **$150**

SWIFT

MAP OF THE TERRITORY OF FLORIDA, FROM ITS NORTHERN BOUNDARY TO LAT: 27 30' N. CONNECTED WITH THE DELTA OF THE MISSISSIPPI [1829] Annexed to report of the Board of Internal Improvement. South to Tampa Bay. 70x169cm (27½x66½") Lt chipping & wear; needs devarnishing & some restoration. Ref: Phillips (M) p.283. [15] £452 **$750**

SWINTON

UNITED STATES SECTION 4. TEXAS, KANSAS, S. NEBRASKA, COLORADO. NEW MEXICO INDIAN TERRITORY ... [c.1880] School geography map with text page. 28x23cm (11x9½") Full color. Good. [16] £30 **$50**

TALLIS

[ATLAS] THE ILLUSTRATED ATLAS AND MODERN HISTORY OF THE WORLD [c.1851] R. Montgomery Martin, ed. Quarto; half calf & marbled boards; 81 maps by Rapkin, OL color. Ref: see *Antique Maps of the 19th Century World*, NY: Portland House, 1989. Phillips (A) 804. [47] £3,500 **$5,804**
AUSTRALIA [1851] From *Illustrated Atlas*. 24x32cm (9½x12½") Orig OL color. Ref: Campbell (Early) ill. p.144-5; Tooley (Landmarks) ill. p.268. Tooley (Australia) 1217. [13] **Aus$540** £245 **$406**
AUSTRALIA [IN SET WITH] NEW SOUTH WALES [AND] VICTORIA OR PORT PHILLIP [AND] SOUTH AUSTRALIA [AND] VAN DIEMENS LAND [AND] WESTERN AUSTRALIA [1851] Complete 6 map Australian set. Bound at side, not middle. [13] **Aus$2,600** £1,181 **$1,958**
AUSTRIA [c.1850] Vignettes. 24x32cm (9½x13") OL color. Minor spot; good (B). [A4] £33 **$55**

TALLIS continued

BRITISH INDIA [c.1860] Table of mutinies & massacres. 33x24cm (13x9½") OL col. VG (A). [A4] £29 **$48**

CABOOL, THE PUNJAB AND BELOOCHISTAN [c.1850] 25x34cm (10x13") OL col. Fine (A+). [A4] £19 **$31**

CHANNEL ISLANDS [c.1850] Maps of Jersey & Guernsey; English Channel inset. 33x24cm (13x9½") OL color. Top trimmed, title surround affected; else fine; VG (A). [A4] £28 **$46**

CHINA [c.1850] Incl Burma. 25x32cm (9½x12½") OL col. Minor soiling at fold; VG (A). [A4] £115 **$190**

EASTERN HEMISPHERE [1851] From *Illustrated Atlas*. 25x34cm (9½x13½") Orig OL color. [13] **Aus$320** £145 **$241**

EGYPT AND ARABIA PETRA [1851] Vignettes. 34x25cm (13½x10") Orig OL color. Fine. [38] £75 **$125**

JAMAICA [1851] 5 vignettes. 25x35cm (10x14") Color. Bit browned. [11] £42 **$70**

JAPAN & COREA [1851] As in *Illustrated Atlas*. 26x34cm (10x13½") Orig OL col. Fine. Ref: Cortazzi pl.90. [4] £145 **$241**

MALAY ARCHIPELAGO OR EAST INDIA ISLANDS [1851] From *Illustrated Atlas*. 24x33cm (9½x13") Orig OL color. [13] **Aus$290** £132 **$218**

MEXICO, CALIFORNIA AND TEXAS [1851] 3 vignettes; outsized CA gold regions in yellow. 22x30cm (9x12") OL color. Fine. Framed. [16] £271 **$450**

NEW SOUTH WALES [1851] From *Illustrated Atlas*. 1st ed with Sydney vignette, not the cove; untitled NSW seal. 33x25cm (13x10") Color. [2nd ed, with Sydney Cove, "The Seal of NSW", Cape Byron & Richmond PO, offered at Aus$ 410] Ref: Tooley (Australia) 1222, pl.188. [13] **Aus$420** £191 **$316**

NORTH AMERICA [1850] 9 vignettes. 36x24cm (14x9½") OL color. Fine. Ref: Goss (NA) #82. [12] £112 **$185**

[SAME TITLE] [c.1850] 10 vignettes. 30x22cm (12x9") Partial color. Good. [16] £136 **$225**

[SAME TITLE] [c.1850] Several vignettes. 36x24cm (14x9½") Orig OL color. Minor foxing spot in Greenland; o/w VG to fine. Ref: Goss (NA) 82. [A2] £265 **$440**

[SAME TITLE] [c.1850] 29x22cm (11½x8½") Full col. Sl toned edges; else clean. Framed. [A10] £90 **$150**

[SAME TITLE] [1851] 9 vignettes. 34x24cm (13½x9½") OL color. Fine (A+). [A4] £214 **$355**

[SAME TITLE] [c.1852] London: Virtue. 9 vignettes. 33x27cm (13x10½") Some col. VG. [25] £109 **$180**

NOVA SCOTIA AND NEWFOUNDLAND [c.1850] With vignettes. 26x33cm (10x13") OL color. Bit of foxing; good (B). [A3] £66 **$110**

PART OF SOUTH AUSTRALIA [1851] From *Illustrated Atlas*. 34x25cm (13½x9½") Orig OL color. Ref: Tooley (Australia) 1231. [13] **Aus$280** £127 **$211**

[SAME TITLE] [c.1850] Vignettes of Adelaide, etc. 33x25cm (13x9½") OL col. Fine (A+). [A4] £80 **$133**

RUSSIA IN ASIA [c.1850] Vignettes. 25x32cm (10x12½") OL color. Fine (A+). [A3] £70 **$116**

THIBET, MONGOLIA AND MANDCHOURIA [c.1850] 6 vignettes. 25x32cm (9½x12½") OL color. Fine (A+). [A3] £107 **$178**

[SAME TITLE] [1851] 25x33cm (9½x13") OL color. By sight, fine. Framed. [A9] £69 **$115**

TURKEY IN EUROPE [c.1850] Vignettes: Constantinople. 25x33cm (10x13") OL & wash col. [39] £60 **$100**

UNITED STATES [1851] 28x38cm (11x15") Some OL color. VG. Ref: Illus: *Antique Maps of the 19th Century World*, p.147. [25] £106 **$175**

[SAME TITLE] [1852] London: J. & F. Tallis. TX incl Santa Fe. 24x34cm (9½x13½") Orig OL color; later color to vignettes. VG. Ref: Illus: *Antique Maps of the 19th Century World*, p.147. [16] £181 **$300**

VAN DIEMEN'S ISLAND OR TASMANIA [1851] From *Illustrated Atlas*. 2nd state; 2 counties. 26x33cm (10x13") Orig OL color. Ref: Tooley (Australia) 1233 & 1552, pl.118. [13] **Aus$295** £134 **$222**

VICTORIA OR PORT PHILLIP [c.1861] Gold regions in yellow. 26x32cm (10x13") Orig OL color. [11] £60 **$100**

WESTERN AUSTRALIA / SWAN RIVER [1851] From *Illustrated Atlas*. 25x33cm (9½x13") Orig OL color. Ref: Tooley (Australia) 1236, pl.91; Clancy (Australis) ill. p.158. [13] **Aus$460** £209 **$346**

TANNER

[ATLAS] A NEW UNIVERSAL ATLAS ... [1841] Imperial quarto, 117 maps on 70 sheets, incl 1838 Bradford Texas. Quarter roan broken, badly worn, waterstained; world map a fragment, lacks NC; most maps undamaged, with sm margin stains. [16] £2,865 **$4,750**

[BOOK WITH MAPS] THE AMERICAN TRAVELLER; OR GUIDE THROUGH THE UNITED STATES [1837] 3rd ed. Sm 12mo; 144 pp, 7 views, 4 city plans & "Map of the Roads, Canals and Rail Roads ..." (18x22") Color by state. Cover rubbed; lt soiled; occas pencil notations; minor map surface loss along outside fold, map separations stabilized with museum tape; good-VG. Ref: Howes (US) T24. [5] £317 **$525**

TANNER continued

A MAP OF THE UNITED STATES OF AMERICA [1823] Appeared in Darby's Edition of Brookes Gazetteer, 3rd ed. 38x33cm (15x13") Full color. Minor repairs verso; bright. [25] £96 **$160**

A NEW MAP OF LOUISIANA WITH ITS CANALS, ROADS AND DISTANCES [1839 (1843)] From 2nd Carey & Hart ed, *New Universal Atlas.* Phila: Carey & Hart. 38 parishes. 27x34cm (10½x13½") Full color. Immaculate. Ref: Phillips (A) 6099-20. [12] £136 **$225**

A NEW MAP OF MAINE [1840] 36x29cm (14½x11½") Orig color by counties. Fine. ["... New York ..." offered at same price] [14] £100 **$165**

A NEW MAP OF MISSISSIPPI WITH ITS ROADS AND DISTANCES [1836] 33x27cm (13x10½") Orig color. Fine. [14] £106 **$175**

A NEW MAP OF OHIO WITH ITS CANALS ROADS & DISTANCES [1841] From *Universal Atlas.* Cincinnati inset; canal profile. 33x27cm (13x10½") Orig color by counties. VG. [14] £96 **$160**

A NEW MAP OF PENNSYLVANIA WITH ITS CANALS, RAIL-ROADS & DISTANCES FROM PLACE TO PLACE ALONG THE STAGE ROADS [1840 (1842-43)] From *New Universal Atlas.* 1st or 2nd Carey & Hart issue. 58 counties. 27x34cm (10½x13½") Color. Immaculate. Ref: Phillips (A) 788-11 or 6099-11. [12] £112 **$185**

AN ALPHABETICAL INDEX TO THE FOUR SHEET MAP OF THE UNITED STATES [c.1839] 1st ed. Rackliff & Jones, Printers, Phila. 12mo, cloth, paper label; viii, 99, 14 pp. Incl catalogue of Tanner maps & atlases. Some foxing; sl wear head of spine; fine. Ref: Sabin 94310. [16] £151 **$250**

CITY OF WASHINGTON [1836 / 1846] From Mitchell's *New Universal Atlas.* 30x39cm (12x15") Full wash color by wards; single green border. Top & bottom margins trimmed close; near fine. Ref: Phillips (A) 3553-16. [35] £72 **$120**

IRELAND [1843] From *Universal Atlas.* 28x22cm (11x9") Orig color by counties. Fine. ["England" & "Scotland" offered at same price] [14] £106 **$175**

MAP OF FLORIDA [1823] From *New American Atlas.* Full color by county. 69x53cm (27x21") Fine. [15] £663 **$1,100**

MAP OF PENNSYLVANIA AND NEW JERSEY [1823] From *New American Atlas.* Full color by county. 50x62cm (19½x24½") Lt foxing; sm split at c'fold; minor chipping bottom edge; fine [15] £422 **$700**

MEXICO & GUATEMALA [1834 / 1844] Incl TX, Southwest, CA & trans-Sierra Timpanagos & Buenaventura Rivers. 29x37cm (11½x14½") Color; 2-color border. [41] £226 **$375**

NEW HAMPSHIRE & VERMONT [1840] 35x28cm (14x11") Orig OL color. Fine [14] £93 **$155**

PERSIA ARABIA &C. [1840] 29x36cm (11½x14") Orig color. Fine. [14] £84 **$140**

SCHUYLKILL COUNTY, PENNSYLVANIA [c.1830] Pocket map in orig cloth folder. Dated from RR presence. Full color by town. 38x51cm (15x20") Minor separations at fold junctions; exc. [15] £302 **$500**

SWEDEN & NORWAY [1836] Incl uncolored Finland. 28x22cm (11x9") Orig color. Fine. [14] £87 **$145**

THE TRAVELER'S GUIDE ... OF THE UNITED STATES [1825] On thin paper; orig folding into boards or slipcase. 46x56cm (18x22") Orig color. Minor repairs. [34] **£450** $746

THE TRAVELER'S GUIDE. A MAP OF THE ROADS, CANALS AND STEAM BOAT ROUTES OF THE UNITED STATES [1825] Folding map in modern morocco folder to replicate orig. OL color by state. 45x56cm (17½x22") Map sl browned; rebacked. Ref: Phillips (M) p.884. [15] £603 **$1,000**

TURKEY IN ASIA [1843] Incl present Iraq, Syria, Jordan, Lebanon, Israel, Cyprus. 28x36cm (11x14") Orig color. Lt surface soiling; o/w VG to fine. [14] £90 **$150**

VIRGINIA MARYLAND AND DELAWARE [1820] 51x73cm (20½x29") Orig wash color. C'fold repair; good. [28] £407 **$675**

TARDIEU

CARTE DE LA CAROLINE MERIDIONALE ET SEPTENTRIONALE ET DE LA VIRGINIE [1797-1801] From Mentelle & Chanlaire *Atlas Universel de Geographie Physique et Politique.* South NJ to North GA. 33x43cm (13x17") OL color. Fine. Ref: Phillips (A) 6011-158. [31] £347 **$575**

CARTE DES ANTILLES [1797] Puerto Rico to Margarita & Tobago. 33x43cm (13x17") Color. Ref: Phillips (A) 6011-163. [18] £136 **$225**

CARTE DU MEXIQUE DRESSE POUR L'INTELLIGENCE DE L'HISTOIRE GENERALE DES VOYAGES DE LA HARPE [1821] North to 42nd parallel. 39x25cm (15½x10") Orig OL color. Lt margin age toning; few lt spots on margin; o/w fine. [A1] £183 **$303**

CARTE MAGNETIQUE DES DEUX HEMISPHERES GRAVE PAR TARDIEU [1810] Double polar hemi. 18x35cm (7½x14") Orig color. [13] **Aus$520** £236 $391

ETATS UNIS DE L'AMERIQUE, CORRIGES ET AUGMENTES EN 1803 [c.1803] Maximum GA. 18x20cm (7x8") Orig red OL color. Fine. [29] £100 **$165**

TARLETON
PLAN OF THE SIEGE OF CHARLESTOWN IN SOUTH CAROLINA [Mar 1,1787] Orig found in *History of the Campaigns of 1780 and 1781*. Cartographer's name not given. 26x29cm (10x11½") Linen backed. Fine. Ref: Nebenzahl (Battle Plans) 83. [32] £543 **$900**

TASSIN
[ATLAS] CARTES GENERALES DES PROVINCES DE FRANCE ET D'ESPAGNE ... [BOUND WITH] PLANS ET PROFILS DES PRINCIPALES VILLES DU DUCHE DE LORRAINE ... [AND] CARTES GENERALES DES ROYAUMES ET PROVINCES DE LA HAUTE ET BASSE ALLEMAGNE ... [1633] Paris: Chez Sebastien Cramoisy. Sm oblong quarto, extravagant gold stamped baroque morocco binding. 142 maps (68+22+52). Exc. Ref: Pastoureau, Tassin IIIAe, IXc, IVAb. [3] £6,634 **$11,000**

TAUNTON
MAP OF THE CITY OF BROOKLYN SHOWING THE RAILROADS, WAREHOUSES, HORSE CAR LINES, CONEY ISLAND AND ROCKAWAY BEACH DEPOTS [1883] S.D.L. Taunton, NY. Folding map printed both sides in orig cloth folder; RRs & water in color. Verso, 3 maps: Hudson R. & L.I. RR; Greenwood Cemetery; Coney Island. 64x50cm (25x19½") [15] £211 **$350**

TAVERNIER
ANTIQUORUM ITALIAE & ILLYRICI ... [1640-1667] Paris: Mariette. Insets: Sicily; Corsica & Sardinia. 36x50cm (14x20") Orig OL color. [34] £360 **$597**
CARTE DE L'AMERIQUE CORRIGEE , ET AUGMENTEE ... [1627] After Hondius. 38x50cm (15x19½") Color. Top c'fold reinforced; VG. Ref: Burden 218. [24] £1,930 **$3,200**
NOVA TOTIUS TERRARUM ORBIS GEOGRAPHICA AC HYDROGRAPHICA TABULA [1643] Double hemi, mileage banners above & below; celestial hemis; insular Calif. Separately published. 38x53cm (15x20½") Color. Ref: Shirley (W) 360; pl.274. [13] **Aus$7,400** £3,361 **$5,572**
PATRIARCHATUS HIEROSOLYMITANI GEOGRAPHICA DESCRIPTIO ... [1640-1667] In *Tables de la Geographie* ... Paris: Mariette. Cyprus to Persian Gulf in Roman times. 35x50cm (13½x19½") Orig OL color. Ref: Laor 768. [34] £260 **$431**

TEESDALE
A NEW CHART OF THE WORLD ON MERCATOR'S PROJECTION ... [1842] H. Teesdale & Co; John Dower, sc. 32 panels laid on linen folding into orig leather boards, with title & gold tooling. 125x192cm (49x75½") Orig wash & OL color. Wear at edges. [11] £286 **$475**
UNITED STATES [(1782) c.1830] To beyond Missouri River. 34x41cm (13x16") OL col. Fine. [1] £106 **$175**

TEGG
TEGG'S NEW PLAN OF LONDON &C. WITH 360 REFERENCES TO THE PRINCIPAL STREETS, &C. 1829 [1829] 44x62cm (17x24½") Color. Tears rt margin just into image; ex lib NYHS. [A7] £208 **$345**

THEVENOT
[AUSTRALIA, NEW ZEALAND & NEW GUINEA] [1663] From *Relation de Diverse Voyages Curieux*. 3rd ed, with rhumb lines, Tropic of Capricorn & Tasman's track. 39x60cm (15½x23½") B&W. Extensive worm holes repaired. Ref: Schilder (Australia) 85; Tooley (Australia) 1247, pl.92; Tooley (Landmarks) ill. p.258. [13] **Aus$5,900** £2,679 **$4,443**
[FAR EAST: CHINA, KOREA, JAPAN, INDO-CHINA, EAST INDIES] [1664] From *Relations de Divers Voyages*. Portolan chart after Teixera. 51x67cm (20½x26½") Sm tear mended; exc. [43] £3,920 **$6,500**
DESCRIPTION DE LA PARTIE DES INDES ORIENTALES QUI EST SOUS LA DOMINATIONS DU GRAND MOGOL [1683] Appeared in *Relations* ... Northern India; 1st published by Purchas, 1625. 27x36cm (10½x14") Few wax stains. [11] £232 **$385**

THOMAS, COWPERTHWAIT & CO. Try *Mitchell (Atlas maps 1859 or earlier)*
[ATLAS] NEW UNIVERSAL ATLAS [1852] By S.A Mitchell; Phila. Folio, orig marble boards, calf label; 122 map & plans. Scuffed; good. Ref: Phillips (A) 807. [3] £1,689 **$2,800**
A NEW MAP OF ALABAMA WITH ITS ROADS AND DISTANCES FROM PLACE TO PLACE, ALONG THE STAGE AND STEAMBOAT ROUTES [1850] From Mitchell's *New Universal Atlas*. 36x29cm (14x11½") Orig color by counties. Sm dark spot in blank area; o/w fine. [A1] £63 **$105**
A NEW MAP OF ARKANSAS WITH ITS CANALS ROADS & DISTANCES [1850] From Mitchell's *New Universal Atlas*. 36x29cm (14x11½") Full color. [22] £45 **$75**

THOMAS, COWPERTHWAIT & CO. continued

A NEW MAP OF GEORGIA WITH ITS ROADS AND DISTANCES ... [1850] From Mitchell's *New Universal Atlas*. 36x29cm (14½x11½") Color. Lt age toning at edges; o/w fine. ["... Alabama ...", "... Kentucky ... ", "... Pennsylvania ..." & "... South Carolina ..." offered at same price] [14] £90 **$150**

A NEW MAP OF ILLINOIS WITH ITS CANALS, ROADS & DISTANCES FROM PLACE TO PLACE ALONG THE STAGE AND STEAM BOAT ROUTES [1850] From Mitchell's *New Universal Atlas*. 37x29cm (14½x11½") Full color. ["A New Map of Michigan ..." & "A New map of Indiana ...", both lt foxed, offered at same price] [22] £72 **$120**

A NEW MAP OF MAINE [1855] Population tables. 38x30cm (15x12") Full color. [40] £48 **$80**

A NEW MAP OF MICHIGAN WITH ITS CANALS, ROADS & DISTANCES [1854] From Mitchell's *New Universal Atlas*. 37x30cm (14½x12") Orig color by counties. Few faint foxing area; o/w fine. ["... Tennessee ..." offered at same price] [14] £93 **$155**

A NEW MAP OF MISSISSIPPI WITH ITS ROADS AND DISTANCES [1850] From Mitchell's *New Universal Atlas*. 36x29cm (14x11½") Full color. [22] £60 **$100**

A NEW MAP OF TENNESSEE WITH ITS ROADS AND DISTANCES FROM PLACE TO PLACE ALONG THE STAGE AND STEAMBOAT ROUTES [1850 (1852)] From 3rd ed, *New Universal Atlas*. 78 counties. 28x39cm (11x15½") Full color. Mint. Ref: Phillips (A) 807-27. [12] £60 **$100**

A NEW MAP OF THE STATE OF CALIFORNIA, THE TERRITORIES OF OREGON & UTAH, AND THE CHIEF PART OF NEW MEXICO [1850] Pre-Gadsden Purchase. 41x32cm (16x12½") Color. Lt even browning; couple minor blemishes; else VG. [9] £256 **$425**

A NEW MAP OF THE STATE OF CALIFORNIA, THE TERRITORIES OF OREGON, WASHINGTON, UTAH & NEW MEXICO [1854] From Mitchell's *New Universal Atlas*. Pre-Gadsden Purchase borders. 40x32cm (15½x12½") Orig color. Lt age toning margin; some faint spots; o/w fine. [A1] £315 **$523**

A NEW MAP OF THE STATE OF MISSOURI [1850] From Mitchell's *New Universal Atlas*. 33x41cm (13x16") Orig color by counties. Fine. [14] £84 **$140**

[SAME TITLE] [1852] 33x41cm (13x16") Full color by counties. [40] £48 **$80**

A NEW MAP OF THE UNITED STATES OF AMERICA [1850] From Mitchell's *New Universal Atlas*. Insets: CA gold region; DC. 40x67cm (16x26½") Full color. Fine. Ref: Wheat (TM) 685. [1] £286 **$475**

A NEW MAP OF THE WORLD ON THE GLOBULAR PROJECTION [1850] From Mitchell's *New Universal Atlas*. 24x36cm (9½x14") Orig color. VG. [14] £118 **$195**

A NEW MAP OF VIRGINIA WITH ITS CANALS, ROADS & DISTANCES FROM PLACE TO PLACE ALONG THE STAGE AND STEAMBOAT ROUTES [1850] From Mitchell's *New Universal Atlas*. 30x37cm (11½x14½") Color. [1] £121 **$200**

[SAME TITLE] [1850] From same source. 30x37cm (11½x14½") Full color. [22] £90 **$150**

CANADA WEST FORMERLY UPPER CANADA [1850] From Mitchell's *New Universal Atlas*. Inset: Toronto area; Niagara area. 32x40cm (12½x15½") Orig color. Lt margin soiling; few faint brown marks top rt; o/w fine. ["Canada East ..." & "The Pacific Ocean including Oceana ..." offered at same price] [14] £90 **$150**

CHINA [1850] 29x36cm (11½x14½") Color. Fine. [38] £51 **$85**

CITY OF NEW YORK [1850] From Mitchell's *New Universal Atlas*. NYC north to 37th St. 37x29cm (14½x11½") Orig color. Extremely lt foxing; o/w VG. [14] £90 **$150**

CITY OF WASHINGTON [1850] From Mitchell's *New Universal Atlas*. With Capitol floor plan; key to buildings. [no dimens] Color. Lt margin time toning; 2 sm margin tears bottom; 2 sm brown spots top margin. [14] £106 **$175**

CONNECTICUT [1850] From *New Universal Atlas*. 3 RRs; Hartford & New Haven area insets. 30x37cm (12x14½") Color. Ref: Thompson (CT) 123. [22] £54 **$90**

FLORIDA [1850] From Mitchell's *New Universal Atlas*. 3 insets. 37x29cm (14½x11½") Full color. [22] £103 **$170**

GREECE [1850] Southern Greece & islands. 30x38cm (12x15") Full color. ["Kingdom of Sardinia" offered at same price] [40] £24 **$40**

IRELAND [1850] 30x24cm (12x9½") Orig color. Some foxing in margin; o/w fine. [A1] £66 **$110**

MAP OF FLORIDA [1854] From Mitchell's *New Universal Atlas*. 3 insets. 37x30cm (14½x12") Orig color. Faint foxing blank areas; o/w fine. [A2] £199 **$330**

MAP OF MINNESOTA TERRITORY [dated 1852] From *New Universal Atlas*. Missouri R. is west boundary. 33x41cm (13x16") Color. Flawless. Ref: cf Karrow (MW) 7-0667. [Cowperthwait, Desilver & Butler, 1854 ed (Karrow (MW) 7-0673) offered at same price] [12] £121 **$200**

MAP OF NEW HAMPSHIRE & VERMONT [1850] From *New Universal Atlas*. 38x30cm (15x12") Full color. Perfect. Ref: Cobb (NH) 192. [22] £42 **$70**

THOMAS, COWPERTHWAIT & CO. continued

MAP OF THE STATE OF TEXAS [1850] Insets: Northern Texas; Galveston area. 32x41cm (13x16") Full color. Fine. Ref: Day (TX) 34. [37] £232 **$385**

MAP OF THE STATE OF TEXAS FROM THE LATEST AUTHORITIES [dated 1853] From *New Universal Atlas*. 90 counties. 32x41cm (12½x16") Full col. Mint. Ref: Phillips (M) p.845; cf Day (TX) 35. [12] £332 **$550**

[SAME TITLE] [1854] By J.H. Young. 35x40cm (14x16") Orig color by counties. VG to fine. Ref: Day (TX) p.56. [A1] £249 **$413**

MEXICO & GUATEMALA [1850] From Mitchell's *New Universal Atlas*. Pre-Gadsden Purchase; 3 isthmus insets. 30x38cm (12x15") Color. Some lt foxing in Mexico; o/w fine. [14] £75 **$125**

[SAME TITLE] [1850] From same source. Extended NM & UT. 30x38cm (12x15") Wash color. Near fine. [35] £112 **$185**

[SAME TITLE] [1852] Pre-Gadsden Purchase border; some detail on U.S. side; 3 insets across top. 30x38cm (12x15") Full color. [40] £54 **$90**

NEW JERSEY REDUCED FROM T. GORDON'S MAP [1850 (1855)] From *New Universal Atlas*. 20 counties. 39x32cm (15½x12½") Full color. Almost perfect. [22] £81 **$135**

NORTH AMERICA [1855] Large U.S. western territories. 39x32cm (15½x12½") Color. [40] £54 **$90**

PERU AND BOLIVIA [1852] Bolivia has Pacific access. 31x38cm (12½x15") Full color. [40] £27 **$45**

WEST INDIES [1850] Colonial possession chart at rt. 30x38cm (12x15") Color. Clean. [40] £36 **$60**

THOMSON

[ATLAS] **A GENERAL ATLAS** [1819] Edinburgh & London. Quarto, half morocco; 2 tables, 40 OL color maps engraved by N.R. Hewitt after Wyld. Covers worn, upper cover detached; some soiling, mainly margins; maps coming loose. [A6] **£267** $443

AMERICA [1813] U.S. only to Mississippi. 46x51cm (18x20") Orig color. Canvas backing. Sl image transfer; lt soiling blank areas; o/w fine. [A1] £126 **$209**

ASIATIC TURKEY [1814] Incl present Iraq, Syria, Jordan, Lebanon, Israel, Cyprus, Georgia, Armenia. 51x59cm (20x23½") Orig color. Fine. [14] £151 **$250**

AUSTRIAN DOMINIONS [1816] Incl Hungary, Romania, Czech Republic, Slovakia, Croatia. 50x59cm (19½x23½") Orig color. Faint image transfer in blank areas; o/w fine. [14] £151 **$250**

BELGIUM OF THE NETHERLANDS [1815] 47x59cm (18½x23") Orig color. Bottom c'fold separation repaired verso with archival tape; VG to fine. [A1] £73 **$121**

CANADA AND NOVA SCOTIA [1814 / 1817] 48x60cm (19x23½") Wash & OL color. Creases near c'fold; near fine. Ref: Phillips (A) 731-54. [35] £106 **$175**

CHART OF THE BAHAMA ISLANDS [ON SHEET WITH] **THE BERMUDAS OR SUMMER ISLANDS** [AND] **ISLAND OF CUBA** [1816] 51x60cm (20x23½") Orig OL color. [34] **£260** $431

EUROPE AFTER THE CONGRESS OF VIENNA [1817] 4 sheets joined, 103x123cm (40½x48½") Color. [A6] **£172** $286

EUROPEAN RUSSIA [1815] Incl Baltics, Finland, Moldavia, Ukraine. 59x50cm (23½x19½") Color. Lt soiling in blank areas; archival tape repair to fold split to border; VG. [14] £121 **$200**

[SAME TITLE] [1815] 65x54cm (25½x21½") Color. [A7] £156 **$258**

[SAME TITLE] [1820] 60x50cm (23½x19½") Full color. [39] £54 **$90**

HINDOOSTAN [1814] 45x61cm (18x24") Color. Sh split c'fold margin; VG. [14] £151 **$250**

HOLLAND [1820] Walled cities, drainage canals, roads. 59x50cm (23½x19½") Full color. [40] £54 **$90**

NORTH AMERICA [1814] 50x60cm (19½x23½") OL color. Fine. [1] £232 **$385**

[SAME TITLE] [c.1816] 50x60cm (19½x23½") Orig OL color. Lower margin trimmed to neatline; lt image transfer in blank areas; o/w fine. [A1] £100 **$165**

PALAESTINA [ON SHEET WITH] **AEGYPTUS ANTIQUA** [1820] 48x66cm (19x26") OL color. [A7] £69 **$115**

POLAND [1814] Incl modern Lithuania. 50x60cm (20x23½") Orig color. Archival tape repair to ½" vert fold separation; lt transfer; o/w VG. [14] £136 **$225**

SOUTHERN PROVINCES OF THE UNITED STATES [dated 1817] From *New General Atlas*. GA to Mississippi River; extend north to NYC & Lake Erie; sm Hudson River scene. 50x56cm (19½x22") Full color. Lf margin extended; faint orig folds; else fine. Ref: Phillips (A) 731-57. [12] £271 **$450**

SPANISH NORTH AMERICA [1814] From *New General Atlas*. Mexico & Southwest. 51x62cm (20x24½") Full color. Fine. Ref: Wheat (TM) 320. [16] £392 **$650**

SPANISH NORTH AMERICA SOUTHERN PART [1816] Yucatan to Panama. 48x65cm (19x25½") Orig OL color. Lt soiling blank areas; VG. [A1] £100 **$165**

THOMSON continued

ST. CHRISTOPHERS ... [ON A SHEET WITH] ST. LUCIA ... [AND] NEVIS [1814] 50x59cm (19½x23½") Orig OL color. Sm pinhole lower rt border; o/w fine. ["Guadaloupe. Mariegalante &c. Antigua" offered as same price] [14] £166 **$275**

THE UNITED STATES OF AMERICA [ON SHEET WITH] THE COURSE OF THE RIVER ST. LAURENCE ... [c.1816] 45x63cm (17½x25") Color. Scattered moderate browning. [A7] £62 **$103**

WEST INDIES [1827] From *New General Atlas*. 48x69cm (19x27") OL color. A lt misfold; else beautiful. Ref: Phillips (A) 750-60. [12] £151 **$250**

THORNTON

A CHART OF THE EASTERNMOST PART OF THE EAST INDIES AND CHINA. FROM CAPE COMORIN TO IAPAN WITH ALL THE ADJACENT ISLANDS ... [c.1685] 43x53cm (17x21") Color. Minor reinforcement lower c'fold split in margin; o/w VF. [4] **£2,350** **$3,897**

TIRINUS

CHOROGRAPHIA TERRE SANCTAE IN AUGUSTIOREM FORMAM REDACTA ET EX VARIIS AUCTORIBUS A MULTIS ERRORIBUS EXPURGATA [c.1750] Later unrecorded version of 1632 map. Sacred objects & places illustrated on three sides. 31x79cm (12½x31") Color. Exc. Framed. Ref: cf Laor 771. [24] £1,327 **$2,200**

TIRION

CARTA ACCURATA DELL'IMPERIO DEL GIAPPONE ... [1738] By Ricciardo. 25x32cm (10x13") Exc. [44] £392 **$650**

[SAME TITLE] [1744] 24x32cm (9½x12½") Color. [A6] £230 **$382**

KAART VAN HET WESTELYK GEDEELTE VAN NIEUW MEXICO EN VAN CALIFORNIA VOLGENS DE LAATSTE ONTDEKKINGEN DER JESUITEN EN ANDEREN. TE AMSTERDAM BY ISAAK TIRION. MDCCLXV [1765] Modern AZ, NM & Sonora. 32x34cm (12½x13½") Orig wash color. Ref: Wheat (TM) 148. [27] £392 **$650**

KAART VAN LONDON ENZ. EN VAN HET NABY GELEGEN LAND ... [1754] After 16-sheet map by Rocque; 48-point key. 29x42cm (11½x16½") Orig body color. Ref: Howgego 102. [47] £250 **$415**

NIEUWE KAART VAN AMERICA UITGEGEVEN ... [1766] 27x32cm (10½x12½") Full color. Faint narrow 2" coloring stain lower rt corner; else clean, fresh. Framed. [A10] £146 **$242**

NUOVA CARTA DEL CIRCOLO DI WESFALIA DIVISO NE' SUOI VESCOVADI, PRINCIPATI, CONTEE, ... [c.1750] 28x33cm (11x13") Sh tear restored. [48] **DM 420** £145 $240

WERELD KAART NA DE ALDERLAATSTE ONTDEKKING IN'T LICHT GEBRACHT ... [1744] Double hemi; 2 sm polar projections. 33x42cm (13x16½") Color. Ref: Phillips (A) 600-1. [19] £353 **$585**

[SAME TITLE] [1744] 36x44cm (14x17½") Orig color. [46] **£680** $1,128

TOWN & COUNTRY MAGAZINE

AN ACCURATE MAP OF THE COUNTRY ROUND BOSTON IN NEW ENGLAND ... [1776] [attribution & reference supplied by editor] 32x42cm (13x16½") OL color. Trimmed close to top border; few chips affect border; browned overall. Ref: Jolly TOWN-2; Sellers & Van Ee 894. [A8] £294 **$488**

THE WEST INDIES, AND GULF OF MEXICO FROM THE LATEST DISCOVERIES AND BEST OBSERVATIONS. [1778] 23x35cm (9x13½") B&W. Trimmed close at binding edge as issued; VG (A). Ref: Jolly TOWN-3 [A3] £128 **$212**

TRUSLER

PLAN OF THE CITY OF MOSCOW [1794] 17-item key. 20x22cm (8x8½") Color. Lt age-toning; sm margins; else VG. [38] £75 **$125**

TRUXTON

A GENERAL CHART OF THE GLOBE, SHEWING THE COURSE OF THE GULPH STREAM ... [1794] Truxton was captain of "London Packet"; helped in Franklin's experiments. 2 sheets, each 46x44cm (18x17½") if joined, 18x35". Sm loss at would-be joinder; repaired tear; good. Ref: Wheat & Brun 22. [2] £2,411 **$3,500**

TUNISON

TUNISON'S SOUTH DAKOTA [1891] From *Peerless ... Atlas ...* 25x32cm (10x12½") Full col. [12] £45 **$75**

TUNISON'S TEXAS AND INDIAN TERRITORY [1887] Verso: AL; NE. 50x33cm (19½x13") Full color. Lt browned; good. [16] £75 **$125**

UNITED STATES GOVERNMENT Try other *U.S.* sub-categories following

[ATLAS] ATLAS DE FILIPINAS COLECCION DE 30 MAPAS [1900] Inside cover, "Atlas of the Philippine Islands". 30 full page colored maps; 30 pp place names index. 38x33cm (15x13") Paper covers partly detached & chipping; last map reattached, margin missing; other maps A+; good (B). [A3] £237 **$393**

[ATLAS] GEOLOGICAL AND TOPOGRAPHICAL ATLAS ACCOMPANYING THE REPORT OF THE GEOLOGICAL EXPLORATION OF THE FORTIETH PARALLEL ... CLARENCE KING [1876] Julius Bien, NY. Double-page folio; 11 maps on 25 loose sheets, incl sketch map of the western cordillera & pairs of geological maps & sections, and topo maps. Geological series colored; brushwork shows altitude on topo maps. Brittle chipped edges; few margin tears; clean, bright, VG. Ref: Wheat (TM) 1270. [5] £452 **$750**

[SAME TITLE] [1876] Folio. 5 sets of two maps, each covering about 105 by 165 miles: 1. Rocky Mountains; II. Green River Basin; III. Utah Basin; IV. Nevada Plateau; V. Nevada Basin. Colored geological maps; topo maps with brushwork. Complete, but covers not present. Edges browned; margin chipping; maps clean, bright. Ref: Wheat (TM) 1270. [7] £724 **$1,200**

[ATLAS] TOPOGRAPHICAL AND GEOLOGICAL ATLAS OF THE BLACK HILLS OF DAKOTA [1879] By Henry Newton & Walter P. Jenney. Atlas accompanying report, with topo and geological maps, each 72x97cm (28½x38") and bird's-eye view. Color on geological map; some on topo map. Edges browned; some margin chipping & water staining. Repaired tear on bird's-eye, no loss. For its type, VG. Ref: Wheat (TM) 1298. [7] £452 **$750**

[BOOK WITH MAPS] NOTES OF A MILITARY RECONNOISSANCE FROM FORT LEAVENWORTH, IN MISSOURI TO SAN DIEGO IN CALIFORNIA INCLUDING PARTS OF THE ARKANSAS, DEL NORTE AND GILA RIVERS [1848] Wash: Wendell & Van Benthuysen. 415 pp; numerous illustrations; large map in pocket, probably never opened. Binding tight, label legible; some foxing in text. Ref: Storm (Graff) 1249. Wagner-Camp 148. [26] £377 **$625**

[BOOK WITH MAPS] REPORT OF A GEOLOGICAL EXPLORATION OF PART OF IOWA, WISCONSIN AND ILLINOIS [1844] David Dale Owen. Sm quarto; half-leather & marbled boards; 199 pp, 25 of 25 maps, sections, views, plates, incl 23x18" geological chart of part of IA, WI & IL. 5 maps in color. Incl 50 pp Locke report of magnetic observations. Spine missing, lt wear, scattered internal foxing; good+. [35] £75 **$125**

[CA: IMPERIAL VALLEY SOIL MAP SHEET] [1903] U.S. Dept of Agriculture; color litho by Bien. Incl Salton Sink & Mexican border; much detail; 1"=mile. 61x43cm (24x17") Embossed stamp; VG (A). [Mason Co., KY (VG); Baker City, OR (3 matching sheets, good); Salem, OR (VG) sold at same price] [A4] £10 **$17**

[CA: SAN JOSE SOIL MAP SHEET] [1903] U.S. Dept of Agriculture; color litho by Bien. North to Menlo Park; much detail; 1"=mile. 47x79cm (18½x31") Embossed stamp; VG (A). [A4] £24 **$40**

[FLORIDA: PENSACOLA] [1834] From vol. 4, *American State Papers* ... Downtown; buildings keyed (but lacks key; title page furnished.) 19x23cm (7½x9") B&W. Fine. [12] £75 **$125**

[IL: MCLEAN COUNTY SOIL MAP SHEET] [1903] U.S. Dept of Agriculture; color litho by Bien. Much detail; 1"=mile. 81x107cm (32x42") Embossed stamp; some fold splits; good (B). [Johnson Co., IL (VG); McNeill Co., MS (VG) sold at same price] [A4] £7 **$11**

[MINNESOTA] [1878] Issued by Northern Boundary Commission. Lake of the Woods, west to Dakota; Indian reservations & villages shown.. 43x53cm (17x21") [40] £30 **$50**

[NORTH DAKOTA] [1878] Issued by Northern Boundary Commission. Ft. Stevenson to MT. 41x54cm (16x21½") [40] £39 **$65**

[UNITED STATES: NORTHERN BOUNDARY, LAKE OF THE WOODS TO ROCKY MOUNTAINS] [c.1875] Set of 6 reconnaissance maps showing topo adjacent to 49th parallel (lacks profile sheet). Each about 39x54cm (15½x21") B&W. Fine (A+). [A3] £66 **$110**

[WESTERN MISSOURI TO ROCKY MOUNTAINS] [1836] Orig appeared in *Report of the Expedition of the Dragoons ... to the Rocky Mountains*. Dodge Expedition. (Kansas, Nebraska and Colorado). 50x88cm (19½x34½") Some OL color. Folded as issued; o/w clean, bright. Ref: Wheat (TM) 421. [7] £271 **$450**

[WESTERN TERRITORY: KANSAS & NEBRASKA, ETC.] [1836] From Lt. J.P. Kingsbury, *Journal of the Expedition ... to the Rocky Mountains ... 1835*. Missouri to Rockies, Taos to Black Hills. 50x89cm (19½x35") Orig OL color. Tiny thin paper spots; o/w flawless. Ref: Wheat (TM) 421; Wagner-Camp 63; Luebke fig. 7.4. [12] £362 **$600**

A MAP OF THE SEAT OF WAR IN FLORIDA 1836 [1861] American State Papers. St. Augustine to Tampa Bay. 38x28cm (15x11") Uncolored. VG. [25] £48 **$80**

ARCHAEOLOGICAL MAP OF PAJARITO PARK, TERRITORY OF NEW MEXICO [1900 (1902)] From *Report of the Governors of New Mexico to the Sec. of the Interior*. Produced by N.M. Normal Univ. Expedition. Jemez Mts to Rio Grande. 53x57cm (21x22½") B&W. Immaculate. [12] £66 **$110**

U.S. GOVERNMENT continued

CHART OF THE COAST OF CHINA AND THE JAPAN ISLANDS INCLUDING THE MARIANES AND A PART OF THE PHILIPPINES COMPILED BY ORDER OF COMMODORE M.C. PERRY, U.S.N. ... [1855] From report of Japan Expedition. 102x91cm (40x36") Uncolored. Exposed fold worn, repair with some loss; some corner repairs. [25] £96 **$160**

CROQUIS DE L'AFRIQUE CENTRAL MIS AU COURANT PAR A.J. WATERS, INSTITUTE NATIONALE DE GEOGRAPHIE, BRUXELLES [1887] Reprinted by U.S. Gov't for 42 pp report by Lt. E.H. Taunt, U.S.N., of 6 months travels in the Congo. 25x38cm (10x15") Full color. VG. [26] £36 **$60**

DEPARTMENT OF THE MISSOURI. SKETCH SHOWING MILITARY ROADS LEADING TO FORT LEWIS, PAGOSA SPRINGS IN CHARGE OF 1ST LT. E.H. RUFFNER [1879] San Luis Valley, CO & NM. Similar to Wheeler map. 57x53cm (22½x21") Uncolored. [41] £81 **$135**

EXPLORATIONS AND SURVEYS SOUTH OF CENTRAL PACIFIC R.R. WAR DEPARTMENT PRELIMINARY TOPOGRAPHICAL MAP EMBRACING IN SKELETON A PORTION ONLY OF THE NOTES FROM SURVEYS ... 1871 [1871] Wheeler map, Tucson to Elko, demonstrating capabilities. 71x56cm (28x22") Repaired tear, no loss; o/w bright, crisp. Ref: Wheat (TM) 1237. [7] £90 **$150**

GENERAL CHART OF ALASKA TO ACCOMPANY REINDEER REPORT [1898] By Sheldon Jackson, General Agent of Education. Missions, settlements, trails, rivers, topo. 64x89cm (25x35") Some color. VG. [25] £90 **$150**

GEOLOGICAL MAP OF THE DISTRICT BETWEEN KEWEENAW BAY AND CHOCOLATE RIVER, LAKE SUPERIOR, MICHIGAN [1849] In Charles T. Jackson geological report for MI; Senate Doc 1, 31st Cong, 1st Sess. 50x61cm (19½x24") Full wash 7-color key. Fine+. Ref: Hazen 5635. [35] £112 **$185**

GEOLOGICAL MAP OF THE TOYABE MOUNTAINS [NV] [1879] From Clarence King's Atlas of the Mining Industry. North at lf. 29x44cm (11½x17½") Printed color. [40] £45 **$75**

GEOLOGICAL MAP OF THE UNITED STATES [1874] From Francis A. Walker's *Statistical Atlas of the United States ... Ninth Census, 1870 ...* Compiled by C.H. Hitchcock & W.P. Blake. Plate 13-14. 9-color chromolitho. 50x71cm (19½x28") One orig vert fold; margin chips; else immaculate. Ref: Marcou 70; Phillips (A) 1330. [12] £136 **$225**

[SAME TITLE] [1874] Compiled by C.H. Hitchcock & W.P. Blake; publ in 1870 census atlas. 9 geological classifications. 50x72cm (19½x28½") Color. [39] £87 **$145**

GEOLOGICAL MAP OF THE WESTERN PART OF THE PLATEAU PROVINCE [1882] From C.E. Dutton's *Atlas ... on the Tertiary History of the Grand Canon District.* Most of UT with northern AZ. 10-color litho. 75x46cm (29½x18") Dampstain trace lf border; else mint. Ref: Moffat (UT) [12] £136 **$225**

GEOLOGICAL MAP OF WESTERN WYOMING ILLUSTRATING THE REPORT OF MR. THEO. B. COMSTOCK [1874] 79x55cm (31x21½") Full color. Old folds; VG. [26] £106 **$175**

HEAD QUARTERS DEPARTMENT OF NEW MEXICO SANTA FE, N.M. ... OFFICIAL COPY OF A MAP ACCOMPANYING THE REPORT OF MAJOR D. FERGUSSON 1ST CAVALRY. ... ON THE ROUTES FROM TUCSON TO LIBERTAD AND LOBOS BAY [1862] 17x36cm (6½x14") Ref: Wheat (TM) 1042. [9] £60 **$100**

HYDROLOGICAL BASIN OF THE UPPER MISSISSIPPI ... BY J.N. NICOLLET ... [1843] Illinois R. to Lake Superior. 2-sheet folding map, joined 97x80cm (38x31½") Minor browning. [A8] £294 **$488**

LAKES OF THE GLACIAL PERIOD [1878] From Vol. I, *Report on the Geological Exploration of the Fortieth Parallel.* King Expedition. Utah Lake to Tahoe, incl Great Salt Lake. 3-color litho. 25x42cm (10x16½") Fine. [12] £45 **$75**

LANAI [HI] [1878] Brown & Monsarrat; Washington. 50x66cm (19½x26") Full color. Repaired tear; else VG. [36] £181 **$300**

LANDS CEDED BY THE SIOUX, SACS, FOXES, OTOES, IOWAYS, &C. IN 1825 [1836] From *Journal of the Expedition ... [under Col. Dodge to the Rockies].* KS, NE, CO with Indian boundaries. 50x88cm (19½x34½") OL color. Invisibly repaired 4" tear lf edge; sh repaired fold separation; faint foxing fold & margins; else clean. [A10] £208 **$345**

LINGUISTIC STOCKS OF AMERICAN INDIANS NORTH OF MEXICO [c.1890] In several BAE reports. 32x24cm (12½x9½") Languages color coded. Mild soiling margin. [25] £45 **$75**

MAP ILLUSTRATING THE GENERAL GEOLOGICAL FEATURES OF THE COUNTRY WEST OF THE MISSISSIPPI RIVER. COMPILED FROM SURVEYS MADE UNDER THE ORDER OF W.H. EMORY AND FROM THE PACIFIC RAILROAD SURVEYS & OTHER SOURCES: BY PROFESSOR JAMES HALL ... [1857] From *United States and Mexican Boundary Survey.* Simplified Emory map for base. Color keyed. 51x56cm (20x22") Misfolds flattened with archival tape; o/w exc. Ref: Wheat (TM) 922. [12] £172 **$285**

[SAME TITLE] [1857] 51x58cm (20x23") Full color. Fine (A+). [A4] £200 **$332**

U.S. GOVERNMENT continued

MAP ILLUSTRATING THE PLAN OF THE DEFENCES OF THE WESTERN & NORTH-WESTERN FRONTIER AS PROPOSED BY CHARLES GRATIOT IN HIS REPORT OF OCT. 31, 1837 ... [1837] Hood. LA, AR, MO delineated; incl Indian lands just west of Mississippi River; with distance table. 54x38cm (21x15") Full color. Fine (A+). Ref: Wheat (TM) 427. [A4] £551 **$913**

[SAME TITLE] [1837] Hood-Gratiot. Shows Indian lands just west of Mississippi River. 53x38cm (21x15") Orig OL color Ref: Wheat (TM) 427. [27] £163 **$270**

MAP ILLUSTRATING THE PLAN OF THE DEFENCES OF THE WESTERN & NORTH-WESTERN FRONTIER, AS PROPOSED BY THE HON. J.R. POINSETT, SEC OF WAR, IN HIS REPORT OF DEC. 30, 1837 ... [1838] Hood. LA, AR, MO delineated; incl Indian lands just west of Mississippi River; no distance table. 55x39cm (21½x15½") Full color. Sm foxing spot; VG (A). Ref: Wheat (TM) 426. [A4] £321 **$532**

MAP NO.1. RIO COLORADO OF THE WEST EXPLORED BY 1ST LT. JOSEPH C. IVES ... [IN SET WITH] MAP NO.2. ... [1858] Geological maps by Newberry. Each 37x87cm (14½x34½") Color. [41] £271 **$450**

MAP NO.4 SHOWING CONTINUATION OF FORT SMITH AND SANTA FE ROUTE FROM TUCUMCARI CREEK TO SANTA FE [1849] By Lt. J.H. Simpson; fourth and last section of set from 31st Cong, 1st Sess, Sen Ex Doc No.12. 28x50cm (11x19½") B&W. Pinhole at fold intersection; minor creases; fine. Ref: Wheat (TM) 640. [12] £96 **$160**

MAP OF A CARRIAGE ROAD IN THE ISTHMUS OF PANAMA DRAWN BY ORDER OF THE GOVERNMENT BY MAURICE FALMARK, 2D COMMANDANT OF ENGINEERS [1838] 38x48cm (15x19") Uncol. VG. [26] £45 **$75**

MAP OF A RECONNAISSANCE BETWEEN BALTIMORE AND PHILADELPHIA EXHIBITING THE SEVERAL ROUTES OF THE MAIL-ROAD CONTEMPLATED BY THE RESOLUTION OF CONGRESS APPROVED ON THE 4TH OF MAY 1826 ... [1827] 27 mile wide corridor. By S. Bernard & W.T. Poussin, in 19th Cong., 2 Sess., House Doc. 94. 23x79cm (9x31") B&W. Lt time-toned; fine. Ref: Maryland Hist Soc 24; Claussen & Friis 7. [12] £196 **$325**

MAP OF A SURVEY AND RECONNAISSANCE OF THE VICINITY OF THE MOUTH OF THE RIO GILA [1849] By Lt. A.W. Whipple & A.B. Gray under John B. Weller. Pre-Gadsden Purchase. 28x42cm (11x16½") Minor foxing; else VG. Ref: Wagner-Camp 189a. [8] £75 **$125**

MAP OF CHARLESTON HARBOR, S.C. [1860] From vol.5, No.591, *American State Papers - Military Affairs*. Printed red depth contours. 44x57cm (17½x22½") Full color. Clean, fresh. [A10] £63 **$104**

MAP OF ILLINOIS WITH PARTS OF INDIANA, OUISCONSIN &C. BY DAVID BURR, DRAUGHTSMAN TO THE HOUSE OF REPS. [1836] 46x33cm (18x13") Uncolored. VG. [26] £45 **$75**

MAP OF INDIAN TERRITORY [1879] Surface text signed by E.C. Budinot, Native American RR lawyer. 41x56cm (16x22") [10] £109 **$180**

MAP OF INDIAN TERRITORY AND OKLAHOMA [1890] Top margin reads "Eleventh Census ... The Five Civilized Tribes". Division is red-lined; corrected text pasted over orig lower lf. 56x74cm (22x29") Color litho. Lower c'fold browning. [A10] £118 **$196**

MAP OF LINGUISTIC STOCKS OF AMERICAN INDIANS CHIEFLY WITHIN THE PRESENT LIMITS OF THE UNITED STATES [1894] From *Indians Taxed and Indians Not Taxed* ... By Sackett & Wilhelms; special report of 11th census; orig issued 3 years prior in 7th Annual Report, Bureau of American Ethnology. 10+ color litho. 51x44cm (20x17½") Narrow lf margin; else mint [12] £75 **$125**

MAP OF THAT PORTION OF THE BOUNDARY BETWEEN THE UNITED STATES AND MEXICO, FROM THE PACIFIC COAST TO THE JUNCTION OF THE GILA AND COLORADO RIVERS ... AND THE RIO GILA FROM NEAR ITS INTERSECTION ... NEGOTIATED BY THE HON. JAMES GADSDEN ... [1855] By Andrew B. Gray. 54x123cm (21½x48½") Uncolored. Exc. Ref: Wheat (TM) vol 3, 821. [41] £317 **$525**

MAP OF THE ARLINGTON ESTATE, VA. [1888] Ft Meyer, Nat'l Cemetery to Alexandria; land owners identified. 69x84cm (27x33") Uncolored. VG. [26] £54 **$90**

MAP OF THE COUNTRY BETWEEN THE FRONTIERS OF ARKANSAS AND NEW MEXICO EMBRACING THE SECTION EXPLORED IN 1849, 50, 51 & 52 BY CAPT. R.B. MARCY ... [1853] 69x150cm (27½x59") Fold browning; misfolding; tears repaired on verso; fair. Ref: Storm (Graff) 2675. [16] £302 **$500**

[SAME TITLE] [1854] Mississippi R. to Colorado R. 70x151cm (27½x59½") Minimal browning & splitting; sm neat line loss at one edge; for age & size, exc. Ref: Wheat (TM) 792. [9] £226 **$375**

MAP OF THE COUNTRY EMBRACING THE VARIOUS ROUTES SURVEYED FOR THE WESTERN & ATLANTIC RAIL ROAD OF GEORGIA UNDER THE DIRECTION OF COL. S.H. LONG [1837] Resulted in RR to Chattanooga. 20x53cm (8x21") Uncolored. VG. [26] £54 **$90**

MAP OF THE COUNTRY UPON THE UPPER RED RIVER EXPLORED IN 1852 BY CAPT. R.B. MARCY ... [1852] 41x86cm (16½x34") Deacidified; lt fold browning; VG. Ref: Day (TX) 900. [16] £166 **$275**

U.S. GOVERNMENT continued

MAP OF THE CUMBERLAND RIVER FROM THE FALLS TO NASHVILLE [dated 1834] After Matthew Rhea's map drawn by Coyle; H. Stansbury, engr. 38x61cm (15x24") B&W. Lt foxing upper rt. Ref: Claussen & Friis 44. [12] £121 **$200**

MAP OF THE CUMBERLAND RIVER FROM THE FALLS TO NASHVILLE. MADE TO ACCOMPANY A REPORT ON THE IMPROVEMENT OF THAT STREAM FOR THE NAVIGATION OF IT BY STEAM BOATS ... [1835] By Howard Stansbury. 46x74cm (18x29") Uncolored. Folded as issued; mild foxing. [26] £72 **$120**

MAP OF THE GREAT SALT LAKE AND ADJACENT COUNTRY IN THE TERRITORY OF UTAH. SURVEYED IN 1849 AND 1850 [1852] From *Exploration and Survey of the Valley of the Great Salt Lake* ... By Capt. Howard Stansbury. 109x76cm (43x30") Blue shaded shore lines. One close edge with some neat line loss; o/w clean, bright. Ref: Wheat (TM) 765, illus. Moffat (UT) 26. [9] £241 **$400**

MAP OF THE INDIAN COLONIES WEST OF MISSOURI AND ARKANSAS [1854] Drawn by Eastman. Extent: Council Bluffs south to Red River. 28x19cm (11x7½") OL color. [41] £87 **$145**

MAP OF THE INDIAN TERRITORY AND OKLAHOMA [1890 (1894)] From *Indians Taxed and Not Taxed* ... 11th Census. Highly detailed; margin notes. 5-color litho. 56x75cm (22x29½") Immaculate. [12] £232 **$385**

MAP OF THE LANDS, GRANTED TO THE CHEROKEE INDIANS, BY THE STATE OF NORTH CAROLINA, UNDER THE ACT OF 1783 [1845] 18x25cm (7x10") Uncolored. [26] £30 **$50**

MAP OF THE NAVAJO INDIAN RESERVATION [1886] 28x39cm (11x15½") Printed OL color. [41] £72 **$120**

MAP OF THE NORTHERN PART OF THE STATE OF MAINE AND OF THE ADJACENT BRITISH PROVINCES SHEWING THE PORTION OF THAT STATE TO WHICH GREAT BRITAIN LAYS CLAIM [1838] 43x41cm (17x16") Color indicates claims. VG. [26] £45 **$75**

MAP OF THE RIVER SABINE FROM ITS MOUTH ON THE GULF OF MEXICO IN THE SEA TO LOGAN FERRY ... [1840] As in *Sen. Doc. 199*. One of 6 maps issued with Texas-U.S. Boundary Survey. 86x18cm (34x7") B&W. Few minor spots; overall fine (A). [A4] £274 **$455**

MAP OF THE ROUTE PASSED OVER BY AN EXPEDITION INTO THE INDIAN COUNTRY IN 1832 TO THE SOURCE OF THE MISSISSIPPI, BY LIEUT. J. ALLEN, U.S. INF. [1834] With accompanying report: 23rd Cong, 1st Sess, House of Reps, No.323 (lacking transmittal page); map folded as issued. 39x48cm (15½x19") Browned. [8] £151 **$250**

[SAME TITLE] [1861] Reduced from 1834 orig by Lt. Drayton. 41x48cm (16x19") Uncolored. Some lt foxing; VG. [26] £45 **$75**

MAP OF THE ROUTE PURSUED BY THE LATE EXPEDITION UNDER THE COMMAND OF COL. S.W. KEARNY, U.S. 1ST DRAGOONS [1846] By W.B Franklin. 22x34cm (8½x13½") Uncol. Cleaned; rebacked. [26] £136 **$225**

MAP OF THE ROUTE PURSUED BY U.S. TROOPS, FROM FORT SMITH, ARKANSAS, TO SANTA FE, NEW MEXICO [SET OF 4 SHEETS] [1849] 10 miles/inch. Each map about 28x48cm (11x19") Evenly browned. Generally clean. Ref: Wheat (TM) 640. [8] £211 **$350**

MAP OF THE SANGRE DE CRISTO GRANT SITUATE IN SAN LUIS VALLE, COLORADO TERRITORY [c.1880's] 44x29cm (17½x11½") Printed in 3 colors. [41] £75 **$125**

MAP OF THE STRAITS OF DETROIT ... [1842] With accompanying report; Sen Doc 393, 27th Cong, 2nd Sess. 91x57cm (36x22½") Uncol. Trimmed within lower neat line. Ref: Claussen & Friis 418. [A10] £90 **$150**

MAP OF THE TERRITORIAL LIMITS OF THE CHEROKEE "NATION OF" INDIANS EXHIBITING THE BOUNDARIES OF THE VARIOUS CESSIONS OF LAND MADE BY THEM ... BY TREATY STIPULATIONS, FROM THE BEGINNING OF THEIR RELATIONS WITH THE WHITES TO THE DATE OF THEIR REMOVAL ... [1884] By C.C. Royce, BAE. 36 cessions color coded. 53x76cm (21x30") Full color. Minor verso repairs to folds & corners. [26] £72 **$120**

MAP OF THE UNITED STATES AND TEXAS BOUNDARY LINE AND ADJACENT TERRITORY ... [1860 (1902)] Incl NM to Rio Grande & Indian Terr. Civil War interrupted publication of MS until later date. 67x100cm (26½x39½") Folded; near fine. Ref: Wheat (TM) 1022 (reproduced in USGS Bul. 194). [10] £136 **$225**

MAP OF THE UNITED STATES AND THEIR TERRITORIES BETWEEN THE MISSISSIPPI AND THE PACIFIC OCEAN AND PART OF MEXICO. COMPILED FROM SURVEYS MADE UNDER THE ORDER OF W. H. EMORY ... [1857] From *Report on the United States and Mexican Boundary Survey*. Large NE, WA, OR, UT & NM territories. 51x58cm (20x23") B&W. Tear repaired verso; VG. Ref: Wheat (TM) 916; Phillips (M) p.907. [26] £196 **$325**

[SAME TITLE] [1857-58] From *Report on the United States and Mexican Boundary Survey*. Compendium map of American West; large NE, WA, OR, UT & NM territories. 52x58cm (20½x23") Folded as issued; some browning; above average. Ref: Wheat (TM) 916; Phillips (M) p.907. [8] £178 **$295**

MAP OF THE UNITED STATES EXHIBITING THE SEVERAL COLLECTION DISTRICTS DRAWN BY DAVID BURR, U.S. SENATE [1856] Issued folded. 84x124cm (33x49") Boundaries in OL color. VG. [26] £75 **$125**

U.S. GOVERNMENT continued

MAP OF THE WABASH AND ERIE CANAL LINE FROM THE MOUTH OF TIPPECANOE TO TERRE-HAUTE AS SURVEYED BY CHARLES T. WHIPPO 1835 [1835] 33x25cm (13x10") Uncolored. VG. [26] £36 **$60**

MAP OF THE YELLOWSTONE NATIONAL PARK [1881] Compiled from Official Explorations & Surveys of the Sup't of the Park and other sources. 43x43cm (17x17") Some color; thermal areas in red. Minor repairs verso. [26] £75 **$125**

MAP SHOWING INDIAN RESERVATIONS IN THE UNITED STATES WEST OF THE 84TH MERIDIAN AND NUMBER OF INDIANS BELONGING THERETO 1883 [1885] GLO. 33x43cm (13x17") Substantial color. VG. [25] £54 **$90**

MAP SHOWING LANDS ASSIGNED TO EMIGRANT INDIANS WEST OF ARKANSAS & MISSOURI [1836 / 1861] Reissue. 48x46cm (19x18") Uncolored. Exc. [26] £75 **$125**

MAP SHOWING THE DIFFERENT ROUTES TRAVELLED OVER BY THE DETACHMENTS OF THE OVERLAND COMMAND IN THE SPRING OF 1855 FROM SALT LAKE CITY, UTAH TO THE BAY OF SAN FRANCISCO [1855] 51x51cm (20x20") B&W. Trimmed to binding side neatline; binding tear repaired; else fine (A). Ref: Wheat (TM) 868. [A4] £88 **$146**

MAP SHOWING THE GENERAL GEOLOGICAL FEATURES OF THE COUNTRY WEST OF THE MISSISSIPPI RIVER ... [1858] From Vol.I, Emory's *Report of the United States and Mexican Boundary Survey*. Did not appear in all copies. By Hall, assisted by Leslie. 12 color geological key on base map of West from Report. 52x58cm (20½x23") Folded as issued; else clean, bright. Ref: Wheat (TM) 922. [8] £196 **$325**

MAP SHOWING THE LOCATION OF THE PUEBLOS OF ARIZONA AND NEW MEXICO [1887] Issued by B.A.E. Coverage from Taos to Hopi villages also showing topo, ruins, etc. 24x30cm (9½x12") Red highlighting. [40] £39 **$65**

MAP SHOWING THE ROUTE PURSUED BY THE EXPLORING EXPEDITION TO NEW MEXICO AND THE SOUTHERN ROCKY MOUNTAINS ... [1845] By Abert & Peck. Ft Laramie south to whole Santa Fe Trail. 50x71cm (19½x28") Folded as issued; else VG. Ref: Wheat (TM) 489. [8] £211 **$350**

MAP SHOWING THE TERRITORY ORIGINALLY ASSIGNED TO THE CHEROKEE "NATION OF" INDIANS WEST OF THE MISSISSIPPI, ALSO THE BOUNDARIES OF THE TERRITORY NOW OCCUPIED OR OWNED BY THEM [1884] By C.C. Royce, BAE. Tracts in OK, KS & AR numbered & color coded. 51x71cm (20x28") Some fold repairs verso; tape removed outside neatline. [26] £72 **$120**

PART OF THE STATE OF INDIANA FROM ACTUAL SURVEY ON FILE IN THE GENERAL LAND OFFICE [1831 (1834)] From *American State Papers ... in Relation to the Public Lands ... Vol. IV*. Sketchy map of northern IN; 4 pp text furnished. 42x36cm (16½x14") B&W. Offsetting near top; else exc. [12] £106 **$175**

PLAT OF A SURVEY OF LAND "FOR MILITARY PURPOSES" AROUND FORT BRADY SAULT ST. MARIE, MICH. [1847] By G.C. Westcott 25x33cm (10x13") B&W. Issued folded; VG. [25] £39 **$65**

PORTION OF THE MAP OF THE INDIAN NATIONS AND TRIBES OF THE TERRITORY OF WASHINGTON AND THE TERRITORY OF NEBRASKA WEST OF THE MOUTH OF THE YELLOWSTONE [1894] Drawn by Isaac Stevens in 1857. Region between Walla Walla & Mt. St. Helens in regard to native fishery claims. 36x36cm (14x14") Some color. [26] £36 **$60**

POSITIONS OF THE UPPER AND LOWER GOLD MINES ON THE SOUTH FORK OF THE AMERICAN RIVER, CALIFORNIA. JULY 20, 1848 [1848] By R.B. Mason. Sutters Fort to Webers Creek. 23x46cm (9½x18½") Minor foxing; trimmed close one edge; o/w VG. Ref: Wheat (Gold) 51. [8] £106 **$175**

[SAME TITLE] [1848] From Mason's *Report*. 24x46cm (9½x18") B&W. Fine. [12] £136 **$225**

PRELIMINARY MAP OF CENTRAL COLORADO SHOWING THE REGION SURVEYED IN 1873 AND 1874 ... [1876] From Hayden Surveys, ... *of the Territories, Embracing Colorado* ... 8th Annual Report. 64x57cm (25x22½") Ref: Wheat (TM) 1246. Schmeckebier p.36. [12] £81 **$135**

RECONNOISSANCES IN THE DACOTA COUNTRY BY G.K. WARREN ... [1856] MO to Ft. Laramie; Platte to Missouri R.. 89x140cm (35x55") Minor browning; an edge trimmed; good. Ref: Storm (Graff) 4546; Howes W118; Wagner-Camp 283. [8] £238 **$395**

[SAME TITLE] [1856] MO to Ft. Laramie. 90x144cm (35x56½") [A8] £121 **$201**

RECONNOISSANCES OF ROUTES FROM SAN ANTONIO DE BEXAR [TO] EL PASO DEL NORTE, &C., &C. ... [1849] By Lt. Col. J.E. Johnston. 62x97cm (24½x38") Browned; fold repairs; good. Ref: Day (TX) 1529; Wheat (TM) 677. [16] £226 **$375**

SABINE PASS ... [IN SET WITH] MAP OF THE RIVER SABINE FROM ITS MOUTH ON THE GULF OF MEXICO IN THE SEA TO LOGAN'S FERRY ...[AND] ... TO 32ND DEGREE ... [AND] A2. ... TO THE 36TH MILE MOUND [AND] B2. ... TO THE 72ND MILE MOUND [AND] .... TO RED RIVER [1840-41] Joint US-Texas Boundary Commission. 6 maps, about 22x18", 7x34", 7x9", last three 11x6". Folded as issued; minor foxing; o/w clean. Ref: Day (TX) 952, 952A, B, C, D, E. [8] £392 **$650**

U.S. GOVERNMENT continued

SKETCH INDICATING THE ADVANCEMENT OF THE SURVEYS OF THE PUBLIC LANDS AND THE MILITARY, TOPOGRAPHICAL AND GEOGRAPHICAL SURVEYS WEST OF THE MISSISSIPPI [1879] From Wheeler Surveys, ... *West of 100th Meridian.* Vol.1, Geographical Report. A summary of western exploration. 4-color litho. 83x113cm (32½x44½") Minor misfolds; fold intersection pinholes repaired; else fine. [12] £136 **$225**

SKETCH OF CAPT. GUNNISON'S ROUTE [1853] Pueblo to Green River; Middle Park to Ft. Massachusetts. 33x51cm (13x20") Folds; VG. [10] £90 **$150**

SKETCH OF GENERAL RILEY'S ROUTE THROUGH THE MINING DISTRICTS JULY AND AUG. 1849 [1850] By Lt. George H. Derby. 53x51cm (21x20") Folded as issued; else near fine. Ref: Wheat (Gold) 79. [8] £299 **$495**

[SAME TITLE] [1850] 51x61cm (20x24") B&W. Folding. No breaks; fine. [27] £256 **$425**

[SAME TITLE] [1850] 53x50cm (21x19½") Uncolored. [41] £271 **$450**

[SAME TITLE] [1850] 51x48cm (20x19") B&W. Deacidified, pressed; trimmed to binding side neatline; VG (A). [A4] £199 **$330**

SKETCH OF PART OF THE MARCH & WAGON ROAD OF LT. COLONEL COOKE FROM SANTA FE TO THE PACIFIC OCEAN, 1846-7 ... [1847] Preview of Gadsden Purchase area. 30x58cm (11½x23") Minor repair, print unaffected; clean, crisp. Ref: Wheat (TM) 505. [7] £90 **$150**

SKETCH OF THE COUNTRY BETWEEN SOUTH PASS & THE GREAT SALT LAKE [1860] 44x55cm (17½x22") Folded' else clean. Ref: Wheat (TM) 958. [7] £54 **$90**

[SAME TITLE] [1858] 55x44cm (21½x17½") B&W. Folds as issued; trimmed to border bottom lf; minor foxing some areas; o/w VG. Ref: Wheat (TM) 958. [14] £106 **$175**

SKETCH OF THE DYEA AND SKAGUA TRAILS ... [1897] By C.B. Talbot, Sitka; Dept. of Interior. 36x23cm (14x9") Uncolored. VG. [25] £30 **$50**

SKETCH OF THE ROUTE OF CAPT. WARNER'S EXPLORING PARTY IN THE SACRAMENTO VALLEY AND SIERRA NEVADA ... 1849 BY R.S. WILLIAMSON [1849 (1850)] 60x27cm (23½x10½") Minor foxing; bottom trimmed close; else VG. Ref: Wheat (TM) 700. Wheat (Gold) 182. [8] £106 **$175**

SKETCH OF THE ROUTE PURSUED BY THE EXPEDITION TO THE RED RIVER OF THE NORTH IN THE SUMMER OF 1849 ... [1850] Bound with Samuel Woods, *Pembina Settlement* ... 39x50cm (15½x19½") Clean, fresh. Ref: Wagner-Camp 193a. [A10] £90 **$150**

TERRITORY OF HAWAII [1918] Dept. of Interior. 76x107cm (30x42") Full color. VG. [26] £54 **$90**

THAT PART OF DISTURNELL'S TREATY MAP IN THE VICINITY OF THE RIO GRANDE AND SOUTHERN BOUNDARY OF NEW MEXICO ... [1851] Incl note: "The Santa Fe Road was laid out in 1825 ..." 22x28cm (8½x11") Folded as issued; else bright, clean. Ref: Wheat (TM) 720; Wagner-Camp 254. [8] £60 **$100**

[SAME TITLE] [1851] From Andrew B. Gray, *Report ... Relative to the Mexican Boundary.* From Sen Ex Doc No.19, 32nd Cong, 1st Sess. 22x27cm (8½x10½") B&W. [12] £81 **$135**

THE GREAT RAILROAD ROUTES TO THE PACIFIC AND THEIR CONNECTION [1869] NY: Amer. Photo-Lithography Co. With accompanying Senate document, Feb. 19, 1869. 34x69cm (13½x27½") Uncolored. Ref: Wheat (TM) 1207. [A10] £90 **$150**

THE SACRAMENTO VALLEY FROM THE AMERICAN RIVER TO BUTTE CREEK [1849] Lt. G.H. Derby. 56x44cm (22x17½") Sh tear one fold, else VG. Ref: Wheat (Gold) 149. [10] £226 **$375**

TOPOCRAPHICAL [SIC] MAP OF THE ROAD FROM FORT SMITH, ARKS. TO SANTA FE, N.M. AND FROM DONA ANA, N.M. TO FORT SMITH [1850] By Capt. R.B. Marcy; 40 miles/inch. 37x71cm (15x28") Folded as issued. Some browning; laid on archival paper. Ref: Wheat (TM) 681, illus. [8] £166 **$275**

[SAME TITLE] [n.d.] By Capt. Randolph B. Marcy; 1850 survey. 37x70cm (14½x27½") Uncolored. Folds reinforced. Ref: Wheat (TM) 681, illus. [41] £166 **$275**

TOPOGRAPHICAL SKETCH OF THE GOLD & QUICKSILVER DISTRICT OF CALIFORNIA, JULY 25TH, 1848 [1848] By Lt. Ord; P. Duval, Lith. Early report of gold. 55x39cm (21½x15½") Folded as issued; minor foxing; else near fine. Ref: Wheat (TM) 565. Wheat (Gold) 54. [8] £256 **$425**

[SAME TITLE] [1848] From Mason's *Report.* By Lt. Ord. 55x39cm (21½x15½") B&W. Fine. Ref: Wheat (TM) 565; Schwartz & Ehrenberg p.278-9. [12] £392 **$650**

[SAME TITLE] [1848] By Lt. Ord; early report of gold. 55x39cm (21½x15½") B&W. Pressed folding map; sl foxing one fold; else fine (A). Ref: Wheat (TM) 565. [A4] £199 **$330**

TOPOGRAPHICAL SKETCH OF THE SOUTHERNMOST POINT OF THE PORT OF SAN DIEGO, ... FOR DETERMINING INITIAL POINT OF BOUNDARY BETWEEN THE UNITED STATES AND MEXICAN REPUBLIC ... IN CONFORMITY WITH ... THE TREATY ... OF GUADALUPE HIDALGO ... 1848 [1849] By A.B. Gray. Incl determination of "Marine League" (5564 meters). About 2 inches/mile. 44x57cm (17½x22½") Ref: Wheat (TM) 616. [8] £151 **$250**

U.S. GOVERNMENT continued

UPPER MINES [ON SHEET WITH] LOWER MINES OR MORMON DIGGINGS [c.1848] From Mason's *Report*. Calif gold field localities. 23x17cm (9x6½") B&W. Fine. [12] £60 **$100**

WESTERN TERRITORY [1836 / 1861] Reissue of Dodge expedition map, Ft. Leavenworth to Rockies, by Steen. 28x43cm (11x17") Uncolored. Issued folded. exc. [26] £84 **$140**

U.S. CIVIL WAR MAPS - Infrequent Publishers

MAP OF BATTLEGROUND OF AUGUST 28TH, 29TH & 30TH, 1862 IN THE VICINITY OF GROVETON, PRINCE WILLIAM CO, VA. [1878] Maj. Gen. G.K. Warren; Newport, R.I. 3 maps: "Accompanying Argument of Petitioner's Counsel" for court martial resulting from defeat at Second Battle of Bull Run. 56x66cm (22x26") Troop positions in color. Browning at folds; good. Each priced at [36] £121 **$200**

U.S. COAST & GEODETIC SURVEY   Try *U.S. Coast Survey*

APPROACHES TO NEW YORK - GAY HEAD TO CAPE HENLOPEN [1891] 4-sheet linen-backed chart. 82x98cm (32x38½") [A7] £34 **$57**

COAST CHART NO.166. FLORIDA REEFS FROM KEY BISCAYNE TO CARYSFORT REEF [1878] Dissected into 4 panels; canvas-backed for use. 100x79cm (39½x31") B&W; buoys colored. Minor offsetting; lt foxing; VG. [35] £196 **$325**

HUDSON RIVER, SHEET NO.1, FROM NEW YORK TO HAVERSTRAW [1863 / 1882] Covers East River. 99x44cm (39x17½") B&W. On heavy paper; folds reinforced with linen verso; 2" fold separation at intersection; image fine. [35] £96 **$160**

HUDSON RIVER, SHEET NO.3, FROM POUGHKEEPSIE TO TROY, NEW YORK [1863 / 1882] 99x50cm (39x19½") B&W. Orig linen-backed folds, lt uplifting lower part; 2" fold separation; VG, image fine. [35] £42 **$70**

PRELIMINARY CHART OF HUDSON RIVER, SHEET NO.2, FROM HAVERSTRAW TO POUGHKEEPSIE, NEW YORK [1861 / 1878] 98x50cm (38½x19½") B&W. Toned; linen reinforcement verso; fold separations; image wrinkled where backed; good. [35] £27 **$45**

U.S. COAST SURVEY

[BOOK WITH MAPS] A REPORT OF THE SUPERINTENDENT OF THE COAST SURVEY, SHOWING THE PROGRESS OF THAT WORK DURING THE YEAR ENDING NOVEMBER, 1850 [1850] Senate Doc 7, 31st Cong, 2nd Sess. Octavo; 134 pp text; 26 maps. Disbound; 1st page soiled; o/w VG. [26] £72 **$120**

[BOOK WITH MAPS] REPORT OF THE SUPERINTENDENT OF THE COAST SURVEY, SHOWING THE PROGRESS OF THE SURVEY ... 1854 [1855] 288 pp; 53 B&W coastal charts, various sizes. Covers rubbed, abraded; maps generally good, occas tears & lt foxing; VG (A). [A4] £166 **$275**

[BOOK WITH MAPS] SKETCHES ACCOMPANYING REPORT OF COAST SURVEY FOR 1851 [1851] 20 folding charts; sm quarto; publisher's cloth. Backstrip lacking. [A7] £62 **$103**

[BOOK WITH MAPS] SKETCHES ACCOMPANYING THE ANNUAL REPORT ... 1851 [1851] Ex Doc 26; 32nd Cong, 1st Sess. Full leather, gold embossed spine; complete with 57 B&W maps, various sizes. All maps VG, mostly unopened, except San Francisco Bay detached & trimmed close at top; fine (A). [A4] £185 **$306**

ATLANTIC COAST OF THE UNITED STATES ... NANTUCKET TO CAPE HATTERAS [1863] Shows Continental Shelf to 100 fathom line & Gulf Stream edges. 60x69cm (23½x27") [17] £54 **$90**

BARNSTABLE HARBOR MASSACHUSETTS ... [1861] Marine & shore detail. 42x57cm (16½x22½") B&W. [a copy with color offered for $140] [17] £75 **$125**

[SAME TITLE] 1861] 41x56cm (16x22") Uncolored. Exc. [25] £45 **$75**

BOSTON HARBOR MASSACHUSETTS [1857] Much land detail; 6 views. 72x91cm (28½x36") B&W. Folded as issued; trimmed close to lf border; couple minor tears along horiz fold end; few fold-point separations; lt age toning along some folds; o/w VG. [14] £166 **$275**

[SAME TITLE] [1857] Topographic details. 73x91cm (29x36") Minor fold restoration. [17] £148 **$245**

COAST OF TEXAS FROM GALVESTON TO CORPUS CHRISTI [1867] Soundings. 55x79cm (21½x31") VG. [16] £151 **$250**

COASTERS HARBOR AND APPROACHES. RHODE ISLAND ... [1862] Newport waters. 26x32cm (10½x12½") Color. [17] £36 **$60**

FROM MONOMOY AND NANTUCKET SHOALS TO MUSKEGET CHANNEL [1888] Coast Chart No.11. Linen-backed. 100x69cm (39½x27") Minor soiling. [A7] £42 **$69**

GALVESTON BAY TEXAS [1898] Coast Chart No.204. Shows city grid. 67x56cm (26½x22") Repaired; VG. [16] £72 **$120**

U.S. COAST SURVEY continued

GALVESTON ENTRANCE TEXAS [1853] Sketch I No.3 by J.M. Wampler. Shows land features. 35x43cm (14x17") VG. [16] £106 **$175**

GENERAL MAP OF CHARLESTON HARBOR SOUTH CAROLINA SHOWING REBEL DEFENCES AND OBSTRUCTIONS [1865] Shows city plan. 55x63cm (22x25") Printed color. Folded as issued. Ref: Stephenson (CW-1) 370. [7] £151 **$250**

GRAND ISLAND PASS, MISSISSIPPI [1857] Pearl River & Heron Bay area. 27x41cm (10½x16") Uncolored. [40] £18 **$30**

GULF COAST OF THE UNITED STATES KEY WEST TO RIO GRANDE [1863] 2-sheet chart; can be joined. 69x130cm (27½x51") Fold browning; some spotting; good. [16] £166 **$275**

HARBOR OF NEW HAVEN ... [1872] Shore side detail; 4"/mile. 77x63cm (30½x25") [17] £81 **$135**

HEMPSTEAD HARBOR LONG ISLAND [1859] By Blunt & Gerdes. Shows roads & houses. 46x37cm (18x14½") [17] £57 **$95**

J. NO.4, PRELIMINARY SURVEYS OF THE HARBORS ON THE WESTERN COAST OF THE UNITED STATES [1854] From annual report. Incl Santa Cruz & Pt Ano Nuevo. 31x32cm (12x12½") VG+. [35] £33 **$55**

MAP OF THE WORLD ON A POLYCONIC DEVELOPMENT OF THE SPHERE 1856 [1856] Bazarre projection. 24x28cm (9½x11") [19] £30 **$50**

MUSKEGET CHANNEL MASSACHUSETTS [1859] Marine & shore detail. 71x53cm (28x20½") [17] £87 **$145**

NANTUCKET HARBOR [1848] 2 recognition views. 36x48cm (14x19") Uncolored. Old folds, minor browning. ["Davis Shoal and Other Dangers", same condition, offered at same price] [26] £45 **$75**

NEW HAVEN HARBOUR [CT] [1838] 94x61cm (37x24") Narrow margin at binding edge; VG. [A9] £111 **$184**

NEW YORK BAY AND HARBOR [1861] Incl NYC detail. 76x69cm (30x27") Uncolored. Folded as issued; exc. [25] £72 **$120**

NORFOLK HARBOR VIRGINIA [1870] 49x39cm (19½x15½") Color. Fine. [31] £87 **$145**

OYSTER BAY TO MATAGORDA BAY (TEXAS). COAST CHART NO.107 [1858] 53x102cm (21x40") Wash color. Folding; lower lf margin trimmed where bound into report. [27] £163 **$270**

PATAPSCO RIVER AND THE APPROACHES ... [1870] 44x69cm (17x27") Toned at folds; VG. [A9] £31 **$52**

PORTLAND HARBOR MAINE ... [1862] Marine & shore detail; profile view; inset of approaches. 73x65cm (29x25½") [17] £75 **$125**

POTOMAC RIVER (IN FOUR SHEETS) [1862] Separate issue; each section linen-backed. 58x272cm (23x107") [15] £814 **$1,350**

PRELIMINARY CHART OF KENNEBEC RIVER MAINE FROM ENTRANCE TO BATH ... [1858] Shows roads, houses; 2"/mile. 69x46cm (27x18") [17] £51 **$85**

PRELIMINARY CHART OF MONOMOY SHOALS MASSACHUSETTS ... [1856] Marine & topo detail. 62x47cm (24½x18½") [17] £75 **$125**

PRELIMINARY CHART OF NANTUCKET SHOALS MASSACHUSETTS [1853] Inc Nantucket Island. 44x49cm (17½x19½") [17] £66 **$110**

PRELIMINARY CHART OF NEW YORK BAY AND HARBOR [1857] Folded map. 76x66cm (30x26") Good. [40] £45 **$75**

PRELIMINARY CHART OF ST. AUGUSTINE HARBOR, FLORIDA ... [1862] Chart & town plan. 52x53cm (20½x21") Uncolored. Minor browning; else VG. [36] £106 **$175**

PRELIMINARY CHART OF THE SEA COAST OF MASSACHUSETTS FROM SAUGHKONNET RIVER TO PLYMOUTH FROM A TRIGONOMETRICAL SURVEY [1856] 90 mile swath incl the cape & islands. 57x80cm (22½x31½") [17] £87 **$145**

PROVINCETOWN HARBOR MASSACHUSETTS [1857] With shore side detail. 38x44cm (15x17½") Color. [17] £66 **$110**

RECONNAISSANCE OF THE WESTERN COAST OF THE UNITED STATES FROM MONTEREY TO THE COLUMBIA RIVER. SHEET NO.3 [1851] Umpqua to Columbia River. [no dimens] B&W. Folds as issue; lt uniform age toning; o/w VG to fine. [14] £90 **$150**

RECONNAISSANCE OF THE WESTERN COAST OF THE UNITED STATES FROM SAN FRANCISCO TO SAN DIEGO [1852] 1st edition. 17 recognition views. 56x58cm (22x23") B&W. Folds as issued; narrow margin lower lf, tear just across border; some lt image transfer; o/w fine. [14] £136 **$225**

RECONNAISSANCE OF WASHINGTON SOUND AND ITS APPROACHES ... [1862] 66x58cm (26x23") Uncolored. Folded as issued; VG. [25] £45 **$75**

SKETCH F. NO.2 SHOWING THE PROGRESS OF THE SURVEY OF THE FLORIDA REEFS [1854] From annual report. Key Biscayne area with insets; triangulation. 29x37cm (11½x14½") Folds; fine. [35] £27 **$45**

U.S. COAST SURVEY continued

SKETCH J NO.6 SHOWING THE PROGRESS OF THE SURVEY OF SAN FRANCISCO BAY AND VICINITY. SECTION X. FROM 1850 TO 1853 [ON SHEET WITH] SKETCH J NO.6 SHOWING THE PROGRESS OF THE SURVEY IN THE BAY OF SAN DIEGO CALIFORNIA [1853] 23x41cm (9x16") B&W. Lt age toning along fold; a lt spot in blank area; o/w fine. [A1] £30 **$50**

SKETCH SHOWING THE PROGRESS OF THE SURVEY IN SECTION IX FROM 1848 TO 1883 [1883] Triangulation of TX coast. 79x93cm (31x37") Fine. [16] £57 **$95**

THE HARBOR OF HOLMES HOLE AND THE HARBOR OF TARPAULIN COVE [MA] [1848] 2 charts on sheet. 36x48cm (14x19") Uncolored. Old folds, minor browning. [26] £36 **$60**

U.S. EXPLORING EXPEDITION

MAP OF THE OREGON TERRITORY ... [1849] C. Wilkes. 21x33cm (8½x13") B&W. Fine. [1] £106 **$175**

MAP OF UPPER CALIFORNIA BY THE U.S. EX. EX. AND BEST AUTHORITIES [1841] From Wilkes *Narrative* ... 20x28cm (8x11") B&W. Fine (A+). Ref: Wheat (TM) 458. [A4] £110 **$182**

U.S. GEOLOGICAL SURVEY

[BOOK WITH MAPS] ECONOMIC GEOLOGY OF THE BINGHAM MINING DISTRICT, UTAH [1905] John Mason Boutwell; USGS PP#38. 412 pp; maps & illus as called for, incl 2 maps in pocket. Cover wraps worn, loose; o/w exc. [26] £54 **$90**

[BOOK WITH MAPS] GEOLOGY AND GOLD DEPOSITS OF THE CRIPPLE CREEK DISTRICT COLORADO [1906] Lingren & Ransome; USGS PP#54. 516 pp; maps & illus as called for, incl 3 maps in pocket. VG. [26] £96 **$160**

[BOOK WITH MAPS] LEAD ZINC AND FLUORSPAR DEPOSITS OF WESTERN KENTUCKY [1905] Ulrich & Smith; USGS PP#36. 218 pp; maps, illus. VG. [26] £24 **$40**

ASPEN SPECIAL SHEET [1898] Geological version; cloth backed, separately issued. 51x41cm (20x16") Minor color. Exc. [26] £72 **$120**

MAP OF TEXAS [1899] Base map at 25 miles/inch; counties, towns, RRs, waterways; 250' contours. 79x89cm (31x35") Folded; fine. [9] £51 **$85**

MAP OF THE WASHOE DISTRICT SHOWING MINING CLAIMS [1883] Orig appeared in *Comstock Mines and Miners*. 76x46cm (30x18") Full color. Some fold repairs verso. [25] £72 **$120**

PANORAMA FROM POINT SUBLIME [AZ] [1882] William Henry Holmes, Dutton Report, Wash. Set of 3 prints presenting wide view of Grand Canyon. Plates fold, each 46x79cm (18x31") Full rich color. Fold unobtrusive; exc. [26] £844 **$1,400**

RECONNAISSANCE MAP OF CIRCLE QUADRANGLE YUKON- TANANA REGION ALASKA [1911] Surveyed 1903-8 by Brooks et al. 91x79cm (36x31") Faint water stains. ["Geological ..." map of same region, color keyed, offered at $35] [40] £18 **$30**

TOPOGRAPHY OF THE DENVER BASIN COLORADO [1888] Boulder to Parker. 56x53cm (22x21") Minor color. VG. ["Areal Geology ..." & "Economic Geology ..." offered at same price] [25] £54 **$90**

UINTA INDIAN RESERVATION & WAGON ROAD FROM HEBER CITY THERETO WITH PART OF UTAH TERRITORY, REPRESENTING IRRIGABLE, TIMBER AND PASTURE LANDS [1878] By C.A.H. McCauley. 41x51cm (16x20") Uncolored. VG. [25] £30 **$50**

YELLOWSTONE NATIONAL PARK AND FOREST RESERVE ... [1903] 46x48cm (18x19") Some color. VG. [25] £54 **$90**

U.S. HYDROGRAPHIC OFFICE

MAP OF THE NORTH POLAR REGION [c.1880] Chart No.68. Wrangell Land inset. Fold out map with canvas backing. [no dimens] Orig OL color. Canvas tear between two map sections, no damage to image; lt soiling; o/w fine. [A1] £183 **$303**

U.S. PACIFIC R.R. SURVEY

EXPLORATIONS AND SURVEYS FOR A RAIL ROAD ROUTE ... NEAR THE 41ST PARALLEL ... MAP NO.1 ... GREEN RIVER TO THE GREAT SALT LAKE [IN SET WITH] NO. 2 ... TO THE HUMBOLDT MOUNTAINS [AND] NO.3 ... TO THE MUD LAKES ... [AND] NO.4 ... TO THE PACIFIC OCEAN [1861] By E.G. Beckwith. Complete set of 4 maps, each about 46x52cm (18x20½") B&W. Lt fold browning; few separations repaired with archival tape; good (B). [A3] £110 **$182**

GEOLOGICAL MAP OF THE ROUTE EXPLORED BY CAPT. JNO. POPE ... NEAR THE 32ND PARALLEL ... FROM THE RED RIVER TO THE RIO GRANDE ... [1854] 25x58cm (10x23") Orig partial col. VG. [16] £90 **$150**

U.S. PACIFIC R.R. SURVEY continued

GEOLOGICAL PLAN OF THE COAST RANGE OF CALIFORNIA FROM SAN FRANCISCO BAY TO LOS ANGELES ... **1855 1856** [1858] Accompanies Thomas Antisell report. 43x30cm (17x12") Geologic color. Old folds as issued. [25] £45 **$75**

LOS ANGELES [1855] 1st published view. 15x23cm (6x9") Tinted litho. [41] £112 **$185**

MAIN CHAIN OF THE ROCKY MOUNTAINS, AS SEEN FROM THE EAST, EXTENDING FROM A POINT NORTH OF THE MARAIS PASS TO NEAR LITTLE BLACKFOOT PASS [c.1854] Panoramic view by Stanley & Sohon. 16x53cm (6½x21") [41] £24 **$40**

MAP NO.1. FROM FORT SMITH TO THE RIO GRANDE ... [1854-57] 35th parallel route; inset: "Sketch of Rio Pecos at Anton Chico". 61x132cm (24x52") Fold repair; VG. [16] £241 **$400**

MAP OF THE SURVEY OF A ROUTE FOR THE PACIFIC RAILROAD NEAR THE 32ND PARALLEL, BETWEEN THE RIO GRANDE & RED RIVER ... BY BVT. CAPT. JNO. POPE ... [1856] From octavo ed. 69x142cm (27x56") Wrinkled, clean; fold repairs; VG. [16] £347 **$575**

MILK R. TO THE CROSSING OF THE COLUMBIA R. ... [1860] Stevens 1853-55 surveys on 47th & 49th parallel. Central MT to Eastern WA. 58x152cm (23x60") Ref: Wheat (TM) 867, illus. [41] £136 **$225**

PRELIMINARY MAP OF THE WESTERN PORTION OF THE RECONNAISSANCE FOR THE PACIFIC RAIL ROUTE NEAR THE 35TH PARALLEL [1858] By E.F. Beale. Albuquerque to Pacific. 66x123cm (26x48½") Some splitting at fold junctions; o/w clean, bright. Ref: Wheat (TM) 939. [9] £90 **$150**

SAINT PAUL [MN] [(1854) 1860] View by John Mix Stanley. 15x23cm (6x9") [41] £36 **$60**

SECTION OF MAP COMPILED IN THE P.R.R. OFFICE WITH ADDITIONS DESIGNED TO ILLUSTRATE LT. WARREN'S REPORT OF MILITARY RECONNAISANCES IN THE DACOTA COUNTRY [1855 (1856)] From 34th Cong, 1st Sess, Sen Exec Doc 76. Shows explorer's routes from Missouri R. to Rockies since Lewis & Clark. 38x48cm (15x19") B&W. Narrow lower 2/3 lf margin; mended sm fold intersection splits; overall exc. Ref: Wheat (TM) 871. Karrow (MW) 1-0185. [12] £166 **$275**

U.S. STATE SURVEYS

A DIAGRAM OF OREGON [1861] GLO. 43x58cm (17x23") Uncolored. Exc. [26] £72 **$120**

[SAME TITLE] [1861] Sen Ex Doc No.1, 37th Cong, 2nd Sess. 57x44cm (22½x17½") B&W. Lt age toning along some folds; a minor fold-point separation; o/w VG. Ref: Wheat (TM) 1036. [A1] £93 **$154**

ARKANSAS [1856] 39x42cm (15x16½") B&W. Lt fold browning repaired with archival tape. [A3] £33 **$55**

DAKOTA TERRITORY. SHOWING PROGRESS OF THE U.S. LAND SURVEY DURING 1861, 62 & 63 [1863] 60x52cm (23½x20½") B&W. Folds as issued; some fold-point separations; lt age toning along a fold; o/w VG. [14] £75 **$125**

DIAGRAM OF THE STATE OF ILLINOIS [1848] By F.R. Conway. 57x36cm (22½x14") B&W. Folds as issued; a few extras; VG. [14] £66 **$110**

DIAGRAM OF THE STATE OF MISSOURI [1849] 7 districts; Indian boundary lines. 44x57cm (17½x22½") OL color. [41] £39 **$65**

INDIAN TERRITORY [1883] GLO. Reservations & leases delineated, referenced to treaties. 61x81cm (24x32") Some printed color. [41] £169 **$280**

INDIAN TERRITORY, 1883 [1883] GLO. Similar to 1879 issue, reduced. Tribal areas delineated, partially color coded. 30x41cm (12x16") Full color. Lf edge trimmed when issued; now replaced. [25] £72 **$120**

MAP OF A PART OF THE TERRITORY OF WASHINGTON TO ACCOMPANY REPORT OF THE SURVEYOR GENERAL 1855 [1855] Western Rockies to Pacific. 37x49cm (14½x19½") Uncolored. Few fold-point separations; faint age toning along folds & margins; o/w VG. Ref: Wheat (TM) 869. [14] £121 **$200**

[SAME TITLE] [1855] Most of present state. 37x49cm (14½x19½") New OL color. Few lt foxing spots; margin split repaired verso; o/w VG. Ref: Wheat (TM) 869. [A2] £159 **$264**

MAP OF A PORTION OF WASHINGTON TERRITORY TO ACCOMPANY REPORT OF THE SURVEYOR GENERAL, 1861 [1861] GLO. 56x66cm (22x26") Uncolored. Issued folded; VG. [26] £72 **$120**

MAP OF LOUISIANA REPRESENTING THE SEVERAL LAND DISTRICTS [1850] From *Annual Report of the Commissioner of [GLO]*. 39x42cm (15½x16½") Wide OL color. Fine. Ref: Phillips (M) p.375. [12] £60 **$100**

MAP OF OKLAHOMA TERRITORY [1898] The actual Territory (W part of present OK). 38x56cm (15x22") Substantial color. VG. [Editions of 1899 (dated 1898), 1900, 1905 & 1906, showing a progression of changes leading to disappearance of Indian Territory, offered at same price] [26] £54 **$90**

[SAME TITLE] [1901] Publ by GLO & Governor of Territory. Guthrie capital. Topo indicated. 37x56cm (14½x22") Printed color. [40] £60 **$100**

U.S. STATE SURVEYS continued

MAP OF PUBLIC SURVEYS WASHINGTON TERRITORY TO ACCOMPANY REPORT OF SURV: GENL: 1863 [1863] From House Ex Doc No.1, 38th Cong, 1st Sess. Within ultimate boundaries. 43x55cm (17x21½"). Uncolored. Folds as issued; few sm fold-point separations; faint age toning along some folds; o/w fine. [14] £100 **$165**

MAP OF PUBLIC SURVEYS IN CALIFORNIA ... [1857] Names 43 "private" surveyed grants, 5 unsurveyed. 91x76cm (36x30"). Minor fold separations, no loss. [10] £87 **$145**

MAP OF PUBLIC SURVEYS IN CALIFORNIA AND NEVADA ... [1863] Folding map; western NV only; 433 CA land grants identified. 75x90cm (29½x35½"). Uncolored. [40] £60 **$100**

MAP OF PUBLIC SURVEYS IN COLORADO TERRITORY [1863] 41x56cm (16x22"). Laid on archival paper; some browning at folds. [8] £151 **$250**

MAP OF RED RIVER WITH ITS BAYOUS AND LAKES IN THE VICINITY OF THE RAFT [1855] North at rt; plantation owner's names; trees indicate forests. 57x113cm (22½x44½"). Uncolored. [40] £36 **$60**

MAP OF THAT PART OF WASHINGTON TERRITORY LYING WEST OF THE CASCADE MOUNTAINS TO ACCOMPANY THE REPORT OF THE SURVEYOR GENERAL 1857 [1857] 34x23cm (13½x9"). Uncolored. Folds as issued; lt age toning along horiz fold; o/w fine. [14] £84 **$140**

MAP OF THE PUBLIC SURVEYS IN CALIFORNIA TO ACCOMPANY REPORT OF SURVEYOR GENERAL [1854] 51x117cm (20x46"). B&W. Lt age toning along folds; occas sm fold separations; trimmed past neatline lower lf. [14] £75 **$125**

MAP OF THE STATE OF MONTANA [1897] GLO. 26 counties. Reservations & coal bearing townships colored. 42x63cm (16½x25"). [10] £75 **$125**

MAP OF THE STATE OF NEVADA [1866] GLO. Topo by hachures; mail route & proposed RR; color highlighted mineral deposits & mining districts indicated. 53x46cm (21x18"). Minor fold browning; o/w bright. [9] £226 **$375**

MAP OF THE UNITED STATES AND TERRITORIES. SHOWING THE EXTENT OF PUBLIC SURVEYS AND OTHER DETAILS CONSTRUCTED FROM THE PLATS AND OFFICIAL SOURCES OF THE GENERAL LAND OFFICE ... [1868] Linen-backed folding map; mining region key. 71x140cm (28x55"). Full color. Some loss at fold intersections; o/w clean, good (B). [A4] £159 **$264**

MAP SHOWING PRIVATE LAND CLAIMS, PATENTED OR UNPATENTED, OR CONFIRMED, IN NEW MEXICO, COLORADO AND ARIZONA, TO JUNE 30, 1883 [1885] GLO. 33x43cm (13x17"). Full color. Some fold repairs verso. [25] £75 **$125**

MAP SHOWING THE EXTENT OF SURVEYS IN THE TERRITORY OF UTAH [1856] Attributable to David Burr. Area north, south & east of Great Salt Lake. 82x39cm (32½x15½"). B&W. Folds as issued; trimmed to border top lf; few fold-point separations; lt age toning along some folds; o/w VG. [14] £87 **$145**

MAP SHOWING THE PROGRESS OF THE PUBLIC SURVEYS IN KANSAS AND NEBRASKA, TO ACCOMPANY ANNUAL REPORT OF THE SURVEYOR GENERAL 1863 [1863] In House Ex Doc No.1, 38th Cong, 1st Sess. 44x46cm (17½x18½"). Lt age toning at folds; minor fold splits repaired with archival tape; o/w fine. [14] £106 **$175**

NEW MEXICO [1861] GLO. Towns, roads, some topo; incl AZ. 51x74cm (20x29"). Uncolored. Folded as issued; VG. [26] £72 **$120**

SKETCH OF PUBLIC SURVEYS IN NEW MEXICO ... [1856] 57x83cm (22½x32½"). Part printed color; modern highlight. VG [16] £166 **$275**

[SAME TITLE] [1859] Incl present AZ, parts of UT & KS Terr. 58x82cm (23x32"). Folds as issued; few minor fold-point separations; lt age toning along some folds; narrow margins; o/w fine. [14] £106 **$175**

SKETCH OF THE PUBLIC SURVEYS IN THE STATE OF WISCONSIN [1866] From *Maps Accompanying the Report of ... the GLO*. Colored nuggets indicate minerals. 43x41cm (17x16"). OL color. Fine. Ref: Phillips (A) 1388-5. [12] £106 **$175**

STATE OF IDAHO [1899] GLO. Shading shows landforms; much detail. 116x74cm (45½x29"). 4-color printing. Minor splitting at fold junctions; o/w good. [9] £90 **$150**

STATE OF MINNESOTA [1879] GLO. 76x66cm (30x26"). Substantial color. Old folds, some repairs verso. [25] £84 **$140**

STATE OF OHIO [1866] Issued by GLO. Old land districts shown: "Virginia Military Lands", "Symmes' Purchase", "Connecticut Reserve", etc. 38x46cm (15x18"). Counties in OL color. On poor paper; some darkening at folds; sl loss at intersections; mulberry paper backing. [Similar AL, AR offered at same price] [39] £90 **$150**

[SAME TITLE] [Oct. 2, 1866] Washington: GLO. Major & Knapp, lith. Earlier grants & purchases appear with all 88 counties. 38x44cm (15x17½"). OL color. Fine. Ref: Karrow (MW) 2-1952; Kelsay p.143. [12] £106 **$175**

U.S. STATE SURVEYS continued

STATE OF OREGON [1879] 43x56cm (17x22") Printed color. Folded as issued. [9] £51 **$85**

[SAME TITLE] [1879] Washington: GLO. 2-color litho. 42x57cm (16½x22½") [12] £136 **$225**

[SAME TITLE] [1884] Dept. of Interior, GLO. 64x74cm (25x29") Substantial color. VG. [26] £136 **$225**

STATE OF WISCONSIN [1866] Issued by GLO. RR land grant limits & mineral regions shown. 43x41cm (17x16") Counties in OL color; mineral symbols highlighted. On poor paper; some darkening at folds; sl loss at intersections; mulberry paper backing. [Similar IA offered at same price] [39] £90 **$150**

TERRITORY OF ARIZONA [1903] GLO. 51x41cm (20x16") Substantial color. VG. [1906 ed offered at same price] [25] £75 **$125**

[SAME TITLE] [1903] GLO. Reservations, grants, claims distinguished with color; topo in sepia. 51x43cm (20½x17") [41] £72 **$120**

[SAME TITLE] [1908] GLO; with governor's report. Shows reservations, RRs, topo & county boundaries in color. 51x43cm (20x17") [9] £72 **$120**

TERRITORY OF DAKOTA [1882] By Roeser; Wash: GLO; Bien & Co., lith. 2-color litho. 74x61cm (29x24") Ref: Karrow (MW) 10-0227; Kelsay p.152. [12] £181 **$300**

TERRITORY OF NEW MEXICO [1903] Incl Leonard Wood County, now Guadalupe; land grants shown. 56x46cm (22x18") Printed OL color. [41] £81 **$135**

U.S. UNION & CONFEDERATE ARMIES ATLAS (1891-1895)

[ATLAS] ATLAS TO ACCOMPANY THE OFFICIAL RECORDS OF THE UNION AND CONFEDERATE ARMIES [1891-95] Washington: GPO. 178 folded plates, some in color as issued in 37 orig parts in fascicles with wrappers. Not perfect; good as obtainable. [33] £1,327 **$2,200**

GENERAL TOPOGRAPHICAL MAP SHEET XXII [E. TEXAS; S.W. LOUISIANA] [1893] Plate CLVII. Sabine Lake to Austin with Gulf coast. 47x75cm (18½x29½") Printed OL color. Good. [16] £90 **$150**

MAP OF SAVANNAH ... AND VICINITY ... [1891-95] Pl.70; operations under Sherman resulting in fall of city Dec. 21, 1864; sm maps of Sherman's march & Selma, AL. 5-color litho. 42x70cm (16½x27½") [12] £54 **$90**

PLATE XLIII [9 BATTLE PLANS: GETTYSBURG (3); KENNESAW MOUNTAIN; TEXAS COAST; ETC.] [1892] Printed OL & highlight color. Sl fold browning; good. [16] £75 **$125**

PLATE LIV MAP OF TEXAS AND PART OF NEW MEXICO ... [1891-95] Map dated 1857. Also maps of New Creek, WV; Pleasant Mills, MD. 42x70cm (16½x27½") Litho OL color. [27] £90 **$150**

PLATE LXV COAST OF TEXAS AND ITS DEFENSES [AND OTHER SMALL MAPS] [1892] Maps of Petersburg, Marietta area, Atlanta area, Chattahoochee, Deep Bottom, James River section. 41x69cm (16x27") Printed color. Couple sm abrasions; else VG (B). [A4] £66 **$110**

PLATE CXIX SECTION OF MAP OF THE STATES OF KANSAS AND TEXAS AND INDIAN TERRITORY, WITH PARTS OF THE TERRITORIES OF COLORADO AND NEW MEXICO [1892] Topo by hachures. 41x70cm (16½x27½") Printed OL color. VG. [16] £106 **$175**

TERRITORY AND MILITARY DEPARTMENT OF UTAH ... 1860 [1892] Covers UT, NV, part of CO, CA; unrelated inset. 41x69cm (16½x27½") Printed browns & blues. [41] £78 **$130**

U.S. WAR DEPARTMENT

[YELLOWSTONE NATIONAL PARK] [1892] From atlas accompanying *Report of the Secretary* ... 52nd Cong, 2nd Sess, House Exec Doc 1. Boundaries not final; 2.65 miles/inch. 70x50cm (27½x19½") B&W. [12] £45 **$75**

APPOMATTOX COURT HOUSE [1867 (c.1872)] Identical to maps in *Military Maps ... Operations of the Armies of the Potomac and James*. Issued separately. 76x58cm (30x23") Uncolored. Top rt corner lost; repaired margin tears. Ref: Stephenson (CW) 525.3. ["High Bridge and Farmville" offered at same price] [25] £72 **$120**

BATTLE OF CERRO GORDO, APRIL 17TH & 18TH 1847 [1847] Capt. McClellan. Troop positions color highlighted. 47x68cm (18½x27") Clean split at ctr vert fold; other sh tears. [A7] £208 **$345**

CHANCELLORVILLE, PREPARED BY BVT. BRIG. GENL. N. MICHLER ... [1867 (c.1872)] Identical to maps in *Military Maps ... Operations of the Armies of the Potomac and James*. Issued separately. 56x64cm (22x25") Lower edge worn; sm margin tears repaired; VG. Ref: Stephenson (CW) 528.3. ["Richmond" offered at same price] [25] £96 **$160**

CHART OF DETROIT RIVER. FROM LAKE ERIE TO LAKE ST. CLAIR. SURVEYED IN 1840, '41, '42 ... W.G. WILLIAMS [1844] 114x74cm (45x29") Sh splits at fold margins; tiny fold intersection splits; faint offsetting; fresh, clean. [A9] £111 **$184**

[SAME TITLE] [c.1843] Two sheets joined, 119x79cm (47x31") Offset. [A8] £225 **$373**

U.S. WAR DEPARTMENT continued

CHART OF THE HEAD OF NAVIGATION OF THE POTOMAC RIVER SHEWING THE ROUTE OF THE ALEXANDRIA CANAL MADE IN PURSUANCE OF A RESOLUTION OF THE ALEX'A CANAL COMPANY OCT. 1838 [1841] Alexandria to Little Falls. 48x91cm (19x36") Narrow lf margin at binding edge, with sh tear; else VG. Ref: Phillips (M) p.97. [A9] £111 **$184**

COHASSET HARBOR, MASS. SURVEY IN ACCORDANCE WITH THE RIVERS & HARBORS ACT ... [1899] C.W. Mason, Hydrographer. 36x68cm (14x27") [17] £30 **$50**

CUSTER'S BATTLE-FIELD (JUNE 25TH, 1876) SURVEYED AND DRAWN UNDER THE PERSONAL SUPERVISION OF LIEUT. EDWARD MAGUIRE ... BY SERGEANT CHARLES BECKER ... [1876] From part three, *Annual Report of the Chief of Engineers to the Secretary ... 1876* Grave site key. With 6 pp text in facsimile. 38x44cm (15x17½") B&W. Sh repaired tears near margin; else exc. Ref: Wheat (TM) 1266. [12] £172 **$285**

EL VADO DE LOS PADRES, COLORADO RIVER [1872, publ 1889] From Wheeler Surveys, ... *West of 100th Meridian*. Vol.I, "Geographical Report". The "Crossing [place] of the Fathers" in 1777. Tinted litho. 15x38cm (6x15") Immaculate. [12] £54 **$90**

EXPLORATIONS AND SURVEYS SOUTH OF CENTRAL PACIFIC R.R. WAR DEPARTMENT PRELIMINARY TOPOGRAPHICAL MAP EMBRACING IN SKELETON A PORTION ONLY OF THE NOTES FROM SURVEYS ... 1871 [1872] From Wheeler Surveys, ... *West of 100th Meridian*. 72x56cm (28½x22") B&W. Repaired fold intersection splits; else superb. Ref: Wheat (TM) 1237. Schmeckebier p.44. [12] £166 **$275**

GALVESTON HARBOR TEXAS ... MAJ. C.J. ALLEN ... [1890] To accompany annual report. Harbor bottom outlined. 27x27cm (10½x10½") Fine. [16] £45 **$75**

HARPERS FERRY, PREPARED BY BVT. BRIG. GENL. N. MICHLER ... 1867 [1869] From *Military Maps ... Operations of the Armies of the Potomac and James*. 57x69cm (22½x27½") B&W; blue highlight. Lt toning; fine. Ref: Phillips (A) 3688-15. [35] £90 **$150**

JETERSVILLE AND SAILORS CREEK [1867 (c.1872)] Identical to maps in *Military Maps ... Operations of the Armies of the Potomac and James*. Issued separately. 53x79cm (21x31") Some color. VG. ["Bermuda Hundred" offered at same price] [25] £84 **$140**

LAND CLASSIFICATION MAP OF EASTERN CALIFORNIA ATLAS SHEET NO.65 (D) [1877] From Wheeler Surveys, ... *West of 100th Meridian*. Panamint & Death Valley; hachured topo. 41x51cm (16x20") Full color. Exc. [25] £60 **$100**

LAND CLASSIFICATION MAP OF PART OF CENTRAL COLORADO, ATLAS SHEET NO.62 (A) [1878] Pikes Peak region. 43x51cm (17x20") Full color. Issued folded. ["Part of Southwestern Colorado, Atlas Sheet No.61 (D)", topo map of San Luis Valley, offered at same price] [25] £60 **$100**

LAND CLASSIFICATION MAP OF PART OF WESTERN COLORADO, ATLAS SHEET NO.61A [c.1882] From Wheeler Surveys, ... *West of 100th Meridian*. With contour lines. 38x49cm (15x19½") Printed greens & browns. [39] £60 **$100**

MAP ILLUSTRATING THE OPERATIONS OF THE SEVENTH DIVISION UNDER BRIG. GENERAL G.W. MORGAN AT CUMBERLAND GAP TENNESSEE DURING A PORTION OF THE YEAR 1862 [1877] 36x30cm (14x12") Some color. Sl faded; tear repaired verso. [25] £84 **$140**

MAP OF THE DELTA OF THE ST. CLAIR [MI] [1842] 119x72cm (47x28½") Lt offsetting. [A9] £77 **$127**

MAP OF THE ROUTE PURSUED IN 1849 BY THE U.S. TROOPS UNDER THE COMMAND OF BVT. LIEUT. COL. JNO. M. WASHINGTON, GOVERNOR OF NEW MEXICO, IN AN EXPEDITION AGAINST THE NAVAJO INDIANS [1849] By Simpson & Kern. 51x71cm (20½x28") Printed on poor paper; mends at several folds, some words obscured, no loss. Ref: Wheat (TM) 641. [7] £256 **$425**

[SAME TITLE] [1849] By Simpson & Kern. 51x71cm (20x28") B&W; route in red. Lt toning along some folds; near mint (A+). Ref: Wheat (TM) 641. [A4] £136 **$226**

MAP OF THE ROUTES EXAMINED AND SURVEYED FOR THE WINCHESTER AND POTOMAC RAILROAD, STATE OF VIRGINIA ... 1831 AND 1832 [1832] Bur. of Topo. Eng. Winchester to Harper's Ferry. 53x69cm (21x27") Uncolored. VG. [26] £45 **$75**

MAP OF THE TERRITORY OF NEW MEXICO [1846-1847] By Abert & Peck, with narrative. Rio Grand valley. 64x50cm (25x19½") Folded as issued. Ref: Howes (US) A11. [7] £196 **$325**

MAP OF THE YELLOWSTONE AND MISSOURI RIVERS AND THEIR TRIBUTARIES, EXPLORED BY CAPT. W.F. RAYNOLDS ... [1867] Northern NE to Rockies. With accompanying report. 71x107cm (28x42") Uncolored. Rebacked to halt deterioration of poor paper; sm loss lf edge & 2 corners. Ref: Storm (Graff) 4303. [26] £256 **$425**

MAP SHOWING LOCATION OF SHERIDAN WYOMING AND SURROUNDING RESERVATIONS [1895] In support of effort to locate military post; color indicates posts, reservations, timber. 33x41cm (13x16") VG. [26] £45 **$75**

U.S. WAR DEPARTMENT continued

MAP SHOWING THE ROUTE OF THE ARKANSAS REGIMENT FROM SHREVEPORT, LA. TO SAN ANTONIO DE BEXAR, TEXAS [1850] From Capt. G.W. Hughes' *Memoir ... of the March ... from San Antonio ... to Saltillo ...* 31st Cong, 1st Sess, Sen Ex Doc 32. East-central TX. 29x43cm (11½x17") B&W. Couple sm spots; else fine. [12] £106 **$175**

MAP SHOWING THE ROUTES TRAVELLED BY THE COMMAND OF MAJR. E. STEEN, U.S. DRAGS., AGAINST THE SNAKE INDIANS IN 1860, BY LIEUT. JOSEPH DIXON ... [1860] From *Topographical Memoir of the Command against the Snake Indians ...* 37th Cong, 2nd Sess, Sen Ex Doc No.1. Julius Bien, lith. 61x85cm (24x33½") B&W. Lt browning at some folds; sh fold intersection splits repaired; overall exc. Ref: Wheat (TM) 1016. [12] £166 **$275**

[SAME TITLE] [1860] Oregon east of Cascades. 61x84cm (24x33"). Uncolored. Folds as issued; several fold-point separations; faint age toning along some folds; o/w VG to fine. [14] £166 **$275**

[SAME TITLE] [1861] 61x81cm (24x32"). Uncolored. Folded; minor repairs verso. Ref: Storm (Graff) 1096. [26] £166 **$275**

MILITARY MAP OF THE UNITED STATES [1857] Prepared by Quartermaster General; shows western army posts. 34x76cm (13½x30") OL color, possibly later. Folded; bright. Ref: Wheat (TM) 929. [9] £151 **$250**

MILITARY RECONNAISSANCE OF THE ARKANSAS RIO DEL NORTE AND RIO GILA BY W.H. EMORY, LIEUT. TOP. ENGRS ... MADE IN 1846-47 ... UNDER THE COMMAND OF BRIG. GEN. STEPHN. W. KEARNEY ... CONSTRUCTED UNDER THE ORDERS OF COL. J.J. ABERT ... TOP. ENGRS. 1847 [1847] Eastern sheet only. 76x64cm (30x25") Reinforced at fold joints with archival tape; good. Ref: Wheat (TM) 544. [16] £332 **$550**

OUTLINE MAP SHOWING A NEW ROUTE FROM TEXAS TO FORT YUMA, CALIFORNIA, FOR CATTLE DROVES AND TRAINS EN ROUTE TO CALIFORNIA. ... BY CAPT. OVERMAN [c.1870] Compiled & drawn by C.W. Pressler. 37x126cm (14½x49½") B&W. Flawless. Ref: Wheat (TM) 1216. [12] £211 **$350**

OWLS HEAD HARBOR MAINE ... 1836 [1838] As in *Internal Improvements ...* Topo & proposed breakwater. 38x32cm (15x12½") Ref: Phillips (A) 1377-136. [17] £57 **$95**

PART OF CENTRAL COLORADO, ATLAS SHEET NO.52D [c.1882] From Wheeler Surveys, ... *West of 100th Meridian*. Denver, Aspen, etc. 41x48cm (16x19") On heavy paper. [39] £84 **$140**

PART OF CENTRAL NEVADA, ATLAS SHEET NO.48D [1882] From Wheeler Surveys, ... *West of 100th Meridian*. 38x48cm (15x19") [39] £60 **$100**

PART OF CENTRAL NEW MEXICO. ATLAS SHEET NO.69(D) [1877] From Wheeler Surveys, ... *West of 100th Meridian*. Incl Santa Fe, Taos, Abiquiu; shows trails, irrigation, timber & grazing lands. 39x51cm (15½x20") Minor splitting & browning; sm loss at fold junctures. [9] £178 **$295**

PART OF CENTRAL NEW MEXICO. ATLAS SHEET NO.77(B) [1877] From Wheeler Surveys, ... *West of 100th Meridian*. Albuquerque region. 39x51cm (15½x20") Minor splitting & browning. [9] £121 **$200**

PART OF NORTH CENTRAL NEW MEXICO. ATLAS SHEET NO.70 [1877] From Wheeler Surveys, ... *West of 100th Meridian*. Ft. Union area. 39x51cm (15½x20") Minor splitting & browning. [9] £106 **$175**

PART OF SOUTHERN CALIFORNIA, ATLAS SHEET NO.73 [1883] From Wheeler Surveys, ... *West of 100th Meridian*. L.A. to beyond San Bernardino & Bakersfield. 38x51cm (15x20½") [39] £84 **$140**

PART OF SOUTH'N COLORADO & NORTH'N NEW MEXICO. ATLAS SHEET NO.69(B) [1877] From Wheeler Surveys, ... *West of 100th Meridian*. Rio Grande gorge & upper Chama River. 39x51cm (15½x20") Minor splitting & browning. ["... Central New Mexico ... Sheet No.77(D)" offered at same price] [9] £72 **$120**

PARTS OF EASTERN CALIFORNIA AND WESTERN NEVADA. ATLAS SHEETS 47 (B) & 47 (D) [c.1878] From Wheeler Surveys, ... *West of 100th Meridian*. 2 sheets published as one. 76x74cm (30x29") Substantial color. Exc. [25] £72 **$120**

PARTS OF EASTERN NEVADA AND WESTERN UTAH, ATLAS SHEET NO.49 [1875-76] From Wheeler Surveys, ... *West of 100th Meridian*. Range & basin topo rendered with shading; many ghost towns. Tinted litho. 37x48cm (14½x19") Unfolded. Ref: Schmeckebier p.61; Phillips (A) 1281-60. [12] £136 **$225**

PARTS OF NORTHERN & NORTH WESTERN ARIZONA & SOUTHERN UTAH, ATLAS SHEET NO.67 [c.1874] From Wheeler Surveys, ... *West of 100th Meridian*. Topographical emphasis; many surface notes. Tinted litho map. 38x50cm (15x19½") Unfolded. Sm spot lf margin; o/w perfect. [another, c.1875, with similar coverage but geological emphasis offered at same price] Ref: Phillips (A) 1281-117. [12] £166 **$275**

PARTS OF SOUTHERN COLORADO AND NORTHERN NEW MEXICO ATLAS SHEET NO. 70(A) [1884] From Wheeler Surveys, ... *West of 100th Meridian*. Geological map; incl Raton & Sangre de Cristos. 38x50cm (15x19½") Color. Folded; good. [10] £90 **$150**

PLAN AND SECTIONS OF FORT FISHER CARRIED BY ASSAULT BY THE U.S. FORCES ... JAN 15TH, 1865 [n.d.] 28x38cm (11x15") Uncolored. Engineer stamp in margin; o/w VG. Ref: Stephenson (CW-1) [25] £45 **$75**

U.S. WAR DEPARTMENT continued

PRELIMINARY CHART OF EASTPORT HARBOR MAINE [1864] U.S.T.E. Lubec & Eastport street plans; incl Campobello. 52x43cm (20½x17"). Color. [17] £57 **$95**

PROGRESS MAP OF THE LINES AND AREAS OF EXPLORATIONS AND SURVEYS CONDUCTED UNDER THE AUSPICES OF THE WAR DEPARTMENT GIVING THE AREA OF THE PUBLIC DOMAIN LYING WEST OF THE 100TH MERIDIAN ... GEO. M. WHEELER ... [1881] Many editions starting 1873. Army explorers trails noted. 41x56cm (16x22") Substantial color. VG. [26] £72 **$120**

PROVINCETOWN HARBOR, MASS. ENGRAVED IN THE ENGINEER DEPT. [1866] Sounding, lighthouse; with "Essayons" logo. 15x23cm (6x9") [17] £21 **$35**

S.W. COLORADO, SAN JUAN MINING REGION - ATLAS SHEET NO.61(C) [c.1876] From Wheeler Surveys, ... *West of 100th Meridian*. Topo map; 1"=2 miles. 3 color litho. 38x50cm (15x19½") Perfect. Ref: Schmeckebier p.61. [12] £136 **$225**

SAN DIEGO FROM THE OLD FORT [1848] From Emory's Notes of a Military Reconnaissance. Early (1st?) publ view of city. 10x18cm (4x7") [41] £27 **$45**

SANTA FE [NM] [1848] From *Examination of New Mexico*. 30th Cong, 1st Sess, Sen Ex Doc No.23. Steel engraved view. 10x18cm (4x7") B&W. [12] £54 **$90**

SHEET NO.2, CAMPAIGN MAP OF THE DEPARTMENT OF THE PLATTE COMPRISING THAT PORTION OF NEBRASKA LYING BETWEEN LONG. 100 - 103 AND LAT 39 30 - 43 30 [1873] 69x43cm (27x17") Uncolored. A corner almost torn off & sm tears repaired verso. [26] £196 **$325**

SKETCH OF THE HARBOUR OF BRUNSWICK [GA] [1837] Sketchy. 33x36cm (13x14") Uncolored. Folded as issued; VG. [26] £45 **$75**

SOUTHWESTERN COLORADO ATLAS SHEET NO.61 (C) [1877-78] From Wheeler Surveys, ... *West of 100th Meridian*. San Juan Mountains; 8 versions of atlas sheet were produced. 43x51cm (17x20") Black on tan. VG. Ref: Phillips (a) 1281. ["... San Juan Mining Region" & "Land Classification ..." of No.61 (C) offered at same price] [25] £75 **$125**

SURVEY OF A VALLEY AND PONDS AUXILIARY TO A CONTEMPLATED CANAL BETWEEN BUZZARDS & BARNSTABLE BAYS, ... MASSACHUSETTS & TOWN OF SANDWICH 1825 [assumed 1825] Searle, Smith & Thompson under Maj. Perrault. 21x36cm (8½x14") Color. [17] £160 **$265**

TERRITORY OF NEW MEXICO [1846-47 (1848)] From *Examination of New Mexico*. By Lt. J.W. Abert & Lt. W.G. Peck; in 30th Cong, 1st Sess, Sen Ex Doc No.23. Rio Grande Valley & adjacent. 38x50cm (15x19½") B&W. Fine Ref: Wheat (TM) 532. [12] £211 **$350**

TOPOGRAPHICAL SKETCH OF THE BATTLEFIELD OF STONE'S RIVER NEAR MURPHREESBORO, TENNESSEE DECEMBER 31ST 1862 TO JAN. 3RD 1863 [1863] 51x58cm (20x23") Uncolored. VG. Ref: Stephenson (CW-1) 441. [26] £75 **$125**

UNIVERSAL MAGAZINE

A NEW AND ACCURATE MAP OF CONNECTICUT AND RHODE ISLAND, FROM THE BEST AUTHORITIES. [1780] 25x33cm (10x13") Uncolored. Minor repairs, but VG. Ref: Jolly UNIV-189. [25] £196 **$325**

A NEW AND ACCURATE MAP OF NEW JERSEY, FROM THE BEST AUTHORITIES. [1780] 33x25cm (13x10") Uncolored. Minor repairs, but VG. Ref: Jolly UNIV-186. [25] £211 **$350**

A NEW AND ACCURATE MAP OF THE COLONY OF MASSACHUSETTS BAY, IN NORTH AMERICA FROM A LATE SURVEY. [1780] 26x32cm (10½x13") B&W. Ref: Jolly UNIV-190. [22] £166 **$275**

[SAME TITLE] [1780] 25x33cm (10x13") Uncolored. Minor repairs but VG. [25] £226 **$375**

A NEW AND ACCURATE PLAN OF THE TOWN OF BOSTON, IN NEW ENGLAND. [ON SHEET WITH] **A NEW PLAN OF BOSTON HARBOR, FROM AN ACTUAL SURVEY.** [1774] 27x35cm (11x13½") B&W. Lt offsetting; else fine. Ref: Jolly UNIV-172. Boston (List) p.49. [12] £211 **$350**

A NEW MAP OF THE PROVINCE OF MARYLAND IN NORTH AMERICA. [1780] 28x33cm (11x13") Color. Mild toning along fold & partial separation; else VG. Framed. Ref: Jolly UNIV-184. [A10] £243 **$403**

[SAME TITLE] [1780] 28x33cm (11x13") Uncolored. Minor repair, but VG. Ref: Jolly UNIV-184. [25] £211 **$350**

AN ACCURATE MAP OF NEW HAMPSHIRE IN NEW ENGLAND, FROM A LATE SURVEY. [1781] 32x28cm (12½x11") Color. VG. Ref: Jolly UNIV-191. [24] £211 **$350**

AN ACCURATE MAP OF NEW YORK IN NORTH AMERICA, FROM A LATE SURVEY. [Aug. 1780] Long Island to Lake Champlain. 33x27cm (13x10½") B&W. Remargined top & lf, restored neatline; good. Ref: Jolly UNIV-187. Phillips (M) p.506; Sellers & Van Ee 1112. [29] £232 **$385**

[SAME TITLE] [1781] 34x28cm (13½x11") Uncol. Folded; VG. Ref: Jolly UNIV-187. [25] £166 **$275**

289

UNIVERSAL MAGAZINE continued

AN ACCURATE MAP OF THE ENGLISH COLONIES IN NORTH AMERICA BORDERING ON THE RIVER OHIO. [1754] ME to MI to Cape Lookout. 20x24cm (8x9½") B&W. Repaired sh tears; good. Ref: Jolly UNIV-41; Sellers & Van Ee 707. [31] £148 **$245**

AN EXACT PLAN OF THE CAPITAL CITY AND PORT OF MALTA, WITH ITS SUBURBS AND DEPENDENCIES. [ON SHEET WITH] AN ACCURATE MAP OF THE ISLANDS OF MALTA AND GOZA, FROM AN ACTUAL SURVEY, PERFORMED UNDER THE PATRONAGE OF THE GRAND OFFICERS OF THE ORDER. [1761] R.W. Seale. 26x17cm (10½x6½") B&W. Toned; fold splits margin, archival tape repair; VG (A). Ref: Jolly UNIV-101. [A4] £66 **$110**

VADIANUS

TYPUS COSMOGRAPHICUS UNIVERSALIS [1534 (1570)] State 3. 24x38cm (9½x15") Exc. Ref: Shirley (W) 70. [45] £3,015 **$5,000**

VALDIS

CARTA ESFERICA DE LA ISLANDE MALLORCA Y SUS ADYACENTES ... [1786] 6 inset views of ports & islets. 81x56cm (32x22") Orig OL col; full color cartouche. Occas lt surface soiling; o/w fine. [A1] £166 **$275**

VALENTINE'S MANUAL

MAP OF NEW YORK I. WITH THE ADJACENT ROCKS AND OTHER REMARKABLE PARTS OF HELL-GATE [1869] Reprint of 1778 Kitchin map in London Magazine. 25x18cm (10x7½") Color. Ref: cf Jolly LOND-322. [22] £39 **$65**

PLAN OF THE CITY OF NEW YORK [1855] Reprint of 1817 Prior & Dunning map. 87 landmarks keyed. 46x36cm (18x14") Uncolored. Narrow margins; folded as issued. [22] £45 **$75**

VALENTYN

ANTHONY VAN DIEMENS LAND [1724-26] As in *Oud en Nieuw Oost Indien, Collection of Voyages* ... Tasmania, with 2 New Zealand views. 18x29cm (7x11½") Color. Ref: Tooley (Australia) 431, pl.217. [13] **Aus$900** £409 **$678**

ATSJIEN [1726] From *Oud en Nieuw Oost Indien*. View of Banda Ache, northern Sumatra city. 27x36cm (10½x14") Uncolored. Fine. [4] **£150** **$249**

BOREELS EYLANDEN [ON SHEET WITH] STORM BAY [AND] ZUYD CAPE [AND] TASMANS EYLAND [1724-26] As in *Oud en Nieuw Oost Indien, Collection of Voyages* ... Tasmania east coast. 15x16cm (6x6½") B&W. [Tasmania: Frederick Hendricks Bay / Marias Island offered at same price] Ref: Tooley (Australia) 1274, map 432, p.348. [13] **Aus$340** £154 **$256**

JUDIA, DE HOOFD-STAD VAN SIAM [1724-26] Ayutthaya, capital of Siam. 27x36cm (10½x14") Exc. [45] £347 **$575**

KAART VAN HET EYLANDT BALI ... [1726] Publ in *Oud en Niew Oost-Indien*. 45x56cm (17½x22") Uncolored. Exc. [4] **£425** **$705**

NIEUWE KAART VAN HET EYLAND SUMATRA ... [1726] From *Oud en Nieuw Oost Indien*. 51x59cm (20x23") Uncolored. Fine. [4] **£850** **$1,410**

TABULA INDIAE ORIENTALIS ET REGNORUM ADJACENTIUM J. VAN BRAAM ET G. ONDER DE LINDEN ... [1724-26] As in *Oud en Nieuw Oost Indien, Collection of Voyages* ... Indian Ocean & adjacent lands.. 50x66cm (19½x26") Color. Ref: Tooley (Australia) 1268. [13] **Aus$3,200** £1,453 **$2,409**

[SAME TITLE] [1724] Appeared in *Oud en Nieuw Oost Indien*. 50x66cm (19½x26") Full color. Exc. Ref: Tooley (Australia) p.211, #68. [24] £1,508 **$2,500**

VALK

AMERICA AUREA PARS ALTERA MUNDI ... [c.1706] G. & L. Valk. Insular Calif. 48x59cm (19x23") Orig full color. Ref: McLaughlin 176. [27] £1,508 **$2,500**

ARTESIAE COMITATUS, COMPLECTENS COMITATUS NOMINE FANUM S. PAULI ... [c.1710] 49x60cm (19½x23½") Orig wash & OL color. Lower edge & margin sl soiled with few sh tears joined & supported on verso. [11] £51 **$85**

BULGARIA ET ROMANIA, DIVISA IN SINGULARES ... [c.1710] 60x49cm (23½x19½") Orig color. [34] £360 **$597**

MAPPE-MONDE GEO-HYDROGRAPHIQUE DU GLOBE [c.1686] Reduced version of larger map; double hemi, sm polar views; insular Calif. 19x23cm (7½x9") B&W. Faint stain at lf; sh tear in sl worn image repaired; VG. Ref: cf Shirley (W) 531. [35] £271 **$450**

VALK continued

MAPPE-MONDE GEO-HYDROGRAPHIQUE OU DESCRIPTION GENERALE DU GLOBE TERRESTRE ET AQUATIQUE EN DEUX-PLANS-HEMISPHERES ... [c.1686] With 2 sm polar hemis & lush surrounds. 48x58cm (19x23") Orig color. Narrow margins as issued; o/w fine. Ref: Shirley (W) 531, pl.373. [4] **£3,750** **$6,218**

NOVUS PLANIGLOBII TERRESTRIS PER UTRUMQUE POLUM CONSPECTUS [c.1672 - c.1695] Polar projection by Blaeu (signature almost erased); insular California. 41x54cm (16x21½") Orig color. Ref: Shirley (W) 459. [34] **£5,200** **$8,622**

ORBIS TERRARUM NOVA ET ACCURATA TABULA ... [c.1700] Double hemi; insular Calif; ornate decor. 48x57cm (19x22½") Orig & later color, gold heightened. 2 fold reinforcements; else exc. Ref: Shirley (W) 638. [23] **£3,015** **$5,000**

VALK & SCHENK

[SOUTH POLAR REGIONS] [c.1700] Reissue of Hondius. 43x48cm (17x19") Orig wash color; cartouche uncolored. Exc. Ref: MCC 66 #732, pl.56; Perry pl.20. [4] **£675** **$1,120**

AEGYPTI RECENTIOR DESCRIPTIO: AEGYPTIUS & TURCIS ESCHIBITH; ARABIBUS MESRE & MISRI HEBRAEIS MITSRAIM [1658 - c.1700] Orig publ by Jansson. 41x49cm (16x19½") Orig color. [34] **£450** **$746**

AETHIOPIA INFERIOR VEL EXTERIOR ... [1705] Reissue of Jansson map. 38x50cm (15x19½") Wash color. [46] **£420** **$697**

AETHIOPIA SUPERIOR VEL INTERIOR; VULGO ABISSINORUM SIVE PRESBITERI IOANNIS IMPERIUM [1705] Jansson reissue from composite atlas. 38x48cm (15x19") Orig wash color. [46] **£320** **$531**

BOURDELOIS, PAYS DE MEDOC, ET LA PREVOSTE DE BORN [c.1700] Orig publ in Jansson's Appendix; appeared in composite atlas with gridlines added. Hamersveldt, sc. 38x50cm (15x19½") Orig wash color. Some creasing at c'fold. [46] **£160** **$266**

HAEMISPHAERIUM STELLATUM BOREALE ANTIQUUM [c.1705] Northern sky. 43x51cm (17x20") Newer color. Sl paper uplifting along vert fold ends repaired; o/w fine. [14] **£2,593** **$4,300**

HUQUANG, KIANGSI, CHEKIANG, AC FOKIEN, PROVIN: SIVE PRAEFECTURAE REGNI SINEN 1658 - c.1700] Reissue of Jansson. Southeastern China. 46x52cm (18x20½") Orig color. [34] **£400** **$664**

[SAME TITLE] [1705] 36x52cm (14½x20½") Orig wash color. Laid on tissue to strengthen verdigris paper weakness. [46] **£280** **$465**

IMPERII SINARUM NOVA DESCRIPTIO [1658 - c.1700] Reissue of Jansson. 46x52cm (18x20½") Orig color. [34] **£800** **$1,327**

[SAME TITLE] [1705] Reissue of Jansson. 47x52cm (18½x20½") Orig wash color. [46] **£620** **$1,028**

INSULA S. IUAN DE PUERTO RICO, CARIBES VEL CANIBASUM INSULAE [c.1720] After Blaeu, Puerto Rico and Windward Is. 40x50cm (16x20") Color. Arsenic hole closed verso; scattered lt browning. [A7] **£173** **$287**

INSULAE FLANDRICAE, OLIM ASORES DICTA [1657 c.1710] 42x53cm (16½x20½") Orig col. [34] **£360** **$597**

IUNNAN QUEICHEU, QUANGSI ET QUAN TUNG PROVINCIAE REGNI SINENSIS [1658 - c.1700] Reissue of Jansson. Southern China. 46x52cm (18x20½") Orig color. [34] **£600** **$995**

NOVA ET ACCURATA IAPONIAE TERRAE ESONIS ... [1658 - c.1700] Republication of Jansson. 45x55cm (18x21½") Orig color. Ref: Walter (Japan) 57. [34] **£2,400** **$3,980**

PECHELI, XANSI, XANTUNG, HONAN, NANKING, IN PLAGA REGNI SINENSIS INTER SEPTENTIONEM AC ORIENTEM CECIAM VERSUS SITAE PROVINCIAE [1658 - c.1700] Reissue of Jansson. NE provinces. 46x52cm (18x20½") Orig color. [34] **£500** **$829**

[SAME TITLE] [1705] Reissue of Jansson map of NE China. 46x52cm (18x20½") Orig wash color. Laid on tissue to strengthen verdigris paper weakness. [46] **£340** **$564**

SUCHUEN; ET XENSI, PROVINCIA SUE PRAEFECTURAE REGNI SINENSIS ... [1658 - c.1700] Reissue of Jansson. Western provinces. 46x52cm (18x20½") Orig color. [34] **£350** **$581**

TABULA MAGELLANICA QUA TIERRAE DEL FUEGO [c.1740] 41x52cm (16x20½") Col. [A7] **£260** **$431**

THEORIA VENERIS ET MERCURII [c.1710] 43x51cm (17x20") Col. 20 sm wormholes seen when held to light. [A7] **£225** **$373**

VENEZUELA, CUM PARTE AUSTRALI NOVAE ANDALUSIAE [1633-1710] Jansson, reissued. 37x48cm (14½x19") Orig color. [34] **£500** **$829**

VAN ADRICHEM

TRIBUS ASER, ID EST, PORTIO ILLA TERRAE SANCTAE, QUAE TRIBUI ASER IN DIVISIONE REGIONIS ATTRIBUTA FUIT. [1590] From *Theatrum Terrae Sanctae*. Publ by Brunius. 22x38cm (8½x15") Uncolored. Couple worm tracks top margin; Lt toning; lt surface soiling & dampstaining; soft creases along vert fold. Ref: Laor 9. [A2] **£150** **$248**

VAN ADRICHEM continued

Tribus Iuda, Id Est, Pars Illa Terrae Sancta, quam in Ingressu Tribus Iuda Consecuta Fuit [1590] From *Theatrum Terrae Sanctae*. Publ by Brunius. 33x42cm (13x16½") Uncolored. Toned; lt soiling, bit of foxing; few margin tears, one to neatline. ["Domidia Tribus Manasse ..." sold at same price] Ref: Laor 13. [A2] £133 **$220**

VAN DE PASSE

[Portrait with world map] **Thomas Cavendish** ... [1598] Commander of 3rd circumnavigation; sm double hemi. 13x10cm (5½x4") Exc. [43] £353 **$585**

VAN DEN KEERE

[Ireland: Southeastern] [c.1599] Probably from Linschoten, *Itinerario*. Inset: West coast. 34x50cm (13½x19½") OL color. Minor loss 3 corners; few sm stains top margin & cartouche; else VG. Framed. [A10] £329 **$546**

Belgii Veteris Typus ... [1619] Lowlands. 38x50cm (15x19½") Full color. Exc. [44] £271 **$450**
Europae Nova Tabula [c.1676] 14x20cm (5½x8") B&W. Fine (A+). [A4] £106 **$176**
Italia [c.1676] 14x20cm (5½x8") B&W. Tiny margin spot; overall fine (A). [A4] £80 **$133**
Leo Belgicus ... [c.1617] 2nd state. Lowlands as Lion. 37x45cm (14½x18") Orig color, probably heightened later. Tear repaired; strengthened with japan paper. Ref: Potter illus p.187. [2] £9,951 **$16,500**

VAN DER AA

[Title page] **Virginien** [1706] Image of humans & angel adorning large globe. With 3 pp text with battle scenes. 42x26cm (16½x10") B&W. Some lt age toning. [A1] £166 **$275**
Bassora en de Land Schappen Tussen de Eufrat en Tiger S'Troom ... Persien ... Indiaanzee [early 18th c.] Appeared in *Cartes des Itineraires et Voiages Modernes*. South Asia, Indian Ocean, most of Africa & some Australia; engraved mock frame. 22x28cm (8½x11") Orig OL color. [34] **£460** $763
De Landschappen Tabasco en Iucatan tussen de Golf van Mexico en de Zuyd Zee Gelegen [1706] 15x23cm (6x9") B&W. Exc. ["Nieuw Spaanje ..." offered at same price] Ref: Kapp (Cent Amer) 27. [20] £148 **$245**
De Straat van Magellan ... [1706] 15x23cm (6x9") B&W. Exc. [20] £118 **$195**
De Vaste Kuste van Chicora tussen Florida en Virginie ... Hispaniola ... [1706] 15x23cm (6x9") B&W. Exc. Ref: Cumming (SE) 141. [20] £136 **$225**
L'Amerique Selon les Nouvelles Observations ... [1713] Insular Calif. 48x66cm (19x26") Fine. Ref: McLaughlin 184; Tooley (Amer) p.129, #71. [24] £2,111 **$3,500**
L'Asie ... [1729] 23x29cm (9x11½") Full color. [41] £151 **$250**
L'Inde de la le Gange ... [c.1710] 22x30cm (9x12") Exc. [45] £196 **$325**
[Same title] [1729] 22x30cm (8½x12") Full color. [41] £136 **$225**
Le Cap de Bonne Esperance [1713] False Bay to Saldanha Bay. 23x30cm (9x12") Color. Ref: Norwich 212. [34] **£350** $581
Le Compte d'Oxford [1714] From *Nouveau Petit Atlas*. Oxfordshire. Printed frame border. 23x40cm (9x15½") [11] £78 **$130**
Le Detroit de Malacca ... [1729] 25x16cm (10x6½") Col. Exc. Ref: Koeman Aa7 (140). [4] **£300** $498
Nicaragua en de Kusten der Zuyd-Zee Noordwaard von Panama ... [1706] 15x22cm (6x9") B&W. Exc. Ref: Kapp (Cent Amer) 30, pl.XI. [20] £166 **$275**
Nova Orbis Terraquei Tabula ... [in set with] **Africae in Praecipuas Ipsius Partes Distributa** ... [and] **America** ... [and] **Asia** ... [and] **Europa** ... [1713] *Le Nouveau Theatre du Monde*. Double hemi world; 2 show insular Calif. All about 50x66cm (19½x26") Color. World reinforced lower c'fold along platemark; continents fine. Ref: McLaughlin 184. Koeman Aa 6. [4] **£9,250** $15,338
Plan de la Ville et du Chateau de Batavia en l'Isle de Iava ... [(1669) 1729] Reissue of Montanus plate. 26x35cm (10x14") Color. Exc. [4] **£325** $539
Plan de Ville du Chateau de Batavia en l'Isle de Iava [1729] Reissue of 1669 Montanus plate. With view. 27x36cm (10½x14") Full color. Exc. [43] **£347 $575**
Reys Togt door Thomas Coryat, van Jerusalem ... Grooten Mogols [early 18th c.] Appeared in *Cartes des Itineraires et Voiages Modernes*. 22x29cm (8½x11") Uncolored. [34] **£260** $431
Reys-Togt van Aleppo, over Ormus, door Indien ... Pegu en Siam [early 18th c.] Appeared in *Cartes des Itineraires et Voiages Modernes*. 22x29cm (8½x11½") Orig OL col. Ref: Tibbetts 185. [34] **£360** $597
Robert Covertes ... **Opper Indien, Persien en Arabie** [early 18th c.] Appeared in *Cartes des Itineraires et Voiages Modernes*. 22x29cm (8½x11") Uncolored. Ref: Tibbetts 186. [34] **£280** $465

VAN DER AA continued

ROBERT COVERTES SWERF-REYSEN NO GELEDE SCHIPBREUK VAN CAMBAYA TE L AND DOOR OPPER ONDIEN, PERSIEN EN ARABIE TIT IN MOGOL GEDAAN [1729] Publ in *Galerie Agreable du Monde*. Picture frame border. 22x29cm (8½x11½") Orig OL color. Margin damp stain. [46] £250 $415

SCHEEPS-TOGT DOOR FERDINAND MAGELLAEN NIR KASTILIEN GEDAAN NA R. DE LA PLATA EN VAN DAAR ZYN ONTDEKTE STRAAT TOT AAN DE MOLUCCAS [1707] Probably from *Cartes des Itineraires et Voyages Moderne*. The Americas & Australia; insular Calif. 15x22cm (6x8½") Col. [13] Aus$1,180 £536 $888

T ZUIDER AMERICA VAN TERRA FIRMA OU GUJANA VOOR BY RIO DE LA PLATA, TOT AN DE STRAAT MAGELLEN EN KUSTEN TEGEN DE ZUID ZEE [1706] 20x30cm (8x12") Uncolored. VG. [25] £136 $225

TERRE SAINTE ... [1729] 23x29cm (9x11½") B&W. [20] £226 $375

VAN DER SCHLEY

PLATTE-GROND VAN AMBOINA, ZOO ALS HET WAS IN DEN JAARE 1718 [1748] Probably after Bellin. 41-item key. 27x28cm (10½x11") [11] £106 $175

VAN JAGEN

[WORLD] [c.1730] Bible map; double hemi; polar hemis; peninsular Calif; flora & fauna landscape background. 30x45cm (12x17½") Color. Good. [11] £754 $1,250

[WORLD] [c.1730] Highly decorative double hemi Dutch bible map after 1663 Visscher map. 29x44cm (11½x17½") Full color. Fine. Ref: cf Shirley (W) 431. [38] £1,809 $3,000

VAN KEULEN

A NEW GRADUALLY INCREASING COMPASS-MAP OF A PART OF THE SEA COASTS OF ENGLAND, IN WHICH IS CONTINUED THE COASTS OF SUSSEX. EXTENDING FROM EASTWARD OF HASTINGS TO ARUNDEL ... [1698] Show 17 coastal towns. 52x59cm (20½x23") Strong impression. [11] £302 $500

NIEUWE PLATTE PAS KAART VAN DE NORD OCCIAAN VAN HITLAND TOT IN DE STRAAT DAVIDS ... [c.1680] North Atlantic. Two sheets joined, 59x100cm (23x39½") Orig wash color. Archival tissue reinforcement of paper cracked by verdi gris. [46] £580 $962

NOORDLYK HALVROND [1798] Gerard Hulst van Keulen. Northern celestial hemi. Separately issued. 66x66cm (26x26") Narrow margins; lacks part of lf margin, sm text loss, no image loss. Ref: Koeman Keu 464. [48] DM 1,980 £684 $1,133

OOST INDIEN. WASSENDE-GRAADE PASKAART VERTOONENDE NEVENS HET OOSTELYCKSTE VAN AFRICA MEEDE DE ZEEKUSTEN VAN ASIA VAN C. DE BONA ESPERANCA TOT ESO. BOVEN JAPAN ... BIJ PIETER GOOS ... [1680] As in *De Groote Nieuwe Vermeerderde Zee-Atlas* .. Indian ocean lands with Australia as then known. 62x88cm (24½x34½") Color. Trimmed at top by binder. Framed. Ref: Perry pl.21; Schilder (Australia) pl.44. [13] Aus$16,800 £7,629 $12,650

PAS KAART VAN DE KUST VAN CAROLINA TUSSCHEN C DE CANAVERAL EN C HENRY ... [1682] Charleston area inset. 51x58cm (20½x23") Exc. Ref: Cumming (SE) 91. [2] £2,714 $4,500

[SAME TITLE] [1684] 51x58cm (20½x23") Full color. 4 sm wormholes patched; else exc. Ref: Cumming (SE) 91. [44] £2,292 $3,800

PAS-KAART VAN DE ZEE-KUSTEN VAN TERRA NOVA, MET DE BYLEGGENDE ZEE-KUSTEN VAN FRANCIA NOVA, CANADA EN ACCADIE ... [1695] From *Groote Nieuwe Vermeerdarde Zee Atlas*. With Grand Banks. 51x58cm (20x23") Sl rubbing & offsetting; o/w fine. Ref: Kershaw (Canada) 189, 3rd state. [21] Can$620 £271 $449

PAS KAART VAN DE ZEE KUSTEN VAN VIRGINIA TUSSCHEN C. HENRY EN T HOOGE LAND VAN RENSELAARS HOEK ... [1684] Based on Hermann; Chesapeake & Delaware Bays. 51x57cm (20½x22½") Uncolored. Fine. [32] £3,377 $5,600

PAS KAART VAN RIO ORONOQUE GOLFO DE PARIA MET D'EYLANDEN TRINIDAD, TABAGO, GRANADA, GRANADILLOS, EN BEQUIA [1683] Tobago inset. 51x58cm (20x23") B&W. Superior condition. Ref: MCC No.2. [20] £1,131 $1,875

PAS-KAART VANDE ZEE KUSTEN VAN NIEW NEDERLAND ANDERS GENAAMT NIEW YORK TUSSCHEN RENSELAARS HOEK EN DE STAATEN HOEK ... [1685] Hudson River detail. 51x56cm (20½x22") Color. Exc. Ref: Stokes (Manhattan) II, p158-9; Deak #68. [24] £4,393 $7,500

PASCAERT VAN'T EYLANDT CEYLON, VOORDEFEN TAPROBANA; BY DE INWOONDERS GENAEMT LANKAUN. BY JOANNES VAN KEULEN ... [1680] As in *Le Grand Nouvel Atlas de la Mer* ... 52x60cm (20½x23½") Period color. Minor repair; narrow margins. Ref: Koeman Keu 2, 29. [42] Aus$2,300 £1,045 $1,732

VAN KEULEN continued

PASCAERT VANDE ZUYD ZEE EN EEN GEDEELTE VAN BRASIL VAN ILHAS DE LADRONES TOT R. DE LA PLATA ... [1680] Insular Calif. 52x59cm (20½x23½") Color. Remargined sides & bottom just shaving lower neatline. Ref: McLaughlin 76. [45] £1,749 **$2,900**

SEPTEMTRIONALIORA AMERICAE A GROENLANDIA, PER FRETA DAVIDIS ET HUDSON AD TERRAM NOVAM [c.1710] 50x57cm (19½x22½") Wash & OL color. Several arsenic thinned portions stabilized. [A7] £451 **$747**

VAN LINSCHOTEN

AFRICAE [c.1594] East Africa coast with Madagascar. 40x56cm (15½x22") Margins probably trimmed. [A7] £381 **$632**

DELINEATIO OMNIUM ORARUM TOTIUS AUSTRALIS PARTIS AMERICAE, DICTAE PERUVIANAE, A R. DE LA PLATA, BRASILIAM, PARIAM, & CASTELLAM ... [(1596) c.1619] Publ in *Itinerario*. Also Dutch title. Arnold van Langren, sc. 39x56cm (15½x22") Color. Usual narrow margins; overall VF. [4] £2,700 **$4,477**

[SAME TITLE] [1599] 38x51cm (15x20½") Color. Lf margin extended, sl loss; close rt margin; else VG. Ref: Tooley (Landmarks) illus at p.216. [23] £2,352 **$3900**

DELINEATIO ORARUM MARITIMARUM, TERRAE VULGO INDIGETATAE TERRA DO NATAL, ITEM SOFALAE, MOZAMBICAE & MELINDAE ... [1596-99] From *Itinerario*. A.F. van Langren, sc. SE Africa & W Indian Ocean. 38x55cm (15x21½") B&W. Tiny hole filled; fine. Ref: Tooley (Africa) p.67; Tooley (Landmarks) ill. pp. 168-9. Norwich 239b. [31] £724 **$1,200**

EXACTA ET ACCURATA DELINEATIO CUM ORARUM MARITIMARUM TUM ETIAM LOCORUM TERRESTRIUM QUAE IN REGIONIBUS CHINA ... [(1596) 1619] From *Itinerario*. Arnold van Langren, sc. 39x52cm (15½x20½") Color. Sm repair lf ctr into image below Korea; o/w VF. Ref: Schilder (Australia) #18; Walter (Japan) #12. [4] £3,500 **$5,804**

GOAE INDIAE ORIENTALIS METROPOLIS & EMPORIJ [1599] Title repeated in German. 38x42cm (15x16½") [A6] £517 **$858**

I. S. LAURENTIJ [c.1596] Madagascar. 9x12cm (3½x5") [11] £45 **$75**

TYPUS ORARUM MARITIMARUM GUINEAE, MANICONGO & ANGOLAE ULTR PROMONTORIUM BONAE SPEI ... [IN SET WITH] DELINEATIO ORARUM MARITIMARUM, TERRAE VULGO INDIGETATAE TERRA DO NATAL, ITEM SOFALA MOZAMBICAE, & MELINDAE ... [1596-] Publ in *Itinerario*. West & east southern Africa. Each 38x53cm (15x21") Color. Fine. Ref: Norwich 239a & 239b. [4] £3,000 **$4,975**

VERA EFFIGIES ET DELINEATIO INSULAE SANCTAE HELENAE ... [1599] Baptista Doetechum, engr. 3 bird's eye approach views. 30x47cm (12x18½") B&W. Sm margins; few faint stains; else VG. [37] £121 **$200**

VAN LOON

IMPERII SINARUM NOVA DESCRIPTIO [1655] 46x51cm (18x20") Full orig color. Oxidized areas reinforced; few stains; good-VG. [23] £905 **$1,500**

ORBIS TERRARUM NOVA ET ACCURATISSIMA TABULA AUCTORE IOANNE A LOON [1666-1680] From Pitt's *English Atlas*. Double hemi; insular Calif; Charles II dedication. 44x53cm (17½x21") Color. Ref: Shirley (W) 439, pl.323. [13] **Aus$9,000** £4,087 **$6,777**

VAN MEURS

[TITLE PAGE] AMERICA [1673] Allegorical scene drawn from Montanus & Ogilby volumes. 30x20cm (11½x8") B&W. Extended margins; fine. [29] £271 **$450**

[TITLE PAGE] ASIA [1672] Allegorical scene. 29x18cm (11½x7") B&W. Fine. [29] £226 **$375**

AFRICAE ACCURATA TABULA ... [1671] 44x55cm (17½x22") OL color. Exc. [45] £513 **$850**

NOVA DELINEATIO TOTIUS ORBIS TERRARUM AUCTORE I. V. MEURS [c.1660] Double hemi; insular Calif. After Colom, reduced. 22x34cm (9x13½") Color. Fine. Ref: Shirley (W) 417. [4] £1,250 **$2,073**

VANCOUVER

COTE NORD-OUEST DE L'AMERIQUE RECONNUE PAR LE CAP.E VANCOUVER. 1E. PARTIE [1800] *A Voyage of Discovery* ... 1st French ed. Calif coast; insets: San Francisco; San Diego. 76x61cm (30x24") Repair in fold; else exc. [24] £724 **$1,200**

COTE NORD-OUEST DE L'AMERIQUE RECONNUE PAR LE CAPE. VANCOUVER. IV PARTIE [1801] From French ed, *A Voyage of Discovery* ... Tardieu the elder, engr. Incl Queen Charlotte Island; S Alaska. 27x22cm (10½x9") B&W. Fine. Ref: Howes V-23; Storm (Graff) 4654. [12] £112 **$185**

VANDERMAELEN

AMER. SEP. NO.41 PARTIE DES ETATS-UNIS [1827] Wisconsin & Minnesota. 47x49cm (18½x19½") Lt image transfer blank areas; some lt foxing; o/w fine. [A1] £265 **$440**

AMER. SEP. NO.42 HAUT CANADA ET MICHIGAN [1827] Shows Great Lakes 47x49cm (18½x19½") Lt image transfer; some lt foxing; o/w fine. [A1] £315 **$523**

AMER. SEP. NO.43 PARTIE DES ETATS-UNIS [1827] New England, MA northward, & upstate NY. 47x49cm (18½x19½") OL color. Lt image transfer blank areas; ½" lower margin tear; some lt foxing; o/w fine. [A1] £332 **$550**

AMER. SEP. NO.46 NOUVELLE CALIFORNIE [1827] From *Atlas Universelle*. Monterey to Oregon. Inset: Acapulco to Mexico City profile. 47x57cm (18½x22½") OL color. Some lt image transfer; some lt foxing; o/w fine. [A1] £189 **$314**

AMER. SEP. NO.47 PARTIE DU MEXIQUE [1827] From *Atlas Universelle* ... Present Utah, etc. 43x34cm (17x13½") with text 18½x22". Partial color. Fine. Ref: Wheat (TM) 378. Moffat 3. [12] £211 **$350**

AMER. SEP. NO.48 PARTIES DES ETATS-UNIS ET DU NOUVEAU MEXIQUE [1827] Parts of NM, CO and KS. 46x57cm (18½x22½") Later OL color. Minor repairs; part of border replaced; still VG. Ref: Wheat (TM) 378. [10] £302 **$500**

AMER. SEP. NO.54 PARTIE DU MEXIQUE [1827] Incl present NM & AZ. 47x49cm (18½x19½") Fine. [A1] £232 **$385**

AMER. SEP. NO.55 PARTIE DES ETATS UNIS [1827] North Texas. 46x49cm (18x19½") Orig color. Some faint image transfer; o/w fine. [A1] £299 **$495**

[SAME TITLE] [1827] North Texas. 46x51cm (18x20") Orig color. [27] £362 **$600**

AMER. SEP. NO.56 PARTIE DES ETATS UNIS [1827] From *Atlas Universelle*. Mississippi, Louisiana; part of Louisiana & Arkansas. 46x48cm (18x19") Lt OL color. Lt foxing & soil with c'fold. [7] £166 **$275**

AMER. SEP. NO.57 PARTIE DES ETATS UNIS [1827] Georgia, South Carolina, half of North Carolina. 46x49cm (18x19½") Margin tear repaired on verso; o/w fine. [A1] £199 **$330**

AMER. SEP. NO.62 FLORIDES ET ILES LUCAYES [1827] 47x49cm (18½x19½") OL color. Faint image transfer; o/w fine. [A1] £630 **$1,045**

AMER. SEP. NO.63 PARTIE DE LA VIELLE CALIFORNIE [1827] As in *Atlas Universelle* ... Colorado River mouth regions. 46x53cm (18½x21") Col, probably later. Some spotting one corner; else VG [10] £286 **$475**

AMER. SEP. NO.66 MERIDA [1827] From *Atlas Universelle* ... Yucatan. 46x53cm (18x21") Wide OL color. Lt mottling; o/w perfect. [12] £136 **$225**

AMER. SEP. NO.75 PETITES ANTILLES [1825] St. Croix to Grenada. 46x55cm (18½x22") Color. [18] £136 **$225**

ILES SANDWICH [1827] 48x55cm (19x21½") Orig color. Exc. [43] £332 **$550**

VAUGHAN

A NEW AND ACCURATE MAPPE OF THE WORLD ... [IN SET WITH] AFRICAE DESCRIPTIO [AND] AMERICAE DESCRIPTIO [AND] ASIA [AND] EUROPA [1628] World, with insular Calif, 14x25cm (5½x10"), continents about 15x20cm (6x7½") Uncolored. Lib stamp traces on verso; exc. Ref: Shirley (W) 326, pl.249. [4] £1,850 $3,068

VAUGONDY See *De Vaugondy*

VIELE

THE WEST END PLATEAU OF THE CITY OF NEW YORK [1879] Egbert L Viele; NY. Upper west side. With orig cloth; 25 pp text. 33x120cm (13x47") Full color. Some minor fold junction separations; fine. Ref: Haskell 1334. [15] £362 **$600**

TOPOGRAPHICAL MAP OF THE CITY OF NEW YORK SHOWING THE ORIGINAL WATER COURSES AND MADE LAND [1865] Printed by Ferd. Mayer, NY. Folding map with covers; 2 sheets joined. 44x154cm (17½x60½") Full orig color. Some splitting at folds; o/w good. Ref: Stokes (Manhattan) variant of 155-b. [32] £905 **$1,500**

VIRTUE

[ATLAS] A NEW COUNTRY ATLAS OF GREAT BRITAIN AND IRELAND CONTAINING SIXTY-EIGHT COLOURED MAPS [c.1871] 186 pp; printed color maps, 30x23cm (12x9") Covers & spine rubbed; contents tight, complete, fine (A). [A4] £164 **$272**

FORTRESS MONROE [VA] ... AND ITS VICINITY [1862] From Charles MacKays' *History of the United States* ... London. Bird's eye view; 20 item key. Hinshelwood, engr. 16x23cm (6x9") B&W. [12] £45 **$75**

VIRTUE continued

NEW ORLEANS...AND ITS VICINITY [1863] Bird's-eye view, with key. 12x19cm (5x7½") B&W. Fine. Ref: Hebert 241. [12] £51 **$85**

RICHMOND ... AND ITS VICINITY [1863] From Charles MacKays' *History of the United States ...* London. Bird's eye view; with key. Hinshelwood, engr. 13x19cm (5x7½") B&W. [12] £36 **$60**

VISSCHER

[ATLAS] **ATLAS MINOR, SIVE TOTUS ORBIS TERRARUM** [after 1680] Amsterdam: Folio, orig gold tooled calf, gilt edges; 64 maps in orig color, including 2 world & 5 American maps. Rebacked. Ref: Koeman Vis 24. [3] £57,294 **$95,000**

AFRICAE ACCURATA TABULA EX OFFICINA NIC. VISSCHER [1690] 43x54cm (17x21½") Full orig wash & OL color. Margins sl soiled. [11] £392 **$650**

ASIAE NOVA DELINEATIO [1690] 43x54cm (17x21½") Full orig wash & OL color. Sh c'fold split joined; lower margin sl soiled. [11] £347 **$575**

BRUXELLENSIS TETRARCHIA ... [c.1690] Brussels-Mechlin region. 58x46cm (22½x18½") Full orig wash & OL color. Lf margin sl soiled; few sh tears, image unaffected. [11] £196 **$325**

CARTE NOUVELLE CONTENANT LA PARTIE D'AMERIQUE LA PLUS SEPTENTRIONALE [c.1700] 60x48cm (24x19") Color. Margins just ample. [A7] £242 **$402**

CARTE PARTICULAIRE DU TERROIR ET DES ENVIRONS DES PARIS ... [c.1680] 57x48cm (22½x19") Full orig color. Little discoloration margins; c'fold splits; minor oxidation; else fine (B). [A3] £239 **$396**

COMITATUS FLANDRIA ... T'AMSTERDAM GEDRUCK BIJ CLAES JANSS VISSCHER ... 1652 [1652] Panels all around; engraved on 2 plates; lower frieze separately printed. 46x56cm (18x22") Color. A sm stain. [A6] £1,840 **$3,051**

DE BESCHRYVINGH VAN DE REYSEN PAULI, EN VAN DE ANDERE APOSTELEN ... [1738] From *Biblia dat Is de Gantsche H. Schrifture.* Eastern Mediterranean regions; religious scenes below. 32x47cm (12½x18½") Recent full color. Couple repaired margin tears; fine (A+). Ref: cf Laor 811. [A4] £150 **$248**

DE STOEL DES OORLOGS IN ITALIEN WAAR IN VERTOONT WERDEN DE STAAT VAN MILANO ... [c.1690] North Italy, on 2 joined sheets 59x74cm (23½x29") Orig OL color. [11] £452 **$750**

DUCATUS BRUNSUICENSIS FEREQUE LUNAEBURGENSIS CUM ADIACENTIBUS EPISCOPATIBUS, COMITATIBUS ET DOMINATIBUS ... [1650] By "Piscator". 42x54cm (16½x21") Color. Tear with small loss; 2 sm c'fold tears restored. Ref: Koeman Vis 21. [48] DM 550 £190 $315

EUROPA DELINEATA ET RECENS EDITA ... [1680] 43x54cm (17x21½") Contemp color. [A6] £184 **$305**

[SAME TITLE] [c.1680] 43x53cm (17x21") Orig color. VG. [24] £573 **$950**

[SAME TITLE] [1690+] From *Atlas Minor.* 43x54cm (17x21½") Full orig wash color. Lower margin sl soiled & reinforced. [11] £256 **$425**

EXACTISSIMA TOTIUS SCANDINAVIAE QUA TAM SUECIAE, DANIAE, ET NORVEGIAE REGNA ... [c.1680] 44x53cm (17½x21") Orig col, later additions. Mend lower margin; creasing; VG. [24] £528 **$875**

[SAME TITLE] [c.1690] Incl Finland, Baltics, NW Russia. Orig wash & OL color. Lower margin bit soiled & strengthened, image unaffected. 44x53cm (17½x21") ["Regnum Hungariae ...", "Cataloniae ... nec non Ruscinonensis et Cerretaniae...", "Regnorum Castellae Veteris..." & "Regiae Celsitudinis Sabaudicae Status" offered at same price] [11] £211 **$350**

FLANDRIA COMITATUS PARS MEDIA ... [c.1690+] Ghent, Ypres, Lille region. Orig wash & OL color. Lower edge & margin sl oil stained & supported on verso. 47x57cm (18½x22½") ["Artesia Comitatus ...", "Comitatus Hannoniae ...", "Flandriae ... Australis ..." & "Leodiensis Episcopatus Pars Media ..." offered at same price] [11] £90 **$150**

FLANDRIAE COMITATUS PARS ORIENTALIS ... [c.1690] Brussels, Antwerp, Ghent region in detail. Full orig wash & OL color. Lower edge & margin sl oil stained; supported on verso. 51x58cm (20x23") ["Flandria ... Septentrionalis ...", "Leodiensis ... Septentrionalis ...", "Lovaniensis Tetrarchia ..." & "Totius Alsatiae ..." offered at same price] [11] £112 **$185**

GALLIAE SEU FRANCIAE TABULA ... [c.1680] 46x56cm (18x22") Orig col. Lt toned; else exc. [24] £332 **$550**

[SAME TITLE] [c.1690+] 46x56cm (18x22") Orig wash & OL color by provinces. Sl soiling lower margin; o/w good. [11] £90 **$150**

GENERALIS LOTHARINGIAE DUCATUS TABULA ... [c.1690] 46x57cm (18x22½") Full orig wash & OL color. Lower margin sl torn & oil stains just affecting map; o/w good. ["Comitatus Namurci ..." & "... Campaniae ..." offered at same price] [11] £106 **$175**

HIBERNIAE REGNUM TAM IN PRAECIPUAS ULTONIAE, CONNACIAE, LAGENIAE, ET MOMONIAE ... [c.1680] 56x48cm (22x19") Color. C'fold reinforced. [46] £520 **$863**

VISSCHER continued

HIBERNIAE REGNUM TAM IN PRAECIPUAS ULTONIAE, CONNACIAE, LAGENIAE, ET MOMONIAE ... [c.1695] 57x46cm (22½x18½") Old color, modern enhancements. Scattered pinholes repaired; c'fold strengthened; else VG. [38] £392 **$650**

INDIAE ORIENTALIS NEC NON INSULARUM ADIACENTIUM NOVA DESCRIPTIO, PER NICOLAUM VISSCHER ... [1670] 46x56cm (18x22") Color. Ref: Koeman, Visscher 183. [42] **Aus$2,500** £1,135 **$1,882**

INSULA CEILON OLIM TAPROBANA INCOLIS TENARISIN ET LANKAWN EXACTISSIME DELINEATA ... [c.1680] Sri Lanka; west oriented. 50x59cm (19½x23") Orig body color. Verdigris weakened paper reinforced with tissue on verso; no apparent damage. [46] **£450** **$746**

INSULAE AMERICANAE IN OCEANO SEPTENTRIONALI AE REGIONES ADIACENTES, A C. DE MAY USQUE AD LINEAM AEQUINOCTIALEM [1680 or later] West Indies & continents from Cape May to equator. 46x56cm (18x22") Orig wash & OL color. Ref: Portinaro & Knirsch 82. [11] £754 **$1,250**

[SAME TITLE] [c.1680] 46x56cm (18½x22") Full orig color. Lt toned; else exc. [24] £1,327 **$2,200**

JAMAICA, AMERICAE SEPTENTRIONALIS AMPLA INSULA, CHRISTOPHORO COLUMBO DETECTA, IN SUAS GUBERNATIONES PERACCURATAE DISTINCTA [1680] 51x60cm (20x23½") Full color. Ref: Kapp (Jamaica) 26. [20] £769 **$1,275**

[SAME TITLE] [c.1680] 51x59cm (20x23½") Full orig col. Few reinforcements; else exc. [24] £452 **$750**

LUXEMBURGENSIS DUCATUS, TAM IN EJUSDEM MINORES, QUAM PRINCIPALES DITIONES PERACCURATE DISTINCTUS [1690+] 2 sheets joined, 71x58cm (28x23") Full orig wash & OL color. ["Tetrarchiae Antverpiensis Pars Meridionalis ..." offered at same price] [11] £151 **$250**

MAGNAE BRITANNIAE TABULA ... [1694+] 46x55cm (18x22") Orig wash & OL col. Sl soiled. [11] £302 **$500**

MAGNAE PRUSSIAE DUCATUS TABULA [1690+] East Prussia & adjacent. 44x53cm (17x21") Full orig color. [11] £106 **$175**

MOSCOVIAE SEU RUSSIAE MAGNAE ... [c.1680] 41x52cm (16x20½") Orig color. Few margin stains; else exc. [24] £452 **$750**

MOSCOVIAE SEU RUSSIAE MAGNAE GENERALIS TABULA ... [1695+] Much of Europe; Denmark to Caspian Sea. 41x52cm (16½x20½") Orig wash & OL color. [11] £106 **$175**

NOVA HAEC TABULA GALLIAE ... [1660] Carte-a-figures on 4 sides. 46x55cm (18x21½") Uncolored. Sm verso repair upper ctr; close margins as issued; dark impression. Ref: MCC 46, #35, pl.13. [4] £1,750 **$2,902**

NOVA TABULA GEOGRAPHICA COMPLECTENS BOREALIOREM AMERICAE PARTEM: IN QUA EXACTE DELINEATAE SUNT CANADA SIVE NOVA FRANCIA, NOVA SCOTIA, NOVA ANGLIA, NOVUM BELGIUM, PENSYLVANIA, VIRGINIA, CAROLINA ET TERRA NOVA, ... [c.1690-1720] Maine to SC. 2 sheets joined. 60x88cm (23½x34½") OL color. Minor offsetting; o/w VF. [A7] £1,526 **$2,530**

[SAME TITLE] [c.1700-10] 58x47cm (23x18½") Orig OL col. Exc. Ref: Morrison fig.28. [24] £1,689 **$2,800**

NOVA TOTIUS TERRARUM ORBIS GEOGRAPHICA AC HYDROGRAPHICA TABULA [1639 (1652)] Carte a figure; panels all around. [no dimens] Contemporary color. Sh c'fold split repaired; overall near fine. Ref: Shirley (W) 350, pl.267. [38] £9,951 **$16,500**

NOVI BELGII NOVAEQUE ANGLIAE NEC NON PARTIS VIRGINIAE TABULA MULTIS IN LOCIS EMENDATA [1655 (c.1659)] 4th state of five. With view of "Nieuw Amsterdam". 47x55cm (18½x21½") Orig color. Good Ref: Burden 315; Tooley (Amer) p.285. [32] £4,222 **$7,000**

[SAME TITLE] [c.1684] With view of New York. 46x55cm (18½x22") Color. Occas lt browning & foxing; o/w VG to fine. Ref: Burden 315; Suarez 50, color illus. [A1] £2,819 **$4,675**

NOVISSIMA ET ACCURATISSIMA TOTIUS AMERICAE DESCRIPTIO PER N. VISSCHER [c.1658] Insular Calif. 43x54cm (17x21½") Contemporary color, possibly refreshed. Repaired c'fold split; else fine. Ref: Burden 332; McLaughlin 48; Tooley (Amer) p.119, #29, pl.41. [38] £1,447 **$2,400**

[SAME TITLE] ... [1670] Insular California. 43x54cm (17x21½") Full orig wash & OL color. Faint oil stain sea area. Ref: Van Ermen 19. [11] £1,176 **$1,950**

[SAME TITLE] [c.1670] 1st issue. Insular California. 43x54cm (17x21½") Orig OL color. Mounted on linen. Few minor margin tears, some into image, sl loss; lt surface soiling. [A2] £1,260 **$2,090**

ORBIS TERRARUM NOVA ET ACCURATISSIMA TABULA [1658+] Double hemi; sm polar hemis; insular Calif; elaborate decor. 47x56cm (18½x22") Orig color, partial additions. Heavy paper; lower margin supported on verso; o/w good. Ref: Shirley (W) 406. [11] £2,865 **$4,750**

ORBIS TERRARUM NOVA ET ACCURATISSIMA TABULA ... [IN SET WITH] AFRICAE ACCURATA TABULAE [AND] ASIAE NOVA DELINEATIO [AND] EUROPA DELINEATA ET RECENS [AND] NOVISSIMA ET ACCURATISSIMA TOTIUS AMERICAE [c.1670] 5 maps: double hemi world; insular Calif on both world & America. All about 46x55cm (18x21½") Color. High quality condition. Ref: Shirley (W) 406, pl.302; McLaughlin 48; Tooley (Amer) p.119, #29, pl.41. [24] £11,459 **$19,000**

VISSCHER continued

ORBIS TERRARUM TABULA RECENS EMENDATA ET IN LUCEM EDITA PER N. VISSCHER [1663, dated 1677] Double-hemi; found in Dutch Bibles; 2nd derivative with Tasman's voyage to New Zealand. 30x47cm (12x18½") Orig color. Ref: Shirley (W) 431; pl.318. [13] **Aus$5,200** £2,361 **$3,915**

ORBIS TERRARUM TYPUS DE INTEGRO IN PLURIMUS EMENDATUS, AUCTUS ET ICUNCULIS ILLUSTRATUS [1657] 1st Visscher bible map; peninsular Calif. pre- & post-Copernican planetary diagrams. 31x47cm (12x18½") Full color. Ref: Shirley (W) 401. [11] £1,659 **$2,750**

[SAME TITLE] [c.1665] Double hemi; peninsular Calif. Unrecorded variant. 36x47cm (14x18½") Color. Ref: cf Shirley (W) 401 & 414. [13] **Aus$7,400** £3,361 **$5,572**

PORTUGALLIAE ET ALGARBIAE REGNA ... [c.1680] 46x55cm (18x22") Full orig color. Lower c'fold reinforced; else exc. [24] £452 **$750**

[SAME TITLE] [c.1690] 46x56cm (18x22") Orig wash & OL color. [11] £226 **$375**

[SAME TITLE] [c.1698] 47x58cm (18½x22½") OL color. 4 sm arsenic holes closed on verso, no visible loss. [A7] £242 **$402**

REGNI DANIAE NOVISSIMA ET ACCURATISSIMA TABULA [c.1690] Incl S Sweden, N Germany. 45x54cm (17½x21½") Orig wash & OL col. ["Hispaniae et Portugalliae Regna" offered at same price] [11] £151 **$250**

REGNUM BOHEMIAE ET QUE ANNEXAE PROVINCIAE ... [1690+] 50x59cm (19½x23") C'fold split joined; lower margin bit soiled & supported on verso. [11] £136 **$225**

S.R.I. BAVARIAE CIRCULUS ATQ. ELECTORATUS ... [c.1690] Full orig wash & OL color. 57x46cm (22½x18") ["... Coloniense Electoratu ...", "... Electoratus Treverensis ...", "... Tabula Sedis Belli Palatinatus ad Rhenum ..." & "... Danubii Fluvii Pars Superior" offered at same price] [11] £166 **$275**

TABULA ELECTORATUS BRANDENBURGICI, MECKELENBURGI, ... POMERANIAE [1630-33] 1st ed of 2nd state. 45x54cm (17½x21½") Uncolored. [34] £460 **$763**

TABULA FRISIAE, GRONINGAE, ET TERRITORIEMDENSIS [c.1690] 110x138cm (43x54½") Full orig color. Two 2cm tears joined; lower margin support. ["Nieuwe Kaart, van t'Land Donawert, en Hochstett &c." offered at same price] [11] £151 **$250**

TABULA NOVA COMPLECTENS PRAEFECTURAS NORMANNIAE ET BRITANNIAE, UNA CUM ANGLIAE ... [1690+] English Channel & adjacent. 47x56cm (18½x22") Orig wash & OL color by counties & provinces. [11] £106 **$175**

TERRA SANCTA, SIVE PROMISSIONIS, OLIM PALESTINA RECENS DELINEATA, ET IN LUCEM EDITA PER NICOLAUM VISSCHER ANNO 1659 [1659] 47x56cm (18½x22") Color. Early MS notation top margin. Ref: Laor 793. [A8] £971 **$1,610**

TOTIUS ITALIAE TABULA [c.1690] Incl Sicily, Sardinia, Corsica. 46x56cm (18x22") Orig wash & OL color. Sl soiling lower margin. [11] £196 **$325**

VIVIEN

CARTE GENERALE DES ETATS UNIS DE L'AMERIQUE SEPTENTRIONALE [1834] Unusual western configurations. 31x41cm (12x16") Old OL color. Strong impression on heavy paper; VG. [38] £136 **$225**

CARTE GENERALE DU MEXIQUE ET DES PROVINCES-UNIES DE L'AMERIQUE CENTRALE OU GUATEMALA [1826] From *Atlas Universel* Incl Southwest & CA. 30x39cm (12x15½") on heavy paper, 16x23". OL color. Pristine. Ref: Phillips (A) 4315-34. [12] £166 **$275**

VON EULER

MAPPA GEOGRAPHICA AMERICAE SEPTENTRIONALIS ... [c.1755] 36x38cm (14x15") Full & OL color. Lt toned. [A8] £381 **$632**

TABULA GEOGRAPHICA HEMISPHAERII AUSTRALIS ... [c.1750] 31x32cm (12x12½") Orig color. [34] £350 **$581**

VON HUMBOLDT

CARTE REDUITE DE LA PARTIE ORIENTALE DE LA NOUVELLE-ESPAGNE DEPUIS LE PLATEAU DE LA VILLE DE MEXICO JUSQU'AU PORT DE LA VERACRUZ [1807] Berlin. 22x62cm (8½x24½") [11] £211 **$350**

VON LEONARD

[ATLAS] GEOLOGISCHER ATLAS ZUR NATURGESCHICHTE DER ERDE [1841] Stuttgart. Oblong 4to; blue marbled paper boards; 26 map pp; Mont Blanc, Aetna, Vesuvius, glaciers, volcanic islands. Color. Board surface & edges rubbed; sl fraying cloth spine some foxing on maps. [A1] £265 **$440**

VON REILLY

[SPAIN: CUENCA] [1799] Province in 4 sheets, each 22x25cm (8½x10") Old color. [48] **DM 150** £52 **$86**

DAS FURSTENTHUM EISENACH [1796] 23x29cm (9x11½") Old color. [48] **DM 240** £83 **$137**

VON REILLY continued

DAS HERZOGTHUM NEUBURG [1792] 19x35cm (7½x14") Old color. [48] **DM 300** £104 $172
DAS HOCHSTIFT SPEYER MIT DER FREYEN REICHSSTADT SPEYER [1793] 22x26cm (9x10½") Old color. [48] **DM 490** £169 $280
DAS HOCHSTIFT WORMS MIT DER FREYEN REICHSSTADT WORMS [1793] 20x28cm (8x11") Old color. [48] **DM 290** £100 $166
DER STAATEN DES LANDGRAFEN ZU HESSEN DARMSTADT NOERDLICHE AEMTER UNTER DER REGIERUNG VON GIESSEN MIT DEN HERRSCHAFTEN NIDDA UND ITTER [1793] 28x31cm (11x12") Old color. ["Die Grafschaft Waldeck" offered at same price] [48] **DM 490** £169 $280
DES KANTONS ZURCH SUDLICHER THEIL [1796] 24x31cm (9½x12") Old color. [48] **DM 880** £304 $504
DES KONIGREICHS SCHWEDEN NORDLICHE PROVINZEN [1789] 22x27cm (8½x10½") Old color. [48] **DM 320** £110 $183
DIE ENGLISCHE KUSTE DEM NORDLICHEN FRANKREICH GEGENUBER [1799] English Channel. 21x32cm (8½x12½") Old color. [48] **DM 80** £28 $46
DIE FURSTENTHUMER GRUBENHAGEN UND BLANKENBURG MIT DER FREYEN REICHSSTADT NORDHAUSEN [1795] 22x29cm (9x11½") Old color. [48] **DM 380** £131 $217
DIE INSEL VIST [1799] Hebrides. 32x20cm (12½x8") Old color. [48] **DM 180** £62 $103
DIE LANDSCHAFT HOLLSTEIN [1795] 22x32cm (9x12½") Old color. [48] **DM 200** £69 $114
DIE SCHWEIZ ODER DIE EIDGENOSSENSCHAFT SAMT DEN DERSELBEN ZUGEWANDTEN ORTEN [1796] 24x28cm (9½x11") Old color. [48] **DM 420** £145 $240
KARTE VON AMERIKA NACH D'ANVILLE UND POWNALL ... [1795] Vienna. Insets: USA; Alaska; Arctic. 62x79cm (24½x31") OL col. Minor dampstaining margins; lt soiling; sh tear lf margin. [A7] £277 **$460**
KARTE VON DER ISELWELT, POLYNESIEN ODER DER FUNFTEN WELTTHEILE NACH DJURBERG UND ROBERTS ... [1795] As in *Deutscher Atlas*. Incl SE Asia, Australia as "Ulimaroa", & New Zealand. 46x64cm (18x25") Color. Ref: Tooley (Australia) 997, pl.146. [13] **Aus$2,600** £1,181 $1,958
OBER KAERNTEN MIT DEN SALZBURGISCHEN ANTHEILEN [1791] 22x31cm (8½x12") Old color. [48] **DM 240** £83 $137

VRIENTS   Try *Ortelius*

ANGLIAE ET HIBERNIAE [c.1606] Basically an Ortelius map with sl changes. 44x58cm (17½x22½") Color. Sl toned overall. [A7] £1,179 **$1,955**

VUILLEMIN

[ATLAS] ATLAS UNIVERSEL [1848] Oblong quarto; complete with 50 maps, all but two in OL color. Disbound; scattered foxing & soiling. [A8] £121 **$201**
NOUVELLE CARTE ILLUSTREE DE L'AMERIQUE DU NORD ... [1860] 16 pictorial side-panels. 60x84cm (23½x33½") Orig OL color. [11] £377 **$625**

WAESBERGER

DE GROOTE ENDE KLEYNE EYLANDEN VAN WEST-INDIEN [1676] From enlarged ed of Mercator Minor Atlas. 18x25cm (7½x10") Full color. [39] £211 **$350**

WAGHENAER

[FACSIMILE ATLAS] SPIEGHEL DER ZEEVAERDT [1964] Folio, 2 volumes in one, quarter morocco; color facsimile of 1584-85 Univ of Utrecht copy. [A8] £156 **$258**
BESCHRIJIUNGHE VANDE ZEE CUSTEN VAN ENGELANDT TUSSCHEN BLACQNEY EN SCHARENBURCH ALSOE DAT LANDT IN ZYN WESEN EN GEDAENTE. ORAE MARITIMAE ANGLIAE INTER BLACGUEYAM ET SCARENBURGUM EXASTISSIMA DESCRIPTIO [c.1586-88] From *Spieghel der Zeevaerdt*. Joannes a Doeticum, sc. Blackney to Scarborough. 32x50cm (13x20") Ref: Koeman IV, p.474 (3rd state). [47] **£780** $1,294
THE OUTTERMOST OR THE FARTHESTE PARTE OF THE EASTERNE SEA. EASTWARDLY, THE WHICH LYETH INCLOSED WITH IN THE COASTES IF EAST FINLAND, RUSLAND, Y LYFFLAND [1588] From Anthony Ashley's English translation of "Mariners Mirrour". 33x51cm (13x20") Color. Sl stain at lower fold. Framed. [A6] **£437** $725
THE SEA COASTS BETWEENE DOVER & ORFORDNES: WHEREIN IS CONTEINED THE MOST FAMOUS RIVER OF THAMES ... [1588] From *The Mariners Mirrour*. 32x50cm (12½x19½") Color. [11] £814 **$1,350**

WALCH

AUSTRALIEN (SUDLAND) AUCH POLYNESIEN ODER INSELWELT ... [1830] Incl East Indies & most all Pacific islands. 48x62cm (19x24½") Full orig wash & OL col. Ref: cf Tooley (Australia) 1309-12. [11] £452 **$750**

WALCH continued

CHARTE VON NORDAMERICA ... [1816] State of Franklin located. 57x49cm (22x19") Orig OL color.
[34] **£460** **$763**

DER ERDE SUDL. [c.1822] South polar area; islands, no continent. 18x23cm (7x9") OL color. Some edge soiling. [26] **£48** **$80**

MAPPA TOTIUS MUNDI [c.1800] Augsburg. Double hemi after De L'Isle, adapted by Lotter; Johann Will, engr. 46x64cm (18x25") OL color. Few soft creases; early ink notes near Australia. [A7] **£555** **$920**

VEREINEGTE STAATEN VON NORD AMERICA [c.1822] Publ Augsburg. West to Oregon. 18x23cm (7x9") Substantial color. Some edge soiling. [26] **£48** **$80**

WALDSEEMULLER

[BRITISH ISLES: PTOLEMAIC] [1535] Lyons: Treschel. Redrawn & reduced version. 30x41cm (11½x16") Margin damage restored; sl affect to verso decoration. Ref: Shirley (BI to 1650) 24. [46] **£780** **$1,294**

DECIMA ASIAE TABULA [1513-1520] Strasbourg: Joannes Schott. Ptolemaic India. 35x52cm (14x20½") Fine. [46] **£780** **$1,294**

DUODECIMA ASIAE TABULA [1513] Ptolemaic Taprobana. 29x25cm (11½x10") Exc. [45] **£513** **$850**

TABU. MODER. ANGLIE & HIBER. [1535] Lyons: Treschel. Redrawn & reduced version. 30x41cm (11½x16") Ref: Shirley (BI to 1650) 25. [46] **£950** **$1,576**

TABULA NOVA ANGLIAE & HIBERNIAE [1541] Vienne. Primitive British Isles. 28x41cm (11x16") Lt browning at fold. Ref: Shirley (BI to 1650) 31. [A6] **£598** **$992**

TABULA NOVA HIBERNIE ANGLIE ET SCOTIE [1513] 38x52cm (15x20½") Ref: Shirley (BI to 1650) 11, pl.8.
[47] **£2,500** **$4,146**

WALKER, H.B.

ARIZONA [1895] From *International Atlas*. Basically a Cram map. 11 counties. 53x41cm (21x16") Hand color. Fine, bright. [12] **£54** **$90**

COLORADO [c.1895] From *International Atlas*. Basically a Cram map. 55 counties. 41x56cm (16x22") Full hand color. Immaculate. [12] **£60** **$100**

MAP OF OKLAHOMA AND INDIAN TERS. [c.1895] From *International Atlas*. Cram licensee. Guthrie capital; population table verso. 41x56cm (16x22") Full hand coloring. Perfect. [12] **£66** **$110**

TEXAS [1895] From *International Atlas*. Basically a hand colored Cram map. 242 counties, incl Greer Co. OK; Panhandle inset. 41x56cm (16x22") [12] **£96** **$160**

WALL

RAILROAD MAP OF PENNSYLVANIA PUBLISHED BY THE DEPARTMENT OF INTERNAL AFFAIRS OF PENNSYLVANIA [1890] Folding map in pocket of orig cloth folder. Litho OL color by county by J. Bien. 76x136cm (30x53½") Unbacked; superb. [15] **£136** **$225**

WALLING

[ATLAS] ATLAS OF THE STATE OF MICHIGAN [1873] Detroit: R.M. & S.T. Tackabury. Folio, half leather & cloth; 84 colored maps, some double page, incl US; Spine worn chipped; tips & front hinge tape repaired; lt narrow dampstains top margin throughout, images unaffected; Some sl toning, soiling, foxing; a map with 4" tear. Ref: LeGear (US) 1754. [A10] **£31** **$52**

MAP OF HAMPDEN COUNTY, MASSACHUSETTS [1855] Phila. Linen-backed wall map with orig rollers; 19 insets. Full color by town. 110x168cm (43½x66") Sl staining near top; exc. [15] **£513** **$850**

MAP OF MERRIMACK COUNTY, NEW HAMPSHIRE [1858] Wall map; 45 insets, 14 views; business directory. Full color by town; borders highlighted. 147x155cm (58x61") Sm hole top border; VF Ref: Cobb (NH) 248; Phillips (M) p.404. [15] **£362** **$600**

MAP OF MIDDLESEX COUNTY, CONNECTICUT [1859] Wall map. Color by town. 152x148cm (60x58½") Damage near top; some tears repaired, a large tear; loss at border top lf; below top 6" exc. Ref: Thompson (CT) 183. [15] **£377** **$625**

MAP OF MIDDLESEX COUNTY, MASSACHUSETTS [1856] Wall map; 70 inset maps, 7 bldg views. Full color by town. 157x157cm (62x62") Sh tear into map at top; minor staining lower rt; exc. Ref: Phillips (M) p.429.
[15] **£573** **$950**

MAP OF OXFORD COUNTY, MAINE [1858] Wall map; 51 town insets. 152x152cm (60x60") Full color. Minor soiling near top; VG. Ref: Phillips (M) p.647. [15] **£482** **$800**

MAP OF THE STATE OF MAINE [1861] 1st ed. Wall map, linen-backed & varnished; 30 insets. Full color by town. 160x154cm (63x60½") Minor tears repaired; fine. Ref: cf Phillips (M) p.385. [15] **£603** **$1,000**

WALLING continued

MAP OF THE STATE OF MAINE   [1861]   Portland: J. Chace.   Rolled wall map; mounts top & bottom. 160x160cm (63x63"). Color. Sm hole in image; sl yellow from shellac.   [A8]   £260   **$431**

TOPOGRAPHICAL MAP OF ESSEX COUNTY, MASSACHUSETTS   [1856]   Wall map; 44 inset maps & views. Full color by town. 152x152cm (60x60")   Wear, chipping, minor loss; fraying at top; mostly good.   Ref: Phillips (M) p.275.   [15]   £362   **$600**

WALLING & GRAY

[ATLAS]   NEW TOPOGRAPHICAL ATLAS OF THE STATE OF PENNSYLVANIA ...   [1872]   Phila: Stedman, Brown & Lyon.   Folio, cloth; colored maps incl US, RR & 4 thematic state maps, 18 of counties, 11 cities. Covers worn, leather spine rubbed & chipped; maps fine.   Ref: LeGear (US) 2995.   [A2]   £212   **$352**

[SAME TITLE]   [1872]   Phila: Stedman, Brown & Lyon.   Folio; 35 maps & city plans.   Orig gold stamped boards respined; exc.   Ref: Phillips (A) 2453; LeGear (US) 2995.   [3]   £271   **$450**

[ATLAS]   OFFICIAL TOPOGRAPHICAL ATLAS OF MASSACHUSETTS   [1871]   Folio, publisher's half morocco; profusion of colored maps of counties, etc. [Editor: there is a version with cities beside Boston and a version without]   Extremities rubbed; scattered browning & soiling.   Ref: LeGear (US) 1551.   [A8]   £191   **$316**

MAP OF THE COMPACT PORTIONS OF PHILADELPHIA AND CAMDEN   [1872]   From *New Topographical Atlas ... of Pennsylvania*. 41x61cm (16x24")   Full color.   Ref: Phillips (A) 2453.   [12]   £75   **$125**

[SAME TITLE]   [dated 1872]   From same source. 41x61cm (16x24")   Full color.   [22]   £30   **$50**

RAILWAY & TOWNSHIP MAP OF MASSACHUSETTS   [1871]   From *Atlas of Massachusetts*. 60 RRs named; every station shown. 37x61cm (14½x24")   Color.   [22]   £33   **$55**

WALTON

A NEW AND ACCURAT MAP OF THE WORLD DRAWNE ACCORDING TO YE TRUEST DESCRIPTIONS LATEST DISCOVERIES & BEST OBSERVATIONS TY HAVE BEENE MADE BY ENGLISH OR STRANGERS   [1656]   2nd issue. Often mistaken for Speed 1627, plate size differs. 39x52cm (15½x20½")   Later color. A tear repaired; good.   Ref: Shirley (W) 397, pl.297.   [2]   £5,729   **$9,500**

A NEW, PLAINE & EXACT MAP OF EUROPE ...   [1668]   Panels all around. 43x53cm (17x21")   Color. 2 mended tears; else exc.   [23]   £2,111   **$3,500**

WARBURTON

[ENGLAND: YORKSHIRE]   [1720]   4 sheets; lacks separate sheet with title, etc.; together, 99x127cm (39x50")   Uncolored.   Ref: Rawnsley, chap.19.   [34]   £1,200   **$1,990**

WARE

A MAP OF THE SACRED GEOGRAPHY TAKEN FROM THE OLD AND NEW TESTAMENT CONTAINING MOST OF YE THEN KNOWN PARTS OF THE WORLD ...   [1725]   From *Sacred Geography Contained in Six Maps*. 36x43cm (14x17")   Heavy crease along lower c'fold; couple minor spots.   Ref: Laor 821.   [21]   **Can$120**   £52   **$87**

A MAP SHEWING THE MOST REMARKABLE PLACES TO WHICH THE APOSTLES TRAVEL'D TO PREACH THE GOSPEL AND ALSO ST. PAUL'S VOYAGE TO ROME ...   [1725]   From *Sacred Geography Contained in Six Maps*. 35x40cm (13½x15½")   Creased lower lf; c'fold wear.   ["A Map of the Holy Land Divided into the XII Tribes ..." offered at same price]   Ref: Laor 824.   [21]   **Can$90**   £39   **$65**

A MAP SHEWING YE SITUATION OF PARADICE AND YE COUNTRY INHABITED BY YE PATRIARCHS   [1725] From *Sacred Geography Contained in Six Maps*. After Mortier's version 36x43cm (14x17")   Creasing long lower c'fold; couple minor spots.   Ref: Laor 822.   [21]   **Can$130**   £57   **$94**

THE LAND OF CANAAN TRAVEL'D OVER BY O:S: JESUS CHRIST AND BY HIS APOSTLES   [1725]   From *Sacred Geography Contained in Six Maps*.   After Visscher rendition. 36x43cm (14x17")   Creasing long lower c'fold; o/w VG.   Ref: Laor 825.   [21]   **Can$130**   £57   **$94**

WARNER & BEERS

MAP OF KANSAS, ARIZONA, COLORADO, NEW MEXICO, UTAH, INDIAN TERRITORY   [c.1874]   Issued with state atlases. 43x61cm (17x24")   Full col. Edge discoloration creeping toward border corner.   [26]   £84   **$140**

MAP OF NEVADA AND CALIFORNIA   [c.1874]   Issued with state atlases. 43x36cm (17x14")   Full color by counties. Edge discoloration creeping toward border corner.   [26]   £48   **$80**

MAP OF THE TERRITORIES OF MONTANA, IDAHO AND WYOMING   [1872]   43x36cm (17x14")   Color. VG.   [26]   £54   **$90**

MAP OF THE TERRITORY OF DAKOTA AND THE STATES OF MINNESOTA AND NEBRASKA   [c.1874]   Issued with state atlases. 43x36cm (17x14")   Full color. Edge discoloration creeping toward border corner.   [26]   £48   **$80**

TEXAS   [1876]   Counties dated 30x42cm (12x16½")   Full color. VG.   [16]   £106   **$175**

WATSON
RAILWAY MAP OF THE MIDDLE AND WESTERN STATES ... [c.1868] Gaylord Watson, NY. Extent: NJ to UT. 29x51cm (11½x20½") Full color. [39] £84 **$140**

WEEKLY DISPATCH
[ATLAS] THE DISPATCH ATLAS [1863] Folio, modern cloth; 245 litho mapsheets incl town plans, some double-page, most in OL color. Few sm tears, some margin fraying & soiling. [A6] £805 $1,335
CALIFORNIA, UTAH, LR. CALIFORNIA AND NEW MEXICO [c.1860] From *Weekly Dispatch Atlas*. Theodor Ettling. 43x30cm (17x11½") OL color. Clipping from atlas pasted verso; MS ink title in top margin; else clean; VG (A). Ref: Wheat (TM) 942. [A4] £100 **$165**
MADRAS &C. [1858] India, from Goa southward. Color indicates governing status. 42x30cm (16½x12") OL color. [40] £18 **$30**
MAP OF THE GREAT SALT LAKE AND ADJACENT COUNTRY IN THE TERRITORY OF UTAH [ON SHEET WITH] THE GREAT SALT LAKE (MORMON) CITY AND SURROUNDING COUNTRY [c.1860] By E. Weller. Overall 43x30cm (17x12") OL color. MS ink title verso; couple sh tears & folds repaired with archival tape verso; good (B). [A3] £113 **$188**
UNITED STATES OF NORTH AMERICA, SOUTHWEST SHEET [JOINED WITH] SOUTH CENTRAL SHEET [1859] AL to NM. 43x61cm (17x24") Broad OL color. [39] £72 **$120**

WEIGEL
[PORTRAIT] CHRISTOPHORUS WEIGELIUS CHALCOGRAPHICUS CELEBERRIMUS NORINBERGAE NATUS ANNO MDCLIIII [1714] Head & shoulders mezzotint by Johann Kupezki; Bernard Vogel, sc. 49x34cm (19½x13½") Uncolored. Exc. [4] £360 $597
NOVI ORBIS SIVE TOTIUS AMERICAE CUM ADIACENTIBUS INSULIS NOVA EXHIBITIO [1725] Insular Calif. 27x34cm (11x13½") Orig color. Exc. Ref: McLaughlin 204. [43] £452 **$750**
UKRANIA SEU COSACORUM REGIO WALACHIA ITEM MOLDAVIA ET TARTARIA [c.1720] 33x39cm (13x15½") Orig color. [34] £300 $498

WEILAND
DIE SUDSPITZE VON AFRICA MIT DER COLONIE VOM VORGEBIRGE DER GUTEN HOFFNUNG ... [1827] Highly detailed. 50x43cm (19½x17") Orig OL color. [46] £230 $382
NORD AMERICA [1820] Fanciful US western borders. 58x54cm (23x21") Orig color. VG to fine. [A2] £564 **$935**

WEIMAR GEOGRAPHISCHES INSTITUT
CHARTE VON DEN INSELN TRINIDAD, TABAGO UND MARGARETHA ... [1814] With paste-on color key. 23x41cm (9x16") Orig OL color. [34] £220 $365
DIE VEREINIGTEN STAATEN VON NORD-AMERICA ... [1837] By C.F. Weiland. 48x63cm (19x24½") Orig OL & border color. Lt toned; VG. [24] £392 **$650**

WELD
AN EYE SKETCH OF THE FALLS OF NIAGARA [1798] From *Travels through ... North America ...* London: Stockdale. 17x23cm (6½x9") B&W. Fine. Ref: Howes (US) W-235. [29] £57 **$95**

WELLER
THE ENVIRONS OF DUBLIN [1862] London: Cassell, Peter & Galpin. Some buildings shown. 43x30cm (17x12") OL col. VG. ["The Environs of Cork" & "The Lakes of Killarney ..." offered at same price] [25] £27 **$45**
THE LEEWARD & WINDWARD ISLANDS [1858] 43x30cm (17x12") Color. [18] £57 **$95**

WELLS
A NEW MAP OF NORTH AMERICA ... [1700] 36x48cm (14x19") [A7] £381 **$632**
A NEW MAP OF NORTH AMERICA SHEWING ITS PRINCIPAL DIVISIONS, CHIEF CITIES, TOWNES, RIVERS, MOUNTAINS &C. [1704] Insular Calif. 37x49cm (14½x19½") Orig color. Lifted off cardboard backing, deacidified; uniformly toned; sm tears into image repaired, sl loss. Ref: McLaughlin 142 (state 4); Tooley (Amer) pl.53; Portinaro & Knirsch pl.104. Lunny (NA) pl.18. [A2] £1,061 **$1,760**
A NEW MAP OF THE EASTERN PARTS OF ASIA MINOR [c.1700] 37x50cm (14½x19½") ["A New Map of the Western Parts of Asia Minor" sold at same price] [A7] £76 **$126**
A NEW MAP OF THE LAND OF CANAAN AND PARTS ADJOINING SHOWING THE DIVISION THEREOF AMONG THE TWELVE TRIBES OF ISRAEL ... [1722] 38x50cm (15x19½") OL color. Ref: Laor 835. [A8] £260 **$431**

WELLS continued

A NEW MAP OF THE MOST CONSIDERABLE PLANTATIONS OF THE ENGLISH IN AMERICA   [1700] 5 insets. 36x48cm (14x19") Fold strengthened; else fine. Ref: Cumming (SE) 130.   [43]   £1,086 **$1,800**
[SAME TITLE]   [1700] 5 insets. 35x48cm (14x18½") Contemp OL col. Sl creased at fold.   [A6]   £529 **$877**
A NEW MAP OF THE NORTH PART OF ANTIENT AFRICA   [c.1700] 37x50cm (14½x19½") Sm tear lower margin.   [A7]   £76 **$126**
A NEW MAP OF THE TERRAQUEOUS GLOBE ACCORDING TO THE LATEST DISCOVERIES AND MOST GENERAL DIVISIONS OF IT INTO CONTINENTS AND OCEANS   [1704] 38x52cm (15x20½") Ref: Shirley (W) 609.   [A8]   £763 **$1,265**
HODIERNAE EUROPAE TABULA   [c.1703] Modern Europe. 9x14cm (3½x5½") Color. VG.   [37]   £60 **$100**
ORBIS TERRARUM COGNITUS ...   [1709] Double hemi; insular Calif. 8x16cm (3x6½") Full color; VG.   [38]   £121 **$200**

WELLS, J.

WASHINGTON, D.C. AND ITS VICINITY   [1862] NY: Virtue & Co. 13x19cm (5x7½") B&W. Perfect.   [12]   £45 **$75**

WHITNEY

MAP OF THE TOWN OF ROXBURY, SURVEYED IN 1848 BY ORDER OF THE TOWN AUTHORITIES   [1848] Charles Whitney, Boston. 16 views. 83x61cm (32½x24") Uncolored. Repaired tears across width & length, no loss except bottom border.   [15]   £121 **$200**

WILKINSON

A MAP OF THE UNITED STATES OF AMERICA WITH PART OF THE ADJOINING PROVINCES FROM THE LATEST AUTHORITIES   [1794] From *New General Atlas*. Condor, sc. 22x28cm (8½x11") Wash & OL color. Sh acid burn; margin foxing; VG+. Ref: Phillips (A) 696-46; Phillips (M) p.873.   [35]   £136 **$225**
[SAME TITEL]   [1794 (1800-02)] From 2nd ed, *General Atlas*. T. Conder, engr. West to Mississippi. 21x27cm (8½x10½") Color. Ref: Phillips (A) 696-46.   [12]   £166 **$275**
A NEW AND ACCURATE MAP OF NEW SOUTH WALES WITH NORFOLK AND LORD HOWES ISLANDS, PORT JACKSON &C. FROM ACTUAL SURVEYS   [1794] 27x23cm (10½x9") Orig OL color.   [11]   £75 **$125**
[SAME TITEL]   [1794] From *New General Atlas*. 23x28cm (9x11") Full color. Near fine. Ref: Tooley (Australia) 1357.   [35]   £112 **$185**
A NEW MAP OF NORTH AMERICA, AGREEABLE TO THE LATEST DISCOVERIES   [1794 / 1800] Condor, sc. 21x25cm (8x10") Wash & OL color. Few spots; lt margin soiling; image near fine. Ref: Phillips (A) 696-45. Phillips (M) p.594.   [35]   £112 **$185**
AFRICA INCLUDING THE MEDITERRANEAN ...   [1800] From *New General Atlas*. 28x25cm (11x10") Full color. Sm spot in ocean area; near fine. Ref: Phillips (A) 696.   [35]   £48 **$80**
AN ACCURATE MAP OF THE WEST INDIES FROM THE LATEST IMPROVEMENTS   [1794] OL color-keyed colonial possessions. 18x25cm (7x9½") Couple faint spots; else fine (A). Ref: Phillips (A) 696-47.   [A4]   £33 **$55**
ASIA DRAWN FROM THE LATEST ASTRONOMICAL OBSERVATIONS ... 1800 ...   [1800] Publ in *A General Atlas* ... 22x28cm (8½x11") Color.   [13]   Aus$390 £177 **$294**
CANAAN OR THE LAND OF PROMISE TO ABRAHAM AND HIS POSTERITY   [1798] 28x22cm (11x8½") Pastel body color. Fine. Ref: Laor 851.   [37]   £75 **$125**
MAP OF THE WORLD FROM THE BEST AUTHORITIES   [1786] Double hemi. 19x36cm (7½x14") Color.   [19]   £66 **$110**
THE UNITED STATES OF AMERICA CONFIRMED BY TREATY 1783   [1806-12] State of Franklin listed. 22x28cm (8½x11") Orig color. Ref: TMC 72, p.17, map 15.1.   [34]   **£360** **$597**
[SAME TITLE]   [dated 1842] From *General Atlas of the World* London: Henry G. Bohn. Way out of date: incl state of "Franklinia" in eastern TN & 2 Indianas, one at WV location. 24x28cm (9½x11") Full color. Mint.   [12]   £172 **$285**

WILLARD

[ATLAS]   ATLAS TO ACCOMPANY A SYSTEM OF UNIVERSAL HISTORY   [1835]   Emma Willard. NY: Huntington. After Quin's English atlas; historical sequence of 5 double page world maps, incl 1492, to 1835 known world. Full color. VG.   [25]   £136 **$225**
CONNECTICUT, FROM ACTUAL SURVEYS OF WARREN & GILLETTE   [1837] Asaph Willard, Hartford. Sm linen-backed wall map with rollers; no text below (after 1833). Full color by county. 54x46cm (21x18") Fine. Ref: cf Thompson (CT).   [15]   £452 **$750**

WILLDEY

A NEW & CORRECT MAP OF ENGLAND & WALES NOW CALLED SOUTH BRITAIN [1717] Side borders of 18 uncolored views; 2 joined sheets, 62x105cm (24½x41½") OL color. Some soiling & browning; few tears. Framed. Ref: Shirley (BI 1650-1750) p.152. [A5] £748 $1,241

ASIA CORRECTED ACCORDING TO THE LATEST DISCOVERIES & OBSERVATIONS COM-MUNICATED TO YE ROYAL SOCIETY AT LONDON & YE ROYAL ACADEMY AT PARIS ... [1714] Emanuel Bowen, sc. 2 sheets joined, 62x98cm (24½x38½") Full color. Repair & verso reinforcement along side folds; sl cropping where joined; sm tears into lower ctr repaired. [4] £1,675 $2,778

WILLIAMS, C.S.

MAP OF TEXAS FROM THE MOST RECENT AUTHORITIES [1845] Shows Le Grand explorations. 29x36cm (11½x14") Full color. Margins browned; good. [16] £467 **$775**

[SAME TITLE] [1845] Incl ephemeral Spring Creek County; inset panhandle beyond Santa Fe. 30x38cm (12x15") Orig wash color. Some browning. [27] £573 **$950**

MAP OF THE UNITED STATES CONSTRUCTED FROM THE LATEST AUTHORITIES ... [1833] New Haven. Folding map in orig boards entitled "William's Travellers' Directory and Map" & sheet with routes & statistics. 54x42cm (21½x16½") Ref: Streeter 3847. [15] £573 **$950**

WILLIAMS, J.D.

MAP OF COLORADO, UTAH, NEW MEXICO AND ARIZONA [1873] 43x36cm (17x14") Full color. Some repaired binding holes in Colorado's extension into margin; VG. [25] £106 **$175**

WILLIAMS, W.

MAP OF THE SOUTHERN AND SOUTH-WESTERN STATES [1849] Carolinas to Florida to Louisiana; insets incl state of TX. 30x44cm (12x17½") Full color. VG. [16] £90 **$150**

THE TRAVELLER'S AND TOURIST'S GUIDE THROUGH THE UNITED STATES, CANADA, ETC. ... ACCOMPANIED BY ... MAP OF THE UNITED STATES [1855] William Williams; Phila: Lippincott, Grambo & Co. 16mo, embossed cloth; 246 pp. 24x29" OL color U.S. map to Rockies; inset of Rockies to Pacific. Map & cover restored; map has japan paper backing. [16] £271 **$450**

WILLIAMSON

MAP OF THE BRITISH PLANTATIONS ON THE CONTINENT OF AMERICA [1755] 34x29cm (13½x11½") Exc. [44] £332 **$550**

WILMORE

MAP OF TEXAS [1885] Publ Richmond, VA. 21x26cm (8½x10½") Full printed col. Good. [16] £33 **$55**

WINCHELL

A GEOLOGICAL MAP OF THE BLACK HILLS BY PROFESSOR N.H. WINCHELL ... [1876] To accompany Capt. Ludlow's report. Substantial geological col. 56x46cm (22x18") Minor browning at folds; VG. [26] £78 **$130**

WINTERBOTHAM

GENERAL MAP OF NORTH AMERICA, DRAWN FROM THE BEST SURVEYS [1795] From Atlas to accompany *History of America*. NY: Smith, Reid, & Wayland. 35x44cm (13½x17½") Uncolored. C'fold repair; 3 LOC stamps lower margin. Ref: Wheat & Brun 56; Wheat (TM) 233. [15] £136 **$225**

WISLIZENUS

MAP OF A TOUR FROM INDEPENDENCE TO SANTA FE, CHIHUAHUA, MONTEREY AND MATAMOROS ... IN 1846 AND 1847 [1847] From ... *Memoir of a Tour to Northern Mexico* ... 30th Cong, 1st Sess, Sen Misc Doc No.26; E. Weber, lith. Covers TX, OK & adjacent. 50x41cm (19½x16") B&W. Lower lf margin extended; fine. Ref: Wheat (TM) 572; Storm (Graff) 4723. [12] £211 **$350**

WOODBRIDGE

ISOTHERMAL CHART OR VIEW OF CLIMATES; SHOWING ALSO THE SITUATION OF THE PRINCIPAL PLANTS & ANIMALS OF THE WORLD [1843] From *Modern Atlas, Physical, Political and Statistical* ... Full col indicates thermal bands; 100+ sm fauna illustrations 22x28cm (8½x11") Minor foxing 2 corners. [12] £96 **$160**

POLITICAL MAP OF NORTH AMERICA ... [1843] From *Modern Atlas, Physical, Political and Statistical* ... Hartford: Belknap & Hamersley. Independent Texas. 22x27cm (8½x10½") Full col. Fine. [12] £66 **$110**

POLITICAL MAP OF THE UNITED STATES, TEXAS, MEXICO AND THE BRITISH PROVINCES ... [dated 1845] From *Modern Atlas, Physical, Political and Statistical* ... Insets: Eastern RR & canals; DC; MI-WI-IA. 28x46cm (11x18") Wide OL color. Fine, bright. [12] £112 **$185**

WYLD

A MAP OF THE PROVINCE OF LOWER CANADA, DESCRIBING ALL THE SEIGNEURIES, TOWNSHIPS, GRANTS OF LAND, &C. [1838] 2nd ed. Dissected, mounted on linen, folds to 8x5" with orig cloth slip case. 57x89cm (22½x35") OL color. Lt toned, faint surface soiling; tack holes corners. Ref: Tooley (Amer) p.66, #28(d). [A10] £194 **$322**

A MAP OF THE PROVINCE OF UPPER CANADA, DESCRIBING ALL THE NEW SETTLEMENTS, TOWNSHIPS, &C. WITH THE COUNTRIES ADJACENT, FROM QUEBEC TO LAKE HURON ... [1838] Dissected, mounted on linen, folds to 8x5" with orig cloth slip case. 57x87cm (22½x34½") OL color. Mild surface soiling; minor foxing; tack holes corners. Ref: Tooley (Amer) p.102, 82(e). [A10] £201 **$334**

AFRICA [1823] 2nd ed. 54x60cm (21½x23½") OL color. Some offsetting; scattered browning; few sh margin tears. [A8] £294 **$488**

GEO-HYDROGRAPHIC SURVEY OF THE ISLAND OF MADEIRA ... [1835] Separately issued. With town plan & view. 56x76cm (22x29½") Uncolored. Sm patch at ctr; no detail missing. [34] £320 **$531**

MAP OF AUSTRALIA, COMPILED FROM THE NAUTICAL SURVEYS, MADE BY ORDER OF THE ADMIRALTY AND OTHER AUTHENTIC DOCUMENTS [1838] 56x81cm (22x32") Orig OL color. Few minor mends; else exc. Ref: Tooley (Australia) #1375; Clancy (Australis) p.159. [24] £513 **$850**

[SAME TITLE] [c.1840] Dissected into 18 panels, linen-backed, folds into 5x7½" marbled paper covers with gold-stamped leather label. 56x80cm (22x31½") Full color settled areas, o/w OL color. Sm splits most fold intersections; lt browned, esp 2 fold lines; VG (A). [A4] £183 **$303**

MAP OF CENTRAL AMERICA, SHEWING THE DIFFERENT LINES OF ATLANTIC & PACIFIC COMMUNICATION [1850] Republished as U.S. Gov't document. 57x80cm (22½x31½") OL col. Folded; VG. [10] £106 **$175**

MAP OF NORTH AMERICA, EXHIBITING THE RECENT DISCOVERIES, GEOGRAPHICAL & NAUTICAL [c.1823] Folding map, dissected, linen-backed, with paper covers. 46x36cm (18x14") Full & OL color. Lt offsetting; covers soiled; else fine; VG (A). [A3] £232 **$385**

MAP OF SOUTH AUSTRALIA, NEW SOUTH WALES, VAN DIEMEN'S LAND. AND SETTLED PARTS OF AUSTRALIA [c.1841] Dissected into 24 panels, linen-backed, folds into 8x5" orig cloth covers; insets: Sydney; Adelaide; dedicated to T.L. Mitchell. 60x94cm (23½x37") Full color. Couple spots; fine for folding map (A). [A3] £274 **$454**

SCANDIA OR SCANDINAVIA COMPREHENDING THE KINGDOM OF SWEDEN INCLUDING NORWAY [1823] After Delarochette. 2nd ed. 74x52cm (29x20½") Area & OL color. Scattered offsetting; minor browning. [A8] £121 **$201**

TASMANIA OR VAN DIEMENS LAND [c.1840] Dissected into 8 panels, linen-backed, folds into 5½x8" marbled paper covers with gold stamped leather label. 54x39cm (21x15½") Full color. 2 sh fold splits & couple intersection splits; VG (A). [A4] £90 **$149**

THE BASIN OF THE PACIFIC [c.1840] Folding map of Pacific & Rim; dissected, linen-backed. 57x84cm (22½x33") OL col. Intersection splits in linen, some soiling verso & edge browning; good (B). [A3] £93 **$154**

WYLD'S MILITARY MAP OF THE UNITED STATES [1861] Dissected, linen-backed, folds into orig quarto slipcase; insets. 86x60cm (33½x23½") [A6] £230 $382

WYTFLIET

CHICA SIVE PATAGONICA ET AUSTRALIS TERRA [(1597) 1611] 2 maps on sheet: Strait of Magellan; southern continent. 23x29cm (9x11½") Uncolored. Exc. Ref: Tooley (Australia) #1430; Clancy (Australis) 8.2. [4] £850 $1,410

[SAME TITLE] [1611] 2 maps: Magellan Strait & southern continent. 23x29cm (9x11½") Ref: Tooley (Australia) p.176. [A6] £437 $725

CHILI PROVINCIA AMPLISSIMA [(1597) 1611] 23x29cm (9x11½") Uncolored. Fine. ["Peruvani Regni Descriptio" offered at same price] [4] £225 $373

CONIBAS REGIO CUM VICINIS GENTIBUS [(1597) 1611] Interior Canada. 23x28cm (9x11") Uncolored. Fine. Ref: Burden 100; Kershaw (Canada) pl.23. [4] £800 $1,327

CUBA INSULA ET IAMAICA [(1597) 1611] 23x28cm (9x11") Uncolored. Fine. [4] £550 $912

ESTOTILANDIA ET LABORATORIS TERRA [(1597) 1611] Canadian Maritimes to Iceland. 23x28cm (9x11") Uncolored. Fine. Ref: Burden 101; Kershaw (Canada) pl.24. [4] £795 $1,319

FLORIDA ET APALCHE [(1597) 1611] 23x29cm (9x11½") Uncolored. Fine. Ref: Burden 104; Cumming (SE) 18; Goss (NA) 20. Schwartz & Ehrenberg, p.83. [4] **£1,275** $2,114

[SAME TITLE] [1597] 23x28cm (9x11") Full color. Rice paper backing with some wrinkling; else VG. Framed. [36] £1,387 **$2,300**

[SAME TITLE] [1597] 23x29cm (9x11½") Exc. [44] £1,689 **$2,800**

WYTFLIET continued

GRANATA NOVA ET CALIFORNIA   [(1597) 1611]   As in *Histoire Universelle des Indes* ...   1st printed map focusing on Calif. 23x29cm (9x11½") Uncol. Exc. Ref: Burden 106; Wheat (TM) 29.   [4]   **£1,400** $2,322

HISPANIA NOVA   [(1597) 1611]   From *Histoire Universelle des Indes* ...   23x28cm (9x11") Uncolored. Fine. Ref: Burden 105.   [4]   **£750** $1,244

HISPANIOLA INSULA   [(1597) 1611]   23x28cm (9x11") Uncolored. Fine.   [4]   **£450** $746

INDIA ORIENTALIS   [ON SHEET WITH]   IAPANIAE REGNUM   [AND]   CHINAE REGNUM   [AND]   INSULAE PHILIPPINAE   [(1597) 1611]   From later editions of *Histoire Universelle des Indes* ...   4 miniature maps on sm folio; each 10x12cm (3½x4½") Uncolored. Old c'fold stitch holes; o/w fine. Ref: Walter (Japan) 21A/B; Campbell (Japan) 8; Quirino p.39 & 79.   [4]   **£1,225** $2,032

IUCATANA REGIO ET FONDURA   [1597]   Central America. 23x30cm (9x12") Exc.   [44]   **£392**   **$650**

LIMES OCCIDENTIS QUIVIRA ET ANIAN   [(1597) 1611]   As in *Histoire Universelle des Indes* ...   1st printed map focusing on Alaska. 23x29cm (9x11½") Uncolored. Sh repaired tear lf margin; Ref: Burden 107. Falk (AK) 1597-1; Wagner (NW) 189; Bancroft (NW) p.82-4.   [4]   **£965** $1,600

[SAME TITLE]   [1597]   23x29cm (9½x11½") Exc. Ref: Verner & Stubbs, p.84.   [24]   **£1,447**   **$2,400**

NORUMBEGA ET VIRGINIA   [(1597) 1611]   23x28cm (9x11") Uncolored. Fine. Ref: Burden 103; Cumming (SE) 19; Schwartz & Ehrenberg pl.40.   [4]   **£1,400** $2,322

[SAME TITLE]   [1597]   23x30cm (9x11½") Few sm filled wormholes; else exc.   [24]   **£1,689**   **$2,800**

NOVA FRANCIA ET CANADA   [(1597) 1611]   2nd state. 23x29cm (9x11½") Uncolored. Fine. Ref: Burden 102; Kershaw (Canada) pl.22.   [4]   **£1,200** $1,990

NOVA FRANCIA ET CANADA 1597   [1597]   State 1. 23x30cm (9x11½") Exc. Ref: Burden 102.   [44]   **£965**   **$1,600**

PLATA AMERICAE PROVINCIA   [(1597) 1611]   23x29cm (9x11½") Uncolored. Fine.   [4]   **£275** $456

RESIDUUM CONTINENTIS CUM ADIACENTIBUS INSULIS   [(1597) 1611]   23x28cm (9x11") Uncolored. Fine.   [4]   **£400** $664

UTRIUSQUE HEMISPHAERII DELINEATIO   [(1597) 1611]   Double-hemi. 23x29cm (9x11½") Color. Fine. Ref: Shirley (W) 207. Koeman Wyt 1A (1).   [4]   **£900** $1,493

ZAHN

FACIES UNA HEMISPHAERII TERRESTRIS   [IN SET WITH]   FACIES ALTERA HEMISPHAERII TERRESTRIS   [1696]   As in *Mundus Mirabili* ...   Nuremberg. Two hemis; insular Calif; zodiac bands above. Each 36x42cm (14x16½") Color. Ref: cf. Shirley (W) 584, pl.403.   [13]   **Aus$7,200**   £3,270 $5,421

[SAME TITLE]   [1696]   From *Mundis Mirabili: Specula Physico-Mathematico-Historiae Notabilium*. 2 hemis, zodiac above, seasons below; insular Calif. Each 36x41cm (14x16½") B&W. Fine. Ref: Shirley (W) 584; McLaughlin 122.   [29]   £1,930   **$3,200**

TABULA GEOGRAPHICO - HYDROGRAPHICA MOTUS OCEANI CURRENTES, ABYSSOS, MONTES IGNIVOMOS IN UNIVERSO ORBE INDICANS ...   [1696]   As in *Mundus Mirabili* ...   Nuremberg. Large title bloc above; Mercator projection; out of date geography. 36x42cm (14x16½") Color. Ref: cf. Shirley (W) 583, pl.405.   [13]   **Aus$5,800**   £2,634 $4,367

[SAME TITLE]   [1696]   Appeared in *Mundus Mirabili* ... *Speculae Physico-Mathematico-Historicae*. Physical features emphasized. 36x42cm (14x16½") Uncolored. Ref: Shirley (W) 583.   [34]   **£880** $1,459

ZATTA

IL CANADA, LE COLONIE INGLESI CON LA LUIGIANA E FLORIDA ...   [1778]   32x42cm (12½x16½") OL color. 4 sm stain spots on image; 3 MS words over top border.   [A8]   **£225**   **$373**

IL PAESE DE SELVAGGI OUTAUACESI E KILISTINESI INTORNO AL LAGO SUPERIORE   [1778]   Florida inset. 32x42cm (12½x16½") B&W. Ref: Portinaro & Knirsch pl.144.   [27]   **£151**   **$250**

ISOLE DI MAJORCA, D'IVICA E DI FORMENTERA ...   [1778]   32x42cm (12½x16½") Orig OL color. C'fold lt discolored.   [46]   **£320** $531

ISOLE FILIPPINE   [1785]   Based on Murillo Velarde map. 41x31cm (16x12½") Orig color. Exc. Ref: Quirino p.91.   [24]   **£724**   **$1,200**

L'EUROPA ...   [1778]   28x38cm (11x15") Full orig color. Fine.   [24]   **£211**   **$350**

L'IMPERO DEL GIAPON DIVISO IN SETTE PRINCIPALI PARTI ...   [1785]   Publ in *Atlante Novissimo*. 32x40cm (13x15½") Orig color, later additions. Exc. Ref: Walter 119; MCC 36. #77.   [4]   **£650** $1,078

LA BAJA D'HUDSON TERRA DI LABRADOR E GROENLANDIA CON LE ISOLE ADIACENTI ...   [dated 1778] From *Atlante Novissimo*. 29x39cm (11½x15½") Color. Immaculate. Ref: Sellers & Van Ee 298; Phillips (A) 650-1,54 or 651-4,40.   [12]   **£241**   **$400**

ZATTA continued

LA GRECIA DIVISA NELLE SUE PROVINCIE ... [1781] Northern part into Albania. 42x32cm (16½x13") OL color. Ref: Zacharakis (1992) 2400. [48] **DM 110** £38 **$63**

LA NUOVA ZELANDA TRASCORSA NEL 1769 E 1770 DAL COOK ... [1778] From *Atlante Novissimo*. 36x45cm (14x17½") Orig color. Ref: Campbell (Early) ill. p.143. Tooley (Australia) 1433, pl.104. [13] **Aus$1,950** £886 **$1,468**

LE INDIE ORIENTALI [c.1784] From *Atlante Novissimo* ... 32x40cm (12½x15½") Orig color. [13] **Aus$580** £263 **$437**

LI CIRCOLI DELL ALTO, E BASSO RENO [1780] Rhine regions. 32x42cm (13x16½") OL color. [48] **DM 190** £66 **$109**

LUIGIANA INGLESE, COLLA PARTE OCCIDENTALE DELLA FLORIDA, DELLA GIORGIA E CAROLINA MERIDIONALE [1778] 32x42cm (12½x16½") Orig OL color. Minor crease. [27] £286 **$475**

[SAME TITLE] [1778] 32x41cm (12½x16") Contemp OL color, modern highlights. Fine. [38] £271 **$450**

PARTE ORIENTALE DELLA FLORIDA, DELLA GIORGIA, E CAROLINA MERIDIONALE [1778] Sheet XI from multi-sheet map. 32x43cm (12½x17") Orig OL color. C'fold sl toned; fine. Ref: Portinaro & Knirsch pl.153. [31] £256 **$425**

ZEESE

WATERTOWN, SOUTH DAKOTA [dated June 1, 1889] Printed 2 sides: city in detail; center of circle of region reaching to St. Paul; text below. 52x41cm (20½x16") [15] £603 **$1,000**

ZURNER

PLANISPHAERIUM TERRESTRE CUM UTROQUE COELESTI HAEMISPHAERIO ... [c.1700] Double hemi; insular Calif; decor of scientific & natural phenomena. 50x58cm (20x22½") Orig color. C'fold reinforcement; else exc. Ref: Shirley (W) 639, pl.440. [23] £2,714 **$4,500**

Abbreviations Used

B&W – black & white	engr – engraver	occas – occasional	sh – short
cf (latin) – compare	esp –especially	OL – outline	sl – slight, slightly
c'fold – centerfold	exc, excel – excellent	orig – original	sm – small
col – color	horiz – horizontal	o/w – otherwise	uncol – uncolored
ctr – center	lf – left	pub – published	vert – vertical
dims – dimensions	litho – lithograph (ic)	Ref: – reference	VF – very fine
deriv – derivative	lt – light, lightly	rev – reverse	VG – very good
ed – edition		rt – right	

Cumulative References Cited

The references listed below have been cited by dealers in their catalogues and reported in the *Price Listing*. If an author is cited more than once, an identifying word or phrase appears in parentheses. If reviewed in this or other volumes of the *Price Record* the date is given in square brackets.

Adams, J.T., editor. *Album of American History* (vols. II & III) 1945-46

Alden, John, editor. *European Americana ... 1493-1776.* 1980

Allen, Phillip, *The Atlas of Atlases - The Map Maker's Vision of the World.* 1992. [reviewed in 1993]

Armstrong, J.C.W., *From Sea unto Sea: Art & Discovery Maps of Canada.* 1982

Bagrow, L., (Russia) *The History of the Cartography of Russia up to 1600.* 1975 [reviewed in 1990]

— (History) *The History of Cartography.* [see "General References"]

Bancroft, Herbert Howe. *History of the North West Coast* (part of multi-volume set) 1882-91

Baynton-Williams, Roger. *Investing in Maps.* 1969

Benes, P., ed. *New England Prospect: Maps, Place Names, and Historical Landscape.* 1982

Birmingham Public Library, *List of 19th Century Maps of the State of Alabama.* 1973

Booth, John (Wales) *Antique Maps of Wales.* 1978, 2nd ed.

Boston Engineering Dept., *List of Maps of Boston Published between 1600 & 1903.* 1903

Buczek, K. *The History of Polish Cartography ...* 1981. [reviewed in 1985]

Brown (Ohio) *Early Maps of the Ohio Valley.*

Burden, Philip D. *The Mapping of America 1511-1670.* 1996. [reviewed in 1997-98]

Burrus, E.J. *Kino and the Cartography of Northwestern New Spain.* 1965

Campbell, J.F., (Navigator & Pilot) *Hist. & Bibliog. of the New Amer. Practical Navigator & the Amer. Coast Pilot.* 1964.

Campbell, T. (Earliest) *The Earliest Printed maps 1472-1500* [reviewed in 1989]

— (Early) *Early Maps.* 1981 [reviewed in 1985]

— (Japan) *Japan, European Printed Maps to 1800.*

Chapin, H., *Contributions to Rhode Island Bibliography No. V. Checklist of Maps of Rhode Island.* 1928.

Chubb, T., *Printed Maps in the Atlases of Great Britain and Ireland: 1579-1870.* 1970.

Clancy, Robert (Australis). *The Mapping of Terra Australis.* 1995

Clancy, R. & A. Richardson. *So They Came South.*

Clark, D., *Index to Maps of the American Revolution in Books and Periodicals.* 1974.

Clark, T.D., (KY) *Historic Maps of Kentucky.* 1979

Clausen, M.P. & H.R. Friis, *Descriptive Catalogue of Maps Published by Cong. 1817-1843.* 1941

Cobb, D.A. (NH) *New Hampshire Maps to 1900: An annotated checklist.* 1981 [reviewed in 1989]

— (VT) "Vermont Maps Prior to 1900: An Annotated Cartobibliography" in *Vermont History*, Vol. XXXIX, Nos 3 & 4. 1971.

Cortazzi, H. (Japan) *Isles of Gold; Antique Maps of Japan.* 1983.

Cumming, W.P. (Colonial Amer) *British Maps of Colonial America.* 1974

— (Discovery) *The Discovery of North America.* 1972

— (SE) *The Southeast in Early Maps.* 1957.

Cumming, W.P. et al, (Exploration) *The Exploration of North America 1630-1776.* 1974.

Day, J.M., compiler, *Maps of Texas 1527-1900.* 1964.
Danforth, S. *The Land of Nurembega.*
Dawson, Joan (NS). The Mapmaker's ... Nova Scotia through Early Maps. 1988
Deak, G.G., *Picturing America: 1497-1899.* 1988.
Dekker, Elly & Peter van der Krogt, *Globes from the Western World.*
Dionne, N.E., *Inventaire Chronologique des Cartes, Plans, Atlas Relatifs a la Nouvelle-France et a la Province de Quebec 1508-1908.* 1909
Ellis, E.H., *Colorado Mapology.* 1983
Falk, M.W. (AK) *Alaskan Maps: A Cartobibliography to 1900.* 1983. [reviewed in 1987]
Fell, R.T. *Early Maps of South-East Asia.* 1991. [reviewed in 1993]
Fite, E.D. & A. Freeman, *A Book of Old Maps Delineating American History from the Earliest Days Down to the Close of the Revolutionary War.* 1926.
Fitzpatrick, G.L. (HI) *The Early Mapping of Hawai'i.* 1987
Freeman, Larry, *Historical Prints of American Cities.* 1952
Gole, S. *Early Maps of India.* 1978
Goss. J. (Grand Atlas) *Blaeu's The Grand Atlas of the 17th-century World.* 1990. [reviewed in 1992]
— (Euro Cities) *The City Maps of Europe; 16th Century Town Plans ...* 1992
— (Art) *The Mapmaker's Art: An Illustrated History of Cartography.* 1993. [reviewed in 1994]
— (NA) *The Mapping of North America: Three Centuries of Map-Making 1500-1860.* 1990.
Gohm, Douglas (Antique) *Antique Maps of Europe, the Americas, West Indies, Australasia, ...* 1972
Guthorn, P. (Amer.Rev.) *British Maps of the American Revolution.*
— (Charts) *United States Coastal Charts, 1783-1861.* 1984.
Harley, J.B. (Encounter) *Maps of the Columbian Encounter; An Interpretive Guide ...* 1990
Haskell, D.C., "Manhattan Maps - A Co-operative List" in *Bulletin of the New York Public Library,* April - October 1930.
Hazen, Robert M. & Margaret H. Hazen. *American Geological Literature, 1669 to 1850.* 1980
Hebert, John R., compiler. *Panoramic Maps of Anglo-American Cities.* 1974
Heidenreich & Dahl. *French Mapping of North America.*
Hellwig, Fritz, Wolfgang Reiniger & Klaus Stopp. *Landkarten der Pfalz am Rhein 1513-1803.* 1984
Holmden, H.R. *Catalogue of Maps, Plans and Charts in the Map Room of the Dominion Archives.* 1912
Howes, W., *U.S.Iana (1650-1950).* 1962.
Howgego, J., *Printed Maps of London circa 1553-1850.* 1978
Howse, D. & M. Sanderson, *Sea Chart, The: An Historical Survey ...* 1973
Humphreys, A.L., *Antique Maps and Charts.* 1989.
Jolly, David. C., *Maps in British Periodicals: Part I* and *Part II.* [reviewed in 1990, 1991]
Johnsen, M.A., compiler (GA) Nineteenth Century Maps on the Collection of the Georgia Surveyor General Department, 1800-1849. 1981
Johnson, Adrian. *America Explored.* 1974
Kapp, K.S. (Cent Amer) *Central America Early Maps up to 1860.* 1974.
— (Panama) *Early Maps of Panama up to 1865.* 1971.
— (Jamaica) *The Printed Maps of Jamaica up to 1825.* 1968.
Karpinski, L.C. (MI) *Bibliography of the Printed Maps of Michigan, 1804-1880.* 1931.
— Carolina) *Early Maps of Carolina and Adjoining Regions.* 1937.

Karpinski, L.C. (FC) *Maps of Famous Cartographers Depicting North America. An Historical Atlas of the Great Lakes and Michigan ...* 1977. 2nd edition of Karpinski (MI) above.

Karrow, R.W., Jr., ed. *Checklist of Printed Maps of the Middle West to 1900.* 1981.

— (16c) *Mapmakers of the Sixteenth Century and Their Maps: Bio-Bibliographies.* 1993. [reviewed in 1994]

Kaufman, K. (Gt. Lakes) *The Mapping of the Great Lakes in the Seventeenth Century.* 1989 [reviewed in 1994]

Kelsay, L.E., *List of Cartographic Records of the General Land Office.* 1964

Kershaw, K.A. *Early Printed Maps of Canada.* 1993. [reviewed in 1994]

Klein, Christopher M. *Maps in Eighteenth-Century British Magazines; A check list.* 1989

Klemp, Egon, *America in Maps Dating from 1500 to 1856.* 1976

Koeman, I.C., *Atlantes Neerlandici: Bibliography of terrestrial, Maritime and celestial atlases and pilot books, published in the Netherlands up to 1880*, 5 vols. 1967-71. [see "General References"]

Koerner, A.G.A., *Detroit and Vicinity before 1900: An Annotated List of Maps.* LOC, 1968

Ladd, R.S., *Maps Showing Explorers' Routes, Trails & Early Roads in the United States.* LOC, 1962.

Lande, Lawrence, The Lawrence Lande Collection of Canadiana in the Redpath Library of McGill University: A Bibliography. 1965.

Landis, D.C., ed., *European Americana: A Chronological Guide to Works Printed in Europe Relating to America, 1493-1776* (several volumes) 1980s

Laor, E., *Maps of the Holy Land: Cartobibliography of Printed Maps, 1475-1900.* [reviewed in 1988]

Lawson, S. & W.J. Faupel, *A Foothold in Florida; The Eye-Witness Account of Four Voyages made by the French to that Region and their attempt at Colonisation 1562-1568.* [reviewed in 1994]

Le Gear, C.E., compiler (US) *United States Atlases: A List of National, State, County, City, and Regional Atlases in the Library of Congress.* 1950.

Leighly, John, *California as an Island.* 1972.

Lemon, D.P. (NS) *Theatre of Empire: Three Hundred Years of Maps of the Maritimes.* 1987

Lépine, Pierre, *Cartes Ancienne: Cartes Originales ou Reproduites.* [reviewed in 1994]

Lowery, W., *A Descriptive List of Maps of the Spanish Possessions within the Present Limits of the United States 1502-1820.* 1912.

Luebke, F.C. et al. *Mapping the North American Plains.* 1987

Lunny, Robert M. *Early Maps of North America.* 1961

Map Collector, The. Tring, England: Map Collector Publications. Quarterly, 1977-1996 [see "General References"]

Map Collectors' Series, London: The Map Collectors' Circle. 110 numbered issues in 11 volumes, 1964-1974. [see "General References"]

Marcou, Jules & J.B. Marcou, *Mapoteca Geologica Americana: A Catalogue of Geological Maps of America (North and South) 1752-1881.* USGS Bulletin 7, 1884

Martin, J.C. & R.S. Martin, *Maps of Texas and the Southwest, 1513-1900.* [reviewed in 1987]

Marshall, D.W. ed., *Research Catalogue of Maps of America to 1860 in the William L Clements Library, University of Michigan* (4 vol.). 1972

Maryland Historical Society. *The Mapping of Maryland 1590-1914: An Overview.* 1982

McCorkle, B.B. *America Emergent; An Exhibition of Maps and Atlases ...* 1985

McCormick, T. *First Views of Australia 1788-1825*

McLaughlin, Glen. The Mapping of California as an Island. 1995 [reviewed in 1996]

Mickwitz, A. (Nordenskiold Col) *The A.E. Nordenskiold Collection ...* 1979- [reviewed in 1986]

Modelski, A.M., compiler. (NA) *Railroad Maps of North America - The First Hundred Years.* 1984

— (US) *Railroad Maps of the United States: A selective annotated bibliography of original 19th-century maps in the Geography and Map Division of the Library of Congress.* [see "Specialized References"]

Moffat, R.M. *Printed Maps of Utah to 1900.* Western Assoc. of Map Libraries, 1981

Moir. *The Early Maps of Scotland.*

Moreland, C. & D. Bannister, *Antique Maps: A collector's handbook.* [reviewed in 1985, 1987]

Morrison, Russell, et al, *On the Map.* 1983.

Nebenzahl, K. (Biblio Amer Rev) *A Bibliography of Printed Battle Plans of the American Revolution.* 1975

— (Amer Rev) *Atlas of the American Revolution.* 1975.

— (Holy Land) *Maps of the Holy Land: Images of Terra Sancta through two millennia* [reviewed in 1988]

Nordenskiöld, A.E., *Facsimile-Atlas: To the Early History of Cartography with Reproductions of ... Maps Printed in the XV and XVI Centuries.* 1973.

(Nordenskiold Col) see Mickwitz.

Norwich, O.I., *Maps of Africa: An illustrated carto-bibliography* [reviewed in 1986]

Pagani, Lelio, ed., *Cities of the World.* 1990

Palmer, M. (Bermuda) *Printed Maps of Bermuda.*

Papenfuse, E.C. & J.M. Coale III, *The Hammond-Harwood House Atlas of Historical Maps of Maryland, 1608-1908.* 1982.

Pastoureau, M. *Les Atlas Francais XVIe-XVIIe Siecles: Repertoire Bibliographique et Etude.* 1984

Paullin, C.O. & J.K. Wright, ed., *Atlas of the Historical Geography of the United States.* 1932

Pedley, M. S., *BEL ET UTILE: The work of the Robert De Vaugondy Family of mapmakers.* [reviewed in 1993]

Perry, T.M., *The Discovery of Australia.* 1982

Perry, T.M. & Dorothy Prescott. *A Guide to Maps of Australia in Books Published 1780-1830.* 1996 [reviewed in 1997-98]

Phillips, Philip L. (A) *A List of Geographical Atlases in the Library of Congress,* Vols. I-IV, continued by Clara Egli LeGear, Vols. 5-8. [see "General References"]

— (Alaska) *Alaska and the N.W. Part of North America, 1588-1898 ...* 1898

— (M) *A List of Maps of America in the Library of Congress Preceded by a List of Works Relating to Cartography.* [see "Specialized References"]

— (Phila) *A Descriptive List of Maps and Views of Philadelphia ... 1683-1865.* 1926.

— (VA) *Virginia Cartography, A Bibliographical Description.* 1896

— (Wash) *Maps & Views of Washington.*

Portinaro, P. & F. Knirsch, *The Cartography of North America 1500-1800.* 1987 [reviewed in 1990]

Potter, J., *Country Life Book of Antique Maps: An introduction to the history of maps and how to appreciate them.* [reviewed in 1990]

Preston, R.W. (ID) *Early Idaho Atlas.* 1978

Quirino, C., *Philippine Cartography, 1320-1899.* 1963.

Rawnsley. *Antique Maps of Yorkshire.*

Reinhartz, Dennis & C.C. Colley, *The Mapping of American Southwest.* 1987

Reps, John W. (Views) *Views & Viewmakers of Urban America: Lithographs of towns and cities in the United States and Canada, notes on the artists and publishers, and a union catalog of their work, 1825-1925*. [see "Specialized References"; reviewed in 1985]

—(Wash) *Washington on View - The Nation's Capital Since 1790*. 1991

—(West) Cities of the American West. 1979

Ristow, W.W., compiler, *A la Carte: Selected Papers on Maps and Atlases*. 1972.

— (Amer M&M) *American Maps and Mapmakers*. 1985

Royal Scottish Geographical Society. *The Early Maps of Scotland to 1850* 1973.

Rumsey, D,M. *Catalogue of the Collection of...* 1995

Sabin, J. *Bibliotheca Americana. A Dictionary of Books Relating to America ...* reprinted 1962.

Sames, J.W., comp, & L.C. Woods, ed., Index of Kentucky & Virginia Maps 1562 to 1900. 1976

Seavey, C.A., "Maps of the American State Papers". *Bulletins 107 & 110*, Spec. Lib. Assoc., 1977

Sanchez-Saavedra, E.M., *A Description of the Country. Virginia's Cartographers and Their Maps, 1607-1881*. 1975

Schilder, Günter. *Australia Unveiled*. 1976

— (Monumenta) Monumenta Cartographica Neerlandica (vol. IV focuses on Blaeu)

Schmeckebier, L.F. *Catalogue and Index of the Hayden, King, Powell, and Wheeler Surveys*. 1904

Schwartz, S.I., & R.E. Ehrenberg, *The Mapping of America*. 1980. [see "Specialized References"]

Sellers, J.R. & P.M. van Ee, *Maps and Charts of North America and the West Indies 1750-1789: A guide to the collections in the Library of Congress*. 1981. [see "Specialized References"]

Shirley, R.W., (BI to 1650) *Early Printed Maps of the British Isles 1477-1650*. [reviewed in 1994]

— (BI 1650-1750) *Printed Maps of the British Isles 1650-1750*. 1988.

— (W) *The Mapping of the World: Early printed world maps 1472-1700* [see "Specialized References"; reviewed in 1985]

Simonetti, M.L., *Descriptive List of the Map Collection in the Pennsylvania State Archives*. 1976.

Skelton, R.A., (County) "*County Atlases of the British Isles, 1579-1850.*" Map Col. Series, 1964

— (Decorative) *Decorative Printed Maps of the 15th to 18th Centuries*. [see "General References"]

Smith, T.H. (OH) *The Mapping of Ohio*. 1977

Snyder, George (Heavens) *Maps of the Heavens*. 1984

Snyder, J.P. (NJ) *The Mapping of New Jersey*. 1973.

Snyder, M.P. (City of Indep.) *City of Independence, Views of Philadelphia before 1800*. 1975.

Society for Hellenistic Cartography. *Cartography of the Shores and Islands of Greece*. 1989

Stephenson, R.W. (CW: 1st or 2nd edition) *Civil War Maps; An Annotated List*. 1961.

Stevens, H.N. (Evans 1749-55) *A Comparative Account of the Original Editions of Lewis Evans' Maps of 1749 and 1755 and their Derivatives*. 1926

— (Ptolemy) *Ptolemy's Geography; A Brief Account of All the Printed Editions ...* 1908 (1972)

Stevens, H. & R.Tree, *Comparative Cartography Exemplified in an Analytical & Bibliographical Description of Nearly One Hundred Maps and Charts of the American Continent Published in Great Britain during the Years 1600 to 1850*, Map Collectors' Circle, No.39, 1967 (Revised 2nd ed.). Revised 3rd ed. appeared as Chapter 2 of R.V. Tooley, *The Mapping of America*, 1980.

Stokes, I.N.P. (Manhattan) *The Iconography of Manhattan Island*. 1967.

Stokes, I.N.P. & Haskell, *American Historical Prints; Early Views of American Cities, ...* 1933.

Storm, Colton, compiler, *A Catalogue of the Everett D. Graff Collection of Western Americana*. 1968

(Streeter) *The Celebrated Collection of Americana Formed by the Late Thomas Winthrop Streeter.* Parke-Bernet, 1966-69.

Stott, C., *Celestial Charts.*

Stylianou. *The History of the Cartography of Cyprus.* 1980

Suarez, T., *Shedding the Veil: Mapping the European discovery of America and the world ... 1434-1865* [reviewed in 1992]

Swem, E.G. *Maps Relating to Virginia in the Virginia State Library.* 1914

Thompson, Edmund (CT) *Maps of Connecticut for the Years of the Industrial Revolution, 1801-1860.* 1942.

Tibbetts, G.R. *Arabia in Early Maps.* 1978.

Tooley, R.V., (Africa) *Collector's Guide to Maps of the African Continent and Southern Africa.* 1969.

— (Amer.) *The Mapping of America.* 1979.

— (Australia) *The Mapping of Australia and Antarctica.*

— (M&M) *Maps and Map-Maker.* [see "General References"]

Tooley, R.V., C. Bricker, & G.R. Crone (Landmarks) *Landmarks of Mapmaking.* [see "General References"]

Trudel, M. *Atlas de la Nouvelle-France. An Atlas of New France.* 1968.

Van den Broecke, Marcel. *Ortelius Atlas Maps.* 1996

Van der Krogt, Peter, *Globi Neerlandici: The Production of Globes in the Low Countries.*

Van Ermen, E. *The United States in Old Maps & Prints.* 1990. [reviewed in 1992]

Verner, Cooley, (N. Pac) *Cook and the Cartography of the North Pacific.* 1978

— (Arctic) "Explorers' Maps of Canadian Arctic: 1818-1860". *Cartographica* Mon. No.6, 1972

— (VA) "Smith's 'Virginia' and its Derivatives ..." 1968. reprinted in Tooley (Amer).

Verner, Cooley & B. Stuart-Stubbs. *The North Part of America.* 1979

Wagner, Henry Raup . (NW) *Cartography of the Northwest Coast of America to the Year 1800.* 1937.

Wagner, Henry Raup & C.L. Camp (Wagner-Camp), *The Plains and the Rockies ...* 4th ed, 1982

Walter, L. *Japan A Cartographic Vision: European Printed Maps ...* 1994. [reviewed in 1995]

Warner, D.J., *The Sky Explored: Celestial cartography, 1500-1800* [see "Specialized References"; reviewed in 1986]

Williams, Gregory W. & Allen S. Johnson. Tar Heel Maps: Colony and State 1590-1995. 1996 [reviewed in 1997-98]

Winearls, J. *Mapping Upper Canada 1780-1867; An Annotated Bibliography ...* 1991

Winsor, Justin (C&N). *Narrative and Critical History of America.* 1889

Wheat, Carl I. (Gold) *The Maps of the California Gold Region 1848-1857.* 1942

— (TM) *Mapping the Transmississippi West 1540-1861*, Vols. 1-5. [see "Specialized References"]

Wheat, James C. & Christian F. Brun, *Maps and Charts Published in America before 1800: A bibliography.* [see "Specialized References"]

Whitfield, Peter. *The Charting of the Oceans: Ten centuries of maritime maps.* 1996

Wolff, H., ed. *America: Early Maps of the World.* 1992.

Yeo, Julie et al (compiler), *Mapping of the Continent of Asia.* 1994

Zacharakis, C., *A Catalogue of Printed Maps of Greece.*

TITLE INDEX

ATLASES and BOOKS WITH MAPS:

Title	Author	Size
[Atlas, Composite]	HOMANN	53x34cm
[Atlas, school exercise]	LOCAL & STATE MAPS	Quarto
A Chronological History of the Civil War in America. ...	JOHNSON	Octavo
A Compendius and Complete System of Modern Geography	MORSE, JEDIDIAH	23x14cm
A Complete Genealogical, Historical, Chronological, and Geographical Atlas	LAVOISNE	Folio
A Comprehensive Atlas Geographical, Historical & Commercial	BRADFORD	Quarto
A Description of the Empire of China and Chinese-Tartary ... Edward Cave	DU HALDE	Folio
A General Atlas	THOMSON	Quarto
A General Gazetteer; or Compendious Geographical Dictionary ...	BROOKES	Octavo
A Geographical Description of the United States, with the Contiguous ...	MELISH	Octavo
A National Geography, for Schools; Illustrated with 220 engravings, and ...	GOODRICH	Quarto
A New and Improved School Atlas ...	OLNEY	Quarto
A New Atlas of the Mundane System; or, of Geography and Cosmography	DUNN	Folio
A New Country Atlas of Great Britain and Ireland Containing Sixty-Eight ...	VIRTUE	30x23cm
A New Gazetteer of the Eastern Continent; or, A Geographical Dictionary	MORSE, JEDIDIAH	Octavo
A New, General and Universal Atlas ...	DURY	Quarto
A New Geographical and Historical Grammar ...	SALMON	Octavo
A New Pocket Atlas and Geography of England and Wales	LUFFMAN	Octavo
A New Universal Atlas ...	TANNER	Quarto
A New Universal Atlas of the World, on an Improved Plan ...Thirty Maps ...	MORSE, SIDNEY	Folio
A Report of the Superintendent of the Coast Survey, Showing the Progress	U.S. COAST SURVEY	Octavo
A School Atlas of Astronomy ...	JOHNSTON	Quarto
A Set of Plans and Forts in America	ROCQUE	Quarto
A Set of Thirty Six New and Correct Maps of Scotland ...	MOLL (Small)	Quarto
A State of the Expedition from Canada ... with a Collection of Authentic ...	BURGOYNE	Octavo
A System of Geography for the Use of Schools	MORSE, SIDNEY	Quarto
America Being the Latest, and Most Accurate Description ...	OGILBY	Folio
Americae Utriusque Descriptio Novus Orbis seu Descriptionis Indiae ...	DE LAET	Folio
An Account of a Voyage in Search of La Perouse	LABILLARDIERE	Quarto
An Easy Grammar of Geography. Intended as a Companion ... for Schools	PHILLIPS	12mo
An Expedition to the Valley of the Great Salt Lake of Utah	STANSBURY	Octavo
An Atlas of Ancient Geography	BUTLER	23x15cm
An Atlas of Ancient Geography Biblical and Classical	SMITH	Folio
An Atlas of Modern Geography for the Use of King's College School	ARROWSMITH	Octavo
An Atlas to Guthrie's Geographical Grammar	GUTHRIE	Octavo
An Illustrated Atlas of Washington County, Maryland	LAKE et al	Folio
Appletons' Illustrated Hand-book of American Travel	APPLETON	12mo
Arbuckles' Illustrated Atlas of Fifty Principal Nations of the World	ARBUCKLE	8x13cm
Arbuckles' Illustrated Atlas of the United States of America	ARBUCKLE	Quarto
Asher & Adams' New Commercial, Topographical, and Statistical Atlas ...	ASHER & ADAMS	Folio
Asher & Adams' New Topographical Atlas and Gazetteer of New York ...	ASHER & ADAMS	Folio
Atlante di Geografica-Storica Universale	MARMOCCHI	Folio
Atlas	DE WIT	Folio
Atlas de Filipinas Coleccion de 30 Mapas	U.S. GOV'T	38x33cm
Atlas de Toutes les Parties Connues du Globe Terrestre	BONNE	Folio
Atlas Designed to Illustrate Burritt's Geography of the Heavens	BURRITT	Folio
Atlas General	LE ROUGE	Folio
Atlas General de la Chine, de la Tartarie Chinoise, et du Tibet: ...	DEZAUCHE	Folio
Atlas Geographique, Statistique, Historique et Chronologique des Deux ...	BUCHON	Folio
Atlas Iuzhnago Moria	KRUSENSTERN	Folio
Atlas Minor ...	HONDIUS	Quarto
Atlas Minor. Das Ist: Ein Kurtze Jedoch Grandliche Beschreibung ...	MERCATOR (Small)	Quarto
Atlas Minor Praecipua Orbis Terrarum Imperia, Regna ... Germaniae ...	SEUTTER	21x33cm
Atlas Minor Praeipua Orbis Terrarum Imperia, Regna ... Germaniae ...	LOTTER	Quarto
Atlas Minor, sive Totus Orbis Terrarum	VISSCHER	Folio
Atlas National Illustre des 86 Departements et des Possessions de la France	LEVASSEUR	Folio
Atlas of Livingston Co. New York	BEERS	Folio
Atlas of Long Island, New York ...	BEERS	Folio

The dimensions given may not always exactly match those given for multiple entries in the *Price Listing*

Entries are based on the spelling given in the dealers' catalogues. Differences from the expected may indicate a variant, or may be due to misspellings in a catalogue that we are unable to correct with confidence.

ATLASES and BOOKS WITH MAPS continued:

Title	Author	Size
Atlas of Luzerne County, Pennsylvania ...	BEERS	Folio
Atlas of Lycoming County Pennsylvania ... Direction of Beach Nichols	POMEROY	no dimens
Atlas of New York and Vicinity	BEERS	Folio
Atlas of Oneida County, New York	BEERS	Folio
Atlas of Seneca County New York ... Direction of Beach Nichols	POMEROY	no dimens
Atlas of the City of Philadelphia, Complete in One Volume	BROMLEY	Folio
Atlas of the Heavens; Showing the Places of the Principal Stars, Clusters...	KENDALL	22x41cm
Atlas of the State of Michigan	WALLING	Folio
Atlas of the State of New York Prepared under the Direction of ... Bien ...	BIEN	Folio
Atlas of Wayne County Pennsylvania	BEERS	Folio
Atlas of Westchester County, New York	BROMLEY	Folio
Atlas of Windsor County. Vermont	BEERS	Folio
Atlas of Worcester County [MA]	BEERS	Folio
Atlas Russicus Mappa una Generali et Underviginti Specialibus ...	DE L'ISLE	Folio
Atlas sive Cosmographie Meditationes de Fabrica Mundi et Fabricati ...	JANSSON	Folio
Atlas to Accompany a System of Universal History	WILLARD	no dimens
Atlas to Accompany Chambers's Encyclopoedia	CHAMBERS	Quarto
Atlas to Accompany the Official Records of the Union and Confederate ...	U.S. UNION & CONFED.	Folio
Atlas to Marshall's Life of Washington	MARSHALL	Octavo
Atlas Tres-Exact des Pais Bas Catholiques	SEUTTER	Quarto
Atlas Universal	DE VAUGONDY	Folio
Atlas Universel	DE VAUGONDY	Folio
Atlas Universel	VUILLEMIN	Quarto
Beschreibung und Contrafactur der Vornembster Staet der Welt [Facsimile]	BRAUN & HOGENBERG	Folio
Black's General Atlas: A Series of Fifty-Four Maps from the latest ...	BLACK	Folio
Bridgens' Atlas of Lancaster County Pennsylvania	BRIDGENS	Folio
Britannia ...	CAMDEN	Folio
Britannia Depicta or Ogilby Improv'd ...	OWEN & BOWEN	Quarto
Britannia: or a Chorographical Description of Great Britain and Ireland, ...	CAMDEN	Folio
Britannia: or a Geographical Account Description of the Flourishing Kingdoms	CAMDEN	Folio
Brookes's General Gazetteer Improved	BROOKES	Octavo
Caldwell's ... Atlas of Clearfield County [PA]	CALDWELL	Folio
Caldwell's ... Atlas of Jefferson County [PA]	CALDWELL	Folio
Carey's General Atlas, Improved and Enlarged: ...	CAREY	Folio
Carta Marina Universalis 1530 [Facsimile]	FRIES	Quarto
Cartes Generales des Provinces de France et d'Espagne ... [with] Plans ...	TASSIN	Quarto
Cary's Actual Survey of the Country Fifteen Miles Round London	CARY	Octavo
Cary's New and Correct English Atlas	CARY	Quarto
Cary's Traveller's Companion, or a Delineation of the Turnpike Roads ...	CARY	Octavo
City Atlas of Schenectady, New York	HOPKINS	Folio
Civitates Orbis Terrarum [Facsimile]	BRAUN & HOGENBERG	Folio
Colton's General Atlas ...	COLTON (Atlas Maps)	Folio
Combination Atlas Map of Dauphin County Pennsylvania	EVERTS & STEWART	Folio
Combination Atlas Map of Washtenaw County, Michigan	EVERTS & STEWART	Folio
Combination Atlas of Lancaster County Pennsylvania ...	EVERTS & STEWART	Folio
Cosmographei oder Beschreibung Aller Laender ...	MUNSTER	Folio
County Atlas of Litchfield [CT]	BEERS	Folio
County Atlas of Middlesex [CT]	BEERS	Folio
County Atlas of Middlesex [MA]	BEERS	Folio
County Atlas of Tioga Pennsylvania	BEERS	Folio
Cram's Superior Atlas of the World. Indexed	CRAM	Folio
Cram's Unrivaled Family Atlas of the World	CRAM	Folio
De Nieuwe en Onbekende Weereld of Beschryving van America ...	MONTANUS	Folio
De Somnium Scipionis ...	MACROBIUS	7x7cm
Description de l'Egypte - Atlas Geographique ... Seconde Edition	PANCKOUCKE	72x55cm
Description Exact des Isles de l'Archipel, et de Chypre, Rhodes, Candie ...	DAPPER	Folio
Description of the Plain of Troy: with a Map of that Region Delineated ...	CHEVALIER	Quarto
Economic Geology of the Bingham Mining District, Utah	U.S. GEOLOGICAL SURVEY	no dimens
England, Wales, Scotland and Ireland Described and Abridged	SPEED	Octavo
Epitome du Theatre du Monde d'Abraham Ortelius ... a Anvers, ...	ORTELIUS (Miniature)	Quarto
Family Cabinet Atlas	CAREY & LEA	Quarto
Fourteen Maps of Ancient and Modern Geography for the Illustration ...	BLAIR	Folio
Geographiae Universae tum Veteris tum Novae Absolvtissimvm...	MAGINI	Octavo
Geography Anatomiz'd: or, the Geographical Grammar ... by Mr. Senex	GORDON	Octavo
Geography Made Easy	MORSE, JEDIDIAH	12mo
Geological and Topographical Atlas ... of the Fortieth Parallel ...	U.S. GOV'T	Folio

ATLASES and BOOKS WITH MAPS continued:

Title	Author/Source	Size
Geologischer Atlas zur Naturgeschichte der Erde	VON LEONARD	Quarto
Geology and Gold Deposits of the Cripple Creek District Colorado	U.S. GEOLOGICAL SURVEY	no dimens
Gerardi Mercatoris Atlas sive Cosmographicae	MERCATOR (Folio)	Folio
Grand Voyages ... Francoforti	DE BRY	Folio
Guthrie's Universal Geography, Improved ...	GUTHRIE	Quarto
Hardesty's Historical and Geographical Encyclopedia, Illustrated	HARDESTY	Folio
Histoire des Troubles de l'Amerique Anglaise	SOULES	Octavo
Histoire Philosophique et Politique des Etablissemens ... dans les Deux Indes	RAYNAL	Quarto + 10 Octavo
Historical Atlas of the World	HARDESTY	Folio
Historical Hand Atlas ... General Survey ... Map of Gallia County ...	HARDESTY	Folio
History of South America and Mexico ... [with] A ... View of Texas	PEASE & NILES	Octavo
Illinois in 1837; A Sketch Descriptive of the Situation ... Also, Suggestions ...	MITCHELL, S.A. (non-atlas)	38x31cm
Illustrated Atlas of Allegan County Michigan	LOCAL & STATE MAPS	Folio
Illustrated Historical Atlas of Berks County, Penna.	DAVIS	no dimens
Isolario di Benedetto Bordone nel qual si Ragiona di Tutte le Isole del Mondo	BORDONE	Folio
Johnson's New Illustrated Family Atlas ...	JOHNSON	Folio
Johnson's New Illustrated (Steel Plate) Family Atlas ...	JOHNSON	Folio
Journal of and Exploring Tour beyond the Rocky Mountains	PARKER	Octavo
Kurzgefassete Geographie ... von Tobias Lobeck ... / Atlas Geographicus ...	LOTTER	Octavo
L'Appendice de l'Atlas de Gerard Mercator et Iudocus Hondius: ...	MERCATOR (Folio)	Folio
L'Isole Piu Famose Del Mondo ... In Venetia MDLXXVI	PORCACCHI	Folio
La Cosmographie Universelle	MUNSTER	Folio
La Geografia di Claudio Tolomeo Alessandrino Nouvamente Tradotta ...	RUSCELLI	Quarto
La Geographia ... Aggiunteui di Meser Iacopo Gastaldi ...	GASTALDI	Octavo
Le Grande Atlas ou Cosmographie Blaviane [Facsimile]	BLAEU	Folio
Le Nouveau et Curieux Atlas Geographique et Historique, ...	CHIQUET	Quarto
Le Petit Neptune Francais; or, French Coasting Pilot	FADEN	Quarto
Lead Zinc and Fluorspar Deposits of Western Kentucky	U.S. GEOLOGICAL SURVEY	no dimens
Liber Chronicarum	SCHEDEL	Folio
Map and Profiles of New-York State Canals	LOCAL & STATE MAPS	57x99cm
Mapa del Peru	RAIMONDI	Folio
Maps, VII P. Rivett	MANUSCRIPT MAPS	Quarto
Mitchell's Ancient Atlas, Classical and Sacred ...	MITCHELL, S.A. (1860 +)	24x30cm
Mitchell's Atlas of Outline Maps	MITCHELL, S.A. (to 1859)	Quarto
Mitchell's New General Atlas ...	MITCHELL, S.A. (1860 +)	Folio
Mitchell's School Atlas	MITCHELL, S.A. (to 1859)	Quarto
Modern History	SALMON	Folio
Narrative of the Texas Santa Fe Expedition	KENDALL	12mo
Neuester Himmels-Atlas ...	GOLDBACH	Quarto
New Century Atlas of the State of New York ...	EVERTS	Folio
New Illustrated Atlas of Lehigh County, Pennsylvania	DAVIS	no dimens
New Topographical Atlas of the State of New York	ASHER & ADAMS	Folio
New Topographical Atlas of the State of Pennsylvania ...	WALLING & GRAY	Folio
New Universal Atlas	MITCHELL, S.A. (to 1859)	Folio
New Universal Atlas	THOMAS, COWPERTHWAIT	Folio
Notes of a Military Reconnoissance from Fort Leavenworth ... to San Diego	U.S. GOV'T	no dimens
Nouvel Atlas de la Chine, de la Tartarie Chinoise, et du Thibet: ... Coree ...	D'ANVILLE	Folio
Novus Atlas Sinensis a Martino Martinio Soc.Iesu Descriptus et Seren ...	BLAEU	Folio
Novus Orbis Regionum ac Insularum Veteribus Incognitarum, ...	GRYNAEUS	31x41cm
Official Topographical Atlas of Massachusetts	WALLING & GRAY	Folio
Olney's School Atlas Containing ... 13 Maps ...	OLNEY	Quarto
Pennsylvania Maps Accompanying the Report of the Secretary of Internal ...	GOV'T: LOCAL & STATE	no dimens
Peter Parley's Geography for Beginners ...	GOODRICH	16mo
Petit Atlas Moderne ou Collection de Cartes Elementaire ...	DELAMARCHE	Octavo
Prima Parte dello Specchio del Mare	CORONELLI	Folio
Provinciarum Europae Geographica Descriptio	BODENEHR	12mo
Rand, McNally & Co.'s Indexed Atlas of the World ...	RAND, McNALLY (atlas maps)	Quarto
Recueil de Cartes Geographiques ... de l'Ancienne Grece ... Anacharsis	BARTHELEMY	Quarto
Recueil des Fortifications Forts et Ports de Mer de France ...	LE ROUGE	Octavo
Report of a Geological Exploration of Part of Iowa, Wisconsin and Illinois	U.S. GOV'T	Quarto
Report of the Exploring Expedition to the Rocky Mountains in the Year ...	FREMONT	Octavo
Report of the Superintendent of the Coast Survey, showing the Progress ...	U.S. COAST SURVEY	Quarto
Richards Standard Atlas of the City of Worcester Massachusetts ...	RICHARDS	Folio
School Atlas to Cummings' Ancient & Modern Geography	CUMMINGS & HILLIARD	Quarto
Schul-Atlas zum Unterricht in der Erdunde	LANGE	Quarto
Sketches Accompanying Report of Coast Survey for 1851	U.S. COAST SURVEY	Quarto

ATLASES and BOOKS WITH MAPS continued:

Title	Author/Publisher	Size
Sketches Accompanying the Annual Report ... 1851	U.S. COAST SURVEY	no dimens
Slater's New British Atlas	SLATER	Folio
Spieghel der Zeevaerdt [Facsimile]	WAGHENAER	Folio
State Atlas of New Jersey	BEERS	Folio
The American Atlas ...	JEFFERYS	Folio
The American Geography ...	MORSE, JEDIDIAH	Quarto
The American Military Pocket Atlas; Being an approved Collection ...	SAYER & BENNETT	Octavo
The American Traveller; or Guide through the United States	TANNER	12mo
The American Universal Geography	MORSE, JEDIDIAH	Octavo
The Diamond Atlas	DIAMOND ATLAS	Quarto
The Dispatch Atlas	WEEKLY DISPATCH	Folio
The English Counties Delineated: or a Topographical Description of England	MOULE	Quarto
The English Pilot for the Southern Navigation: Describing the Sea-Coasts ...	MOUNT & PAGE	Folio
The English Pilot The Fourth Book Describing the West India Navigation ...	MOUNT & PAGE	Folio
The Historie of the World	RALEIGH, W.	Folio
The History of New England Containing an Impartial Account of the Civil ...	NEAL	23x53cm
The Illustrated Atlas and Modern History of the World	TALLIS	Quarto
The National Atlas of Historical, Commercial, and Political Geography ...	JOHNSTON	Folio
The Parliamentary Gazetteer of England and Wales ... Forming a Complete	FULLARTON	Octavo
The Theatre of the Empire of Great Britain ... together with a Prospect ...	SPEED	Folio
The Travelling Atlas of England and Wales	COLLINS, H.G.	Octavo
The Universal Gazetteer: or, a Description of the ... Known World	MARTIN	Octavo
Theatrum Orbis Terrarum	ORTELIUS (Folio)	Folio
Theatrum Orbis Terrarum [Facsimile]	ORTELIUS (Folio)	Folio
Topographia Circuli Burgundici [bound with] Topographia Galliae. Part 1	MERIAN	30x20cm
Topographia Galliae. Parts 2 - 8	MERIAN	Quarto
Topographia Germaniae [Facsimile atlas]	MERIAN	Quarto
Topographical and Geological Atlas of the Black Hills of Dakota	U.S. GOV'T	72x97cm
Voyage au Pole Sud et dans l'Oceanie	DUMONT D'URVILLE	Folio
Voyage autour du Monde sur la Fregate La Venus	DEPOT DE LA MARINE	Folio
Voyage dans les Quatre Principales Isles des Mers d'Afrique	BORY de SAINT-VINCENT	Folio
Voyage de la Corvette l'Astrolabe	DUMONT D'URVILLE	Folio

GLOBES and GLOBE GORES:

Title	Author/Publisher	Size
[12 inch globe]	GLOBES	Diam: 30cm
[Advertisement for Globes]	RAND, McNALLY (atlas maps)	46x32cm
[Globe]	GLOBES	Diam: 3cm
[Globe]	GLOBES	Diam: 5cm
[Globe Gore: Africa, Southeast, & Madagascar]	CORONELLI	41x28cm
[Globe Gore: Africa, Southern]	CORONELLI	45x37cm
[Globe Gore: Australia]	CORONELLI	41x28cm
[Globe Gore: Australia, Eastern]	CORONELLI	47x30cm
[Globe Gore: Australia, Northern]	CORONELLI	23x28cm
[Globe Gore: North America, Central; Hudson's Bay to Gulf of Mexico]	CORONELLI	42x28cm
[Globe Gore: North America, Eastern; Delaware to Canadian Arctic]	CORONELLI	43x25cm
[Globe Gore: North America: Insular California & Southwest U.S.]	CORONELLI	47x30cm
[Globe Gore: North America, New England to Northern South America]	CORONELLI	42x28cm
[Globe Gore: Pacific, New Zealand]	CORONELLI	44x29cm
[Globe Gore: South America, southern]	CORONELLI	46x27cm
[Globe Gores: Asia & Pacific: Japan, Philippines, western Micronesia]	CORONELLI	46x28cm
[Globe Gores: Asia & Pacific, set of 3 covering Far East	CORONELLI	46x28cm
[Globe Gores: North America, Set of Three]	CORONELLI	41x25cm
A New American Terrestrial Globe, on Which the Principal Places ...	GLOBES	Diam: 33cm
Geographia 8 inch Terrestrial Globe	GLOBES	Diam: 20cm
Kunstlicher Mechanischer Globus zum Gebrauch des Kleinen Geographer	GLOBES	Diam: 12cm
Malby's Terrestrial Globe Compiled from the Globes of the S.D.U.K.	GLOBES	Diam: 8cm
New Eight-Inch Terrestrial Globe	GLOBES	Diam: 20cm
Newton's New & Improved Terrestrial Globe. ... by Newton, Son & Berry	NEWTON & BERRY	Diam: 8cm
To the Honorable Sir Joseph Banks ... This New British Terrestrial Globe ...	BARDIN	Diam: 46cm

TITLE PAGES, FRONTISPIECES, PORTRAITS, PUZZLES etc.

Title	Author/Publisher	Size
[Frontispiece] Lapponum Mores, Habitus, et Conversandi ac Vivendi Ratio	SCHERER	24x20cm
[Frontispiece] Planisphere Representant Toute l'Entendue du Monde ...	RENARD	43x26cm
[Portrait] Abrahamus Ortelius Antverpianus Cosmographicus ...	ORTELIUS (Miniature)	14x10cm
[Portrait] Aet. M Viri Clarissimi Joannis Speed ...	SPEED	no dimens
[Portrait] Christophorus Weigelius Chalcographicus Celeberrimus ...	WEIGEL	49x34cm
[Portrait] Gerardus Mercator ... ludocus Hondius ...	HONDIUS	39x46cm

TITLE PAGES, FRONTISPIECES, PORTRAITS, etc, continued:

[Portrait] Ioannes Baptista Homann Sac. Caes. Rego. Cath. Maj. ...	HOMANN	38x27cm
[Portrait] Petrus Bertius Collegii Illustr.ordinum Regens	BERTIUS	14x10cm
[Portrait] Spectandum Dedit Ortelius Mortalib.orbem Orbi Spectandum ...	ORTELIUS (Folio)	32x21cm
[Portrait] Vinc. Coronelli Min: Con Cosmografo della Serenis Repub di ...	CORONELLI	39x29cm
[Portrait with world map] Thomas Cavendish ...	VAN DE PASSE	13x10cm
[Puzzle] A New Map of Ireland, Divided into Its Provinces and Counties ...	CARY	47x52cm
[Puzzle] Bacon's Geographical Establishment	PUZZLES & GAMES	20x25cm
[Puzzle] England and Wales	PUZZLES & GAMES	43x34cm
[Puzzle] Europe	PUZZLES & GAMES	56x68cm
[Puzzle] Europe	PUZZLES & GAMES	46x49cm
[Puzzle] Europe	GALL & INGLIS	32x38cm
[Puzzle] Map of the World on Mercators Projection	GALL & INGLIS	47x52cm
[Puzzles: Set of 8 - World, 5 continents, Oceania, France]	FREMIN	34x46cm
[Tarot card] Carta VI Seguono le Colonie Inglesi	ARTIFACTS	10x6cm
[Title page: Atlantic and adjacent lands]	DE BRY	9x14cm
[Title page]	STRADANUS	20x27cm
[Title page] America	VAN MEURS	30x20cm
[Title page] American Atlas	COLTON (Atlas Maps)	46x36cm
[Title page] Asia	VAN MEURS	29x18cm
[Title page] Atlantic Neptune	DES BARRES	67x51cm
[Title page] Le Neptune Francois	MORTIER	51x37cm
[Title page] New Universal Atlas ...	DESILVER	43x35cm
[Title page] Theatrum Orbis Terrarum	BLAEU	no dimens
[Title page] Virginien	VAN DER AA	42x26cm

UNTITLED MAPS:

[Africa]	DE BRY	28x41cm
[Africa]	RAMUSIO	22x14cm
[Americas]	FRIES	29x37cm
[Americas: Eastern, with Atlantic]	FRIES	29x43cm
[Arizona]	ARBUCKLE	8x11cm
[Armillary Sphere]	FRIES	27x27cm
[Asia]	KIP	25x38cm
[Asia]	PORRO	18x24cm
[Asia: East]	FRIES	29x46cm
[Asia: Southern]	FRIES	29x44cm
[Asia: Southwest]	RAMUSIO	28x38cm
[Australia, New Zealand & New Guinea]	THEVENOT	39x60cm
[Austria: Voralberg; Tirol. & Liechtenstein]	HILDBURGHAUSEN BIBLIO	16x21cm
[Bali]	DE BRY	14x18cm
[Balkans]	MUNSTER	15x19cm
[British Isles]	FRIES	28x41cm
[British Isles: Ptolemaic]	WALDSEEMULLER	30x41cm
[CA: Imperial Valley soil map sheet]	U.S. GOV'T	61x43cm
[CA: San Jose soil map sheet]	U.S. GOV'T	47x79cm
[Chesapeake Bay Entrance]	BLUNT	18x21cm
[China & Japan: Complete set of 17 folio maps]	BLAEU	Folio
[Chios, Greece]	DE BRUYN	29x124cm
[Continents, 4 maps on single sheet: Africa, Americas; Asia; Europe]	HOMANN	17x21cm
[England: Somersetshire]	GREENWOOD	131x178cm
[England: The Severn or Channell of Bristoll]	COLLINS, G.	45x56cm
[England: Yorkshire]	WARBURTON	99x127cm
[Estate Plan of the] Landes of William Hunt of Dalehill in ... of Tisehurst ...	MANUSCRIPT MAPS	58x72cm
[Europe]	MUNSTER	12x15cm
[Europe]	PORRO	11x15cm
[Europe as a Woman]	MUNSTER	25x17cm
[Europe: Central and Northern]	SCHEDEL	40x58cm
[Far East: China, Korea, Japan, Indo-China, East Indies]	THEVENOT	51x67cm
[Florida: Pensacola]	U.S. GOV'T	19x23cm
[France: Rouen]	RAUW	7x9cm
[Geocentric Universe]	ANONYMOUS	18x16cm
[Geographical symbols]	BELL	23x18cm
[Germany: Aachen]	RAUW	7x9cm
[Germany: Mainz]	RAUW	7x9cm
[Germany: Philippsburg]	MERIAN	18x26cm
[Germany: Rostock]	RAUW	7x9cm

UNTITLED MAPS continued:

[Great Lakes, 7 charts: one of each lake; Mackinac Strait; River St. Mary]	BRITISH ADMIRALTY	54x96cm
[Gulf of Mexico]	OTTENS	45x57cm
[Holy Land]	KIP	28x38cm
[IL: McLean County soil map sheet]	U.S. GOV'T	81x107cm
[Ireland: Carlingford Lough]	COLLINS, G.	42x32cm
[Ireland: Dublin Bay]	COLLINS, G.	45x56cm
[Ireland: Southeastern]	VAN DEN KEERE	34x50cm
[Isle of Man]	COLLINS, G.	45x56cm
[Japan: Kyoto]	JAPANESE CARTOGRAPHY	58x88cm
[Jerusalem]	SCHONSPERGER	10x20cm
[Kansas]	RAND, McNALLY (non-atlas)	33x51cm
[Korea]	MANUSCRIPT MAPS	29x34cm
[Little Egg Harbor, NJ]	BLUNT	13x21cm
[London: Improvements to the Docks around the Tower of London]	LOCAL & STATE MAPS	54x61cm
[London: View from South Bank of Thames looking North]	ILLUS. LONDON NEWS	29x119cm
[Massachusetts: Boston view]	LOCAL & STATE MAPS	28x35cm
[Massachusetts: Nantucket, Martha's Vineyard, Elizabeth Islands ...	DES BARRES	74x107cm
[Mexico City]	RAMUSIO	27x17cm
[Middle East]	KIP	30x38cm
[Minnesota]	U.S. GOV'T	43x53cm
[New France]	RAMUSIO	30x39cm
[New York City] Map Showing All the Farm and Boundary ... Apthorpes ...	HOLMES	69x98cm
[New York City view]	ILLUS. LONDON NEWS	24x36cm
[New York City view with Brooklyn Bridge]	ILLUS. LONDON NEWS	21x30cm
[Newport Harbor, RI]	BLUNT	20x22cm
[North America: Eastern]	CLOUET	32x56cm
[North Dakota]	U.S. GOV'T	41x54cm
[North Polar regions]	S.D.U.K.	28x28cm
[Northeastern North America: Canada & New England]	RAMUSIO	27x37cm
[Ohio, Indiana & Illinois]	RAILROAD COMPANY	13x24cm
[Pacific Ocean & northern rim]	SCHERER	23x43cm
[Pacific Ocean & northern rim]	SCHERER	23x34cm
[Pennsylvania: Bedford County]	MANUSCRIPT MAPS	20x31cm
[Poland: Wroclaw. (Breslau, Silesia)]	RAUW	7x9cm
[Ptolemaic World]	FRIES	30x46cm
[South Polar regions]	VALK & SCHENK	43x48cm
[Southeast Asia & East Indies]	FRIES	30x43cm
[Southern Hemisphere]	DE WIT	43x48cm
[Spain: Cuenca]	VON REILLY	22x25cm
[Sri Lanka: Candy]	DE BRY	27x35cm
[Staffordshire]	PLOT	65x54cm
[Switzerland: Zurich]	RAUW	7x10cm
[Tennessee: Memphis with Chattanooga]	RAND, McNALLY (atlas maps)	22x15cm
[Texas: western part]	HARDESTY	49x33cm
[Texas: western part]	RAND, McNALLY (atlas maps)	49x32cm
[Tibet]	DU HALDE	no dimens
[United States: 15 City Plans]	BRADFORD	25x19cm
[United States: Great Lakes and Missouri area]	ANONYMOUS	30x39cm
[United States: Northern Boundary, Lake of the Woods to Rocky Mts]	U.S. GOV'T	39x54cm
[United States: West]	STIELER	36x41cm
[West Indies: St. Croix & Antiqua to Dominica]	BORDONE	10x15cm
[Western Hemisphere]	BURNET	Diam: 20cm
[Western Missouri to Rocky Mountains]	U.S. GOV'T	50x88cm
[Western Territory: Kansas & Nebraska, etc.]	U.S. GOV'T	50x89cm
[World]	BOWEN, EMANUEL	18x30cm
[World]	FRIES	31x47cm
[World]	HALLEY	52x144cm
[World]	VAN JAGEN	30x45cm
[World] ... La Carta da Navigare	PORCACCHI	10x14cm
[World] Nansenbushu Bankoku Shoka No Zu	JAPANESE CARTOGRAPHY	114x142cm
[World: Circular, Korean title]	MANUSCRIPT MAPS	29x34cm
[World in set with 4 maps of Terra Australis]	HALL	no dimens
[World on silk]	ANONYMOUS	42x64cm
[World: Medieval]	ANONYMOUS	Diam: 31cm
[World. Set of two hemispheres]	HAPPEL	29x29cm
[Yellowstone National Park]	U.S. WAR DEPARTMENT	70x50cm

319

TITLED MAPS:

Title	Publisher/Source	Size
1905 Revised and Reduced Edition ... County of Santa Clara, California	LOCAL & STATE WALL	100x144cm
A Chart of New South Wales, Van Diemen's Land &c [with] Surveys in ...	ASPIN	50x60cm
A Chart of New York Harbour ...	MOUNT & PAGE	61x46cm
A Chart of the Arabian Gulf or Red Sea ... James Capper	FADEN	117x88cm
A Chart of the Baltic Sea, Gulfs of Finland and Bothnia ...	GENTLEMAN'S MAGAZINE	24x26cm
A Chart of the Channel in the Philipne Islands, through which the Manila ...	LONDON MAGAZINE	25x21cm
A Chart of the Easternmost Part of the East Indies and China. ... to Iapan	THORNTON	43x53cm
A Chart of the Entrance Into St. Mary's River [with] ... Amelia Island ...	JEFFERYS	51x61cm
A Chart of the Entrance of the Red Sea	SAYER & BENNETT	33x65cm
A Chart of the Gulf Stream	AMER. PHILOSOPHICAL SOC.	20x25cm
A Chart of the Inner Passage, between the Coast of Africa ... Madagascar	SAYER & BENNETT	61x72cm
A Chart of the North Sea from the Forelands to North Bergen ... Shetlands	MOUNT & PAGE	88x100cm
A Chart of the Nth. West Coast of America, & the Nth. East Coast of Asia	MORSE, JEDIDIAH	18x29cm
A Chart of the Pacific Ocean from the Equinoctial to the Latitude of 39½	ANSON	30x89cm
A Chart of the Red Sea from Geddah to Suez ...	SAYER & BENNETT	50x68cm
A Chart of the Sea Coast of New Foundland, New Scotland, New England	MOUNT & PAGE	47x59cm
A Chart of the Sea Coasts of New England, ... to Cape Hatteras ...	SELLER	43x53cm
A Chart of the Southern Part of the North Sea Shewing the Navigation ...	NORIE	126x79cm
A Chart of the Straits of Magellan	JEFFERYS	52x70cm
A Chart of the Straits of Malacca and Sincapore ...	LAURIE & WHITTLE	61x83cm
A Chart of the West Indies, from the Latest Marine Journals and Surveys	CAREY	28x40cm
A Chart of ye East Indies. With the Coast of Persia, China, also the Philipina	MOLL (Small)	30x43cm
A Chart Showing the Track of the Centurion Round the World	ANSON	23x41cm
A Compleat Map of the British Isles	KITCHIN	64x50cm
A Correct Chart of Hispaniola with the Windward Passage ... C. Price ...	MOUNT & PAGE	48x60cm
A Correct Chart of the Caribbee Islands ...	MOUNT & PAGE	43x53cm
A Correct Draught of the North Pole and of All the Countries hitherto	BOWEN, EMANUEL	39x44cm
A Correct Map of the Georgia Western Territory	MORSE, JEDIDIAH	18x15cm
A Correct Map of the Island of Jamaica.	KITCHIN	11x19cm
A Diagram of Oregon	U.S. STATE SURVEYS	43x58cm
A Draught of the City of Jerusalem	LE BRUYN	8x22cm
A Draught of the Great Bay, Back Bay and Harbour of Trincomalay ...	NICHELSON	91x98cm
A Draught of the Harbour of Halifax in Nova Scotia by an Officer ...	LOTTERY MAGAZINE	17x23cm
A Draught of the Harbours of Port Royal and Kingston, in Jamaica ...	POLITICAL MAGAZINE	26x38cm
A Draught of the Sea Coast and Rivers of Virginia, Maryland	BLOME	20x25cm
A General and Particular Description of America ...	MOLL (Small)	18x19cm
A General Chart of the Globe, Shewing the Course of the Gulph Stream ...	TRUXTON	46x44cm
A General Chart of the Indian and part of the Pacific Oceans ...	HOBBS	110x199cm
A General Chart of the South Sea from the River Plate to Dampier's ...	SELLER	43x57cm
A General Map of Ireland to Accompany the Report of the Railway ...	GOV'T MAPS: NATIONAL	180x146cm
A General Map of North America Drawn from the Best Surveys ...	RUSSELL	36x47cm
A General Map of North America from the Best Authorities	MORSE, JEDIDIAH	20x23cm
A General Map of North America from the Latest Observations	RUSSELL	28x41cm
A General Map of the Discoveries of Admiral de Fonte ...	GENTLEMAN'S MAGAZINE	19x25cm
A General Map of the Northern British Colonies in America ...	SAYER & BENNETT	66x48cm
A General Map of the Northewestern Part of the Dominion of Canada	CANADIAN GOV'T	91x122cm
A General Stereographic Map on the Plane of the Meridian	HARRISON	14x19cm
A General View of the City of Lisbon, the Capital of the Kingdom of Portugal	COLE	15x28cm
A Generall Mapp of Carolina. Describeing Its Sea Coast and Rivers	BLOME	15x22cm
A Geographically Correct Map of the State of Texas ...	RAILROAD COMPANY	46x51cm
A Geological Map of the Black Hills by Professor N.H. Winchell ...	WINCHELL	56x46cm
A Geological Map of the United States	HINTON	25x39cm
A Large Chart Describing ye Streights of Malacca and Sincapore ...	MOUNT & PAGE	44x54cm
A Large Draft of the Island Antegua	MOUNT & PAGE	33x25cm
A Map Exhibiting All the New Discoveries in the Interior Parts of North Amer	ARROWSMITH	122x140cm
A Map of a Large Country Newly Discovered in the Northern America ...	HENNEPIN	37x43cm
A Map of America, Between Latitudes 40 and 70 North, and Longitudes ...	MacKENZIE	45x79cm
A Map of Antient Egypt	SEALE	24x21cm
A Map of Boston County of Suffolk and the Adjacent Towns	BOWEN	31x31cm
A Map of Cape Cod, and the Parts Adjacent	HILL	32x27cm
A Map of Connecticut and Rhode Island, with Long Island Sound, &c.	GENTLEMAN'S MAGAZINE	17x23cm
A Map of Essex	KITCHIN	12x14cm
A Map of Georgia, Also the Two Floridas, from the Best Authorities	MORSE, JEDIDIAH	19x32cm
A Map of Guadeloupe One of the Caribby Islands in the West Indies ...	LONDON MAGAZINE	13x20cm
A Map of India on the West Side of the Ganges ...	BOWEN, EMANUEL	32x23cm
A Map of Ireland. Warranted Perfect Improved Dissected Maps ...	PUZZLES & GAMES	no dimens

Title	Author/Source	Size
A Map of Louisiana and the River Mississipi	SENEX	49x57cm
A Map of Mr. Bell's Journey from Moscow to Pekin	ANONYMOUS	25x66cm
A Map of New England & ye Country Adjacent, Extending Northward ...	GENERAL MAG. OF ARTS	20x18cm
A Map of New England and New York ...	SPEED	39x51cm
A Map of New France Containing Canada, Louisiana &c. in Nth. Americ	MOLL (Small)	19x26cm
A Map of North America by J. Palairet with Considerable Alterations ...	PALAIRET	48x58cm
A Map of North America from the Latest Aurthorities	PAYNE	20x22cm
A Map of North America from the Latest Surveys and Maps	BLAIR	42x58cm
A Map of North America with the European Settlements & ... West Indies	SEALE	37x47cm
A Map of Old & New Castile from the Observations of Rodrigo Mendes ...	SENEX	44x55cm
A Map of Pennsylvania Exhibiting Not Only the Improved Parts of That ...	SCULL	66x131cm
A Map of Philadelphia and Parts Adjacent, by N. Scull and G. Heap	GENTLEMAN'S MAGAZINE	34x29cm
A Map of Switzerland	MOLL (Small)	18x19cm
A Map of That Part of America Which Was the Principal Seat of War ...	GENTLEMAN'S MAGAZINE	22x34cm
A Map of that Part of Bucks County Released by the Indians ... Delaware	MANUSCRIPT MAPS	63x43cm
A Map of the British & French Plantations in North America.	LONDON MAGAZINE	21x26cm
A Map of the British American Plantations, Extending from Boston ...	GENTLEMAN'S MAGAZINE	22x27cm
A Map of the British Empire in America ... [4 sheets: NY to Labrador]	POPPLE	100x98cm
A Map of the British Empire In America ... [key sheet]	POPPLE	50x48cm
A Map of the British Empire in America ... [Lower left quadrant]	POPPLE	68x49cm
A Map of the British Empire in America, from Hudsons Bay ... Georgia ...	MAGAZINE OF MAGAZINES	26x32cm
A Map of the Brittish Plantations on the Continent of America	OSBORNE	34x30cm
A Map of the Circle of Lower Saxony	KITCHIN	22x26cm
A Map of the City of Philadelphia	LOCAL & STATE MAPS	102x76cm
A Map of the Coast of New England, from Staten Island to ... Breton ...	MOUNT & PAGE	62x80cm
A Map of the Countrey and Citty of Panama ...	ESQUEMELING	17x28cm
A Map of the Country Round Philadelphia Including Part of New Jersey ...	GENTLEMAN'S MAGAZINE	18x22cm
A Map of the Country which Was the Scene of Operations of the Northern	MARSHALL	25x19cm
A Map of the County of Kent	HARRIS	57x82cm
A Map of the Discoveries Made by Captn. Willm. Dampier in the Roebuck	BOWEN, EMANUEL	20x32cm
A Map of the Discoveries Made by Capts. Cook & Clerke ...	CAREY	19x28cm
A Map of the East Indies from the Latest Authorities and Observations	BLAIR	42x56cm
A Map of the Island of Jamaica.	GENTLEMAN'S MAGAZINE	11x20cm
A Map of the Kingdom of Ireland from ye Latest & Best Observations	BOWEN, EMANUEL	48x38cm
A Map of the Kingdome of Ireland ...	ROCQUE	122x96cm
A Map of the Most Inhabited Part of New England ...	JEFFERYS	104x99cm
A Map of the Most Inhabited Part of New England Containing the Provinces	LE ROUGE	101x97cm
A Map of the Most Inhabited Part of New England Containing the Provinces	BOWLES	64x52cm
A Map of the Most Inhabited Part of New England Containing the Provinces	LOTTER	102x97cm
A Map of the New Governments, of East & West Florida.	GENTLEMAN'S MAGAZINE	20x25cm
A Map of the North Pole and the Parts Adjoining	PITT	46x58cm
A Map of the North Pole with All the Territories that Lye Near It ...	MOLL (Small)	20x28cm
A Map of the North Western Territory	MORSE, JEDIDIAH	24x18cm
A Map of the Old Colony Railroad and Connections	MORRILL	100x97cm
A Map of the Principal Rivers ... and Comparative Lengths	S.D.U K.	39x31cm
A Map of the Province of Lower Canada, Describing All the Seigneuries...	WYLD	57x89cm
A Map of the Province of Upper Canada, Describing All the New Settlements	WYLD	57x87cm
A Map of the Provinces of New-York and New-Jersey, with a Part of Penn...	LOTTER	74x57cm
A Map of the Rhine from Dusseldorf to Mainz or Mayence	PHILLIPS	14x24cm
A Map of the River Gambia from Eropina to Barrakunda by ... John Leach	KITCHIN	20x32cm
A Map of the Sacred Geography Taken from the Old and New Testament	WARE	36x43cm
A Map of the Seat of War in Florida 1836	U.S. GOV'T	38x28cm
A Map of the South Pole, with the Track of His Majesty's Sloop Resolution	GENTLEMAN'S MAGAZINE	22x21cm
A Map of the State of Kentucky and the Tennessee Government ... Harris	MORSE, JEDIDIAH	20x29cm
A Map of the State of Pennsylvania	HOWELL	54x84cm
A Map of the Tennessee Government Formerly Part of North Carolina ...	CAREY	24x52cm
A Map of the United States of America	MORSE, JEDIDIAH	14x14cm
A Map of the United States of America	TANNER	38x33cm
A Map of the United States of America with Part of the Adjoining ...	WILKINSON	22x28cm
A Map of the United States: Compiled Chiefly from the State Maps ...	CAREY	64x90cm
A Map of the West Indies and Middle Continent of America from the Latest	KITCHIN	41x57cm
A Map of the West Indies and Middle Continent of America from the Latest	BLAIR	42x58cm
A Map of the West Indies or the Islands of America in the North Sea ...	MOLL (Large)	59x110cm
A Map of the Western Parts of the Colony of Virginia.	LONDON MAGAZINE	19x12cm
A Map of the Wondrous Isle of Manhattan	LOCAL & STATE MAPS	64x102cm
A Map of the World from the Best Authorities	BROOKES	15x28cm
A Map of the World, on Mercators Projection.	GENTLEMAN'S MAGAZINE	18x28cm

Title	Author	Size
A Map of the World with the Latest Discoveries ...	BLAIR	41x70cm
A Map of Virginia and Maryland ...	SPEED	38x50cm
A Map of ye Holy Land	LE BRUYN	28x54cm
A Map Shewing the Most Remarkable Places to Which the Apostles ...	WARE	35x40cm
A Map Shewing ye Situation of Paradice and ye Country Inhabited by ...	WARE	36x43cm
A Map to Explain the History of the Assyrians ... & Persians	GIBSON	24x21cm
A Mapp of Italy	BLOME	29x39cm
A Mapp of Jerusalem ...	LEA	32x47cm
A Mapp of the Five Zones	SELLER	11x12cm
A Mapp of the Kingdome of Ireland	BLOME	37x38cm
A Mapp of the Sommer Ilands Once Called the Bermudas ...	SPEED	40x53cm
A Mercator Chart of the World ...	BOWEN, THOMAS	34x45cm
A Missionary Map Representing the Evangelical Condition of the World ...	AMER. SUNDAY SCHOOL	32x54cm
A Movable Planisphere of the Heavens at Every Minute ...	ARTIFACTS	Diam: 38cm
A New & Accurate Chart of the World ...	BOWEN, EMANUEL	36x57cm
A New & Accurate Map of All the Known World ...	BOWEN, EMANUEL	31x54cm
A New & Accurate Map of Asia Drawn from Actual Surveys ...	BOWEN, EMANUEL	34x42cm
A New & Accurate Map of China, Drawn from Surveys Made by the Jesuit	KITCHIN	34x41cm
A New & Accurate Map of Louisiana, with Part of Florida and Canada ...	BOWEN, EMANUEL	34x42cm
A New & Accurate Map of North America ...	BOWEN, THOMAS	27x43cm
A New & Accurate Map of Scotland or North Britain	BOWEN, EMANUEL	43x36cm
A New & Accurate Map of the Island of Antigua or Antego ...	BOWEN, EMANUEL	32x23cm
A New & Accurate Map of the Islands of Newfoundland, Cape Breton ...	BOWEN, EMANUEL	35x43cm
A New & Accurate Map of the North Pole, with All the Countries ...	BOWEN, EMANUEL	38x43cm
A New & Correct Chart of Cuba, Streights of Bahama, Windward Passage	MOUNT & PAGE	46x64cm
A New & Correct Map of England & Wales Now Called South Britain	WILLDEY	62x105cm
A New & Correct Map of the Netherlands or Low Countries ...	BOWEN, EMANUEL	43x34cm
A New & Correct Map of the Whole World ...	MOLL (Large)	46x70cm
A New & Exact Mapp of the Island of Jamaica ...	BOCHART & KNOLLIS	56x42cm
A New & Exact Mapp of ye Isle of Iamaica As It Was Lately Surveyed ...	BLOME	28x33cm
A New and Accurat Map of the World ...	OVERTON	39x52cm
A New and Accurat Map of the World Drawne According to ye Truest ...	WALTON	39x52cm
A New and Accurate Chart of the Harbour of Boston, in New England ...	POLITICAL MAGAZINE	22x17cm
A New and Accurate Chart of the West Indies with the Adjacent Coasts	BOWEN, EMANUEL	37x45cm
A New and Accurate Chart of the Western or Atlantic Ocean ...	BOWEN, EMANUEL	37x45cm
A New and Accurate Chart of the Western or Atlantic Ocean ...	BOWEN, THOMAS	21x27cm
A New and Accurate Map of Africa Drawn & Engraved ...	GIBSON	20x23cm
A New and Accurate Map of America ... Exhibiting the Course of the Trade	BOWEN, EMANUEL	36x44cm
A New and Accurate Map of America Drawn from the Most Approved ...	BOWEN, EMANUEL	35x45cm
A New and Accurate Map of Connecticut and Rhode Island, from the ...	UNIVERSAL MAGAZINE	25x33cm
A New and Accurate Map of East and West Florida, Drawn from the ...	PROCKTER	19x20cm
A New and Accurate Map of Europe ...	BOWEN, EMANUEL	37x45cm
A New and Accurate Map of Italy Drawn from the Latest and Best ...	BOWEN, EMANUEL	31x22cm
A New and Accurate Map of New Jersey, from the Best Authorities.	UNIVERSAL MAGAZINE	33x25cm
A New and Accurate Map of New South Wales with Norfolk and Lord ...	WILKINSON	27x23cm
A New and Accurate Map of North America Drawn & Engraved ...	GIBSON	15x20cm
A New and Accurate Map of Paraguay, Rio de la Plata ...	BOWEN, EMANUEL	36x43cm
A New and Accurate Map of Portugal Comprised from the Latest ...	BOWEN, EMANUEL	31x22cm
A New and Accurate Map of Switzerland with Its Allies and Subjects ...	BOWEN, EMANUEL	32x22cm
A New and Accurate Map of Terra Firma and the Caribbe Islands ...	BOWEN, EMANUEL	36x43cm
A New and Accurate Map of the British Dominions in America ... Treaty ...	KITCHIN	52x63cm
A New and Accurate Map of the Colony of Massachusetts Bay ...	UNIVERSAL MAGAZINE	25x33cm
A New and Accurate Map of the Empire of Japan ...	BOWEN, EMANUEL	36x43cm
A New and Accurate Map of the Kingdom of Hungary and ...Transilvania	BOWEN, EMANUEL	34x42cm
A New and Accurate Map of the Kingdoms of Naples & Sicily ...	BOWEN, EMANUEL	31x22cm
A New and Accurate Map of the Provinces of Pensilvania, Virginia ...	GIBSON	28x34cm
A New and Accurate Map of the World Drawn from the Best Authorities	BOWEN, EMANUEL	29x55cm
A New and Acurate Map of the World, Comprehending All the New ...	BALDWIN	29x46cm
A New and Accurate Mappe of the World ... [in set with 4 continents]	VAUGHAN	15x20cm
A New and Accurate Plan of the Town of Boston, in New England ...	UNIVERSAL MAGAZINE	27x35cm
A New and Correct Chart of All the Known World ... Mercator's Projection	BOWEN, EMANUEL	36x46cm
A New and Correct Chart of the North Part of America from New Found ...	MOUNT & PAGE	43x55cm
A New and Correct Chart of the Sea Coast of New England ... Cape Codd	MOUNT & PAGE	50x118cm
A New and Correct Chart of the Western and Southern Oceans Showing	MOUNT & PAGE	58x71cm
A New and Correct Map of Africa Drawn from the Most Approved ...	BOWEN, EMANUEL	37x45cm
A New and Correct Map of North America ... West India Islands	BOWEN, EMANUEL	102x115cm
A New and Correct Map of Scotland or North Britain	KITCHIN	128x107cm

Title	Publisher	Size
A New and Correct Map of Scotland or North Britain	LAURIE & WHITTLE	129x108cm
A New and Correct Map of the World ...	SENEX	15x29cm
A New and Correct Map of the World Projected upon the Plane of the ...	PRICE	64x102cm
A New and Correct Map of the World, Laid Down According to the ...	MOLL (Large)	57x97cm
A New and Exact Map of Asia ...	BOWEN, EMANUEL	37x46cm
A New and Exact Map of the Dominions of the King of Great Britain on ...	MOLL (Large)	101x61cm
A New and Exact Map of the Island of Antigua in America ...	BOWLES	114x142cm
A New and Exact Map of the Island of St. Chistopher in America ...	BOWLES	114x142cm
A New and Exact Plan of the City of London and Suburbs thereto ...	OVERTON	58x147cm
A New Chart of Holland with the Entrances to the Scheld, &c. ...	HEATHER	63x79cm
A New Chart of the Carribean Isles Called Also the Windward & Leeward	NORIE	63x93cm
A New Chart of the Cattegat and Baltic or East Sea ...	HEATHER	94x123cm
A New Chart of the Coast of North America from Port Royal Entrance ...	LAURIE & WHITTLE	72x51cm
A New Chart of the Gulf of Finland Surveyed by Order ...	HEATHER	no dimens
A New Chart of the River St. Lawrence from the Island of Anticosti to ...	SCOTS MAGAZINE	18x25cm
A New Chart of the Vast Atlantic or Western Ocean	BOWLES	46x56cm
A New Chart of the World on Mercator's Projection ...	TEESDALE	125x192cm
A New Chart of the World on Mercator's Projection; Exhibiting the Tracks	CARY	46x51cm
A New Description of Carolina ...	SPEED	39x51cm
A New General Map of America, Drawn from Several Accurate ...	BOWEN, EMANUEL	35x42cm
A New Generall Chart for the West Indies of E. Wright's Projection ...	MOUNT & PAGE	45x57cm
A New Gradually Increasing Compass-Map of ... Sea Coasts of England ...	VAN KEULEN	52x59cm
A New Map of Africa, from the Latest Authorities	CARY	47x53cm
A New Map of Alabama with Its Roads & Distances from Place to Place ...	MITCHELL, S.A. (to 1859)	36x29cm
A New Map of Alabama with Its Roads and Distances from Place to Place	THOMAS, COWPERTHWAIT	36x29cm
A New Map of America	CARY	46x52cm
A New Map of America from the Latest Observations Revis'd ...	SENEX	48x56cm
A New Map of Arkansas with Its Canals Roads & Distances	THOMAS, COWPERTHWAIT	36x29cm
A New Map of Arkansas with Its Counties Towns, Post Offices, &c.	COWPERTHWAIT, DESILVER	38x32cm
A New Map of Barkshire with All the Hundreds, Parkes ...	HOLLAR	37x50cm
A New Map of Carolina ...	MORDEN	12x13cm
A New Map of Carolina by Philip Lea ...	LEA	54x45cm
A New Map of China, from the Latest Authorities	CARY	47x51cm
A New Map of England Divided into Its Counties ...	KITCHIN	36x33cm
A New Map of France, Agreeable to Its Division into Provinces ...	CARY	46x52cm
A New Map of Georgia with Its Roads and Distances ...	THOMAS, COWPERTHWAIT	36x29cm
A New Map of Georgia with Part of Carolina, Florida, and Louisiana ...	BOWEN, EMANUEL	36x48cm
A New Map of Germany Divided Into Circles	ROLLOS	20x29cm
A New Map of Illinois with Its Canals, Roads & Distances from Place ...	THOMAS, COWPERTHWAIT	37x29cm
A New Map of India & China	SENEX	50x59cm
A New Map of Ireland ...	PRINALD	28x19cm
A New Map of Ireland Divided into Provinces, Counties &c.	KITCHIN	64x56cm
A New Map of Ireland from the Latest Observations	SENEX	59x49cm
A New Map of Ireland, Divided into Its Provinces and Counties	CARY	50x56cm
A New Map of Jamaica ... from Actual Surveys Made by Mr. Sheffield ...	BROWNE	68x127cm
A New Map of Kansas	HOLMES	42x69cm
A New Map of Louisiana with Its Canals, Roads and Distances	TANNER	27x34cm
A New Map of Louisiana with It's Canals, Roads and Distances ...	MITCHELL, S.A. (to 1859)	31x39cm
A New Map of Maine	TANNER	36x29cm
A New Map of Maine	THOMAS, COWPERTHWAIT	38x30cm
A New Map of Mexico, California & Oregon	JAMES	33x23cm
A New Map of Michigan	DESILVER	33x41cm
A New Map of Michigan with Its Canals, Roads & Distances	THOMAS, COWPERTHWAIT	37x30cm
A New Map of Mississippi with Its Roads and Distances	TANNER	33x27cm
A New Map of Mississippi with Its Roads and Distances	THOMAS, COWPERTHWAIT	36x29cm
A New Map of Nebraska Showing Counties, Cities, Towns, Railways ...	GAST & CO.	22x40cm
A New Map of North America	CARVER	43x55cm
A New Map of North America	HARRISON	19x27cm
A New Map of North America ...	WELLS	36x48cm
A New Map of North America According to the Newest Observations	MOLL (Small)	18x26cm
A New Map of North America from the Latest Discoveries. 1763.	LONDON MAGAZINE	27x37cm
A New Map of North America Shewing All the New Discoveries	MORSE, JEDIDIAH	19x23cm
A New Map of North America Shewing All the New Discoveries, 1791	ARROWSMITH	20x24cm
A New Map of North America, Agreeable to the Latest Discoveries	WILKINSON	21x25cm
A New Map of North America, from the Best Authorities	LODGE	33x36cm
A New Map of North America, with the West India Islands ... 1783	LAURIE & WHITTLE	102x117cm
A New Map of Nova Scotia ...	JEFFERYS	32x42cm

323

A New Map of Nova Scotia, Newfoundland ...	CARY	46x52cm
A New Map of Ohio with Its Canals Roads & Distances	TANNER	33x27cm
A New Map of Ohio with its Canals, Roads & Distances	MITCHELL, S.A. (to 1859)	36x29cm
A New Map of Our Country Present and Prospective ...	GASTON & JOHNSON	142x156cm
A New Map of Part of the United States of North America ... New York ...	CARY	52x58cm
A New Map of Pennsylvania with Its Canals, Rail-Roads & Distances ...	TANNER	27x34cm
A New Map of Rome Showing Its Ancient and Present Situation	BROWNE	49x58cm
A New Map of Swisserland, Divided into Its Cantons and Dependencies ...	CARY	46x52cm
A New Map of Tennessee with Its Roads and Distances from Place ...	THOMAS, COWPERTHWAIT	28x39cm
A New Map of Texas Oregon and California with the Regions Adjoining ...	MITCHELL, S.A. (non-atlas)	51x47cm
A New Map of the City of Amsterdam	SENEX	49x58cm
A New Map of the Eastern Parts of Asia Minor	WELLS	37x50cm
A New Map of the Kingdom of Poland	KITCHIN	50x66cm
A New Map of the Land of Canaan and Parts Adjoining Showing the ...	WELLS	38x50cm
A New Map of the Most Considerable Plantations of the English in America	WELLS	36x48cm
A New Map of the North Part of Antient Africa	WELLS	37x50cm
A New Map of the North Parts of America Claimed by France ...	MOLL (Large)	60x100cm
A New Map of the Northern States Containing the Kingdoms of Sweden ...	KITCHIN	50x66cm
A New Map of the Province of Maryland in North America	UNIVERSAL MAGAZINE	28x33cm
A New Map of the Province of Quebec in North America ...	LONDON MAGAZINE	17x22cm
A New Map of the Russian Empire, Divided into Its Governments ...	CARY	46x100cm
A New Map of the State of California, the Territories of Oregon & Utah, ...	THOMAS, COWPERTHWAIT	41x32cm
A New Map of the State of California, the Territories of Oregon, Wash. ...	THOMAS, COWPERTHWAIT	40x32cm
A New Map of the State o Illinois	DESILVER	39x33cm
A New Map of the State of Missouri	THOMAS, COWPERTHWAIT	33x41cm
A New Map of the State of South Carolina	DESILVER	33x39cm
A New Map of the Terraqueous Globe According to the Latest Discoveries	WELLS	38x52cm
A New Map of the United States of America	DESILVER	39x67cm
A New Map of the United States of America	THOMAS, COWPERTHWAIT	40x67cm
A New Map of the United States of America, from the Latest Authorities	CAREY	32x43cm
A New Map of the United States of America, from the Latest Authorities	CARY	46x51cm
A New Map of the West India Isles ...	CARY	46x51cm
A New Map of the West Indies for the History of the British Colonies	STOCKDALE	70x112cm
A New Map of the Whole Continent of America	SAYER	104x118cm
A New Map of the World	MITCHELL, S.A. (to 1859)	24x36cm
A New Map of the World ...	MOLL (Small)	18x28cm
A New Map of the World According to the New Observations ...	MOLL (Small)	18x28cm
A New Map of the World from the Latest Observations ...	SENEX	42x52cm
A New Map of the World on the Globular Projection	THOMAS, COWPERTHWAIT	24x36cm
A New Map of the World with the Latest Discoveries ...	DUNN	34x50cm
A New Map of Upper and Lower Canada from the Latest Authorities ...	CARY	46x51cm
A New Map of Virginia with Its Canals, Roads & Distances from Place ...	THOMAS, COWPERTHWAIT	30x37cm
A New Map, or Chart ... of Part of Europe, Asia and Africa	HERBERT	62x79cm
A New Map, or Chart ... of the Ethiopic Ocean with Part of Africa ...	HERBERT	62x79cm
A New Map, or Chart ... of the Western or Atlantic Ocean ...	HERBERT	62x79cm
A New Mapp of the Citty of London Much Inlarged ...	OVERTON	56x94cm
A New Mapp of the Kingdom of England Showing Its Antient and Present	BROWNE	Quarto
A New Mappe of the Romane Empire ...	SPEED	38x51cm
A New Projection of the Eastern Hemisphere of the Earth ...	GENTLEMAN'S MAGAZINE	21x21cm
A New Projection of the Western Hemisphere of the Earth ...	GENTLEMAN'S MAGAZINE	21x23cm
A New, Plaine & Exact Map of Europe ...	WALTON	43x53cm
A Newe Mape of Tartary ...	SPEED	39x50cm
A Particular Map of the American Lakes, Rivers etc. par le Sr. D'Anville ...	HARRISON	51x71cm
A Particular Map, to Illustrate Gen. Amhersts, Expedition, to Montreal ...	GENTLEMAN'S MAGAZINE	18x23cm
A Physical Planisphere Wherein Are Represented All the Known Lands ...	BUACHE	31x29cm
A Plan of Bridge Town, in the Island of Barbadoes.	GENTLEMAN'S MAGAZINE	10x19cm
A Plan of Captain Carver's Travels in the Interior Parts of North America ...	CARVER	26x34cm
A Plan of Iuan Fernandes Island in the South Sea ...	SEALE	23x49cm
A Plan of New York Island with Part of Long Island, Staten Island ...	FADEN	52x44cm
A Plan of Port Royal in South Carolina. Survey'd by Capn. John Gascoigne	JEFFERYS & FADEN	71x58cm
A Plan of Quebec, Metropolis of Canada in North America	LONDON MAGAZINE	13x20cm
A Plan of the Attack of Fort Sullivan, near Charles Town in South Carolina	FADEN	29x37cm
A Plan of the City and Environs of Philadelphia	LOTTER	60x46cm
A Plan of the City of Batavia	ANDREWS	17x23cm
A Plan of the City of Canton on the River Ta Hoo	HARRIS	28x21cm
A Plan of the City of Quebec	ANDREWS	18x23cm
A Plan of the Harbour of Chebucto and Town of Halifax.	GENTLEMAN'S MAGAZINE	22x27cm

Title	Publisher	Size
A Plan of the Operations of the King's Army ... in New York and ... Jersey	FADEN	72x48cm
A Plan of the Siege of the Havana, Drawn by an Officer on the Spot ...	GENTLEMAN'S MAGAZINE	20x25cm
A Plan of the Surprise of Stoney Point by a Detachment of the American ...	FADEN	50x70cm
A Plan of the Town and Chart of the Harbour of Boston ...	GENTLEMAN'S MAGAZINE	26x34cm
A Plan of the Town of Newport in Rhode Island ...	FADEN	33x36cm
A Plan Shewing the Direct Roads ... from the City of Bristol	DOUGLAS	23x23cm
A Prospect of the City of Genoa	HARRIS	18x37cm
A Reduced Map of the Empire of Germany, Holland, the Netherlands, ...	STOCKDALE	47x81cm
A Topographical Chart of the Bay of Narraganset ...	FADEN	93x63cm
A Travelling Game of India Designed to Afford Instruction and Amusement	PUZZLES & GAMES	60x47cm
A View of Amsterdam	GENTLEMAN'S MAGAZINE	17x39cm
A View of Amsterdam	JEFFERYS	17x39cm
A View of Madrid the Capital of Spain	MIDDLETON	15x25cm
A View of the City of Mexico	RUSSELL	18x20cm
A View of the City of Vienna ...	MIDDLETON	16x26cm
A View of the Grand Harbour of Malta. With Part of the City of La Valetta	BARKER	22x26cm
A View of the Town and Castle of St. Augustine, and the English Camp ...	GENTLEMAN'S MAGAZINE	30x17cm
A View of ye General & Coasting Trade-Winds, Monsoons or ye Shifting ...	MOLL (Small)	19x53cm
Abissinorum Imperium	BERTIUS	8x13cm
Abissinorum Regnu	MERCATOR (Small)	15x18cm
Abissinorum sive Pretiosi Ioannis Imperiu	MERCATOR (Folio)	34x49cm
Abrahami Patriarchae Peregrinatio et Vita ...	ORTELIUS (Folio)	35x46cm
Abriss der Stadt Franckenthal, Wie Solche von dem Vice General Don Go ...	BELLUS	27x32cm
Accurata Delineatio Celeberrimae Regionis Ludovicianae vel Gallice Louisiane	SEUTTER	49x57cm
Accurata Designatio Celebris Freti Prope Andalusiae Castellum Gibraltar	SEUTTER	50x58cm
Accurate Geographische Delineation des Zudem Chursaechsischen ...	SCHENK	47x56cm
Accurate Vorstellung der Hoch Furstl. Bischoffl. Residenz ... Wurtzburg ...	HOMANN	49x58cm
Accurater Grundriss u: ... Haupt und Residenz-Stadt London ...	HOMANN	50x59cm
Accuratissima Dominii Veneti in Italia, Ducatus Parmae ... Lombardia ...	DE WIT	50x62cm
Accuratissima Totius Asiae Tabula ...	DE WIT	49x58cm
Achaia Quae et Hellas Hodie Livadia	CLUVER	20x25cm
Aden, Arabiae Foelicis Emporium Celeberrimi Nominis, quo ex India, ...	BRAUN & HOGENBERG	33x47cm
Adirondack Map, 1909	GOV'T: LOCAL & STATE	84x76cm
Aebudae Insulae sive Hebrides	BLAEU	38x53cm
Aegypti Recentior Descriptio: Aegyptius & Turcis Eschibith; Arabibus ...	VALK & SCHENK	41x49cm
Aegyptus	HONDIUS	15x18cm
Aegyptus Antiqua	FULLER	30x34cm
Aegyptus Antiqua	JANSSON	38x52cm
Aegyptus Antiqua	ORTELIUS (Folio)	36x51cm
Aelst. - Alostum, Urbs Flandriae Imperatoriae Firmissima	BRAUN & HOGENBERG	33x42cm
Aeneae Troiani Navigatio ...	ORTELIUS (Folio)	35x48cm
Aeneae Troiani Navigatio ad Virgilij Sex Priores Aeneidos	JANSSON	40x50cm
Aethiopia Inferior Vel Exterior ...	JANSSON	38x50cm
Aethiopia Inferior Vel Exterior ...	VALK & SCHENK	38x50cm
Aethiopia Inferior, vel Exterior ...	BLAEU	38x50cm
Aethiopia Superior vel Interior; Vulgo Abissinorum sive Presbiteri Ioannis	BLAEU	39x50cm
Aethiopia Superior vel Interior; Vulgo Abissinorum sive Presbiteri Ioannis	VALK & SCHENK	38x48cm
Aevi Veteris usque ad Annum Salutis non Agesimum supra Milles ...	CORONELLI	46x62cm
Afbeeldinge van de Veertich-Jaarige Reyse der Kinderen Israels	DANCKERTS	35x51cm
Africa	BRADFORD	19x25cm
Africa	CARY	23x29cm
Africa	CRAM	24x32cm
Africa	GRANT	56x41cm
Africa	MAGINI	13x17cm
Africa	WYLD	54x60cm
Africa, Lybia, Morenlandt mit Allen Koenigreichen ... [and variations]	MUNSTER	31x36cm
Africa / Lybia / Morlandt ... [and variations]	MUNSTER	27x35cm
Africa ex Magna Orbis Terre Descriptione Gerardi Mercatoris Desumpta ...	MERCATOR (Folio)	38x46cm
Africa from the Best Authorities	PAYNE	18x22cm
Africa including the Mediterranean ...	WILKINSON	28x25cm
Africa mit Seinem Befundern Laendern Thieren und Wunderbelichen ...	MUNSTER	13x16cm
Africa Nova Tabula	GASTALDI	13x17cm
Africa Nuova Tavola	RUSCELLI	18x25cm
Africa Secundum Legitimas Projectionis Stereographicae Regulas ...	HOMANN	47x56cm
Africa Tertia Pars Terrae	BUNTING	26x34cm
Africa Tertia Pars Terrae Septentrio	BUNTING	26x34cm
Africa Vetus	SANSON (Folio)	40x55cm

Title	Author	Size
Africae	VAN LINSCHOTEN	40x56cm
Africae Accurata Tabula ...	VAN MEURS	44x55cm
Africae Accurata Tabula ex Officina Nic. Visscher	VISSCHER	43x54cm
Africae Antiquae ... Europae Asiaeque Adiacentium Regionum ...	JANSSON	38x53cm
Africae, Described, the Manners of their Habits, and Buildings: Newly ...	SPEED	40x52cm
Africae Nova Descriptio ...	BLAEU	41x56cm
Africae Nova Tabula	HONDIUS	41x55cm
Africae Pars Australis	SCHERER	23x35cm
Africae Pars Borealis 1699	SCHERER	24x36cm
Africae Propriae Tabula	ORTELIUS (Folio)	34x48cm
Africae Tabula Nova	ORTELIUS (Folio)	38x50cm
Afrique	BRION DE LA TOUR	28x27cm
Afrique	LEVASSEUR	30x46cm
Afrique ...	BONNE	21x32cm
Afrique Centrale	DUFOUR	25x32cm
Alabama	BRADFORD	36x29cm
Alabama	BRADFORD	24x19cm
Alabama	FINLEY	29x22cm
Alameda County, California	REAL ESTATE MAPS	38x56cm
Albany & New York Day Steamers	AMER. BANK NOTE CO.	51x20cm
Aldenburg	MUNSTER	12x16cm
Alexandria, Vetustissimum Aegypti Emporium, Amplissima Civitas ...	BRAUN & HOGENBERG	36x48cm
Algerie, Colonie Francaise	LEVASSEUR	29x43cm
Alsatia Superior	MERCATOR (Small)	14x18cm
Alten Stettin	BRAUN & HOGENBERG	34x48cm
Amer. Sep. No.41 Partie Des Etats-Unis	VANDERMAELEN	47x49cm
Amer. Sep. No.42 Haut Canada et Michigan	VANDERMAELEN	47x49cm
Amer. Sep. No.43 Partie des Etats-Unis	VANDERMAELEN	47x49cm
Amer. Sep. No.46 Nouvelle Californie	VANDERMAELEN	47x57cm
Amer. Sep. No.47 Partie du Mexique	VANDERMAELEN	43x34cm
Amer. Sep. No.48 Parties des Etats-Unis et du Nouveau Mexique	VANDERMAELEN	46x57cm
Amer. Sep. No.54 Partie du Mexique	VANDERMAELEN	47x49cm
Amer. Sep. No.55 Partie des Etats Unis	VANDERMAELEN	46x51cm
Amer. Sep. No.56 Partie des Etats Unis	VANDERMAELEN	46x48cm
Amer. Sep. No.57 Partie des Etats Unis	VANDERMAELEN	46x49cm
Amer. Sep. No.62 Florides et Iles Lucayes	VANDERMAELEN	47x49cm
Amer. Sep. No.63 Partie de la Vielle Californie	VANDERMAELEN	46x53cm
Amer. Sep. No.66 Merida	VANDERMAELEN	46x53cm
Amer. Sep. No.75 Petites Antilles	VANDERMAELEN	46x55cm
America	CARY	28x23cm
America	D'ANANIA	18x24cm
America	HONDIUS	38x51cm
America	MAGINI	13x17cm
America	MOLL (Small)	17x19cm
America	RUSCELLI	19x25cm
America	THOMSON	46x51cm
America 1841	HILDBURGHAUSEN BIBLIO	26x21cm
America Aurea Pars Altera Mundi ...	VALK	48x59cm
America Borealis	SCHERER	24x36cm
America Meridionale ...	CORONELLI	61x92cm
America Meridionalis	HONDIUS	36x49cm
America Noviter Delineata	JANSSON	38x50cm
America Noviter Delineata	MERIAN	36x44cm
America Noviter Delineata	MERIAN	28x36cm
America Noviter Delineata ...	HONDIUS	38x50cm
America Noviter Delineata Auct: Judoco Hondio	HONDIUS	41x54cm
America Septentrionalis	JANSSON	47x57cm
America Septentrionalis a Domino D'Anville in Gallis Edita Nunc in Anglia	HOMANN	48x52cm
America Septentrionalis, Concinnata juxta Observationes ... De L'Isle ...	LOTTER	45x57cm
America Settentrionale	NAYMILLER & ALLODI	42x33cm
America Settentrionale Colle Nuove Scoperte fin all' Anno 1688 ...	CORONELLI	60x88cm
America sive India Nova ad Magnae Gerardi Mercatoris Avi Universalis ...	MERCATOR (Folio)	37x46cm
America with Those Known Parts in That Unknowne World ...	SPEED	39x51cm
Americae ...	HOMANN	50x58cm
Americae Descrip.	HONDIUS	15x20cm
Americae Descriptio	JANSSON	14x20cm
Americae Descriptio Nova [in set with] Africae [&] Asiae [&] Europae	CHETWIND	34x33cm

Title	Author	Size
Americae Mappa Generalis ...	HOMANN	49x56cm
Americae Nova Tabula	BLAEU	36x46cm
Americae Nova Tabula. Auct: Guiljelmo Blaeuw	BLAEU	41x56cm
Americae Pars Magis Cognita. Chorographia Nobilis & Opulentae Peruanae	DE BRY	36x44cm
Americae Pars, Nunc Virginia Dicta, Primum ab Anglis ...	DE BRY	30x42cm
Americae Septentrionalis Circuitus	MORISOT	13x17cm
Americae sive Indiae Occidentalis Tabula Generalis	DE LAET	28x35cm
Americae sive Novi Orbis, Nova Descriptio	ORTELIUS (Folio)	36x48cm
Americae sive Novi Orbis, Nova Descriptio ...	MUNSTER	32x37cm
Americae tam Septentrionalis quam Meridionalis in Mappa Geographica ...	SCHENK	49x57cm
Americque Septentrionale ...	SANSON (Small)	20x24cm
Amerika [in set with] Ap'rike [&] Asia [&] Ewropia	ARMENIAN CARTOGRAPHY	46x60cm
Amerique	DESNOS	29x24cm
Amerique du Nord	DUFOUR	90x64cm
Amerique du Nord ...	DUFOUR	76x55cm
Amerique Meridionale	BELLIN (Small)	31x20cm
Amerique Meridionale	BONNE	32x22cm
Amerique Meridionale	LEVASSEUR	30x46cm
Amerique Meridionale ...	SANSON (Folio)	40x56cm
Amerique Meridionale Divisee en Ses Principales Parties ou Sont Distingues	JAILLOT	46x64cm
Amerique ou Indes Occidentales	DE VAUGONDY	52x64cm
Amerique ou le Nouveau Continent ...	NOLIN	46x69cm
Amerique Septentrionale	FREMIN	22x30cm
Amerique Septentrionale	LEVASSEUR	30x46cm
Amerique Septentrionale	MALLET	17x11cm
Amerique Septentrionale ...	BONNE	22x32cm
Amerique Septentrionale ...	DE VAUGONDY	48x59cm
Amerique Septentrionale ...	DE VAUGONDY	20x16cm
Amerique Septentrionale ...	ELWE	48x60cm
Amerique Septentrionale avec les Routes, Distences en Miles, Villages ...	LE ROUGE	132x48cm
Amerique Septentrionale Divisee en Ses Principales Parties ...	JAILLOT	45x63cm
Amerique Septentrionale Divisee en Ses Principales Parties ...	JAILLOT	55x88cm
Amerique Suivant le R. P. Charlevoix Jte. Mr. de la Condamine et ...	LE ROUGE	49x64cm
Amorfortia Dioecesis Ultrarectensis Oppidum ...	LASOR A VAREA	9x13cm
Amplissimae Regionis Mississipi seu Provinciae Ludovicianae a R.P. ...	HOMANN	49x58cm
Amstelodamum ...	BRAUN & HOGENBERG	27x39cm
Amstelredamum, Nobile Inferioris Germaniae Oppidum ...	BRAUN & HOGENBERG	33x48cm
Amsterdam	S.D.U.K.	32x38cm
An Accurate Chart of the Mediterranean and Adriatic Seas ... Black Sea	BOWEN, EMANUEL	29x59cm
An Accurate Map of Italy ...	BOWEN, EMANUEL	24x22cm
An Accurate Map of New Hampshire in New England, from a Late Survey	UNIVERSAL MAGAZINE	32x28cm
An Accurate Map of New York in North America, from a Late Survey.	UNIVERSAL MAGAZINE	34x28cm
An Accurate Map of North America Drawn from the Sieur Robert ...	ROLLOS	19x29cm
An Accurate Map of North and South Carolina with Their Indian Frontiers	MOUZON	100x141cm
An Accurate Map of Paraguay, Tucumania, Chaco, Rio de la Plata ...	GENERAL MAG. OF ARTS	28x42cm
An Accurate Map of the Caribby Islands, with the Crowns, &c. ...	LONDON MAGAZINE	25x19cm
An Accurate Map of the Country Round Boston in New England ...	TOWN & COUNTRY MAG.	32x42cm
An Accurate Map of the County of Surrey ...	BOWEN, EMANUEL	36x72cm
An Accurate Map of the East Indies Exhibiting the Course of the European	BOWEN, EMANUEL	37x45cm
An Accurate Map of the English Colonies in North America ... River Ohio	UNIVERSAL MAGAZINE	20x24cm
An Accurate Map of the Morea together with ... Greece; Also the Islands	BOWEN, EMANUEL	22x32cm
An Accurate Map of the Two Sicilies, Particularly Shewing the Places ...	POLITICAL MAGAZINE	32x24cm
An Accurate Map of the West Indies	BOWEN, EMANUEL	36x42cm
An Accurate Map of the West Indies. Exhibiting Not Only All the Islands ...	GENTLEMAN'S MAGAZINE	29x39cm
An Accurate Map of the West Indies from the Latest Improvements	WILKINSON	18x25cm
An Accurate Map of the World Laid Down from the Most Approved ...	BOWEN, EMANUEL	15x25cm
An Alphabetical Index to the Four Sheet Map of the United States	TANNER	12mo
An Ancient or Bible Map, Designed for the Use of Bible Classes ...	ANDRUS & JUDD	32x48cm
An East Prospect of the City of Philadelphia	COGGINS	56x90cm
An East Prospect of the City of Philadelphia; Taken by George Heap ...	JEFFERYS	49x91cm
An Exact Chart of the River St. Lawrence ...	JEFFERYS	59x92cm
An Exact Ground-Plot of ye City of Worcester, As it Stood Fortifyd ...	SEILE	28x36cm
An Exact Map of New England, New York, Pennsylvania & New Jersey ...	RUSSELL	19x25cm
An Exact Map of New Jersey, Pensylvania, New York, Maryland & Virginia	RUSSELL	19x25cm
An Exact Map of North America from the Best Authorities	RUSSELL	25x38cm
An Exact Map of North and South Carolina, & Georgia with East and West	RUSSELL	19x25cm
An Exact Map of the Crim, (Formerly Taurica Chersonesus) ...	GENTLEMAN'S MAGAZINE	23x32cm

Title	Author/Publisher	Size
An Exact Map of the Five Great Lakes with Part of Pensilvania, New York	RUSSELL	19x25cm
An Exact Map of the Province of Quebec with Part of New York ...	RUSSELL	19x25cm
An Exact Plan of the Capital City and Port of Malta [with] Malta and Goza	UNIVERSAL MAGAZINE	26x17cm
An Eye Sketch of the Falls of Niagara	WELD	17x23cm
Anciens Royaumes de Kent, d'Essex, et de Sussex ...	SANSON (Folio)	36x48cm
Anglia	MERCATOR (Small)	15x18cm
Anglia Scotia et Hibernia	MERCATOR (Small)	15x18cm
Anglia, Scotia et Hibernia	MERCATOR (Folio)	33x41cm
Angliae et Hiberniae	VRIENTS	44x58cm
Angliae Regni Florentissimi Nova Descriptio, Auctore Humeredo Lhuyd ...	QUAD	18x27cm
Angliae Regni Florentissimi Nova Descriptio, Auctore Humfredo Lhuyd ...	ORTELIUS (Folio)	38x48cm
Angliae, Scotiae, et Hiberniae, sive Britannicar:Insularum Descriptio	ORTELIUS (Folio)	34x50cm
Angra	MALLET	14x9cm
Annandia Praefectura	BLAEU	58x51cm
Anthony Van Diemens Land	VALENTYN	18x29cm
Antigua Surveyed by Robert Baker, Surveyor General of That Island	JEFFERYS	50x62cm
Antiquae Ierusalem Vera Icnographia ...	ARIAS MONTANUS	28x24cm
Antiquae Urbis Romae Imago Accuratiss: ...	BRAUN & HOGENBERG	69x50cm
Antiquorum Italiae & Illyrici ...	TAVERNIER	36x50cm
Antorff	MEISNER	10x15cm
Antwerp	S.D.U.K.	30x40cm
Anverpia	BRAUN & HOGENBERG	34x48cm
Aphrica	QUAD	21x30cm
Aphricae Tabula IIII	MUNSTER	28x36cm
Appomattox Court House	U.S. WAR DEPARTMENT	76x58cm
Approaches to New York - Gay Head to Cape Henlopen	U.S. COAST & GEODETIC	82x98cm
Aquarius, Piscis Notus and Capricornus	BUTLER	17x22cm
Arabia	CARY	23x28cm
Arabia ...	MOLL (Small)	19x26cm
Archaeological Map of Pajarito Park, Territory of New Mexico	U.S. GOV'T	53x57cm
Archipel des Indes Orientales Qui Comprend les Isles de la Sonde, ...	DE VAUGONDY	48x59cm
Archipelagi Americani Delineatio Geographica	SCHERER	24x34cm
Archipelagi Insularum Aliquot Descrip.	ORTELIUS (Folio)	36x50cm
Archipelague du Mexique ou Sont les Isles de Cuba, Espagnole, Iamaique ...	NOLIN	45x60cm
Archipelague du Mexique ou Sont les Isles de Cuba, Espagnole, Iamaique ...	COVENS & MORTIER	60x99cm
Argentina [Strasbourg, France]	LASOR A VAREA	8x12cm
Argow cum Parte Merid Zurichgow	BLAEU	38x50cm
Argyllshire	FADEN	148x120cm
Arizona	RAND, McNALLY (atlas maps)	48x33cm
Arizona	WALKER, H.B.	53x41cm
Arizona and New Mexico	MITCHELL, S.A. (1860+)	28x36cm
Arkansas	BRADFORD	28x36cm
Arkansas	BURR	27x32cm
Arkansas	COLTON (Atlas Maps)	32x41cm
Arkansas	CRAM	41x57cm
Arkansas	GREENLEAF	28x32cm
Arkansas	U.S. STATE SURVEYS	39x42cm
Arkansas, Mississippi, and Louisiana	JOHNSON	61x44cm
Arles	LEMERCIER	29x44cm
Armenian Map of Asia [Armenian titled]	ARMENIAN CARTOGRAPHY	46x64cm
Arnheim. in Geldern	MEISNER	10x15cm
Arnhem	GUICCIARDINI	23x34cm
Arragonia Regnum	JANSSON	41x51cm
Arragonia Regnum ...	BLAEU	41x52cm
Arras. Atrebatum, Fertilissimae Artesia Urbs Primaria, Elegantissimo Situ ...	BRAUN & HOGENBERG	35x47cm
Arrow Airways, Inc.	AERONAUTICAL MAPS	36x51cm
Artesia cum Finitimis Locis Velut Sedes Ac Theatrum Belli ...	SEUTTER	49x58cm
Artesiae Comitatus, Complectens Comitatus Nomine Fanum S. Pauli ...	VALK	49x60cm
Arx Carolina	OGILBY	28x35cm
Aschaffenburg	MERIAN	11x32cm
Asher & Adams' California & Nevada Northern Portion	ASHER & ADAMS	42x58cm
Asher & Adams' California & Nevada Southern Portion	ASHER & ADAMS	42x58cm
Asher & Adams' Colorado	ASHER & ADAMS	40x47cm
Asher & Adams' Dakota	ASHER & ADAMS	58x41cm
Asher & Adams' Kentucky & Tennessee	ASHER & ADAMS	41x58cm
Asher & Adams' Texas	ASHER & ADAMS	57x41cm
Asher & Adams' Texas Western Portion	ASHER & ADAMS	57x41cm

Asher & Adams' Washington	ASHER & ADAMS	39x57cm
Asher & Adams' Wyoming	ASHER & ADAMS	41x57cm
Asia	ARROWSMITH	63x75cm
Asia	BLACK	42x54cm
Asia	BOTERO	20x24cm
Asia	BURCKHARDT	33x38cm
Asia	HAFFNER	27x34cm
Asia	MAGINI	13x17cm
Asia ...	LOTTER	48x58cm
Asia and Its Islands	LAURIE & WHITTLE	102x119cm
Asia Corrected According to the Latest Discoveries & Observations ...	WILLDEY	62x98cm
Asia cum Omnibus Imperiis Provinciis Statibus et Insulis ...	SEUTTER	50x58cm
Asia cum Omnis Imperiis Provinciis, Statibus et Insulis ...	SEUTTER	49x57cm
Asia Drawn from the Latest Astronomical Observations ... 1800 ...	WILKINSON	22x28cm
Asia ex Magna Orbis Terrae Descriptione Gerardi Mercatoris Desumpta ...	MERCATOR (Folio)	38x46cm
Asia Noviter Delineata Auctore Guiljelmo Blaeuw	BLAEU	42x55cm
Asia Partiu Orbis Maxima	QUAD	21x30cm
Asia Recens Summa Cura Delineata. Auct Iud Hondio	HONDIUS	38x49cm
Asia Secunda Pars Terrae in Forma Pegasir	BUNTING	24x35cm
Asia Secundum Legitimas Projectionis Stereographicae ...	HOMANN	50x56cm
Asia Vetus ...	SANSON (Folio)	40x56cm
Asia with the Islands Adioyning Described ...	SPEED	39x51cm
Asiae Nova Delineatio	VISSCHER	43x54cm
Asiae Nova Descriptio	DE WIT	44x56cm
Asiae Nova Descriptio	ORTELIUS (Folio)	37x49cm
Asiae Nova Descriptio Auctore Jodoco Hondio ... Anian Fretum et ...	HONDIUS	38x50cm
Asiae Nova Discriptio ... Allard ... 1679	ALLARD	44x54cm
Asiae Novissima Tabula	DE JODE	34x44cm
Asiae Tabula Prima	PTOLEMY (1522-1541)	30x46cm
Asiatic Archipelago	S.D.U.K.	31x41cm
Asiatic Turkey	THOMSON	51x59cm
Asie	LEVASSEUR	29x43cm
Asie ...	SANSON (Folio)	39x56cm
Aspen and Its Surroundings - From a Photograph by W.H. Jackson ...	HARPER'S WEEKLY	38x51cm
Aspen Special Sheet [CO]	U.S. GEOLOGICAL SURVEY	51x41cm
Astronomische Hemel Spiegel	OTTENS	46x62cm
Athens	S.D.U.K.	34x40cm
Atlantic Coast of the United States ... Nantucket to Cape Hatteras	U.S. COAST SURVEY	60x69cm
Atlantis Insula, a Nicolao Sanson Antiquitati Restituta nunc demun Majori ...	SANSON (Folio)	39x56cm
Atlas General a l'Usage des Colleges et Maisons d'Education ... 1783 ...	NOLIN	Quarto
Atlas Map of Texas ...	MAST, CROWELL ...	30x43cm
Atsjien	VALENTYN	27x36cm
Audienca de Guadalajara, Nova Mexico, California &c.	SANSON (Small)	20x24cm
Audience de Guadalajara, Nouveau Mexique, Californie, &c. ...	SANSON (Small)	20x24cm
Augustodunum [with] Noviodunum	BRAUN & HOGENBERG	34x42cm
Australia	JOHNSTON	23x30cm
Australia	TALLIS	24x32cm
Australia [in set with 5 regions]	TALLIS	no dimens
Australian Colonies and New Zealand XLVII	GALL & INGLIS	47x58cm
Australien (Sudland) auch Polynesien oder Inselwelt ...	WALCH	48x62cm
Austria	COLTON (Atlas Maps)	32x40cm
Austria	TALLIS	24x32cm
Austria Archiduc	MERCATOR (Small)	15x18cm
Austriae Descrip. per Wolfgangum Lazium	ORTELIUS (Folio)	35x48cm
Austriae Ducatus Chorographia, Wolfgango Lazio Auctore ...	ORTELIUS (Folio)	34x47cm
Austrian Dominions	THOMSON	50x59cm
Bacon's New Map of the Seat of War in Virginia and Maryland. ...	BACON	60x46cm
Bacon's New Plan of Brighton and Hove	BACON	58x94cm
Bahama and Windward Passage	MOUNT & PAGE	43x53cm
Baie de Almerie	ROUX	13x20cm
Baltia, Quae et Scandia, Finningia ...	SANSON (Folio)	40x52cm
Barbados	MOUNT & PAGE	29x27cm
Barbariae et Biledulgerid, Nova Descriptio	ORTELIUS (Folio)	33x50cm
Barcelona, Barcino, que vulgo Barcelona Dicitur [with] Ecija	BRAUN & HOGENBERG	32x47cm
Barnstable Harbor Massachusetts ...	U.S. COAST SURVEY	42x57cm
Baronia Udrone in Comitatu Catherloughe	BLAEU	38x25cm
Basilea	BRAUN & HOGENBERG	37x38cm

Title	Author/Source	Size
Basiliensis Territorii Descriptio Nova, Auctore Sebastiano Munstero ...	ORTELIUS (Folio)	32x24cm
Basin of the Baltic	JOHNSTON	44x57cm
Basse Partie de l Evesche de Munster, et le Comte de Benthem	JAILLOT	44x57cm
Bassora en de Land Schappen tussen de Eufrat en Tiger S'Troom ... Persien	VAN DER AA	22x28cm
Battenberg	MERIAN	9x17cm
Battle of Brandywine in which the Rebels Were Defeated ...	FADEN	54x44cm
Battle of Cerro Gordo, April 17th & 18th 1847	U.S. WAR DEPARTMENT	47x68cm
Bavaria	SCHEDEL	23x23cm
Bavariae Circulus et Electorat	HOMANN	56x47cm
Bay of Seven Islands	DES BARRES	76x54cm
Bedford Shire	MORDEN	32x40cm
Belagerung und Eroberung der Vostung Demin ... zu Brandenburg ...	MERIAN	26x36cm
Belgii Novi, Angliae Novae, et Partis Virginiae Novissima Delineatio	JANSSON	44x51cm
Belgii Pars Septentrionalis ... vulgo Hollandia ...	SCHENK	48x60cm
Belgii Veteris Typus ...	VAN DEN KEERE	38x50cm
Belgii Veteris Typus ex Conatibus Geographicis ...	JANSSON	39x48cm
Belgium	FINLEY	22x28cm
Belgium Foederatum ...	SEUTTER	50x57cm
Belgium of the Netherlands	THOMSON	47x59cm
Benedict Arias Montanus Sacrae Geographiae Tabulam ex Antiquissimorum	ARIAS MONTANUS	33x52cm
Berlin	MEYER	25x34cm
Berlin	S.D.U.K.	29x37cm
Berlin [Germany]	LOCAL & STATE MAPS	36x56cm
Berry	MERCATOR (Small)	13x17cm
Beschrijiunghe vande Zee Custen van Engelandt tusschen Blacqney ...	WAGHENAER	32x50cm
Bird's Eye View of Boston Harbor and South Shore to Provincetown ...	LOCAL & STATE MAPS	48x38cm
Bird's Eye View of Cairo Looking North East	GRAPHIC, THE	41x56cm
Bird's-Eye View of Fulton, N.Y.	LOCAL & STATE MAPS	61x76cm
Bird's Eye View of Philadelphia	LOCAL & STATE MAPS	50x70cm
Bird's Eye View Placerville, Cal. ...	ELLIOTT	52x72cm
Birdseye View of the City of Washington, with the Capitol ...	ILLUS. LONDON NEWS	34x51cm
Biturigum Exactiss: Descriptio per D. Ioannem Calamaeum	ORTELIUS (Folio)	31x31cm
Black's Road & Railway Traveling Map of England	BLACK	81x66cm
Blanchard's Guide Map of Chicago ...	BLANCHARD, R.	69x48cm
Blick vom Telegraph Hill auf die Stadt, den Hafen und die Bay	HILDBURGHAUSEN BIBLIO	no dimens
Block 16 G.H. & S.A. Ry. Foley County ...	MANUSCRIPT MAPS	50x65cm
Bohemia ...	SPEED	42x52cm
Bohemia in suas Partes Geographice Distincta ...	JANSSON	41x47cm
Bohemiae Nova Descriptio Tabula XVII	MUNSTER	29x38cm
Boreels Eylanden [with] Storm Bay [&] Zuyd Cape [&] Tasmans Eyland	VALENTYN	15x16cm
Borussiae Regnum ...	SEUTTER	50x58cm
Boston and Adjacent Cities	GRAY	no dimens
Boston and Maine Railroad and Connections	RAND, AVERY & CO.	95x113cm
Boston Bay	BLUNT	10x18cm
Boston et Ses Environs	MARSHALL	21x32cm
Boston Harbor Massachusetts ...	U.S. COAST SURVEY	73x91cm
Boston Harbour ...	BLUNT	21x26cm
Boston with Charlestown and Roxbury	S.D.U.K.	37x29cm
Bourdeaux	MERIAN	24x68cm
Bourdelois, Pays de Medoc, et la Prevoste de Born	VALK & SCHENK	38x50cm
Boussole des Vents	MORTIER	37x37cm
Bowles's European Geographical Amusement, or Game of Geography ...	BOWLES	48x68cm
Bowles's New Pocket Map of the ... States of North America ... Evans	BOWLES	50x64cm
Brandeburgum Marchionatus, cum Ducatibus Pomeraniae et Mekelenburgi	BLAEU	40x53cm
Brasil Nova Tabula	RUSCELLI	20x26cm
Brasil Nuova Tavola	RUSCELLI	18x25cm
Brasilien	HILDBURGHAUSEN BIBLIO	25x20cm
Breisach wie Es Ao. 1697 bey Schliessung des Ryswyckischen Fridens ...	BODENEHR	17x33cm
Brightstowe	BRAUN & HOGENBERG	34x44cm
Brightstowe in Engellandt	MEISNER	10x15cm
Britain As It Was Devided in the Tyme of the Englishe-Saxons ... Heptarchy	SPEED	38x50cm
Britanicae Insulae	MAGINI	13x17cm
Britannia Antiqua	BARBIE DU BOCAGE	24x18cm
Britannia Prout Divisa suit Temporibus Anglo-Saxorum ... Heptarchia	BLAEU	42x53cm
Britannia Prout Divisa suit Temporibus Anglo-Saxorum ... Heptarchia	JANSSON	41x53cm
Britannia Romana	MORDEN	36x43cm
Britannicarum Insularum Typus ...	ORTELIUS (Folio)	36x50cm

Title	Author	Size
Britisches Nord-America	HILDBURGHAUSEN BIBLIO	22x26cm
British Columbia, Vancouver Island, &c.	S.D.U.K.	32x38cm
British Dominions in America Agreeable to the Treaty of 1763 ...	KITCHIN	44x54cm
British India	TALLIS	33x24cm
British Islands to Petshora Bay [Chart No.1] Scotland to Norway ...	IMRAY	106x139cm
British Possessions in North America	CAREY & LEA	25x36cm
Brookland and Additions [DC]	REAL ESTATE MAPS	53x43cm
Brussel, die Haupt-Stadt des Hertzogtums - Brabant, und Residentz ...	MERIAN	19x28cm
Bruxella, Urbs Aulicorum Frequentia, Fontium Copia, Magnificentia ...	BRAUN & HOGENBERG	34x48cm
Bruxellensis Tetrarchia ...	VISSCHER	58x46cm
Buckingamiae Comitatus cum Bedfordiensi; vulgo Buckinghamshire and ...	JANSSON	40x50cm
Buckingham, Both Shyre and Shiretowne Describ.	SPEED	38x51cm
Buda Civitas	CUSTODIS	54x40cm
Bulgaria et Romania, Divisa in Singularis ...	VALK	60x49cm
Burgundiae Duca.	MERCATOR (Small)	14x18cm
Burgundiae Inferioris, quae Ducatus Nomine Censetur, Des. 1584	ORTELIUS (Folio)	37x46cm
Burgundiae Inferioris quae Ducatus Nomine Censetur Desc.	QUAD	19x26cm
Burgundische Crais. Westphalische Crais.	LOTTER	10x12cm
Byzantium, nunc Constantinopolis	BRAUN & HOGENBERG	32x48cm
Caarte van de Beyde Afgelegenste Colonien Drakensteen	KOLB	30x40cm
Caarte van de Colonie van de Kaap	KOLB	30x40cm
Caarte van de Colonie van Stellenbosch	KOLB	30x40cm
Caarte van de Kaap Goede Hoop	KOLB	30x40cm
Caarte van de Oost-Kust van Africa ... aan Kaap de Goede Hoop	KOLB	30x40cm
Caarte vande Kaap de Goede Hoop Leggende in't Zuyder Gedeelte van Africa	KOLB	30x38cm
Cabool, the Punjab and Beloochistan	TALLIS	25x34cm
Cairus, quae olim Babylon; Aegypti Maxima Urbs	BRAUN & HOGENBERG	33x48cm
Calaris Sardiniae Caput	MUNSTER	18x18cm
Calcutta	S.D.U.K.	31x40cm
Caliaecia Regnum	BLAEU	38x50cm
California	CRAM	47x30cm
California	RAND, McNALLY (atlas maps)	23x30cm
California & Nevada (Northern Portion)	ASHER & ADAMS	42x58cm
California and Nevada	GRAY	66x41cm
California and Other Western States of the United States	CASSELL	43x30cm
California, Lastest Map of the State	RAILROAD COMPANY	43x38cm
California, Oregon, Idaho, Utah, Nevada, Arizona and Washington	MITCHELL, S.A. (1860+)	28x22cm
California, Utah, Lr. California and New Mexico	WEEKLY DISPATCH	43x30cm
Californien, Texas, und die Territorien New Mexico u. Utah	MEYER	23x28cm
Cambalu or Peking	MALLET	14x9cm
Cambria sive Wallia	HONDIUS	15x20cm
Cambriae Typus	ORTELIUS (Folio)	37x49cm
Cambridge Shire, Divided into Hundreds	BOWEN, EMANUEL	32x23cm
Cambridgshire Described with the Devision of the Hundreds, the Townes	SPEED	38x52cm
Canaan ...	SPEED	39x52cm
Canaan or the Land of Promise to Abraham and His Posterity	WILKINSON	28x22cm
Canaan, with Part of Egypt, during the Residence of the Israelites ...	LAVOISNE	25x24cm
Canada	DU VAL	10x12cm
Canada	FINLEY	22x28cm
Canada and Nova Scotia	THOMSON	48x60cm
Canada et Louisiane	LE ROUGE	62x51cm
Canada Orientale nell'America Settentrionalie ...	CORONELLI	45x60cm
Canada West Formerly Upper Canada	MITCHELL, S.A. (to 1859)	32x38cm
Canada West Formerly Upper Canada	THOMAS, COWPERTHWAIT	32x40cm
Canada West or Upper Canada	COLTON (Atlas Maps)	32x40cm
Canada, Louisiane et Terres Angloises	D'ANVILLE	48x54cm
Canada, Louisiane, Etats-Unis ... Corriges par le Cen. Lamarche ...	DELAMARCHE	24x29cm
Canada, Louisiane, Possessions Angl? ...	DE VAUGONDY	24x29cm
Candia	MERCATOR (Small)	15x18cm
Candia [with] La Cita de Corphu	BRAUN & HOGENBERG	no dimens
Candia cum Insulis Aliquot Circa Graeciam	MERCATOR (Folio)	34x48cm
Cangoxuma	MONTANUS	28x57cm
Canibales Insulae	BLAEU	42x53cm
Cantebrigia	BRAUN & HOGENBERG	33x45cm
Canton [with] Macao [and] Sketch of the River from Macao to Canton	S.D.U.K.	30x38cm
Canton Zurich	KELLER	55x40cm
Cantuarbury	BRAUN & HOGENBERG	29x43cm

Title	Author	Size
Cape Ann Harbour Surveyed by The Rev. C. Fetch & T. Mallone ...	BLUNT	22x19cm
Cape of Good Hope	ARROWSMITH	48x60cm
Cape of Good Hope	CARY	23x28cm
Cape Poge and Adjacent Shoals [MA]	BLUNT	10x18cm
Capland und Angrenzende Gebeite	ANDREES	34x43cm
Caribbean Sea	IMRAY	104x206cm
Carlow	LEWIS, SAMUEL & CO.	30x24cm
Carolina By H. Moll Geographer	MOLL (Small)	20x28cm
Carolinae Floridae nec non Insularum Bahamensium ...	SELIGMANN	43x58cm
Carreck-Fergus	COLLINS, G.	46x56cm
Carta Accurata dell'Imperio del Giappone ...	TIRION	25x32cm
Carta Cosmographica, con los Nombres, Propriedad, y Virtud de los Vientos	APIANUS	23x31cm
Carta de Parte de las Costas del Nuevo Santander ... y Yucatan ...	DIRECCION DE HIDROGRAFIA	61x100cm
Carta della Nuova Inghilterra, Nuova Yorke, Pensilvania	BELLIN (Small)	22x32cm
Carta Esatta Rappresentante il Corso del Fiume Paraguay ...	GAZZETTIERE AMERICANO	23x26cm
Carta Esferica de la Islande Mallorca y Sus Adyacentes ...	VALDIS	81x56cm
Carta Esferica de las Costas Orientales de la America Setentrional ...	DIRECCION DE HIDROGRAFIA	63x92cm
Carta Esferica de las Costas Orientales de los Estados Unidos ...	DIRECCION DE HIDROGRAFIA	61x90cm
Carta Geografica del Messico o sia della Nuova Spagna	ALBRIZZI	33x42cm
Carta Geographica ... lo Stato della Republica di Genova ... Der Staat ...	HOMANN	51x58cm
Carta Hydrographica oder Algemeine Welt und Commercien Carte	BODENEHR	15x23cm
Carta Marina Nova Tabula	GASTALDI	13x18cm
Carta Marina Nova Tabula	RUSCELLI	19x24cm
Carta Marina Nuova Tavola	RUSCELLI	18x24cm
Carta Maritima de la Isla de Cuba ... Filipina, la Havana ...	LOPEZ	37x84cm
Carta Particolare del Isole di Iava ... Sumatra e Burneo	DUDLEY	48x75cm
Carta Particolare della Barberia Occidentale che Comincia con il Capo Gruer	DUDLEY	48x74cm
Carta Particolare della Costa Australe Scoperta dall' Olandesi ...	DUDLEY	38x47cm
Carta Particolare della Malacca ... Sumatra ... Burneo	DUDLEY	49x75cm
Carta Prima Generale della Asia	DUDLEY	24x38cm
Carta Quinta Generale di Europa	DUDLEY	37x47cm
Carta Rappresentante il Porto di Boston	GAZZETTIERE AMERICANO	22x18cm
Carta Terza Generale del' Asia	DUDLEY	48x38cm
Carte Contenant le Royaume du Mexique et la Floride ...	CHATELAIN	40x52cm
Carte d'Afrique	DE L'ISLE	52x64cm
Carte d'Afrique	FRICX	48x61cm
Carte d'Afrique	LAPIE	43x56cm
Carte d'Amerique	FRICX	48x60cm
Carte d'Amerique ...	DE L'ISLE	50x62cm
Carte d'Amerique, Dressee pour l'Instruction ... Delisle ... Buache ...	DEZAUCHE	47x60cm
Carte d'Amerique, pour l'Instruction. Dressee sur la Mem Echelle ...	DEZAUCHE	47x59cm
Carte d'un Nouveau Monde, entre le Nouveau Mexique et la Mer Glacialle	HENNEPIN	29x47cm
Carte d'une Partie de l'Amerique Septentrionale ... Pretentions des Anglois ...	BELLIN (Small)	36x46cm
Carte d'une Partie de la Mer du Sud Contenant les Decouvertes ...	COOK	37x67cm
Carte de l'Amerique	DUFOUR	52x77cm
Carte de l'Amerique ...	FREMIN	86x60cm
Carte de l'Amerique Corigee et Augmentee ...	BEREY	40x51cm
Carte de l'Amerique Corigee et Augmentee ... par P. Bertius 1662	BERTIUS	27x36cm
Carte de l'Amerique Corrigee , et Augmentee ...	TAVERNIER	38x50cm
Carte de l'Amerique et des Mers Voisines	BELLIN (Small)	46x30cm
Carte de l'Amerique Meridionale	DELAMARCHE	43x30cm
Carte de l'Amerique Septentrionale	LAPIE	53x41cm
Carte de l'Amerique Septentrionale depuis le 28 Degre de Latitude ...	BELLIN (Large)	58x89cm
Carte de l'Archipel de St. Lazare ou les Isles Marianes ...	BELLIN (Small)	23x15cm
Carte de l'Egypt de la Nubie de l Abissinie &c.	DE L'ISLE	50x58cm
Carte de l'Empire de la Chine, de la Tartarie Chinoise ... Isles du Japon	BONNE	32x21cm
Carte de l'Empire du Japon ...	BELLIN (Small)	22x32cm
Carte de l'Empire du Mexique	BELLIN (Small)	20x29cm
Carte de l'Entree de la Riviere de Canton ...	BELLIN (Small)	26x20cm
Carte de l'Eta du Royaume de Dannemarck ...	CHATELAIN	33x44cm
Carte de l'Etat du Monde vers la Fin du XVeme Siecle	DELAMARCHE	29x44cm
Carte de l'Hemisphere Austral ...	COOK	54x53cm
Carte de l'Ile de la Jamaique Extraite des Cartes Topographiques ...	DEPOT DE LA MARINE	58x86cm
Carte de l'Isle Cayenne	LAGNIET	31x40cm
Carte de l'Isle d'Hayti Aujourd'hui l'Espagnole, ou l'Isle de St. Dominique	BELLIN (Small)	22x33cm
Carte de l'Isle d'Otahiti par le Lieutenant J. Cook. 1769	COOK	23x41cm
Carte de l'Isle de Ceylon	BELLIN (Small)	26x20cm

Title	Author	Size
Carte de l'Isle de Java Partie Occidentale, Partie Orientale ...	CHATELAIN	38x87cm
Carte de l'Isle de la Grenade	BELLIN (Small)	22x17cm
Carte de l'Isle de la Jamaique	BELLIN (Small)	21x32cm
Carte de l'Isle de la Jamaique	BONNE	22x32cm
Carte de l'Isle de la Martinique Colonie Francoise des Isles Antilles ...	DE L'ISLE	47x60cm
Carte de l'Isle de la Martinique Dressee par Mr. Bellin ...	HOMANN	47x56cm
Carte de l'Isle de St. Domingue une des Grandes Antilles ...	BONNE	21x31cm
Carte de l'Isle de Taiti, par le Lieutenant J. Cook, 1769	COOK	23x39cm
Carte de l'Italie	LAPIE	56x43cm
Carte de l'Oceanie Contenant l'Australie, la Polynesie et les Iles Asiatiques	LAPIE	39x54cm
Carte de la Baye de Hudson	BELLIN (Small)	21x29cm
Carte de la Californie et des Pays Nord-Ouest Separes de l'Asie ...	DIDEROT	29x37cm
Carte de la Californie Suivant I. Carte Manuscrit 1604, II. Sanson 1656 ...	DIDEROT	29x36cm
Carte de la Caroline Meridionale et Septentrionale et de la Virginie	TARDIEU	33x43cm
Carte de la Colonie de Stellenbosch	KOLB	30x38cm
Carte de la Floride, de la Louisiane ...	BELLIN (Small)	22x30cm
Carte de la Hongrie ...	DE L'ISLE	47x65cm
Carte de la Louisiane, et de la Floride	BONNE	32x21cm
Carte de la Louisiane et du Cours du Mississipi ...	DE L'ISLE	48x65cm
Carte de la Louisiane et du Cours du Mississipi ... De L'Isle	COVENS & MORTIER	44x60cm
Carte de la Louisiane et Pays Voisins ...	BELLIN (Small)	23x30cm
Carte de la Manche ...	JAILLOT	59x79cm
Carte de la N'le. Galles Merid'le ... N'le Hollande ...	COOK	36x77cm
Carte de la Nle Zelande Visitee en 1769 et 1770 par le Lieutenant J. Cook	COOK	48x38cm
Carte de la Nouvelle Angleterre, Nouvelle York, Nouvelle Jersey et ...	DE LAPORTE	18x22cm
Carte de la Nouvelle France, ou Se Voit le Cours des Grandes Rivieres ...	CHATELAIN	50x55cm
Carte de la Palestine ou Terre Sainte	LAPIE	56x43cm
Carte de la Partie ... du Royaume de Suede ...	CHATELAIN	39x45cm
Carte de la Partie Nord, des Etats Unis, de l'Amerique Septentrionale	BONNE	22x33cm
Carte de la Partie Orientale de la Nouvelle France ou du Canada ...	BELLIN (Large)	40x56cm
Carte de la Partie Sud des Etats Unis de l'Amerique Septentrionale	BONNE	22x32cm
Carte de la Plata du Chili et de la Patagonie	LAPIE	53x39cm
Carte de la Riviere de la Plata	BELLIN (Small)	19x28cm
Carte de la Terre Ferme, du Perou, du Bresil ...	DE L'ISLE	47x63cm
Carte de la Terre Sainte Divisee selon les Douze Tribus d'Israel	HOMANN	50x75cm
Carte de la Virginie et du Mariland	DE LAPORTE	18x22cm
Carte de la Virginie et du Mariland	LAPORTE	18x22cm
Carte de la Virginie et du Maryland ... Josue Fry et Pierre Jefferson	DE VAUGONDY	48x64cm
Carte de Partie Nord et Est de l'Asie qui Comprend les Cotes ...	DIDEROT	30x38cm
Carte de Pologne et des Etats qui en Dependent	DU VAL	40x52cm
Carte de Savoye	DU VAL	36x48cm
Carte de Suisse	DE L'ISLE	49x62cm
Carte des Antilles	TARDIEU	33x43cm
Carte des Antilles du Golfe du Mexique et d'une Partie des Etats Voisons	LAPIE	43x56cm
Carte des Antilles Francoises et des Isles Voisines ...	DE L'ISLE	59x44cm
Carte des Antilles Francoises et des Isles Voisines ...	CHATELAIN	48x33cm
Carte des Costes de l'Asie sur l'Ocean Contenant les Bancs Isles ...	MORTIER	58x87cm
Carte des Costes de la Floride Francoise	BELLIN (Small)	20x14cm
Carte des Costes, de Perse, Gusarat, et Malabar ... l'Ocean Oriental	BELLIN (Small)	25x20cm
Carte des Cotes de Barbarie	BONNE	32x46cm
Carte des Cotes Orientales de Chine ...	DEPOT DE LA MARINE	88x59cm
Carte des Decouvertes ... la Mer Pacifique ... par le Captaine Cook ...	LA HARPE	36x46cm
Carte des Decouvertes Faites en 1787 dans les Mers de Chine et de ...	LA PEROUSE	49x68cm
Carte des Deux Regions Polaires jusqu'au 45 de Latitude	DE BEAURAIN	44x23cm
Carte des Deux Regions Polaires jusqu'au 45 de Latitude	DE BEAURAIN	19x28cm
Carte des Etats Unis d'Amerique	LAPIE	39x55cm
Carte des Etats-Unis d'Amerique et du Cours du Mississipi ...	BRION DE LA TOUR	23x27cm
Carte des Etats-Unis d'Amerique, du Canada, du Nouveau Brunswick ...	LAPIE	39x53cm
Carte des Etats-Unis du Mexique	LAPIE	53x39cm
Carte des Havres de Kingstown et de Port Royal	BELLIN (Small)	25x37cm
Carte des Indes et de la Chine ...	DE L'ISLE	62x62cm
Carte des Indes Orientales par P. Du Val Geographe Ordinaires du Roy	DU VAL	39x54cm
Carte des Isles Antilles dans l'Amerique Septentrionale ...	BRION DE LA TOUR	52x75cm
Carte des Isles Antilles ou du Vent avec la Partie Orientale des Isles sous ...	BONNE	32x21cm
Carte des Isles de Java, Sumatra, Borneo &c., les Detroits de la Sonde ...	BELLIN (Small)	25x29cm
Carte des Isles de l'Amerique et de Plusieurs Pays de Terre Ferme ...	D'ANVILLE	31x44cm
Carte des Lacs du Canada ...	BELLIN (Small)	29x46cm

Carte des Nouvelles Decouvertes au Nord de la Mer du Sud ...	BUACHE	46x65cm
Carte des Parties des Iles Sandwich ... [with] Carte des Iles Sandwich ...	LA PEROUSE	69x50cm
Carte des Parties Nord et Ouest de l'Amerique ...	DIDEROT	30x38cm
Carte des Pays Bas Comprenant le Brabant, Gueldre, Limbourg, ...	LAPORTE	18x22cm
Carte des Possessions Angloise & Francoises du Continent de l'Amerique	PALAIRET	41x57cm
Carte des Possessions Angloises & Francoises du Continent de l'Amerique	OTTENS	46x56cm
Carte des Possessions Angloises dans l'Amerique Septentrionale ...	IMBERT	56x75cm
Carte des Possessions Francoises et Angloises dans le Canada ...	LONGCHAMPS	54x75cm
Carte des Postes d'Allegmane et de Pays Voisins. Neue Vermehrte ...	HOMANN	44x56cm
Carte des Provinces de Nicaragua et Costa Rica	BELLIN (Small)	20x17cm
Carte des Provinces Meridionales des Etats-Unis ...	MARSHALL	35x51cm
Carte des Regions et des Lieux Dont Il Est Parle dans le Nouveau Testament	BONNE	30x44cm
Carte des Royaumes d'Angleterre d'Ecosse et d'Irlande ...	JAILLOT	64x85cm
Carte des Terres Australes ...	BUACHE	24x30cm
Carte des Troubles de l'Amerique ... New York ... New Jersey	LE ROUGE	71x52cm
Carte du Canada ...	CHATELAIN	41x52cm
Carte du Canada ou de la Nouvelle France ...	DE L'ISLE	49x57cm
Carte du Canal de Mozambique, Contenant l'Isle de Madagascar ...	BONNE	21x32cm
Carte du Congo et du Pays des Cafres	COVENS & MORTIER	50x61cm
Carte du Cours du Fleuve de St. Laurent depuis Quebec jusqu'au Lac...	BELLIN (Small)	19x28cm
Carte du Cours du Fleuve de St. Laurent depuis Son Embouchure ...	BELLIN (Small)	19x30cm
Carte du Detroit de Malacca	DAMPIER	15x27cm
Carte du Duche de Bourgogne et des Comtez en Dependans	DE L'ISLE	48x64cm
Carte du Globe Terrestre ou les Terres de l'Hemisphere Meridl. ...	BUACHE	25x33cm
Carte du Golphe du Mexique et des Isles de l'Amerique	BELLIN (Small)	27x38cm
Carte du Gouvernment de Guienne et Gascogne, avec celui de Bearn ...	BONNE	41x29cm
Carte du Greenland	LA HARPE	19x25cm
Carte du Mexique Dresse pour l'Intelligence de l'Histoire Generale ...	TARDIEU	39x25cm
Carte du Mexique et de la Floride des Terres Angloises et des Isles Antilles	DE L'ISLE	48x65cm
Carte du Mexique et des Etats Unis d'Amerique ...	DEZAUCHE	48x65cm
Carte du Plan du Venise, l'Etat de Sa Noblesse, ...	CHATELAIN	38x47cm
Carte du Royaume de France	DE VAUGONDY	49x53cm
Carte du Royaume de Siam ...	JOLLAIN	48x33cm
Carte du Texas pour les Mission et Voyages de l'Abbe Em Domenech ...	DE CORDOVA	44x36cm
Carte du Theatre de la Guerre entre les Anglais et les Americains ...	BRION DE LA TOUR	75x51cm
Carte Genealogique por Conduire a l'Historique des Rois du Nord ...	CHATELAIN	38x97cm
Carte General de la Caroline	MORTIER	57x46cm
Carte Generale d'une Partie de la Cote du Nord-Ouest de l'Amerique ...	LA PEROUSE	68x49cm
Carte Generale de Canada	LA HONTAN	23x39cm
Carte Generale de l'Amerique Divisee en Ses Principaux Etats ...	DELAMARCHE	53x59cm
Carte Generale de l'Ocean Atlantique	DEPOT DE LA MARINE	62x90cm
Carte Generale de la Caroline Dresse sur les Memoires le Plus Nouveaux ...	SANSON (Folio)	56x47cm
Carte Generale de la Cote Septentrionale de la Nouvelle Guinee ...	DUMONT D'URVILLE	58x87cm
Carte Generale de la Terre ou Mappemonde ... [with 4 continents]	DANET	49x72cm
Carte Generale de Toutes les Costes du Monde ...	MORTIER	58x50cm
Carte Generale des Decouvertes de l'Amiral de Fonte et autres ...	DIDEROT	30x38cm
Carte Generale des Decouvertes de l'Amiral de Fonte Representant ...	DIDEROT	29x37cm
Carte Generale des Etats Unis de l'Amerique Septentrionale ...	VIVIEN	31x41cm
Carte Generale des Indes Orientales et des Isles Adiacentes	SANSON (Folio)	39x48cm
Carte Generale des Indes Orientales Indiquant les Possessions Anglaises	ANDRIVEAU-GOUJON	38x51cm
Carte Generale des Isles ... [Bourbon; Isle de France; Rodrigues]	BONNE	21x32cm
Carte Generale des Royaumes d'Espagne & de Portugal ...	OTTENS	48x58cm
Carte Generale du Canada, de la Louisiane, de la Floride, de la Caroline ...	SANTINI	no dimens
Carte Generale du Globe Terrestre	BRUE	163x246cm
Carte Generale du Marquisat de Moravie	COVENS & MORTIER	51x64cm
Carte Generale du Mexique et des Provinces-Unies de l'Amerique Centrale	VIVIEN	30x39cm
Carte Generale du Royaume de France	CHATELAIN	13x17cm
Carte Generale et Routiere du Royaume de France	HERISSON	131x186cm
Carte Geo-Hydrographique du Golfe du Mexique et de Ses Isles	RIZZI-ZANNONI	31x45cm
Carte Geographique du Comte de la Marck	LOTTER	49x58cm
Carte Geographique, Statistique et Historique de l'Indiana	BUCHON	28x21cm
Carte Geographique, Statistique et Historique de la Georgie	BUCHON	28x23cm
Carte Geographique, Statistique et Historique de Michigan	BUCHON	36x27cm
Carte Geographique, Statistique et Historique du Connecticut	BUCHON	24x29cm
Carte Geographique, Statistique et Historique du New Hampshire	BUCHON	30x24cm
Carte Geographique, Statistique et Historique du Territoire d'Arkansas	BUCHON	36x36cm
Carte Magnetique des Deux Hemispheres Grave par Tardieu	TARDIEU	18x35cm

Title	Author	Size
Carte Nouvelle Contenant la Partie d'Amerique la Plus Septentrionale	VISSCHER	60x48cm
Carte Nouvelle de l'Amerique Angloise ...	LOTTER	60x49cm
Carte Nouvelle de l'Amerique Angloise Contenant la Virginie ... Jorck ...	MORTIER	59x91cm
Carte Nouvelle de Tout l'Empire de la Grande Russie	OTTENS	47x65cm
Carte Nouvelle des Possessions Angloises en Amerique Dressee pour ...	MOITHEY	49x70cm
Carte Particulaire de l'Isle et des Environs de Cayenne, Colonie Francaise	DESNOS	38x55cm
Carte Particulaire du Terroir et des Environs des Paris ...	VISSCHER	57x48cm
Carte Particuliere de Isthmus ou Darien qui Comprend le Golfe de Panama	MORTIER	62x86cm
Carte Particuliere de l'Amerique Septentrionale ou Sont Compris le ...	MORTIER	60x84cm
Carte Particuliere de la Caroline ...	MORTIER	48x60cm
Carte Particuliere de la Caroline Dresse Sur les Memoires le Plus Nouveaux ...	SANSON (Folio)	48x59cm
Carte Particuliere de la Cote du Nord-Ouest de l'Amerique ... en 1786 ...	LA PEROUSE	50x69cm
Carte Particuliere de la Cote Occidentale de l'Afrique depuis le Cap Blanc	D'ANVILLE	70x100cm
Carte Particuliere de la Hongrie de la Transilvanie de la Croatie ...	DE L'ISLE	48x57cm
Carte Particuliere de la Mer Rouge ...	MORTIER	55x76cm
Carte Particuliere de Virginie, Maryland, Pennsilvanie, la Nouvelle Jarsey ...	MORTIER	54x84cm
Carte Particuliere des Costes du Cap de Bone Esperance ...	MORTIER	57x80cm
Carte Particuliere des Environs de Dunkerque, Bergues, Furnes ...	FRICX	44x56cm
Carte Particuliere du Havre de Boston	DEPOT DE LA MARINE	58x86cm
Carte Physique et Politique des Etats-Unis, Canada et Partie du Mexique	DRIOUX & LEROY	29x42cm
Carte pour Servir a l'Itineraire Pittoresque du Fleuve Hudson et des Parties	MILBERT	50x43cm
Carte pour Servir l'Intelligence de l'Histoire de Gustave Adolphe ...	CHATELAIN	35x44cm
Carte Reduite de l'Isle d'Antigue ...	BELLIN (Large)	56x42cm
Carte Reduite de l'Isle de Saint Christophe	BELLIN (Large)	61x95cm
Carte Reduite de l'Ocean Occidental	DEPOT DE LA MARINE	55x80cm
Carte Reduite de la Mer des Indes ... de Celle du Sud	BARBIE DU BOCAGE	48x70cm
Carte Reduite de la Mer du Sud pour Servir a l'Histoire Generale ...	BELLIN (Small)	21x36cm
Carte Reduite de la Partie Orientale de la Nouvelle-Espagne depuis ...	VON HUMBOLDT	22x62cm
Carte Reduite des Costes Orientales de l'Amerique Septentrionale ...	BELLIN (Large)	55x89cm
Carte Reduite des Cotes Orientales de l'Amerique Septentrionale ...	SARTINE	59x88cm
Carte Reduite des Detroits de Malacca Sincapour et du Gouverneur ...	BELLIN (Large)	55x89cm
Carte Reduite des Iles Antilles [with] Carte ... de St. Domingue ...	DEPOT DE LA MARINE	88x56cm
Carte Reduite des Isles Britanniques ... Contenant l'Ireland	BELLIN (Large)	86x55cm
Carte Reduite des Mers Comprises entre l'Asie et l'Amerique Apelees ...	BELLIN (Large)	56x84cm
Carte Reduite des Parties Septentrionales du Globe, Situees Entre l'Asie...	BELLIN (Small)	21x34cm
Carte Reduite des Terres Australes	BELLIN (Small)	20x28cm
Carte Reduite du Globe Terrestre	BELLIN (Small)	22x34cm
Carte Reduite du Golphe du Mexique et des Isles de l'Amerique	BELLIN (Small)	23x32cm
Carte Tres Curieuse de la Mer du Sud Contenant des Remarques Nouvelles	CHATELAIN	81x140cm
Carte Universelle de Ptolomee	BOURGOIN	14x19cm
Carte Universelle du Monde ... [Terres Australes; Amerique Meridionale]	DU VAL	41x58cm
Carte van de Colonie van de Kaap	KOLB	30x38cm
Cartes de supplement pour les Isles Antilles	BONNE	24x35cm
Cary's New Map of England and Wales, with Part of Scotland	CARY	219x196cm
Cary's New Pocket Plan of London, Westminster and Southwark ...	CARY	40x60cm
Cassel	LASOR A VAREA	9x13cm
Cassell's Large Map of London. New Edition, Corrected to the Present ...	CASSELL	Folio
Castiliae Novae Parts Orientalis Provincias Ceunca et Guadalaxara	HOMANN	52x44cm
Ceilon Insula	MERCATOR (Small)	15x18cm
Central America	COLTON (Atlas Maps)	41x69cm
Central America and the West Indies from the Best Authorities	COPLEY	33x50cm
Central America and the West Indies from the Latest ...	HALL, SIDNEY	31x51cm
Central America and West India Islands	JOHNSTON	23x30cm
Central America II. Including Texas, California and the Northern ... Mexico	S.D.U.K.	31x39cm
Cercle de Franconie ...	SANSON (Folio)	40x52cm
Cette Carte de Californie et du Nouveau Mexique ...	DE FER (Small)	24x34cm
Champagne	JANSSON	36x49cm
Chancellorville, Prepared by Bvt. Brig. Genl. N. Michler ...	U.S. WAR DEPARTMENT	56x64cm
Channel Islands	TALLIS	33x24cm
Chapman's Sectional Map of the Surveyed Part of Minnesota	CHAPMAN	72x64cm
Chapman's Township Map of Wisconsin	CHAPMAN	69x53cm
Charleston and Adjacent Country	MELISH	17x10cm
Chart of Detroit River, from Lake Erie to Lake St. Clair ...	U.S. WAR DEPARTMENT	119x79cm
Chart of New-Zealand Explored in 1769 and 1770 ... Endeavor	COOK	50x38cm
Chart of Part of the Coast of New South Wales from Cape Tribulation ...	COOK	30x35cm
Chart of the Antarctic Polar Circle, with the Countries Adjoining ...	GENTLEMAN'S MAGAZINE	20x22cm
Chart of the Bahama Islands [with] The Bermudas ... [&] ... Cuba	THOMSON	51x60cm

335

Title	Author	Size
Chart of the Bay of Bengal, Including Plans of the Principal Harbours	IMRAY	102x171cm
Chart of the Coast of China and the Japan Islands Including the Marianes	U.S. GOV'T	102x91cm
Chart of the Gulf of Mexico and Windward Passages ... Cuba, Haiti ...	IMRAY	105x192cm
Chart of the Head of Navigation of the Potomac River ... Alexandria Canal	U.S. WAR DEPARTMENT	48x91cm
Chart of the New Discoveries East of New Holland and New Guinea	MORSE, JEDIDIAH	16x24cm
Chart of the Parts of the Sandwich Islands [with] Chart of the Sandwich I.	LA PEROUSE	50x38cm
Chart of the Sacramento & San Joaquin Rivers Showing All Landings ...	LOCAL & STATE WALL	66x85cm
Chart of the Sandwich Islands	COOK	21x34cm
Chart Prepared by James B. Moore ... Communication with China, Japan ...	MOORE	71x97cm
Charta Cosmographica cum Ventorum Propria Natura et Operatione	GEMMA FRISIUS	20x29cm
Charta Cosmographica, cum Ventorum Propria Natura et Operatione	APIANUS	19x27cm
Charte der XV Vereinigten Staaten von Nord-America ...	GUSSEFELD	47x52cm
Charte Uber die XIII Vereinigten Staaten von Nord-America ...	GUSSEFELD	45x58cm
Charte von Australien ...	STREIT	48x65cm
Charte von den Inseln Trinidad, Tabago und Margaretha ...	WEIMAR GEOG. INSTITUT	23x41cm
Charte von Nordamerica ...	WALCH	57x49cm
Chattanooga and Vicinity	HOPKINS	53x74cm
Chemins de Fer de l'Europe Centrale	LANEE	46x64cm
Chersonesi quae Hodie Natolia Descriptio	CLUVER	20x26cm
Chesapeake Bay Entrance	BLUNT	18x21cm
Chica sive Patagonica et Australis Terra	WYTFLIET	23x29cm
Chicago Investments	BLANCHARD, R.	43x31cm
Chicago, Milwaukee, St. Paul and Pacific Railroad	RAILROAD COMPANY	107x157cm
Chili	OGILBY	29x36cm
Chili Maggellans-Land ...	MOLL (Small)	16x18cm
Chili Provincia Amplissima	WYTFLIET	23x29cm
China	CLOPPENBURGH	18x25cm
China	COLTON (Atlas Maps)	32x40cm
China	HONDIUS	34x46cm
China	JOHNSTON	50x60cm
China	MERCATOR (Folio)	34x46cm
China	MERCATOR (Small)	15x18cm
China	PURCHAS	15x18cm
China	TALLIS	25x32cm
China	THOMAS, COWPERTHWAIT	29x36cm
China According to the Newest and Most Exact Observations	MOLL (Small)	18x26cm
China and the Tributary Kingdom of Corea	LAVOISNE	22x27cm
China, Japan &c.	BRADFORD	20x25cm
China Veteribus Sinarum Regio ...	MERIAN	28x35cm
China Veteribus Sinarum Regio nunc Incolis Tame Dicta	BLAEU	41x50cm
Chinae, olim Sinarum Regionis, Nova Descriptio. Auctore Ludovico Georgio	ORTELIUS (Folio)	37x47cm
Chorographia Terre Sanctae in Augustiorem Formam Redacta et ex Variis ...	TIRINUS	31x79cm
Cincinnati, Covington & Newport	ANONYMOUS	26x39cm
Circuli Franconiae Pars Orientalis ...	HOMANN	56x49cm
Circumjacent the North Pole	S.D.U.K.	27x27cm
Circumjacent the South Pole	S.D.U.K.	27x27cm
Citta di Venetia ...	CORONELLI	50x77cm
City and University of Oxford	MOULE	24x19cm
City of Baltimore	COLTON (Atlas Maps)	33x39cm
City of Fort Scott [KS]	LOCAL & STATE MAPS	69x79cm
City of New Orleans [with] City of Louisville	COLTON (Atlas Maps)	39x33cm
City of New York	MITCHELL, S.A. (to 1859)	38x30cm
City of New York	THOMAS, COWPERTHWAIT	37x29cm
City of Washington	MITCHELL, S.A. (to 1859)	30x38cm
City of Washington	TANNER	30x39cm
City of Washington	THOMAS, COWPERTHWAIT	no dimens
Civitas Colonie	MUNSTER	17x37cm
Civitas Exoniae	BRAUN & HOGENBERG	31x40cm
Civitas Florentina ...	MUNSTER	22x36cm
Civitas Francko fordiana	MUNSTER	25x40cm
Civitas Loandae S. Pauli	MERIAN	30x38cm
Civitas Venetio ...	MUNSTER	24x39cm
Civitatis Avenionis Omnimq Viarum et Aedificiorum eius Perfecta ... 1635	MERIAN	27x34cm
Civitatis Essensis Exactiss. Descrip.	BRAUN & HOGENBERG	14x42cm
Clark's Map of Litchfield Cty, Connecticut. From Actual Surveys ...	CLARK	155x135cm
Clason's Guide Map of Nebraska	CLASON MAP CO.	36x71cm
Clemens' Map of Ohio	PUZZLES & GAMES	29x37cm

Title	Publisher	Size
Coast Chart No.166. Florida Reefs from Key Biscayne to Carysfort Reef	U.S. COAST & GEODETIC	100x79cm
Coast of France and Italy from La Napoule to Villafranca	FADEN	23x31cm
Coast of France from Cape La Hague to Isle Brehat ...	FADEN	31x23cm
Coast of Texas from Galveston to Corpus Christi	U.S. COAST SURVEY	55x79cm
Coast of the United States from New York to Cape Fear	COPLEY	124x90cm
Coast to Coast Map of the Denver & Rio Grande Railroad	RAILROAD COMPANY	24x84cm
Coasters Harbor and Approaches. Rhode Island ...	U.S. COAST SURVEY	26x32cm
Coburg in Sachsen	MEISNER	10x15cm
Coeli Stellati Christiani Haemisphaerium Prius ...	CELLARIUS	43x51cm
Cohasset Harbor, Mass. Survey in Accordance with the Rivers & Harbors ...	U.S. WAR DEPARTMENT	36x68cm
Col. N.M., Arizona and Utah	RAND, McNALLY (atlas maps)	32x25cm
Collin's Standard Map of London	COLLINS & SON	74x85cm
Colonies Francaises (en Afrique)	LEVASSEUR	28x42cm
Colonies Francaises (en Amerique)	LEVASSEUR	30x43cm
Colonies Francaises, Martinique, Amerique du Sud	LEVASSEUR	30x46cm
Colorado	BRADLEY	42x57cm
Colorado	CRAM	46x64cm
Colorado	CRAM	26x33cm
Colorado	MITCHELL, S.A. (1860+)	29x38cm
Colorado	WALKER, H.B.	41x56cm
Colossus Monarchicus Status Danielis	LOTTER	58x49cm
Colton's The United States of America	COLTON (Atlas Maps)	39x66cm
Colton's California	COLTON (Atlas Maps)	39x32cm
Colton's City of Baltimore ...	COLTON (Atlas Maps)	32x39cm
Colton's Common School Geography Reference Map of the United States	COLTON (Atlas Maps)	30x24cm
Colton's Common School Geography. Map No.12. United States	COLTON (Atlas Maps)	26x21cm
Colton's Delaware and Maryland	COLTON (Pocket & Wall)	28x40cm
Colton's Georgetown and the City of Washington ...	COLTON (Atlas Maps)	33x41cm
Colton's Hawaiian Group or Sandwich Islands	COLTON (Atlas Maps)	40x32cm
Colton's Illinois	COLTON (Atlas Maps)	40x32cm
Colton's Illinois	COLTON (Pocket & Wall)	39x32cm
Colton's Indiana	COLTON (Atlas Maps)	40x33cm
Colton's Kansas	COLTON (Pocket & Wall)	39x57cm
Colton's Kansas and Nebraska	COLTON (Atlas Maps)	64x43cm
Colton's Kentucky and Tennessee	COLTON (Atlas Maps)	32x42cm
Colton's Kentucky and Tennessee	COLTON (Pocket & Wall)	35x42cm
Colton's Louisiana	COLTON (Pocket & Wall)	32x38cm
Colton's Maine	COLTON (Atlas Maps)	39x32cm
Colton's Map of Boston and Adjacent Cities	COLTON (Atlas Maps)	40x32cm
Colton's Map of the State of Texas	COLTON (Pocket & Wall)	38x39cm
Colton's Massachusetts and Rhode Island	COLTON (Pocket & Wall)	32x39cm
Colton's Michigan [in set with] Colton's Lake Superior	COLTON (Atlas Maps)	41x34cm
Colton's New Brunswick, Nova Scotia, Prince Edward Id., & Cape Breton	COLTON (Pocket & Wall)	42x59cm
Colton's New Map of Missouri, Compiled from the U.S. Surveys ...	COLTON (Pocket & Wall)	53x69cm
Colton's New Railroad and County Map of the United States	COLTON (Pocket & Wall)	74x102cm
Colton's New Topographical Map of the States of Virginia, West Virginia	COLTON (Pocket & Wall)	80x113cm
Colton's Oregon, Washington, Idaho, Montana and British Columbia	COLTON (Atlas Maps)	42x69cm
Colton's Pennsylvania	COLTON (Pocket & Wall)	32x40cm
Colton's Persia and Arabia	COLTON (Atlas Maps)	32x39cm
Colton's Railroad & Township Map of Massachusetts, Rhode Island ...	COLTON (Pocket & Wall)	55x64cm
Colton's Railroad & Township Map of the Western States ...	COLTON (Pocket & Wall)	84x100cm
Colton's Railroad and Township Map of New England ...	COLTON (Pocket & Wall)	134x116cm
Colton's Road Map of the Counties of Putnam and Duchess New York	COLTON (Pocket & Wall)	64x32cm
Colton's South Carolina	COLTON (Atlas Maps)	41x34cm
Colton's Territories of New Mexico Arizona Colorado Nevada and Utah	COLTON (Atlas Maps)	33x39cm
Colton's Territories of New Mexico and Utah	COLTON (Atlas Maps)	32x39cm
Colton's Texas	COLTON (Atlas Maps)	46x71cm
Colton's Texas	COLTON (Atlas Maps)	32x27cm
Colton's Township Map of the State of Minnesota	COLTON (Pocket & Wall)	58x43cm
Colton's United States of America	COLTON (Atlas Maps)	39x67cm
Colton's Washington and Oregon	COLTON (Atlas Maps)	32x41cm
Colton's Wisconsin	COLTON (Atlas Maps)	40x33cm
Columbus [OH] Showing Terminal Facilities of the Norfolk & Western ...	RAILROAD COMPANY	39x60cm
Comitatus Flandria ... t'Amsterdam Gedruck bij Claes Janss Visscher ...	VISSCHER	46x56cm
Comitatus Flandriae	PEETERS	15x18cm
Comitatus Glatz Authore Jona Sculteto	BLAEU	41x50cm
Comitatus Holandiae	PEETERS	15x18cm

Title	Author	Size
Comitatus Lancastrensis. The Countie Palatine of Lancaster	JANSSON	38x51cm
Comites Tirolenses ...	CUSTODIS	54x40cm
Conibas Regio cum Vicinis Gentibus	WYTFLIET	23x28cm
Connachtia Vulgo Connaughty	BLAEU	38x50cm
Connecticut	ARROWSMITH & LEWIS	20x25cm
Connecticut	FINLEY	23x28cm
Connecticut	MITCHELL, S.A. (to 1859)	30x37cm
Connecticut	THOMAS, COWPERTHWAIT	30x37cm
Connecticut ...	SOTZMANN	38x47cm
Connecticut, from Actual Surveys of Warren & Gillette	WILLARD	54x46cm
Connecticut from the Best Authorities	CAREY	30x37cm
Connecticut with Portions of New York and Rhode Island	COLTON (Atlas Maps)	32x39cm
Constantinople	S.D.U.K.	32x39cm
Constantinopolis	MERIAN	20x70cm
Constantinopolis ...	SCHEDEL	39x53cm
Constantinopolis Amplissima, Potentissima, et Magnificentissima ...	SEUTTER	49x57cm
Constantinopolitanae Urbis Effigies ...	MUNSTER	20x38cm
Contado di Zara, Parte della Dalmatia Descritto ...	CORONELLI	46x60cm
Contruseheung der Surnemmen Statt Venizig ...	MUNSTER	27x38cm
Corectissima nec non Novissima Dominii et Provinciae Groningae et ...	DE WIT	49x58cm
Cornwall	SELLER	12x14cm
Cornwall	SPEED	38x51cm
Corsica	QUAD	24x32cm
Corso del Fiume dell Amazoni ...	CORONELLI	27x46cm
Costes et Rivieres de Virginie, de Mariland et de Nouvelle Angleterre	MICHAULT	19x24cm
Cote Nord-Ouest de l'Amerique Reconnue par le Cap.e Vancouver. 1e ...	VANCOUVER	76x61cm
Cote Nord-Ouest de l'Amerique Reconnue par le Cape. Vancouver. IV ...	VANCOUVER	27x22cm
County and Township Map of Arizona and New Mexico	MITCHELL, S.A. (1860+)	34x52cm
County and Township Map of Dakota	BRADLEY	36x29cm
County and Township Map of Montana Idaho and Wyoming	BRADLEY	37x55cm
County and Township Map of Oregon and Washington	MITCHELL, S.A. (1860+)	51x37cm
County and Township Map of Utah & Nevada	MITCHELL, S.A. (1860+)	36x55cm
County Map of California	MITCHELL, S.A. (1860+)	34x27cm
County Map of Colorado, Utah, New Mexico, and Arizona	LLOYD, H.H.	41x36cm
County Map of Colorado, Wyoming, Dakota, Montana	MITCHELL, S.A. (1860+)	50x36cm
County Map of England and Wales	MITCHELL, S.A. (1860+)	34x26cm
County Map of Florida [with] ... North Carolina [&] ... South Carolina	MITCHELL, S.A. (1860+)	29x35cm
County Map of Florida [with] Map of South Carolina	MITCHELL, S.A. (1860+)	29x35cm
County Map of Georgia and Alabama	MITCHELL, S.A. (1860+)	27x34cm
County Map of Massachusetts, Connecticut, and Rhode Island	MITCHELL, S.A. (1860+)	29x36cm
County Map of Michigan and Wisconsin	MITCHELL, S.A. (1860+)	27x34cm
County Map of Nova Scotia, New Brunswick, Cape Breton Id. and [P.E.I.]	MITCHELL, S.A. (1860+)	34x27cm
County Map of Texas	MITCHELL, S.A. (1860+)	28x35cm
County Map of Texas and Indian Territory	LLOYD, H.H.	42x39cm
County Map of Texas, New Mexico, and Indian Territory	PAGE	37x56cm
County Map of Texas, Showing Also Portions of the Adjoining States ...	MITCHELL, S.A. (1860+)	36x54cm
County Map of the State of California	MITCHELL, S.A. (1860+)	53x37cm
County Map of the State of Illinois	MITCHELL, S.A. (1860+)	34x28cm
County Map of the State of Texas, Showing Also Portions of the Adjoining	MITCHELL, S.A. (1860+)	36x54cm
County Map of Utah and Nevada	MITCHELL, S.A. (1860+)	29x36cm
County Map of Virginia and West Virginia	MITCHELL, S.A. (1860+)	27x34cm
Cours du Danube de Belgrade jusques au Pont Euxin	SANSON (Folio)	40x52cm
Cours du Fleuve Maragnon autrement Dit des Amazones	FRITZ	21x33cm
Cours du Mississipi et la Louisiane	DE VAUGONDY	20x16cm
Course of the River Mississippi, from the Balise to Fort Chartres ...	SAYER	112x34cm
Cram's Township and Rail Road Map of Illinois	CRAM	58x41cm
Creta Iovis Magni, Medio Jacet Insula Ponto ...	JANSSON	38x49cm
Croquis de l'Afrique Central Mis au Courant par A.J. Waters ...	U.S. GOV'T	25x38cm
Cruchley's New Plan of London Shewing All the ... Improvements ...	CRUCHLEY	46x86cm
Cuba	COLTON (Atlas Maps)	33x41cm
Cuba Insul [with] Hispaniola [&] Havana [&] Iamaica [&] I.S. Ioannis [&] ...	MERCATOR (Small)	14x19cm
Cuba Insula et Iamaica	WYTFLIET	23x28cm
Cuba, Jamaica and Porto Rico	COLTON (Pocket & Wall)	31x39cm
Culiacanae Americae Regionis Descriptio ... [with] Hispaniolae, Cubae ...	ORTELIUS (Folio)	36x50cm
Cumberland	SPEED	38x50cm
Custer's Battle-Field (June 25th, 1876) ... by Sergeant Charles Becker ...	U.S. WAR DEPARTMENT	38x44cm
Cypri Insulae Nova Descript.	ORTELIUS (Folio)	36x50cm

Cyprus Insula	BLAEU	38x51cm
Cyprus, Insula Laeta Choris, Bladorum et Mater Amorum	JANSSON	34x47cm
Daenmark mit Holstein	STIELER	29x34cm
Dakota [Northern Portion]	RAND, McNALLY (atlas maps)	32x47cm
Dakota Territory. Showing Progress of the U.S. Land Survey during 1861 ...	U.S. STATE SURVEYS	60x52cm
Dallas, Texas	CRAM	33x25cm
Damiata	SCHEDEL	14x24cm
Dane Marck et Sud-Gothlande	PEETERS	13x16cm
Danorum Marca, ues Cimbricum, aut Daniae Regnum ...	BRAUN & HOGENBERG	38x46cm
Dantzig	BERTIUS	15x20cm
Danubii Fluvii sive Turcici Imperii	DE WIT	50x61cm
Daphne	ORTELIUS (Folio)	36x48cm
Das Caspische Meer [with] Das Land Kamtzadalie sonst Jedso	HOMANN	50x58cm
Das Erst General Inhaltend ...	MUNSTER	28x37cm
Das Erst General Inhaltend die Beschreibung und den Circkel des Gantzen ...	MUNSTER	26x38cm
Das Furstenthum Eisenach	VON REILLY	23x29cm
Das Heilig Judisch Landt mit Auszteilung der Zwolff Geschlechter	MUNSTER	26x34cm
Das Herzogthum Neuburg	VON REILLY	19x35cm
Das Heylig Judisch Landt mit Auszteilung der Zwolff Geschlechter	MUNSTER	28x35cm
Das Hochstift Speyer mit der Freyen Reichsstadt Speyer	VON REILLY	22x26cm
Das Hochstift Worms mit der Freyen Reichsstadt Worms	VON REILLY	20x28cm
Das Kunigreich Engellandt mit dem Anstossenden Rich Schottlandt ...	MUNSTER	27x35cm
Das Schloss Brandeyss in Bohme, und Verschantzungen des Schwedische	MERIAN	21x32cm
Das Vorgebirg der Guten Hofnung Verfasst von Herrn L.S. De La Rochette	SCHRAEMBL	51x33cm
Dawson's Map of the Dominion of Canada	DAWSON	54x81cm
De Beschryvingh van de Reysen Pauli, en van de Andere Apostelen ...	VISSCHER	32x47cm
De Carybsche Eylanden van de Barbados tot de Bocht van Mexico ...	COLOM	53x64cm
De Comitatus Flandriae	MUNSTER	12x15cm
De Cordova's Map of the State of Texas ... by Robert Creuzbaur ...	DE CORDOVA	85x78cm
De Gelegentheyt van't Paradys en't Landt Canaan	DANCKERTS	35x51cm
De Groote Ende Kleyne Eylanden van West-Indien	WAESBERGER	18x25cm
De Hemelsche Cloot	HONDIUS	9x13cm
De l'Empire de la Chine	LE ROUGE	31x32cm
De la Cosmographie Florence ...	MUNSTER	25x36cm
De Landschappen Tabasco en Iucatan tussen de Golf van Mexico ...	VAN DER AA	15x23cm
De Reyse des Apostels Pauli na Roomen	DANCKERTS	37x52cm
De Stadt Jerusalem	DANCKERTS	35x51cm
De Stoel des Oorlogs in Italien Waar in Vertoont Werden ... Milano ...	VISSCHER	59x74cm
De Straat van Magellan ...	VAN DER AA	15x23cm
De Vaste Kuste van Chicora tussen Florida en Virginie ... Hispaniola ...	VAN DER AA	15x23cm
De West Custen van Yerlandt beginnende van Corckbeg tot Aen Slynhooft	GOOS	44x43cm
Decima Asiae Tabula	WALDSEEMULLER	35x52cm
Delaware	ARROWSMITH & LEWIS	25x20cm
Delaware	BRADFORD	36x29cm
Delaware	FINLEY	29x22cm
Delaware and Maryland	JOHNSON	32x41cm
Delaware from the Best Authorities	CAREY	41x23cm
Delineatio Nova et Vera Partis Australis Novi Mexici cum Australi Parte ...	SCHERER	24x36cm
Delineatio Omnium Orarum Totius Australis Partis Americae, Dictae Peru...	VAN LINSCHOTEN	38x51cm
Delineatio Orarum Maritimarum, Terrae Vulgo Indigetatae Terra do Natal ...	VAN LINSCHOTEN	38x55cm
Delineatio Praelii inter ser. Suecorum Regem et ...	GOTTFRIED	27x38cm
Denver & Rio Grande Railroad System	RAILROAD COMPANY	37x46cm
Departement du Mont Blanc ... Decrete ... le 27 Novembre 1792	LONGCHAMPS	64x50cm
Department of the Missouri. Sketch Showing Military Roads ... Fort Lewis	U.S. GOV'T	57x53cm
Dept. de la Seine	LEVASSEUR	30x46cm
Der Erde Sudl.	WALCH	18x23cm
Der Gantze Welt Krets in Seinen Zwey Grossen Begrissen ...	BODENEHR	15x13cm
Der Noerdliche Theil des Grossenwelt Meeres ...	REICHARD	51x67cm
Der Staaten des Landgrafen zu Hessen Darmstadt Noerdliche Aemter ...	VON REILLY	28x31cm
Der Statt Metz Circkel, Mawren und Porten und Furnemeste ...	MUNSTER	16x21cm
Der Sudliche Theil von Sud-America	STIELER	31x41cm
Des Kantons Zurch Sudlicher Theil	VON REILLY	24x31cm
Des Konigreichs Schweden Nordliche Provinzen	VON REILLY	22x27cm
Des Mers on Appelle Mer cette Vaste Etendue ... de la Surface de la Terre	CLOUET	32x56cm
Des Zones les Tropiques et les Cercles Polaires Divisent la Terre ...	CLOUET	32x56cm
Descripcion de las Yndias de Norte	DE HERRERA	21x29cm
Descriptio Acurata Terrae Promissae per Sortes XII ... [with] Terre Sainte ...	DE FER (Large)	46x72cm

Title	Author	Size
Descriptio Hydrographica Accomodata ad Battavorum Navigatione in Javam	DE BRY	36x66cm
Descriptio Perigrinationis D. Pauli, Apostoli, Exhibens Loca Fere Omnia ...	JANSSON	36x51cm
Description de l'Isthme de Darien ... la Ville de Panama ...	CHATELAIN	37x43cm
Description de la Partie des Indes Orientales qui Est sous la Dominations ...	THEVENOT	27x36cm
Description de la Tartarie Tiree ed Partie de Plusieurs Cartes	SANSON (Folio)	36x57cm
Description del Destricto del Audiencia de la Espanola 3	DE HERRERA	22x30cm
Description des Isles Bermudas / Mappa Aetivarum Insularum	CLOPPENBURGH	19x25cm
Description Nouvelle d'Europe	MUNSTER	25x34cm
Description Nouvelle des Gaules	MUNSTER	25x34cm
Descrittione del Mappamondo	PORCACCHI	11x15cm
Designatio Orbis Christiani	MERCATOR (Small)	15x19cm
Det Sydlige Norge [in set with] Det Nordlige Norge	PONTOPPIDAN	53x69cm
Detailed Map of the Revd. Dr. Livingstone's Route across Africa ...	ARROWSMITH	29x64cm
Devonia ...	BLAEU	39x50cm
Devonshire	SELLER	12x14cm
Devonshire with Excester Described	SPEED	38x51cm
Di Hungaria et Transilvania	RUSCELLI	14x20cm
Di Hungaria et Transilvania Tavola Novissima	LASOR A VAREA	14x20cm
Diagram of the State of Illinois	U.S. STATE SURVEYS	57x36cm
Diagram of the State of Missouri	U.S. STATE SURVEYS	44x57cm
Die Belagerung von Colberg Angegriffen durch den Russischen General ...	KILIAN, G.C.	16x24cm
Die Capitein Drake die Statt S. Dominico in der Insel Hispaniola ...	DE BRY	15x21cm
Die Eigentliche und Warhafftige Gestalt der Erden und des Meers ...	BUNTING	27x36cm
Die Englische Kuste dem Nordlichen Frankreich Gegenuber	VON REILLY	21x32cm
Die Erst General Tafel Die Beschzeibung und den Circkel des Gantzen ...	MUNSTER	31x36cm
Die Furstenthumer Grubenhagen und Blankenburg mit ... Nordhausen	VON REILLY	22x29cm
Die Gegend um Prag, oder der Alte Prager Kreys ...	HOMANN	51x58cm
Die Grosseren der Viti - oder Fiji Inseln	PETERMANN	20x24cm
Die Insel Vist	VON REILLY	32x20cm
Die Inseln Malta und Gozzo	HOMANN	50x59cm
Die Laender Asie nach Ihrer Gelegenheit bisz in India Werden ...	MUNSTER	25x33cm
Die Lander Aste nach Ihzer Gelegenh it Bisz in India / Werden in Diser Tafel	MUNSTER	29x37cm
Die Landschaft Hollstein	VON REILLY	22x32cm
Die Neuwe Inselen / So zu Unsern Zeiten durch die Kunig von Hispania ...	MUNSTER	28x35cm
Die Neuwen Inseln / So Hinder Hispaniam Gegen Orient / Bey Dem Landt ...	MUNSTER	26x34cm
Die Republik Polen nach Ihrem Bestande im Jahre 1772 ... 1815	HILDBURGHAUSEN BIBLIO	18x25cm
Die Schweiz oder die Eidgenossenschaft samt den Derselben Zugewandten	VON REILLY	24x28cm
Die Staaten von Maine, New Hampshire, Massachusetts, Vermont, Conn...	MEYER	27x20cm
Die Statt Aygsburg	MUNSTER	26x35cm
Die Statt Franckfurt	MUNSTER	20x29cm
Die Statt Genff	MUNSTER	15x36cm
Die Statt Heydelberg	MUNSTER	25x72cm
Die Statt Montpellier	MUNSTER	10x31cm
Die Statt Paris ...	MUNSTER	28x35cm
Die Statt Zurich	MUNSTER	18x39cm
Die Sudspitze von Africa mit der Colonie vom Vorgebirge der Guten ...	WEILAND	50x43cm
Die Vereinigten Staaten von Amerika in 6 Blattern - Bl.4	STIELER	33x41cm
Die Vereinigten Staaten von Nord-America ...	WEIMAR GEOG. INSTITUT	48x63cm
Die Viti - oder Fiji Inselen ...	PERTHES	43x51cm
Diepe	MERIAN	12x32cm
Dierechte See-Karte von der Zelegenheit der Landes Iapan	CARON	14x23cm
Dimida Tribus Manasse ... Tribus Ruben, et Gad ... [& other tribes]	JANSSON	85x178cm
Dinant [Belgium]	MORTIER	21x28cm
Discorso Intorno alla Carta da Navigare	PORCACCHI	11x14cm
Disretione Vera de Lantica Cita di Gierusalem	AMICO	23x29cm
Dissected Outline Map of the United States of America	PUZZLES & GAMES	25x36cm
Diversi Globi Terr-Aquei Statione Variante et Visu Intercedente ...	SEUTTER	50x57cm
Diversi Globi Terraquei ...	SEUTTER	49x57cm
Domestic Air Mail Service in the United States	AERONAUTICAL MAPS	46x71cm
Dominia Anglorum in America Septentrionali. Specialibus Mappis Londini ...	HOMANN	50x55cm
Dorcet Shire:	SPEED	8x12cm
Dortmundt. in Westphalen	MEISNER	10x15cm
Draft of Mathewern Bay, on the North Side of the Island of Diego Rayes ...	NICHELSON	85x129cm
Drainage Map of Colorado	HAYDEN, F.V.	65x89cm
Draughts and Plans of Some of the Principal Towns and Harbours ...	BOWEN, EMANUEL	36x43cm
Dresden	S.D.U.K.	32x38cm
Drew's New Map of the State of Florida Showing the Townships ...	DREW	61x64cm

Title	Author	Size
Driving Map of Allegheny County Pennsylvania	HOPKINS	85x85cm
Du Destroit de Magellan	CLOPPENBURGH	18x25cm
Dublin	LEWIS, SAMUEL & CO.	30x24cm
Dublin	S.D.U.K.	29x40cm
Ducato Ouero Territorio di Milano	BLAEU	38x51cm
Ducatus Brunsuicensis Fereque Lunaeburgensis cum Adiacentibus ...	VISSCHER	42x54cm
Ducatus Brunsuicensis in Tres Suos Principatus Calenbergicum ...	HOMANN	51x60cm
Ducatus Lutzenburgici Tabula Nuperrime in Lucem Edita ...	DE WIT	46x56cm
Ducatus Lutzenburgicus	JANSSON	12x17cm
Ducatus Prussiae tam Polono Regiae, quam Brandenburgo ...	DE WIT	46x59cm
Ducatus Silesiae Ligniciensis.	JANSSON	39x48cm
Ducatus Stiriae	HOMANN	50x59cm
Dunedin, N.Z.	LOCAL & STATE MAPS	35x65cm
Duodecima Asiae Tabula	WALDSEEMULLER	29x25cm
Durham	BOWEN, EMANUEL	22x32cm
Eastern Frontier of the Colony of the Cape of Good Hope ... from Algoa Bay	ARROWSMITH	49x59cm
Eastern Half of Texas	CRAM	41x56cm
Eastern Half of Texas [in set with] Western Half of Texas	CRAM	34x52cm
Eastern Hemisphere	TALLIS	25x34cm
Eastern Hemisphere [in set with] Western Hemisphere	S.D.U.K.	34x67cm
Eboracum Lincolnia ...	MERCATOR (Small)	13x17cm
Economic Map of Colorado	HAYDEN, F.V.	76x94cm
Edenburck in Schottl.	MEISNER	10x15cm
Edenburg	BRAUN & HOGENBERG	34x45cm
Egypt and Arabia Petra	TALLIS	34x25cm
Eigentliche Contrafactur der Statt Breysach, wie Solche von Mittag ...	MERIAN	22x34cm
Eigentliche Verzeichnus, dieses im ... Jahr 1618 ...	HERSBACH	30x25cm
Eigentlicher Grundtriss der Statt Eger wie Dieselbe von ... Carol Gustaff ...	MERIAN	30x38cm
Einsidlen in Schweitz	MEISNER	10x15cm
El Vado de Los Padres, Colorado River	U.S. WAR DEPARTMENT	15x38cm
Empire of Japan	S.D.U.K.	39x31cm
England	MORDEN	36x43cm
England & Scotland - Coast Northward of Flamborough head	IMRAY	105x203cm
England and Wales	BLACK	41x56cm
England and Wales	COLTON (Pocket & Wall)	62x41cm
England and Wales	LOCKHEAD	23x21cm
England and Wales Drawn from the Most Accurate Surveys	ROCQUE	146x98cm
Ensign's Traveller's Guide and Map of the United States ...	ENSIGN	65x96cm
Entrances to Auckland Harbour	BRITISH ADMIRALTY	46x62cm
Environs of New York [with 5 other urban regions]	OLNEY	27x23cm
Episcop. Ultraiectinus	PITT	38x48cm
Erfordiae Primariae Thuringiae Urbis ... Erfurth, der Haupt Stadt ...	HOMANN	52x58cm
Ertz-Hertzogthumb Oesterreich ... Archiduche d'Austriche ...	SANSON (Folio)	40x52cm
Eryn. Hiberniae, Britannicae Insulae, Nova Descriptio. Irlandt	ORTELIUS (Folio)	36x48cm
Erythraei sive Rubri Maris Periplus ...	JANSSON	40x47cm
Essay d'une Carte Reduite, Contenant les Parties Connuees du Globe ...	BELLIN (Large)	52x71cm
Essexia Comitatus	BLAEU	42x53cm
Estats et Royaumes de Fez et Maroc	SANSON (Folio)	36x52cm
Estotilandia et Laboratoris Terra	WYTFLIET	23x28cm
Etats du Grand-Seigneur en Asie, Empire de Perse ...	DE VAUGONDY	48x55cm
Etats Unis de l'Amerique, Corriges et Augmentes en 1803	TARDIEU	18x20cm
Etats Unis et Grandes Antilles	LA HARPE	30x23cm
Etats-Unis	BINET	19x24cm
Etats-Unis	DUFOUR	24x38cm
Etats-Unis	DUVOTENAY	23x30cm
Etats-Unis	PERROT	14x18cm
Etats-Unis d'Amerique	BUCHON	43x53cm
Etats-Unis de l'Amerique Septentrionale ...	LAPIE	22x29cm
Etats-Unis Region des Territoires	DUFOUR	32x24cm
Ethnographical Map of North America in the Earliest Times, Illustrative ...	PRICHARD	61x48cm
Ethnographical Map of the Indian Tribes of the United States A.D. 1600	SCHOOLCRAFT	23x30cm
Ethnographische Karte von Nordamerica	PERTHES	29x39cm
Europa	BURCKHARDT	33x37cm
Europa	MAGINI	13x17cm
Europa	STIELER	29x36cm
Europa Christiani Orbis Domina ...	HOMANN	48x57cm
Europa das ein Drittheil der Erden ...	MUNSTER	25x37cm

Title	Author	Size
Europa Delineata et Recens Edita ...	VISSCHER	43x54cm
Europa / die Erst Tafel desz Ersten Buche	STUMPF	29x39cm
Europa Exactissime Descripta ...	HONDIUS	38x50cm
Europa Prima Nova Tabula	MUNSTER	27x34cm
Europa Prima Pars Terrae In Forma Virginis	BUNTING	26x37cm
Europa Recens Descripta ...	BLAEU	41x55cm
Europa Regnorum	LOTTER	50x58cm
Europae	ORTELIUS (Folio)	34x46cm
Europae Nova Tabula	VAN DEN KEERE	14x20cm
Europae Tabula V	RUSCELLI	18x25cm
Europae Tabula VI	RUSCELLI	18x24cm
Europam, sive Celticam Veterem	JANSSON	36x47cm
Europe	COLTON (Atlas Maps)	32x40cm
Europe	COLTON (Pocket & Wall)	65x83cm
Europe	KITCHIN	107x125cm
Europe	LEVASSEUR	30x46cm
Europe	MOLL (Small)	17x19cm
Europe after the Congress of Vienna	THOMSON	103x123cm
Europe for the Elucidation of the Abbe Gaultiers' Geographical Games	PUZZLES & GAMES	33x41cm
European Russia	THOMSON	60x50cm
Exacta et Accurata Delineatio cum Orarum Maritimarum tum Etiam ... China	VAN LINSCHOTEN	39x52cm
Exactissima Totius Scandinaviae ...	VISSCHER	44x53cm
Exactissima Totius Scandinaviae Tabula, qua tam Sueciae, Daniae, et ...	VISSCHER	44x53cm
Explorations and Surveys for a Rail Road Route [4 maps: Green R.-Pacific]	U.S. PACIFIC R.R. SURVEY	46x52cm
Explorations and Surveys South of Central Pacific R.R. ... 1871	U.S. GOV'T	71x56cm
Explorations and Surveys South of Central Pacific R.R. ... Preliminary ...	U.S. WAR DEPARTMENT	72x56cm
Expositioni [Armillary sphere]	RUSCELLI	13x18cm
Extrema Americae Versus Boream, Ubi Terra Nova Nova Francia ...	BLAEU	46x56cm
Facies Una Hemisphaerii Terrestris [with] ... Altera Hemisphaerii ...	ZAHN	36x42cm
Ferdinandus Sotto Treibt Graffe Buteren in der Landtschasst Florida	DE BRY	15x19cm
Figura del Mondo Universale	MUNSTER	28x35cm
Figure du Port Royal en la Nouvelle France	LESCARBOT	14x24cm
Firenza la Capitale di Toscana	LOTTER	50x58cm
Flandria Comitatus Pars Media ...	VISSCHER	47x57cm
Flandria Nova Descriptio	PITT	48x56cm
Flandriae Comitatus Descriptio	ORTELIUS (Folio)	37x49cm
Flandriae Comitatus Pars Orientalis ...	VISSCHER	51x58cm
Flandriae Teutonicae Pars Orientalior	BLAEU	38x50cm
Florence	S.D.U.K.	28x38cm
Florencia	SCHEDEL	25x50cm
Florida	BRADFORD	36x29cm
Florida	COLTON (Atlas Maps)	41x34cm
Florida	CRAM	30x25cm
Florida	DU VAL	9x11cm
Florida	MORSE & BREESE	36x28cm
Florida	THOMAS, COWPERTHWAIT	37x29cm
Florida et Apalche	WYTFLIET	23x29cm
Florida et Regiones Vicinae	DE LAET	28x36cm
Florida Strait, North Part	BRITISH ADMIRALTY	99x66cm
Floridae Americae Provinciae Recens & Exactissima Descriptio ...	DE BRY	37x45cm
Floridae Americae Provinciae Recens & Exactissima Descriptio ...	LE MOYNE	37x46cm
Fori Iulii Accurata Descriptio	ORTELIUS (Folio)	36x48cm
Fort Bend County [TX]	GOV'T: LOCAL & STATE	46x53cm
Fortress Monroe [VA] ... and Its Vicinity	VIRTUE	16x23cm
Fortress Monroe, Old Point Comfort and Hygeia Hotel, Va.	MAGNUS, C.	46x71cm
France	MANUSCRIPT MAPS	36x50cm
Francfordia	LASOR A VAREA	9x14cm
Francfurt am Mayn	GOTTFRIED	18x30cm
Franciae Orientalis (Vulgo Franckenlant) Descriptio	ORTELIUS (Folio)	36x25cm
Franckfurt an der Oder Anno Dni. 1548	MUNSTER	21x30cm
Frankreich	HILDBURGHAUSEN BIBLIO	20x26cm
Freiberg in Meissen	BERTIUS	15x20cm
Freiburg im Brisgow	BODENEHR	16x29cm
Fretum Magellani	MERCATOR (Small)	15x18cm
Freyburg der Furnemmen Statt in Uchtlandt wahre Abcontrafactur	MUNSTER	11x29cm
Friesland	OTTENS	33x42cm
From Monomoy and Nantucket Shoals to Muskeget Channel	U.S. COAST SURVEY	100x69cm

Title	Author	Size
Gallia	MERCATOR (Folio)	36x41cm
Gallia	ORTELIUS (Folio)	40x48cm
Gallia IIII Nova Tabula	MUNSTER	27x34cm
Gallia Vetus	ORTELIUS (Folio)	36x46cm
Gallia Vetus ...	BLAEU	38x50cm
Galliae Antiquae	MORTIER	44x54cm
Galliae Regionis Nova Descriptio	MUNSTER	25x34cm
Galliae Regni Potentiss: Nova Descriptio, Ioanne Ioliveto Auctore	ORTELIUS (Folio)	34x46cm
Galliae Regnum	MAGINI	13x17cm
Galliae seu Franciae Tabula ...	VISSCHER	46x56cm
Galveston Bay Texas	U.S. COAST SURVEY	67x56cm
Galveston Entrance Texas	U.S. COAST SURVEY	35x43cm
Galveston Harbor Texas ... Maj. C.J. Allen ...	U.S. WAR DEPARTMENT	27x27cm
Galway	LEWIS, SAMUEL & CO.	30x24cm
Game of Uncle Sam's Mail	PUZZLES & GAMES	48x86cm
Gegend am Rhein im Clevischen, wo die Alliirte Armee ...	KILIAN, G.C.	16x26cm
Gemeine Beschreibung Aller Mitnachtigen Lander / Schweden / Gothen / ...	MUNSTER	25x34cm
Gendt. in Flandern	MEISNER	10x15cm
General Chart of Alaska to Accompany Reindeer Report	U.S. GOV'T	64x89cm
General Chart on Mercator's Projection	PAYNE	18x23cm
General Charte von den Mitternachte America und ... Franzos Colonien ...	KILIAN, G.C.	17x25cm
General Map of Charleston Harbor South Carolina Showing Rebel ...	U.S. COAST SURVEY	55x63cm
General Map of North America	COLLOT	58x84cm
General Map of North America, Drawn from the Best Surveys	WINTERBOTHAM	35x44cm
General Map of the World, or Terraqueous Globe ...	DUNN	108x125cm
General Map Showing the Countries Explored & Surveyed by [US & Mexico]	COLTON (Pocket & Wall)	39x49cm
General Map Showing the Countries Explored & Surveyed by [US & Mexico]	BARTLETT, J.R	38x49cm
General Topographical Map Sheet XXII [E. Texas; S.W. Louisiana]	U.S. UNION & CONFED.	47x75cm
Generalis Lotharingiae Ducatus Tabula ...	VISSCHER	46x57cm
Geo-Hydrographic Survey of the Island of Madeira ...	WYLD	56x76cm
Geographia Mosaica Generalis cum Novissima Orbis Terraquei Facie et ...	ANONYMOUS	32x36cm
Geographia Sacra, or New & Compendious Maps of the Holy Land	OVERTON	60x102cm
Geographiae Sacra	SANSON (Folio)	40x51cm
Geographiae Sacrae ex Veteri, et Novo Testamento	SANSON (Folio)	40x52cm
Geographica Sacra. Ophiram Regionem ...	JANSSON	36x48cm
Geographical Topographical and Railroad Map of California	LOCAL & STATE MAPS	64x50cm
Geographical and Historical Map of Africa	LAVOISNE	29x30cm
Geographical and Statistical Map of England	LAVOISNE	38x34cm
Geographical and Statistical Map of Ireland	LAVOISNE	35x33cm
Geographical and Statistical Map of Poland	LAVOISNE	30x28cm
Geographical and Statistical Map of Scotland	LAVOISNE	34x31cm
Geographical Map of the World with the Tracks of the Most Celebrated ...	LAVOISNE	27x51cm
Geographical, Historical and Statistical Map of America	CAREY & LEA	42x52cm
Geographical, Historical and Statistical Map of America	LAVOISNE	41x55cm
Geographical, Statistical and Historical Map of Brazil	CAREY & LEA	30x22cm
Geographical, Statistical and Historical Map of Colombia	CAREY & LEA	30x22cm
Geographical, Statistical and Historical Map of Connecticut	CAREY & LEA	25x29cm
Geographical, Statistical and Historical Map of Hayti, Formerly Hispaniola	CAREY & LEA	42x52cm
Geographical, Statistical and Historical Map of Indiana	CAREY & LEA	28x22cm
Geographical, Statistical and Historical Map of Jamaica	CAREY & LEA	29x31cm
Geographical, Statistical and Historical Map of Kentucky	CAREY & LEA	29x46cm
Geographical, Statistical and Historical Map of Louisiana	CAREY & LEA	29x32cm
Geographical, Statistical and Historical Map of Massachusetts	CAREY & LEA	30x47cm
Geographical, Statistical and Historical Map of Mexico	CAREY & LEA	38x37cm
Geographical, Statistical and Historical Map of Michigan Territory	CAREY & LEA	37x27cm
Geographical, Statistical and Historical Map of Mississippi	CAREY & LEA	29x23cm
Geographical, Statistical and Historical Map of New Hampshire	CAREY & LEA	30x22cm
Geographical, Statistical and Historical Map of New Jersey	CAREY & LEA	29x23cm
Geographical, Statistical and Historical Map of New York	CAREY & LEA	30x46cm
Geographical, Statistical and Historical Map of North America	CAREY & LEA	35x34cm
Geographical, Statistical and Historical Map of Ohio	CAREY & LEA	42x52cm
Geographical, Statistical and Historical Map of Rhode Island	CAREY & LEA	29x21cm
Geographical, Statistical and Historical Map of the District of Columbia	CAREY & LEA	27x27cm
Geographical, Statistical and Historical Map of the Leeward Islands	CAREY & LEA	42x52cm
Geographical, Statistical and Historical Map of Upper and Lower Canada	CAREY & LEA	25x52cm
Geographical, Statistical and Historical Map of Vermont	CAREY & LEA	31x24cm
Geography [World]	BLOME	24x38cm

Title	Author	Size
Geography. A Map of the World in Three Sections Describing the Polar ...	PHIPPS	23x42cm
Geological Map of New Jersey	BIEN	89x62cm
Geological Map of Scotland, Lochs, Mountains, Islands	KNIPE	107x81cm
Geological Map of the British Isles and Part of France	KNIPE	161x138cm
Geological Map of the District between Keweenaw Bay and Chocolate River	U.S. GOV'T	50x61cm
Geological Map of the Route Explored by Capt. Jno. Pope ... Red River ...	U.S. PACIFIC R.R. SURVEY	25x58cm
Geological Map of the Toyabe Mountains [NV]	U.S. GOV'T	29x44cm
Geological Map of the United States	U.S. GOV'T	50x72cm
Geological Map of the Western Part of the Plateau Province	U.S. GOV'T	75x46cm
Geological Map of Western Wyoming Illustrating the Report of ... Comstock	U.S. GOV'T	79x55cm
Geological Plan of the Coast Range of California from San Francisco Bay...	U.S. PACIFIC R.R. SURVEY	43x30cm
Geometrical Survey of the Gulf of Naples Made by Order of the King ...	FADEN	23x36cm
Georgetown and the City of Washington	JOHNSON	32x38cm
Georgetown and the City of Washington, the Capital of the United States	COLTON (Pocket & Wall)	35x40cm
Georgia	ARROWSMITH & LEWIS	22x27cm
Georgia	BRADFORD	36x32cm
Georgia	FINLEY	29x22cm
Georgia	LUCAS	27x21cm
Georgia and Alabama	JOHNSON	40x57cm
Georgie, Armenie	SANTINI	38x56cm
Germania	HONDIUS	15x19cm
Germania	MAGINI	14x17cm
Germania	ORTELIUS (Folio)	36x51cm
Germania Antiqua	BARBIE DU BOCAGE	18x24cm
Germania New Teutschlande ...	MUNSTER	31x36cm
Germania Nova Tabula	GASTALDI	13x17cm
Germania VI Nova Tabula	MUNSTER	29x37cm
Germaniae Nova ac Accurata Descriptio ...	CLOPPENBURGH	45x56cm
Germaniae Veteris Nova Descriptio	JANSSON	38x47cm
Germaniae Veteris Typus	BLAEU	38x48cm
Globi Coelestis in Tabulas Planas Redacti [5 parts]	DOPPELMAYR	50x60cm
Globus Terrestris ex Probatissimis Recentiorum Geographorum ...	DE AEFFERDEN	16x24cm
Gloucestershire	SPEED	38x51cm
Goa	MERIAN	28x36cm
Goa Fortissima Indiae Urbs in Christianorum [with] Dui [&] Azaamurum ...	BRAUN & HOGENBERG	33x46cm
Goae Indiae Orientalis Metropolis & Emporij	VAN LINSCHOTEN	38x42cm
Golfe du Mexique Assujetti aux Observations Astronomiques	LAPORTE	18x22cm
Goritiae, Karstii, Chaczeolae, Carniolae, Histriae, et Windorum Marchae ...	ORTELIUS (Folio)	34x23cm
Gouvernement General d'Orleans	SANSON (Folio)	40x53cm
Gouvernement General du Dauphine Divise par Bailliages	DE VAUGONDY	49x51cm
Government Map of Nicaragua from the Latest Surveys ...	GOV'T MAPS: NATIONAL	80x64cm
Graecia	HONDIUS	36x47cm
Graecia	MAGINI	13x17cm
Graecia	MERCATOR (Small)	14x18cm
Graeciae Antiquae ...	SANSON (Folio)	41x55cm
Graeciae pars Septentrionalis	LAURIE & WHITTLE	48x64cm
Graeciae Universae Secundum Hodie R'num Situm Neoterica Descriptio	ORTELIUS (Folio)	36x50cm
Granata et Murcia Regna	BLAEU	38x50cm
Granata in Hispania	MEISNER	10x15cm
Granata Nova et California	WYTFLIET	23x29cm
Grand Island Pass, Mississppi	U.S. COAST SURVEY	27x41cm
Grande Oceano ouvero Quinta Parte del Mondo	ROSSI, L.	20x25cm
Gray's Atlas Map of Texas [on leaf with] ... Arkansas	GRAY	31x38cm
Gray's New Map of Baltimore	GRAY	38x30cm
Gray's New Map of Massachusetts Rhode Island and Connecticut	GRAY	39x64cm
Gray's New Map of Richmond ...	GRAY	34x43cm
Gray's New Map of Saint Louis	GRAY	41x33cm
Gray's New Map of Texas and the Indian Territory	GRAY	43x66cm
Greece	SPEED	39x50cm
Greece	THOMAS, COWPERTHWAIT	30x38cm
Greece, Archipelago and Part of Anadoli	FADEN	53x74cm
Greece with the Northern Provinces near the Danube	GIBSON	20x18cm
Grenada Divided into Its Parishes, Surveyed by Order of ... Governor Scott	JEFFERYS	46x61cm
Grund Riss und Kon. Preuss. Belagerung der Stadt Breslau ...	KILIAN, G.C.	18x28cm
Grundriss des Hafens von Acapulco	BELLIN (Small)	19x15cm
Grundriss von Neu-Orleans nach den Manuscripten in dem Schatze der ...	BELLIN (Small)	19x28cm
Grundriss von Port Royal in Accadia ... Annapolis Royale [Nova Scotia]	BELLIN (Small)	19x28cm

Title	Author	Size
Guiana sive Amazonium Regio	BLAEU	37x49cm
Guiana sive Amazonum Regio	JANSSON	38x50cm
Guide Map of Minneapolis Minnesota	LOCAL & STATE POCKET	61x43cm
Guide through Ohio, Michigan, Indiana, Illinois, Missouri, Wisconsin, Iowa ...	COLTON (Pocket & Wall)	51x70cm
Guinea	BLAEU	39x53cm
Guineae Nova Descriptio	HONDIUS	35x49cm
Gulf Coast of the United States Key West to Rio Grande	U.S. COAST SURVEY	69x130cm
H. & T.C. RW. Co.'s Blocks Nos. 6, 7 & 8. In Presidio Co. [TX]	MANUSCRIPT MAPS	68x62cm
Haage. in Hollandt	MEISNER	10x15cm
Haec Est Nobilis & Florens Illa Neapolis ...	BRAUN & HOGENBERG	33x46cm
Haemisphaerium Stellatum Australe Aequali Sphaerarum Proportione	CELLARIUS	43x51cm
Haemisphaerium Stellatum Australe Antiquum	CELLARIUS	44x52cm
Haemisphaerium Stellatum Boreale Antiquum	VALK & SCHENK	43x51cm
Haemisphaerium Stellatum Boreale cum Subjecto Haemisphaerio Terrestri	CELLARIUS	43x51cm
Haiti	IMRAY	64x100cm
Hall in Sachsen	MEISNER	10x15cm
Hall in Schwaben	MEISNER	10x15cm
Hamborg, Ville Imperiale d'Allemagne	MORTIER	22x30cm
Hampshire	MORDEN	36x42cm
Hampshire	MOULE	20x26cm
Hannover	HILDBURGHAUSEN BIBLIO	16x14cm
Harbor of New Haven ...	U.S. COAST SURVEY	77x63cm
Harbour of Annis Squam in Ipswich Bay	BLUNT	11x18cm
Harmonie or Correspondance du Globe ...	SANSON (Folio)	38x52cm
Harpers Ferry, Prepared by Bvt. Brig. Genl. N. Michler ... 1867	U.S. WAR DEPARTMENT	57x69cm
Hassia	MERCATOR (Small)	14x18cm
Haute Allemagne, Divisee par ses Estats ...	SANSON (Folio)	40x52cm
Haute Ethiopie Ou Sont l'Empire des Abissins, la Nubie.	SANSON (Folio)	36x52cm
Haute ou Petite Pologne ...	SANSON (Folio)	40x52cm
Haute Partie de la Basse Saxe ...	SANSON (Folio)	40x52cm
Hawaii	RAND, McNALLY (atlas maps)	31x48cm
Hawaii [in set with maps of 5 other islands]	GOV'T: LOCAL & STATE	various dimens
Hayward's Map of the City of Brooklyn	HAYWARD	34x49cm
Head Quarters Department of New Mexico ... Routes from Tucson to ...	U.S. GOV'T	17x36cm
Hellas seu Graecia Sophani	BLAEU	36x50cm
Hellas, seu Graecia Universa ...	JANSSON	46x56cm
Helsinge, Medelpadie Angermannie, Iemptie, Dalecarlie ...	SANSON (Folio)	40x52cm
Helvetia	MAGINI	13x17cm
Helvetia Prima et VIII	MUNSTER	32x40cm
Helvetiae Descriptio ...	ORTELIUS (Folio)	34x46cm
Helvetiae Moderna Descriptio	MUNSTER	26x35cm
Hemisphaerii Borealis Coeli et Terrae Sphaeri Cascenographia	CELLARIUS	43x50cm
Hemisphaerium Coeli Australi	HOMANN	50x60cm
Hemisphaerium Orbis Antiqui cum Zonis Circulis et Situ Populorum Diverso	CELLARIUS	41x51cm
Hemisphere Occidental du Globe Tertre Veu en Convex [with] ... Concave	SANSON (Folio)	23x21cm
Hemisphere Occidental ou du Nouveau ... par le S'r D'Anville ...	D'ANVILLE	65x61cm
Hemisphere Oriental	BRION DE LA TOUR	27x30cm
Hemisphere Septentrional ... [in set with] Hemisphere Meridional ...	DE L'ISLE	47x47cm
Hemisphere Septentrional pour Voir Plus Distinctement les Terres Arctiques	DE L'ISLE	Diam: 45cm
Hempstead Harbor Long Island	U.S. COAST SURVEY	46x37cm
Hertzothumb Pommern ...	SANSON (Folio)	40x52cm
Hessiae seu Cattorum Noblissimorum ac Bellicosissimorum ...	DE JODE	36x46cm
Het Beloofde Landt Canaan	DANCKERTS	35x51cm
Het Beloofde Landt Canaan ...	STOOPENDAAL	36x46cm
Het Beloofde Landt Canaan door wandelt van Onsen Salichmaeker ...	STOOPENDAAL	32x46cm
Hibernia	BERTIUS	9x12cm
Hibernia Regnum Vulgo Ireland	BLAEU	38x50cm
Hibernia V. Tabula	MERCATOR (Small)	15x18cm
Hiberniae Britanicae Insulae Nova Descriptio. Eryn	QUAD	22x30cm
Hiberniae Regnum	HOMANN	58x49cm
Hiberniae Regnum tam in Praecipuas Ultoniae, Connaciae, Laceniae ...	HOMANN	57x48cm
Hiberniae Regnum tam in Praecipuas Ultoniae, Connaciae, Laceniae et ...	VISSCHER	57x46cm
Hierosolima	SCHEDEL	19x23cm
Hierosolyma, Clarissima Totius Orientis Civitas Iudaee Metropolis	BRAUN & HOGENBERG	34x49cm
Highway Map of Colorado	HIGHWAY MAPS	41x66cm
Hindoostan	THOMSON	45x61cm
Hindoostan or British India	COLTON (Atlas Maps)	40x32cm

Title	Author	Size
Hispania	PURCHAS	15x18cm
Hispania Nova	MERCATOR (Small)	15x18cm
Hispania Nova	WYTFLIET	23x28cm
Hispania Nova Tabula	GASTALDI	13x17cm
Hispania Regnum	MERIAN	27x36cm
Hispaniae Nova ... 1579	ORTELIUS (Folio)	34x50cm
Hispaniae Novae Nova Descriptio	MERCATOR (Folio)	38x51cm
Hispaniae Novae Nova Descriptio	CLOPPENBURGH	19x25cm
Hispaniae Novae Nova Descriptio	HONDIUS	13x19cm
Hispaniae Regionis Nova Descriptio	MUNSTER	25x34cm
Hispaniae Regnum	MAGINI	13x17cm
Hispaniae Veteris Descriptio	JANSSON	37x50cm
Hispaniola Insula	WYTFLIET	23x28cm
Hispaniolae, Cubae, Aliarumque Insularum Circumiacientium ...	ORTELIUS (Folio)	35x50cm
Histoire de la Decouverte des Monde Nouveau et Inconnu ... 1761	BRION DE LA TOUR	38x52cm
Historical and Military Map of the Border and Southern States	PHELPS & WATSON	49x89cm
Hodiernae Europae Tabula	WELLS	9x14cm
Holbrook's Map of the City of Newark New Jersey	LOCAL & STATE POCKET	51x46cm
Holland	THOMSON	59x50cm
Hollande et Belgium	DELAMARCHE	41x29cm
Hollandia	MERCATOR (Small)	15x18cm
Holyoke and South Hadley Falls [MA] ... No.13	BACHELDER, J.B.	25x39cm
Homburg. Nassaw Sarbr.	MEISNER	10x15cm
Honolulu	MEYER	11x16cm
Horizon de Paris ...	ST. ALBIN	60x81cm
Hudson River, Sheet No.1, From New York to Haverstraw	U.S. COAST & GEODETIC	99x44cm
Hudson River, Sheet No.3, From Poughkeepsie to Troy, New York	U.S. COAST & GEODETIC	99x50cm
Hungaria	MERCATOR (Small)	15x18cm
Hungaria Regnum	SANSON (Folio)	40x52cm
Hungaria Regnum ...	JANSSON	42x51cm
Hungaria Regnum Sumptibus Henrici Hondy per Gerardum Mercatorem ...	MERCATOR (Folio)	37x44cm
Hungariae Descriptio, Wolfgango Lazio Auct.	ORTELIUS (Folio)	36x50cm
Hungariae Regnum	PITT	42x51cm
Huquang, Kiang Si, Che Kiang, ac Fokien ...	VALK & SCHENK	46x52cm
Huquang, Kiangsi, Chekiang, ac Fokien, Provin: sive Praefecturae Regni ...	JANSSON	36x52cm
Husenum	LASOR A VAREA	9x13cm
Hydrological Basin of the Upper Mississippi ... by J.N. Nicollet ...	U.S. GOV'T	97x80cm
Hydrophylacium Africae ...	KIRCHER	34x41cm
I. de St. Helene	MALLET	15x10cm
I. S. Laurentij	VAN LINSCHOTEN	9x12cm
Iapan	LANGENES	9x13cm
Iaponia	CLOPPENBURGH	18x24cm
Iaponia	HONDIUS	34x45cm
Iaponiae Insulae Descriptio ...	ORTELIUS (Folio)	35x48cm
Iaponiae Nova Descriptio	JANSSON	34x44cm
Iava Maior	DE RENEVILLE	15x20cm
Ichnography of Charleston ... for the Use of the Phoenix Fire Company ...	PETRIE	49x69cm
Idaho	CRAM	30x25cm
Il Canada, le Colonie Inglesi con la Luigiana e Florida ...	ZATTA	32x42cm
Il Paese de Selvaggi Outauacesi e Kilistinesi Intorno al Lago Superiore	ZATTA	32x42cm
Il Situ de' Curzolari	PORCACCHI	9x14cm
Ile de New-York. Partie de Long-Island ou de l'Ile Longue, et Positions ...	MARSHALL	41x26cm
Iles Sandwich	VANDERMAELEN	48x55cm
Illinois	LUCAS	30x23cm
Illyricum	ORTELIUS (Folio)	37x48cm
Imperii Sinarum Nova Descriptio	VALK & SCHENK	47x52cm
Imperii Sinarum Nova Descriptio	VAN LOON	46x51cm
Imperii Sinarum Nova Descriptio. Auctore Joh van Loon	JANSSON	47x52cm
Imperium Japonicum ...	SEUTTER	49x58cm
Imperium Romanum Auth Phil. Briete Societ Iesu	JANSSON	38x52cm
Imperium Russicum Omnisque Tartaria	LOTTER	10x12cm
Imperium Turcicum in Europa, Asia et Africa	HOMANN	51x61cm
India Extrema XXIIII. Nova Tabula	MUNSTER	29x37cm
India Orientalis	CLOPPENBURGH	19x26cm
India Orientalis	HONDIUS	36x49cm
India Orientalis	MAGINI	13x18cm
India Orientalis	MERCATOR (Folio)	36x48cm

Title	Cartographer	Size
India Orientalis	MERCATOR (Small)	15x18cm
India Orientalis [with] Iapaniae ... [&] Chinae ... [&] ... Philippinae	WYTFLIET	10x12cm
India Orientalis cum Adiacentibus Insulis Nova Delineatione ...	SEUTTER	48x57cm
India Orientalis et Insulae Adiacentes	MERIAN	27x36cm
India quae Orientalis Dicitur et Insulae Adiacentes	BLAEU	41x50cm
India quae Orientalis Dicitur et Insulae Adiacentes	JANSSON	40x50cm
India quae Orientalis Dicitur, et Insulae Adiacentes	HONDIUS	40x49cm
Indiae Orientalis Insularumque Adiacientium Typus	ORTELIUS (Folio)	35x50cm
Indiae Orientalis nec non Insularum Adiacentium Nova Descriptio ...	DE WIT	50x60cm
Indiae Orientalis nec non Insularum Adiacentium Nova Descriptio ...	VISSCHER	46x56cm
Indiae Orientalis Nova Descriptio	JANSSON	39x50cm
Indian Territory	U.S. STATE SURVEYS	61x81cm
Indian Territory, 1883	U.S. STATE SURVEYS	30x41cm
Indiana	COLTON (Atlas Maps)	39x32cm
Indiana	FINLEY	29x22cm
Indiana	RAND, McNALLY (atlas maps)	66x48cm
Insprugk in Tyrol	MEISNER	10x15cm
Insula Candia Ejusque Fortificatio ...	DE WIT	46x54cm
Insula Candia olim Creta	MERIAN	31x42cm
Insula Ceilon olim Taprobana Incolis Tenarisin et Lankawn Exactissime ...	VISSCHER	50x59cm
Insula Corsica ...	COVENS & MORTIER	56x49cm
Insula Creta Hodie Candia ...	HOMANN	48x58cm
Insula d. Helenae ...	DE BRY	21x28cm
Insula S. Iuan de Puerto Rico, Caribes vel Canibasum Insulae	VALK & SCHENK	40x50cm
Insulae Americanae in Oceano Septentrionali ...	BLAEU	38x52cm
Insulae Americanae in Oceano Septentrionali ... C. de May ... Lineam ...	VISSCHER	46x56cm
Insulae Americanae in Oceano Septentrionali, cum Terris Adiacentibus	OGILBY	28x36cm
Insulae Americanae Nempe: Cuba, Hispaniola, Jamaica, Pto Rico ...	DANCKERTS	50x58cm
Insulae Balearides et Pytivsae	BLAEU	39x51cm
Insulae Borneo et Occidentalis pars Celebes ...	JANSSON	42x53cm
Insulae Corsicae	HOMANN	56x50cm
Insulae Cuba Hispaniola &c.	MERCATOR (Small)	15x18cm
Insulae Flandricae, olim Asores Dicta	VALK & SCHENK	42x53cm
Insulae Iavae cum Parte Insularum Borneo Sumatrae ...	JANSSON	42x52cm
Insulae Indiae Orientalis	HONDIUS	14x20cm
Insulae Indiae Orientalis	MERCATOR (Small)	15x18cm
Insulae Indiae Orientalis Praecipuae in Quibus Moluccae Celeberrimae ...	HONDIUS	35x48cm
Insulae Indicae cum Terris Circumvicinis	SCHERER	24x36cm
Insular Aliquot Aegean ...	ORTELIUS (Folio)	no dimens
Insularum Aliquot Maris Mediterranei Descriptio	ORTELIUS (Folio)	36x48cm
Insularum Melitae vulgo Maltae Gozae et Comini Correctissima Descriptio	DE WIT	46x56cm
Insularum Moluccarum Nova Descriptio	JANSSON	38x50cm
Investissiment et Attaque d'York, dans la Virginie	MARSHALL	21x23cm
Iowa	COLTON (Atlas Maps)	30x41cm
Iowa	MITCHELL, S.A. (to 1859)	41x34cm
Iowa and Wisconsin	BRADFORD	36x29cm
Iowa and Wisconsin Chiefly from the Map of J.N. Nicollet	MORSE & BREESE	30x38cm
Ireland	BLACK	51x41cm
Ireland	CARY	28x23cm
Ireland	LOCKHEAD	23x19cm
Ireland	RAND, McNALLY (atlas maps)	65x48cm
Ireland	S.D.U.K.	41x33cm
Ireland	TANNER	28x22cm
Ireland	THOMAS, COWPERTHWAIT	30x24cm
Irlandia	MERCATOR (Small)	15x18cm
Irlandia Regnum	MERCATOR (Folio)	34x42cm
Irlandiae Regnum	MERCATOR (Folio)	34x48cm
Island of Luzon - Philippine Islands	RAND, McNALLY (atlas maps)	31x23cm
Island of St. Lucia [with] ... St. Vincent [&] ... Windward Is. ...	LONDON MAGAZINE	25x19cm
Islandia	MERCATOR (Small)	15x18cm
Islandia	QUAD	22x29cm
Islands in the Indian Ocean	S.D.U.K.	32x39cm
Islands in the Pacific Ocean - Sheet 8	JOHNSTON	50x61cm
Isle d'Auphine ... Nommee ... Madagascar	SANSON (Folio)	58x45cm
Isle de la Guadeloupe ...	SANSON (Folio)	32x43cm
Isle de la Jamaique	LAPORTE	18x22cm
Isle de Madagascar autrement Isle de St. Laurent	BELLIN (Small)	29x23cm

Isle du Japon	MALLET	14x10cm
Isle et Royaume de Sicile	DE FER (Small)	23x33cm
Isle Molucoues	MALLET	15x10cm
Isle Royale	DE VAUGONDY	16x24cm
Isles Caribes	MALLET	15x10cm
Isles des Larrons	MALLET	14x9cm
Isles Moluques	LE ROUGE	20x27cm
Isles of Shoals [NH]	BLUNT	23x19cm
Isola Cuba Nova	GASTALDI	13x17cm
Isola Cuba Nova	RUSCELLI	18x25cm
Isola de lames, a Giamaica, Possedutta dal Re Britannico Divisa in ...	CORONELLI	22x29cm
Isola de' Rhodi	BERTELLI	20x15cm
Isola de Zante	BERTELLI	20x15cm
Isole dell' India Cioe le Molucche le Filippine e della Sonda ...	ROSSI	45x58cm
Isole di Majorca, d'Ivica e di Formentera ...	ZATTA	32x42cm
Isole Filippine	ZATTA	41x31cm
Isothermal Chart or View of Climates; ... Plants & Animals of the World	WOODBRIDGE	22x28cm
Itala Name Tellus Graecia Maior Erat.	ORTELIUS (Folio)	34x48cm
Italia	MERCATOR (Folio)	37x47cm
Italia	VAN DEN KEERE	14x20cm
Italia mit den Dreyen Furnempften Inseln Corsica, Sardinia und Sicilia	MUNSTER	27x34cm
Italia Nova	CLUVER	26x30cm
Italiae Antiquae Nova Delineatio ...	JANSSON	38x50cm
Italiae Gallicae sive Galliae Cisalpinae	CLUVER	20x25cm
Italiae Novissima Descriptio ...	ORTELIUS (Folio)	36x51cm
Italy	BRADFORD	25x20cm
Italy	KITCHIN	60x52cm
Iucatana Regio et Fondura	WYTFLIET	23x30cm
Iudaea seu Palaestina ob Sacratissima Redemtoris Vestigia Hodie ...	HOMANN	48x56cm
Iudaea seu Terra Sancta ...	JAILLOT	54x85cm
Iudaeae seu Terrae Israelis Tabula Geographica; in qua Locorum in Veteri ...	JANSSON	36x48cm
Iunnan Queicheu, Quangsi et Quan Tung Provinciae Regni Sinensis	VALK & SCHENK	46x52cm
Iustissimae Causae Heroica Virtute Propugnatae Gloriosiss: Triumphi ...	SEUTTER	50x58cm
J.H. Colton's Colorado and New Mexico	COLTON (Atlas Maps)	28x22cm
J.H. Colton's Map of Florida	COLTON (Atlas Maps)	28x20cm
J.H. Colton's Map of Nebraska, Dakota and Montana	COLTON (Atlas Maps)	28x20cm
J. No.4, Preliminary Surveys of the Harbors on the Western Coast ...	U.S. COAST SURVEY	31x32cm
Jamaica	TALLIS	25x35cm
Jamaica, Americae Septentrionalis Ampla Insula, Christophoro Columbo ...	VISSCHER	51x60cm
Jamaica from the Latest Surveys	JEFFERYS	46x61cm
Japan & Corea	TALLIS	26x34cm
Japan Nippon, Kiusiu, Sikok, Yesso and the Japanese Kuriles	JOHNSON	32x39cm
Jetersville and Sailors Creek	U.S. WAR DEPARTMENT	53x79cm
Johnson's Asia	JOHNSON	39x55cm
Johnson's Australia and East Indies	JOHNSON	57x43cm
Johnson's California Territories of New Mexico and Utah	JOHNSON	43x61cm
Johnson's California, Territories of New Mexico, Arizona, Colorado, ...	JOHNSON	43x62cm
Johnson's California, with Utah, Nevada, Colorado, New Mexico and ...	JOHNSON	43x61cm
Johnson's Cuba Jamaica and Porto Rico	JOHNSON	33x40cm
Johnson's Delaware and Maryland	JOHNSON	32x40cm
Johnson's Europe	JOHNSON	42x57cm
Johnson's Florida	JOHNSON	32x39cm
Johnson's Globular World	JOHNSON	41x59cm
Johnson's Japan	JOHNSON	32x39cm
Johnson's Maine	JOHNSON	39x32cm
Johnson's Map of New York and the Adjacent Cities	JOHNSON	41x65cm
Johnson's Map of the Vicinity of Richmond, and Peninsular Campaign ...	JOHNSON	45x67cm
Johnson's Map of the World on Mercator's Projection.	JOHNSON	41x64cm
Johnson's Mexico	JOHNSON	31x39cm
Johnson's Minnesota and Dakota	JOHNSON	32x39cm
Johnson's Nebraska, Dakota, Colorado & Kansas	JOHNSON	32x39cm
Johnson's Nebraska, Dakota, Colorado, Idaho & Kansas	JOHNSON	32x40cm
Johnson's Nebraska, Dakota, Idaho and Montana	JOHNSON	43x59cm
Johnson's New Jersey	JOHNSON	40x32cm
Johnson's New Map of the State of Texas	JOHNSON	41x62cm
Johnson's New Military Map of the United States Showing the Forts ...	JOHNSON	43x61cm
Johnson's North America	JOHNSON	56x44cm

Title	Author	Size
Johnson's Ontario, of the Dominion of Canada	JOHNSON	42x58cm
Johnson's Texas	JOHNSON	39x55cm
Johnson's Western Hemisphere [&] Johnson's Eastern Hemisphere	JOHNSON	38x67cm
Johnson's World on Mercator's Projection	JOHNSON	41x58cm
Judia, de Hoofd-Stad van Siam	VALENTYN	27x36cm
Kaart van Basses Straat	FLINDERS	48x69cm
Kaart van de Geheele Wereld	DE LAT	18x29cm
Kaart van het Eylandt Bali ...	VALENTYN	45x56cm
Kaart van het Westelyk Gedeelte van Nieuw Mexico en van California ...	TIRION	32x34cm
Kaart van het Zuider Halfrond Vertoonende de Koersen van Enige ...	COOK	53x53cm
Kaart van London Enz. en van het Naby Gelegen Land ...	TIRION	29x42cm
Kaart van Van Diemens Land Opgenoomen door Kapitein Furneaux ...	COOK	21x14cm
Kaartje van het Noorder-Deel van America	DE LAT	17x23cm
Kamtschatskisches Meer ...	CHAPPE D'AUTEROCHE	17x27cm
Kansas	COLTON (Atlas Maps)	42x61cm
Kansas City	MEYER	11x17cm
Kansas, Colorado, Texas, &c.	CORNELL	25x21cm
Karta ofvar Sodra Delen af Sverige och Orrige ...	FORSELL	231x163cm
Karta ofver Sverige och Norrige	HAELLSTROM	92x64cm
Karte von Accadia ...	BELLIN (Small)	20x32cm
Karte von Amerika nach D'Anville und Pownall ...	VON REILLY	62x79cm
Karte von dem Deutschen Meere und den Angranzenden Theilen ...	HILDBURGHAUSEN BIBLIO	28x22cm
Karte von dem Eylande Hayti Heutiges Tages Espagnola oder die Insel ...	BELLIN (Small)	22x33cm
Karte von dem Fluss Richelieu und dem See Champlain ...	BELLIN (Small)	30x14cm
Karte von den Kusten des Franzosischen Florida	BELLIN (Small)	20x14cm
Karte von den Laender Nicaragua und Costa Rica	BELLIN (Small)	20x17cm
Karte von den Umliegenden Gegenden der Stadt Mexico	BELLIN (Small)	20x16cm
Karte von der Erdenge Panama und den Provinzen Veragua, Terra Firma ...	BELLIN (Small)	20x29cm
Karte von der Hudsons Bay	BELLIN (Small)	20x28cm
Karte von der Insel Montreal ...	BELLIN (Small)	24x31cm
Karte von der Iselwelt, Polynesien oder der Funften Welttheile nach ...	VON REILLY	46x64cm
Karte von l'Isle Royale	BELLIN (Small)	18x26cm
Karte von Luisiana, dem Laufe des Mississipi ...	BELLIN (Large)	39x55cm
Karte von Mexico	BELLIN (Small)	20x29cm
Karte von Nord-America ...	BELLIN (Small)	28x35cm
Kent	SPEED	38x50cm
Kentucky	ARROWSMITH & LEWIS	22x27cm
Kentucky	BRADFORD	29x37cm
Kentucky	CAREY	26x48cm
Kentucky and Tennessee	JOHNSON	42x58cm
Kerry	LEWIS, SAMUEL & CO.	30x24cm
Koishikawa	JAPANESE CARTOGRAPHY	46x51cm
Konigreich Boheim ...	SANSON (Folio)	40x52cm
Kremlenagrad, Castellum Urbis Moskvae	BLAEU	38x49cm
L'Afrique ...	DE L'ISLE	45x58cm
L'Afrique Divisee Suivant l'Estendue de Ses Principales Parties ... Sanson	JAILLOT	56x86cm
L'Afrique Dressee sur les Relations les Plus Recentes et Rectifices ...	NOLIN	122x136cm
L'Afrique ou Lybie Ulterieure ...	SANSON (Folio)	36x52cm
L'Amerique	BRION DE LA TOUR	22x34cm
L'Amerique Divisee en Ses Principaux Etats, Assujetie aux Observations	JANVIER	47x65cm
L'Amerique Divisee par Grands Etats ...	JANVIER	30x44cm
L'Amerique, Dresse sur les N:Observations Faites en Toutes les Parties ...	COVENS & MORTIER	112x130cm
L'Amerique Meridionale ...	DE L'ISLE	48x58cm
L'Amerique Meridionale et Septentrionale ...	DANET	48x70cm
L'Amerique, Meridionale, et Septentrionale ...	DE FER (Large)	46x60cm
L'Amerique Meridionale et Septentrionale ...	DE FER (Small)	23x34cm
L'Amerique Meridionale et Septentrionale ...	DESNOS	50x72cm
L'Amerique Selon les Nouvelles Observations ...	VAN DER AA	48x66cm
L'Amerique Septentrionale ...	COVENS & MORTIER	48x58cm
L'Amerique Septentrionale Dressee sur les Observations ...	DE L'ISLE	44x58cm
L'Amerique Septentrionale Suivant Mr. DeLisle de l'Acadamie des Sciences	CHATELAIN	14x17cm
L'Ancien et le Nouveau Mexique, avec la Floride et la Basse Lousiane. ...	BONNE	35x23cm
L'Ancien Monde et le Nouveau en Deux Hemispheres	BONNE	23x42cm
L'Asie	FRICX	44x58cm
L'Asie ...	VAN DER AA	23x29cm
L'Asie Suivant les Nouvelles Decouvertes dont les Point Principaux ...	DE FER (Small)	22x32cm

Title	Publisher	Size
L'Electorat de Hannover ou les Domaines du Roi ...	COVENS & MORTIER	59x52cm
L'Empire d'Allemagne Divisee en Tous Ses Etats	OTTENS	48x61cm
L'Empire de la Chine avec les Isles du Japon	DE LAPORTE	18x22cm
L'Empire de la Chine d'apres l'Atlas Chinois, avec les Isles du Japon	BONNE	31x45cm
L'Empire du Japon ...	DE VAUGONDY	48x54cm
L'Empire du Japon Tire des Cartes des Japonnois ...	CHATELAIN	36x44cm
L'Espagne ...	DE L'ISLE	48x60cm
L'Europa ...	ZATTA	28x38cm
L'Europe [should read "L'Asie"] Divisee selon l'Etendue de ses Principales	DE FER (Large)	105x154cm
L'Europe Divisee Suivant ...	JAILLOT	51x87cm
L'Hemisphere Meridional pour Voir Plus Distinctement les Terres Australes	COVENS & MORTIER	47x53cm
L'Hemisphere Septentrional pour Voir Plus Distinctement les Terres Arctiques	DE L'ISLE	20x46cm
L'Hydrographie ou Description de l'Eau c'est a Dire des Mers, Golfes, ...	SANSON (Folio)	40x54cm
L'Impero del Giapon Diviso in Sette Principali Parti ...	ZATTA	32x40cm
L'Inde de la le Gange ...	VAN DER AA	22x30cm
L'Inde deca et dela le Gange, Ou Est l'Empire du Grand Mogol ...	SANSON (Folio)	35x55cm
L'Irlande	DE VAUGONDY	24x22cm
L'Irlande	LE ROUGE	28x21cm
L'Isle de Cuba	BONNE	21x32cm
L'Isle de Martinique	DE VAUGONDY	16x19cm
L'Isle St. Domingue ou Espagnole Decouverte l'An 1492. Par les Espagnols	DE FER (Large)	43x58cm
L'Italie	DEZAUCHE	52x65cm
L'Italie	JANVIER	32x46cm
La Baja d'Hudson Terra di Labrador e Groenlandia con le Isole Adiacenti ..	ZATTA	29x39cm
La Barbade ... [with] Isle St. Christophle ...	LE ROUGE	27x20cm
La Basse Guinee Contenant les Royaumes de Loango, de Congo, d'Angola	BONNE	36x23cm
La Chine Royaume ...	SANSON (Folio)	41x54cm
La Citta di Treveri, Capitale dell' Arcivescovato	SALMON	16x22cm
La Florida [with] Guastecan	ORTELIUS (Folio)	15x23cm
La Florida [with] Peruviae Auriferae Regionis Typus [&] Guastecan Reg.	ORTELIUS (Folio)	34x46cm
La Floride	MALLET	15x11cm
La Floride par N. Sanson d'Abbeville ...	SANSON (Small)	18x25cm
La Grande Tartarie	SANSON (Small)	19x25cm
La Grecia Divisa Nelle sue Provincie ...	ZATTA	42x32cm
La Guadeloupe ...	LE ROUGE	47x55cm
La Jamaique aux Anglois ... [with] La Bermude aux Anglois ...	CREPY	20x27cm
La Judee ou Palestine Dresse pour l'Intelligence de l'Histoire Sainte	BRION DE LA TOUR	28x32cm
La Judee ou Terre Sainte, Divisee en Ses Douze Tribes	DE VAUGONDY	48x59cm
La Livonie Duche Divisee en Ses Principles Parties Esten, et Letten	SANSON (Folio)	41x53cm
La Lorraine, Qui Comprend les Duches de Lorraine et de Bar, et les Balliages	SANSON (Folio)	55x88cm
La Martinique par les Ingenieurs Anglais lorsqu'ils en Etoient Possesseurs	LE ROUGE	46x60cm
La Nuova Francia	RAMUSIO	31x40cm
La Nuova Olanda e la Nuova Guinea ...	CASSINI	35x48cm
La Nuova Zelanda Trascorsa nel 1769 e 1770 dal Cook ...	ZATTA	36x45cm
La Partie Orientale de l'Asie ou se Trouvent le Grand Empire des Tartares ...	DE FER (Small)	23x33cm
La Plus Grande Partie de la Manche, qui Contient les Cotes D'Angleterre ...	LOTTER	49x57cm
La Presqu'Isle de l'Inde au dela du Gange	BONNE	24x35cm
La Provence	JAILLOT	46x64cm
La Riviere du Detroit depuis le Lac Sainte Claire jusqu'au Lac Erie	BELLIN (Small)	20x32cm
La Russie d'Europe	LAPORTE	18x23cm
La Souabe ...	SANSON (Folio)	40x52cm
La Suisse	RIZZI-ZANNONI	33x47cm
La Table de la Region Orientale Comprenant les Dernieres Terres ... d'Asie	MUNSTER	28x36cm
La Table des Isles Neusues, lesquelles on Appelle Isles d'Occident & d'Indie	MUNSTER	25x33cm
La Table du Pays de Pomeran, selon les Principautez, les Villes les Plus ...	MUNSTER	24x38cm
La Terra de Hochelaga nella Nova Francia	RAMUSIO	27x37cm
La Terre et les Isles Magellaniques ...	SANSON (Folio)	37x49cm
La Terre Sainte Divisee en Ses Douze Tribus	NOLIN	46x66cm
La Terre Sainte. Tiree des Memoires de M. de la Rue	DE FER (Small)	24x31cm
La Vera e Reale Cita di Gierusalem come Si Trova Ogi	AMICO	23x29cm
Laconia und die Insel Cythera	BARBIE DU BOCAGE	26x20cm
Lacus Agnianus [with] La Caverna di Sibylla Cumana	BRAUN & HOGENBERG	33x47cm
Lagenia Anglis Leinster	BLAEU	39x50cm
Lake Superior and the Northern Part of Michigan	COLTON (Atlas Maps)	33x40cm
Lakes of the Glacial Period	U.S. GOV'T	25x42cm
Lambach [Austria]	MEISNER	10x15cm
Lanai [HI]	U.S. GOV'T	50x66cm

Title	Author	Size
Land Classification Map of Eastern California Atlas Sheet No.65 (D)	U.S. WAR DEPARTMENT	41x51cm
Land Classification Map of Part of Central Colorado, Atlas Sheet No.62 (A)	U.S. WAR DEPARTMENT	43x51cm
Land Classification Map of Part of Western Colorado, Atlas Sheet No.61A	U.S. WAR DEPARTMENT	38x49cm
Landau	BODENEHR	16x22cm
Lands Ceded by the Sioux, Sacs, Foxes, Otoes, Ioways, &c. in 1825	U.S. GOV'T	50x88cm
Lands of the Maxwell Irrigated Land Co. [NM]	REAL ESTATE MAPS	15x25cm
Latium	ORTELIUS (Folio)	36x46cm
Lauenau	MERIAN	20x38cm
Lauere Depintura di Colmaria Citta, & del Campo, che la Circonde	MUNSTER	23x34cm
Le Beau Port	CHAMPLAIN	15x25cm
Le Bermude [with] Frislanda [&] Isola di Mayen [&] Isola di Terra Nuova	CORONELLI	46x61cm
Le Canada ou Nouvelle France ...	SANSON (Folio)	40x54cm
Le Canada, ou Nouvelle France, la Floride, la Virginie ... Riviere de Misisipi	DE FER (Small)	24x34cm
Le Canada ou Partie de la Nouvelle France, Contenant la Terre de Labrador	MORTIER	57x79cm
Le Cap de Bonne Esperance	VAN DER AA	23x30cm
Le Cercle de Westphalie Divise en Tous les Estats ...	JAILLOT	60x45cm
Le Chili Divise en Ses Treize Iurisdictions ...	SANSON (Folio)	40x46cm
Le Compte d'Oxford	VAN DER AA	23x40cm
Le Danemark Divise par Provinces et Dioceses	BRION DE LA TOUR	24x25cm
Le Danemark Suivant Dernier Relations	DE FER (Small)	18x14cm
Le Detroit de Malacca ...	VAN DER AA	25x16cm
Le Duche d'Aniou	JANSSON	37x49cm
Le Duche de Luxembourg ...	JAILLOT	58x69cm
Le Globe Terrestre Represente en Deux Plans ...	CHIQUET	16x22cm
Le Globe Terrestre Vu en Connexe par les Deux Poles, l'Equateur Servant ...	MOITHEY	23x41cm
Le Golfe de Mexique, et les Isles Voisine. Dresse sur les Relations les ...	MORTIER	60x85cm
Le Gouvernement de Champagne. i.e. Praefectura Generalis Campaniae ...	SEUTTER	58x50cm
Le Gouvernement de l'Isle de France	BLAEU	41x52cm
Le Gouvernement General de Normandie Divise en Haute et Basse	DE FER (Large)	47x66cm
Le Gouvernement General du Daufine, et des Pays ... ou Sont la Savoye	SANSON (Folio)	36x43cm
Le Gouvernment General de Champagne et la Provinci de Brie	DE FER (Large)	61x52cm
Le Indie Orientali	ZATTA	32x40cm
Le Nouveau Mexique, et la Floride ...	SANSON (Folio)	32x55cm
Le Plan de Paris Ses Faubourgs et Ses Environs ...	SEUTTER	50x57cm
Le Planisphere autrement la Carte du Monde Terrestre	DU VAL	41x80cm
Le Poste della Francia	ROSSI	67x56cm
Le Royaume de Hongrie	JAILLOT	55x86cm
Le Royaume de Siam ...	MORTIER	48x55cm
Le Royaume de Siam avec les Royaumes qui Luy Sont Tributaires ...	MORTIER	79x55cm
Le Sette Chiese di Roma ... Die Sieben Kitchen von Rom, mit Ihren ...	SEUTTER	50x58cm
Leo Belgicus ...	VAN DEN KEERE	37x45cm
Leodiensis Diocesis Typus	ORTELIUS (Folio)	38x49cm
Leodiensis Dioecesis	BLAEU	38x50cm
Leonard Tract, Town of Berkeley, Sale, Thursday, 16th May, 1878	REAL ESTATE MAPS	45x56cm
Les Costes aux Environs de la Riviere de Misisipi ...	DE FER (Small)	22x33cm
Les Costes des Royaumes de Fez, Alger, Tunis et Tripoli en Barbarie	DU VAL	22x75cm
Les Couronnes du Nord Comprenant les Royaumes du Suede, Norwege ...	LAPORTE	18x22cm
Les Deserts d'Egypte, de Thebaide d'Arabie, de Sirie	MICHALET	57x78cm
Les Deux Poles Arctique ou Septentrional, et Antarcticque ou Meridional	SANSON (Folio)	39x53cm
Les Environs de Vienne en Austriche ...	DE FER (Small)	17x51cm
Les Etats de la Couronne de Castille, ... Andalousie, Granade, et Murcie	SANSON (Folio)	40x52cm
Les Etats de la Couronne de Portugal en Espagne	SANSON (Folio)	52x40cm
Les Etats Unis de l'Amerique Septentrionale Partie Occidentale ...	BONNE	35x23cm
Les Indes	CHATELAIN	13x17cm
Les Indes Orientales et Leur Archipel	DE LAPORTE	18x22cm
Les Isles Antilles ...	DE VAUGONDY	16x22cm
Les Isles Antilles et le Golfe du Mexique	BONNE	21x32cm
Les Isles Britannique ...	OTTENS	47x59cm
Les Isles Britanniques	DE FER (Large)	85x107cm
Les Isles Britanniques ou Sont le Royaumes d'Angleterre ...	DE L'ISLE	45x57cm
Les Isles Philippines [with] Islas de los Ladrones ou Isle des Larrons ...	SANSON (Small)	19x25cm
Les Isles Philippines, Celle de Formose, le Sud de la Chine ... Cochinchine	BONNE	21x32cm
Les Lacs du Canada et Nouvelle Angleterre	DE VAUGONDY	17x22cm
Leyda, Batavorum Lugdunum, Vulgo Leyden	BRAUN & HOGENBERG	34x48cm
Li Circoli dell Alto, e Basso Reno	ZATTA	32x42cm
Lier. - Lira, Elegans et Amoenum Brabantiae Opp.	BRAUN & HOGENBERG	32x40cm
Lieut. Wheeler's Expedition nach New-Mexico & Arizona, 1873	PETERMANN	25x19cm

Title	Author	Size
Lille. Insula. Ryssele	BRAUN & HOGENBERG	33x43cm
Limes Occcidentis et Quivira Anian	METELLUS	18x22cm
Limes Occidentis Quivira et Anian	WYTFLIET	23x29cm
Lincolne Shire:	SPEED	8x12cm
Linguistic Stocks of American Indians North of Mexico	U.S. GOV'T	32x24cm
Lisbon	S.D.U.K.	31x38cm
Lithuania	MERCATOR (Small)	14x18cm
Little Egg Harbor [NJ]	BLUNT	12x20cm
Littora Brasiliae. Pascaert van Brasil	DE WIT	49x56cm
Livonia	MERCATOR (Small)	15x18cm
Livonia vulgo Lyefland	BLAEU	38x50cm
Livoniae et Curlandiae Ducatus cum Insulis Adjacentib.	LOTTER	49x58cm
Lloyd's New Map of United States, the Canadas and New Brunswick ...	LLOYD	95x126cm
Lloyd's Railroad, Telegraph & Express Map of the Eastern States ...	LLOYD	66x95cm
Londinum Feracissimi Angliae Regni Metropolis	BRAUN & HOGENBERG	33x48cm
Londinum Urbs Praecipua Regni Anglae	AVELINE	37x50cm
London	BLOME	17x28cm
London	MERIAN	23x70cm
London	S.D.U.K.	39x66cm
London, from the South Side of the Thames	ILLUS. LONDON NEWS	43x131cm
Londonderry	LEWIS, SAMUEL & CO.	30x24cm
Lorraine. Lotharingiae Nova Descriptio	ORTELIUS (Folio)	34x50cm
Los Angeles	U.S. PACIFIC R.R. SURVEY	15x23cm
Lotharingia Ducatus; Vulgo Lorraine	BLAEU	38x50cm
Lotharingia Septentr.	MERCATOR (Small)	13x20cm
Louisiana	ARROWSMITH & LEWIS	25x20cm
Louisiana	BRADFORD	29x36cm
Louisiana	COLTON (Atlas Maps)	32x39cm
Louisiana	FINLEY	22x28cm
Louisiana [in set with] British Possessions in America [&] Spanish ...	ARROWSMITH & LEWIS	27x22cm
Louisiana, Mississippi, Arkansas and part of Texas	SMITH, ROSWELL C.	30x25cm
Lower Canada, New Brunswick, Nova Scotia ... Newfoundland	ARROWSMITH	61x48cm
Lubec	GOTTFRIED	7x13cm
Lubrecht's California	LUBRECHT	32x28cm
Lugdunum Batavorum ...	LOCAL & STATE MAPS	79x88cm
Luigiana Inglese, Colla Parte Occidentale della Florida, della Giorgia e ...	ZATTA	32x42cm
Lumen Historiarum per Occidentem ex Conatibus Fran. Haraei Antverpiae	JANSSON	38x48cm
Lunden [with] Abilltung vie Konigliche Maistat in Engelandt ...	ANONYMOUS	27x32cm
Lutetia Vulgari Nomine Paris, Urbs Galliae Maxima ...	BRAUN & HOGENBERG	33x47cm
Lutzenburgensis Ducatus Veriss. Descript.	ORTELIUS (Folio)	36x49cm
Luxemburgensis Ducatus, Tam in Ejusdem Minores, quam Principales ...	VISSCHER	71x58cm
Madras &c.	WEEKLY DISPATCH	42x30cm
Madrid, Ville Considerable de la Nouvelle Castille ...	DE FER (Small)	23x33cm
Magnae Britanniae et Hiberniae Tabula	BLAEU	39x50cm
Magnae Britanniae et Hiberniae Tabula ... 1631	HONDIUS	38x50cm
Magnae Britanniae et Hiberniae Tabulae	MERIAN	28x36cm
Magnae Britanniae Tabula ...	VISSCHER	46x55cm
Magnae Prussiae Ducatus Tabula	VISSCHER	44x53cm
Magni Ducatus Lithuaniae	DE WIT	45x52cm
Magni Ducatus Lithuaniae ...	BLAEU	44x53cm
Magni Mogolis Imperium	BLAEU	41x52cm
Magnus Ducatus Lithuania ...	LOTTER	48x57cm
Maiestas Austriaca	SEUTTER	50x58cm
Main Chain of the Rocky Mountains, As Seen from the East ...	U.S. PACIFIC R.R. SURVEY	16x53cm
Maine	LUCAS	30x24cm
Maine and Part of Quebec	ASHER & ADAMS	41x56cm
Mainz	MERIAN	30x41cm
Malay Archipelago or East India Islands	TALLIS	24x33cm
Map and Description of the Principal Mountains, &c. Throughout the World	CAREY & LEA	42x52cm
Map Exhibiting the Experimental and Located Lines for the [NY & NH RR]	RAILROAD COMPANY	47x315cm
Map Illustrating Baldwin Mollhausen's Travels from the Mississippi to ...	MOLLHAUSEN	20x44cm
Map Illustrating the General Geological Features ... West of the Mississippi	U.S. GOV'T	51x58cm
Map Illustrating the Operations ... under ... Morgan at Cumberland Gap ...	U.S. WAR DEPARTMENT	36x30cm
Map Illustrating the Plan of the Defences of the Western & North-Western ...	U.S. GOV'T	55x39cm
Map Illustrating the Plan of the Defenses of the Western Frontier ... Gaines ...	BURR	60x37cm
Map Illustrating the System of Parcs ... of the Great Plains ...	GILPIN	53x57cm
Map No.1. From Fort Smith to the Rio Grande ...	U.S. PACIFIC R.R. SURVEY	61x132cm

Title	Source	Size
Map No.1. Rio Colorado of the West Explored by 1st Lt. Joseph C. Ives ...	U.S. GOV'T	37x87cm
Map No.10. United States	SMITH, ROSWELL C.	28x23cm
Map No.3 Map of North America ... to Illustrate Mitchell's School and ...	MITCHELL, S.A. (to 1859)	26x20cm
Map No.4 Map of the United States and Texas ... [with] ... Mexico ...	MITCHELL, S.A. (to 1859)	26x42cm
Map No.4 Showing Continuation of Fort Smith and Santa Fe Route ...	U.S. GOV'T	28x50cm
Map of a Carriage Road in the Isthmus of Panama Drawn by Order ...	U.S. GOV'T	38x48cm
Map of a Part of the Territory of Washington to Accompany Report ...	U.S. STATE SURVEYS	37x49cm
Map of a Portion of Washington Territory to Accompany Report ... 1861	U.S. STATE SURVEYS	56x66cm
Map of a Reconnaissance Between Baltimore and Philadelphia Exhibiting ...	U.S. GOV'T	23x79cm
Map of a Section of Twelve Miles of the Scioto Valley, ...	AMER. ETHNOLOG. SOC.	25x19cm
Map of a Survey and Reconnaissance of the Vicinity of the ... Rio Gila	U.S. GOV'T	28x42cm
Map of a Tour from Independence to Santa Fe, Chihuahua, Monterey ...	WISLIZENUS	50x41cm
Map of Africa ...	OLNEY	22x28cm
Map of Africa, Showing Its Most Recent Discoveries	MITCHELL, S.A. (1860+)	27x34cm
Map of Alabama	RAND, McNALLY (atlas maps)	66x48cm
Map of an Exploring Expedition to the Rocky Mountains ...	FREMONT	130x80cm
Map of Anglesea, Five Mile Beach, Cape May Co., N.J.	REAL ESTATE MAPS	82x56cm
Map of Australia, Compiled from the Nautical Surveys, Made by Order ...	WYLD	56x81cm
Map of Basic City, Augusta County, Virginia. November 1st, 1890	REAL ESTATE MAPS	36x50cm
Map of Battleground ... in the Vicinity of Groveton, Prince William Co, Va.	U.S. CIVIL WAR MAPS	56x66cm
Map of Bexar County	GOV'T: LOCAL & STATE	57x66cm
Map of Boston and Adjacent Cities	COLTON (Atlas Maps)	37x30cm
Map of Boston (as it should be) and the Country Adjacent ...	DUTTON	44x62cm
Map of Brazil, Bolivia, Paraguay and Uruguay [with] Chili	MITCHELL, S.A. (1860+)	27x34cm
Map of Bucks County, Pennsylvania	LOCAL & STATE POCKET	63x41cm
Map of Canada	OLNEY	22x28cm
Map of Canada and New-York	OLNEY	27x44cm
Map of Canada East and West	ENSIGN, BRIDGMAN ...	65x51cm
Map of Canada West in Counties	MITCHELL, S.A. (1860+)	32x39cm
Map of Cape Ann [with Gloucester, MA]	SAMPSON, DAVENPORT	31x52cm
Map of Cape May City and Sea Grove [NJ]	LOCAL & STATE POCKET	85x48cm
Map of Central America, Shewing the Different Lines of Atlantic & Pacific	WYLD	57x80cm
Map of Charleston Harbor, S.C.	U.S. GOV'T	44x57cm
Map of Cheshire Co., New Hampshire	LOCAL & STATE WALL	139x142cm
Map of Chicago and Its Southern & Western Suburbs	REAL ESTATE MAPS	69x48cm
Map of Colorado, Utah, New Mexico and Arizona	WILLIAMS, J.D.	43x36cm
Map of Dakota 1885	RAND, McNALLY (non-atlas)	34x49cm
Map of Delaware County, Pennsylvania	SMITH	105x142cm
Map of Eastland Co. [TX]	RAND, AVERY & CO.	57x55cm
Map of England and Wales, Showing the Railways, Canals ...	ARROWSMITH	42x70cm
Map of Fairfield County, Connecticut	CLARK	132x150cm
Map of Florida	RAND, McNALLY (atlas maps)	48x66cm
Map of Florida	TANNER	69x53cm
Map of Florida	THOMAS, COWPERTHWAIT	37x30cm
Map of Florida [and] Southern Railway System	RAILROAD COMPANY	76x46cm
Map of Florida according to the Latest Authorities	FINLEY	41x25cm
Map of French & English Grants on Lake Champlain	PEASE	59x37cm
Map of Gilpin Co., Colo.	MINING MAPS	63x101cm
Map of Hampden County, Massachusetts	WALLING	110x168cm
Map of Harrisburg City	BRION	79x111cm
Map of Illinois	COLTON (Pocket & Wall)	39x30cm
Map of Illinois with Parts of Indiana, Ouisconsin, &c.	BURR	44x33cm
Map of Illinois with Parts of Indiana, Ouisconsin &c. by David Burr ...	U.S. GOV'T	46x33cm
Map of Indian Territory	U.S. GOV'T	41x56cm
Map of Indian Territory and Oklahoma	U.S. GOV'T	56x74cm
Map of Kansas, Arizona, Colorado, New Mexico, Utah, Indian Territory	WARNER & BEERS	43x61cm
Map of Kansas, Nebraska and Colorado, Showing Also the Eastern ... Idaho	MITCHELL, S.A. (1860+)	29x36cm
Map of Kings County Showing the Avenues, Streets, Basins, Bulkhead ...	McELROY, SON & BROWN	77x64cm
Map of Lake George & Vicinity	BEERS	79x55cm
Map of Lancaster City, Pa. and Suburbs	LOCAL & STATE POCKET	61x50cm
Map of Leicestershire	PRIOR	112x120cm
Map of Linguistic Stocks of American Indians Chiefly within the Present ...	U.S. GOV'T	51x44cm
Map of Long Island	LOCAL & STATE POCKET	no dimens
Map of Louisiana Representing the Several Land Districts	U.S. STATE SURVEYS	39x42cm
Map of Louisiana, Mississippi and Alabama ...	FINLEY	43x55cm
Map of Louisiana, Mississippi, and Arkansas	MITCHELL, S.A. (1860+)	34x27cm
Map of Madison and the Four Lake Country [WI]	LOCAL & STATE MAPS	43x69cm

Map of Maine, New Hampshire and Vermont	HINTON	36x25cm
Map of Maine, New Hampshire and Vermont ...	FINLEY	43x53cm
Map of Manitoba	CANADIAN GOV'T	91x122cm
Map of Manitoba Shewing Provincial Government Lands for Sale	CANADIAN GOV'T	91x122cm
Map of Massachusetts, Connecticut and Rhode Island ...	ENSIGN & THAYER	64x86cm
Map of Merrimack County, New Hampshire	WALLING	147x155cm
Map of Mexico, Central America, and the West Indies	MITCHELL, S.A. (1860+)	33x53cm
Map of Michigan, Wisconsin and Minnesota	OLNEY	22x28cm
Map of Middlesex County, Connecticut	WALLING	152x148cm
Map of Middlesex County, Massachusetts	WALLING	157x157cm
Map of Minnesota Territory	COWPERTHWAIT, DESILVER	33x41cm
Map of Minnesota Territory	THOMAS, COWPERTHWAIT	33x41cm
Map of Moosehead Lake and Northern Maine, Embracing the Headwaters	LOCAL & STATE MAPS	58x47cm
Map of Nevada and California	WARNER & BEERS	43x36cm
Map of New Hampshire & Vermont	THOMAS, COWPERTHWAIT	38x30cm
Map of New Haven County, Connecticut	LOCAL & STATE WALL	141x139cm
Map of New Jersey Compiled from the Latest Authorities	DESILVER	38x31cm
Map of New London and Windham Counties in Conn. from Actual Survey	LESTER	82x70cm
Map of New Mexico	HARDESTY	51x36cm
Map of New South Wales and Victoria	ALLAN	64x53cm
Map of New York I. with the Adjacent Rocks and ... Parts of Hell-Gate	VALENTINE'S MANUAL	25x18cm
Map of North America	OLNEY	28x22cm
Map of North America ...	FINLEY	53x43cm
Map of North America, Exhibiting the Recent Discoveries, Geographical ...	WYLD	46x36cm
Map of North America Showing Its Political Divisions, and Recent ...	MITCHELL, S.A. (1860+)	34x27cm
Map of North America to Illustrate Olney's School Geography	OLNEY	27x22cm
Map of North and South Carolina	MORSE, JEDIDIAH	20x24cm
Map of North and South Carolina and Georgia ...	FINLEY	43x55cm
Map of North West Territories [Canada]	RAND, McNALLY (atlas maps)	31x48cm
Map of Oklahoma and Indian Ters.	WALKER, H.B.	41x56cm
Map of Oklahoma Territory	U.S. STATE SURVEYS	38x56cm
Map of Oregon	RAILROAD COMPANY	51x66cm
Map of Oregon and Upper California from the Surveys ... Fremont	FREMONT	84x67cm
Map of Oregon and Upper California from the Surveys ... Fremont	FREMONT	50x42cm
Map of Oregon Showing the Location of Indian Tribes	SCHOOLCRAFT	21x25cm
Map of Oregon Territory	PARKER	36x58cm
Map of Oregon, Washington, and Part of British Columbia	MITCHELL, S.A. (1860+)	27x34cm
Map of Oregon, Washington, Idaho and Part of Montana	MITCHELL, S.A. (1860+)	27x34cm
Map of Oxford County, Maine	WALLING	152x152cm
Map of Part of the Province of Ontario, Canada	CANADIAN GOV'T	47x70cm
Map of Pennsylvania and New Jersey	TANNER	50x62cm
Map of Poland, Prussia and Hungary, Indicating ... Sieges and Battles	LAVOISNE	29x29cm
Map of Property Belonging to Nich.s Luquer in the 6th Ward ... Brooklyn ...	LOCAL & STATE MAPS	46x61cm
Map of Public Surveys in California ...	U.S. STATE SURVEYS	91x76cm
Map of Public Surveys in California and Nevada ...	U.S. STATE SURVEYS	75x90cm
Map of Public Surveys in Colorado Territory	U.S. STATE SURVEYS	41x56cm
Map of Public Surveys Washington Territory to Accompany ... 1863	U.S. STATE SURVEYS	43x55cm
Map of Red River with Its Bayous and Lakes in the Vicinity of the Raft	U.S. STATE SURVEYS	57x113cm
Map of Rockingham County, New Hampshire	CHACE	144x143cm
Map of Routes to the Principal Mining Districts in ... Mexico	HALL, SIDNEY	41x55cm
Map of San Jacinto Co. [TX]	GAST & CO.	53x44cm
Map of San Saba Co. [TX]	GAST & CO.	48x56cm
Map of Saratoga Co. New York	GEIL	145x96cm
Map of Savannah ... and Vicinity ...	U.S. UNION & CONFED.	42x70cm
Map of Silver Bow County, Montana - July 1st, 1897	BAKER & HARPER	56x88cm
Map of South America	LAVOISNE	41x32cm
Map of South Australia, New South Wales, Van Diemen's Land ...	WYLD	60x94cm
Map of Texas	RAND, McNALLY (atlas maps)	22x25cm
Map of Texas	U.S. GEOLOGICAL SURVEY	79x89cm
Map of Texas	WILMORE	21x26cm
Map of Texas ...	MITCHELL, S.A. (to 1859)	30x38cm
Map of Texas Compiled from Surveys on Record in the General Land Office	HUNT & RANDEL	80x61cm
Map of Texas, Compiled from Surveys Recorded in the Land Office of Texas	ARROWSMITH	60x50cm
Map of Texas from the Most Recent Authorities	WILLIAMS, C.S.	30x38cm
Map of Texas, Oklahoma and Indian Territory	HUNT & EATON	29x23cm
Map of Texas Published by H.R. Page & Co.	PAGE	66x42cm
Map of That Part of Washington Territory Lying West of the Cascade ...	U.S. STATE SURVEYS	34x23cm

Title	Publisher	Size
Map of That Portion of the Boundary Between the United States and Mexico	U.S. GOV'T	54x123cm
Map of the Adirondack Forest and Adjoining Territory Compiled from ...	LOCAL & STATE WALL	174x143cm
Map of the Adirondack Wilderness	STODDARD	77x61cm
Map of the All-Water Route from the Mississippi to New York ...	RAND, McNALLY (non-atlas)	53x67cm
Map of the Arlington Estate, Va.	U.S. GOV'T	69x84cm
Map of the Battlefield of Gettysburg July 1st 2nd 3rd 1863 [3 maps]	BACHELDER, J.B.	74x69cm
Map of the British Plantations on the Continent of America	WILLIAMSON	34x29cm
Map of the Central Pacific Railroad. The Western Portion of the Main Trunk	COLTON (Pocket & Wall)	19x76cm
Map of the Chesapeake and Ohio Rail Road and Its Connections	COLTON (Pocket & Wall)	39x108cm
Map of the Chicago, Burlington and Quincy Railroad and Its Connections	RAILROAD COMPANY	51x74cm
Map of the Chief Part of the Western States and Part of Virginia	MITCHELL, S.A. (to 1859)	26x41cm
Map of the Cities of Pittsburgh, Allegheny, and the Adjoining Boroughs	HOPKINS	48x60cm
Map of the City of Albany	MAGNUS, C.	13x20cm
Map of the City of Bridgeport, Conn. from Original Surveys by Sidney ...	COLLINS & CLARK	94x90cm
Map of the City of Brooklyn and Village of Williamsburgh ...	LOCAL & STATE POCKET	78x120cm
Map of the City of Brooklyn Showing the Railroads, Warehouses, Horse ...	TAUNTON	64x50cm
Map of the City of Buffalo	LOCAL & STATE POCKET	64x43cm
Map of the City of Milwaukee	CHAPMAN	51x44cm
Map of the City of New York	SHANNON	97x20cm
Map of the City of New York, with Adjacent Cities ...	ENSIGN & THAYER	41x51cm
Map of the City of New York, with Street Directory ...	DRIPPS	70x50cm
Map of the City of Staunton, Augusta County, Virginia	REAL ESTATE MAPS	52x67cm
Map of the City of Troy, New York	LOCAL & STATE WALL	213x180cm
Map of the City of Washington ..	LOCAL & STATE MAPS	42x50cm
Map of the City of Washington, District of Columbia	REAL ESTATE MAPS	36x46cm
Map of the Compact Portions of Philadelphia and Camden	WALLING & GRAY	41x61cm
Map of the Cotton Belt Route	RAILROAD COMPANY	34x70cm
Map of the Country Between the Frontiers of Arkansas and New Mexico ...	U.S. GOV'T	70x151cm
Map of the Country Bordering the Buffalo & Mississippi and Other Lake RRs	RAILROAD COMPANY	37x99cm
Map of the Country Drained by the Mississippi	JAMES	38x52cm
Map of the Country Embracing the Various Routes ... Rail Road of Georgia	RAILROAD COMPANY	19x55cm
Map of the Country Embracing the Various Routes ... Rail Road of Georgia	U.S. GOV'T	20x53cm
Map of the Country upon the Upper Red River Explored in 1852 by Capt. ...	U.S. GOV'T	41x86cm
Map of the County of Cambridge from an Actual Survey ...	GREENWOOD	57x72cm
Map of the County of Somerset from Actual Survey ...	GREENWOOD	132x185cm
Map of the Cumberland River from the Falls to Nashville	U.S. GOV'T	38x61cm
Map of the Cumberland River from the Falls to Nashville. Made to ...	U.S. GOV'T	46x74cm
Map of the Delta of the St. Clair [MI]	U.S. WAR DEPARTMENT	119x72cm
Map of the Dominion of Canada and Part of the United States	CANADIAN GOV'T	91x122cm
Map of the Elk Mountains Colorado from Survey by G.B. Chittenden ...	HAYDEN, F.V.	48x25cm
Map of the Goldfield Mining District, Nye and Esmeralda Counties, Nevada	MINING MAPS	61x58cm
Map of the Great Salt Lake and Adjacent Country ... of Utah [with SLC]	WEEKLY DISPATCH	43x30cm
Map of the Great Salt Lake and Adjacent Country in the Territory of Utah	U.S. GOV'T	109x76cm
Map of the Indian Colonies West of Missouri and Arkansas	U.S. GOV'T	28x19cm
Map of the Indian Territory and Oklahoma	U.S. GOV'T	56x75cm
Map of the Islands of Martinico, Dominico, Guardalupe, St. Christophers ...	POLITICAL MAGAZINE	24x28cm
Map of the Lands, Granted to the Cherokee Indians, by the State of [NC]	U.S. GOV'T	18x25cm
Map of the Lands Included in the Central Park, from a Topographical ...	LOCAL & STATE MAPS	111x57cm
Map of the Lands Owned by the New York & Texas Land Company ...	GAST & CO.	no dimens
Map of the Lima Toledo Railroad Company and Connections	RAILROAD COMPANY	51x56cm
Map of the Main Portion of Boston	RAND, McNALLY (atlas maps)	23x30cm
Map of the Missouri Pacific Railway	RAILROAD COMPANY	23x16cm
Map of the Navajo Indian Reservation	U.S. GOV'T	28x39cm
Map of the New and Popular St. Louis and Texas Short Line!	RAILROAD COMPANY	48x80cm
Map of the North Polar Region	GRAPHIC, THE	62x79cm
Map of the North Polar Region	U.S. HYDROGRAPHIC OFF.	no dimens
Map of the North West from Explorations by the United States Engineers	RAILROAD COMPANY	38x107cm
Map of the Northern Part of the State of Maine and of the Adjacent British	U.S. GOV'T	43x41cm
Map of the Oklahoma Country in the Indian Territory	CRAM	29x24cm
Map of the Oregon Railroad and Navigational Company and the [SP] ...	RAILROAD COMPANY	61x53cm
Map of the Oregon Territory ...	U.S. EXPLORING EXPED.	21x33cm
Map of the Public Surveys in California to Accompany Report of Surveyor ...	U.S. STATE SURVEYS	51x117cm
Map of the Railroads of Pennsylvania and New Jersey and Parts of ...	ANDERSON	81x120cm
Map of the Republic of Switzerland	FADEN	58x60cm
Map of the River Sabine from Its Mouth on the Gulf of Mexico in the Sea ,,,	U.S. GOV'T	86x18cm
Map of the Route Passed over by an Expedition into the Indian Country ...	U.S. GOV'T	41x48cm
Map of the Route Pursued by the Late Expedition under... Kearny ...	U.S. GOV'T	22x34cm

355

Title	Author/Source	Size
Map of the Route Pursued by U.S. Troops, from Fort Smith ... to Santa Fe	U.S. GOV'T	28x48cm
Map of the Route Pursued in 1849 by the U.S. Troops ... against the Navajo	U.S. WAR DEPARTMENT	51x71cm
Map of the Routes Examined ... for the Winchester and Potomac Railroad	WAR DEPARTMENT	53x69cm
Map of the Sangre de Cristo Grant Situate in San Luis Valle, Colorado ...	U.S. GOV'T	44x29cm
Map of the Shoshone Geyser Basin ... Yellowstone National Park	HAYDEN, F.V.	61x88cm
Map of the Sources of the Snake River, with Its Tributaries ...	HAYDEN, F.V.	28x25cm
Map of the South Western and Part of the Western States	OLNEY	46x27cm
Map of the Southern and South-Western States	WILLIAMS, W.	30x44cm
Map of the Southern Parts of the United States of America ...	MORSE, JEDIDIAH	20x38cm
Map of the Southern States	OLNEY	27x44cm
Map of the St Louis Iron Mountain and Southern Railway	RAILROAD COMPANY	27x36cm
Map of the State of Alabama	BURR	32x27cm
Map of the State of Connecticut	BEERS	116x127cm
Map of the State of Kentucky; with the Adjoining Territories	RUSSELL	38x46cm
Map of the State of Maine	WALLING	160x160cm
Map of the State of Missouri	HINTON	25x37cm
Map of the State of Missouri and Territory of Arkansas ...	FINLEY	43x55cm
Map of the State of Montana	U.S. STATE SURVEYS	42x63cm
Map of the State of Nevada	U.S. STATE SURVEYS	53x46cm
Map of the State of New Jersey	BEERS	56x36cm
Map of the State of New York, Showing the Boundaries of the Counties ...	SMITH, J.C.	48x61cm
Map of the State of Texas	MITCHELL, S.A. (to 1859)	27x20cm
Map of the State of Texas	MITCHELL, S.A. (to 1859)	20x28cm
Map of the State of Texas from the Latest Authorities	COWPERTHWAIT, DESILVER	33x40cm
Map of the State of Texas from the Latest Authorities	THOMAS, COWPERTHWAIT	32x41cm
Map of the States of Kentucky and Tennessee	HINTON	25x39cm
Map of the States of Kentucky and Tennessee ...	MITCHELL, S.A. (non-atlas)	45x53cm
Map of the States of Missouri and Illinois	HINTON	28x37cm
Map of the States of North & South Carolina	HINTON	25x40cm
Map of the States of Ohio Indiana & Illinois and Part of Michigan ...	FINLEY	43x55cm
Map of the States of Pennsylvania and New Jersey	HINTON	25x39cm
Map of the Straits of Detroit ...	U.S. GOV'T	91x57cm
Map of the Survey of a Route for the Pacific Railroad ... Rio Grande & Red ...	U.S. PACIFIC R.R. SURVEY	69x142cm
Map of the Surveyed Part of Michigan	FARMER	84x58cm
Map of the Territorial Limits of the Cherokee "Nation of" Indians Exhibiting ...	U.S. GOV'T	53x76cm
Map of the Territories	MITCHELL, S.A. (to 1859)	16x14cm
Map of the Territories of Montana, Idaho and Wyoming	WARNER & BEERS	43x36cm
Map of the Territory of Dakota and the States of Minnesota and Nebraska	WARNER & BEERS	43x36cm
Map of the Territory of Florida, from Its Northrn Boundary to Lat: 27 30'	SWIFT	70x169cm
Map of the Territory of New Mexico	U.S. WAR DEPARTMENT	64x50cm
Map of the Texas & Pacific Railway & Connections	RAILROAD COMPANY	17x28cm
Map of the Texas and Pacific Railway and Connections	RAILROAD COMPANY	39x71cm
Map of the Town of Bristol, Hartford County, Connecticut ...	CLARK	106x84cm
Map of the Town of Norwalk, Fairfield County, Conn.	CLARK	113x90cm
Map of the Town of Roxbury, Surveyed in 1848 by Order of the Town ...	WHITNEY	83x61cm
Map of the United States	CASE, TIFFANY & CO.	62x65cm
Map of the United States	CRAM	30x46cm
Map of the United States	RANNEY	48x74cm
Map of the United States and Canada Designed to Accompany Smith's ...	SMITH, ROSWELL C.	27x45cm
Map of the United States and Territories ...	MITCHELL, S.A. (1860+)	34x53cm
Map of the United States and Territories. Showing the Extent of Public ...	U.S. STATE SURVEYS	71x140cm
Map of the United States, and Texas	COPLEY	44x58cm
Map of the United States and Texas	HARPER	44x57cm
Map of the United States and Texas ...	BRADFORD	27x45cm
Map of the United States and Texas Boundary Line and Adjacent Territory	U.S. GOV'T	67x100cm
Map of the United States and Their Territories between the Mississippi ...	U.S. GOV'T	52x58cm
Map of the United States, Canada, Texas and Part of Mexico	OLNEY	27x44cm
Map of the United States, Constructed from the Latest Authorities	FINLEY	43x56cm
Map of the United States Constructed from the Latest Authorities ...	WILLIAMS, C.S.	54x42cm
Map of the United States Drawn from the Most Approved Surveys	SCHOYER	42x52cm
Map of the United States Exhibiting the Several Collection Districts ...	U.S. GOV'T	84x124cm
Map of the United States, Mexico, &c. Showing the Various Land ...	COLTON (Pocket & Wall)	32x51cm
Map of the United States of America and Nova Scotia, &c. &c.	HINTON	25x39cm
Map of the United States of America Including Canada and ... of Texas	SMITH, J.C.	160x208cm
Map of the United States Showing Land Grants for Rail and Wagon Roads	DAILY GRAPHIC	35x52cm
Map of the United States Showing the Principal Geological Formations ...	GRAY	41x66cm
Map of the United States Showing the Principal Travelling, Turnpike & ...	MITCHELL, S.A. (non-atlas)	59x45cm

Map	Publisher	Size
Map of the United States Showing the St. Louis, Iron Mountain & Southern	RAILROAD COMPANY	26x36cm
Map of the United States Territory of Oregon West of the Rocky Mountains	HOOD	44x52cm
Map of the United States, the Canadas ...	COLTON (Pocket & Wall)	74x62cm
Map of the United States to Illustrate Olney's School Geography	OLNEY	25x43cm
Map of the Upper Sound Country Comprising Parts of the Counties of Pierce	REAL ESTATE MAPS	62x81cm
Map of the Village of Niagara Falls Made for the Proprietor	ENDICOTT & CO.	16x23cm
Map of the Wabash and Erie Canal Line from the Mouth of Tippecanoe ...	U.S. GOV'T	33x25cm
Map of the Washoe District Showing Mining Claims	U.S. GEOLOGICAL SURVEY	76x46cm
Map of the West - Burlington Route	RAILROAD COMPANY	109x155cm
Map of the Western and Middle Portion of North America	GREENHOW	57x65cm
Map of the Western States	ATWOOD	45x58cm
Map of the White Mountains	LOCAL & STATE MAPS	22x27cm
Map of the Windward Islands; Comprising Barbados, St. Vincent, Grenada ...	ARROWSMITH	61x46cm
Map of the World from the Best Authorities	PAAS	19x36cm
Map of the World from the Best Authorities	WILKINSON	19x36cm
Map of the World on a Polyconic Development of the Sphere 1856	U.S. COAST SURVEY	24x28cm
Map of the World on Globular Projection [with] A Chart of the World ...	OLNEY	30x47cm
Map of the Yellowstone and Missouri Rivers and Their Tributaries ...	U.S. WAR DEPARTMENT	71x107cm
Map of the Yellowstone National Park	U.S. GOV'T	43x43cm
Map of the Yukon Territory	CANADIAN GOV'T	91x122cm
Map of Tolland County Connecticut, from Actual Surveys	LOCAL & STATE WALL	141x131cm
Map of Ulster County, New York	FRENCH	147x147cm
Map of Upper California by the U.S. Ex. Ex. and Best Authorities	U.S. EXPLORING EXPED.	20x28cm
Map of Vermont & New Hampshire	LOCAL & STATE WALL	73x58cm
Map of Virginia and Maryland Constructed from the Latest Authorities	FINLEY	43x55cm
Map of Washington County, New York	LOCAL & STATE WALL	145x99cm
Map of Washington Ter.	PAGE	41x66cm
Map of Western Canada, Manitoba, Alberta, Saskatchewan and Part [BC]	RAILROAD COMPANY	109x74cm
Map of Wisconsin Published by the State Board of Immigration	GOV'T: LOCAL & STATE	51x58cm
Map Shewing the Railroads between Lake Erie, New York & Boston ...	RAILROAD COMPANY	42x55cm
Map Showing a Division of Part of the Real Estate Late of N... Stuyvesant	DOUGHTY	54x76cm
Map Showing Indian Reservations in the United States West of the 84th ...	U.S. GOV'T	33x43cm
Map Showing Lands Assigned to Emigrant Indians West of Arkansas & ...	U.S. GOV'T	48x46cm
Map Showing Location of Sheridan Wyoming and Surrounding ...	U.S. WAR DEPARTMENT	33x41cm
Map Showing Private Land Claims, ... New Mexico, Colorado and Arizona	U.S. STATE SURVEYS	33x43cm
Map Showing the Different Routes Travelled ... Salt Lake City ... San Fran	U.S. GOV'T	51x51cm
Map Showing the Extent of Surveys in the Territory of Utah	U.S. STATE SURVEYS	82x39cm
Map Showing the General Geological Features of the Country West of...	U.S. GOV'T	52x58cm
Map Showing the Location of the Pueblos of Arizona and New Mexico	U.S. GOV'T	24x30cm
Map Showing the Pacific Railways and Their Branches ...	COLTON (Pocket & Wall)	57x84cm
Map Showing the Progress of the Public Surveys in Kansas and Nebraska	U.S. STATE SURVEYS	44x46cm
Map Showing the Route of the Arkansas Regiment from Shreveport, La. ...	U.S. WAR DEPARTMENT	29x43cm
Map Showing the Route of the Champlain Transportation Co's Steamers ...	LOCAL & STATE MAPS	69x41cm
Map Showing the Route Pursued by the Exploring Expedition to New Mexico	U.S. GOV'T	50x71cm
Map Showing the Routes Travelled ... against the Snake Indians ... Dixon	U.S. WAR DEPARTMENT	61x84cm
Map Showing the Territory Originally Assigned to the Cherokee "Nation of"	U.S. GOV'T	51x71cm
Map to Illustrate an Exploration of the Country Lying between the Missouri	FREMONT	36x83cm
Map to Illustrate Capt. Bonneville's Adventures among the Rocky Mountains	COLTON (Pocket & Wall)	28x46cm
Map to Illustrate Capt. Bonneville's Adventures among the Rocky Mountains	BONNEVILLE	28x45cm
Map to Illustrate the Narrative of Robt. Adams' Route in Africa	MURRAY	50x37cm
Map to Illustrate the Route of Prince Maximilian of Wied in the Interior ...	MAXIMILIAN OF WIED	42x80cm
Map to Illustrate the Sketches of David Roberts, Esq: R.A. in Egypt ...	ROBERTS	20x15cm
Mapa de la Ciudad de la Habana y Loblaciones de Sus Alrdedores ...	MANUSCRIPT MAPS	30x44cm
Mapa de la Republicas de America Centrale	SONNENSTERN	96x108cm
Mapa Historico Pintoresco Moderno de la Isla de Cuba	MIALHE	43x56cm
Mapa Oficial del Estado de Sonora [Mexico]	LOCAL & STATE MAPS	107x94cm
Mapp Geographiae Naturalis ...	SEUTTER	50x57cm
Mappa Aestivarum Insularum ...	OGILBY	29x36cm
Mappa Aestivarum Insularum Alias Barmudas ...	HONDIUS	40x52cm
Mappa Aestivarum Insularum Alias Barmudas Dictarum ...	MERCATOR (Small)	20x25cm
Mappa Aestivarum Insularum Alias Barmudas ...	SPEED	40x52cm
Mappa Aestivarum Insularum, Alias Barmudas Dictarum ...	BLAEU	40x53cm
Mappa Aestivarum Insularum, Alias Barmudas Dictarum ...	JANSSON	40x52cm
Mappa Circuli Rhenani Superioris ...	SEUTTER	49x57cm
Mappa Fluxus et Reflxu Rationes in Isthmo America; No in Freto Magellanico	KIRCHER	34x41cm
Mappa Geographica ... Indiae Occidentalis ...	HOMANN	58x48cm
Mappa Geographica Americae Septentrionalis ...	VON EULER	36x38cm

Title	Author	Size
Mappa Geographica Exhibens Electoratum Brandenburgensem ...	LOTTER	50x58cm
Mappa Geographica Provinciae Novae Eboraci ab Anglis New York ...	HOMANN	76x58cm
Mappa Geographica Regionem Mexicanam et Floridam Terraeque ...	SEUTTER	47x57cm
Mappa Specialis Itineris ... ab Urbe Nangasaki ... [maps to] ... Urbem Iedo	KAEMPFER	30x30cm
Mappa Specialis Principatus Halberstadiensis ...	HOMANN	50x56cm
Mappa Totius Mundi	WALCH	46x64cm
Mappae Imperii Moscovitici pars Septentrionalis	SEUTTER	49x57cm
Mappe Monde Historique	RENOUARD	28x57cm
Mappe Monde ou Description du Globe Terrestre ...	DE VAUGONDY	46x70cm
Mappe Monde ou Description du Globe Terrestre et Aquatique	ELWE	46x61cm
Mappe Monde qui Comprend les Nouvelles Decouvertes [with 5 continents]	LE ROUGE	22x30cm
Mappe Monde qui Represente les Deux Hemispheres	HOMANN	46x55cm
Mappe Monde Suivant la Projection de Cartes Reduites	DE VAUGONDY	24x39cm
Mappe-Monde Dressee Suivant les Nouvelles Relations ...	DE VAUGONDY	47x74cm
Mappe-Monde en Deux Hemispheres	DELAMARCHE	29x43cm
Mappe-Monde Geo-Hydrographique du Globe	VALK	19x23cm
Mappe-Monde Geo-Hydrographique ou Description Generale du Globe ...	VALK	48x58cm
Mappe-Monde Geo-Hydrographique, ou Description Generale du Globe ...	JAILLOT	53x91cm
Mappe-Monde Geo Spherique ou Nouvelle Carte Ideale ...	LATTRE	50x74cm
Mappe-Monde ou Carte Generale de la Terre ...	DE FER (Small)	23x34cm
Mappe-Monde ou Carte Generale de la Terre Divisee en Deux Hemispheres	DE FER (Large)	77x109cm
Mappe-Monde ou Carte Universelle ...	DE FER (Small)	23x8cm
Mappe-Monde ou Description du Globe Terrestre	DE LAPORTE	18x22cm
Mappe-Monde ou Description du Globe Terrestre ...	JANVIER	30x44cm
Mappe-Monde par Robert de Vaugondy ... Corrigee par Delamarche ...	DELAMARCHE	26x43cm
Mappe-Monde Planispherique Physique et Hydrographique ...	DUFOUR	55x75cm
Mappe-Monde sur la Projection Reduite de Mercator Grave par...	CHAMOUIN	29x45cm
Mappemonde a l'Usage du Roi ...	DEZAUCHE	45x65cm
Mappemonde a l'Usage du Roy par Guillaume Delisle ...	DE L'ISLE	44x67cm
Mappemonde en Deux Hemispheres ... Barbie du Bocage	PUZZLES & GAMES	24x33cm
Mappemonde ou Description du Globe Terrestre ...	DE VAUGONDY	46x70cm
Mappemonde ou Description Generale du Globe Terrestre	CHATELAIN	34x44cm
Maps of the Wharves and Piers of the East [& Hudson] River	EWEN	50x46cm
Mar del Zur Hispanis Mare Pacificum	JANSSON	44x54cm
Marchionatus Misniae	SEUTTER	50x59cm
Marchionatus Moraviae ... Hondius	HONDIUS	38x54cm
Marchionatus Moraviae Circuli Znoymensis et Iglaviensis	HOMANN	50x59cm
Marchionatus Moraviae Circulus Olomucensis	HOMANN	50x58cm
Mare del Nord ...	CORONELLI	46x60cm
Mare del Norte ...	CORONELLI	46x60cm
Mare del Sud detto Altrimenti Mare Pacifico ...	CORONELLI	45x60cm
Margaritin	CAMOCIO	17x21cm
Maris Pacifici, (Quod Vulgo Mar del Zur) cum Regionibus Circumiacentibus	ORTELIUS (Folio)	35x50cm
Maryland	BRADFORD	29x36cm
Maryland	LUCAS	29x50cm
Maryland, Delaware and the District of Columbia	GRAY	41x67cm
Massachusetts	DORR, HOWLAND & CO.	18x30cm
Massachusetts	FINLEY	23x29cm
Massachusetts	RAND, McNALLY (atlas maps)	48x66cm
Massachusetts and Rhode Island	COLTON (Atlas Maps)	33x41cm
Massachusetts and Rhode Island	COLTON (Pocket & Wall)	31x40cm
Massachusetts, Rhode Island & Connecticut	CRAM	24x29cm
McCulloch County [TX]	GOV'T: LOCAL & STATE	53x41cm
Meklenburg Ducatus	JANSSON	36x48cm
Mendenhall's Road Map of Wisconsin	MENDENHALL	61x51cm
Mer du Sud, ou Pacifique Contenant l'Isle de Californie, les Costes de ...	MORTIER	61x75cm
Messico o Nuova Spagna	KITCHIN	28x37cm
Mexico	ARROWSMITH	59x48cm
Mexico	ARROWSMITH	20x25cm
Mexico	BLACK	25x37cm
Mexico	BLACKIE	34x50cm
Mexico	COLTON (Atlas Maps)	33x39cm
Mexico	MORSE & BREESE	30x38cm
Mexico & Guatemala	DESILVER	31x38cm
Mexico & Guatemala	TANNER	29x37cm
Mexico & Guatimala	LOTHIAN	29x37cm
Mexico and Guatemala	THOMAS, COWPERTHWAIT	30x38cm

Title	Author/Source	Size
Mexico and Guatimala	CAREY & LEA	9x14cm
Mexico and Guatimala	GRIGG	20x25cm
Mexico and Guatimala. Corrected from Original Information ...	HALL, SIDNEY	41x51cm
Mexico including California and Texas	BETTS	38x30cm
Mexico or New Spain Divided into the Audiance of Guadalayara, Mexico ...	MOLL (Small)	17x18cm
Mexico or New Spaine	MORDEN	11x12cm
Mexico und Centro-America	STIELER	30x36cm
Mexico, California and Texas	TALLIS	22x30cm
Mexico, Central America and the West Indies	MITCHELL, S.A. (1860+)	33x55cm
Mexico, from the Azotea of the House of H.M.s Mission, San Cosme.	LOCAL & STATE MAPS	18x39cm
Mexico, Regia et Celebris Hispaniae Novae Civitas ...	BRAUN & HOGENBERG	27x23cm
Mexico, Regia et Celebris Hispaniae Novae Civitas ... [with] Cusco	BRAUN & HOGENBERG	27x48cm
Mexico, Texas, Guatimala & West Indies	GOODRICH	11x16cm
Mexique	BINET	24x19cm
Mexique	MALLET	15x10cm
Mexique Antilles et Californie	DUFOUR	55x75cm
Mexique Antilles, Etats-Unis ...	DUFOUR	55x74cm
Mexique ou Nouvelle Espagne	MALLET	15x10cm
Mexique, ou Nouvelle Espagne, Nouv.lle Gallice, lucatan &c. et Autres ...	SANSON (Folio)	37x55cm
Meydenburg	MUNSTER	12x15cm
Michigan	BURR	32x27cm
Michigan	COLTON (Atlas Maps)	62x44cm
Michigan and Wisconsin	JOHNSON	44x61cm
Middle-Sex:	SPEED	8x12cm
Middlesex	MOULE	20x26cm
Middlesex	PIGOT	23x35cm
Middletown, Conn. Revised 1877 Edition	BAILEY, O.H.	60x71cm
Midle-Sex Described with the Most Famous Cities of London and ...	SPEED	40x51cm
Midlesex	MORDEN	37x43cm
Military Map of the United States	U.S. WAR DEPARTMENT	34x76cm
Military Reconnaissance of the Arkansas Rio del Norte and Rio Gila ...	U.S. WAR DEPARTMENT	76x64cm
Milk R. to the Crossing of the Columbia R. ...	U.S. PACIFIC R.R. SURVEY	58x152cm
Miller's New Map of the City of New York	PHELPS	38x69cm
Milwaukee	RAND, McNALLY (atlas maps)	48x31cm
Minnesota	COLTON (Atlas Maps)	33x41cm
Minnesota	COLTON (Pocket & Wall)	32x37cm
Minnesota and Dacotah	MITCHELL, S.A. (1860+)	27x34cm
Minnesota and Dakota	JOHNSON	31x40cm
Minnesota Farm Land Company	REAL ESTATE MAPS	53x66cm
Mississippi	BRADFORD	37x29cm
Mississippi	COLTON (Atlas Maps)	37x29cm
Mississippi	FINLEY	28x22cm
Mississippi & Alabama	BRADFORD	20x25cm
Mississippi Territory	ARROWSMITH & LEWIS	22x27cm
Missouri	BRADFORD	29x36cm
Missouri	COLBY	15x13cm
Missouri	FINLEY	29x22cm
Missouri and Kansas	JOHNSON	43x58cm
Missouri, Kansas & Texas Railway and Connections	RAND, McNALLY (non-atlas)	21x29cm
Mitchell's National Map of the American Republic, or the United States ...	MITCHELL, S.A. (non-atlas)	64x88cm
Mitchell's National Map of the American Republic, or United States ...	MITCHELL, S.A. (non-atlas)	93x115cm
Mitchell's New Traveler's Guide through the United States, Showing ...	MITCHELL, S.A. (non-atlas)	56x73cm
Mitchell's Travelers Guide Through the United States. A Map of Roads ...	MITCHELL, S.A. (non-atlas)	42x53cm
Moderna Discrizzione dell' Europa	MUNSTER	27x35cm
Moderna Europae Descriptio	MUNSTER	26x34cm
Moluccae Insulae	BERTIUS	9x13cm
Moluccae Insulae Celeberrimae	BLAEU	37x49cm
Momonia ... Anglice Mounster	BLAEU	38x50cm
Monachium Utriusque Bavariae Civitas Primar	BRAUN & HOGENBERG	28x49cm
Monk's New American Map Exhibiting the Larger Portion of North America	MONK	122x155cm
Mons	BRAUN & HOGENBERG	36x46cm
Montana	CRAM	46x64cm
Montana (Eastern Portion)	ASHER & ADAMS	41x57cm
Montana, Idaho and Wyoming	BRADLEY	38x56cm
Montgomeria Comitatus et Comitatus Mervinia	BLAEU	38x50cm
Morant Point to Port Royal	BRITISH ADMIRALTY	65x99cm
Moschovia Nuova Tavola	RUSCELLI	18x24cm

Title	Author/Publisher	Size
Moscovia, Urbs, Regionis eius de Nominis Metropolitica ...	LASOR A VAREA	9x14cm
Moscoviae Imperium	MAGINI	13x17cm
Moscoviae seu Russiae Magnae ...	VISSCHER	41x52cm
Moscow	S.D.U.K.	33x36cm
Mountains & Rivers	JOHNSON	42x61cm
Mouvemens Apparens du Soleil, Theorie des Saisons	ANDRIVEAU-GOUJON	46x58cm
Munden - Mundensis, ad Visurgum Flu. Saxoniae Urbis, Genuina Delineatio	BRAUN & HOGENBERG	30x48cm
Munich	S.D.U.K.	31x38cm
Muskeget Channel Massachusetts ...	U.S. COAST SURVEY	71x53cm
Namur cum Elegantissima ad Mosae Flume Civitas	BRAUN & HOGENBERG	34x43cm
Nantucket Harbor	U.S. COAST SURVEY	36x48cm
National Map of the United States	MITCHELL, S.A. (non-atlas)	86x62cm
Natolia Nuova Tavola	RUSCELLI	19x26cm
Natolia, quae Olim Asia Minor	BLAEU	38x50cm
Natoliae, quae olim Asia Minor, Nova Descriptio [with] Aegypti ...	ORTELIUS (Folio)	32x49cm
Navigationes Praecipuae Europaeorum ad Exteras Nationes	SCHERER	23x34cm
Neapel	MEYER	35x39cm
Neapolitanum Regnum	MAGINI	13x17cm
Nebraska and Kansas	COLTON (Pocket & Wall)	69x51cm
Nebraska and Kanzas	COLTON (Atlas Maps)	32x39cm
Nebraska, Kansas, Dakota and Colorado	McNALLY	23x28cm
Negroponte in Morea	MEISNER	10x15cm
Nell's Map of Colorado	NELL	72x99cm
Neu Vermehrte Post Charte durch Gantz Teutschland	HOMANN	49x58cm
Neu Vermehrter Curioser Meilen-Zeiger der Vornehmsten Staedte ...	HOMANN	47x56cm
Neue Welt-Karte Welche auf Zwoo Kugelslaschen die Haupt Theile der Erde	HOMANN	48x56cm
Neues Panorama des Rhein von Mannheim bis Coln ...	LOCAL & STATE MAPS	Octavo
Neueste Karte von Florida	MEYER	37x30cm
Neueste Karte von Georgia	MEYER	37x30cm
Neueste Karte von Louisiana	MEYER	29x37cm
Neueste Karte von Mexico ...	MEYER	29x36cm
Neueste Karte von Nord Carolina mit Seinen Canaelen, Strassen und Routen	MEYER	30x37cm
Neueste Karte von Nordamerika in 4 Blattern	HILDBURGHAUSEN BIBLIO	34x43cm
Neueste Karte von Tennessee	MEYER	30x37cm
Neueste Karte von Virginia	MEYER	30x37cm
Neueste Special-Karte der Westlichen u. Sudlichen Theile von Nord Amerik	SCHMOLDER	43x57cm
Neuew Griechenlandt	MUNSTER	26x34cm
Neuvie me Plan de Paris ... sours le Regne de Louis XV ...	DELAGRIVE, J.	62x84cm
Neuw India / mit Vilen Anstossenden Lendern / Besunder Scythia / Parthia	MUNSTER	28x25cm
Nevada	CRAM	56x41cm
Nevada	GRAY	38x30cm
New & Accurate Map of North America Including Nootka Sound: ...	BOWEN, THOMAS	26x43cm
New England and New York by Robt. Morden	MORDEN	11x13cm
New England, New York, New Jersey, and Pensilvania	MOLL (Small)	19x26cm
New Guide Map of the United States & Canada with Railroads ...	COLTON (Pocket & Wall)	77x93cm
New Hampshire	BRADFORD	36x29cm
New Hampshire	LUCAS	27x21cm
New Hampshire & Vermont	TANNER	35x28cm
New Hampshire by Recent Survey ...	CARRIGAIN, P.	155x117cm
New Hampshire, Vermont, &c.	GORDON, WILLIAM	36x34cm
New Hartford, Conn.	BAILEY, O.H.	50x62cm
New Haven (from Perry Hill)	LADIES REPOSITORY	11x20cm
New Haven Harbour [CT]	U.S. COAST SURVEY	94x61cm
New Holland and New Zealand	GREENLEAF	28x33cm
New Jersey	ARROWSMITH & LEWIS	27x22cm
New Jersey	RAND, McNALLY (atlas maps)	50x32cm
New Jersey and Eastern Pennsylvania	COLBY	15x13cm
New Jersey Reduced from T. Gordon's Map	THOMAS, COWPERTHWAIT	39x32cm
New Map of Brooklyn and Vicinity, Published for the Brooklyn Directory	LOCAL & STATE POCKET	67x55cm
New Map of Florida, 1880	GOV'T: LOCAL & STATE	50x32cm
New Map of That Portion of North America, Exhibiting the United States ...	MONK	142x150cm
New Map of the American Overland Route Showing Its Connections ...	RAND, McNALLY (non-atlas)	45x90cm
New Map of the State of Texas ...	COLTON (Atlas Maps)	41x66cm
New Map of the State of Texas As It Is in 1875	COLTON (Pocket & Wall)	49x65cm
New Map of the United States Showing the Complete Railway System ...	RAND, McNALLY (non-atlas)	67x112cm
New Mexico	RAND, McNALLY (atlas maps)	48x33cm
New Mexico	U.S. STATE SURVEYS	51x74cm

Title	Author	Size
New Mexico New Spain with the West Indies	LOCKHEAD	23x16cm
New Military Map of the United States Showing the Forts, Military Posts ...	JOHNSON	44x60cm
New National Map, Exhibiting the United States	MITCHELL, S.A. (non-atlas)	159x152cm
New Orleans ... and Its Vicinity	VIRTUE	12x19cm
New Orleans from the Lower Cotton Press	LADIES REPOSITORY	11x18cm
New Physical, Historical ... Map of England & Wales	STOCKDALE	133x162cm
New Pocket Map of the City of Philadelphia from the Latest City Surveys	SMITH	83x67cm
New Port Harbor [RI]	BLUNT	21x19cm
New Rail Road & County Map of Nebraska	CRAM	22x33cm
New Rail Road and County Map of Southern California and Arizona	CRAM	29x53cm
New Railroad and County Map of Indian Territory and Northern Part of Texas	CRAM	32x44cm
New Railroad and County Map of Southern Part of Idaho	CRAM	29x24cm
New Sectional, Township and County Map of Washington	GILL	70x53cm
New South Wales	S.D.U.K.	39x33cm
New South Wales	TALLIS	33x25cm
New South Wales and Van Dieman's Land	BELL	28x35cm
New Topographical Map of the State of Connecticut	CLARK & TACKABURY	220x138cm
New Township Map of the State of Arkansas	RAILROAD COMPANY	36x39cm
New Township Map of the State of Florida	COLTON (Pocket & Wall)	69x68cm
New York	ARROWSMITH & LEWIS	22x27cm
New York	BRADFORD	28x36cm
New York	BRADFORD	20x25cm
New York	BURR	25x32cm
New York	FINLEY	23x28cm
New York	S.D.U.K.	29x37cm
New York and Its Environs	ROGERS & JOHNSTON	19x17cm
New York and the Adjacent Cities	JOHNSON	41x66cm
New York Bay and Harbor	U.S. COAST SURVEY	76x69cm
New York Central Lines	RAILROAD COMPANY	41x66cm
New York City Map	PHELPS	42x74cm
New York Island, & Parts Adjacent	GORDON, WILLIAM	26x17cm
New York State Reservation at Niagara	GOV'T: LOCAL & STATE	33x33cm
New York to Norwalk Islands, Long Island Sound	HURD	43x69cm
Newark [NJ] (East of Mulberry St. 1820-5)	LOCAL & STATE MAPS	65x51cm
Newport to Halifax, Chart K	ELDRIDGE	96x108cm
Newton's New & Improved Terrestrial Globe. Published by Newton, Son...	NEWTON & BERRY	Diam: 8cm
Nicaragua en de Kusten der Zuyd-Zee Noordwaard von Panama ...	VAN DER AA	15x22cm
Nieuw Algemeene Kaart van Groenland et Straet Davids	OTTENS	48x115cm
Nieuwe Caarte van Kaap de Goede Hoop ... van Africa ...	OTTENS	44x56cm
Nieuwe Kaart van America Uitgegeven ...	TIRION	27x32cm
Nieuwe Kaart van het Eyland Sumatra ...	VALENTYN	51x59cm
Nieuwe Platte Pas Kaart van de Nord Occiaan van Hitland ... Straat Davids	VAN KEULEN	59x100cm
Nle. Carte d'Amerique	DESNOS	112x117cm
N'lle Galles Merid'le ou Cote Orientale de la Nouvelle Hollande ...	BONNE	24x35cm
Nobilis Fluvius Albis ...	MERIAN	18x104cm
Non ex Quovis Ligno fit Mercurius - Amacao in Chyna	MEISNER	10x15cm
Nona Asie Tabula	PTOLEMY (1482-1486)	no dimens
Noordlyk Halvrond	VAN KEULEN	66x66cm
Nord America	WEILAND	58x54cm
Nord-Americanische Freistaaten	MEYER	29x36cm
Nordlicher Theil des Grossen Sud Meers	CHAPPE D'AUTEROCHE	23x16cm
Nordovicum, Angliae Civitas	BRAUN & HOGENBERG	29x42cm
Norfolk and Western Railroad and Connections	RAILROAD COMPANY	19x44cm
Norfolk Harbor Virginia	U.S. COAST SURVEY	49x39cm
Norfolk Showing the Property and Lines of the Norfolk and Western RR ...	RAILROAD COMPANY	29x44cm
North America	BETTS	36x41cm
North America	BRADFORD	37x28cm
North America	BURR	32x27cm
North America	COLTON (Atlas Maps)	40x34cm
North America	FISHER	18x23cm
North America	HALL, SIDNEY	37x26cm
North America	JOHNSON	56x43cm
North America	JOHNSTON	60x50cm
North America	JOHNSTON	30x23cm
North America	KITCHIN	18x23cm
North America	PLAYFAIR	44x53cm
North America	S.D.U.K.	39x30cm

Title	Author	Size
North America	SMITH, C.	27x35cm
North America	SMITH, ROSWELL C.	27x22cm
North America	TALLIS	30x22cm
North America	THOMAS, COWPERTHWAIT	39x32cm
North America	THOMSON	50x60cm
North America ...	POSTLETHWAIT	43x33cm
North America. ... By the Sieur D'Anville.	BOLTON	81x85cm
North America Agreeable to the Most Approved Maps and Charts	CONDER	33x38cm
North America Sheet IV Lake Superior Reduced from the Admiralty ...	S.D.U.K.	32x39cm
North America Sheet V Parts of Wisconsin and Michigan	S.D.U.K.	30x38cm
North America Sheet V The North West and Michigan Territories	S.D.U.K.	30x38cm
North America Sheet VII Pennsylvania, New Jersey, Maryland, Delaware	S.D.U.K.	37x32cm
North-America Sheet VIII Ohio, with Parts of Kentucky, Virginia and ...	S.D.U.K.	35x32cm
North America Sheet X Parts of Missouri, Illinois, Kentucky, Tennessee ...	S.D.U.K.	31x39cm
North America Sheet XI Parts of North and South Carolina	S.D.U.K.	37x34cm
North America Sheet XIV Florida	S.D.U.K.	41x30cm
North America Sheet XV Utah, New Mexico, Texas, California ...	S.D.U.K.	31x39cm
North America Sheet XVI The Southern Part of Mexico ... Costa Rica	S.D.U.K.	32x39cm
North and South Carolina	GREENLEAF	27x32cm
North and South Carolina	JOHNSON	43x61cm
North Britain or Scotland 1708. A New Mapp of Scotland ...	BROWNE	56x48cm
North Carolina	COLTON (Atlas Maps)	32x40cm
North Carolina	MORSE & BREESE	30x43cm
North Dakota	RAND, McNALLY (atlas maps)	34x57cm
North-Western Colorado and Part of Utah	HAYDEN, F.V.	57x88cm
Northern America - British, Russian & Danish Possessions ...	COLTON (Atlas Maps)	32x40cm
Northern California	HARDESTY	48x34cm
Northern Circumpolar Map for Each Month in the Year [with] Southern ...	BURRITT	Diam: 30cm
Northern Hemisphere [with] Southern Hemisphere [&] Western ... [&]	RAND, McNALLY (atlas maps)	32x23cm
Northern Pacific Railroad	RAILROAD COMPANY	33x69cm
Northumberland	MORDEN	42x36cm
Northumbr. Cumberladia	MERCATOR (Small)	14x19cm
Northwestern America Showing the Territory Ceded by Russia to the [US]	MITCHELL, S.A. (1860+)	29x37cm
Norumbega et Virginia	WYTFLIET	23x30cm
Norvegia et Suecia	BERTIUS	14x18cm
Norvegia Regnum ...	DANCKERTS	58x50cm
Norwalk Islands to Southwest Ledge Long Island Sound	HURD	43x69cm
Nottingham Shire	MORDEN	35x43cm
Nottingham Shire	SPEED	8x12cm
Nouvaux Mappemonde ou Globe Terrestre avec des Tables et des ...	CHATELAIN	46x66cm
Nouveau Mexique et Californie	MALLET	14x10cm
Nouveau Mexique, Louisiane, Canada et Nlle. Angleterre	BRION DE LA TOUR	27x30cm
Nouveau Paris Monumental. Itineraire Pratique de l'Etranger dans Paris	GARNIER	53x69cm
Nouveau Plan de Moscou	DE LAVAUR	56x64cm
Nouveau Plan Routier de la Ville et Fauxbourgs de Paris	LOCAL & STATE MAPS	56x79cm
Nouvelle Angleterre Nlle York, Nlle Jersey, Pensilvanie Mariland et Virginie	DE VAUGONDY	19x16cm
Nouvelle Carte de l'Amerique Septentrionale ...	CHATELAIN	47x59cm
Nouvelle Carte de l'Archipel ...	MICHELOT	47x63cm
Nouvelle Carte des Mers ... le Detroit de Banca ... de Malac	DELAHAYE	49x67cm
Nouvelle Carte Illustree de l'Amerique du Nord ...	VUILLEMIN	60x84cm
Nouvelle Carte Particuliere de l'Amerique ou Sont Exactement Marquees ...	COVENS & MORTIER	57x52cm
Nouvelle Descriptio du Pays de Souysse	MUNSTER	25x34cm
Nouvelle Description du Pais de Souysse	MUNSTER	31x40cm
Nouvelle Mappe Monde Dediee au Progres de Nos Connoissances ...	SANTINI	46x64cm
Nouvelle Mappemonde ...	BAILLEUL	52x72cm
Nova & Accurata Tusciae Antiquae Discriptio ,,,	JANSSON	35x50cm
Nova Aegypti Tabula	BLAEU	44x54cm
Nova Anglia Novum Belgium et Virginia	DE LAET	28x36cm
Nova Anglia Septentrionali Americae Implantata Anglorumque Coloniis ...	HOMANN	49x58cm
Nova Barbariae Descriptio	JANSSON	35x52cm
Nova Belgica et Anglia Nova	BLAEU	39x50cm
Nova Belgica et Anglia Nova	JANSSON	39x50cm
Nova Delineatio Totius Orbis Terrarum Auctore I. V. Meurs	VAN MEURS	22x34cm
Nova Delineatio Urbis et Templi Hierosolymarum ...	HOFMANN	19x28cm
Nova et Accurata Iaponiae Terrae Esonis ...	VALK & SCHENK	45x55cm
Nova et Accurata Poli Arctici ...	JANSSON	41x52cm
Nova et Accurata Regni Hungariae ...	COVENS & MORTIER	46x57cm

Title	Author	Size
Nova et Accurata Tabula Regnorum Sup. et Inf. Hungariae It. Sclavoniae ...	PROBST	50x59cm
Nova et Accurata Totius Regni Scotiae ...	SEUTTER	58x49cm
Nova et Accuratissima Maris Caspii ...	SEUTTER	49x57cm
Nova et Accuratissima Totius Terrarum Orbis Tabula ...	BLAEU	40x54cm
Nova Europae Descriptio	DE WIT	44x56cm
Nova Europae Descriptio ...	HONDIUS	38x50cm
Nova Francia et Canada	WYTFLIET	23x29cm
Nova Haec Tabula Galliae ...	VISSCHER	46x55cm
Nova Hispania et Nova Galicia	JANSSON	34x48cm
Nova Mappa Geographica Americae Septentrionalis ...	PROBST	58x51cm
Nova Mappa Geographica Totius Ducatus Silesiae ...	LOTTER	48x58cm
Nova Maris Caspii Et Regionis Usbeck ...	HOMANN	49x59cm
Nova Orbis Tabula ...	DE WIT	48x56cm
Nova Orbis Terraquei Tabula ... [in set with 4 continents]	VAN DER AA	50x66cm
Nova Persiae, Armeniae Natoliae et Arabiae ...	DE WIT	47x56cm
Nova Scotia and Newfoundland	TALLIS	26x33cm
Nova Tabula Geographica Complectens Borealiorem Americae Partem: ...	VISSCHER	60x88cm
Nova Tabula Geographica Complectens Borealiorem Americae Partem: ...	VISSCHER	58x47cm
Nova Tabula India Orientalis Hugo Allardt Excudit ...	ALLARD	45x56cm
Nova Tabula Insularum Iava, Sumatrae, Borneonis et Aliarum Mallaccam ...	DE BRY	36x43cm
Nova Totius Americae Descriptio Auct F. de Wit	DE WIT	44x55cm
Nova Totius Germaniae Descriptio	CLUVER	26x33cm
Nova Totius Terrarum Orbis Geographica ac Hydrographica ...	COLOM	39x53cm
Nova Totius Terrarum Orbis Geographica ac Hydrographica Tabula	BLAEU	41x55cm
Nova Totius Terrarum Orbis Geographica ac Hydrographica Tabula	CAVAZZA	35x55cm
Nova Totius Terrarum Orbis Geographica ac Hydrographica Tabula	HONDIUS	38x54cm
Nova Totius Terrarum Orbis Geographica ac Hydrographica Tabula	MERIAN	26x35cm
Nova Totius Terrarum Orbis Geographica ac Hydrographica Tabula	PITT	40x53cm
Nova Totius Terrarum Orbis Geographica ac Hydrographica Tabula	TAVERNIER	38x53cm
Nova Totius Terrarum Orbis Geographica ac Hydrographica Tabula	VISSCHER	no dimens
Nova Totius Terrarum Orbis Tabula ...	DANCKERTS	50x58cm
Nova Totius Terrarum Orbis Tabula Auctore D.D.	DAVIDSZOON	40x58cm
Nova Totius Terrarum Orbis Tabula ex Officina L. Renard Amstelodami	RENARD	48x56cm
Nova Virginiae Tabula	BLAEU	38x48cm
Nova Virginiae Tabula	HONDIUS	38x49cm
Nova Virginiae Tabula	OGILBY	29x36cm
Nova Virginiae Tabula ...	MERCATOR (Small)	18x25cm
Nova Zemla, Waygats, Fretum Nassovicum, et Terra Samoiedum ...	JANSSON	41x50cm
Novae Insulae XXVI Nova Tabula	MUNSTER	27x34cm
Novi Belgii Novaeque Angliae nec non Partis Virginiae Tabula ...	VISSCHER	46x55cm
Novi Belgii Novaeque Angliae nec non Pennsylvaniae et Partis Virginiae ...	DANCKERTS	46x54cm
Novi Belgii, quod nunc Novi Jorck Vocatur, Novae qe Angliae & Partis...	OGILBY	29x36cm
Novi Orbis Pars Borealis, America Scilicet, Complectens Floridam, ...	QUAD	23x30cm
Novi Orbis sive Totius Americae cum Adiacentibus Insulis Nova Exhibitio	WEIGEL	27x34cm
Novissima ac Prae Caeteris ... Regni et Insulae Hiberniae Delineato ...	DE WIT	58x49cm
Novissima et Accuratissima Barbados. Descriptio per Johannem ...	OGILBY	29x36cm
Novissima et Accuratissima Delineatio Status Ecclesiae et ... Hetruriae	SEUTTER	50x58cm
Novissima et Accuratissima Helvetiae ...	LOTTER	49x57cm
Novissima et Accuratissima Helvetiae ...	OTTENS	48x57cm
Novissima et Accuratissima Jamaicae Descriptio per Johannem ...	OGILBY	43x54cm
Novissima et Accuratissima Septentrionalis ac Meridionalis Americae	DE WIT	44x54cm
Novissima et Accuratissima Totius Americae Descriptio ...	VISSCHER	43x54cm
Novissima et Accuratissima Totius Angliae, Scotiae et Hiberniae Tabula ...	DANCKERTS	50x57cm
Novissima et Accuratissima Totius Italiae Corsicae et Sardiniae	DANCKERTS	50x58cm
Novissima Ichnographica Delineatio Munitissimae Urbis ... Ostendae ...	SEUTTER	50x58cm
Novissima Islandiae Tabula	PITT	38x49cm
Novus Orbis sive America Meridionalis et Septentrionalis ...	SEUTTER	49x57cm
Novus Planiglobii Terrestris per Utrumque Polum Conspectus	VALK	41x54cm
Novus XVII Inferioris Germaniae Provinciarum Typus	BLAEU	40x50cm
Nth Carolina	LUCAS	28x48cm
Nueva Hispania Tabula Nova	GASTALDI	13x17cm
Nullus in Orbe Locus Baiis Praelucet Amoenis	BRAUN & HOGENBERG	34x49cm
Nuova Carta del Circolo di Wesfalia Diviso ne' suoi Vescovadi, Principati ...	TIRION	28x33cm
Nuova Carta dell' Italia ...	RIZZI-ZANNONI	122x92cm
Nuova e Corretta Carta dell'Indie Occidentali ...	GAZZETTIERE AMERICANO	27x34cm
Nuova ed Esatta Carta della America Ricavata dalle Mappe ...	GAZZETTIERE AMERICANO	34x28cm
Nuova Esatta Carta dell' Asia ...	BOWEN, EMANUEL	34x42cm

Nuremberga [with Vienna]	SCHONSPERGER	10x20cm
Nurnbergk	MEISNER	10x15cm
Ober Kaernten mit den Salzburgischen Antheilen	VON REILLY	22x31cm
Occidentalis Americae Partis, Velearum Regionum Quas ...	DE BRY	32x42cm
Oceani Occidentalis seu Terrae Novae Tabula	FRIES	29x43cm
Oceanie	LEVASSEUR	30x42cm
Oceanie Dressee par A.H. Dufour	DUFOUR	55x75cm
Octava Europae Tabula	PTOLEMY (1511)	39x46cm
Ofen [Buda] in Ungarn	MEISNER	10x15cm
Official Map of El Paso Texas	GAST & CO.	130x140cm
Official Map of the Union Pacific Railway	RAILROAD COMPANY	41x109cm
Ohio	ARROWSMITH & LEWIS	26x21cm
Ohio	COLBY	15x13cm
Ohio	MADISON	59x58cm
Oklahoma and Indian Territory	CENTURY ATLAS	27x38cm
Oklahoma / Indian Territory	RAND, McNALLY (atlas maps)	30x48cm
Omaha	CRAM	33x27cm
One Hundred & Fifty Miles Around Richmond	MAGNUS, C.	66x77cm
Oost Indien. Wassende-Graade Paskaart ... Oostelyckste van Africa ... Japan	VAN KEULEN	62x88cm
Oosterdeel van Oost Indien ...	DONCKER	53x61cm
Operations in Georgia and Tennessee	DAVIS	22x19cm
Operations in Mississippi	DAVIS	20x17cm
Opulentissimum Sinarum Imperium ...	SEUTTER	49x57cm
Opulentissimum Sinarum Imperium juxta Recentissimam Delineationem ...	LOTTER	50x57cm
Orbis Descriptio	RUSCELLI	18x26cm
Orbis Terrae Compendiosa Descriptio	ROSACCIO	17x25cm
Orbis Terrae Compendiosa Descriptio ...	MERCATOR (Folio)	29x52cm
Orbis Terrae Compendiosa Descriptio ... Mercator ...	MAGINI	15x24cm
Orbis Terrae Compendiosa Descriptio quam ex Magna Universali ...	MERCATOR (Folio)	36x52cm
Orbis Terrae Novissima Descriptio	LE CLERC	33x52cm
Orbis Terrarum Cognitus ...	WELLS	8x16cm
Orbis Terrarum Nova et Accurata Tabula ...	VALK	48x57cm
Orbis Terrarum Nova et Accuratissima Tabula	VISSCHER	47x56cm
Orbis Terrarum Nova et Accuratissima Tabula Auctore Ioanne a Loon	PITT	44x53cm
Orbis Terrarum Nova et Accuratissima Tabula Auctore Ioanne a Loon	VAN LOON	44x53cm
Orbis Terrarum Nova et Accuratissima Tabula ... [with 4 continents]	VISSCHER	46x55cm
Orbis Terrarum Tabula Recens Emendata et in Lucem Edita	STOOPENDAAL	36x47cm
Orbis Terrarum Tabula Recens Emendata et in Lucem Edita per N. Visscher	VISSCHER	30x47cm
Orbis Terrarum Typus de Integro in Plurimis Emendatus, Auctus et Icunculis	VISSCHER	36x47cm
Orbis Terrarum Typus de Integro Multis in Locis Emendatus	MERCATOR (Folio)	29x52cm
Orbis Terrarum Veteribus Cogniti Typus Geographicus	JANSSON	40x51cm
Orbis Veteribus Noti Tabula Nova ... 1714	DE L'ISLE	49x48cm
Orbis Vetus in Ultraque Continente juxta Mentem Sansonianam Distinctus	DE VAUGONDY	46x71cm
Orcadum et Schetlandiae Insularum Accuratissima Descriptio	BLAEU	40x53cm
Oregon & Washington Ter.	GILL	88x69cm
Oregon and California	SWANSTON	23x15cm
Oregon, and the Territory of Washington.	LLOYD, H.H.	38x29cm
Oregon Territory	BURR	27x32cm
Oregon Territory	GREENLEAF	27x32cm
Oregon, Washington, California, Colorado, Nevada, Utah, New Mexico ...	COLTON (Atlas Maps)	32x27cm
Orientaliora Indiarum Orientalium cum Insulis Adiacentibus ... Iapan	DU VAL	44x54cm
Orientaliora Indiarum Orientalium cum Insulis Adjacentibus ... ad Iapan ...	OTTENS	44x54cm
Osterreichische Crais. Churf. u. Hertzogt. Bayern	LOTTER	10x13cm
Our Nation's Campground	ENSIGN, BRIDGMAN ...	62x39cm
Outline Map of the United States	PUZZLES & GAMES	41x51cm
Outline Map Showing a New Route from Texas to Fort Yuma, California ...	U.S. WAR DEPARTMENT	37x126cm
Owls Head Harbor Maine ... 1836	U.S. WAR DEPARTMENT	38x32cm
Oxford Shire	MORDEN	42x36cm
Oxford Shire	SELLER	12x14cm
Oxfordshire Described with ye Citie and the Armes of the Colledges ...	SPEED	38x52cm
Oyster Bay to Matagorda Bay (Texas). Coast Chart No.107	U.S. COAST SURVEY	53x102cm
Pacific States and Territories	LLOYD, H.H.	66x37cm
Paderbornensis Episcopatus Descriptio Nova	BLAEU	38x50cm
Page's Map of Colorado	PAGE	41x66cm
Page's Map of Kansas	PAGE	41x67cm
Palacios City Matagorda County Texas	REAL ESTATE MAPS	40x40cm

Title	Author	Size
Palaestina [with] Aegyptus Antiqua	THOMSON	48x66cm
Palaestina in XII Tribus Divisa cum Terris Adiacentibus Denuo Revisa & ...	HOMANN	44x52cm
Palaestina, vel Terra Sancta	MAGINI	13x17cm
Palaestinae Accurata Descriptio Geographica ...	SEUTTER	50x58cm
Palaestinae sive Totius Terrae Promissionis Nova Descriptio ...	ORTELIUS (Folio)	35x46cm
Palatinatus ad Rhenum	BLAEU	41x50cm
Palatinatus Rheni	MERCATOR (Small)	15x18cm
Palestina sive Terrae Sanctae Descriptio ...	JANSSON	44x56cm
Palestinae sive Totius Terrae Promissionis ...	MAGINI	13x17cm
Palestine	LIZARS	23x18cm
Palestine with the Hauran ...	S.D.U.K.	39x31cm
Palestine with the Hauran and the Adjacent Districts [with] Ancient ...	S.D.U.K.	39x32cm
Panorama du Mont-Righi ... vom Rigiberg ...	LOCAL & STATE MAPS	53x53cm
Panorama from Point Sublime [AZ]	U.S. GEOLOGICAL SURVEY	46x79cm
Panorama of the City of Mexico	ILLUS. LONDON NEWS	17x99cm
Panorama of the Mississippi Valley and Its Fortifications ...	MAGNUS, C.	60x64cm
Panoramic View from Bunker Hill Monument	CROSMAN & MALLORY	15x112cm
Panoramic View of the City of Toronto, Canada West	HARPER'S WEEKLY	23x34cm
Paradisus	HONDIUS	15x19cm
Paradisus	MERCATOR (Small)	15x18cm
Paraguay, O Prov. de Rio de la Plata cum Regionibus Adiacentibus ...	BLAEU	37x48cm
Paraquaria vulgo Paraguay cum Adjacentibus	OGILBY	29x37cm
Paris	MUNSTER	25x32cm
Paris	PROBST	34x97cm
Pars Flandriae Teutonicae Occidentalior	BLAEU	40x50cm
Pars Regni Moab	FULLER	28x33cm
Part of Central Colorado, Atlas Sheet No.52D	U.S. WAR DEPARTMENT	41x48cm
Part of Central Nevada, Atlas Sheet No.48D	U.S. WAR DEPARTMENT	38x48cm
Part of Central New Mexico. Atlas Sheet No.69(D)	U.S. WAR DEPARTMENT	39x51cm
Part of Central New Mexico. Atlas Sheet No.77(B)	U.S. WAR DEPARTMENT	39x51cm
Part of Central Wyoming	HAYDEN, F.V.	65x85cm
Part of North America, Containing Canada, the North Parts of New England	DE VAUGONDY	21x29cm
Part of North Central New Mexico. Atlas Sheet No.70	U.S. WAR DEPARTMENT	39x51cm
Part of South Australia	TALLIS	34x25cm
Part of Southern California, Atlas Sheet No.73	U.S. WAR DEPARTMENT	38x51cm
Part of South'n Colorado & North'n New Mexico. Atlas Sheet No.69(B)	U.S. WAR DEPARTMENT	39x51cm
Part of the State of Indiana from Actual Survey on File in the [GLO]	U.S. GOV'T	42x36cm
Parte Alpestre dello Stato di Milano con il Lago Maggiore di Lugano e di Como	BLAEU	38x51cm
Parte de I Africa	RAMUSIO	28x38cm
Parte della Nuova Spagne, o del Mexico ...	CORONELLI	45x60cm
Parte Meridionale del Regno d'Inghilterra [in set with] Parte Settentrionale	CORONELLI	91x61cm
Parte Orientale della Florida, della Giorgia, e Carolina Meridionale	ZATTA	32x43cm
Parte Settentrionale dell'Irelanda Descritta ... / Irlanda Parte Meridional ...	CORONELLI	90x62cm
Partie de l'Amerique Septent? qui Comprend la Nouvelle France ou le ...	DE VAUGONDY	48x58cm
Partie de l'Amerique Septentrionale, qui Comprend le Cours de l'Ohio ...	DE VAUGONDY	48x62cm
Partie de l'Etat de Rhode-Island, et Position des Armees Americaine ...	MARSHALL	44x26cm
Partie de la Barbarie ou Est le Royaume d'Alger	SANSON (Folio)	36x53cm
Partie de la Carte du Capitaine Cluny ...	DIDEROT	21x41cm
Partie de la Nouvelle France ...	JAILLOT	46x64cm
Partie de Lithuánie ... Minsk ...	SANSON (Folio)	40x52cm
Partie de Terre Ferme ou Sont Guiane et Caribane ...	SANSON (Folio)	40x54cm
Partie du Canada ou Se Trouvent le Fleuve St Laurent et la Nouvelle Ecosse	DE VAUGONDY	16x21cm
Partie du Duche de Milan, La Principaute de Piemont ...	JAILLOT	46x64cm
Partie du Mexique ... Ou Se Trouve ... Californie &c.	DE VAUGONDY	16x20cm
Partie du Nord de l'Amerique Septentrionale pour Servir a l'Histoire ...	BONNE	28x21cm
Partie Meridio.le du Royaume d'Irlande	SANSON (Folio)	40x50cm
Partie Meridional do Reyno de Portugal	SANSON (Folio)	40x52cm
Partie Meridionale d'Afrique ou Se Trouvent le Bassee Guinee ...	DE FER (Small)	22x32cm
Partie Meridionale de l'Ancien Mexique ou de la Nouvle Espagne	BONNE	21x32cm
Partie Meridionale de l'Inde en Deux Presqu'Isles l'une deca ... le Gange ...	SANSON (Folio)	38x52cm
Partie Meridionale de la Riviere de Missisipi ...	DE FER (Large)	46x64cm
Partie Occidentale de la Nouvelle France ou du Canada ...	BELLIN (Large)	41x52cm
Partie Occidentale de la Nouvelle France ou du Canada. Par Mr. Bellin ...	HOMANN	44x55cm
Partie Occidentale del Mediterraneo ...	CORONELLI	40x51cm
Partie Occidentale du Canada Contenent les Cinq Grands Lacs ...	BONNE	21x31cm
Partie Orientale de la Lapponie Suedoise ...	SANSON (Folio)	40x52cm
Partie Septentrie du Royaume d'Irlande	SANSON (Folio)	40x49cm

Title	Author	Size
Partie Septentr.le du Royaume d'Irlande ... [with] Partie Meridio.le	SANSON (Folio)	40x49cm
Partie Septentrionale de l'Ocean Pacifique ou l'On A Marque les ...	POIRSON	35x46cm
Partie Septentrionale du New-Jersey, et Positions des Armees Americaine	MARSHALL	40x26cm
Partie Septentrionale du Royaume de Naples	DE VAUGONDY	49x60cm
Parts of Eastern California and Western Nevada. Atlas Sheets 47 (B) ...	U.S. WAR DEPARTMENT	76x74cm
Parts of Eastern Nevada and Western Utah, Atlas Sheet No.49	U.S. WAR DEPARTMENT	37x48cm
Parts of Northern & North Western Arizona & Southern Utah, Atlas Sheet ...	U.S. WAR DEPARTMENT	38x50cm
Parts of Southern Colorado and Northern New Mexico Atlas Sheet No. 70(a)	U.S. WAR DEPARTMENT	38x50cm
Parys	MERIAN	26x69cm
Pas Kaart van de Kust van Carolina Tusschen C de Canaveral en C Henry	VAN KEULEN	51x58cm
Pas Kaart van de Zee Kusten van Virginia tusschen C. Henry en t Hooge ...	VAN KEULEN	51x57cm
Pas Kaart van Rio Oronoque Golfo de Paria met d'Eylanden Trinidad, ...	VAN KEULEN	51x58cm
Pas-Kaart van de Zee-Kusten van Terra Nova ... Francia Nova, Canada ...	VAN KEULEN	51x58cm
Pas-Kaart vande Zee Kusten van Niew Nederland ... en de Staaten Hoek ...	VAN KEULEN	51x56cm
Pascaart vertoonende de Zeecusten van Chili, Peru ... en California	DONCKER	43x54cm
Pascaert vande Caribes Eylanden; Curiooslyck Betrocken ...	GERRITZ	50x70cm
Pascaert vande Zuyd Zee en een Gedeelte van Brasil van Ilhas de Ladrones	VAN KEULEN	51x60cm
Pascaert van't Eylandt Ceylon, Voordefen Taprobana; by de Inwoonders ...	VAN KEULEN	52x60cm
Passage par Terre a La Californie Decouvert par le Rev. Pere ... Kino ...	KINO	23x20cm
Passaw. in Nieder Bayern	MEISNER	10x15cm
Patapsco River and the Approaches ...	U.S. COAST SURVEY	44x69cm
Patriae Antiquae inter July et Caroli Magni	JANSSON	48x61cm
Patriarchatus Hierosolymitani Geographica Descriptio ...	TAVERNIER	35x50cm
Patriarchatus Ierosolymitanus Comprehendebat Tres Provincias ...	SCHERER	23x36cm
Paye Situe entr Frog's Point et Croton River, et Position des Armees ...	MARSHALL	42x23cm
Pays des Caribes de Guiane	MALLET	15x10cm
Pecheli, Xansi, Xantung, Honan, Nanking, in Plaga Regni Sinensis	VALK & SCHENK	46x52cm
Peloponnesus nunc Morea	CLUVER	21x25cm
Penigk Misniae Oppidum	BRAUN & HOGENBERG	33x46cm
Pennsylvania	FINLEY	22x28cm
Pensylvania Nova Jersey et Nova York cum Regionibus ad Fluvium Delaware	LOTTER	57x50cm
Pensylvania Nova Jersey et Nova York cum Regionibus ad Fluvium Delaware	SEUTTER	57x49cm
Per Inclyti Circuli Suevici ... Sueviae Universae Descriptionem	HOMANN	144x135cm
Perchensis Comitatus [with] Comitatus Blesensis	BLAEU	38x23cm
Peregrinnatio Israelitaru in Deserto	MERCATOR (Small)	15x18cm
Perigrinatie ofte Veertich larige Reyse der Kinderen Israels	DAPPER	39x47cm
Perigrinatie Veertich-larize Reyse der Kinderen Israels ...	KEUR	30x45cm
Perigrinatio Pauli in qua et Omnia Loca Quorum Fit Mentio in Actis et ...	MERCATOR (Small)	15x19cm
Perrine's New Topographical War Map of the South	PERRINE	71x92cm
Persia Arabia &c.	TANNER	29x36cm
Persici vel Sophorum Regni Tipus	CLOPPENBURGH	19x26cm
Persici vel Sophorum Regni Typus	HONDIUS	36x50cm
Persicum Regnum	MERCATOR (Small)	14x19cm
Peru and Bolivia	THOMAS, COWPERTHWAIT	31x38cm
Phaenomena in Planetis Primariis	DOPPELMAYR	49x57cm
Phelps & Ensign's Map of the City of New York	PHELPS	42x51cm
Phelps & Ensign's Traveller's Guide through the United States: Containing ...	PHELPS & ENSIGN	55x43cm
Phelps & Ensign's Traveller's Guide through the United States: Containing ...	PHELPS & ENSIGN	43x97cm
Phelps and Watson's Historical and Military Map of the Border & Southern	PHELPS & WATSON	64x89cm
Phelps New-York City Guide and Conductor	PHELPS	44x39cm
Phelps's National Map of the United States, A Travellers Guide ...	PHELPS	53x64cm
Philadelphia	BRADFORD	36x28cm
Philadelphia	COLTON (Atlas Maps)	40x32cm
Philadelphia	S.D.U.K.	29x38cm
Philippine Islands Agreeable to Modern History	MOLL (Small)	20x26cm
Philipsburg zu Braubach	MEISNER	10x15cm
Piacenza in Italia	MEISNER	10x15cm
Piano di Porto Bello	GAZZETTIERE AMERICANO	20x25cm
Pianta della Citta di Roma	MONALDINI	75x112cm
Pianta della Citta e Fortezza d'Atene ...	CORONELLI	45x60cm
Pic de Lantao, Pres de l'Entree du Bocca Tigris ...	MEARES	17x23cm
Piccola Tartaria	LASOR A VAREA	10x15cm
Pittsburgh and Allegheny	LADIES REPOSITORY	11x18cm
Pixix Nautica or the Marriner Compas Shewing the names of the Points	SELLER	12x14cm
Plan and Sections of Fort Fisher Carried by Assault by the U.S. Forces ...	U.S. WAR DEPARTMENT	28x38cm
Plan d' York en Virginie avec les Attaques et les Campemes de l'Armee ...	SOULES	29x38cm
Plan de Jedo.	KAEMPFER	32x32cm

Title	Author	Size
Plan de l'Isle Spine Longue sur l'Isle Candie	ROUX	12x19cm
Plan de la Baye de Manille	ANSON	20x25cm
Plan de la Baye de Rio-Janeiro	BELLIN (Large)	51x34cm
Plan de la Baye de Rio-Janeiro	BELLIN (Small)	21x32cm
Plan de la Baye de St. Yago dans l'Isle de Cube	BELLIN (Small)	21x16cm
Plan de la Baye et Port de Rio Janeiro, Situe a la Coste de Bresil ...	DEZAUCHE	73x51cm
Plan de la Riviere du Cap Fear depuis la Barre jusques a Brunswick	SARTINE	58x42cm
Plan de la Ville & du Fort de St. Petersbourg ...	COVENS & MORTIER	48x57cm
Plan de la Ville ... Vienne ...	MOLLO	37x44cm
Plan de la Ville de Boston et Ses Environs	BELLIN (Small)	17x27cm
Plan de la Ville de Buenos-Ayres	BELLIN (Small)	18x27cm
Plan de la Ville de Louisbourg dans l'Isle Royale	BELLIN (Small)	20x34cm
Plan de la Ville de Quebec	BELLIN (Small)	20x28cm
Plan de la Ville et du Chateau de Batavia en l'Isle de Iava ...	VAN DER AA	26x35cm
Plan de la Ville et du Port de Macao	BELLIN (Small)	21x17cm
Plan de la Ville et Rade de Cartagene et du Fort de St. Lazare	MANUSCRIPT MAPS	53x74cm
Plan de Longuvy	MANUSCRIPT MAPS	42x56cm
Plan de Paris Commence l'Annee 1734 ...	BRETEZ	Folio
Plan de Stuttgart	MALTE-BRUN	24x33cm
Plan de Ville du Chateau de Batavia en l'Isle de Iava	VAN DER AA	27x36cm
Plan der Belagerung u. Einnahme der Stadt u. Vestung Wolffenbuttel ...	SEYFART	20x28cm
Plan des Vielles et Nouvelle Fortifications de Malthe	MORTIER	22x29cm
Plan du Bassin de Quebec et de Ses Environs	BELLIN (Small)	20x28cm
Plan du Port de la Ville et des Forteresses de Carthagene ...	COVENS & MORTIER	50x60cm
Plan du Port et Ville de Louisbourg dans l'Isle Royale	BELLIN (Small)	19x28cm
Plan General de Paris en Quatre Divisions ... [in set with 4 divisions]	MOITHEY	28x42cm
Plan Nouveau & Tres Exact de la Ville d'Amsterdam	COVENS & MORTIER	no dimens
Plan of Acarron Bay Situated at the East Point of the Malouine Islands ...	BOUGAINVILLE	26x24cm
Plan of Cape Girardo	COLLOT	27x16cm
Plan of Coblentz with the Citadel of Ehrenbreistein and the Fortifications ...	MANUSCRIPT MAPS	78x94cm
Plan of Falmouth Heights. Falmouth, Mass.	LOCAL & STATE MAPS	53x83cm
Plan of Philadelphia	MITCHELL, S.A. (1860+)	28x33cm
Plan of Portland Harbour.	BLUNT	18x10cm
Plan of Portsmouth Harbour	BLUNT	18x19cm
Plan of Portsmouth Harbour	BLUNT	10x18cm
Plan of St. Lucia, in the West Indies: Shewing the Positions ...	GENTLEMAN'S MAGAZINE	19x25cm
Plan of the Battle of Waterloo, or, Mont St. Jean, June 18th, 1815	LEIGH	44x51cm
Plan of the City and Environs of Quebec, with its Siege and Blockade ...	FADEN	44x62cm
Plan of the City and Harbour of Havanna.	GENTLEMAN'S MAGAZINE	11x20cm
Plan of the City and Harbour of the Havana	JEFFERYS	22x27cm
Plan of the City of London, Distinguishing the Several Wards ...	FADEN	64x152cm
Plan of the City of Moscow	TRUSLER	20x22cm
Plan of the City of New York	VALENTINE'S MANUAL	46x36cm
Plan of the City of New York, with Recent and Intended Improvements	MAVERICK, P.	31x33cm
Plan of the City of Philadelphia and Camden	MITCHELL, S.A. (1860+)	37x56cm
Plan of the City of Washington	MITCHELL, S.A. (1860+)	28x36cm
Plan of the City of Washington ...	ELLICOTT	39x50cm
Plan of the City of Washington ...	ELLICOTT	22x26cm
Plan of the City of Washington and the Territory of Columbia	LIZARS	34x35cm
Plan of the City of Washington, in the Territory of Columbia, Ceded by ...	RUSSELL	40x53cm
Plan of the Country from Frogs Point to Cotton River Shewing the Positions	MARSHALL	41x22cm
Plan of the Encampment and Position of the Army under ... Burgoyne ...	FADEN	32x34cm
Plan of the House, Gardens, Park & Hermitage of the Majesties, at Richmond	ROCQUE	58x90cm
Plan of the Operations of General Washington ... in New Jersey ...	FADEN	29x39cm
Plan of the Position Taken by Gen. Burgoyne on the 10th of Octr. 1777 ...	ANALECTIC MAGAZINE	22x36cm
Plan of the Siege of Charlestown in South Carolina	STEDMAN	25x29cm
Plan of the Siege of Charlestown in South Carolina	TARLETON	26x29cm
Plan of the Town and Fortifications of Gibraltar	RAPIN	39x60cm
Plan of the Town of Patterson, on the Line of the Pennsylvania RR ...	DUVAL	44x57cm
Plan Topographique de la Campagne de Rome ...	SICKLER	56x87cm
Planisfero del Mondo Nuovo, Descritto dal P. Coronelli ...	CORONELLI	46x61cm
Planisfero del Mondo Vecchio Descritto dal P. Coronelli	CORONELLI	55x62cm
Planisphaerium Braheum	CELLARIUS	42x42cm
Planisphaerium Coeleste ...	SCHENK	48x56cm
Planisphaerium Terrestre cum Utroque Coelesti Haemisphaerio ...	ZURNER	50x58cm
Planisphere Physique ou l'On Voit du Pole Septentrionale ...	BUACHE	36x44cm
Plano de la Ria y Puerto del Ferrol	MANUSCRIPT MAPS	44x112cm

Title	Source	Size
Plano del Porto e degli Stabilimenti di Pensacola	GAZZETTIERE AMERICANO	20x27cm
Plano Geometrico del Puerto Capital de la Isla de Puerto Rico ...	CHURRUCA	44x58cm
Plans of the Old & New City of North Peking ye Metropolis of China	HARRIS	32x20cm
Planta della Citta di Sant' Iago Capitale del Regno del Chili	GAZZETTIERE AMERICANO	23x20cm
Plat Book of Nodaway County Missouri	NORTHWEST PUBL.	Folio
Plat of a Survey of Land "For Military Purposes" around Fort Brady [MI]	U.S. GOV'T	25x33cm
Plat of Boise City, Capital of Idaho	LOCAL & STATE MAPS	56x74cm
Plat of Columbia Heights	REAL ESTATE MAPS	91x51cm
Plat of Grammar's Addition to Takoma Park [MD]	REAL ESTATE MAPS	28x51cm
Plat of the Seven Ranges of Townships Being Part of the Territory [US]	CAREY	61x34cm
Plata Americae Provincia	WYTFLIET	23x29cm
Plate XLIII [9 battle plans: Gettysburg (3); Kennesaw Mt; Texas Coast; etc.]	U.S. UNION & CONFED.	Folio
Plate LIV. Map of Texas and Part of New Mexico ...	U.S. UNION & CONFED.	42x70cm
Plate LXV Coast of Texas and Its Defenses [and other small maps]	U.S. UNION & CONFED.	41x69cm
Plate CXIX Section of Map of the States of Kansas and Texas and Indian	U.S. UNION & CONFED.	41x70cm
Platte-Grond van Amboina, zoo als het Was in den Jaare 1718	VAN DER SCHLEY	27x28cm
Platte Grond van de Sterke Vesting Rhynberk, den 7den February 1703 ...	RATELBAND	16x28cm
Plymouth to the Rt. Hon.ble Arthur Earle of Torrington	COLLINS, G.	45x56cm
Pocket Map and Shippers Guide of Kansas	LOCAL & STATE POCKET	38x66cm
Pocket Map and Shippers' Guide of Texas	RAND, McNALLY (non-atlas)	66x94cm
Poland	THOMSON	50x60cm
Political Map of New Jersey	HARPER'S WEEKLY	36x24cm
Political Map of North America ...	WOODBRIDGE	22x27cm
Political Map of the United States, Texas, Mexico and the British Provinces	WOODBRIDGE	28x46cm
Polonia et Silesia	MERCATOR (Small)	14x18cm
Poloniae ...	ORTELIUS (Folio)	37x50cm
Poloniae et Ungariae Nova Descriptio	MUNSTER	26x34cm
Poloniae Finitimarumque' Locorum Descriptio. Auctore Wenceslao ...	ORTELIUS (Folio)	38x50cm
Poloniae Nova et Acurata Descriptio	JANSSON	39x50cm
Poloniae Regnum	MAGINI	13x17cm
Polus Antarcticus Henricus Hondius Excudit	HONDIUS	43x49cm
Polus Arcticus cum Vicinis Regionibus	MERCATOR (Small)	13x19cm
Polus Arcticus sive Tract, Septentrionalis. Coloniae ... Bussemechers	QUAD	21x28cm
Polynesien (Inselwelt) oder der Funfte Welttheil ... Schraembl ...	DJURBERG	47x71cm
Polynesien und der Grosse Ocean	STIELER	33x41cm
Polynesien und der Grosse Ocean ... zur Ethnographischen Übersicht ...	PERTHES	25x43cm
Pompeii	S.D.U.K.	31x39cm
Port Fortune [Chatham, MA]	CHAMPLAIN	20x25cm
Port Royal and Kingston Harbours	BRITISH ADMIRALTY	65x94cm
Portion of the Map of the Indian Nations and Tribes of the Territory of [WA]	U.S. GOV'T	36x36cm
Portland Harbor Maine ...	U.S. COAST SURVEY	73x65cm
Portland Harbour for Blunt's Coast Pilot	BLUNT	20x11cm
Portland, Maine	LADIES REPOSITORY	13x20cm
Porto Rico	OGILBY	28x34cm
Portugallia et Algarbia quae olim Lusitania	BLAEU	38x50cm
Portugallia et Algarbiae Regna ...	SEUTTER	49x56cm
Portugalliae et Algarbiae Regna ...	VISSCHER	46x56cm
Portugalliae que olim Lusitania, Novissima et Exactissima ...	QUAD	18x26cm
Portus Acupulco	OGILBY	28x36cm
Positions of the Upper and Lower Gold Mines on the South Fork of the ...	U.S. GOV'T	24x46cm
Post-Kanal-und Eisenbahnkarte der Vereinigten Staaten von Nord-Amerika	BROMME	55x67cm
Potomac River (In Four Sheets)	U.S. COAST SURVEY	58x272cm
Praga Celeberrima et Maxima Totius Bohemiae ...	SEUTTER	49x57cm
Praga Regni Bohemiae Metropolis / Palatium Imperatorum Pragae ...	BRAUN & HOGENBERG	36x49cm
Preliminary Chart of Eastport Harbor Maine	U.S. WAR DEPARTMENT	52x43cm
Preliminary Chart of Hudson River ... Haverstraw to Poughkeepsie ...	U.S. COAST & GEODETIC	98x50cm
Preliminary Chart of Kennebec River Maine from Entrance to Bath ...	U.S. COAST SURVEY	69x46cm
Preliminary Chart of Monomoy Shoals Massachusetts ...	U.S. COAST SURVEY	62x47cm
Preliminary Chart of Nantucket Shoals Massachusetts	U.S. COAST SURVEY	44x49cm
Preliminary Chart of New York Bay and Harbor	U.S. COAST SURVEY	76x66cm
Preliminary Chart of St. Augustine Harbor, Florida ...	U.S. COAST SURVEY	52x53cm
Preliminary Chart of the Sea Coast of Massachusetts from Saughkonnet ...	U.S. COAST SURVEY	57x80cm
Preliminary Map of Central Colorado Showing the Region ...	HAYDEN, F.V.	64x56cm
Preliminary Map of Central Colorado Showing the Region Surveyed in ...	U.S. GOV'T	64x57cm
Preliminary Map of the Eastern Base of the Rocky Mountains ...	HAYDEN, F.V.	122x28cm
Preliminary Map of the Western Portion of the Reconnaissance for the ...	U.S. PACIFIC R.R. SURVEY	66x123cm
Premiere Partie de la Carte de la Louisiane [with] ... l'Interior de la Louisiane	PIKE, ZEBULON	43x41cm

Title	Author/Publisher	Size
Presbiteri Iohannis, sive Abissinorum Imperii Descriptio	ORTELIUS (Folio)	37x44cm
Preussen	MUNSTER	10x14cm
Prima Tavola [Africa]	RAMUSIO	27x39cm
Principatus Cataloniae nec non Comitatuum Ruscinonensis et Cerretanaie	HOMANN	48x56cm
Principatus Walliae pars Borealis Vulgo North Wales	JANSSON	41x51cm
Principaute de Catalogne ...	JAILLOT	46x64cm
Profil de la Ville de Quebec et de Ses Environs Attaquee par les Angloise ...	LA HONTAN	19x20cm
Progress Map of the Lines and Areas of Explorations ... West of the 100th	U.S. WAR DEPARTMENT	41x56cm
Prospect der Statt undt Vestung Harburg	MERIAN	26x74cm
Prospect und Grund-Riss der Kayserl Residenz-Stadt Wein ...	HOMANN	50x58cm
Prospect und Grundriss der Weltberuhinten Konigliche Haubt Stadt Paris	HOMANN	49x57cm
Prospectus Templi Cathedralis ... Prospect des Munsters ... Basel	MERIAN	21x32cm
Province de New-York ... par Montresor ... 1777	LE ROUGE	144x66cm
Province de New-York ... par Montresor ... 1777	LE ROUGE	141x91cm
Provincetown Harbor Massachusetts	U.S. COAST SURVEY	38x44cm
Provincetown Harbor, Mass. Engraved in the Engineer Dept.	U.S. WAR DEPARTMENT	15x23cm
Provinciae Borealis Americae Non Ita Pridem Detectae Aut Magis Ab ...	SCHERER	23x34cm
Prussia	BLACK	26x38cm
Prussia ...	BLAEU	38x50cm
Prussia Accurate Descripta ...	BLAEU	38x50cm
Ptolemaei Typus	MAGINI	13x17cm
Ptolemaisch General Tafel ...	MUNSTER	25x34cm
Ptolemeisch General Tafel ...	MUNSTER	30x36cm
Ptolemeisch General Tafel [with 4 continents]	MUNSTER	31x36cm
Quarta Pars Brabantiae Cujus Caput Sylvaducis	BLAEU	41x52cm
Quebec, Ville de l'Amerique Septentrionale dans la Nouvelle France	MORTIER	20x29cm
Quivirae Regnu cum Alijs versus Borea	DE JODE	35x23cm
Radio Stations Map of the United States and Mexico ...	CONCEPT MAPS	46x61cm
Ragusi	CORONELLI	13x16cm
Rail Road & Township Map of Nebraska	CRAM	42x55cm
Railroad and County Map of Dakota and Manitoba	CRAM	56x41cm
Railroad and County Map of Louisiana	CRAM	41x56cm
Railroad and County Map of Maine	CRAM	56x41cm
Railroad and County Map of Montana	CRAM	41x56cm
Railroad and County Map of Nebraska	CRAM	41x56cm
Railroad and County Map of New Jersey	CRAM	57x41cm
Railroad and County Map of Texas	CRAM	42x57cm
Railroad and County Map of Utah	CRAM	41x56cm
Railroad and County Map of Washington	CRAM	39x56cm
Railroad Map of New England and Eastern New York	GOLDTHWAIT	60x50cm
Railroad Map of Ohio	GOV'T: LOCAL & STATE	80x71cm
Railroad Map of Pennsylvania Published by the Department of Internal ...	WALL	76x136cm
Railroad Map of the United States Together with the Various Steamship ...	BRADLEY	37x58cm
Railway & Township Map of Massachusetts	WALLING & GRAY	37x61cm
Railway Map of the Middle and Western States ...	WATSON	29x51cm
Rambles through Our Country, An Instructive Geographical Game ...	PUZZLES & GAMES	64x89cm
Rand McNally ... Map of New Orleans	RAND, McNALLY (atlas maps)	50x32cm
Rand McNally ... Map of St. Paul, Minneapolis and Environs	RAND, McNALLY (atlas maps)	66x48cm
Rand-McNally & Cos. Indexed County and Township Pocket Map ... [KS]	RAND, McNALLY (non-atlas)	48x66cm
Rand-McNally & Cos. Indexed County and Township Pocket Map ... [SD]	RAND, McNALLY (non-atlas)	32x47cm
Rand, McNally & Co.'s Indexed Map of Massachusetts	RAND, McNALLY (non-atlas)	51x41cm
Rand McNally & Co's Indexed Pocket Map of Alaska	RAND, McNALLY (non-atlas)	48x48cm
Rand McNally World Map for the Air Age	AERONAUTICAL MAPS	112x112cm
Rand McNally's Pocket Map and Shipper's Guide of Arizona	RAND, McNALLY (non-atlas)	48x32cm
Recens Edita Totius Novi Belgii, in America Septentrionali Siti ...	LOTTER	50x58cm
Recens Edita Totius Novi Belgii, in America Septentrionali Siti ...	SEUTTER	50x58cm
Recentis Romae Ichnographia et Hypsographia sive Planta et Facies ...	RUBEIS	69x88cm
Recentisima Nova Orbis sive Americae Septentrionalis et Meridionalis ...	ALLARD	50x59cm
Recentisima Novi Orbis sive Americae Septentrionalis et Meridionalis ...	DE WIT	50x58cm
Reconnaissance Map of Circle Quadrangle Yukon- Tanana Region Alaska	U.S. GEOLOCICAL SURVEY	91x79cm
Reconnaissance of the Western Coast ... Monterey to the Columbia River	U.S. COAST SURVEY	no dimens
Reconnaissance of the Western Coast ... San Francisco to San Diego	U.S. COAST SURVEY	56x58cm
Reconnaissance of Washington Sound and Its Approaches ...	U.S. COAST SURVEY	66x58cm
Reconnoissances in the Dacota Country by G.K. Warren ...	U.S. GOV'T	90x144cm
Reconnoissances of Routes from San Antonio de Bexar [to] El Paso ...	U.S. GOV'T	62x97cm
Regenspurg. - Ratisbona. Regenspurg	MERIAN	29x36cm

Title	Author	Size
Reges Navarrae ...	CUSTODIS	40x25cm
Regiones Sub Polo Arctico	BLAEU	41x53cm
Regionum Circum Polarium Lapponiae Islandiae et Groenlandiae, Novae ...	SCHERER	23x35cm
Regna Portugalliae et Algarbiae, cum Adjacentibus Hispaniae Provinciis	LOTTER	58x49cm
Regni Bohemiae Descriptio	ORTELIUS (Folio)	34x52cm
Regni Bohemiae, Ducatus Silesiae, Marchionatus Moraviae et Lusatiae	HOMANN	47x56cm
Regni Bohemiae Nova Descriptio	CLOPPENBURGH	39x50cm
Regni Daniae Accuratissima Delineatio	CLUVER	21x25cm
Regni Daniae Novissima et Accuratissima Tabula	VISSCHER	45x54cm
Regni Galliae seu Franciae et Navarrae ...	HOMANN	48x57cm
Regni Japoniae Nova Mappa Geographica ...	SEUTTER	48x56cm
Regni Mexicani Novae Hispaniae, Floridae, Novae Angliae, Carolinae, ...	HOMANN	48x57cm
Regni Mexicani seu Novae Hispaniae Ludovicianae, N. Angliae, Carolinae ...	HOMANN	48x57cm
Regni Navarrae Accurata Tabula	DE WIT	38x50cm
Regni Poloniae et Ducatus Lithuaniae, Voliniae, Podoliae, Ucraniae ...	DE WIT	35x50cm
Regni Suiciae ...	HOMANN	49x56cm
Regni Valentiae Typus	HONDIUS	34x47cm
Regnorum Castellae Novae, Andalusiae, Granadae, Valentiae, et Murciae	DE WIT	50x59cm
Regnorum Hispaniae et Portu Galliae Tabula Generalis de l'Islnana	HOMANN	47x57cm
Regnorum Hungariae, Dalmatia, Croatiae, Sclavoniae, Bosniae, Serviae ...	HOMANN	48x57cm
Regnum Bohemiae et que Annexae Provinciae ...	VISSCHER	50x59cm
Regnum Chinae	BOTERO	15x21cm
Regnum Hiberniae Divisum in Quatour Partes quae Partes sunt Ultonia ...	DE WIT	58x50cm
Regnum Judeorum in Filios Herodis Magni per Tatrarchias ...	DE LA RUE	41x54cm
Regnum Portugalliae Divisum in Quinque Provincias Majores ...	HOMANN	59x45cm
Reims in Champanien	MEISNER	10x15cm
Rendsburgum Chilonium et Bordesholma	BLAEU	41x61cm
Repraesentatio Geographica Iteneris Maritimi Navis Victoriae ...	SCHERER	23x36cm
Repraesentatio Pugnae qua Ill.mus Luneburgensium Dux Georgius. ...	MERIAN	36x93cm
Representation du Cours Ordinaire des Vents de Traverse qui Regnent ...	DAMPIER	15x29cm
Representation Symbolique ... Les Attaques de l'Amour	SEUTTER	50x57cm
Residuum Continentis cum Adiacentibus Insulis	WYTFLIET	23x28cm
Revised Map of Belmont Terrace, Town of Babylon, Suffolk Co. N.Y. ...	LOCAL & STATE MAPS	46x130cm
Reys Togt door Thomas Coryat, van Jerusalem ... Grooten Mogols	VAN DER AA	22x29cm
Reys-Togt van Aleppo, over Ormus, door Indien ... Pegu en Siam	VAN DER AA	22x29cm
Rice's Map of Minneapolis Minnesota	RICE, G.J.	71x56cm
Richmond ... and Its Vicinity	VIRTUE	13x19cm
Riviera di Genova di Levante	BLAEU	40x50cm
Road Map of Hennepin and Ramsey Counties ... Minnesota	HIGHWAY MAPS	43x53cm
Robert Covertes ... Opper Indien, Persien en Arabie	VAN DER AA	22x29cm
Robert Covertes Swerf-Reysen no Gelede Schipbreuk van Cambaya ...	VAN DER AA	22x29cm
Rock Island City [IL]	MEYER	11x17cm
Roma	BRAUN & HOGENBERG	33x49cm
Roma	MERIAN	30x70cm
Roma	SCHEDEL	23x54cm
Roma Antiqua Triumphatrix ...	ROSSI	48x74cm
Romanae Urbis Situs, quem hoc Christi Anno 1549 habet.	MUNSTER	24x36cm
Romandiola cum D. Parmensi	MERCATOR (Small)	14x18cm
Romani Imperii Imago	MERCATOR (Small)	15x19cm
Rostochium	MERIAN	14x36cm
Rotelandiae	MORDEN	29x36cm
Round the World with Nellie Bly	PUZZLES & GAMES	41x42cm
Route of the Western Rail Road. West of Connecticut River	RAILROAD COMPANY	48x65cm
Royaume d'Irlande Divise en Ses Provinces. Subdivise en Shireries ou...	JAILLOT	89x62cm
Royaume de Norwege ...	SANSON (Folio)	52x40cm
Royaume de Portugal	DE FER (Small)	18x14cm
Rufach	BERTIUS	14x19cm
Rugia	MERCATOR (Small)	14x16cm
Russia cum Confinijs	MERCATOR (Folio)	36x46cm
Russia in Asia	TALLIS	25x32cm
Russia In Europe [Part I throught Part VIII]	S.D.U.K.	39x32cm
Russiae et Novae Zemlae Maritimae	OTTENS	49x56cm
Russiae, Moscoviae et Tartariae Descriptio ...	ORTELIUS (Folio)	35x45cm
Russiae, vulgo Moscovia ...	JANSSON	42x54cm
Russiae vulgo Moscovia Dictae Pars Australis	BLAEU	39x53cm
Russiae vulgo Moscovia Dictae Partes Septentrionalis et Orientalis	BLAEU	42x54cm

Title	Author	Size
S.R.I. Bavariae Circulus atq. Electoratus ...	VISSCHER	57x46cm
S.R.I. Circulus Rhenanus Inferior Sive Electorum Rheni Complectens ...	HOMANN	58x49cm
S.W. Colorado, San Juan Mining Region - Atlas Sheet No.61(C)	U.S. WAR DEPARTMENT	38x50cm
Sabaudia Ducatus ...	BLAEU	38x48cm
Sabine Pass ... [set of 6 maps] ... to Red River	U.S. GOV'T	various dimens
Saint Paul [MN]	U.S. PACIFIC R.R. SURVEY	15x23cm
Sale Map No.3 - Salt Marsh and Tide lands ... San Francisco ...	ALLARDT	52x59cm
Salisburgensis Jurisdictionis	ORTELIUS (Folio)	34x44cm
Saltzburg	JANSSON	38x48cm
San Diego from the Old Fort	U.S. WAR DEPARTMENT	10x18cm
San Francicso	GRAY	38x30cm
San Francisco	MEYER	11x16cm
San Joaquin, The Gateway County of California	LOCAL & STATE MAPS	64x48cm
Sant Juan del Foratche ... Jerenna ...	BRAUN & HOGENBERG	38x49cm
Santa Fe [NM]	U.S. WAR DEPARTMENT	10x18cm
Sardinia Insula	MUNSTER	26x15cm
Sarmatia et Scythia Russia et Tartaria Europaea	CLUVER	23x25cm
Savoy and Piedmont	MOLL (Small)	21x18cm
Saxoniae Inferioris Circulus juxta Principatus ...	SEUTTER	50x58cm
Scandia or Scandinavia Comprehending the Kingdom of Sweden including ...	WYLD	74x52cm
Scandia sive Regiones Septentrionales	MAGINI	13x17cm
Scandinavia Complectens Sueciae Daniae & Norvegiae Regna ...	HOMANN	48x57cm
Scavonia	MERCATOR (Small)	14x19cm
Scheeps-Togt door Ferdinand Magellaan nir Kastilien Gedaan na R. de la Plata	VAN DER AA	15x22cm
Schels van de Donkere Baai in Nieuw Zeeland 1773	COOK	20x38cm
Schlavoniae, Croatiae, Carniae, Istriae, Bosniae ...	ORTELIUS (Folio)	33x46cm
Schonladia Nuova	RUSCELLI	18x25cm
Schuylkill County, Pennsylvania	TANNER	38x51cm
Scientia Terrarum et Coelorum, or the Heavens and Earth ...	DUNN	104x124cm
Scilam	BORDONE	8x14cm
Sclavonia, Croatia, Bosnia cum Dalmatiae Parte	MERCATOR (Folio)	36x46cm
Scotia Parte Meridionale [in set with] Parte Settentrionale	CORONELLI	91x62cm
Scotia Tabula II	MERCATOR (Small)	15x18cm
Scotiae Tabula II	MERCATOR (Small)	14x19cm
Scotiae Tabula III	MERCATOR (Small)	15x19cm
Scotland with the Principal Roads from the Best Authorities	CAREY	36x28cm
Scotland with the Roads, from the Latest Survey ...	KITCHIN	36x33cm
Scythia et Serica	CLUVER	20x30cm
Section of Map Compiled in the P.R.R. Office ... the Dacota Country	U.S. PACIFIC R.R. SURVEY	38x48cm
Sectional Map No.2 of the Lands and the Line of the Texas & Pacific Ry ...	RAILROAD COMPANY	36x52cm
Sectional Map of Iowa	CRAM	69x76cm
Sectional Map of Minnesota	CHAPMAN	74x56cm
Secunda Etas Mundi	SCHEDEL	31x44cm
Secunda Europae Tabula	PTOLEMY (1511)	41x57cm
Secunda Pars Brabantiae Cuius Urbs Primaria Bruxellae	BLAEU	42x52cm
Sena	SCHEDEL	20x22cm
Septemtrionaliora Americae a Groenlandia, per Freta Davidis et Hudson ...	VAN KEULEN	50x57cm
Septentrionalium Partium Nova Tabula	RUSCELLI	18x24cm
Septentrionalium Regionum Descrip.	ORTELIUS (Folio)	36x50cm
Septentrionalium Terrarum Descriptio	CLOPPENBURGH	18x25cm
Septentrionalium Terrarum Descriptio per Gerardum Mercatorem cum ...	MERCATOR (Folio)	37x39cm
Serio-Comic War Map for the Year 1877. By F.W.R.	BACON	43x47cm
Sexta Asie Tabula	PTOLEMY (1482-1486)	29x55cm
Shaker Heights, The Van Sweringen Company	REAL ESTATE MAPS	43x61cm
Sheet No.2, Campaign Map of the Department of the Platte ... Nebraska ...	U.S. WAR DEPARTMENT	69x43cm
Shropshire	MOULE	26x20cm
Sicilia	MERCATOR (Small)	14x19cm
Sicilia Colla Distenzione, delle Nove Diocesi ...	ANONYMOUS	49x71cm
Siciliae Insulae	MORTIER	44x56cm
Siciliae Veteris Typus	JANSSON	38x48cm
Sicily	CARY	23x28cm
Siege de Charleston	MARSHALL	21x32cm
Sige de Breda. Israel Silvestre ex Parisijs ...	CALLOT	120x140cm
Silesiae Typus Descriptus et Editus a Martino Heilwig ... 1561	ORTELIUS (Folio)	28x38cm
Sitten	BERTIUS	14x19cm
Situs Terrae Circulis Coelestibus Circundatae	CELLARIUS	43x51cm
Situs Terrae Promissionis	JANSSON	38x50cm

Title	Author/Source	Size
Situs Urbis Romae	MUNSTER	29x44cm
Sketch F. No.2 Showing the Progress of the Survey of the Florida Reefs	U.S. COAST SURVEY	29x37cm
Sketch Indicating the Advancement of the Surveys ... West of the Miss...	U.S. GOV'T	83x113cm
Sketch J No.6 Showing the Progress of the Survey of San Francisco Bay	U.S. COAST SURVEY	23x41cm
Sketch Map of the Province of Southland, New Zealand	BAKER	82x52cm
Sketch of Capt. Gunnison's Route	U.S. GOV'T	33x51cm
Sketch of General Riley's Route Through the Mining Districts ... 1849	U.S. GOV'T	53x51cm
Sketch of Part of the Himma-Leh Mountains ... Paper by Capt. Johnson	ROYAL GEOG. SOC.	20x17cm
Sketch of Part of the March & Wagon Road of Lt. Colonel Cooke from ...	U.S. GOV'T	30x58cm
Sketch of Public Surveys in New Mexico ...	U.S. STATE SURVEYS	58x82cm
Sketch of Sydney Cove, Port Jackson in the County of Cumberland ...	STOCKDALE	45x52cm
Sketch of the Battle of Hobkirks Hill, Near Camden, on the 25th April ...	STEDMAN	43x29cm
Sketch of the Country Between South Pass & the Great Salt Lake	U.S. GOV'T	44x55cm
Sketch of the Country Illustrating the Late Engagement in Long Island.	GENTLEMAN'S MAGAZINE	20x31cm
Sketch of the Dyea and Skagua Trails ...	U.S. GOV'T	36x23cm
Sketch of the Harbour of Brunswick [GA]	U.S. WAR DEPARTMENT	33x36cm
Sketch of the Public Surveys in the State of Wisconsin	U.S. STATE SURVEYS	43x41cm
Sketch of the Route of Capt. Warner's Exploring Party in the Sacramento ...	U.S. GOV'T	60x27cm
Sketch of the Route Pursued by the Expedition to the Red River of the North	U.S. GOV'T	39x50cm
Sketch of the States of Massachusetts, Connecticut and Rhode Island ...	GOV'T: LOCAL & STATE	46x51cm
Sketch Showing the Progress of the Survey in Section IX from 1848 to ...	U.S. COAST SURVEY	79x93cm
Societas Iesu per Universum Mundum Diffusa Praedicat Christi Evangelium	SCHERER	23x36cm
Solothurensis Civitatis ...	MUNSTER	23x30cm
Somerset-shire Described: Ad in to Hundreds Devided, with ... Bathe	SPEED	38x51cm
Sous's Chart of the Cattegat	HEATHER	64x78cm
South Africa	S.D.U.K.	31x39cm
South America	COLTON (Atlas Maps)	39x33cm
South America Performed under the Patronage of Louis	BOLTON	120x75cm
South Atlantic	IMRAY	100x158cm
South Carolina	ARROWSMITH & LEWIS	22x27cm
South Carolina	BRADFORD	29x37cm
South Carolina	CAREY	15x19cm
South Carolina	MORSE & BREESE	30x38cm
South Carolina	SCOTT	15x18cm
South Dakota	CRAM	26x33cm
South West View of Fort George with the City of New York	RUSSELL	18x20cm
Southern Provinces of the United States	THOMSON	50x56cm
Southern States	SMITH, ROSWELL C.	27x42cm
Southwestern Colorado Atlas Sheet No.61 (C)	U.S. WAR DEPARTMENT	43x51cm
Spaine ...	SPEED	42x54cm
Spaine Newly Described with Many Additions, both in the Attires ...	SPEED	42x54cm
Spallato	CAMOCIO	15x20cm
Spanien und Portugal	HILDBURGHAUSEN BIBLIO	21x26cm
Spanish Dominions in N. America	MacPHERSON	19x24cm
Spanish North America	THOMSON	51x62cm
Spanish North America Southern Part	THOMSON	48x65cm
St. Christophers ... [with] St. Lucia ... [&] Nevis	THOMSON	50x59cm
St. George Harbr. ... [Grenada]	BRITISH ADMIRALTY	64x99cm
St. Jago	DAPPER	13x15cm
St. Joseph Missouri ... the Queen City of the Missouri Valley	RAND, McNALLY (non-atlas)	51x74cm
St. Louis World's Fair, Louisiana Purchase Exposition ...	LOCAL & STATE POCKET	25x46cm
St. Omer mitt Nahe Anliegender Gegend	BODENEHR	16x27cm
Stadt St Domingo	PREVOST D'EXILES	18x26cm
Standard Railway Map of South Africa ...	JUTA	96x75cm
Stanford's Map of the Seat of War in America (Sheet 1)	STANFORD	69x56cm
State Highway Department's ... State of Oregon	HIGHWAY MAPS	33x51cm
State of Idaho	U.S. STATE SURVEYS	116x74cm
State of Minnesota	U.S. STATE SURVEYS	76x66cm
State of Ohio	U.S. STATE SURVEYS	38x46cm
State of Oregon	U.S. STATE SURVEYS	64x74cm
State of Oregon	U.S. STATE SURVEYS	43x56cm
State of Sequoyah	GAST & CO.	41x38cm
State of Wisconsin	U.S. STATE SURVEYS	43x41cm
Status Mutinensis in Suas Ditiones ...	HOMANN	48x51cm
Statuum Moroccanorum ...	HOMANN	49x55cm
Statuum Totius Italiae ...	HOMANN	49x57cm
Stellarum Fixarum Hemisphaerium Boreale ... [with] ... Australe ...	SENEX	Diam: 65cm

Title	Author	Size
Stockholm	GOTTFRIED	7x14cm
Stockholm	S.D.U.K.	33x40cm
Stockholm / Stocholm	BRAUN & HOGENBERG	32x47cm
Strasburg	BERTIUS	14x20cm
Street and Road Map of San Jose and Vicinity, California	LOCAL & STATE POCKET	38x51cm
Street Guide Map of Chicago	RAND, McNALLY (atlas maps)	70x48cm
Street Number Map of Chicago	LOCAL & STATE POCKET	86x61cm
Suchuen; et Xensi, Provincia sue Praefecturae Regni Sinensis ...	VALK & SCHENK	46x52cm
Sud-Gotlande, et Pays Circomvoisins	SANSON (Folio)	40x52cm
Suecia et Norwegia	MERCATOR (Small)	15x18cm
Suede Norvege et Danemark	MONIN	40x28cm
Suevia et Bavaria XI Nova Tabula	MUNSTER	27x34cm
Suevia quae cis Codanum Suitsinum	CLUVER	18x25cm
Sueviae Circulus sive Liga Vulgo Schwabische Kraiss. David Seltzlin ...	ORTELIUS (Folio)	32x24cm
Suffolke, Described ...	SPEED	38x52cm
Suite des Isles Antilles 1 Partie	BELLIN (Small)	22x16cm
Sumatra	RAMUSIO	27x37cm
Sumatra ein Grosse Insel ...	MUNSTER	30x36cm
Sumatrae ...	JANSSON	43x52cm
Sumatrae et Insularum Locorumque ... Circumiacentium Tabula Nova	JANSSON	42x52cm
Superior et Inferior Hassiae Landgraviatus ...	SEUTTER	49x56cm
Surrey	MORDEN	36x43cm
Surrey	PIGOT	23x35cm
Survey of a Valley and Ponds Auxiliary ... Canal between Buzzards & ...	U.S. WAR DEPARTMENT	21x36cm
Sussex	MORDEN	34x42cm
Sussex	ROCQUE	16x20cm
Sussex	SPEED	39x51cm
Sweden & Norway	TANNER	28x22cm
Sweden and Norway	MOLL (Small)	17x18cm
Swedish Pomerania, with the Island of Rugen	FADEN	58x60cm
Syria Cypern Palestina Mesopotamia Babylonia Chaldea und Zwey Arabia ...	MUNSTER	25x33cm
Systems Planetaires	LAPIE	41x81cm
ΘPAKH. Thraciae Veteris Typus	JANSSON	36x48cm
'T Gebiedt van Guadalajara, Niew Mexico en California ...	SANSON (Small)	20x23cm
T Zuider America van Terra Firma ou Gujana voor by Rio de la Plata ...	VAN DER AA	20x30cm
Tab. XII. Asiae. Tabrobanam Repraesentans	MERCATOR (Folio)	35x36cm
Tab. XII. Asiae. Taprobanam Repraesentans	PTOLEMY (1578-1730)	34x36cm
Tabor Civitas Anno 1621 Obsessa et Capta	JANSSON	34x46cm
Tabu. Moder. Anglie & Hiber.	WALDSEEMULLER	30x41cm
Tabu. Moder. Indiae	FRIES	34x44cm
Tabu. Nova Asiae Mi.	FRIES	26x38cm
Tabu. Nova Partis Aphri	FRIES	32x40cm
Tabula Anemographica seu Pyxis Nautica Ventorum Nomina Sex Linguis	JANSSON	44x56cm
Tabula Anemographica seu Pyxis Nautica, vulgo Compass Charte	LOTTER	50x58cm
Tabula Aphricae I	MAGINI	13x17cm
Tabula Aphricae II	RUSCELLI	19x25cm
Tabula Aphricae III	RUSCELLI	18x25cm
Tabula Aphricae IIII	RUSCELLI	19x25cm
Tabula Asia I	MUNSTER	26x34cm
Tabula Asia IX	RUSCELLI	19x24cm
Tabula Asiae IIII	GASTALDI	14x18cm
Tabula Asiae IIII	MAGINI	13x17cm
Tabula Asiae IIII	RUSCELLI	18x24cm
Tabula Asiae V	RUSCELLI	19x25cm
Tabula Asiae VI	MAGINI	13x17cm
Tabula Asiae VI	RUSCELLI	18x23cm
Tabula Asiae IX	MAGINI	13x17cm
Tabula Asiae X	MUNSTER	26x34cm
Tabula Asiae XI	MAGINI	13x17cm
Tabula Asiae XI	MUNSTER	25x34cm
Tabula Asiae XII	MAGINI	13x17cm
Tabula Asiae XII	MUNSTER	26x34cm
Tabula Cananaeae ...	PURCHAS	15x18cm
Tabula Comitatus Artesiae	DE WIT	46x55cm
Tabula Electoratus Brandenburgici, Meckelenburgi, ... Pomeraniae	VISSCHER	45x54cm
Tabula Europae Prima	MAGINI	13x17cm
Tabula Europae I	MUNSTER	30x33cm

Tabula Europae I	RUSCELLI	18x25cm
Tabula Europae II	GASTALDI	13x17cm
Tabula Europae II	MUNSTER	27x34cm
Tabula Europae IIII	MAGINI	13x17cm
Tabula Europae V	RUSCELLI	18x26cm
Tabula Europae VI	MAGINI	13x18cm
Tabula Europae VI	RUSCELLI	15x18cm
Tabula Europae VIII	MUNSTER	27x34cm
Tabula Europae X	MAGINI	13x17cm
Tabula Frisiae, Groningae, et Territoriemdensis	VISSCHER	110x138cm
Tabula Geodoborica Itinerum a Varijs in Cataium ...	KIRCHER	27x35cm
Tabula Geogra. Regni Congo	DE BRY	31x38cm
Tabula Geograph in qua Europa, Africa, Asiaq. et Circumiacentium ...	HONDIUS	27x42cm
Tabula Geographica Hemisphaerii Australis ...	VON EULER	31x32cm
Tabula Geographica, in qua Lisraelitarum, ab Aegypto ad Kenahanaeam ...	CLOPPENBURGH	29x50cm
Tabula Geographica in qua Omnes Regiones Urbes, Oppida, Loca et Fluvii ...	CLOPPENBURGH	28x50cm
Tabula Geographica, in qua Paradisus, nec non Regiones, Urbes Oppida ...	PLANCIUS	29x33cm
Tabula Geographica, in qua Paradisus, nec non Regiones, Urbes Oppida ...	PLANCIUS	29x49cm
Tabula Geographica Terrae Sanctae	BONFRERIUS	39x115cm
Tabula Geographico - Hydrographica Motus Oceani Currentes, Abyssos ...	ZAHN	36x42cm
Tabula Greaciae	MUNSTER	25x32cm
Tabula I Asiae	FRIES	29x44cm
Tabula Indiae Orientalis ...	DE WIT	46x57cm
Tabula Indiae Orientalis et Regnorum Adjacentium J. van Braam ...	VALENTYN	50x66cm
Tabula Islandiae	HONDIUS	38x49cm
Tabula Islandiae Auctore Georgio Carolo Flandro	BLAEU	38x50cm
Tabula Magellanica Qua Tierrae del Fuego	JANSSON	41x53cm
Tabula Magellanica qua Tierrae del Fuego	VALK & SCHENK	41x52cm
Tabula Magellanica, qua Tierrae de Fuego ...	OGILBY	29x36cm
Tabula Magellanica, qua Tierrae del Fuego ...	BLAEU	42x54cm
Tabula Marchionatus Brandenburgici Et Ducatus Pomeraniae ...	HOMANN	48x56cm
Tabula Moderna Terra Sanctae	PTOLEMY (1482-1486)	25x53cm
Tabula Nova Angliae & Hiberniae	WALDSEEMULLER	28x41cm
Tabula Nova Complectens Praefecturas Normanniae et Britanniae ...	VISSCHER	47x56cm
Tabula Nova Hibernie Anglie et Scotie	WALDSEEMULLER	38x52cm
Tabula Nova Partis Africae	PTOLEMY (1522-1541)	28x40cm
Tabula Nova Totius Regni Poloniae ...	SANSON (Folio)	42x55cm
Tabula Novissima Accuratissima Regnorum Angliae, Scotiae Hiberniae	SEUTTER	58x50cm
Tabula Orbis cum Descrizzione Ventorum	FRIES	34x48cm
Tabula Regni Poloniae, Ducatus Lithuaniae ...	JAILLOT	47x60cm
Tabula Russia vulgo Moscovia ...	DE WIT	45x56cm
Tabula Terrae Novae Zemblae ...	DE BRY	18x24cm
Tabula Terre Sanctae	FRIES	27x41cm
Tabula Totius Orbis Terrarum	HALLEY	20x48cm
Tabula VI Asiae	FRIES	31x46cm
Tabulam Hanc Aegypti, Si Aequus ac Dilignes Lecot, cum Alys ...	DE BRY	55x41cm
Tartaria	HONDIUS	36x49cm
Tartaria	MERCATOR (Folio)	34x50cm
Tartaria sive Magni Chami Imperium	BLAEU	39x50cm
Tartariae Imperium	MAGINI	13x17cm
Tartariae sive Magni Chami Regni Typus	ORTELIUS (Folio)	36x48cm
Tasmania or Van Diemens Land	WYLD	54x39cm
Taurica Cheronesus	MERCATOR (Small)	13x17cm
Tavola, & Discrizzione Universale di Tutta l'Africa	MUNSTER	30x40cm
Tavola dell'Isole Nuove ...	MUNSTER	32x41cm
Tavola della Oriental Regione dell' Asia	MUNSTER	25x33cm
Tavola Nuova d'Italia	RUSCELLI	19x25cm
Tavola Nuova di Germania	RUSCELLI	18x25cm
Tegg's New Plan of London &c. with 360 References to the Principal ...	TEGG	44x62cm
Tempe	ORTELIUS (Folio)	36x48cm
Temperance Map	CONCEPT MAPS	31x35cm
Tennessee	ARROWSMITH & LEWIS	22x27cm
Tennessee & Kentucky	BRADFORD	20x25cm
Terra Antarctica	DU VAL	10x12cm
Terra Australis Incognita	JANSSON	43x49cm
Terra Firma and the Caribbe Islands &c.	MOLL (Small)	16x19cm
Terra Nova	BERTIUS	9x12cm

Title	Author	Size
Terra Nova ac Maris Tractus Circa Novam Franciam ... Venezuela	DE WIT	49x57cm
Terra Promissa in Sortes seu Tribus XII ...	SANSON (Folio)	40x52cm
Terra Promissa in Sortes seu Tribus XII Distincta seu Tabula ad Librum ...	DE LA RUE	41x51cm
Terra Sancta a Petro Laicstain Perlustrata, et ab Eius Ore et Schedis ...	ORTELIUS (Folio)	37x50cm
Terra Sancta quae in Sacris Terra Promissionis olim Palestina	BLAEU	38x50cm
Terra Sancta XXIII Nova Tabula	MUNSTER	31x40cm
Terra Sancta, sive Promissionis, olim Palestina Recens Delineata ...	VISSCHER	47x56cm
Terrae Israel	FULLER	34x50cm
Terrae Yemen Maxima Pars, seu Imperii Imami, Principatus Kaukeban ...	LOTTER	57x37cm
Terre Artiche ...	CORONELLI	46x61cm
Terre Sainte ...	VAN DER AA	23x29cm
Terrestrial Globe [with] Celestial Globe	MIDDLETON	16x26cm
Territories of New Mexico and Utah	COLTON (Atlas Maps)	32x41cm
Territories of Washington and Oregon	COLTON (Atlas Maps)	34x41cm
Territorii Bergensis Accuratissima Descriptio	BLAEU	42x55cm
Territorio di Cremona	JANSSON	38x48cm
Territorium Metense ... Le Pais Messin	BLAEU	39x50cm
Territory and Military Department of Utah ... 1860	U.S. UNION & CONFED.	41x69cm
Territory of Arizona	U.S. STATE SURVEYS	51x43cm
Territory of Dakota	U.S. STATE SURVEYS	74x61cm
Territory of Hawaii	U.S. GOV'T	76x107cm
Territory of Idaho	MITCHELL, S.A. (1860+)	36x27cm
Territory of New Mexico	U.S. STATE SURVEYS	56x46cm
Territory of New Mexico	U.S. WAR DEPARTMENT	38x50cm
Tetrachia Ducatus Geldriae Neomagensis	DE WIT	45x56cm
Texas	ASHER & ADAMS	56x41cm
Texas	BRADFORD	36x29cm
Texas	COLTON (Atlas Maps)	32x40cm
Texas	COLTON (Pocket & Wall)	32x38cm
Texas	CRAM	33x44cm
Texas	McNALLY	21x27cm
Texas	MORSE & GASTON	16x13cm
Texas	MORSE, SIDNEY	13x14cm
Texas	RAND, McNALLY (atlas maps)	48x66cm
Texas	SAVAGE	12x20cm
Texas	SMITH, ROSWELL C.	25x22cm
Texas	STEDMAN, BROWN & LYONS	29x38cm
Texas	WALKER, H.B	41x56cm
Texas	WARNER & BEERS	30x42cm
Texas ...	MEYER	29x36cm
Texas and Indian Territory	COLTON (Atlas Maps)	20x17cm
Texas and Part of Mexico & the United States Showing ... Santa Fe Exped...	KENDALL	41x29cm
Texas Engraved for the People's Publishing Co.	CRAM	30x43cm
Texas in 1836	KEMBLE	21x24cm
Texas, New Mexico, & Indian Territory ...	BARTHOLOMEW	29x41cm
Texas, Western Part and Panhandle	CENTURY ATLAS	38x27cm
That Part of Disturnell's Treaty Map in the Vicinity of the Rio Grande ...	U.S. GOV'T	22x28cm
The ... Russian Empire	KITCHIN	50x128cm
The Antilles or West-India Islands	S.D.U.K.	30x39cm
The Artificial Sphere	MOLL (Small)	13x10cm
The Atlantic Ocean	PHILIP, G.	60x50cm
The Australian Colonies.	S.D.U.K.	40x68cm
The Austrian & French Netherlands Agreeable to the Barrier ...	GENTLEMAN'S MAGAZINE	11x20cm
The Bahama Banks and Gulf of Florida	BLUNT	97x124cm
The Barritt-Serviss Star and Planet Finder. Northern Hemisphere	ARTIFACTS	38x38cm
The Basin of the Pacific	WYLD	57x84cm
The Battle Front of the Drys	CONCEPT MAPS	69x107cm
The Bay and River of Delaware	BLUNT	18x21cm
The British & French Dominions in North America ...	BOWLES	43x56cm
The British Colonies in North America ...	GUTHRIE	33x33cm
The British Governments in Nth. America Laid Down Agreeable ...	GENTLEMAN'S MAGAZINE	20x23cm
The British Islands in the West Indies	S.D.U.K.	32x39cm
The British Isles, Compiled from Government Ordnance	DAW	153x141cm
The Caribbe Islands and Guayana ...	FADEN	74x60cm
The Citty Osacco - De Stadt Osacco	OGILBY	26x70cm
The Coast of New England	DES BARRES	106x74cm
The Coast of the United States, Sheet No.2 from Cape Lookout to Cape ...	BLUNT	78x118cm

Title	Author/Publisher	Size
The Coast of West Florida and Louisiana, by Thos. Jefferys Geographer ...	JEFFERYS	48x63cm
The Coast of West Florida and Louisiana, by Thos. Jefferys Geographer ...	JEFFERYS	47x122cm
The Countie and Citie of Lyncoln Described with the Armes of Them ...	SPEED	39x52cm
The Countie of Nottingham Described, the Shire Townes Situation ...	SPEED	39x51cm
The Countye Palatine of Chester with That Most Ancient Citie Described	SPEED	39x51cm
The Dominions of Moscovy or Russia	MOLL (Small)	18x25cm
The East Indies Drawn from the Latest Discoveries ...	GENTLEMAN'S MAGAZINE	23x26cm
The East Indies with the Roads	LAURIE & WHITTLE	106x136cm
The East Part of India or India beyond the R. Ganges ...	MOLL (Small)	18x26cm
The English Empire in America, Newfound-Land, Canada, Hudsons Bay ...	MOLL (Small)	22x18cm
The Environs of Dublin	WELLER	43x30cm
The Environs of London	COLTON (Atlas Maps)	33x41cm
The Environs of London Reduced from an Actual Survey in 16 Sheets ...	ROCQUE	44x66cm
The Gallapagos Islands Discovered and Described by Capt. Cowley ...	BOWEN, EMANUEL	32x21cm
The Geography of the Great Solar Eclipse of July, 14. MDCCXLVIII ...	GENTLEMAN'S MAGAZINE	30x44cm
The Gold and Coal Fields of Alaska ... Steamer Routes and Trails	EMMONS	60x72cm
The Great Province of Rio de la Plata	MOLL (Small)	17x19cm
The Great Railroad Routes to the Pacific and Their Connection	U.S. GOV'T	34x69cm
The Harbor of Holmes Hole and the Harbor of Tarpaulin Cove [MA]	U.S. COAST SURVEY	36x48cm
The Holy Land and Its Borders	JOHNSON	57x47cm
The Invasions of England and Ireland with Al Their Civill Wars ...	SPEED	38x51cm
The Irish or St. George's Channel Compiled from the Most Recent Surveys	IMRAY	189x103cm
The Island of Cuba with Part of the Bahamas Banks & the Martyrs	JEFFERYS	50x63cm
The Isle of California, New Mexico, Louisiane, the River Misisipi ... Canada	MOLL (Small)	16x19cm
The Isles of Montreal, As They Have Been Survey'd by the French ...	LONDON MAGAZINE	23x33cm
The Jerseys, &c.&c.	GORDON, WILLIAM	30x23cm
The Kingdom of Korea [called by the Chinese Kau-Li-Quae ...]	DU HALDE	51x35cm
The Kingdome of China ...	SPEED	40x51cm
The Kingdome of England	SPEED	40x52cm
The Kingdome of Great Britaine and Ireland	SPEED	38x51cm
The Kingdome of Persia with the Cheef Citties and Habites ...	SPEED	40x51cm
The Kingdome of Scotland	SPEED	38x51cm
The Land of Canaan Travel'd over by O:S: Jesus Christ and by His Apostles	WARE	36x43cm
The Leeward & Windward Islands	WELLER	43x30cm
The Mape of Hungari ...	SPEED	40x51cm
The Moqui Mesas	HAYDEN, F.V.	19x34cm
The National Map of the Territory of the United States, from the Mississippi	KEELER	124x151cm
The North Part of America Conteyning Newfoundland ... Island of California...	PURCHAS	29x36cm
The North Prospect of the City of Edinburgh	SLEZER	44x107cm
The North-West-Coast of North America and Adjacent Territories ...	BURR	41x54cm
The Northwest Presents the Greatest Opportunities for Settlers of Any ...	RAILROAD COMPANY	62x52cm
The Only Correct Map of the City of Cleveland Issued in 1876	LOCAL & STATE POCKET	50x73cm
The Outtermost or the Fartheste Parte of the Easterne Sea. Eastwardly ...	WAGHENAER	33x51cm
The Pacific Region	GOODRICH	18x15cm
The Part of Virginia Which Was the Seat of Action	GORDON, WILLIAM	18x25cm
The Phat Boy's Delineations of the St. Lawrence River	LOCAL & STATE POCKET	16x240cm
The Philippine Islands and Other of the East Indies	MOLL (Small)	18x26cm
The Plan of Constantinople	SALMON	17x28cm
The Plan of Edenburgh Exactly Done ...	DE WIT	42x105cm
The Plan of the City and Castle of Edinburgh	EDGAR	30x60cm
The Position of the Yukon Goldfields ... Canada	STANFORD	51x64cm
The Principal Islands of the East Indies According to ye Newest ...	MOLL (Small)	17x26cm
The Principal Transportation Lines West of Chicago, St. Louis & New O...	RAILROAD COMPANY	52x58cm
The Province of Leinster Surveyed ...	BERRY	44x56cm
The Provinces of New York and New Jersey, with Part of Pensilvania, ...	SAYER	136x54cm
The Provinces of New York and New Jersey, with Part of Pensilvania, ...	SAYER & BENNETT	103x52cm
The River of Thames from London to the Buoy of ye Noure	MOUNT & PAGE	47x59cm
The Road from Bristol ... to Exeter ...	OGILBY	33x43cm
The Road from Tinmouth ... to ... Carlisle	OGILBY	33x43cm
The Road from Welshpool ... to ... Carnarvan ...	OGILBY	33x43cm
The Sacramento Valley from the American River to Butte Creek	U.S. GOV'T	56x44cm
The Scots Settlement in America Called New Caledonia	MOLL (Small)	25x20cm
The Sea Coasts betweene Dover & Orfordnes: ...River of Thames ...	WAGHENAER	32x50cm
The Seige of Vicksburg. Major General U.S. Grant, Commanding ...	MATHEWS	35x60cm
The Seven United Provinces with the Dutch and Austrian Netherlands	LOCKHEAD	23x17cm
The Siege of Rhode Island, Taken from Mr. Brindley's House ...	GENTLEMAN'S MAGAZINE	13x22cm
The Smaller Islands in the British Ocean	MORDEN	36x42cm

Title	Author	Size
The South Eastern Portion of Australia	ARROWSMITH	52x64cm
The State of Connecticut, with All the New Towns, Including Parts of ...	STEBBINS	74x99cm
The State of Maryland, from the Best Authorities. By Samuel Lewis	CAREY	28x42cm
The State of New Hampshire Compiled Chiefly from Actual Surveys	PAYNE	30x18cm
The State of New Jersey	BIEN	89x63cm
The State of New Jersey, Compiled from the Most Authentic Information	CAREY	47x30cm
The State of New York, from New & Original Surveys	FRENCH & SMITH	168x183cm
The State of Virginia from the Best Authorities. 1799	PAYNE	19x25cm
The Straits of Sincapore with Those of Drion, Sabon, Mandol, &ca ...	LAURIE & WHITTLE	43x58cm
The Telegraph Hill Observatory, San Francisco, California	BRITTON & REY	41x64cm
The Territories of New Mexico & Utah	COLTON (Atlas Maps)	30x37cm
The Territories of Washington and Oregon	COLTON (Atlas Maps)	33x39cm
The Tourist Pocket Map of Pennsylvania Exhibiting Its Internal ...	MITCHELL, S.A. (non-atlas)	32x38cm
The Tourists Ideal Route, Rome, Watertown & Ogdensburg Railroad ...	RAILROAD COMPANY	18x61cm
The Tourist's Map of the State of Ohio	MITCHELL, S.A. (non-atlas)	39x32cm
The Tourist's Pocket Map of the State of Ohio Exhibiting Its Internal ...	MITCHELL, S.A. (non-atlas)	38x32cm
The Tourist's Pocket Map of the State of Tennessee	MITCHELL, S.A. (non-atlas)	32x39cm
The Traveler's Guide ... of the United States	TANNER	46x56cm
The Traveler's Guide. A Map of the Roads, Canals and Steam Boat Routes	TANNER	45x56cm
The Traveller's and Tourist's Guide through the United States, Canada, etc.	WILLIAMS, W.	61x74cm
The Travellers Guide. A New and Correct Map of the United States ...	LEWIS	75x105cm
The Turkish Empire	SPEED	40x52cm
The United States, 1861	ANONYMOUS	11x18cm
The United States No.12	LETTS	32x39cm
The United States of America	CARY	28x23cm
The United States of America	COLTON (Atlas Maps)	41x66cm
The United States of America	COLTON (Pocket & Wall)	48x71cm
The United States of America	GORDON, WILLIAM	29x29cm
The United States of America [with] The Course of the River St. Laurence	THOMSON	45x63cm
The United States of America, According to the Treaty of Peace of 1784	GUTHRIE	18x20cm
The United States of America Confirmed by Treaty 1783	WILKINSON	24x28cm
The United States, of North America. (General Map)	BLACKIE	34x50cm
The United States of North America, Pacific States [with North Atlantic]	BLACKIE	34x25cm
The United States of North America with the British Territorys ... Treaty ...	LOCKHEAD	23x20cm
The West End Plateau of the City of New York	VIELE	33x120cm
The West India Islands	CARY	23x28cm
The West Indies and Gulf of Mexico from the Latest Discoveries ...	RUSSELL	23x36cm
The West Indies, and Gulf of Mexico from the Latest Discoveries ...	TOWN & COUNTRY MAG.	23x35cm
The West Indies Exhibiting the English, French, Spanish, Dutch & Danish ...	MIDDLETON	19x28cm
The West Indies from the Best Authorities	GUTHRIE	19x32cm
The Windward or South Caribbean Islands	LOWRY	47x34cm
The Windward Passage with the Several Passages, from the East End ...	JEFFERYS	50x64cm
The World. ... by S. Hall	HALL, SIDNEY	22x39cm
The World Agreeable to the Latest Discoveries	POWELL	16x26cm
The World Agreeable to the Latest Discoveries ...	JEFFERYS	19x39cm
The World, Based on Mercator's Projection ...	BURR	43x53cm
The World from the Best Authorities	KITCHIN	18x37cm
The World from the Best Authorities	PAYNE	Diam: 19cm
The World from the Discoveries & Observations Made in the Latest ...	ARROWSMITH	23x45cm
The World in Hemispheres	GUYOT	20x27cm
The World in Hemispheres	JOHNSTON	39x57cm
The World in Hemispheres with ... Mountains and ... Rivers ...	FULLARTON	43x53cm
The World in Hemispheres with Other Projections &c. &c.	MITCHELL, S.A. (1860+)	28x33cm
The World in Planisphere	MOLL (Small)	16x19cm
The World Including the Discoveries Made by Capt. Cook	BOWEN, EMANUEL	27x45cm
The World Including the Discoveries of Capt. Cook and Other ...	BOWEN, THOMAS	34x46cm
The World, Including the Late Discoveries, by Captn. Cook and Other ...	BOWEN, THOMAS	27x46cm
The World on an Equatorial Projection [with] The World on a Polar ...	MITCHELL, S.A. (to 1859)	29x20cm
The World on Mercator's Projection	FINLEY	22x28cm
The World on Mercator's Projection	S.D.U.K.	39x66cm
The World with the Latest Discoveries	LOCKHEAD	23x40cm
The World with the Latest Discoveries to the Present Year 1808	RUSSELL	22x43cm
The World with the Tracks & Discoveries of the Latest Navigators	FINDLAY	23x43cm
Theatre des Operations de l'Armee du Nord et Desert que le General Arnold ...	MARSHALL	25x22cm
Theatre des Operations des Armees Americaine et Britannique ... Maryland	MARSHALL	25x39cm
Theatre des Operations les Plus Importantes de l'Armee du Sud ... Virginie ...	MARSHALL	36x26cm
Theatrum Belli ... in Partibus Regnorum Serviae et Bosniae	HOMANN	54x57cm

Title	Author	Size
Theatrum Belli in America Septentrionali	RHODE	57x80cm
Theatrum Belli Russorum Victoriis ... Turcicarum et Tartaricum ...	SEUTTER	49x57cm
Theatrum Historicum	DE L'ISLE	48x65cm
Theoria Veneris et Mercurii	VALK & SCHENK	43x51cm
Thibet, Mongolia and Mandchouria	TALLIS	25x32cm
This Chart Exhibiting the Tracks of the Discovery and Antelope ... Paracels	MANUSCRIPT MAPS	64x64cm
This Chart of Kingsale Harbour	COLLINS, G.	45x58cm
Thuringia	QUAD	22x27cm
Tierra Nova	GASTALDI	13x17cm
Tierra Nueva	GASTALDI	13x17cm
Tierra Nueva	RUSCELLI	19x26cm
Tijpus Freti Magellanici quod Georgius Spilbergius cum Classe Lustravit	COMMELIN	15x43cm
Tipus Orbis Terrarum	SOLIS	34x50cm
Tirolis Comitatus Continens Episcop. Tridentinum et Brixiensem ...	LOTTER	49x58cm
To Evan Neapean ... This Chart of the Sound and Grounds ...	HEATHER	64x77cm
To Her Most Sacred Majesty Carolina Queen ... This Map of Europe ...	MOLL (Large)	58x96cm
To Sir Watkin Williams Wynn, Bart., This Map of North Wales ...	EVANS	73x62cm
To the Merchants & Ship Owners ... Chart of the Indian & Pacific Oceans	BLACHFORD	98x181cm
To the Merchants and Masters ... Chart of the East Coast of England ...	HEATHER	63x74cm
To the Most Noble Thomas Holles Pelham ... County of Middlesex ...	SEALE	52x71cm
To the Officers of the Army ... of the [US] ... Upper and Lower Canada ...	KENSETT	35x46cm
To the Right Honorable Charles Earl of Sunderland ... South America ...	MOLL (Large)	57x96cm
To the Right Honorable Lord Duncan ... Chart of the Coasts of Holland ...	HEATHER	64x77cm
To the Right Honorable The Master ... Chart of the Downs and Margate ...	HEATHER	62x78cm
To the Right Honourable John Lord Sommers ... Map of North America ...	MOLL (Large)	58x97cm
To the Right Honourable William Lord Cowper, ... This Map of Asia ...	MOLL (Large)	58x96cm
Toledo	LASOR A VAREA	8x13cm
Tolosa	SCHEDEL	20x22cm
Topocraphical [sic] Map of the Road from Fort Smith, Arks. to Santa Fe ...	U.S. GOV'T	37x71cm
Topographic Map of Colorado, 1913	LOCAL & STATE WALL	97x140cm
Topographical Map of Essex County, Massachusetts	WALLING	152x152cm
Topographical Map of the City of New York Showing the Original Water ...	VIELE	44x154cm
Topographical Map Showing the Locations of the Sutro Tunnel ...	GOV'T: LOCAL & STATE	36x28cm
Topographical Sketch of the Battlefield of Stone's River near ...	U.S. WAR DEPARTMENT	51x58cm
Topographical Sketch of the Gold & Quicksilver District of California ...	U.S. GOV'T	55x39cm
Topographical Sketch of the Southernmost Point of the Port of San Diego	U.S. GOV'T	44x57cm
Topography of the Denver Basin Colorado	U.S. GEOLOGICAL SURVEY	56x53cm
Torino Metropoli del Piamonte	LASOR A VAREA	12x18cm
Toscana Nuova Tabula	RUSCELLI	17x25cm
Totius Americae ...	HOMANN	48x58cm
Totius Americae Septentrionalis et Meridionalis ...	HOMANN	49x57cm
Totius Europae Littora Novissime Edita ...	RENARD	71x89cm
Totius Flumines Rheni ...	DE WIT	46x53cm
Totius Italiae Tabula	VISSCHER	46x56cm
Totius Orbis Cogniti Universalis Descriptio	MERULA	30x50cm
Tours	MUNSTER	25x34cm
Town Site of La Gloria [Cuba]	REAL ESTATE MAPS	61x67cm
Township, County and Railroad Map of Dakota	RAND, McNALLY (non-atlas)	53x46cm
Tractuum Borussiae, circa Gedanum et Elbingam ab Incolis Werder ...	JANSSON	41x49cm
Trajectum. - Traiectum Clara et Vetus Est Episcopalis Civitas	BRAUN & HOGENBERG	33x48cm
Transylvania XXI Nova Tabula	MUNSTER	26x34cm
Trapano in Sicilien	BODENEHR	16x19cm
Travelers Guide through the United States ...	MITCHELL, S.A. (non-atlas)	46x56cm
Tribus Aser, Id Est, Portio Illa Terrae Sanctae, quae Tribui Aser in Divisione ...	VAN ADRICHEM	22x38cm
Tribus Iuda, Id Est, Pars Illa Terrae Sancta, quam in Ingressu Tribus Iuda ...	VAN ADRICHEM	33x42cm
Tubingen	MERIAN	19x29cm
Tunison's South Dakota	TUNISON	25x32cm
Tunison's Texas and Indian Territory	TUNISON	50x33cm
Turcici Imperii Descriptio	ORTELIUS (Folio)	38x50cm
Turcici Imperii Imago	CLOPPENBURGH	19x25cm
Turcici Imperii Imago	HONDIUS	15x20cm
Turcicum Imperium	BLAEU	41x52cm
Turcicum Imperium	JANSSON	42x52cm
Turkey in Asia	TANNER	28x36cm
Turkey in Europe	TALLIS	25x33cm
Turquie d'Asie, Arabie, Perse, Tartarie Independante	DE VAUGONDY	23x21cm
Tuscia	MAGINI	13x17cm

Typus Choro-Topographicus Regiae ... Lutetiae Parisiorum ...	SEUTTER	50x58cm
Typus Chorographicus, Celebrium Locorum in Regno Iudae et Israhel ...	ORTELIUS (Folio)	36x46cm
Typus Cosmographicus Universalis	VADIANUS	24x38cm
Typus Frisiae Orientalis ...	JANSSON	38x50cm
Typus Orarum Maritimarum Guineae, Manicongo & Angolao ... Bonae Spei	VAN LINSCHOTEN	38x53cm
Typus Orbis Descriptione Ptolemaei	FRIES	30x46cm
Typus Orbis Terrarum	BERTIUS	10x13cm
Typus Orbis Terrarum	CLOPPENBURGH	19x26cm
Typus Orbis Terrarum	HONDIUS	14x20cm
Typus Orbis Terrarum	JANSSON	15x20cm
Typus Orbis Terrarum	MUNSTER	34x50cm
Typus Orbis Terrarum	ORTELIUS (Folio)	36x49cm
Typus Orbis Terrarum [in set with 4 continents]	ORTELIUS (Folio)	36x48cm
Typus Orbis Terrarum, ad Imitationem Universalis Gerhardi Mercatoris ...	QUAD	22x32cm
Typus Orbis Universalis	MUNSTER	26x38cm
Typus Totius Orbis Terraquei Geographice Delineatus ...	SCHERER	22x35cm
Tyrus	MUNSTER	10x11cm
Ubersicht von Nord-America ...	BERGHAUS	33x41cm
Uinta Indian Reservation & Wagon Road from Heber City ... Utah Terr...	U.S. GEOLOGICAL SURVEY	41x51cm
Ukrania quae et Terrae Cosaccorum cum Vicinis Walachiae, Moldaviae ...	HOMANN	47x56cm
Ukrania seu Cosacorum Regio Walachia item Moldavia et Tartaria	WEIGEL	33x39cm
Ulrichstein am Vogel	MEISNER	10x15cm
Ultonia, Conatia, et Media	MERCATOR (Small)	14x20cm
Ultonia; Hibernis Cuj-Gujlly; Anglis Ulster	BLAEU	38x50cm
Ultraiectum Dominium	BLAEU	38x50cm
Undecima Asiae Tabula	PTOLEMY (1511)	41x46cm
Ungariae Loca Praecipua Recens Emendata atque Edita, per Ioannem ...	ORTELIUS (Folio)	35x50cm
Union Pacific System of the Rocky Mountain National (Estes) Park ...	RAILROAD COMPANY	81x64cm
United States	ARROWSMITH	20x25cm
United States	BLACKIE	48x37cm
United States	BRADFORD	8x10cm
United States	BRADFORD	36x58cm
United States	BRADFORD	20x25cm
United States	BURR	44x53cm
United States	CRAM	29x46cm
United States	FINLEY	28x22cm
United States	GOODRICH	25x38cm
United States	GRAY	39x69cm
United States	HALL, SIDNEY	19x26cm
United States	JOHNSON	42x58cm
United States	LUCAS	29x48cm
United States	MITCHELL, S.A. (to 1859)	27x42cm
United States	MORSE, SIDNEY	24x42cm
United States	SMITH, C.	36x36cm
United States	SMITH, ROSWELL C.	27x43cm
United States	TALLIS	28x38cm
United States	TEESDALE	34x41cm
United States ... South Central Section Comprising Texas, Louisiana ...	SWANSTON	41x53cm
United States and Texas	JOHNSTON	50x61cm
United States of America	ARROWSMITH & LEWIS	22x27cm
United States of America	CAREY & LEA	42x54cm
United States of America	COLTON (Atlas Maps)	39x66cm
United States of America	GRAY	39x67cm
United States of America	LIZARS	40x46cm
United States of America Compiled from the Latest & Best Authorities ...	MELISH	43x54cm
United States of North America (Western States)	JOHNSTON	44x57cm
United States of North America, Southwest Sheet [joined with] S Central	WEEKLY DISPATCH	43x61cm
United States, Exhibiting the Railroads & Canals	BRADFORD	19x25cm
United States Section 4. Texas, Kansas, S. Nebraska, Colorado. New ...	SWINTON	28x23cm
United States, West & Mexico, North	LETTS	32x40cm
Universale della Parte del Mondo Nuovamente Ritrovata	RAMUSIO	32x42cm
Universale della Parte del Mondo Nuovamente Ritrovata	RAMUSIO	29x30cm
Universale Novo	GASTALDI	13x17cm
Universalis Cosmographia Tiguri Ive MDXLVI	HONTER	13x16cm
Universalis Orbis Descriptio; Cogimur e Tabula Pictos Ediscere Mundos	MYRITIUS	27x40cm
Universi Orbis Descriptio	MAGINI	13x17cm
Universi Orbis Descriptio ad Usum Navigantium	MAGINI	13x17cm

Title	Author	Size
Upper Canada &c. ...	ARROWSMITH	63x50cm
Upper Geyser Basin, Fire Hole River ... 1871	HAYDEN, F.V.	28x25cm
Upper Mines [with] Lower Mines or Mormon Diggings	U.S. GOV'T	23x17cm
Upper Territories of the United States	CAREY	20x15cm
Urbis Moskvae	BLAEU	38x48cm
Urbis Romae	JANSSON	38x51cm
Urbis Romae Veteris Accurata Delineatio	HOMANN	48x58cm
Utah and Nevada	BRADLEY	38x57cm
Utah, and the Overland Routes to It, from the Missouri River	RICHARDS	29x47cm
Utriusque Frisiorum Regionis Noviss Descriptio 1568	ORTELIUS (Folio)	34x51cm
Utriusque Hemisphaerii Delineatio	WYTFLIET	23x29cm
Valenchiennes. - Valencena, Quondam Cygnorum Vallis ...	BRAUN & HOGENBERG	36x39cm
Valentia Regnum	BLAEU	39x50cm
Valentia Regnum. Cotestini. Ptol. Edentani Plin.	JANSSON	35x48cm
Valesiae Prior et Vi Nova Tabula	MUNSTER	26x36cm
Van Dieman's Land	DOWER	34x41cm
Van Diemen's Island or Tasmania	TALLIS	26x33cm
Van Diemen's Land ...	ARROWSMITH	61x50cm
Venetia	BRAUN & HOGENBERG	36x50cm
Venetia	MERIAN	29x71cm
Venetia Potentissima ...	SEUTTER	50x57cm
Venezuela cum Parte Australi Novae Andalusiae	OGILBY	29x36cm
Venezuela, cum Parte Australi Novae Andalusiae	VALK & SCHENK	37x48cm
Venezuela, cum Partis Australis Novae Andalusiae	BLAEU	37x48cm
Venice	S.D.U.K.	38x59cm
Vera Effigies et Delineatio Insulae Sanctae Helenae ...	VAN LINSCHOTEN	30x47cm
Vereinegte Staaten von Nord America	WALCH	18x23cm
Vereinigte Staaten von Nord-America	STIELER	30x39cm
Vereinigte Staaten von Nord-America und Mexico	HILDBURGHAUSEN BIBLIO	19x26cm
Vergleichende Ubersicht Bekannter Hohen und Orte der Erde ...	HILDBURGHAUSEN BIBLIO	22x26cm
Vermont	BRADFORD	36x29cm
Vermont	COLTON (Atlas Maps)	40x32cm
Vermont	FINLEY	28x22cm
Vermont from the Latest Authorities	REID	42x34cm
Versucheiner Topographie von Sparta ...	BARBIE DU BOCAGE	31x19cm
Veteris Orbis Climata ex Strabone	SEALE	20x30cm
Vetus Descriptio Daciarum nec non Moesiarum. Petrus Kaerius Caelavit	JANSSON	36x48cm
Vetus Mexico	DAPPER	28x34cm
Veue des Dardanelles de Constantinople	DE FER (Small)	23x34cm
Victoria or Port Phillip	TALLIS	26x32cm
Vienna	S.D.U.K.	34x37cm
Vienna Austria Metropolis ...	BRAUN & HOGENBERG	15x48cm
View of Castle Garden, and New York Bay	APPLETON	20x65cm
View of Rockville, Conn. 1877	BAILEY, O.H.	50x65cm
Vindelicia, Rhaetia, Niricum, Pannonia et Lillyricum	BARBIE DU BOCAGE	19x24cm
Virginia	BRADFORD	29x38cm
Virginia	COLTON (Atlas Maps)	32x40cm
Virginia and Maryland By H. Moll Geographer	MOLL (Small)	27x20cm
Virginia Erforshet und Beschriben durch Captain Iohan Schmidt	DE BRY	29x36cm
Virginia et Florida	MERCATOR (Small)	15x19cm
Virginia et Florida	PURCHAS	15x18cm
Virginia et Insulae Bermudes	DU VAL	10x12cm
Virginia Maryland and Delaware	TANNER	51x73cm
Virginia, Marylandia et Carolina in America Septentrionali ...	HOMANN	48x58cm
Virginiae Item et Floridae Americae Provinciarum ...	HONDIUS	34x49cm
Virginiae Item et Floridae Americae Provinciarum Nova Descriptio	CLOPPENBURGH	19x25cm
Virginiae Item et Floridae Americae Provinciarum, Nova Descriptio	MERCATOR (Folio)	34x43cm
Virginiae Partis Australis, et Floridae Partis Orientalis ...	BLAEU	39x50cm
Virginiae Partis Australis, et Floridae Partis Orientalis ...	MONTANUS	29x36cm
Virginiae Partis Australis, et Floridae Partis Orientalis ...	OGILBY	29x36cm
Virginiae Partis Australis et Floridae Partis Orientalis Interjacentiumq ...	JANSSON	39x50cm
Von dem Banerlandt	MUNSTER	6x13cm
Von dem Elsass	MUNSTER	9x13cm
Von dem Preussen Landt	MUNSTER	9x13cm
Voyage du Cap'n Dampier, a la N. Hollande &c in 1699 &c.	DAMPIER	16x28cm
Vue de l'Entree du Bocca Tigris ...	MEARES	17x23cm
Vue de l'Ile Tiger ...	MEARES	17x23cm

Title	Author	Size
Vue de la Ville de Macao	MEARES	25x49cm
Vue de Stockholm &c.	CHATELAIN	35x45cm
Vue General de la Maison du Plaisance, de sa Majeste le Roy de Prusse ...	MERIAN	49x70cm
Vue Generale de la Havane	DEROY	37x50cm
Vue Perspective de la Ville de Nice	LOCAL & STATE MAPS	29x42cm
W. & N.B.R.R Extension from Nordmont to Dohm's Summit	RAILROAD COMPANY	20x38cm
Wahre Contrafactur der Churfurstlichen Residentz Statt Heidelberg	MERIAN	27x36cm
Wahrer Abriss der Beyden Koniglichen Haubt Alt und Newstatt Prag ...	MERIAN	30x58cm
Wales	SPEED	38x50cm
Wallis's New Geographical Game Exhibiting a Voyage Round the World ...	PUZZLES & GAMES	48x64cm
Warborch. Warburgum, Elegans Westphaliae Opp.	BRAUN & HOGENBERG	18x48cm
Warwick Shire	MORDEN	37x42cm
Washington [with] Cincinnati [and] New Orleans [and] Louisville	BRADFORD	29x36cm
Washington and Oregon	COLTON (Atlas Maps)	29x38cm
Washington, D.C. and Its Vicinity	WELLS, J.	13x19cm
Washington, Oregon and Idaho	JOHNSON	31x39cm
Watertown, South Dakota	ZEESE	52x41cm
Weinmar. - Winmaria, Fertiliss. Thuringiae Urbs ...	BRAUN & HOGENBERG	35x48cm
Wereld Kaart na de Alderlaatste Ontdekking in't Licht Gebracht ...	TIRION	33x42cm
Werelt Caert	STOOPENDAAL	30x43cm
West Indies	MITCHELL, S.A. (to 1859)	30x38cm
West Indies	THOMAS, COWPERTHWAIT	30x38cm
West Indies	THOMSON	48x69cm
West Indies, Agreeable to the Most Approved Maps & Charts	KITCHIN	34x38cm
West Indies from the Best Authorities	MORSE, JEDIDIAH	19x32cm
West Indies, with part of Guatemala	BURR	48x58cm
West Virginia	RAND, McNALLY (atlas maps)	33x50cm
Western Australia	BETTS	29x38cm
Western Australia / Swan River	TALLIS	25x33cm
Western Half of Texas	CRAM	56x42cm
Western Hemisphere	HALL, SIDNEY	Diam: 42cm
Western Hemisphere	S.D.U.K.	Diam: 33cm
Western Hemisphere [in set with] Eastern Hemisphere	BRADFORD	Diam: 29cm
Western Hemisphere [in set with] Eastern Hemisphere	CRAM	Diam: 23cm
Western Hemisphere [in set with] Eastern Hemisphere	FINDLAY	22x41cm
Western Hemisphere [in set with] Eastern Hemisphere	FINLEY	32x25cm
Western Territories of the United States	OLNEY	28x44cm
Western Territory	U.S. GOV'T	28x43cm
Westphaliae Totius	ORTELIUS (Folio)	35x50cm
Wetteravia cum Omnibus Inclusis Principatibus ...	SEUTTER	50x58cm
Wetzslar	MEISNER	10x15cm
Wexford	LEWIS, SAMUEL & CO.	30x24cm
Wilmington and Cape Fear River, North Carolina	ILLUS. LONDON NEWS	34x24cm
Wilt Shire	MORDEN	34x42cm
Wiltshire	MOULE	27x21cm
Wirtenberg	MERCATOR (Small)	15x19cm
Wisconsin	MITCHELL, S.A. (to 1859)	41x34cm
Wismar	BODENEHR	16x23cm
Wittenberg	GOTTFRIED	8x14cm
World. Engraved for Walker's Geography ...	DARTON	18x34cm
Wormbs	RAUW	7x9cm
Wright's Map of Kansas City	LOCAL & STATE POCKET	61x51cm
Wyld's Military Map of the United States	WYLD	86x60cm
Wyoming	CRAM	41x56cm
Xaintonge et Angoumois	BLAEU	39x50cm
Xuntien alias Quinzay	JANSSON	42x52cm
Yellowstone National Park	CRAM	29x23cm
Yellowstone National Park	HAYDEN, F.V.	109x61cm
Yellowstone National Park and Forest Reserve ...	U.S. GEOLOGICAL SURVEY	46x48cm
Yorktown and Gloucester Point as Besieged by the Allied Army	GORDON, WILLIAM	29x21cm
Zeelandia Comitatus ...	BLAEU	38x50cm
Zeelandica Comitatus	BLAEU	38x50cm
Zurych. Tigarum sive Turegum, Caesari, ut Plerique Existimant, Tigurinus ...	BRAUN & HOGENBERG	37x48cm
Zuyd America - L'Amerique Meridionale	RATELBAND	14x19cm

GEOGRAPHICAL INDEX

The world has been divided into hemispheres, continents, polar, oceans, and a few miscellaneous categories. Each item is listed in only one location. Where there is more than one item by a particular map-maker, their number is indicated in square brackets [ ].

The embracing concept of the Geographical Index is to start with the *general* and end with the *particular.* Accordingly, the first heading is the **World**. Next comes **Hemispheres**; then the **Continents** in alphabetical order, and within North America there is further subdivision into Canada, Mexico and Central America, the United States, and the West Indies; followed by **Polar** regions. The **Oceans** are next, in alphabetical order. And finally, **Celestial** and **Miscellaneous**. Similarly, national categories may be subdivided into regions, then provinces or states, and then cities.

Maps of regions of what is now the United States are listed under the main heading of *North America* if before about 1770, and under *United States* if after about 1770. An exception is in the case of a single colony which became a state -- Pennsylvania, for example -- which would appear under *United States*. Generally when a U.S. map shows two or three states, it is listed under the one occurring first alphabetically. Maps of the Americas -- North and South America together -- are listed in the *Hemisphere* section under *The Americas; Western Hemisphere*. Many maps showing the northwest coast of North America are listed under *Pacific Ocean, North*. Major geographical features such as Chesapeake Bay or the Gulf of Mexico may be under *North America* rather than *United States*. North American cities are listed under their respective countries and states, regardless of age, rather than under North America.

To help locate items, the order of the major headings is listed below:

WORLD: World & continents, sets of continents, sets of globe gores, globes
HEMISPHERES of the WORLD: includes two Americas
AFRICA
ASIA: includes the Holy Land, Persian Gulf, and the East Indies
AUSTRALIA
EUROPE: includes the Mediterranean
NORTH AMERICA: The whole continent and U.S. regions before Independence
    CANADA
    MEXICO and CENTRAL AMERICA
    UNITED STATES: Cities from all periods
    WEST INDIES
SOUTH AMERICA
POLAR
OCEANS:
    ATLANTIC
    INDIAN includes Red Sea
    PACIFIC includes the Philippines
CELESTIAL & MISCELLANEOUS: includes allegorical, oddities, portraits, title pages, etc.

WORLD

ANCIENT WORLD: Jansson [3]; Manuscript Maps; Seale
- **(ATLASES):** Butler; Macrobius; Mitchell, S.A. (Atlas maps 1860 & later) [2]; Smith

GLOBE, TERRESTRIAL: Globes [8]; Newton & Berry
GLOBE PAIR, TERRESTRIAL & CELESTIAL: Bardin
GLOBE DEPICTIONS: Middleton
GLOBE GORES, TERRESTRIAL: Coronelli [8]; Scherer
MODERN WORLD: Aeronautical Maps; American Sunday School Union; Anonymous or unknown [3]; Anson; Apianus [2]; Arias Montanus [2]; Arrowsmith; Bailleul; Baldwin; Bellin (Large); Bellin (Small); Bertius; Blaeu [4]; Blair; Blome; Bodenehr [2]; Bonne [4]; Bowen, E. [7]; Bowen, T. [3]; Brion de la Tour; Brookes; Brue; Buache; Bunting; Burr; Cary; Cavazza; Chamouin; Chatelain [3]; Chiquet; Cloppenburgh; Clouet [2]; Colom; Danckerts; Darton; Davidszoon; De Aefferden; De Beaurain [2]; De Fer (Large) [2]; De Fer (Small) [2]; De L'Isle [2]; De Laporte; De Lat; De Vaugondy [6]; De Wit [2]; Delamarche [3]; Dezauche; Du Val; Dufour; Dunn [4]; Elwe; Findlay; Finley [3]; Fries [2]; Fullarton; Gastaldi [2]; Gemma Frisius; Gentleman's Magazine; Guyot; Hall; Hall, S.; Halley [2]; Harrison; Homann & Homann Heirs [3]; Hondius [6]; Honter; Jaillot [2]; Jansson [2]; Janvier [2]; Japanese Cartography; Jefferys; Johnson [4]; Johnston; Kitchin; Lattre; Lavoisne [2]; Le Clerc [2]; Lockhead; Magini [4]; Mercator (Folio) [4]; Mercator (Small); Merian; Merula; Mitchell, S.A. (Atlas maps 1859 & earlier) [2]; Mitchell, S.A. (Atlas maps 1860 & later) [2]; Moithey; Moll (Large) [2]; Moll (Small) [5]; Moore; Mortier; Munster [8]; Myritius; Olney; Ortelius (Folio) [8]; Ottens; Overton; Paas; Payne [2]; Phipps; Pitt [2]; Porcacchi [3]; Powell; Price; Puzzles & games [2]; Quad [2]; Rand, McNally (Atlas maps); Renard [2]; Renouard; Rosaccio; Ruscelli [3]; Russell; Sanson (Folio) [5]; Santini; Scherer [4]; Senex [2]; Seutter [3]; S.D.U.K.; Solis; Stoopendaal [5]; Tardieu; Tavernier; Teesdale; Thomas, Cowperthwait; Tirion [2]; Truxton; U.S. Coast Survey; Vadianus; Valk [4]; Van De Passe; Van Jagen [2]; Van Loon; Van Meurs; Visscher [5]; Walch; Walton; Wells [2]; Wilkinson; Woodbridge; Wytfliet; Zahn [3]; Zurner

- **(ATLASES):** Arbuckle; Arrowsmith; Black; Blair; Bonne; Bordone; Bradford; Brookes [2]; Butler; Carey [2]; Carey & Lea; Chambers; Chiquet; Colton (Atlas maps) [2]; Cram [3]; Cummings & Hilliard; De Vaugondy [3]; De Wit; Delamarche; Diamond Atlas; Dunn; Dury; Gastaldi [2]; Goodrich [2]; Gordon; Grynaeus; Guthrie [2]; Hardesty [2]; Homann & Homann Heirs; Hondius; Jansson; Johnson [9]; Johnston; Lange; Lavoisne; Le Rouge; Lotter; Magini; Manuscript Maps; Marmocchi; Martin; Mercator (Folio) [2]; Mercator (Small) [3]; Mitchell, S.A. (Atlas maps 1859 & earlier) [5]; Mitchell, S.A. (Atlas maps 1860 & later) [9]; Morse, J. [3]; Morse, S. [2]; Munster [2]; Nolin; Olney [2]; Ortelius (Folio) [2]; Ortelius (Miniature); Phillips; Porcacchi; Raleigh, W.; Rand, McNally (Atlas maps) [2]; Raynal; Ruscelli [2]; Salmon [2]; Speed; Tallis; Tanner; Thomas, Cowperthwait; Thomson; Visscher; Vuillemin; Weekly Dispatch; Willard

- **(FACSIMILE ATLASES):** Blaeu; Braun & Hogenberg [2]; Fries; Ortelius (Folio)

PTOLEMAIC WORLD: Fries [4]; Magini [2]; Munster [4]; Schedel
SET OF 2 HEMISPHERES: Bradford [2]; Coronelli; Cram; De L'Isle [2]; Findlay; Finley [2]; Gentleman's Magazine; Happel; Sanson (Folio); S.D.U.K.; Zahn
SET OF 4 CONTINENTS: Chetwind; Homann & Homann Heirs; Puzzles & games
WORLD & 4 CONTINENTS: Armenian Cartography; Danet; Munster; Ortelius (Folio); Van Der Aa; Vaughan; Visscher
WORLD & 5 CONTINENTS: Le Rouge
WORLD, UNCLASSIFIED: Puzzles & games; Seller
- **(ATLASES):** Depot De La Marine; Dumont D'urville; Schedel; Von Leonard

HEMISPHERES of the WORLD:

The AMERICAS; WESTERN HEMISPHERE: Allard; Bellin (Small); Berey; Bertius; Blaeu [3]; Bowen, E. [3]; Brion De La Tour; Burnet; Carey & Lea; Cary [2]; Chatelain; Coronelli; Covens & Mortier; D'anania; D'Anville; Danet; De Fer (Large); De Fer (Small) [2]; De Herrera; De L'Isle [2]; De Laet; De Vaugondy; De Wit [4]; Delamarche; Desnos [3]; Dezauche [2]; Dufour; Fremin; Fricx; Fries; Gazzettiere Americano; Hall, S.; Hildburghausen Biblio; Homann & Homann Heirs [9]; Hondius [9]; Jansson [2]; Janvier [3]; Kircher; Lavoisne [2]; Le Rouge; Magini [2]; Mercator (Folio) [3]; Merian [3]; Moll (Small) [2]; Morisot; Munster [10]; Nolin; Ortelius (Folio) [3]; Ramusio [3]; Ruscelli; Sanson (Folio) [3]; Sanson (Small); Sayer; Schenk; Senex; Seutter [5]; S.D.U.K.; Speed [5]; Stradanus; Tavernier; Thomson; Tirion; Valk; Van Der Aa; Visscher [3]; Von Euler; Von Reilly; Weigel

- **(ATLASES):** Buchon; De Bry; De Laet; Montanus; Mount & Page; Ogilby; Pease & Niles

EASTERN HEMISPHERE: Barbie Du Bocage; Bourgoin; Brion De La Tour; Cellarius; Coronelli; Dampier; De Bry; De L'Isle; Gentleman's Magazine [2]; Herbert; Hondius; Tallis
- **(ATLASES):** Morse, J. [2]

NORTHERN HEMISPHERE: Buache [2]; De L'Isle; St. Albin

SOUTHERN HEMISPHERE: Buache; Cook [2]; Covens & Mortier; De Wit; Du Val [2]; Gentleman's Magazine [2]; Jansson; Von Euler; Wytfliet

AFRICA:

AFRICA: Blaeu [2]; Bonne; Bowen, E.; Bradford; Brion De La Tour; Bunting [2]; Cary [2]; Cram; De Bry [2]; De L'Isle [2]; Fricx; Gibson; Grant; Homann & Homann Heirs; Hondius; Jaillot; Lapie; Lavoisne [2]; Levasseur; Local & State Maps & Views; Magini [3]; Mercator (Folio); Mitchell, S.A. (Atlas maps 1860 & later); Munster [8]; Nolin; Olney; Ortelius (Folio) [7]; Payne; Quad; Ramusio [4]; Sanson (Folio); Speed; Van Meurs; Visscher; Wilkinson; Winterbotham; Wyld
- **REGIONS - CENTRAL:** Blaeu; Dufour; Sanson (Folio); U.S. Gov't.; Valk & Schenk
  - **(CENTRAL, PRESTER JOHN):** Blaeu [2]; Mercator (Folio); Ortelius (Folio)
  - **EAST:** Van Linschoten
  - **NORTH:** Fries [2]; Jansson; Ptolemy (1522-1541 Strassburg); Ruscelli [2]; Scherer; Wells
  - **NORTHEAST:** De L'Isle
  - **NORTHWEST:** Dudley; Magini; Murray
  - **SOUTH:** Arrowsmith; Blaeu [2]; Bonne [2]; Coronelli; Covens & Mortier; De Fer (Small); Fries; Gastaldi; Jansson; Kircher; Munster; Ottens; Ruscelli [2]; Scherer; Valk & Schenk; Van Linschoten
  - **SOUTHEAST:** Sayer & Bennett; Van Linschoten
  - **WEST:** D'Anville
  - **(MISCELLANEOUS):** Levasseur
    - **(ATLAS):** Bory De Saint-Vincent

ABYSSINIA: Bertius; Mercator (Small); Ortelius (Folio)

ALGERIA: Levasseur

ANGOLA: Merian

BARBARY: Bonne; Du Val; Jansson; Ortelius (Folio); Sanson (Folio)

CONGO: De Bry

EGYPT: Blaeu; Fuller; Hondius; Jansson; Ortelius (Folio); Ruscelli; Seale; Tallis; Valk & Schenk
- **(ATLAS):** Panckoucke
- **CITIES:** Braun & Hogenberg [3]; Graphic, The; Schedel

GAMBIA: Kitchin

GUINEA: Blaeu; Hondius

LIBYA: Sanson (Folio)

MADAGASCAR: Bellin (Small); Coronelli; Sanson (Folio); Van Linschoten

MOROCCO: Homann & Homann Heirs; Sanson (Folio)

NILE RIVER: Roberts

SOUTH AFRICA: Andrees; Arrowsmith [2]; Cary; Juta; Kolb [8]; Mortier [2]; Schraembl; S.D.U.K.; Van Der Aa; Weiland

ASIA

ASIA: Allard; Armenian Cartography; Arrowsmith; Black; Blaeu [2]; Botero; Bowen, E. [3]; Burckhardt; De Fer (Large); De Fer (Small); De Jode; De Wit [3]; Fricx; Haffner; Homann & Homann Heirs; Hondius [2]; Johnson; Kip; Kircher; Laurie & Whittle; Levasseur [3]; Lotter; Magini [2]; Mercator (Folio) [2]; Moll (Large) [2]; Munster [6]; Ortelius (Folio) [2]; Porro; Quad; Sanson (Folio) [3]; Seutter [2]; Speed; Van Der Aa; Visscher; Wilkinson; Willdey
- **REGIONS - CENTRAL:** Cluver; Homann & Homann Heirs
  - **EAST:** Fries; Magini
  - **SOUTH:** Bellin (Small); Dudley; Fries [2]; Jansson; Moll (Small); Munster; Ramusio; Tallis; Van Der Aa
  - **SOUTHEAST:** Andriveau-Goujon; Blair; Cloppenburgh; Hondius [3]; Magini; Mercator (Folio); Mercator (Small); Moll (Small); Mortier; Munster [2]; Ptolemy (1511 Venice); Sanson (Folio); Senex; Van Der Aa [2]
  - **SOUTHEAST & EAST INDIES:** Blaeu [3]; Bonne [2]; Bowen, E.; Chatelain; De L'Isle [2]; De Laporte; De Wit [2]; Doncker; Du Val; Fries; Hondius [2]; Jansson [6]; Laurie & Whittle; Magini; Mercator (Small); Merian; Mortier [2]; Ortelius (Folio) [5]; Ottens; Sanson (Folio); Seutter; S.D.U.K.; Thevenot; Thornton; Van Linschoten; Visscher; Wytfliet
    - **(ATLAS):** Labillardiere

ASIA: REGIONS - SOUTHWEST: Colton (Atlas maps); De Wit; Magini; Tanner; Van Der Aa [2]
ARABIA: Cary; Fries [2]; Magini; Moll (Small); Ptolemy (1482-1486 Ulm); Ruscelli
ASIA MINOR see Turkey: Fries
- **(ATLAS):** Chevalier
BAY OF BENGAL: Imray
CASPIAN SEA: Homann & Homann Heirs; Seutter
CAUCASUS REGION: Santini
CEYLON, see Taprobana: Bellin (Small); Bordone; De Bry; Magini; Mercator (Small) [2]; Munster; Nichelson; Ptolemy (1578-1730 Mercator); Van Keulen; Visscher; Waldseemuller
CHINA: Bonne; Botero; Cary; Colton (Atlas maps) [2]; Harris; Johnston; Le Rouge; Mercator (Folio); Mercator (Small); Moll (Small); Ortelius (Folio); Purchas; Sanson (Folio); Tallis; Thomas, Cowperthwait; Valk & Schenk
- **(ATLASES):** D'Anville; Du Halde
- **PROVINCES:** Bellin (Small); Jansson; Tallis; Valk & Schenk [5]
- **CITIES:** Bellin (Small); Harris; Jansson; Mallet; S.D.U.K.
- **(MISCELLANEOUS):** Meares [3]
CHINA & JAPAN: Bradford; Hondius; Speed [2]; Valk & Schenk
- **(ATLAS):** Blaeu
CHINA & KOREA: Bonne; De Laporte; Depot De La Marine; Jansson; Kitchin [2]; Lavoisne; Lotter; Seutter; Valk & Schenk; Van Loon
CHINA, JAPAN & KOREA: Blaeu [2]; Bonne; Cloppenburgh; De Fer (Small); Hondius; Merian [2]; Speed [3]
CYPRUS: Blaeu; Jansson; Ortelius (Folio) [2]
EAST INDIES, see Indonesia: De Vaugondy; De Wit; Dudley; Gentleman's Magazine; Hondius [2]; Mercator (Small); Moll (Small) [2]; Mortier; Rossi; Scherer; Tallis; Valentyn; Zatta
- **AMBOINA:** Van Der Schley
- **BORNEO:** Jansson
- **MALACCA STRAIT:** Dampier; Laurie & Whittle; Mount & Page; Van Der Aa
- **MOLUCCAS:** Bertius [2]; Blaeu; Jansson [2]; Le Rouge; Mallet
- **NEW GUINEA:** Bowen, E.; Dumont D'urville
HOLY LAND: Blaeu [?]; Bonfrerius; Brion De La Tour; Cloppenburgh [2]; Danckerts [2]; Dapper; De Fer (Large); De Fer (Small); De La Rue [2]; De Vaugondy; Fries; Fuller [2]; Gastaldi; Homann & Homann Heirs [4]; Jaillot [2]; Jansson [5]; Johnson; Keur; Kip; Lapie; Lavoisne; Le Bruyn; Lizars; Magini [3]; Mercator (Small) [2]; Munster [4]; Nolin; Ortelius (Folio) [8]; Overton; Plancius; Ptolemy (1482-1486 Ulm); Purchas; Sanson (Folio) [3]; Scherer; Seutter; S.D.U.K. [2]; Speed; Stoopendaal [2]; Thomson; Tirinus; Van Adrichem [2]; Van Der Aa; Visscher; Ware; Wells; Wilkinson
- **JERUSALEM:** Amico [2]; Arias Montanus; Braun & Hogenberg [2]; Danckerts; Hofmann; Le Bruyn; Lea; Schedel; Schonsperger
- **(OTHER CITIES):** Munster
INDIA: Blaeu; Bowen, E.; Colton (Atlas maps); Royal Geographical Society; S.D.U.K.; Tallis; Thevenot; Thomson; Waldseemuller; Weekly Dispatch
- **GOA:** Braun & Hogenberg; Merian; Van Linschoten
INDIA & SOUTHEAST ASIA: Sanson (Folio)
INDONESIA: Bellin (Small); De Bry; Dudley
- **BALI:** De Bry; Valentyn
- **JAVA:** Andrews; Chatelain; De Reneville; Jansson; Van Der Aa [2]
- **SUMATRA, see Taprobana:** Jansson [2]; Ramusio [2]; Valentyn [2]
JAPAN: Bellin (Small) [2]; Bowen, E.; Caron; Chatelain [2]; De Vaugondy; Hondius; Jansson; Johnson; Kaempfer; Langenes; Mallet; Montanus; Ortelius (Folio) [2]; Seutter [3]; S.D.U.K.; Tirion [2]; Zatta
JAPAN & KOREA: Cloppenburgh; Hondius [2]; Ortelius (Folio); Tallis; Valk & Schenk
- **TOKYO:** Japanese Cartography; Kaempfer
- **(OTHER CITIES):** Japanese Cartography; Ogilby
KOREA: Du Halde; Manuscript Maps
MACAO: Bellin (Small); Meares; Meisner
MIDDLE EAST: Bonne [2]; Danckerts; Gibson; Kip; Michalet; Munster; Plancius; Ruscelli; Tavernier; Van Der Aa; Ware; Wells
- **(with EASTERN MEDITERRANEAN):** Ware [2]

OTTOMAN EMPIRE, see Turkey (in Europe & Asia): Blaeu; Cloppenburgh; De Vaugondy; Homann & Homann Heirs; Jansson; Ortelius (Folio); Speed
PAKISTAN: Ptolemy (1482-1486 Ulm); Ruscelli
PERSIA: Cloppenburgh; Hondius; Mercator (Small) [2]; Ruscelli; Speed [3]
RUSSIA (ASIAN): Anonymous or unknown; Tallis
- **KAMTCHATKA:** Homann & Homann Heirs
SINGAPORE: Bellin (Large) [2]; Delahaye; Laurie & Whittle
TABROBANA, see Ceylon; Sumatra: Mercator (Folio); Munster
TARTARY: Blaeu [2]; Hondius [2]; Magini [2]; Mercator (Folio); Ortelius (Folio) [6]; Sanson (Folio); Sanson (Small); Speed
THAILAND: Jollain; Valentyn
TIBET: Du Halde; Tallis
TURKEY, see Asia Minor; Turkey in Europe: Blaeu; Cluver; De Vaugondy; Fries; Hondius; Munster; Ortelius (Folio) [2]; Ptolemy (1522-1541 Strassburg); Ruscelli; Tanner; Thomson
YEMEN: Braun & Hogenberg; Lotter

AUSTRALIA and NEW ZEALAND

AUSTRALIA: Bellin (Small); Cassini; Coronelli; Johnston; S.D.U.K.; Tallis [2]; Wyld [2]
- **REGIONS:** Allan; Aspin; Bell; Betts; Bonne; Coronelli; Wyld
- **NEW SOUTH WALES:** Arrowsmith; Cook [2]; S.D.U.K.; Stockdale; Tallis; Wilkinson [2]
- **SOUTH AUSTRALIA:** Tallis [2]
- **TASMANIA:** Arrowsmith; Cook [2]; Dower; Flinders; Tallis; Valentyn [2]; Wyld
- **VICTORIA:** Tallis
- **WESTERN AUSTRALIA:** Tallis
- **(MISCELLANEOUS):** Dudley
AUSTRALIA & EAST INDIES: Johnson; Streit
AUSTRALIA & NEW ZEALAND: Gall & Inglis; Greenleaf; Johnston; Thevenot
NEW ZEALAND: Baker; British Admiralty; Cook [5]; Coronelli; Local & State Maps & Views; Zatta

EUROPE

EUROPE: Blaeu; Bowen, E.; Bowles; Burckhardt; Colton (Atlas maps); Colton (Pocket & Wall Maps); Danckerts; De L'Isle; De Wit; Homann & Homann Heirs; Hondius [4]; Jaillot; Jansson [3]; Johnson; Kitchin; Lanee; Levasseur; Lotter; Magini [2]; Mercator (Small); Moll (Large); Moll (Small); Munster [10]; Ortelius (Folio) [2]; Porro; Puzzles & games [2]; Renard; Stieler; Stumpf; Thomson; Van Den Keere; Visscher [3]; Walton; Wells; Zatta
- **(ATLASES):** Bodenehr; Mount & Page
- **(FACSIMILE ATLASES):** Braun & Hogenberg [4]; Waghenaer
- **REGIONS - CENTRAL:** Barbie Du Bocage; Chatelain; Schedel; Stockdale
- **EAST:** Munster [2]; Ptolemy (1511 Venice); Visscher
- **NORTH:** Ruscelli [2]
- **(MISCELLANEOUS):** Bacon
ADRIATIC SEA & COAST: Coronelli
ADRIATIC STATES: Ortelius (Folio)
AEGEAN SEA: Michelot
AUSTRIA: Colton (Atlas maps); Lotter; Mercator (Small); Ortelius (Folio) [2]; Sanson (Folio); Seutter; Tallis; Thomson
- **TIROL:** Lotter
- **(OTHER PROVINCES):** Hildburghausen Biblio; Homann & Homann Heirs; Ortelius (Folio); Von Reilly
- **VIENNA:** Braun & Hogenberg; De Fer (Small); Homann & Homann Heirs; Middleton; Mollo; S.D.U.K. [2]
- **(OTHER CITIES):** Custodis; Jansson; Meisner [2]
BALKANS: Homann & Homann Heirs; Mercator (Folio); Munster; Ruscelli; Sanson (Folio); Valk
BALTIC COUNTRIES: Blaeu; Johnston; Lotter; Sanson (Folio)
BALTIC SEA: Gentleman's Magazine; Heather
BELGIUM: Finley; Laporte; Thomson
- **(ATLAS):** Seutter
- **PROVINCES - FLANDERS:** Blaeu [3]; Munster; Ortelius (Folio); Peeters; Pitt; Visscher [3]

BELGIUM: PROVINCES - LIEGE: Blaeu; Ortelius (Folio)
 -**NAMUR:** Braun & Hogenberg
 -**(OTHER PROVINCES):** Blaeu
 - **CITIES - ANTWERP:** Braun & Hogenberg; Meisner; S.D.U.K.
 -**BRUSSELS:** Braun & Hogenberg [2]; Merian; Visscher
 -**(OTHER CITIES):** Braun & Hogenberg [3]; Meisner; Mortier; Seutter
 -**WATERLOO ATLAS:** Leigh
BELORUS: Sanson (Folio)
BOHEMIA, see Czech Republic: Cloppenburgh; Jansson; Merian [2]; Munster; Ortelius (Folio); Speed; Visscher
BRITISH ISLES: Barbie Du Bocage; Blaeu; Danckerts; Daw; De Fer (Large); De L'Isle; Fries; Hondius; Jaillot; Kitchin; Knipe; Magini; Mercator (Folio); Mercator (Small) [2]; Merian; Morden; Munster [3]; Ortelius (Folio) [5]; Ottens; Ruscelli; Seutter; Speed [3]; Visscher; Vrients; Waldseemuller [4]
 -**(ATLASES):** Camden [2]; Slater; Speed; Virtue
 - **IRISH SEA:** Imray
CROATIA: Camocio
CZECH REPUBLIC, see Bohemia: Homann & Homann Heirs; Jansson; Sanson (Folio)
 - **PRAGUE:** Braun & Hogenberg; Homann & Homann Heirs; Merian; Seutter
DENMARK: Braun & Hogenberg; Brion De La Tour; Cluver; De Fer (Small); Heather [2]; Peeters; Stieler; Visscher
 -**COPENHAGEN:** Chatelain
ENGLAND: Browne; Kitchin; Lavoisne; Mercator (Small) [2]; Morden; Munster; Quad; Speed [2]; Waghenaer
 - **(ATLASES):** Camden; Cary [2]; Moule; Owen & Bowen
 - **REGIONS - NORTH:** Mercator (Small) [2]
 -**SOUTHEAST:** Sanson (Folio)
 - **COUNTIES - BERKSHIRE:** Hollar
 -**BUCKINGHAMSHIRE:** Jansson; Speed
 -**CAMBRIDGESHIRE:** Bowen, E.; Braun & Hogenberg; Greenwood; Speed
 -**CORNWALL:** Seller; Speed
 -**DEVONSHIRE:** Blaeu; Collins, G.; Seller; Speed [2]
 -**DORSETSHIRE:** Speed
 -**DURHAM:** Bowen, E.
 -**ESSEX:** Blaeu [2]; Kitchin
 -**HAMPSHIRE:** Morden; Moule
 -**KENT:** Harris; Speed
 -**LANCASHIRE:** Jansson
 -**LEICESTERSHIRE:** Prior
 -**LINCOLNSHIRE:** Speed [2]
 -**MIDDLESEX:** Morden; Moule; Pigot; Seale; Speed [2]
 -**NOTTINGHAMSHIRE:** Morden; Speed [2]
 -**OXFORDSHIRE:** Morden; Moule; Seller; Speed; Van Der Aa
 -**SHROPSHIRE:** Moule
 -**SOMERSETSHIRE:** Greenwood [2]; Speed
 -**STAFFORDSHIRE:** Plot
 -**SURREY:** Bowen, E.; Morden; Pigot
 -**SUSSEX:** Morden; Rocque; Speed
 -**WILTSHIRE:** Morden; Moule
 -**YORKSHIRE:** Warburton
 -**(OTHER COUNTIES):** Morden [4]; [ ]Speed [4]
 - **CITIES - LONDON:** Anonymous or unknown; Arrowsmith; Aveline; Blome; Braun & Hogenberg [3]; Cary; Cassell; Collins & Son; Colton (Atlas maps); Cruchley; Faden; Homann & Homann Heirs [5]; Illustrated London News [2]; Local & State Maps & Views; Merian [2]; Overton [2]; Rocque [2]; S.D.U.K. [2]; Tegg; Tirion. **(ATLAS):** Cary
 -**(OTHER CITIES):** Bacon; Braun & Hogenberg [4]; Meisner; Seile
 - **ISLANDS:** Morden
 -**CHANNEL ISLANDS:** Tallis
 -**ISLE OF MAN:** Collins, G.

ENGLAND: PHYSICAL & CULTURAL FEATURES
- **BRISTOL CHANNEL:** Collins, G.
- **COAST:** Collins, G.; Heather [2]; Van Keulen
- **ROADS:** Ogilby [2]
- **THAMES RIVER:** Mount & Page; Waghenaer
- **(MISCELLANEOUS):** Manuscript Maps

ENGLAND & SCOTLAND: Heather; Imray

ENGLAND & WALES: Black [2]; Cary; Colton (Pocket & Wall Maps); Coronelli; Douglas; Lockhead; Mercator (Small); Mitchell, S.A. (Atlas maps 1860 & later); Ortelius (Folio) [2]; Puzzles & games; Rocque; Stockdale; Willdey
- **(ATLASES):** Cary; Collins, H.G.; Fullarton; Luffman

ENGLISH CHANNEL: Dudley; Jaillot; Lotter; Visscher; Von Reilly

FRANCE: Blaeu [2]; Cary; Chatelain; De Vaugondy; Herisson; Hildburghausen Biblio; Homann & Homann Heirs; Le Rouge; Magini; Manuscript Maps; Mercator (Folio); Mortier; Munster [3]; Ortelius (Folio) [3]; Rossi; Visscher [3]
- **(ATLASES):** Levasseur; Merian [2]; Tassin
- **REGIONS - NORTH:** Fricx
  - **SOUTHEAST:** Blaeu
  - **SOUTHWEST:** Valk & Schenk
- **PROVINCES - ALSACE:** Munster
  - **ANJOU:** Blaeu; Jansson
  - **ARTOIS:** De Wit; Seutter; Valk
  - **BORDEAUX:** Merian
  - **BURGUNDY:** De L'Isle; Mercator (Small); Ortelius (Folio); Quad
  - **CHAMPAGNE:** De Fer (Large); Jansson; Seutter
  - **CORSICA:** Covens & Mortier; Homann & Homann Heirs; Quad
  - **DAUPHINE:** De Vaugondy
  - **ISLE DE FRANCE:** Blaeu
  - **LORRAINE:** Blaeu; Mercator (Small); Ortelius (Folio); Sanson (Folio); Visscher
  - **NORMANDY:** De Fer (Large)
  - **PROVENCE:** Jaillot
  - **(OTHER PROVINCES & REGIONS):** Blaeu [3]; Bonne; Longchamps; Mercator (Small); Ortelius (Folio); Sanson (Folio) [2]
- **CITIES - PARIS:** Braun & Hogenberg [3]; Bretez; Delagrive, J.; Garnier; Homann & Homann Heirs; Levasseur; Local & State Maps & Views; Merian; Moithey; Munster [2]; Probst; Seutter [3]; Visscher
  - **(OTHER CITIES):** Bertius [2]; Bodenehr; Braun & Hogenberg [5]; Lasor A Varea; Lemercier; Local & State Maps & Views; Manuscript Maps; Meisner; Merian [2]; Munster [4]; Rauw; Schedel
- **NAUTICAL - (CHART):** Faden [2]; **(ATLAS):** Faden

GERMANY: Barbie Du Bocage; Blaeu [2]; Cloppenburgh; Cluver; Gastaldi; Homann & Homann Heirs [2]; Hondius; Jansson; Magini [3]; Munster [2]; Ortelius (Folio); Ottens; Rollos; Ruscelli
- **(ATLASES):** Lotter; Seutter
- **(FACSIMILE ATLAS):** Merian
- **REGIONS - EAST:** Schenk
  - **NORTH:** Cluver; Sanson (Folio); Visscher
  - **SOUTH:** Homann & Homann Heirs; Munster; Sanson (Folio)
- **STATES, PROVINCES, REGIONS and their CITIES:**
  - **ANHALT (CITIES):** Gottfried; Homann & Homann Heirs; Meisner; Munster
  - **BADEN-WURTTEMBURG (CITIES):** Bodenehr [2]; Braun & Hogenberg; Malte-Brun; Meisner; Merian [4]; Munster; Ratelband
  - **BAVARIA:** Homann & Homann Heirs; Munster; Schedel; Visscher; Von Reilly
    - **MUNICH:** Braun & Hogenberg; S.D.U.K.
    - **(OTHER CITIES):** Meisner [3]; Merian [2]; Munster; Schonsperger
  - **BRANDENBURG:** Blaeu; Homann & Homann Heirs; Lotter
    - **(CITIES):** Lasor A Varea; Munster [2]
  - **BERLIN:** Local & State Maps & Views; Merian; Meyer; S.D.U.K.
  - **EAST FRISIA:** Jansson; Visscher
  - **EAST PRUSSIA:** Blaeu [2]; Munster; Visscher
  - **FRANCONIA:** Homann & Homann Heirs; Ortelius (Folio); Sanson (Folio)

GERMANY: – **HAMBURG:** Merian [2]; Mortier
 – **HESSE:** De Jode; Mercator (Small); Merian; Seutter [3]; Von Reilly
  – **FRANKFORT:** Gottfried
  – **(OTHER CITIES):** Lasor A Varea; Meisner [2]; Munster
 – **LOWER SAXONY:** Covens & Mortier; Homann & Homann Heirs; Jaillot; Kitchin; Seutter; Visscher; Von Reilly
  – **(CITIES):** Braun & Hogenberg; Hildburghausen Biblio; Merian [2]; Munster; Seyfart
 – **MECKLENBURG:** Jansson; Mercator (Small)
  – **(CITIES):** Bodenehr; Braun & Hogenberg; Kilian, G.C.; Merian [2]; Rauw
 – **NORTH RHEIN-WESTPHALIA:** Blaeu; Kilian, G.C.; Lotter; Tirion
  – **(CITIES):** Braun & Hogenberg; Meisner; Rauw
 – **POMERANIA:** Faden; Munster; Sanson (Folio)
 – **PRUSSIA:** Black; Jansson; Munster; Seutter
 – **RHEINLAND-PFALZ:** Blaeu [2]; Homann & Homann Heirs; Mercator (Small); Von Reilly [2]
  – **(CITIES):** Bellus; Bodenehr; Manuscript Maps; Meisner; Merian; Munster; Rauw [2]; Salmon
 – **SAARLAND:** Meisner
 – **SAXONY:** Seutter
  – **(CITIES):** Bertius; Braun & Hogenberg; Gottfried; S.D.U.K.
 – **SCHLESWIG-HOLSTEIN:** Blaeu; Von Reilly
  – **(CITIES):** Gottfried; Lasor A Varea
 – **SWABIA:** Ortelius (Folio); Sanson (Folio)
 – **THURINGEN:** Quad; Von Reilly
  – **(CITIES):** Braun & Hogenberg; Homann & Homann Heirs
 – **WESTPHALIA:** Jaillot; Ortelius (Folio)
 – **WURTTEMBERG:** Mercator (Small)
GIBRALTAR: Rapin; Seutter
GREAT BRITAIN: Blaeu [2]; Jansson [2]; Magini; Munster; Speed
 – **(ATLAS):** Owen & Bowen
GREECE: Blaeu; Cluver; Faden; Gibson; Hondius; Jansson; Laurie & Whittle; Magini [2]; Mercator (Small); Munster [2]; Ortelius (Folio); Sanson (Folio); S.D.U.K.; Speed [2]; Thomas, Cowperthwait
 – **(ATLAS):** Barthelemy
 – **PROVINCES:** Bowen, E.; Cluver; Ortelius (Folio); Porcacchi, Zatta
 – **CITIES:** Barbie Du Bocage; Camocio; Coronelli; De Bruyn; Meisner; S.D.U.K.
 – **ISLANDS:** Bertelli [2]; **(ATLAS):** Dapper
  – **AEGEAN ISLANDS:** Ortelius (Folio)
  – **CRETE:** Braun & Hogenberg; De Wit; Homann & Homann Heirs; Jansson; Mercator (Folio); Mercator (Small); Merian; Ortelius (Folio); Roux
GULF OF FINLAND: Heather; Waghenaer
HUNGARY: Bowen, E.; Covens & Mortier; Custodis; De L'Isle; Jansson; Lasor A Varea; Meisner; Mercator (Folio); Mercator (Small); Ortelius (Folio) [2]; Pitt; Ruscelli; Speed [2]
HUNGARY & BALKANS: De L'Isle; Homann & Homann Heirs; Jaillot; Probst
IRELAND: Bellin (Large); Bertius; Black; Blaeu [2]; Blome; Bowen, E.; Cary [2]; Coronelli [2]; De Vaugondy; De Wit [2]; Government Maps: National; Homann & Homann Heirs [3]; Jaillot; Kitchin; Lavoisne; Le Rouge; Lockhead; Mercator (Folio) [2]; Mercator (Small); Ortelius (Folio); Prinald; Puzzles & games; Quad [2]; Rand, McNally (Atlas maps); Rocque [2]; Sanson (Folio); Senex; S.D.U.K.; Tanner; Thomas, Cowperthwait; Visscher [2]
 – **REGIONS & PROVINCES:** Blaeu [2]; Mercator (Small) [2]; Sanson (Folio) [2]; Van Den Keere
  – **CONNAUGHT:** Blaeu
  – **LEINSTER:** Berry; Blaeu [2]
  – **MUNSTER:** Blaeu
  – **ULSTER:** Blaeu
 – **COUNTIES:** Lewis, Samuel & Co. [5]
 – **DUBLIN:** Lewis, Samuel & Co.; S.D.U.K. [2]; Weller
 – **NAUTICAL (CHART):** Collins, G. [3]; Goos
ITALY: Blome; Bowen, E. [2]; Bradford; Cluver; Danckerts; Dezauche; Homann & Homann Heirs [2]; Jansson; Janvier; Kitchin; Lapie; Magini [2]; Mercator (Folio); Munster; Ortelius (Folio) [2]; Rizzi-Zannoni; Ruscelli [4]; Tavernier; Van Den Keere; Visscher

ITALY: REGIONS - NORTH: Blaeu; Cluver; De Wit; Mercator (Small); Moll (Small); Ortelius (Folio); Visscher
  - **SOUTH:** Bowen, E.; Ortelius (Folio); Political Magazine
- **PROVINCES - LOMBARDY:** Jansson
  - **PAPAL STATES:** Seutter
  - **PIEDMONT:** Jaillot
  - **SARDINIA:** Munster [2]
  - **SAVOY:** Du Val
  - **SICILY:** Anonymous or unknown; Cary; Coronelli; De Fer (Small); Jansson [2]; Mercator (Small); Mortier
  - **TUSCANY:** Jansson; Magini; Ruscelli
  - **(OTHER PROVINCES):** Barbie Du Bocage
- **CITIES - FLORENCE:** Lotter; Munster [2]; Schedel; S.D.U.K.
  - **GENOA:** Blaeu; Harris; Homann & Homann Heirs
  - **MILAN:** Blaeu; S.D.U.K.
  - **MODENA:** Homann & Homann Heirs
  - **NAPLES:** Braun & Hogenberg; De Vaugondy; Faden; Magini; Meyer
  - **ROME:** Braun & Hogenberg [4]; Browne; Homann & Homann Heirs; Jansson; Merian; Monaldini; Munster [2]; Ortelius (Folio); Rossi; Rubeis; Schedel; Seutter; Sickler
  - **TURIN:** Lasor A Varea
  - **VENICE:** Braun & Hogenberg; Chatelain; Coronelli; Merian; Munster [2]; Seutter; S.D.U.K.
  - **(OTHER CITIES):** Bodenehr; Braun & Hogenberg; Meisner; Schedel; S.D.U.K.
- **(MISCELLANEOUS):** Braun & Hogenberg
LAPPLAND: Scherer
LITHUANIA: Blaeu; De Wit; Lotter; Mercator (Small) [2]
LIVONIA: Mercator (Small)
LOW COUNTRIES, LEO BELGICUS: Van Den Keere
LUXEMBURG: De Wit; Jaillot; Jansson; Ortelius (Folio) [2]; Visscher
MALTA: Barker; De Wit; Homann & Homann Heirs; Mortier; Universal Magazine
MEDITERANEAN SEA: Bowen, E. [2]
  - **(ATLAS):** Coronelli
- **EASTERN:** Andrus & Judd; Jansson [3]; Mercator (Small); Ortelius (Folio) [2]; Visscher
- **WESTERN:** Coronelli
- **(MISCELLANEOUS):** Ortelius (Folio) [3]
MORAVIA: Covens & Mortier; Homann & Homann Heirs [2]; Hondius
NETHERLANDS & BELGIUM: Blaeu; Bowen, E.; Delamarche; Jansson; Lockhead; Van Den Keere
NETHERLANDS: Heather; Schenk; Seutter
- **PROVINCES - FRISIA:** Ortelius (Folio); Ottens
  - **GRONINGEN:** De Wit
  - **HOLLAND:** Mercator (Small); Peeters; Thomson
  - **NORTH BRABANT:** Blaeu
  - **ZEELAND:** Blaeu [2]
  - **(OTHER PROVINCES):** De Wit
- **CITIES: - AMSTERDAM:** Braun & Hogenberg [2]; Covens & Mortier; Gentleman's Magazine; Jefferys; Senex; S.D.U.K.
  - **UTRECHT:** Blaeu; Braun & Hogenberg; Pitt
  - **(OTHER CITIES):** Blaeu; Braun & Hogenberg; Callot; Guicciardini; Lasor A Varea; Local & State Maps & Views; Meisner [2]
NETHERLANDS, BELGIUM & LUXEMBOURG: Gentleman's Magazine; Lotter
NORTH SEA: Heather; Imray; Mount & Page; Norie
NORWAY: Danckerts; Pontoppidan; Sanson (Folio)
POLAND: Du Val; Hildburghausen Biblio; Jansson; Kitchin; Lavoisne [2]; Magini [2]; Mercator (Small); Ortelius (Folio) [2]; Sanson (Folio) [2]; Thomson
- **PROVINCES - SILESIA:** Blaeu; Jansson; Lotter; Ortelius (Folio)
- **CITIES:** Bertius; Kilian, G.C.; Rauw
POLAND & LITHUANIA: De Wit [2]; Jaillot
PORTUGAL: Blaeu; Bowen, E.; De Fer (Small); Homann & Homann Heirs; Lotter; Quad; Sanson (Folio); Seutter; S.D.U.K.; Visscher [3]

PORTUGAL: LISBON: Cole
RHINE RIVER: De Wit; Local & State Maps & Views; Mercator (Small); Ortelius (Folio); Phillips; Zatta
ROMAN EMPIRE: Jansson; Speed [2]
ROMANIA: Jansson
RUSSIA: Blaeu; Cluver; De Wit; Jansson; Laporte; Magini; Mercator (Folio); Moll (Small); Ortelius (Folio); Ruscelli; S.D.U.K.; Thomson [3]; Visscher
 –REGIONS - Seutter
  –ARCTIC: Jansson
  –CRIMEA: Gentleman's Magazine; Lasor A Varea
  –NOVAYA ZEMLYA: De Bry; Ottens
  –SOUTH: Blaeu [2]
 – CITIES - MOSCOW: Blaeu [2]; De Lavaur; Lasor A Varea; S.D.U.K.; Trusler
  –ST. PETERSBURG: Covens & Mortier
RUSSIA in EUROPE & ASIA: Cary; Lotter; Ottens
 – (ATLAS): De L'Isle
SCANDINAVIA: Bertius; Chatelain; Forsell; Haellstrom; Homann & Homann Heirs [2]; Kitchin; Laporte; Mercator (Small); Moll (Small); Monin; Munster; Sanson (Folio); Tanner; Visscher [2]; Wyld
 – (MISCELLANEOUS): Sanson (Folio)
SCOTLAND: Bowen, E. [2]; Browne; Carey; Coronelli; Kitchin [2]; Knipe; Laurie & Whittle; Lavoisne; Seutter; Speed
 (ATLAS): Moll (Small)
 – REGIONS: Mercator (Small) [3]
  –COUNTIES - ARGYLESHIRE: Faden
  –DUMFRIES SHIRE: Blaeu
  –EDINBURGHSHIRE: Braun & Hogenberg
 – EDINBURGH: De Wit; Edgar; Meisner; Slezer
 – ISLANDS: Blaeu [2]; Von Reilly
SPAIN: Gastaldi; Purchas; Speed
 – PROVINCES - ARAGON: Jansson
  –CATALONIA: Homann & Homann Heirs; Jaillot
  –GRANADA: Blaeu
  –VALENCIA: Blaeu; Hondius; Jansson
  –(OTHER PROVINCES): Blaeu; De Wit [2]; Homann & Homann Heirs; Sanson (Folio); Senex; Von Reilly
 – CITIES - MADRID: De Fer (Small) [2]; Middleton
  –(OTHER CITIES): Braun & Hogenberg [2]; Custodis; Lasor A Varea; Manuscript Maps; Meisner; Roux
 – BALEARIC ISLANDS: Blaeu [2]; Valdis; Zatta
SPAIN & PORTUGAL: De L'Isle; Gastaldi; Hildburghausen Biblio; Homann & Homann Heirs; Jansson; Magini; Merian; Munster [3]; Ottens; Ptolemy (1511 Venice); Sanson (Folio); Speed [2]
SWEDEN: Chatelain; S.D.U.K.
 – REGIONS: Sanson (Folio) [2]; Von Reilly
 – STOCKHOLM: Braun & Hogenberg; Chatelain; Gottfried; S.D.U.K.
SWITZERLAND: Blaeu; Bowen, E.; Cary; De L'Isle; Faden; Lotter; Magini; Moll (Small); Munster [5]; Ortelius (Folio) [2]; Ottens; Rauw; Rizzi-Zannoni
 – CANTONS: Local & State Maps & Views; Von Reilly
 – CITIES - GENEVA: Munster
  –(OTHER CITIES): Bertius; Braun & Hogenberg [2]; Keller; Meisner; Merian; Munster [3]; Von Reilly
THRACE: Jansson
TRANSYLVANIA: Munster
TURKEY IN EUROPE: De Wit; Tallis
 – CONSTANTINOPLE: Braun & Hogenberg; Merian; Munster; Salmon; Schedel; S.D.U.K.; Seutter
 – DARDANELLES: De Fer (Small)
UKRAINE: Homann & Homann Heirs; Mercator (Small); Seutter [2]; Weigel
WALES: Hondius; Ortelius (Folio); Speed [2]
 – COUNTIES: Blaeu; Evans; Jansson
 – (MISCELLANEOUS): Ogilby
YUGOSLAVIA, FORMER (PROVINCES): Mercator (Small); Ortelius (Folio) [2]; Seutter

NORTH AMERICA: General & Pre-Independence U.S. Regions

NORTH AMERICA: Arrowsmith; Arrowsmith & Lewis; Bellin (Large) [3]; Bellin (Small); Berghaus; Betts; Blair; Bolton; Bonne [3]; Bowen, T. [3]; Bradford; Brion De La Tour; Burr; Carey & Lea [2]; Chatelain [2]; Collot; Colton (Atlas maps) [2]; Conder; Coronelli [2]; Covens & Mortier; De L'Isle [2]; De Lat; De Vaugondy [4]; Diderot; Dufour [3]; Elwe [2]; Finley; Fisher; Fremin; Gaston & Johnson; Gibson; Hall, S.; Harrison; Hennepin; Hildburghausen Biblio [2]; Jaillot [5]; Jansson [3]; Johnson [2]; Johnston [2]; Kilian, G.C.; Kitchin; Lapie; Laurie & Whittle; Levasseur [7]; Lodge; London Magazine; Lotter; Mallet [2]; Mitchell, S.A. (Atlas maps 1859 & earlier); Mitchell, S.A. (Atlas maps 1860 & later); Mitchell, S.A. (Maps not from atlases); Moll (Large) [6]; Moll (Small); Morse, J. [2]; Naymiller & Allodi; Olney [3]; Palairet; Payne; Perthes; Playfair; Prichard; Probst; Purchas; Quad [2]; Rollos; Russell [2]; Scherer [2]; Schoolcraft; Seale; Smith, C.; Smith, Roswell C.; S.D.U.K.; Tallis [6]; Thomas, Cowperthwait; Thomson [2]; U.S. Gov't. [2]; Vuillemin; Weiland; Wells [2]; Wilkinson; Woodbridge; Wyld
- **REGIONS - CENTRAL:** Bellin (Small) [3]; Bowen, E.; Coronelli; Covens & Mortier; De L'Isle [2]; De Vaugondy; Hennepin; Homann & Homann Heirs [2]; Sanson (Folio); Senex
- **EAST:** Bellin (Large); Bonne; Bowles; Carver; Chatelain [3]; Clouet; D'Anville; De Fer (Small) [2]; De L'Isle; De Vaugondy [5]; De Wit; Delamarche; Gastaldi; Gentleman's Magazine [4]; Harrison; Homann & Homann Heirs [5]; Kitchin [2]; Le Rouge; Longchamps [2]; Lotter; Moithey; Moll (Large); Moll (Small) [3]; Mortier; Osborne; Ottens; Palairet; Popple [2]; Rhode; Russell; Santini; Seutter; Visscher; Williamson; Wytfliet [2]; Zatta
- **(ATLASES):** Jefferys; Sayer & Bennett; Rocque
- **EAST COAST:** Direccion de Hidrografia; Mount & Page [2]; Sartine; Seller; Van Keulen
- **NORTH:** Diderot; Van Keulen
- **NORTHEAST:** Bellin (Large); Bellin (Small); Du Val; London Magazine; Michault; Ogilby; Ramusio [2]; Ruscelli [2]; Sayer; Sayer & Bennett [2]; Visscher
- **NORTHWEST:** Burr; De Jode; Diderot [3]; La Perouse; Metellus; Vancouver; Wytfliet [2]
- **SOUTH:** Bonne; De Herrera; De L'Isle [2]; Moll (Small)
- **SOUTHEAST:** De Fer (Large); Homann & Homann Heirs [2]; Mallet; Popple; Seligmann; Van Der Aa; Wytfliet [3]
- **SOUTHWEST:** Lockhead; Postlethwait
- **WEST COAST:** Chappe D'auteroche; La Perouse; Vancouver
- **WEST:** Coronelli; Greenhow; Moll (Small) [2]; Sanson (Small) [4]
- **(MISCELLANEOUS):** De Bry

NORTH AMERICA & WEST INDIES: Bowen, E.; Homann & Homann Heirs; Monk [3]; Walch

ARCTIC: Bowen, E.

CALIFORNIA: De Fer (Small); Diderot [3]; Wytfliet

CALIFORNIA & NEW MEXICO: De Fer (Small) [2]; Kino; Mallet [2]; Tirion

CAROLINA: Blome; Lea; Moll (Small); Montanus; Morden; Mortier [2]; Mouzon; Ogilby; Sanson (Folio) [5]; Sartine; Speed; Van Keulen [2]

CAROLINA & FLORIDA: Bellin (Small)

CAROLINA, MARYLAND & VIRGINIA: Homann & Homann Heirs

ENGLISH POSSESSIONS: Magazine Of Magazines

FLORIDA: Bellin (Small); De Bry; De Laet; Du Val; Jefferys [2]; Le Moyne [2]; Ortelius (Folio) [3]; Prockter; Sanson (Small)

FLORIDA & LOUISIANA: Bonne

FLORIDA & MEXICO: Chatelain; Seutter

FLORIDA & VIRGINIA: Blaeu [5]; Cloppenburgh; Hondius [4]; Jansson [3]; Mercator (Folio); Mercator (Small); Ogilby [2]; Purchas

GREAT LAKES: Bellin (Large); Bellin (Small); Bonne [3]; British Admiralty; De Vaugondy; Homann & Homann Heirs [2]; La Hontan; Russell; S.D.U.K.; Vandermaelen; Zatta

GULF COAST: De Fer (Small) [2]

LOUISIANA: Covens & Mortier; De L'Isle

MARYLAND & VIRGINIA: De Vaugondy [3]; Moll (Small) [2]; Speed

MIDDLE BRITISH COLONIES: Du Val; Gibson; London Magazine; Lotter [2]

NEW ENGLAND: Blaeu [2]; Eldridge; General Magazine Of Arts & Sciences; Jefferys [2]; Morden; Neal

NEW FRANCE: Bellin (Large); Chatelain [3]; De L'Isle; Ramusio [2]; Sanson (Folio); Wytfliet [2]

NIAGARA RIVER: Government Maps: Local & State

NORTHERN BRITISH COLONIES: Blaeu; Blome; Danckerts; De Laet; Gentleman's Magazine; Homann & Homann Heirs [2]; Jansson [3]; Lotter; Moll (Small); Seutter; Speed [3]; Van Keulen; Visscher [2]; Wells [2]
SOUTHERN BRITISH COLONIES: Speed [3]
SOUTHWESTERN USA & MEXICO: Bartlett, J.R; Binet; Blackie; Grigg; Kitchin; Tallis
- **(ATLAS):** Kendall
UNITED STATES, PRESENT: Scherer
UNITED STATES & CANADA: Kensett
VIRGINIA: Blaeu [5]; De Bry; Hondius [2]; Mercator (Small); Ogilby

NORTH AMERICA: CANADA

CANADA: Canadian Governments; Colton (Atlas maps) [2]; Dawson; Hildburghausen Biblio; Mackenzie
- **REGIONS - CENTRAL:** Cary; Wytfliet
  - **EAST:** Arrowsmith; Blaeu; Carey & Lea [2]; Coronelli; De L'Isle [3]; De Vaugondy [3]; Finley; Guthrie; Jaillot; Mortier; Mount & Page; Olney; Thomson; Wyld; Wytfliet
  - **NORTH:** Mortier; Zatta
  - **NORTHWEST:** Canadian Governments [2]; Stanford
  - **WEST:** Railroad Company Maps; Rand, McNally (Atlas maps); S.D.U.K.
BRITISH COLUMBIA: S.D.U.K.
CAPE BRETON ISLAND: Bellin (Small); De Vaugondy
- **LOUISBURG:** Bellin (Small) [2]
HUDSON BAY: Bellin (Small) [2]
MANITOBA: Canadian Governments [2]
MARITIME PROVINCES: Bowen, E.; Cary; Colton (Pocket & Wall Maps); De Vaugondy; Mitchell, S.A. (Atlas maps 1860 & later); Tallis; Visscher
NEWFOUNDLAND: Bertius; Van Keulen
NOVA SCOTIA: Bellin (Small) [2]; Jefferys; Lescarbot
- **HALIFAX:** Gentleman's Magazine [2]; Lottery Magazine
ONTARIO: Arrowsmith; Canadian Governments; Colton (Atlas maps); Ensign, Bridgman & Fanning; Johnson; Mitchell, S.A. (Atlas maps 1859 & earlier); Mitchell, S.A. (Atlas maps 1860 & later); Thomas, Cowperthwait; Wyld
- **TORONTO:** Harper's Weekly
QUEBEC: London Magazine; Russell
- **MONTREAL:** Bellin (Small); London Magazine; Ramusio [2]
- **QUEBEC CITY:** Andrews; Bellin (Small) [2]; Faden; La Hontan; London Magazine [2]; Mortier
ST. LAWRENCE RIVER: Bellin (Small) [3]; Des Barres; Jefferys; Local & State Pocket Maps; Scots Magazine

NORTH AMERICA: MEXICO and CENTRAL AMERICA

CENTRAL AMERICA: Bellin (Small); Colton (Atlas maps); Sonnenstern; Wyld; Wytfliet
COSTA RICA: Bellin (Small)
MEXICO: Albrizzi; Bellin (Small) [2]; Cloppenburgh; Colton (Atlas maps); Coronelli; Gastaldi; Hondius; Jansson; Johnson; Mallet; Mercator (Folio); Mercator (Small); Ortelius (Folio); Vandermaelen; Wytfliet
- **REGIONS:** Direccion De Hidrografia; Hall, S.; Local & State Maps & Views; Scherer; Von Humboldt
- **MEXICO CITY:** Bellin (Small); Braun & Hogenberg [3]; Dapper; Illustrated London News; Local & State Maps & Views; Mallet; Ramusio; Russell
- **(OTHER CITIES):** Bellin (Small); Ogilby; U.S. War Dep't
MEXICO & CENTRAL AMERICA: Bonne [2]; Sanson (Folio) [2]; S.D.U.K.; Thomson; Van Der Aa
MEXICO & GUATEMALA: Desilver; Thomas, Cowperthwait [2]
MEXICO & PRESENT U.S. SOUTHWEST: Arrowsmith [2]; Black; Blackie; Carey & Lea [2]; De Vaugondy; Goodrich; Hall, S.; Lapie [4]; Lothian; Macpherson; Morden; Morse & Breese; Stieler; Tardieu; Thomas, Cowperthwait; Thomson; Vivien
MEXICO & WEST INDIES: Lapie; Mitchell, S.A. (Atlas maps 1860 & later) [2]
NICARAGUA: Government Maps: National; Van Der Aa
PANAMA: Bellin (Small); Chatelain; Esquemeling; Gazzettiere Americano; Moll (Small); Mortier; U.S. Gov't

NORTH AMERICA: UNITED STATES

UNITED STATES: Aeronautical Maps; Anonymous or unknown; Binet; Blackie [2]; Bradford [4]; Bradley; Braun & Hogenberg; Bromme; Buchon; Carey & Lea; Case, Tiffany & Co.; Colton (Atlas maps) [5]; Colton (Pocket & Wall Maps) [3]; Concept Maps [2]; Copley; Cram [2]; Daily Graphic; Desilver [2]; Drioux & Leroy; Dufour; Duvotenay; Ensign [2]; Finley; Goodrich; Gray [3]; Hall, S.; Harper; Hinton [3]; Homann & Homann Heirs; Johnson [4]; Johnston; Kitchin; Lapie [4]; Lewis; Lucas [2]; Melish; Meyer; Mitchell, S.A. (Atlas maps 1859 & earlier); Mitchell, S.A. (Atlas maps 1860 & later); Mitchell, S.A. (Maps not from atlases) [8]; Morse, S.; Olney; Perrot; Phelps; Phelps & Ensign; Puzzles & games [4]; Railroad Company Maps [6]; Rand, McNally (Pocket & Wall Maps); Ranney; Sanson (Folio); Schoyer; Smith, J.C.; Smith, Roswell C.; Stieler; Tallis [2]; Thomas, Cowperthwait; Thomson; U.S. Gov't. [4]; U.S. State Surveys; U.S. War Dep't; Vivien; Walch; Watson; Weimar Geographisches Institut; Wilkinson [2]; Williams, W.; Wyld

(ATLASES): Appleton; Arbuckle; Asher & Adams; Hardesty; Local & State Maps & Views; Melish; Morse, J.; Tanner; U.S. Coast Survey [4]; U.S. Union & Confederate Armies Atlas

- **REGIONS - CENTRAL:** Bonne; Buchon; Colton (Pocket & Wall Maps); Cornell; Fremont; James; Olney [2]; Pike, Zebulon; Railroad Company Maps [2]; S.D.U.K.; Swinton; U.S. Gov't. [5]
- **EASTERN:** Arrowsmith; Arrowsmith & Lewis; Blair; Bradford; Brion De La Tour; Burr; Carey [2]; Cary [2]; Colton (Pocket & Wall Maps) [2]; Finley; Gordon, William; Gussefeld [2]; Guthrie; Imbert; La Harpe; Le Rouge; Lizars; Mitchell, S.A. (Atlas maps 1859 & earlier); Mitchell, S.A. (Maps not from atlases) [5]; Morse, J.; Phelps & Ensign; Railroad Company Maps; Rand, McNally (Pocket & Wall Maps); Schoyer; Smith, C.; Tanner [3]; Tardieu; Teesdale; Thomson Wilkinson [2]; Williams, C.S.
  - **(ATLASES):** Marshall; Soules
- **EAST COAST:** Blunt; Copley; Direccion De Hidrografia; Laurie & Whittle; U.S. Coast & Geodetic Survey; U.S. Coast Survey
- **GREAT PLAINS:** Colton (Atlas maps) [2]; Fremont; Johnson [6]; Letts; McNally; Mitchell, S.A. (Atlas maps 1860 & later) [2]; U.S. Gov't. [8]; U.S. Pacific R.R. Survey; U.S. Union & Confederate Armies Atlas; U.S. War Dep't; Vandermaelen; Warner & Beers
- **GULF COAST:** Ottens; U.S. Coast Survey
- **MIDDLE ATLANTIC:** Bacon; Colton (Pocket & Wall Maps); Ensign, Bridgman & Fanning; Gentleman's Magazine; Marshall; Mortier; Russell; S.D.U.K. [3]; Tardieu
- **MIDWEST, see Northwest Territory:** Anonymous or unknown; Atwood; Carey [2]; Carver; Colton (Pocket & Wall Maps); Finley; Mitchell, S.A. (Atlas maps 1859 & earlier); Morse, J. [2]; Railroad Company Maps [2]; U.S. Gov't. [2]
  - **(ATLAS):** U.S. Gov't
- **MOUNTAIN WEST:** Colton (Atlas maps) [2]; Fremont; Railroad Company Maps; U.S. Gov't. [2]; U.S. Pacific R.R. Survey [2]
  - **(ATLASES):** U.S. Gov't. [2]
- **NEW ENGLAND:** Des Barres; Jefferys; Le Rouge; Lotter; Marshall; Meyer; Mount & Page
- **NEW ENGLAND & NEW YORK:** Bellin (Small); Bowles; Colton (Pocket & Wall Maps); Goldthwait; Olney; Railroad Company Maps; Russell; Vandermaelen
- **NORTH:** Maximilian Of Wied
- **NORTHEAST:** Bellin (Small); Bonne [2]; Bowles; Brion De La Tour; Cary [2]; De Laporte; Laporte; Le Rouge; Lloyd; Lotter [4]; Marshall; Milbert; Railroad Company Maps; Stanford; Universal Magazine
- **NORTHEAST & EASTERN CANADA:** Rand, Avery & Co.; Sartine
- **NORTHWEST:** Colton (Atlas maps) [2]; Mitchell, S.A. (Atlas maps 1860 & later) [2]; Railroad Company Maps; U.S. Pacific R.R. Survey; U.S. War Dep't
- **SOUTH:** Finley; Johnson; Mitchell, S.A. (Atlas maps 1860 & later); Perrine; Phelps & Watson [4]; Smith, Roswell C.; Swanston; Vandermaelen; Weekly Dispatch; Williams, W.
  - **(ATLAS):** Johnson
- **SOUTHEAST:** Bonne [5]; Bowen, E.; Finley [2]; Marshall [2]; Morse, J. [2]; Olney; Russell; Smith, Roswell C.; U.S. Gov't.; Vandermaelen; Zatta [5]
- **SOUTHWEST:** Bartholomew; Colton (Atlas maps) [3]; Lloyd, H.H.; Meyer; Rand, McNally (Atlas maps); Stieler; U.S. Gov't. [7]; U.S. Pacific R.R. Survey [2]; U.S. Union & Confederate Armies Atlas; U.S. War Dep't [3]; Vandermaelen; Warner & Beers; Williams, J.D.
- **SOUTHWEST & CALIFORNIA:** Fremont; Johnson [4]; S.D.U.K.; Tanner; U.S. Exploring Expedition; Vandermaelen
- **SOUTHWEST & MEXICO:** Betts; Colton (Pocket & Wall Maps); Letts; Meyer [4]; S.D.U.K. [2]; Weekly Dispatch; Wislizenus

UNITED STATES – WEST: Arrowsmith & Lewis; Blackie; Bonneville; Burr; Cassell; Colton (Atlas maps) [2]; Colton (Pocket & Wall Maps) [3]; Dufour; Fremont [2]; Gilpin; Goodrich; James; Johnson; Johnston; Keeler; Lloyd, H.H.; Mitchell, S.A. (Atlas maps 1859 & earlier); Mitchell, S.A. (Atlas maps 1860 & later); Mitchell, S.A. (Maps not from atlases); Mollhausen; Olney [2]; Railroad Company Maps [4]; Rand, McNally (Pocket & Wall Maps); Richards; Smith, Roswell C.; Stieler; Swanston [2]; Thomas, Cowperthwait [2]; U.S. Gov't. [8]; U.S. War Dep't
 – **(ATLASES):** Fremont; Parker; Stansbury; U.S. Gov't
 – **(CITIES, MISCELLANEOUS):** Bowen, E.; Bradford [2]; Olney
UNITED STATES & CANADA: Arrowsmith; Colton (Pocket & Wall Maps); Lloyd; Lockhead; Olney; Railroad Company Maps; Smith, Roswell C.
UNITED STATES & MEXICO: Dezauche; Dufour [2]; Homann & Homann Heirs; Mitchell, S.A. (Atlas maps 1859 & earlier); Schmolder; Woodbridge

LISTING BY STATES

ALABAMA: Bradford [3]; Burr; Finley; Mitchell, S.A. (Atlas maps 1859 & earlier); Rand, McNally (Atlas maps); Thomas, Cowperthwait [2]
ALABAMA & GEORGIA: Johnson [2]; Mitchell, S.A. (Atlas maps 1860 & later)
ALABAMA & MISSISSIPPI: Arrowsmith & Lewis; Bradford; Morse, J.
ALASKA: Emmons; Mitchell, S.A. (Atlas maps 1860 & later) [2]; Rand, McNally (Pocket & Wall Maps); U.S. Gov't. [2]; U.S. Geological Survey
ARIZONA: Arbuckle; Cram; Hayden, F.; Rand, McNally (Atlas maps); Rand, McNally (Pocket & Wall Maps); U.S. Gov't. [3]; U.S. Geological Survey; U.S. State Surveys [3]; U.S. War Dep't; Walker, H.B.
ARIZONA & NEW MEXICO: Mitchell, S.A. (Atlas maps 1860 & later) [2]; Petermann; U.S. Gov't. [2]; U.S. Pacific R.R. Survey; U.S. State Surveys [3]; U.S. War Dep't
ARKANSAS: Bradford; Burr; Colton (Atlas maps) [2]; Cowperthwait, Desilver & Butler; Cram; Greenleaf; Railroad Company Maps; Thomas, Cowperthwait; U.S. State Surveys
ARKANSAS & MISSOURI: Finley [2]
CALIFORNIA: Colton (Atlas maps); Cram; Elliott; Hardesty; Local & State Maps & Views [2]; Local & State Pocket Maps; Local & State Wall Maps [2]; Lubrecht; Mitchell, S.A. (Atlas maps 1860 & later) [2]; Railroad Company Maps; Rand, McNally (Atlas maps); Real Estate & Promotional Maps [2]; U.S. Gov't. [15]; U.S. Coast Survey [3]; U.S. Pacific R.R. Survey; U.S. State Surveys [2]; U.S. War Dep't [3]; Vandermaelen
 – **LOS ANGELES:** U.S. Pacific R.R. Survey
 – **SAN FRANCISCO:** Allardt; Britton & Rey; Gray; Hildburghausen Biblio; Meyer
CALIFORNIA & NEVADA: Asher & Adams [3]; Gray; U.S. State Surveys; U.S. War Dep't; Warner & Beers
CALIFORNIA & OREGON: Fremont
COLORADO: Asher & Adams; Bradley; Cram [3]; Harper's Weekly; Hayden, F. [9]; Highway Maps; Local & State Wall Maps; Mining Maps; Mitchell, S.A. (Atlas maps 1860 & later) [2]; Nell; Page; Railroad Company Maps; U.S. Gov't. [3]; U.S. Geological Survey [2]; U.S. State Surveys; U.S. War Dep't [5]; Walker, H.B.
COLORADO & NEW MEXICO: Colton (Atlas maps); U.S. Gov't.; U.S. War Dep't
COLORADO & UTAH: Railroad Company Maps
 – **(ATLAS):** U.S. Geological Survey
CONNECTICUT: Arrowsmith & Lewis; Bailey, O.H., & Co. [3]; Beers; Buchon; Carey [2]; Carey & Lea; Clark [4]; Clark & Tackabury; Collins & Clark; Colton (Atlas maps); Finley [2]; Hurd; Ladies Repository; Lester; Local & State Wall Maps [2]; Mitchell, S.A. (Atlas maps 1859 & earlier); Sotzmann; Stebbins; Thomas, Cowperthwait; U.S. Coast Survey [2]; Walling; Willard
 – **(ATLASES):** Beers [2]
CONNECTICUT & NEW YORK: Railroad Company Maps
CONNECTICUT & RHODE ISLAND: Gentleman's Magazine; Universal Magazine
DAKOTA TERRITORY: Asher & Adams; Bradley; Cram; Rand, McNally (Pocket & Wall Maps) [2]; U.S. State Surveys
DAKOTA TERRITORY & MINNESOTA: Colton (Atlas maps); Johnson [3]; Mitchell, S.A. (Atlas maps 1860 & later)
DELAWARE: Arrowsmith & Lewis; Bradford; Carey; Finley
DELAWARE & MARYLAND: Colton (Pocket & Wall Maps); Gray; Johnson [4]
DELAWARE & NEW JERSEY: Blunt

DISTRICT OF COLUMBIA: Carey & Lea; Colton (Atlas maps); Colton (Pocket & Wall Maps); Ellicott [4]; Illustrated London News; Johnson [2]; Lizars; Local & State Maps & Views; Mitchell, S.A. (Atlas maps 1859 & earlier); Mitchell, S.A. (Atlas maps 1860 & later); Real Estate & Promotional Maps [3]; Russell; Tanner; Thomas, Cowperthwait; U.S. War Dep't; Wells, J.

FLORIDA: Blunt; Bradford; British Admiralty; Colton (Atlas maps) [2]; Colton (Pocket & Wall Maps); Cram; Drew; Finley; Gentleman's Magazine; Government Maps: Local & State; Jefferys [2]; Johnson; Meyer; Mitchell, S.A. (Atlas maps 1860 & later); Morse & Breese; Railroad Company Maps; Rand, McNally (Atlas maps); S.D.U.K. [3]; Swift; Tanner; Thomas, Cowperthwait [2]; U.S. Gov't.; U.S. Coast & Geodetic Survey; U.S. Coast Survey; Vandermaelen

- **PENSACOLA:** Gazzettiere Americano; U.S. Gov't
- **ST. AUGUSTINE:** Gentleman's Magazine [3]; U.S. Coast Survey

GEORGIA: Arrowsmith & Lewis; Bradford [2]; Buchon; Davis; Finley; Lucas; Meyer [2]; Railroad Company Maps; U.S. Gov't.; U.S. Union & Confederate Armies Atlas; U.S. War Dep't

HAWAII: Colton (Atlas maps); Cook; Government Maps: Local & State; La Perouse [3]; Meyer; Rand, McNally (Atlas maps); U.S. Gov't. [2]; Vandermaelen

IDAHO: Cram [2]; Local & State Maps & Views; Mitchell, S.A. (Atlas maps 1860 & later) [2]; U.S. State Surveys

IDAHO, MONTANA & WYOMING: Bradley [2]; Warner & Beers

ILLINOIS: Burr; Colton (Atlas maps); Colton (Pocket & Wall Maps) [2]; Cram; Desilver; Lucas; Meyer; Mitchell, S.A. (Atlas maps 1860 & later); Mitchell, S.A. (Maps not from atlases) Thomas, Cowperthwait; U.S. Gov't. [2]; U.S. State Surveys

- **CHICAGO:** Blanchard, R. [2]; Local & State Pocket Maps; Rand, McNally (Atlas maps); Real Estate & Promotional Maps

ILLINOIS & MISSOURI: Hinton

INDIAN TERRITORY, see Oklahoma: Gast & Co.

INDIANA: Buchon; Carey & Lea; Colton (Atlas maps) [2]; Finley; Rand, McNally (Atlas maps); U.S. Gov't. [2]

INDIANA & OHIO: Railroad Company Maps

IOWA: Colton (Atlas maps); Cram; Mitchell, S.A. (Atlas maps 1859 & earlier) [3]

IOWA & WISCONSIN: Bradford; Morse & Breese

KANSAS: Colton (Atlas maps); Colton (Pocket & Wall Maps); Holmes; Local & State Maps & Views; Local & State Pocket Maps; Meyer; Page; Rand, McNally (Pocket & Wall Maps) [2]

KANSAS & MISSOURI: Johnson

KANSAS & NEBRASKA: Colton (Atlas maps); Colton (Pocket & Wall Maps); U.S. State Surveys

KENTUCKY: Arrowsmith & Lewis; Bradford; Carey; Carey & Lea; Russell

- **(ATLAS):** U.S. Geological Survey

KENTUCKY & TENNESSEE: Asher & Adams; Bradford; Colton (Atlas maps); Colton (Pocket & Wall Maps); Hinton; Johnson; Mitchell, S.A. (Maps not from atlases); Morse, J.; U.S. Gov't

LOUISIANA: Bradford; Carey & Lea; Colton (Atlas maps); Colton (Pocket & Wall Maps); Cram; Finley; Meyer; Mitchell, S.A. (Atlas maps 1859 & earlier); Tanner; U.S. State Surveys [2]

- **NEW ORLEANS:** Bellin (Small); Colton (Atlas maps); Ladies Repository; Rand, McNally (Atlas maps); Virtue

MAINE: Asher & Adams; Blunt [2]; Colton (Atlas maps); Cram; Johnson; Ladies Repository; Local & State Maps & Views; Lucas; Tanner; Thomas, Cowperthwait; U.S. Gov't.; U.S. Coast Survey [2]; U.S. War Dep't [2]; Walling [3]

MARYLAND: Bradford [2]; Carey; Lucas [2]; Real Estate & Promotional Maps; U.S. Gov't.; U.S. Coast Survey; Universal Magazine [2]

- **(ATLAS):** Lake et al
- **BALTIMORE:** Colton (Atlas maps) [2]; Gray

MARYLAND & VIRGINIA: De Bry; De Laporte; De Vaugondy; Finley [2]; Laporte; U.S. Coast Survey

MASSACHUSETTS: Bachelder, J.B.; Beers; Blunt [4]; Carey & Lea; Champlain [2]; Dorr, Howland & Co.; Finley [2]; Hill; Local & State Maps & Views; Morrill; Railroad Company Maps; Rand, McNally (Atlas maps); Rand, McNally (Pocket & Wall Maps); Sampson, Davenport & Co.; U.S. Coast Survey [10]; U.S. War Dep't [3]; Universal Magazine; Walling [3]; Walling & Gray

- **(ATLASES):** Beers [2]; Richards; Walling & Gray
- **BOSTON:** Bellin (Small); Blunt [2]; Bowen - Generally, Blunt [2]; Bowen; Colton (Atlas maps) [2]; Crosman & Mallory; Depot De La Marine; Dutton; Gazzettiere Americano; Gentleman's Magazine; Gray; Local & State Maps & Views [2]; Marshall; Political Magazine; Rand, McNally (Atlas maps); S.D.U.K.; Town & Country Magazine; U.S. Coast Survey [2]; Universal Magazine; Whitney

MASSACHUSETTS, CONNECTICUT & RHODE ISLAND: Colton (Pocket & Wall Maps); Ensign & Thayer; Government Maps: Local & State; Gray; Mitchell, S.A. (Atlas maps 1860 & later)
MASSACHUSETTS & RHODE ISLAND: Colton (Atlas maps) [2]; Colton (Pocket & Wall Maps) [3]; Cram; Des Barres; Universal Magazine
MICHIGAN: Bellin (Small); Buchon; Burr; Carey & Lea; Colton (Atlas maps) [3]; Desilver; Farmer; Thomas, Cowperthwait; U.S. Gov't. [3]; U.S. War Dep't [3]
- **(ATLASES):** Everts & Stewart; Local & State Maps & Views; Walling
MICHIGAN & WISCONSIN: Johnson; Mitchell, S.A. (Atlas maps 1860 & later); Olney; S.D.U.K.
MINNESOTA: Chapman [2]; Colton (Atlas maps) [2]; Colton (Pocket & Wall Maps) [2]; Cowperthwait, Desilver & Butler; Highway Maps; Local & State Pocket Maps; Rand, McNally (Atlas maps); Real Estate & Promotional Maps; Rice, G.J.; Thomas, Cowperthwait; U.S. Gov't. [4]; U.S. Pacific R.R. Survey; U.S. State Surveys
MINNESOTA & WISCONSIN: Vandermaelen
MISSISSIPPI: Bradford; Carey & Lea; Colton (Atlas maps); Davis; Finley; Mathews; Tanner; Thomas, Cowperthwait; U.S. Coast Survey
MISSISSIPPI RIVER: Burr; Magnus, C.; Sayer
MISSOURI: Bradford; Colby; Collot; Colton (Pocket & Wall Maps); Finley [2]; Hinton; Local & State Pocket Maps; Northwest Publishing Co.; Rand, McNally (Pocket & Wall Maps); Thomas, Cowperthwait [2]; U.S. State Surveys
- **ST. LOUIS:** Gray; Local & State Pocket Maps
MONTANA: Asher & Adams; Baker & Harper; Cram [3]; U.S. Pacific R.R. Survey; U.S. State Surveys; U.S. War Dep't
NEBRASKA: Clason Map Co.; Cram [4]; Gast & Co.; U.S. War Dep't
NEVADA: Cram; Government Maps: Local & State; Gray; Mining Maps; U.S. Gov't.; U.S. Geological Survey; U.S. State Surveys; U.S. War Dep't [2]
NEVADA & UTAH: Bradley; Mitchell, S.A. (Atlas maps 1860 & later) [2]; Vandermaelen
NEW HAMPSHIRE: Blunt [3]; Bradford [2]; Buchon; Carey & Lea; Carrigain, P.; Chace; Local & State Maps & Views; Local & State Wall Maps; Lucas; Payne; Universal Magazine; Walling
NEW HAMPSHIRE & VERMONT: Local & State Wall Maps; Tanner; Thomas, Cowperthwait
NEW HAMPSHIRE, VERMONT & MAINE: Finley; Gordon, William; Hinton
NEW JERSEY: Aeronautical Maps; Anderson; Arrowsmith & Lewis; Beers [2]; Bien [2]; Blunt [2]; Carey [2]; Carey & Lea; Cram; Desilver; Faden; Gordon, William; Harper's Weekly; Johnson; Local & State Maps & Views; Local & State Pocket Maps [2]; Marshall; Rand, McNally (Atlas maps); Real Estate & Promotional Maps; Thomas, Cowperthwait; Universal Magazine
- **(ATLAS):** Beers
NEW JERSEY & PENNSYLVANIA: Colby; Hinton; Seutter; Tanner
NEW MEXICO: Hardesty; Rand, McNally (Atlas maps); Real Estate & Promotional Maps; U.S. Gov't. [4]; U.S. State Surveys [2]; U.S. War Dep't [7]
NEW YORK: American Bank Note Co.; Analectic Magazine; Arrowsmith & Lewis; Beers [2]; Bradford [2]; Bromley; Burr; Carey & Lea; Colton (Pocket & Wall Maps); Endicott & Co.; Faden [3]; Finley; French; French & Smith; Geil; Gentleman's Magazine; Government Maps: Local & State; Homann & Homann Heirs; Hurd; Le Rouge [2]; Local & State Maps & Views [2]; Local & State Pocket Maps [2]; Local & State Wall Maps [3]; Magnus, C.; Marshall [3]; Pease; Railroad Company Maps; Smith, J.C.; Stoddard; U.S. Coast & Geodetic Survey [3]; U.S. Coast Survey; Universal Magazine [2]; Weld
- **(ATLASES):** Asher & Adams [3]; Beers [3]; Bien [3]; Burgoyne; Everts; Hopkins; Local & State Maps & Views; Pomeroy
- **NEW YORK CITY:** Appleton; Doughty; Dripps; Ensign & Thayer; Ewen; Faden [3]; Gentleman's Magazine; Gordon, William; Hayward; Holmes; Illustrated London News [2]; Johnson [2]; Local & State Maps & Views [3]; Local & State Pocket Maps [2]; Marshall; Maverick, P.; Mcelroy, Son & Brown [2]; Mitchell, S.A. (Atlas maps 1859 & earlier); Mount & Page; Phelps [4]; Rogers & Johnston; Russell; Shannon; S.D.U.K.; Taunton; Thomas, Cowperthwait; U.S. Coast Survey [2]; Valentine's Manual [2]; Viele [2]
NORTH CAROLINA: Colton (Atlas maps) [3]; Illustrated London News; Lucas; Meyer; Morse & Breese; U.S. Gov't.; U.S. War Dep't
NORTH CAROLINA & SOUTH CAROLINA: Greenleaf; Hinton; Johnson; Mitchell, S.A. (Atlas maps 1860 & later); Morse, J. [2]; S.D.U.K.
NORTH CAROLINA & VIRGINIA: De Bry
NORTH DAKOTA: Rand, McNally (Atlas maps) [2]; U.S. Gov't
NORTH DAKOTA & SOUTH DAKOTA: U.S. State Surveys

NORTHWEST TERRITORY: S.D.U.K.

OHIO: American Ethnological Society; Arrowsmith & Lewis [2]; Carey; Carey & Lea [2]; Colby; Government Maps: Local & State; Local & State Pocket Maps; Madison; Mitchell, S.A. (Atlas maps 1859 & earlier); Mitchell, S.A. (Maps not from atlases) [2]; Puzzles & games; Railroad Company Maps; Real Estate & Promotional Maps; S.D.U.K.; Tanner; U.S. State Surveys [2]

- **CINCINNATI:** Anonymous or unknown

OKLAHOMA, see Indian Territory: Century Atlas; Cram; Rand, McNally (Atlas maps); U.S. Gov't. [4]; U.S. State Surveys [4]; Walker, H.B.

OREGON: Highway Maps; Railroad Company Maps [2]; U.S. Coast Survey; U.S. State Surveys [5]; U.S. War Dep't [2]

OREGON TERRITORY: Burr; Greenleaf; Hood [2]; Parker; Schoolcraft; U.S. Exploring Expedition

OREGON & WASHINGTON: Colton (Atlas maps) [3]; Gill; Lloyd, H.H.; Mitchell, S.A. (Atlas maps 1860 & later); Railroad Company Maps; U.S. War Dep't

OREGON, WASHINGTON & IDAHO: Johnson [2]

PENNSYLVANIA: Bachelder, J.B.; Brion; Colton (Pocket & Wall Maps); Duval; Faden; Finley [2]; Hopkins [2]; Howell [2]; Ladies Repository; Local & State Pocket Maps [2]; Manuscript Maps [2]; Mitchell, S.A. (Maps not from atlases); Railroad Company Maps; Scull; Smith; Tanner [2]; U.S. Union & Confederate Armies Atlas; Wall

- **(ATLASES):** Beers [3]; Bridgens; Caldwell [2]; Davis [2]; Everts & Stewart [2]; Government Maps: Local & State; Pomeroy; Walling & Gray [2]

- **PHILADELPHIA:** Bradford; Coggins; Colton (Atlas maps); Gentleman's Magazine; Jefferys; Local & State Maps & Views [2]; Lotter [4]; Mitchell, S.A. (Atlas maps 1860 & later) [3]; Smith; S.D.U.K.; Walling & Gray [2]

-**(ATLAS):** Bromley

RHODE ISLAND: Blunt [2]; Carey & Lea; Faden [3]; Gentleman's Magazine [2]; Marshall; U.S. Coast Survey

SOUTH CAROLINA: Arrowsmith & Lewis; Bradford [3]; Carey; Colton (Atlas maps); Desilver; Jefferys & Faden; Morse & Breese; Scott; Stedman

- **CHARLESTON:** Faden; Marshall; Melish; Petrie; Stedman; Tarleton; U.S. Gov't.; U.S. Coast Survey

SOUTH DAKOTA: Cram; Rand, McNally (Pocket & Wall Maps); Tunison; Winchell; Zeese

- **(ATLAS):** U.S. Gov't

TENNESSEE: Arrowsmith & Lewis; Carey; Hopkins; Meyer [2]; Mitchell, S.A. (Maps not from atlases); Rand, McNally (Atlas maps); Thomas, Cowperthwait; U.S. Gov't.; U.S. War Dep't [2]

TEXAS: Arrowsmith; Asher & Adams [3]; Bradford; Century Atlas; Colton (Atlas maps) [9]; Colton (Pocket & Wall Maps) [3]; Cowperthwait, Desilver & Butler; Cram [7]; De Cordova [2]; Gast & Co. [4]; Government Maps: Local & State [3]; Gray [2]; Hardesty; Hunt & Randel; Johnson [6]; Kemble; Kendall; Manuscript Maps [2]; Mast, Crowell & Kirkpatrick; McNally; Mitchell, S.A. (Atlas maps 1859 & earlier) [6]; Mitchell, S.A. (Atlas maps 1860 & later) [7]; Morse & Gaston; Morse, S.; Page; Railroad Company Maps [3]; Rand, Avery & Co.; Rand, McNally (Atlas maps) [5]; Rand, McNally (Pocket & Wall Maps) [2]; Real Estate & Promotional Maps; Savage; Smith, Roswell C.; Stedman, Brown & Lyons; Thomas, Cowperthwait [3]; U.S. Gov't. [5]; U.S. Coast Survey [5]; U.S. Geological Survey; U.S. Pacific R.R. Survey; U.S. Union & Confederate Armies Atlas [3]; U.S. War Dep't [2]; Vandermaelen [2]; Walker, H.B.; Warner & Beers; Williams, C.S. [2]; Wilmore

TEXAS & OKLAHOMA: Colton (Atlas maps) [2]; Cram; Gray [2]; Hunt & Eaton; Lloyd, H.H.; Mitchell, S.A. (Atlas maps 1860 & later); Page; Tunison; U.S. Gov't

UTAH: Cram; U.S. Gov't. [2]; U.S. Geological Survey; U.S. State Surveys; U.S. War Dep't; Weekly Dispatch

- **(ATLAS):** U.S. Geological Survey

VERMONT: Bradford; Carey & Lea; Colton (Atlas maps) [2]; Finley [2]; Reid

- **(ATLAS):** Beers

VIRGINIA: Blunt [2]; Bradford; Colton (Atlas maps) [3]; Gordon, William [2]; Gray; Johnson; Magnus, C. [2]; Marshall; Meyer; Payne; Railroad Company Maps [2]; Real Estate & Promotional Maps [2]; Soules; Thomas, Cowperthwait [2]; U.S. Gov't.; U.S. Civil War Maps; U.S. Coast Survey; U.S. War Dep't [4]; Virtue [2]

VIRGINIA & WEST VIRGINIA: Bradford; Mitchell, S.A. (Atlas maps 1860 & later)

VIRGINIA, MARYLAND & DELAWARE: Tanner

WASHINGTON: Asher & Adams; Cram; Gill; Page; Real Estate & Promotional Maps; U.S. Gov't.; U.S. Coast Survey; U.S. State Surveys [5]

WASHINGTON & OREGON: Colton (Atlas maps)

WEST VIRGINIA: Rand, McNally (Atlas maps); U.S. War Dep't
WISCONSIN: Chapman [2]; Colton (Atlas maps) [3]; Government Maps: Local & State; Local & State Maps & Views; Mendenhall; Mitchell, S.A. (Atlas maps 1859 & earlier) [2]; Rand, McNally (Atlas maps); U.S. State Surveys [2]
WYOMING: Asher & Adams; Cram [3]; Hayden, F. [5]; U.S. Gov't. [2]; U.S. Geological Survey; U.S. War Dep't [2]

NORTH AMERICA: WEST INDIES

WEST INDIES: Bellin (Small) [5]; Blaeu [5]; Blair; Bonne; Bowen, E. [2]; Brion De La Tour; Burr; Carey; Cary [2]; Colom; Copley; Covens & Mortier; D'Anville; Danckerts; De Bry; De Herrera; De Vaugondy; Gazzettiere Americano; Gentleman's Magazine; Guthrie; Hall, S.; Homann & Homann Heirs; Imray; Johnston; Kitchin [2]; Laporte; Middleton; Mitchell, S.A. (Atlas maps 1859 & earlier); Moll (Large) [2]; Morse, J.; Mortier; Nolin; Ogilby; Ortelius (Folio) [2]; Rizzi-Zannoni; Russell; Scherer; S.D.U.K.; Stockdale; Thomas, Cowperthwait; Thomson; Town & Country Magazine; Visscher [2]; Waesberger; Wilkinson
  - **(MISCELLANEOUS):** Levasseur
ANTIGUA: Bellin (Large); Bowen, E.; Bowles; Jefferys; Mount & Page
ANTILLES: Depot De La Marine; Mount & Page; S.D.U.K.
BAHAMAS: Jefferys
BARBADOS: Gentleman's Magazine; Le Rouge; Mount & Page; Ogilby
CARIBBEAN SEA: Imray; Scherer
CARIBBEE ISLANDS: London Magazine; Mount & Page
CAYENNE: Desnos; Lagniet
CUBA: Bellin (Small); Bonne; Gastaldi; Jefferys; Lopez; Mercator (Small); Mialhe; Real Estate & Promotional Maps
  - **HAVANA:** Deroy; Gentleman's Magazine [2]; Jefferys; Manuscript Maps
CUBA & JAMAICA: Colton (Atlas maps); Colton (Pocket & Wall Maps); Johnson [2]; Ruscelli; Wytfliet
DOMINICAN REPUBLIC: De Bry; Prevost D'exiles
FLORIDA, CUBA & BAHAMAS: Mount & Page
GREATER ANTILLES: Mercator (Small) [2]; Mount & Page
GRENADA: Bellin (Small); British Admiralty; Jefferys
GUADELOUPE: Le Rouge; London Magazine; Sanson (Folio)
HISPANIOLA: Bellin (Small) [2]; Bonne [2]; Carey & Lea; De Fer (Large); Imray; Mount & Page; Wytfliet
JAMAICA: Bellin (Small); Blome [2]; Bochart & Knollis; Bonne [2]; British Admiralty [2]; Browne; Carey & Lea; Coronelli; Depot De La Marine; Gentleman's Magazine; Jefferys; Kitchin; Laporte; Ogilby; Political Magazine; Tallis; Visscher [2]
  - **KINGSTON:** Bellin (Small)
LEEWARD ISLANDS: Bordone; Carey & Lea
LESSER ANTILLES: Bellin (Small); Blaeu; Bonne [2]; Chatelain; De L'Isle [3]; Faden; Gerritz; London Magazine; Mallet [2]; Norie; Tardieu; Valk & Schenk; Vandermaelen; Weller
MARTINIQUE: De L'Isle [2]; De Vaugondy; Homann & Homann Heirs; Le Rouge; Levasseur; Political Magazine
PUERTO RICO: Churruca; Ogilby
ST. KITTS: Bellin (Large); Bowles; Thomson
ST. LUCIA: Gentleman's Magazine
WINDWARD ISLANDS: Arrowsmith; Lowry; Van Keulen; Weimar Geographisches Institut
WINDWARD PASSAGE: Jefferys

SOUTH AMERICA

SOUTH AMERICA: Bellin (Small); Bolton; Bonne; Colton (Atlas maps); Coronelli [2]; De Bry; De L'Isle; Delamarche; Gastaldi; Hondius; Jaillot; Lavoisne; Levasseur; Moll (Large); Ratelband; Sanson (Folio); Seale; Van Der Aa; Van Linschoten [2]
 - **REGIONS - CENTRAL:** Mitchell, S.A. (Atlas maps 1860 & later)
  - **NORTH:** Bowen, E.; Coronelli; De L'Isle; Fritz; Moll (Small); Sanson (Folio); Wytfliet
  - **SOUTH:** Blaeu; Bowen, E.; Coronelli; General Magazine Of Arts & Sciences; Lapie; Moll (Small); Ogilby; Stieler
  - **WEST:** Thomas, Cowperthwait

ARGENTINA: Bellin (Small); Moll (Small)
BRAZIL: Bellin (Large); Bellin (Small); Carey & Lea; De Wit; Dezauche; Hildburghausen Biblio; Mitchell, S.A. (Atlas maps 1860 & later); Ruscelli [2]
CHILE: Dapper; Gazzettiere Americano; Ogilby; Sanson (Folio); Wytfliet
COLOMBIA: Carey & Lea
- **CARTAGENA:** Covens & Mortier; Manuscript Maps
GUIANA: Blaeu; Jansson; Sanson (Folio)
LA PLATA BASIN & RIVER: Bellin (Small); Gazzettiere Americano; Wytfliet
MAGELLAN STRAITS & TIERRA DEL FUEGO: Blaeu [3]; Cloppenburgh; Commelin; Jansson; Jefferys; Mercator (Small); Ogilby; Sanson (Folio); Valk & Schenk; Van Der Aa; Wytfliet
PERU: Raimondi
VENEZUELA: Blaeu; Ogilby; Valk & Schenk

POLAR

ANTARCTICA: Hondius; S.D.U.K.; Walch
ARCTIC REGIONS: Bellin (Small); Blaeu; Bowen, E.; Cloppenburgh; Coronelli; De L'Isle; Graphic, The; Jansson; Mercator (Folio) [4]; Mercator (Small); Moll (Small); Ottens; Pitt; Quad; Scherer [2]; S.D.U.K. [2]; U.S. Hydrographic Office; Valk & Schenk

OCEANS: ATLANTIC

ATLANTIC OCEAN: American Philosophical Society; Bowen, E.; Bowen, T. [2]; Bowles; Coronelli [2]; De Bry; Depot De La Marine; Fries [2]; Herbert; Hildburghausen Biblio; Mount & Page [2]; Philip, G.
- **REGIONS - NORTH:** Depot De La Marine; Magini [2]; Ortelius (Folio) [3]; Ruscelli; Van Keulen
  - **SOUTH:** Herbert; Imray
  - **(MISCELLANEOUS):** Coronelli
- **ISLANDS & ISLAND GROUPS:**
  - **AZORES:** Mallet; Valk & Schenk
  - **BERMUDA:** Blaeu; Cloppenburgh; Crepy; Hondius [2]; Jansson [2]; Mercator (Small); Ogilby; Speed [3]; Thomson
  - **FALKLAND ISLANDS:** Bougainville
  - **GREENLAND:** La Harpe
  - **ICELAND:** Blaeu [2]; Hondius; Mercator (Small); Pitt; Quad [2]
  - **MADEIRA ISLANDS:** Wyld
  - **ST. HELENA:** De Bry; Mallet; Van Linschoten

OCEANS: PACIFIC

PACIFIC OCEAN: Anson; Bellin (Large); Bellin (Small); Coronelli; Dampier; Dudley; Dufour; Jansson [2]; Krusenstern; Levasseur; Mortier [3]; Ortelius (Folio) [5]; Rossi, L.; Seller; Stieler; Van Der Aa; Van Keulen; Walch; Wyld
- **REGIONS - EAST:** Doncker [2]
  - **NORTH:** Buache [2]; Carey; Chappe D'auteroche; Diderot [3]; Gentleman's Magazine; Morse, J.; Poirson; Reichard; Scherer [2]
  - **SOUTH:** Barbie Du Bocage; Cook [2]; Djurberg; Morse, J.; Von Reilly
  - **WEST:** La Perouse; Lapie; U.S. Gov't
  - **(MISCELLANEOUS):** La Harpe;
    - **(ATLAS):** Dumont D'Urville
- **OCEANIA:** Lapie; Levasseur
- **POLYNESIA:** Perthes
- **ISLAND & ISLAND GROUPS:**
  - **FIJI:** Perthes; Petermann
  - **GALAPAGOS ISLANDS:** Bowen, E.
  - **MARIANAS ISLANDS:** Bellin (Small); Mallet
  - **PHILIPPINE ISLANDS:** Anson; Bonne; London Magazine; Moll (Small); Rand, McNally (Atlas maps); Sanson (Small); Zatta
    - **(ATLAS):** U.S. Gov't
  - **TAHITI:** Cook [2]
  - **(OTHER ISLANDS):** Manuscript Maps; Seale

OCEANS: INDIAN

INDIAN OCEAN: Allard; Blachford; Du Val; Hobbs; Valentyn; Van Der Aa; Van Keulen
- **ISLANDS:** Bonne; Nichelson; S.D.U.K.
- **RED SEA:** Faden; Mortier [2]; Sayer & Bennett [2]

CELESTIAL

ARMILLARY SPHERE: Fries; Moll (Small); Ruscelli
ASTRONOMICAL DIAGRAMS: Andriveau-Goujon; Anonymous or unknown; Cellarius [2]; Doppelmayr; Lapie; Valk & Schenk
CELESTIAL ATLASES: Burritt [2]; Goldbach; Johnston; Kendall
CELESTIAL CHARTS: Artifacts [3]; Burritt; Butler; Cellarius [5]; Doppelmayr; Hersbach; Homann & Homann Heirs; Schenk; Senex; Valk & Schenk; Van Keulen

MISCELLANEOUS

ADVERTISEMENT: Rand, McNally (Atlas maps)
COMPASS ROSE: Lotter; Seller
GAMES: Puzzles & games [2]
IMAGINARY LANDS: Concept Maps; Seutter
MOUNTAINS: Carey & Lea; Hildburghausen Biblio
MOUNTAINS & RIVERS: Johnson
ODDITIES: Bunting [3]; Lotter
PARADISE: Hondius; Mercator (Small)
PLAYING CARDS: Artifacts
PORTRAITS: Bertius; Coronelli; Homann & Homann Heirs; Hondius [2]; Ortelius (Folio); Ortelius (Miniature); Speed; Weigel
PUZZLES: Cary; Fremin; Gall & Inglis [2]
RIVERS: S.D.U.K.
TITLE PAGES: Blaeu; Colton (Atlas maps); Des Barres; Desilver; Mortier; Renard; Van Der Aa; Van Meurs [2]
UNCLASSIFIED: Bell, Homann & Homann Heirs [2]; Jansson; Mortier; Seutter; Tanner

ORDERING INFORMATION

The *Price Record* may be ordered directly from Kimmel Publications. A single copy of the 1997-1998 *Price Record* is **$46.00**, plus shipping. Checks from foreign customers should be payable in U.S. Dollars and drawn on a U.S. bank. Postal money orders in U.S. Dollars are acceptable. Massachusetts residents should add 5% to the merchandise total for Sales Tax.

Purchasers placing a new standing order will receive a 10% discount. New subscribers should pay in advance. Thereafter an invoice will accompany each annual shipment. Payment must be made within 30 days of receipt to maintain a standing order.

Order from: **KIMMEL PUBLICATIONS, P.O Box 12, Amherst, MA 01004, USA**
For inquiries: Tel **(413) 256-8900**, Fax **(413) 256-6291**, E-mail: **navigateur@aol.com**

Price Record Shipping Charges

	Book Rate/Surface Mail		First Class/Air Mail	
	First copy	Each additional copy	First copy	Each additional copy
U.S.	$2.50	$0.75	$4.00	$2.50
Canada	3.00	2.00	5.00	3.00
Western Hemisphere	3.00	2.00	9.00	5.00
Europe	3.00	2.00	13.00	10.00
Asia, Africa & Pacific Rim	3.00	2.00	17.00	14.00

Alternative carriage may be arranged at the cost of shipping and handling, with a minimum charge of $6.00.

Available Volumes of *Antique Map Price Record & Handbook*

Volumes 1 through 10, (1983) through (1992), are all *out of print*

Volume 11 (1993) ISBN 0-9638100-0-6	$40.00
Volume 12 (1994) ISBN 0-9638100-1-4	$40.00
Volume 13 (1995) ISBN..0-9638100-2-2	$40.00
Volume 14 (1996) ISBN 0-9638100-3-0	$42.00
Volume 15 (1997-1998) ISBN 0-9638100-4-9 (current volume)	$46.00

Payment should accompany order. Make check payable to *Kimmel Publications*. Massachusetts residents must include 5% sales tax. Foreign customers should pay by check drawn on a U.S. bank and payable in U.S. Dollars, or by postal money order in U.S. dollars.

For the convenience of customers, payment by VISA or MasterCard for *single copies of the current edition at the list price of $46.00 each, plus tax and shipping*, may be made through Amherst Antiquarian Maps, P.O. Box 12, Amherst, MA 01004, USA; Fax (413) 256-6291.

Prices and shipping charges are subject to change without notice.

(advertisement)

David Jolly's Carto-Bibliographies are Available
MAPS IN BRITISH PERIODICALS: PART I and *PART II*

Together, they are the definitive collation of maps published in British Periodicals from 1669 to 1800. These are the magazines that kept literate English society informed of global events, especially during the tumultuous Eighteenth Century.

> *Part I* describes all 1100 maps in the major monthlies, including *Gentleman's Magazine*, *London Magazine*, *Political Magazine*, *Scots Magazine* and *Universal Magazine*. Part II is a continuation of the first book, covering over 1100 maps from more than 50 different annuals & magazines, mostly before 1800, such as *Annual Register*, *British Magazine*, *General Magazine of Arts & Sciences*, *Gentleman's and London Magazine* or *Exshaw's Magazine*, *Grand Magazine of Magazines*, *Royal Magazine*, *Imperial Magazine*, *Naval Chronicle*, and many others.

A complete bibliographical description is given with each entry, including full title, dimensions, publisher's imprint, engraver's signature, and other reference works in which the map is mentioned. Entries are arranged chronologically for each periodical with the widely accepted "Jolly" reference number. Each entry is fully indexed by title, geographical region, engraver, personal name, and reference cited.

> Part I. ISBN 0-911775-51-X 1990 6 x 9 inches 1 illus. 256 pages.
> Part II. ISBN 0-911775-52-8 1991 6 x 9 inches 1 illus. 320 pages.

Part I is available only as a pair with Part II for $85.00
Part II may be purchased separately for $35.00

> Carriage additional:
> Book Rate postage: U.S.A. $3.00; All other countries: $4.00
> First Class Mail or Airmail at cost.

MAILING LISTS AVAILABLE

Mailing lists are available from the publisher. These lists do *not* include the names of individuals who have written to order this book. Those names are treated as confidential to protect the privacy of individual customers. The lists are furnished for *one time use* on laser printed, self-adhesive labels. Both lists have been completely overhauled in 1998 and are current. They are updated as soon as we receive any information suggesting additions, changes or deletions. The U.S. entries are zip-sorted. Overseas entries are sorted by country, with Canada on a separate sheet.

> List 1. *United States Dealers*. About 200 dealers. **$40**
> List 2. *International Dealers*. About 150 dealers in the rest of the world. **$35**
> Lists 1 & 2, **World-wide Dealers**. About 350 names. **$70**

Prices include first class postage to the U.S. and Canada. Please add $6.00 for airmail elsewhere.

CURRENCY CONVERSION TABLE

These exchange rates were in effect at **mid-year 1997**, and were used in the compilation of the price listing.

Country (Unit)	Value in U.S. Dollars	Number per U.S. Dollar	Percent change '95-'97*	'97-'98†
Argentina *(Peso)*	1.0014	0.9986	0.1	- 0.1
Australia *(Dollar)*	0.7530	1.328	6.1	- 14.3
Austria *(Schilling)*	0.0814	12.280	- 20.8	- 3.6
Belgium *(Franc)*	0.0278	35.97	- 21.0	- 3.2
Canada *(Dollar)*	0.7252	1.379	0.3	- 3.4
Czech Republic (Koruna)	0.0309	32.38	- 19.3	- 3.2
Denmark *(Krone)*	0.1507	6.6361	- 18.4	- 3.3
Finland *(Mark)*	0.1928	5.1862	- 17.6	- 5.5
France *(Franc)*	0.1699	5.8845	- 17.8	- 2.5
Germany (Mark)	0.5725	1.7467	- 20.8	- 3.0
Great Britain *(Pound)*	1.6581	0.6031	4.0	0.8
Greece *(Drachma)*	0.003636	275.02	- 18.3	- 12.2
Hong Kong *(Dollar)*	0.1291	7.7455	0.1	0.0
Hungary *(Forint)*	0.0053	186.97	- 32.9	- 11.3
Ireland (Punt)	1.5095	0.6625	- 7.8	- 7.4
Israel *(Shekel)*	0.2781	3.5953	- 17.5	- 3.4
Italy *(Lira)*	0.000588	1700.5	- 3.9	- 4.6
Japan *(Yen)*	0.008705	114.88	- 26.2	- 13.1
Mexico *(Peso)*	0.12628	7.919	- 21.1	- 6.5
Netherlands (Guilder)	0.5095	1.9626	- 21.0	- 3.3
New Zealand *(Dollar)*	0.6781	1.4747	1.6	- 17.6
Norway *(Krone)*	0.1366	7.319	- 15.9	- 2.0
Poland *(Zloty)*	0.3040	3.29	- 27.7	- 3.5
Portugal *(Escudo)*	0.005672	176.29	-17.1	- 4.5
Saudi Arabia (Riyal)	0.2667	3.750	0.0	0.0
Singapore *(Dollar)*	0.6996	1.4293	- 2.2	- 10.6
Spain *(Peseta)*	0.006771	147.68	- 17.6	- 3.5
Sweden *(Krona)*	0.1292	7.740	- 5.9	0.1
Switzerland *(Franc)*	0.6825	1.4653	- 21.6	- 2.1
Venezuela *(Bolivar)*	0.0021	486.75	- 65.1	- 8.6

Source: *New York Times*.   * from July 1, '95 to July 1, '97   † from July 1, '97 to Apr 20, '98

Up to the moment exchange rates between any currencies can be obtained on the internet from **The Universal Currency Converter**™ at: http://www.xe.net/currency

CATALOGUE CODES

The numbers below in square brackets correspond to the dealer or auctioneer codes in the main "Price Listing". Map dealers are listed first with only numerals. Auction houses follow the dealer listing and have the prefix "A" as in [A..] See "Directory of Dealers" for a general listing of antiquarian map dealers. For an explanation of the information in parentheses, see endnotes.

Map Dealer Catalogues

Acquitania Gallery, 158 Carl Street, San Francisco, CA 94117
[1] Catalogue 10 (33/36/84; 16 pp; some illustrations)

Richard B. Arkway, Inc., 59 E. 54th St., Suite 62, New York, NY 10022
[2] Fine Antique Maps - Catalog 47 (111/134; 38 pp; near fully illustrated, cover in color)
[3] Atlases - Catalog 48 (37/42; 38 pp; near fully illustrated by examples, some in color)

Roderick M. Barron, 21 Bayham Road, Sevenoaks, Kent TN13 3XD, England
[4] Catalogue 29 - Van Wytfliet (129/165+; 84 pp; some illustrations; prices in sterling)

Cartographics of Vermont, P.O. Box 145, East Middlebury, VT 05740
[5] Occasional List No. 22 - Americana (33/67; 8 pp; no illustrations)
[6] Occasional List No. 23 - A Summer Miscellany (20/39; 6 pp; no illustrations)

Dumont Maps & Books of the West, 301 E. Palace Avenue, P.O. Box 10250, Santa Fe, NM 87504
[7] Catalogue #38 - January/February 1997 - Rare Western Americana (25/29/225; 42 pp; maps near fully illustrated)
[8] Catalogue #39 - March/April 1997 - Rare Western Americana (26/30/225; 42 pp; maps near fully illustrated)
[9] Catalogue #40 - June 1997 - Rare Western Americana (28/30/190; 34 pp; maps near fully illustrated)
[10] Catalogue #43 - November 1997 Rare Western Americana (25/37/190; 34 pp; some map illustrations)

W.J. Faupel, 3 Halsford Lane, East Grinstead, West Sussex RH19 1NY, England
[11] Faupel's Catalogue 111 (323/544; 44 pp; some illustrations; "Bargain Basement" addenda not included; prices in US$)

Richard Fitch, Old Maps & Prints & Books, 2324 Calle Halcon, Santa Fe, NM, 87505
[12] Americana - Catalogue No. 54 (253/373; 174 pp; many illustrations)

Gowrie Galleries, 316 Oxford St., Woollahra, 2025, Australia
[13] The Printed World II; An exhibition of antique maps of the World, Australia & S.E. Asia, 16th century to 19th century (113/179; 37 pp; some illustrations, about half in color; prices in $Aus. [Exhibition mounted July 1997 at Sydney Cove Prints and Maps, The Rocks])

Heritage Map Museum, 55 N. Water St., P.O. Box 412, Lititz, PA 17543
[14] Antique Map Catalogue - October 1997 (172/203; 27 pp. few color illustrations)
 [see *Auction Catalogues* also]

High Ridge Books, Inc., P.O. Box 286, Rye, NY 10580
[15] Catalogue 35 - Rare Maps and Prints from 19th Century America ... (174/212; 30 pp; few illustrations)

Murray Hudson Antiquarian Books & Maps, 109 S. Church St., P.O. Box 163, Halls, TN 38040
[16] Catalogue 24 - Texas; Maps, Books & Prints 1769-1990 (136/344; 58 pp; 2 illustrations)

Kit S. Kapp, Antiquarian Maps, P.O. Box 64, Osprey, FL 34229
[17] New England - Navigational Charts - Fall 1997 (30/70; 5 pp; some illustrations)
[18] Lesser Antilles - Winter 1997/98 (23/39; 3 pp; some illustrations. [also, 12 pp of several island specific sections not included])
[19] World in Hemispheres - Winter 1997/98 (47/51; 5 pp; some illustrations)

Kauai Fine Arts, P.O. Box 1079, Lawai, Kauai, HI 96765
[20] Antique Maps & Prints - Spring 1997 (51/84+; 30 pp; many illustrations, some in color; all items in good condition unless noted otherwise. [also, 131 sale list items on 2 pp not included])

Neil D. MacDonald Fine Books, 27 Davies Avenue, Suite 2B, Toronto, Ontario M4M 2A9, Canada
[21] Fine Atlases, Maps, and Prints (69/97; 22 pp; some illustrations; maps uncolored & good condition unless otherwise stated; prices in Can$)

Maps of Antiquity, Lynn Vigeant, 160 Midland Avenue, Montclair, NJ 07042; 1022 Route 6A, West Barnstable, MA 02668
[22] Maps of Antiquity, Catalog 12 (82/165 plus some related books; 12 pp; some illustrations; minor defects may be present, significant defects noted)

Martayan Lan, 48 East 57th Street, New York, NY 10022
[23] Fine Antique Maps - Catalogue 21 (81/87; 35 pp; fully illustrated, some in color)
[24] Fine Antique Maps, City Views & Atlases - Catalogue 23 (176/221; 71 pp; many illustrations, some in color)

The Old Map Gallery, Paul F. Mahoney, 1746 Blake Street, Denver, CO 80202
[25] Catalogue # 26 Antique Maps and Books (138/233+; 56 pp; some illustrations)
[26] Catalogue # 27 Antique Maps and Books (134/198; 53 pp; some illustrations)

Old Maps and Prints, P.O. Box 2234, Fort Worth, TX 76113
[27] Fine Maps and Prints (75/110; 18 pp; few illustrations; minor imperfections of age not noted. [also many soil maps not included])

The Old Print Gallery, 1220 31st St. N.W., Washington, DC 20007
[28] Showcase; Volume XXIV, Number 1; March 1997 (17/79; 24 pp; 17 cartographic items fully illustrated; VG to fine except as noted)
[29] Showcase; Volume XXIV, Number 2; July 1997 (25/63; 24 pp; fully illustrated; VG to fine except as noted)
[30] Showcase; Volume XXIV, Number 3; October 1997 (70/123/204; 24 pp; some illustrations; VG to fine except as noted)
[31] Showcase; Volume XXIV, Number 4; December 1997 (20/88; 24 pp; cartographic items fully illustrated; VG to fine except as noted)

The Old Print Shop, 150 Lexington Avenue, New York, NY 10016
[32] Portfolio, Map Issue - Volume LVI, Number 7 (49/96 ; 28 pp; fully illustrated [other than sets])

The Philadelphia Print Shop, Ltd., 8441 Germantown Avenue, Philadelphia, PA 19118
[33] Rare & Reference Books (18/40/254; 34 pp; no illustrations; volumes collate completely unless noted)

Jonathan Potter Ltd., 125 New Bond Street, London W1Y 9AF, England
[34] Choice Items from Stock - 13 (244/306; 32 pp; some illustrations; condition good to fine unless otherwise stated; prices in sterling)

Primitive Pieces. 537 West Franklin St., Slatington, PA 18080
[35] Catalog No.7 - 15th thru 20th Century - Autumn 1997 (77/132; 43pp; cover illus)

Ridler Page Rare Maps, 205 King Street, Suite 102, Charleston, SC 29401
[36] Spring 1997 Catalog (95/143; 51 pp; many illustrations; maps good for their age with defects noted)

George Ritzlin, Maps & Prints, 469 Roger Williams Avenue, Highland Park, IL 60035
[37] Catalog 16 (72/95; 31 pp; some illustrations)
[38] Catalog 17 (74/91; 36 pp; some illustrations)

G. Robinson Old Prints and Maps, 124-D Bent St., Taos, NM 87571
[39] Catalogue 70 - Winter, 1996-'97 (67/103; 16 pp; cartographic items fully illustrated; most in excellent condition, faults described)
[40] Catalogue #72 - Summer, 1997 - One Hundred Inexpensive Maps (80/100; 10 pp; 2 illustrations; all excellent condition, with faults described)
[41] Catalogue 73 - Fall 1997 (70/100; 16 pp; fully illustrated; most excellent, flaws described)

Spencer Scott Sandilands, 546 High Street, Prahran, Melbourne, Victoria, Australia 3181
[42] Old Maps - A Miscellany of Sixteenth and Seventeenth Century Maps (77/108; 56 pp; some illustrations, all in color; prices in Aus$)

Thomas & Ahngsana Suarez, 225 Warren Avenue, Hawthorne, NY 10532
[43] A Selection of Fine Early Maps and Books - Late Winter, 1997 (49/66; 26 pp; many illustrations)
[44] A Selection of Fine Maps & Views - Late Summer 1997 (54/69; 26 pp; fully illustrated)
[45] A Selection of Fine Maps & Views - Autumn 1997 (40/52; 26 pp; fully illustrated, some in color)

Tooley Adams & Co., Antiquarian Maps and Atlases, 13 Cecil Court, Charing Cross Road, London WC2N 4EZ, England
[46] Map Catalogue Summer 1997 (110/113 plus reference books; 25 pp; near fully illustrated; each item good, but some with minor imperfections, serious flaws noted; prices in sterling)
[47] Recent Acquisitions (75/82; 10 pp; some illustrations; good condition, serious flaws noted; prices in sterling)

H. Th. Wenner, Buch- und Kunstantiquariat, Heger Strasse 2 - 3, D 4907 Osnabrück, Germany

[48] Graphik (#419) (238/1174; 110 pp.; few illustrations; dimensions sometimes from publishers information; prices in Deutsche Mark)

Auction Catalogues

Heritage Map Museum, 55 N. Water St., P.O. Box 412, Lititz, PA 1754.
[see *Map Dealer Catalogues* also]

[A1] 16th to 19th Century Rare Map & Book Auction: VIII - June 14, 199" (113/132; 32 pp; some color illustrations)

[A2] 10th Anniversary Antique Map and Atlas Auction: - December 6th, 199" (92/153; 48 pp; some color illustrations)

Old World Mail Auctions, 671 Hwy 179, Suite C2, Sedona, AZ 86336

[A3] Auction No.80 - September 6, 1997 (147/311/457; 51 pp; few illustrations condition by letter grades)

[A4] Auction No.81 - December 6, 1997 (154/361/508; 55 pp; few illustrations condition by letter grades)

Phillips, 101 New Bond Street, London W1Y 0AS

[A5] Books, Manuscripts, Photographs, Atlases & Maps - 13th November 1997; Sale 30,423 (25/41/371; 137 pp; some cartographic illustrations; prices in sterling)

Sotheby's, 34-35 New Bond Street, London W1A 2AA, England

[A6] Printed Books and Maps - 27 November 1997; Sale LN7638 (96/386/716; 100 pp; few illustrations; prices in sterling)

Swann Galleries, Inc., 104 East 25th Street, New York, NY 10010

[A7] Maps & Atlases Map Reference Decorative Graphics Ephemera - Sale 1741, December 5, 1996 (210/343/645; 106 pp; few illustrations)

[A8] Maps & Atlases Map Reference Decorative Graphics Ephemera - Sale 1774, December 4, 1997 (165/305/604; 104 pp; few illustrations)

Waverly Auctions, Inc., 4931 Cordell Ave., Bethesda, MD 20814

[A9] Fine Books Maps & Atlases ... - Sale 139; June 19, 1997 (41/84/498; 61 pp; few illustrations)

[A10] Fine Books Americana ... Maps & Atlases ... - Sale 142; November 13, 1997 (60/115/670; 78 pp; few illustrations)

The first number after the parentheses refers to the number of items from the catalogue which are represented in the "Price Listing". The number after the slash (/) is the total number of items in the catalogue (which may vary according to enumeration method). If three numbers appear, the first refers to number of items in the "Price Listing", the second is the number of cartographic items, the third is the total number in the catalogue.

Illustration quantification is as follows: *fully*, 100%; *near fully*, over 90%; *many*, more than 50% but less than 90%; *some*, more than 20% but less than 50%; *few*, less than 20%; *not illustrated*, none. In some cases only cartographic items are counted.

Where "blanket" condition statements are provided, note is made here rather than in the "Price listing".